C000000134

EasyReaa
Birmingham
and West Midlands

First published in 2004 by

Philip's, a division of
Octopus Publishing Group Ltd
2-4 Heron Quays, London E14 4JP

Second edition 2006
First impression 2006

ISBN-10   0-540-08995-8
ISBN-13   978-0-540-08995-6

© Philip's 2006

This product includes mapping data licensed
from Ordnance Survey® with the permission of
the Controller of Her Majesty's Stationery Office.
© Crown copyright 2006. All rights reserved.
Licence number 100011710.

Printed by Toppan, China

Contents

III	**Key to map symbols**
IV	**Key to map pages**
VI	**Route planning**
VIII	**Administrative and Postcode boundaries**
1	**Street maps**
163	**Enlarged street maps centres of Wolverhampton, Birmingham and Coventry**
166	**Index** of towns and villages
168	**Index** of streets, hospitals, industrial estates, railway stations, schools, shopping centres, universities and places of interest

Digital Data

The exceptionally high-quality mapping found in this atlas is available as digital data in TIFF format, which is easily convertible to other bitmapped (raster) image formats.

The index is also available in digital form as a standard database table. It contains all the details found in the printed index together with the National Grid reference for the map square in which each entry is named.

For further information and to discuss your requirements, please contact Philip's on 020 7644 6932 or james.mann@philips-maps.co.uk

PHILIP'S MAPS
the Gold Standard for drivers

◆ **Philip's street atlases cover every county in England, Wales and much of Scotland**

- ◆ Every named street is shown, including alleys, lanes and walkways
- ◆ Thousands of additional features marked: stations, public buildings, car parks, places of interest
- ◆ Route-planning maps to get you close to your destination
- ◆ Post codes on the maps and in the index
- ◆ Widely used by the emergency services, transport companies and local authorities

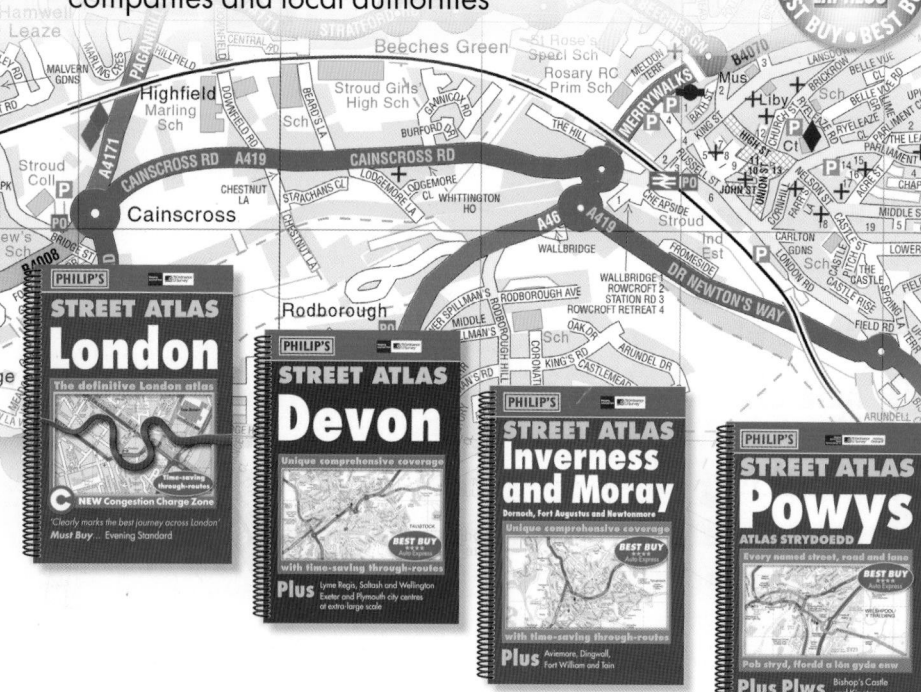

Street atlases currently available

England
Bedfordshire	West Sussex
Berkshire	Tyne and Wear
Birmingham and West Midlands	Warwickshire
	Birmingham and West Midlands
Bristol and Bath	Wiltshire and Swindon
Buckinghamshire	Worcestershire
Cambridgeshire	East Yorkshire Northern Lincolnshire
Cheshire	
Cornwall	North Yorkshire
Cumbria	South Yorkshire
Derbyshire	West Yorkshire
Devon	
Dorset	**Wales**
County Durham and Teesside	Anglesey, Conwy and Gwynedd
Essex	Cardiff, Swansea and The Valleys
North Essex	
South Essex	Carmarthenshire, Pembrokeshire and Swansea
Gloucestershire	
Hampshire	Ceredigion and South Gwynedd
North Hampshire	
South Hampshire	Denbighshire, Flintshire, Wrexham
Herefordshire Monmouthshire	
	Herefordshire Monmouthshire
Hertfordshire	Powys
Isle of Wight	
Kent	**Scotland**
East Kent	Aberdeenshire
West Kent	Ayrshire
Lancashire	Dumfries and Galloway
Leicestershire and Rutland	Edinburgh & East Central Scotland
Lincolnshire	Fife and Tayside
London	Glasgow West Central Scotland
Greater Manchester	
Merseyside	Inverness & Moray
Norfolk	Lanarkshire
Northamptonshire	Scottish Borders
Northumberland	
Nottinghamshire	**Northern Ireland***
Oxfordshire	County Antrim and County Londonderry
Shropshire	
Somerset	County Armagh and County Down
Staffordshire	
Suffolk	Belfast
Surrey	County Tyrone and County Fermanagh
East Sussex	

*Publishing autumn 2006

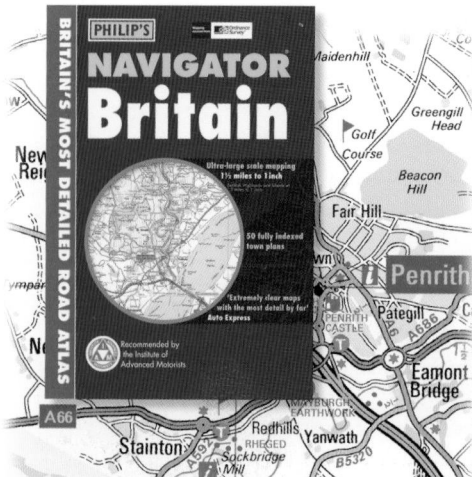

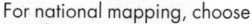

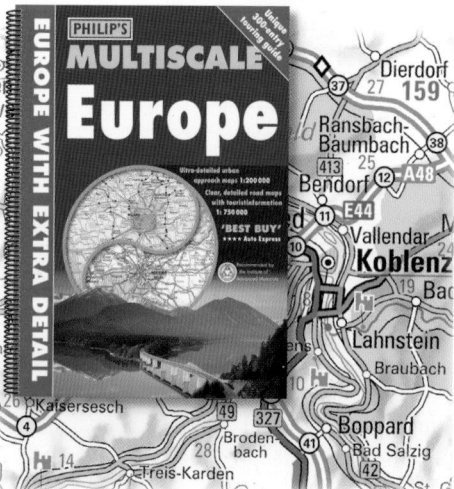

For national mapping, choose
Philip's Navigator Britain –
the most detailed road atlas available of England, Wales and Scotland. Hailed by Auto Express as 'the ultimate road atlas', this is the only one-volume atlas to show every road and lane in Britain.

For European mapping, choose
Philip's Multiscale Europe –
This best-selling atlas contains clear, detailed road maps of the whole of Europe, large-scale approach maps and street-level city centre plans of major cities.

How to order
Philip's maps and atlases are available from bookshops, motorway services and petrol stations.

You can order direct from the publisher by phoning **01903 828503** or online at **www.philips-maps.co.uk**

For bulk orders only, phone 020 7644 6940

Symbol	Description
(22a)	**Motorway** with junction number
	Primary route – dual/single carriageway
	A road – dual/single carriageway
	B road – dual/single carriageway
	Minor road – dual/single carriageway
	Other minor road – dual/single carriageway
	Road under construction
	Tunnel, covered road
	Rural track, private road or narrow road in urban area
	Gate or obstruction to traffic (restrictions may not apply at all times or to all vehicles)
	Path, bridleway, byway open to all traffic, road used as a public path
	Pedestrianised area
DY7	**Postcode boundaries**
	County and unitary authority boundaries
	Railway, tunnel, railway under construction
	Tramway, tramway under construction
	Miniature railway
Walsall	**Railway station**
	Private railway station
South Shields	**Metro station**
	Tram stop, tram stop under construction
	Bus, coach station

Symbol	Description
◆	**Ambulance station**
◆	**Coastguard station**
◆	**Fire station**
◆	**Police station**
+	**Accident and Emergency entrance to hospital**
H	**Hospital**
+	**Place of worship**
i	**Information Centre** (open all year)
	Shopping Centre
P P&R	**Parking, Park and Ride**
PO	**Post Office**
	Camping site, caravan site
	Golf course, picnic site
Prim Sch	**Important buildings, schools, colleges, universities and hospitals**
	Built up area
	Woods
River Medway	**Water name**
	River, weir, stream
	Canal, lock, tunnel
	Water
	Tidal water
Church	**Non-Roman antiquity**
ROMAN FORT	**Roman antiquity**
87 / 237	**Adjoining page indicators and overlap bands** The colour of the arrow and the band indicates the scale of the adjoining or overlapping page (see scales below)

	Academy				
Acad	**Academy**	Inst	**Institute**	Recn Gd	**Recreation Ground**
Allot Gdns	**Allotments**	Ct	**Law Court**		
Cemy	**Cemetery**	L Ctr	**Leisure Centre**	Resr	**Reservoir**
C Ctr	**Civic Centre**	LC	**Level Crossing**	Ret Pk	**Retail Park**
CH	**Club House**	Liby	**Library**	Sch	**School**
Coll	**College**	Mkt	**Market**	Sh Ctr	**Shopping Centre**
Crem	**Crematorium**	Meml	**Memorial**	TH	**Town Hall/House**
Ent	**Enterprise**	Mon	**Monument**	Trad Est	**Trading Estate**
Ex H	**Exhibition Hall**	Mus	**Museum**	Univ	**University**
Ind Est	**Industrial Estate**	Obsy	**Observatory**	W Twr	**Water Tower**
IRB Sta	**Inshore Rescue Boat Station**	Pal	**Royal Palace**	Wks	**Works**
	Boat Station	PH	**Public House**	YH	**Youth Hostel**

■ The small numbers around the edges of the maps identify the 1 kilometre National Grid lines
■ The dark grey border on the inside edge of some pages indicates that the mapping does not continue onto the adjacent page

Enlarged mapping only

Symbol	Description
	Railway or bus station building
	Place of interest
	Parkland

The scale of the maps on the pages numbered in blue is 6 cm to 1 km • 3⅘ inches to 1 mile • 1: 16 666

0 | ¼ | ½ | ¾ | 1 mile
0 | 250m | 500m | 750m | 1 kilometre

The scale of the maps on pages numbered in red is 12 cm to 1 km • 7⅗ inches to 1 mile • 1: 8 333

0 | 220 yards | 440 yards | 660 yards | ½ mile
0 | 125m | 250m | 375m | ½ kilometre

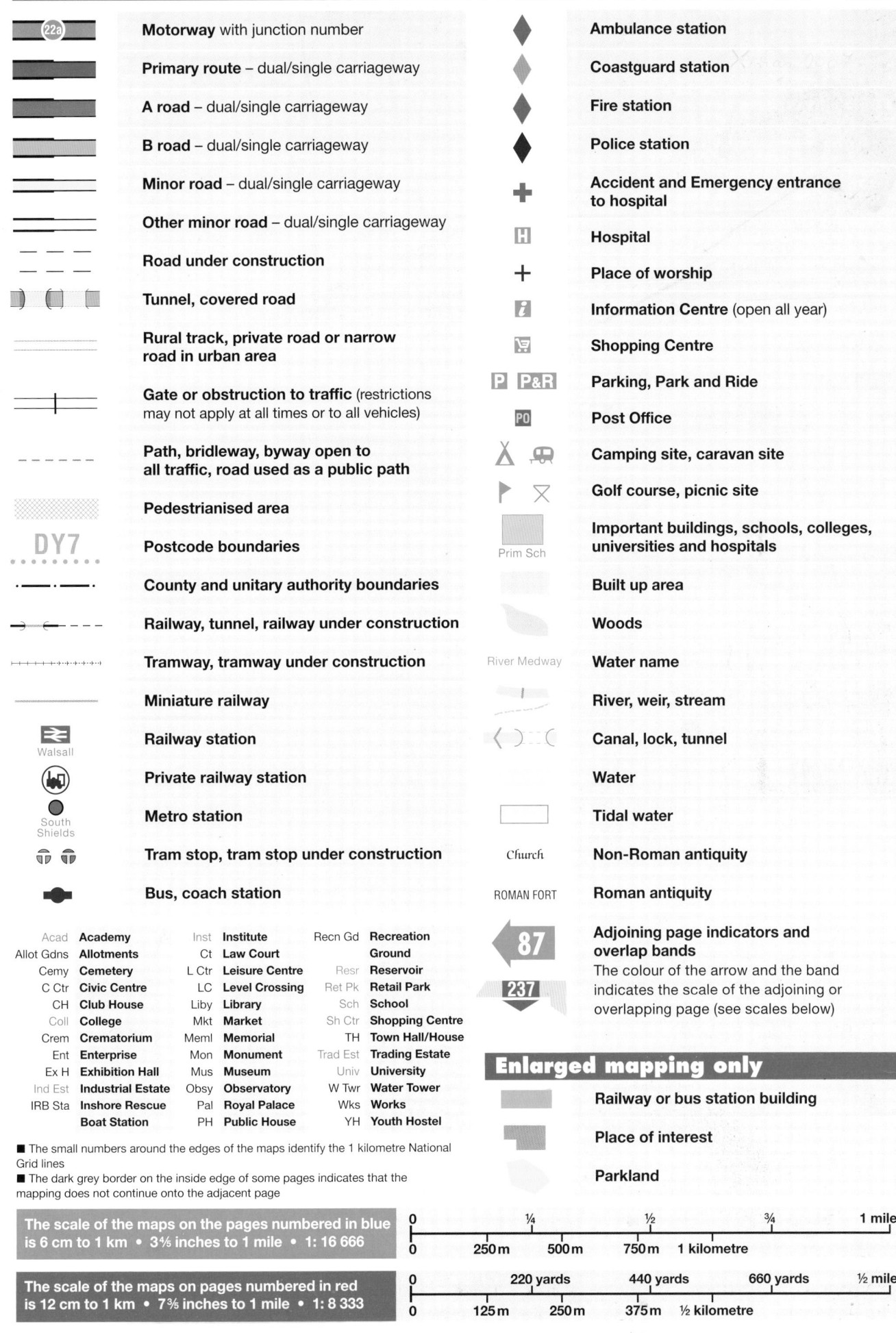

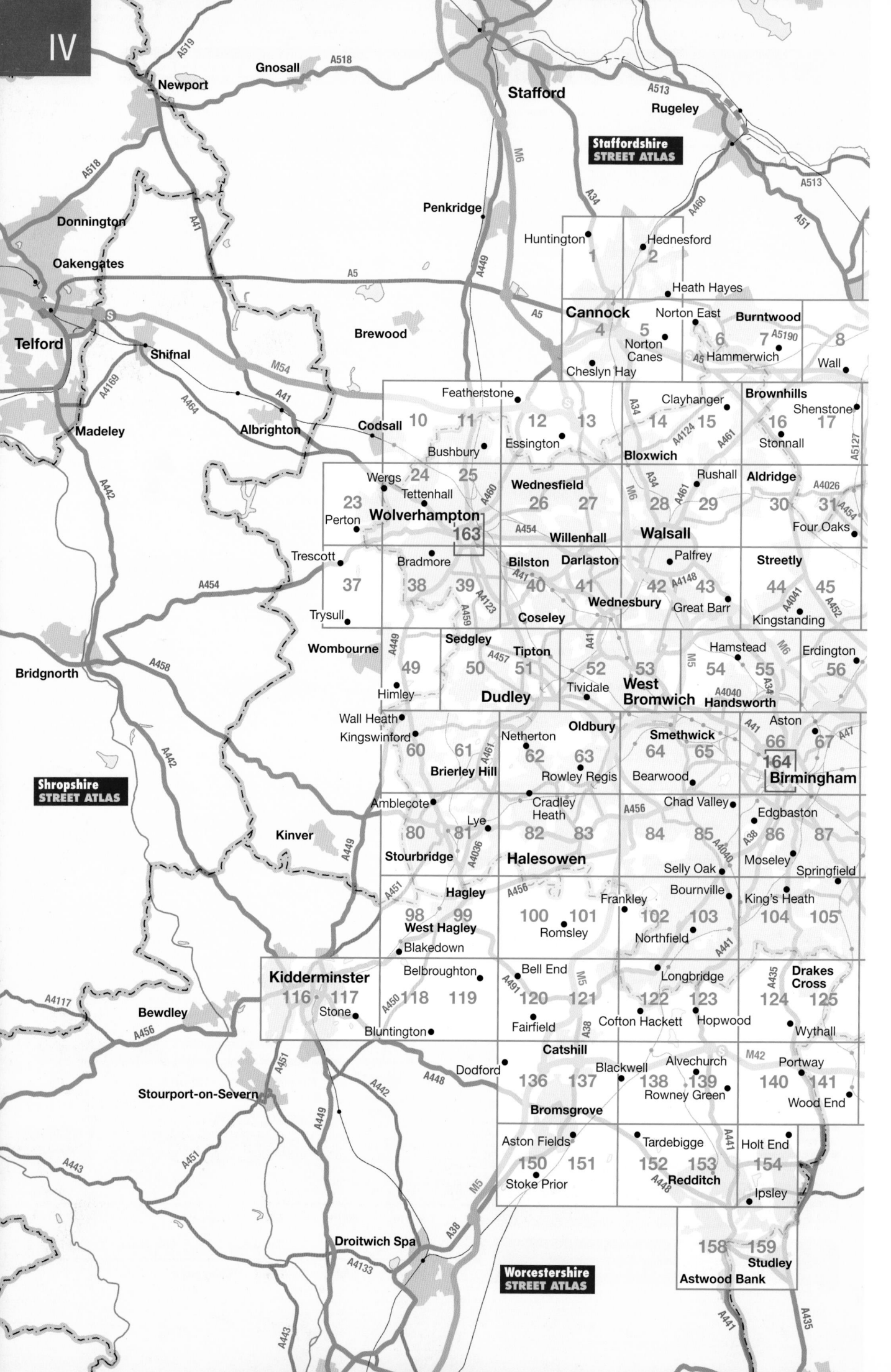

IV

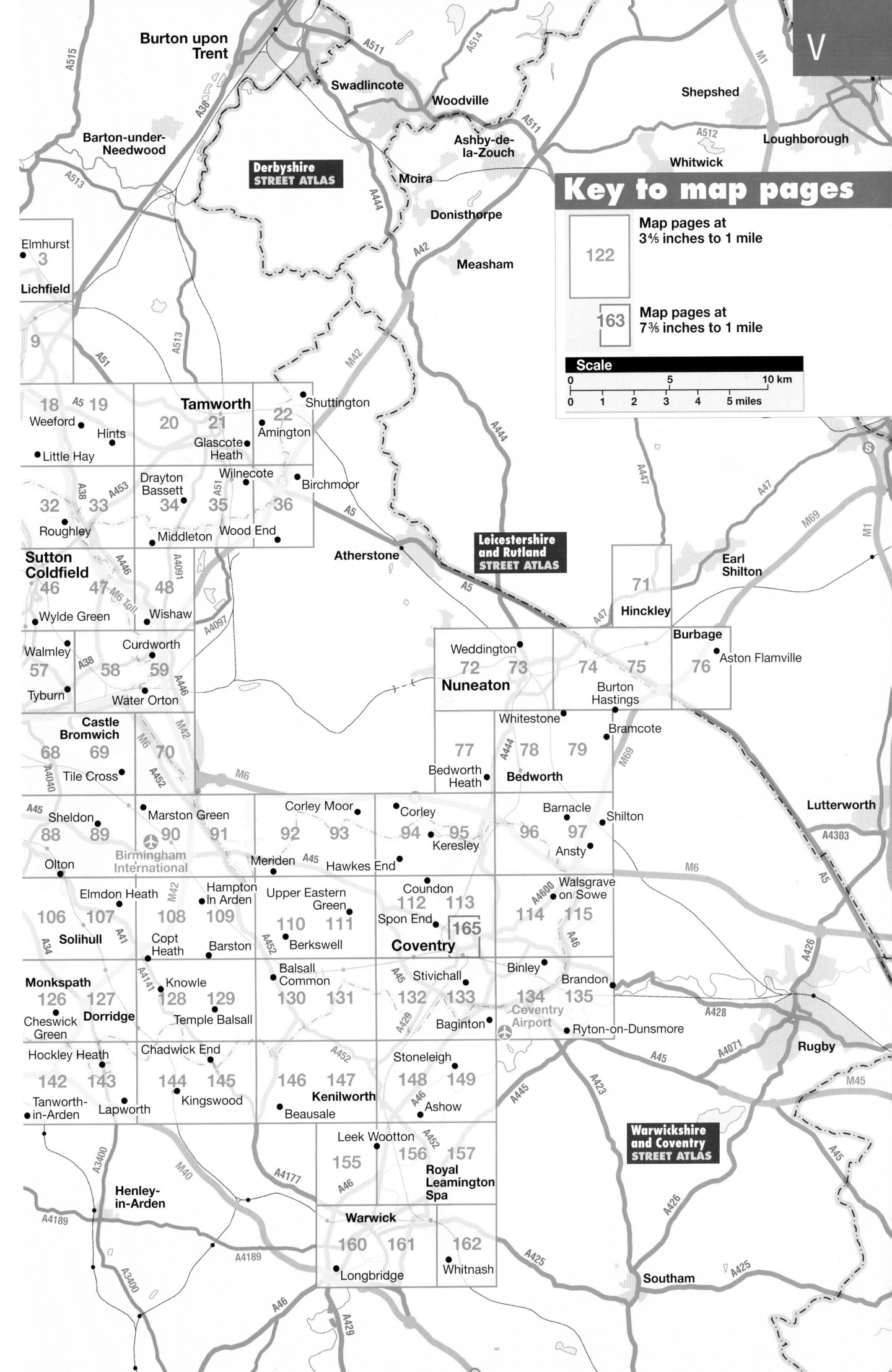

V

Burton upon Trent

Swadlincote

Woodville

Shepshed

Ashby-de-la-Zouch

Whitwick

Loughborough

Barton-under-Needwood

Derbyshire STREET ATLAS

Moira

Donisthorpe

Measham

Key to map pages

122	Map pages at 3⅘ inches to 1 mile
163	Map pages at 7⅗ inches to 1 mile

Scale
0   5   10 km
0   1   2   3   4   5 miles

Elmhurst
3

Lichfield
9

Shuttington

18 A5 **19**   **Tamworth**
Weeford   **20** **21**   **22**
    Hints   Amington
  Little Hay   Glascote
                  Heath

Drayton   Wilnecote
Bassett   Birchmoor
32 **33** **34** **35** **36**
Roughley   Middleton   Wood End

**Sutton
Coldfield**
46 **47** **48**
Wylde Green   Wishaw

Atherstone

**Leicestershire
and Rutland**
STREET ATLAS

71

Earl
Shilton

Hinckley

Burbage

Walmley   Curdworth
57 **58** **59**
Tyburn   Water Orton

72 **73**   **74** **75**   **76**
Weddington   Aston Flamville
Nuneaton   Burton
              Hastings

**Castle
Bromwich**
68 **69** **70**
Tile Cross

Whitestone
Bramcote

77   **78** **79**
Bedworth
Heath   **Bedworth**

Lutterworth

Sheldon   Marston Green
88 **89** **90** **91**
Olton
**Birmingham
International**

Corley Moor   Corley
92 **93** **94** **95** **96** **97**
          Keresley   Ansty
Meriden A45 Hawkes End

Barnacle
Shilton

Elmdon Heath Hampton Upper Eastern
              in Arden   Green
106 **107** **108** **109** **110** **111**
Solihull
Copt   Barston Berkswell
Heath

Coundon
112 **113**
Spon End
Coventry

165

Walsgrave
on Sowe
114 **115**

Binley

Monkspath
126 **127** **128** **129** **130** **131** **132** **133** **134** **135**
Cheswick **Dorridge** Knowle   Balsall   Stivichall   Brandon
Green   Common
          Temple Balsall   Baginton **Coventry
                                              Airport** Ryton-on-Dunsmore

Rugby

Hockley Heath   Chadwick End
142 **143** **144** **145** **146** **147** **148** **149**
Tanworth-   Kingswood   Stoneleigh
in-Arden Lapworth   Beausale   Ashow
                                  Kenilworth

Leek Wootton
155 **156** **157**
**Royal
Leamington
Spa**

**Warwickshire
and Coventry**
STREET ATLAS

Henley-
in-Arden

Warwick
160 **161** **162**
Longbridge   Whitnash

Southam

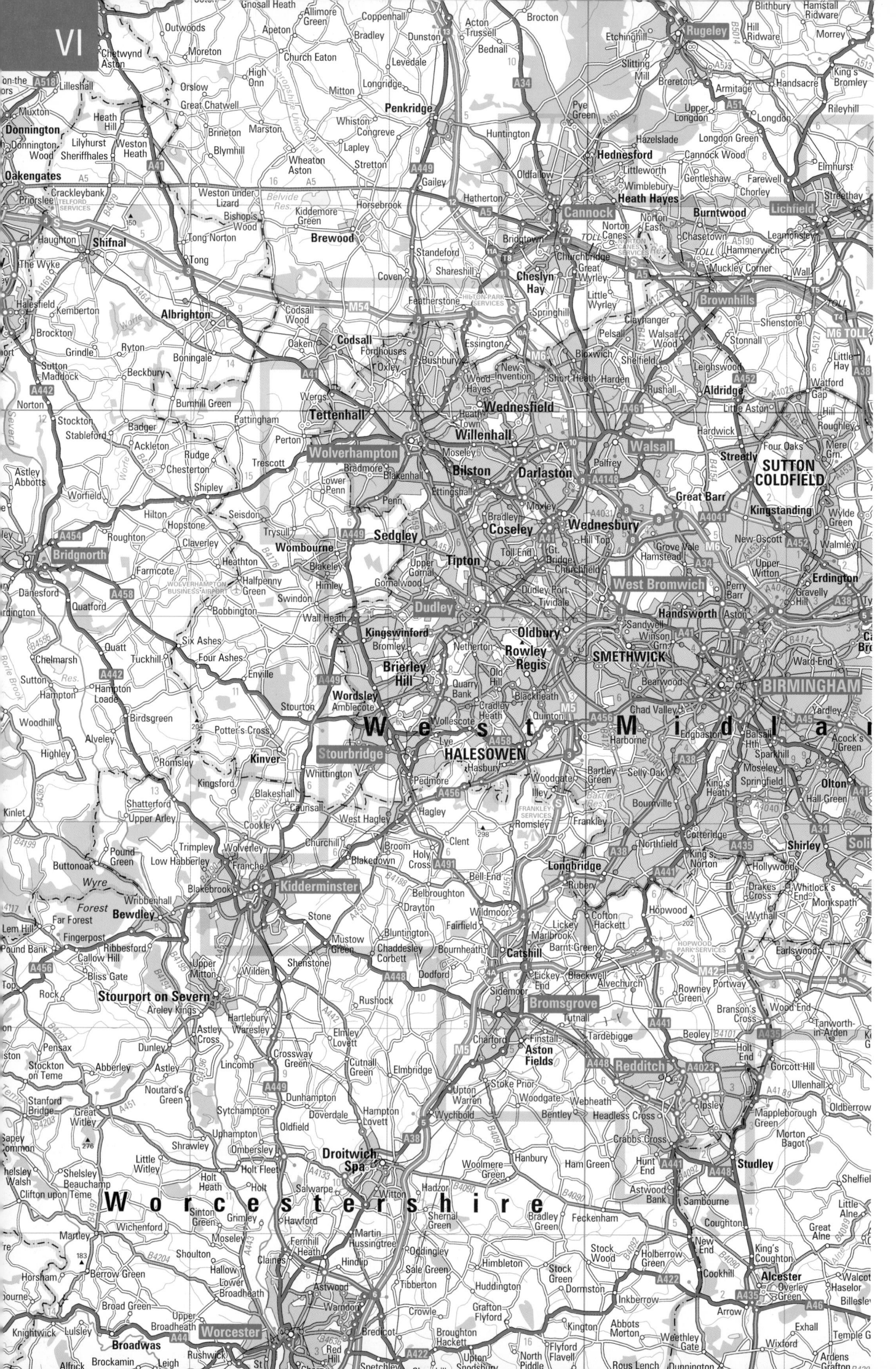

Scale
0   5   10 km
0   1   2   3   4   5 miles

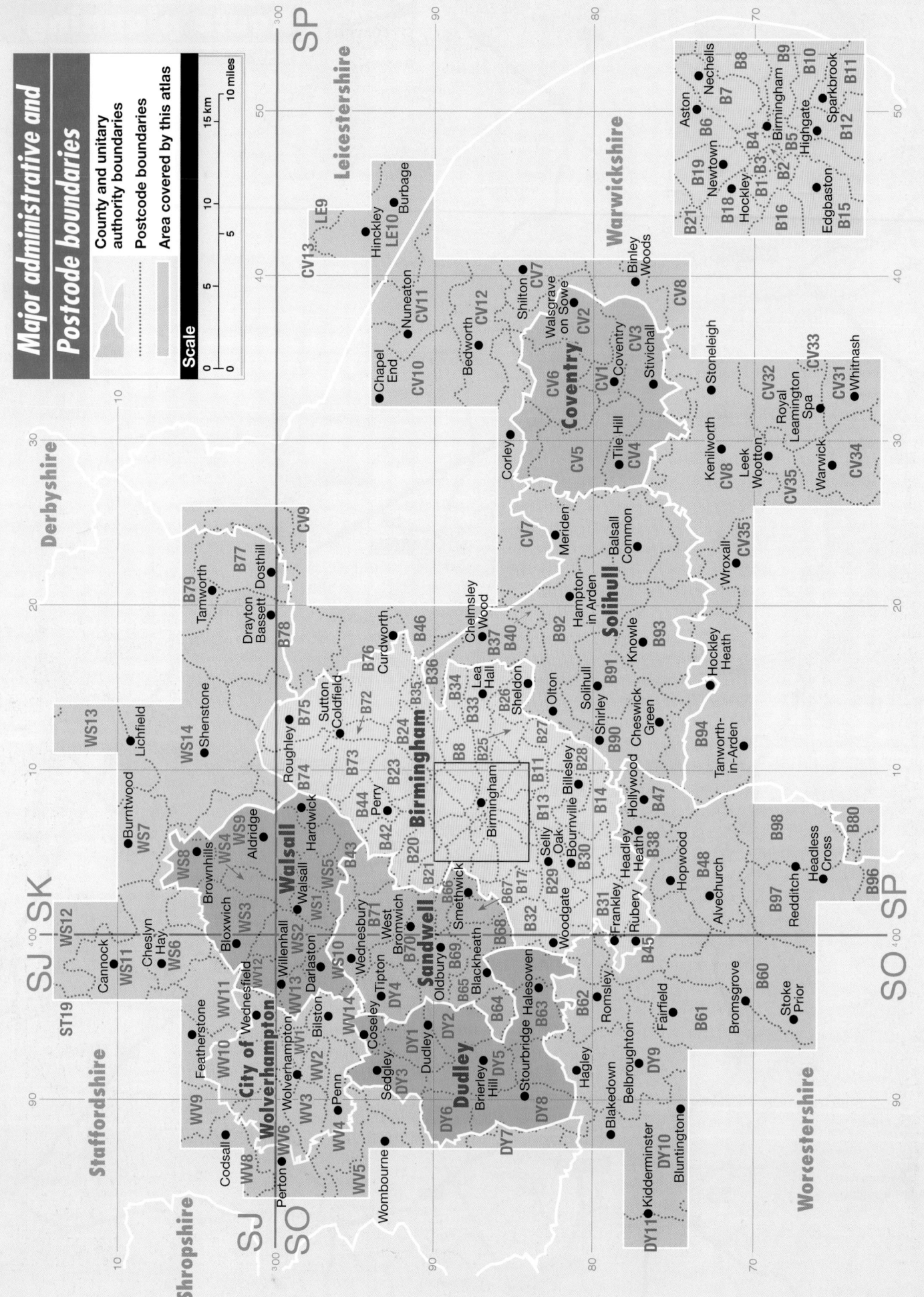

Major administrative and Postcode boundaries

- County and unitary authority boundaries
- Postcode boundaries
- Area covered by this atlas

Scale

0   5   10   15 km
0   5   10 miles

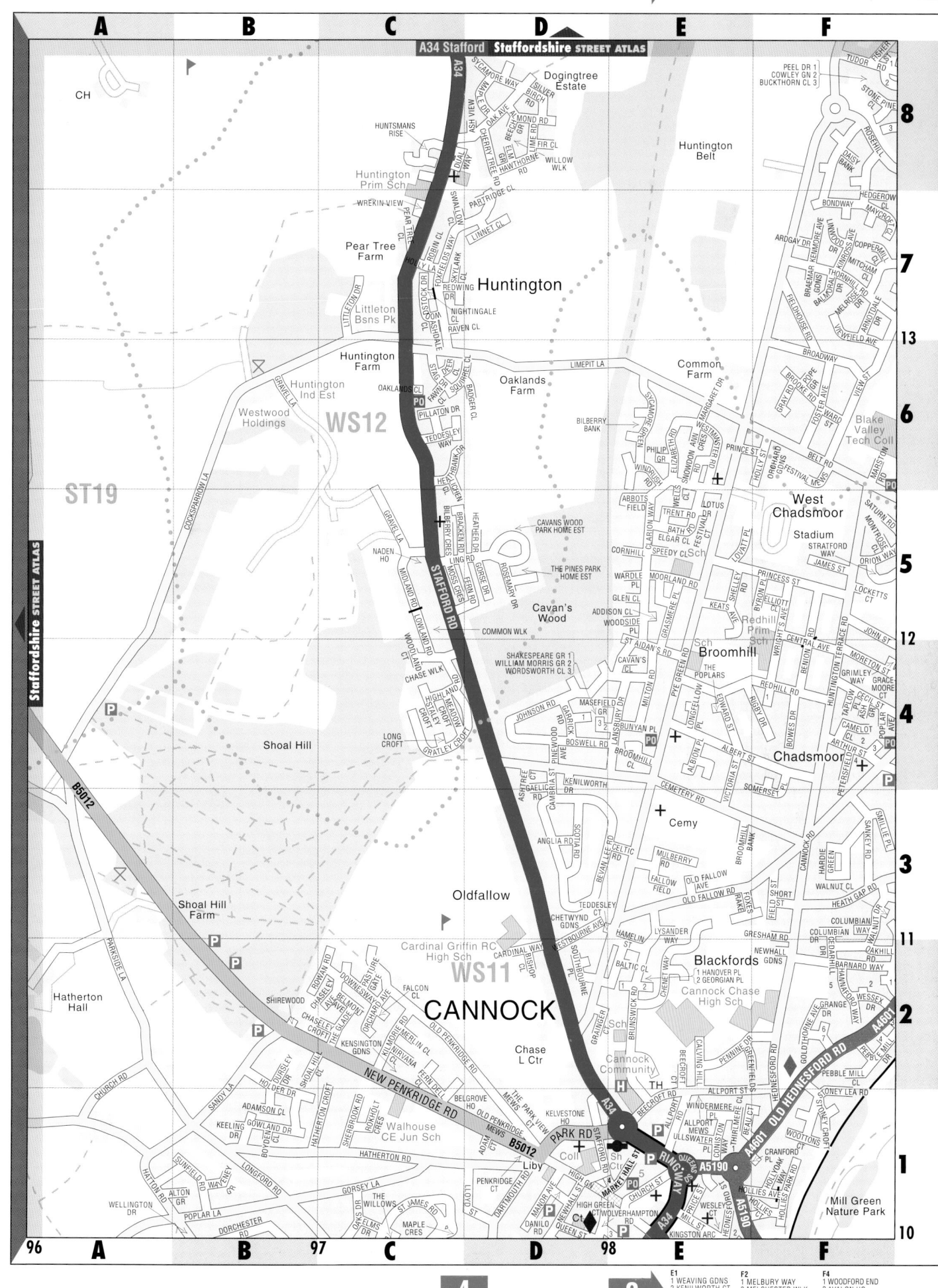

A34 Stafford **Staffordshire** STREET ATLAS

2

4

2

E1
1 WEAVING GDNS
2 KENILWORTH CT
3 BACKCROFTS
4 MARKET PL
5 The Forum

F2
1 MELBURY WAY
2 MELCHESTER WLK
3 STONEYFIELDS CL
4 MILLBROOK CL
5 EXONBURY WLK
6 STRATHMORE PL
7 HAWKESVILLE DR

F4
1 WOODFORD END
2 AVALON HO
3 HORTON CL
4 BETHANY MEWS

A2
1 D'UBERVILLE WLK
2 MARSHWOOD CL
3 RIDINGS BROOK DR
4 THE FIRS MOBILE HOME PK

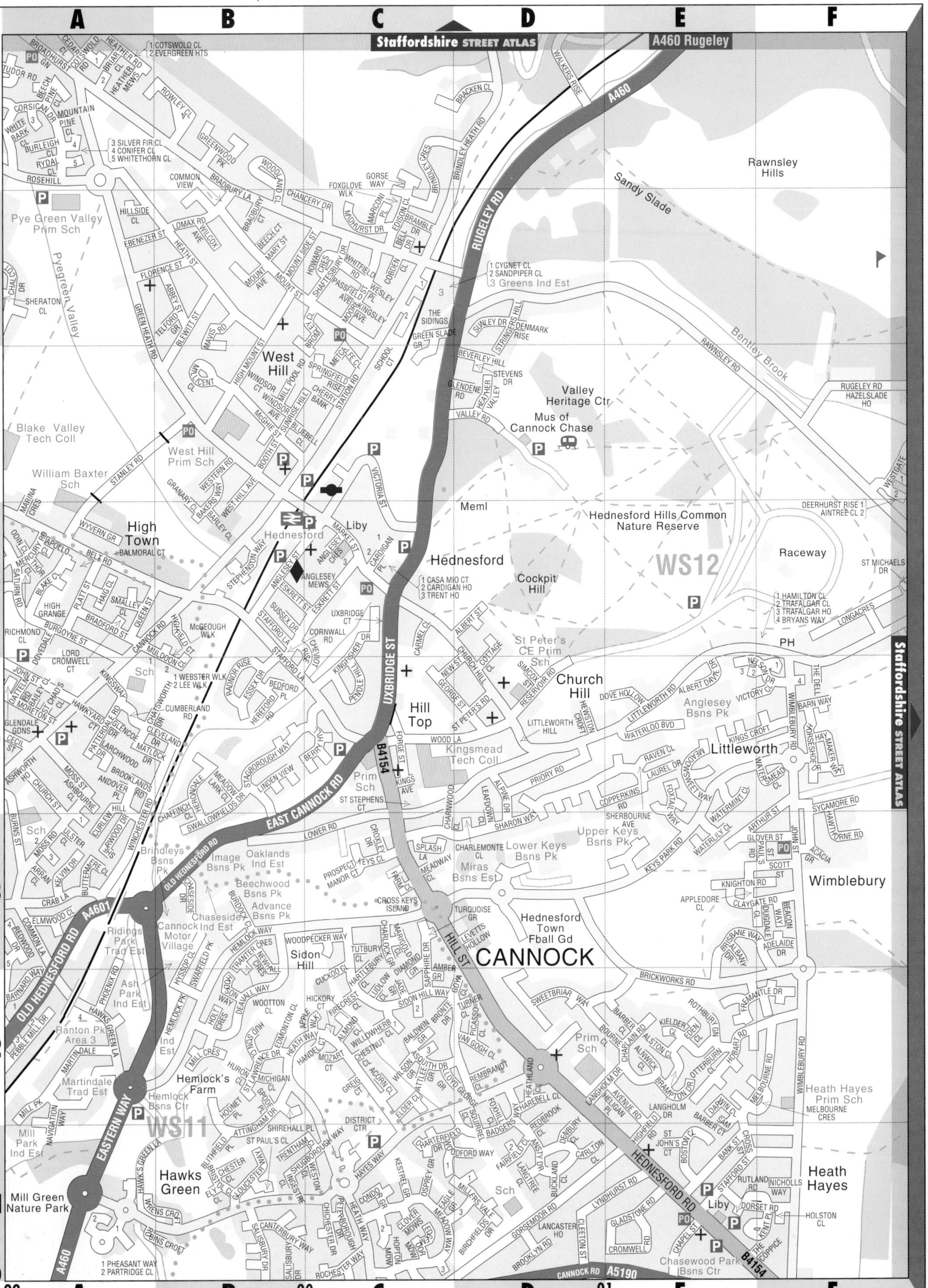

A3
1 GLENDAWN CL
2 PATRICK HO
3 FIRCROFT CL
4 VERMONT GN
5 MEADOW HILL DR

C1
1 WHEATLANDS CL
2 GREEN MDWS
3 BUCKINGHAM PL
C2
1 PRIMROSE MDW
2 ROSE BAY MDW
3 CALLAGHAN GR

D1
1 SPINDLEWOOD CL
2 LAWNSWOOD CL
3 THISTLEDOWN DR

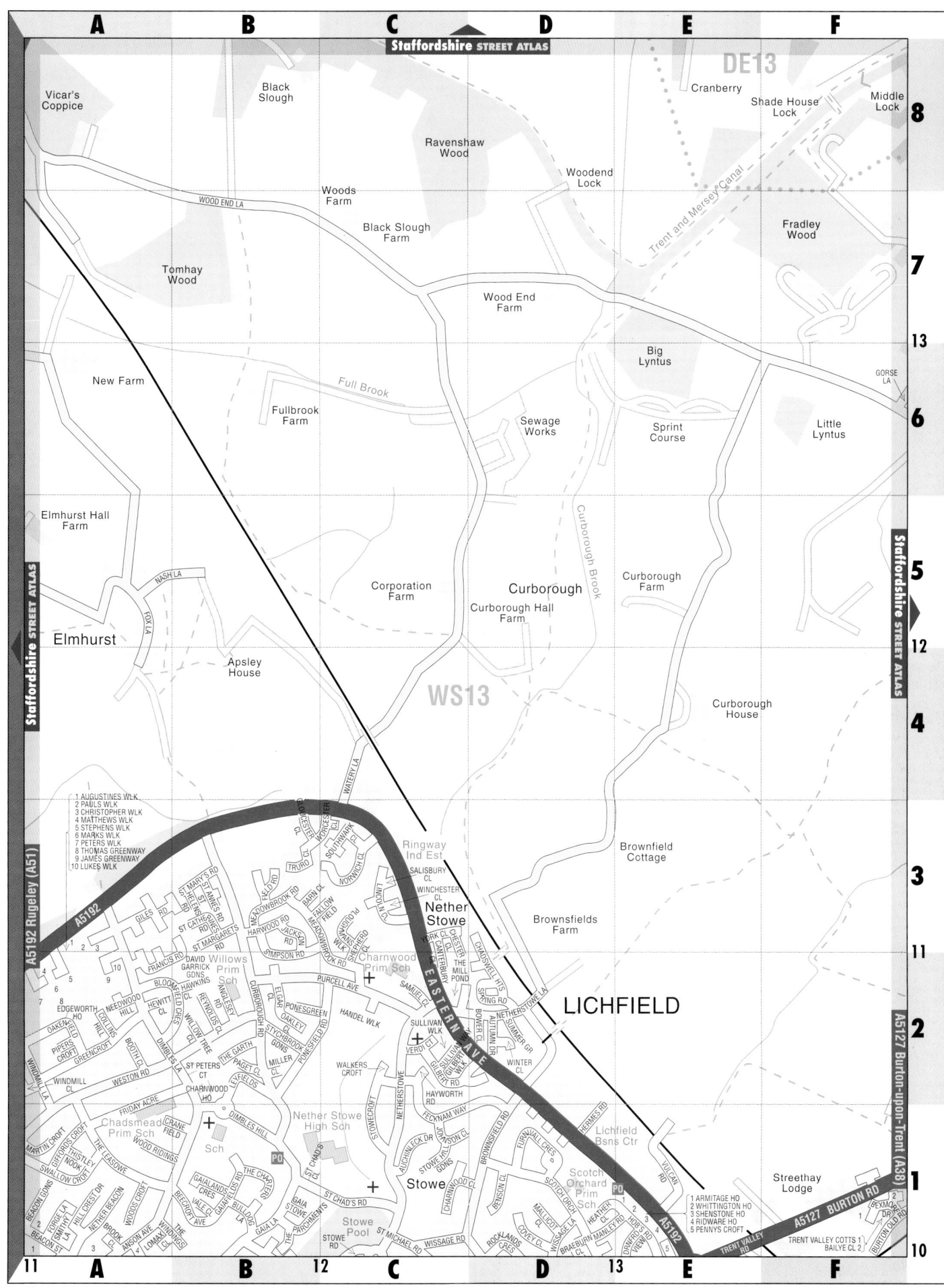

DE13

Cranberry

Shade House
Lock

Middle
Lock

8

Vicar's
Coppice

Black
Slough

Ravenshaw
Wood

Woodend
Lock

Trent and Mersey Canal

Fradley
Wood

WOOD END LA

Woods
Farm

Black Slough
Farm

Wood End
Farm

7

Tomhay
Wood

13

GORSE
LA

New Farm

Full Brook

Big
Lyntus

6

Fullbrook
Farm

Sewage
Works

Sprint
Course

Little
Lyntus

Elmhurst Hall
Farm

NASH LA

Curborough Brook

Curborough
Farm

5

FOX LA

Elmhurst

Corporation
Farm

Curborough

Curborough Hall
Farm

Curborough
House

12

Apsley
House

WS13

4

WATERY LA

Ringway
Ind Est

Brownfield
Cottage

Staffordshire STREET ATLAS

1 AUGUSTINES WLK
2 PAULS WLK
3 CHRISTOPHER WLK
4 MATTHEWS WLK
5 STEPHENS WLK
6 MARKS WLK
7 PETERS WLK
8 THOMAS GREENWAY
9 JAMES GREENWAY
10 LUKES WLK

GLOUCESTER CL

SOUTHWARK

WORCESTER CL

TRURO

NORWICH CL

SALISBURY
CL

WINCHESTER
CL

Nether
Stowe

Brownsfields
Farm

3

A5192 Rugeley (A51)

A5192

ST MARY'S RD

ST JAMES RD

ST HELENS RD

ST CATHERINES RD

GILES RD

MELFORD

MEADOWBROOK RD

FALLOW
FIELD

BARN CL

PLOUGH

SHEPHERD
WLK

YORK CL
CANTERBURY
CL

CHESTER
CL

CHADSWELL HYS

THE
MILL
POND

11

FRANCIS RD

ST MARGARETS
RD

HARWOOD RD

JACKSON
RD

SIMPSON RD

MEADOWBROOK RD

Charnwood
Prim Sch

SAMUEL CL

SPRING RD

NETHERSTOWE LA

David Willows
Prim Sch

GARRICK
GDNS

HEWITT
CL

ANGLESEY

PURCELL AVE

ELGAR

HANDEL WLK

Sullivan
WLK

EASTERN AVE

BOWER CL

LICHFIELD

2

EDGEWORTH
HO

NEEDWOOD
HILL

BLOOMFIELD CRES

HAWKINS

WILLOW TREE CL

OAKLEY

STYCHBROOK GDNS

PONESGREEN

VERDI CT

SULLIVAN
WLK

GILBERT
CT

SUMMER GR

AUTUMN DR

COLLINS
HILL

BOOTH CL

REYNOLDS CL

CURBOROUGH RD

PONESFIELD RD

MILLER
CL

NETHERSTOWE

GILBERT RD

WINTER
CL

PIPERS
CROFT

GREENCROFT

OAKENFIELD

DIMBLES LA

ST PETERS
CT

THE GARTH

PAGET CL

LEYFIELDS

WALKERS
CROFT

NETHERSTOWE

HAYWORTH
RD

TECKNAM WAY

HERMES RD

VULCAN
RD

WINDMILL LA

WESTON RD

CHARNWOOD
HO

FRIDAY ACRE

DIMBLES HILL

Nether Stowe
High Sch

STOWECROFT

STOWE HILL
GDNS

JOHNSON CL

BROWNSFIELD RD

FURALL CRES

Lichfield
Bsns Ctr

Streethay
Lodge

1

MARTIN CROFT

GIFFORDS CROFT

THISTLEY
NOOK

HILL CREST DR

NETHER BEACON

THE LEASOWE

WOOD RIDINGS

CRANE
FIELD

Sch

Chadsmead
Prim Sch

ST CHADS

Scotch
Orchard
Prim
Sch

A5127 Burton-upon-Trent (A38)

BURTON RD

A5127

BEXMORE
DR

BURTON OLD RD

SWALLOW
CROFT

BEACON LDNS

FORGE LA

SMITHY
LA

NETHER BEACON

ANSON AVE

WINDINGS

BROOK

LOMAX CL

WOODS CROFT

VALE CL

GAIALANDS CRES

BEECROFT
AVE

BULLDOG
LA

GAIA LA

ST CHAD'S RD

THE PARCHMENTS

DANFORD

STOWE HILL

Stowe

ROCKLANDS
CRES

AUCHINLECK DR

STOWE HILL
GDNS

BENSON CL

MALLICOT
CL

COVEY CL

SAGE LA

BRAEBURN

MANLEY RD

HEATHER

HOBS
VIEW

Scotch
Orchard
Prim
Sch

Trent Valley
Rd

Armitage Ho
Whittington Ho
Shenstone Ho
Ridware Ho
Pennys Croft

TRENT VALLEY COTTS 1
BAILYE CL 2

A5192

10

BEACON ST

GAIA
STOWE

Stowe
Pool

STOWE
RD

ST MICHAEL RD

WISSAGE RD

1 ARMITAGE HO
2 WHITTINGTON HO
3 SHENSTONE HO
4 RIDWARE HO
5 PENNYS CROFT

PO

PO

A1
1 LANGTON CT
2 CLEAVELAND MEWS
3 LITTLE BARROW WLK
4 DARWIN CL

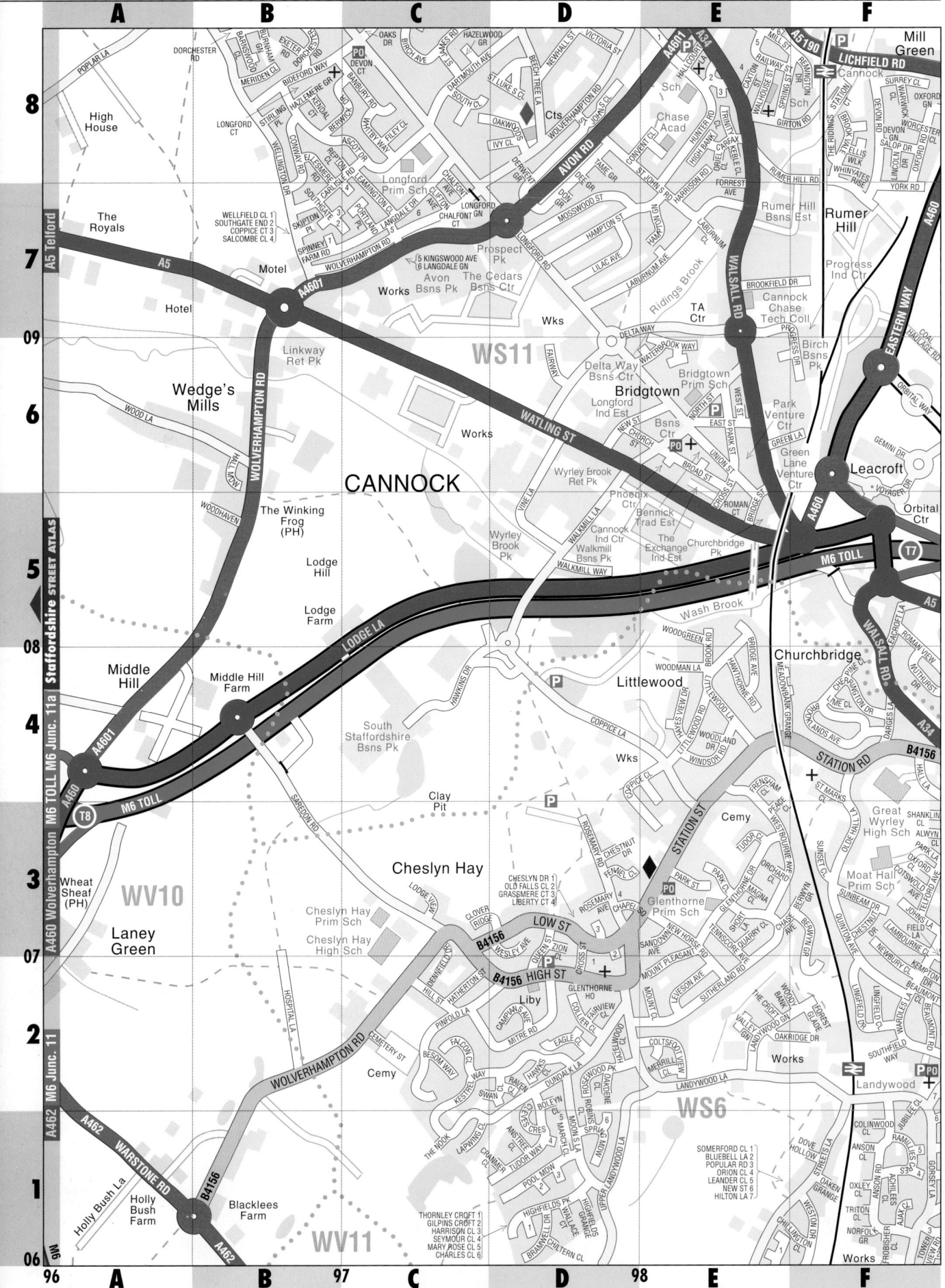

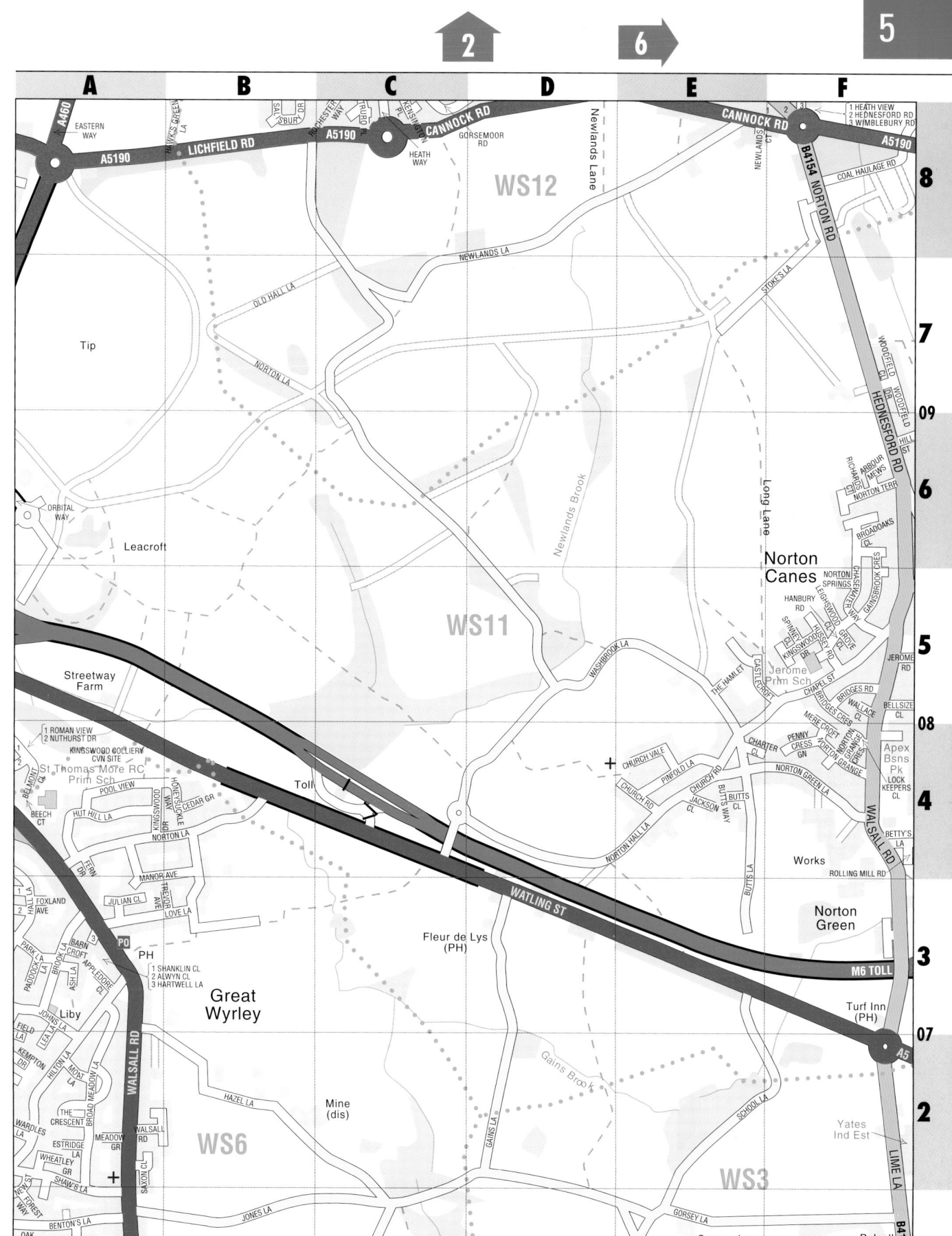

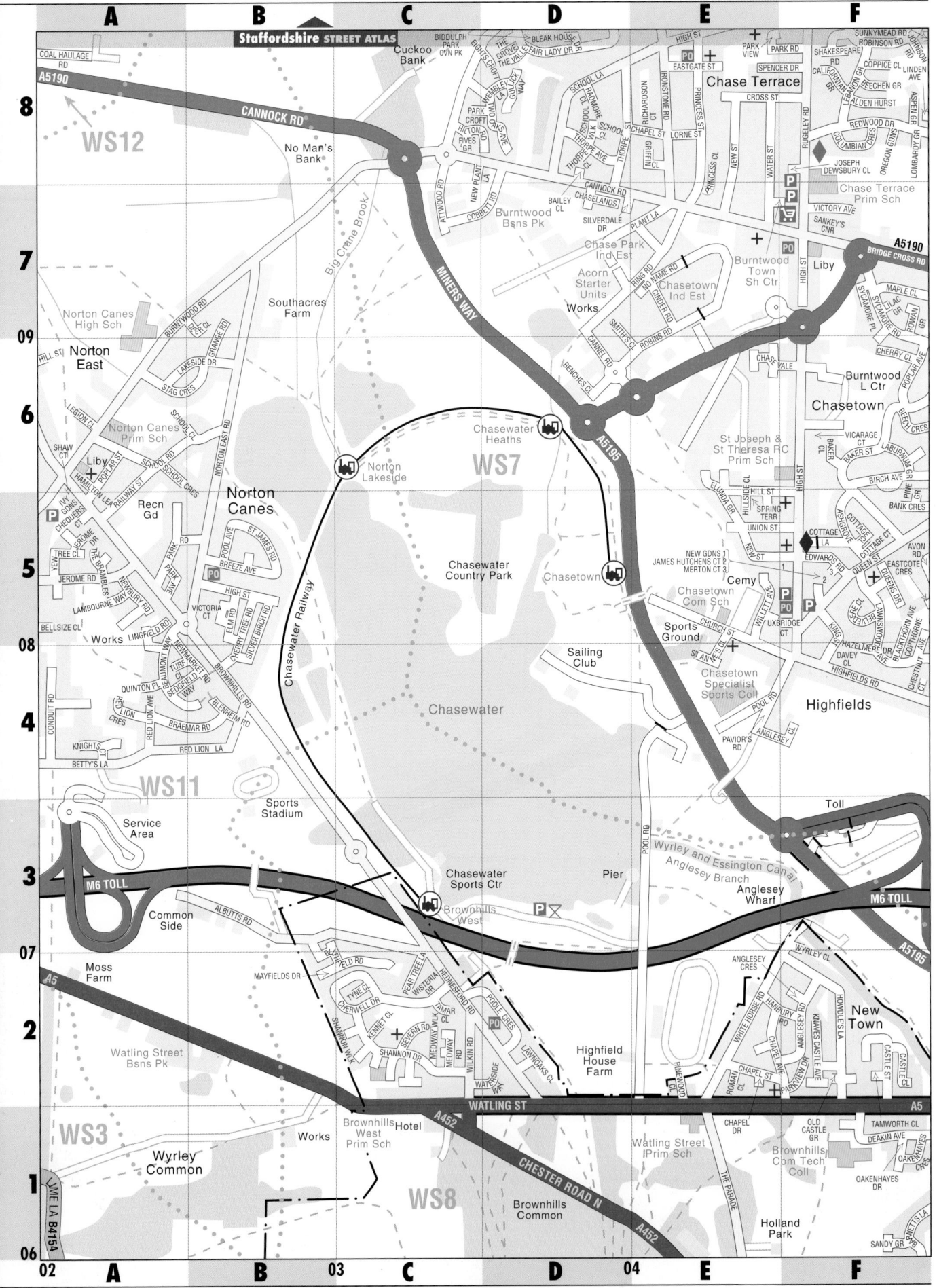

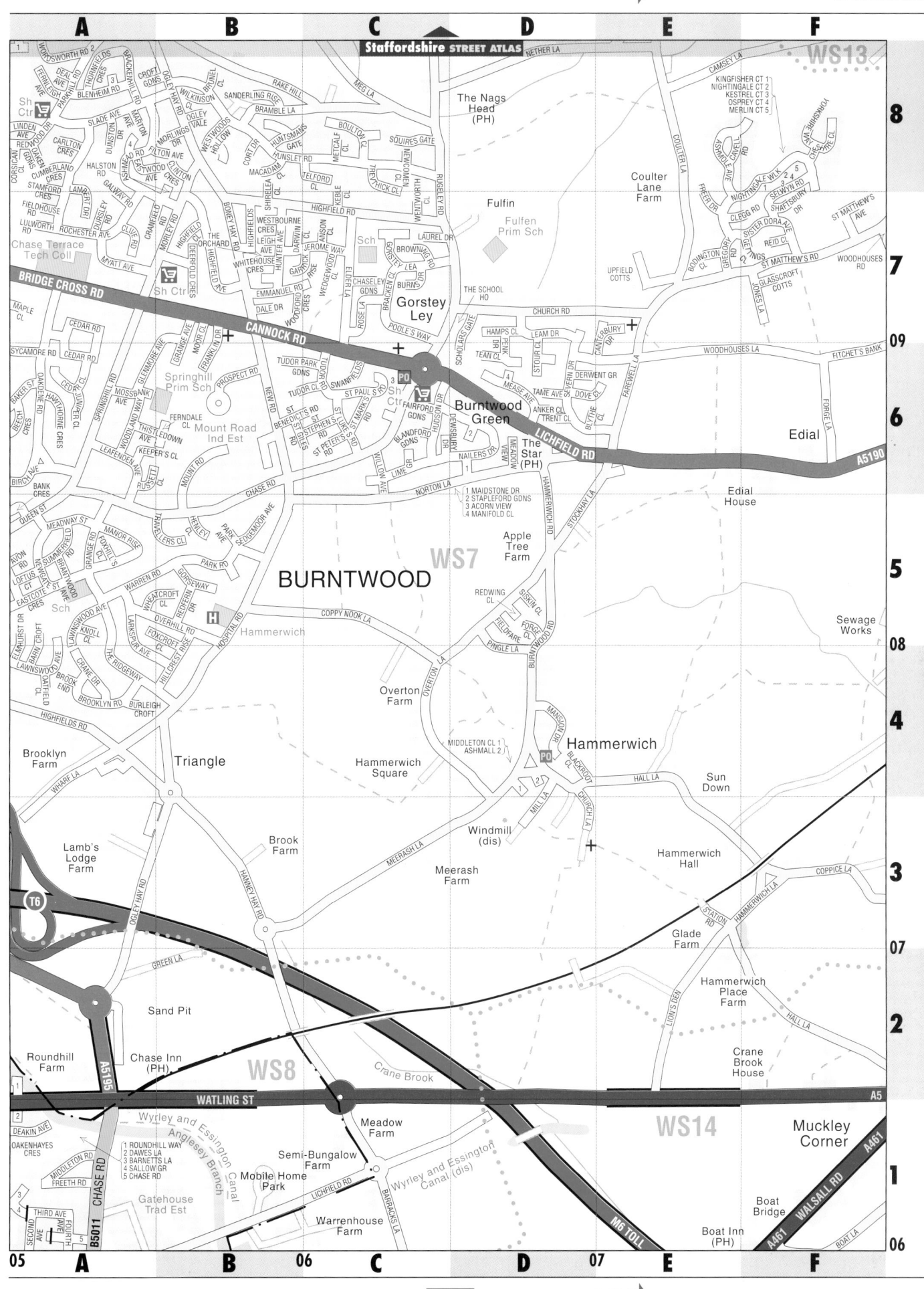

8 →

A8
1 SUNNYMEAD RD
2 SHELLEY RD
3 RYECROFT DR
4 BAMPTON AVE

Staffordshire STREET ATLAS

WS13

A   B   C   D   E   F

KINGFISHER CT 1
NIGHTINGALE CT 2
KESTREL CT 3
OSPREY CT 4
MERLIN CT 5

The Nags
Head
(PH)

Coulter
Lane
Farm

8

Fulfin

Fulfen
Prim Sch

7

Chase Terrace
Tech Coll

BRIDGE CROSS RD

CANNOCK RD

Gorstey
Ley

The School
HO

Upfield
Cotts

CHURCH RD

WOODHOUSES LA

FITCHET'S BANK

09

Springhill
Prim Sch

Mount Road
Ind Est

Burntwood
Green

LICHFIELD RD

Edial

A5190

6

1 MAIDSTONE DR
2 STAPLEFORD GDNS
3 ACORN VIEW
4 MANIFOLD CL

The
Star
(PH)

Edial
House

Apple
Tree
Farm

WS7

BURNTWOOD

5

Hammerwich

COPPY NOOK LA

REDWING
CL

Sewage
Works

08

Brooklyn
Farm

Triangle

Overton
Farm

Hammerwich
Square

MIDDLETON CL 1
ASHMALL 2

Hammerwich

Sun
Down

HALL LA

4

Lamb's
Lodge
Farm

T6

Brook
Farm

MEERASH LA

Meerash
Farm

Windmill
(dis)

Hammerwich
Hall

COPPICE LA

3

GREEN LA

STATION
RD

Glade
Farm

07

Sand Pit

LION'S DEN

HALL LA

Hammerwich
Place
Farm

2

Roundhill
Farm

Chase Inn
(PH)

A5195

WS8

Crane Brook

WS14

Crane
Brook
House

Muckley
Corner

A461

WATLING ST

Meadow
Farm

Wyrley and Essington
Canal

Anglesey
Branch

1 ROUNDHILL WAY
2 DAWES LA
3 BARNETTS LA
4 SALLOW GR
5 CHASE RD

Semi-Bungalow
Farm

Mobile Home
Park

Wyrley and Essington
Canal (dis)

M6 TOLL

WALSALL RD

Boat
Bridge

A461

1

DEAKIN AVE

OAKENHAYES
CRES

MIDDLETON RD

CHASE RD

FREETH RD

B5011

Gatehouse
Trad Est

Warrenhouse
Farm

LICHFIELD RD

BARRACKS LA

Boat Inn
(PH)

BOAT LA

06

SECOND AVE
THIRD AVE

05   A   B   06   C   D   07   E   F

↓ 16

8 →

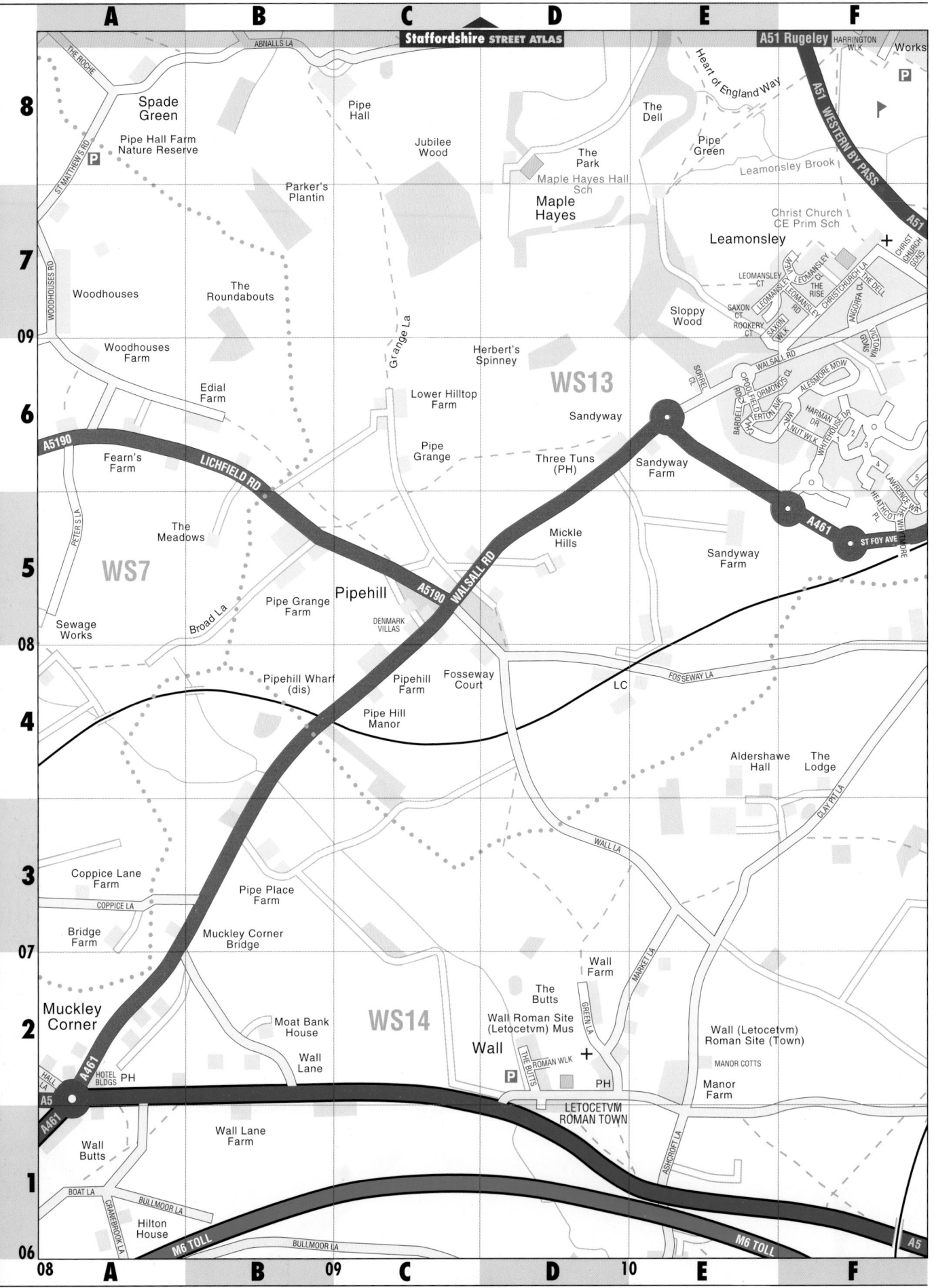

F6
1 BROADBENT CL
2 CATERBANCK WAY
3 COLLINS DR
4 MADDOCKE WLK
5 ALLINGTON AVE

Staffordshire STREET ATLAS

A51 Rugeley

HARRINGTON WLK

Works

A51 WESTERN BY PASS

Spade Green

Pipe Hall Farm
Nature Reserve

St MATTHEW S RD

THE ROCHE

Pipe
Hall

Jubilee
Wood

The Dell

Heart of England Way

Pipe
Green

Leamonsley Brook

Christ Church
CE Prim Sch

A51

CHRIST CHURCH GDNS

The Park

Maple Hayes Hall
Sch

Maple
Hayes

Leamonsley

LEOMANSLEY CT
LEOMANSLEY WLK
LEOMANSLEY
LEOMANSLEY PK
LEOMANSLEY RD
THE RISE
THE DELL
CHRISTCHURCH LA

Parker's
Plantin

WOODHOUSES RD

Woodhouses

The
Roundabouts

Sloppy Wood

SAXON CT
ROOKERY CT
SAXON WLK

ANGORRA CL
VICTORIA
VICTORIA GDNS

Woodhouses
Farm

Grange La

Herbert's
Spinney

WS13

WALSALL RD
SORREL CL
BARDELL CROFT
MIDDLETON CL
ORMONDS CL
EVERTON AVE
ALESMORE MDW
HARMAN DR
KNUT WLK
WHITEHOUSES DR
WATERLOO CL

Edial
Farm

Lower Hilltop
Farm

Sandyway

Pipe
Grange

Three Tuns
(PH)

Sandyway
Farm

HEATHCOT PL
LAWRENCE WAY
THE WHITMORE

A461

St FOY AVE

A5190

LICHFIELD RD

Fearn's
Farm

PETER S LA

The
Meadows

Mickle
Hills

WALSALL RD

Sandyway
Farm

WS7

Pipehill

Pipe Grange
Farm

DENMARK
VILLAS

A5190

Broad La

Sewage
Works

Pipehill Wharf
(dis)

Pipehill
Farm

Fosseway
Court

LC

FOSSEWAY LA

Pipe Hill
Manor

Aldershawe
Hall

The
Lodge

CLAY PIT LA

Coppice Lane
Farm

Pipe Place
Farm

WALL LA

Wall La

COPPICE LA

Bridge
Farm

Muckley Corner
Bridge

Wall
Farm

MARKET LA

GREEN LA

Muckley
Corner

A461

HOTEL
BLDGS
PH

Moat Bank
House

WS14

The
Butts

Wall Roman Site
(Letocetvm) Mus

Wall (Letocetvm)
Roman Site (Town)

MANOR COTTS

HALL LA

A5

Wall
Lane

THE BUTTS
ROMAN WLK

Wall

PH

Manor
Farm

Wall
Butts

Wall Lane
Farm

LETOCETVM
ROMAN TOWN

ASHCROFT LA

BOAT LA

BULLMOOR LA

Hilton
House

CRANEBROOK LA

M6 TOLL

BULLMOOR LA

M6 TOLL

A5

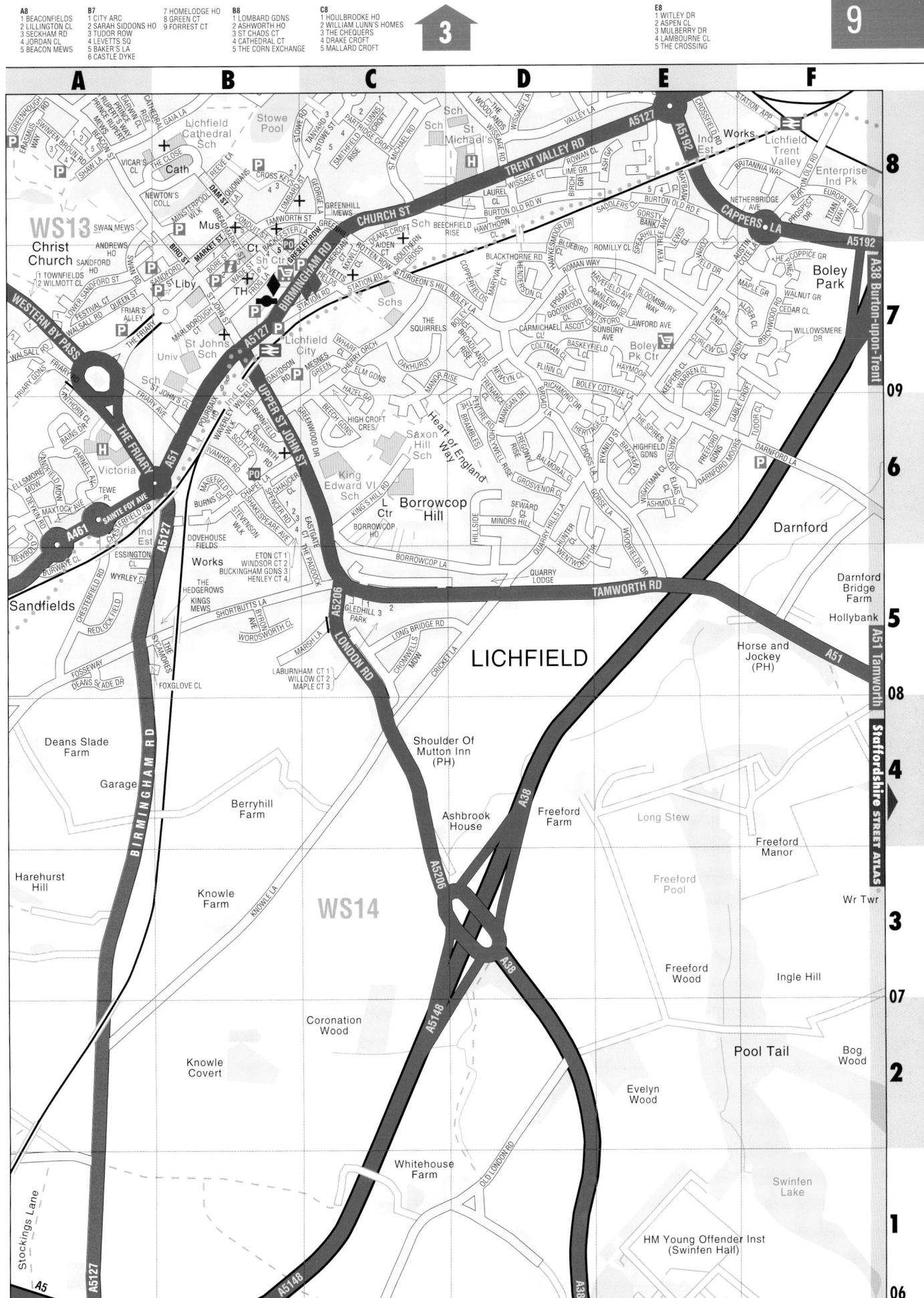

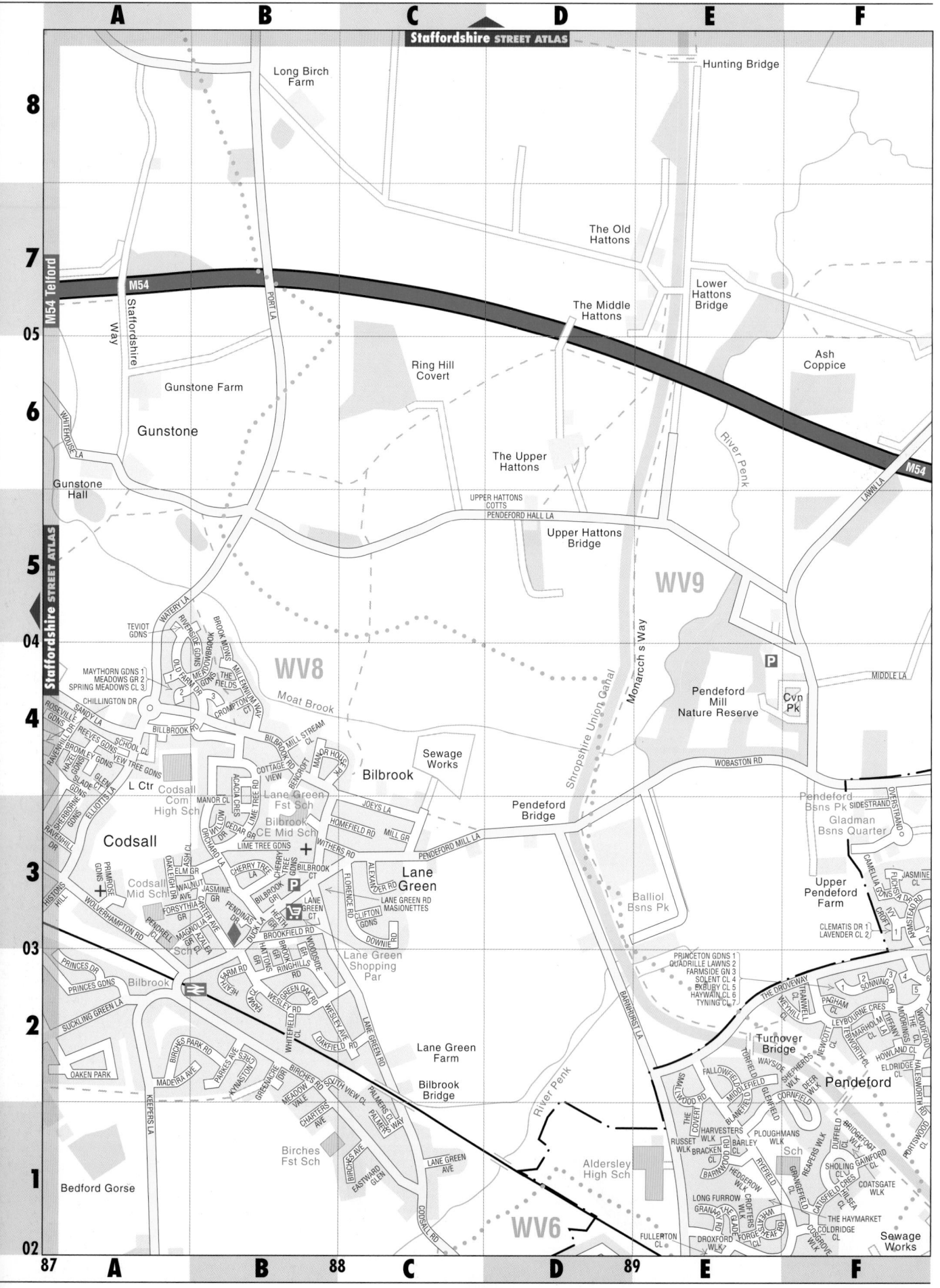

A B C D E F

8
7
05
6
5
04
4
03
3
03
2
1
02

87 A 88 B C 88 D 89 E F

Staffordshire STREET ATLAS

M54 Telford

Hunting Bridge

Long Birch Farm

The Old Hattons

Lower Hattons Bridge

The Middle Hattons

M54

Staffordshire Way

Ash Coppice

Ring Hill Covert

River Penk

Gunstone Farm

Gunstone

WV9

The Upper Hattons

WHITEHOUSE LA

Gunstone Hall

UPPER HATTONS COTTS
PENDEFORD HALL LA

Upper Hattons Bridge

Pendeford Mill Nature Reserve

Cvn Pk

MIDDLE LA

WATERY LA

TEVIOT GDNS

WV8

Moat Brook

Monarch's Way

P

MAYTHORN GDNS 1
MEADOWS GR 2
SPRING MEADOWS CL 3
CHILLINGTON DR

OLD FARM DR

MILLENNIUM WAY
THE FIELDS
CROMPTON CT

Sewage Works

Shropshire Union Canal

WOBASTON RD

Pendeford Bsns Pk
SIDESTRAND

Gladman Bsns Quarter

SANDY LA

ROSEVILLE GDNS
REEVES GDNS
BROMLEY GDNS
GLEN GDNS
SLADE GDNS
ELLIOTTS GDNS
SHERBORNE GDNS
RAVENHILL DR

SCHOOL CL

BILLBROOK RD

L Ctr
Codsall Com High Sch

MANOR CL

LIME TREE RD

ACACIA GDNS

BILLBROOK MDWS
MILL STREAM

COTTAGE VIEW

BENCROFT

MANOR HOUSE LA

Bilbrook

Lane Green Fst Sch

JOEYS LA

Pendeford Bridge

OVERSTRAND

CAMELIA LA

Upper Pendeford Farm

FUCHSIA CL
JASMINE CL
AMBER DR
CROFT

Codsall

CEDAR GR

Bilbrook CE Mid Sch

LIME TREE GDNS

HOMEFIELD RD

MILL GR

WITHERS RD

PENDEFORD MILL LA

Balliol Bsns Pk

CLEMATIS DR 1
LAVENDER CL 2

HISTONS HILL

PRIMROSE GDNS

Codsall Mid Sch

ELM GR
WALNUT
JASMINE AVE
FORSYTHIA GR

CHERRY TREE LA

OAK LEIGH DR

BILLBROOK GR
CHERRY TREE GDNS

CARTER AVE

Lane Green

ALEXANDER RD

LANE GREEN RD MAISONETTES

CLIFTON GDNS

WOLVERHAMPTON RD

PENDRELL CL

MAGNOLIA GR

PENDINAS DR

AZALEA GR

DUKA LA

BROOKFIELD RD

WOODSIDE

DOWNIE

FLORENCE RD

PRINCETON GDNS 1
QUADRILLE LAWNS 2
FARMSIDE GN 3
SOLENT CL 4
EXBURY CL 5
HAYWAIN CL 6
TYNING CL 7

SONNING

THE DROVEWAY

MEXHILL

PAGHAM

PRINCES DR
PRINCES GDNS

Bilbrook

HEATH FARM RD

FARM RD

RINGHILLS RD

Lane Green Shopping Par

BRANDHURST LA

TRANWELL

LEYBOURNE CRES

TIFFANY LA
TENWORTH

Turnover Bridge

WOODFORD
THE CL
MOORINGS

NEWCOTT

HALESWORTH RD

Pendeford

SUCKLING GREEN LA

BIRCHES PARK RD

PARKS AVE

ASH CL

KYNASTON

WESLEY DR

WESLEY RD

WHITEFIELD CL

GREEN OAK RD

OAKFIELD

LANE GREEN RD

Lane Green Farm

SHEPHERDS WLK

WAYSIDE

SMALL CL

FALLOWFIELD

TORFIELD
GLENFIELD

MIDDLEFIELD

BLANEFIELD
CORNFIELD

DEEP WLK

MARHOLM

HOWLAND CL

ELDRIDGE CL

MADEIRA AVE

GREENACRE DR

BIRCHES RD

MEADOW VALE

SOUTH VIEW CL

PALMERS CL

PALMERS WAY

PALMERS CL

Bilbrook Bridge

River Penk

Bilbrook Bridge

THE COVERT

HARVESTERS

RUSSET WLK

BARLEY

BRACKEN

PLOUGHMANS WLK

REAPERS WLK

SHOLING GAINFORD CL

DUFFIELD

BRIDGEFOOT

Sch

CHELSEA

COATSGATE WLK

Oaken Park

KEEPERS LA

CHARTERS AVE

BOBBIN AVE

EASTWARD GLEN

Birches Fst Sch

CODSALL RD

LANE GREEN AVE

Aldersley High Sch

LONG FURROW

GRANARY RD

THE GLADE

BARNFIELD

HEDGEROW WLK

CROFTERS WLK

RYEFIELD

THE FORGE

CATSHILL

COSGROVE WLK

GRANGEFIELD CL

COLDRIDGE CL

THE HAYMARKET

PORTSWOOD

Bedford Gorse

WV6

FULLERTON CL

DROXFORD WLK

Sewage Works

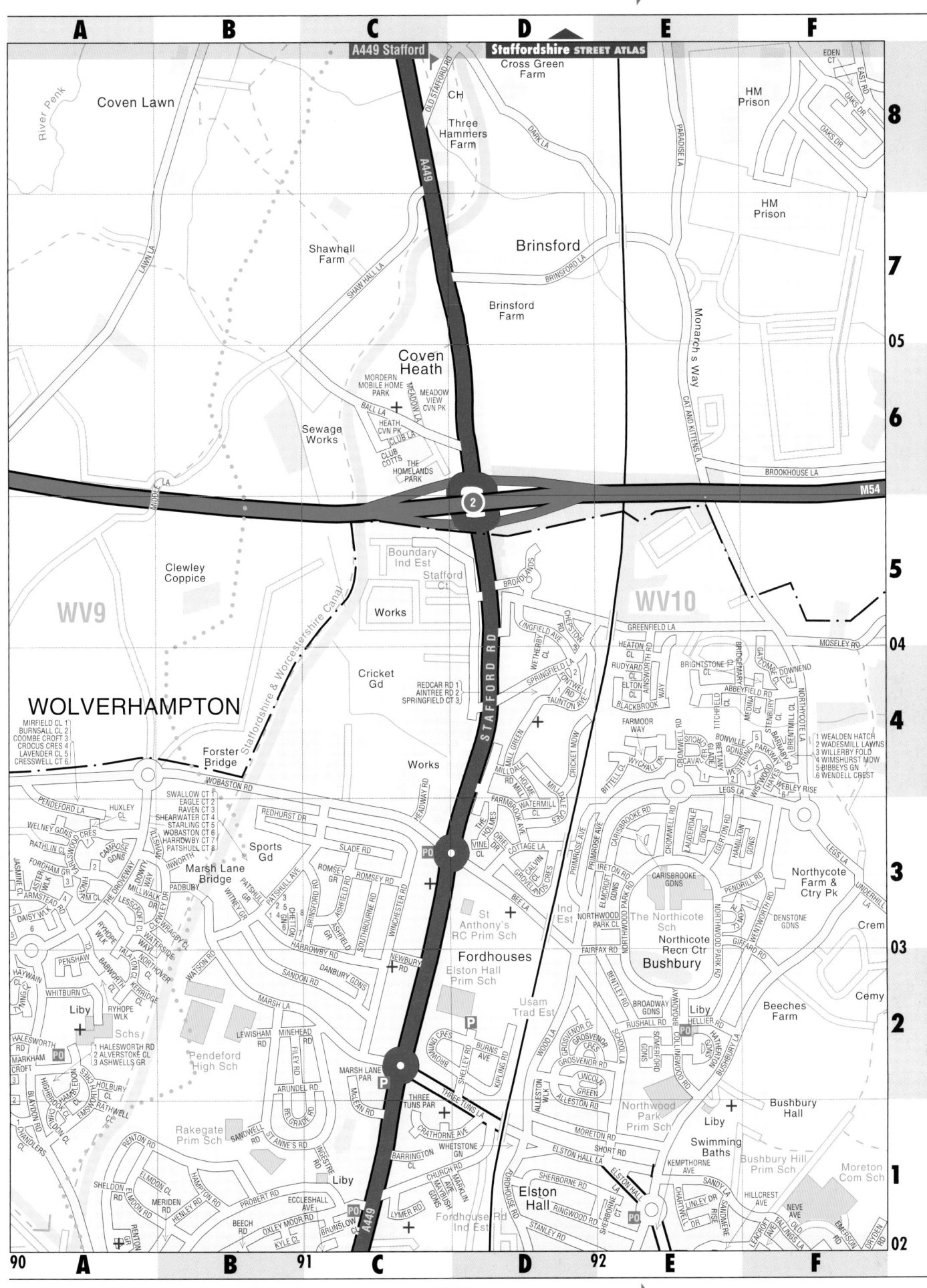

A449 Stafford

Staffordshire STREET ATLAS

Cross Green Farm

HM Prison

8

CH

Three Hammers Farm

HM Prison

Coven Lawn

River Penk

Shawhall Farm

Brinsford

7

Brinsford La

05

Brinsford Farm

LAWN LA

SHAW HALL LA

Coven Heath

Monarch s Way

6

MORDERN MOBILE HOME PARK

MEADOW VIEW CVN PK

CAT AND KITTENS LA

Sewage Works

HEATH CVN PK

CLUB LA

BROOKHOUSE LA

CLUB COTTS

THE HOMELANDS PARK

M54

MIDDLE LA

PARADISE LA

2

Clewley Coppice

5

WV9

Boundary Ind Est

WV10

Stafford Cl

BROADLANDS

GREENFIELD LA

MOSELEY RD

04

Works

CHEPSTON

HEATON CL

BRIGHTSTONE CL

DOWNEND

Cricket Gd

LINGFIELD AVE

RUDYARD CL

AINSWORTH

ABBEYFIELD RD

NORTHCOTE LA

1 WEALDEN HATCH
2 WADESMILL LAWNS
3 WILLERBY FOLD
4 WIMSHURST MDW
5 BIBBEYS GN
6 WENDELL CREST

4

REDCAR RD 1
AINTREE RD 2
SPRINGFIELD CT 3

WETHERBY LA

SPRINGFIELD LA

FONTWELL

ELTON CL

TITCHFIELD

STENBURY CL

BRENTMILL CL

WOLVERHAMPTON

MIRFIELD CL 1
BURNSALL CL 2
COOMBE CROFT 3
CROCUS CRES 4
LAVENDER CL 5
CRESSWELL CT 6

STAFFORD RD

FARMOOR WAY

BLACKBROOK

BONVILLE GDNS

BETTANY GLADE

CRESSWELL

WESTERING

WEBLEY RISE

Staffordshire & Worcestershire Canal

Forster Bridge

MILL GREEN

TAUNTON AVE

CRICKET MDW

HAYES

LEGS LA

WOBASTON RD

MILL DALE CRES

WATERMILL CL

CROMWELL RD

LAUDERDALE

HAMILTON

Northycote Farm & Ctry Pk

3

PENDEFORD LA

SWALLOW CT 1
EAGLE CT 2
RAVEN CT 3
SHEARWATER CT 4
STARLING CT 5
WOBASTON CT 6
HARROWBY CT 7
PATSHULL CT 8

REDHURST DR

MILLDALE RD

HOLME MILL

FARMBROOK AVE

THE HOLMES

ORIEL CL

VINE CL

COTTAGE LA

CALVIN

PRIMROSE AVE

PRIMROSE LA

CARISBROOKE RD

CARISBROOKE GDNS

PENDRILL RD

DENSTONE GDNS

UNDERHILL LA

LEGS LA

WELNEY GDNS

HUXLEY CL

Sports Gd

SLADE RD

ROMSEY RD

BEE LA

ELSTON HALL

The Northicote Sch

Crem

RATHLIN CL

CAMROSE GDNS

Marsh Lane Bridge

PATSHULL

ASHFIELD

WINCHESTER RD

GROVELANDS CRES

IRETON RD

ELMCROFT GDNS

NORTHWOOD PARK RD

NORTHWOOD PARK CL

Ind Est

FAIRFAX RD

Northicote Recn Ctr

GIRFARD RD

Bushbury

03

JASMINE CL

ARMSTEAD

FORDHAM GR

THE DROVEWAY

MILLWALK DR

INWORTH

PADBURY

BRINSFORD RD

CHETTON

HARROWBY RD

SOUTHBOURNE RD

NEWBURY RD

St Anthony's RC Prim Sch

Fordhouses

Elston Hall Prim Sch

BROADWAY GDNS

Liby

HELLIER RD

NORTHWOOD PARK RD

WHITWORTH RD

Cemy

Beeches Farm

2

DAISY WLK

THE LESSCROFT

WRAGBY CL

WATSON RD

DANBURY GDNS

SANDON RD

MARSH LA

Usam Trad Est

RUSHALL RD

SOMERFORD GDNS

COLLINGWOOD DR

HATHERTON

BISSBURY LA

Bushbury Hall

PENSHAW

TALON CT

KERRIDGE

LEWISHAM RD

MINEHEAD RD

GROSVENOR CL

GROSVENOR CRES

SCHOOL LA

Northwood Park Prim Sch

Liby

HAYWAIN CL

BABWORTH

RYHOPE WLK

NORTHOVER

FILEY RD

P

WOOD LA

LINCOLN GREEN

ALLESTON WLK

ALLESTON RD

Swimming Baths

Bushbury Hill Prim Sch

Moreton Com Sch

1

WHITBURN CL

Liby

RYHOPE WLK

Schs

1 HALESWORTH RD
2 ALVERSTOKE CL
3 ASHWELLS GR

Pendeford High Sch

BELGRAVE

Rakegate Prim Sch

SANDWELL

ST ANNE'S RD

INGESTRE RD

Liby

MCLEAN RD

Marsh Lane Par

THREE TUNS PAR

CRATHORNE AVE

WHETSTONE GN

MORETON RD

SHORT RD

ELSTON HALL LA

KEMPTHORNE AVE

SANDY LA

HILLCREST AVE

NEVE AVE

HALESWORTH RD

MARKHAM CROFT

PO

HOLBURY CL

RATHWELL

HIGHBROOK CL

CHAMELEDON

HELDON CL

BLAXTON CL

EMSCOTE

RENTON RD

SHELDON RD

ELMDON CL

MERIDEN RD

HAMPTON RD

PROBERT RD

ECCLESHALL AVE

BARRINGTON CL

MARKLIN AVE

CHURCH RD

SHERBORNE RD

RINGWOOD RD

STANLEY RD

SHERBORNE RD

LINLEY DR

CHARTWELL

RISE

SANDMERE

HILLCREST AVE

Elston Hall

PO

LACROFT

FALLINGS LA

OLD FALLINGS LA

EMERSON RD

DRYDEN RD

02

CHANDLERS

A449

BRUNSLOW

LYMER RD

MAYBUSH GDNS

Fordhouse Rd Ind Est

90

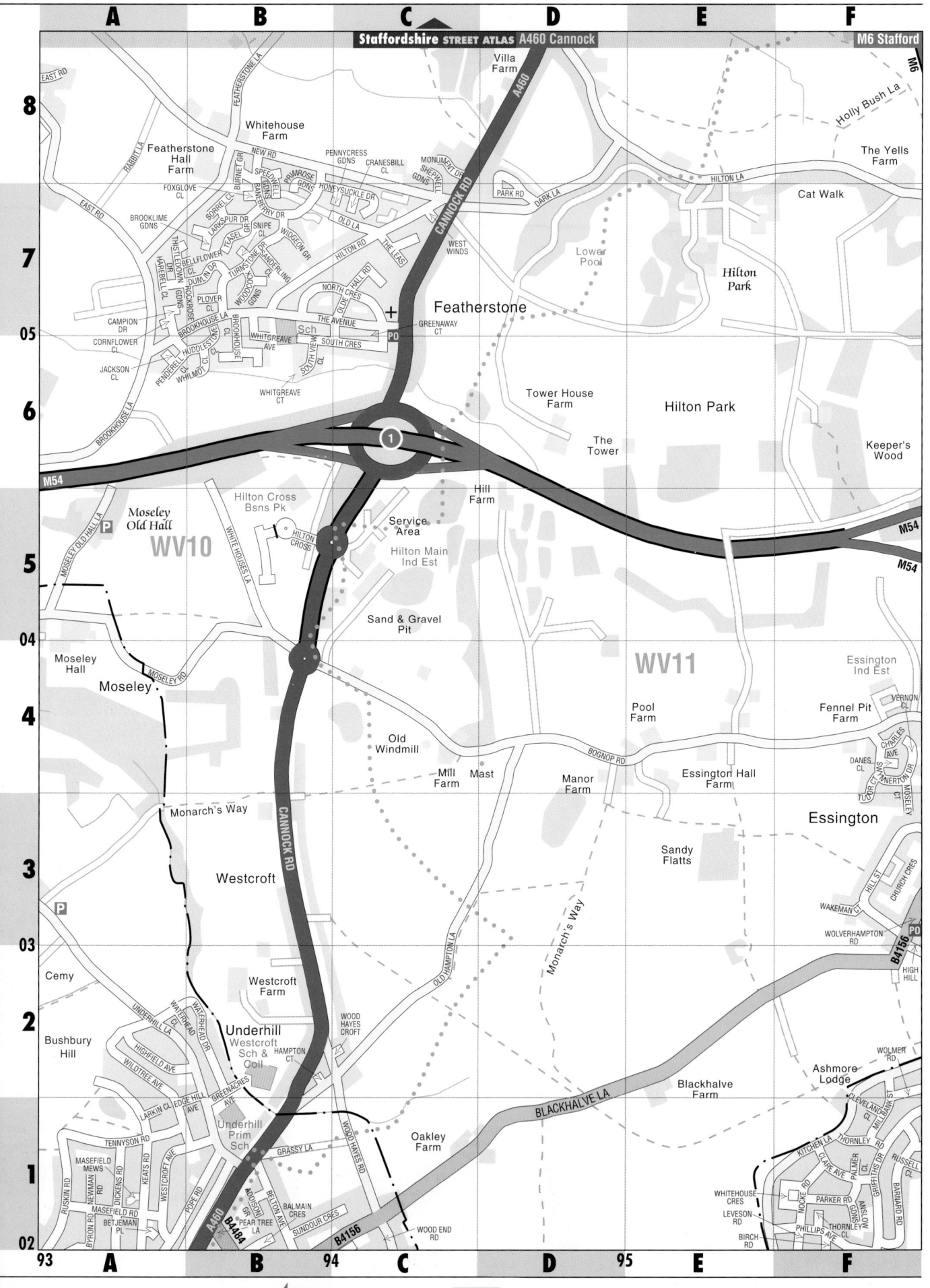

Staffordshire STREET ATLAS A460 Cannock

M6 Stafford

A B C D E F

WV10

Works

Warstone

Sewage
Wks

Hilton La

Hilton Park
Service Areas

Clay
Pit

Ride
Farm

Burns
Wood

Holly Bank
Farm

Mast

Chapel
Farm

Springhill

PH

Springhill
Covert

WV11

CH

Wood Farm
Golf Range

School
Farm

St John's CE
Prim Sch

PH

COXMOOR CL 1
TREVOSE CL 2
COALMEADOW CL 3
ROMSEY WAY 4
BOLTON WAY 5
FURNESS CL 6
TURNBERRY RD 7
FOUNTAINS WAY 8
PERSHORE WAY 9
EASBY WAY 10
MARGAM WAY 11
MARGAM TERR 12
GLASTONBURY WAY 13
SNEYD HALL RD 14

Bloxwich
North

Abbey
Prim Sch

Sneyd
Farm

Mast

WITHYWOOD CL 1
BROCKERIDGE CL 2
FALCONDALE RD 3
CRANLEIGH CL 4
DORCHESTER RD 5
DORCHESTER CL 6
FAIRLAWN WAY 7
ARGYLL CT 8

Holly
Bank
House

Ashmore
Park

Farbrook
Farm

Sneyd
Com Sch

BLOXWICH

Sneyd
Resr

WV12

Somerford
Cl

Landywood
Ent Pk

Holly
Hill

Landywood
Prim Sch

LILAC LA 1
PENNY CT 2

Upper
Landywood

WS6

The White
House

Long Lane
Bridge

WS3

Sneyd
Ho

96 A 97 B C 98 D E F

8
7
05
6
5
04
4
3
03
2
1
02

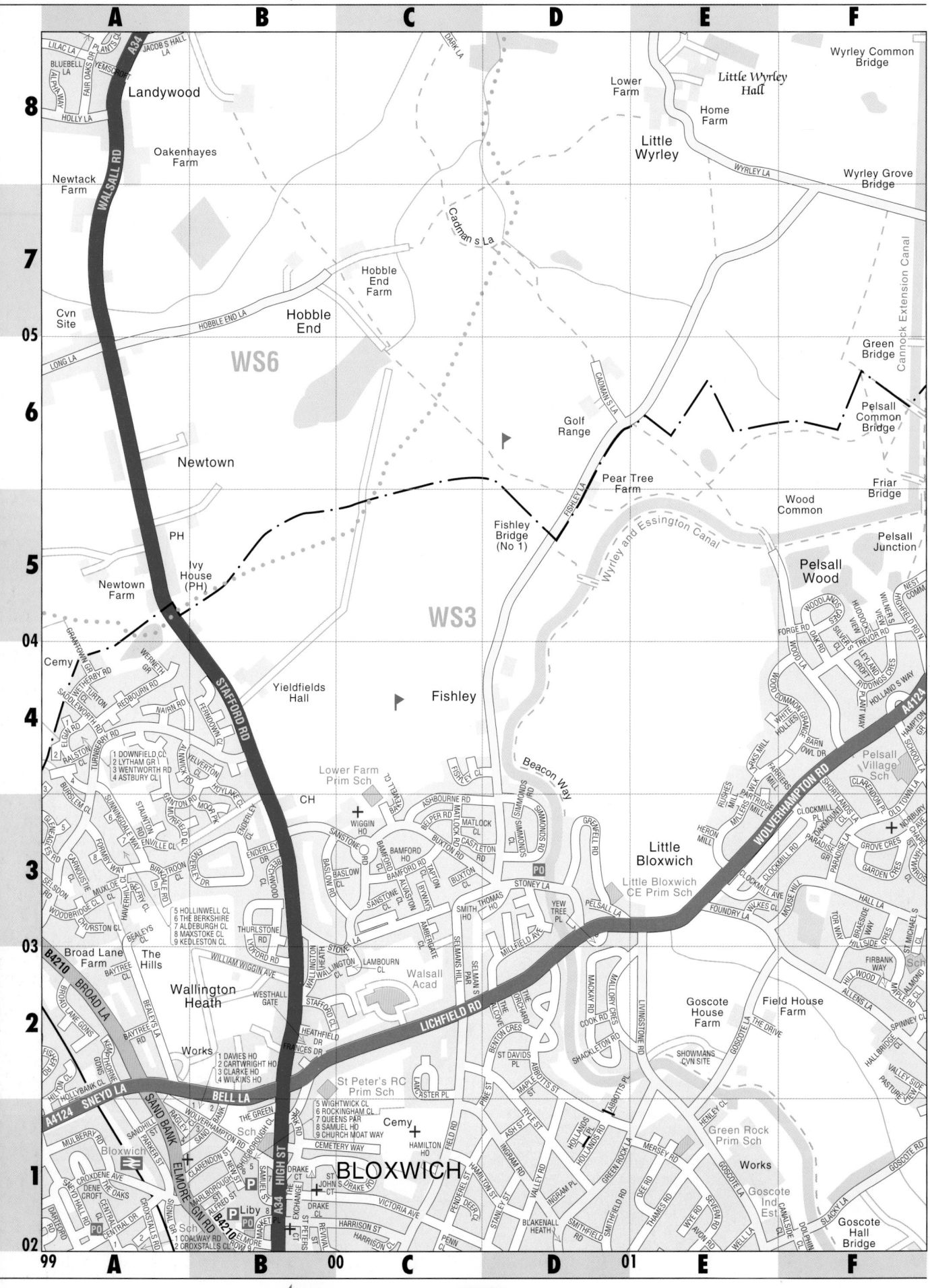

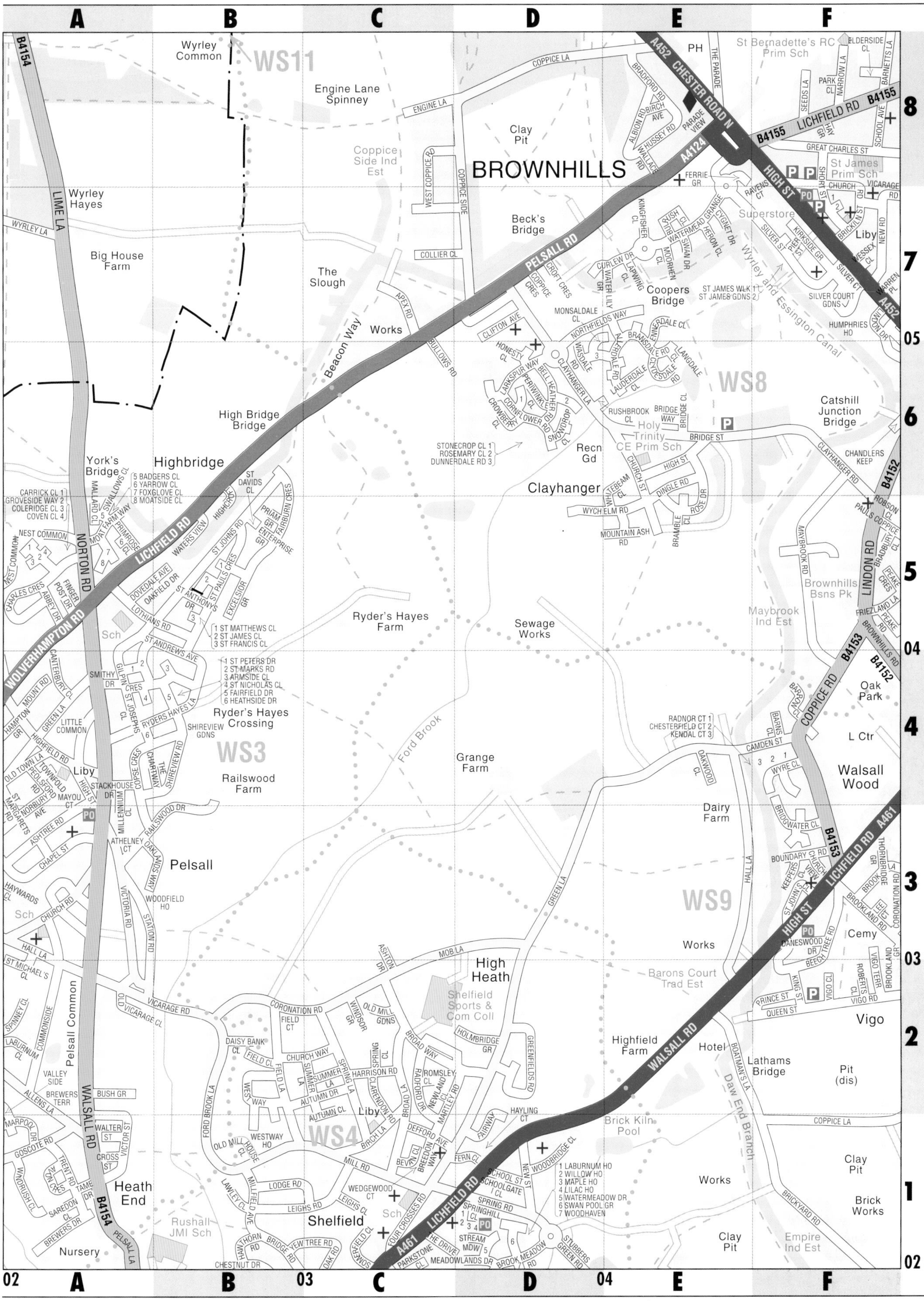

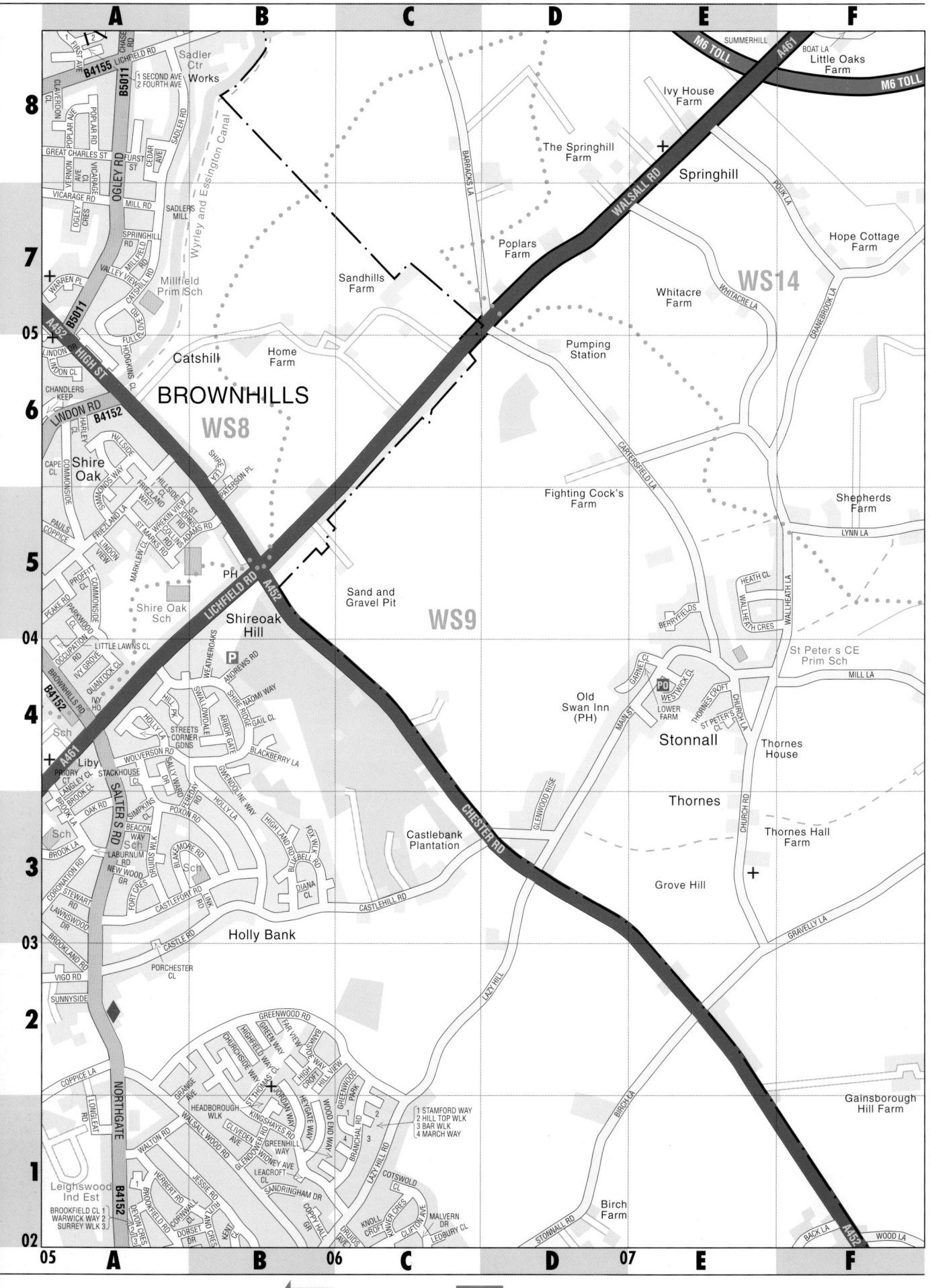

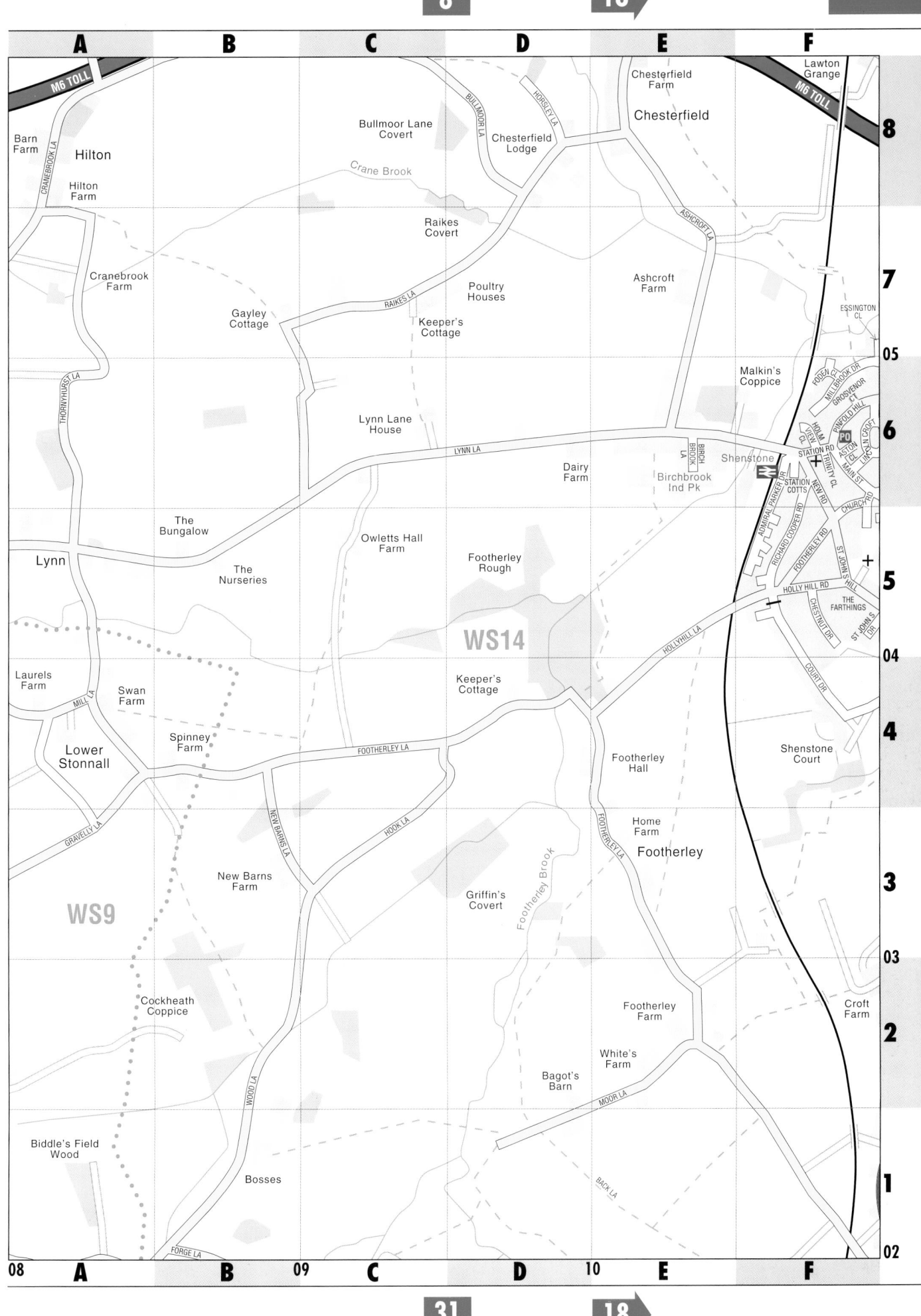

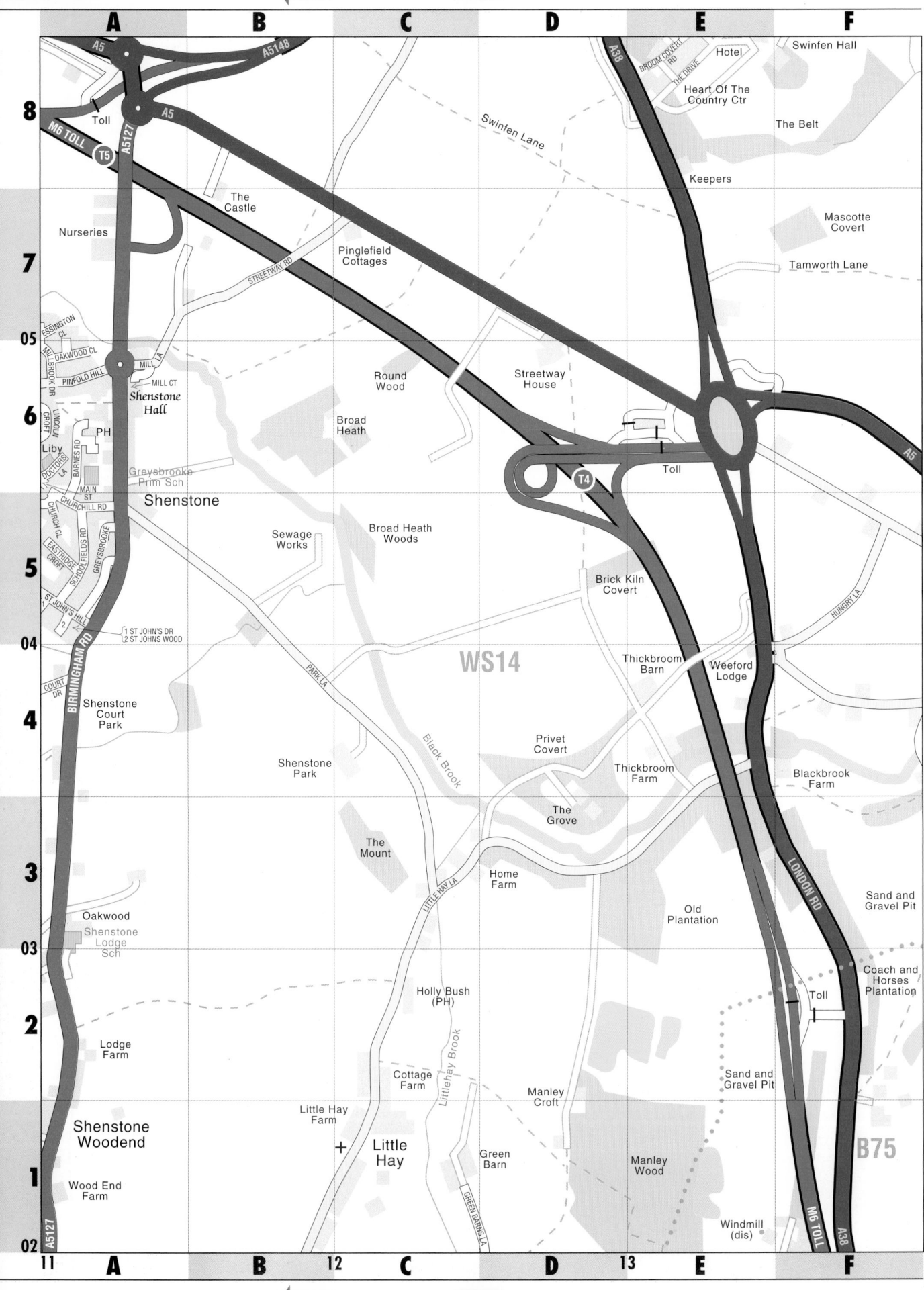

A B C D E F

8

7

05

6

Liby

Shenstone

5

04

WS14

4

3

03

2

1

02

11 A B 12 C D 13 E F

A5
A5148
Toll
M6 TOLL
T5
A5127
The Castle
Nurseries
ESSINGTON CL
OAKWOOD CL
MILL LA
PINFOLD HILL
MILL CT
Shenstone Hall
MILLBROOK DR
CROFT
LINCOLN CROFT
PH
BARNES RD
Greysbrooke Prim Sch
DOCTORS
MAIN ST
CHURCHILL RD
CHURCH CL
EASTRIDGE CROFT
SCHOOLFIELDS RD
GREYSBROOKE
ST JOHN'S HILL
1
2
BIRMINGHAM RD
COURT DR
1 ST JOHN'S DR
2 ST JOHNS WOOD
Shenstone Court Park
Oakwood
Shenstone Lodge Sch
Lodge Farm
Shenstone Woodend
Wood End Farm
A5127
STREETWAY RD
Pinglefield Cottages
Round Wood
Broad Heath
Broad Heath Woods
Sewage Works
Shenstone Park
PARK LA
The Mount
Black Brook
LITTLE HAY LA
Home Farm
Holly Bush (PH)
Cottage Farm
Little Hay Farm
Little Hay
Littlehay Brook
Green Barn
GREEN BARNS LA
Manley Croft
Manley Wood
Swinfen Lane
Streetway House
Brick Kiln Covert
T4
Toll
Privet Covert
The Grove
Thickbroom Barn
Weeford Lodge
Thickbroom Farm
Old Plantation
Manley Wood
A38
BROOM COVERT RD
THE DRIVE
Hotel
Heart Of The Country Ctr
Keepers
Swinfen Hall
The Belt
Mascotte Covert
Tamworth Lane
A5
HUNGRY LA
Blackbrook Farm
LONDON RD
Sand and Gravel Pit
Coach and Horses Plantation
Toll
Sand and Gravel Pit
Windmill (dis)
M6 TOLL
A38
B75

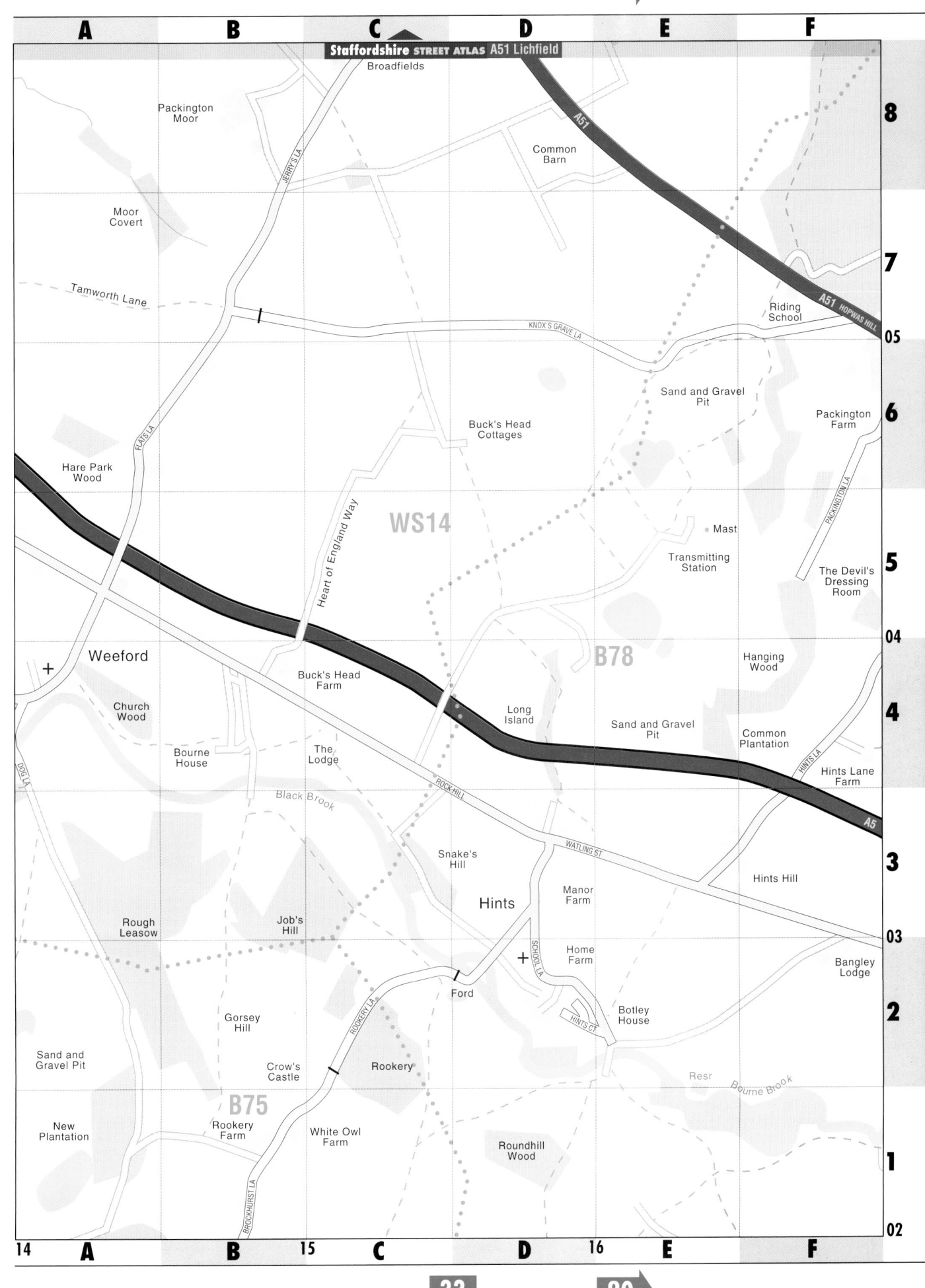

Staffordshire STREET ATLAS A51 Lichfield

Broadfields

Packington
Moor

Common
Barn

A51

8

Moor
Covert

Tamworth Lane

JERRY'S LA

KNOX'S GRAVE LA

A51 HOPWAS HILL

7

Riding
School

05

Sand and Gravel
Pit

6

Packington
Farm

Hare Park
Wood

FLATS LA

Buck's Head
Cottages

WS14

Mast

PACKINGTON LA

Transmitting
Station

5

The Devil's
Dressing
Room

Heart of England Way

B78

04

Weeford

Hanging
Wood

Church
Wood

Buck's Head
Farm

Long
Island

Sand and Gravel
Pit

Common
Plantation

HINTS LA

4

Bourne
House

The
Lodge

ROCK HILL

Hints Lane
Farm

A5

DOG LA

Black Brook

WATLING ST

Snake's
Hill

Hints Hill

3

Hints

Manor
Farm

03

Rough
Leasow

Job's
Hill

SCHOOL LA

Home
Farm

Bangley
Lodge

Ford

HINTS CT

Botley
House

2

Gorsey
Hill

ROOKERY LA

Sand and
Gravel Pit

Crow's
Castle

Rookery

Resr

Bourne Brook

B75

New
Plantation

Rookery
Farm

White Owl
Farm

Roundhill
Wood

1

BROCKHURST LA

02

14

A

B

15

C

D

16

E

F

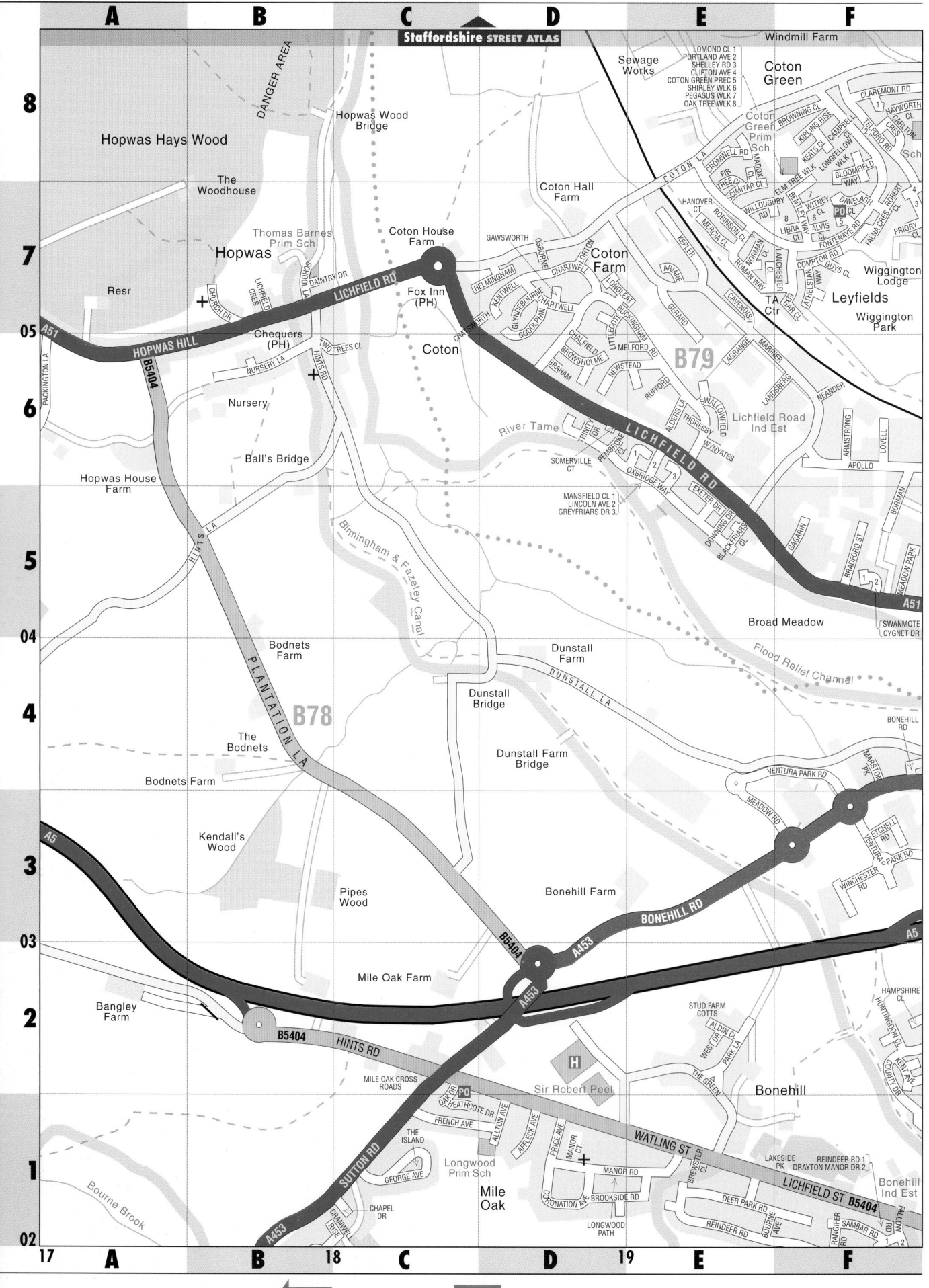

Staffordshire STREET ATLAS

A   B   C   D   E   F

8

Hopwas Hays Wood

DANGER AREA

Hopwas Wood Bridge

Sewage Works

LOMOND CL 1
PORTLAND AVE 2
SHELLEY RD 3
CLIFTON AVE 4
COTON GREEN PREC 5
SHIRLEY WLK 6
PEGASUS WLK 7
OAK TREE WLK 8

Windmill Farm

Coton Green

CLAREMONT RD

HAYWORTH CL

The Woodhouse

Thomas Barnes Prim Sch

Coton Hall Farm

Coton Green Prim Sch

BROWNING CL
KIPLING RISE
KEATS CL
CAMPBELL
LONGFELLOW
ELM TREE WLK
WLK
BLOOMFIELD
WAY
DANEWAY

CARLTON
TELFORD RD
Sch

7

Hopwas

Resr

CHURCH DR
SCHOOL LA
LICHFIELD CRES
DAINTRY DR

LICHFIELD RD

Coton House Farm

Fox Inn (PH)

GAWSWORTH

HELMINGHAM
KENTWELL
GLYNDEBOURNE
GODOL PHIN

OSBORNE
CHARTWELL
CHARTWELL
CHATSWORTH

Coton Farm

CROMWELL RD
FIR
TREE CL
SCIMITAR CL

COTON LA

HANOVER CT

ROBINSON CL

MADOX

MERCIA CL

NORMAN
CL

WILLOUGHBY
BENTLEY AVE
LIBRA
CL

WITNEY
FONTENAYE RD

PO
CL

FALNA CRES
PRIORY

ROBERT
CL

Wiggington Lodge

05

A51

HOPWAS HILL

B5404

Chequers (PH)

NURSERY LA

TWO TREES CL
HINTS RD

Coton

Braham

LONGLEAT
BUCKINGHAM RD
LITTLECOTE

CHALFIELD
BROWSHOLME
NEWSTEAD
MELFORD

RUFFORD

ARUNE

GERARD

KEPLER

COMPTON RD

ROMAN WAY

LANCHESTER
WAY

GUYS CL

CAVENDSH

ATHELSTAN
WAY

FAR CL

B79

Leyfields

Wiggington Park

6

Nursery

Ball's Bridge

Hopwas House Farm

HINTS LA

River Tame

TRINITY
DR

SOMERVILLE
CT

PEMBROKE

ALDERS LA
THORESBY
SWALLOWFIELD

WYNYATES

LICHFIELD RD

Lichfield Road Ind Est

ARMSTRONG

LOVELL

NEANDER

MARINER
LAGRANGE

LANDSBERG

APOLLO

BORMAN

MEADOW PARK

5

Birmingham & Fazeley Canal

MANSFIELD CL 1
LINCOLN AVE 2
GREYFRIARS DR 3

OXBRIDGE WAY

EXETER DR
DOWNING
DE
BLACKFRIARS
CL

GAGARIN

BRADFORD ST

1 2

A51

04

Bodnets Farm

B78

Dunstall Farm

DUNSTALL LA

Broad Meadow

Flood Relief Channel

SWANMOTE
CYGNET DR

4

The Bodnets

PLANTATION LA

Dunstall Bridge

Dunstall Farm Bridge

BONEHILL RD

VENTURA PARK RD

MEADOW RD

MANSTON
PK

ETCHELL RD

VENTURA
S PARK RD

WINCHESTER
RD

BONEHILL RD

3

A5

Bodnets Farm

Kendall's Wood

Pipes Wood

Bonehill Farm

B5404

A453

BONEHILL RD

A5

HAMPSHIRE
CL

03

Bangley Farm

Mile Oak Farm

A453

STUD FARM COTTS

ALDIN CL
WEST DR
PARK LA

THE GREEN

HUNTINGDON DR

KENT AVE
COUNTY DR

2

B5404
HINTS RD

MILE OAK CROSS ROADS

PO

H

Sir Robert Peel

Bonehill

1

SUTTON RD

THE ISLAND

GEORGE AVE

CHAPEL DR

OAK DR
HEATHCOTE DR
FRENCH AVE

ALLTON AVE

AFFLECK AVE

PRICE AVE
MANOR CT
MANOR RD

Longwood Prim Sch

Mile Oak

BROWSTER CL

BREWSTER CL

LAKESIDE PK

REINDEER RD 1
DRAYTON MANOR DR 2

WATLING ST

Bonehill Ind Est

02

A453

CRANWELL RISE

COTON AVE

BROOKSIDE RD

LONGWOOD PATH

CORONATION AVE

DEER PARK RD

REINDEER RD

BOURNE AVE

LICHFIELD ST

RANGER RD
SAMBAR RD

B5404

FALLOW

1 2

Bourne Brook

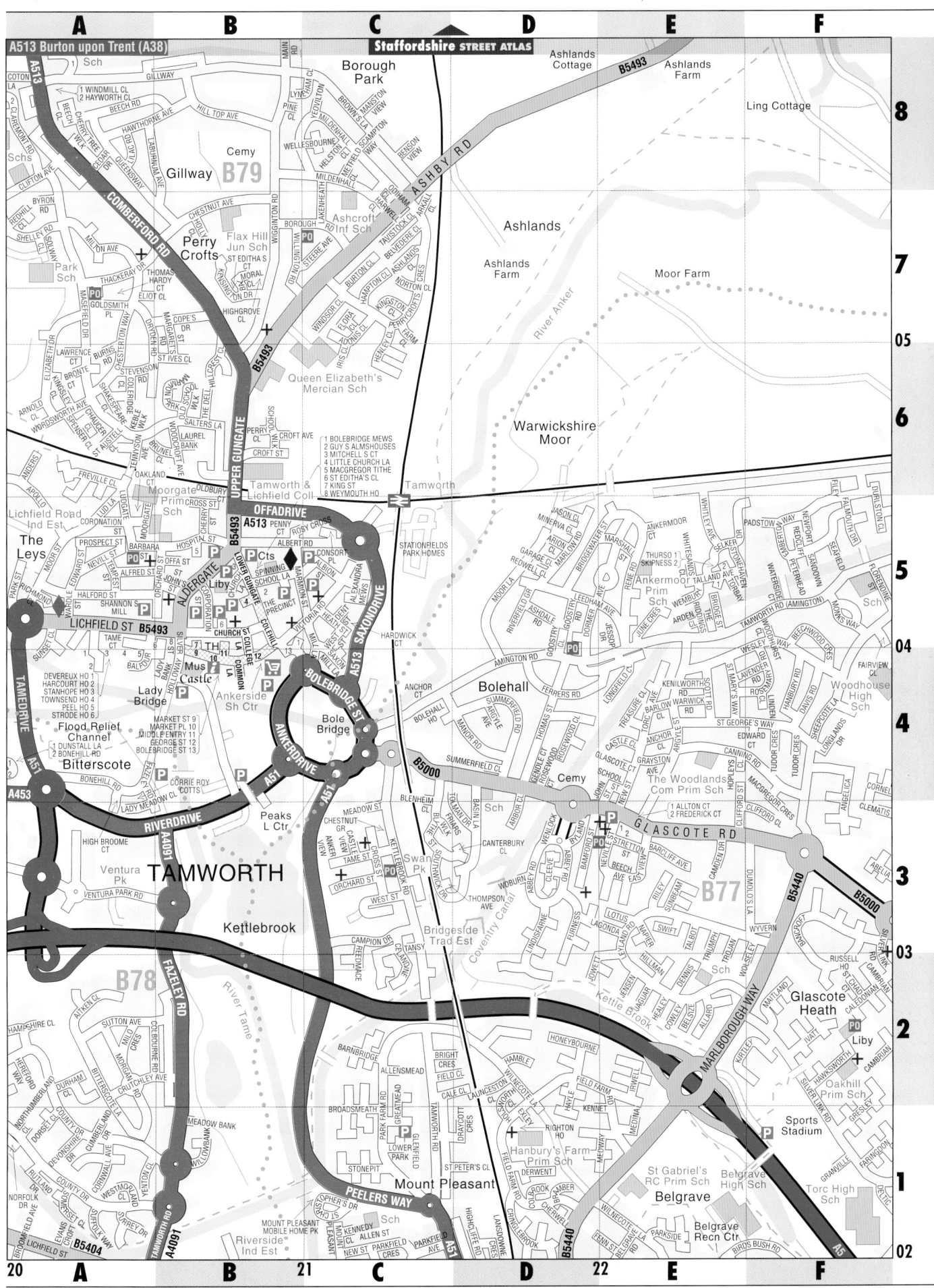

21

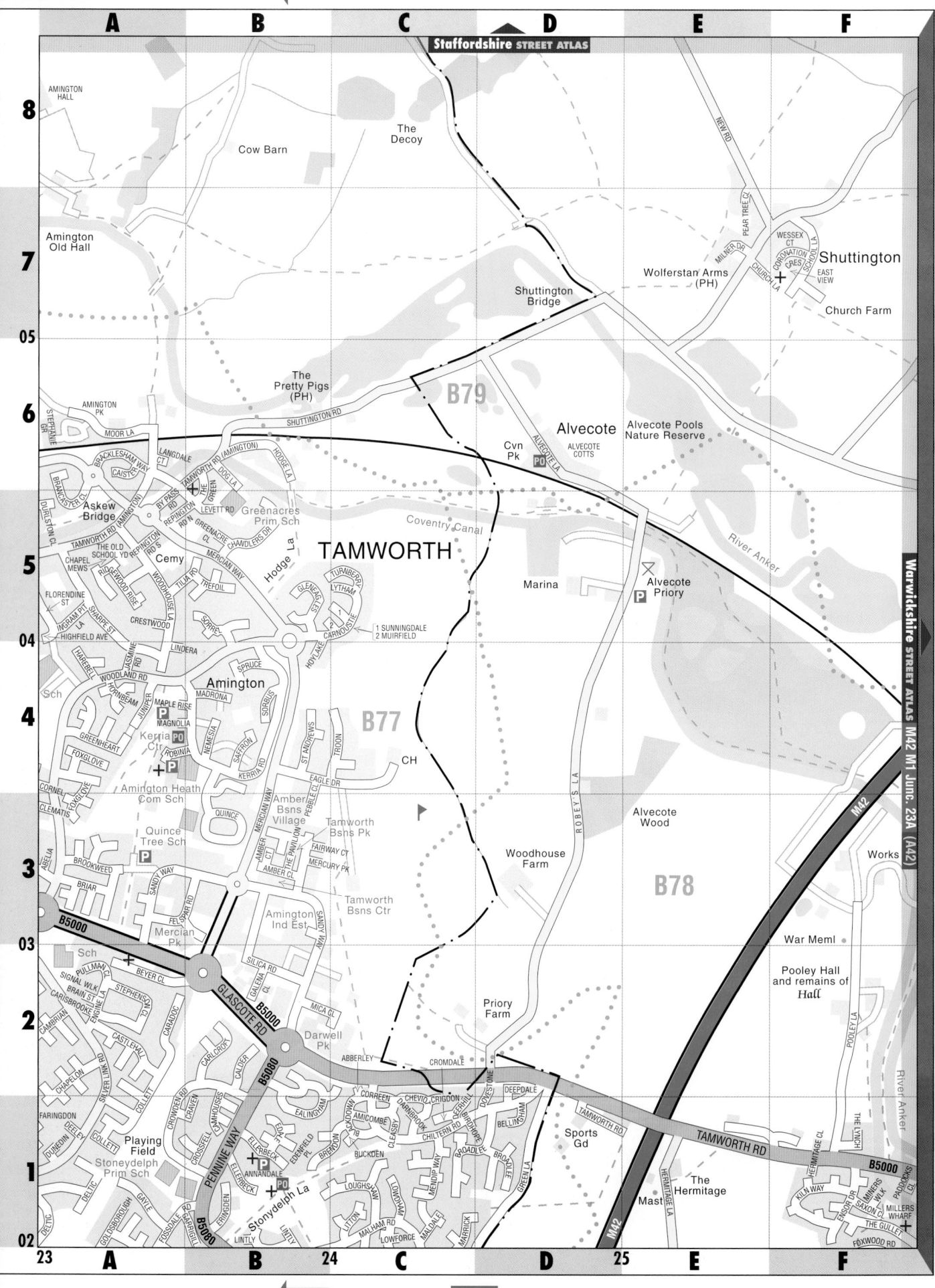

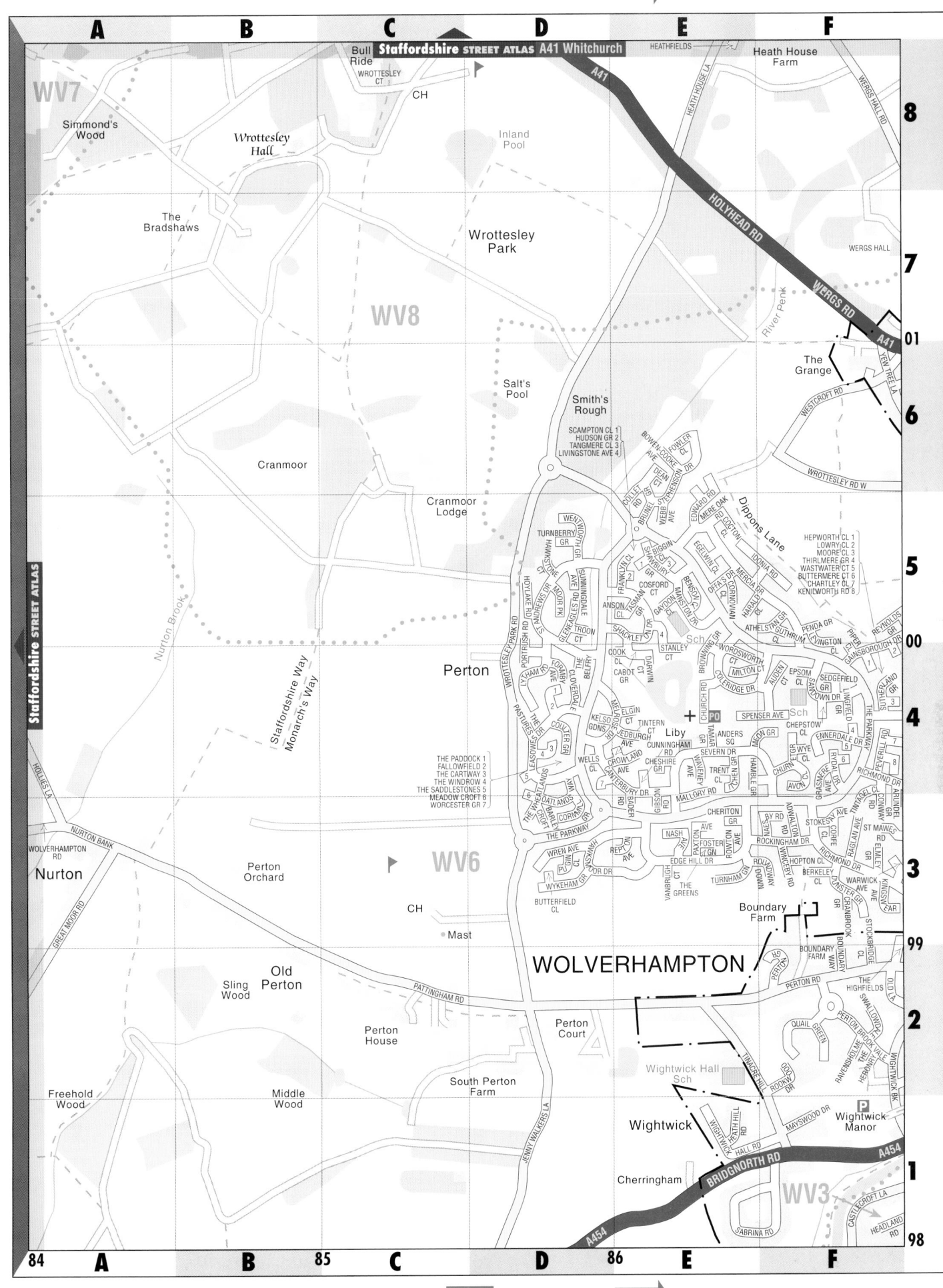

Staffordshire STREET ATLAS A41 Whitchurch

WV7

Simmond's Wood

The Bradshaws

Wrottesley Hall

Bull Ride

WROTTESLEY CT

CH

Inland Pool

Wrottesley Park

WV8

HEATHFIELDS

Heath House Farm

HEATH HOUSE LA

A41

HOLYHEAD RD

WERGS HALL RD

WERGS HALL

8

7

River Penk

WERGS RD

A41

01

The Grange

WESTCROFT RD

YEW TREE LA

6

Salt's Pool

Smith's Rough

SCAMPTON CL 1
HUDSON GR 2
TANGMERE CL 3
LIVINGSTONE AVE 4

BOWEN-COOKE AVE

FOWLER

DEAN RD

COLLEY

STEVENSON DR

MERE OAK RD

COLTON

Dipons Lane

WROTTESLEY RD W

HEPWORTH CL 1
LOWRY CL 2
MOORE CL 3
THIRLMERE CT 4
WASTWATER CT 5
BUTTERMERE CT 6
CHARTLEY CL 7
KENILWORTH RD 8

Cranmoor

Cranmoor Lodge

TURNBERRY GR

WENTWORTH GR

HAWKSTONE

MOOR PK

ST ANDREW'S RD

SUNNINGDALE

BRUNEL CL

WEBB

EDWARD RD

BIGGIN CL

FRANKLYN CL

SANDBURY CL

OFFA'S DR

CORNWALL

EGELWIN CL

MERCIA DR

HARALD

IDONIA RD

ATHELSTAN

GUTHRUM CL

PENDA GR

IVINGTON

PIPER

GAINSBOROUGH DR

REYNOLDS

5

COSFORD CL

ANSON CL

SHACKLETON CT

TROON CT

MAISTON CL

GAYDON DR

BROWNING

WORDSWORTH

COLERIDGE DR

MILTON CT

STANLEY CT

Sch

AUDEN GR

EPSOM GR

SPENSER AVE

SANSOME CT

SEDGEFIELD GR

OWN DR

LINGFIELD

Chepstow

CL

LELAND RD

00

Perton

WROTTESLEY PARK RD

PORTRUSH RD

LYE HAM RD

PASTURES

THE CLOVERDALE

COLVER GR

FOXLEY AVE

COOK CL

CABOT GR

DARWIN CT

Liby

CHURCH RD

TAMAR GR

ANDERS SQ

MEON GR

WYE

CHURN

ENNERDALE DR

RYDAL CT

The Parkway

RICHMOND DR

ARUNDEL CL

PETERFIELD RD

4

THE PADDOCK 1
FALLOWFIELD 2
THE CARTWAY 3
THE WINDROW 4
THE SADDLESTONES 5
MEADOW CROFT 6
WORCESTER GR 7

KELSO GDNS

JEDBURGH AVE

LEASOWES DR

THE MEADLANDS

WELLS CL

CROWLAND AVE

CHESHIRE CL

CUNNINGHAM RD

CANTERBURY DR

GIBSON

SEVERN DR

TRENT CL

WINNEY

MALLORY RD

HAMBLE GR

AVON

GRASMERE GR

RICHMOND DR

ST MAWES

ELMLEY

KINGSV AR

3

ELGIN CT

TINTERN CT

BADER

NASH GR

FOSTER

PAXTON

ROWTON AVE

CHERITON GR

BY RD

STOKESEY CL

COFFE

ADWALTON DR

ROCKINGHAM DR

CRANBROOK

MINSTER GR

WARWICK AVE

OLD LN

STOCKBRIDGE

Perton Orchard

WREN AVE

PJ CL

OUR DR

NAYSMITH

WYKEHAM GR

BUTTERFIELD CL

REPT

CL

EDGE HILL RD

HOPTON CL

TURNHAM GN

ROW

WINCKEY RD

BERKELEY CL

ST MAWES

THE GREENS

CH

Mast

WV6

VANBRUGH

WOLVERHAMPTON RD

NURTON BANK

Nurton

GREAT MOOR RD

HOLLIES LA

Staffordshire Way
Monarch's Way

Perton Orchard

PATTINGHAM RD

Sling Wood

Old Perton

Perton House

Perton Court

South Perton Farm

JENNY WALKERS LA

WOLVERHAMPTON

Boundary Farm

PERTON RD

BOUNDARY FARM WAY

BOUNDARY

QUAIL GREEN

PERTON BROOK VALE

THE HIGHFIELDS

SWALLOWDALE

OLD LN

RAVENSHOLME

HEBRIDEAN

WIGHTWICK BK

99

2

Wightwick Hall Sch

TINACRE HILL

ROOKE DR

MAYSWOOD DR

Wightwick Manor

P

A454

Freehold Wood

Middle Wood

Wightwick

WIGHTWICK HALL RD

HEATH HILL RD

Cherringham

BRIDGNORTH RD

A454

SABRINA RD

WV3

CASTLECROFT LA

HEADLAND RD

1

98

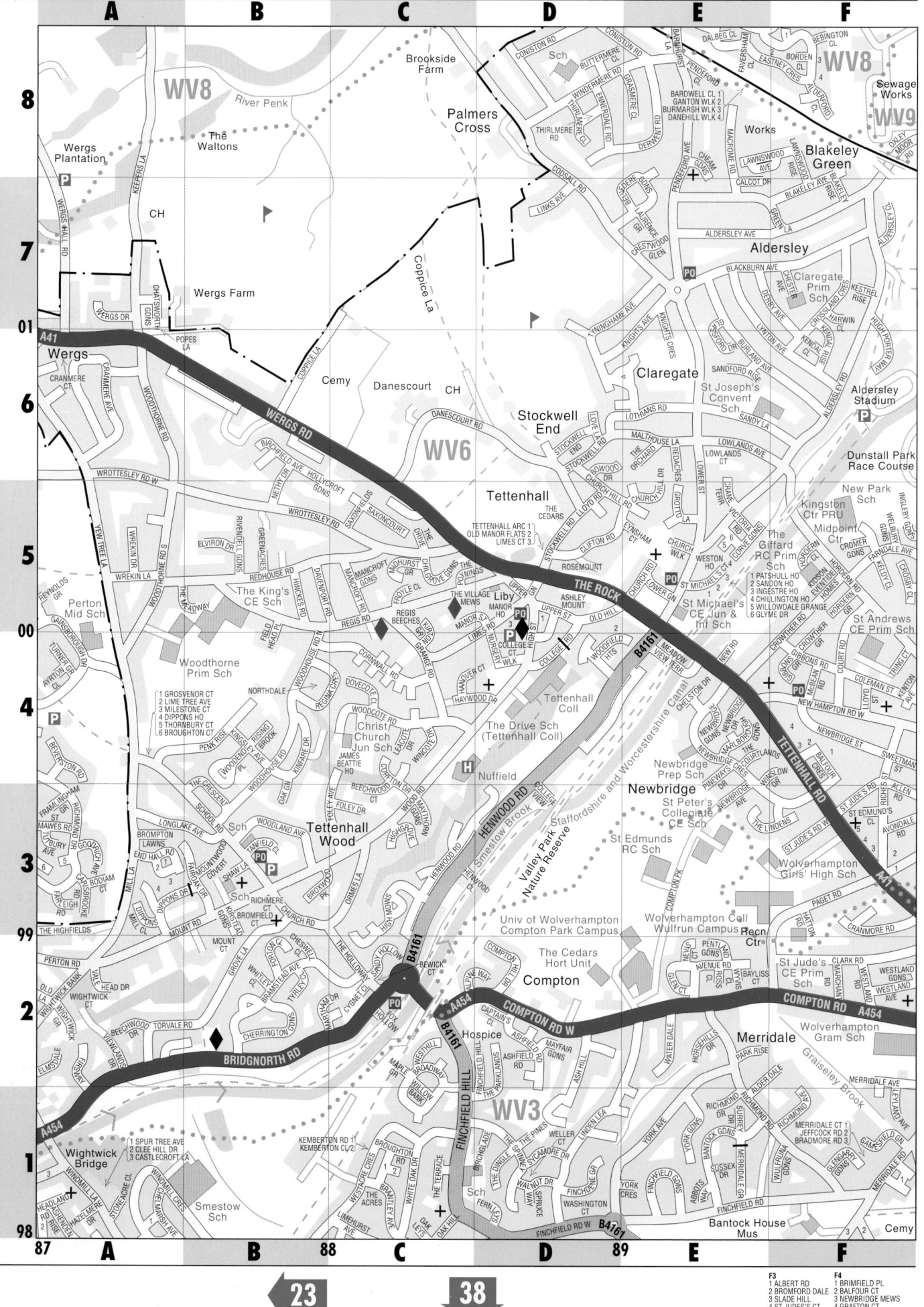

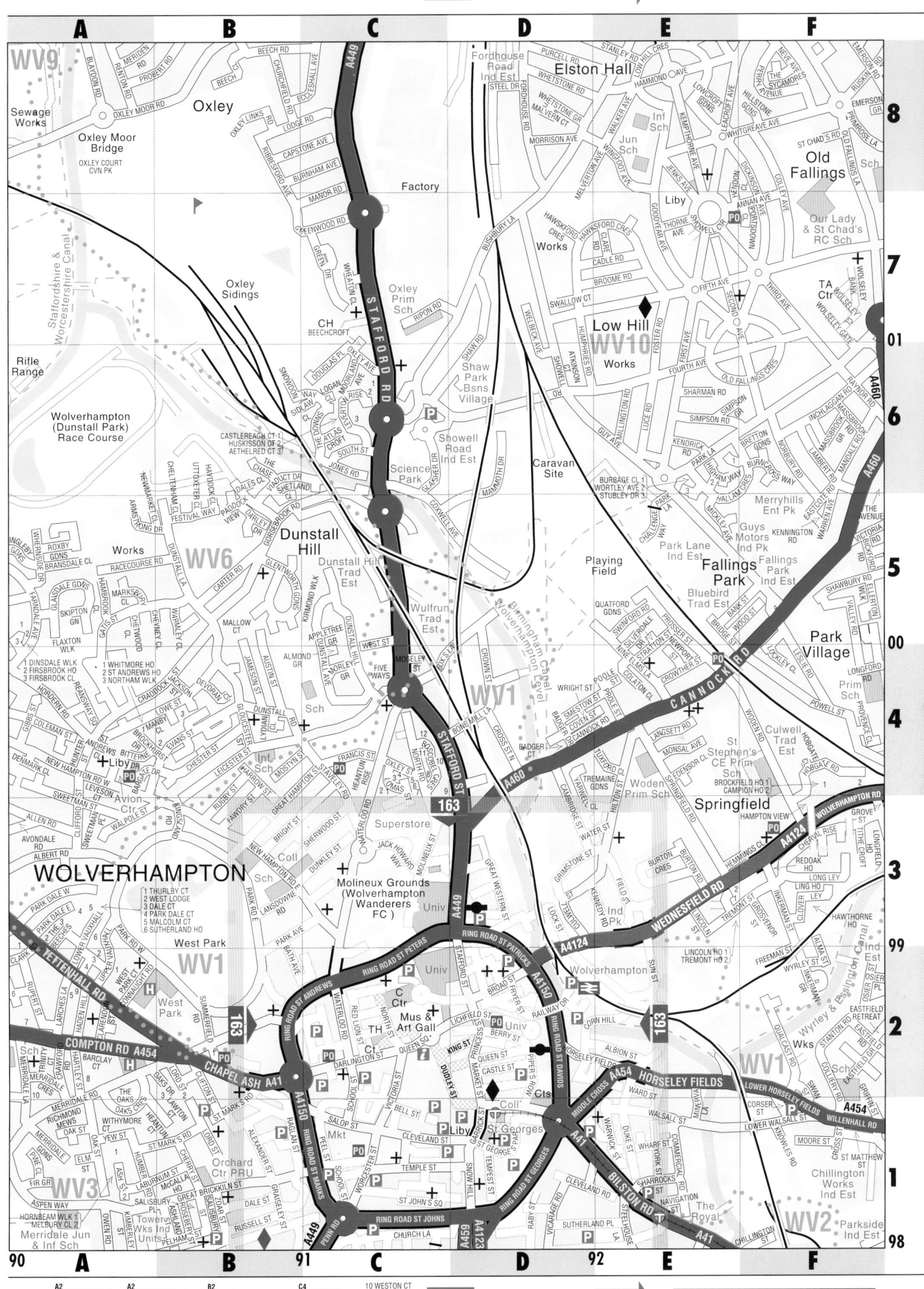

WV9

Sewage Works

Oxley

Oxley Moor Bridge

OXLEY COURT CVN PK

MERIDEN
PROBERT RD

OXLEY MOOR RD

LODGE RD

BEECH RD

BEECH

CHURCHFIELD RD
ECCLESHALL AVE

RIBBESFORD AVE

CAPSTONE AVE

BURNHAM AVE

MANOR RD

GREENWOOD RD

A449

Factory

STAFFORD RD

Elston Hall

Fordhouse Road Ind Est

STEEL DR
FORDHOUSE RD

PURCELL RD
WHETSTONE RD
MALVERN CT
MORRISON AVE

STANLEY RD   LOW HILL CRES
HAMMOND AVE

WHITGREAVE AVE

WALKER AVE

Inf Sch

Jun Sch

KEMPTHORNE AVE

THE SYCAMORES

NEVE AVE

RUSKIN AVE

EMERSON RD

PRIMROSE LA

HILLSTONE GDNS

ST CHAD'S RD

Old Fallings

Sch

8

01

7

6

5

00

4

3

99

2

1

98

Rifle Range

Staffordshire & Worcestershire Canal

Wolverhampton (Dunstall Park) Race Course

Oxley Sidings

CH BEECHCROFT

Oxley Prim Sch

RIPON RD

BUSHBURY LA

Shaw Park Bsns Village

Caravan Site

HAWKSFORD CRES
HAWKSFORD CRES
CLARE RD
CADLE RD
BROOME RD

SWALLOW CT
WELBECK RD

Low Hill
WV10

Works

SHOWELL

HUMPHRES RD
ATKINSON RD

FIFTH AVE
FOSTER AVE
SECOND AVE
THIRD AVE
FOURTH AVE

SHARMAN RD

LICE RD

SIMPSON RD

GUY AVE

PURCELL AVE
WINGFORD AVE
MELVERTON AVE

Liby

GOODYEAR AVE

HENDON RD
DICKINSON RD

ANNAN AVE
PORTLOCK

COLLY AVE

THORNE AVE

OLD FALLINGS CRES

Our Lady & St Chad's RC Sch

TA Ctr

WOLSELEY BANK
WOLSELEY RD
WOLSELEY GATE

LEACROFT AVE

A460

WV6

Works

NEWMARKET CT
UTTOXETER CT
HAVELOCK

RACECOURSE RD
DUNSTALL LA
CARTER RD
GLENTWORTH GDNS

MARKSBY CL
CHELWOOD

DEVORAN CL

PADDOCK VIEW
FESTIVAL WAY

DIXLEY RD
GORSEBROOK RD

MALLOW CT

APPLETREE GR
NORLEY GR
ALMOND GR

Dunstall Hill

Dunstall Hill Trad Est

WEST ST

Wulfrun Trad Est

Five Ways

MOSELEY ST

OXLEY'S LA

CROWN ST

Birmingham Canal / Wolverhampton Level

Playing Field

QUATFORD GDNS

SWINFORD RD
SILVERDALE RD
NINE ELMS LA

NEWPORT RD
CROWTHER ST

WRIGHT ST

COLTON CL

Fallings Park

Bluebird Trad Est

Fallings Park Ind Est

SHAWBURY RD
ELLERTON WLK
VALLEY RD

Park Village

LONGFORD

Prim Sch

POWELL ST

PROVENCE CL

CULWELL Trad Est

St Stephen's CE Prim Sch

BROCKFIELD HO 1
CAMPION HO 2

Springfield

CANNOCK RD

WV1

WOLVERHAMPTON

West Park

WV1

TETTENHALL RD

COMPTON RD A454

CHAPEL ASH A41

WEDNESFIELD RD

A4124

WOLVERHAMPTON RD

RING ROAD ST PATRICKS

A4150

Molineux Grounds (Wolverhampton Wanderers FC)

Univ

Superstore

163

A449

163

Univ
C Ctr
Mus & Art Gall

A4124

Wolverhampton

HORSELEY FIELDS

A454

LOWER HORSELEY FIELDS

WILLENHALL RD

A454

WV1

A460

Chillington Works Ind Est

WV2

Parkside Ind Est

BILSTON RD A41

RING ROAD ST JOHNS

A449

PENN RD

A459

A4123

CHURCH LA

WV3

A2
1 CONNAUGHT HO
2 VAUXHALL HO
3 VAUXHALL AVE
4 MIDDLE VAUXHALL
5 HADEN CT
6 WESTLAND GDNS
7 COMPTON CT
8 BRIGHTON MEWS
9 TETTENHALL GATE

A2
10 BEECHWOOD HO

B2
1 MEADOW ST
2 ROTARY CT
3 OAKLEIGH CT

C4
1 DURHAM HO
2 ESSEX HO
3 FLINT HO
4 GLOUCESTER HO
5 ARGYLL HO
6 BEDFORD HO
7 CUMBERLAND HO
8 LANE CT
9 TONG CT

10 WESTON CT
11 BIRCH CT
12 KILSALL CT

For full street detail of the highlighted area see page 163.

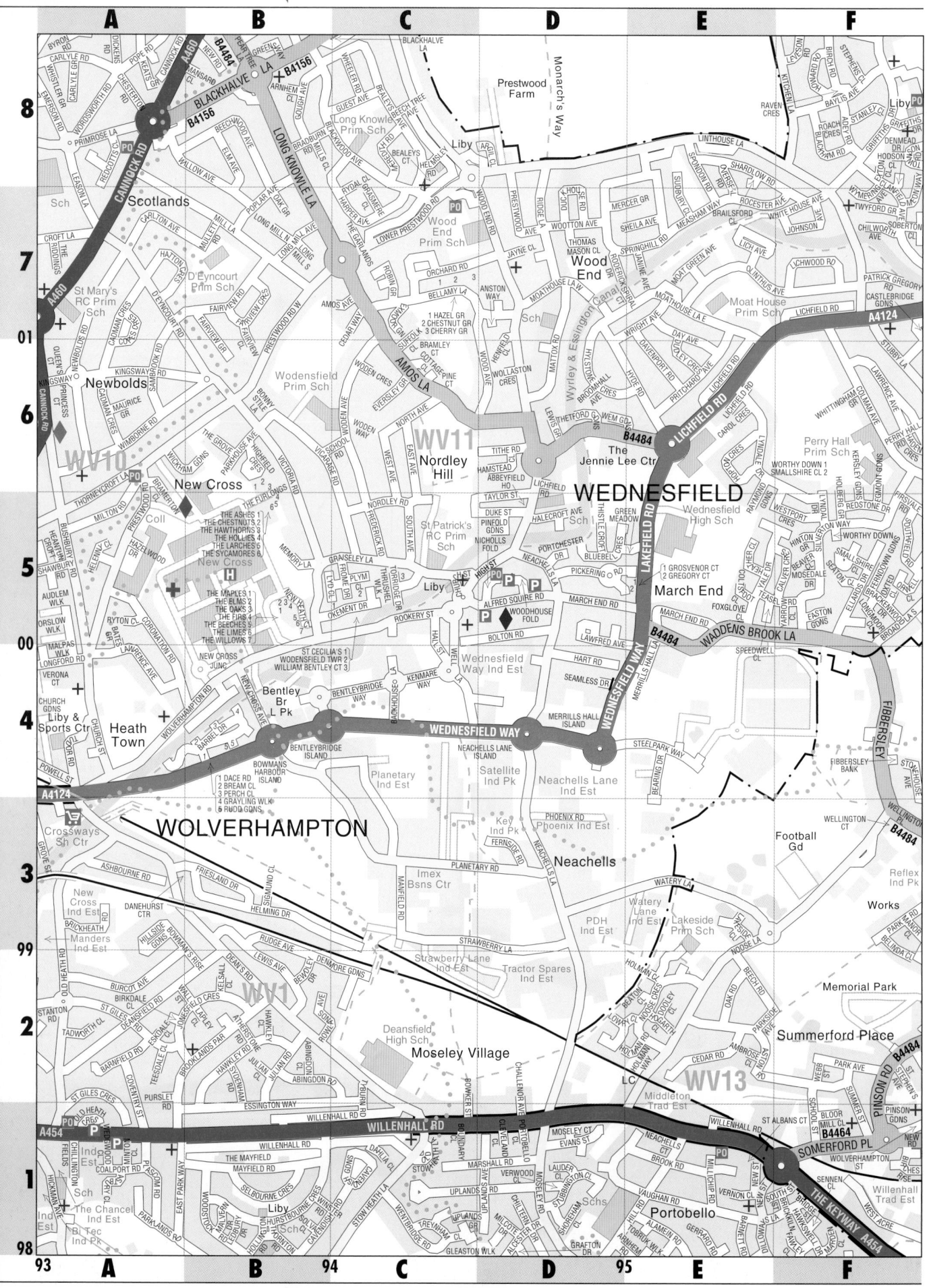

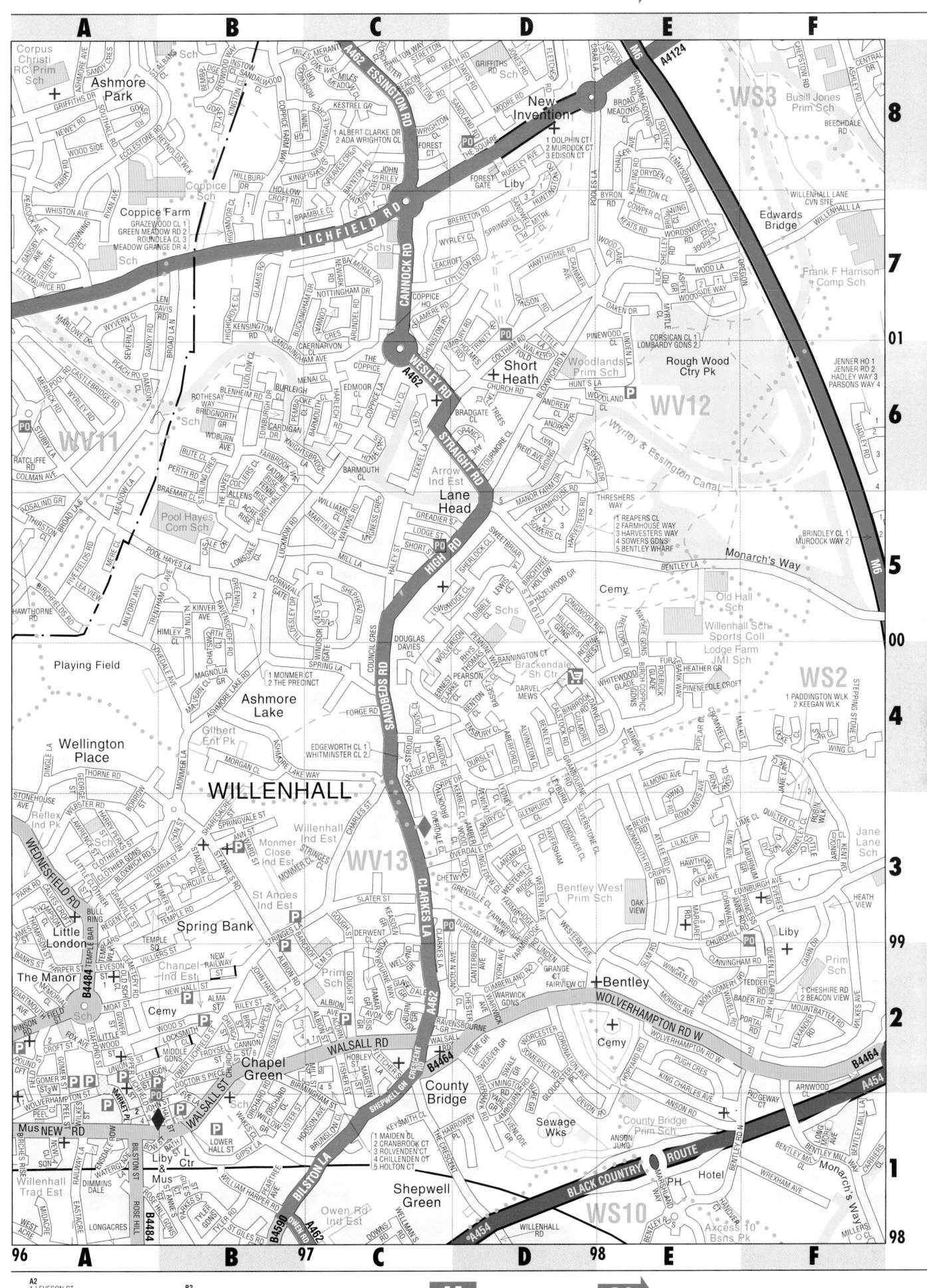

13
28

WS3

WV12

WV11

WV13

WV2

WS2

WS10

WILLENHALL

New Invention

Short Heath

Lane Head

Ashmore Park

Coppice Farm

Ashmore Lake

Wellington Place

Little London

The Manor

Spring Bank

Chapel Green

County Bridge

Shepwell Green

Bentley

Edwards Bridge

Rough Wood Ctry Pk

Playing Field

Frank F Harrison Comp Sch

Busill Jones Prim Sch

Jane Lane Sch

Black Country Route

Monarch's Way

Wyrley & Essington Canal

41
28

A2
1 LEVESON CT
2 CROFT APARTMENTS
3 ST MARY'S CT
A1
1 ST STEPHEN'S GDNS
2 CROSS ST
3 CHEAPSIDE
4 ATLANTIC CT

B2
1 FREDERICK WILLIAM ST
2 CHARLES HOLLAND ST
3 KNIGHTS CL
4 SQUIRES GATE RD
5 WITTERSHAM CT
6 KING ST

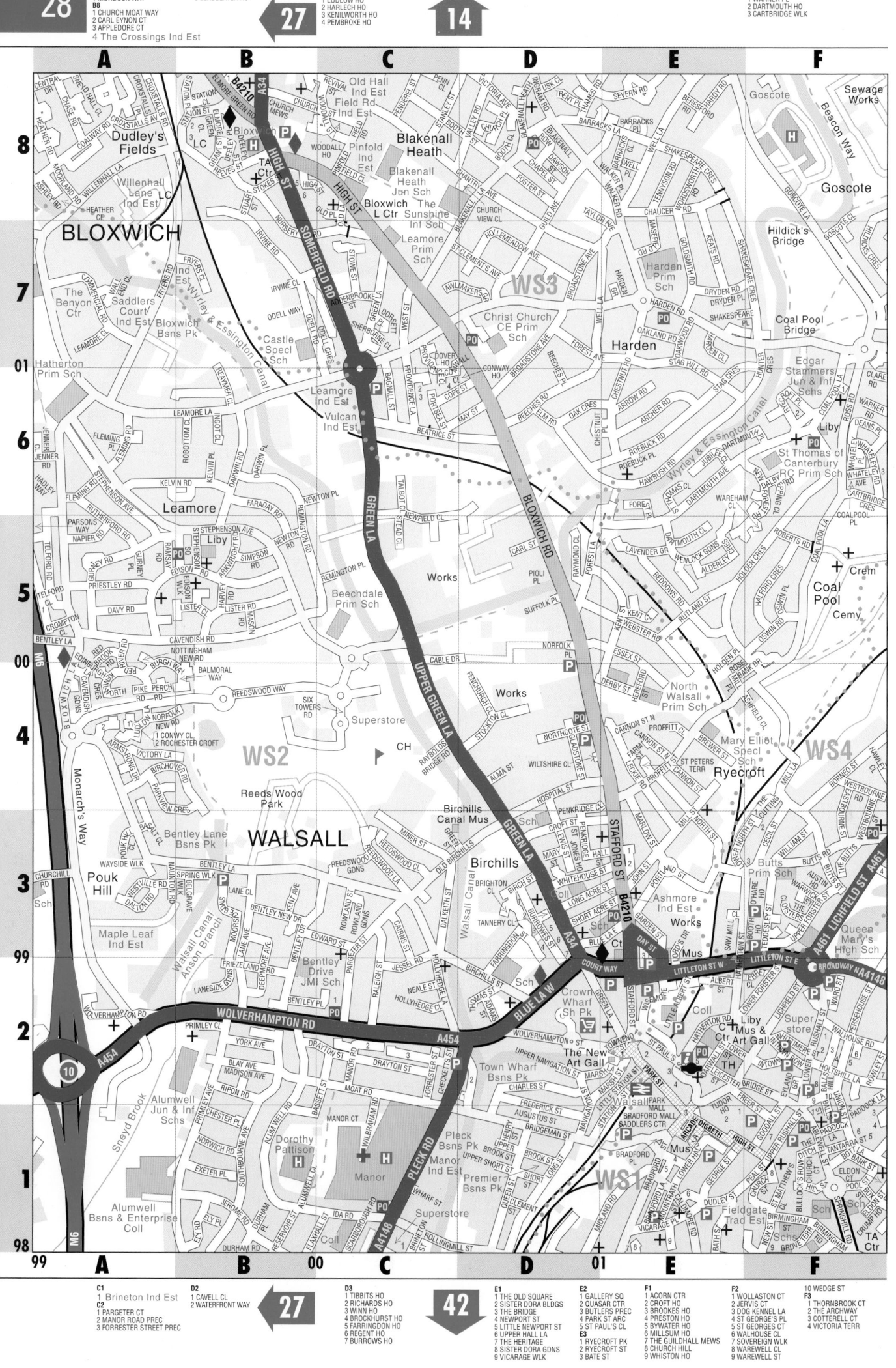

A   B   C   D   E   F

8
7
01
6
5
00
4
3
99
2
1
98

B4154

Sewage Works

HILDICKS CRES
MIDDLE LA
GOSCOTE LODGE CRES
HILDICKS PL

WS3

PELSALL LA
SCHOLARS WLK
WESTMINSTER RD

Liby
NEWCOMEN CT
STANLEY CL
WYATT CL
PO
STATION RD
LICHFIELD RD
B4154

CHESTNUT DR
SYCAMORE CL
HANDY DR
GRANGE CRES
MAPLE DR
BURTON AVE
DEEPWOOD CL

WILLOWS RD
COALHEATH LA
HIGHFIELD AVE
MEADOW

A461

WILSFORD CL
PARKSTONE CL
BROOK MEADOW RD
BROADHEATH DR
GLEBSEY
STREAMSIDE WAY
WATERMERE
MERE VIEW
WILLOWSIDE

Greenfield Prim Sch

BRIARBECK
THE PARKWAY
FENBOURNE
HARRINGWORTH CT

Shelfield

RISCHALE WAY

PO
QUEENS RD

DEAN RD
LINLEY RD
BARNS LA
EARLS RD
YORK RD
KINGS RD

POOL VIEW
SHERWOOD WLK
BALMORAL CL
EDINBURGH DR
WELBECK RD
WINDSOR WAY
BLENHEIM
CULSWORTH

Stubber's Green

STUBBERS GREEN RD
DUMBLEDERRY LA

RUXFORD WAY
WHARF APP
LOCKSIDE

Empire Ind Pk
EMPIRE CL
BRICKYARD RD

8

HARDEN RD
CLARE RD
WARNER RD
SCOTTS

YEMS CROFT

CARTBRIDGE LA
CARTBRIDGE WLK
CARTBRIDGE CRES

Cemy

Works

The Radleys Prim Sch
WINTERLEY LA
RICKLEY RD
RADLEY RD

Rushall

COUNTESS DR

The Longcroft
ABBOTS CL
FRIARY CRES
SPRINGFIELDS
NEW ST
ROWLEY PL
OLD WELL RD
HOLME WAY
KING GEORGE CRES
STANLEY PL
LIME GR
DAW END LA

Rushall Com Coll

FLOYDS LA
ORCHARD CL
LIMEHURST
PARK RD

Daw End Sch

Daw End

WS4

Rushall Hall
HARPUR CL
HARPUR RD

1 GILBERTS CT
2 BIRCH CT
3 LICHFIELD CT
4 WESTBOURNE RD
5 WESLEYAN CL
6 WESTBOURNE CT
7 MELLISH CT
8 LEIGH CT

Park Pits

Park Lime Pits Country Park

Dales La
Daw End Branch

DAW END

College Farm

Riddian Bridge

Beacon Way

WS9

Berryfields Farm

Middlemore La W
Middlemore Bsns Pk

Redhouse JMI Sch

ANGLIAN RD

Linley Lodge Ind Est
Westgate Trad Est
VINTAGE WAY
WESTGATE

Hopley's Bridge
Mast

Redhouse Ind Est

MIDDLEMORE LA

THE MEADOWS
LINLEY WOOD RD
GORSEY WAY
HIGH RIDGE
BERRYFIELDS
THE LEASOW
LINLEY
HEARTHCOTE CRES
LEA VIEW
HIGH RIDGE
PO
MYATT AVE
CROPTHORNE
RED HOUSE LA
WESTBROOK AVE

BOWKER
GRETTON RD
STAPLETON
DILKE RD
DUMBLEDERRY

HONITON WAY
WHITEHOUSE WAY
QUICKSALL LA

A454
B4154

BOSTY LA

WALSALL RD

Bosty Lane Farm

BORNEO ST
SOMERSET RD

LEIGH RD
HARFIELD CL
WORTH

TETLEY AVE
RUSHALL MANOR CL
REGINA DR
PELSALL MANOR RD
STENCILLS RD
KINGSBURY CT
PARK LIME DR
STENCILLS DR
BUTTON FARM RD
MELLISH RD

LEIGH CL
MELROSE CT

A454
MELLISH RD

MOSS CL
DERFIELDS CL
CAMPBELL CL
GLEN CL
RUSHWOOD CL
BUCHANAN CL
CAMERON RD
ARGYLE CL

Stencill's Farm

Longwood Bridge
ALDRIGE RD
AIRFIELD DR

P
Nature Trail

Sports Ground

VICTORIA TERR
VICTORIA MEWS
BUCHANAN AVE
ARBORETUM RD
MARK CT
CRANE CT

Hydesville Tower Sch

Calder Fields Farm

Walsall Arboretum

PH
Whitby Stables

CH

Hayhead Wood Nature Reserve

Hayhead Farm
LONGWOOD LA

ROWLEY ST
WALHOUSE RD
CHARLOTTE ST
THE LIMES
CRABTREE RD
CALDER AVE
NUTMEG GR

BROADWAY N

Sch
TANTARRA ST
LIME ST
SELBORNE ST
WALSINGHAM ST
MONCRIEFFE ST
FLORENCE ST
SELBORNE
OLD MASTERS RD
LINCOLN RD
TONG ST
PRINCES AVE
B4148

The Chuckery

WS1

Playing Fields

KING GEORGE VI AVE

Rushall Canal

WS5

SUTTON RD
B4151

PH

Three Crowns Sch

BERNARD ST
DOVE CL
KINNERLEY ST
LIMLEY RD
LORINERS GR
SHRUBBERY CL
BEACONSFIELD CT
PO

1 BURLEIGH ST
2 RICHMOND ST
3 LANGFORD CL
THE CRESCENT

GROVE HILL
DOWNHAM CL
B4151
LONGMEADOW RD
FALLOWFIELD
ELMSTEAD
ELMSTEAD WOOD
SKIP

02   A   B   03   C   D   04   E   F

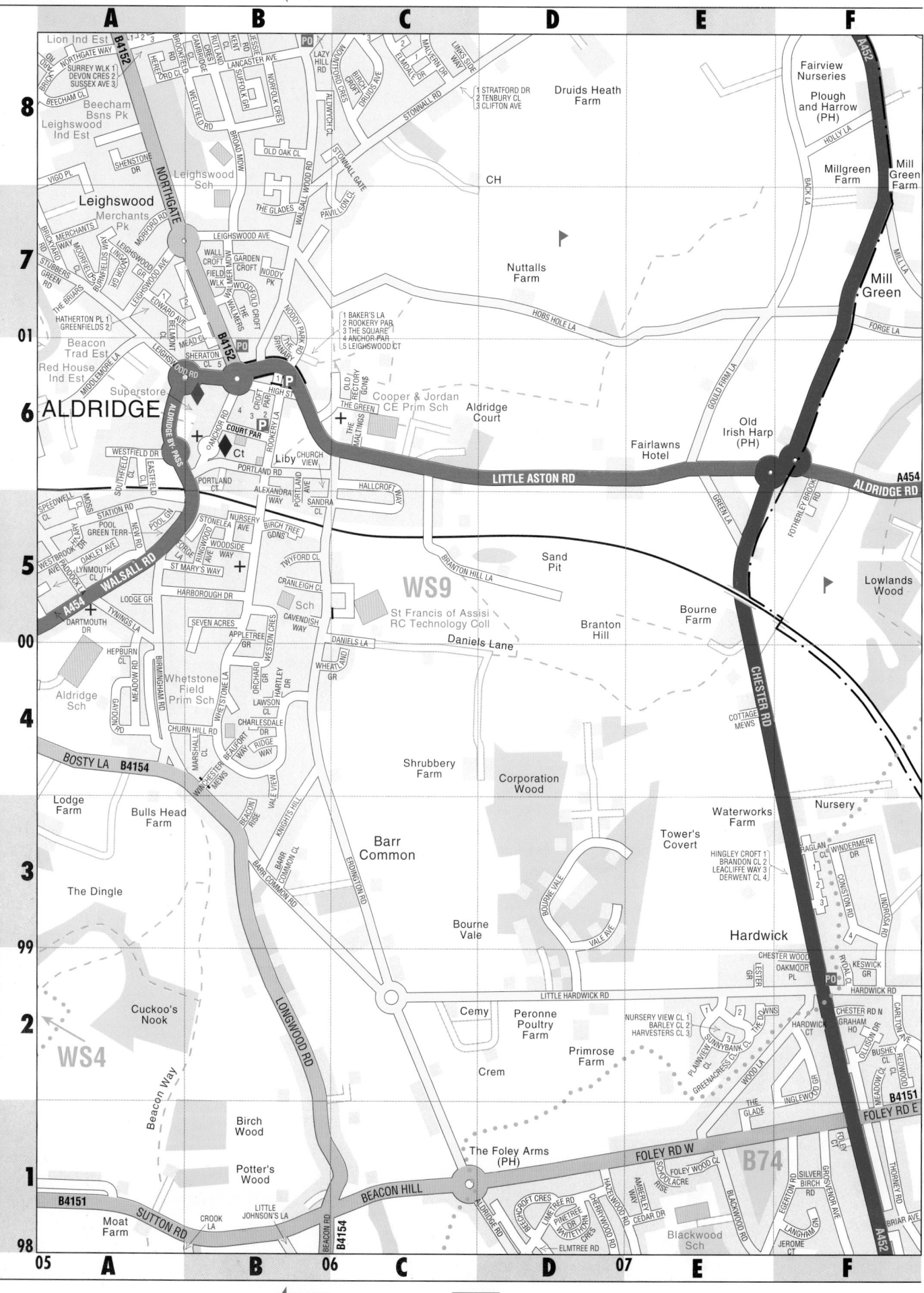

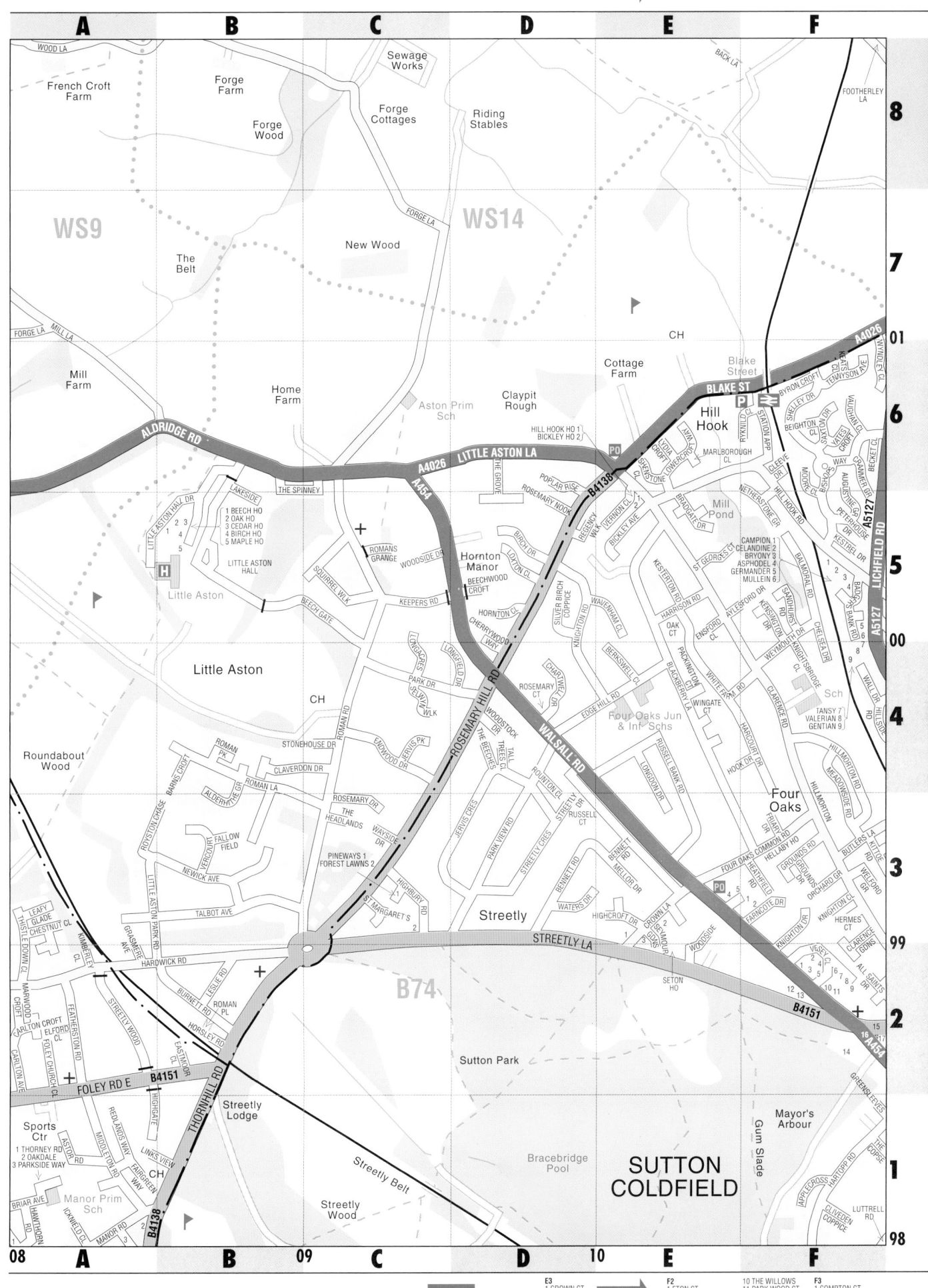

A B C D E F

8

7

01

6

5

00

4

3

99

2

1

98

A5127 BIRMINGHAM RD

A5127 LICHFIELD RD

WS14

B74

Joburns Cottages

Alder Farm

Brookfield

GREEN BARNS LA

LITTLE HAY LA

The Highwayman (PH)

WOODLAND CT

SMARTS AVE

Blossom Hill Farm

Camp Farm

BLAKE ST

WATFORD GAP RD

Biddles Farm

WATFORD GAP

Wyndley Manor

HILLWOOD COMMON RD

Hill Common

Hill Farm

Mast

Television Station

Hill

HAYCROFT DR

BYRON

A5127

HATHAWAY RD

HILLSIDE RD

GRESLEY CL

Oakland Ho

KEATING GDNS

STRINGER

BEECH CL

WARDLE CL

DUNTON CL

DUNTON CV

WESTFIELD

DAWNEY DR

HIGHOVER DR

GLANVILLE DR

1 CHEVIOT CT
2 CHILTERN CT
3 BREDON CT
4 COTSWOLD CT

Hill Wood Farm

Hillside Farm

Manorial Farm

HILLWOOD RD

Hill Wood

B75

Manorial Wood

Camp Road

Hovel Covert

Pine Tree Cottage

Springhill Farm

Springhill Plantation

Spreading Tree Hill

WORCESTER LA

1 PLOUGHMANS PL
2 TILLER GR
3 SOWERS CT
4 COMBINE CL

Dale Farm

Piggery

Woodside Farm

DUTTON'S LA

Hilltop Farm

Black Fir Wood

Green Wood

Weeford Park Farm

A38

M6 TOLL

LONDON RD

A38

TURF PITTS LA

WEEFORD RD

B4151

M6 TOLL

Little Sutton Prim Sch

MAYALL DR

HOMESTEAD DR

ST JOHNS CL

LOXLEY CL

ARLINGTON

WOODSIDE CL

WORCESTER

EDWARDS CL

ST BLASE RD

WILLMOTT CL

WILLMOTT CL

Roughley

WHEATSHEAF CL

HARVEST FIELDS WAY

RECROW LA

HARVEST FIELDS WAY

CANWELL GATE

ROUGHLEY FARM RD

CROFTERS WAY

SLADE RD

PH

BISHOPS CROFT

BRADWELL CROFT

BODICOTE GR

BLAYDON AVE

BUCKTON CL

E3
1 MARLPIT RISE
2 WEEFORD DELL
3 WHEATCROFT CL
4 SHEARERS PL
5 WOODMAN GR
6 FARM HOUSE LA
7 BLACKSMITH DR
8 WEAVER CT

MARLPIT LA

SHERIFOOT LA

BUTLERS LA

Butlers Lane

HENLEY DR

PEGASUS CT

CROCKFORD DR

DUNCALFE DR

DUGDALE CRES

DOVEDALE

KINGS CT

THE DOVECOTES

BRENTNALL WALCOT

TOWER RD

DODWELLS RD

GIBBONS RD

PUDSEY DR

RANDLE DR

GRANGE LA

CARTWRIGHT DR

REDNAL DR

HURST RD

CLARENDON RD

GRANGE AVE

ROUGHLEY DR

HARVEY DR

COBURN DR

LICHFIELD RD

LADRAVTN

HOLLY

RED CL

HARLAND

HOBART CT 1
BALFOUR CT 2

BEATON RD

KITTOE RD

SARA CL

The Arthur Terry Sch

PO

Mere Green

CHURCH TERR

WILMCOTE DR

ELISABETH CT

Mere Green Comb Sch

ALL SAINTS DR 1 2

CLARENCE RD

BELWELL DR

B4151

BELWELL LA

BELWELL GDNS

NURSERY LA

ALSTON CL

MIDDLETON

LE MORE

THE FORDROUGH

B74

A454

FOUR OAKS RD

Ley Hill

HARTOPP RD

Greensleeves

CRESSINGTON DR

THE COPSE

LUTTRELL RD

BEECHCROFT CT

HANSON MAN

FOXTON CL

HAWKESFORD

FOUR OAKS CT

LADYWOOD RD

HAZELMERE DR

CEDARWOOD

LAUREATES WLK

PINE LEIGH

A5127

A454

RIDGEWOOD DR

Coppice Prim Sch

MERE DR

CREMORNE RD

CREMORNE WLK

FARM BOROUGH CT

KINGSLEIGH CROFT

JORDAN RD

DOWER RD

QUEENS RD

DEVEREUX RD

TRINITY RD

LITTLE SUTTON LA

GROSVENOR CL

LOCKHART DR

WENT

JORDAN

WORTH

ST JAMES CL

MERE GREEN RD

WHEATLEY CL

HARWELL

STREATHER RD

HEATH CROFT RD

Moor Hall

ESSEX RD

ROWALLAN RD

Little Sutton Rd

HOMER RD

HOLTE DR

Moor Hall Prim Sch

SHARRAT FIELD

PEROTT DR

CLIVE RD

FERRERS RD

BROCKHURST RD

WYRLEY RD

CH

MOOR HALL DR

Hotel

SUTTON COLDFIELD

Ashfurlong Hall

PO

MORDAUNT DR

MAIN CL

AULTON RD

WARING CL

CHARNLEY

MERE POOL RD

SHEPHERDS POOL RD

WEEFORD DR

Fox Hill RD

Fox Hill Farm

A453 TAMWORTH RD

1 DEVONSHIRE CT
2 HARBOROUGH CT
3 TUDOR CT

CARLTON HO

Liby

Hill

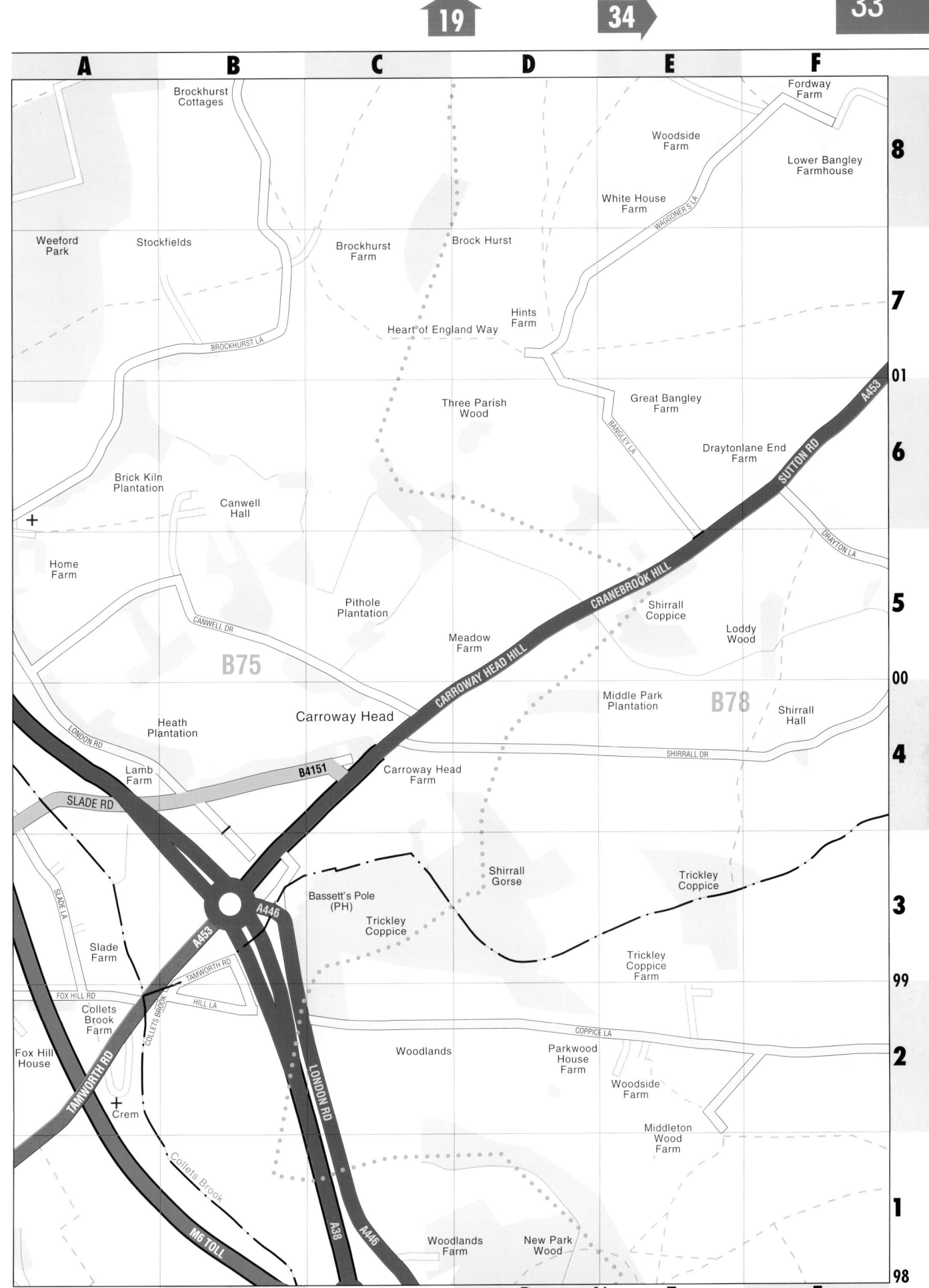

8

7

01

6

5

00

4

3

99

2

1

98

Fordway Farm

Woodside Farm

Lower Bangley Farmhouse

White House Farm

Brockhurst Cottages

Weeford Park

Stockfields

Brockhurst Farm

Brock Hurst

Hints Farm

Heart of England Way

BROCKHURST LA

WAGGONER'S LA

Three Parish Wood

Great Bangley Farm

BANGLEY LA

Draytonlane End Farm

SUTTON RD

A453

DRAYTON LA

Brick Kiln Plantation

Canwell Hall

Home Farm

CANWELL DR

Pithole Plantation

Shirrall Coppice

Loddy Wood

B75

Meadow Farm

CRANEBROOK HILL

CARROWAY HEAD HILL

Middle Park Plantation

B78

Shirrall Hall

Heath Plantation

Carroway Head

LONDON RD

Lamb Farm

B4151

Carroway Head Farm

SHIRRALL DR

SLADE RD

Shirrall Gorse

Trickley Coppice

SLADE LA

Slade Farm

A453

A446

Bassett's Pole (PH)

Trickley Coppice

Trickley Coppice Farm

FOX HILL RD

HILL LA

TAMWORTH RD

Collets Brook Farm

COLLETS BROOK

Fox Hill House

Crem

COPPICE LA

Woodlands

Parkwood House Farm

Woodside Farm

Middleton Wood Farm

Collets Brook

LONDON RD

M6 TOLL

A38

A446

Woodlands Farm

New Park Wood

14

15

16

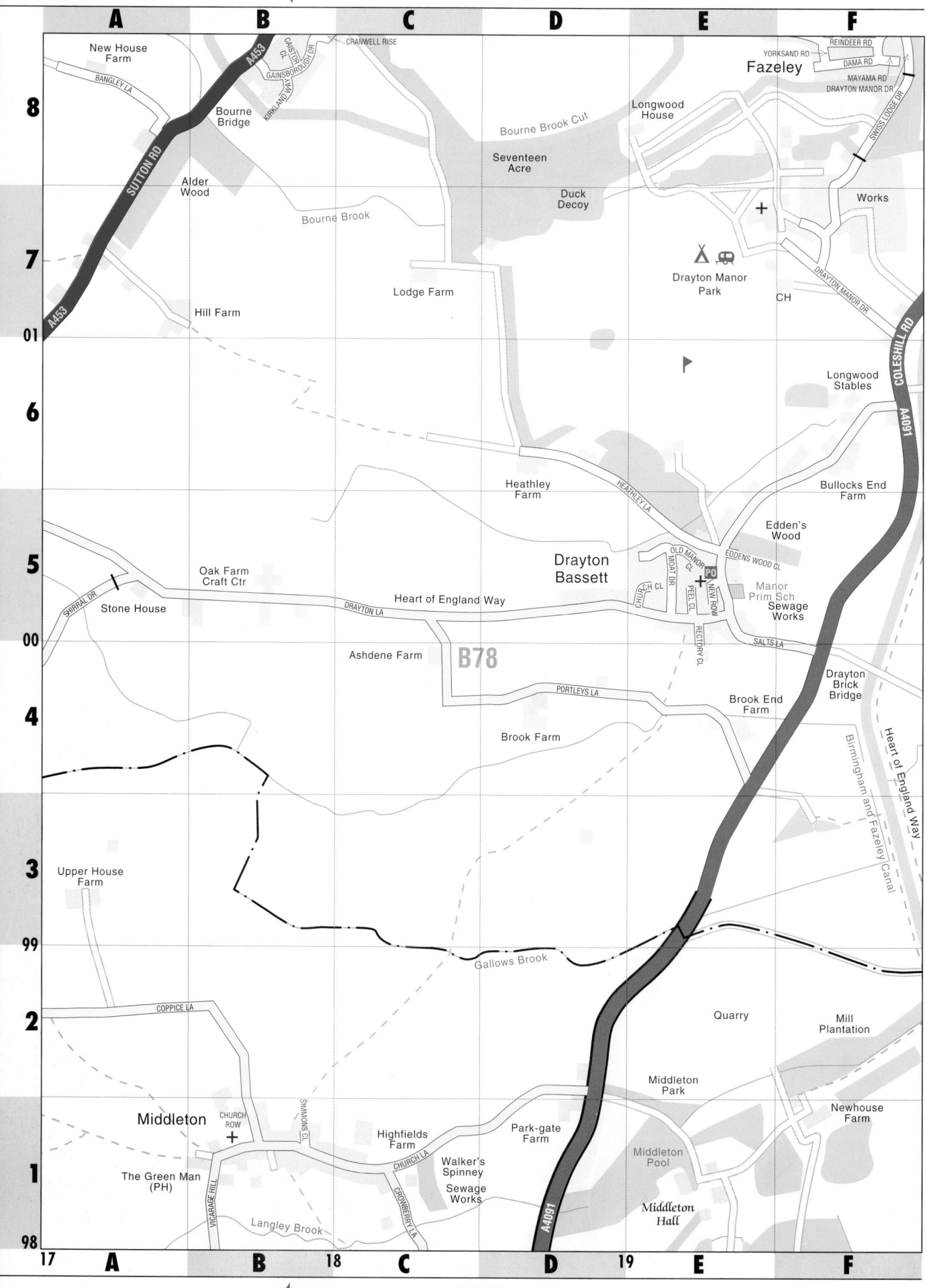

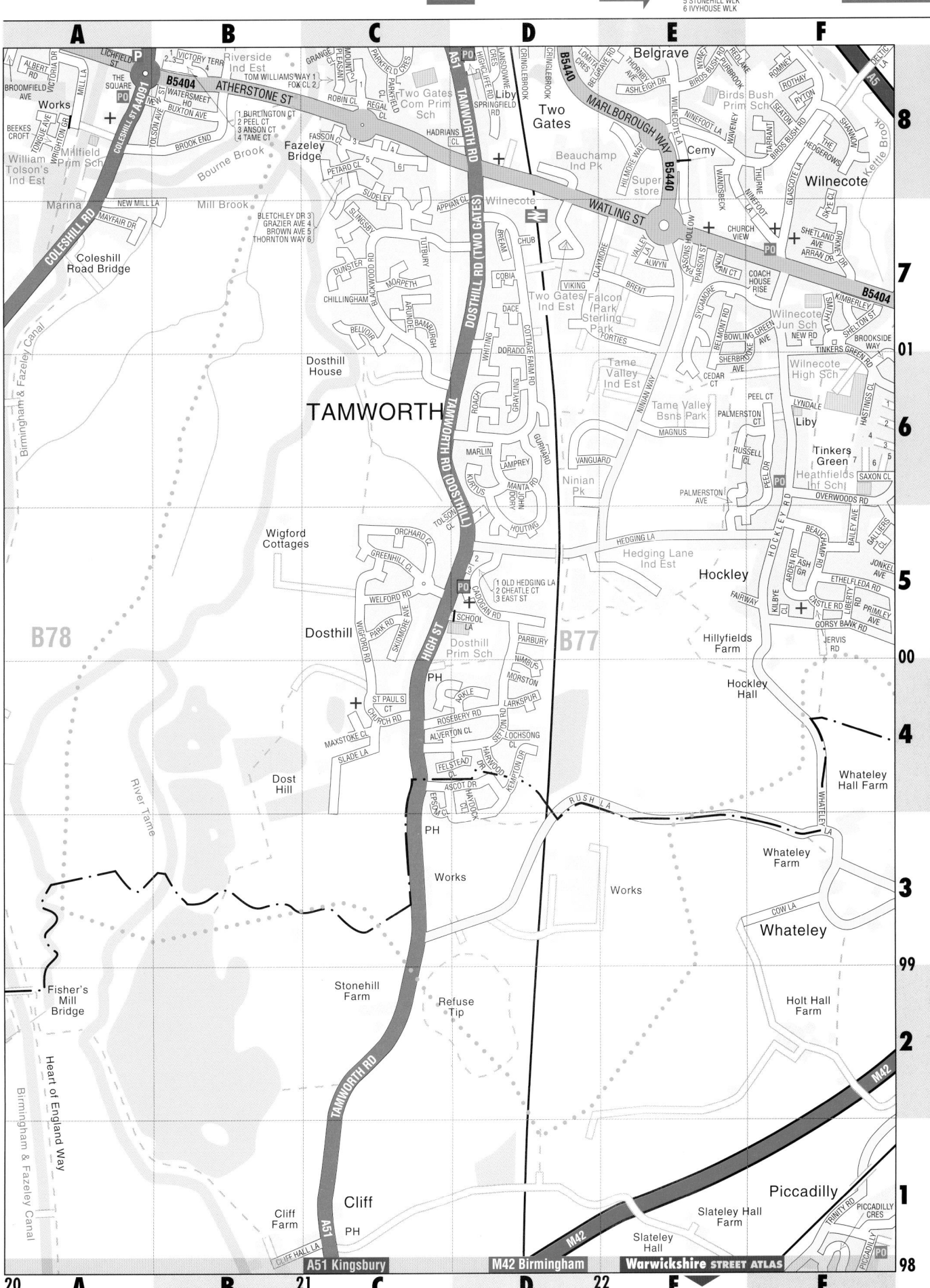

21

36

F6
1 BAKERS WLK
2 CALLIS WLK
3 LINTHOUSE WLK
4 COTTAGE WLK
5 STONEHILL WLK
6 IVYHOUSE WLK

7 LEISURE WLK

35

A B C D E F

ALBERT RD
VICTORIA DR
BROOMFIELD AVE
LICHFIELD ST
THE SQUARE
P
PO
VICTORY TERR 4
1
RIVERSIDE IND EST
TOM WILLIAMS WAY 1
FOX CL 2
GRANGE
PLEASANT
MOUNT
PARKFIELD CRES
LANSDOWNE CRES
HIGHCLIFFE
SPRINGFIELD
CRINGLEBROOK
Belgrave
B5440
LOMITA CRES
BELGRAVE RD
THORNBY AVE
ASHLEIGH DR
WILNECOTE LA
BIRDS BUSH RD
PURBROOK
NINEFOOT LA
WAVENEY
FEDLAKE
ROMNEY
ROTHAY
RYTON

8

Works
BEEKES CROFT
TAME CT
TONGUE LA
WRIGHTON DR
MILL LA
TOLSON AVE
BUXTON AVE
BROOK END
William Tolson's Ind Est
Milfield Prim Sch
FASSON CL
Fazeley Bridge
ROBIN CL
REGAL CL
1 BURLINGTON CT
2 PEEL CT
3 ANSON CT
4 TAME CT
HADRIANS CL
Two Gates Com Prim Sch
Wilnecote
Two Gates
Watling St
WANDSBECK
HILMORE WAY
Super store
Cemy
Birds Bush Prim Sch
THE HEDGEROWS
THURNE
GLASCOTE LA
SHANNON
SEATON
Wilnecote
B5404

Marina
NEW MILL LA
MAYFAIR DR
Mill Brook
BLETCHLEY DR 3
GRAZIER AVE 4
BROWN AVE 5
THORNTON WAY 6
SUDELEY
SLINGSBY
APPIAN CL
Wilnecote
BREAM
CHUB
CLAYMORE
VALLEY
ALWYN
BRENT
CHURCH VIEW
PO
BOWLING GREEN AVE
NEW RD
Wilnecote Jun Sch
KIMBERLEY
SMITH'S LA
SHELTON ST
BROOKSIDE WAY
B5404

7

Coleshill Road Bridge
Birmingham & Fazeley Canal
COLESHILL RD
Bourne Brook
DUNSTER
CHILLINGHAM
BLACKWOOD RD
MORPETH
TUTBURY
BELVOIR
ARUNDEL
BAMBURGH
WHITING
COBIA
DACE
DORADO
COTTAGE FARM RD
Two Gates Ind Est
Falcon Park Sterling Park
FORTIES
VIKING
Tame Valley Ind Est
SYCAMORE
BELMONT RD
RYMAN CT
CEDAR CT
PEEL CT
SHERBROKE AVE
Wilnecote High Sch
HASTINGS CL
Liby
01

6

Dosthill House
TAMWORTH
ROACH
MARLIN
LAMPREY
GURNARD
MANTA
JOHN DORY
HOUTINGS
Tame Valley Bsns Park
MAGNUS
NINIAN WAY
Ninian Pk
VANGUARD
PALMERSTON CT
RUSSELL CT
PALMERSTON AVE
Liby
Tinkers Green
Heathfields Inf Sch
SAXON CL
OVERWOODS RD
TAMWORTH RD (DOSTHILL)
DOSTHILL RD (TWO GATES)
TAMWORTH RD

KURTUS
TOLSON CL
Wigford Cottages
ORCHARD CL
GREENHILL CL
Dosthill
WELFORD RD
Dosthill Prim Sch
2
1 OLD HEDGING LA
2 CHEATLE CT
3 EAST ST
CADOGAN CL
SCHOOL LA
PARBURY
NIMBUS
PH
St PAUL'S CT
CHURCH RD
MORSTON
LARKSPUR
AKLE
ROSEBERY RD
ALVERTON CL
LOCHSONG CL
HEDGING LA
Hedging Lane Ind Est
Hockley
HOCKLEY RD
FAIRWAY
ARDER RD
ASH GR
BEAUCHAMP RD
BAILEY AVE
GALLIERS CL
ETHELFLEDA RD
GORSY BANK RD
JONKEL AVE
PRIMLEY AVE
CASTLE RD
LIBERTY RD
KILBYE CL
B78
B77
Hillyfields Farm
JERVIS RD
5

00

Dost Hill
MAXSTOKE CL
SLADE LA
FELSTEAD CL
HARTWOOD
EPSOM CL
ASCOT DR
KEMPTON DR
HADDOCK RD
Hockley Hall
Whateley Hall Farm
WHATELEY LA
4

River Tame
PH
Works
RUSH LA
Works
Whateley Farm
COW LA
Whateley
3

Fisher's Mill Bridge
Stonehill Farm
Refuse Tip
Holt Hall Farm
99

Heart of England Way
Birmingham & Fazeley Canal
TAMWORTH RD
HIGH ST
M42
2

Cliff
Cliff Farm
CLIFF HALL LA
A51
PH
M42
Slateley Hall
Slateley Hall Farm
Piccadilly
PICCADILLY CRES
TRINITY RD
PICCADILLY RD
PO
1

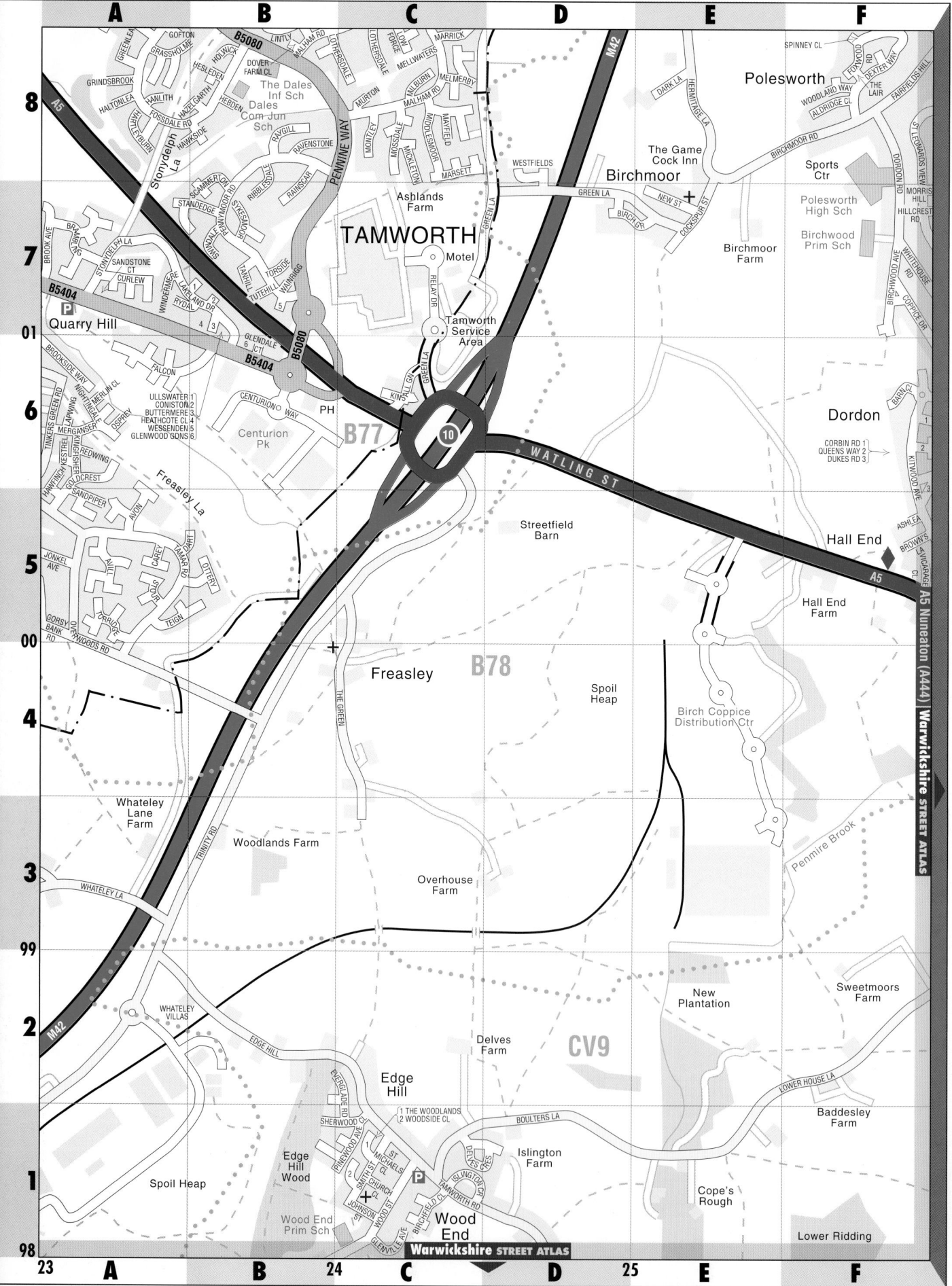

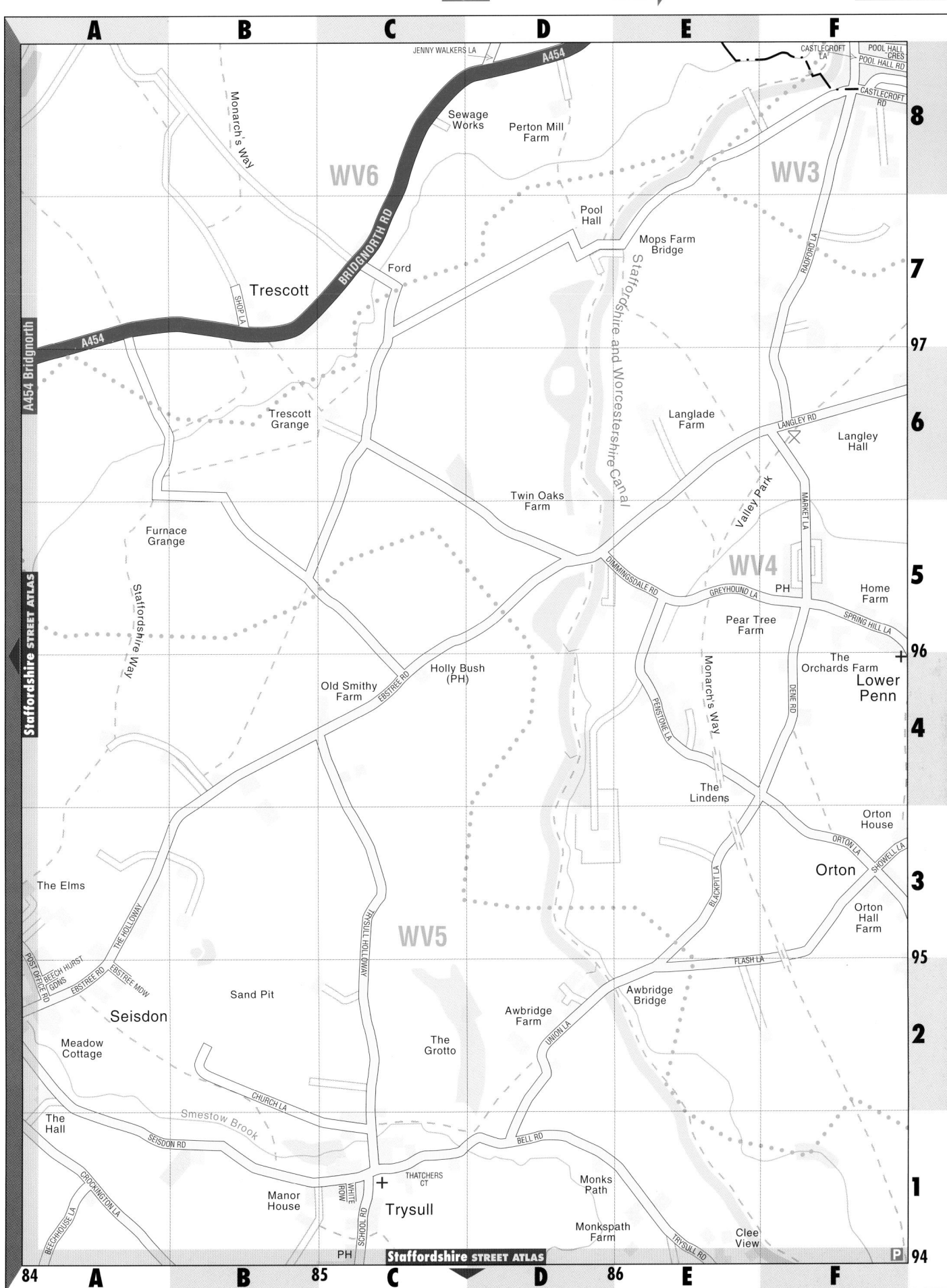

A   B   C   D   E   F

JENNY WALKERS LA

A454

CASTLECROFT
LA
POOL HALL
CRES
POOL HALL RD

CASTLECROFT
RD

8

Sewage
Works

Perton Mill
Farm

WV6

WV3

Monarch's Way

BRIDGNORTH RD

Pool
Hall

Mops Farm
Bridge

7

Ford

Trescott

SHOP LA

97

Staffordshire and Worcestershire Canal

RADFORD LA

A454 Bridgnorth

A454

Trescott
Grange

Langlade
Farm

LANGLEY RD

6

Langley
Hall

Furnace
Grange

Twin Oaks
Farm

Valley Park

MARKET LA

WV4

5

Home
Farm

DIMMINGSDALE RD

GREYHOUND LA

PH

SPRING HILL LA

Staffordshire Way

Pear Tree
Farm

The
Orchards Farm

96

Lower
Penn

Old Smithy
Farm

EBSTREE RD

Holly Bush
(PH)

PENSTONE LA

Monarch's Way

DENE RD

4

Staffordshire STREET ATLAS

The
Lindens

Orton
House

ORTON LA

SHOWELL LA

The Elms

THE HOLLOWAY

BLACKPIT LA

Orton

3

TRYSULL HOLLOWAY

WV5

Orton
Hall
Farm

FLASH LA

95

POST OFFICE RD

BEECH HURST
GDNS

EBSTREE RD

EBSTREE MDW

Sand Pit

Awbridge
Bridge

Seisdon

Awbridge
Farm

2

Meadow
Cottage

The
Grotto

UNION LA

The Hall

CHURCH LA

Smestow Brook

SEISDON RD

BELL RD

Monks
Path

1

BEECHHOUSE LA

CROCKINGTON LA

Manor
House

WHITE
ROW

SCHOOL RD

Trysull

THATCHERS
CT

Monkspath
Farm

TRYSULL RD

Clee
View

PH

94

84   A   B   85   C   D   86   E   F

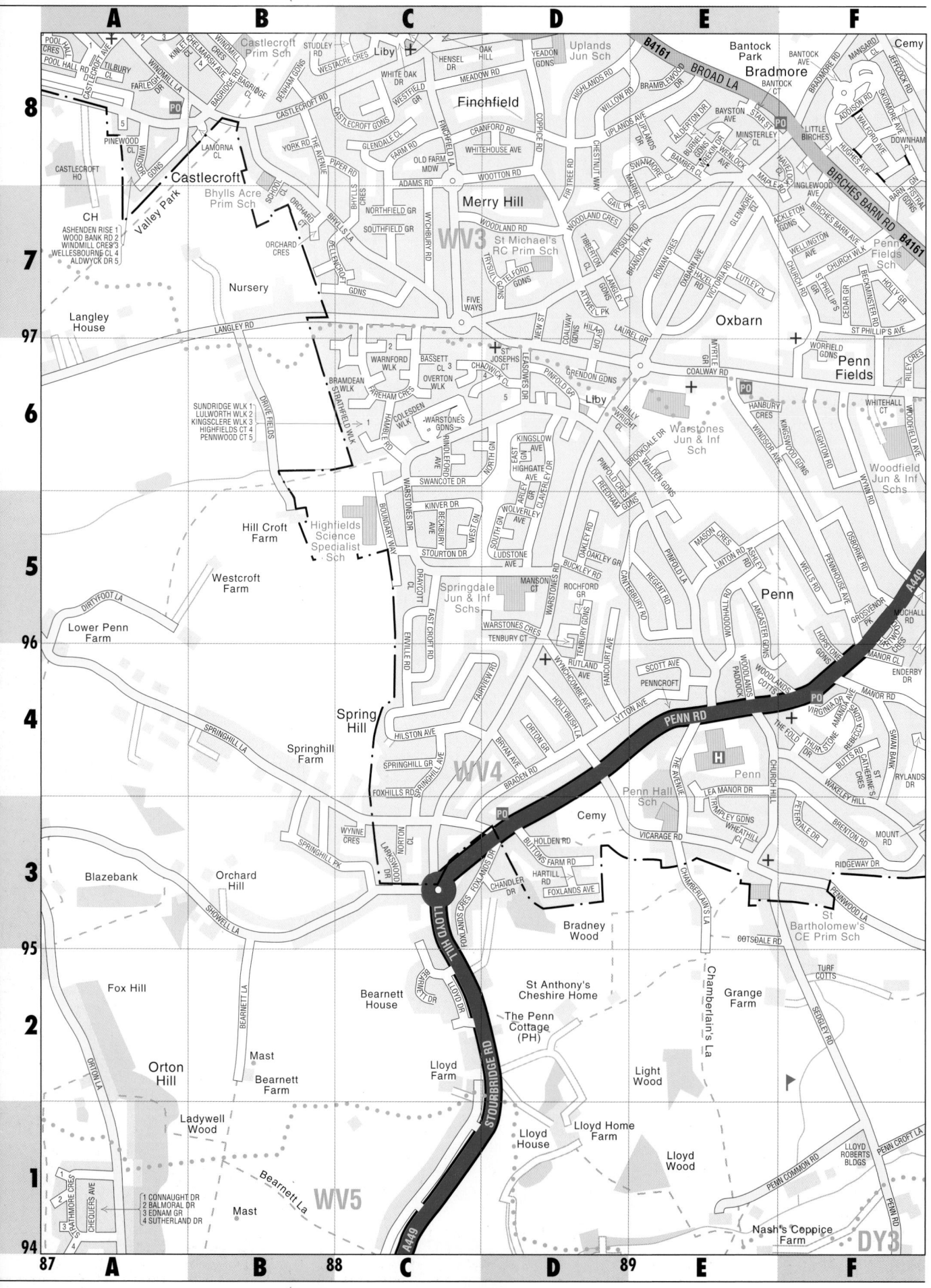

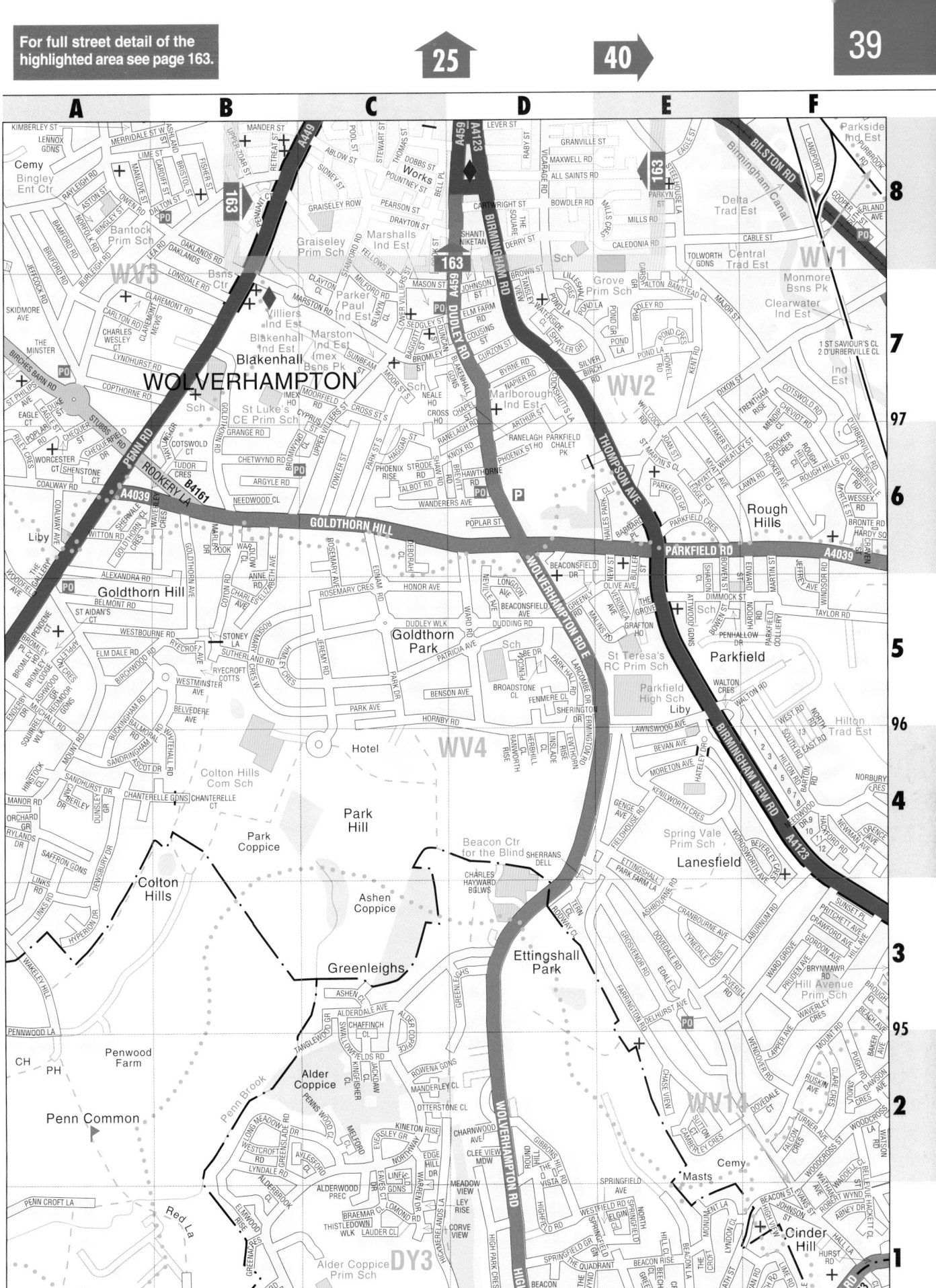

For full street detail of the highlighted area see page 163.

25 40 39

F4
1 ELLIOT CT
2 HARDIE CT
3 MERIDEN CT
4 MORRIS CT
5 WESLEY CT
6 WARWICK CT
7 RYLCROFT
8 AVONCROFT
9 FIRCROFT
10 HOLMCROFT
11 GENTHORN CL
12 ASHCROFT
13 CENTRAL AVE

F8
1 CHARLECOTE RISE
2 RAGLEY DR
3 PETWORTH CL

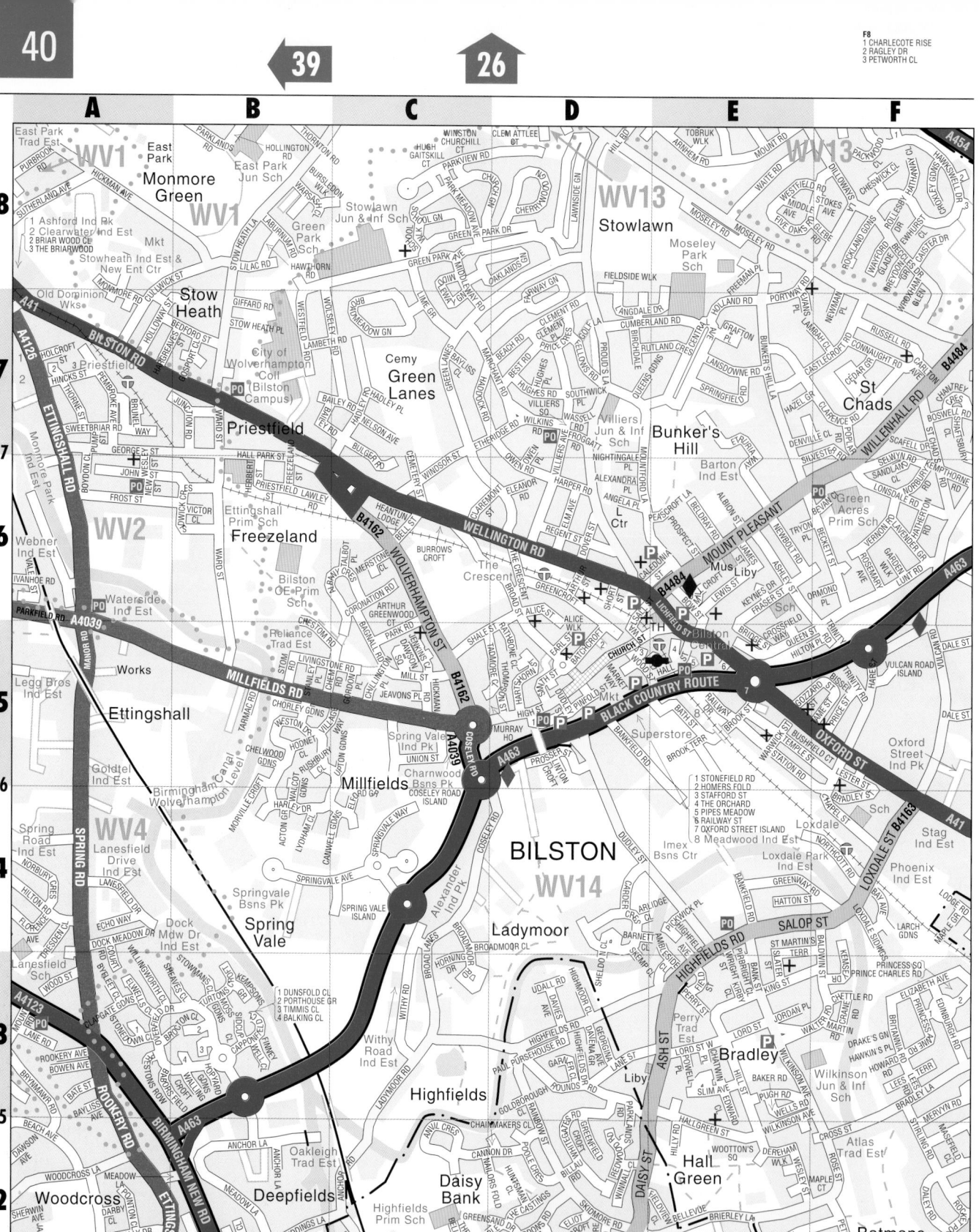

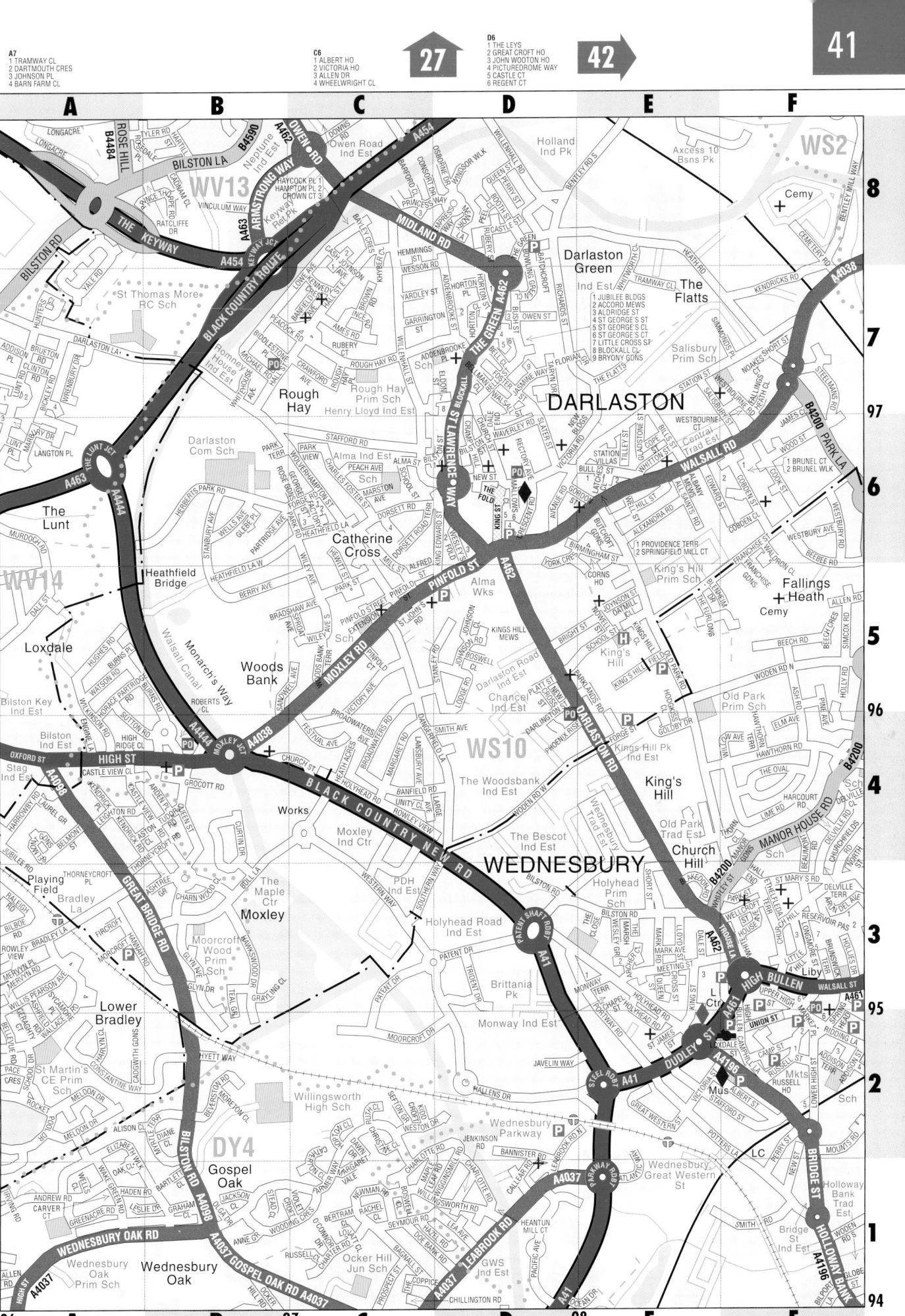

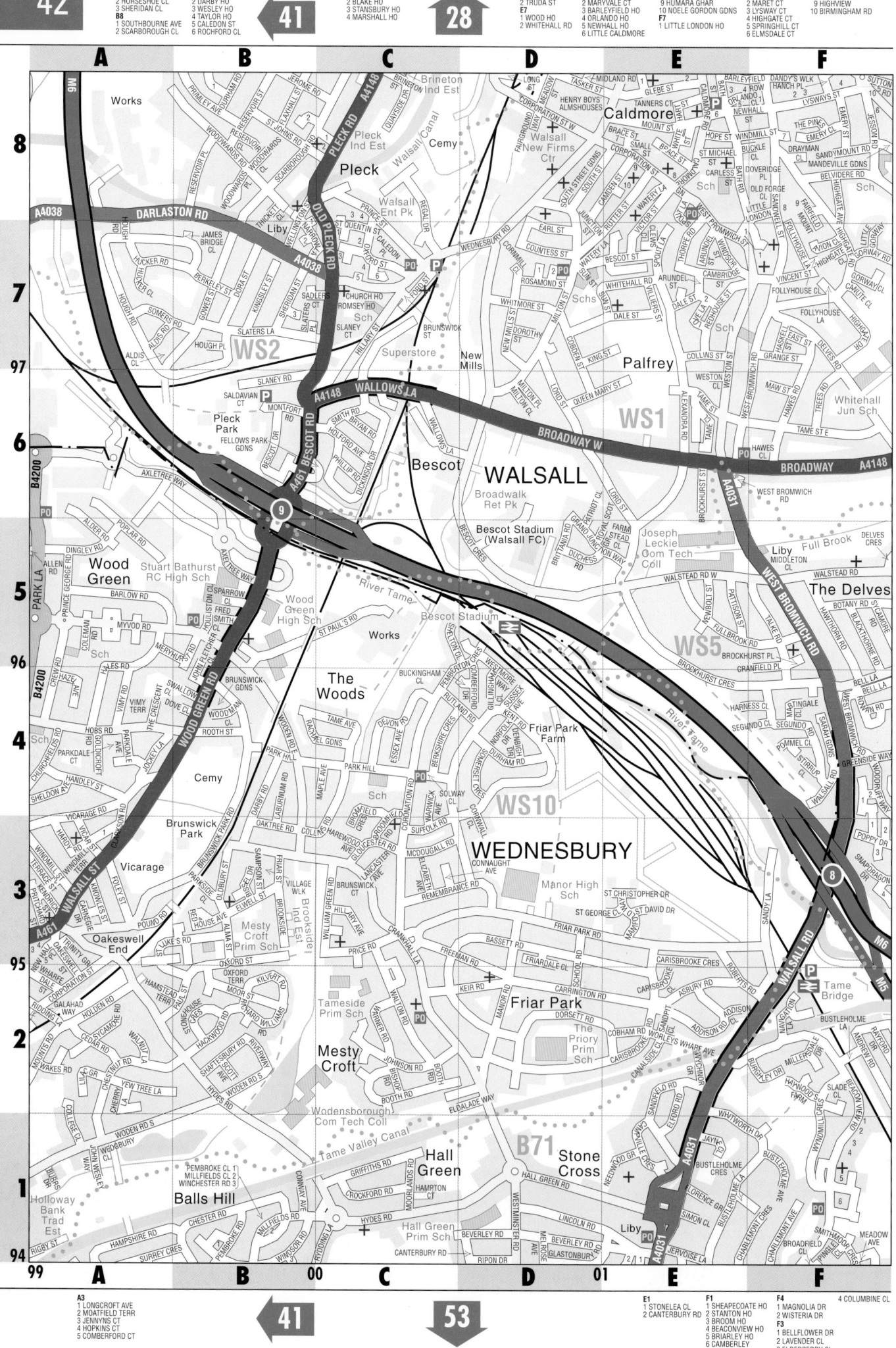

B7
1 DAWLEY CL
2 HORSESHOE CL
3 SHERIDAN CL
B8
1 SOUTHBOURNE AVE
2 SCARBOROUGH CL

C7
1 SCRIMSHAW HO
2 DARBY HO
3 WESLEY HO
4 TAYLOR HO
5 CALEDON CL
6 ROCHFORD CL

C8
1 VICARAGE TERR
2 BLAKE HO
3 STANSBURY HO
4 MARSHALL HO

D7
1 THELMA ST
2 TRUDA ST
E7
1 WOOD HO
2 WHITEHALL HO

E8
1 SISTER DORA GDNS
2 MARYVALE CT
3 BARLEYFIELD HO
4 ORLANDO HO
5 NEWHALL HO
6 LITTLE CALDMORE

7 HAYDN SANDERS SQ
8 THE WHITE HART
9 HUMARA GHAR
10 NOELE GORDON GDNS

F8
1 SANDWELL HO
2 MARET CT
3 LYSWAY CT
4 HIGHGATE CT
5 SPRINGHILL CT
6 ELMSDALE CT
F7
1 LITTLE LONDON HO

7 RIDGEWOOD CL
8 SANDWELL WLK
9 HIGHVIEW
10 BIRMINGHAM RD

41   28

A3
1 LONGCROFT AVE
2 MOATFIELD TERR
3 JENNYNS CT
4 HOPKINS CT
5 COMBERFORD CT

E1
1 STONELEA CL
2 CANTERBURY RD

F1
1 SHEAPECOATE HO
2 STANTON HO
3 BROOM HO
4 BEACONVIEW HO
5 BRIARLEY HO
6 CAMBERLEY

F4
1 MAGNOLIA DR
2 WISTERIA DR
F3
1 BELLFLOWER DR
2 LAVENDER CL
3 ELDERBERRY CL

4 COLUMBINE CL

29
44

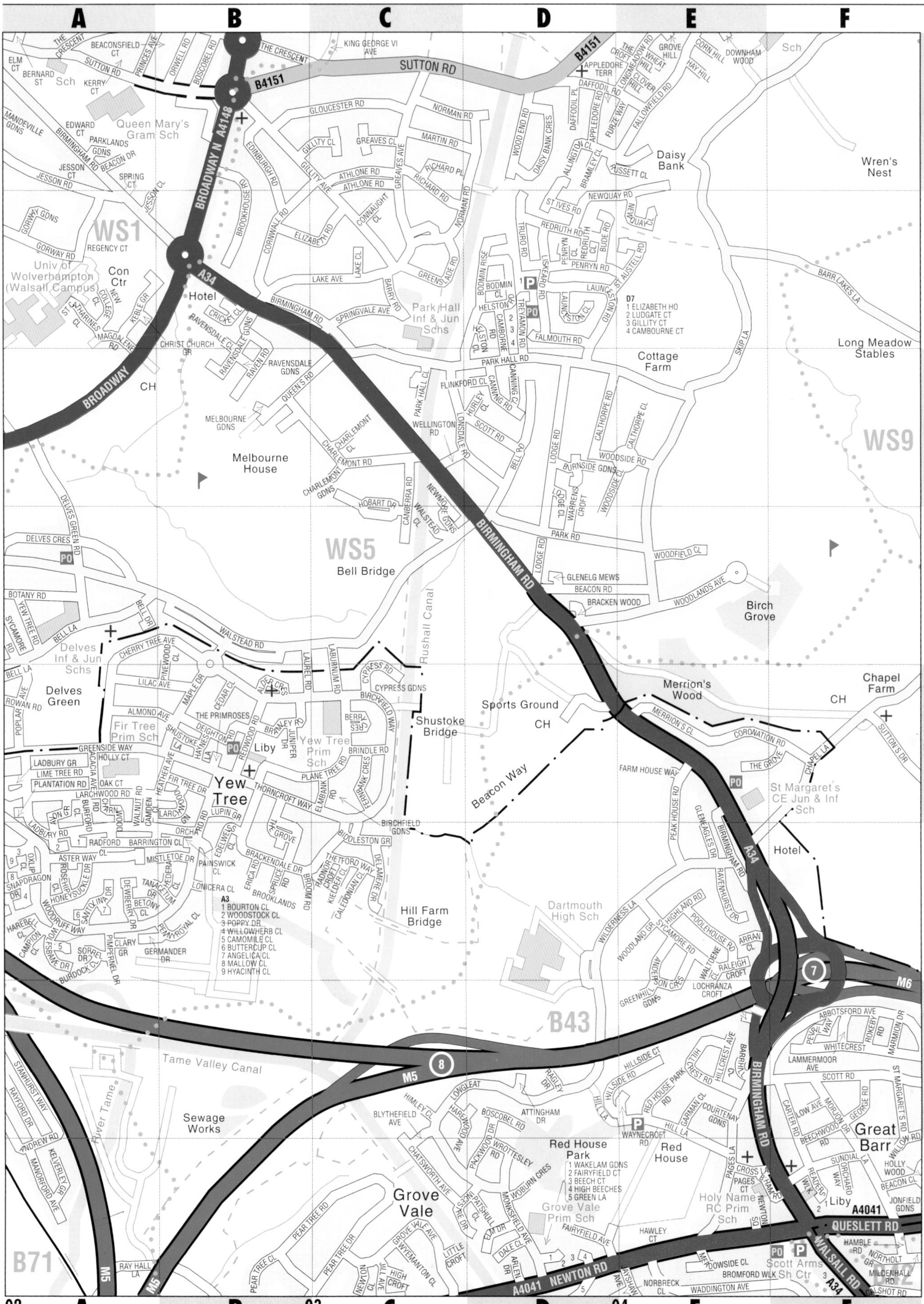

54
44

F1
1 BEACON MEWS
2 BEACON CT
3 SANDRINGHAM CT

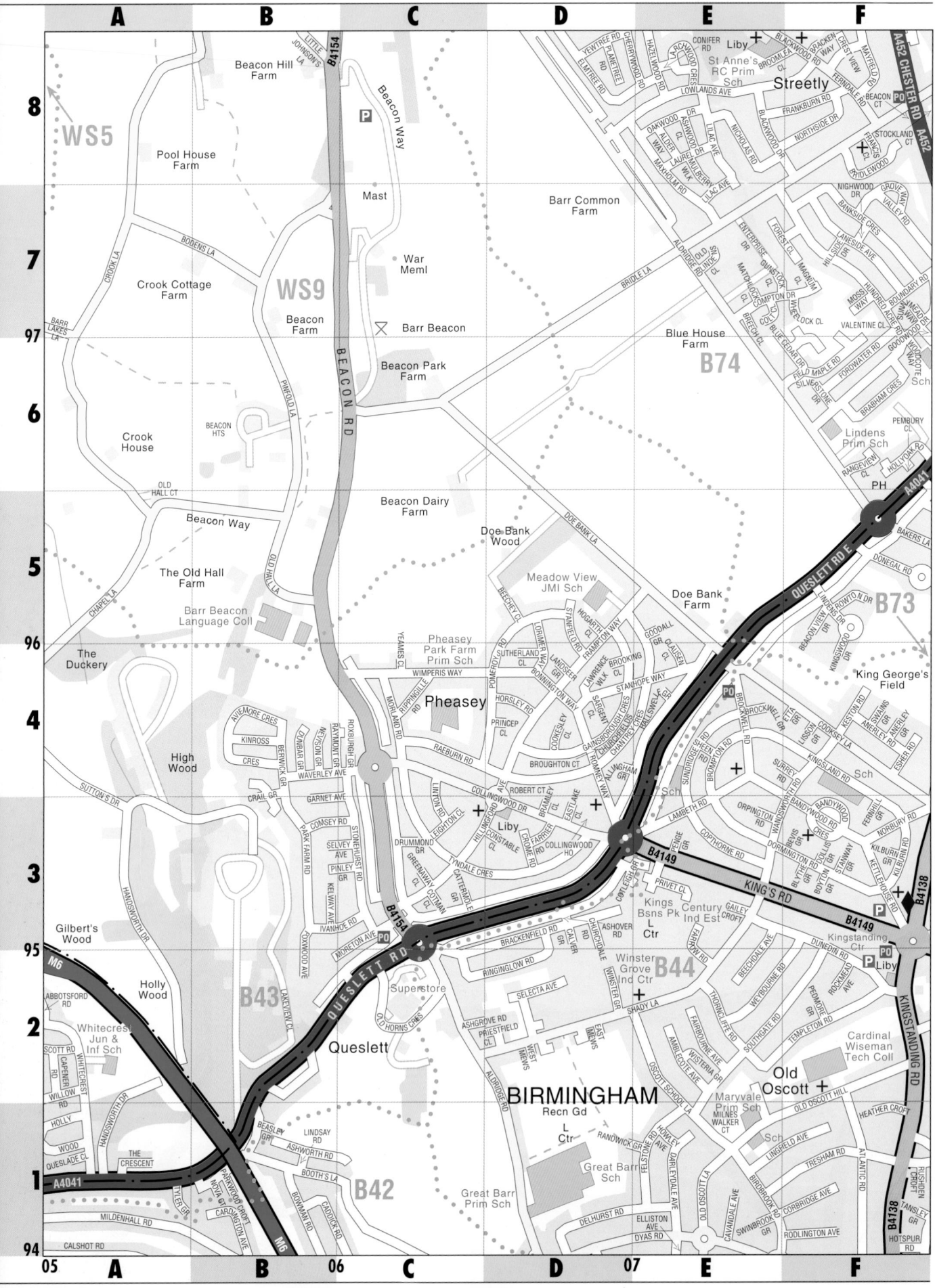

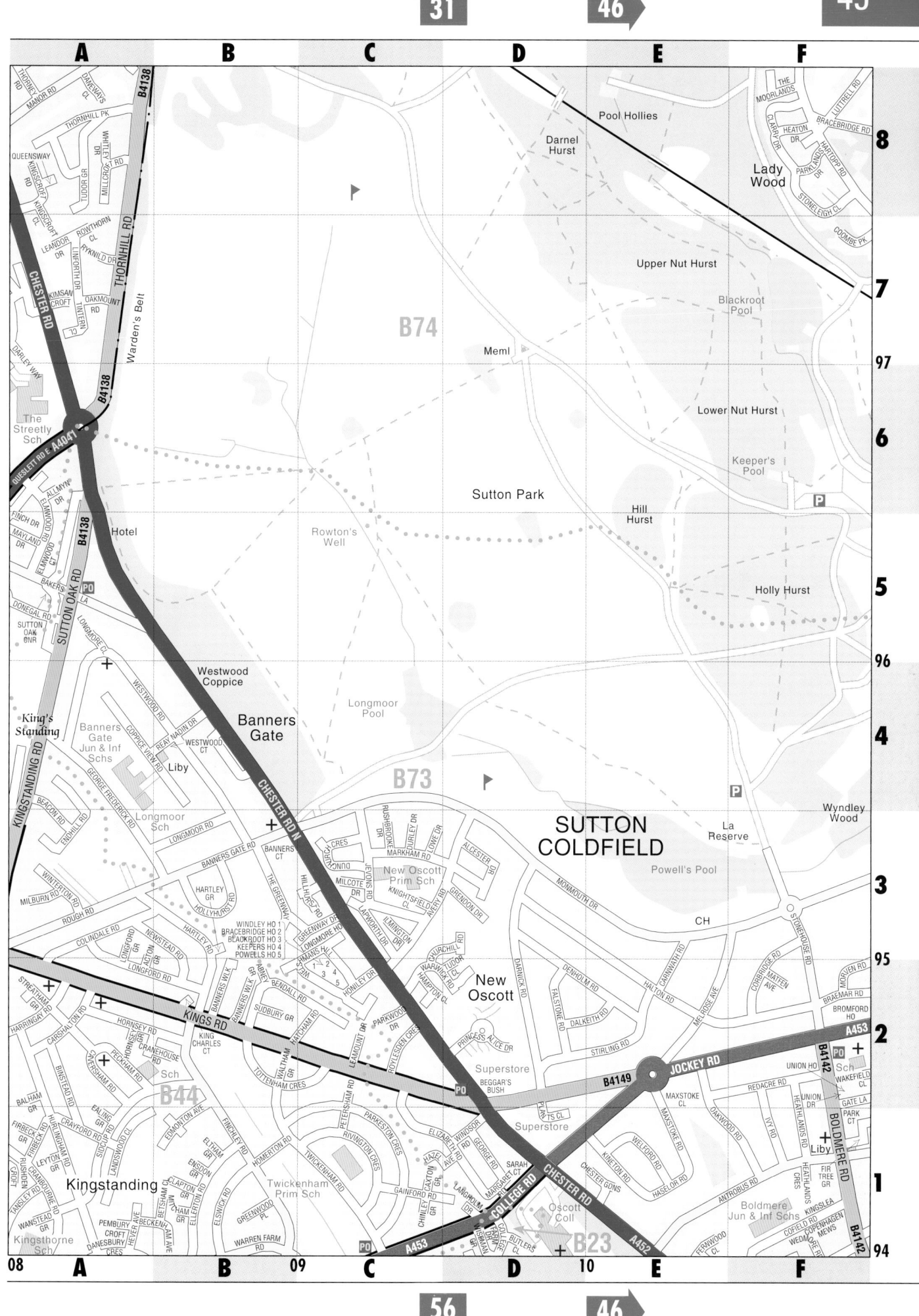

31
46
56
46

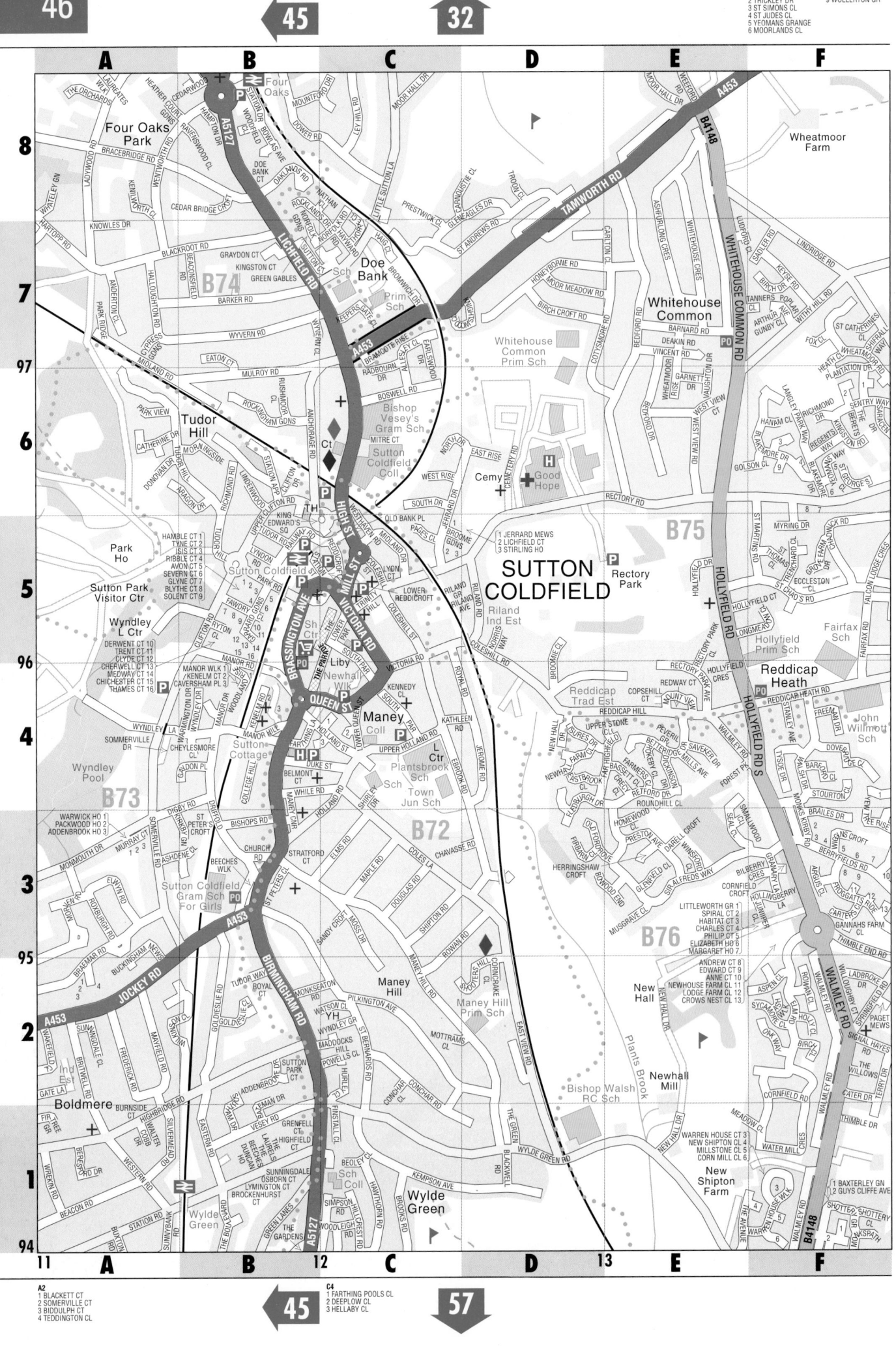

F6
1 ALDERMORE DR
2 TRICKLEY DR
3 ST SIMONS CL
4 ST JUDES CL
5 YEOMANS GRANGE
6 MOORLANDS CL

7 RECTORY PARK CT
8 WHITEHOUSE CT
9 WOLLERTON GR

A   B   C   D   E   F

SUTTON
COLDFIELD

Four Oaks
Park

Tudor
Hill

Park
Ho

Sutton Park
Visitor Ctr

Wyndley
L Ctr

Wyndley
Pool

B73

Boldmere

Doe
Bank

Bishop
Vesey's
Gram Sch

Sutton
Coldfield
Coll

King
Edward's
Sq

Sutton Coldfield

Maney
Coll

Maney
Hill

Wylde
Green

B74

Whitehouse
Common

Whitehouse
Common
Prim Sch

Cemy

Good
Hope

B75

Rectory
Park

Riland
Ind Est

Reddicap
Trad Est

Reddicap
Heath

Hollyfield
Prim Sch

Fairfax
Sch

B72

B76

New
Hall

Newhall
Mill

Bishop Walsh
RC Sch

New
Shipton
Farm

Wheatmoor
Farm

John
Willmott
Sch

Plants Brook

A2
1 BLACKETT CT
2 SOMERVILLE CT
3 BIDDULPH CT
4 TEDDINGTON CL

C4
1 FARTHING POOLS CL
2 DEEPLOW CL
3 HELLABY CL

8 7 97 6 5 96 4 3 95 2 1 94

11   12   13

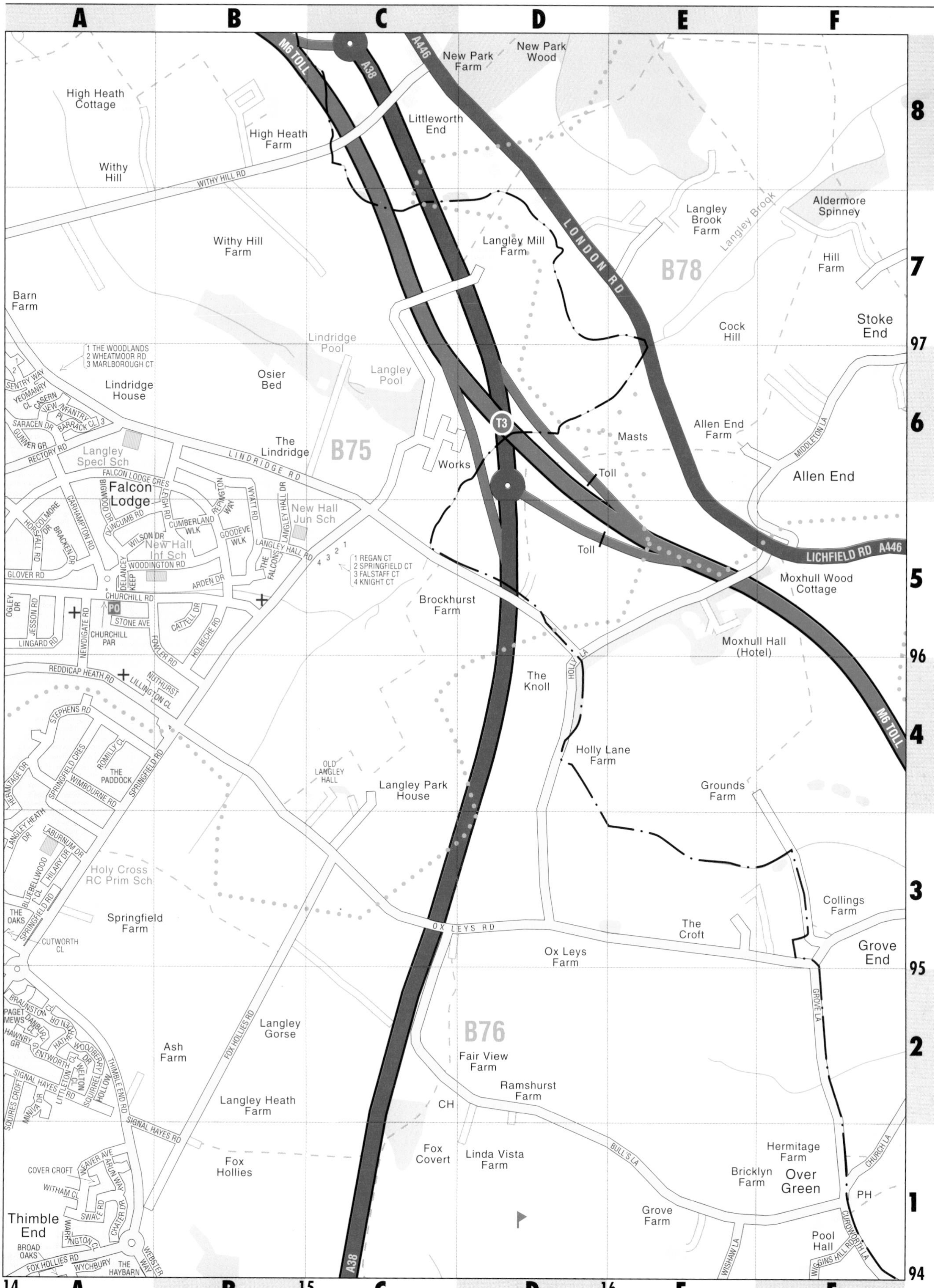

A B C D E F

8
7
97
6
5
96
4
3
95
2
1
94

14 A 15 B C 16 D E F

High Heath Cottage
High Heath Farm
Withy Hill
Withy Hill Farm
Withy Hill Rd
Barn Farm
1 THE WOODLANDS
2 WHEATMOOR RD
3 MARLBOROUGH CT
Lindridge House
Lindridge Pool
Osier Bed
Langley Pool
Langley Specl Sch
The Lindridge
B75
LINDRIDGE RD
Falcon Lodge
Falcon Lodge Cres
Leigh Rd
Wyatt Rd
Ripington Way
New Hall Jun Sch
New Hall Inf Sch
Cumberland Wlk
Goodeve Wlk
Langley Hall Rd
Langley Hall Dr
Woodington Rd
The Falcons
4 3 2 1
1 REGAN CT
2 SPRINGFIELD CT
3 FALSTAFF CT
4 KNIGHT CT
Arden Dr
Glover Rd
Churchill Rd
Stone Ave
Holbeche Rd
Fowler Rd
Cattell Dr
Brockhurst Farm
Reddicap Heath Rd
Nuthurst
Lillington Cl
Churchill Par
Stephens Rd
Springfield Cres
Romilly Cl
Wimborne Rd
Springfield Rd
The Paddock
Hermitage Dr
Langley Heath Dr
Laburnum Dr
Bluebellwood Cl
Hilary Dr
Springer Rd
The Oaks
Holy Cross RC Prim Sch
Springfield Farm
Cutworth Cl
Old Langley Hall
Langley Park House
Ox Leys Rd
Langley Gorse
Langley Heath Farm
Fox Hollies Rd
Braunston Cl
Paget Mews
Hawnby Gr
Wentworth Dr
Signal Hayes Rd
Squires Croft
Minster Dr
Little Hollow
Squirrel Hollow
Thimble End Rd
Ash Farm
Cover Croft
Saer Ave
Arun Way
Witham Cl
Warrington Dr
Swan Cl
Chafer Dr
Webster Way
Broad Oaks
Fox Hollies Rd
Wychbury
The Haybarn
Thimble End
Fox Hollies
Fox Covert
Linda Vista Farm
Fair View Farm
Ramshurst Farm
CH
B76
Ox Leys Farm
Grove Farm
Bull's La
Bricklyn Farm
Over Green
Hermitage Farm
Wishaw La
PH
Pool Hall
Church La
Wiggins Hill Rd
Grove End
Grove La
Collings Farm
The Croft
Grounds Farm
Holly Lane Farm
The Knoll
Holt La
Moxhull Hall (Hotel)
Moxhull Wood Cottage
Lichfield Rd A446
Allen End
Allen End Farm
Masts
Toll
Toll
Works
T3
M6 Toll
A38
A446
London Rd
New Park Farm
New Park Wood
Littleworth End
Langley Mill Farm
Langley Brook Farm
Langley Brook
B78
Cock Hill
Hill Farm
Aldermore Spinney
Stoke End
M6 Toll
Middleton La

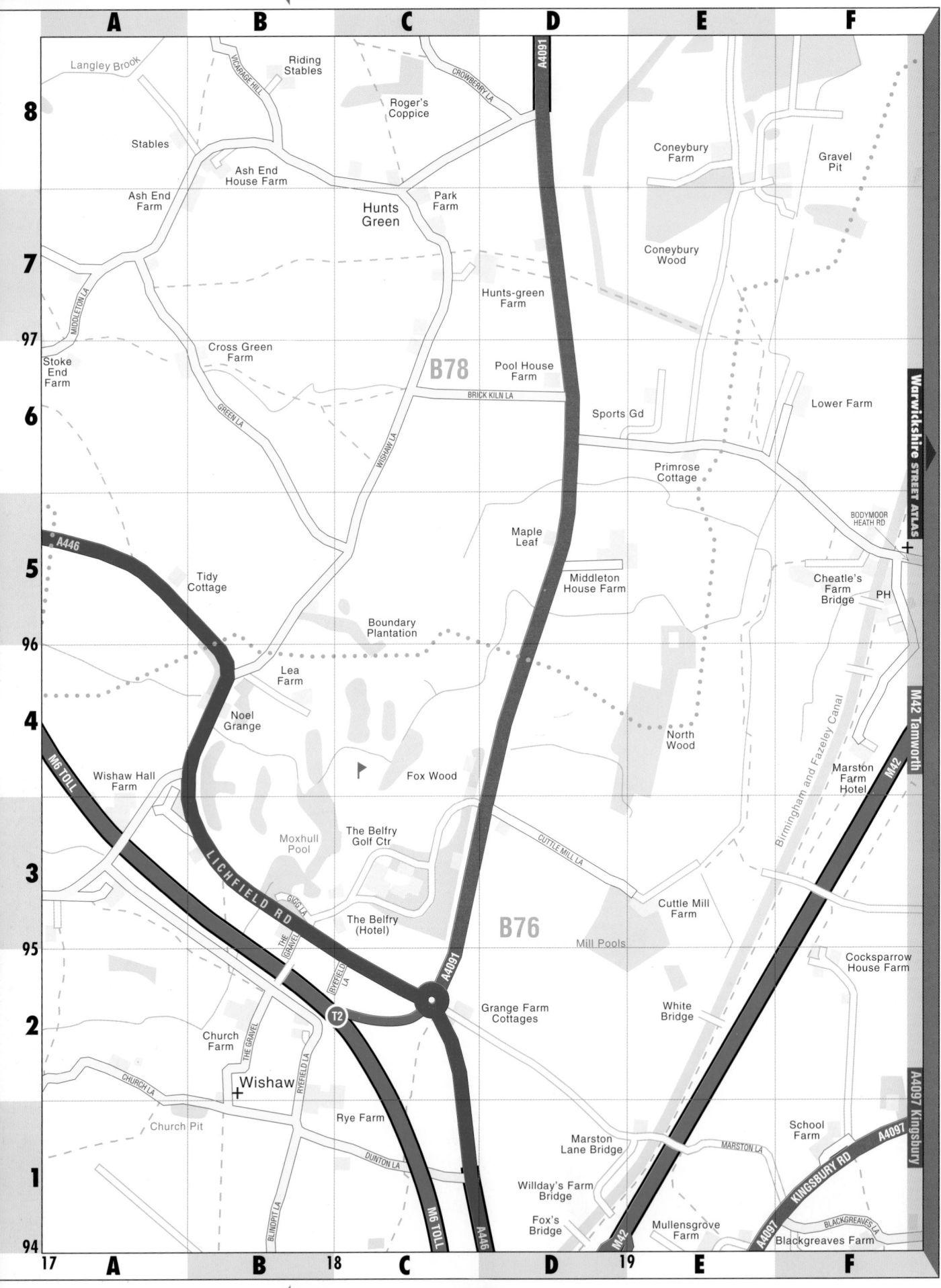

47
34

A B C D E F

8

7

97

6

5

96

4

3

95

2

1

94

17 A B 18 C D 19 E F

Langley Brook

VICARAGE HILL

Riding Stables

Roger's Coppice

CROWBERRY LA

A4091

Stables

Ash End House Farm

Park Farm

Coneybury Farm

Gravel Pit

Ash End Farm

Hunts Green

Coneybury Wood

MIDDLETON LA

Hunts-green Farm

Cross Green Farm

B78

Pool House Farm

BRICK KILN LA

Sports Gd

Lower Farm

Warwickshire STREET ATLAS

Stoke End Farm

GREEN LA

WISHAW LA

Primrose Cottage

BODYMOOR HEATH RD

A446

Tidy Cottage

Boundary Plantation

Maple Leaf

Middleton House Farm

Cheatle's Farm Bridge

PH

Lea Farm

Noel Grange

North Wood

Birmingham and Fazeley Canal

M6 TOLL

Wishaw Hall Farm

Fox Wood

CUTTLE MILL LA

Marston Farm Hotel

M42 Tamworth

LICHFIELD RD

Moxhull Pool

The Belfry Golf Ctr

B76

Cuttle Mill Farm

Cocksparrow House Farm

BIGG LA

The Belfry (Hotel)

Mill Pools

THE GRAVEL

BYEFIELD LA

T2

Grange Farm Cottages

White Bridge

A4091

Church Farm

RYEFIELD LA

Wishaw

A4097 Kingsbury

Church LA

Rye Farm

Marston Lane Bridge

MARSTON LA

School Farm

A4097

Church Pit

BLINDPIT LA

DUNTON LA

Willday's Farm Bridge

KINGSBURY RD

BLACKGREAVES LA

Fox's Bridge

M6 TOLL

A446

M42

Mullensgrove Farm

A4097

Blackgreaves Farm

47
59

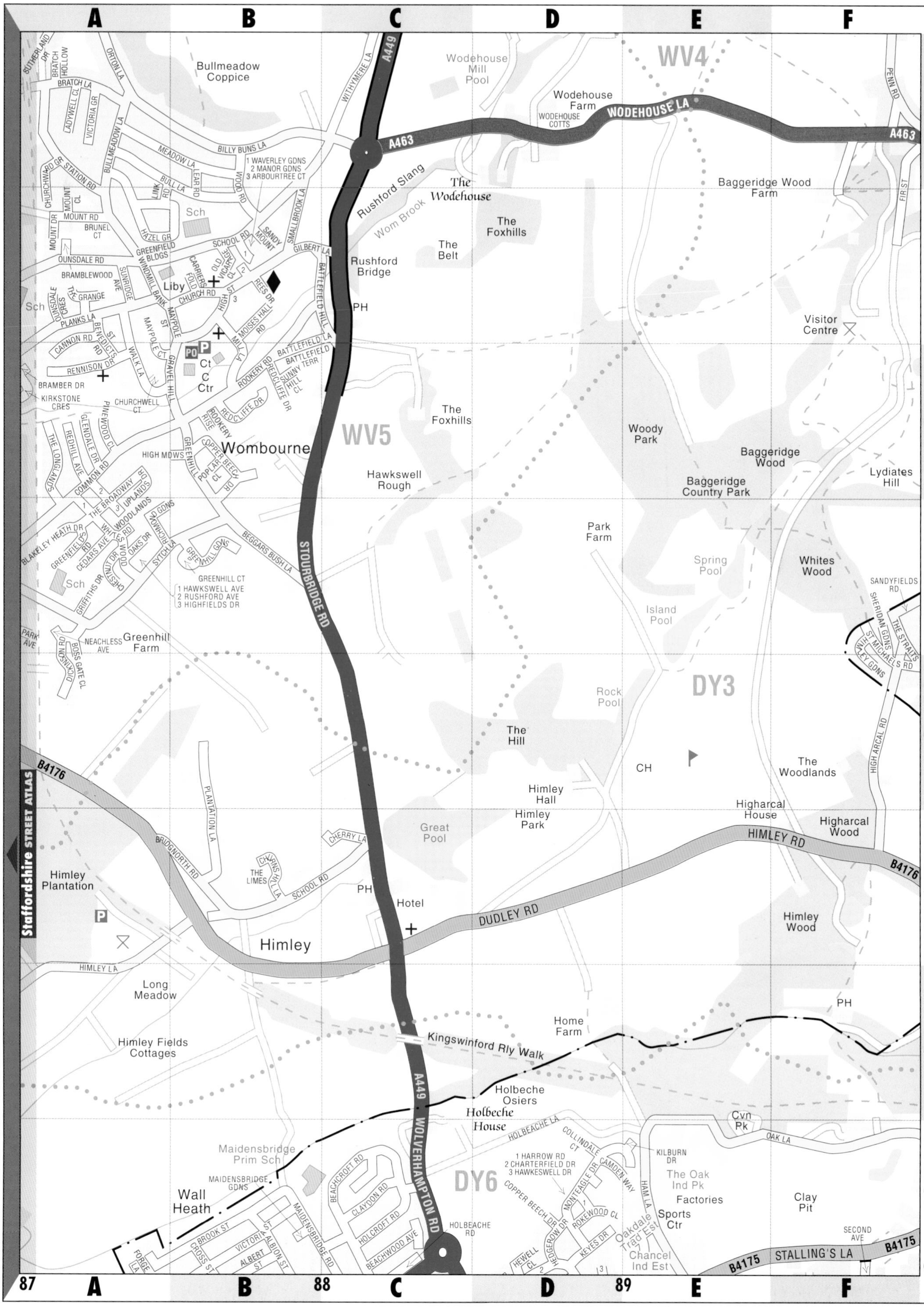

A B C D E F

8
7
93
6
5
92
4
3
91
2
1
90

87 A 88 B C 89 D E F 90

WV4
WV5
DY3
DY6

Wombourne
Himley
Wall Heath

Staffordshire Street Atlas

A449
A463
B4176
B4175

WODEHOUSE LA
HIMLEY RD
DUDLEY RD
STOURBRIDGE RD
WOLVERHAMPTON RD
STALLING'S LA

Bullmeadow Coppice
Wodehouse Mill Pool
Wodehouse Farm
Wodehouse Cotts
Baggeridge Wood Farm
The Wodehouse
Wom Brook
Rushford Slang
Rushford Bridge
The Foxhills
The Belt
The Foxhills
Woody Park
Baggeridge Wood
Baggeridge Country Park
Lydiates Hill
Visitor Centre
PENN RD
FIRS ST
Hawkswell Rough
Park Farm
Spring Pool
Whites Wood
SANDYFIELDS RD
Island Pool
Rock Pool
The Hill
CH
The Woodlands
Himley Hall
Himley Park
Higharcal House
Higharcal Wood
Great Pool
Hotel
Himley Wood
Himley Plantation
Long Meadow
Himley Fields Cottages
Kingswinford Rly Walk
Home Farm
PH
Cvn Pk
Holbeche Osiers
Holbeche House
Maidensbridge Prim Sch
Maidensbridge Gdns
Clay Pit
Sports Ctr
The Oak Ind Pk
Factories
Chancel Ind Est
Oakdale Trad Est
KILBURN DR
OAK LA
HIGH ARCAL RD
SHERIDAN GDNS
THE STRAITS
ST MICHAELS RD
SECOND AVE

Greenhill Farm
Neachless Ave
Greenhill Ct
1 Hawkswell Ave
2 Rushford Ave
3 Highfields Dr
1 Waverley Gdns
2 Manor Gdns
3 Arbourtree Ct
1 Harrow Rd
2 Charterfield Dr
3 Hawkeswell Dr

SOMERLAND DR
BRATCH HOLLOW
BRATCH LA
ORTON LA
LADYWELL CL
VICTORIA GR
BULLMEADOW LA
CHURCHWARD GR
STATION RD
MEADOW LA
BILLY BUNS LA
BULL LA
LEAR RD
LINN
HAZEL GR
MOUNT DR
MOUNT RD
MOUNT CL
BRUNEL CT
OUNSDALE RD
BRAMBLEWOOD
GREENFIELD BLDGS
SANDY MOUNT
SCHOOL RD
GILBERT LA
WINDMILL BANK
CHURCH RD
HIGH ST
REES DR
MOISES HALL RD
BATTLEFIELD HILL
BATTLEFIELD LA
SUNNY TERR
REDCLIFFE DR
REDCLIFFE CL
ROOKERY RD
WALK LA
GRAVEL HILL
CANNON RD
RENNISON DR
BRAMBER DR
KIRKSTONE CRES
CHURCHWELL CT
ROOKERY RISE
COPPER BEECH CL
POPLAR CL
HIGH MDWS
THE LONGLANDS
REDHILL RD
GLENDALE RD
PINEWOOD CT
COMMON RD
THE BROADWAY
UPLANDS
WOODLANDS
GREEN GDNS
BLAKELEY HEATH DR
GREENFIELD
CEDARS AVE
CHESTNUT WLK
OAKS DR
WELLS DR
SYCAMORE
GRIFFITHS DR
PARK AVE
BOSS GATE CL
DINGLE
BEGGARS BUSH LA
GREENHILL LA
PLANTATION LA
BRIDGNORTH RD
THE LIMES
CHAPEL VW LA
CHERRY LA
SCHOOL RD
HIMLEY LA
BEECHCROFT RD
CLAYDON RD
HOLCROFT RD
BEACHWOOD AVE
BROOK ST
CROSS ST
FORGE LA
ALBERT ST
VICTORIA ST
ST ALBON ST
MAIDENSBRIDGE RD
HOLBEACHE RD
HOLBEACHE LA
COLLINDALE CT
CAMDEN WAY
COPPER BEECH DR
HEDGEROW DR
MONTEAGLE DR
HAM LA
ROKEWOOD CL
KEYES DR
HEWELL CL
CHURCHWELL CT
CHAPEL VW

Sch
Liby
PH
PO
P
Ct
C Ctr

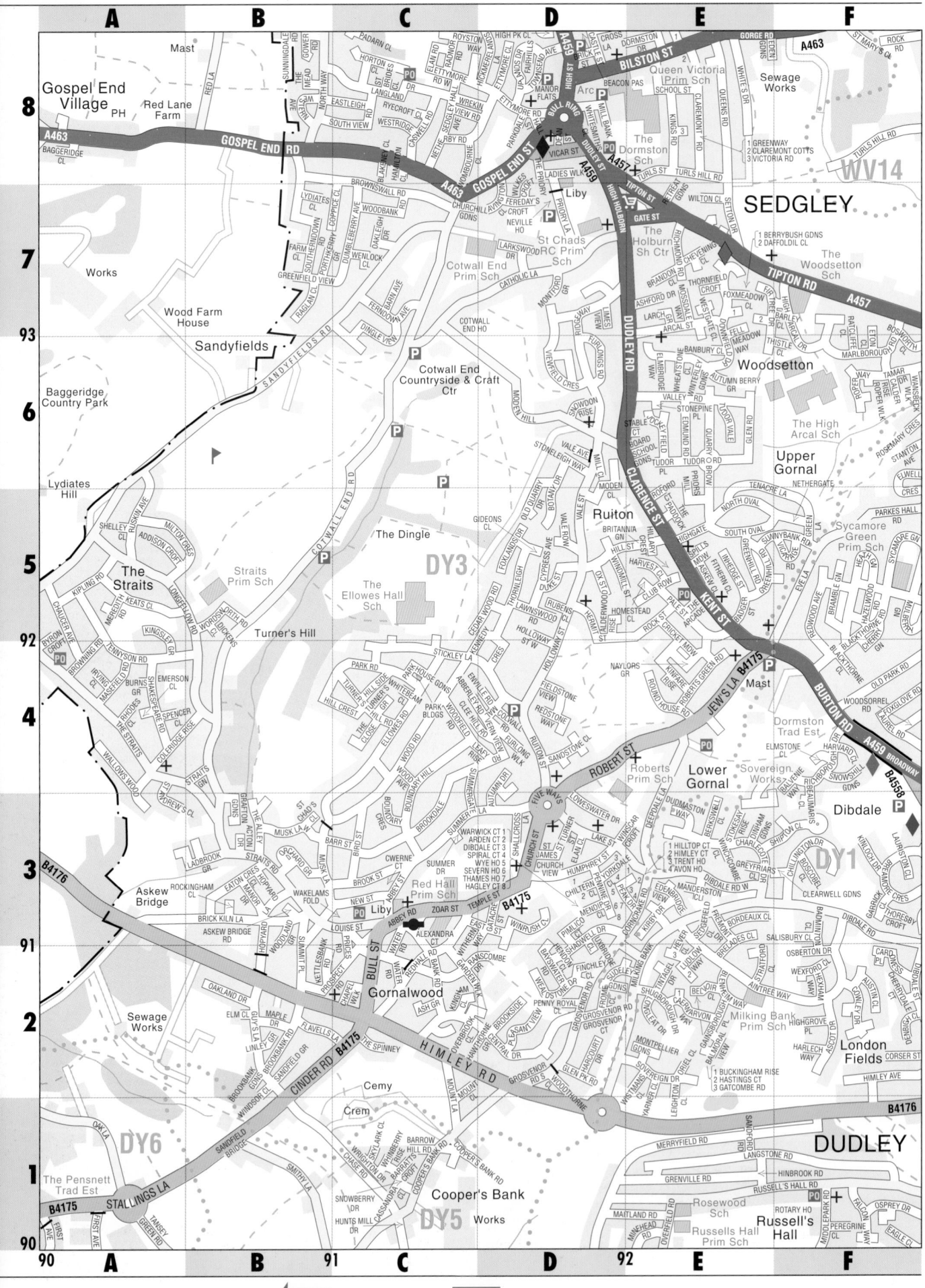

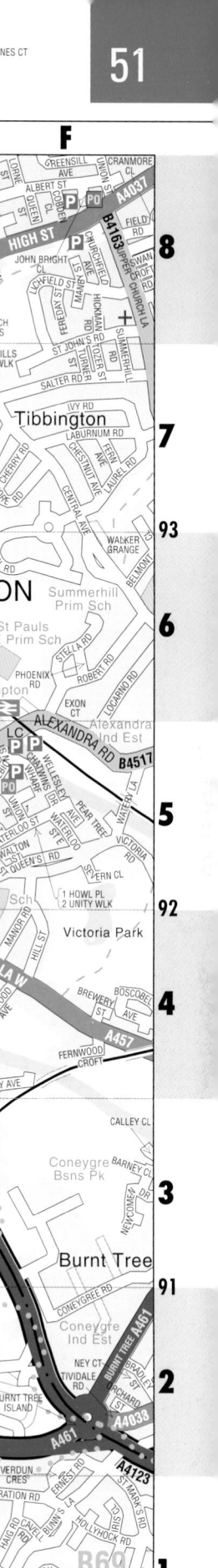

C8
1 COSELEY HALL
2 SCHOOL ST W
3 JACK NEWELL CT
4 ROSEVILLE CT
5 ROSEVILLE PREC
6 GROUCOTT ST

E5
1 Eclipse Ind Est
2 CAMPION CT
3 WADES CL
4 BEEHIVE WLK
5 BRINDLEY CT
6 HORSESHOE WLK
7 DOWNES CT

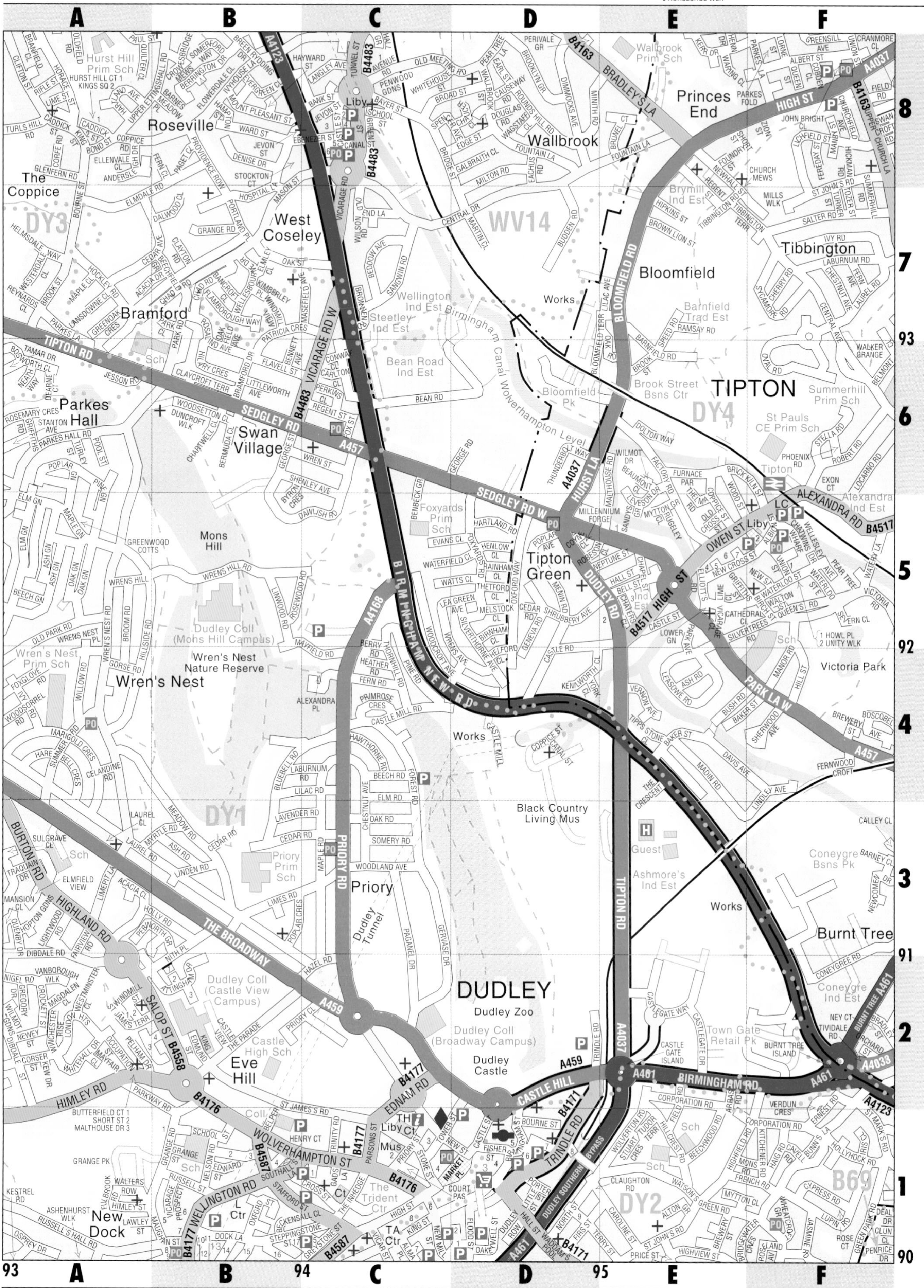

B1
1 GRANGE CT
2 ALEXANDRA ST
3 EDWARD CT
4 CHARLTON CT
5 CLENT CT
6 CLAVERLEY CT
7 FARTHINGS LODGE
8 HOLLAND ST
9 SWANCOTE RD
10 DOCK LA
11 LUDGATE ST
12 TURNER ST
13 Dock Lane Ind Est
14 CLEVELAND ST
15 CHARLOTTE ST
16 GREYSTONE PAS
17 PITFIELD ROW

B2
1 KING EDMUND ST

2 NORTHGATE CL
3 SOUTHGATE WAY
4 THE SHRUBBERY

C1
1 TINCHBOURNE ST
2 HERALD CT
3 PRIORY CT
4 FOUNTAIN ARC
5 PITFIELD ST
6 UNION ST

C1
7 NEW KING ST
8 RUTLAND PAS

D1
1 THE MINORIES
2 KING STREET PAS
3 Churchill Sh Ctr
4 BIRDCAGE WLK
5 GATEHOUSE FOLD
6 PORTERS FIELD
7 ST JOSEPH ST

D1
8 CLAUGHTON ROAD N
9 PORTER STREET S

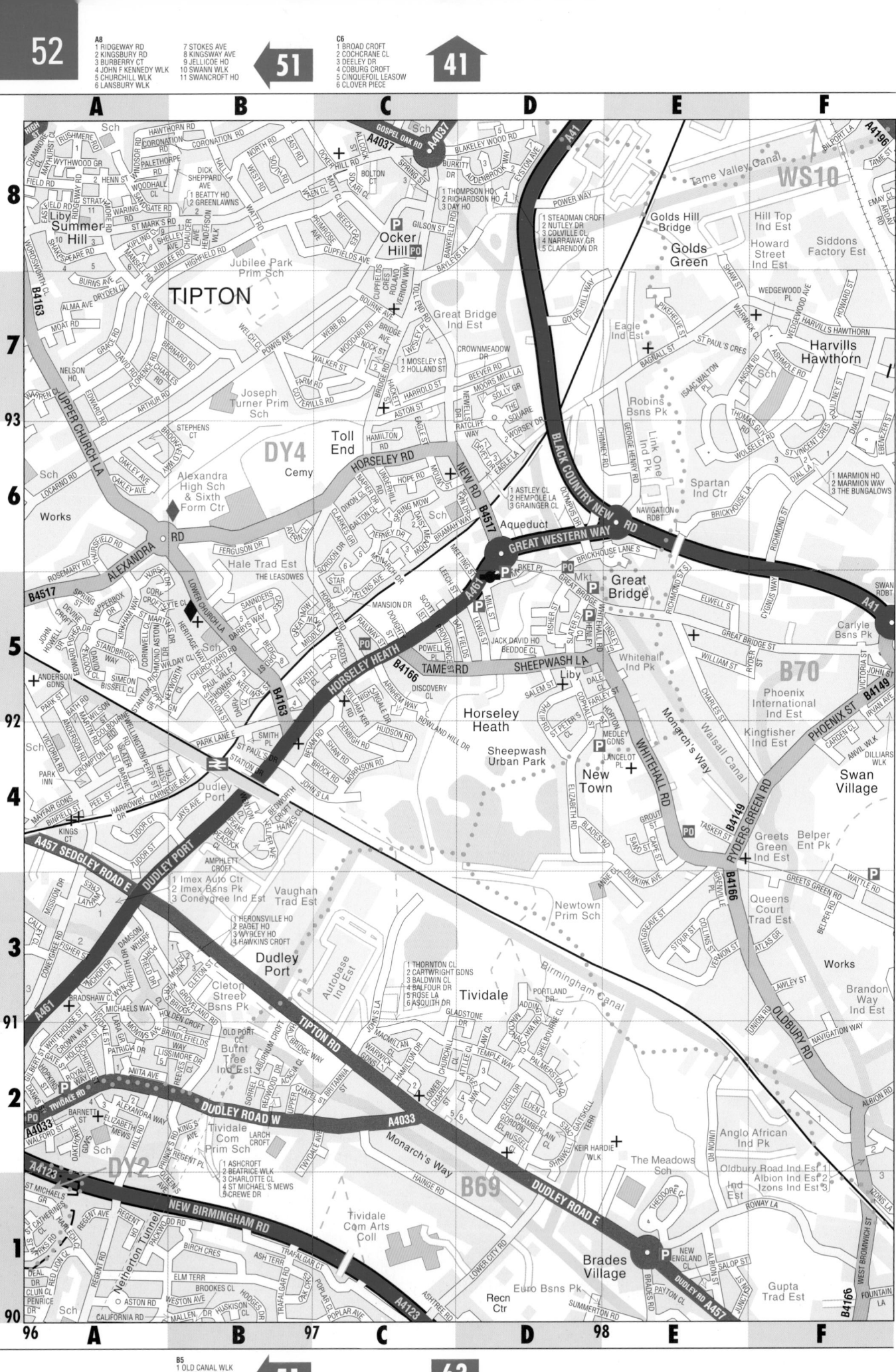

A8
1 RIDGEWAY RD
2 KINGSBURY RD
3 BURBERRY CT
4 JOHN F KENNEDY WLK
5 CHURCHILL WLK
6 LANSBURY WLK
7 STOKES AVE
8 KINGSWAY AVE
9 JELLICOE HO
10 SWANN WLK
11 SWANCROFT HO

C6
1 BROAD CROFT
2 COCHCRANE CL
3 DEELEY DR
4 COBURG CROFT
5 CINQUEFOIL LEASOW
6 CLOVER PIECE

51

41

B5
1 OLD CANAL WLK
2 JORDAN LEYS
3 RYLAND CL
4 MILLWRIGHT CL
5 NEAR HIGH DR
6 FAR HIGH DR
7 JEVONS DR
8 POTTERS BROOK

51

63

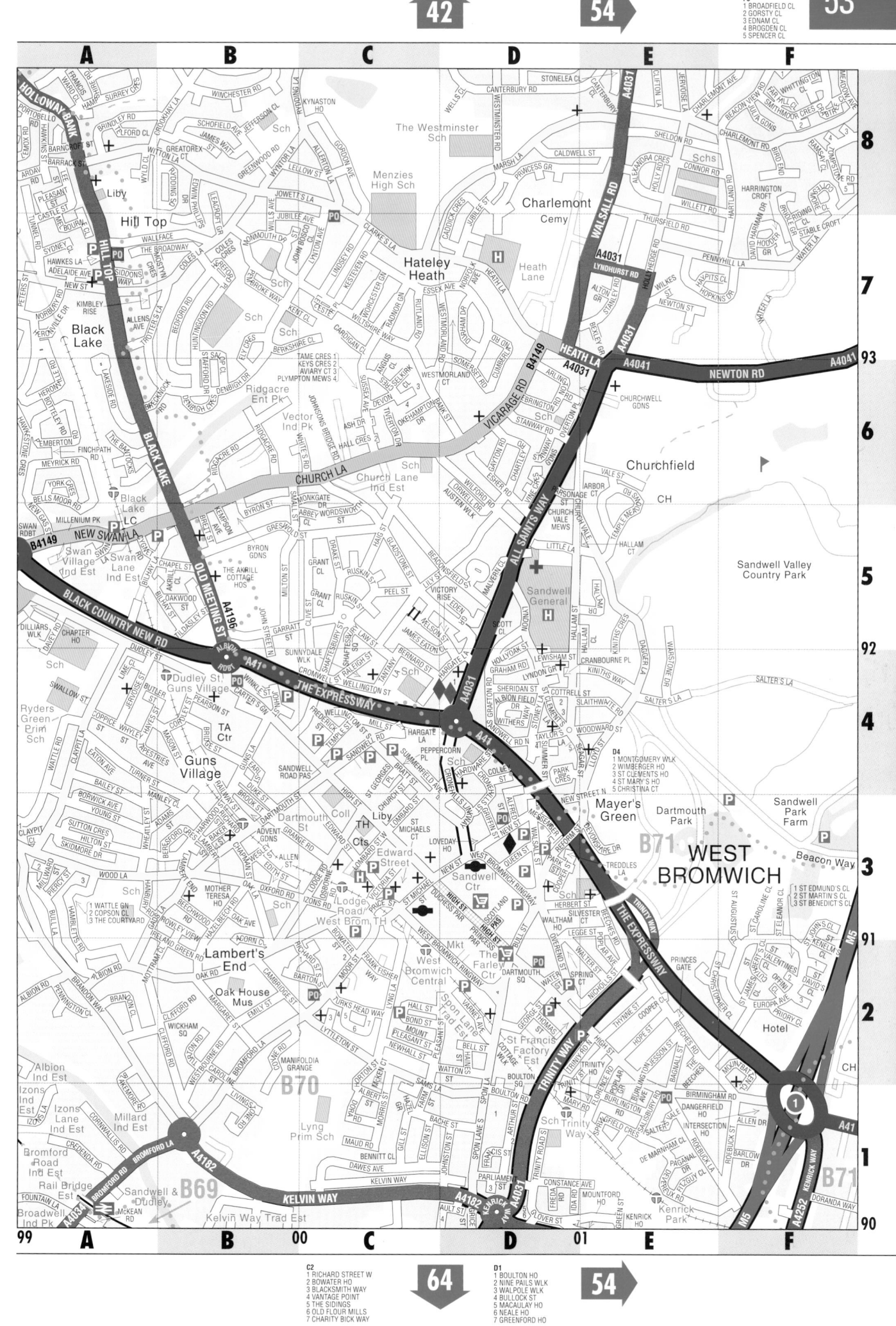

A **B** **C** **D** **E** **F**

WALSALL RD
A34

CHARLEMONT RD
HORSECROFT DR
CEDAR CT
RAY HALL LA
BISHOP ASBURY CRES
PEAR TREE CT
A4041
NEWTON RD
B4167
Bishop Asbury's Cottage

WIGMORE LA
NATER LA
TURNERS CROFT
COMPSTONE RD

8

Newton
B43

HEATHER RD
BROOMHILL CL
GREEN LA
NIXON CROFT
CHUDLEIGH GR
ROUSDON GR
STANTON RD
AMBURY WAY
CELBURY WAY
JAYSHAW AVE
GORSTIE CROFT
CALVERTON GR
SHENSTONE RD
CHADWICK CT
EASTWOOD RD
Ferndale Prim Sch
HOLLYWOOD
CEDARWOOD CROFT
B4124

Crem
Haypits

7

Tame Valley Canal
HAMSTEAD RD
HIGHFIELD RD
GREENFIELD RD
TANHOUSE AVE
HEMUS CRES
VALERIE RD
VALLEY RD
Hamstead Jun & Inf Sch
Hamstead
HAMSTEAD HO 1
SCOTT HO 2
GROVE CT 3
WATERSIDE
COLERIDGE
SOUTH VIEW
WEST RD
BANKSIDE
LANGDALE RD
GRASMERE RD
ENNERDALE CRES
BRADFORD RD
OLD WALSALL RD
CHARNWOOD RD
DYAS AVE
B42

93
A4041

Forge La
Forge Farm
Forge Mill Farm
Sandwell Valley Nature Ctr
EADGAR CT
P
BROOKSIDE
AMBERLEY GN
Garden Grove
WOODEND
GREENWAY
Superstore
B4167
RICHMOND CROFT
KINGSDOWN AVE
RAILWAY TERR
Hamstead Wks
ROCKY LA

6

FARRAN WAY 1
CROMANE SQ 2
FREEMOUNT SQ 3
LATHAM AVE 4
STAFFORD CT 5
RUSHALL CT 6
ALLEN HO 7
PEPYS CT 8
SUTTON CT 9
BOLDMERE CT 10
Hamstead Hall Sch
ACFOLD RD
CHALCOT GR
PARKSIDE
THE CROFTWAY
HAMSTEAD HALL AVE
BEACHAMP AVE
MILLFIELD RD
LEOPOLD RD
DEERHURST RD
MANWAY CL

Sandwell Valley Country Park
B71
Beacon Way
River Tame
P

5

CAMPIN CRES
ELMBANK GR
UNDERWOOD RD
GREENRIDGE RD
CRAYTHORNE AVE
SEDGLEY GR
BENLYS GR
WEST AVE
HAMSTEAD HILL
92

Swan Pool
Park Farm
CH
WESTOVER RD
VERNON AVE
The Grange
LEY HILL RD
PARK HILL DR
ST DAVIDS GR
ST ANNES CL
ST CHRISTOPHERS
Liby
Grestone Prim Sch
B20
MEDCROFT AVE
HAMSTEAD HALL RD
THE SPINNEY
BEECH
FRIARY CL
Brown's Green

4

CH
Sports Gd
P PARK LA
SILVERCROFT AVE
BROSIL AVE
BEECHWOOD
MENTONE CT
WHITLEY CL
WHEATON VALE
HIGH ST
HAWTHORN PK
MAY TREE GR
GRESTONE AVE
SHIRELAND
ASHCOMBE AVE
WOODCROFT AVE
BROWNS GN
ENGLESTEDE CL
TAVERNERS GN
HANDSWORTH WOOD RD
B4124

3

Allot Gdns
CRADLEY CROFT
WILKS GN
POSEY CL
THE LEVER
CRESS
Hamstead Campus
Handsworth Hall
FRIARY RD
LOFTHOUSE RD
SILVERCROFT AVE
DEVONSHIRE RD
OAKLANDS
DEVON CL
Sch

91
B70

OXHILL RD
OXHILL RD
CHURCH LA A4040
Cemy
B21
COPTHALL RD
LINCHMERE RD
LARCH AVE
FRIARY GDNS
STOCKWELL RD
COLLEGE RD
WINDERMERE RD
CORNWALL RD
MILTON RD
COLLEGE RD
SOMERSET RD
ROSEDENE DR
CALDER DR
GRIVELDON
Sch

2

CAMPA LA
FELL GR
LANDGATE RD
CRANBROOK RD
St John Wall RC Sch
St Augustine's RC Prim Sch
SANDWELL RD
GREENHILL RD
FARNHAM RD
UPLANDS RD
NEWCOMBE RD
HEADINGLEY RD
ELMHURST RD
MOUNT PLEASANT AVE
LAUREL GDNS
GROVE GDNS
ORCHARD RD
GROVE HILL RD
PHILIP VICTOR RD
GOLDEN CROFT
HINSTOCK RD
PIKE CL

Recn Gd
Handsworth
FARCROFT RD
FARCROFT GR
BUSH GR
AVENUE RD
MERVYN RD
ASTLEY RD
FORD RD
ALBION RD
ROOKERY RD
Rookery Sch
ANTROBUS RD
Wilkes Green Sch

1

A41
BIRMINGHAM RD
B66
B71
B21
Park Lane Ind Est
Raleigh Ind Est
RALEIGH RD
The Hawthorns (West Bromwich Albion FC)
HOLYHEAD RD
A4040 ISLAND RD
A41
SAMPSON RD
AUSTIN RD
DOWNING RD
NIJON CL
St James CE Prim Sch
ONIBURY RD
GRAFTON RD
HOLLYCROFT
CLEMENT RD
ALBION RD
FARCROFT AVE
WESTBOURNE RD
CARLTON AVE
MAPLE CL
ALBERT RD
BRUNSWICK RD
BRUNSWICK GDNS

COLLIERY RD
HALFORDS LA
BOUNDARY
WILLOW DR
MALVERN RD 1
PADDINGTON RD 2

90

02 **A** **B** 03 **C** **D** 04 **E** **F**

F3
1 HAWTHORN PARK DR
2 CASSOWARY RD
3 QUORN HO
4 ALBRIGHTON HO
5 MEYNELL HO
6 PYTCHLEY HO
7 COTTESMORE HO

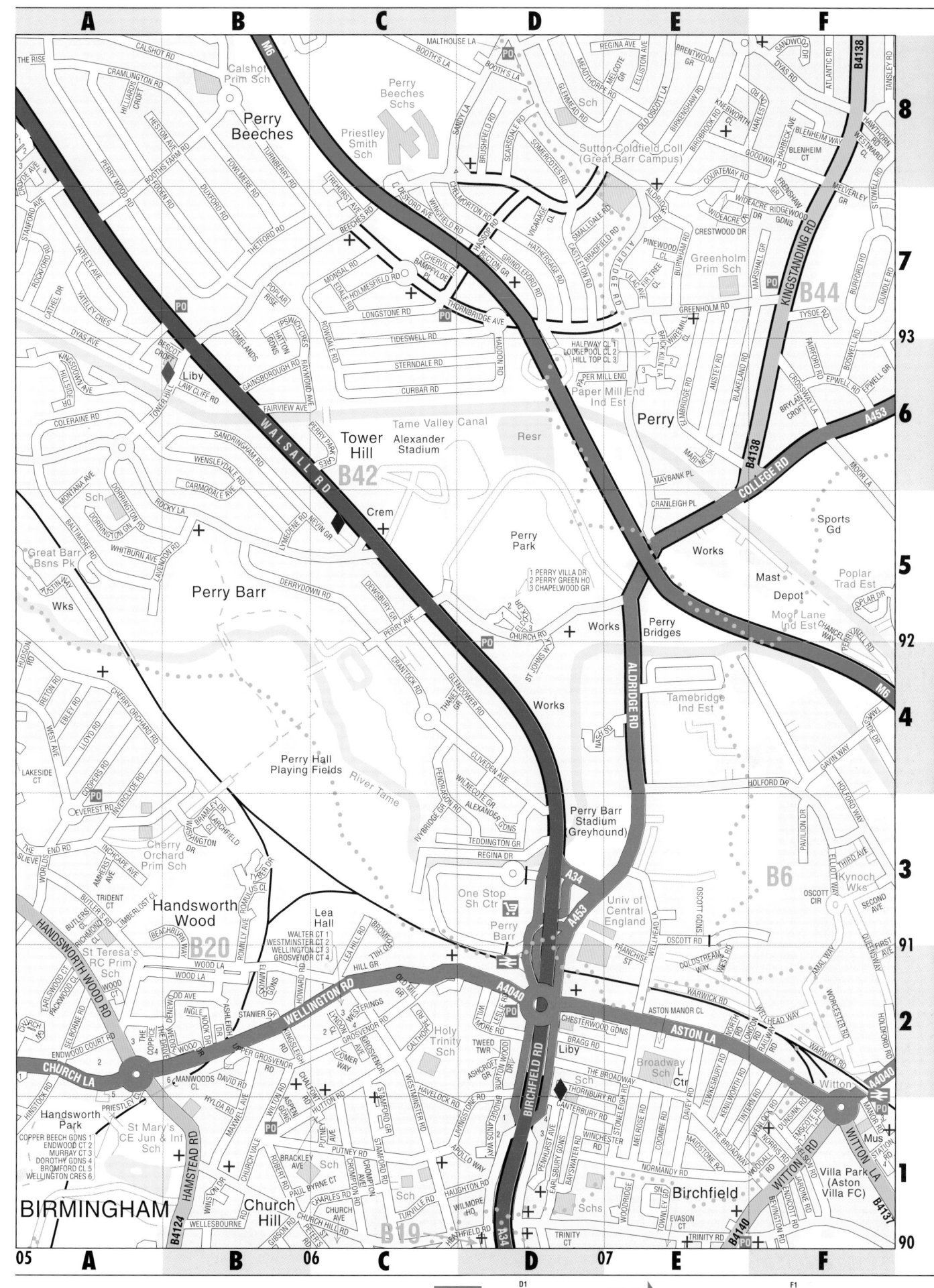

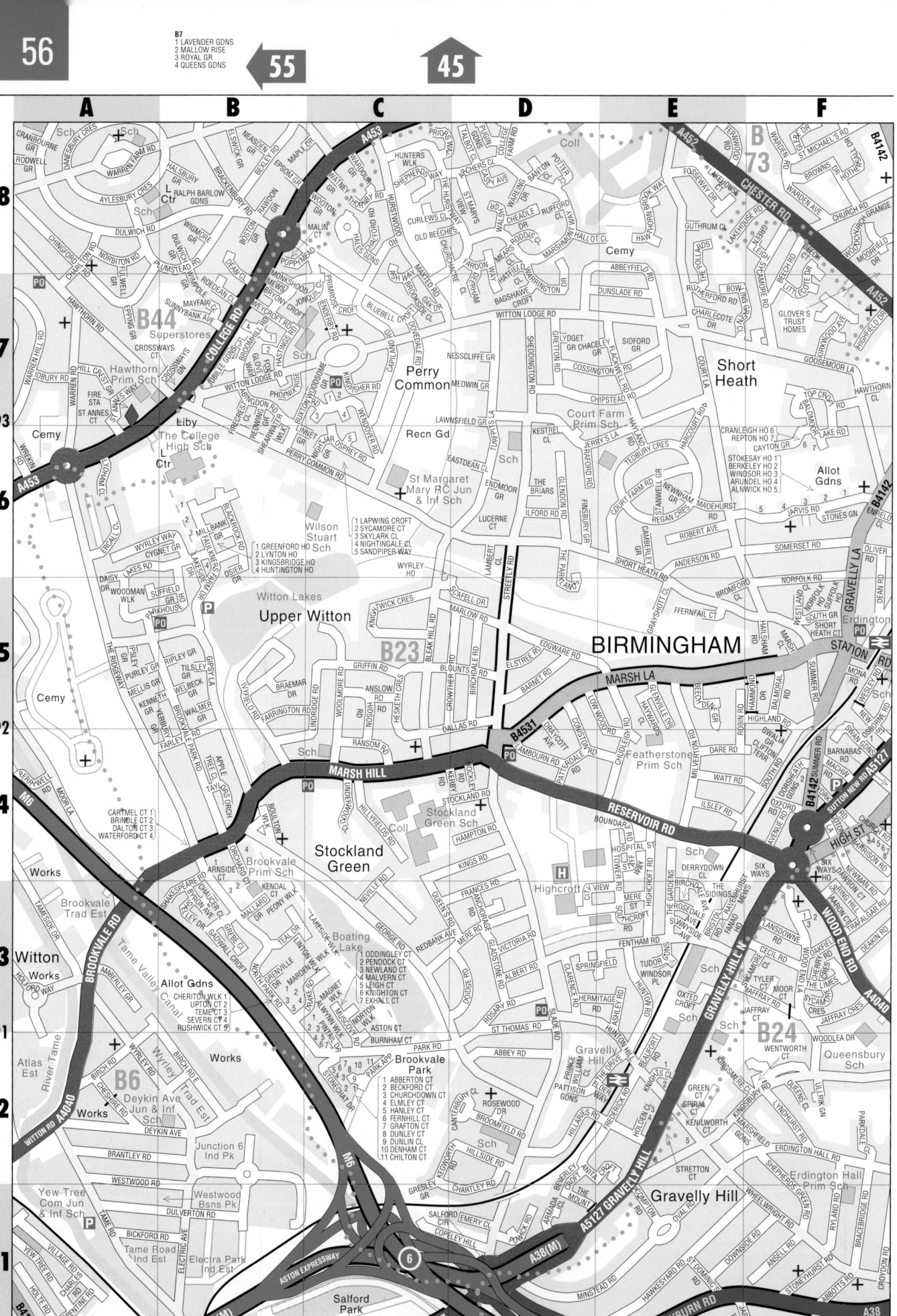

E2
1 CHISWICK CT
2 HUNTON CT
3 WOODVILLE CT
4 GRAVELLY CT
5 WHEELWRIGHT CT
6 NEWCHURCH GDNS

F3
1 COPPICE CL
2 MAPLE CT
3 RESWOOD CT

F4
1 OSBORNE RD S
2 POPLAR AVE
3 SALISBURY HO
4 GLOUCESTER HO
5 TALBOT HO
6 WARWICK HO
7 BEDFORD HO
8 EXETER HO

B6
1 ADRIAN CT
2 ABBEY MANS
3 SUTTON CT
4 KENTMERE TWR
5 GLENDALE TWR

B7
1 The Lanes Sh Ctr
2 RICHMOND CT
3 HERON CT
4 FLORENCE DR
5 FLORENCE AVE

A B C D E F

8 7 93 6 5 92 4 3 91 2 1 90

SUTTON COLDFIELD

Walmley

B73
1 GRANGEWOOD CT
2 CHESTER CT
3 HAZELMEAD CT
4 YEW TREE VILLAS
5 HELLABY CT
6 ANSTEY CT
7 Arena Studios

B72
1 CHARTWELL CT
2 ARDEN CT
3 BLAKELEY CT
4 GREENHILL CT
5 BEECH HILL CT
6 OAKHURST CT
7 HILTON CT

1 CHATSWORTH CL
2 HAYES MDW
3 CATTOCK HURST DR
4 HAWTHORNDEN CT

ULLENHALL RD 1
LINGARD HO 2
PACKENHAM DR 3
PAKENHAM HO 4
BENTLEY CT 5
BERKELEY HO 6
WALMLEY PARK CT 7
WALMLEY ASH CT 8
HARGREAVE CL 9

The Deanery CE Prim Sch

B76

B23

The Abbey RC Sch

St Edmund Campion RC Sch

ORCHARD CT 1
GROSVENOR HO 2
HOLLY CT 3

STONNAL GR 1
STANDLEYS TWR 2
NORMANTON TWR 3
FAIRBOURNE TWR 4

Chester Road

Wylde Green Prim Sch

Erdington

B24

Pype Hayes

Pype Hayes Hall

Pype Hayes Park

1 PADSTOW RD
2 CHESTERGATE CROFT
3 EDINBURGH CT
4 PYPE HAYES CL
5 ASHFORD CL
6 SPENCER CT
7 WINDFALL CT
8 NEWCOME CL

1 AINSDALE GDNS
2 CHESTER HAYES CT
3 BLITHFIELD GR
4 PLANTS GR

Paget Prim Sch

St Barnabas CE Prim Sch

Birches Green Jun & Inf Schs

St Peter & St Paul RC Prim Sch

Birches Green

Tyburn

Gunter Prim Sch

Tyburn Works

1 OAKMEADOW AVE
2 SORREL HO
3 FREEMANTLE HO
4 ASHCOMBE GDNS
5 OAKMEADOW WAY
6 SPRINGSLADE DR
7 KINGSBURY AVE
8 SMALLWOOD CL

Key Bsns Pk

Kingsbury Sch & Sports Coll L Ctr

Holly Park Ind Est

Butler's Bridge

Spitfire Pk

Tyburn Trad Est

Castle Vale Ret Pk

RAF COTTS 1
COLTISHALL CL 2

B35

Works

Hastingwood Ind Pk

Works

The Fort Sh Pk

Bromford

FORT PARKWAY

B36

1 CHILLINGHOME RD
2 KILMORE CROFT

The Fort Ind Pk

Bsns Pk

River Tame

CHILLINGHOME TWR

M6

A B C D E F
11 12 13

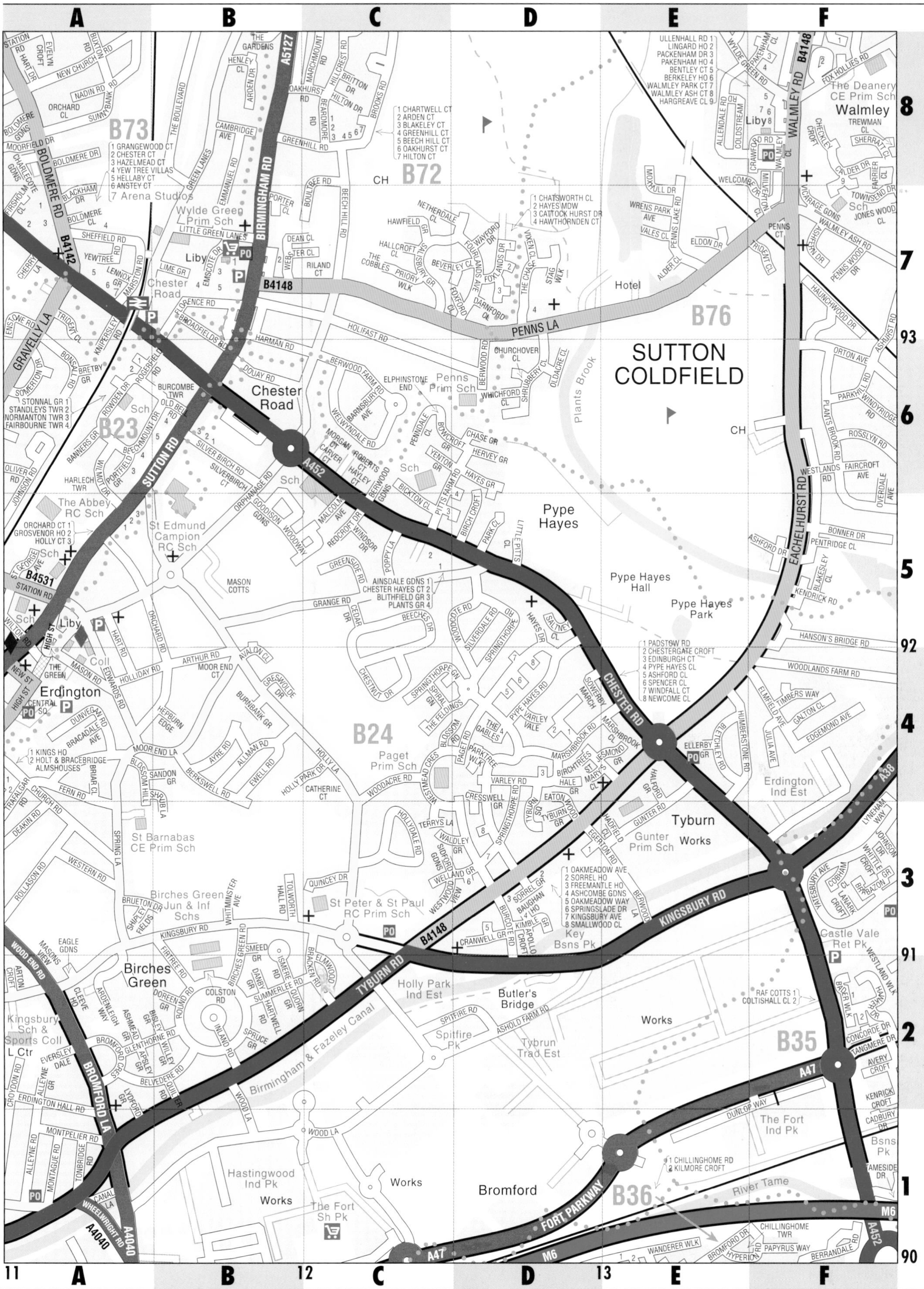

68 58

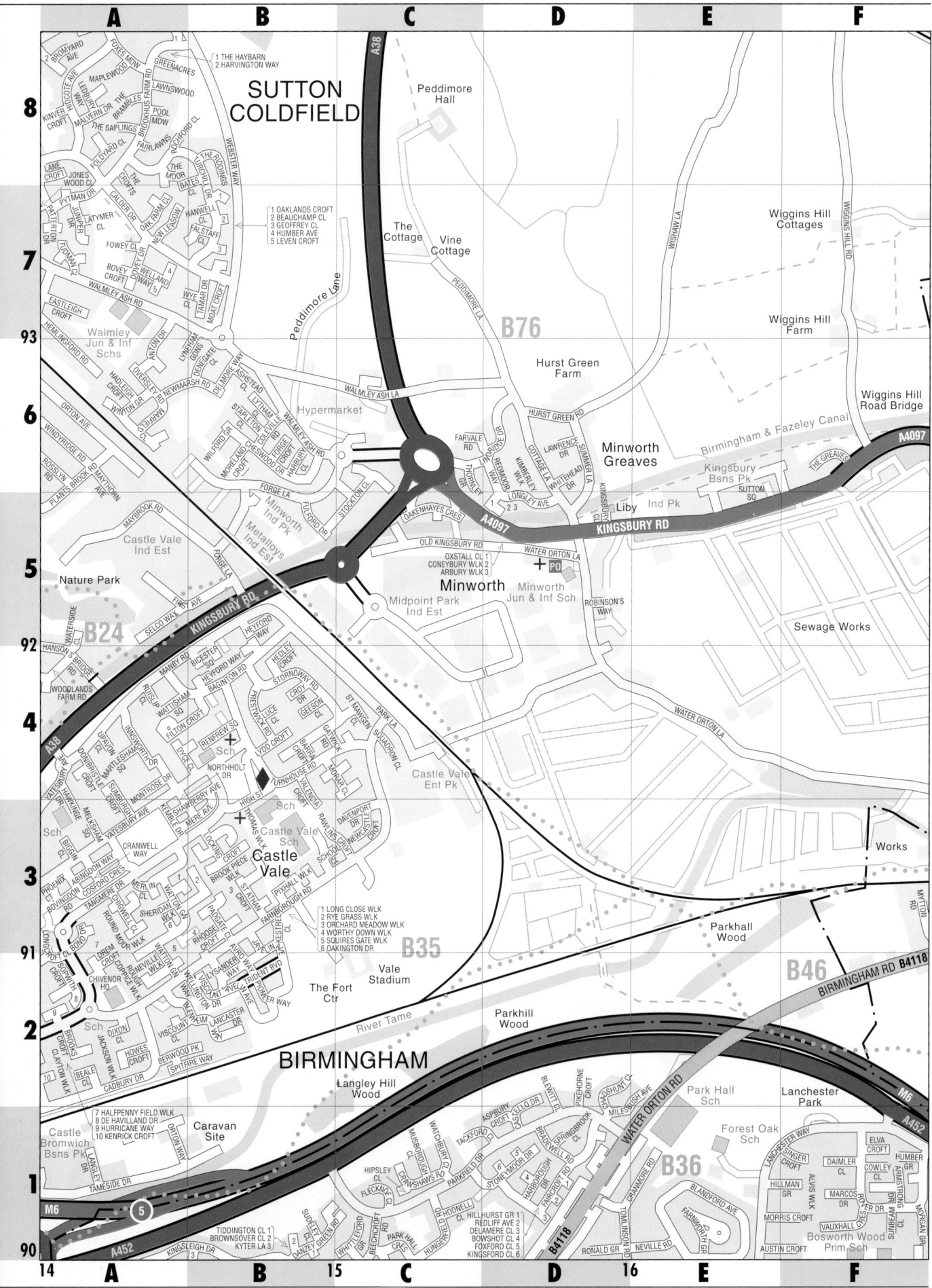

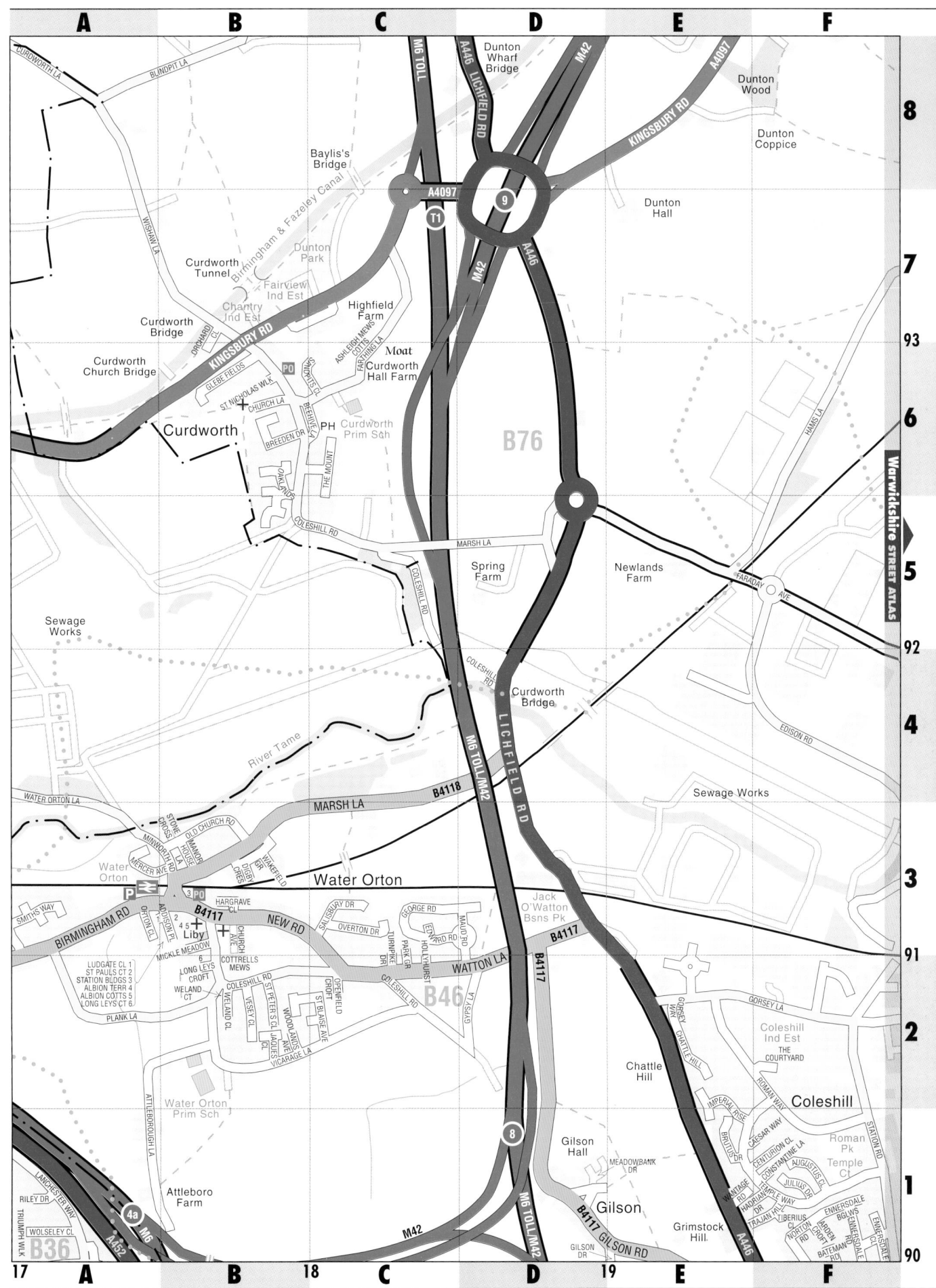

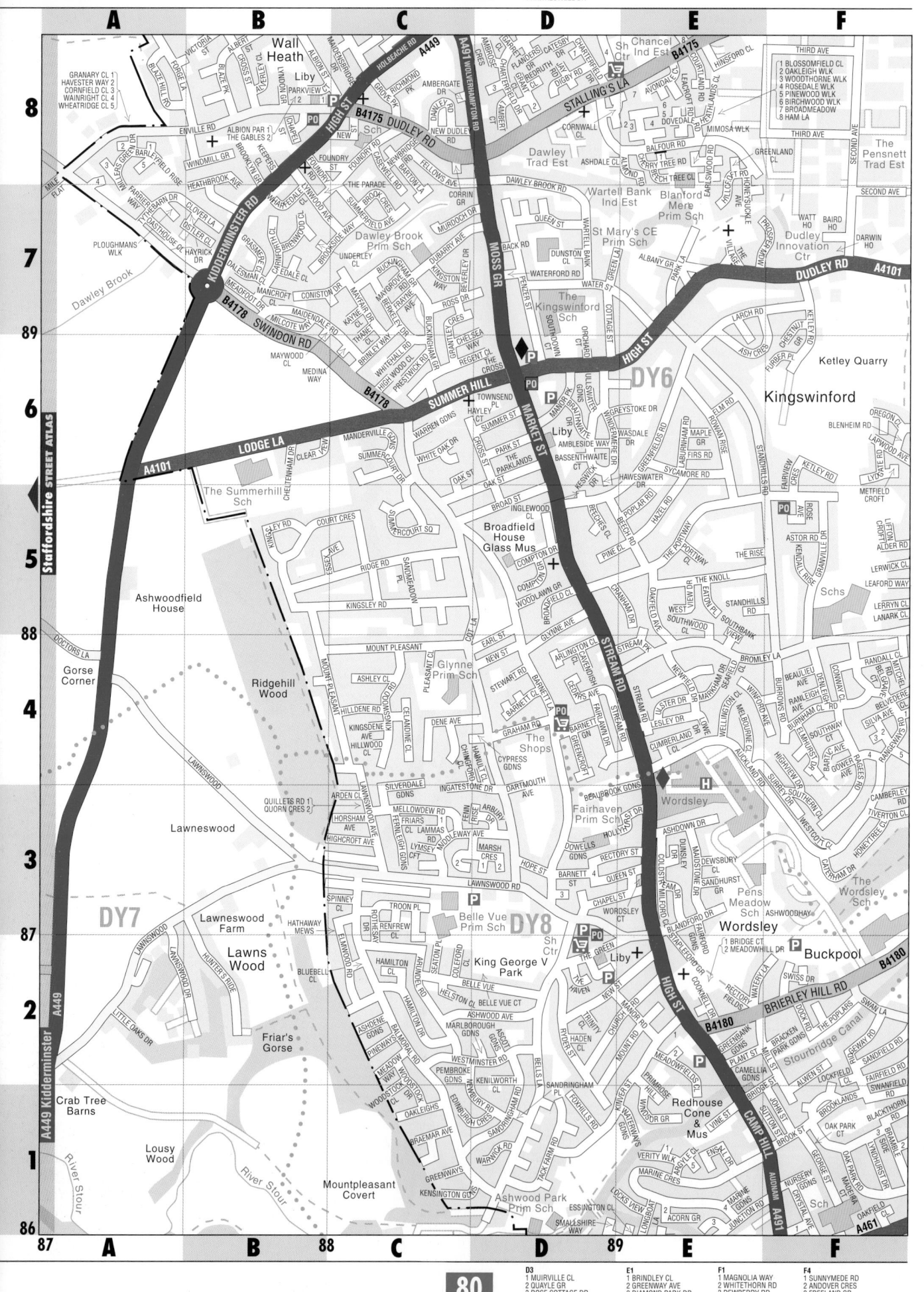

80

D3
1 MUIRVILLE CL
2 QUAYLE GR
3 ROSE COTTAGE DR
4 CROSS ST

E1
1 BRINDLEY CL
2 GREENWAY AVE
3 DIAMOND PARK DR
4 SWEETBRIER DR
5 GILBEYS CL

F1
1 MAGNOLIA WAY
2 WHITETHORN RD
3 DEWBERRY RD

F4
1 SUNNYMEDE RD
2 ANDOVER CRES
3 FREELAND GR
4 GRANGE LA
5 MADELEY RD

E8
1 ESK HO
2 AVON HO
3 BRENT HO
4 FROME HO
5 KENNET HO
6 LEA HO
7 CAM HO
8 DEE HO

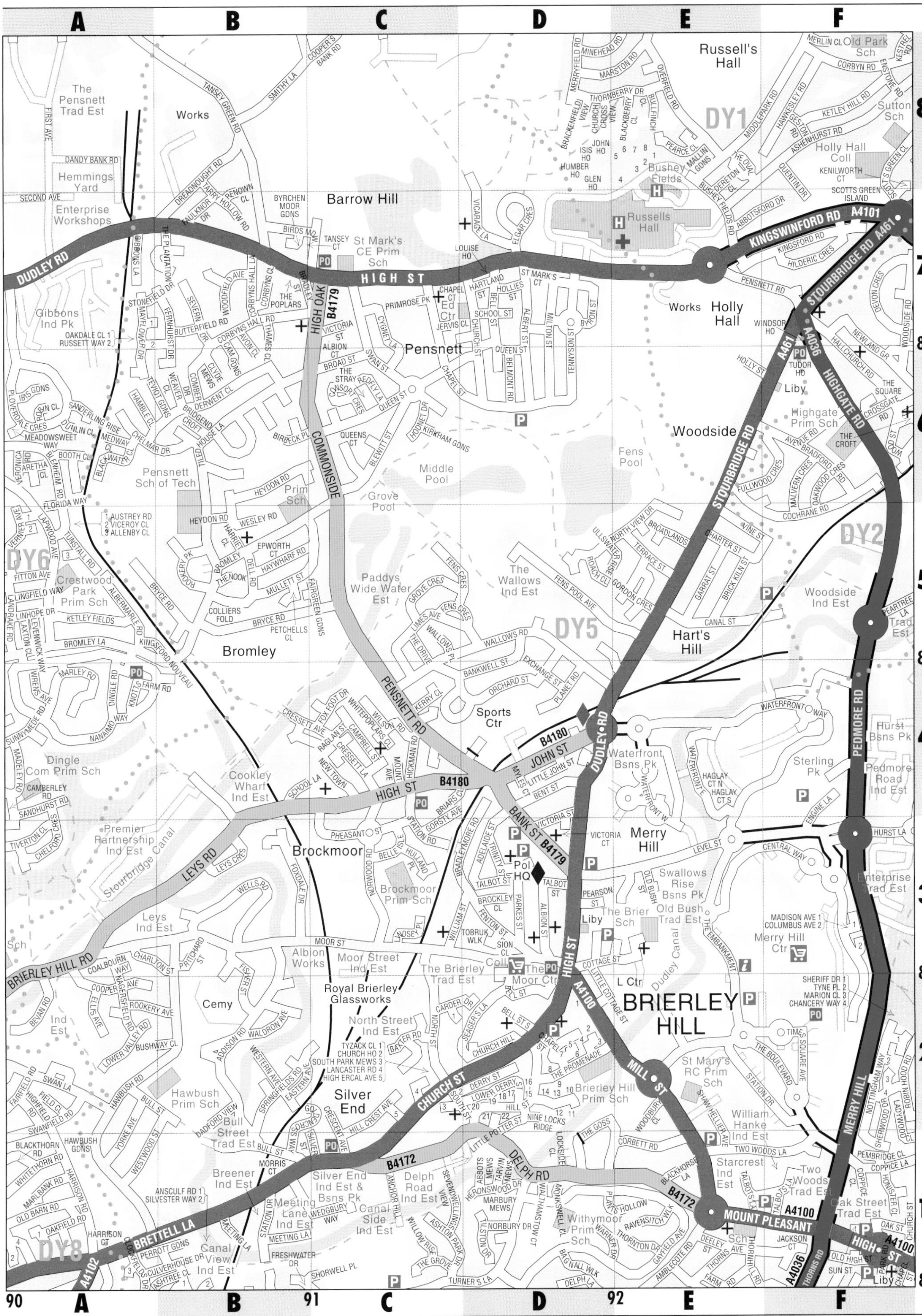

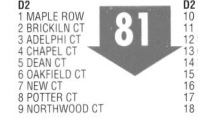

A1
1 SYCAMORE PADDOCK
2 OAK TREE GDNS
3 AMELAS CL
4 OAK PARK RD

D2
1 MAPLE ROW
2 BRICKILN CT
3 ADELPHI CT
4 CHAPEL CT
5 DEAN CT
6 OAKFIELD CT
7 NEW CT
8 POTTER CT
9 NORTHWOOD CT

D2
10 LOWTHER CT
11 KNOTT CT
12 ST MARYS CT
13 GIFFORD CT
14 BRIAR CT
15 YEOVIL CT
16 BODMIN CT
17 BOOTH CT
18 BURNHAM CT

19 PLANT CT
20 ST JOHNS CT
21 RAVEN CT
22 WESTBURY CT

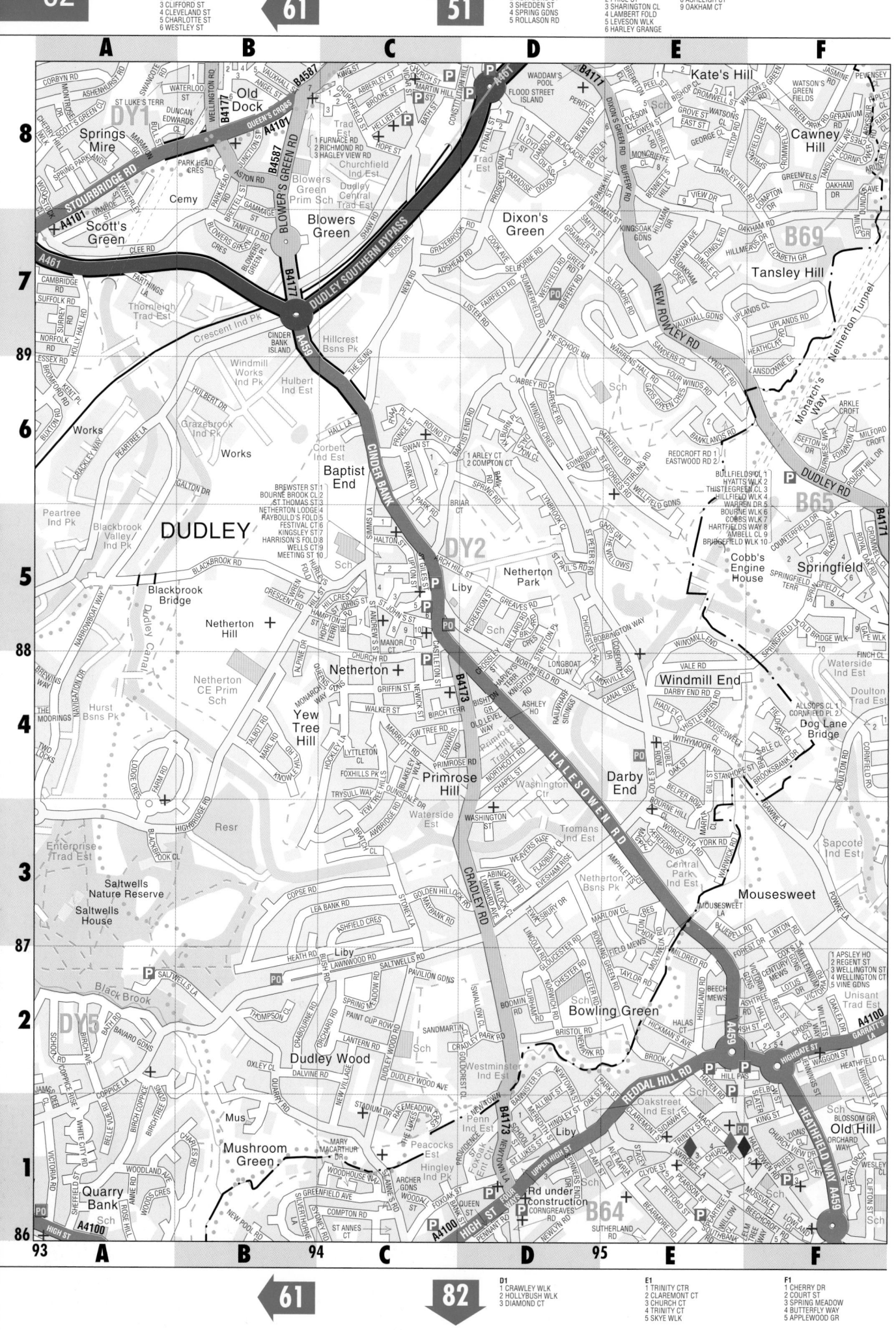

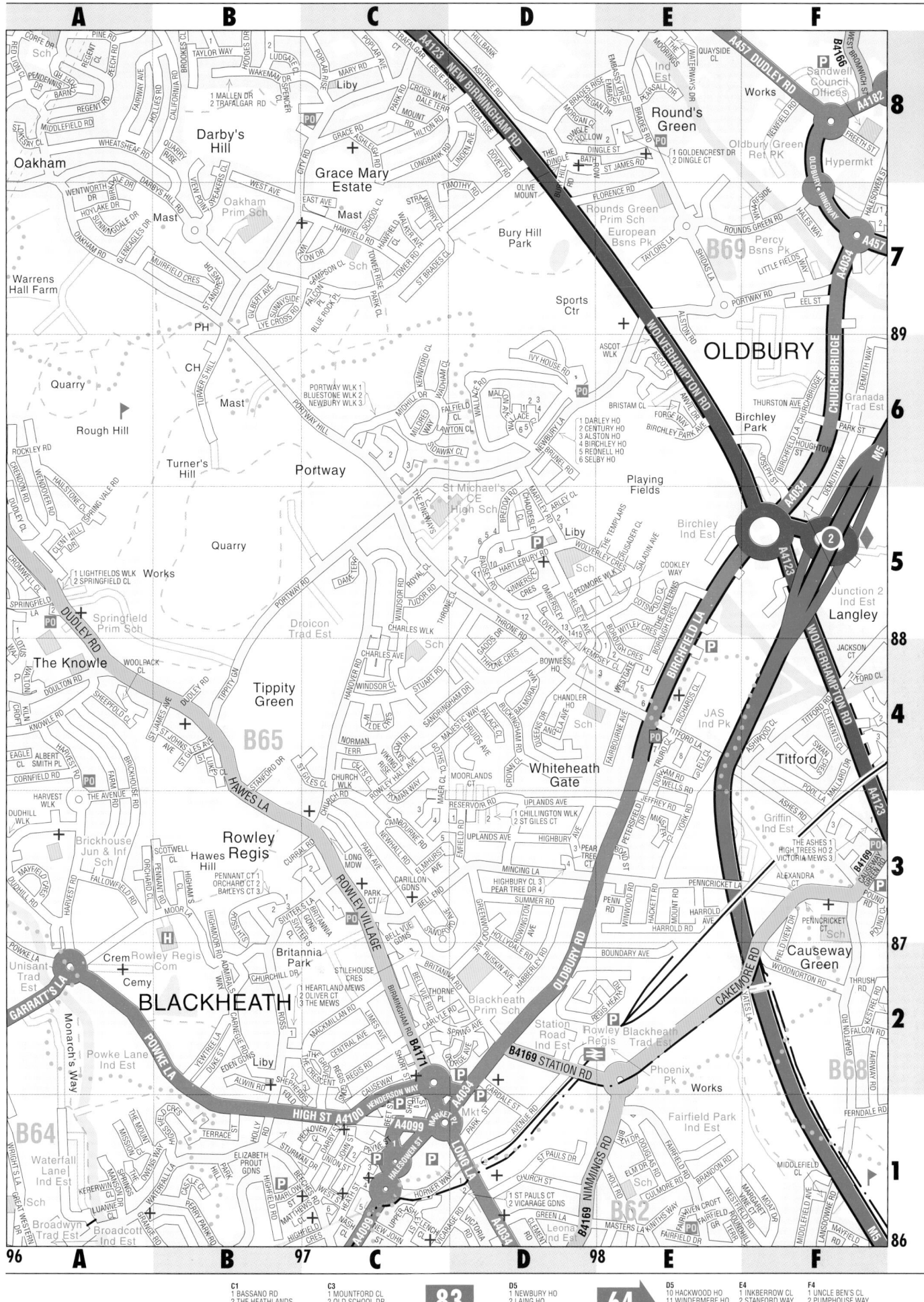

C1
1 BASSANO RD
2 THE HEATHLANDS
3 BEN WILLETTS WLK
4 CROSS ST
5 FRANK TOMMEY CL
6 DOWNING CL

C3
1 MOUNTFORD CL
2 OLD SCHOOL DR
3 RAGLEY WLK
4 HADEN WLK
5 HARVINGTON WLK

D5
1 NEWBURY HO
2 LAING HO
3 JAMES CLIFT HO
4 ULLSWATER HO
5 DERWENT HO
6 RYDAL HO
7 CONISTON HO
8 WALLACE HO
9 HARRY PRICE HO

D5
10 HACKWOOD RD
11 WINDERMERE HO
12 BURNETT HO
13 GRASMERE HO
14 KESWICK HO
15 KENDALL HO

E4
1 INKBERROW CL
2 STANFORD WAY
3 RICHARDS HO
4 BLAKEDOWN WAY
5 STAULTON GN
6 WHITEHEATH CT
7 LANCASTER HO
8 WINCHESTER CL
9 CANTERBURY CL

F4
1 UNCLE BEN'S CL
2 PUMPHOUSE WAY
3 ST MICHAEL'S CRES

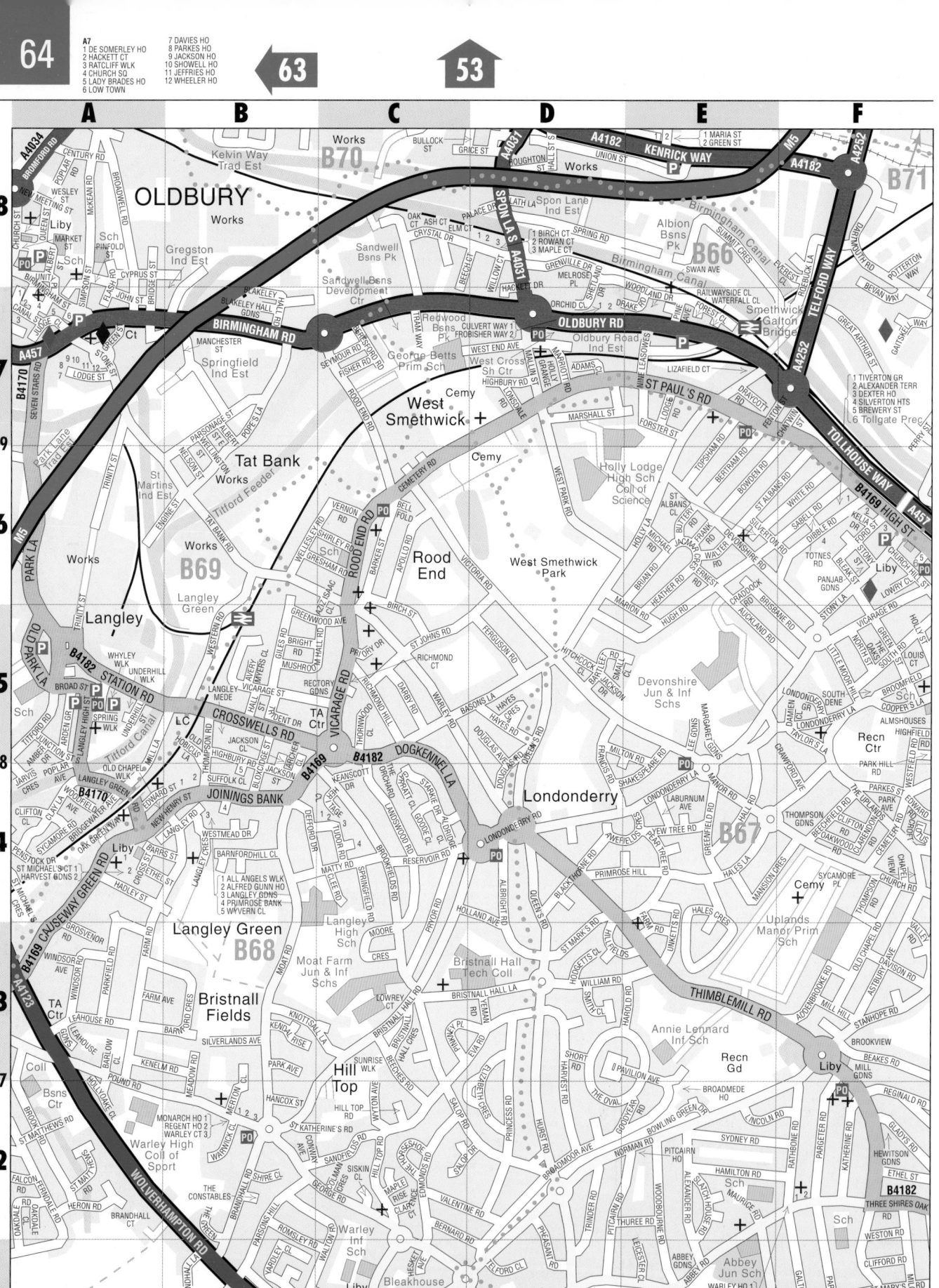

64

A7
1 DE SOMERLEY HO
2 HACKETT CT
3 RATCLIFF WLK
4 CHURCH SQ
5 LADY BRADES HO
6 LOW TOWN
7 DAVIES HO
8 PARKES HO
9 JACKSON HO
10 SHOWELL HO
11 JEFFRIES HO
12 WHEELER HO

63

53

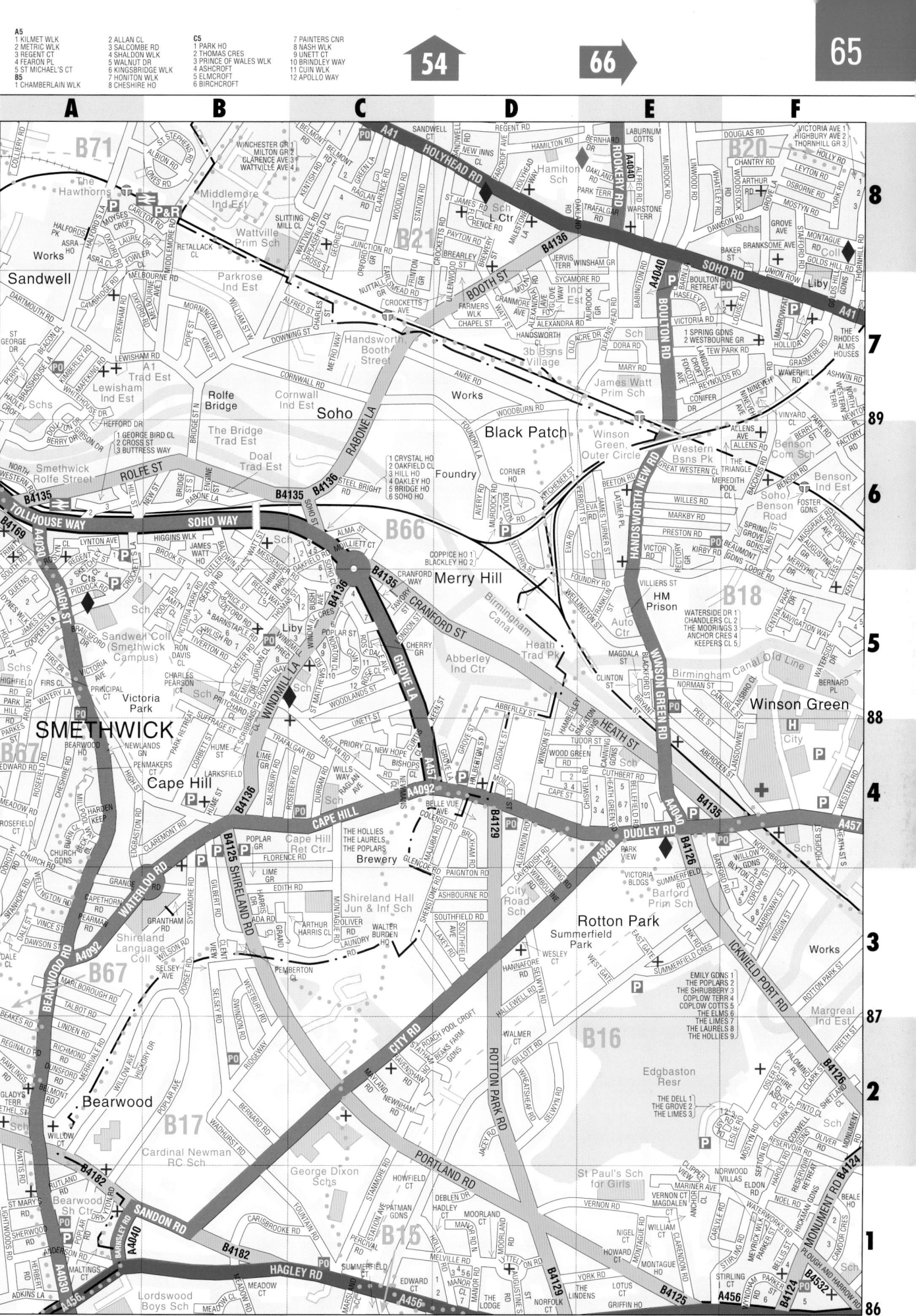

54
66
85
66

A5
1 KILMET WLK
2 METRIC WLK
3 REGENT CT
4 FEARON PL
5 ST MICHAEL'S CT
B5
1 CHAMBERLAIN WLK

2 ALLAN CL
3 SALCOMBE WLK
4 SHALDON WLK
5 WALNUT DR
6 KINGSBRIDGE WLK
7 HONITON WLK
8 CHESHIRE HO

C5
1 PARK HO
2 THOMAS CRES
3 PRINCE OF WALES WLK
4 ASHCROFT
5 ELMCROFT
6 BIRCHCROFT

7 PAINTERS CNR
8 NASH WLK
9 UNETT CT
10 BRINDLEY WAY
11 CUIN WLK
12 APOLLO WAY

D1
1 MELVILLE HALL
2 WESTFIELD HALL
3 ST MICHAEL HO
4 ST HELLIER HO
5 ST DENNIS HO
6 ST LAWRENCE HO
7 HOLLY MOUNT

D4
1 SHIRELAND BROOK GDNS
2 WEST HEATH RD
3 BEWDLEY VILLAS
4 ARLEY VILLAS

E4
1 VICTORIA GR
2 FLORENCE GR
3 PEARL GR
4 HEATH GREEN GR
5 SUMMERFIELD GR
6 DUDLEY GR
7 HALIFAX GR
8 ASHOVER GR

9 ENDERBY GR
10 BELLEFIELD AVE
F1
1 BARROW HO
2 BALFOUR HO
3 CLAYTON HO
4 EDGWOOD CT
5 WINDSOR TERR
6 MONUMENT HO

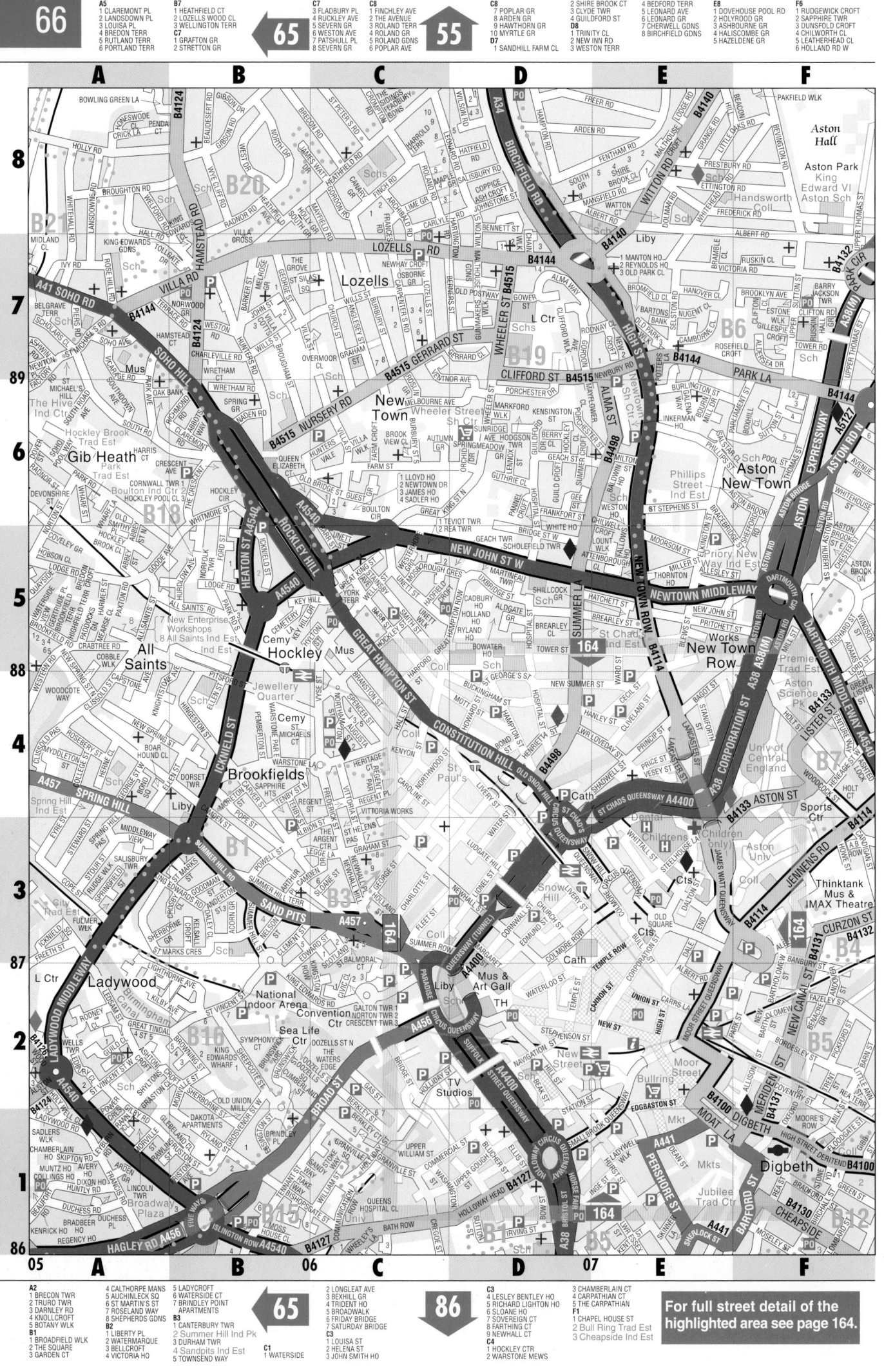

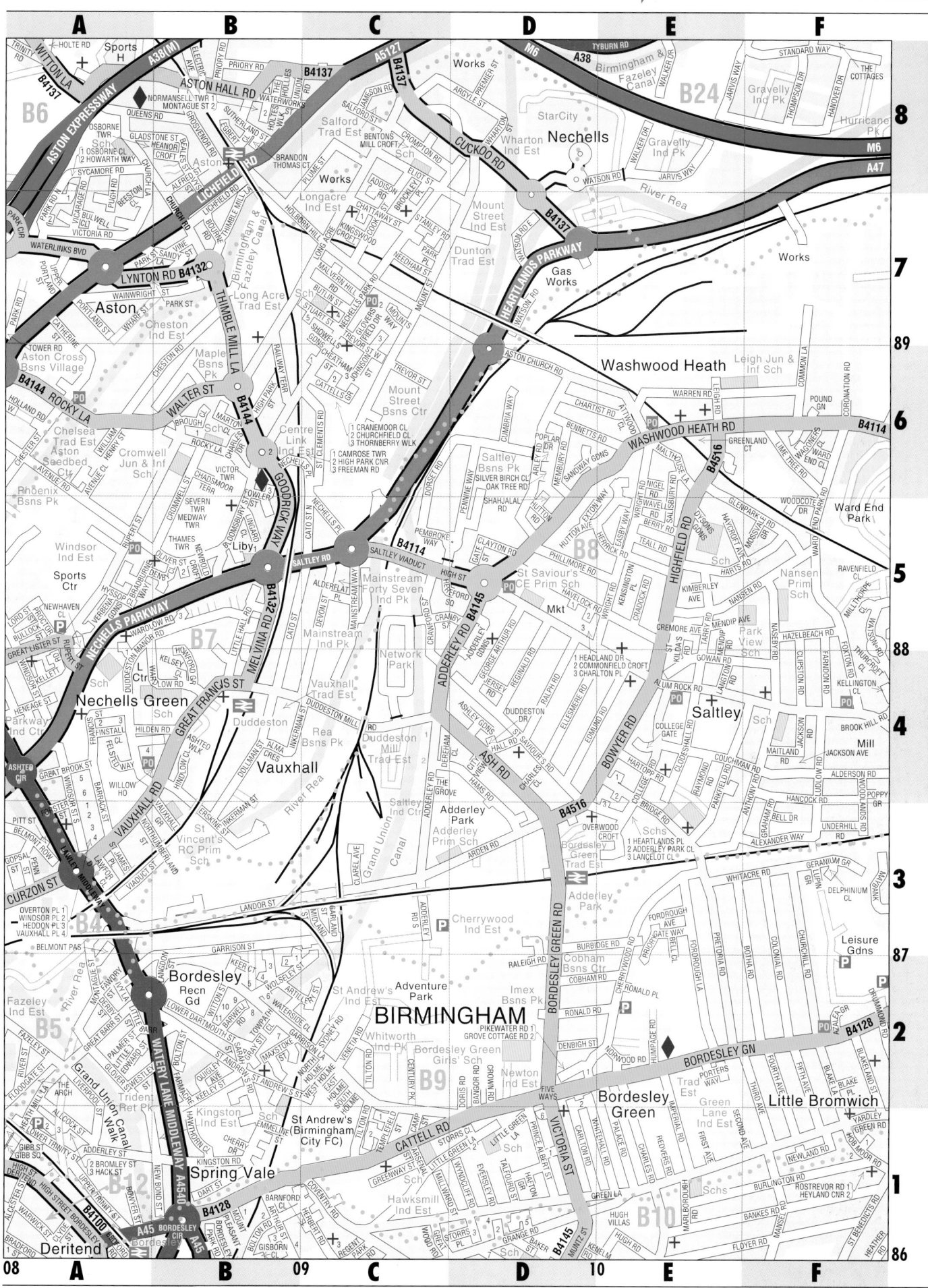

56
68

B5
1 BLOOMSBURY WLK
2 BODMIN GR
3 LITTLE FRANCIS GR

C7
1 RAMSEY RD
2 OLD STABLES WLK
3 LITTLE CLOVER CL
4 JAMES MEML HOMES THE
5 ROBERTSONS GDNS

A1
1 RENAISSANCE CT
A4
1 HOBART CROFT
2 HUMBER TWR
3 TRENT TWR
4 REVESBY WLK
5 MOORCROFT PL
6 HENEAGE PL

B1
1 MOUNT PLEASANT CT
2 ST ANDREWS CT
3 DARNEL CROFT
4 PRITCHETT TWR
B2
1 ISBOURNE WAY
2 MEASE CROFT
3 MILL BURN WAY

4 ALPORT CROFT
5 GORDON ST
6 HOFF BECK CT
7 BORDSLEY CT
8 BARWELL CT
9 GARRISON CT
10 PARK VILLAS
11 ASH GR

C1
1 BROSELEY BROOK CL
2 TEMPLEFIELD GDNS
3 HARMONY HO
C4
1 Cornwall Ind Est
2 Adderley Trad Est

D1
1 NORTH WARWICK ST
2 EVERSLEY RD
3 HOLMWOOD RD
4 GRANEFIELD CT
5 BERTRAM RD
6 REGENCY CL
7 HAWKES ST

87
68

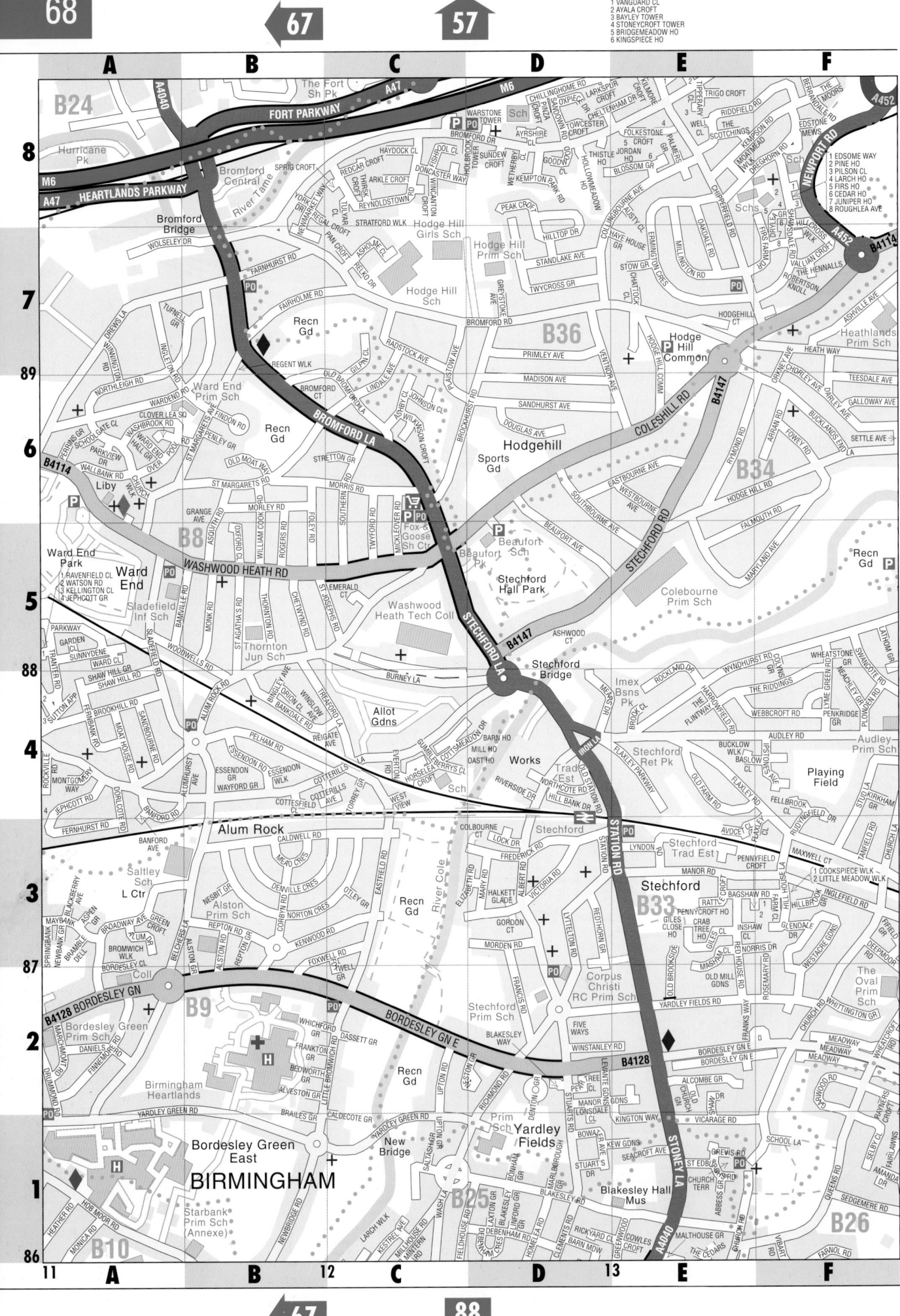

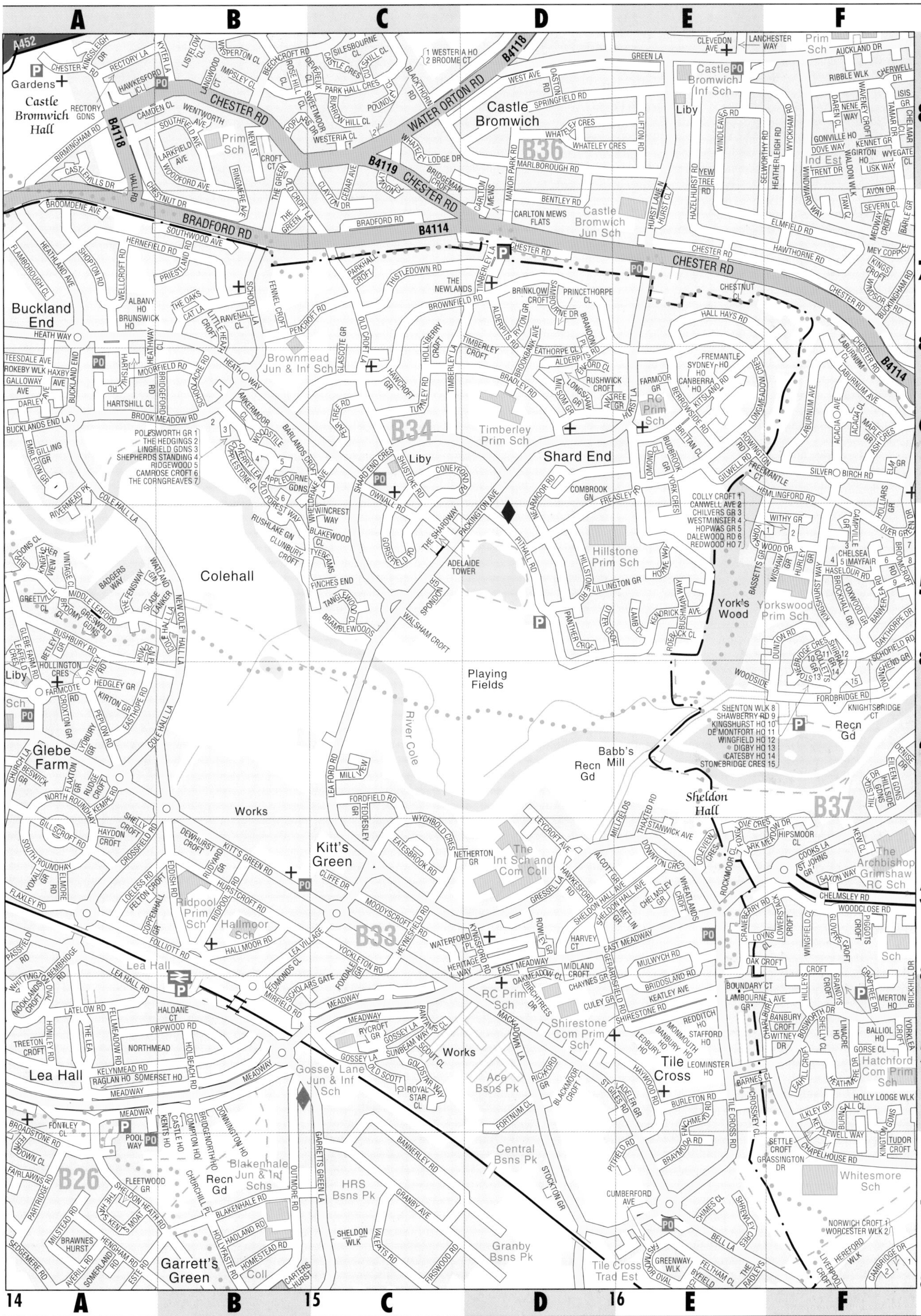

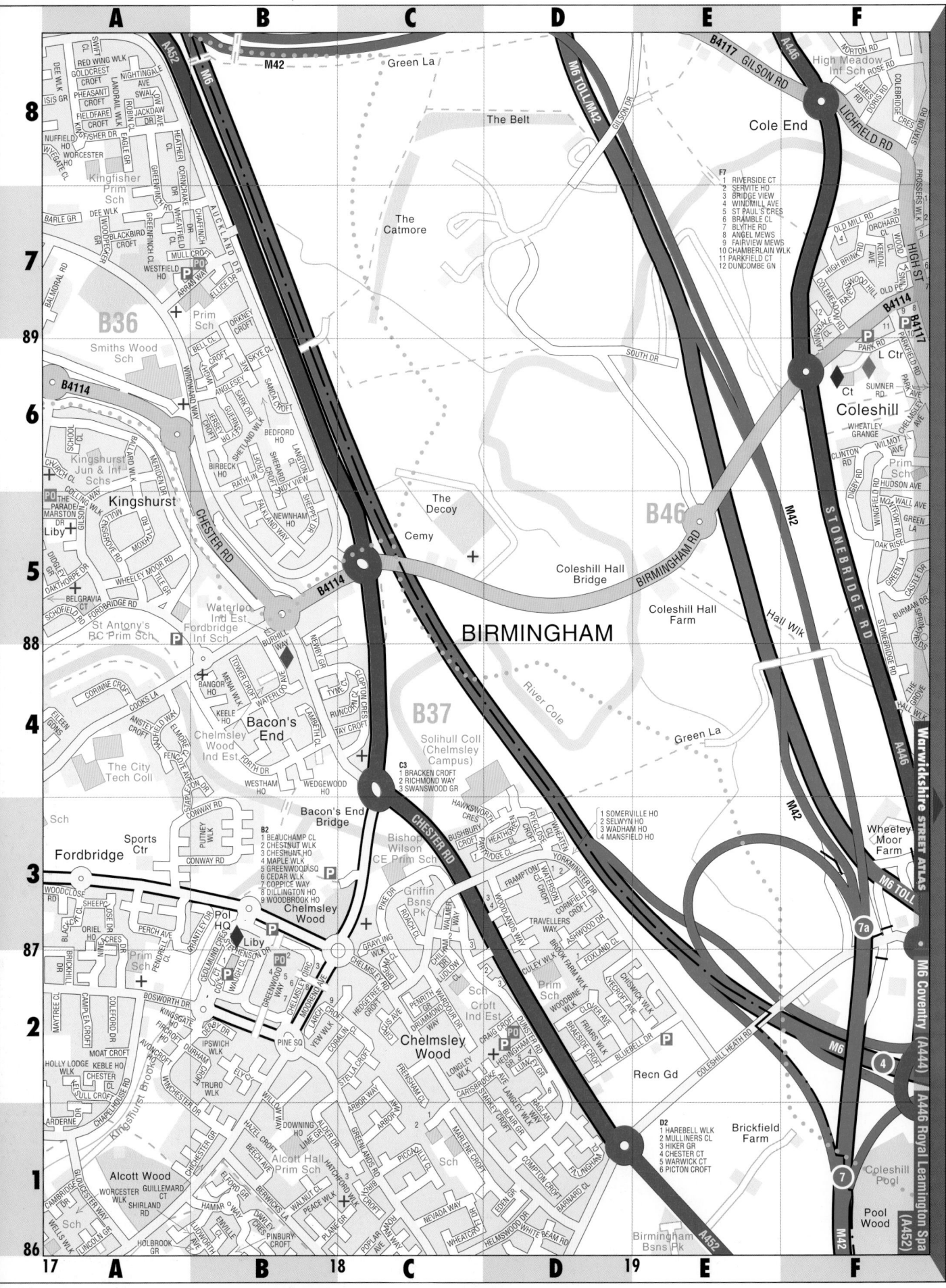

A B C D E F

8
7
89
6
5
88
4
3
87
2
1
86

M42

Green La

The Belt

The Catmore

B36

Smiths Wood Sch

Kingfisher Prim Sch

SWIFT WLK
RED WING WLK
GOLDCREST CROFT
NIGHTINGALE AVE
PHEASANT CROFT
FIELDFARE WLK
ROBIN WLK
JACKDAW
SWAL LOW
KINGFISHER DR
EAGLE GR
DEE WLK
ISIS GR
NUFFIELD HO
WYEGATE CL
WORCESTER
BARLE GR
BALMORAL RD
CHURCH CL
DINGLEY DR
OAKTHORPE DR
SCHOFIELD RD
BELGRAVIA CT
EILEEN GDNS
CORINNE CROFT
COOKS LA
ANSTEE CROFT
THE CITY TECH COLL
FORDBRIDGE RD
ST ANTONY'S R.C. PRIM SCH
WATERLOO IND EST
FORDBRIDGE INF SCH

B4114

Kingshurst

Kingshurst Jun & Inf Schs

THE PARADE
MARSTON DR
Liby

CHESTER RD

Waterloo Ind Est
Fordbridge Inf Sch
BURHILL WAY
MEWBY GR

B4114

BIRMINGHAM

The Decoy
Cemy

B37

Solihull Coll (Chelmsley Campus)

River Cole

Bishop Wilson CE Prim Sch

Bacon's End
Bacon's End Bridge

B2
1 BEAUCHAMP CL
2 CHESTNUT WLK
3 CHESHUNT HO
4 MAPLE WLK
5 GREENWOOD SQ
6 CEDAR WLK
7 COPPICE WAY
8 DILLINGTON HO
9 WOODBROOK HO

C3
1 BRACKEN CROFT
2 RICHMOND WAY
3 SWANSWOOD GR

1 SOMERVILLE HO
2 SELWYN HO
3 WADHAM HO
4 MANSFIELD HO

CHESTER RD

Griffin Bsns Pk

Fordbridge
Sports Ctr

Chelmsley Wood

Pol HQ
Liby
Prim Sch

Chelmsley Wood

D2
1 HAREBELL WLK
2 MULLINERS CL
3 HIKER GR
4 CHESTER CT
5 WARWICK CT
6 PICTON CROFT

Recn Gd

Brickfield Farm

Alcott Wood

Alcott Hall Prim Sch

Birmingham Bsns Pk

A452

Cole End

B4117 GILSON RD
A446

High Meadow Inf Sch

F7
1 RIVERSIDE CT
2 SERVITE HO
3 BRIDGE VIEW
4 WINDMILL AVE
5 ST PAUL'S CRES
6 BRAMBLE CL
7 BLYTHE RD
8 ANGEL MEWS
9 FAIRVIEW MEWS
10 CHAMBERLAIN WLK
11 PARKFIELD CT
12 DUNCOMBE GN

LICHFIELD RD

B4114

B46

Coleshill

Coleshill Hall Bridge

BIRMINGHAM RD

Coleshill Hall Farm

Green La

M42

STONEBRIDGE RD

Wheeley Moor Farm

M6 TOLL

7a

4

7

Coleshill Pool

Pool Wood

M42

Warwickshire street ATLAS

M6 Coventry (A444)

A446 Royal Leamington Spa (A452)

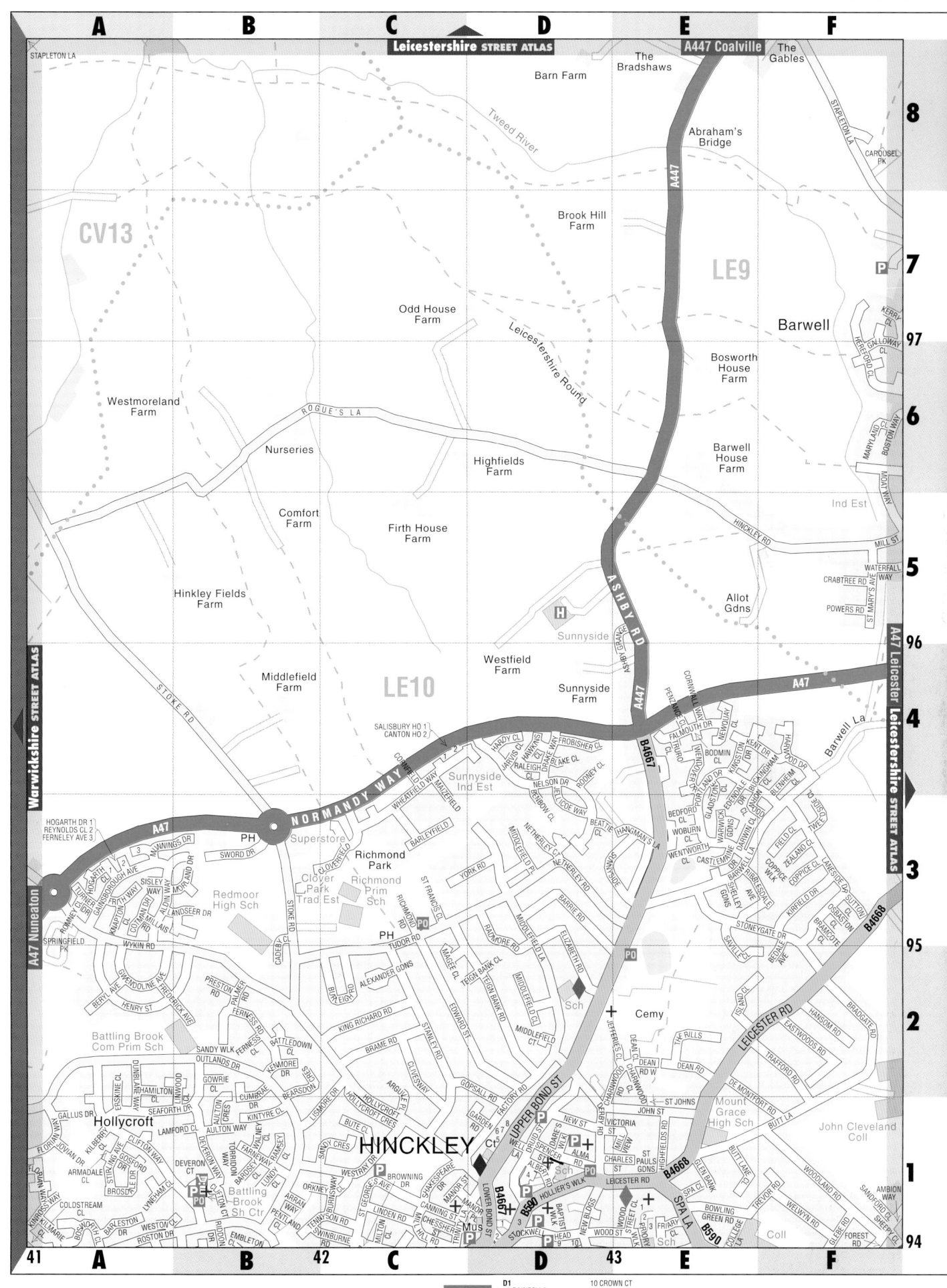

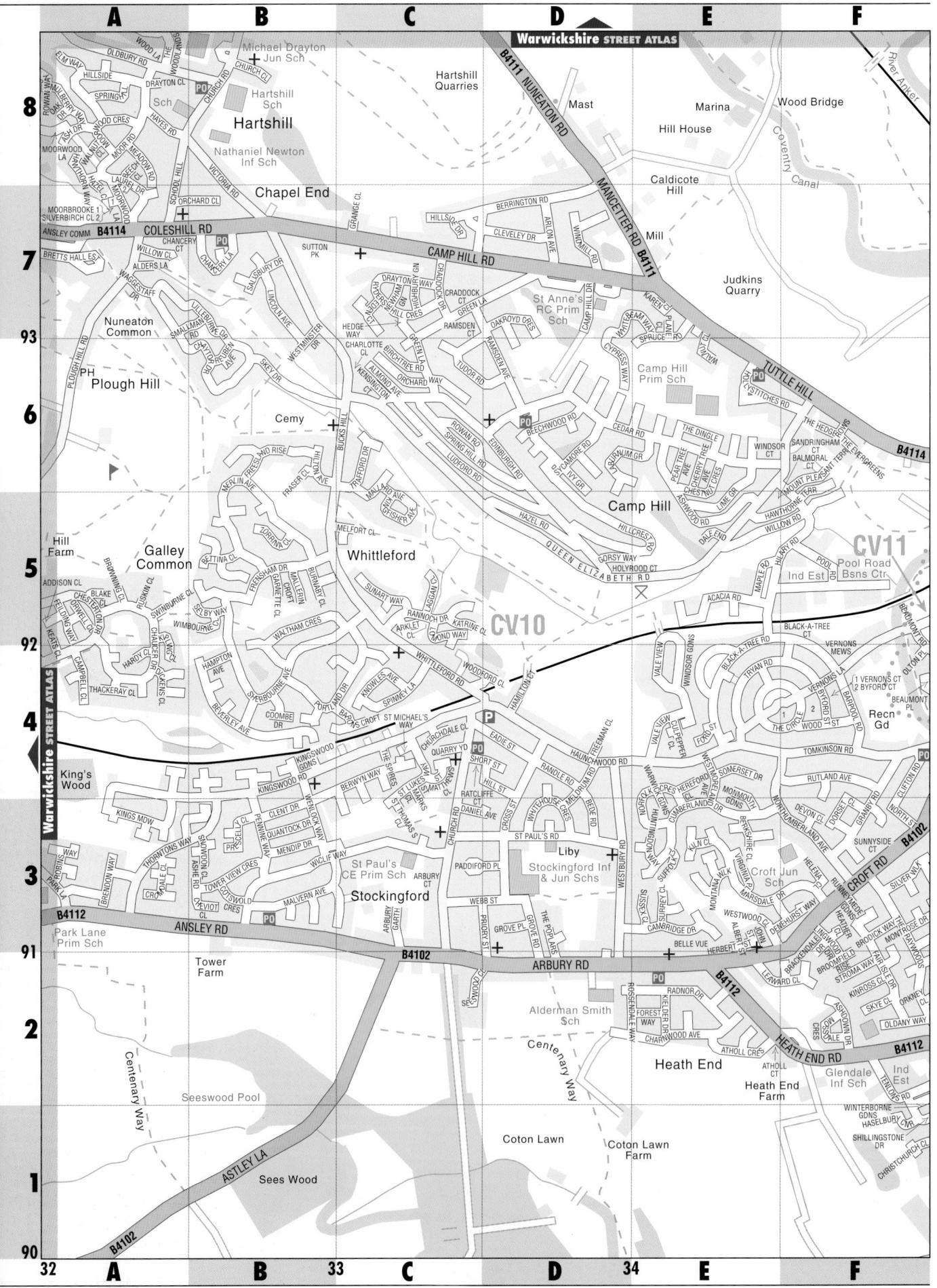

Warwickshire STREET ATLAS

Warwickshire STREET ATLAS

8

7

93

6

5

92

4

3

91

2

1

90

A   B   C   D   E   F

32   **33**   **34**

Elm Way
Oldbury Rd
Hillside
Drayton Cl
Springy
Wood Cres
Hayes Rd
Michael Drayton Jun Sch
Church Cl
Church Rd
Sch
Hartshill Sch
PO

Rowan Way
Mulberry Way
Dr
Sir Dr
Wood La
Moorwood La
Hawthorn Hazel Cl
Laurel Dr
Meadow Rd
Willow Dr
Orchard Cl
School Hill
Victoria Rd

Hartshill

Nathaniel Newton Inf Sch

Moorbrooke
Silverbirch Cl
Ansley Comm   **B4114**

Chapel End

Grange Cl

Hartshill Quarries

B4111 NUNEATON RD

Mast

Marina
Hill House

Wood Bridge

COLESHILL RD

Chancery Ct
Chancery La
Willow Cl
Alders La
PO

Sutton Pk

Hillside Dr
Berrington Rd
Cleveley Dr
Arlon Ave
Windmill Rd

Caldicote Hill

Mill

Coventry Canal

Bretts Hall Est

Wagstaff Dr

Lincoln Ave
Isambury Dr
Westminster Dr

CAMP HILL RD

Drayton Way
Rydersham Way
Cresswell Cres
Craddock Ct
Green La
Ramsden Ct
Ramsden Ave

Karen Cl
Diane St
Whitten Ct
Spruce

St Anne's RC Prim Sch

Camp Hill Rd

Judkins Quarry

TUTTLE HILL

Nuneaton Common

Smallburn Rd
Chattock Cl
Reuben La

Charlotte Cl
Hedge Way
Birchtree Rd
Green La
Almond Ave
Kensington Ct
Orchard Way
Tudor Rd

Cypress Way

Camp Hill Prim Sch

Hollystitches Rd

The Hedges
Sandringham Ct
The Evergreens
Balmoral Ct
Windsor Ct
Mount Pleasant Terr

PH
Plough Hill

Merlin Ave
Freshند Rise
Hill
Fraser Cl
Tithe Ave
Bucks Hill

Rifford Dr
Mallard Ave
Kingfisher Ave

Rowan Rd
Spring Hill La
Ludford Rd
Edinburgh Rd

Beechwood Rd
Sycamore Rd
Ivy Gr

Laburnum Gr
Pear Tree
Cherry Tree
Chestnut
Lime Gr
Hazel Cres

Cedar Rd
The Dingle

Mount Pleasant Terr

Hawthorne Cl

B4114

Cemy

Hill Farm

Galley Common

Browning Cl
Bettina Cl
Rankin Cl
Swinburne Dr
Frensham Dr
Mallerin Croft
Garnette Cl
Burhary Cl
Zorrina Cl

Melfort Cl

Whittleford

Sunart Way

Hazel Rd
Queen Elizabeth Rd
Hillcrest Rd
Gorsy Way
Holyrood Ct
Dale End

Camp Hill

Willow Rd

Maple Rd
Hilary Rd

Pool Ind Est

CV11
Pool Road Bsns Ctr

Addison Cl
Blake Cl
Chesterton Dr
Felding Way
Dorney Cl
Keyes Cl
Campbell Cl
Chaucer Dr
Dickens Cl
Thackeray Cl
Hardy Cl
Wimbourne Cl
Waltham Cres

Rannoch Dr
Arklet Cl
Jagson Dr
Katrine Cl
Almond Way

Woodford Cl

CV10

Windsor Gdns
Vale View
Acacia Rd
Black-A-Tree Ct

Black-A-Tree Rd

Vernons Mews
1 Vernons Ct
2 Byford St
Beaumont Pl

Beaumont Rd

King's Wood

Hampton Ave
Sherbourne Dr
Coombe Dr
Beverley Ave
Portland Dr
Baxters Croft
Knowles Ave
Spinney La

WHITTLEFORD RD

Hamilton Dr

Vale View
Culpepper Cl
Ford St
Tryan Rd

The Circle
Byford St
Barpool Rd
Olton Pl

The Wood
Recn Gd

PO

Kings Mdw
Thorntons Way
Snowdon Cl
Tower View Cres
Ashe Rd
Cheviot Cl
Cotswold Cres
Malvern Ave

Kingswood Gdns
Clent Dr
Wenlock Way
Quantock Dr
Mendip Way
Wiclif Way
The Spires
Berwyn Way
Pennine Way
Pryse Cl

St Luke's
St Matthews
St Thomas's Cl
Ratcliffe Cl
Daniel Ave
Church Rd
Hill Cl
Short St
Eadie St
Quarry Yd
Churchdale Cl

Randle Rd
Cross St
St Paul's Rd
Whitehouse Cres
Belde Rd
Millburn Rd
Haunchwood Rd
Freeman St

Hereford Cl
Somerset Dr
Norfolk Cres
Cumberland Dr
Cumberlands Dr
Monmouth Gdns
Westmoreland Ave

Berkshire Dr
Virginia Rd
Montana Wlk
Marsdale Dr
Westwood Rd

Tomkinson Rd
Rutland Ave
Devon Cl
Dorset Cl
Grange Rd
North St
Sunnyside Ct

CROFT RD

B4102

Silver Wlk

St Paul's CE Prim Sch

Robins Way
Brendon Way
Park La
Arbury Garth
Arbury Ct
Paddiford Pl
Webb St
Priory St
Grove Pl
Grove Rd
The Poplars

Stockingford

B4112

Park Lane Prim Sch

ANSLEY RD

PO

B4102

ARBURY RD

Liby
Stockingford Inf & Jun Schs

Westbury Rd

Croft Jun Sch

Belle Vue
Herbert St
Albert St

Brackendale Way
Broomfield Rise
Stroma Way
Cambridge Dr
Sussex Cl
Surrey Cl

Leaward Cl
Radnor Dr
Forest Way
Kielder Dr
Rosendale Way
Charnwood Ave

Demehurst Way
Helena Ct
Running Mdw
Lingwood
Brodick Way
Kinross Cl
Skye Cl
Ramsden
Montrose Dr
Raywoods
Ashorne Dr
Orkney Cl
Oldany Way

Ind Est

Tower Farm

Centenary Way

Seeswood Pool

Alderman Smith Sch

Centenary Way

Atholl Cres

Heath End

Atholl Ct

Heath End Farm

HEATH END RD

B4112

Glendale Inf Sch

Winterborne Gdns
Haselbury Dr
Shillingstone Dr
Christchurch Rd

Coton Lawn

Coton Lawn Farm

River Anker

B4112

CV11

B4111

MANCETTER RD

Astley La
Sees Wood
B4102

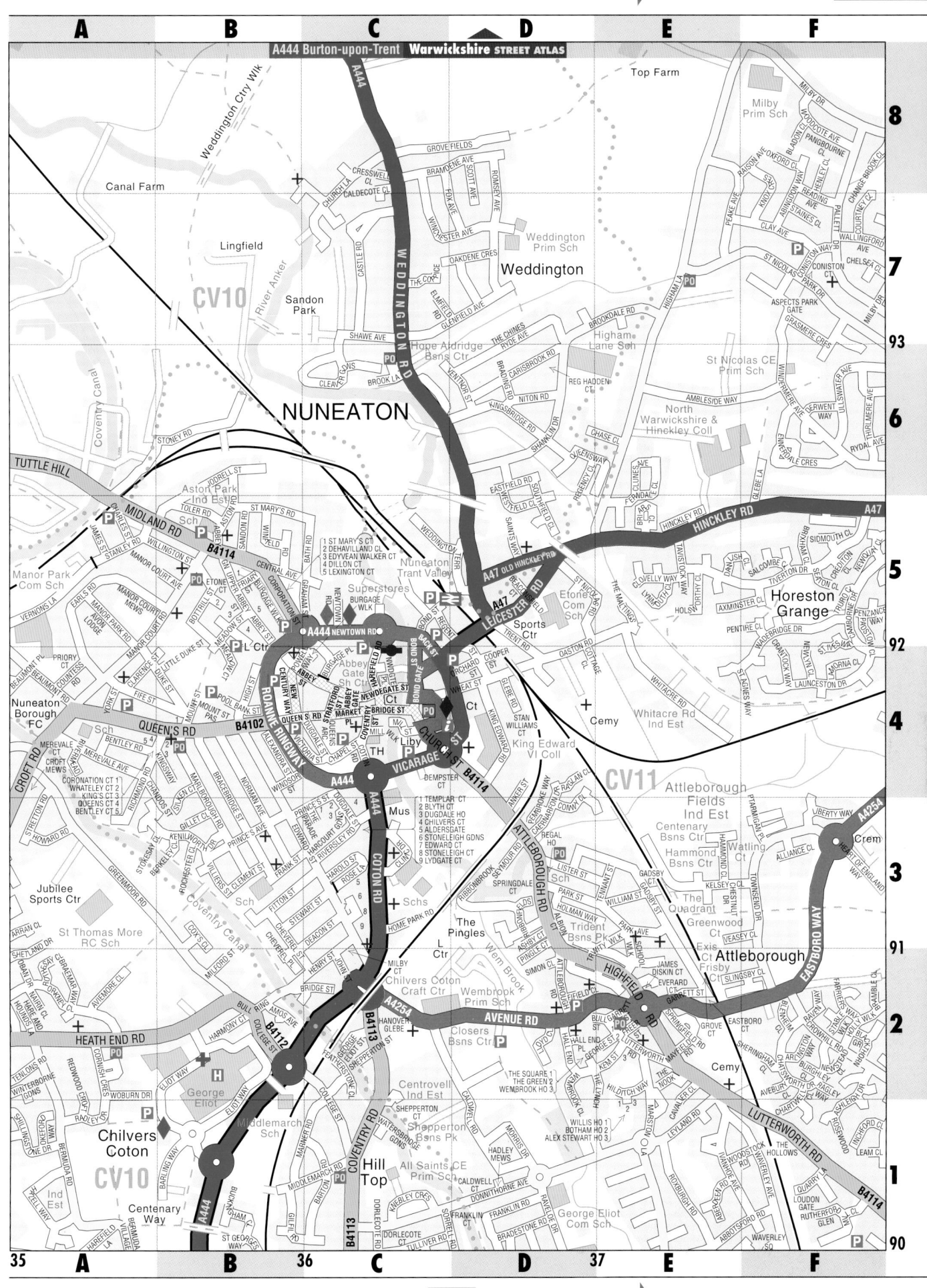

74
78
74

A444 Burton-upon-Trent **Warwickshire** STREET ATLAS

CV10

NUNEATON

Weddington

Top Farm

Milby
Prim Sch

CV11

Horeston
Grange

Attleborough
Fields
Ind Est

Attleborough

Chilvers
Coton

CV10

Hill
Top

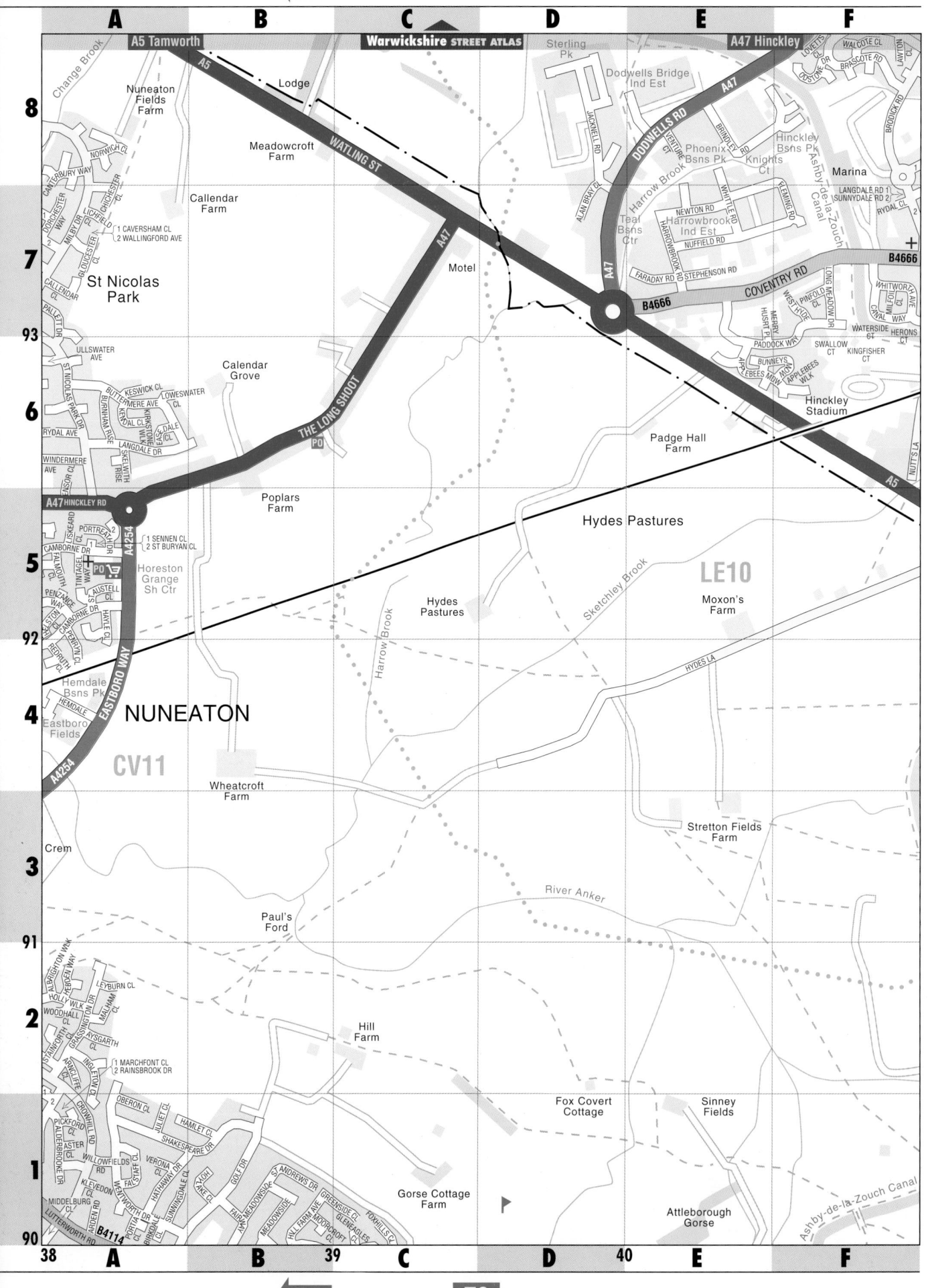

Warwickshire STREET ATLAS

A5 Tamworth

A47 Hinckley

NUNEATON

CV11

LE10

St Nicolas Park

Hydes Pastures

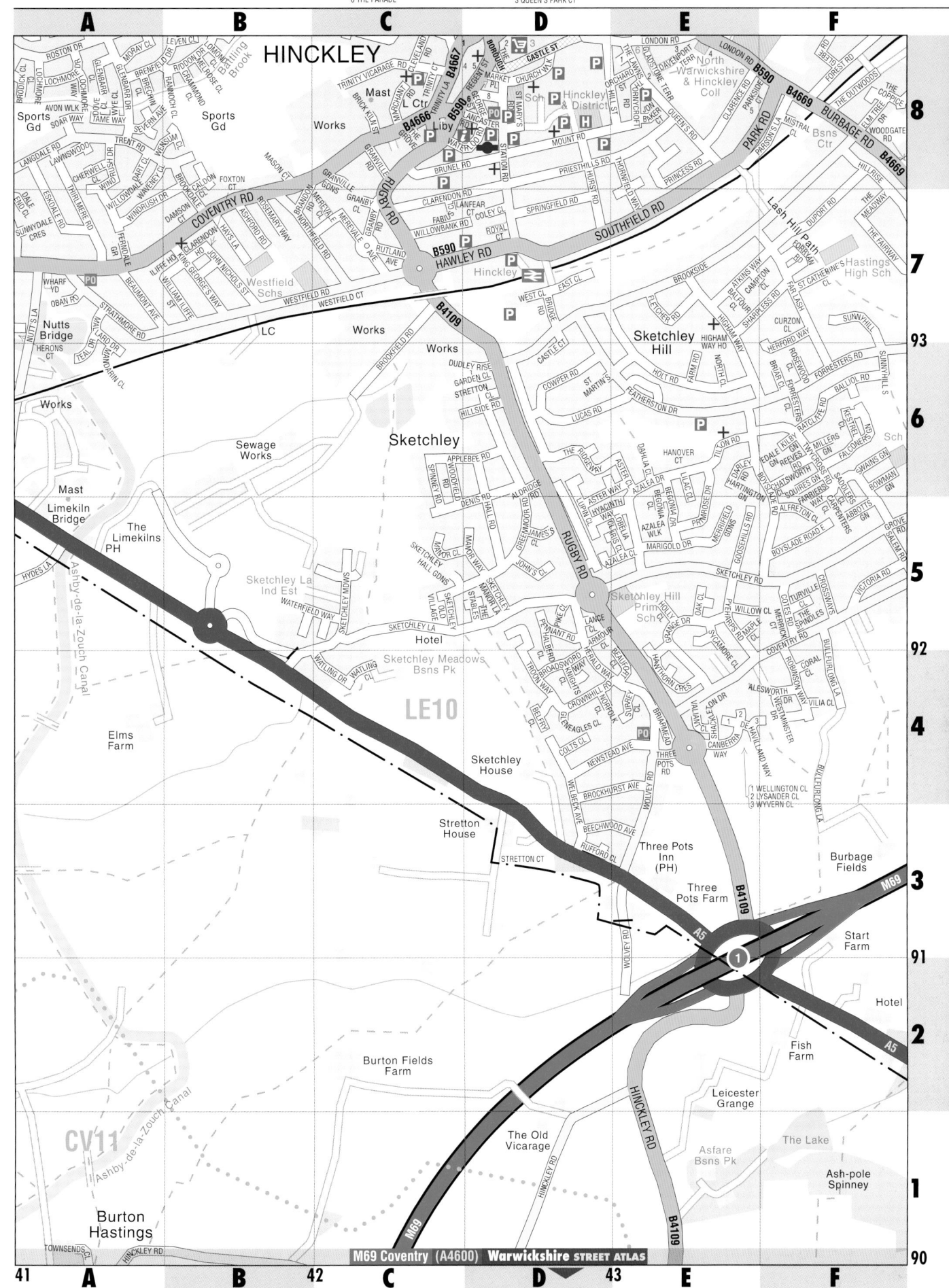

D8
1 MANSION ST
2 HANSOM CT
3 Brittania Sh Ctr
4 BLOCKLEY'S YD
5 REGENT CT
6 THE PARADE

71

D8
7 Edwards Ctr
8 THE HORSEFAIR
E8
1 THE NARROWS
2 QUEEN'S PARK FLATS
3 QUEEN'S PARK CT

76

4 QUEEN S PARK TERR
5 CLARENCE CT
6 The Lawns Bsns Ctr

75

HINCKLEY

Sports Gd

Sports Gd

Nutts Bridge

Works

Limekiln Bridge

Mast

The Limekilns PH

Sketchley La Ind Est

Waterfield Way

Elms Farm

Sewage Works

Sketchley

Works

Works

Works

Sketchley Meadows Bsns Pk

LE10

Sketchley House

Sketchley Hall Gdns

Old Vilage

Hotel

Stretton House

Stretton Ct

Burton Fields Farm

CV11

The Old Vicarage

Burton Hastings

Sketchley Hill

Sketchley Hill Prim Sch

Three Pots Inn (PH)

Three Pots Farm

Burbage Fields

Start Farm

Hotel

Fish Farm

Leicester Grange

Asfare Bsns Pk

The Lake

Ash-pole Spinney

North Warwickshire & Hinckley Coll

Hastings High Sch

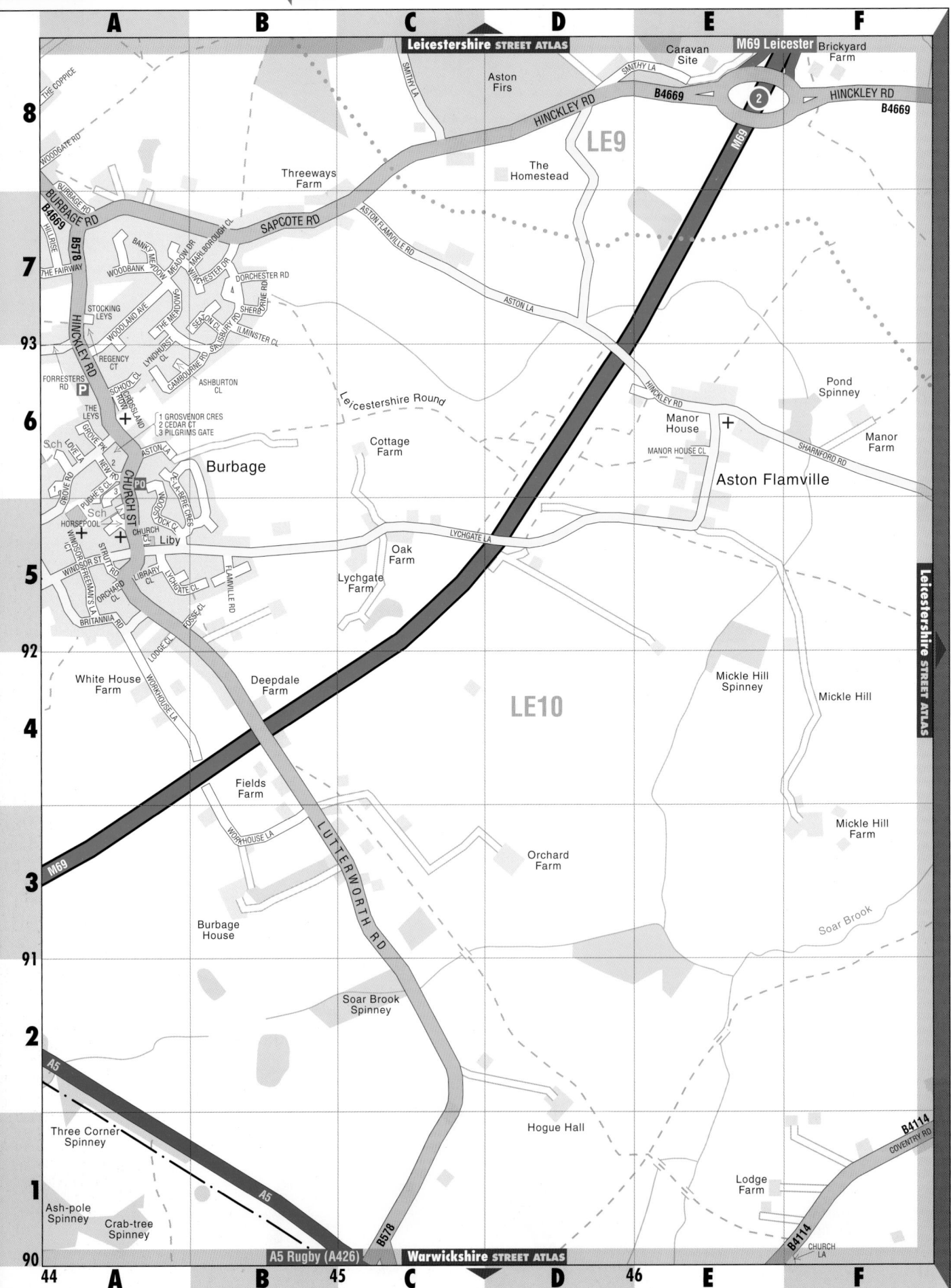

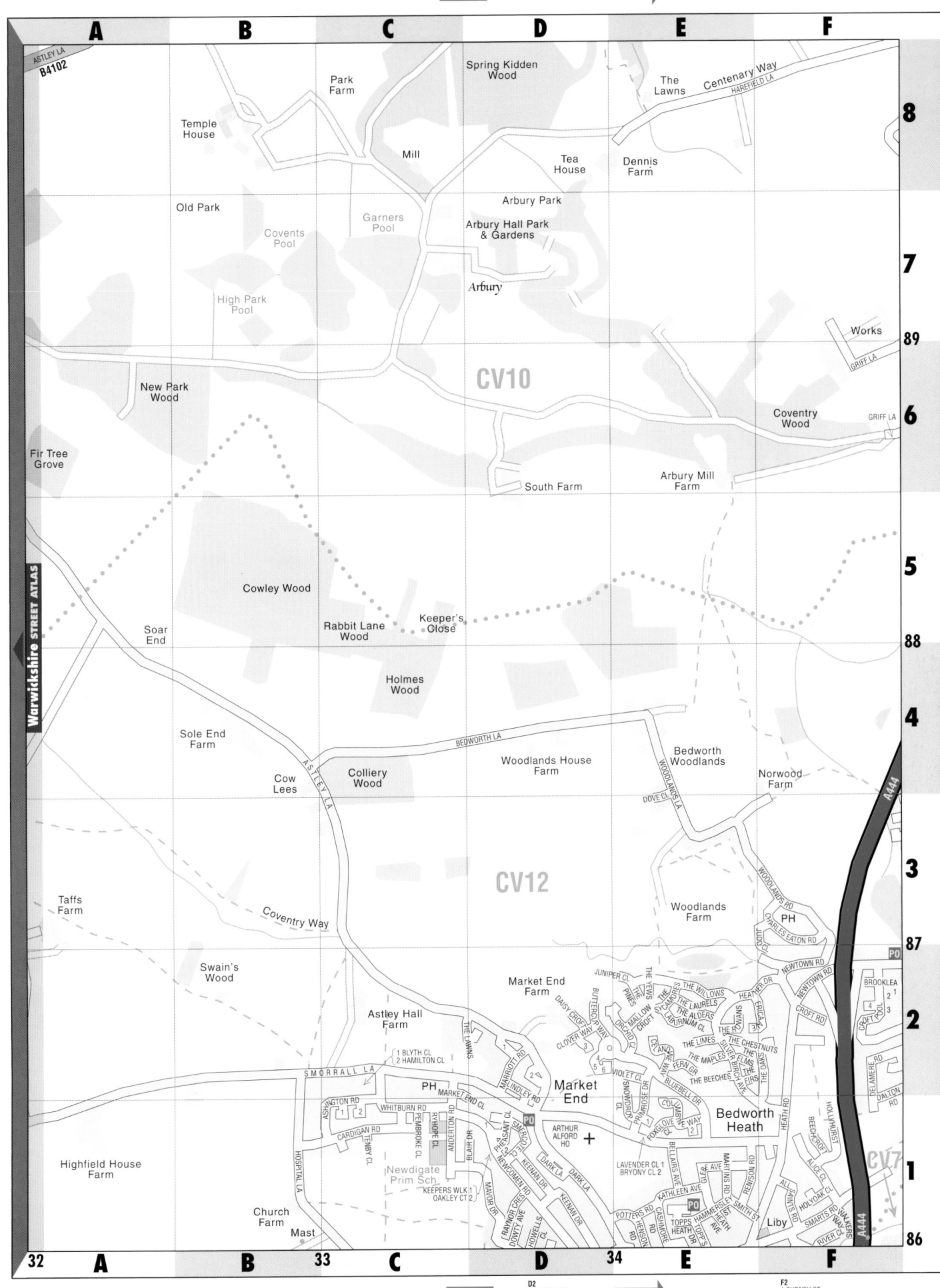

ASTLEY LA
B4102

Warwickshire STREET ATLAS

A B C D E F

8

7

89

6

5

88

4

3

87

2

1

86

Spring Kidden Wood

Park Farm

Temple House

Mill

Old Park

Garners Pool

Covents Pool

High Park Pool

CV10

Arbury Park

Arbury Hall Park & Gardens

Arbury

The Lawns

Centenary Way

HAREFIELD LA

Tea House

Dennis Farm

Works

GRIFF LA

New Park Wood

Coventry Wood

GRIFF LA

Fir Tree Grove

South Farm

Arbury Mill Farm

Cowley Wood

Keeper's Close

Soar End

Rabbit Lane Wood

Holmes Wood

Bedworth La

Sole End Farm

Cow Lees

Colliery Wood

ASTLEY LA

Woodlands House Farm

Bedworth Woodlands

WOODLANDS LA

DOVE CL LA

Norwood Farm

CV12

Taffs Farm

Coventry Way

Woodlands Farm

WOODLANDS RD

CHARLES EATON RD

PH

JUDD CL

NEWTOWN RD

A444

PO

BROOKLEA

Swain's Wood

Market End Farm

JUNIPER CL

THE WILLOWS

THE PINES

THE YEWS

THE SYCAMORES

THE LAURELS

THE ALDERS

HEATHER DR

FRIGA CL

NEWTOWN RD

CROFT RD

CROFT POOL

DELAMERE RD

DALTON RD

Astley Hall Farm

THE LAWNS

MARRIOTT RD

LINDLEY RD

DAISY CROFT

BUTTERCUP WAY

CLOVER WAY

ORCHID CL

THE MALLOW

CAMPION CL

LABURNUM CL

THE LIMES

THE MAPLES

SILVER BIRCH AVE

THE CHESTNUTS

THE ELMS

THE FIRS

THE OAKS

THE BEECHES

HEATH RD

HOLLYHURST

BEECH CROFT

ALICE CL

CV7

1 BLYTH CL
2 HAMILTON CL

PH

ASHINGTON RD

WHITBURN RD

CARDIGAN RD

TENBY CL

PEMBROKE CL

MARKET END CL

RYHOPE CL

ANDERTON RD

BLAIR DR

PHEASANT CL

SMARTS RD

PO

Market End

FERN GR

VIOLET CL

BLUEBELL DR

PRIMROSE DR

COLUMBINE WAY

FOXGLOVE WAY

ARTHUR ALFORD HO

LAVENDER CL 1
BRYONY CL 2

BELLAIRS AVE

MARTINS RD

RENISON RD

ST SE AVE

Bedworth Heath

ALL SAINTS RD

HOLYOAK CL

Highfield House Farm

HOSPITAL LA

SMORRALL LA

Newdigate Prim Sch

KEEPERS WLK 1
OAKLEY CT 2

RAYNOR CRES

DOWTY AVE

MAYOR DR

NEWCOMEN RD

KENNAN DR

HOWELLS CL

KENNAN DR

DARK LA

DARK LA

POTTERS RD

HENSON RD

CASHMORE AVE

PO

TOPPS HEATH

HAMMERSLEY ST

SMITH ST

HEATH DR

Liby

SMARTS RD

WALKERS

RIVER CL

A444

Church Farm

Mast

D2
1 WILDEY RD
2 HIMLEY RD
3 CAMPION WAY
4 DAFFODIL DRIVE
5 LARKSPUR GR
6 SPEEDWELL CL

F2
1 SYDNEY CT
2 CANBERRA CT
3 MELBOURNE CT
4 QUEENSLAND GDNS

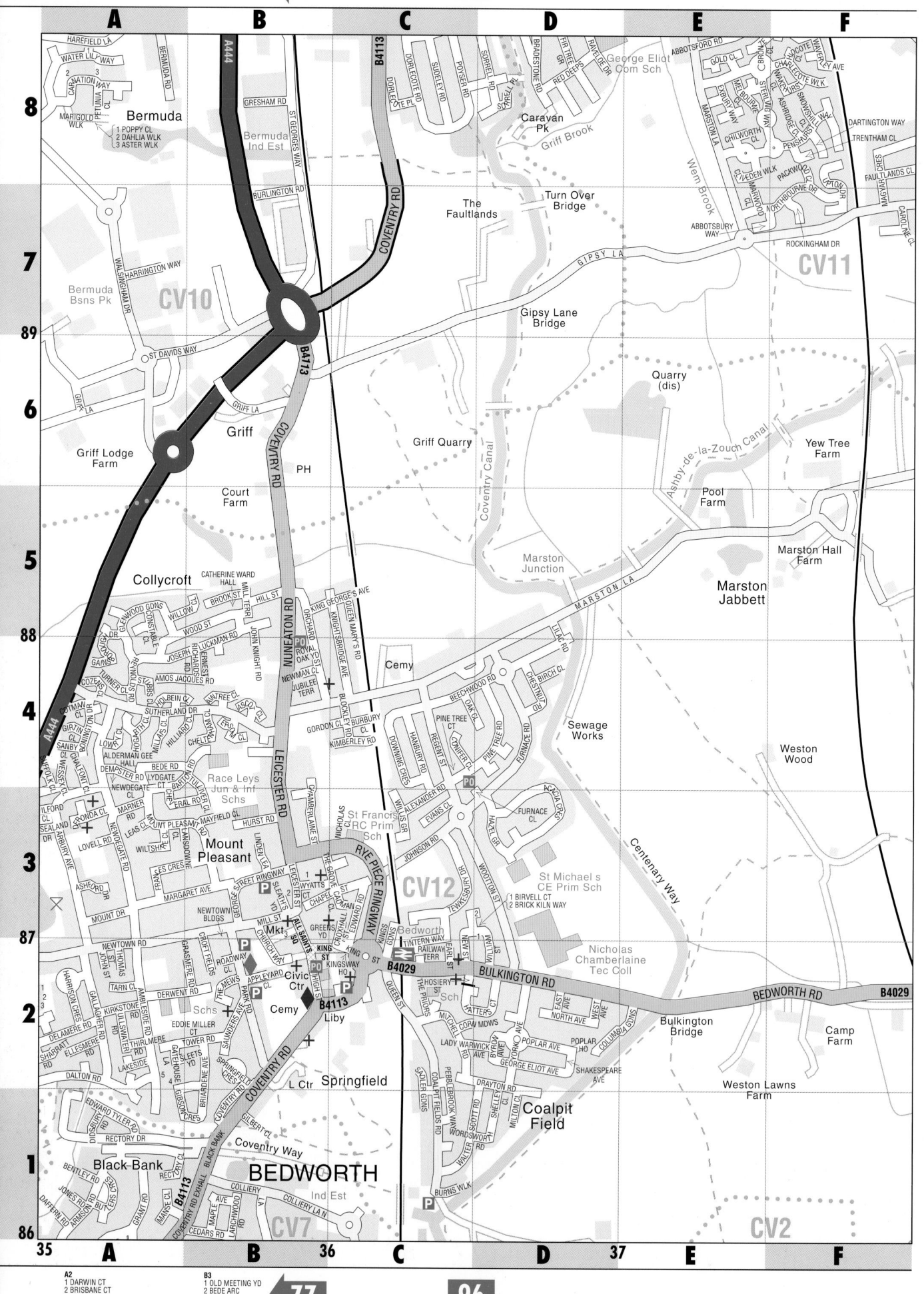
A   B   C   D   E   F

8

HAREFIELD LA
WATER LILY WAY
CARNATION WAY
MARIGOLD WLK
PETUNIA

BERMUDA RD

BERMUDA
1 POPPY CL
2 DAHLIA WLK
3 ASTER WLK

A444

GRESHAM RD

ST GEORGES WAY

Bermuda Ind Est

BURLINGTON RD

B4113

COVENTRY RD

DORLECOTE PL
DORLECOTE RD

SUDELEY RD

POYSER RD
SORRELL RD
SORRELL RD

BRADESTONE RD
FIR TREE
RED DEEPS
RAVEN CL RD

George Eliot Com Sch

ABBOTSFORD RD
GOLD CL

CEDRON
CHAPELCOTE WLK
WAVERLEY AVE

MARSTON LA
CHILWORTH CL

EXBURY WAY
ASHRIDGE CL
PENSHURST WAY

DARTINGTON WAY
TRENTHAM CL

MAYFIELDS CRES
FAULTLANDS CL
CAROLINE CL

7

WALSINGHAM DR

HARRINGTON WAY

CV10

Bermuda Bsns Pk

Caravan Pk

Griff Brook

Turn Over Bridge

The Faultlands

GIPSY LA

Wem Brook

ABBOTSBURY WAY

NORTHBOURNE DR
PACKWOOD
EDEN WLK
MARLWOOD
UPTON DR

ROCKINGHAM DR

CV11

89

ST DAVIDS WAY

B4113

Gipsy Lane Bridge

6

GRIFF LA
GRIFF LA

Griff

COVENTRY RD

Griff Lodge Farm

PH

Court Farm

Griff Quarry

Coventry Canal

Ashby-de-la-Zouch Canal

Quarry (dis)

Pool Farm

Yew Tree Farm

5

Collycroft

CATHERINE WARD HALL

Marston Junction

MARSTON LA

Marston Jabbett

Marston Hall Farm

88

GLENWOOD GDNS
CONSTABLE CL
WILLOW
WOOD ST
HILL TERRI
HILL ST
BROOKIST
MILL TERRI
JOHN KNIGHT RD
ORCHARD
KING GEORGE'S AVE
QUEEN MARY'S RD
KNIGHTSBRIDGE AVE

NUNEATON RD

ROYAL OAK YD
JUBILEE TERR

Cemy

BEECHWOOD RD
CHESTNUT CL
OAK CL
BIRCH CL

LILAC RD

Sewage Works

Weston Wood

4

COTMAN DR
GIRTIN
TURNER CL
COZENS
GAINS
REYNOLDS RD
AMOS JACQUES RD
JOSEPH
LUCKMAN RD
ERNEST RD
RICHARDS ST
KIMTREE CL
ASCO CL

A444

SUTHERLAND DR
HILLIARD CL
CHELT
TERO

GORDON CL
BLOCKLEY CL
KIMBERLEY RD

BURBURY CL

LEICESTER RD

PINE TREE CT
HABURY RD
DOWNING CRES
REGENT ST
CONIFER CL
PINE TREE RD
FURNACE RD

Pine Tree Ct

ACACIA CRES

FURNACE CL

Centenary Way

Weston Wood

3

GIRTIN
WESSEX
SANBY CL
ILFORD CL
SEALAND
ARBURY AVE
RONDA CL
LOVELL RD
NEWDEGATE CL
LEAS CL
WILTSHIRE
MOUNT PLEASANT

ALDERMAN GEE HALL
DEMPSTER CT
NEWDEGATE CL
BEDE RD
LYDGATE
MARNER RD
ERAL CL
BIRTO
MAYFIELD CL
HURST RD

Race Leys Jun & Inf Schs

Mount Pleasant

LINDEN LEA

STREET RINGWAY
LEICESTER CT
THE GROVE
WYATTS
CHAPEL ST
CHAMBERLAINE ST

RYE PIECE RINGWAY

NICHOLAS ST
St Francis RC Prim Sch

JOHNSON RD
G GR
ALEXANDER CL
EVANS CL
NEWTON RD

CV12

WOOTTON ST

St Michael s CE Prim Sch
1 BIRVELL CT
2 BRICK KILN WAY

87

MARGARET RD
MOUNT DR
NEWTOWN RD

NEWTOWN BLDGS

Mkt

All SAINTS SQ

KING ST

Bedworth
Railway Stn

TINTERN WAY

EARL ST
WILLIAM ST

Nicholas Chamberlaine Tec Coll

2

HARRISON CRES
JOHN ST
THOMAS ST
GALLAGHER RD
KIRKSTONE CL
AMBLESIDE RD
ULLSWATER RD
DELAMERE RD
ELLESMERE RD

CROFT FIELDS
GRASMERE RD
DERWENT RD

GREENS YD
MILL ST

ROADWAY CL

Schs

APPLEYARD CL

SAUNDERS AVE
THE MEWS
PARK RD
Civic Ctr

Cemy

B4113
Liby

KINGSWAY
KING ST
KINGS HO

HIGH ST

B4029

HOSIERY
HATTERS

Sch

BULKINGTON RD

EAST AVE
NORTH AVE
WEST AVE

COLUMBIA GDNS

Bulkington Bridge

BEDWORTH RD

B4029

Camp Farm

1

BENTLEY RD
JONES RD
DAFFERN RD
ARMSON RD

EDWARD TYLER RD
DICKENS RD
RECTORY DR

Black Bank

THIRLMERE CL
TOWER RD
GATEHOUSE
SLEETS YD
DALTON RD
LAKESIDE
EDDIE MILLER CT

GIBSON CRES
BRIARDENE AVE
SPRINGFIELD CRES

GILBERT CL

COVENTRY RD

Springfield

L Ctr

RECTORY RD
GRANT RD
MARYS RD
BUTLERS
CEDARS RD

COLLIERY RD
BLACK BANK
MAPLE AVE
DOWNING LA
COLLIERY LA
COLLIERY LA N

Coventry Way

B4113

BEDWORTH

CV7

Ind Est

SADLER GDNS
COALPIT FIELDS RD
PEBBLEBROOK WAY
WATER RD
SCOTT RD
SHELLEY RD
MILTON CL
WORDSWORTH RD

MICHEL
CORN MDWS
LADY WARWICK AVE
YORK AVE
POPLAR AVE
POPLAR HO

GEORGE ELIOT AVE
SHAKESPEARE AVE

DRAYTON RD

Coalpit Field

BURNS WLK

Weston Lawns Farm

86

CV2

35   A   B   36   C   D   37   E   F

A2
1 DARWIN CT
2 BRISBANE CT
3 ADELAIDE CT
4 OLD PENN'S YD
5 BUCKLER'S YD

B3
1 OLD MEETING YD
2 BEDE ARC
3 CONGREVE WLK

77   96

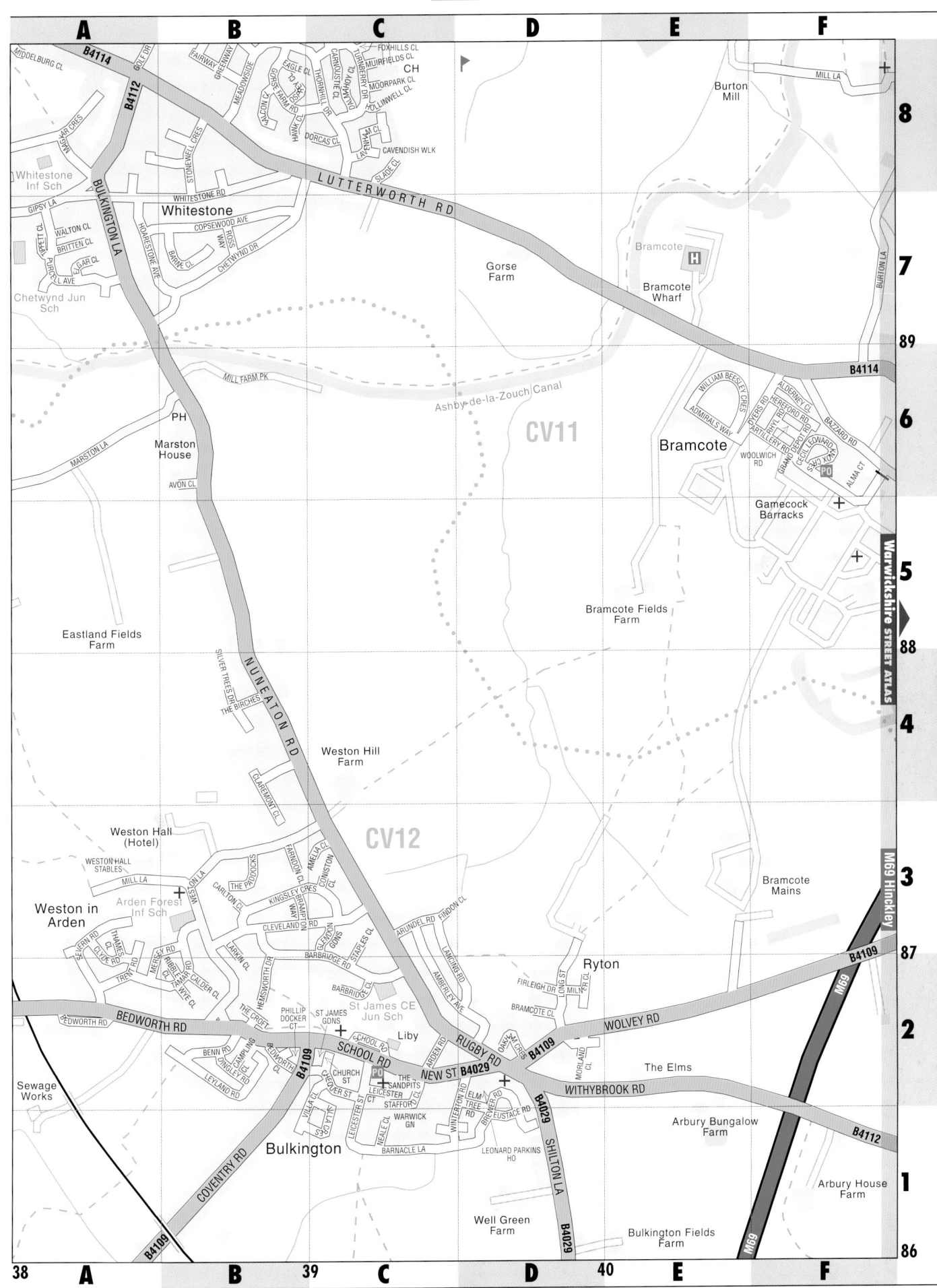

60

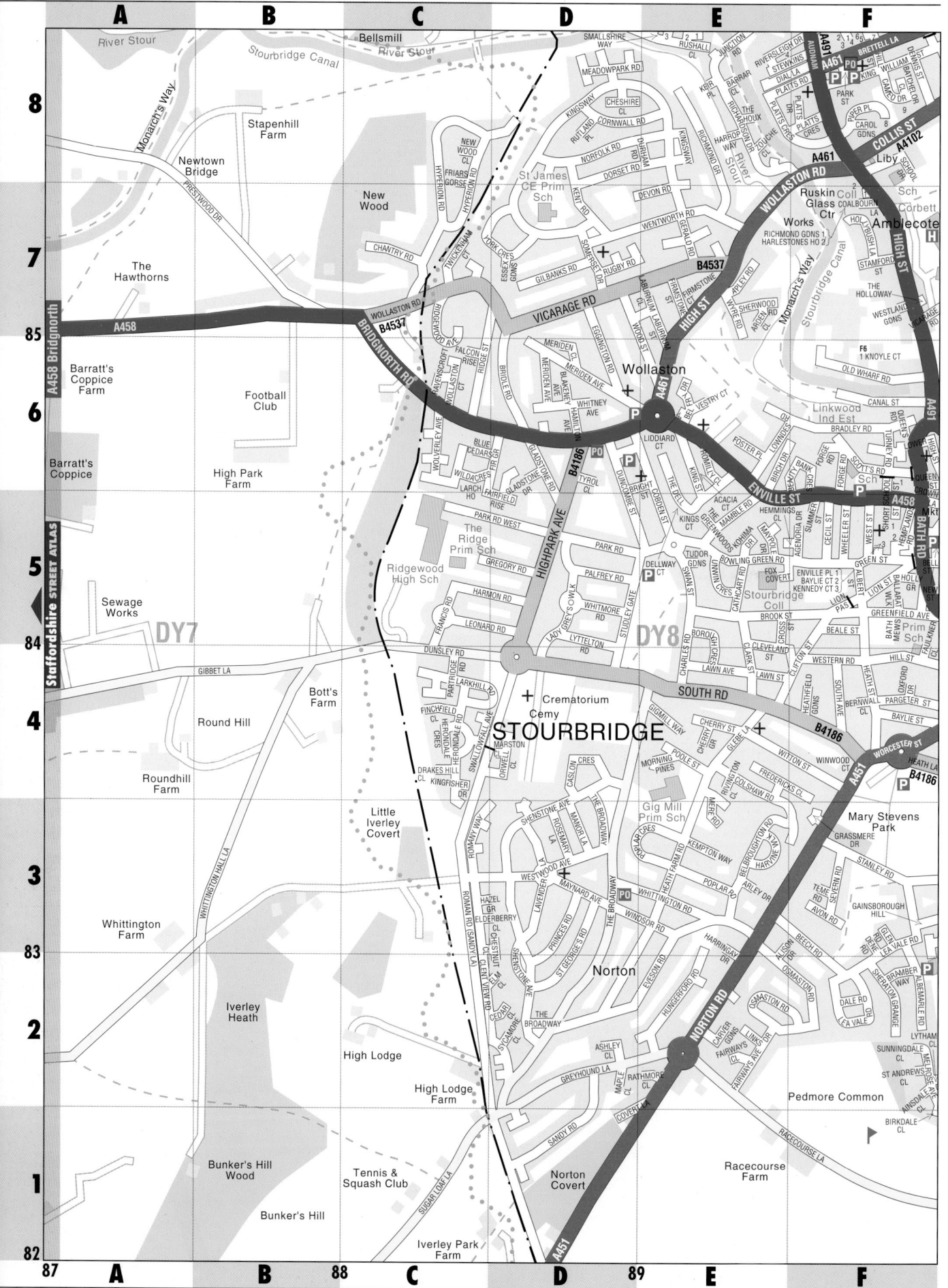

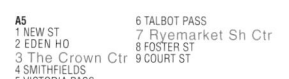

A5
1 NEW ST
2 EDEN HO
3 The Crown Ctr
4 SMITHFIELDS
5 VICTORIA PASS
6 TALBOT PASS
7 Ryemarket Sh Ctr
8 FOSTER ST
9 COURT ST

61
82

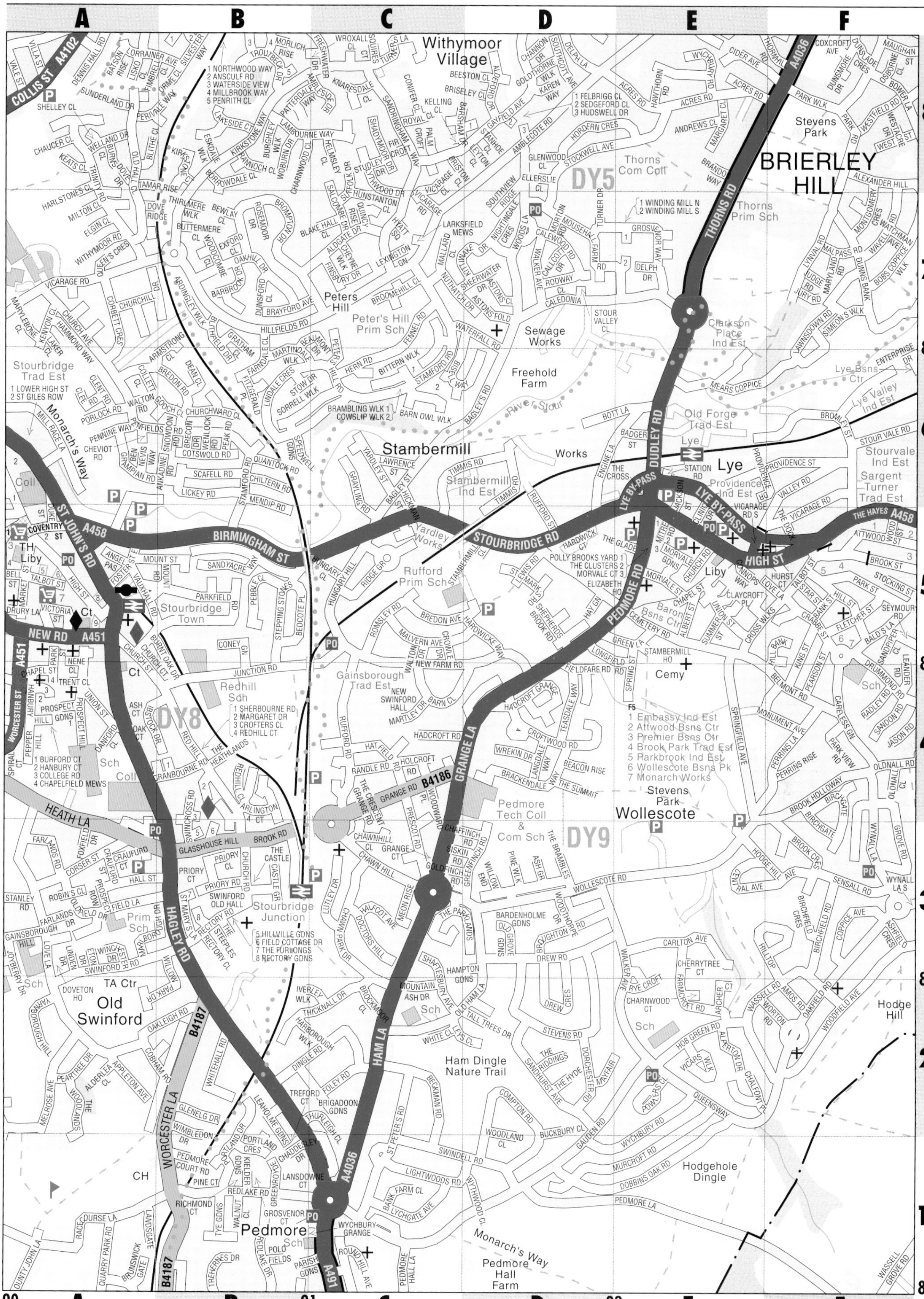

99
82

82

A8
1 QUEEN STREET PAS
2 CHAPEL ST
3 HAMPDEN CL

E8
1 MORGAN CL
2 DELINGPOLE WLK
3 DOROTHY ADAMS CL

F8
1 SHERWOOD HO
2 EDGEWOOD CL
3 ADDENBROOK HO
4 WESLEY CT
5 MEADOW ST
6 PENN ST

81

62

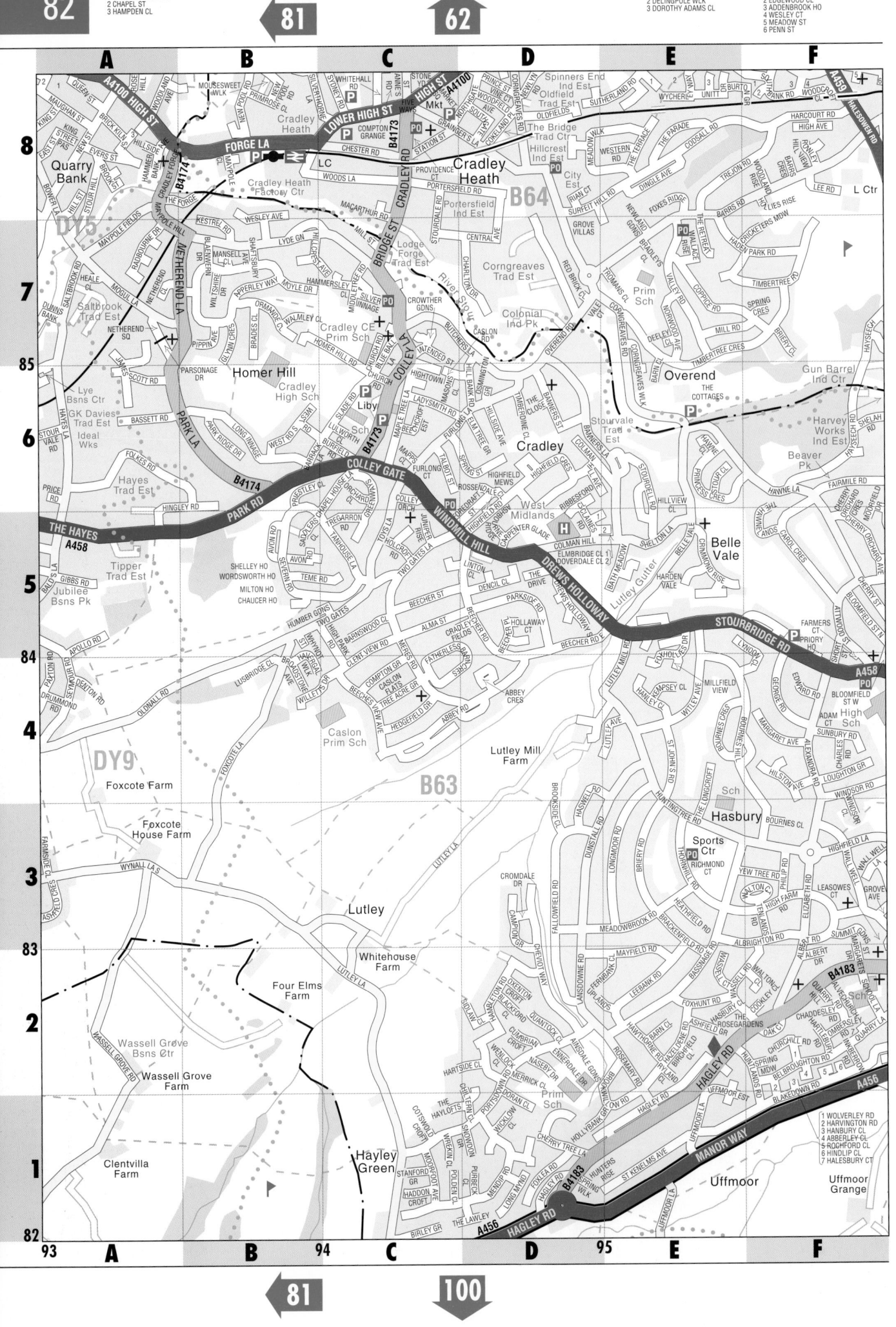

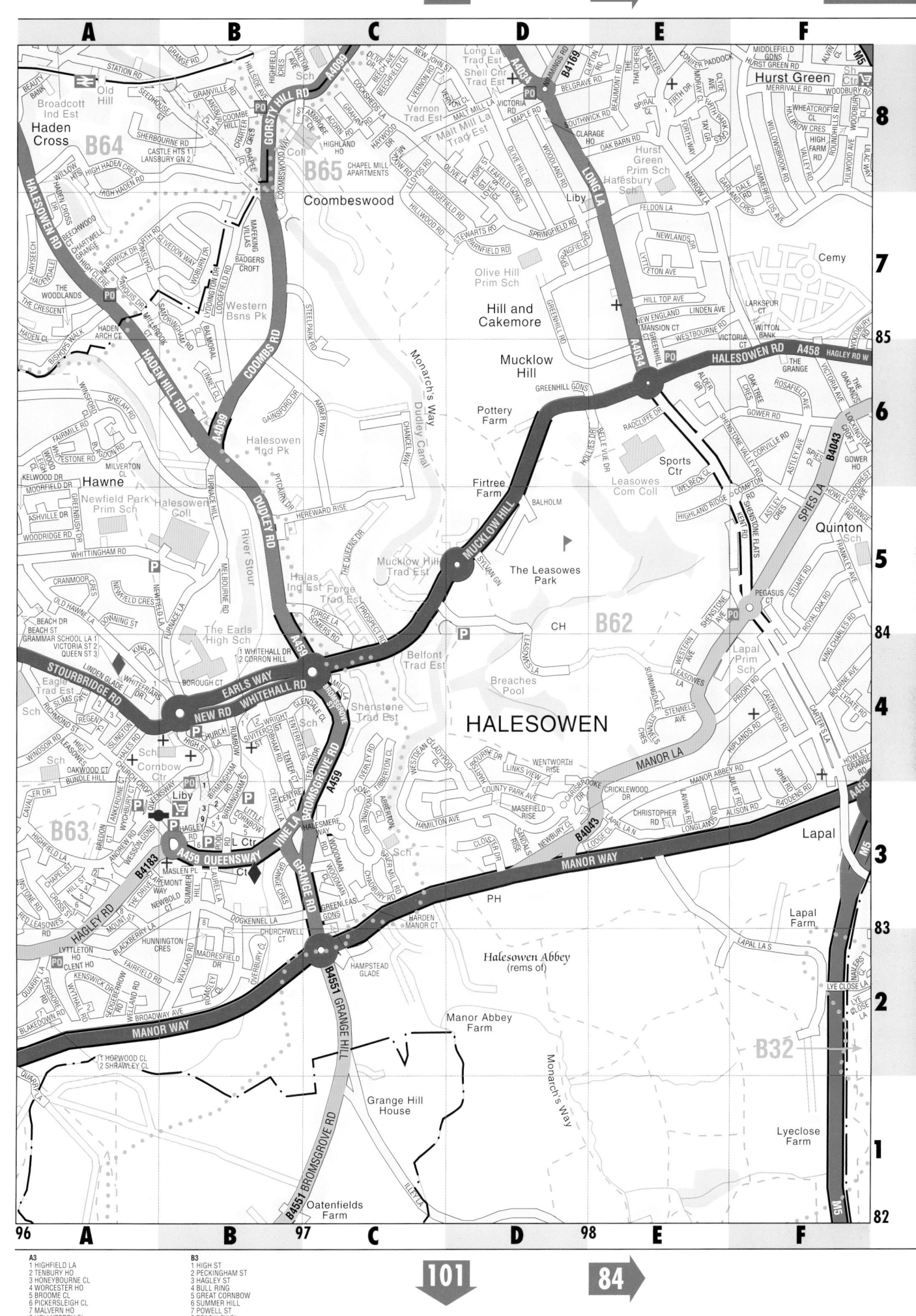

Hurst Green

Haden Cross

Coombeswood

Hill and Cakemore

Mucklow Hill

Hawne

HALESOWEN

Halesowen Abbey
(rems of)

Manor Abbey Farm

Grange Hill House

Lapal

Quinton

96   97   98

A   B   C   D   E   F

A3
1 HIGHFIELD LA
2 TENBURY HO
3 HONEYBOURNE CL
4 WORCESTER HO
5 BROOME CL
6 PICKERSLEIGH CL
7 MALVERN HO
8 HOLLYBERRY CL

B3
1 HIGH ST
2 PECKINGHAM ST
3 HAGLEY ST
4 BULL RING
5 GREAT CORNBOW
6 SUMMER HILL
7 POWELL ST
8 PEACHLEY CL
9 SOMERS SQ

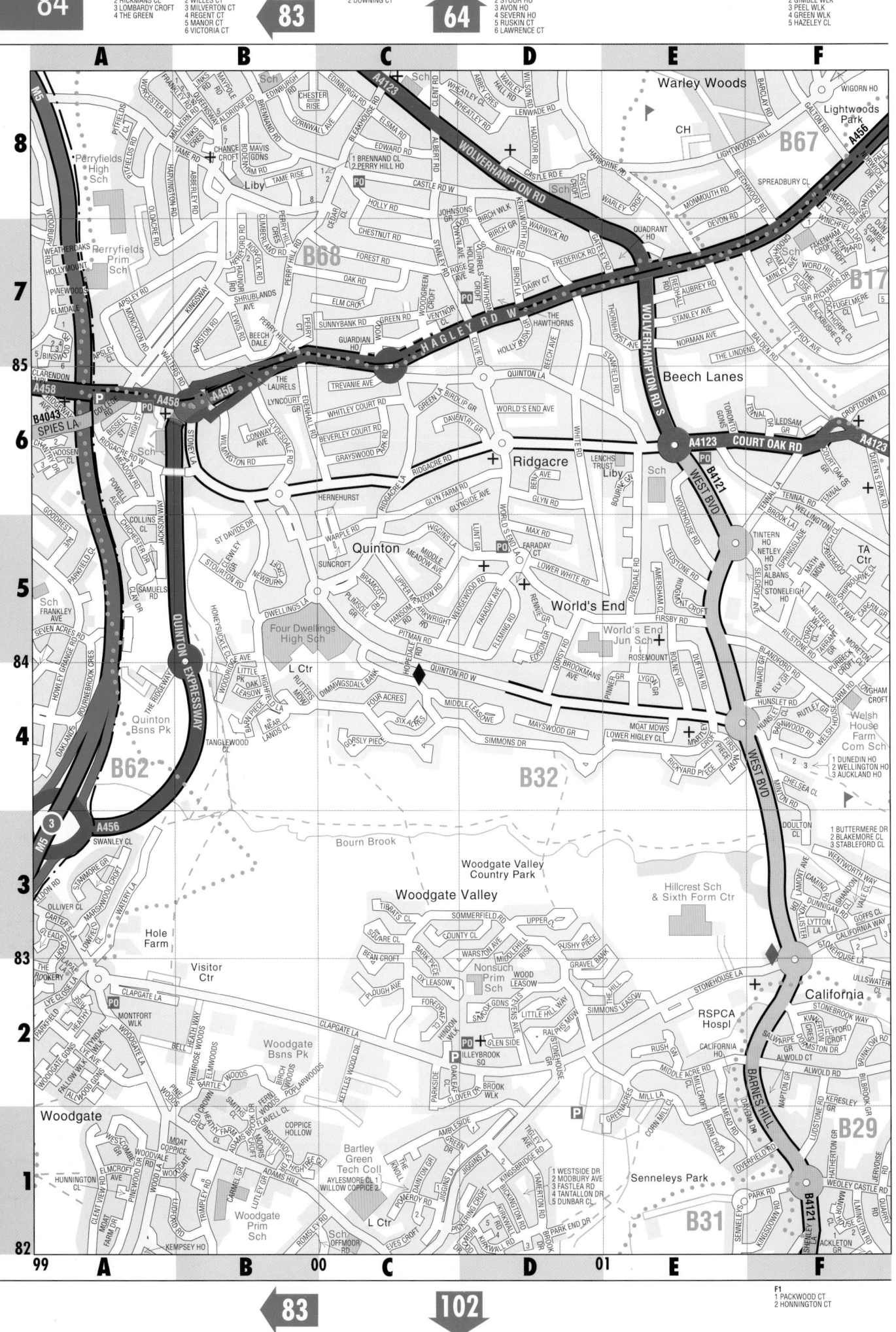

A6
1 BEVERLEY CT
2 HICKMANS CL
3 LOMBARDY CROFT
4 THE GREEN

A7
1 ALBANY CT
2 WILLES CT
3 MILVERTON CT
4 REGENT CT
5 MANOR CT
6 VICTORIA CT

83

B7
1 ASTBURY CT
2 DOWNING CT

64

B8
1 ARROW HO
2 STOUR HO
3 AVON HO
4 SEVERN HO
5 RUSKIN CT
6 LAWRENCE CT

7
7 HENDERSON CT
8 OLD CRESCENT CT

F7
1 WALMEAD CROFT
2 GIMBLE WLK
3 PEEL WLK
4 GREEN WLK
5 HAZELEY CL

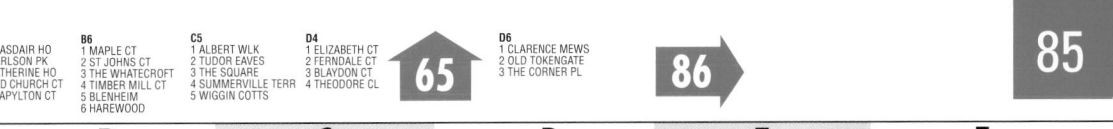

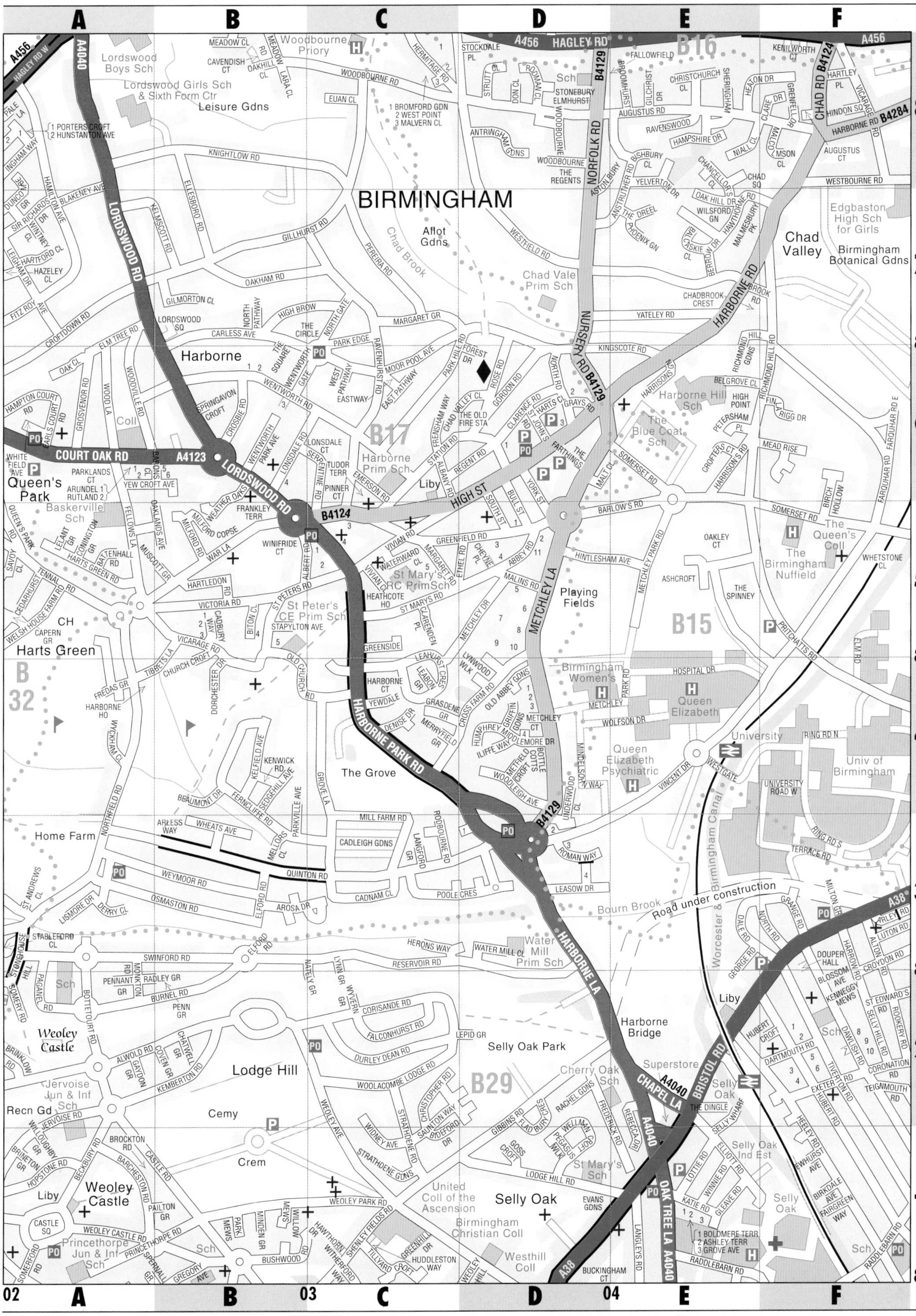

C8
1 AUDLEIGH HO
2 CHISWICK HO
3 LEOFRIC CT
4 ALFRYTH CT
5 FARADAY HO
6 HOGARTH HO

7 BRADSHAW CL
8 Bell Barn Sh Ctr
9 WATERSIDE
D7
1 ST LAWRENCE CL
2 OTTAWA TWR

85

D8
1 HADDON TWR
2 NEWHOPE CL
3 KERRIA CT

66

E5
1 CANNON HILL PL
2 CANNON HILL GR
3 BEACONSFIELD CRES
E7
1 EARLSWOOD HO
2 ELMSTEAD TWR

3 CUMBERLAND AVE
E8
1 HIGHGATE HO
2 CHARLBURY TWR
3 WELLESBOURNE TWR
4 DUNCHURCH HO

F5
1 PARK AVE
2 HEATH CT
F7
1 WILLIAM EDWARD ST
2 CANTLOW HO

3 LENCH'S TRUST ALMSHOUSES
4 BRINKLOW TWR
5 WILMCOTE TWR
6 UPPER CONYBERE ST
7 JAMES SAMUEL PL
8 THOMAS BENSON PL
9 Highgate Sq Craft Ctr

F8
1 HANWOOD HO
2 DARFIELD WLK
3 RADCLIFFE TWR
4 CANBERRA WAY

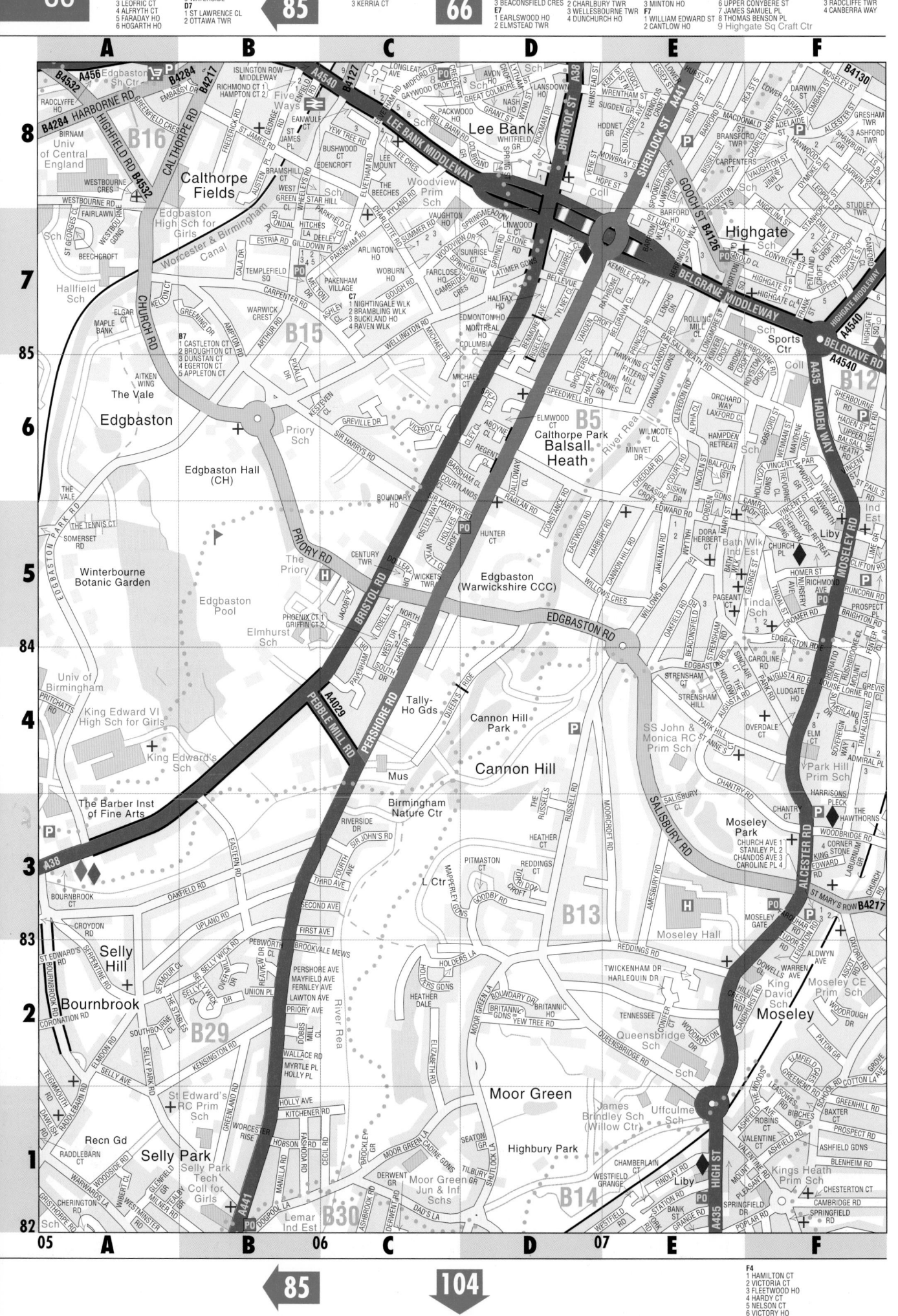

F4
1 HAMILTON CT
2 VICTORIA CT
3 FLEETWOOD HO
4 HARDY CT
5 NELSON CT
6 VICTORY HO
7 WILLIAM CT
8 HELEN DIXON CT

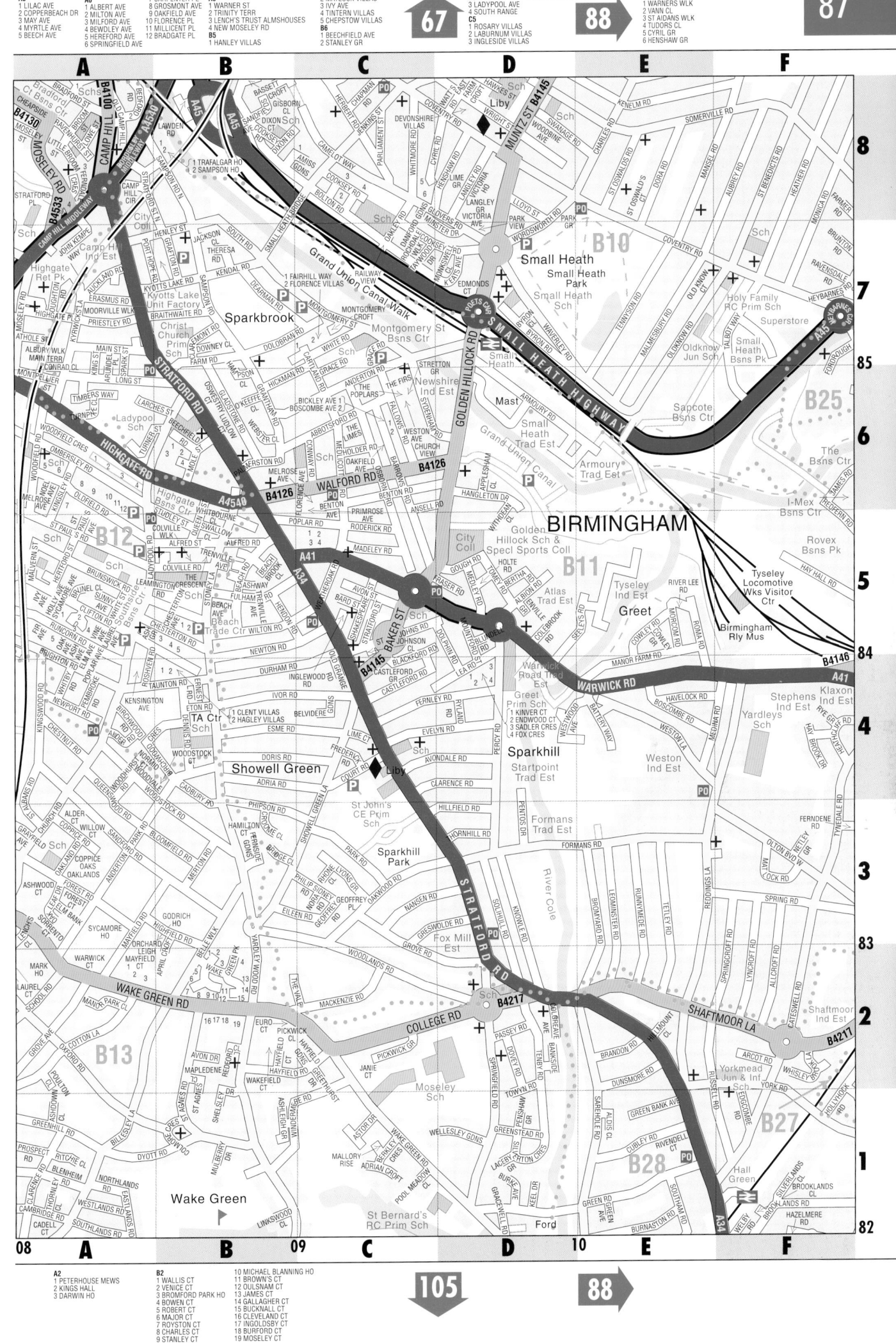

67
88

105
88

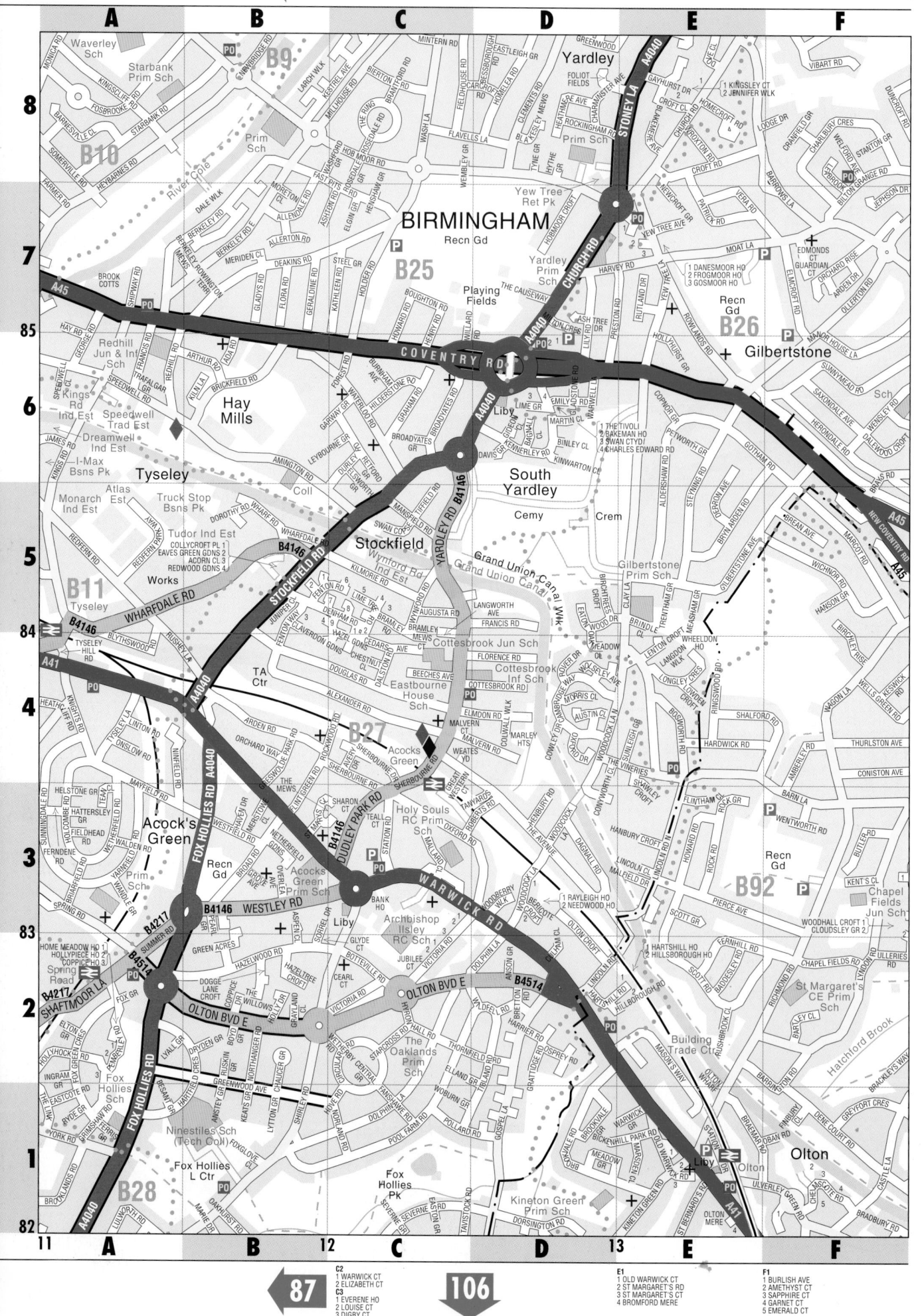

C5
1 SYCAMORE WAY
2 CYPRESS SQ
3 LAUREL GDNS
4 ASH MEWS
5 CHERRY TREE CROFT
6 SNOWBERRY GDNS
87

C5
7 RYE CROFT
8 HONEYSUCKLE GR
9 BLOSSOMVILLE WAY
68

BIRMINGHAM

Yardley

B25

B26

Gilbertstone

B10

Hay Mills

Tyseley

South Yardley

Stockfield

Grand Union Canal

Gilbertstone Prim Sch

B11
Tyseley

B27

Acocks Green

B92

Acock's Green

Archbishop Ilsley RC Sch

Olton

B28

Fox Hollies Pk

Kineton Green Prim Sch

87

C2
1 WARWICK CT
2 ELIZABETH CT
C3
1 EVERENE HO
2 LOUISE CT
3 DIGBY CT

106

E1
1 OLD WARWICK CT
2 ST MARGARET'S RD
3 ST MARGARET'S CT
4 BROMFORD MERE

F1
1 BURLISH AVE
2 AMETHYST CT
3 SAPPHIRE CT
4 GARNET CT
5 EMERALD CT

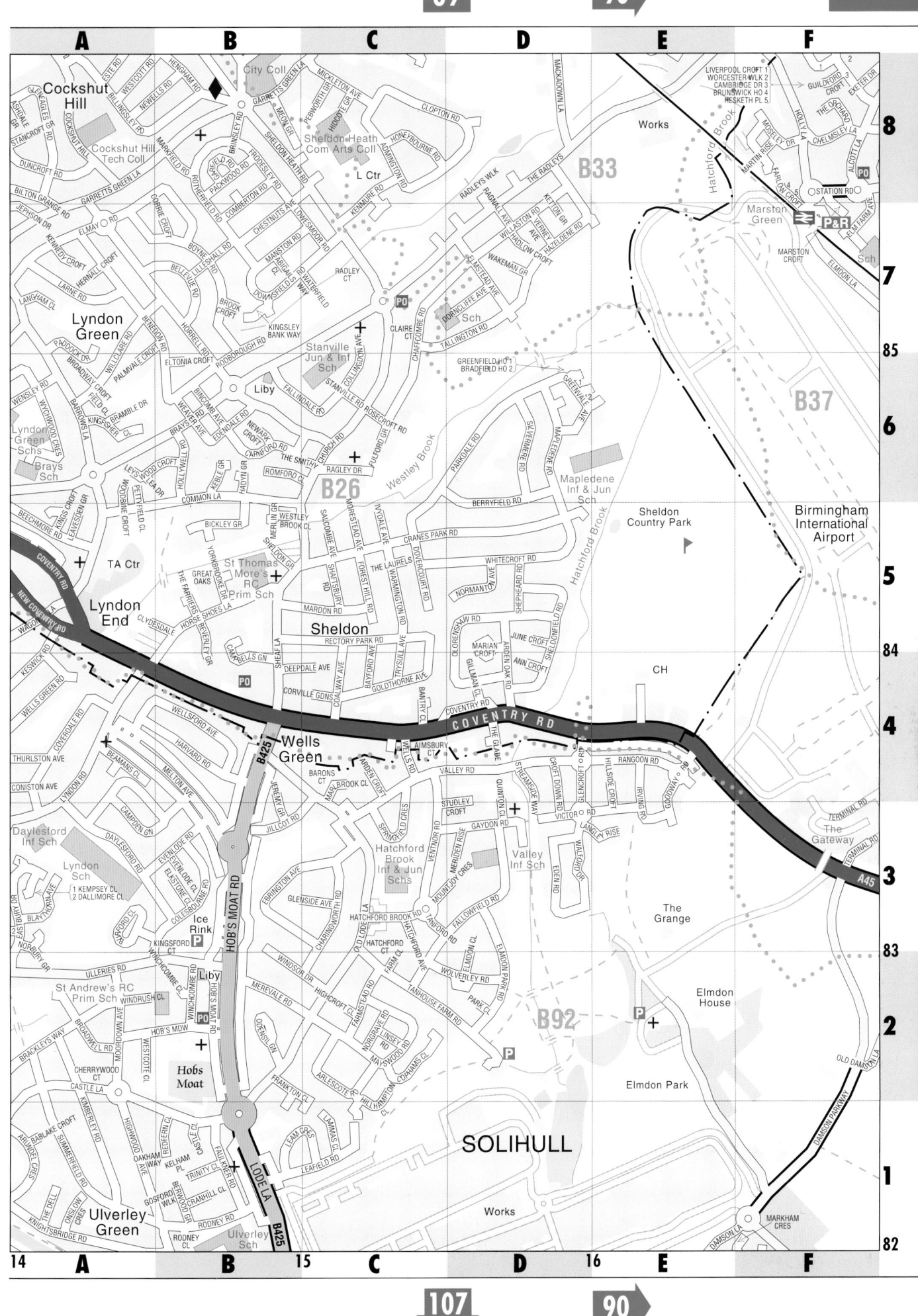

89
70

A B C D E F

8

7

85

6

B46

5

84

4

3

83

2

1

82

17 A B 18 C D 19 E F

Moorend Ave
1 Exeter Dr
2 Wells Wlk
Marston Green
Marston Green Jun & Inf Schs
Liby
St Leonards
Marston Green
School Rough
1 Rotherby Gr
2 Wolverton Rd
B37
Bickenhill Rd
Cemy
Pinewood Bsns Pk
Coleshill Rd
Sports Ctr
Coleshill Heath
John Black Day
1 Newington Rd
2 Fulwell Mews
Poplar Ave
Aspen Dr
Cornel
Irowan Way
Helmswood Dr
Box Rd
Tulip Wlk
White Beam Rd
Heath Farm
The Crescent
Solihull Parkway
Trident Ct
Bishop S Ct
Knights Ct
Birmingham Bsns Pk
Park Sq
The Pavilions
A452
M42
Chester Rd
B4438
A452
Hotel
Blackfirs La
Bickenhill Parkway
Hotel
Bickenhill Plantations
B40
National Exhibition Ctr (The NEC)
North Ave
Northway
Starley Way
Century Pk
Elmdon Trad Est
Low Brook
The Foxgrift
Digby Dr
Newlands La
Century Pk
Bickenhill La
Ramp The Herald Way
Trident Rd
Comet Rd
Concorde Rd
Ambassador Rd 1
Vanguard Rd 2
Station Link Rd 3
Birmingham International Airport
B26
Exhibition Way
Third Exhibition Ave
Second Exhibition Ave
First Exhibition Ave
Perimeter Rd
Birmingham International
The Underpass
Perimeter Rd
Harbet Dr
Pendigo Way
East Car Park Rd
Hotel
Pendigo Lake
Pendigo Way
Forum Rd
Southcar Park Rd
South Way
Eastway
6
A45
Hermes Rd
Airport Way
Depot
Coventry Rd
Bickenhill La
B4438
Trinity Pk
Hotel
Wyckhams Close
The Clock Inn (PH)
Clock La
Catherine De Barnes La
B92
Avon Park Cvn Pk
Bickenhill Green Ct
Pitt La
Church La
Dunston Farm
The Jungle
Castle Hills
Old Damson La
CH
Mast
Elmdon La
Hotels
Hanger Rd
Commissary Rd
Edward Rd
Work Rd
Grange Farm
St Peters
B4438
Bickenhill
Old Station Rd
M42
Carters Cl
Elmdon Ct
Hall Dr
Land La
Canterbury Dr
Elmdon La
The Greenway
Hemlingford Croft
Aylesford Dr
The Rise
Elmdon Rd
Somerton Dr
Farndon Ave
Oaklands
Larowe Croft
Hidcote Gr
Chelmsley La
Wavers Marston
Wagstaff
Wagstaff Gr
Clarkland Gr
Sycamore Cres
Ludworth Ave
Cog Lock Cl
Hamar Way
Maple
Leaf Dr
Harby Cl
Byford Way
Nash Croft
Brooklands Way
Radlow Cres
Malthouse La
Station Rd
Wayside
Ivy Lodge Cl
Brook Croft
Lymington Croft

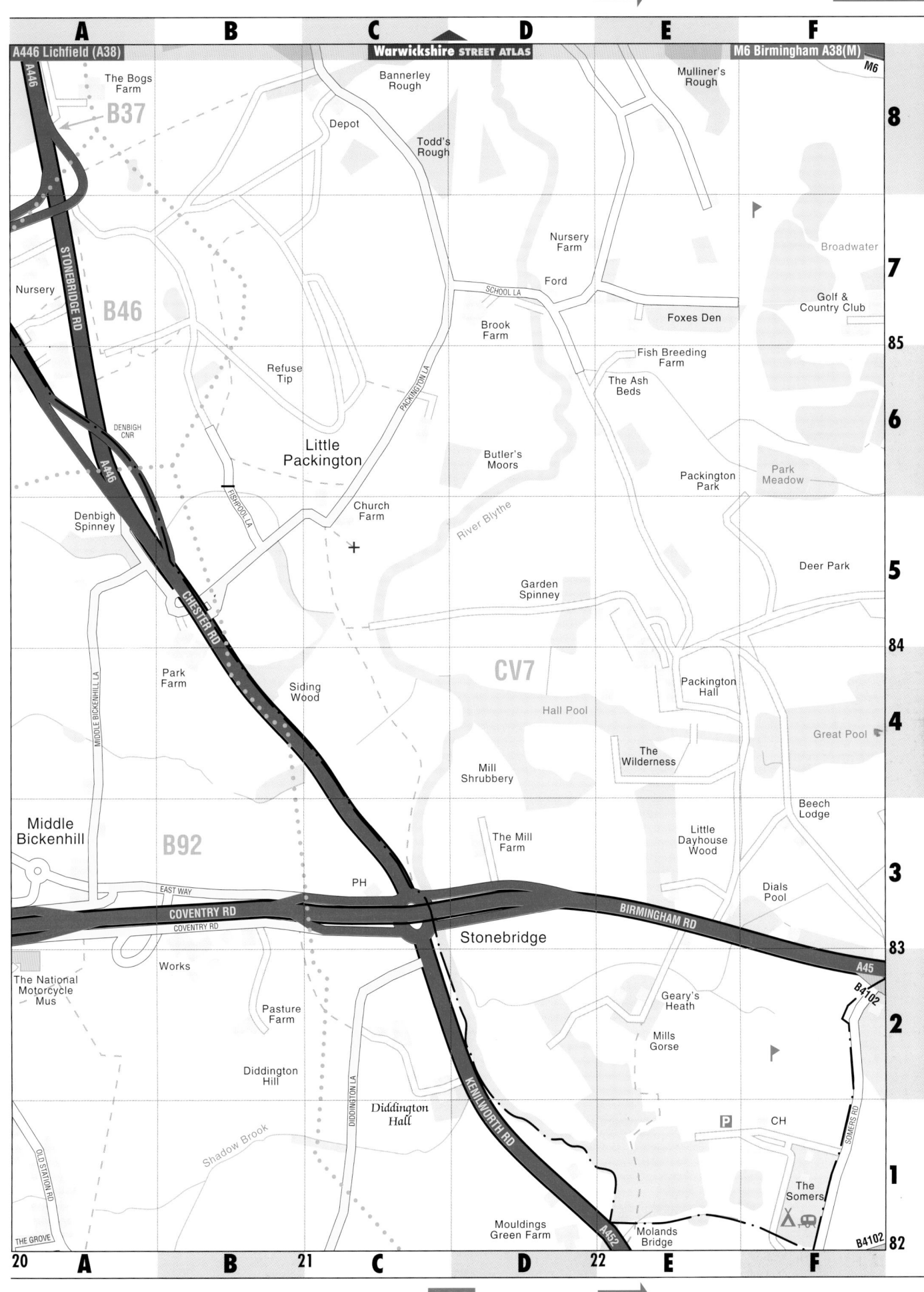

Warwickshire STREET ATLAS

A446 Lichfield (A38)

M6 Birmingham A38(M)

M6

8

The Bogs Farm

B37

Bannerley Rough

Mulliner's Rough

Depot

Todd's Rough

7

Nursery

B46

Nursery Farm

Ford

Broadwater

STONEBRIDGE RD

Golf & Country Club

School La

Foxes Den

85

Refuse Tip

Brook Farm

Fish Breeding Farm

A446

The Ash Beds

6

DENBIGH CNR

PACKINGTON LA

Little Packington

Butler's Moors

Packington Park

Park Meadow

Denbigh Spinney

Church Farm

River Blythe

5

FISHPOOL LA

+

Garden Spinney

Deer Park

CHESTER RD

84

Park Farm

CV7

Packington Hall

4

MIDDLE BICKENHILL LA

Siding Wood

Hall Pool

The Wilderness

Great Pool

Mill Shrubbery

Beech Lodge

3

Middle Bickenhill

B92

The Mill Farm

Little Dayhouse Wood

EAST WAY

PH

Dials Pool

COVENTRY RD

Stonebridge

BIRMINGHAM RD

83

COVENTRY RD

A45

Works

Geary's Heath

B4102

The National Motorcycle Mus

Pasture Farm

Mills Gorse

2

Diddington Hill

KENILWORTH RD

SOMERS RD

DIDDINGTON LA

P

CH

Diddington Hall

The Somers

1

Shadow Brook

Mouldings Green Farm

A452

Molands Bridge

B4102

82

THE GROVE

OLD STATION RD

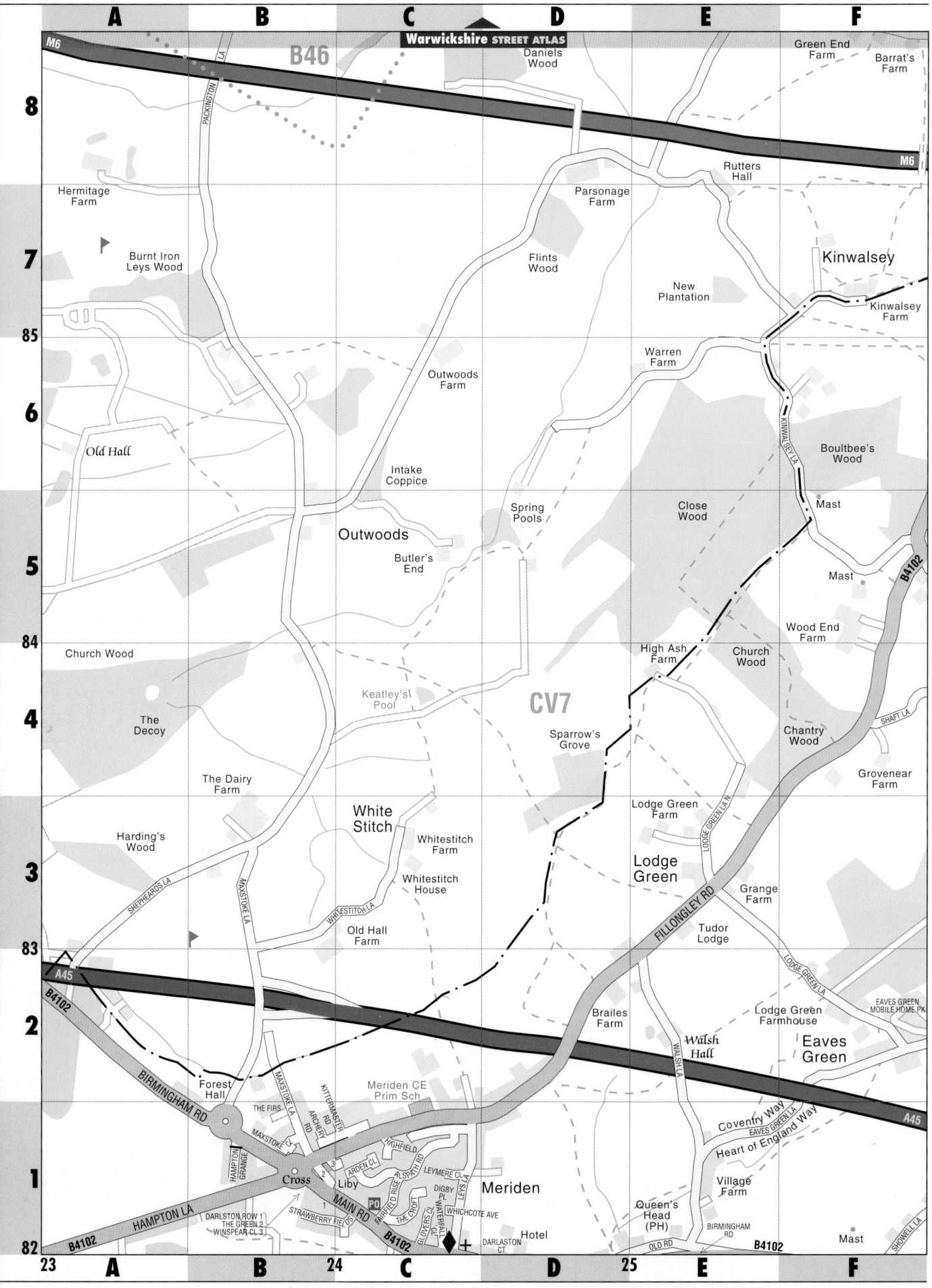

Warwickshire STREET ATLAS

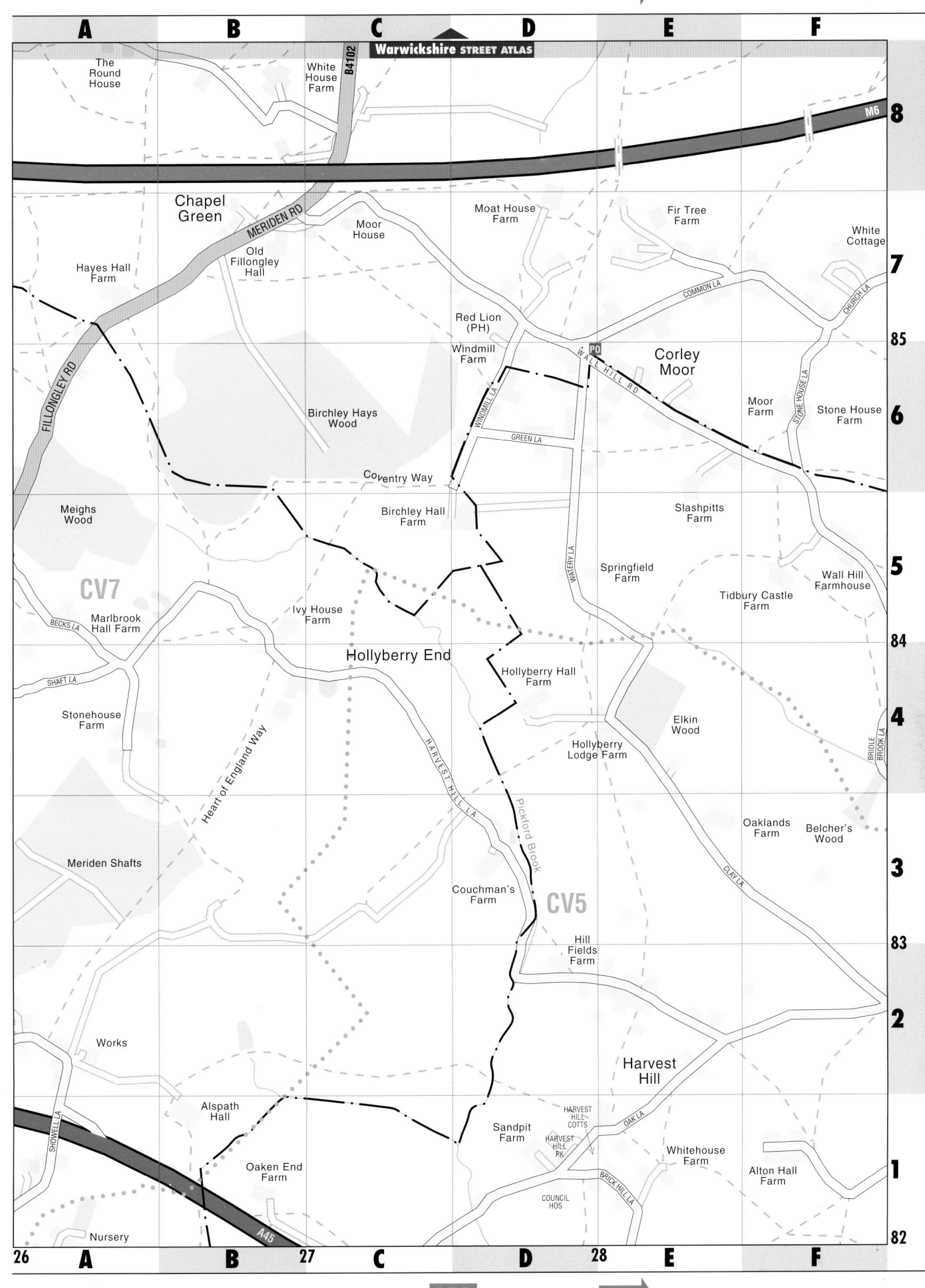

Warwickshire STREET ATLAS

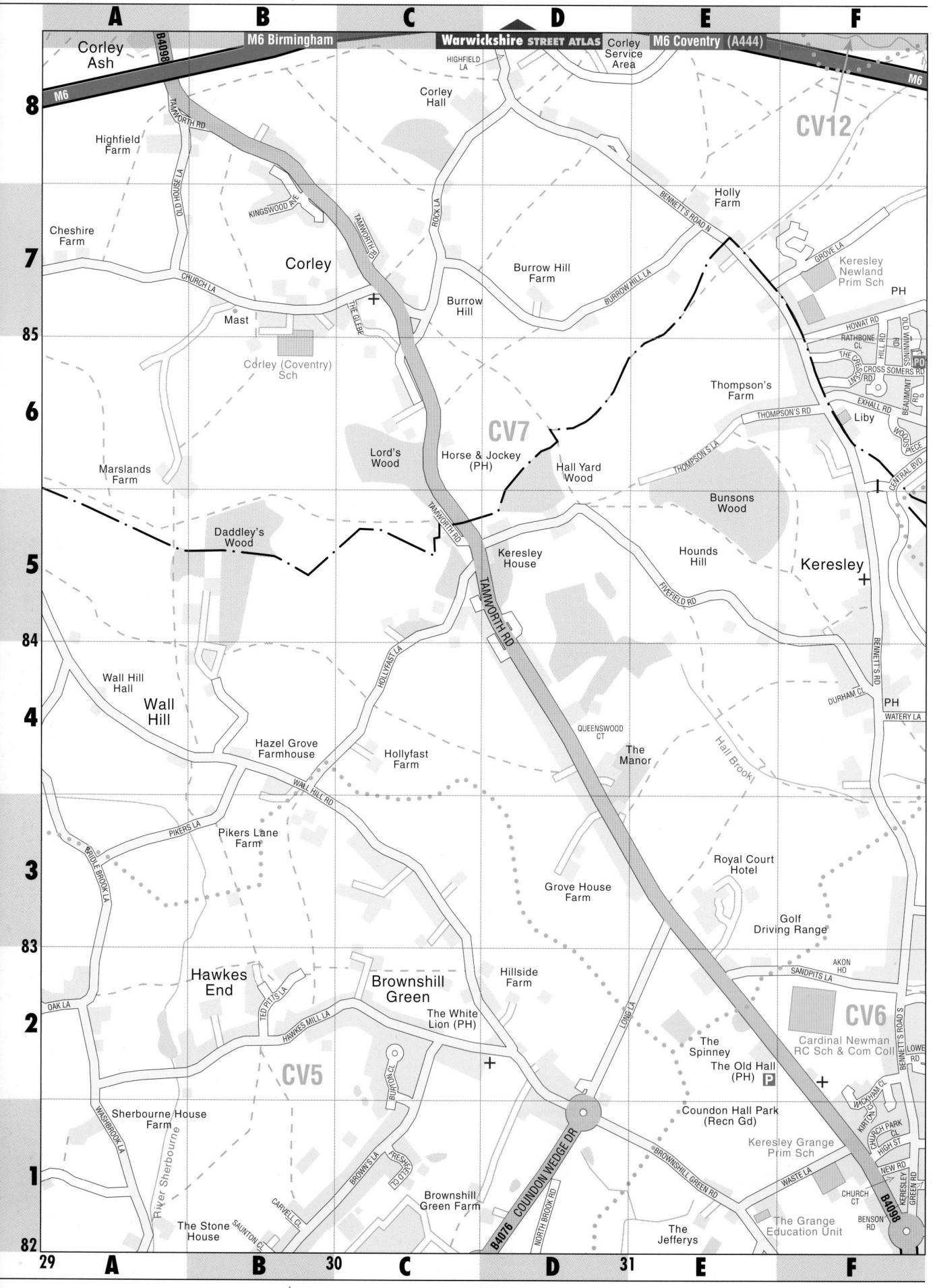

Corley
Ash

M6 Birmingham

Warwickshire STREET ATLAS

Corley
Service
Area

M6 Coventry (A444)

M6

M6

CV12

Highfield Farm

HIGHFIELD LA

Corley
Hall

Holly
Farm

Cheshire
Farm

Kingswood Ave

Corley

TAMWORTH RD

ROCK LA

Burrow Hill
Farm

BENNETT'S ROAD N

GROVE LA

Keresley
Newland
Prim Sch

PH

CHURCH LA

Mast

THE GLEBE

Burrow
Hill

BURROW HILL LA

HOWAT RD

HILL RD

RATHBONE
CL

THE CRES

CROSS RD

SOMERS RD

PO

Corley (Coventry)
Sch

CV7

Thompson's
Farm

THOMPSON'S RD

EXHALL RD

BEAUMONT RD

Liby

Marslands
Farm

Lord's
Wood

Horse & Jockey
(PH)

Hall Yard
Wood

THOMPSON'S LA

Bunsons
Wood

CENTRAL BVD

Daddley's
Wood

TAMWORTH RD

Keresley
House

Hounds
Hill

Keresley

BENNETT'S RD

Wall Hill
Hall

Wall
Hill

HOLLYFAST LA

TAMWORTH RD

FIVEFIELD RD

DURHAM CL

PH

WATERY LA

Hazel Grove
Farmhouse

Hollyfast
Farm

QUEENSWOOD
CT

The
Manor

Hall Brook

WALL HILL RD

PIKERS LA

Pikers Lane
Farm

Royal Court
Hotel

BRIDLE BROOK LA

Grove House
Farm

Golf
Driving Range

AKON
HO

SANDPITS LA

OAK LA

Hawkes
End

TED PITTS LA

Brownshill
Green

Hillside
Farm

LONG LA

The
Spinney

The Old Hall
(PH) P

CV6

Cardinal Newman
RC Sch & Com Coll

BENNETT'S ROAD S

LOWE
RD

HAWKES MILL LA

The White
Lion (PH)

BRITON CL

WACKHAM CL

CV5

KIRTLAND CL

Coundon Hall Park
(Recn Gd)

Keresley Grange
Prim Sch

CHURCH PARK
CL

HIGH ST

WASHBROOK LA

Sherbourne House
Farm

BROWN'S LA

FRESH
FD CFT

COUNDON WEDGE DR

BROWNSHILL GREEN RD

WASTE LA

NEW RD

B4098

KERESLEY

CHURCH
CT

River Sherbourne

The Stone
House

CARVELL CL

SAUNTON CL

Brownshill
Green Farm

B4076

NORTH BROOK RD

The
Jefferys

The Grange
Education Unit

BENSON
RD

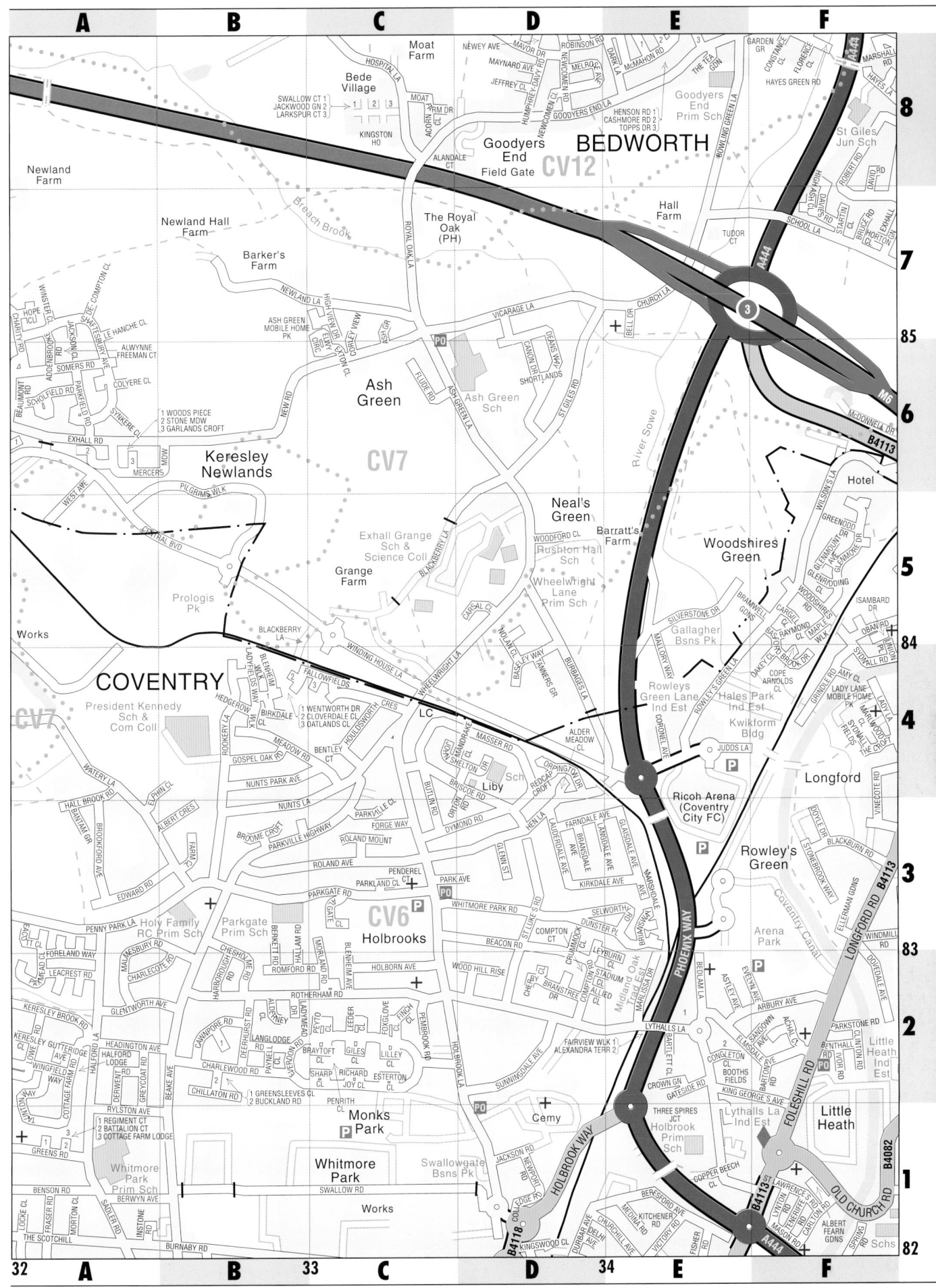

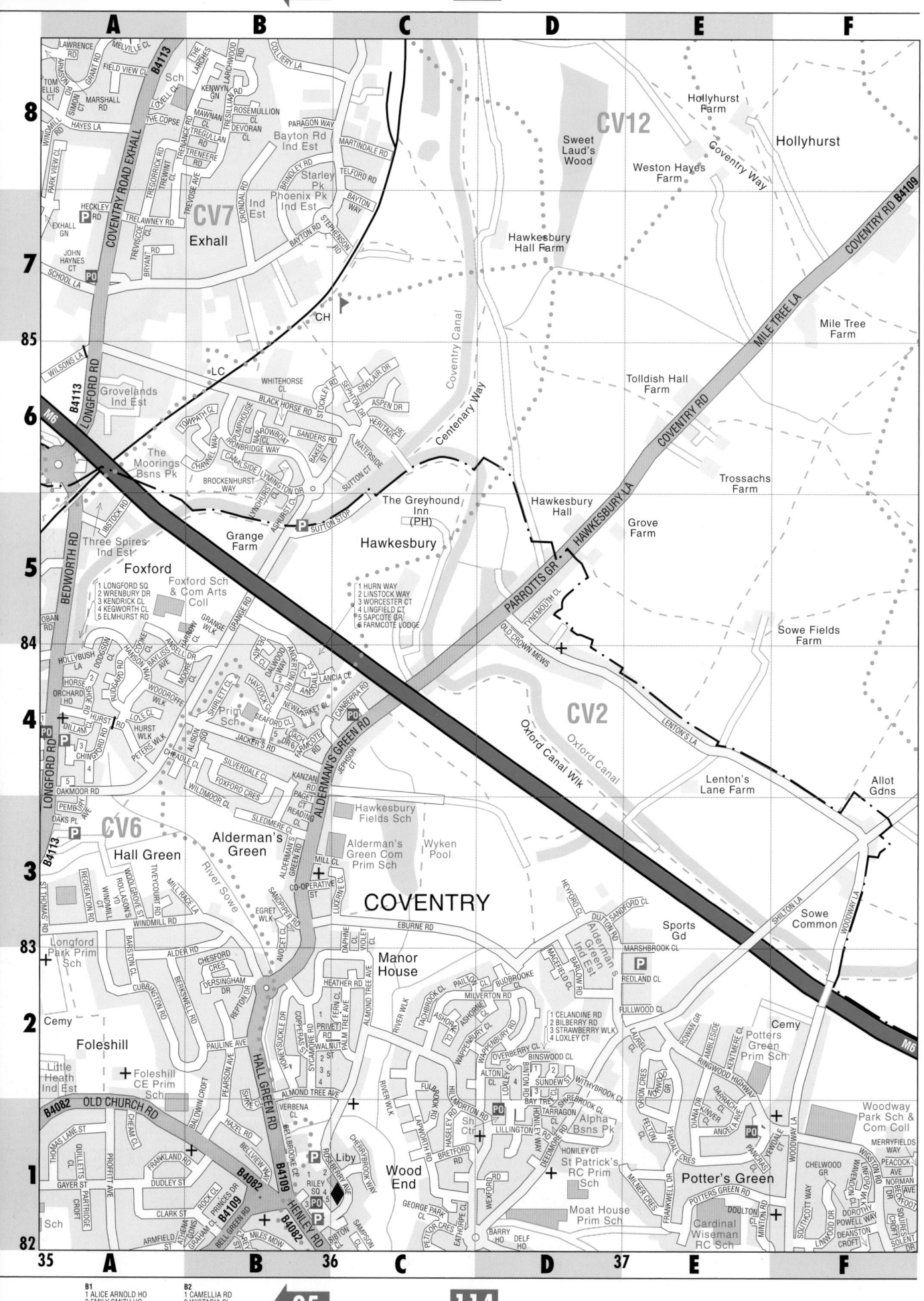

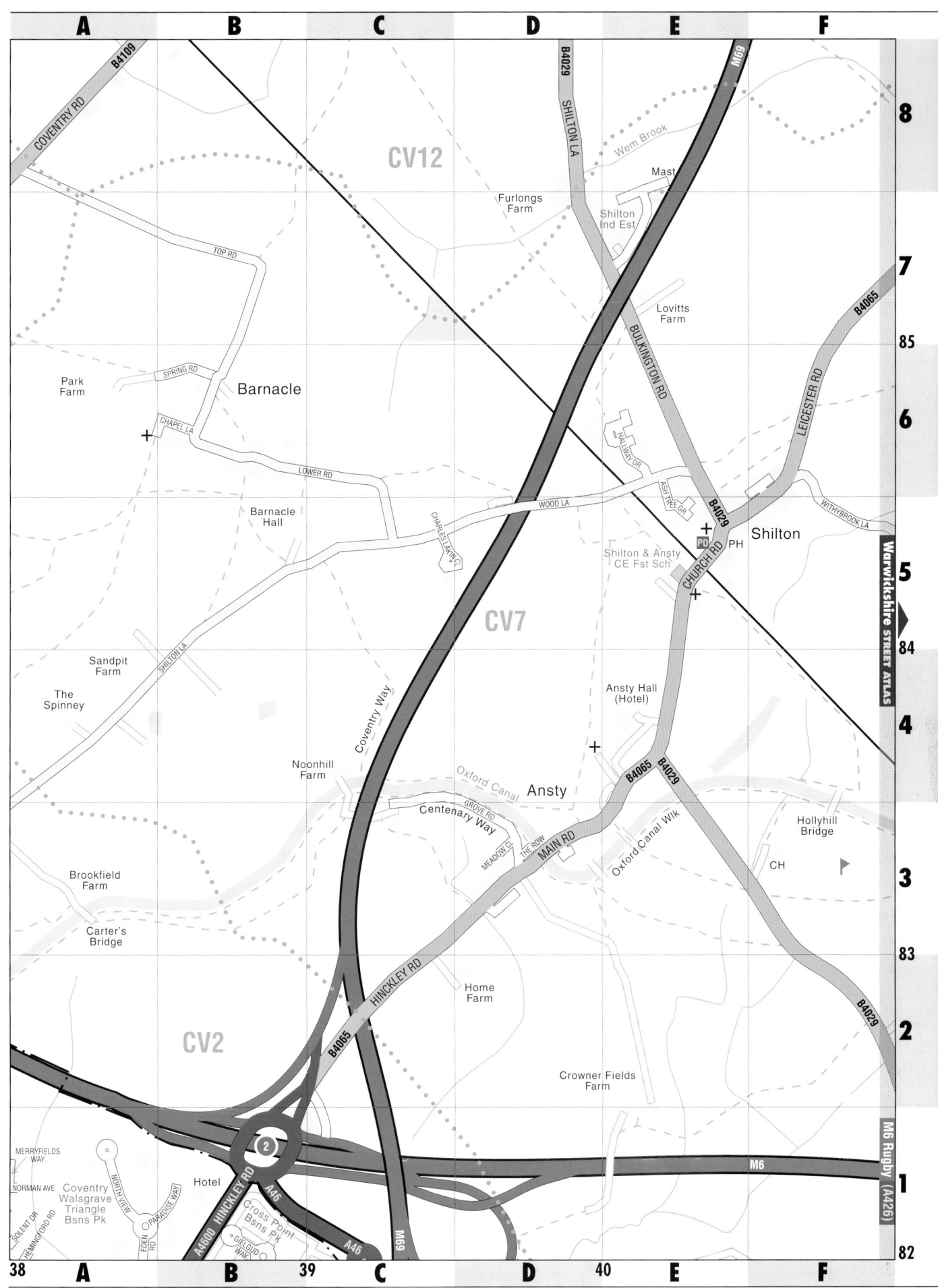

A B C D E F

8

7

85

6

5

84

4

3

83

2

1

82

38 A B 39 C D 40 E F

Warwickshire STREET ATLAS

M6 Rugby (A426)

CV12

CV7

CV2

Barnacle

Shilton

Ansty

COVENTRY RD
B4109
TOP RD
SPRING RD
Park Farm
CHAPEL LA
LOWER RD
Barnacle Hall
CHARLES LAKIN CL
Sandpit Farm
SHILTON LA
The Spinney
Coventry Way
Noonhill Farm
Brookfield Farm
Carter's Bridge
HINCKLEY RD
B4065
Home Farm
Oxford Canal
Centenary Way
GROVE RD
MEADOW CL
THE ROW
MAIN RD
Crowner Fields Farm
MERRYFIELDS WAY
NORMAN AVE
SOLENT DR
HEMINGFORD RD
NORTH VIEW
EDEN RD
PARADISE WAY
GIELGUD WALK
Coventry Walsgrave Triangle Bsns Pk
Hotel
Cross Point Bsns Pk
A4600 HINCKLEY RD
A46
M69
B4029
SHILTON LA
Wem Brook
Furlongs Farm
Mast
Shilton Ind Est
BULKINGTON RD
M69
Lovitts Farm
HALLWAY DR
ASH TREE GR
B4029
WOOD LA
PO
PH
CHURCH RD
Shilton & Ansty CE Fst Sch
LEICESTER RD
B4065
WITHYBROOK LA
Ansty Hall (Hotel)
B4065
B4029
Oxford Canal Wlk
Hollyhill Bridge
CH
M6
B4029

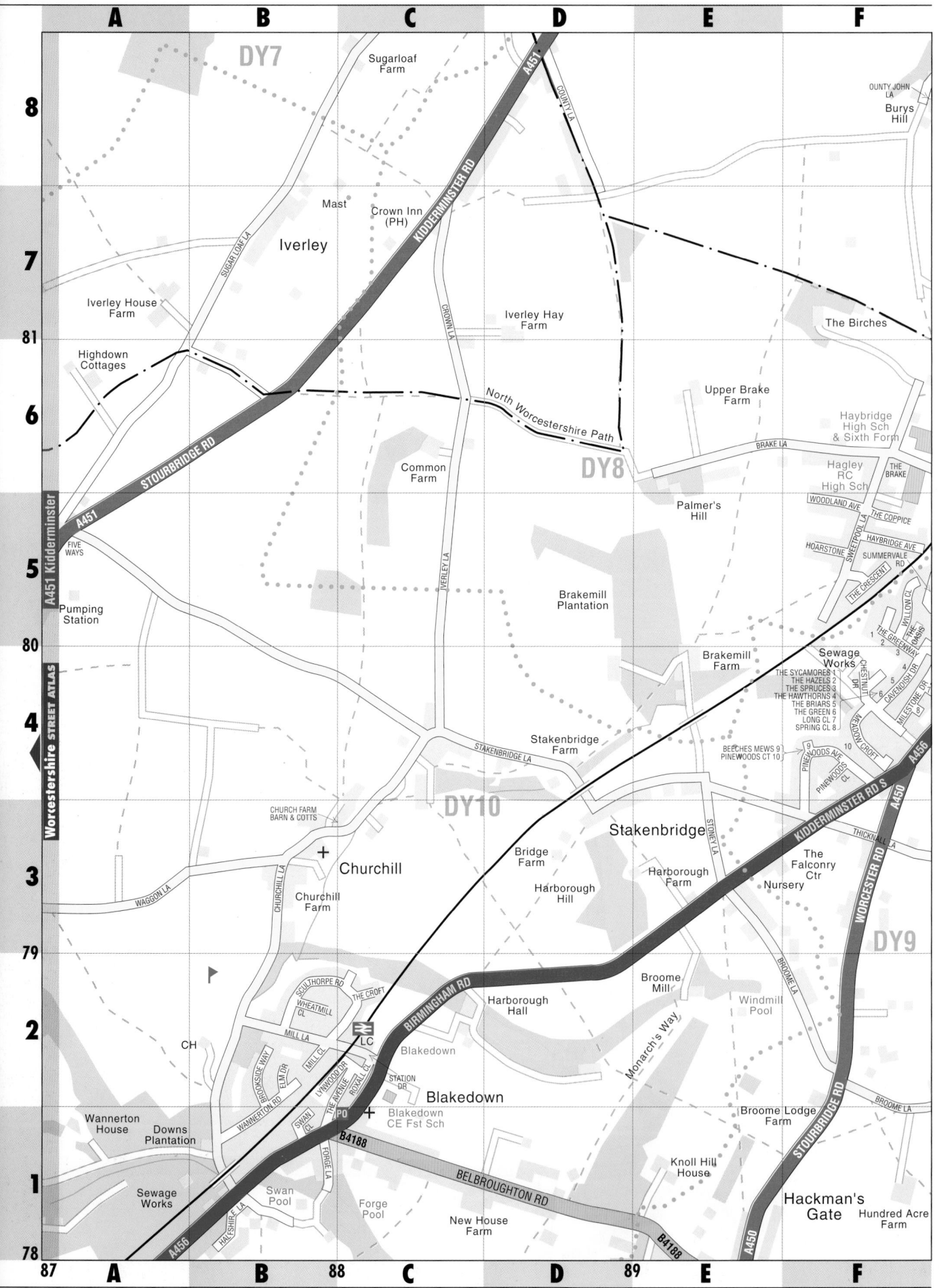

Worcestershire STREET ATLAS

A451 Kidderminster

DY7

Sugarloaf Farm

Mast

Crown Inn (PH)

Iverley

KIDDERMINSTER RD

COUNTY LA

OUNTY JOHN LA

Burys Hill

SUGAR LOAF LA

Iverley House Farm

CROWN LA

Iverley Hay Farm

The Birches

Highdown Cottages

STOURBRIDGE RD

North Worcestershire Path

DY8

Upper Brake Farm

Haybridge High Sch & Sixth Form

BRAKE LA

Hagley RC High Sch

THE BRAKE

WOODLAND AVE

THE COPPICE

A451

FIVE WAYS

Pumping Station

Common Farm

IVERLEY LA

Palmer's Hill

HOARSTONE

SWEETPOOL LA

HAYBRIDGE AVE

SUMMERVALE RD

THE CRESCENT

WILLOW CL

THE OAKS

Brakemill Plantation

Brakemill Farm

Sewage Works

CHESTNUT DR

THE GREENWAY

MILESTONE DR

THE SYCAMORES 1
THE HAZELS 2
THE SPRUCES 3
THE HAWTHORNS 4
THE BRIARS 5
THE GREEN 6
LONG CL 7
SPRING CL 8

MEADOW CROFT

CAVENDISH DR

A456

Stakenbridge Farm

STAKENBRIDGE LA

BEECHES MEWS 9
PINEWOODS CT 10

PINEWOODS AVE

PINEWOODS CL

KIDDERMINSTER RD S

A450

DY10

CHURCH FARM BARN & COTTS

Churchill

Bridge Farm

Stakenbridge

STONEY LA

The Falconry Ctr

WORCESTER RD

THICKNALL LA

DY9

WAGGON LA

CHURCHILL LA

Churchill Farm

Harborough Hill

Harborough Farm

Nursery

SCULTHORPE RD

THE CROFT

WHEATMILL CL

MILL LA

Birmingham Rd

Harborough Hall

Broome Mill

BROOME LA

Windmill Pool

CH

MILL CL

ELM DR

BROOKSIDE WAY

LYNWOOD DR

ROXALL CL

LC

STATION DR

Blakedown

Monarch's Way

STOURBRIDGE RD

BROOME LA

Wannerton House

Downs Plantation

WANNERTON RD

THE AVENUE

SWAN CL

PO

Blakedown CE Fst Sch

Broome Lodge Farm

B4188

FORGE LA

Swan Pool

Forge Pool

New House Farm

BELBROUGHTON RD

Knoll Hill House

Hackman's Gate

Hundred Acre Farm

Sewage Works

A456

HALESHIRE LA

B4188

A450

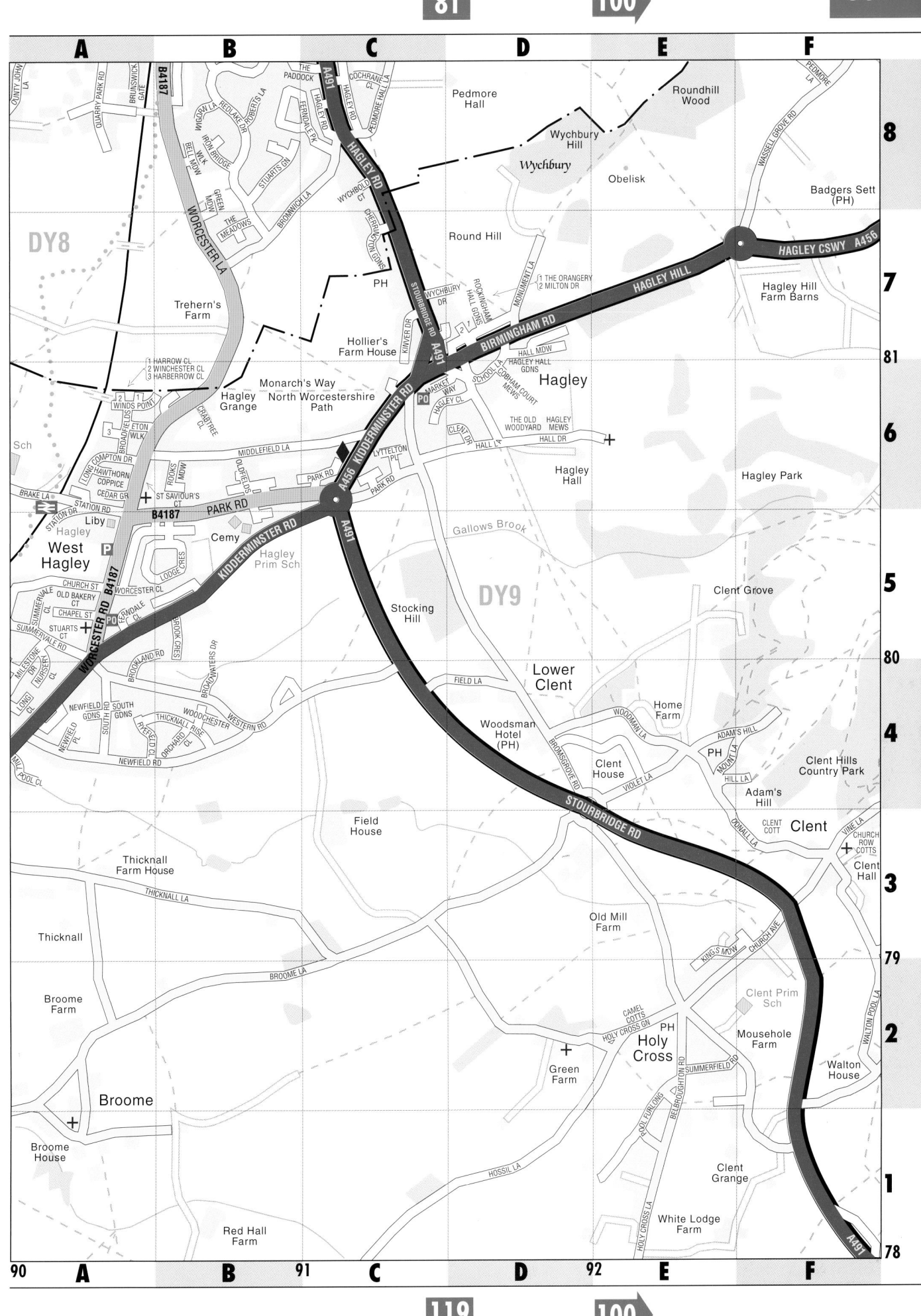

A B C D E F

8
81
7
81
6
5
80
4
79
2
1
78

90   A   91   B   C   92   D   E   F

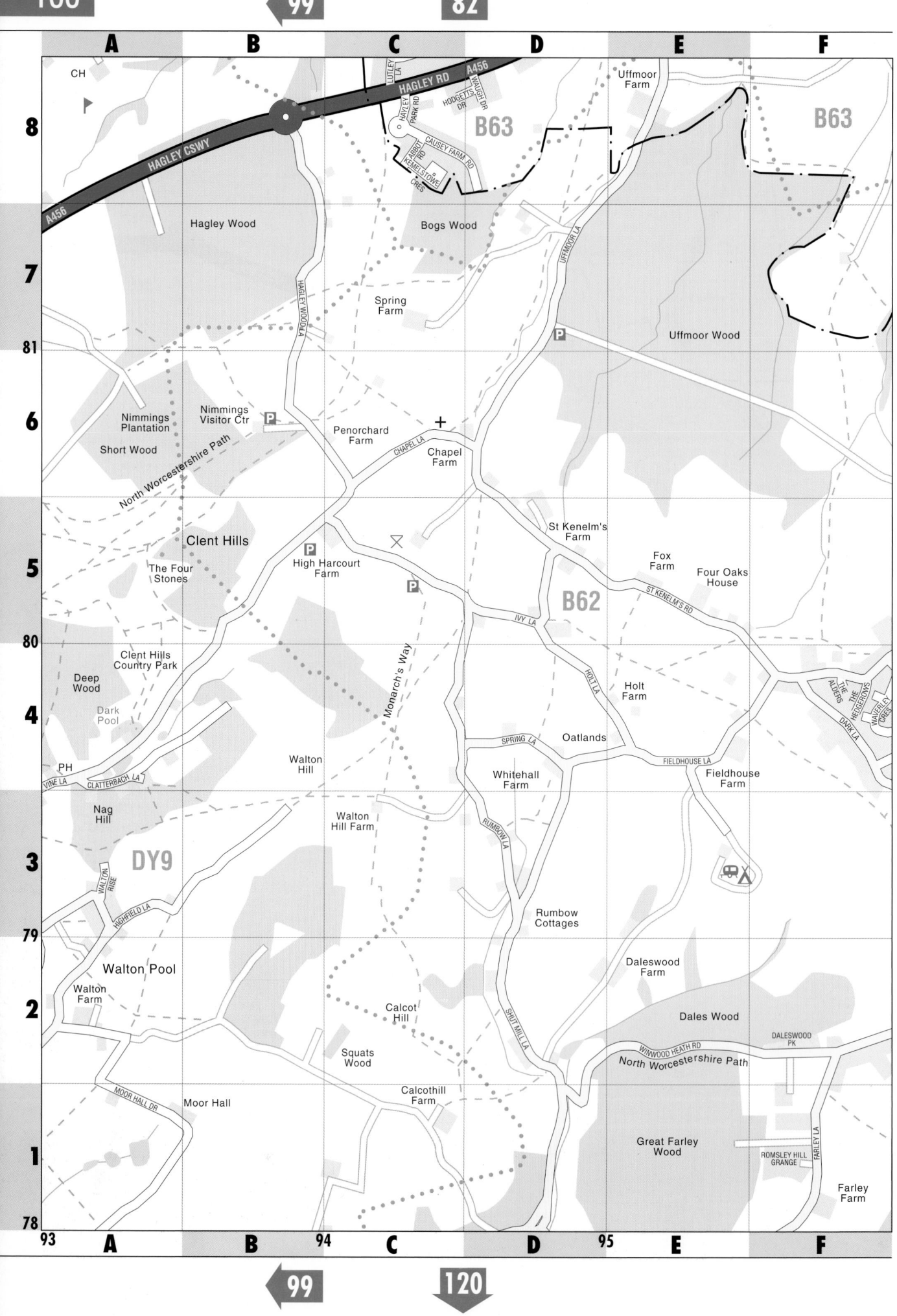

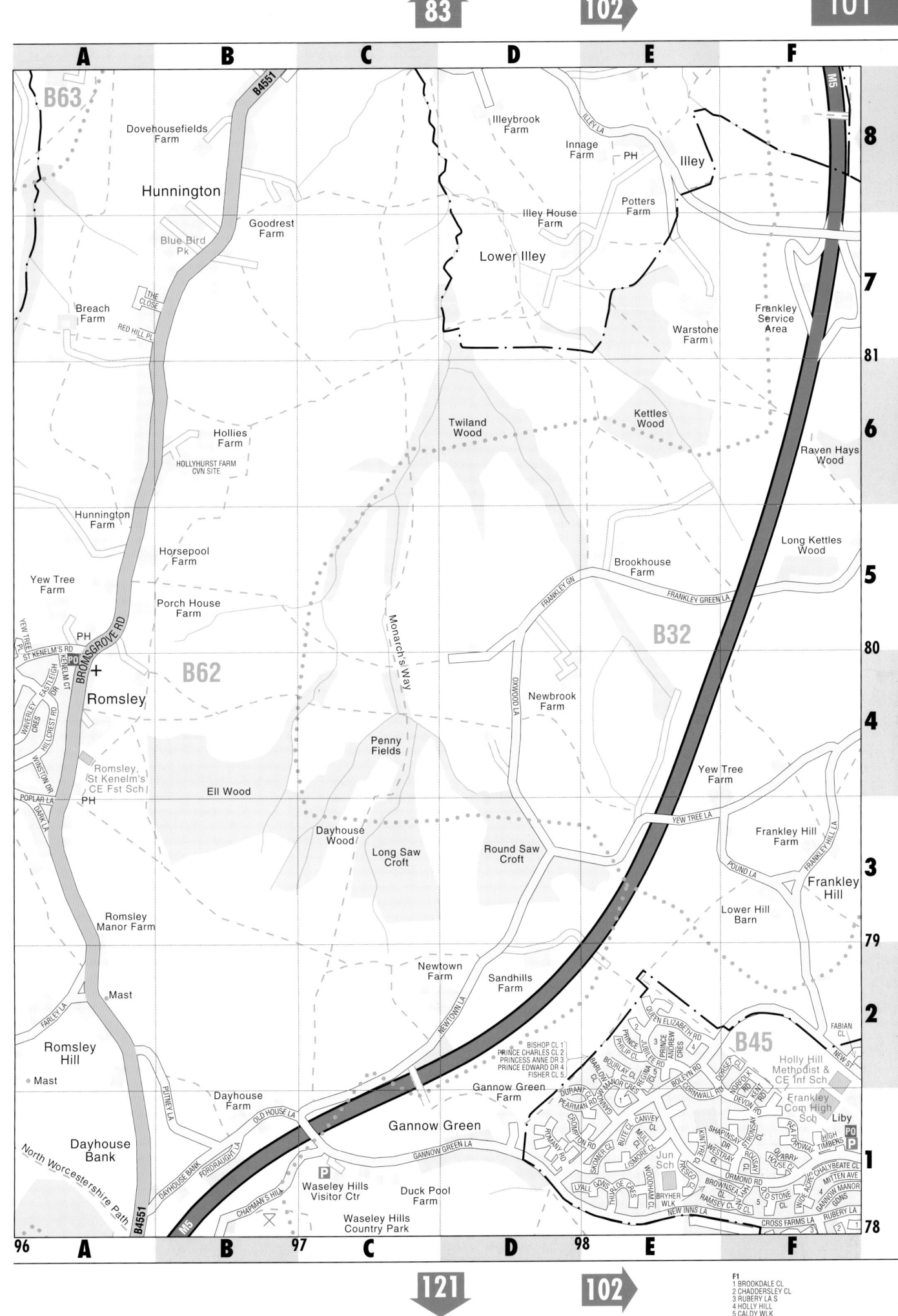

B63

A   B   C   D   E   F

8

Dovehousefields Farm

Illeybrook Farm

Innage Farm

PH

Illey

B4551

Hunnington

Goodrest Farm

Illey House Farm

Potters Farm

Blue Bird Pk

Lower Illey

Frankley Service Area

7

THE CLOSE

Breach Farm

RED HILL PL

81

Hollies Farm

Twiland Wood

Kettles Wood

Warstone Farm

Raven Hays Wood

6

HOLLYHURST FARM CVN SITE

Hunnington Farm

Horsepool Farm

Long Kettles Wood

Yew Tree Farm

Porch House Farm

Brookhouse Farm

FRANKLEY GREEN LA

5

YEW TREE PL

ST KENELM'S RD

PH

KENELM CT

PO

BROMSGROVE RD

FRANKLEY GN

B32

80

WAVERLEY CRES

EASTLEIGH DR

HILLCREST RD

WINSTON DR

B62

Romsley

OXWOOD LA

Monarch's Way

Newbrook Farm

4

POPLAR LA

DARK LA

PH

Romsley, St Kenelm's CE Fst Sch

Ell Wood

Penny Fields

Yew Tree Farm

YEW TREE LA

Frankley Hill Farm

FRANKLEY HILL LA

POUND LA

3

Dayhouse Wood

Long Saw Croft

Round Saw Croft

Frankley Hill

79

Romsley Manor Farm

Lower Hill Barn

FARLEY LA

Mast

Newtown Farm

Sandhills Farm

NEWTOWN LA

FABIAN CL

2

Romsley Hill

Mast

BISHOP CL 1
PRINCE CHARLES CL 2
PRINCESS ANNE DR 3
PRINCE EDWARD DR 4
FISHER CL 5

NEW ST

QUEEN ELIZABETH RD

PRINCE ANDREW CRES

B45

PUTNEY LA

Dayhouse Farm

OLD HOUSE LA

Gannow Green Farm

Gannow Green

GANNOW GREEN LA

Holly Hill Methodist & CE Inf Sch

Frankley Com High Sch

Liby

1

North Worcestershire Path

DAYHOUSE BANK

FORDRAUGHT LA

P

Waseley Hills Visitor Ctr

Duck Pool Farm

Jun Sch

Dayhouse Bank

B4551

M5

CHAPMAN'S HILL

Waseley Hills Country Park

NEW INNS LA

CROSS FARMS LA

RUBERY LA

78

96   A   B   97   C   D   98   E   F

F1
1 BROOKDALE CL
2 CHADDERSLEY CL
3 RUBERY LA S
4 HOLLY HILL
5 CALDY WLK

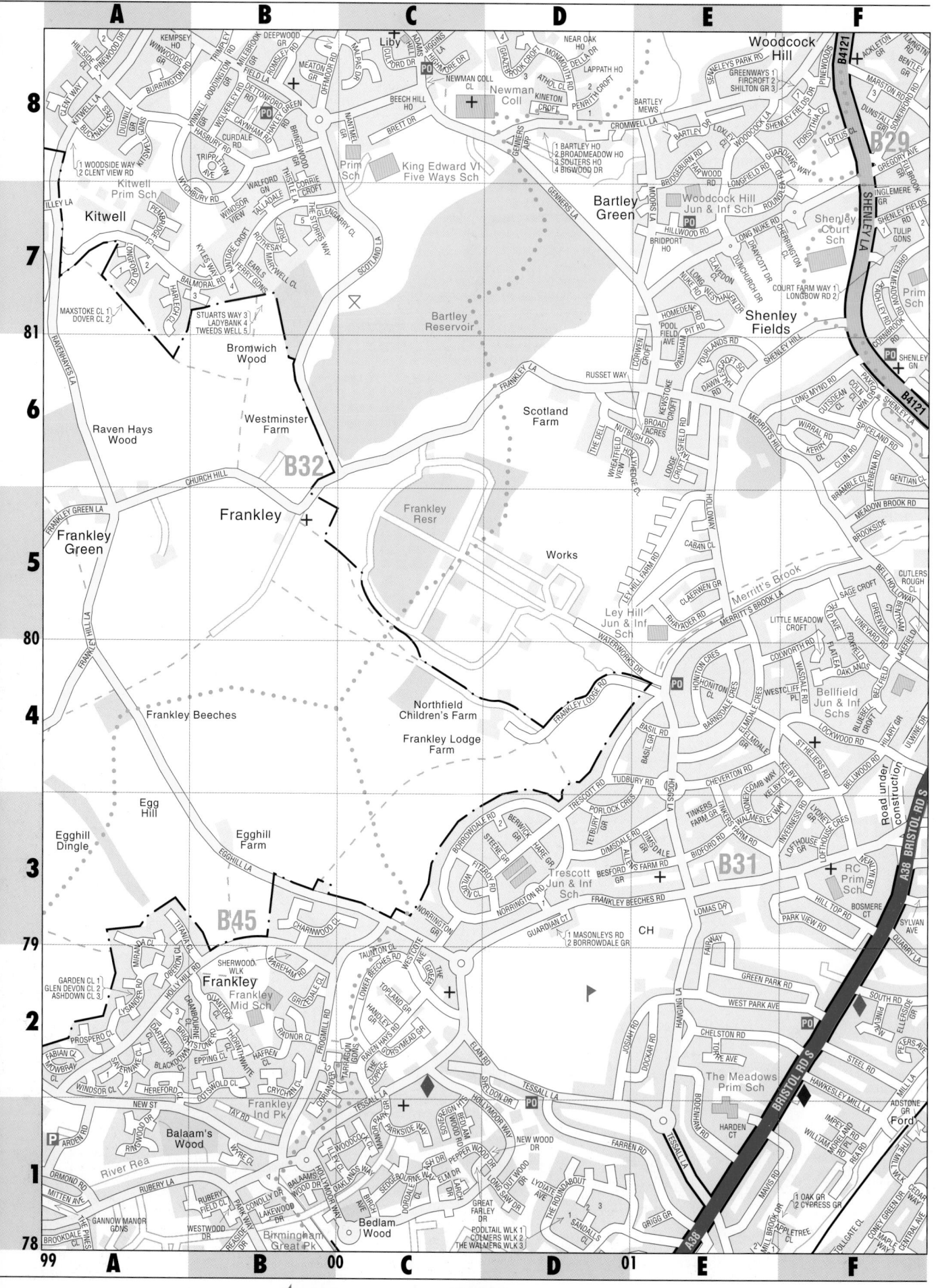

85
104

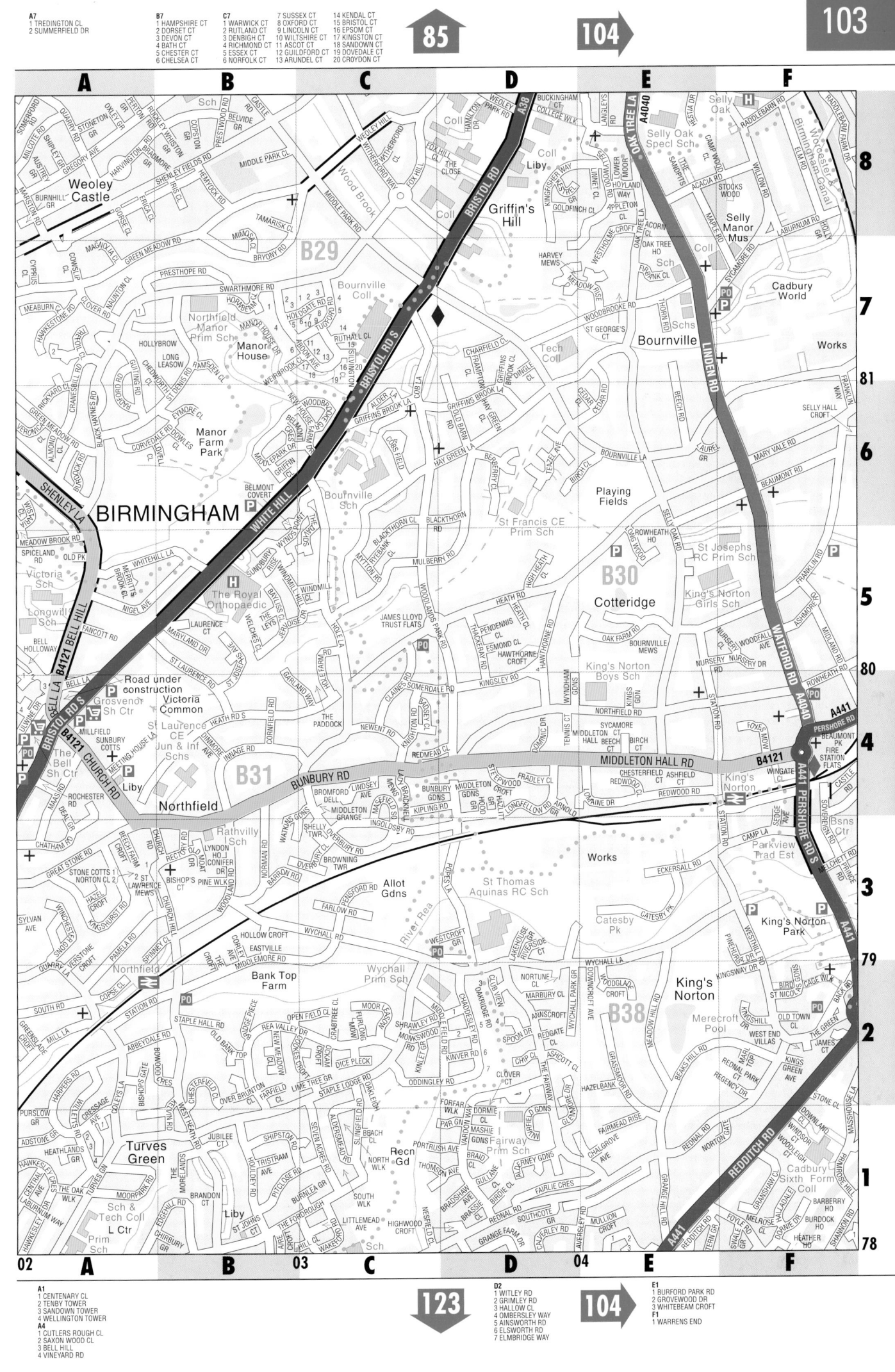

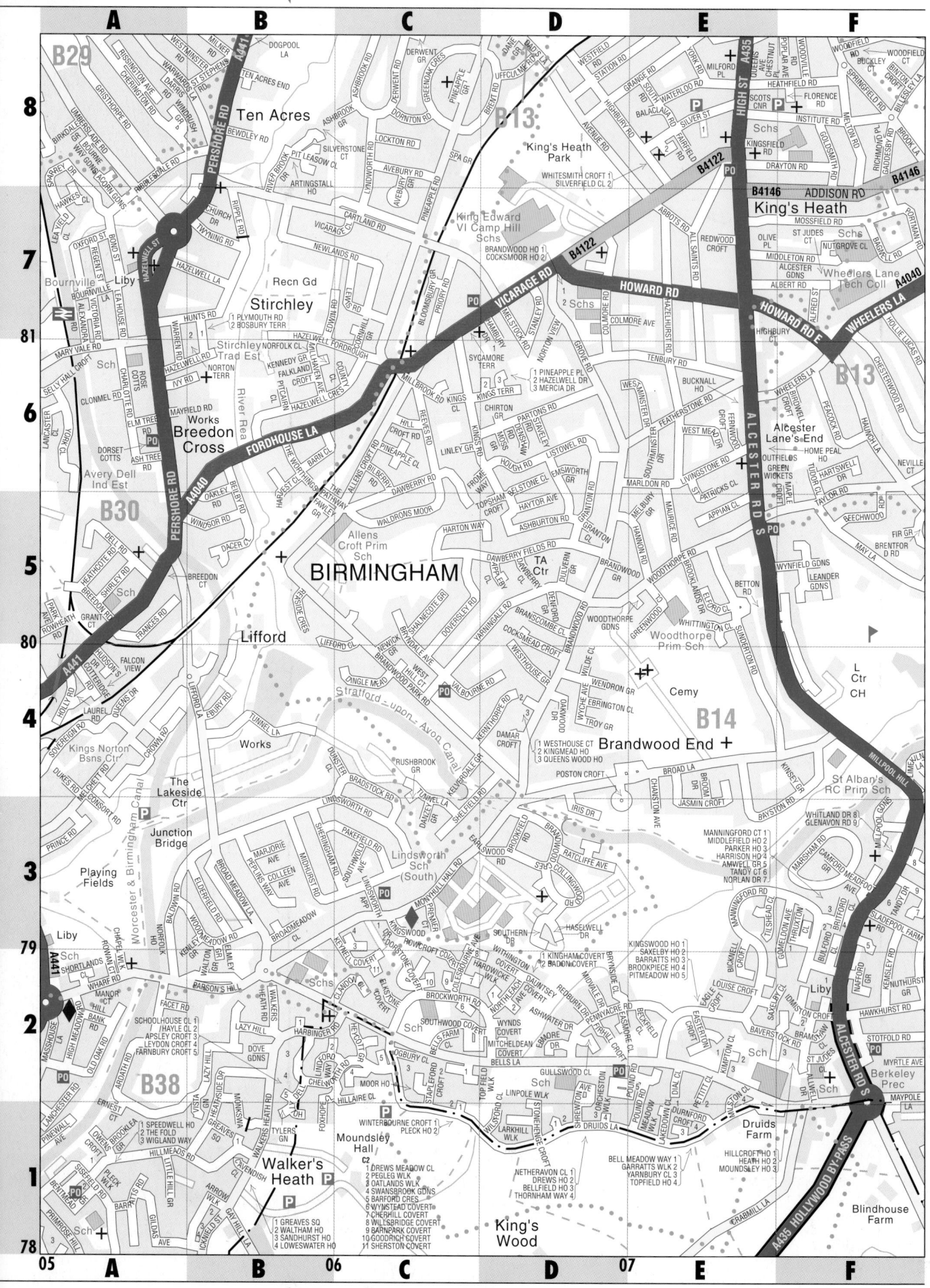

103
86
124

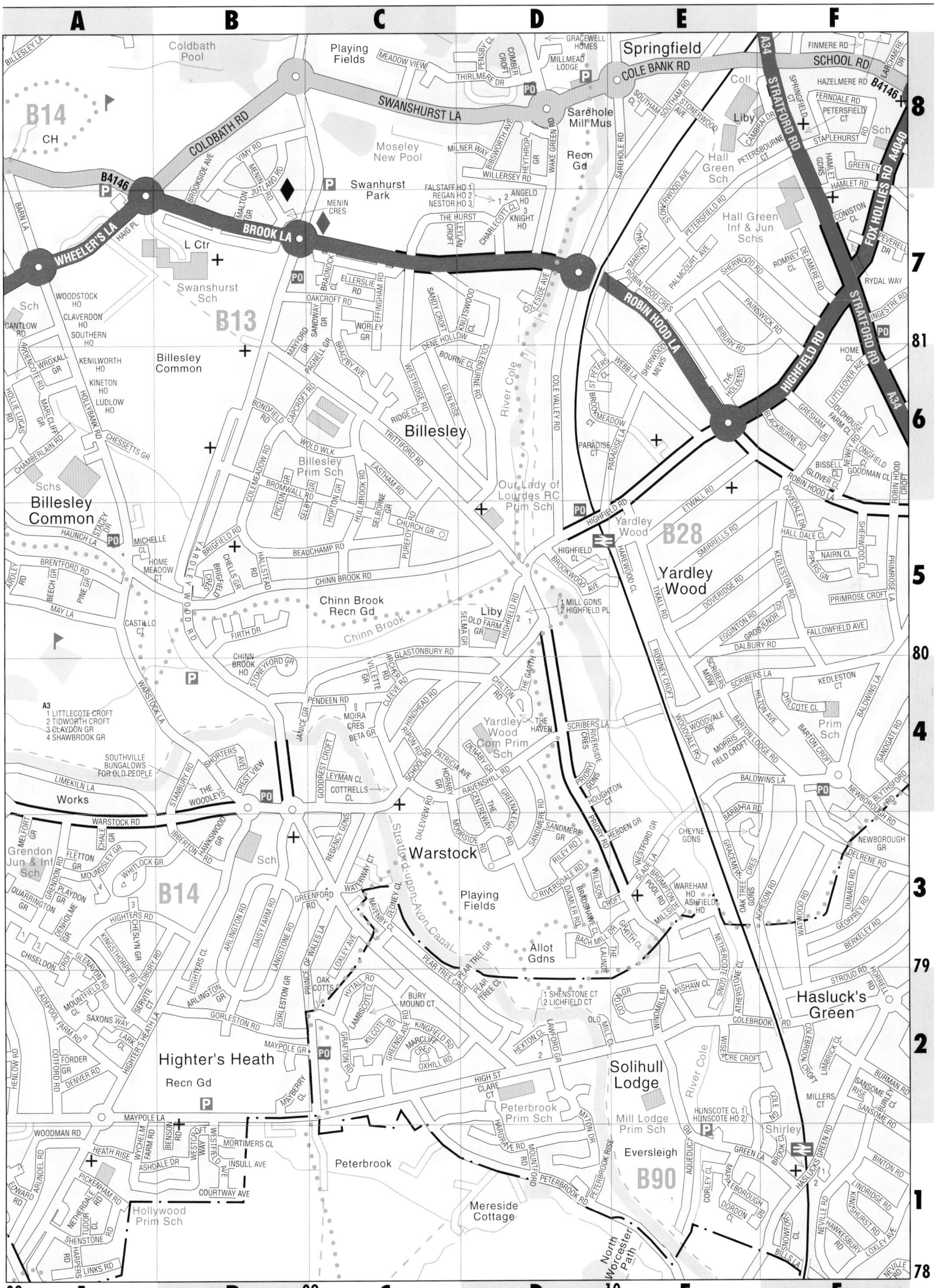

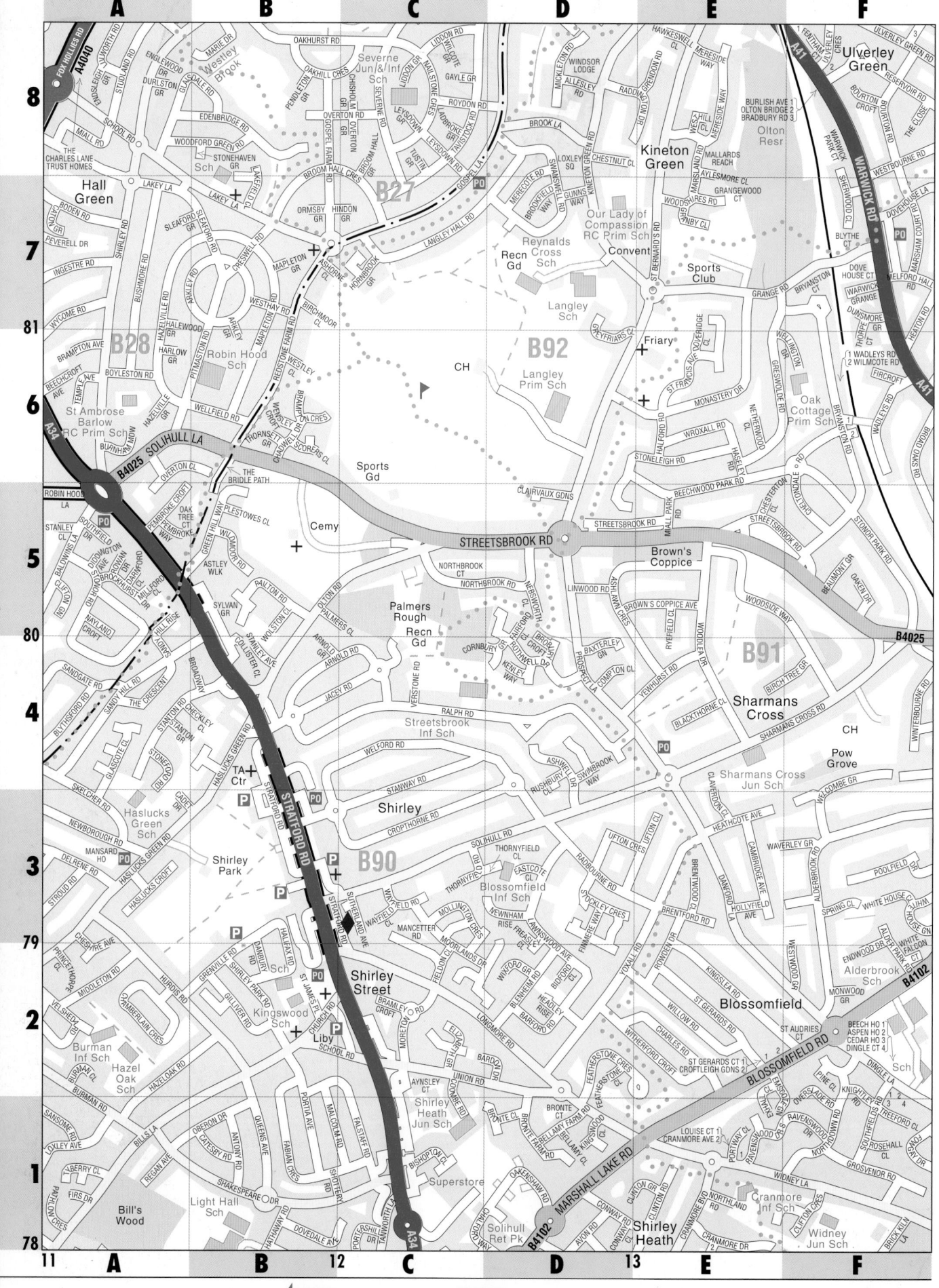

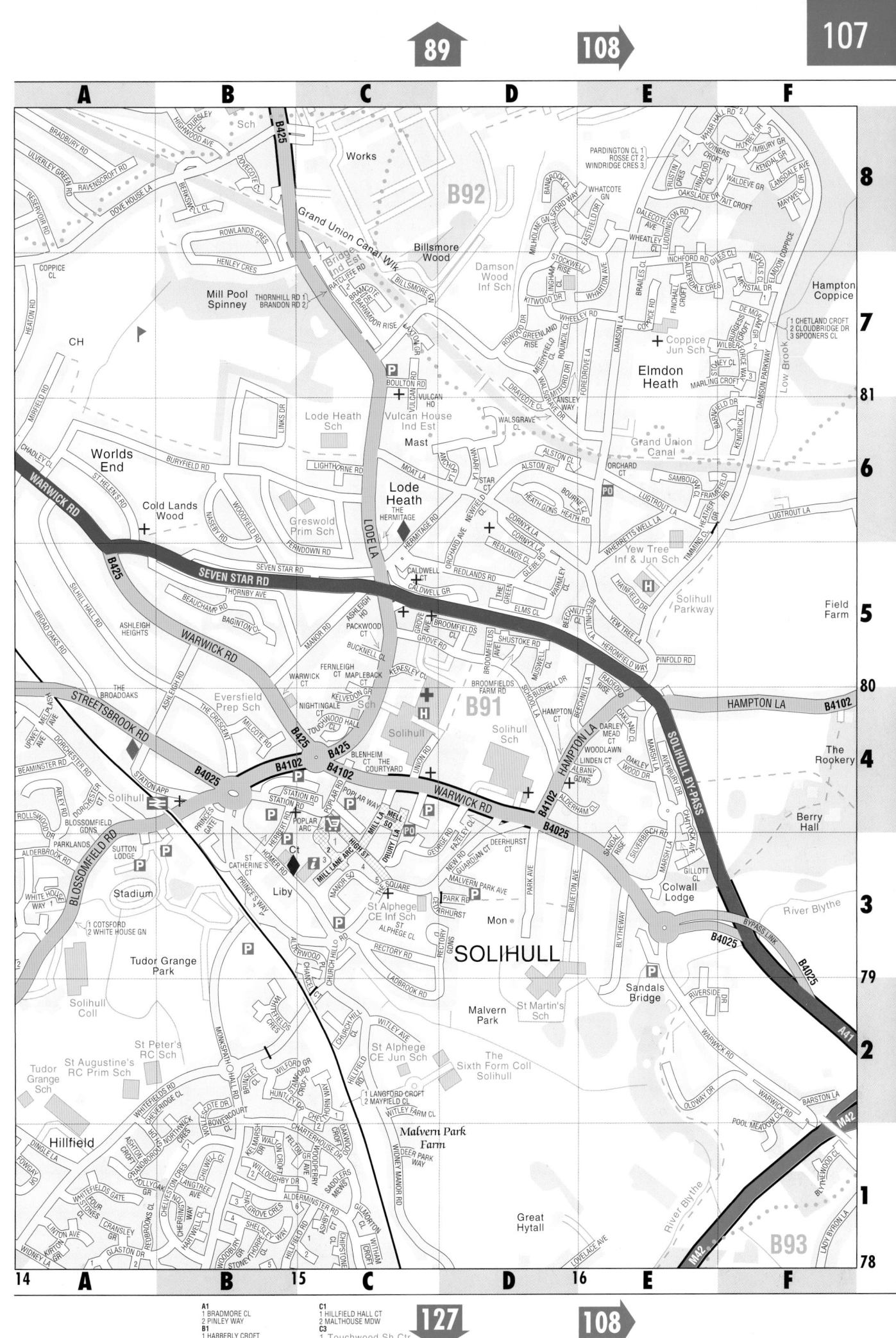

	A	B	C	D	E	F

8
7
81
6
5
80
4
3
79
2
1
78

14   A   B   15   C   D   16   E   F

A1
1 BRADMORE CL
2 PINLEY WAY
B1
1 HABBERLY CROFT
2 HAZELTON CL
3 ALDERTON CL
4 BRANTHILL CROFT
5 MAYTHORN GR
6 CRANFORD GR

C1
1 HILLFIELD HALL CT
2 MALTHOUSE MDW
C3
1 Touchwood Sh Ctr
2 CRESCENT ARC
3 LIBRARY SQ
4 MANOR WLK
5 WARWICK CT

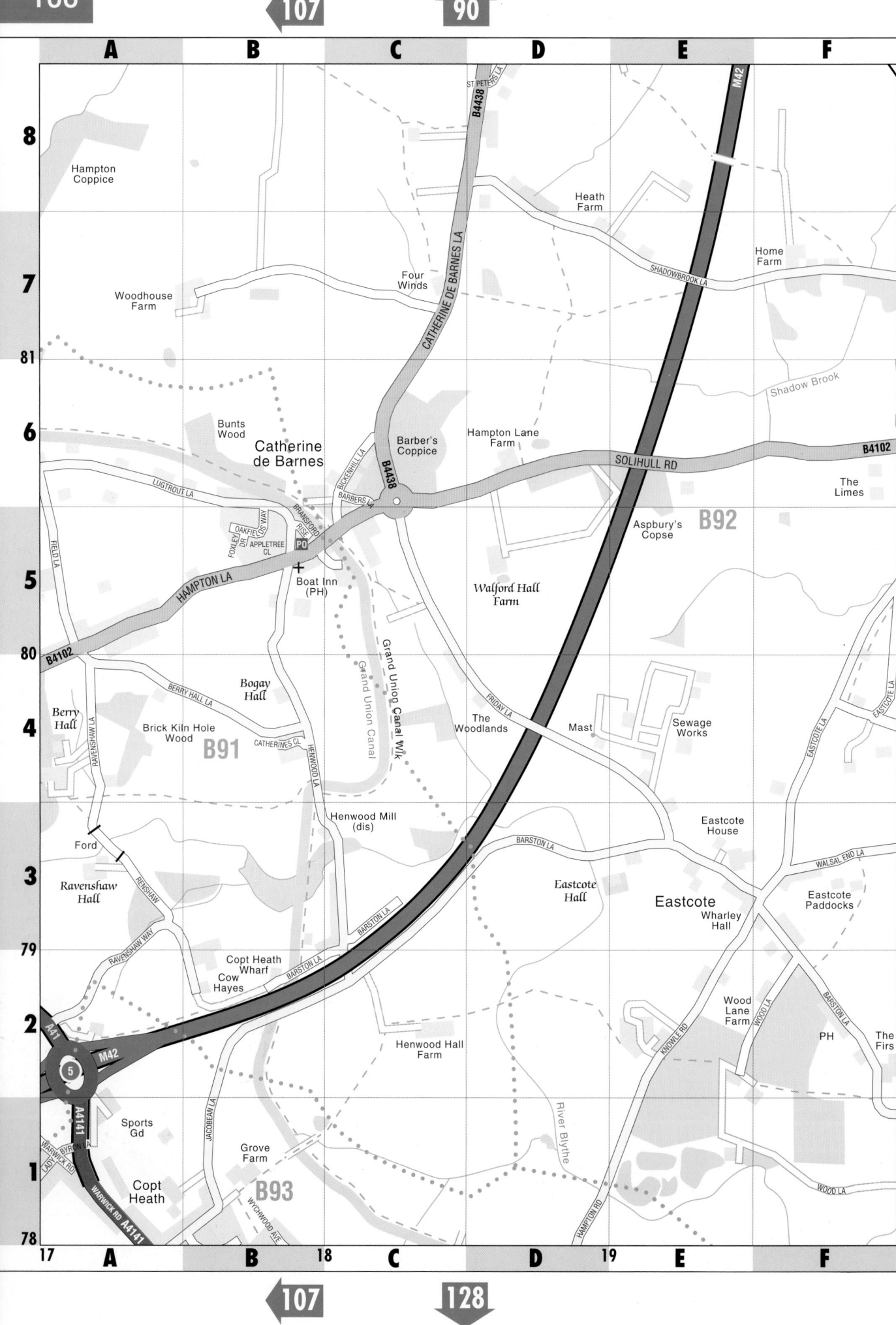

A   B   C   D   E   F

8

7

81

6

5

80

4

79

2

1

78

17   A   B   18   C   D   19   E   F

Hampton
Coppice

Woodhouse
Farm

Four
Winds

Heath
Farm

Home
Farm

Shadow Brook

SHADOWBROOK LA

B4438

ST PETERS LA

CATHERINE DE BARNES LA

M42

Bunts
Wood

Catherine
de Barnes

Barber's
Coppice

Hampton Lane
Farm

SOLIHULL RD

B4102

The
Limes

LUGTROUT LA

BICKENHILL LA

BARBERS LA

B4438

Aspbury's
Copse

B92

FIELD LA

FOXLEY DR

OAKFIELD

LDS WAY

BRANSFORD RISE

APPLETREE CL

PO

+

Boat Inn
(PH)

Walford Hall
Farm

HAMPTON LA

B4102

80

Berry
Hall

Bogay
Hall

BERRY HALL LA

Grand Union Canal Wlk

Grand Union Canal

FRIDAY LA

The
Woodlands

Mast

Sewage
Works

EASTCOTE LA

Brick Kiln Hole
Wood

B91

CATHERINES CL

HENWOOD LA

RAVENSHAW LA

Ford

RENSHAW

Ravenshaw
Hall

Henwood Mill
(dis)

BARSTON LA

Eastcote
House

Eastcote
Hall

Eastcote

WALSAL END LA

Eastcote
Paddocks

RAVENSHAW WAY

Copt Heath
Wharf

Cow
Hayes

BARSTON LA

BARSTON LA

Wharley
Hall

KNOWLE RD

Wood
Lane
Farm

WOOD LA

BARSTON LA

PH

The
Firs

A41

M42

5

A4141

Sports
Gd

JACOBEAN LA

Grove
Farm

Henwood Hall
Farm

River Blythe

WARWICK RD

BYRON LA

Copt
Heath

B93

WYCHWOOD AVE

HAMPTON RD

WOOD LA

A4141

91
110

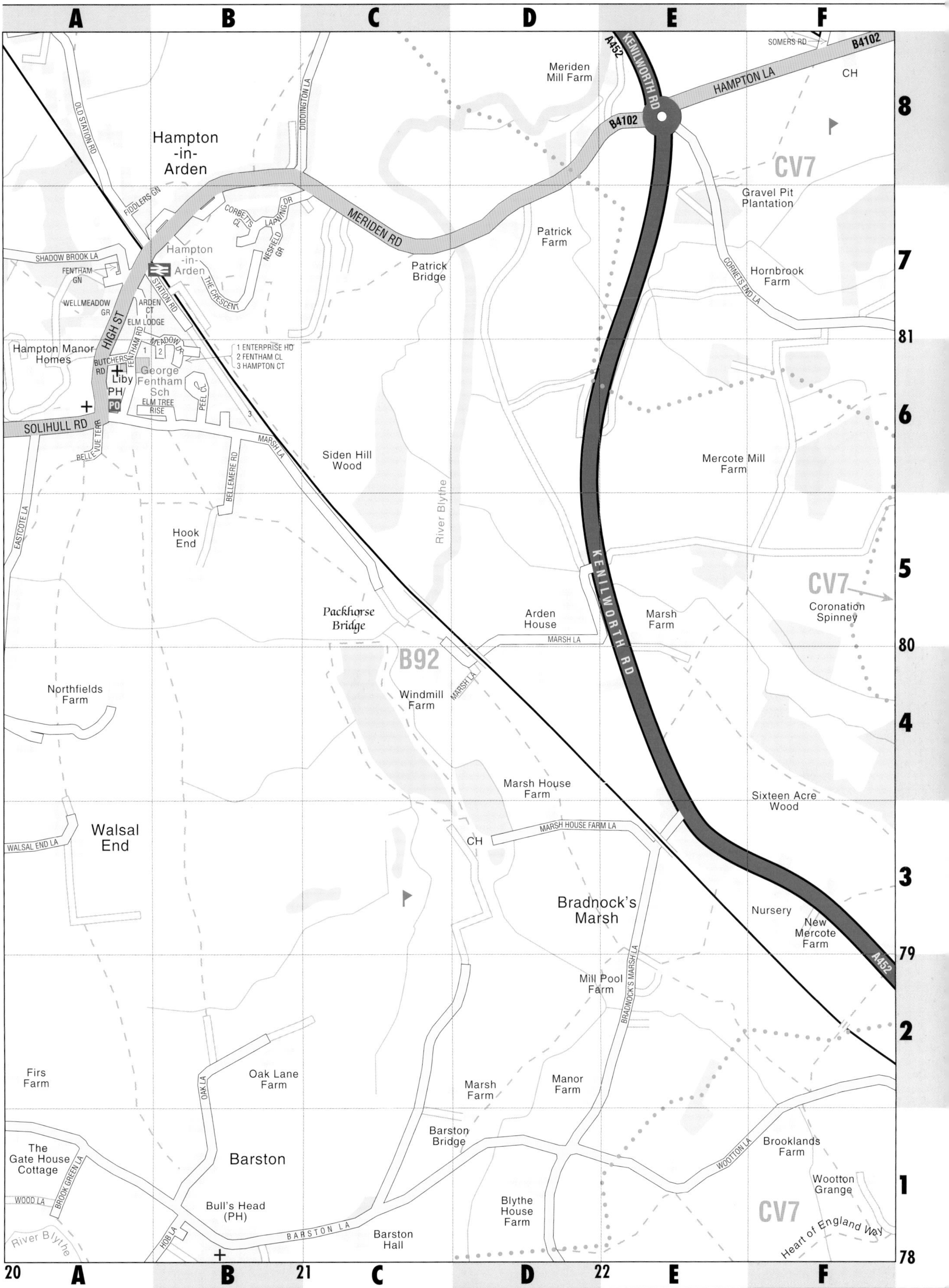

A **B** **C** **D** **E** **F**

8

SOMERS RD
B4102
CH
A452
KENILWORTH RD
Meriden
Mill Farm
HAMPTON LA
CV7
B4102
Gravel Pit
Plantation
7
Hampton
-in-
Arden
DIDDINGTON LA
FIDDLERS GN
Patrick
Farm
CORNET'S END LA
Hornbrook
Farm
SHADOW BROOK LA
CORBETTS CL
LAPWING DR
Hampton
-in-
Arden
MERIDEN RD
81
FENTHAM GN
NESFIELD GR
Patrick
Bridge
WELLMEADOW GR
THE CRESCENT
ARDEN CT
ELM LODGE
Hampton Manor
Homes
HIGH ST
STATION RD
MEADOW RD
1 ENTERPRISE HO
2 FENTHAM CL
3 HAMPTON CT
6
BUTCHERS RD
Liby
PH
PO
George
Fentham
Sch
ELM TREE RISE
PEEL CL
Mercote Mill
Farm
SOLIHULL RD
FENTHAM RD
BELLE VUE TERR
MARSH LA
3
Siden Hill
Wood
River Blythe
KENILWORTH RD
EASTCOTE LA
BELLEMERE RD
5
Hook
End
Arden
House
Marsh
Farm
CV7
Coronation
Spinney
80
Packhorse
Bridge
MARSH LA
Northfields
Farm
B92
Windmill
Farm
MARSH LA
4
Marsh House
Farm
Sixteen Acre
Wood
Walsal
End
WALSAL END LA
CH
MARSH HOUSE FARM LA
3
Bradnock's
Marsh
Nursery
New
Mercote
Farm
79
OAK LA
Mill Pool
Farm
BRADNOCK'S MARSH LA
A452
2
Firs
Farm
Oak Lane
Farm
Marsh
Farm
Manor
Farm
WOOTTON LA
Brooklands
Farm
The
Gate House
Cottage
Barston
Bridge
Wootton
Grange
1
WOOD LA
BROOK GREEN LA
Barston
Bull's Head
(PH)
HOB LA
BARSTON LA
Barston
Hall
Blythe
House
Farm
CV7
Heart of England Way
River Blythe
78

20 **A** **B** 21 **C** **D** 22 **E** **F**

129
110

	A	B	C	D	E	F

8

Heath Farm

Sewage Works

B4102   MAIN RD   OLD RD   MERIDEN HILL   BIRMINGHAM RD   B4102

Meriden Hall

DARLASTON CT

MERIDEN PARK HOMES

Meriden House

Alspath House

Church Farm

CHURCH LA

Moat House Farm

CV5

7

Works

Keeper's Cottage

Berry Fields Farm

BERKSWELL RD

Coventry Way

Crow Wood

81

Cornets End Farm

Cornets End

Wad Barn Farm

Jack Pit

Greenways Farm

6

Four Oaks

Holloway Farm

CORNET'S END LA

BACK LA

Rock Farm

Back Lane Farm

5

Park Farm

Four Oaks Farm

80

Park Pool

CV7

Home Farm

Blind Hall Farm

Coventry Way

Hill House Farm

4

The Bogs

THE STABLES

MERIDEN RD

BLIND LA

Garden Wood

Fir Tree Farm

COVENTRY RD

BERKSWELL HALL

Berkswell

The Moat

3

B92

Berkswell CE Prim Sch

Berkswell

Benton Green

Benton Green Lane Farm House

Berkswell Mus

PH

POUND LA

CHURCH LA

79

Marlowes

A452

Heart of England Way

The Roughs

BENTON GREEN LA

Benton Lane Farm

2

KENILWORTH RD

PARK LA

LAVENDER HALL LA

Priory Orchard

Lower Farm

Victoria Farm

Wootton Green Farm

Skew Bridge

Lodge Farm

SPENCER'S LA

1

WOOTTON LA

GREEN LA

Wootton Green

Fern Bank

Lavender Hall

Ram Hall

BAULK LA

Yew Tree House

Beechcote

A452

PH

78

23	A	B	24	C	D	25	E	F

93
112

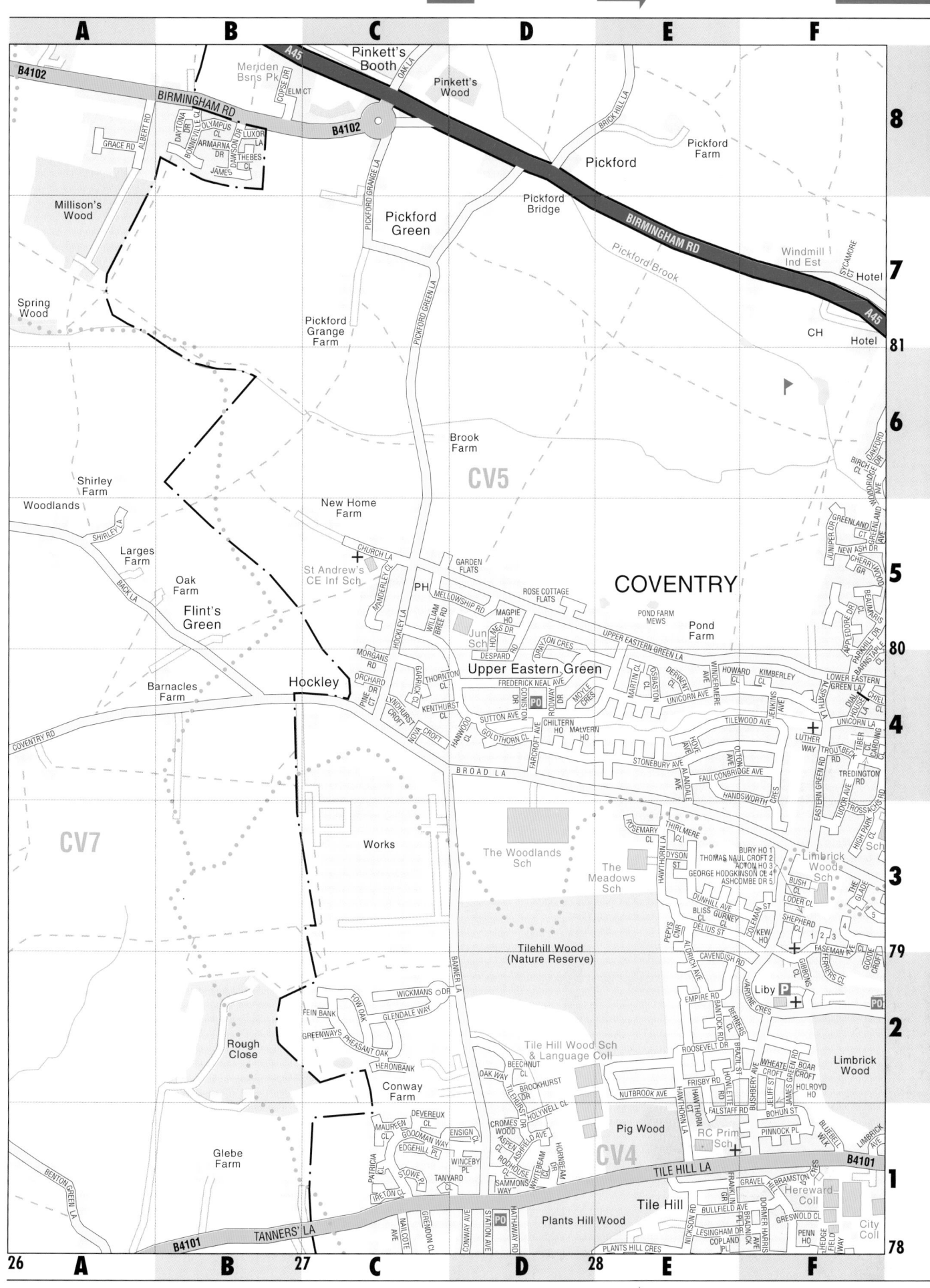

131
112

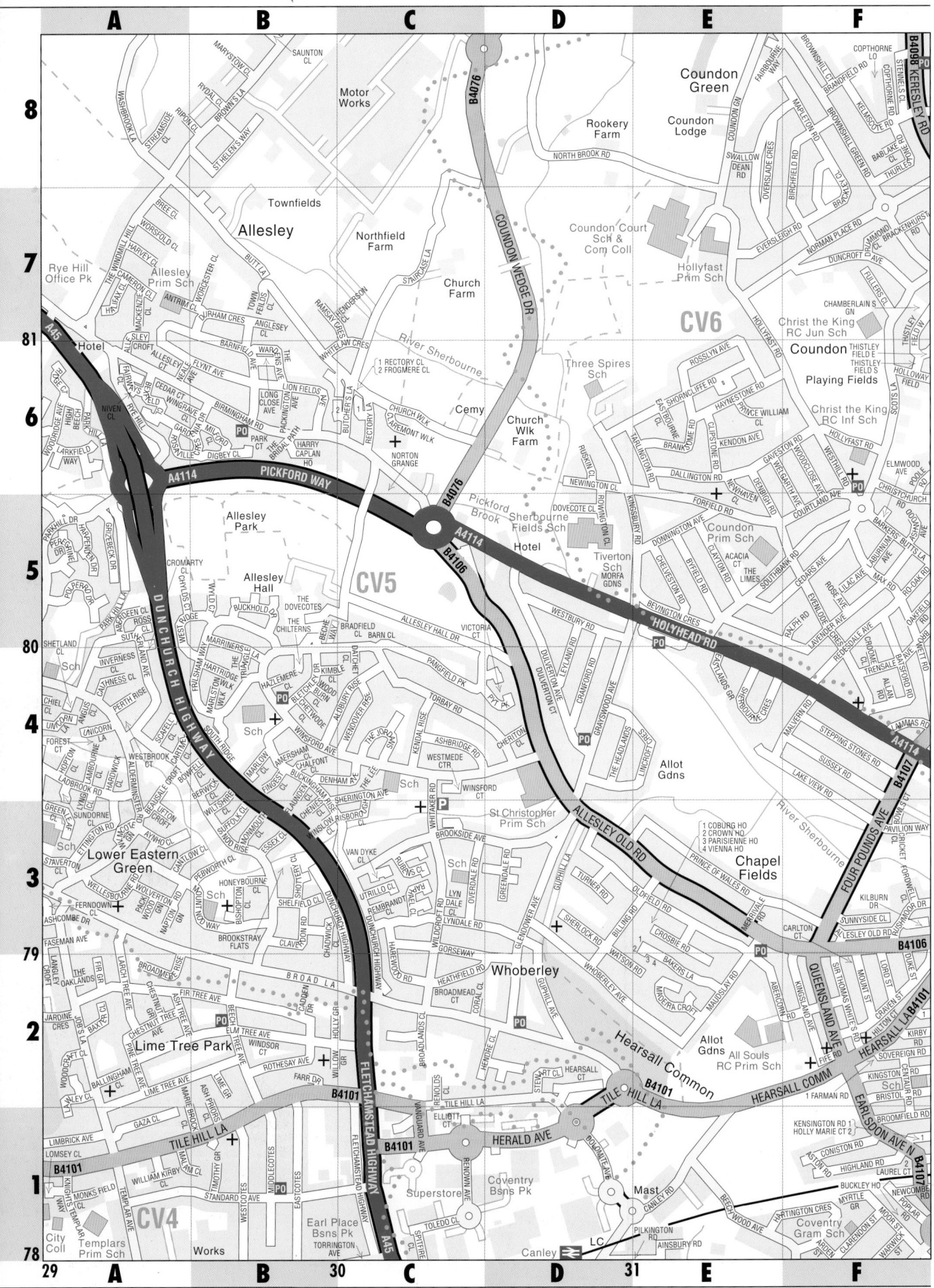

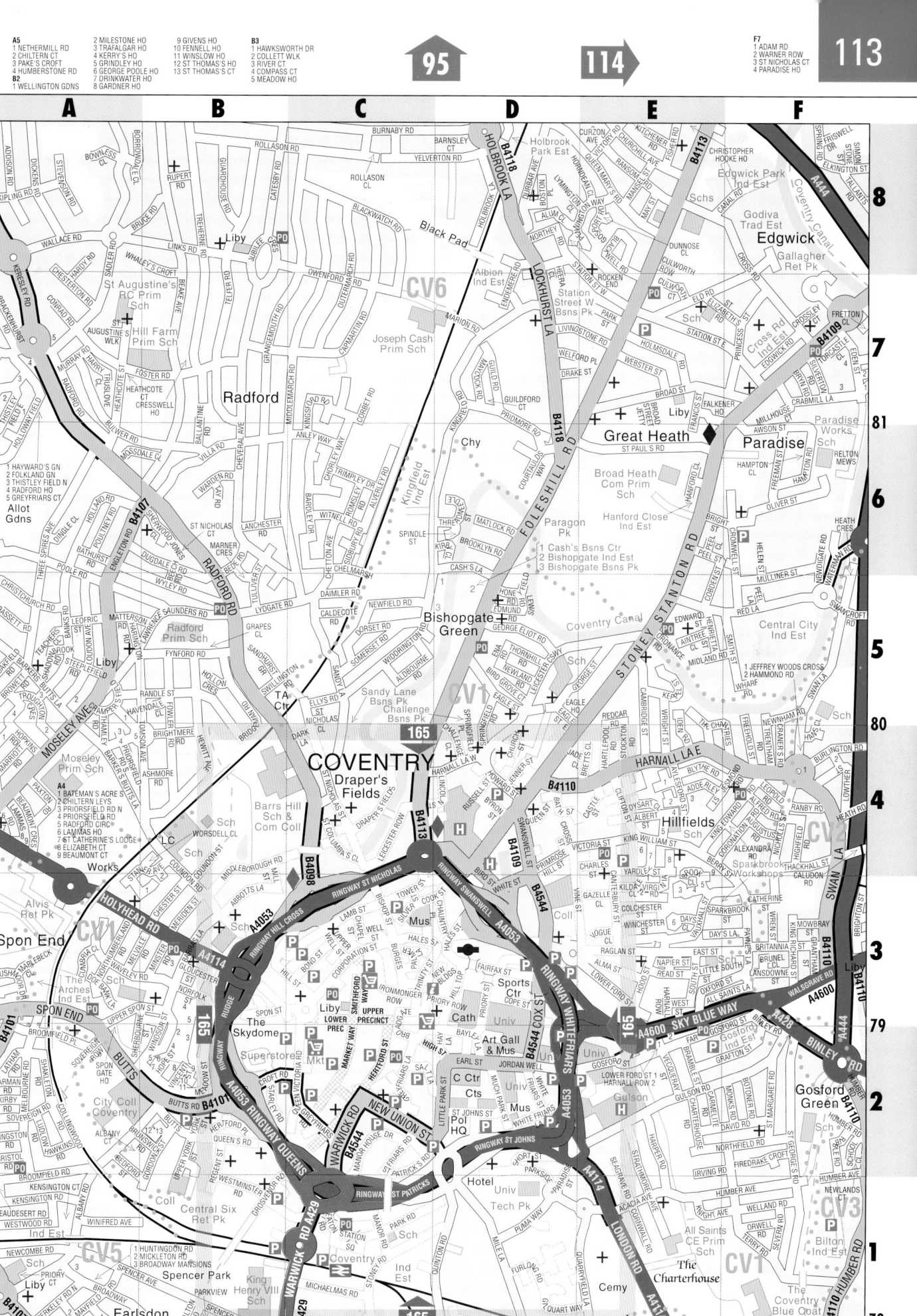

A5
1 NETHERMILL RD
2 CHILTERN CT
3 PAKE'S CROFT
4 HUMBERSTONE RD

B2
1 WELLINGTON GDNS

2 MILESTONE HO
3 TRAFALGAR CT
4 KERRY'S HO
5 GRINDLEY HO
6 GEORGE POOLE HO
7 DRINKWATER HO
8 GARDNER HO

9 GIVENS HO
10 FENNELL HO
11 WINSLOW HO
12 ST THOMAS'S HO
13 ST THOMAS'S CT

B3
1 HAWKSWORTH DR
2 COLLETT WLK
3 RIVER CT
4 COMPASS CT
5 MEADOW HO

F7
1 ADAM RD
2 WARNER ROW
3 ST NICHOLAS CT
4 PARADISE HO

95   114

For full street detail of the highlighted area see page 165.

133   114

E3
1 HILLFIELDS HO
2 JEPHCOTT HO
3 GILBERT CL
4 VAUXHALL CL
5 VERNON CL
6 SPRING CL
7 RAGLAN CT

E4
1 CAWTHORNE CL
2 PENSILVA WAY
3 JACQUARD HO
4 LEIGH ST
5 CLARENCE ST
6 THOMAS KING HO
7 NELSON CL
8 WATERLOO ST
9 VERNON CT

D8
1 LYNE HO
2 HARRY EDWARDS HO
3 FRISWELL HO

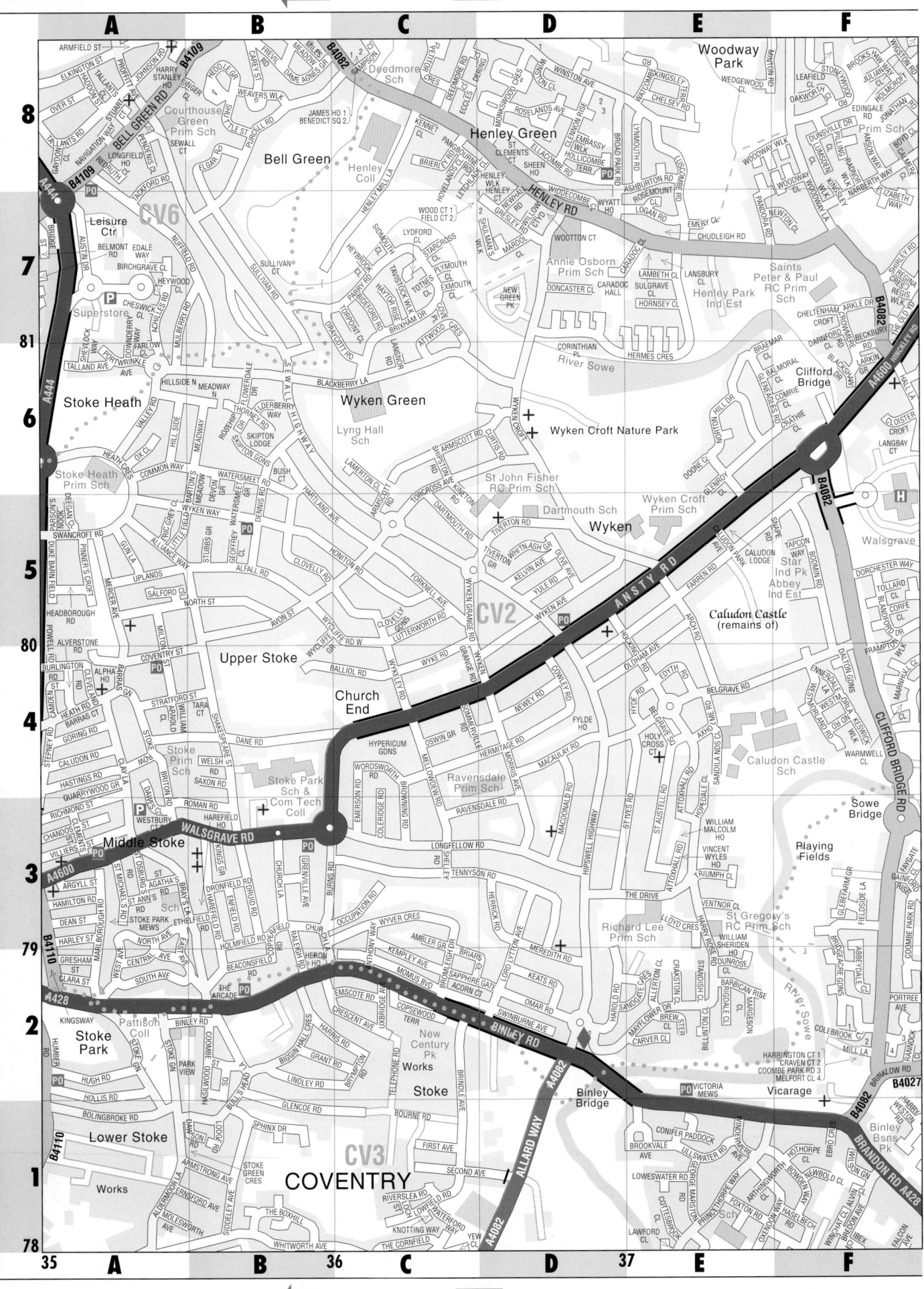

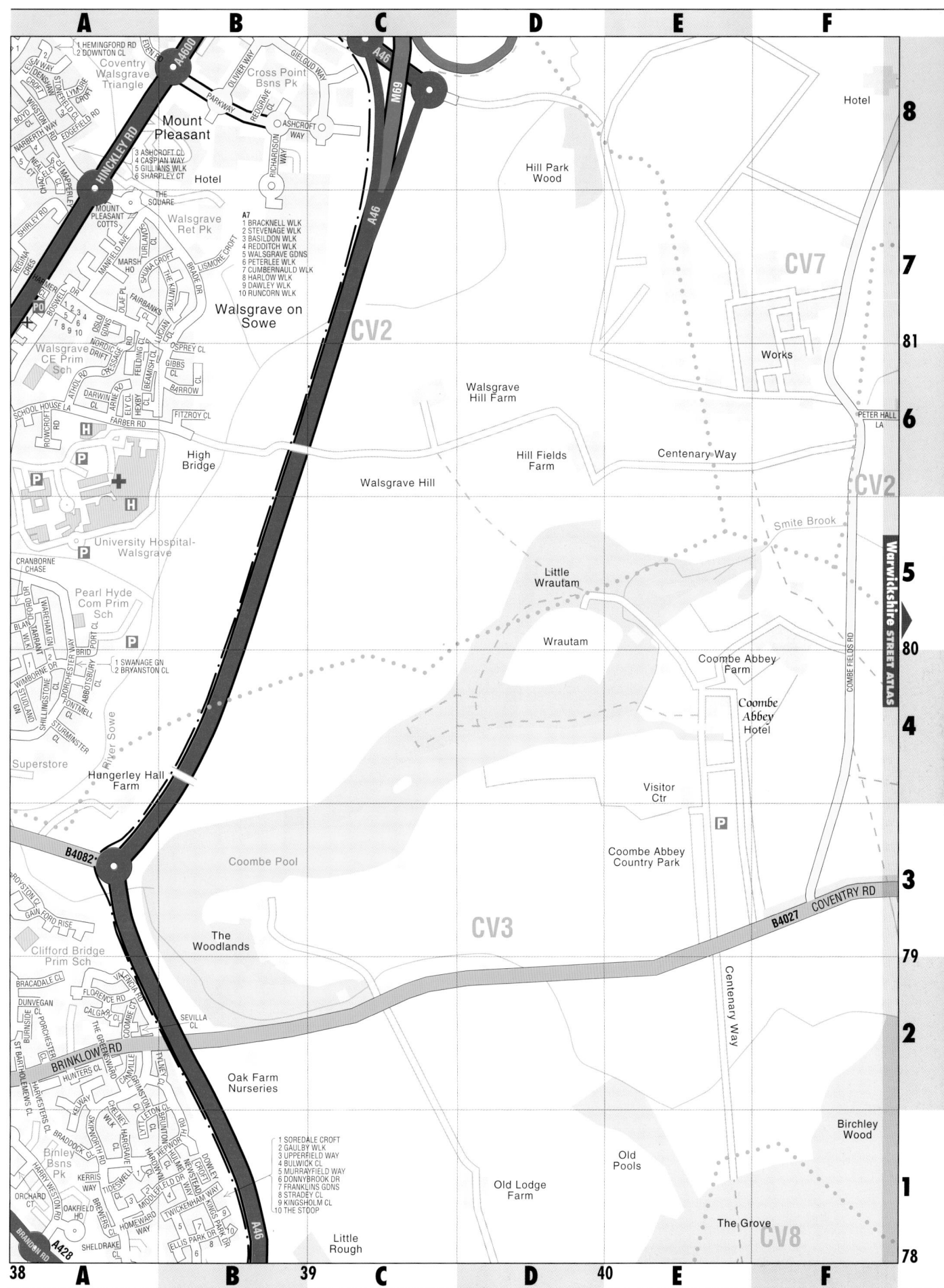

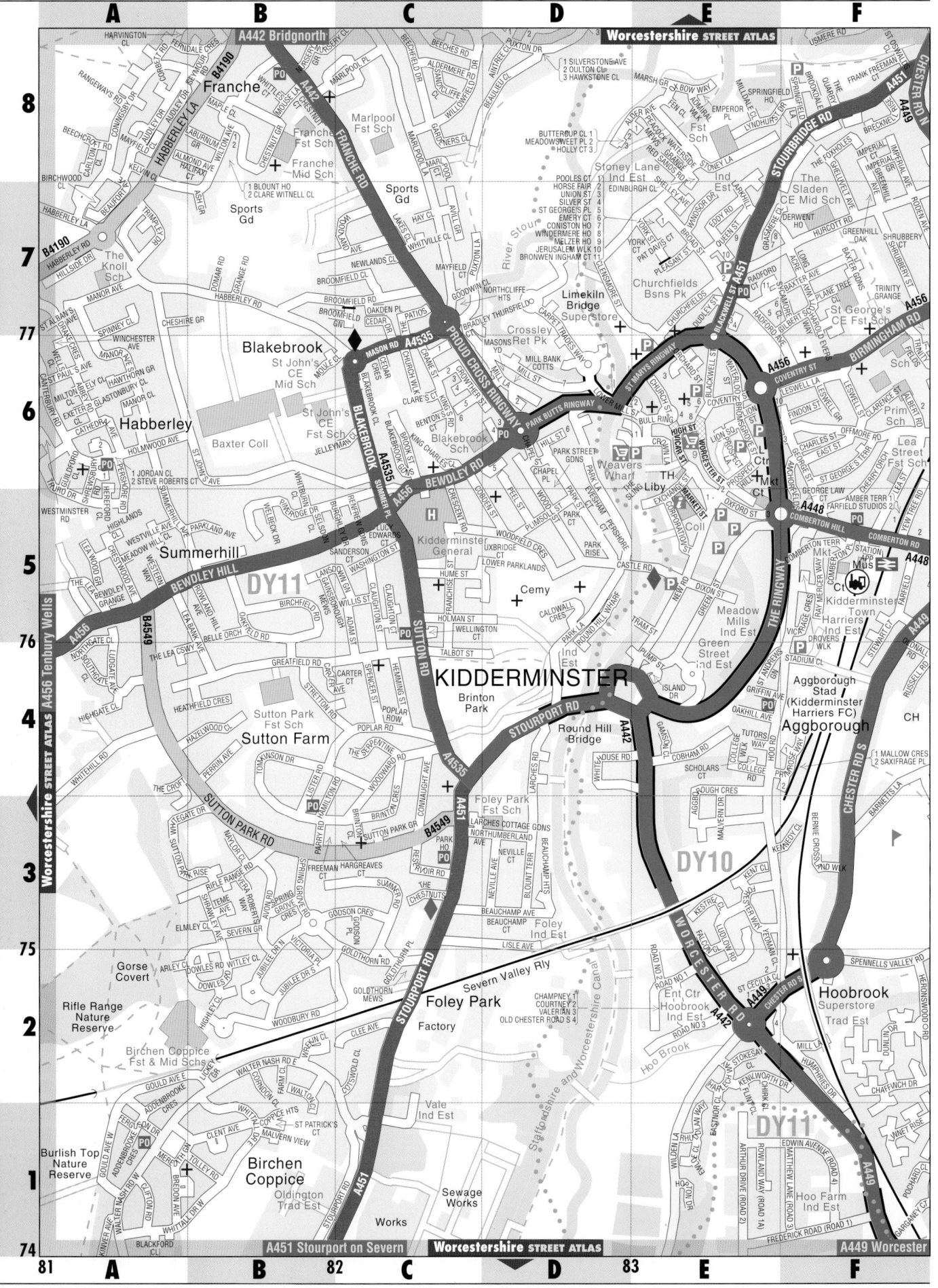

C6
1 HABBERLEY ST
2 BENNETT ST
3 ADAMS HO
4 WOODFIELD ST
5 ST JOHN'S ST
6 ST JOHN'S CL

D6
1 MILLERS CT
2 MILLFIELD GDNS
3 RUTH CHAMBERLAIN CT
4 PATERNOSTER ROW
5 PERRETT WLK
6 ROCK COTTS

7 IDEAL BLDGS
E5
1 BRIDGE ST
2 MARLBOROUGH ST
3 WORCESTER CROSS
E6
1 BLACK HORSE LA

2 CALLOWS LA
3 FREDA EDDY CT
4 KING CHARLES SQ
5 DERICK BURCHER'S MALL
6 SIR GEORGE'S MALL
7 SWAN CTR
8 SIR WALTER'S MALL

9 ROWLAND HILL CTR
10 ST GEORGES CT
F6
1 TRINITY CT
2 VICTORIA CT
3 SOUTH ST

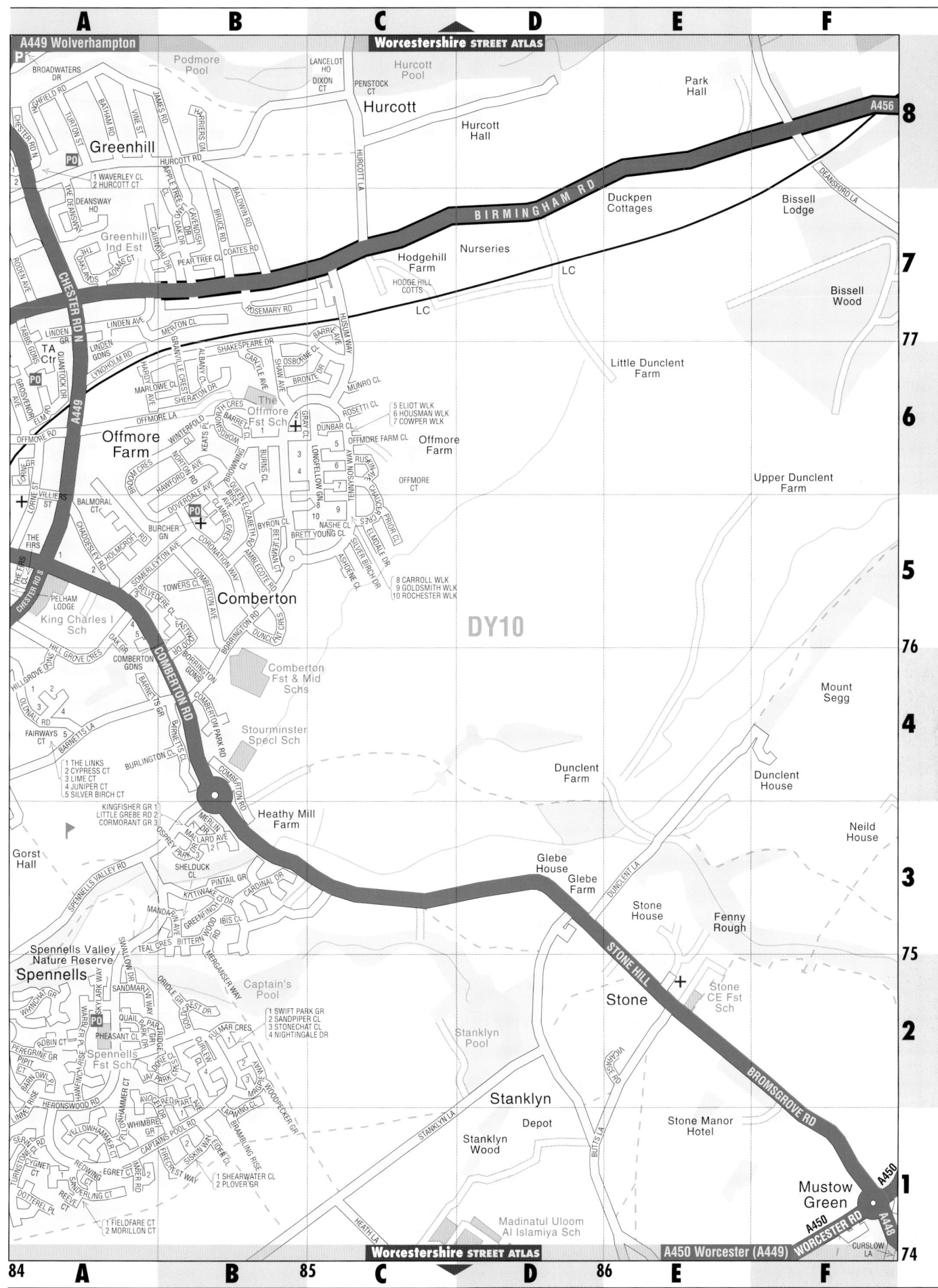

A5
1 THE HAWTHORNS
2 CHADDESLEY GDNS
3 SOMERLEYTON CT
4 COMBERTON MANS
5 COMBERTON CT

B6
1 MASEFIELD GDNS
2 GEORGE DANCE CL
3 KIPLING WLK
4 CHATTERTON WLK

Worcestershire STREET ATLAS

A449 Wolverhampton

Greenhill

Hurcott

Park Hall

A456

Podmore Pool

LANCELOT HO

DIXON CT

PENSTOCK CT

Hurcott Pool

Hurcott Hall

BIRMINGHAM RD

Duckpen Cottages

Bissell Lodge

DEANSFORD LA

Bissell Wood

BROADWATERS DR

HIGHFIELD RD

CHESTER RD N

TURTON ST

BATHAM RD

VINE ST

JAMES RD

HARRIERS GN

HURCOTT RD

APPLE TREE CL

OAK DR

BALDWIN RD

BRUCE WAY

COATES RD

PEAR TREE CL

HURCOTT LA

Hodgehill Farm

Nurseries

HODGE HILL COTTS

LC

LC

Little Dunclent Farm

DEANSWAY HO

1 WAVERLEY CL
2 HURCOTT CT

Greenhill Ind Est

ROSEMARY RD

LC

THE DEANSWAY

RODEN AVE

OAKLANDS

HILL

ADAMS CT

CAIRNDHU DR

MEYTON CL

SHAKESPEARE DR

BARRY LA

HUSUM WAY

CHESTER RD N

A449

LINDEN GR

LINDEN AVE

GRANVILLE CRES

ALBANY CL

SHAW AVE

OSBORNE CL

BRONTE DR

MUNRO CL

5 ELIOT WLK
6 HOUSMAN WLK
7 COWPER WLK

TARBS GDNS

QUANTOCK DR

LINDEN GDNS

LYNDHOLM RD

HARDY AVE

MARLOWE AVE

SHERATON DR

KEATS PL

NORTH CRES

BARRET PL

WORDSWORTH

CASTLE AVE

DUNBAR CL

ROSETTI CL

OFFMORE FARM CL

TA Ctr

Offmore Farm

OFFMORE LA

The Offmore Fst Sch

GRAY CL

Offmore Farm

GROSVENOR AVE

ELM CL

BROOM CRES

HAWFORD AVE

NORTON AVE

BROWNING

BURNS CL

QUEEN ELIZABETH RD

LONGFELLOW GN

RUSKIN

PRIOR CL

EMDALE DR

OFFMORE CT

OFFMORE RD

LORNE GR

VILLIERS ST

BALMORAL CT

DOVERDALE AVE

BYRON CL

CAINES CRES

NASHE CL

CHAUCER CL

ASHDINE CL

SILVER BIRCH DR

BRETT YOUNG CL

THE FIRS

CHADDESLEY RD

HOLMCROFT RD

BURCHER GN

CORONATION WAY

AMBLECOTE RD

BENJAMIN CL

8 CARROLL WLK
9 GOLDSMITH WLK
10 ROCHESTER WLK

Comberton

DY10

THE FIRS CL

CHESTER RD S

PELHAM LODGE

SOMERLEYTON AVE

BELVEDERE CL

TOWERS CL

COMBERTON AVE

BORRINGTON RD

DUNCLET CRES

King Charles I Sch

HILL GROVE CRES

OAK GR

COMBERTON GDNS

EASTW

BORRINGTON GDNS

Comberton Fst & Mid Schs

Mount Segg

HILLGROVE CRES

GLENALL RD

BARNETTS LA

COMBERTON RD

BARNETTS GR

Stourminster Specl Sch

FAIRWAYS CT

BARNETTS LA

COMBERTON PARK RD

Dunclent Farm

Dunclent House

1 THE LINKS
2 CYPRESS CT
3 LIME CT
4 JUNIPER CT
5 SILVER BIRCH CT

BURLINGTON CL

COMBERTON RD

KINGFISHER GR 1
LITTLE GREBE RD 2
CORMORANT GR 3

OSPREY PARK

MERLIN DR

MALLARD AVE

Heathy Mill Farm

Glebe House

Glebe Farm

DUNCLENT LA

Neild House

Gorst Hall

SHELDUCK CL

PINTAIL GR

CARDINAL DR

Stone House

Fenny Rough

SPENNELLS VALLEY RD

KITIWAME

GREENFINCH CL DR

IBIS CL

Spennells Valley Nature Reserve

MANDAR

TEAL CRES

BITTERN RD

STONE HILL

Stone CE Fst Sch

Spennells

SWALLOW DR

SANDMAR

Captain's Pool

MERGANSER WAY

Stone

WHINCHAT GR

LARK

WAY

QUAIL GR

OROLE GR

CREST DR

FULMAR CRES

1 SWIFT PARK GR
2 SANDPIPER CL
3 STONECHAT CL
4 NIGHTINGALE DR

Stanklyn Pool

LARKHILL

PHEASANT CL

PARTRIDGE

CURLEW

Stanklyn Wood

Stone Manor Hotel

RDBIN CT

PEREGRINE GR

PIPIT

BARN OWL

DENE

HERONSWOOD RD

JAY PARK CRES

AVON

WOODPECKER GR

WICKHAM

Stanklyn

Depot

BROMSGROVE RD

A450

LINNET RISE

SERIN CT

YELLOWHAMMER RD

REDSTART AVE

SISKIN CL

LAPWING

BRAMBLING RISE

ELDER CT

STANKLYN LA

BUTTS LA

Mustow Green

A450

TURNSTONE CT

CYGNET CT

REDWING CT

EGRET CT

MERLIN CT

FIRCREST WAY

1 SHEARWATER CL
2 PLOVER GR

1 FIELDFARE CT
2 MORILLON CT

HEATH LA

Madinatul Uloom Al Islamiya Sch

WORCESTER RD

A448

CURSLOW LA

DOTTEREL PL

REEVE

SANDERLING CT

Worcestershire STREET ATLAS

A450 Worcester (A449)

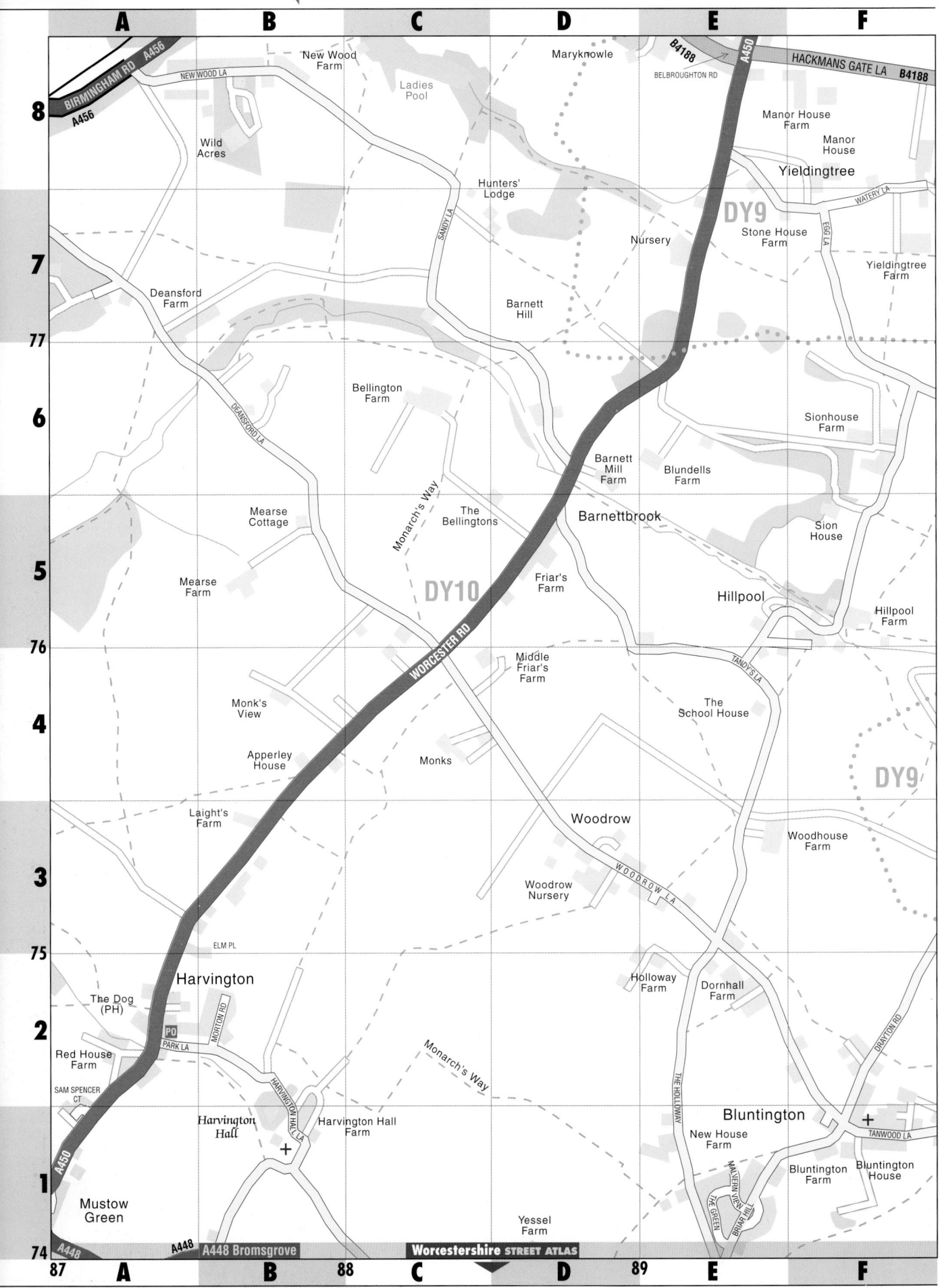

Worcestershire STREET ATLAS

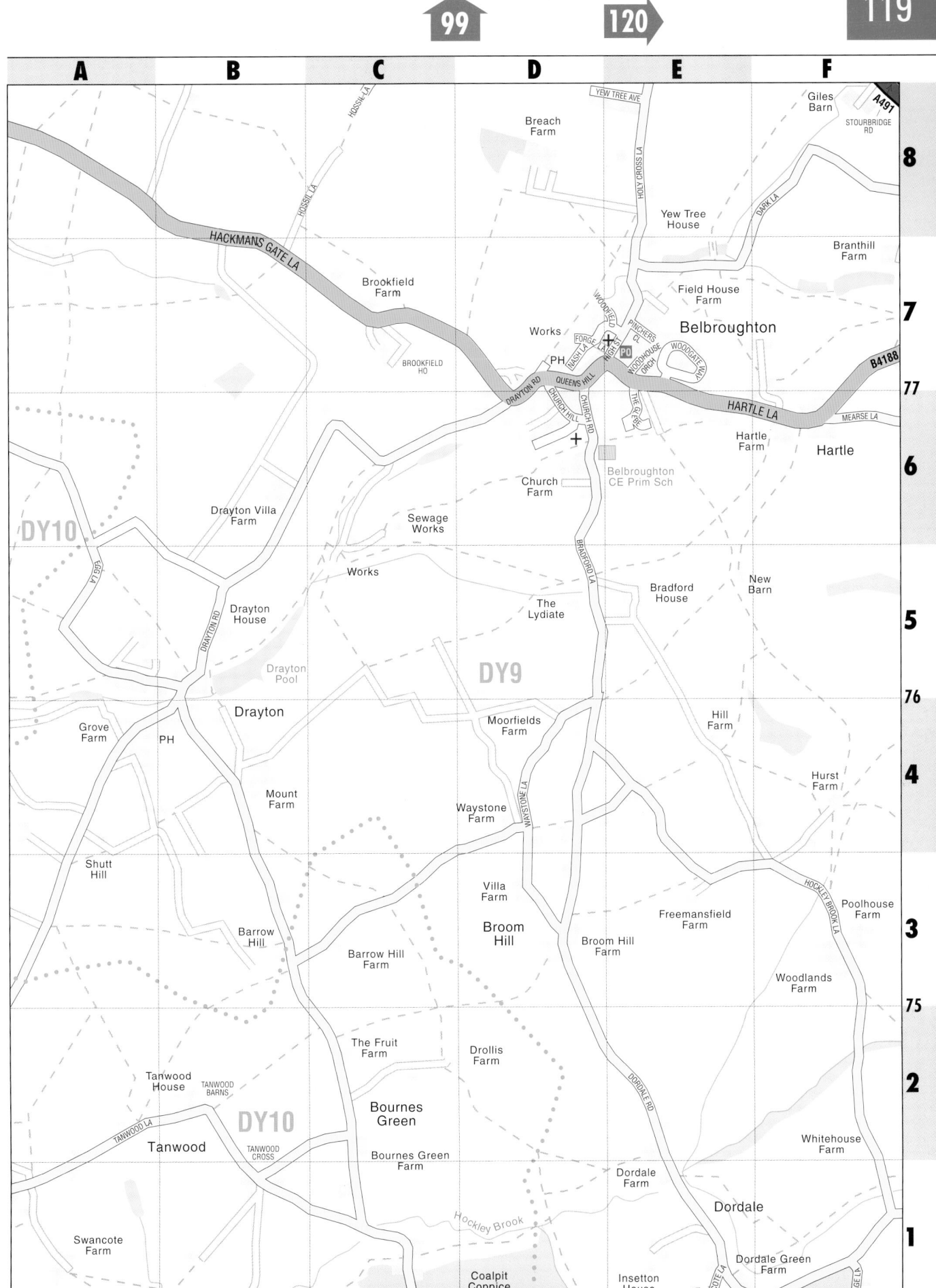

A B C D E F

YEW TREE AVE

Giles
Barn

A491

STOURBRIDGE
RD

8

HOSSILL LA

Breach
Farm

HOLY CROSS LA

Yew Tree
House

DARK LA

Branthill
Farm

HACKMANS GATE LA

Brookfield
Farm

WOODFIELD

Field House
Farm

Belbroughton

7

Works

PINCHERS
CL

Brookfield
HO

PH

FORGE
LA

NASH LA

HIGH ST

PO

WOODHOUSE

WOOGATE WAY

ORCH

B4188

77

DRAYTON RD

QUEENS HILL

HARTLE LA

MEARSE LA

CHURCH HILL

CHURCH RD

THE GLEBE

Hartle
Farm

Hartle

6

DY10

Drayton Villa
Farm

Church
Farm

Belbroughton
CE Prim Sch

Sewage
Works

BRADFORD LA

Bradford
House

New
Barn

A 483 LA

Works

The
Lydiate

5

Drayton
House

DY9

76

Drayton
Pool

Moorfields
Farm

Hill
Farm

Grove
Farm

PH

Drayton

WAYSTONE LA

HOCKLEY BROOK LA

Poolhouse
Farm

Hurst
Farm

4

Mount
Farm

Waystone
Farm

Villa
Farm

Freemansfield
Farm

Shutt
Hill

Barrow
Hill

Barrow Hill
Farm

Broom
Hill

Broom Hill
Farm

Woodlands
Farm

3

75

The Fruit
Farm

Drollis
Farm

DORDALE RD

Whitehouse
Farm

2

Tanwood
House

TANWOOD
BARNS

DY10

Bournes
Green

Tanwood

TANWOOD LA

TANWOOD
CROSS

Bournes Green
Farm

Dordale
Farm

WOODCOTE LA

Dordale

Swancote
Farm

Hockley Brook

Coalpit
Coppice

Insetton
House

Dordale Green
Farm

HARBAGE LA

1

74

90 A B 91 C D 92 E F

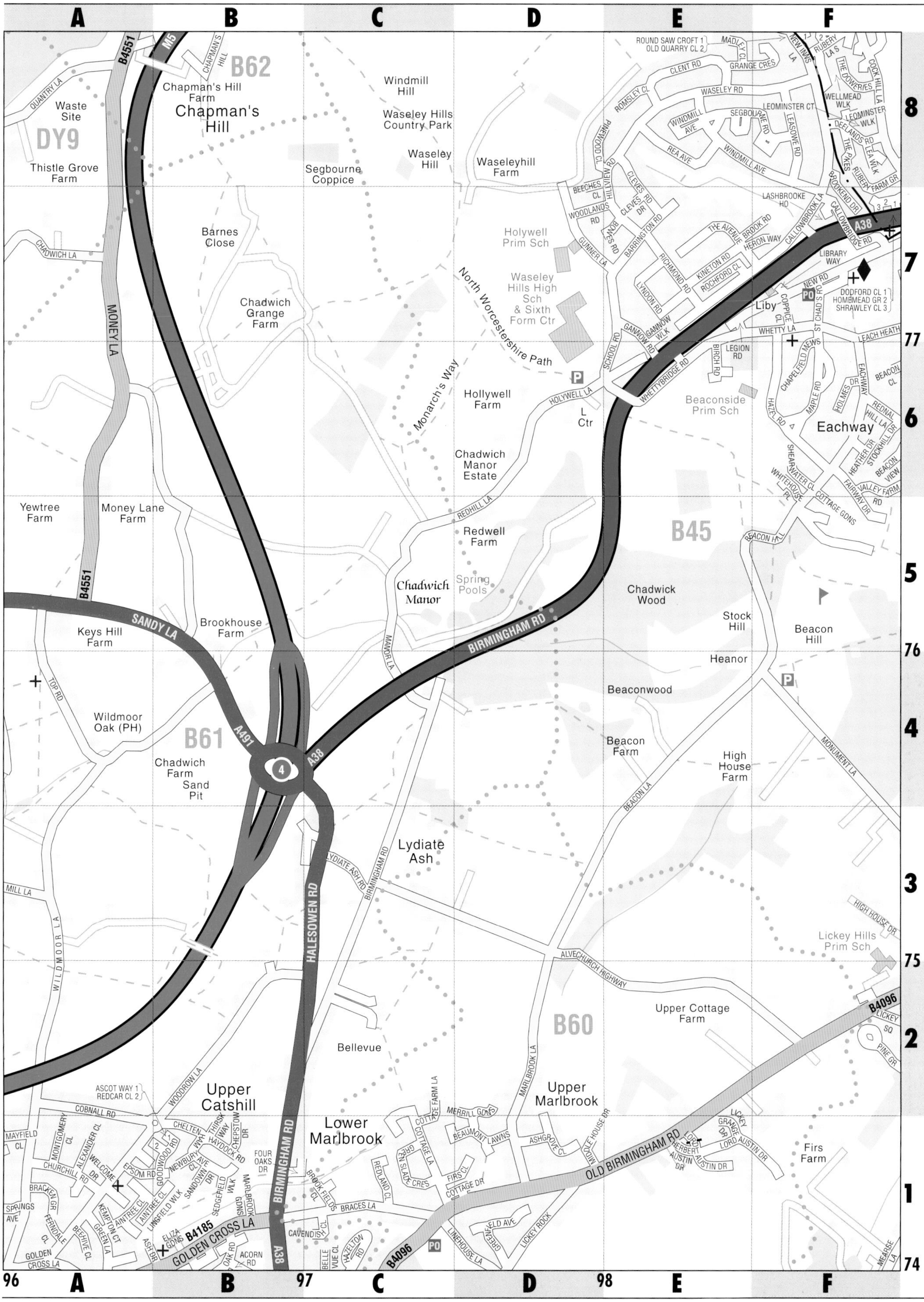

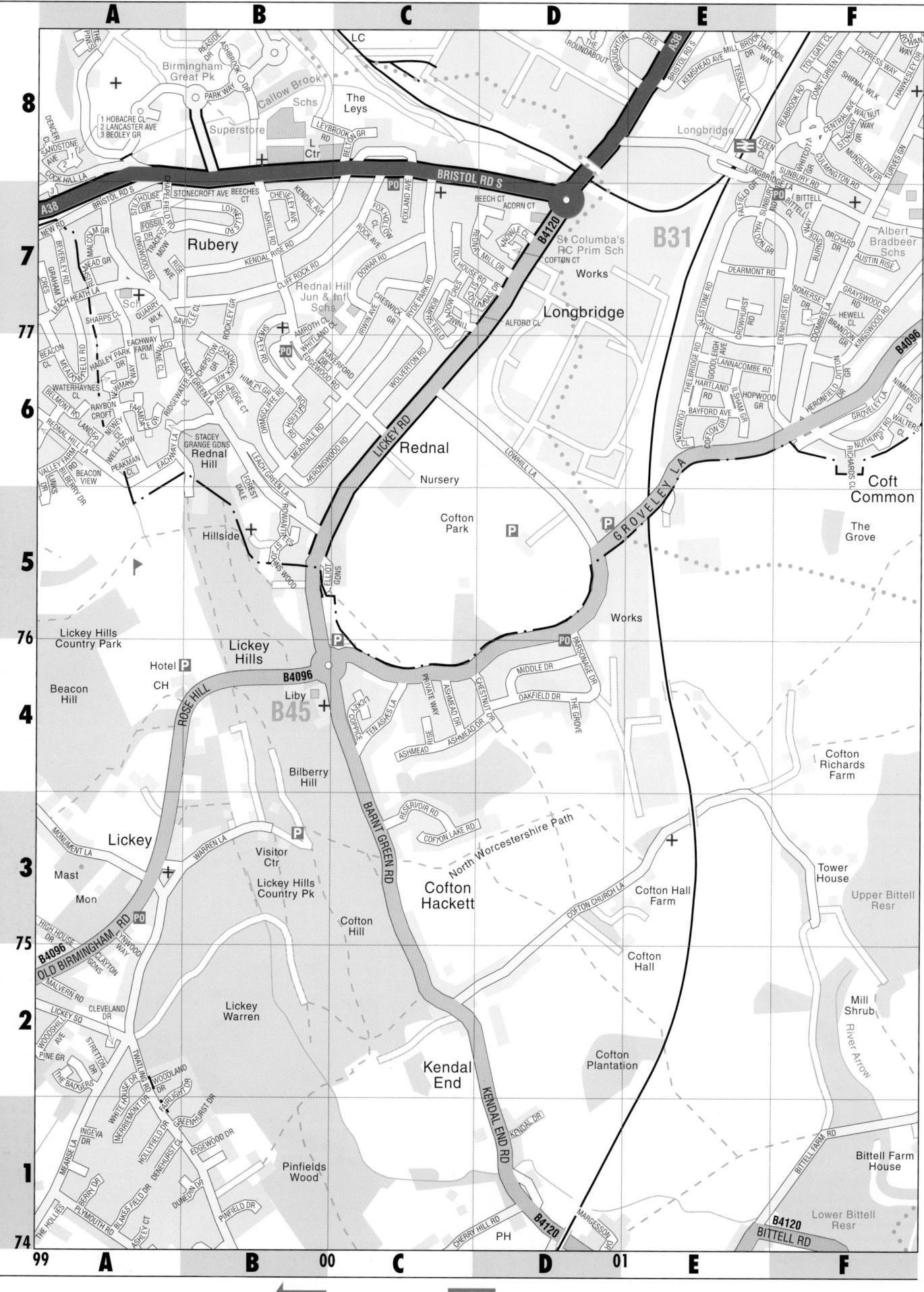

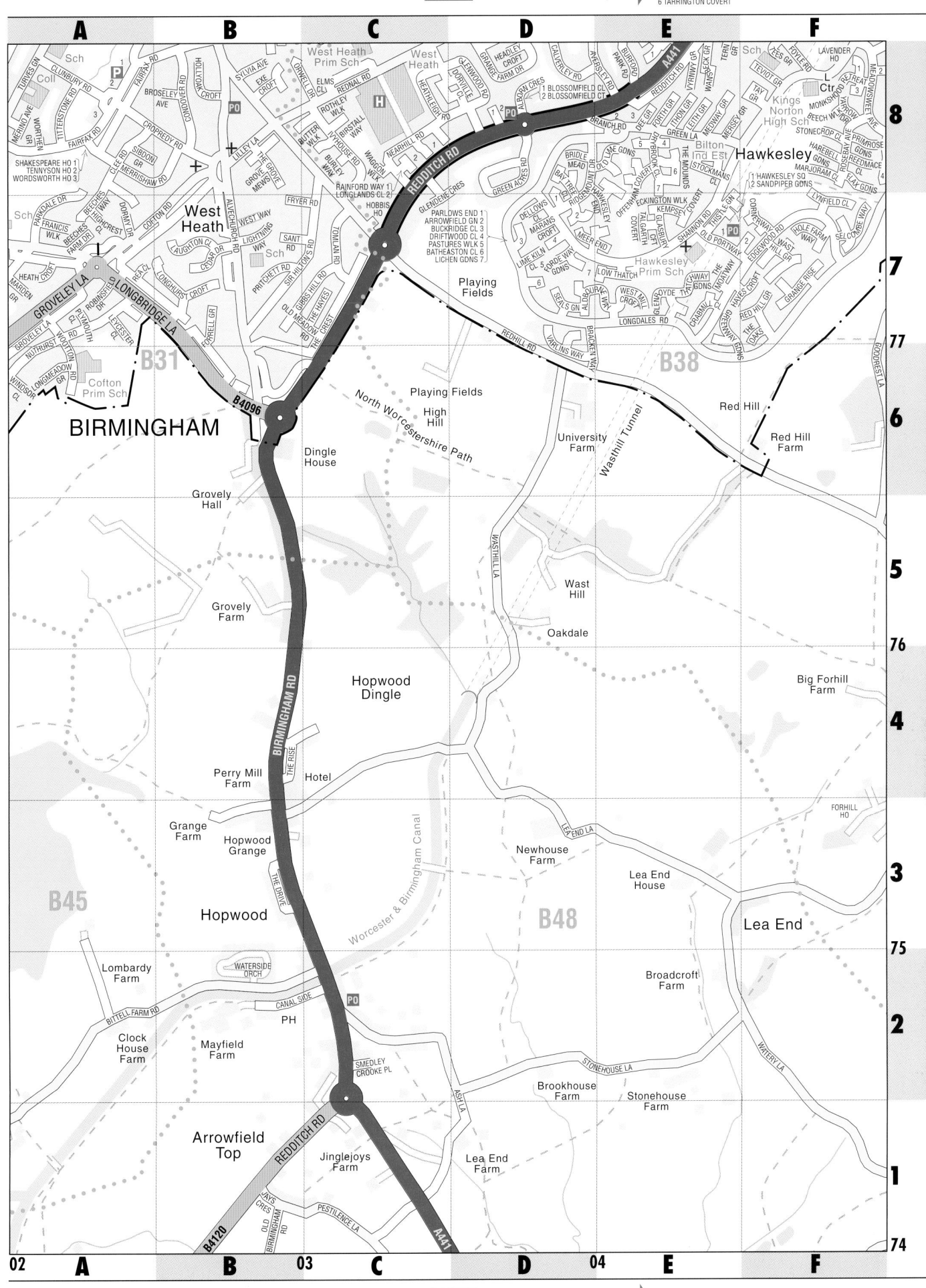

124 →
E8
1 BEECH HURST
2 CAMPION HO
3 SAFFRON HO
4 SEDGEBERROW COVERT
5 LYDBROOK COVERT
6 TARRINGTON COVERT

7 REDBROOK COVERT
F8
1 COWSLIP CL
2 MANITOBA CROFT
3 CAMPION CL
4 WILLMORE CL

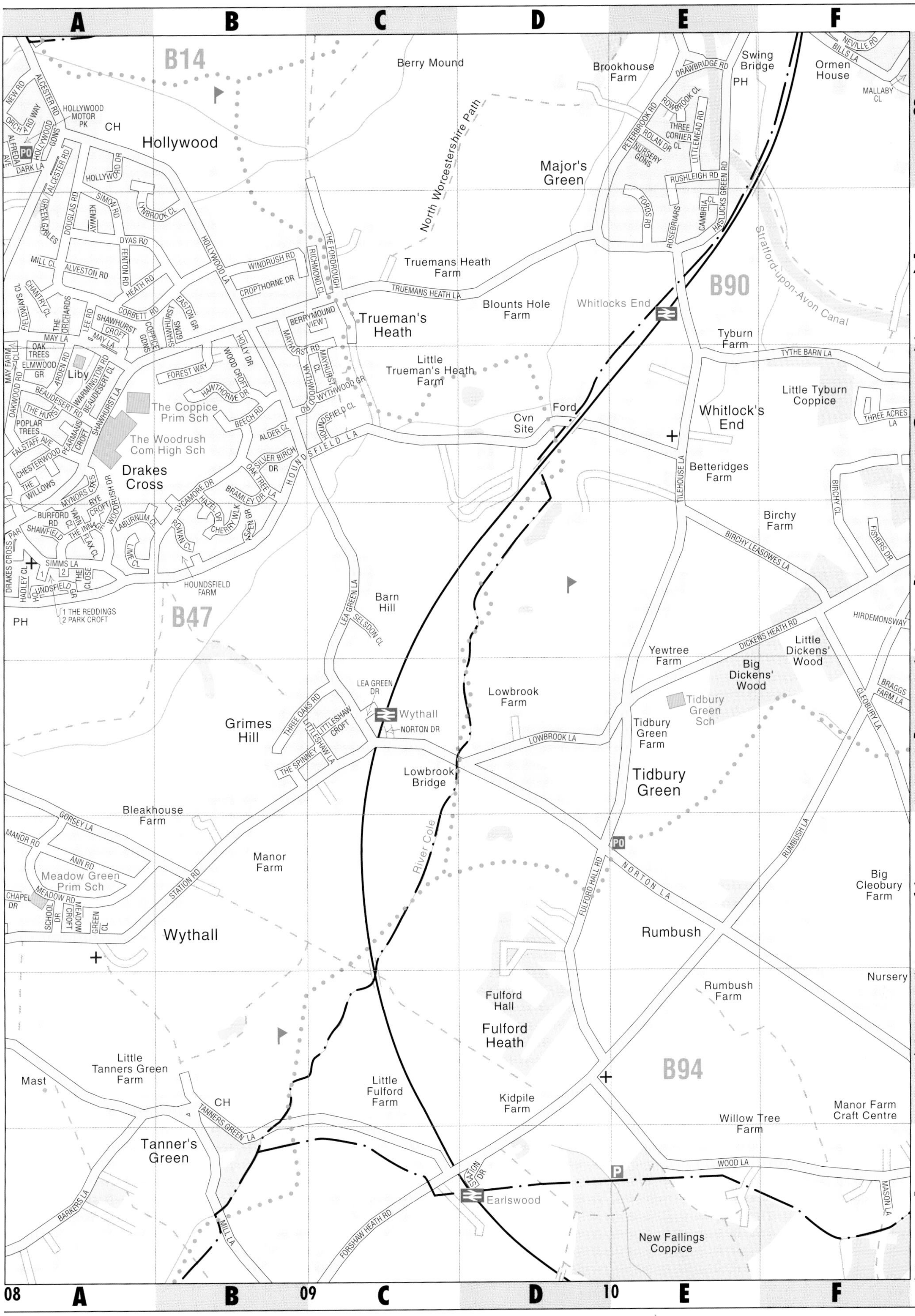

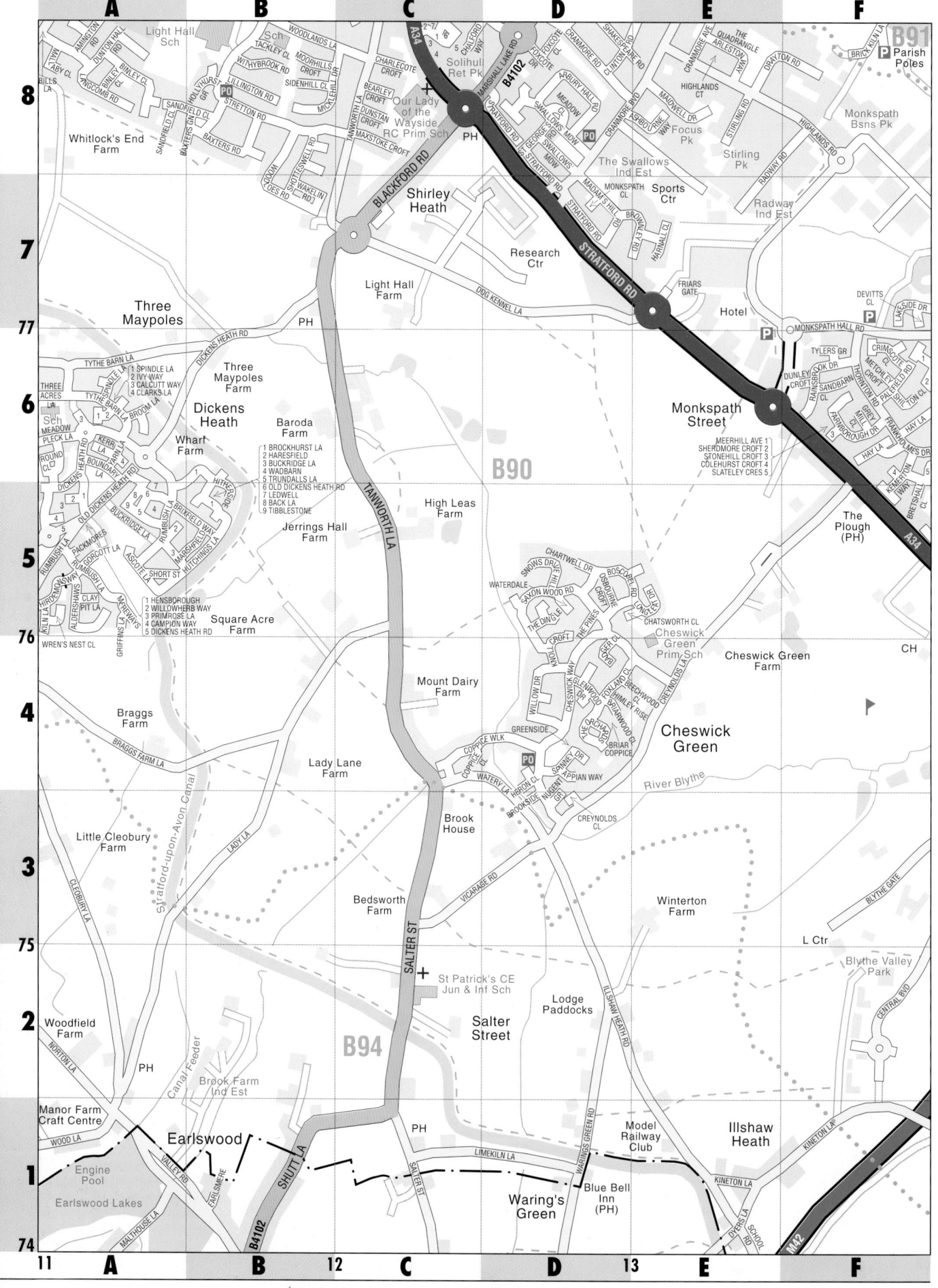

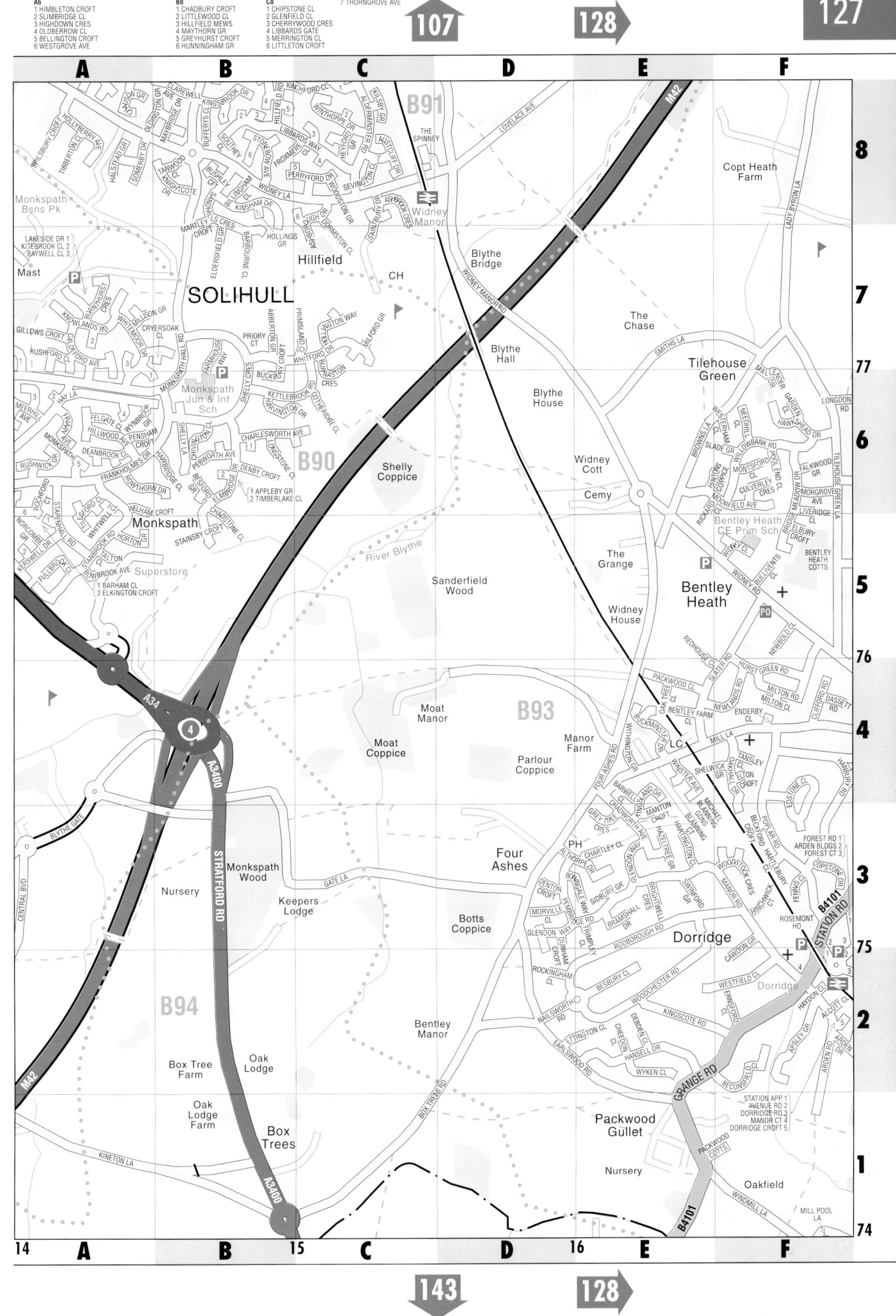

A6
1 HIMBLETON CROFT
2 SLIMBRIDGE CL
3 HIGHDOWN CRES
4 OLDBERROW CL
5 BELLINGTON CROFT
6 WESTGROVE AVE

B8
1 CHADBURY CROFT
2 LITTLEWOOD CL
3 HILLFIELD MEWS
4 MAYTHORN GR
5 GREYHURST CROFT
6 HUNNINGHAM GR

C8
1 CHIPSTONE CL
2 GLENFIELD CL
3 CHERRYWOOD CRES
4 LIBBARDS GATE
5 MERRINGTON CL
6 LITTLETON CROFT

7 THORNGROVE AVE

107   128

SOLIHULL

Hillfield

Monkspath

Monkspath Wood

Box Trees

Shelly Coppice

Sanderfield Wood

Moat Manor

Moat Coppice

Parlour Coppice

Four Ashes

Botts Coppice

Bentley Manor

Widney Manor

Blythe Bridge

Blythe Hall

Blythe House

Widney Cott

Widney House

The Grange

The Chase

Tilehouse Green

Bentley Heath

Dorridge

Packwood Gullet

Oakfield

Copt Heath Farm

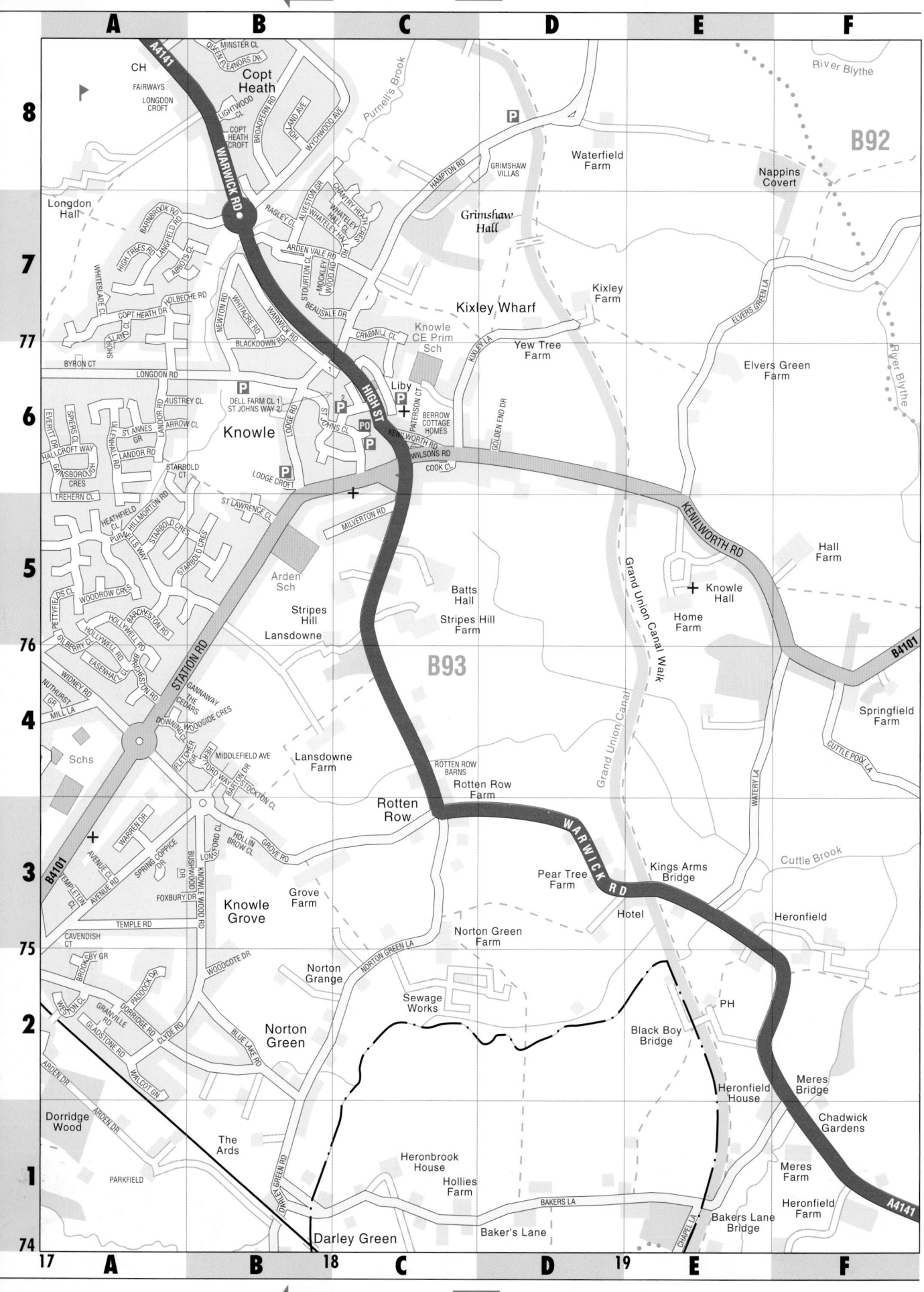

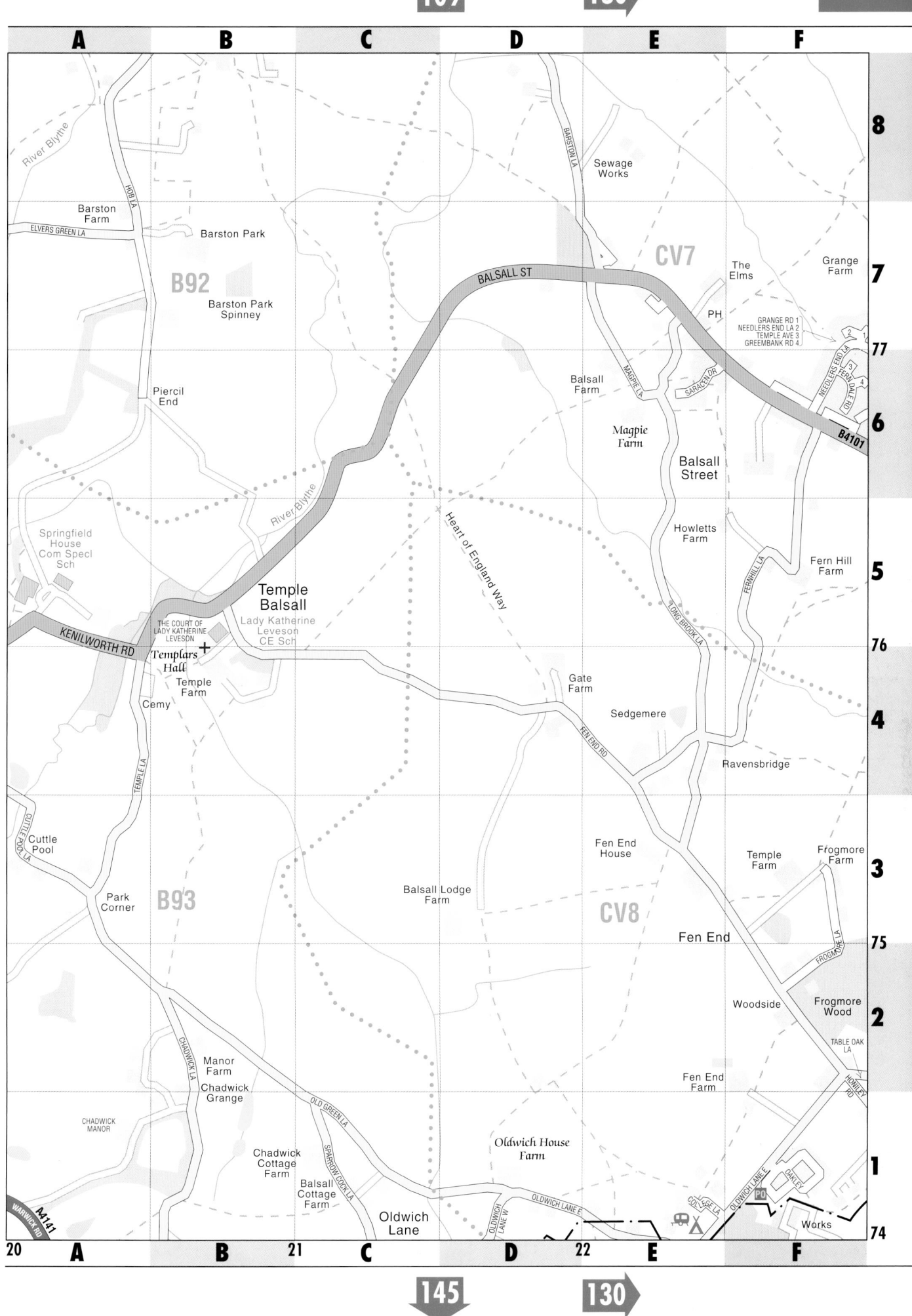

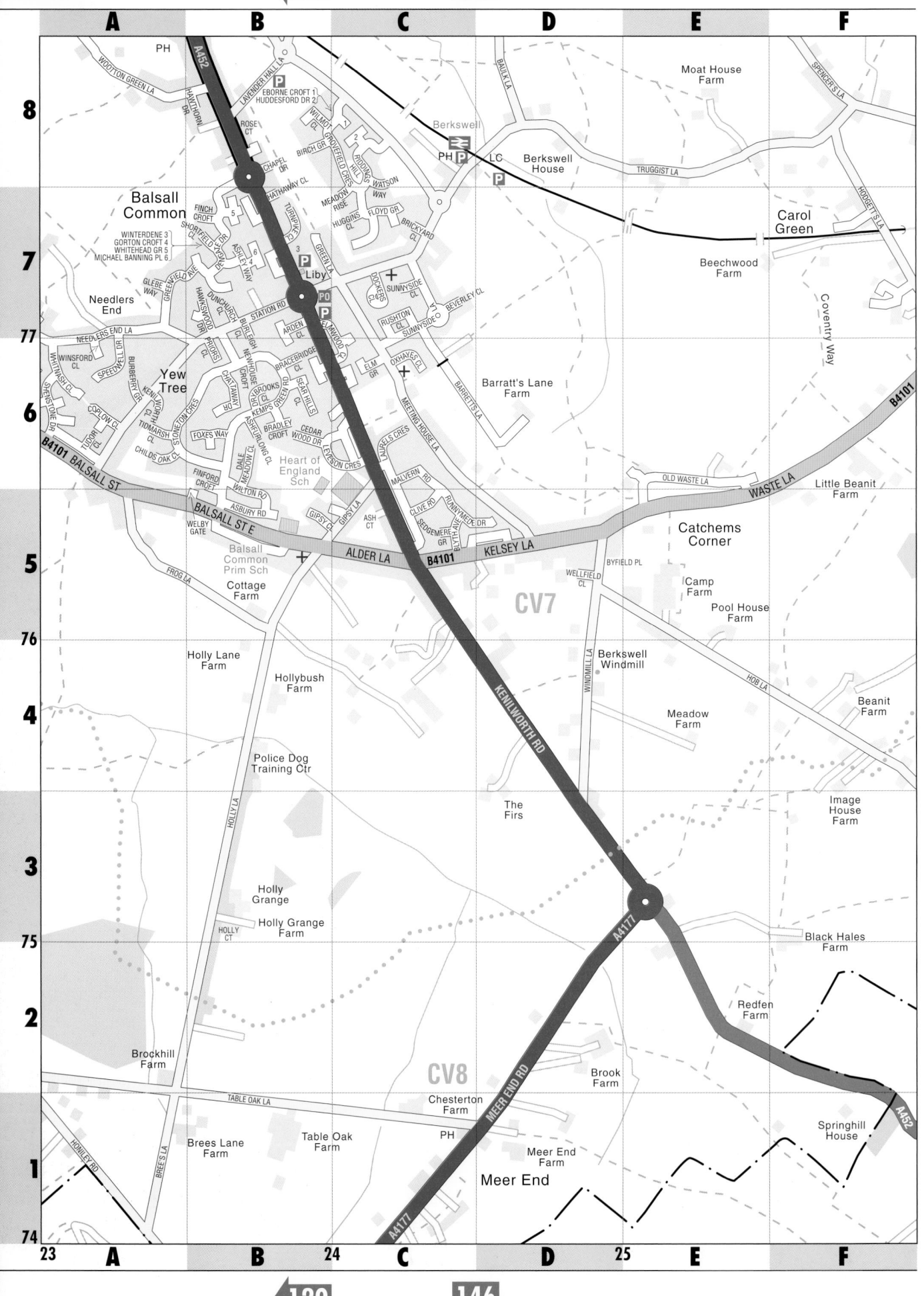

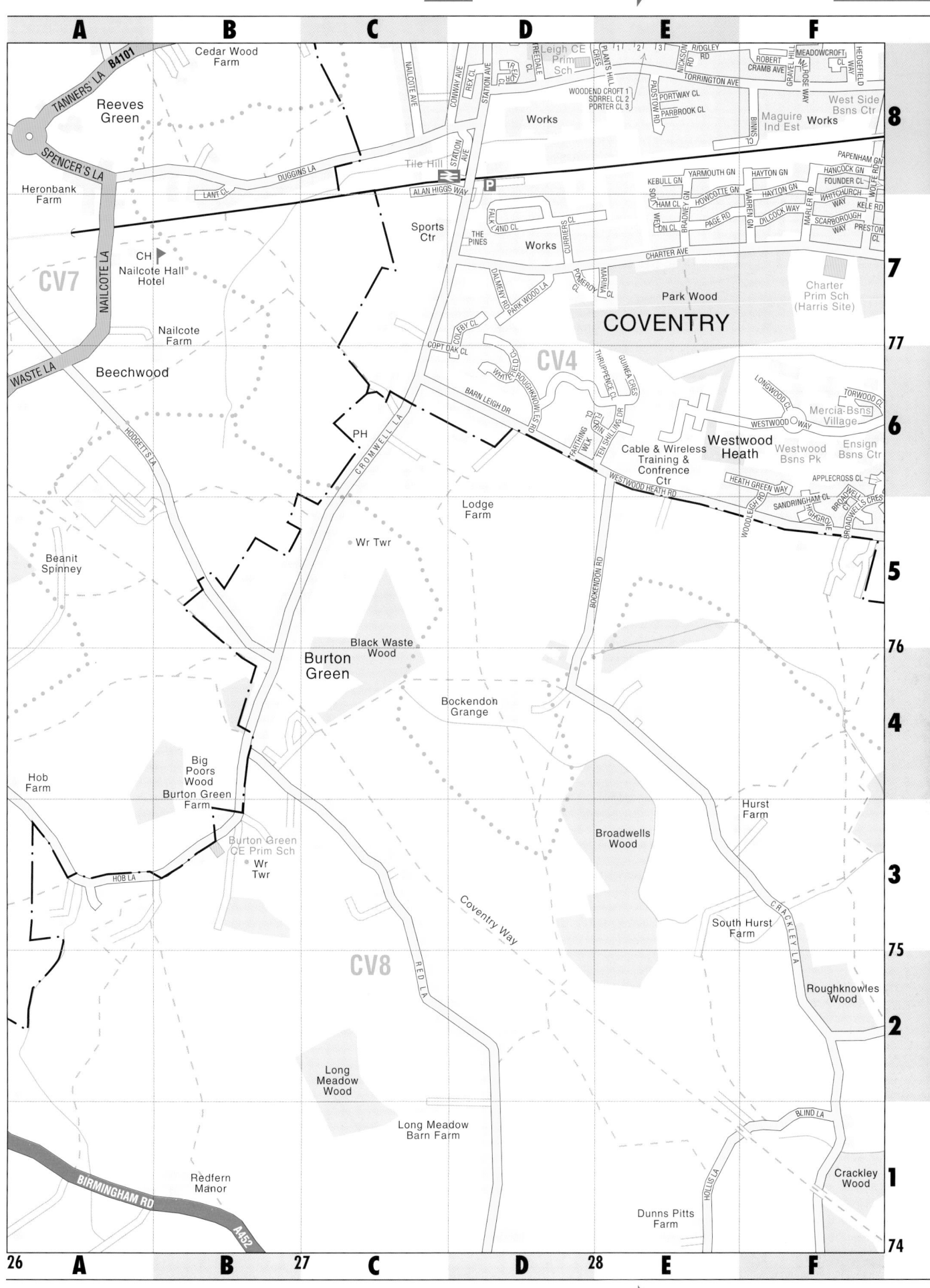

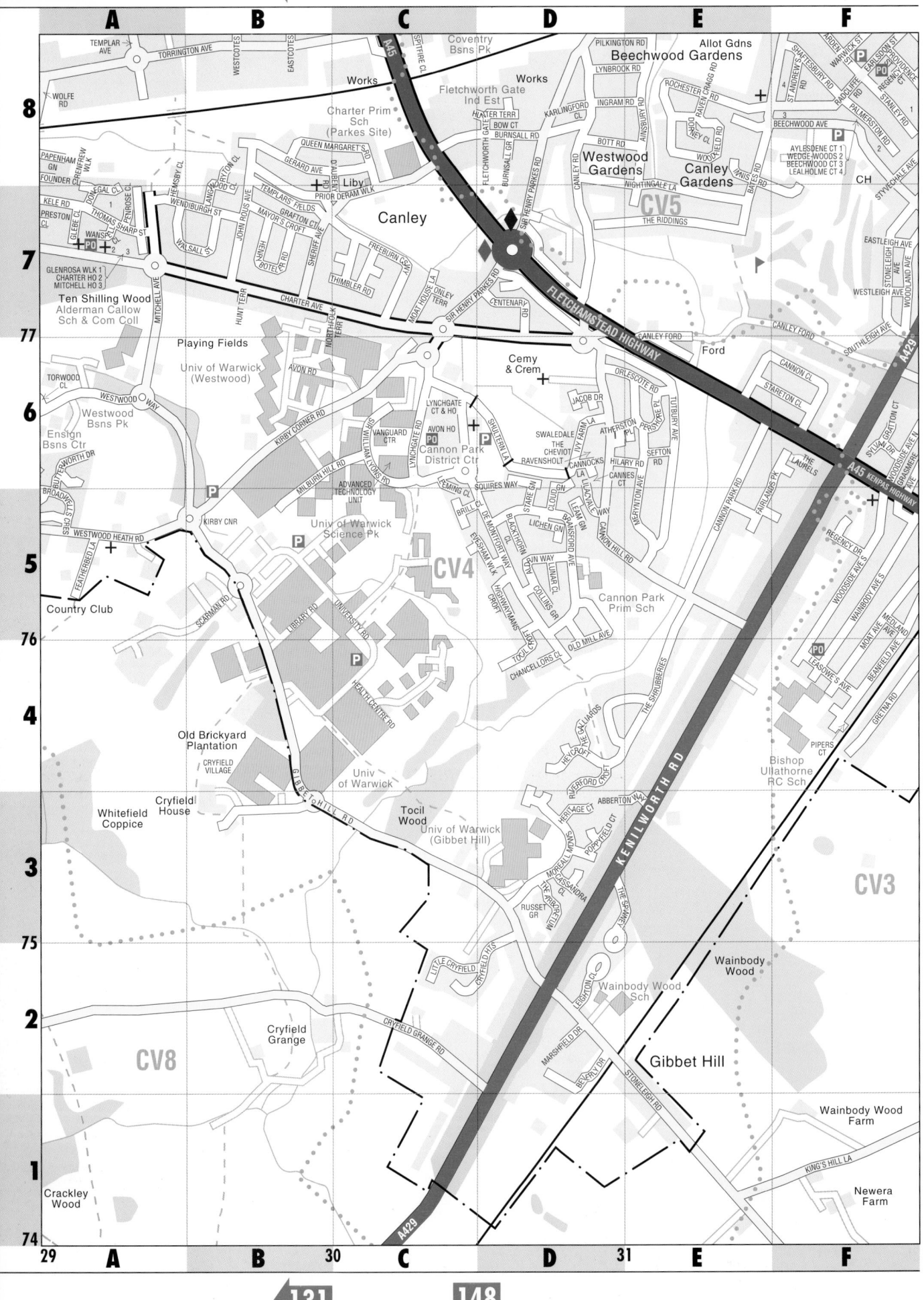

A B C D E F

8
7
77
6
5
76
4
3
75
2
1
74

29 30 31

TEMPLAR AVE
TORRINGTON AVE
WESTCOTES
EASTCOTES
WOLFE RD
Works
Coventry Bsns Pk
Charter Prim Sch (Parkes Site)
Works
Fletchworth Gate Ind Est
PILKINGTON RD
Allot Gdns
Beechwood Gardens
LYNBROOK RD
INGRAM RD
AINSBURY RD
SHAFTESBURY RD
WARWICK ST
ARDEN
EARL SDON ST
PROVIDENCE
ST ANDREW'S RD
RADCLIFF RD
REGENCY CT
STANLEY RD
PALMERSTON RD
STYVECHALE AVE
PAPENHAM GN
ANDREW WLK
CREW
FOUNDER
DALBENY
GERARD AVE
PRIOR DERAM WLK
QUEEN MARGARET'S D
TEMPLARS FIELDS
HUNTER TERR
BOW CT
BURNSALL RD
FLETCHWORTH GATE
BURNSALL RD
KARLINGFORD CL
BOTT RD
CANLEY RD
NIGHTINGALE LA
ROCHESTER RD
RAVEN CRAGG RD
WOODFIELD RD
WEDGE WOODS 2
BEECHWOOD CT 3
LEALHOLME CT 4
AYLESDENE CT 1
BEECHWOOD AVE
CH
Liby
Canley
Westwood Gardens
Canley Gardens
CV5
THE RIDDINGS
EASTLEIGH AVE
STONELEIGH AVE
WOODLAND AVE
WESTLEIGH AVE
KELE RD
PRESTON CL
GLEBE CL
REGAL CL
PENROSE CL
THOMAS SHARP ST
WANSO
WENDIBURGH ST
WALSALL ST
JOHN ROUS AVE
MAYOR'S CROFT
GRAFTON CT
HENRY
BOTEL
SHERIFF AVE
THIMBLER RD
FREEBURN CSY
MOAT HOUSE LA
ONLEY TERR
CENTENARY RD
SIR HENRY PARKES RD
FLETCHAMSTEAD HIGHWAY
CANLEY FORD
Ford
CANLEY FORD
SOUTHLEIGH AVE
A429
GLENROSA WLK 1
CHARTER HO 2
MITCHELL HO 3
Ten Shilling Wood
Alderman Callow Sch & Com Coll
MITCHELL AVE
HUNT TERR
CHARTER AVE
NORTHFOLK TERR
Playing Fields
Univ of Warwick (Westwood)
AVON RD
KIRBY CORNER RD
Cemy & Crem
ORLESCOTE RD
JACOB DR
ATHERSTON PL
TUTBURY AVE
STARETON CL
CANNON CL
CANNON PARK RD
TORWOOD CL
WESTWOOD WAY
Westwood Bsns Pk
Ensign Bsns Ctr
BUTTERWORTH DR
BROADWELLS CRES
SIR WILLIAM LYONS RD
VANGUARD CTR
LYNCHGATE CT & HO
AVON HO
SHULTERN LA
SWALEDALE
THE CHEVIOT
RAVENSHOLT
IVY FARM LA
PERSHORE PL
SEFTON RD
HILARY RD
CANNES CT
LYCHGATE RD
MILBURN HILL RD
Cannon Park District Ctr
FLEMING CL
SQUIRES WAY
CANNOCKS LA
CANNON PK
THE LAURELS
FAIRLANDS PK
WOODSIDE AVE N
GROSMERE AVE
A45 KENPAS HIGHWAY
FEATHERBED LA
WESTWOOD HEATH RD
KIRBY CNR
ADVANCED TECHNOLOGY UNIT
Univ of Warwick Science Pk
BRILL CL
DE MONTFORT WAY
EVESHAM WLK
BLACKTHORN CL
STARE GN
CLOUD GN
LICHEN GN
STANSFORD AVE
LEAM GN
LILAC AVE
CANNON HILL RD
Cannon Park Prim Sch
REGENCY DR
WOODSIDE AVE S
WAINBODY AVE N
MEDLAND AVE
MOAT AVE
BEANFIELD AVE
CV4
SCARMAN RD
LIBRARY RD
UNIVERSITY RD
HEALTH CENTRE RD
AN WAY
LUNAR CL
COLLINS GR
OLD MILL AVE
TOCIL CROFT
HIGHWAYMANS CROFT
CHANCELLORS CL
Country Club
PIPERS CT
WAINBODY AVE S
MEDINA
GRETNA RD
LEASOWES AVE
P0
Old Brickyard Plantation
CRYFIELD VILLAGE
Cryfield House
Whitefield Coppice
GIBBET HILL RD
Univ of Warwick
Tocil Wood
Univ of Warwick (Gibbet Hill)
HELCROFT
RIVERFORD CROFT
ABBERTON WAY
HERITAGE CT
POPPYFIELD CT
THE SHRUBBERIES
KENILWORTH RD
Bishop Ullathorne RC Sch
CV3
MOREALL MDWS
CASSANDRA
THE ABERATION
RUSSET GR
THE SOWREY
LITTLE CRYFIELD
CRYFIELD HTS
LEIGHTON CL
Wainbody Wood Sch
Wainbody Wood
CV8
Cryfield Grange
CRYFIELD GRANGE RD
MARSHFIELD DR
BEVERLY DR
STONELEIGH RD
Gibbet Hill
Wainbody Wood Farm
KING'S HILL LA
Crackley Wood
A429
Newera Farm

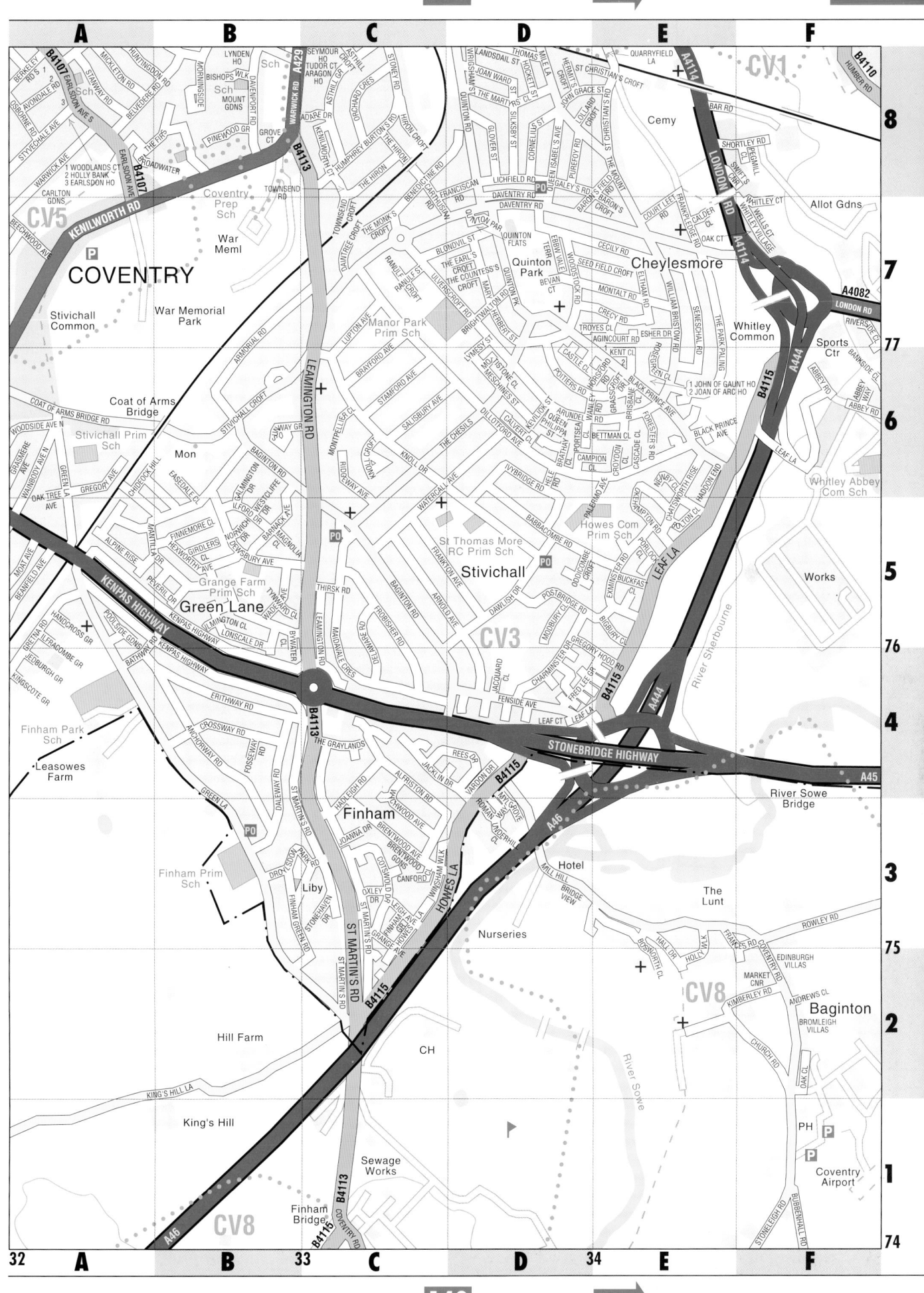

F8
1 CARDALE CROFT
2 KESTREL CROFT
3 RUTLAND CROFT
4 JIM FORREST CL
5 WILLOWHERB CL
6 WASPERTON CL
7 JOE WILLIAMS CL
8 DEERDALE TERR

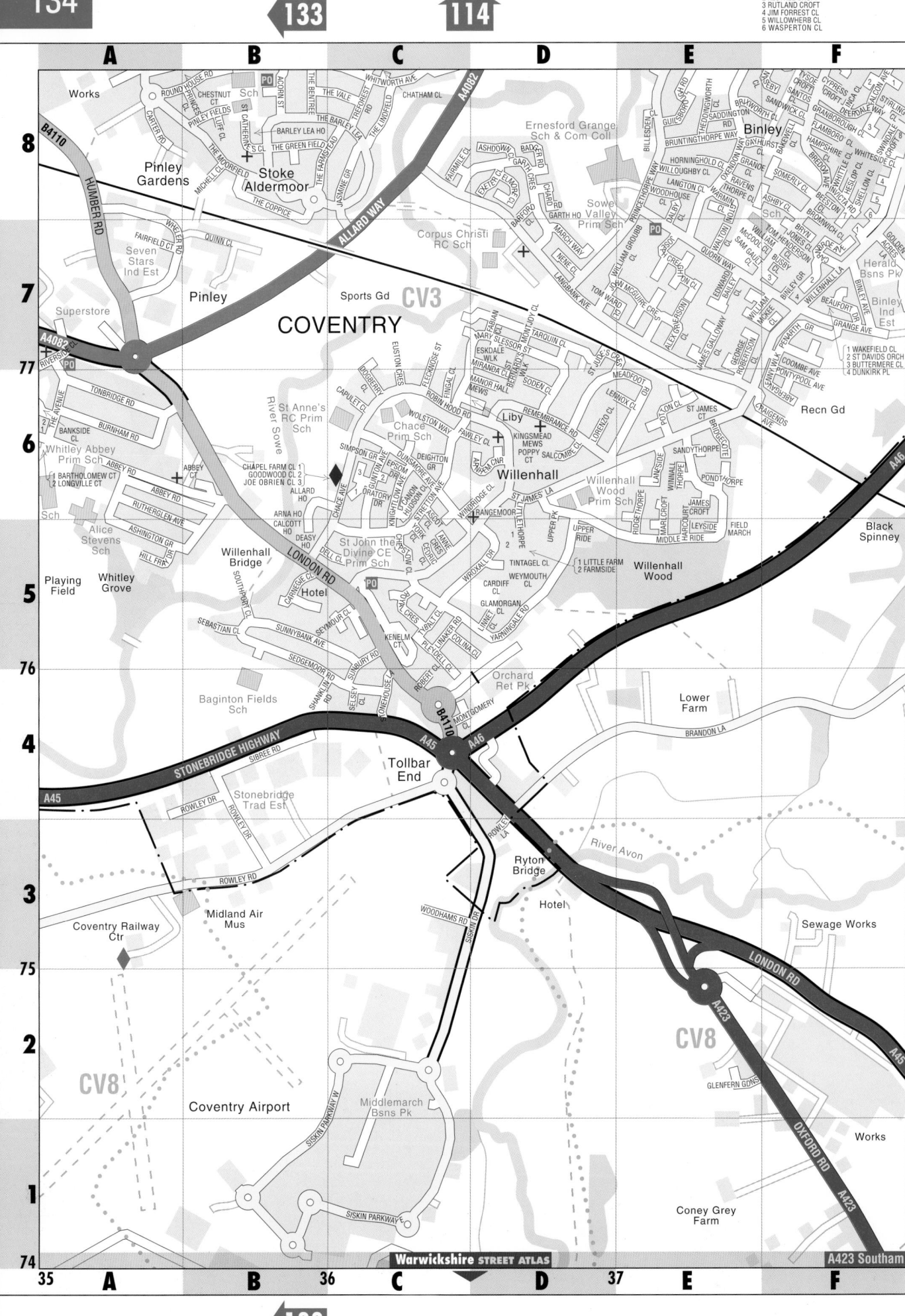

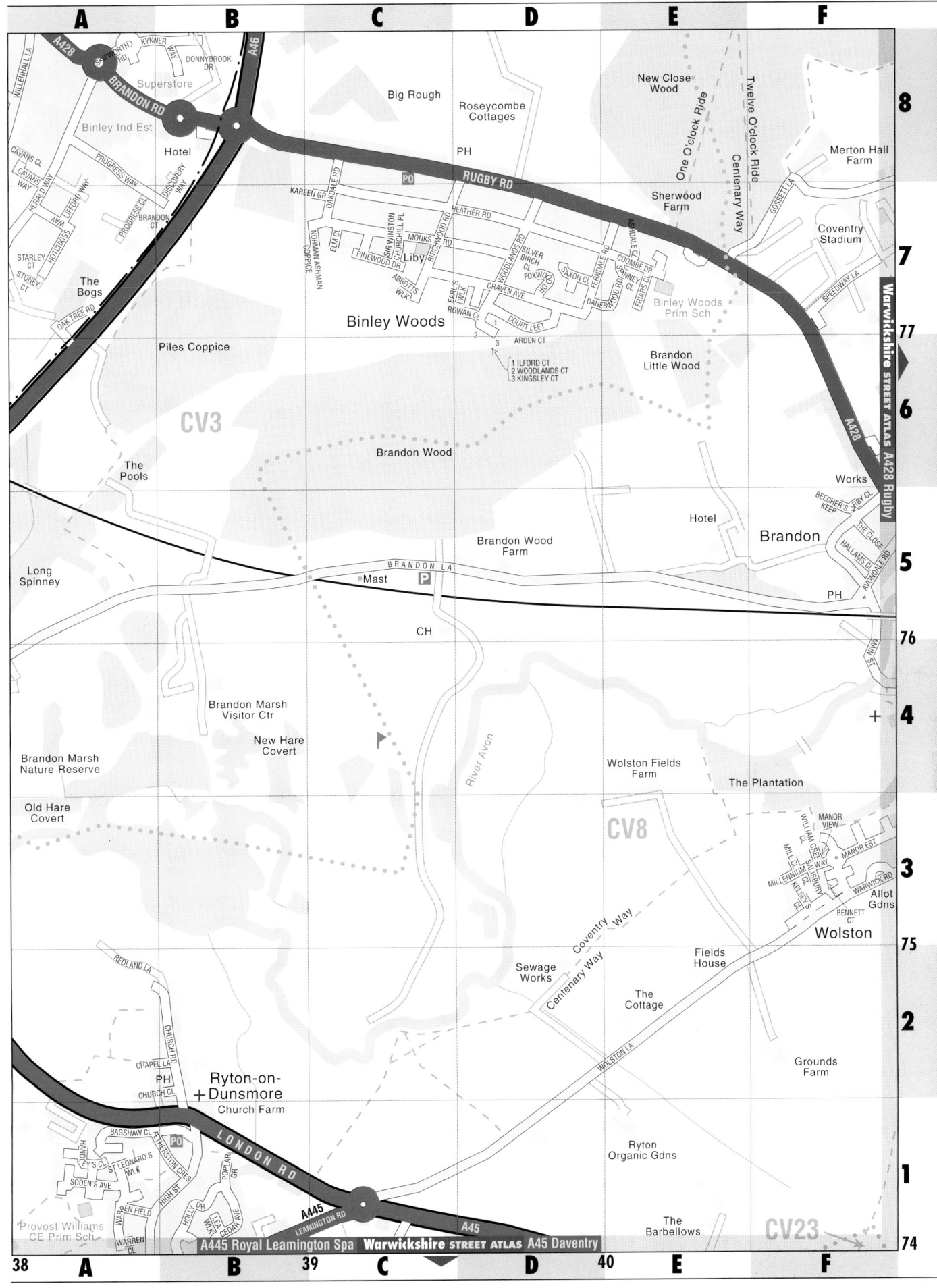

A B C D E F

8

7

77

6

5

76

4

75

3

2

1

74

Warwickshire STREET ATLAS A428 Rugby

A428

A46

BRANDON RD

Superstore

Hotel

Binley Ind Est

(WORTH)

KYNNER WAY

DONNYBROOK DR

CAVANS CL

CAVANS WAY

HERALD WAY

LIFFORD WAY

HOTCHKISS

PROGRESS WAY

PROGRESS CL

BRANDON CT

STARLEY CT

STONEY CT

The Bogs

OAK TREE RD

DISCOVERY WAY

Big Rough

Roseycombe Cottages

PH

PO

RUGBY RD

KAREEN GR

OAKDALE RD

ELM CL

NORMAN ASHMAN COPPICE

PINEWOOD CL

SIR WINSTON CHURCHILL PL

MONKS RD

BIRCHWOOD RD

HEATHER RD

ABBOTTS WLK

EARL'S WLK

ROWAN CL

CRAVEN AVE

WOODLANDS RD

SILVER BIRCH

FOXWOOD RD

COURT LEET

ARDEN CT

1
2
3

Liby

Binley Woods

DANES WOOD RD

SAXON CL

COOMBE DR

TRIARS CL

SPINNEY CL

FERNDALE RD

ASHDALE CL

1 ILFORD CT
2 WOODLANDS CT
3 KINGSLEY CT

New Close Wood

One O'clock Ride

Twelve O'clock Ride

Centenary Way

Sherwood Farm

Binley Woods Prim Sch

Merton Hall Farm

GOSSETT LA

Coventry Stadium

SPEEDWAY LA

Piles Coppice

CV3

Brandon Little Wood

A428

Brandon Wood

The Pools

Works

BEECHER'S KEEP

FBY CL

THE CLOSE

HALLAMS CL

AVONDALE RD

Hotel

Brandon

Long Spinney

BRANDON LA

Mast

P

Brandon Wood Farm

PH

MAIN ST

CH

Brandon Marsh Visitor Ctr

New Hare Covert

River Avon

Wolston Fields Farm

The Plantation

Brandon Marsh Nature Reserve

Old Hare Covert

CV8

MANOR VIEW

WILLIAM BREE RD

SALISBURY CL

MILLENNIUM WAY

KELSEY'S

MILL CL

MANOR EST

WARWICK RD

Allot Gdns

BENNETT CT

Wolston

Coventry Way

Centenary Way

Sewage Works

Fields House

The Cottage

Grounds Farm

REDLAND LA

CHURCH RD

CHAPEL LA

PH

CHURCH CL

Ryton-on-Dunsmore

Church Farm

WOLSTON LA

Ryton Organic Gdns

BAGSHAW CL

PO

PETHERSTON CRES

LONDON RD

HANDLEY'S CL

ST LEONARD'S WLK

SODEN'S AVE

WARREN FIELD

POPLAR GR

HIGH ST

HOLLY DR

CEDAR AVE

WARREN CL

Provost Williams CE Prim Sch

A445

LEAMINGTON RD

A45

The Barbellows

CV23

A445 Royal Leamington Spa Warwickshire STREET ATLAS A45 Daventry

38 A 39 B C 40 D E F

38 A B 39 C D 40 E F

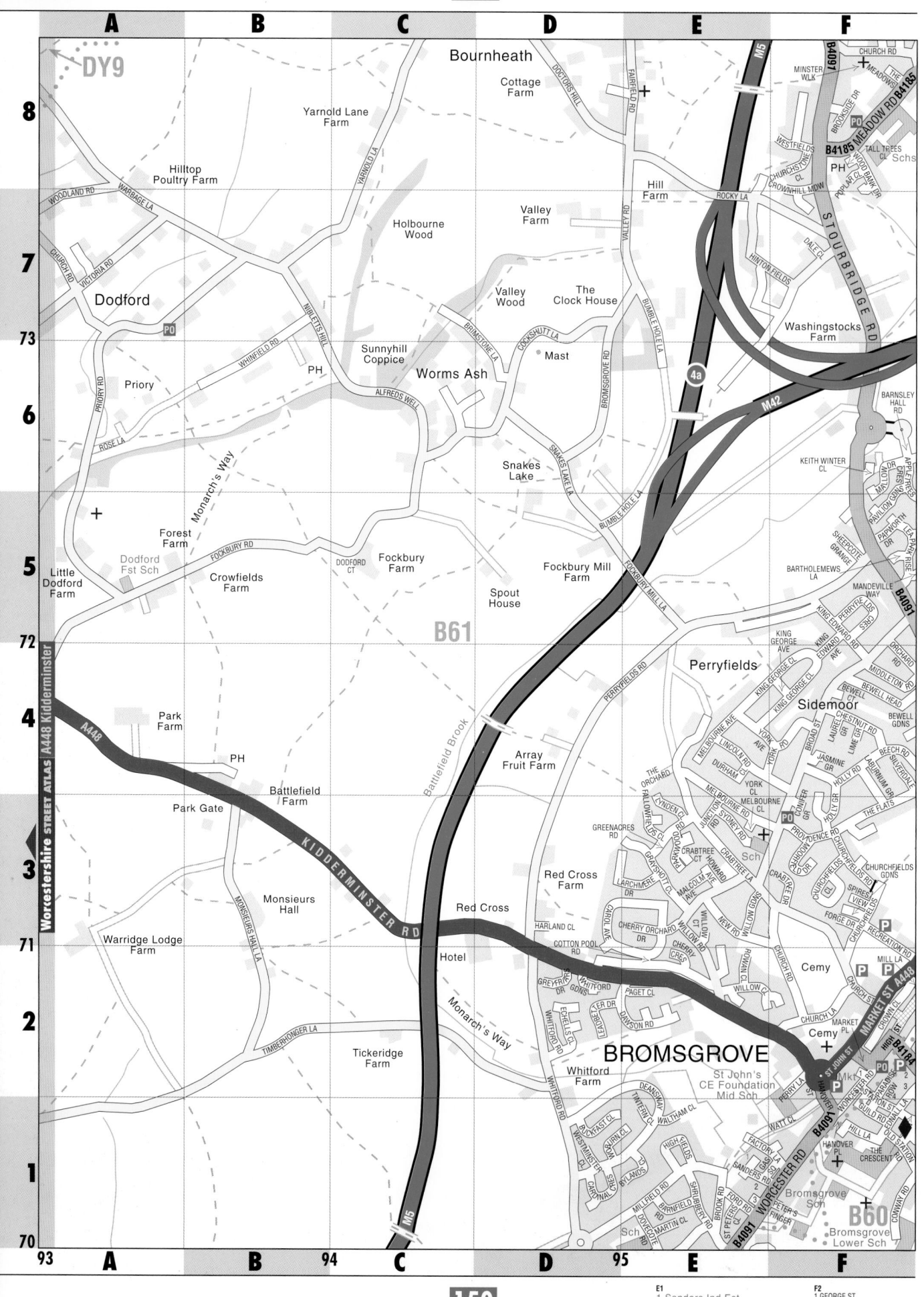

E1
1 Sanders Ind Est
2 WESTBOURNE TERR
3 WESTBOURNE CL

F2
1 GEORGE ST
2 ELGAR MEWS
3 NAILERS CT
4 GUILD CT

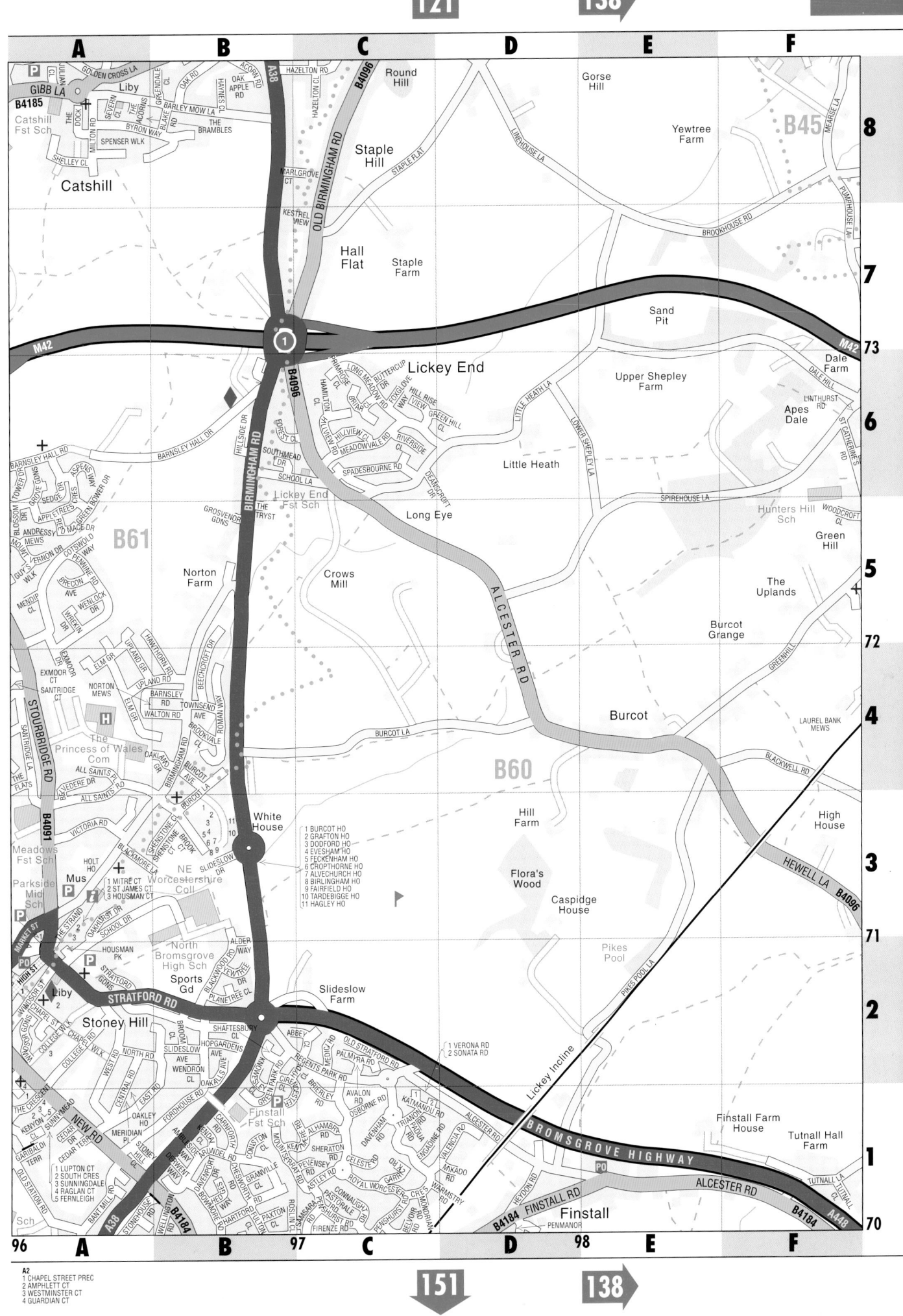

A2
1 CHAPEL STREET PREC
2 AMPHLETT CT
3 WESTMINSTER CT
4 GUARDIAN CT

137
122

A	B	C	D	E	F

8

PLYMOUTH DR 1
GORSE MEADOW DR 2

WOOD END DR
PLYMOUTH RD
THE HAVEN
TWATLING RD

WOODSIDE DR
SHEPLEY MDW

Brook House

WILLOW TREE DR 1
ROSE TERR 2
COACH COTTS 3
VICTORIA MEWS 4

Barnt Green

B4120
PENZER DR
LAUREL GDNS
BITTELL RD

BITTELL RD
B4120

GREENBANK
POPLAR DR
ORCHARD CROFT
St Andrew's CE Fst Sch

CHERRY HILL RD
CHERRY GR
BROOKWOOD DR
BEECH PARK DR
OAKMORE DR
CHERRY HILL AVE

Fiery Hill

CHERRY HILL RD
FIERY HILL RD

STATION APP
HEWELL RD
PO
SANDHILLS RD
BITTELL LA

The Paddocks

BROOKHOUSE RD
SHEPLEY RD

Barnt Green

ROSEWOOD DR

B45

HEWELL LA

SANDHILLS LA

7

BILLY LA

LINTHURST RD

Linthurst Court

THE LONGLANDS

SANDHILLS GN

Sandhills Farm

AQUEDUCT LA
M42

73

PIKE HILL
M42

COOPERS HILL

Uplands

6

PIKE HILL

THE AVENUE

Linthurst
Linthurst Fst Sch

Masts

High Croft

LOCK KEEPERS REACH
BIRCHES LA

Withybed Green

REAR COTTS
FRONT COTTS
WITHYBED LA
P
FORWARD COTTS

ST CATHERINES CL
THE GLEN
BADGERS WAY
FOXES CL
TANGLEWOOD CL
Blackwell
LINTHURST NEWTOWN

Foxhill BARNS

B48

5

ST CATHERINE'S RD
PO
KIMBOLTON DR
CORNEL GDNS
GLENEAGLES DR
BIRKDALE AVE
FAIRWAYS DR
WENTWORTH DR
STATION RD

Foxhill House

FOXHILL LA

Gorsey Lane Farm

SCARFIELD HILL

Scarfields Farm

72

STATION COTTS
CH

AGMORE RD

BLACKWELL RD

Wheeley Farm

WHEELEY RD

COBLEY HILL

Scarfields Dingle

4

Blackwell Court

Cobley Hill

3

B60

Vigo

HOLLOWTREE LA

Hollow Tree Farm

Cattespool

Mast
Cobley Hill Farm

Andrew's Coppice

GRANGE LA

71

B4096

Robin Hill Farm

AGMORE LA

STONEY LA

Stoney Lane Farm

Sunny Bank Farm

2

HEWELL LA

Stoney Lane Cottage

Worcester & Birmingham Canal

Shortwood Rough Grounds

The Lower House

WHARF LA

Tunnel

Little Shortwood

1

TUTNALL LA
TUTNALL GRANGE

H
Bromsgrove Private

Broad Green

Works

Oxleasows Farm

B97

70

B4096
BROCKHILL LA

99	A		00	B	C		D	01	E		F

137
152

123
140

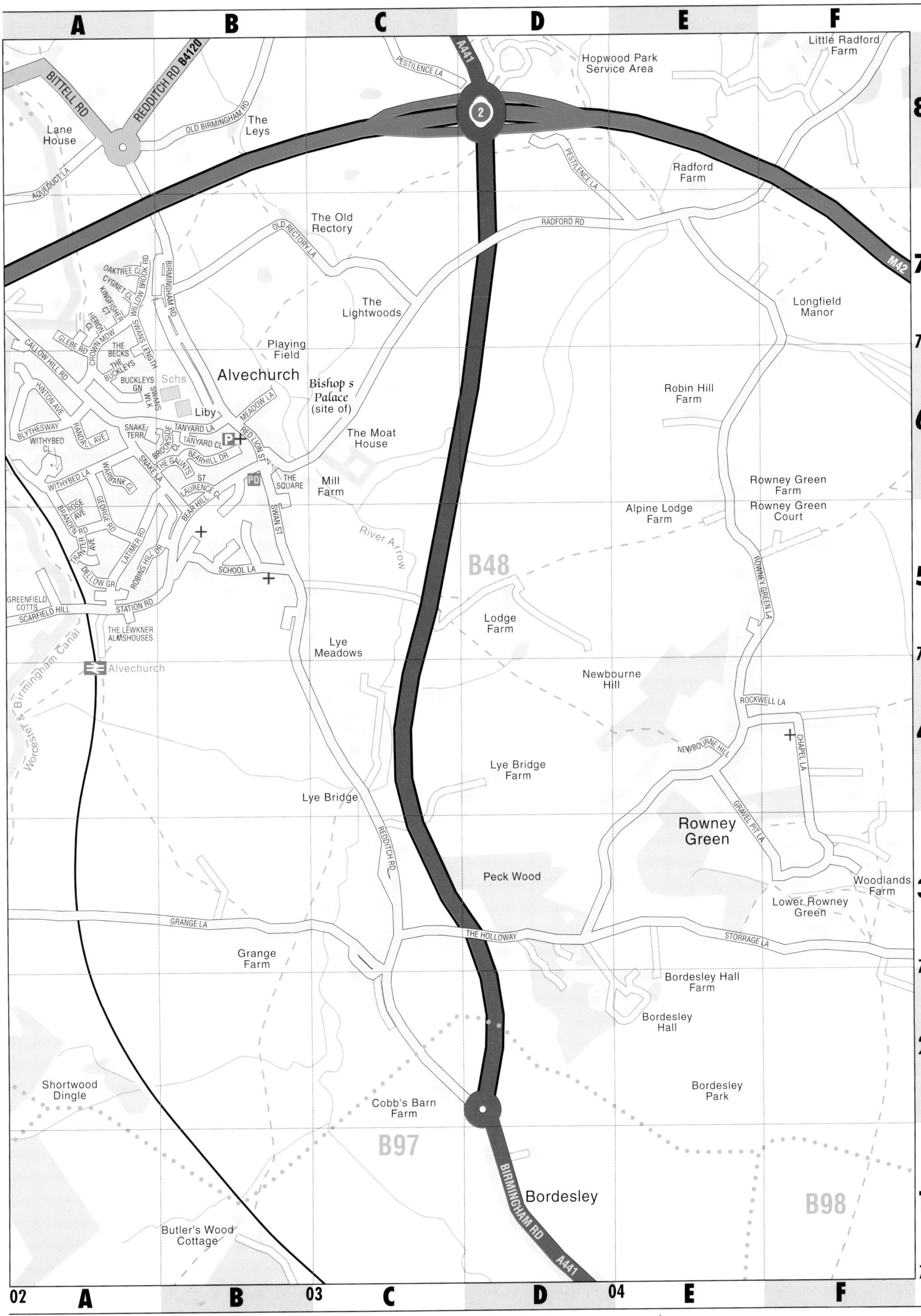

A   B   C   D   E   F

8
7
73
6
5
72
4
3
71
2
1
70

BITTELL RD
REDDITCH RD B4120
Lane House
AQUEDUCT LA
OLD BIRMINGHAM RD
The Leys

PESTILENCE LA
A441
2
Hopwood Park Service Area
Little Radford Farm

PESTILENCE LA
Radford Farm

RADFORD RD

M42

Longfield Manor

OLD RECTORY LA
The Old Rectory

The Lightwoods

OAKTREE CL
CYGNET CL
KINGFISHER CT
HERON CL
WILLOW BROOK RD
BIRMINGHAM RD
SWANS LENGTH
Schs
GLEBE RD
CALLOW HILL RD
CROWN MDW
THE BECKS
THE BUCKLEYS
BUCKLEYS GN
SWANS WLK
Alvechurch
Liby

HINTON AVE
BLYTHESWAY
RANDLE AVE
WITHYBED CL
SNAKE TERR
JUBILEE RD
BROOK LA
TANYARD LA
MEADOW LA
P
TANYARD CL
RED LION ST
Bishop's Palace (site of)

Robin Hill Farm

ROBIN HILL DR

Rowney Green Farm
Rowney Green Court

ROWNEY GREEN LA

Alpine Lodge Farm

Playing Field

The Moat House

WITHYBED LA
WARBANK CL
ROSE AVE
BRANDEN RD
TRATFER AVE
GEORGE RD
LATIMER RD
DELLOW GR
PO
ST LAURENCE CL
BEAR HILL LA
BEAR HILL DR
THE GAUNTS
THE SQUARE
ST LAURENCE
SNAKE LA
SWAN ST
SCHOOL LA

Mill Farm
River Arrow

B48

Newbourne Hill

ROCKWELL LA

GREENFIELD COTTS
SCARFIELD HILL
STATION RD
THE LEWKNER ALMSHOUSES
Alvechurch

Lye Meadows

Lodge Farm

CHAPEL LA
NEWBOURNE HILL

Worcester & Birmingham Canal

Lye Bridge

Lye Bridge Farm

Rowney Green

GRAVEL PIT LA

Woodlands Farm

REDDITCH RD

Peck Wood

Lower Rowney Green

GRANGE LA

THE HOLLOWAY

STORRAGE LA

Grange Farm

Bordesley Hall Farm

Bordesley Hall

Shortwood Dingle

Cobb's Barn Farm

B97

BIRMINGHAM RD

Bordesley Park

Bordesley

B98

Butler's Wood Cottage

A441

153
140

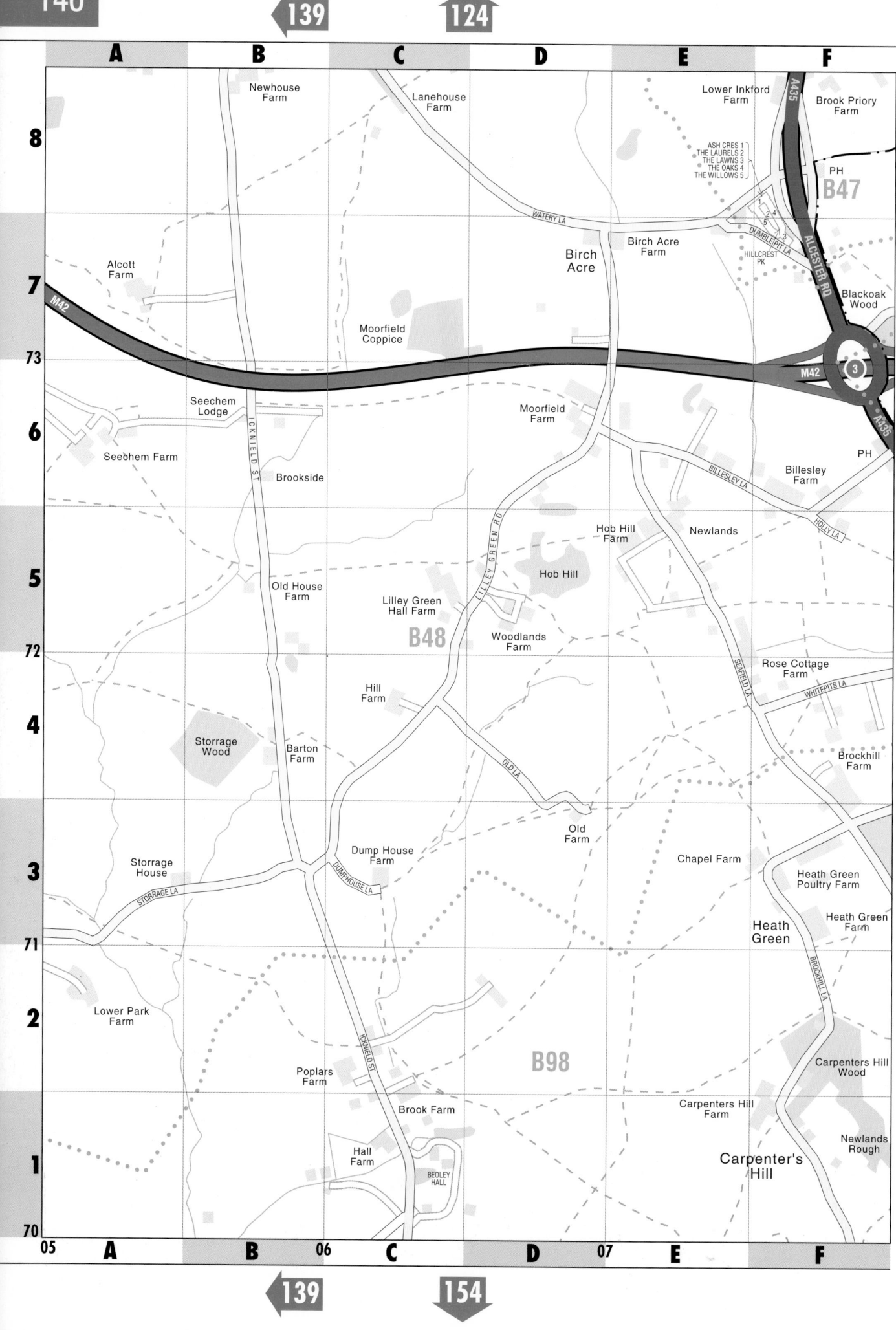

139
124

A   **B**   **C**   **D**   **E**   **F**

8

Newhouse Farm

Lanehouse Farm

Lower Inkford Farm

Brook Priory Farm

A435

ASH CRES 1
THE LAURELS 2
THE LAWNS 3
THE OAKS 4
THE WILLOWS 5

PH

B47

WATERY LA

Birch Acre Farm

DUMBLEPIT LA

HILLCREST PK

ALCESTER RD

Alcott Farm

Birch Acre

7

M42

Blackoak Wood

Moorfield Coppice

73

M42

3

A435

Seechem Lodge

Moorfield Farm

6

Seechem Farm

ICKNIELD ST

Brookside

BILLESLEY LA

Billesley Farm

PH

HOLLY LA

Hob Hill Farm

Newlands

5

Old House Farm

LILLEY GREEN RD

Hob Hill

Lilley Green Hall Farm

B48

Woodlands Farm

72

SEAFIELD LA

Rose Cottage Farm

WHITEPITS LA

Hill Farm

4

Storrage Wood

Barton Farm

OLD LA

Brockhill Farm

3

Storrage House

Dump House Farm

DUMPHOUSE LA

Old Farm

Chapel Farm

Heath Green Poultry Farm

STORRAGE LA

Heath Green Farm

71

Heath Green

BROOKHILL LA

2

Lower Park Farm

B98

Carpenters Hill Wood

ICKNIELD ST

Poplars Farm

Carpenters Hill Farm

Newlands Rough

Brook Farm

1

Hall Farm

BEOLEY HALL

Carpenter's Hill

70

139
154

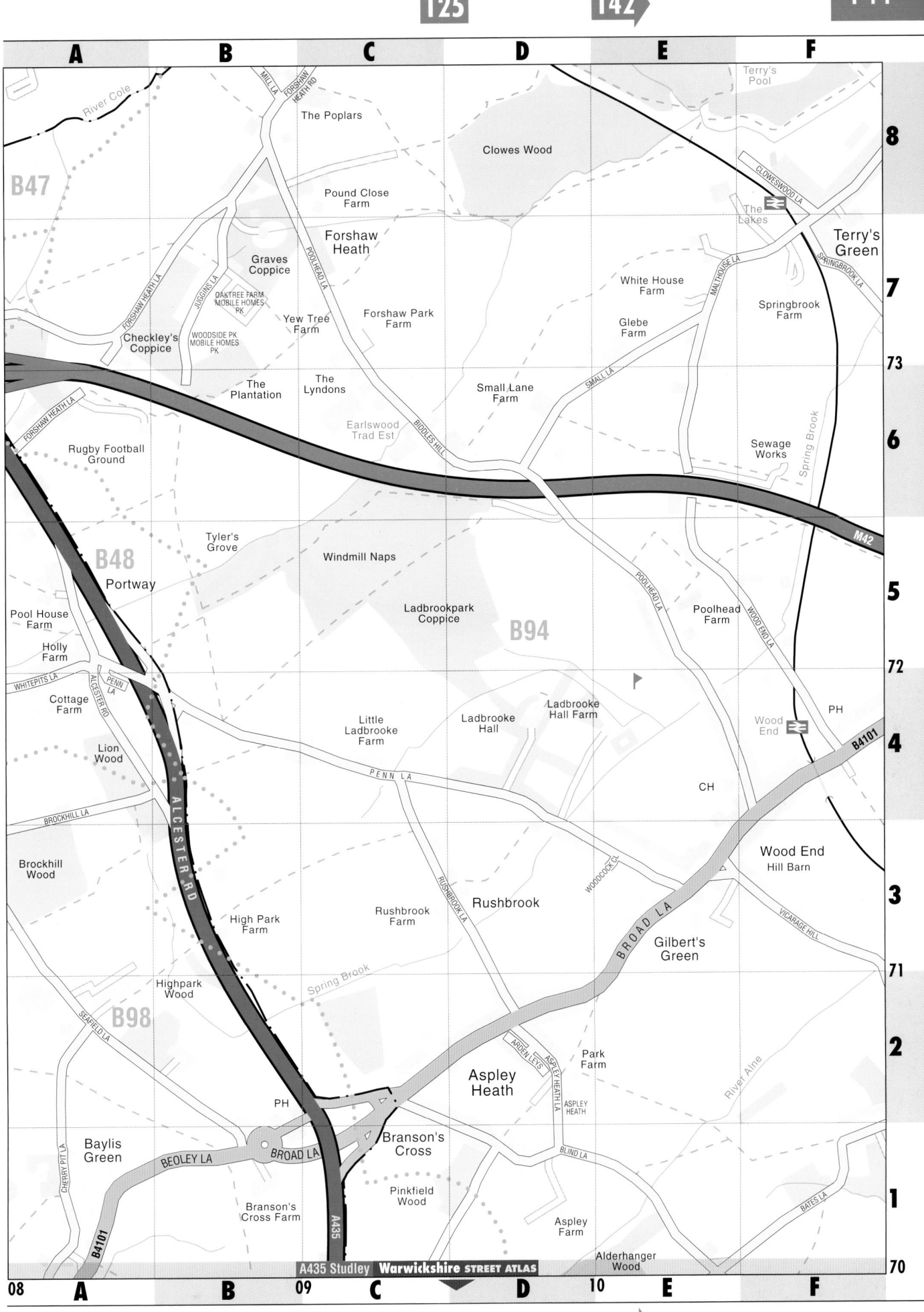

A B C D E F

8

7

73

6

5

72

4

3

71

2

1

70

B47

River Cole

The Poplars

Clowes Wood

Terry's Pool

The Lakes

CLOWESWOOD LA

Terry's Green

MILL LA

FORSHAW HEATH RD

Pound Close Farm

Forshaw Heath

Graves Coppice

POOLHEAD LA

FORSHAW HEATH LA

JUGGINS LA

OAKTREE FARM MOBILE HOMES PK

Yew Tree Farm

Forshaw Park Farm

White House Farm

MALTHOUSE LA

Springbrook Farm

SPRINGBROOK LA

Checkley's Coppice

WOODSIDE PK MOBILE HOMES PK

The Plantation

The Lyndons

Earlswood Trad Est

BIDDLES HILL

Small Lane Farm

Glebe Farm

SMALL LA

Spring Brook

Sewage Works

B48

Portway

Rugby Football Ground

Tyler's Grove

Windmill Naps

Ladbrookpark Coppice

B94

Poolhead Farm

POOL HEAD LA

WOOD END LA

M42

Pool House Farm

Holly Farm

WHITEPITS LA

PENN LA

ALCESTER RD

Cottage Farm

BROCKHILL LA

Lion Wood

Little Ladbrooke Farm

Ladbrooke Hall

Ladbrooke Hall Farm

PENN LA

CH

Wood End

PH

B4101

Brockhill Wood

High Park Farm

Rushbrook Farm

RUSHBROOK LA

Rushbrook

WOODCOCK CL

BROAD LA

Gilbert's Green

Wood End

Hill Barn

VICARAGE HILL

Highpark Wood

Spring Brook

B98

SEAFIELD LA

PH

Baylis Green

CHERRY PIT LA

BEOLEY LA

BROAD LA

Branson's Cross

ARDEN LEYS

Aspley Heath

ASPLEY HEATH LA

Park Farm

River A025

Branson's Cross Farm

A435

Pinkfield Wood

BLIND LA

Aspley Farm

Alderhanger Wood

BATES LA

B4101

8

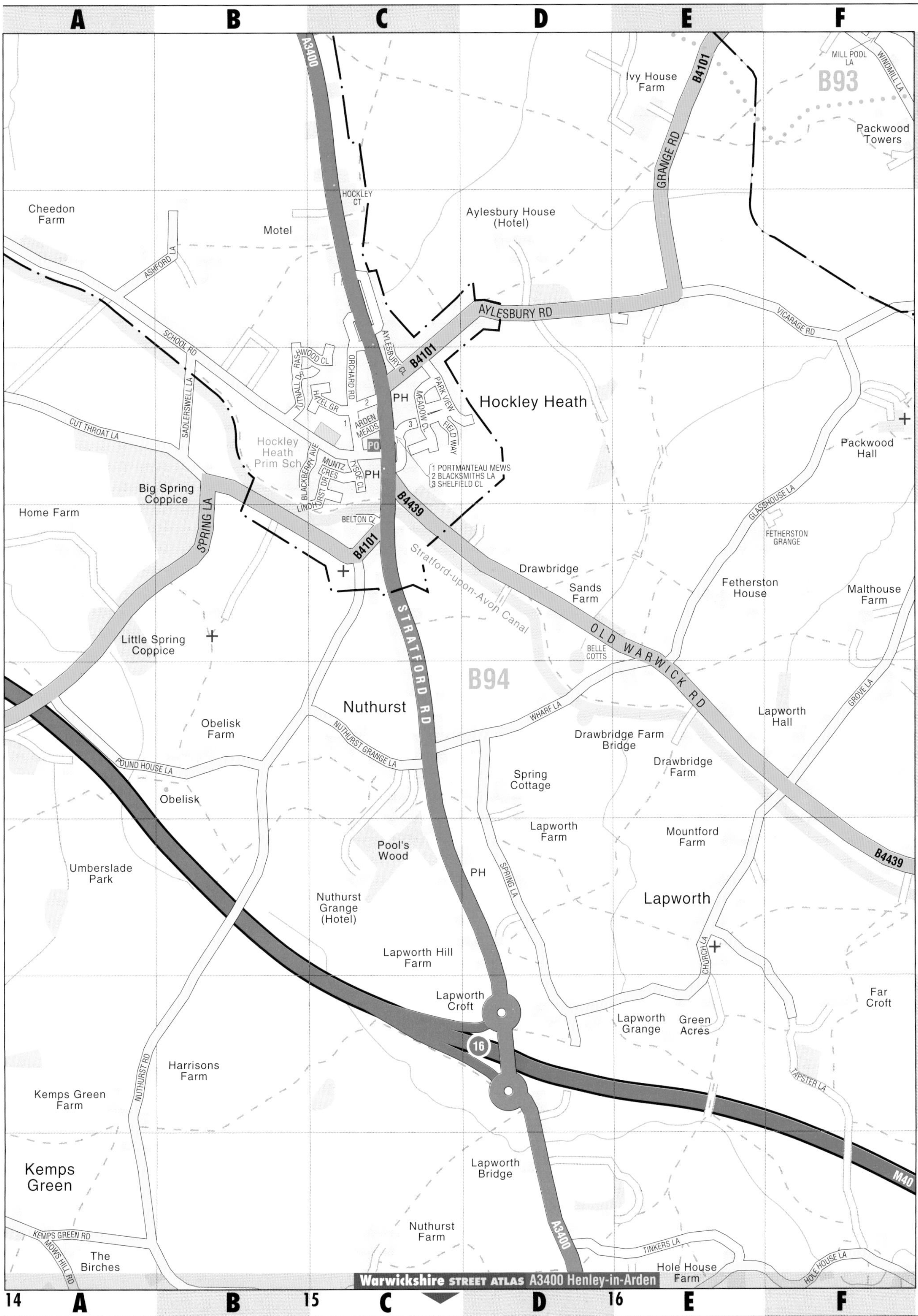

7

73

6

5

72

4

3

71

2

1

70

A B C D E F

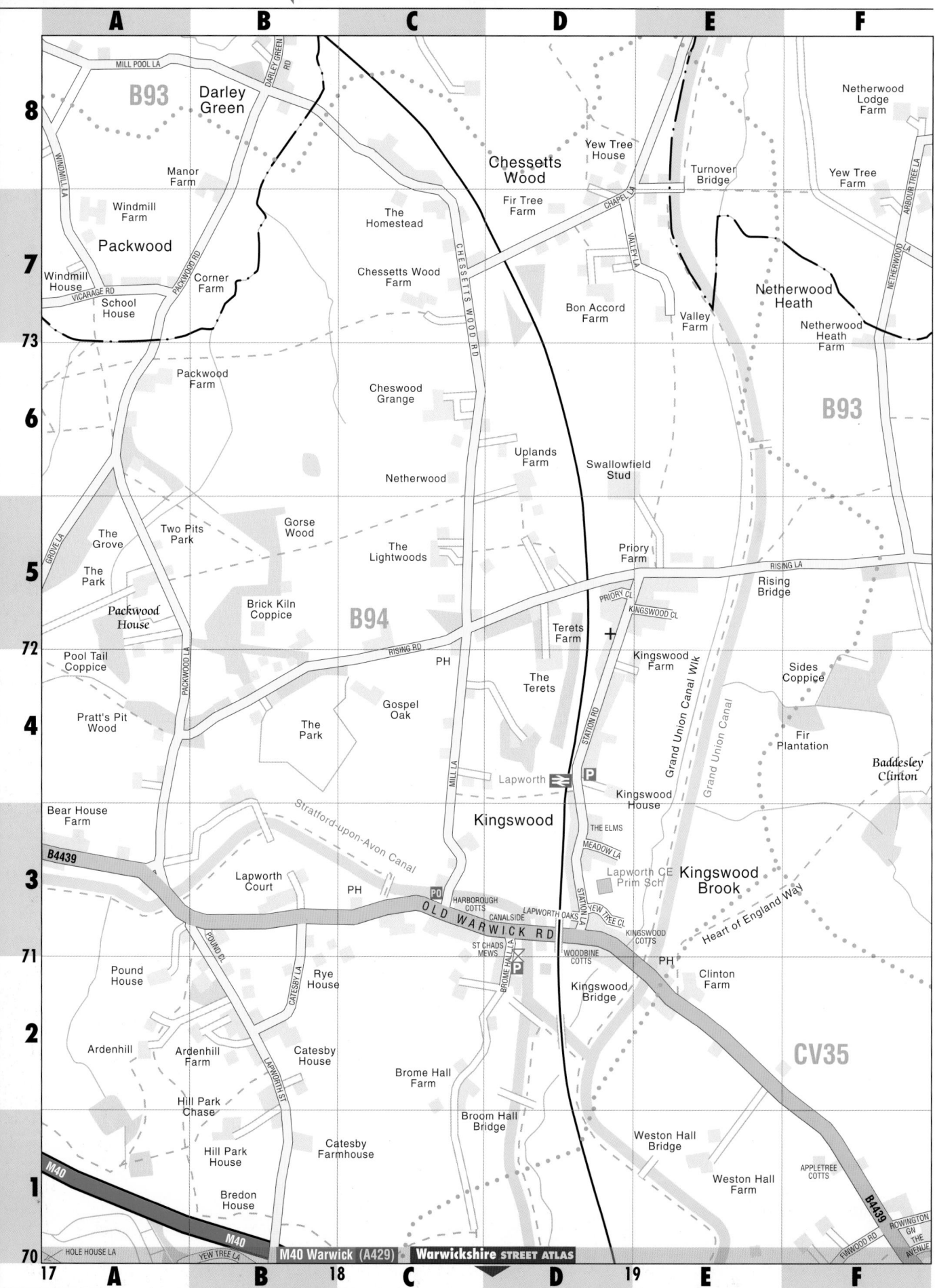

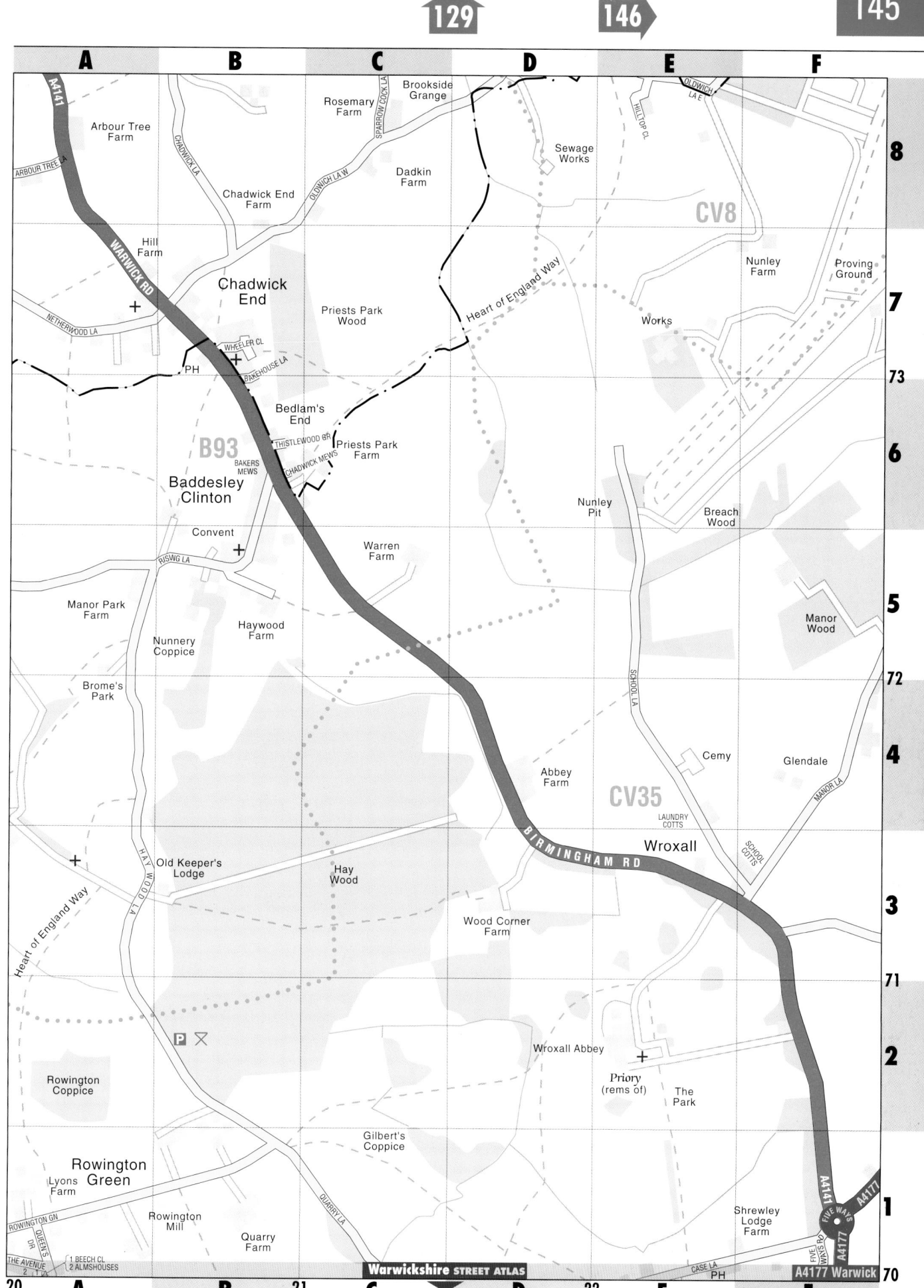

A   B   C   D   E   F

A4141

Arbour Tree Farm

ARBOUR TREE LA

Rosemary Farm

Brookside Grange

SPARROW COCK LA

Sewage Works

OLDWICH LA E

HILL TOP CL

CV8

8

Dadkin Farm

Chadwick End Farm

CHADWICK LA

OLDWICH LA W

Nunley Farm

Proving Ground

Hill Farm

WARWICK RD

NETHERWOOD LA

Chadwick End

Priests Park Wood

Heart of England Way

Works

7

73

PH

WHEELER CL

BAKEHOUSE LA

Bedlam's End

THISTLEWOOD GR

CHADWICK MEWS

Priests Park Farm

6

B93

BAKERS MEWS

Baddesley Clinton

Nunley Pit

Breach Wood

Convent

RISWG LA

Warren Farm

5

Manor Park Farm

Haywood Farm

Manor Wood

Nunnery Coppice

SCHOOL LA

72

Brome's Park

Cemy

Glendale

4

Abbey Farm

CV35

MANOR LA

LAUNDRY COTTS

BIRMINGHAM RD

Wroxall

SCHOOL COTTS

Heart of England Way

HAY WOOD LA

Old Keeper's Lodge

Hay Wood

3

Wood Corner Farm

71

P ✕

Wroxall Abbey

2

Rowington Coppice

Priory (rems of)

The Park

Gilbert's Coppice

Shrewley Lodge Farm

A4141

FIVE WAYS

A4177

1

Rowington Green

Lyons Farm

ROWINGTON GN

QUEEN'S DR

THE AVENUE

1. BEECH CL
2. ALMSHOUSES

Rowington Mill

QUARRY LA

Quarry Farm

FIVE WAYS RD

CASE LA

PH

A4177 Warwick

70

20   A   B   21   C   D   22   E   F

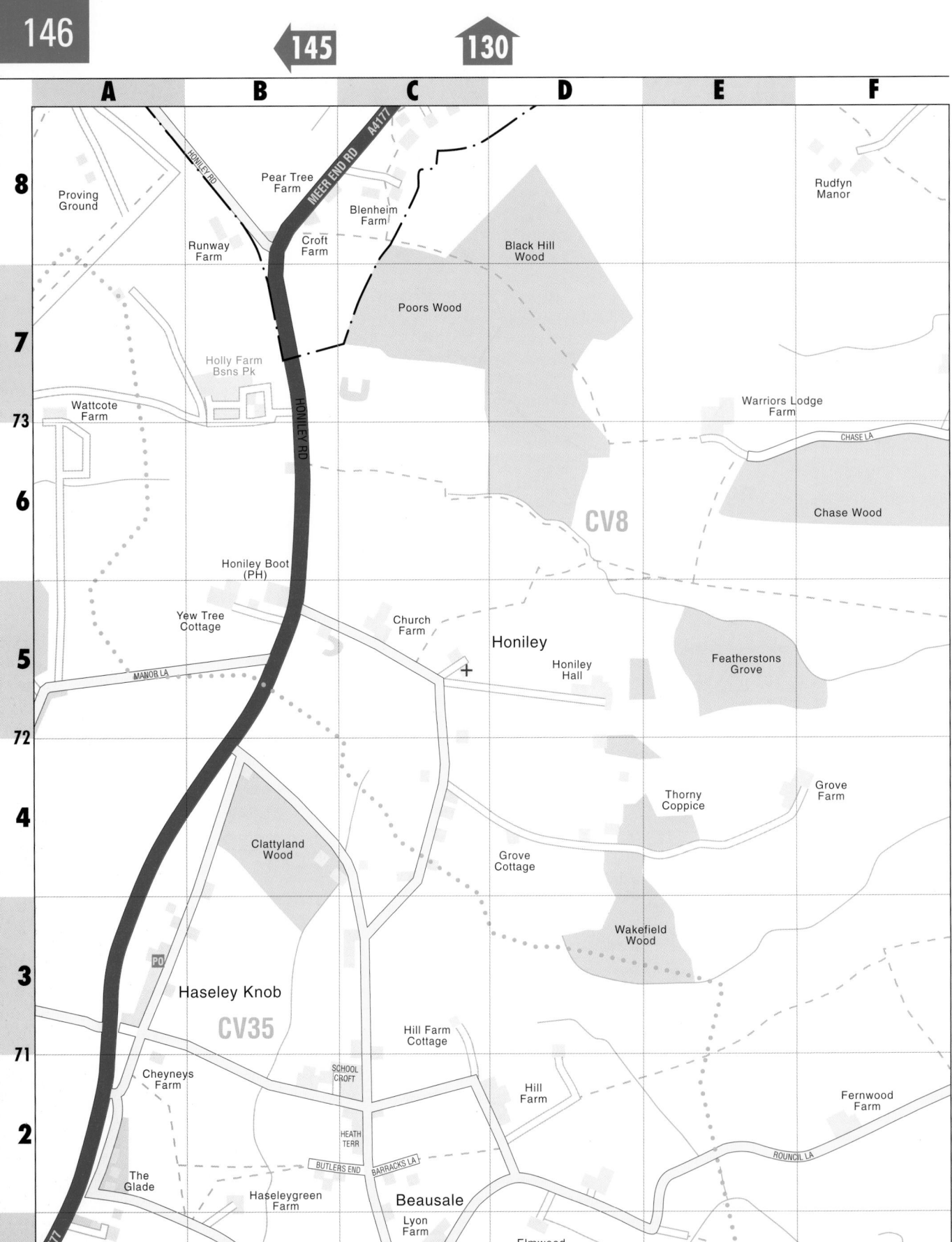

A   B   C   D   E   F

8

Proving
Ground

HONILEY RD

Pear Tree
Farm

MEER END RD   A4177

Blenheim
Farm

Black Hill
Wood

Rudfyn
Manor

Runway
Farm

Croft
Farm

Poors Wood

7

Holly Farm
Bsns Pk

Warriors Lodge
Farm

73

Wattcote
Farm

CHASE LA

6

CV8

Chase Wood

HONILEY RD

Honiley Boot
(PH)

Yew Tree
Cottage

Church
Farm

Honiley

Featherstons
Grove

5

MANOR LA

Honiley
Hall

+

72

Thorny
Coppice

Grove
Farm

4

Clattyland
Wood

Grove
Cottage

3

Haseley Knob

Wakefield
Wood

CV35

Hill Farm
Cottage

71

PO

Cheyneys
Farm

SCHOOL
CROFT

Hill
Farm

Fernwood
Farm

2

HEATH
TERR

ROUNCIL LA

The
Glade

BUTLERS END   BARRACKS LA

Haseleygreen
Farm

Beausale

Lyon
Farm

Elmwood
Farm

A4177

1

Holly
Farm

BEAUSALE LA

KITES NEST LA

Camphill
Farm

70

23   A   B   24   C   D   25   E   F

131   148

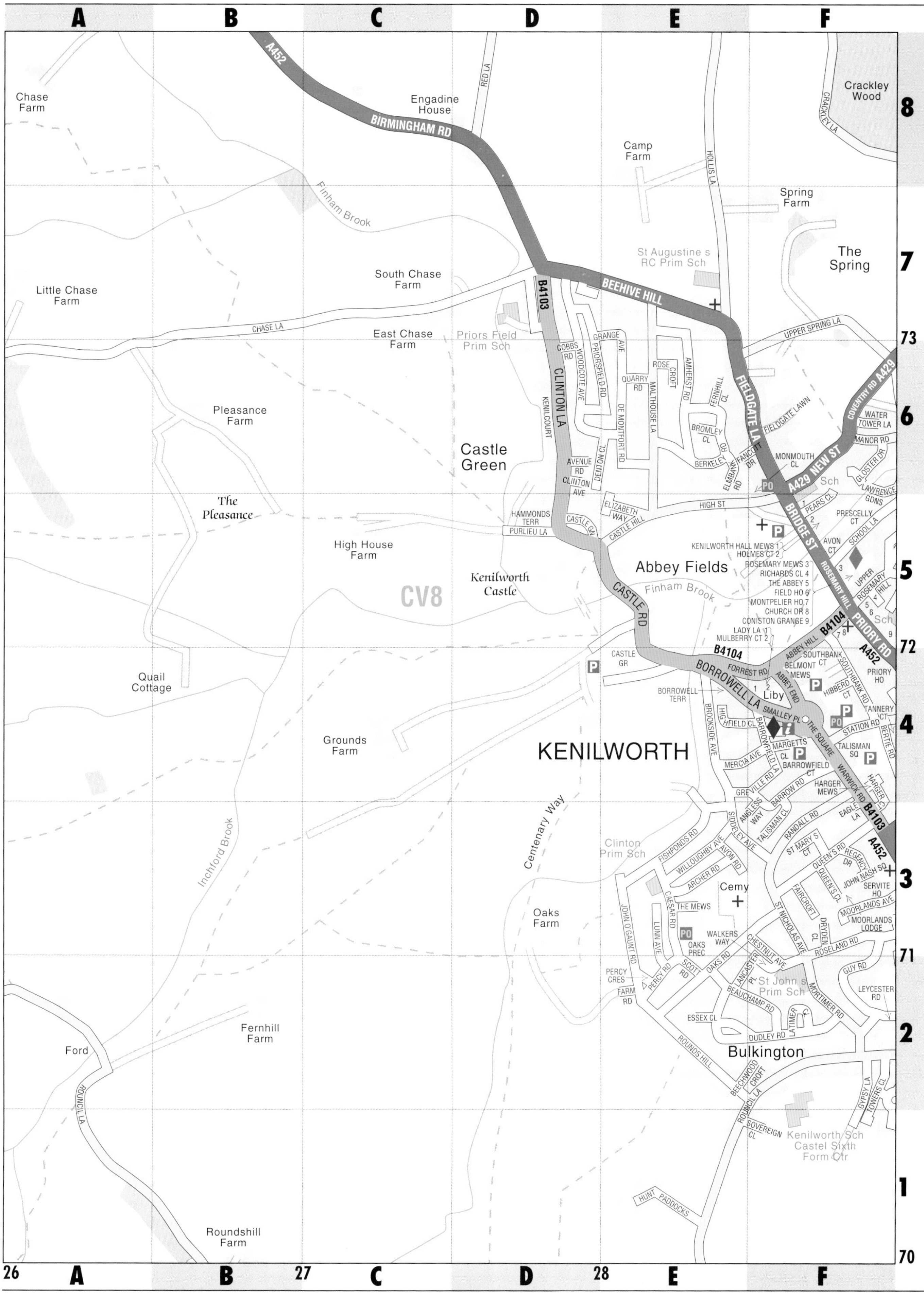

A   B   C   D   E   F

8
Chase Farm
Crackley Wood
A452
Engadine House
RED LA
Camp Farm
BIRMINGHAM RD
Finham Brook
Spring Farm
The Spring   7
St Augustine's RC Prim Sch
HOLLIS LA
South Chase Farm
B4103
BEEHIVE HILL
Little Chase Farm
UPPER SPRING LA   73
CHASE LA
East Chase Farm
Priors Field Prim Sch
COBBS RD
WOODCOTE AVE
PRIORSFIELD RD
GRANGE AVE
ROSE CROFT
AMHERST RD
FERNHILL CL
FIELDGATE LAWN
COVENTRY RD A429
WATER TOWER LA   6
Pleasance Farm
CLINTON LA
KENILCOURT
QUARRY RD
DE MONTFORT RD
MALTHOUSE LA
BROMLEY CL
FIELDGATE LA
A429 NEW ST
MANOR RD
GLUSTER DR
Castle Green
AVENUE RD
CLINTON AVE
BERKELEY RD
ELMBANK RD
FANCOTT DR
MONMOUTH CL
BRIDGE ST
PO
A429
Sch
LAWRENCE GDNS
The Pleasance
HAMMONDS TERR
PURLIEU LA
CASTLE GN
ELIZABETH WAY
CASTLE HILL
HIGH ST
PEARS CL
AVON
SCHOOL LA
PRESCELLY CT   5
High House Farm
Kenilworth Castle
Abbey Fields
Finham Brook
ROSEMARY HILL
Kenilworth Hall Mews 1
HOLMES CT 2
ROSEMARY MEWS 3
RICHARDS CL 4
THE ABBEY 5
FIELD HO 6
MONTPELIER HO 7
CHURCH DR 8
CONISTON GRANGE 9
UPPER ROSEMARY HILL
Sch
CV8
CASTLE RD
LADY LA
MULBERRY CT 2
B4104
PRIORY RD
A452   72
CASTLE GR
FORREST RD
B4104
BORROWELL LA
ABBEY HILL
ABBEY END
SOUTH BANK RD
SOUTHBANK CT
BELMONT MEWS
HIBBERD CT
PRIORY HO
TANNERY CT
Quail Cottage
BORROWELL TERR
Liby
HIGHFIELD CT
BARROWFIELD LA
SMALLEY PL
THE SQUARE
MARGETTS CL
BARROWFIELD CT
STATION RD
PO
BERTIE RD
TALISMAN SQ
HARGER CT   4
Grounds Farm
KENILWORTH
BROOKSIDE AVE
MERCIA AVE
GREVILLE RD
BARROW RD
WARWICK RD
HARGER MEWS
B4103
Centenary Way
ANGLESS WAY
SIDDELEY AVE
TALISMAN CL
RANDALL RD
ST MARY'S RD
EAGLE LA
A452
Clinton Prim Sch
FISHPONDS RD
WILLOUGHBY AVE
ARCHER RD
AVON RD
QUEEN'S RD
QUEEN'S CL
FAIRCROFT
REGENT DR
JOHN NASH SQ
SERVITE HO   3
Cemy
Oaks Farm
CAESAR RD
THE MEWS
ST NICHOLAS AVE
DRYDEN CL
MOORLANDS AVE
ROSELAND RD
MOORLANDS LODGE
JOHN O' GAUNT RD
LUNN AVE
PO OAKS PREC
WALKERS WAY
CHESTNUT AVE
GUY RD
LEYCESTER RD   71
PERCY CRES
FARM RD
PERCY RD
SCOTT RD
OAKS RD
LANCASTER CL
BEAUCHAMP RD
St John's Prim Sch
MORTIMER RD
LATIMER RD   2
Ford
Fernhill Farm
COUNCIL LA
ESSEX CL
DUDLEY RD
ROUNDS HILL
Bulkington
BEECHWOOD CROFT
ROUNDS HILL
COUNCIL LA
SOVEREIGN CL
GYPSY LA
TOWERS CL
Kenilworth Sch Castel Sixth Form Ctr   1
HUNT PADDOCKS
Roundshill Farm
Inchford Brook
70
26   A   B   27   C   D   28   E   F

155   148

A   B   C   D   E   F

8

7

73

6

5

72

4

3

71

2

1

70

Kenilworth / Crackley area map

Coventry Way
Crackley Cres
KENILWORTH RD A429
Crackley Farm
Crackley Cotts
Crackley
Ind Est
Millburn Grange
CV4
CV3
Westley Bridge
Kingswood House
The Dalehouse
Ladyes Hills
COVENTRY RD
Crackley Hall Sch
HERITAGE CT
MONNINGTON HO
COMMON LA
HIGHLAND RD
INCHBROOK RD
Ind Est
Finham Brook
Four Winds
Kingswood Riding School
A429
UPPER LADYES HILLS
HAWKESWORTH DR
Mill End
THE DEER LEAP
NORTHVALE CL
LULWORTH PK
BUTLER CL
WHITEHEAD DR
GARLICK DR
BEST AVE
DALEHOUSE LA
Centenary Way
THE CLOSE
FINHAM
DALEHOUSE FLATS
GREENSWARD CL
FAIRWAY RISE
KNOWLE HILL
ADMIRAL GDNS
FRYTHE CL
CH
Park Hill
CREW LA
South Crest
STURLEY CRES
FINHAM FLATS
Park Hill Jun Sch
HIDCOTE RD
DENEWOOD
PENRHYN CL
Southcrest Farm
KENILWORTH
CV8
Crewe Gardens
Crewe Farm
B4115
Whitemoor
Kenilworth Sch
THE GARDENS
LEYES LA
WISLEY GR
CORNHILL
CAMELOT GR
ARDGE CRES
Woodside
River Avon
PRIORY RD
A452
Bridge Works Ind Est
WYNCOTE
TULIP TREE AVE
SUNNINGDALE AVE
SEEKINGS DR
JACKSON GR
INVERARAY CL
DUNNEGAN
Glasshouse Wood
Grecian Lodges
STATION RD
WAVERLEY RD
A452
Thorns Com Inf Sch
BROOKE RD
ASHOW
KINGS RD
WORDSWORTH DR
GLASSHOUSE LA
WARWICK RD
A452
BLACKTHORNE RD
NEWFIELD AVE
ORCHARD CL
KNIGHTLOW
NEVILLE CROFT
Stoneleigh Abbey
Windy Arbour
CLARENDON RD
HERMITAGE WAY
WALNUT TREE CL
BIRCHES LA
CANTERBURY CL
ROCKY LA
The Grove
OAKLANDS CT
LEYCESTER RD
THICKTHORN ORCHS
Thickthorn Mews
Thickthorn Wood
Abbey Farm
Ashow
Grove Farm House
ROUNCIL LA
SUNSHINE CL
LINDSEY CRES
WARWICK RD
GARDNER WAY
LEAMINGTON RD
Bullimore Wood
A46
A452
B4115
Dial House Farm
Bericote Farm
CV32
Wootton Grange
River Avon

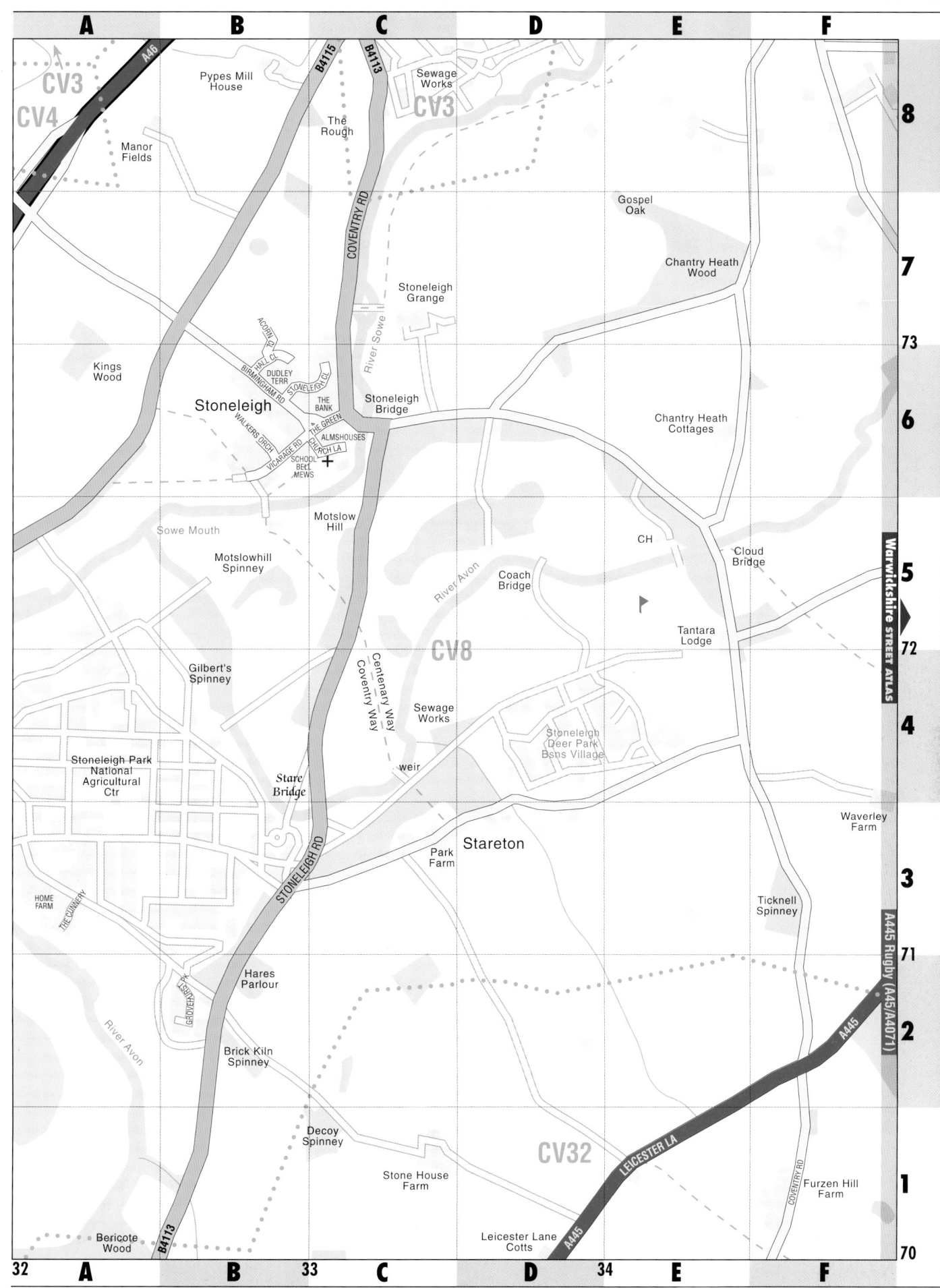

A B C D E F

8 7 73 6 5 72 4 3 71 2 1 70

32 33 34

CV3
CV4

CV3

Pypes Mill House

The Rough

Gospel Oak

Chantry Heath Wood

Stoneleigh Grange

Manor Fields

COVENTRY RD

B4115

B4113

River Sowe

Chantry Heath Cottages

Kings Wood

ACORN CL
HALL CL
DUDLEY TERR
BIRMINGHAM RD
STONELEIGH CL
THE BANK
THE GREEN
ALMSHOUSES
CHURCH LA
WALKERS ORCH
VICARAGE RD
SCHOOL BELL MEWS

Stoneleigh

Stoneleigh Bridge

CH

Cloud Bridge

Sowe Mouth

Motslow Hill

Motslowhill Spinney

River Avon

Coach Bridge

Tantara Lodge

CV8

Gilbert's Spinney

Centenary Way
Coventry Way

Sewage Works

Stoneleigh Deer Park Bsns Village

Waverley Farm

Stoneleigh Park National Agricultural Ctr

Stare Bridge

weir

STONELEIGH RD

Park Farm

Stareton

Ticknell Spinney

HOME FARM
THE CULVERY

Hares Parlour

GROVEHURST

Brick Kiln Spinney

River Avon

Decoy Spinney

CV32

Stone House Farm

LEICESTER LA

A445

COVENTRY RD

Furzen Hill Farm

Bericote Wood

B4113

Leicester Lane Cotts

A445

Sewage Works

Warwickshire STREET ATLAS

A46

A445 Rugby (A45/A071)

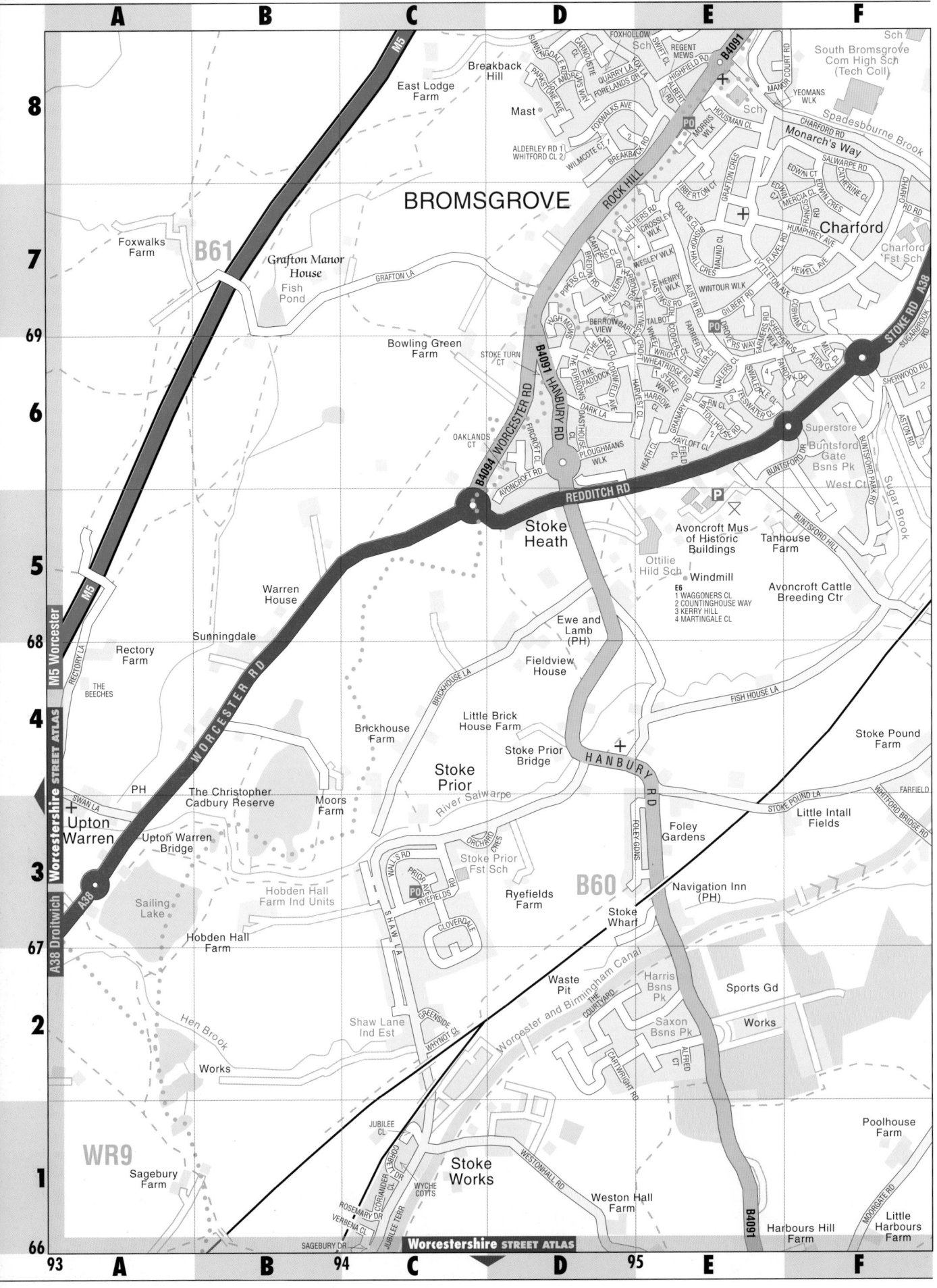

BROMSGROVE

Charford

Stoke Heath

Stoke Prior

Stoke Works

Upton Warren

WR9

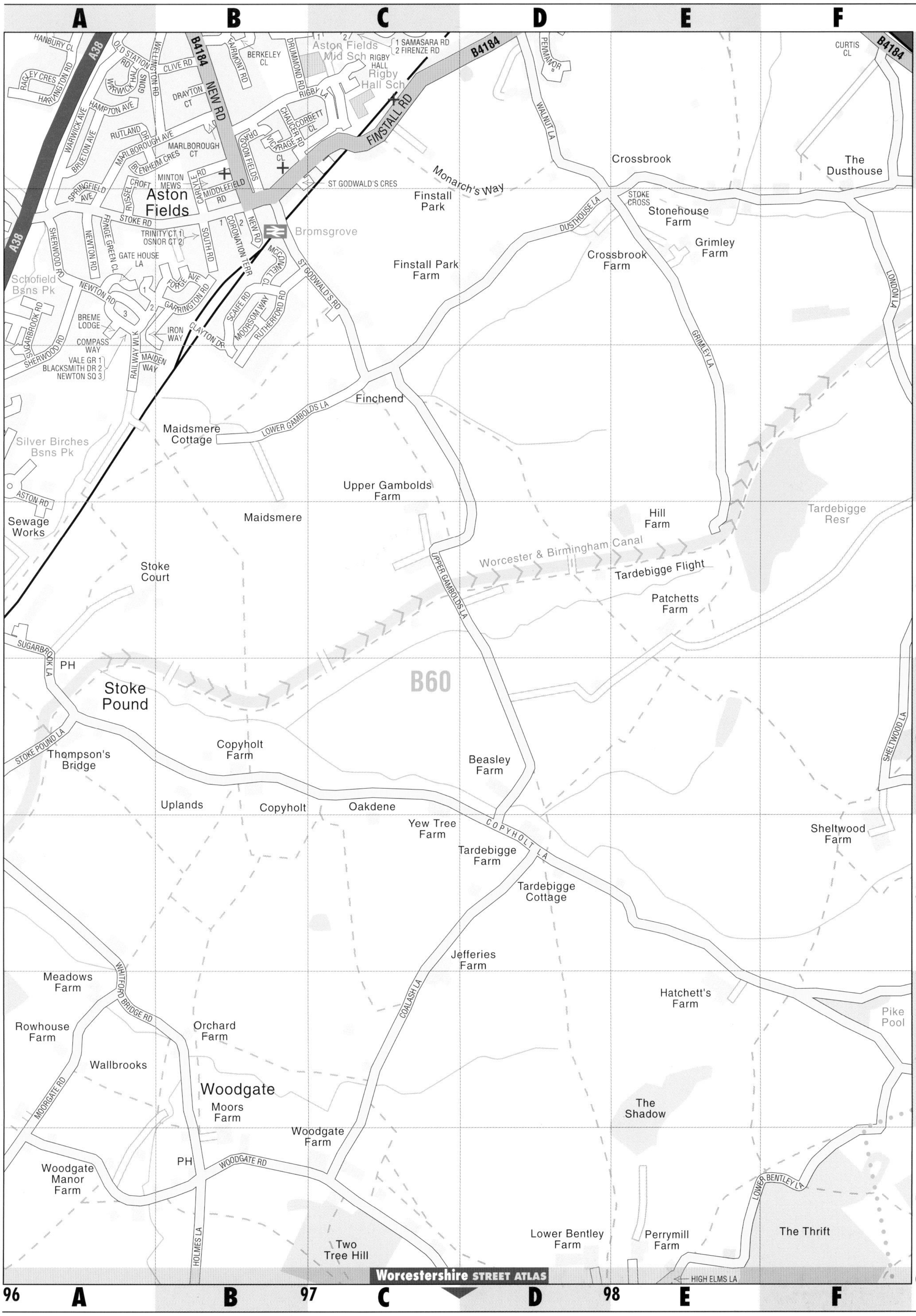
A
B
C
D
E
F
8
7
69
6
5
68
4
3
67
2
1
66
96
97
98
Aston Fields
Aston Fields Mid Sch
Rigby Hall Sch
Bromsgrove
Schofield Bsns Pk
Silver Birches Bsns Pk
Sewage Works
Finstall Park
Finstall Park Farm
Monarch's Way
Crossbrook
Crossbrook Farm
Stonehouse Farm
Grimley Farm
The Dusthouse
Finchend
Maidsmere Cottage
Upper Gambolds Farm
Maidsmere
Hill Farm
Tardebigge Resr
Worcester & Birmingham Canal
Tardebigge Flight
Stoke Court
Patchetts Farm
PH
Stoke Pound
B60
Thompson's Bridge
Copyholt Farm
Beasley Farm
Uplands
Copyholt
Oakdene
Yew Tree Farm
Tardebigge Farm
Sheltwood Farm
Tardebigge Cottage
Jefferies Farm
Meadows Farm
Hatchett's Farm
Pike Pool
Rowhouse Farm
Orchard Farm
Wallbrooks
Woodgate
Moors Farm
The Shadow
Woodgate Farm
Woodgate Manor Farm
Two Tree Hill
Lower Bentley Farm
Perrymill Farm
The Thrift
A38
B4184
NEW RD
FINSTALL RD
HANBURY CL
RAGLEY CRES
HARRINGTON RD
OLD STATION RD
WARWICK HALL GDNS
WELLINGTON RD
CLIVE RD
DRAYTON CT
FAIRMONT RD
BERKELEY CL
DRUMMOND RD
1 SAMASARA RD
2 FIRENZE RD
RIGBY HALL
RIGBY LA
HAMPTON AVE
WARWICK AVE
BRUETON AVE
RUTLAND DR
MARLBOROUGH AVE
MARLBOROUGH CT
BLENHEIM CRES
SPRINGFIELD AVE
RUSSELL CROFT
MINTON MEWS
CARLYLE RD
MIDDLEFIELD RD
DRAGOON FIELDS
VICARAGE CL
CHAUCER RD
CORBETT CL
ST GODWALD'S CRES
STOKE RD
TRINITY CT 1
OSNOR CT 2
SOUTH RD
CORONATION TERR
NEW RD
McCONNELL CL
ST GODWALD'S RD
SHERWOOD RD
NEWTON RD
FRINGE GREEN CL
GATE HOUSE LA
FORGE AVE
GARRINGTON RD
SCAIFE RD
MOORSOM WAY
RUTHERFORD RD
BREME LODGE
COMPASS WAY
IRON WAY
CLAYTON DR
RAILWAY WLK
MAIDEN WAY
SUGARBROOK RD
SHERWOOD RD
VALE GR 1
BLACKSMITH DR 2
NEWTON SQ 3
PENNAMOR
WALNUT LA
DUSTHOUSE LA
STOKE CROSS
GRIMLEY LA
CURTIS CL
LONDON LA
LOWER GAMBOLDS LA
ASTON RD
UPPER GAMBOLDS LA
SUGARBROOK LA
STOKE POUND LA
SHELTWOOD LA
COPYHOLT LA
COALASH LA
WHITFORD BRIDGE RD
MOORGATE RD
WOODGATE RD
HOLMES LA
LOWER BENTLEY LA
HIGH ELMS LA

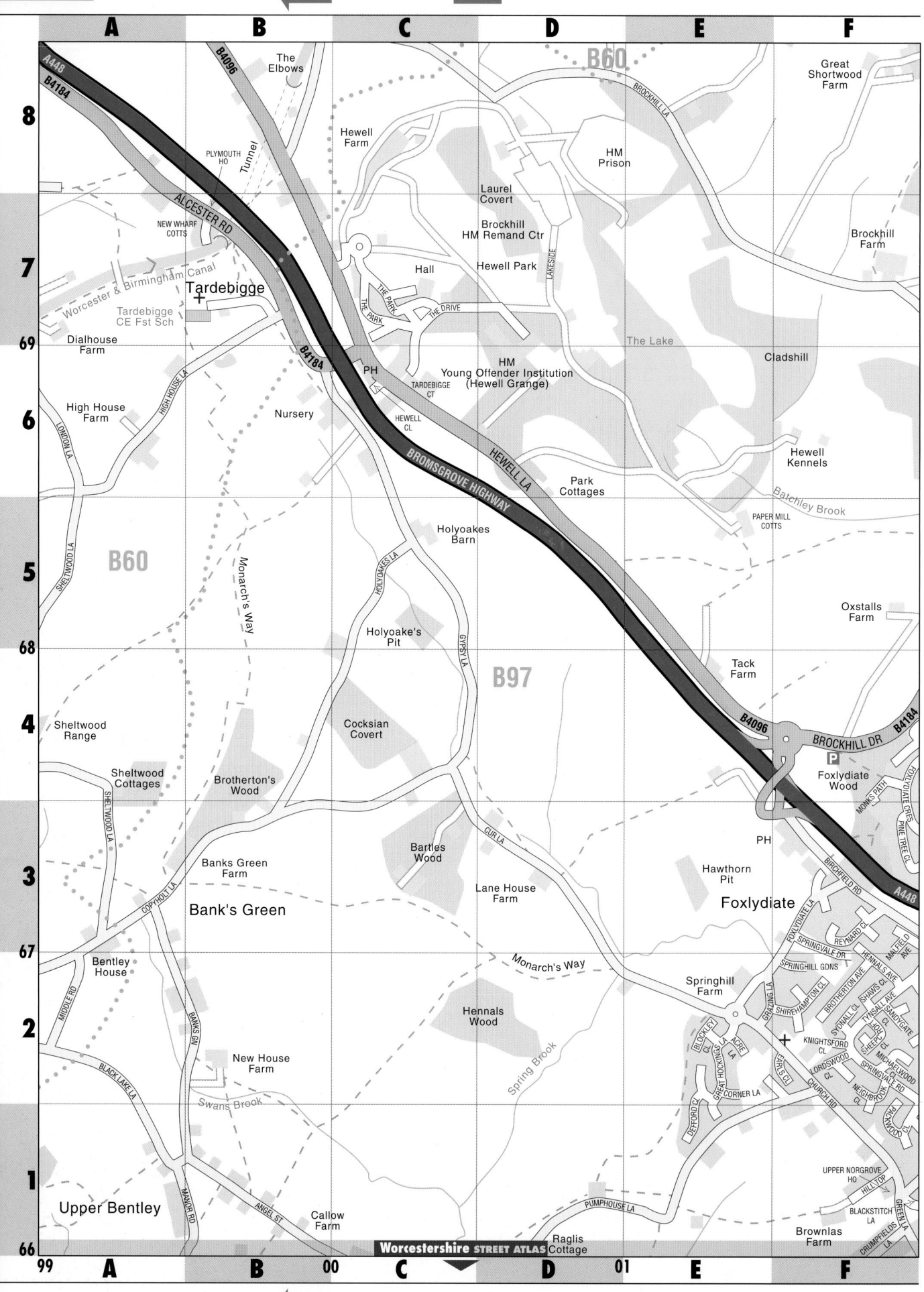

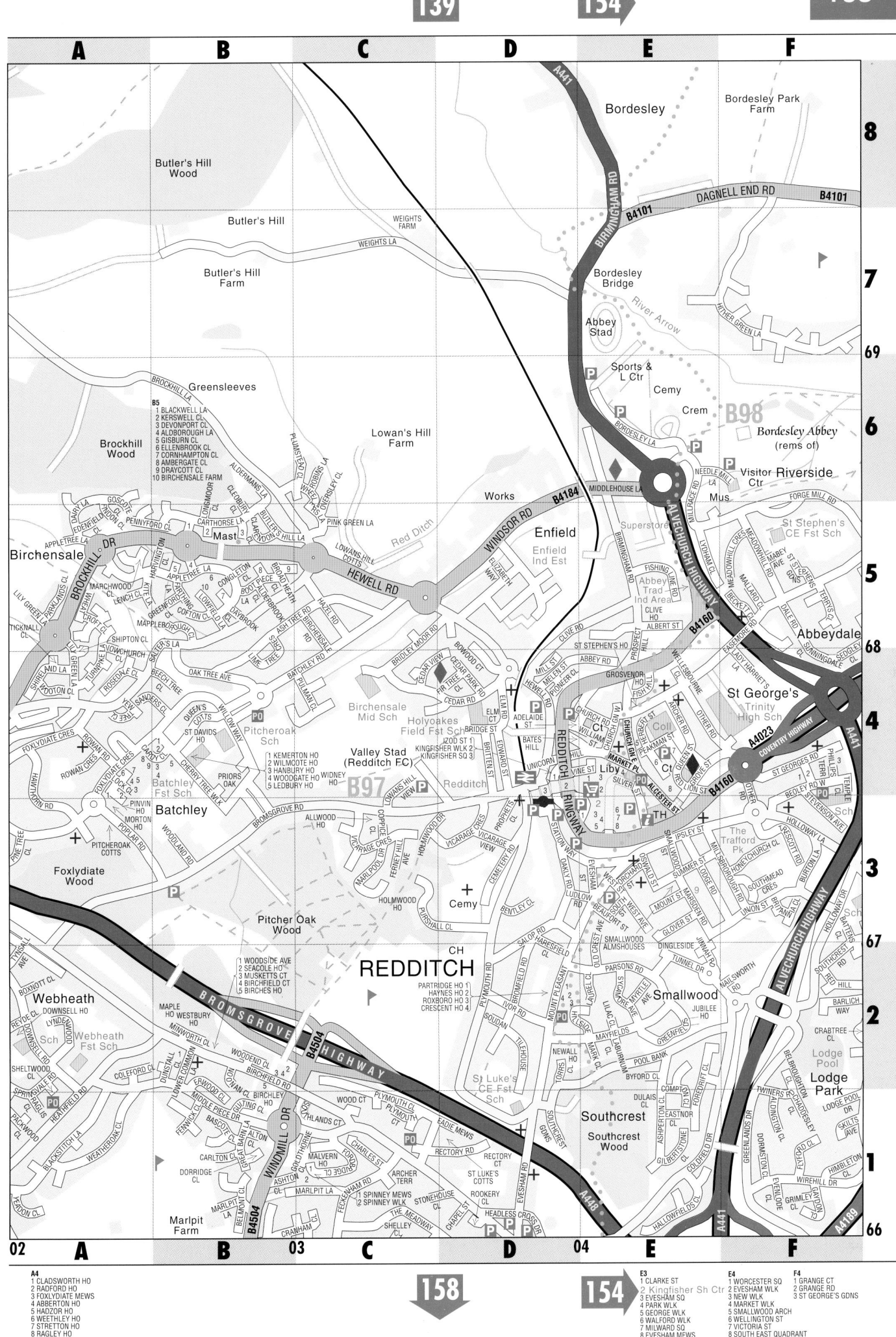

139
154
158
154

Bordesley
Bordesley Park Farm

DAGNELL END RD B4101

BIRMINGHAM RD

B4101

Butler's Hill Wood

Butler's Hill

Butler's Hill Farm

WEIGHTS FARM

WEIGHTS LA

Bordesley Bridge

River Arrow

Abbey Stad

HITHER GREEN LA

Sports & L Ctr

Cemy

Crem

B98

Bordesley Abbey (rems of)

Greensleeves

BROCKHILL LA

B5
1 BLACKWELL LA
2 KERSWELL CL
3 DEVONPORT CL
4 ALDBOROUGH LA
5 GISBURN CL
6 ELLENBROOK CL
7 CORNHAMPTON CL
8 AMBERGATE CL
9 DRAYCOTT CL
10 BIRCHENSALE FARM

Lowan's Hill Farm

Brockhill Wood

NEEDLE MILL LA

Visitor Ctr Riverside

FORGE MILL RD

Mus

St Stephen's CE Fst Sch

MEADOWHILL CRES

MILLRACE RD

LYDHAM RD

Works

WINDSOR RD

B4184

MIDDLEHOUSE LA

Superstore

ALVECHURCH HIGHWAY

Enfield

Enfield Ind Est

Red Ditch

Mast

HEWELL RD

Birchensale

BROCKHILL DR

ELIZABETH WAY

Abbey Trad Ind Area

FISHING LINE RD

CLIVE HO

CLIVE RD

ST STEPHEN'S HO

PROSPECT HILL

B4160

WELLESBOURNE

Abbeydale

St George's Trinity High Sch

A4023

COVENTRY HIGHWAY

A441

Birchensale Mid Sch

Holyoakes Field Fst Sch

Valley Stad (Redditch FC)

B97

LOWAN'S HILL VIEW

Redditch

REDDITCH RINGWAY

B4160

ALVECHURCH HIGHWAY

1 KEMERTON CL
2 WILMCOTE HO
3 HANBURY HO
4 WOODGATE HO
5 LEDBURY HO

Batchley Fst Sch

Batchley

BROMSGROVE RD

Cemy

Pitcher Oak Wood

Foxlydiate Wood

REDDITCH

1 WOODSIDE AVE
2 SEACOLE HO
3 MUSKETTS CT
4 BIRCHFIELD CT
5 BIRCHES HO

PARTRIDGE HO 1
HAYNES HO 2
ROXBORO HO 3
CRESCENT HO 4

Smallwood

Webheath

Webheath Fst Sch

BROMSGROVE HIGHWAY

B4504

Smallwood Almshouses

Lodge Pool

Lodge Park

Marlpit Farm

WINDMILL DR

B4504

St Luke's CE Fst Sch

Southcrest

Southcrest Wood

St Luke's Cotts

HEADLESS CROSS DR

A448

A441

A4188

1 SPINNEY MEWS
2 SPINNEY MEWS

THE MEADWAY

A4
1 CLADSWORTH HO
2 RADFORD HO
3 FOXLYDIATE MEWS
4 ABBERTON HO
5 HADZOR HO
6 WEETHLEY HO
7 STRETTON HO
8 RAGLEY HO
9 ELMLEY HO

E3
1 CLARKE ST
2 Kingfisher Sh Ctr
3 EVESHAM SQ
4 PARK WLK
5 GEORGE WLK
6 WALFORD WLK
7 MILWARD SQ
8 EVESHAM MEWS
9 Tudor Bsns Ctr

E4
1 WORCESTER SQ
2 EVESHAM WLK
3 NEW WLK
4 MARKET WLK
5 SMALLWOOD WLK
6 WELLINGTON ST
7 VICTORIA ST
8 SOUTH EAST QUADRANT

F4
1 GRANGE CT
2 GRANGE RD
3 ST GEORGE'S GDNS

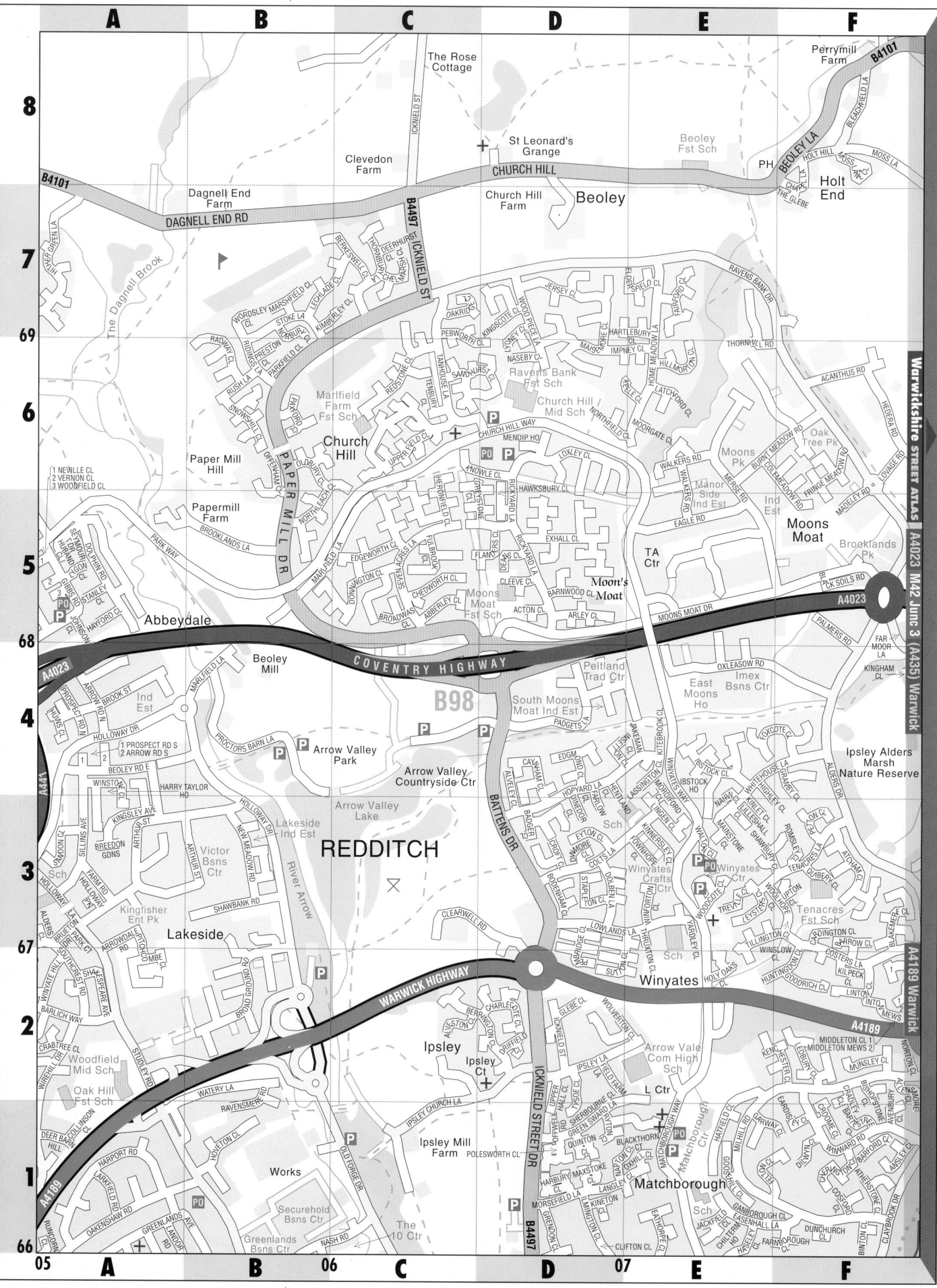

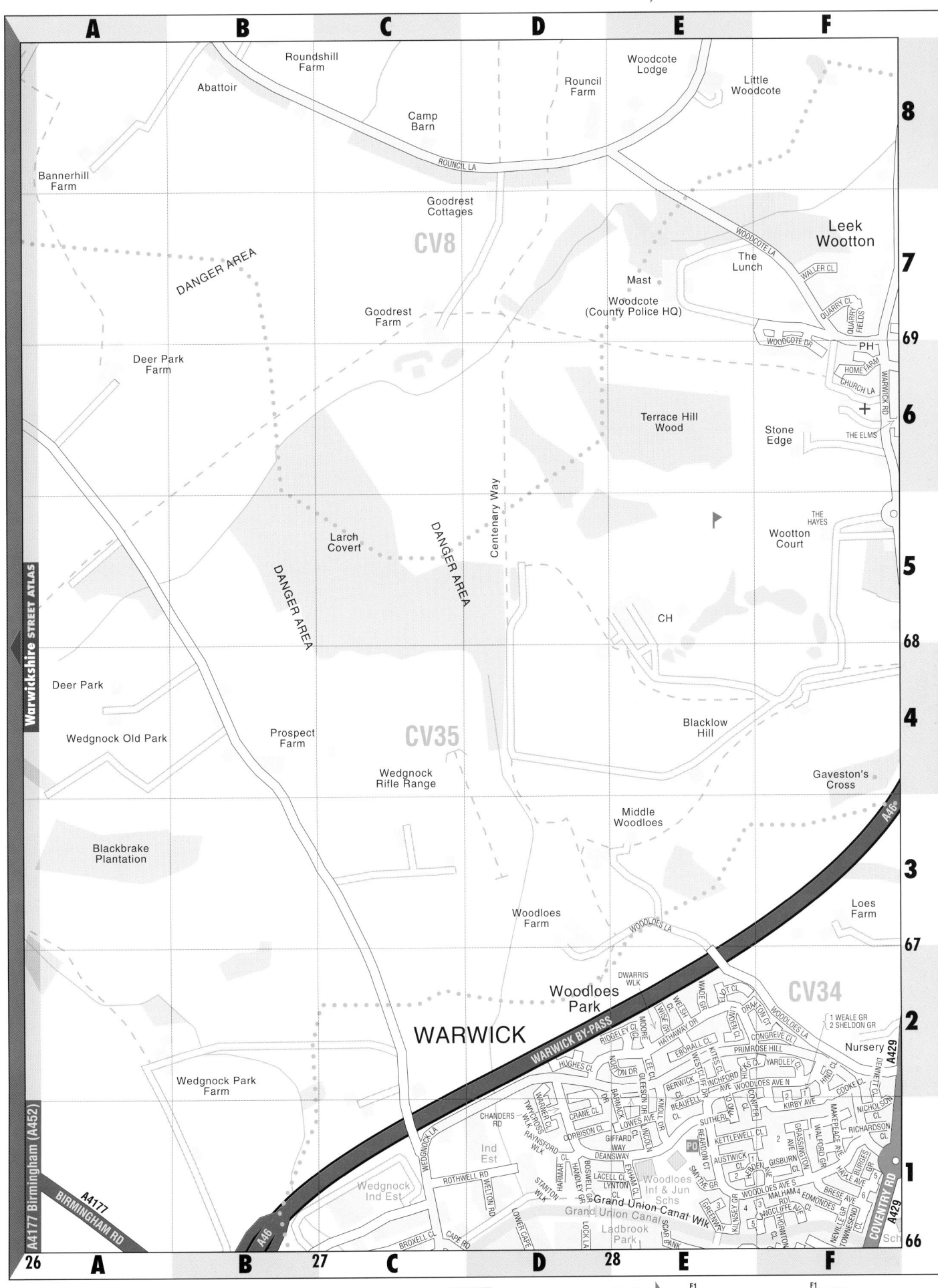

Roundshill
Farm

Abattoir

Camp
Barn

Woodcote
Lodge

Rouncil
Farm

Little
Woodcote

8

ROUNCIL LA

Bannerhill
Farm

Goodrest
Cottages

CV8

Leek
Wootton

DANGER AREA

Mast

The
Lunch

WOODCOTE LA

WALLER CL

7

Goodrest
Farm

Woodcote
(County Police HQ)

WOODCOTE DR

QUARRY CL
QUARRY FIELDS

69

Deer Park
Farm

PH

HOME FARM

CHURCH LA

WARWICK RD

6

Terrace Hill
Wood

Stone
Edge

THE ELMS

Warwickshire STREET ATLAS

Centenary Way

DANGER AREA

Larch
Covert

THE
HAYES

Wootton
Court

5

DANGER AREA

CH

68

Deer Park

Wedgnock Old Park

CV35

Prospect
Farm

Blacklow
Hill

4

Wedgnock
Rifle Range

Gaveston's
Cross

Middle
Woodloes

A46

Blackbrake
Plantation

3

Woodloes
Farm

WOODLOES LA

Loes
Farm

67

A4177 Birmingham (A452)

DWARRIS
WLK

Woodloes
Park

CV34

WELSH CL

WADE GR

WT CL

DRAYTON CL

WOODLOES LA

LODER CL

MOORE

WISE GR

HATHAWAY DR

WESTCLIFF

CONGREVE CL

PRIMROSE HILL

1 WEALE GR
2 SHELDON GR

Nursery

A429

2

WARWICK

WARWICK BY-PASS

RIDGELEY CL

HUGHES CL

NORTON DR

EBORALL CL

KYTES CL

INCHFORD

YARDLEY CL

HINDI CL

WARNER CL

LEE CL

GLESSON DR

BERWICK

BEAUFEL

WOODLOES AVE N

KIRBY AVE

COOKE CL

NICHOLSON CL

RICHARDSON CL

A429 COVENTRY RD

A4177

A46

Wedgnock Park
Farm

TWICROSS WLK

CRANE CL

BARNACK

KNOLL DR

LOWES AVE

LINCOLN

SUTHERLAND

COOPER CL

MAKEPEACE AVE

GRASSINGTON AVE

WALFORD GR

HALE AVE

BURGES

CHANDERS
RD

CORBISON CL

GIFFARD
WAY

REARDON CT

KETTLEWELL CL

AUSTWICK

EDEN

GISBURN CL

KINSLY GR

BRESE AVE

NEVILLE GR

TOWNSEND

Ind
Est

RAYNSFORD
WLK

HARWAR

DEANSWAY

PO

SMITE GR

WOODLOES AVE S

THORNTON

EDMONDES

WEDGNOCK LA

ROTHWELL RD

WELTON RD

STANTON
WLK

HANDLEY GR

BOSWELL GR

LACELL CL

LYNTON
CL

Woodloes
Inf & Jun
Schs

Grand Union Canal WLK

SCAR BANK

GREENWAY

3

MALHAM RD

Sch

Wedgnock
Ind Est

BROXELL CL

CAPE RD

LOWER CAPE

LOCK LA

Grand Union Canal

Ladbrook
Park

66

E1
1 NEWSHOLME CL
2 ADDINGHAM CL
3 WATSON CL
4 RYLSTONE WAY
5 KILDWICK WAY

F1
1 HETTON CL
2 BUCKDEN CL
3 LEYBURN CL
4 ARNCLIFFE WAY
5 HUDDISDON CL
6 PHILLIPPES RD

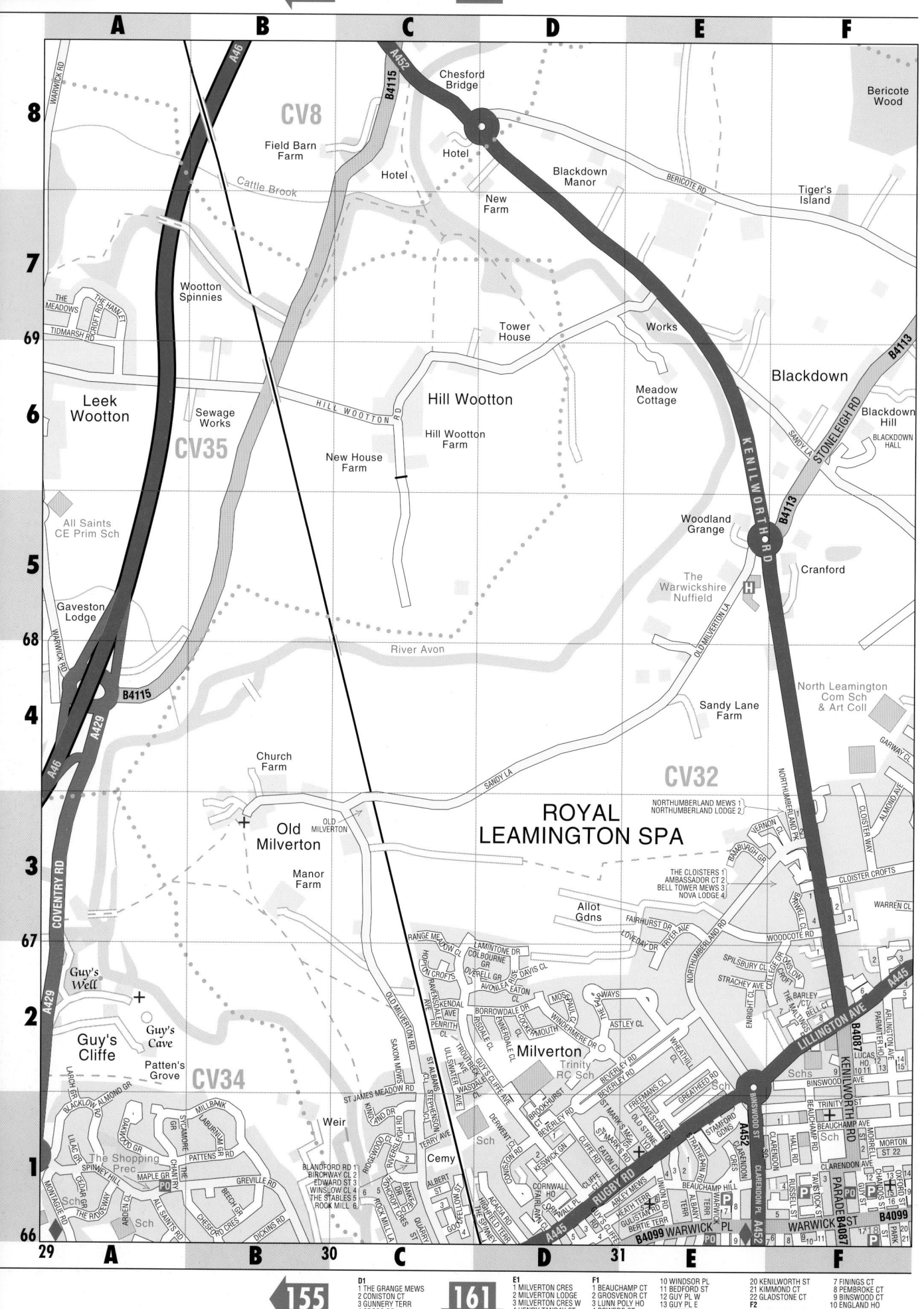

A B C D E F

8

7

69

6

5

68

4

3

67

2

1

66

29 A B 30 C D 31 E F

CV8

Field Barn Farm

Chesford Bridge

Hotel

Hotel

New Farm

Blackdown Manor

BERICOTE RD

Bericote Wood

Tiger's Island

Cattle Brook

Wootton Spinnies

Tower House

Works

Blackdown

B4113

THE MEADOWS
THE HAMLET
CROFT RD
WARWICK RD
TIDMARSH RD

Leek Wootton

Sewage Works

HILL WOOTTON RD

Hill Wootton

Meadow Cottage

Blackdown Hill

STONELEIGH RD
SANDY LA

BLACKDOWN HALL

CV35

Hill Wootton Farm

New House Farm

KENILWORTH RD

B4113

All Saints CE Prim Sch

Woodland Grange

Cranford

Gaveston Lodge

The Warwickshire Nuffield

H

WARWICK RD

River Avon

OLD MILVERTON LA

North Leamington Com Sch & Art Coll

B4115

A429

A46

Sandy Lane Farm

GARWAY CL

Church Farm

OLD MILVERTON

SANDY LA

CV32

NORTHUMBERLAND PK

ALMOND AVE

CLOISTER WAY

COVENTRY RD

Old Milverton

Manor Farm

ROYAL LEAMINGTON SPA

NORTHUMBERLAND MEWS 1
NORTHUMBERLAND LODGE 2

VERNON CT

BAMBURGH GR

CLOISTER CROFTS

WARREN CL

THE CLOISTERS 1
AMBASSADOR CT 2
BELL TOWER MEWS 3
NOVA LODGE 4

Allot Gdns

FAIRHURST DR
LOVEDAY DR
FRYER AVE

WOODCOTE RD

BRANKLE CL
DONEGAL CL

RANGE MEADOW CL

LAMINTONE DR
COLBOURNE GR

HIPTON CROFTS

OVERELL GR

AVONLEA RISE
DAVIS CL
EATON CT

SPILSBURY CL
STRACHEY AVE

NORTHUMBERLAND RD

BARLEY CT
BELL CT
THE MALINGS

A445

A429

Guy's Well

Guy's Cliffe

Guy's Cave

Patten's Grove

CV34

KENDAL AVE
BORROWDALE DR
ENNERDALE CL
RISDALE CL
PENRITH CL

MOSS PL
COCKERMOUTH CL

WINDERMERE DR

ASTLEY CL

WHEATHILL CL

ENRIGHT CL
BARLEY CT

LILLINGTON AVE
B4087
KENILWORTH RD
LUCAS CT

PARMITER HO
ARLINGTON HO

SCHS
BINSWOOD END

MONTAGUE RD
LARCH GR
BLACKLOW RD
OAKWOOD GR
ALMOND GR
SYCAMORE GR
LABURNUM GR
MILLBANK
PATTENS GR
THE
ST JAMES MEADOW RD

Weir

ST ALBANS RD
WASDALE CL
TROUTBECK AVE
ULLSWATER AVE
GUY'S CLIFFE AVE

Milverton

Trinity RC Sch

BEVERLEY RD

BEVERLEY RD

FREEMANS CL

GREATHEED RD

ST MARK'S RD
ST MARK'S MEWS

BINSWOOD AVE

MORTON ST
MORRELL ST

BEAUCHAMP AVE

Sch

TRINITY ST

CLARENDON AVE

The Shopping Prec

LILAC GR
CEDAR GR
SPINNEY HILL
MAPLE GR
CHANTRY
BEECH GR
ARDEN CL
ALL SAINTS RD
CHESFORD CRES
GREVILLE RD
DICKINS RD

BLANDFORD RD 1
BIRCHWAY CL 2
EDWARD ST 3
WINSLOW CL 4
THE STABLES 5
ROOK MILL 6

RIDGEWAY CL
RIVERSIDE
KING RD
QUEEN RD

Cemy

ALBERT ST

SAXON MEWS
ROCK MILL LA

DERWENT CL
BROOKHURST
BEVERLEY GDNS
CLIFFE CT

OLD STONE

CARLSTON RD
GLADSTONE RD

Sch

CLIFFE RD
RUGBY RD

CORNWALL
CHAIRLAWN
ACACIA RD
HIGHFIELD TERR
THE SPINNEY

A445

ARLEY MEWS
HEATH TERR
ALBANY TERR
WARWICK ST

COSMO RD

GULISTAN RD
BERTIE TERR

BEAUCHAMP HILL

B4099
WARWICK PL

STAMFORD GDNS
BINSWOOD ST
ARENDON CRES

CLARENDON PL
A452
A452

RUSSELL TERR
TAVISTOCK ST

WARWICK ST
CLARENDON AVE

CHANDOS ST
GUY ST
BEAUCHAMP AVE

B4087
WARWICK ST
B4099

D1
1 THE GRANGE MEWS
2 CONISTON CT
3 GUNNERY TERR
4 CROSS RD
5 PERCY TERR

E1
1 MILVERTON CRES
2 MILVERTON LODGE
3 MILVERTON CRES W
4 HENRY TANDAY CT
5 VODENA CT
6 GULISTAN CT
7 STUART CT
8 UPPER GROVE ST
9 GROVE ST

F1
1 BEAUCHAMP CT
2 GROSVENOR CT
3 LUNN POLY HO
4 POWERS CT
5 WATERLOO PL
6 CLARENCE TERR
7 CLARENCE HO
8 KILWORTH HO
9 THE CORNER HO
10 WINDSOR PL
11 BEDFORD ST
12 GUY PL W
13 GUY PL E
14 OXFORD PL
15 CHANDOS CT
16 OXFORD ROW
17 WHITEHEADS CT
18 Royal Priors
19 ALVESTON PL
20 KENILWORTH ST
21 KIMMOND CT
22 GLADSTONE ST

F2
1 CLEVELAND CT
2 ARLINGTON CT
3 RIPLINGHAM
4 WHITE ROSE HO
5 ARLINGTON MEWS
6 WOOTTON CT
7 FININGS CT
8 PEMBROKE CT
9 BINSWOOD CT
10 ENGLAND HO
11 SAUNDERS HO
12 OAKFIELD HO
13 NORWOOD HO
14 BINSWOOD MANS
15 DORMER HO

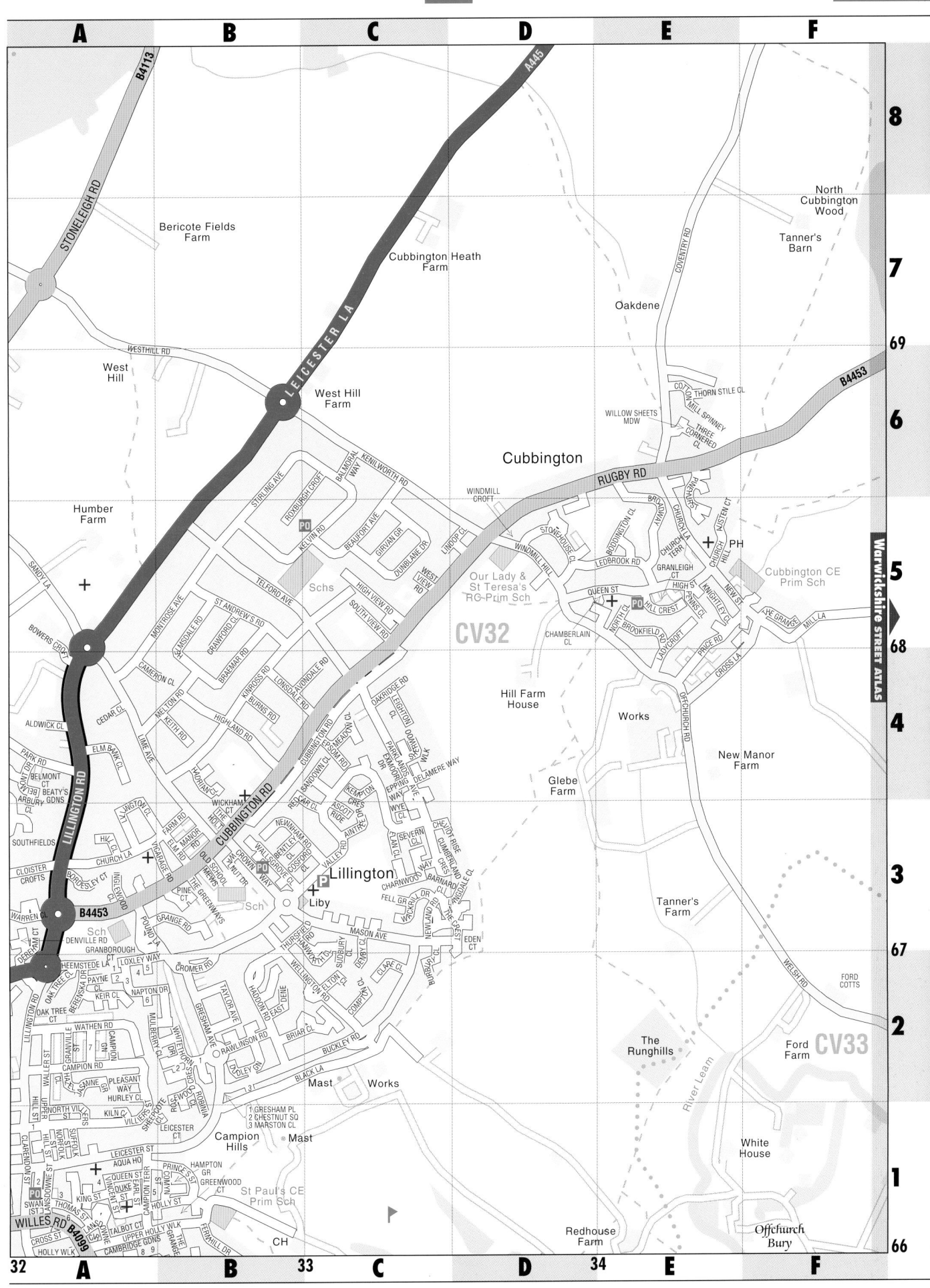

A B C D E F

8

North Cubbington Wood

Bericote Fields Farm

Tanner's Barn

Cubbington Heath Farm

7

B4113

STONELEIGH RD

Oakdene

WESTHILL RD

69

West Hill

COVENTRY RD

B4453

West Hill Farm

THORN STILE CL
COTTON MILL SPINNEY

6

LEICESTER LA

Cubbington

WILLOW SHEETS MDW

THREE CORNERED CL

Humber Farm

RUGBY RD

Warwickshire STREET ATLAS

SANDY LA

STIRLING AVE
ROXBURGH CROFT
KELVIN RD
BALMORAL WAY
KENILWORTH RD
BEAUFORT AVE
GIRVAN GR

WINDMILL CROFT

STONEHOUSE CL
BRADWAY
BODDINGTON CL
PURCHAST
CHURCH LA
AUSTEN CT

BOWERS CROFT

PO

Schs
DUMBLANE DR

LINDOP CL
WEST VIEW RD
HIGH VIEW RD

Our Lady & St Teresa's RC-Prim Sch

WINDMILL HILL
LEDBROOK RD
GRANLEIGH CT
CHURCH TERR
CHURCH HILL
PH

Cubbington CE Prim Sch

5

ALDWICK CL

MONTROSE AVE
KILMSDALE RD
CRANFORD RD
ST ANDREW'S RD
TELFORD AVE
BRAEMAR RD
SOUTH VIEW RD

QUEEN ST
PO
HILL CREST
HIGH
KNIGHTLEY CL
NEW ST
THE GRANGE
MILL LA

68

CEDAR CL
CAMERON CL
MELTON RD
KEITH RD
KINROSS RD
LONSDALE RD
HIGHLAND RD
BURNS RD
AVONDALE RD

CV32

CHAMBERLAIN CL

NORTH CL
PRICE RD
BROOKFIELD
LADYCROFT
CROSS LA
OFFCHURCH RD

4

ELM BANK CL
LIME AVE

OAKRIDGE RD
LEIGHTON CL
DOWNING CRES

CUBBINGTON RD

REDCAR CL
SANDOWN CL
ROSEMEADOW CL

EPPING WAY
EXMOOR DR
PARKLANDS AVE

Hill Farm House

Works

New Manor Farm

PARK RD
BELMONT CT
BEATY'S
ARBURY CL
BELL

LILLINGTON RD

WICKHAM CT
FARM RD
HOLT
MANOR RD

KEMPTON CRES
ASCOT RIDE
AINTREE
DELAMERE WAY
WYE CL

CHEVIOT RISE
CUMBERLAND CRES
DUNDALE CL

Glebe Farm

Tanner's Farm

SOUTHFIELDS

VINGTON CL
VICARAGE RD
OLD SCHOOL

NEWNHAM RD
BENTLEY RD
WALLGROVE CL
COSFORD
SEVERN CL
ALAN CL

WELSH RD

3

CLOISTER CROFTS
WARREN CL

B4453

PINE CT
MEWS
CROWN WAY

PO

Lillington
Liby

CHARNWOOD DR
FELL GR
WACKLIN
VALLEY RD
NEWLAND RD
BARNARD CL
THE CREST
EDEN CT

FORD COTTS

67

BERESFORD AVE
DENVILLE RD
GRANBOROUGH

Sch

GRANGE RD
FOUNDRY LA
LOXLEY WAY
CROMER RD

THURSFIELD
HANWORTH
SUDBURY
DERBY CT
CLARE CL
COMPTON CL

BURFORD
NEWBOLD
EDEN CT

Ford Farm

CV33

2

OAK TREE CL
PAYNE CL
KEIR CL
NAPTON DR

TAYLOR AVE
HADDON RD
DEENE
GRESHAM AVE
RAWLINSON RD
WELLINGTON RD
ELTON CL
BRIAR CL
BUCKLEY RD

The Runghills

River Leam

HEEMSTEDE LA
WATHEN RD
CAMPION GN
MULBERRY CL
WHITTON CL
DOLEY CL
ROBINIA

Mast

BLACK LA

Works

White House

1

LILLINGTON RD
GRANVILLE CT
CAMPION RD
JASMINE GR
PLEASANT WAY
HURLEY CL
KILN CL
SHERBOTE
LEICESTER

1 GRESHAM PL
2 CHESTNUT SQ
3 MARSTON CL

Mast

WALLER ST
NORTH VIL
SUFFOLK CL
HILL ST
NORFOLK CL
LEICESTER ST
AQUA HO
QUEEN ST
PRINCE'S ST
CAMPION TERR
HAMPTON GR
GREENWOOD CT

Campion Hills

St Paul's CE Prim Sch

Redhouse Farm

Offchurch Bury

66

CLARENDON ST
PO
SWAN ST
LANSDOWNE ST
THOMAS ST
DUKE ST
VINCENT ST
KING ST
HOLLY ST
TALBOT ST
PRINCES ST
CAMPION TERR
NAPIER
UPPER HOLLY WLK
THE GRANGE
FERNHILL DR

WILLES RD
B4090
CROSS ST
HOLLY WLK
CAMBRIDGE GDNS

CH

32 A 33 B C 34 E F

A1
1 LOWER VILLIERS ST
2 LANSDOWNE RD
3 KENNEDY SQ
4 ST PAUL'S SQ
5 MERCHANTS CT
6 LANSDOWNE CRES
7 WILLIAM THOMAS HO
8 HANOVER GDNS
9 WHITTLE CT

A2
1 ACORN CT
2 STOCKTON GR
3 WHITACRE RD
4 CHARLES WATSON CT
5 SHUCKBURGH GR
6 HELLIDON CL
7 BROWNLOW ST

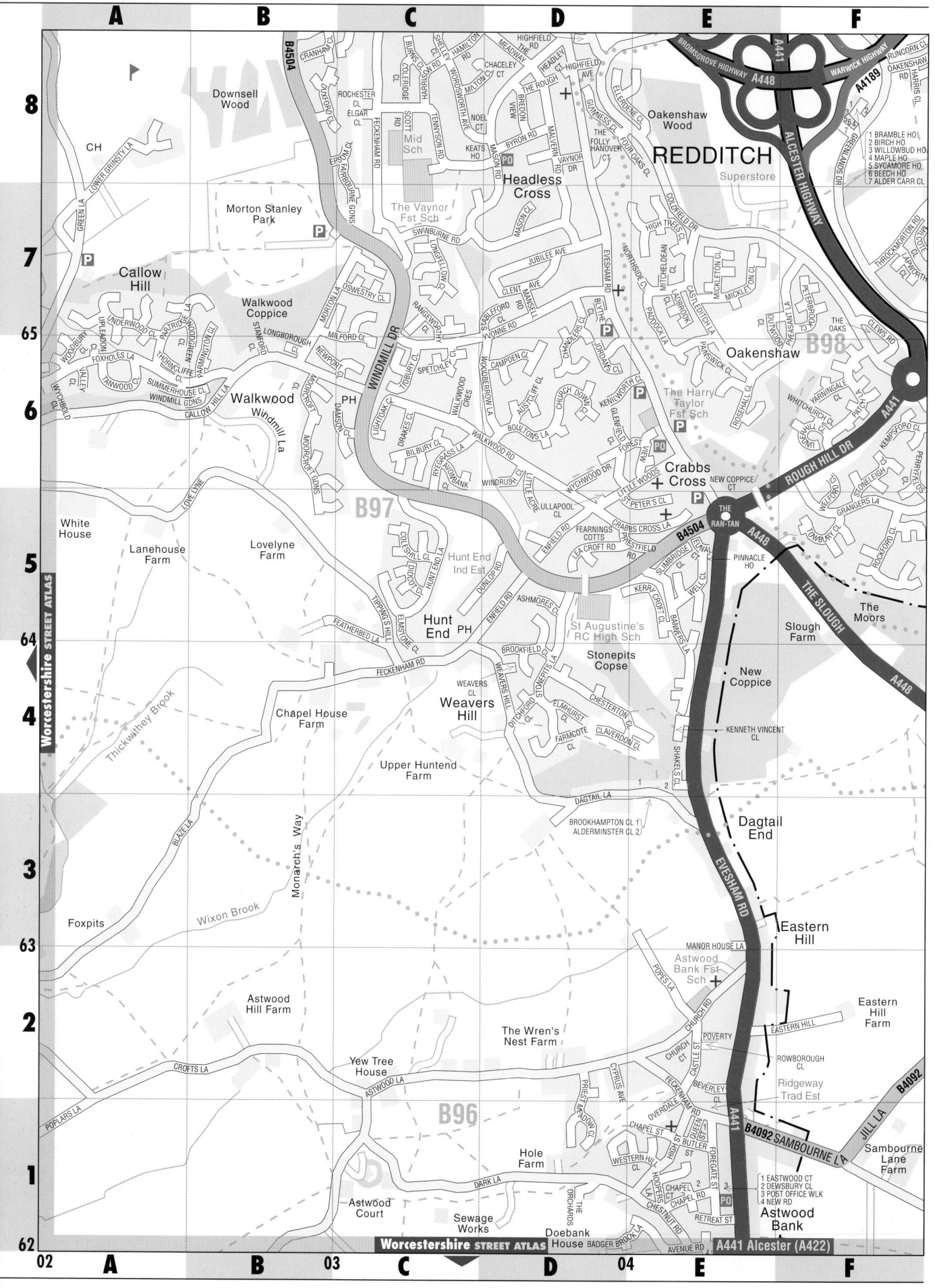

153

8

CH

Downsell Wood

B4504 CRANHAM

ROCHESTER CL ELGAR CL COLERIDGE HAMILTON DR SHELLEY CL HIGHFIELD RD THE RD CHACELEY CL HEADLEY HIGHFIELD AVE

OXFORD RD FARBURNE RD FECKENHAM RD EPSOM RD FARBOURNE GDNS SCOTT RD TENNYSON RD KEATS HO BYRON RD BREDON VIEW NOEL CT MASON CT MALVERN VAYNOR DR THE ROUGH GUINNESS CL ELLERDENE CL FOUR OAKS CL THE FOLLY HANOVER CT

Mid Sch

REDDITCH
Superstore

Oakenshaw Wood

1 BRAMBLE HO
2 BIRCH HO
3 WILLOWBUD HO
4 MAPLE HO
5 SYCAMORE HO
6 BEECH HO
7 ALDER CARR CL

A441 A448 WARWICK HIGHWAY A4189 BROMSGROVE HIGHWAY

RUNCORN CL OAKENSHAW RD HARRIS CL THROCKMORTON RD CARNWORTH PETERBROOK CARPWORTH

Morton Stanley Park

P

The Vaynor Fst Sch

Headless Cross

P

ALCESTER HIGHWAY

THE OAKS CLEWS RD

7

P

Callow Hill

Walkwood Coppice

SWINBURNE RD LONGFELLOW CT JUBILEE AVE

EVESHAM RD NORTHSIDE CL HIGH TREES CL COLEFIELD DR MITCHELDEAN CL CASTLEDITCH LA MICKLETON CL LADBROOK MICKLETON CL

B98

65

WOODBURY CL UNDERWOOD CL PARTRIDGE CL SPENNODGREEN MORTON LA OSWESTRY CL MILFORD CL NEWPORT LA LONGBOROUGH CL STAMFORD CL CLENT AVE RANGEWORTHY YVONNE RD STABLEFORD CL BLYTHE CL PADDOCK LA JORDANS CL KENILWORTH CL CASTLECROFT LA PAINSWICK CL

The Harry Taylor Fst Sch ROSEHALL CL WHITCHURCH CL YARNINGALE CL UNSER KEMPSFORD CL PERRYFIELD

Oakenshaw

65

UPLADBROOK FOXHOLES LA THORNCLIFFE CL PARMINGTON CL CALLOW HILL LA SUMMERHOUSE CL WINDMILL GDNS WINDMILL DR MOORCROFT JAMESON CL PH TOBURY CL SPETCHLEY CL CAMPDEN CL WOODBERROW LA AUSTCLIFF CL CHURCH DOWN CHANDLERS CL GLENFIELD WYCHWOOD DR FOREST VIEW

Walkwood Windmill La DRAKES CL WALKWOOD CRES KENILWORTH CL P PO

6

ANWOOD WYCHBOLD CL VALLEY CL LIGHTOAK CL BILBURY CL RYEGRASS LA AUTUMBANK WALKWOOD RD BOULTONS LA LITTLE ACRE WINDRUSH LITTLE WOODS ST PETER'S CL NEW COPPICE CT PO Crabbs Cross

ROUGH HILL DR STONELEIGH GRANGERS LA A441 ROCKFORD CL

6

B97 ULLAPOOL CL ENFIELD RD WYCHWOOD DR CRABBS CROSS LA THE RAN-TAN A448 WELFORD LOWBURY CL

White House

Lanehouse Farm

Lovelyne Farm

LOVE LYNE COLLIERS CL DIDCOT CL HUNT END LA DUNLOP RD Hunt End Ind Est LEA CROFT RD FEARNINGS COTTS PRIESTFIELD SLIMBRIDGE CL KERRY CL CROFT CL PINNACLE HO THE SLOUGH The Moors

5

B4504 CANAL BANNERS LA

5

64 FEATHERBED LA TIPPINGS HILL ELMSTONE CL ENFIELD RD ASHMORES CL St Augustine's RC High Sch Slough Farm

64

Thickwithey Brook

Chapel House Farm

FECKENHAM RD BROOKFIELD WEAVERS CL WEAVERS HILL STONEPITS LA ELMHURST CL CHESTERTON CL New Coppice KENNETH VINCENT CL

Weavers Hill DITCHFORD FARMCOTE CL CLAVERDON CL SHAKELS CL

4

BLAZE LA Upper Huntend Farm DAGTAIL LA Dagtail End

4

Foxpits Monarch's Way Wixon Brook BROOKHAMPTON CL 1 ALDERMINSTER CL 2 EVESHAM RD Eastern Hill

3

3

63 Astwood Hill Farm MANOR HOUSE LA Astwood Bank Fst Sch Eastern Hill Eastern Hill Farm

63

CROFTS LA Yew Tree House The Wren's Nest Farm ASTWOOD LA CHURCH RD POVERTY CASTLE ST Eastern Hill ROWBOROUGH CL

2

POPLARS LA B96 CYPRUS AVE CHURCH CT BEVERLEY CL Ridgeway Trad Est JILL LA B4092

2

Hole Farm PRIEST MEADOW CL CHAPEL ST OVERDALE CL A441 B4092 SAMBOURNE LA Sambourne Lane Farm

Astwood Court DARK LA WESTERN HILL CL QUEEN ST BUTLER ST HOOPERS CL CHAPEL RD CHAPEL CL

1 Sewage Works THE ORCHARDS CHESTNUT RD RETREAT ST PO 1 EASTWOOD CT 2 DEWSBURY CL 3 POST OFFICE WLK 4 NEW RD

1

Doebank House BADGER BROOK AVENUE RD Astwood Bank

62

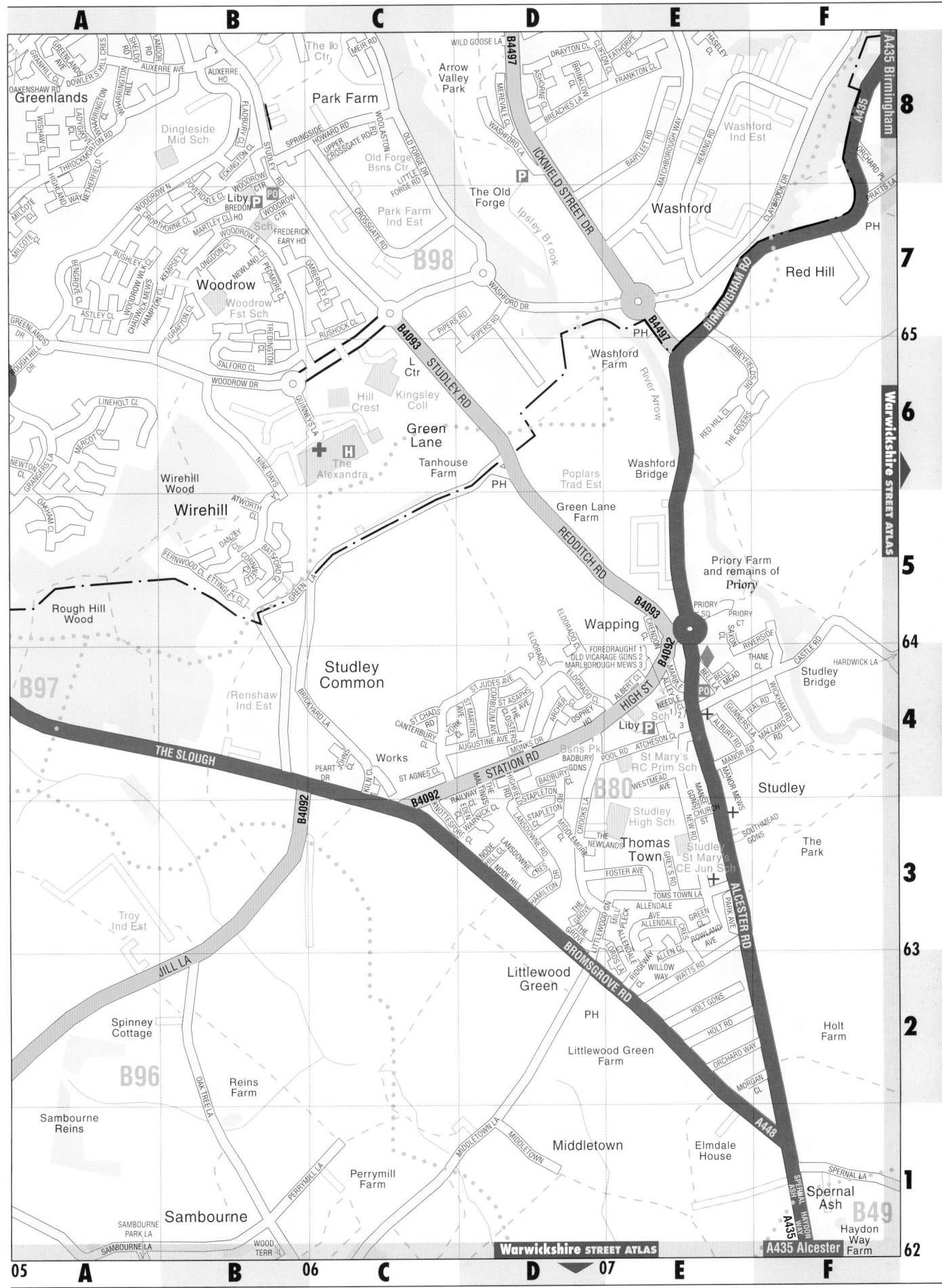

E6
1 GERRARD ST
2 ALMSHOUSES
3 EASTGATE MEWS
4 EASTGATE HO
5 NEVILLE CT
6 CASTLE MEWS

7 MARKS MEWS
8 TIBBITS CT
9 THE WOOLPACK
10 WESTGATE HO
11 PUCKERINGS LA
12 LEYCESTER PL
13 LEYCESTER CT

F7
1 ALEXANDER CT
2 COACH HOUSE MEWS
3 BARTLETT CL
4 ST JOHN'S CT
5 CASTLEGATE MEWS
6 AVERY CT

7 FAIRFAX CT
8 BROOKE MEWS
9 GOODWAY CT
10 PRIORY WLK
11 CROSS ST
12 YEOMANRY CL
13 GREVILLE HO

F8
1 PEMBROKE CL
2 ARUNDEL CL
3 CORNWALL CL
4 CROSS FIELDS RD
5 MULBERRY DR
6 ROWAN DR

7 GAVESTON CL

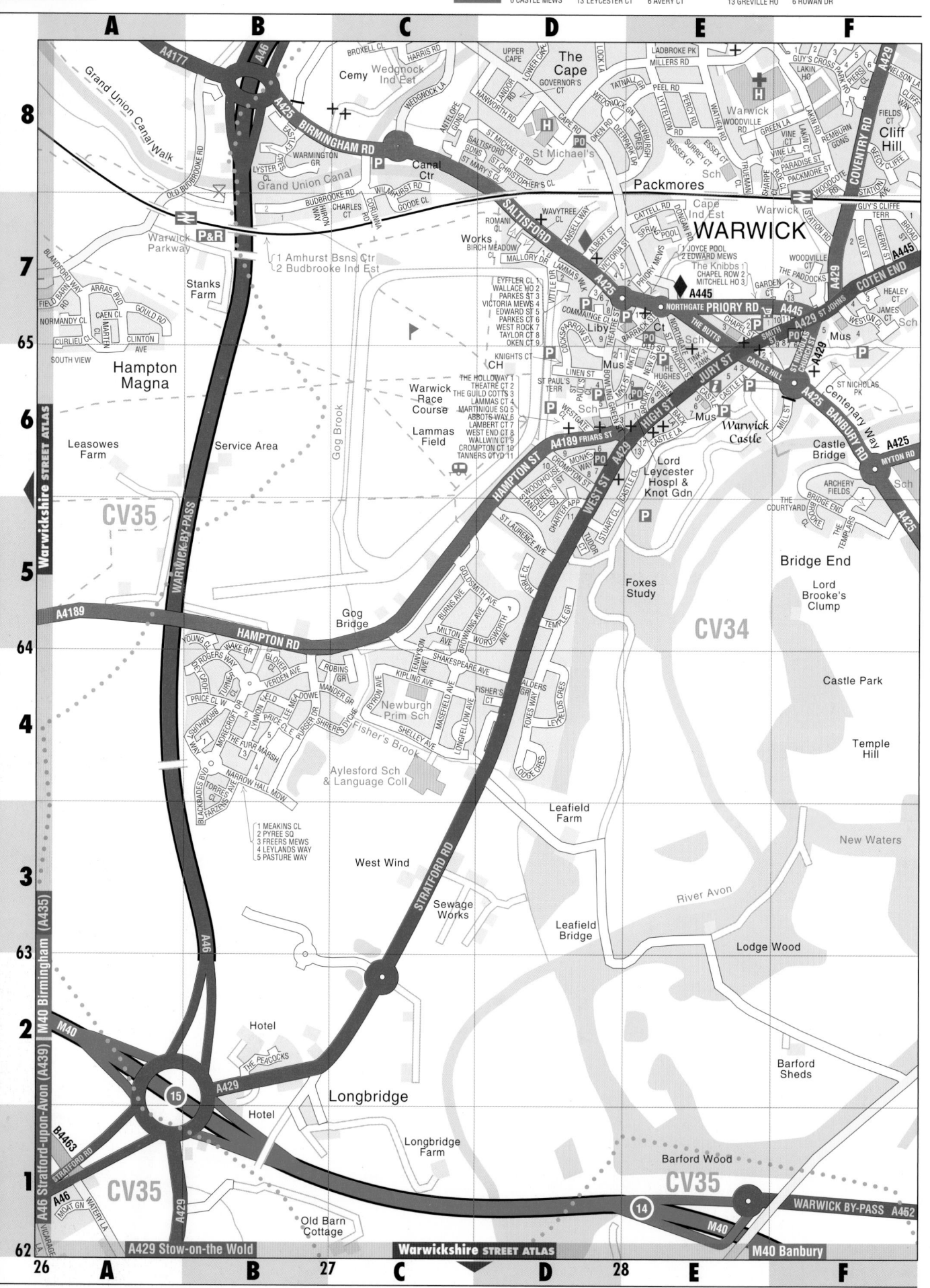

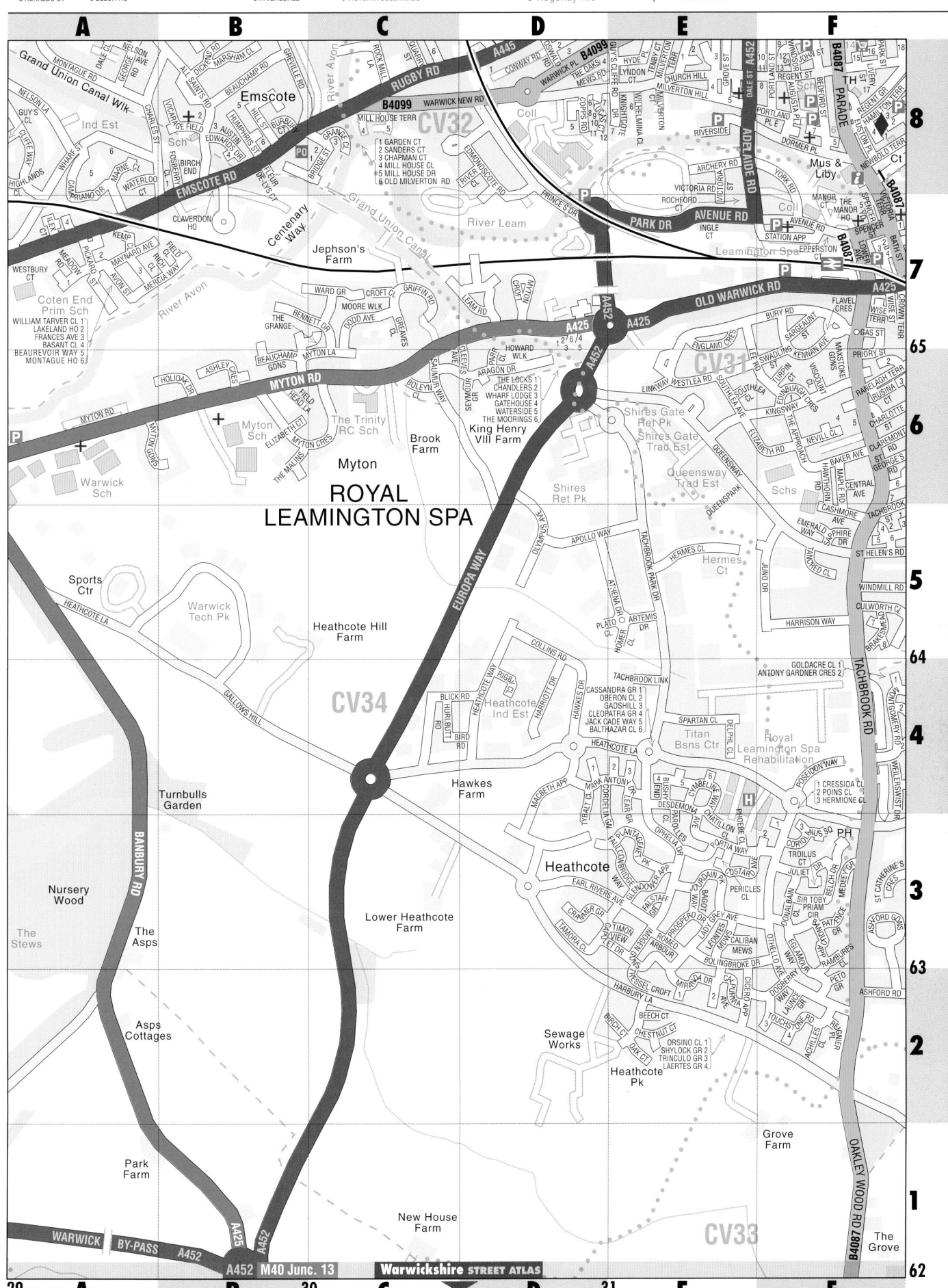

B8
1 CHARLES CT
2 ST EDITH'S HO
3 ST EDITH'S GN
4 WHITTINGTON CL
5 PACKWOOD MEWS
6 HERALDS CT

D8
1 WESTGROVE TERR
2 CROSS RD
3 THE CEDARS MEWS
4 PENDINE CT
5 GOODWAY HO
6 BEECH HO

7 OAK HO
8 BROOKLANDS HO
9 LEAM SIDE HO
10 SOUTHBANK HO
11 WILLOW HO
12 ALDER HO

E8
1 WOODBINE ST
2 WOODBINE COTTS
3 NEW BROOK ST
4 SOMERS PL
5 PORTLAND PL W
6 RIVERSDALE

7 CEDAR HO
F7
1 CHURCH WLK
2 SMITH ST
3 BATH PL
4 ABBOTTS ST
5 VICTORIA COLONNADE

156

F8
1 EUSTON SQ
2 ROSEFIELD ST
3 ROSEFIELD WLK
4 ROSEFIELD PL
5 BEDFORD PL
6 Regency Arc

162

F8
7 ST PETER'S RD
8 CARLTON HO
9 PORTLAND CT
10 PORTLAND MEWS
11 CHURCHILL HO
12 WINDSOR CT

13 CHAPEL CT
14 Royal Priors
15 SATCHWELL CT
16 SATCHWELL WLK
17 DENBY BLDGS
18 KENILWORTH ST

161

F5
1 YEW TREE CT
2 GINKGO WLK
3 CONIFER GR
4 SPRUCE GR
5 SILVER BIRCH GR
6 WYCH ELM DR
7 BONNIKSEN CL
8 LOCKHEED CL

F6
1 PHILIP CT
2 FRANCES HAVERGAL CL
3 PRINCE REGENT CT
4 FETHERSTON CT
5 TATCHBROOK CT
6 CHARLES GARDNER RD
7 MARKET CNR

A6
1 SOUTHBOROUGH TERR
2 GROVE PL
3 PRINCE REGENT CT
4 LISLE CT
5 DUGDALE CT
6 RADCLIFFE GDNS

A6
7 AYLESFORD CT
8 BEAUMONT CT
9 CHRISTINE LEDGER SQ
10 ST GEORGE'S RD
11 CHARLES GARDNER RD
12 MAURICE MEAD CT
13 ST JOHN'S TERR

◄ 161

A6
14 CHARLES CT

A7
1 CHURCH TERR
2 CLINTON ST
3 GLOUCESTER ST
4 REGENT PL
5 CHAPEL ST
6 PACKINGTON PL

▲ 157

A7
7 RUSSELL CT
8 ASH LAWN HO
9 WARNEFORD MEWS
10 BAXTER ST
11 Victoria Bsns Ctr
12 MOSS ST

13 NEILSTON ST
14 CUMMING ST
15 Althorpe Ind Est
16 TOWER ST
17 WEST ST

B7
1 SQUIRHILL PL
2 WILLES CT
3 JEPHSON PL
4 TRAFFORD LODGE
5 CLIFTON CT
6 RICHMOND CT

7 NORTHCOTE ST
8 SOUTHLANDS
9 RUSHMORE TERR

Map labels

ROYAL LEAMINGTON SPA

CV32

Red House Farm

Newbold Comyn Park

Floodgate Spinney

CV33

Willes Bridge

River Leam

Grand Union Canal Wlk

Grand Union Canal

Works

Radford Hall

Sydenham

Radford Semele CE Prim Sch

Radford Semele

A425 Southam

Warwickshire STREET ATLAS

Whitnash

Campion Sch Hastang & Com Coll

Superstore

The Shopping Ctr

Whitnash Prim Sch

CV31

Radford Barn

Radford Barn

Hill Farm

Valley Farm

Crown Hill

The Meadow

Mollington Hill

Pounce Hill Farm

Mollington Hill Farm

Frizmore Hill

Mallory Court Hotel

Tatchbrook Mallory

CV33

A4
1 FRANCIS GIBBS GDNS
2 MONTGOMERY RD
3 COBHAM GN
4 COX'S ORCHARD
5 ANTONY GARDNER CRES
6 WEILERWIST DR
7 OSBOURNE CT

◄ 161

C6
1 FRESHWATER GR
2 ST GOVAN'S CL
3 CONINGSBY CL
4 NEWBURY CL
5 WESTON CL
6 BLADON WLK
7 HARVEST HILL CL
8 FOXDALE WLK
9 MAYFIELD CL

10 LYNWOOD WLK
11 RANDOLPH CL
12 BISSET CRES
13 BURFORD MEWS
14 STANDLAKE MEWS
15 WAVERTON MEWS
16 ALDERTON MEWS
17 LONGLEAT GR

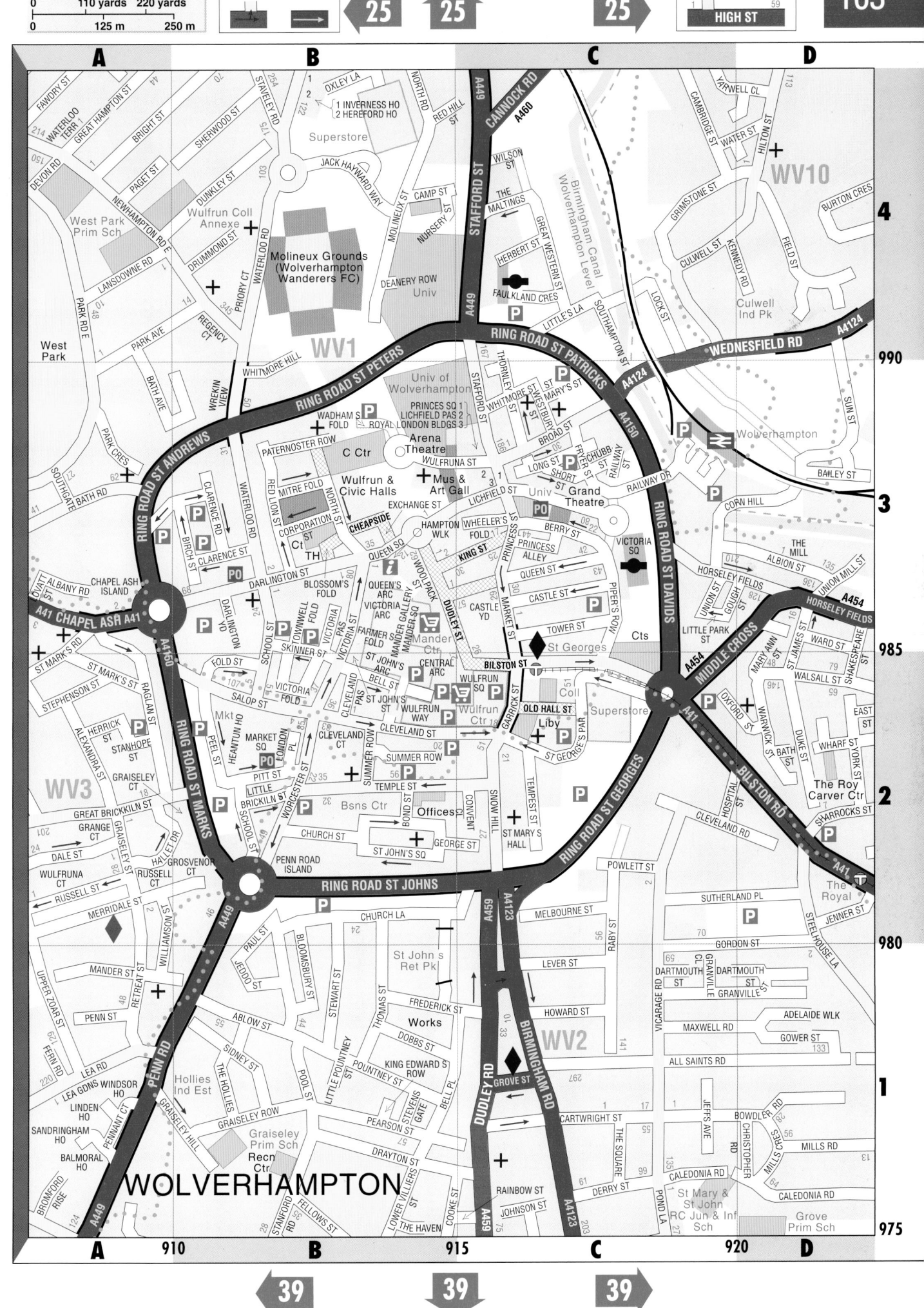

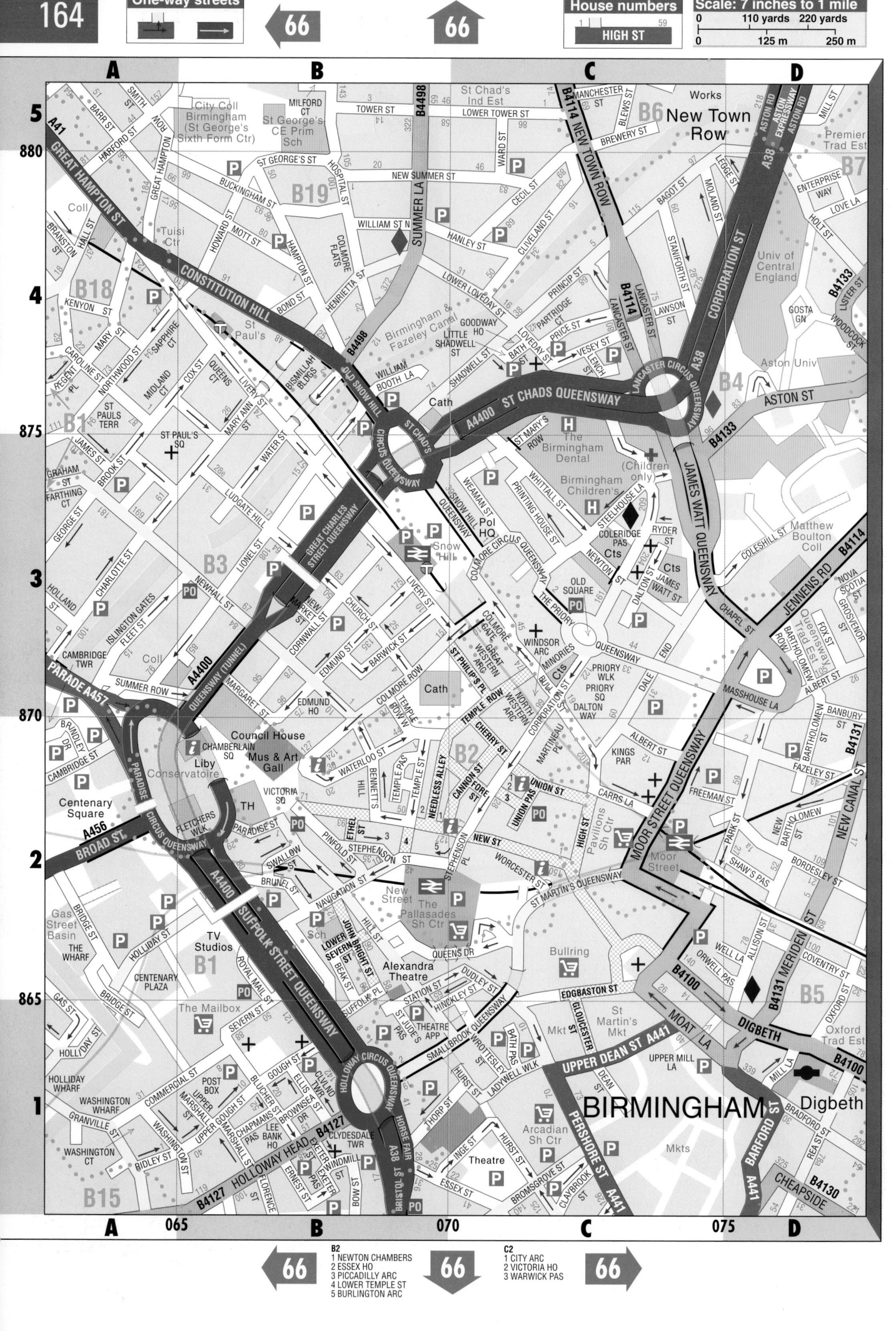

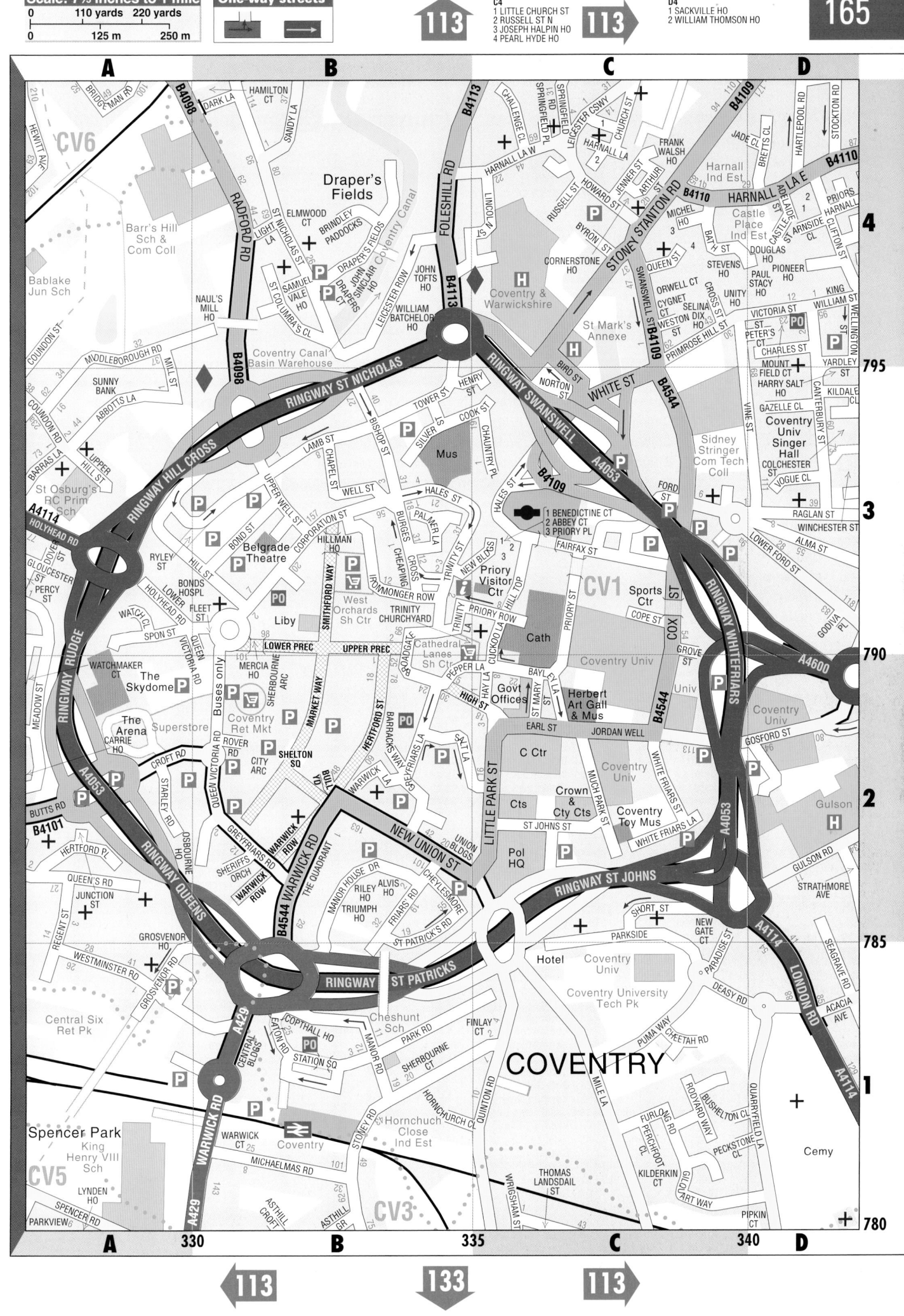

Scale: 7⅝ inches to 1 mile

0   110 yards   220 yards
0   125 m   250 m

One-way streets

113

C4
1 LITTLE CHURCH ST
2 RUSSELL ST N
3 JOSEPH HALPIN HO
4 PEARL HYDE HO

113

D4
1 SACKVILLE HO
2 WILLIAM THOMSON HO

165

COVENTRY

Index

Place name May be abbreviated on the map

Location number Present when a number indicates the place's position in a crowded area of mapping

Locality, town or village Shown when more than one place has the same name

Postcode district District for the indexed place

Page and grid square Page number and grid reference for the standard mapping

→ **Church Rd** 6 Beckenham BR2.........**53** C6

Public and commercial buildings are highlighted in magenta **Places of interest** are highlighted in blue with a star★

Abbreviations used in the index

Acad	**Academy**	Cnr	**Corner**	Dro	**Drove**	HQ	**Headquarters**	Mkt	**Market**
App	**Approach**	Coll	**College**	Ed	**Education**	Hts	**Heights**	Mus	**Museum**
Arc	**Arcade**	Com	**Community**	Emb	**Embankment**	Ind	**Industrial**	Orch	**Orchard**
Ave	**Avenue**	Comm	**Common**	Est	**Estate**	Inst	**Institute**	Pal	**Palace**
Bglw	**Bungalow**	Cott	**Cottage**	Ex	**Exhibition**	Int	**International**	Par	**Parade**
Bldg	**Building**	Cres	**Crescent**	Gd	**Ground**	Intc	**Interchange**	Pas	**Passage**
Bsns Bus	**Business**	Cswy	**Causeway**	Gdn	**Garden**	Junc	**Junction**	Pk	**Park**
Bvd	**Boulevard**	Ct	**Court**	Gn	**Green**	L	**Leisure**	Pl	**Place**
Cath	**Cathedral**	Ctr	**Centre**	Gr	**Grove**	La	**Lane**	Prec	**Precinct**
Cir	**Circus**	Ctry	**Country**	H	**Hall**	Liby	**Library**	Prom	**Promenade**
Cl	**Close**	Cty	**County**	Ho	**House**	Mdw	**Meadow**	Rd	**Road**
		Dr	**Drive**	Hospl	**Hospital**	Meml	**Memorial**	Recn	**Recreation**

Ret	**Retail**
Sh	**Shopping**
Sq	**Square**
St	**Street**
Sta	**Station**
Terr	**Terrace**
TH	**Town Hall**
Univ	**University**
Wk, Wlk	**Walk**
Wr	**Water**
Yd	**Yard**

Index of localities, towns and villages

A

Abbeydale 153 F5
Abbey Fields 147 E5
Acock's Green 88 B3
Aggborough 116 F4
Alderman's Green .. 96 B3
Aldersley 24 F7
Aldridge 30 A6
Allen End 47 F6
Allesley 111 B7
All Saints 66 A5
Alum Rock 68 B3
Alvechurch........ 139 B6
Alvecote 22 D6
Amblecote 80 F7
Amington 22 B4
Ansty 97 D4
Arrowfield Top 123 B1
Ash Green 95 C6
Ashmore Lake 27 B4
Ashmore Park...... 27 A8
Ashow 148 E1
Aspley Heath...... 141 D2
Aston 67 A7
Aston Fields 151 B7
Aston Flamville 76 E6
Aston New Town..... 66 F4
Astwood Bank..... 158 F1
Attleborough.......73 F2

B

Bacon's End 70 B4
Baddesley Clinton.. 145 B6
Baginton 133 F2
Balls Hill 42 B1
Balsall Common.. 130 A7
Balsall Heath...... 86 D6
Balsall Street 129 E6
Bank's Green..... 152 A3
Banners Gate 45 B4
Baptist End 62 C6
Barnacle........ 97 B6
Barnetbrook..... 118 D5
Barnt Green..... 138 A4
Barr Common..... 30 C3
Barrow Hill....... 61 C7

Barston........... 109 B1
Bartley Green 102 D7
Barwell 71 F7
Batchley 153 B3
Bateman's Green .. 124 F6
Batmans Hill 40 F2
Baylis Green 141 A1
Bearwood........... 65 A2
Beausale......... 146 C2
Bedworth 78 B1
Bedworth Heath.... 77 E1
Beech Lanes 84 E6
Beechwood 131 A6
Beechwood
   Gardens 132 E8
Belbroughton 119 E7
Belgrave 21 E1
Bell End 120 C7
Belle Vale 82 E5
Bell Green Coventry .. 114 B8
   Hollywood...... 124 B5
Bell Heath 120 E8
Bentley 27 E2
Bentley Heath 127 E5
Benton Green 110 E3
Beoley 154 D7
Berkswell 110 D3
Bermuda 78 A8
Bescot 42 C6
Bickenhill 90 D1
Bilbrook 10 C4
Billesley 105 C6
Billesley Common .. 105 A5
Bilston 40 D4
Binley.......... 134 E8
Binley Woods 135 C7
Birch Acre 140 D7
Birchen Coppice .. 116 B1
Birchensale 153 A5
Birches Green..... 57 A2
Birchfield 55 E1
Birchills 28 D3
Birchmoor 36 E8
Birmingham 164 C1
Bishopgate Green .. 113 D5
Bitterscote 21 A4
Black Bank 78 A1
Blackdown 156 F6

Blackfords 1 E2
Blackheath........ 63 B2
Black Lake 53 A7
Black Patch 65 D6
Blackwell 138 A5
Blakebrook 116 B6
Blakedown...... 98 C2
Blakeley Green..... 24 F8
Blakenall Heath ... 28 C8
Blakenhall 39 B7
Bloomfield 51 E7
Blossomfield 106 E2
Blowers Green 62 C7
Bluntington 118 E1
Boldmere 46 A1
Bolehall 21 D4
Boley Park 9 F7
Bonehill 20 E2
Bordesley Birmingham. 67 B2
   Redditch 139 D1
Bordesley Green 67 E2
Bordesley Green
   East 68 B1
Borough Park 21 C8
Borrowcop Hill 9 C6
Bournbrook 86 A2
Bournes Green 119 C2
Bournheath 136 D8
Bournville........ 103 E7
Bowling Green 62 E2
Box Trees 127 B1
Brades Village..... 52 E1
Bradley 40 E3
Bradmore 38 E8
Bradnock's Marsh .. 109 D3
Bramcote 79 E6
Bramford 51 A7
Brandon 135 F5
Brandwood End ... 104 E4
Branson's Cross ... 141 C2
Breedon Cross 104 B6
Bridge End 160 F5
Bridgtown 4 E6
Brierley Hill 61 E2
Brinsford 11 D7
Bristnall Fields 64 B3
Broad Green 138 B1
Brockmoor 61 C3

Bromford 57 D1
Bromley 61 B5
Bromsgrove 136 E2
Brookfields 66 B4
Broome 99 A2
Broomhill..........1 E4
Broom Hill 119 D3
Brownhills 16 B6
Brown's Green 54 F4
Brownshill Green.... 94 C2
Buckland End 69 A7
Buckpool.........60 F2
Bulkington 79 B1
Bunker's Hill 40 E7
Burbage 76 B6
Burcot 137 E4
Burnt Tree 51 F3
Burntwood..........7 C5
Burntwood Green ... 7 D6
Burton Green 131 C4
Burton Hastings..... 75 A1
Bushbury 11 E2

C

Caldmore 42 E8
California..........84 F2
Callow Hill 158 A7
Calthorpe Fields ... 86 B8
Camp Hill 72 E5
Canley 132 C7
Canley Gardens 132 E8
Cannock 1 D2
Cannon Hill 86 D4
Cape Hill 65 B4
Carol Green 130 F7
Carpenter's Hill ... 140 F1
Carroway Head..... 33 C4
Castle Bromwich ... 69 D8
Castlecroft......... 38 B8
Castle Green 147 D6
Castle Vale 58 B3
Catchems Corner... 130 E5
Catherine Cross ... 41 C6
Catherine de
   Barnes 108 B6
Catshill Bromsgrove . 137 A8
   Brownhills....... 16 A6

Causeway Green 63 F2
Cawney Hill 62 F8
Chadsmoor 1 F4
Chad Valley 85 F7
Chadwick End 145 B7
Chapel End 72 B7
Chapel Fields 112 E3
Chapel Green
   Coventry 93 B7
   Willenhall 27 B2
Chapman's Hill ... 121 B8
Charford 150 F7
Charlemont 53 D8
Chase Terrace 6 E8
Chasetown 6 F6
Chelmsley Wood ... 70 C2
Cheslyn Hay 4 C3
Chessetts Wood ... 144 D8
Chesterfield........ 17 E8
Chester Road 57 B6
Cheswick Green ... 126 E4
Cheylesmore 133 E7
Chilvers Coton 73 A1
Christ Church.......9 A8
Churchbridge........4 F4
Church End 114 C4
Churchfield 53 E6
Church Hill
   Birmingham 55 B1
   Redditch 154 C6
   Wednesbury 41 E4
Churchill.......... 98 C3
Cinder Hill 39 F1
Claregate 24 E6
Clayhanger 15 D6
Clent 99 F3
Cliff 35 C1
Cliff Hill 160 F8
Coalpit Field 78 D1
Coal Pool 28 F5
Cobley Hill 138 E4
Cockshut Hill 89 A8
Codsall 10 A3
Coft Common 122 F6
Cole End 70 E8
Colehall 69 B5
Coleshill.........70 F6
Coleshill Heath.... 90 C8

Collycroft 78 A5
Colton Hills 39 B3
Comberton....... 117 B5
Compton......... 24 D2
Coombeswood 83 C7
Cooper's Bank 50 C1
Copt Heath....... 108 A1
Corley 94 B7
Corley Ash 94 A8
Corley Moor 93 E6
Cornets End 110 B6
Coseley 40 C1
Coton 20 C6
Coton Green 20 F8
Cotteridge 103 E5
Coundon 112 F6
Coundon Green ... 112 E8
County Bridge..... 27 C2
Coven Heath 11 C6
Coven Lawn 11 A8
Coventry 165 C1
Crabbs Cross 158 E6
Crackley 148 B7
Cradley 82 D6
Cradley Heath..... 82 D8
Cubbington 157 D6
Curborough 3 D5
Curdworth 59 B6

D

Dagtail End 158 E3
Daisy Bank 40 C2
Darby End 62 E4
Darby's Hill 63 B8
Darlaston 41 E7
Darlaston Green.... 41 E8
Darley Green 144 B8
Darnford..........9 F4
Daw End 29 C5
Dayhouse Bank ... 101 A1
Deepfields 40 B2
Deritend 67 A1
Dibdale 50 F3
Dickens Heath 126 B6
Digbeth........ 164 D1
Dixon's Green 62 D7
Dodford......... 136 A7

Doe Bank 46 C7
Dordale 119 E1
Dordon 36 F6
Dorridge 127 E3
Dosthill 35 C5
Drakes Cross 125 A6
Draper's Fields ... 165 B4
Drayton 119 B4
Drayton Bassett 34 D5
Dudley 51 D2
Dudley Port 52 B3
Dudley's Fields 28 A8
Dudley Wood 62 C2
Dunstall Hill 25 C5

E
Eachway 121 F6
Earlsdon 113 A1
Earlswood 126 B1
Eastcote 108 E3
Eastern Hill 158 F3
Eaves Green 92 F2
Edgbaston 86 A6
Edge Hill 36 C2
Edgwick 113 F8
Edial 7 F6
Elmdon Heath 107 E7
Elmhurst 3 A5
Elston Hall 25 D8
Emscote 161 B8
Enfield 153 D5
Erdington 57 A4
Essington 12 F3
Ettingshall 40 A5
Ettingshall Park 39 D3
Eve Hill 51 B2
Exhall 96 B7

F
Fairfield 120 D3
Falcon Lodge 47 A6
Fallings Heath 41 F5
Fallings Park 25 E5
Fazeley 34 E8
Featherstone 12 C7
Fen End 129 E3
Finchfield 38 D8
Finham 133 C3
Finstall 137 D1
Fishley 14 C4
Flint's Green 111 B5
Foleshill 96 A2
Foley Park 116 C2
Footherley 17 F3
Fordbridge 70 A3
Fordhouses 11 D2
Forshaw Heath ... 141 C7
Four Ashes 127 C3
Four Oaks Meriden ... 110 C6
   Sutton Coldfield 31 F3
Four Oaks Park 46 A8
Foxford 96 A5
Foxlydiate 152 F3
Franche 116 B8
Frankley Birmingham ... 102 B2
   Frankley Green ... 102 B5
Frankley Green 102 A5
Frankley Hill 101 F3
Freasley 36 C4
Freezeland 40 B6
Friar Park 42 F2
Fulford Heath 125 D2

G
Galley Common 72 A5
Gannow Green 101 C1
Garrett's Green ... 69 B1
Gibbet Hill 132 F2
Gib Heath 66 A6
Gilbert's Green ... 141 E3
Gilbertstone 88 F6
Gillway 21 B8
Gilson 59 D1
Glascote Heath ... 21 F2
Glebe Farm 69 A4
Golds Green 52 E8
Goldthorn Hill 39 A5
Goldthorn Park 39 C5
Goodyers End 95 D8
Gornalwood 50 C2
Gorsty Ley 7 C7
Goscote 28 F8
Gosford Green ... 113 F2
Gospel End Village .. 50 A8
Gospel Oak 41 B1
Grace Mary Estate .. 63 C8
Gravelly Hill 56 E1

Great Barr 43 F2
Great Bridge 52 E6
Great Heath 113 E6
Great Wyrley 5 B3
Greenhill 117 A8
Green Lane Coventry ... 133 B5
   Redditch 159 C6
Green Lanes 40 C7
Greenleighs 39 C3
Greet 87 E5
Griff 78 B6
Griffin's Hill 103 D8
Grimes Hill 125 B4
Grove End 47 F3
Grove Vale 43 C1
Gunstone 10 A6
Guns Village 53 B4
Guy's Cliffe 156 A2

H
Habberley 116 A6
Hackman's Gate 98 F1
Haden Cross 83 A8
Hagley 99 D6
Halesowen 83 D4
Hall End 36 F5
Hall Flat 137 C7
Hall Green Bilston ... 40 E2
   Birmingham 106 A7
   Coventry 96 A3
   Wednesbury 42 C1
Hammerwich 7 D4
Hampton-in-Arden .. 109 B8
Hampton Magna ... 160 A6
Hamstead 54 E6
Handsworth 54 C1
Handsworth Wood ... 55 B3
Harborne 85 B6
Harden 28 E7
Hardwick 30 E3
Hartle 119 F6
Harts Green 85 A5
Hartshill 72 B8
Hart's Hill 61 E5
Harvest Hill 93 E2
Harvills Hawthorn ... 52 F7
Harvington 118 B2
Hasbury 82 E3
Haseley Knob 146 A3
Hasluck's Green ... 105 F2
Hateley Heath 53 C7
Hawkesbury 96 C5
Hawkes End 94 B2
Hawkesley 123 F8
Hawks Green 2 B1
Hawne 83 A6
Hayley Green 82 C1
Hay Mills 88 B6
Headless Cross ... 158 D8
Headley Heath 124 C6
Heathcote 161 D3
Heath End Bloxwich ... 15 A1
   Nuneaton 72 E2
Heath Green 140 F3
Heath Hayes 2 F1
Heath Town 26 A4
Hednesford 2 D5
Henley Green 114 D8
Highbridge 15 B6
Highfields Burntwood ... 6 F4
   Coseley 40 C3
Highgate 86 F7
High Heath 15 D2
Highter's Heath ... 105 B2
High Town 2 A5
Hill 32 A4
Hill and Cakemore .. 83 D7
Hillfield 107 A1
Hillfields 113 E4
Hill Hook 31 E6
Hillpool 118 E5
Hill Top Cannock 2 C4
   Nuneaton 73 C1
   Oldbury 64 C3
   West Bromwich 53 A7
Hill Wood 32 C5
Hill Wootton 156 C6
Hilton 17 A8
Himley 49 B3
Hinckley 75 B8
Hints 19 D3
Hobble End 14 B7
Hockley Birmingham ... 66 B5
   Coventry 111 C4
   Tamworth 35 E5
Hockley Heath 143 D6
Hodgehill 68 D6
Holbrooks 95 C3
Holly Bank 16 B3

Hollyberry End 93 C4
Hollycroft 71 A1
Holly Hall 61 E7
Hollyhurst 96 F8
Hollywood 125 B8
Holt End 154 F8
Holy Cross 99 E2
Homer Hill 82 B6
Honiley 146 D5
Hoobrook 116 F2
Hopwas 20 B7
Hopwood 123 B3
Horeston Grange ... 73 F5
Horseley Heath 52 D5
Hunnington 101 B8
Hunt End 158 C5
Huntington 1 D7
Hunts Green 48 C7
Hurcott 117 C8
Hurst Green 83 F8
Hurst Hill 40 A1

I
Illey 101 E8
Illshaw Heath 126 E1
Inkford 124 F1
Ipsley 154 C2
Iverley 98 B7

K
Kate's Hill 62 E8
Kemps Green 143 A1
Kenilworth 148 D5
Keresley 94 F5
Keresley Newlands .. 95 B6
Kettlebrook 21 B3
Kidderminster 116 D4
Kineton Green 106 E8
King's Heath 104 F7
King's Hill 41 E4
Kingshurst 70 A5
Kingstanding 45 A1
Kingswinford 60 F6
Kingswood 144 D3
King's Wood 104 D1
Kingswood Brook .. 144 E3
Kinwalsey 92 F7
Kitt's Green 69 C3
Kitwell 102 A7
Kixley Wharf 128 C7
Knowle 128 B6
Knowle Grove 128 B3

L
Ladyes Hills 148 A7
Ladymoor 40 D4
Ladywood 66 A2
Lady Wood 45 F8
Lakeside 154 B3
Lambert's End 53 B2
Landywood 14 A8
Lane Green 10 C3
Lane Head 27 D5
Lanesfield 39 E4
Laney Green 4 A3
Langley 64 A5
Langley Green 64 B3
Lapal 83 F3
Lapworth 143 E3
Lawns Wood 60 B2
Lea Hall 69 A2
Lea Bank 86 D8
Leamonsley 8 E7
Leamore 28 B6
Lee Bank 86 D8
Leek Wootton 155 F7
Leighswood 30 A7
Leyfields 20 F7
Ley Hill 32 B1
Lichfield 9 D5
Lickey End 137 C6
Lifford 104 B5
Lillington 157 C3
Lime Tree Park ... 112 A2
Linthurst 138 A6
Little Aston 31 B4
Little Bloxwich ... 14 E3
Little Bromwich 67 F2
Little Hay 18 C1
Little Heath 95 F1
Little London 27 A3
Little Packington .. 91 C6
Littlewood 14 E4
Littlewood Green .. 159 D2
Littleworth 2 E4
Little Wyrley 14 E8
Lode Heath 107 C6

Lodge Green 92 E3
Lodge Hill 85 B2
Lodge Park 153 F2
Londonderry 64 D4
London Fields 50 F2
Longbridge 160 C2
Longford 95 F4
Lower Bradley 41 A2
Lower Clent 99 D4
Lower Eastern Green ... 112 A3
Lower Gornal 50 E4
Lower Illey 101 D7
Lower Marlbrook .. 121 C1
Lower Penn 37 F4
Lower Stoke 114 A1
Lower Stonnall 17 A4
Low Hill 25 E7
Loxdale 41 A5
Lozells 66 C7
Lutley 82 C3
Lydiate Ash 121 C3
Lye 81 E6
Lyndon End 89 A5
Lyndon Green 89 A7

M
Madeley Heath 120 E7
Major's Green 125 D8
Maney 46 C4
Manor House 96 C2
March End 26 E5
Market End 77 D2
Marston Green 90 A8
Marston Jabbett ... 78 E5
Matchborough 154 E1
Mayer's Green 53 E3
Meer End 130 D1
Mere Green 32 B3
Meriden 92 D1
Merridale 24 E2
Merry Hill Brierley Hill ... 61 E3
   Smethwick 65 D5
   Wolverhampton ... 38 D7
Mesty Croft 42 C2
Middle 4 A4
Middle Bickenhill ... 91 A3
Middle Stoke 114 A3
Middleton 34 A1
Middletown 159 D1
Mile Oak 20 D1
Mill End 148 A6
Millfields 40 C5
Mill Green Aldridge ... 30 F7
   Cannock 4 F8
Milverton 156 D2
Minworth 58 C5
Minworth Greaves .. 58 D6
Monks Park 95 C1
Monkspath 127 B5
Monkspath Street .. 126 E6
Monmore Green 40 A8
Moons Moat 154 F5
Moor Green 86 D1
Moor Hall 32 D1
Moseley 86 F2
Moseley Village ... 26 C2
Mount Pleasant Bedworth ... 78 B3
   Coventry 115 B8
   Tamworth 21 C1
Mousesweet 62 F3
Moxley 41 B3
Muckley Corner 8 A2
Mucklow Hill 83 D6
Mushroom Green ... 62 B1
Mustow Green 117 F1

N
Neachells 26 D3
Neal's Green 95 D5
Nechells 67 D8
Nechells Green ... 67 A4
Nether Stowe 3 C3
Netherton 62 C4
Newbolds 26 A6
Newbridge 24 E3
New Cross 26 B6
New Dock 51 A1
New Invention 27 D8
New Oscott 45 D2
Newton 54 C8
Newtown 14 B6
New Town Birmingham ... 66 C6
   Brownhills 6 F2
   Tipton 52 D4
New Town Row 164 C5

Nordley Hill 26 C6
Northfield 103 B4
Norton 80 D2
Norton Canes 5 C6
Norton East 6 A6
Norton Green 128 B2
Nurton 23 A3
Nuthurst 143 C4

O
Oakenshaw 158 E6
Oakham 63 A8
Ocker Hill 52 C8
Offmore Farm 117 A6
Oldbury 63 F6
Old Dock 62 B8
Old Fallings 25 F8
Oldfallow 1 D3
Old Hill 62 F1
Old Milverton 156 B3
Old Oscott 44 F2
Old Perton 23 B2
Old Swinford 81 A2
Oldwich Lane 129 C1
Olton 88 F1
Orton 37 F3
Outwoods 92 C5
Overend 82 E6
Over Green 47 F1
Oxbarn 38 E7
Oxley 25 B8

P
Packmores 160 E8
Packwood 144 A8
Packwood Gullet .. 127 E1
Palfrey 42 E7
Palmers Cross 24 D8
Paradise 113 F6
Parkes Hall 51 A6
Park Farm 159 C8
Parkfield 39 E5
Park Hill 148 C6
Park Village 25 F5
Pedmore 81 B1
Pelsall 15 B3
Pelsall Wood 14 F5
Pendeford 10 F2
Penn 38 E5
Penn Fields 38 F6
Pensett 61 C6
Pensnett 61 C6
Perry 55 E6
Perry Barr 55 B5
Perry Beeches 55 B8
Perry Common 56 C7
Perry Crofts 21 B7
Perryfields 136 E4
Perton 23 C4
Pheasey 44 C4
Piccadilly 35 F7
Pickford 111 E8
Pickford Green ... 111 C7
Pinkett's Booth ... 111 C8
Pinley 134 B7
Pinley Gdns 134 A8
Pipehill 8 C5
Pleck 42 C8
Plough Hill 72 A6
Polesworth 36 F8
Portobello 26 E1
Portway Oldbury ... 63 C6
   Redditch 141 A5
Potter's Green 96 E1
Pouk Hill 28 A3
Priestfield 40 B7
Primrose Hill 62 C4
Princes End 51 E8
Priory 51 C3
Pype Hayes 57 D5

Q
Quarry Bank 82 A8
Quarry Hill 36 A7
Queslett 44 C2
Quinton 84 C5

R
Radford 113 B7
Radford Semele ... 162 E5
Reddicap Heath ... 46 F4
Redditch 153 C2
Rednal 122 C6
Reeves Green 131 A8
Ridgacre 84 D6

Riverside 153 F6
Romsley 101 A4
Romsley Hill 101 A2
Rood End 64 C6
Roseville 51 B8
Rotten Row 128 C3
Rotton Park 65 E3
Rough Hay 41 C7
Rough Hills 39 F6
Roughley 32 D3
Round's Green 63 E8
Rowington Green .. 145 A1
Rowley Regis 63 B3
Rowley's Green ... 95 E3
Rowney Green 139 E3
Royal Leamington Spa ... 156 D3
Rubery 122 B7
Ruiton 50 D5
Rumbush 125 E3
Rumer Hill 4 F7
Rushall 29 C6
Rushbrook 141 D3
Russell's Hall 61 E8
Ryecroft 28 E4
Ryton 79 D2
Ryton-on-Dunsmore ... 135 B2

S
St Chads 40 F7
St George's 153 F4
St Nicolas Park ... 74 A7
Salter Street 126 D2
Saltley 67 E4
Sambourne 159 B1
Sandfields 9 A5
Sandwell 65 A7
Sandyfields 50 B6
Scotlands 26 A7
Scott's Green 62 A7
Sedgley 50 F7
Seisdon 37 A2
Selly Hill 86 A2
Selly Oak 85 D1
Selly Park 86 A1
Shard End 69 D6
Sharmans Cross ... 106 E4
Sheldon 89 C5
Shelfield 15 C1
Shenley Fields ... 102 E7
Shenstone 18 A5
Shenstone Woodend .. 18 A1
Shepwell Green ... 27 C1
Shilton 97 F5
Shire Oak 16 A6
Shireoak Hill 16 B5
Shirley 106 C3
Shirley Heath 126 C7
Shirley Street 106 C2
Short Heath Birmingham ... 56 E7
   Willenhall 27 D6
Showell Green 87 B4
Shuttington 22 F7
Sidemoor 136 F4
Silver End 61 C2
Silver Street 124 F5
Sketchley 75 C6
Sketchley Hill 75 E7
Small Heath 87 D7
Smallwood 153 E2
Smethwick 65 A4
Snuff Hill 120 C7
Soho 65 C7
Solihull 107 D3
Solihull Lodge 105 E2
Southcrest 153 E1
South Yardley 88 D6
Spade Green 8 A8
Sparkbrook 87 B7
Sparkhill 87 D4
Spencer Park 165 B4
Spennells 117 A2
Spernal Ash 159 F1
Spon End 113 A3
Spring Bank 27 B3
Springfield Bedworth ... 78 C2
   Birmingham 105 E8
   Rowley Regis 62 F5
   Wolverhampton ... 25 E3
Springhill 16 E8
Spring Hill 38 C4
Springs Mire 62 A8
Spring Vale Bilston ... 40 B4
   Birmingham 67 B1
Stakenbridge 98 E3
Stambermill 81 C6
Stanklyn 117 D2

Staple Hill 137 C8
Stareton 149 D3
Stechford 68 E3
Stirchley 104 B7
Stivichall 133 C3
Stockfield 88 C5
Stockingford 72 C3
Stockland Green 56 C4
Stockwell End...... 24 D6
Stoke 114 C2
Stoke Aldermoor ... 134 B8
Stoke End .... .47 F7
Stoke Heath
  Bromsgrove 150 D5
  Coventry 114 A6
Stoke Park 114 A2
Stoke Pound 151 A4
Stoke Prior 150 C4
Stoke Works 150 C1
Stone 117 E2
Stonebridge 91 D3
Stone Cross 42 D1
Stoneleigh 149 B6
Stoney Hill 137 A2
Stonnall 16 E4
Stourbridge 80 D4
Stowe 3 C1
Stow Heath 40 B7
Stow Lawn 40 D8
Streetly .... .44 F8
Stubber's Green 29 E8
Studley 159 F4
Studley Common ... 159 C4
Summerford Place ..26 F2
Summerhill 116 B5
Summer Hill 52 A8
Sutton Coldfield.... 46 D5
Sutton Farm 116 B4
Swan Village Dudley .. 51 B6
  West Bromwich 52 F4
Sydenham 162 D5

T
Tamworth 21 B3
Tanner's Green 125 B1
Tansley Hill 62 F7
Tanwood 119 B2
Tanworth-In-Arden 142 B2
Tardebigge........ 152 B7
Tat Bank 64 B6
Tatchbrook Mallory. 162 A1
Temple Balsall 129 B5
Ten Acres 104 B8
Terry's Green 141 F7
Tettenhall 24 D5
Tettenhall Wood.... 24 C3
The Cape 160 D8
The Chuckery 29 A1
The Coppice 51 A7
The Delves .... .42 F5
The Flatts 41 E7
The Knowle 63 A4
The Leys 21 A5
The Lunt 41 A6
The Manor 27 A2
The Straits 50 A5
The Woods 42 C4
Thimble End 47 A1
Thomas Town 159 E3
Thornes........... 16 E3
Three Maypoles ... 126 A7
Tibbington .... .51 F7
Tidbury Green...... 125 E4
Tile Cross 69 E2
Tile Hill 111 E1
Tilehouse Green ... 127 F6
Tippity Green 63 B4
Tipton .... .51 F6
Tipton Green 51 D5
Titford .... .63 F4
Tividale 52 D3
Tollbar End 134 C4

Toll End.......... 52 C6
Tower Hill........ 55 C6
Trescott.......... 37 B7
Triangle.......... .7 B4
Trueman's Heath .. 125 C7
Trysull 37 C1
Tudor Hill 46 B6
Turves Green 103 A1
Two Gates 35 B8
Tyburn 57 E3
Tyseley........... 88 A6

U
Uffmoor 82 E1
Ulverley Green 89 A1
Underhill 12 B2
Upper Bentley..... 152 A1
Upper Catshill..... 121 B2
Upper Eastern
  Green 111 D4
Upper Gornal......50 F6
Upper Landywood ... 13 E8
Upper Marlbrook .. 121 D2
Upper Stoke 114 B4
Upper Witton 56 B5
Upton Warren 150 A3

V
Vauxhall 67 B4
Vigo .... .15 F2

W
Wake Green........ 87 B1
Walker's Heath.... 104 B1
Walkwood 158 B6
Wall 8 D2
Wallbrook......... 51 D8
Wall Heath 60 B8

Wall Hill 94 A4
Wallington Heath... 14 B2
Walmley .... .57 F8
Walsal End 109 A3
Walsall 28 B3
Walsall Wood ..... .15 F4
Walsgrave on Sowe 115 B7
Walton Pool...... 100 A2
Wapping 159 E5
Ward End 68 A5
Waring's Green ... 142 D8
Warley Woods..... 84 E8
Warstock 105 C3
Warstone 13 C8
Warwick 160 E7
Washford 159 E7
Washwood Heath... 67 E6
Water Orton 59 C3
Weatheroak Hill ... 124 B1
Weavers Hill 158 C4
Webheath........ 153 A2
Weddington 73 D7
Wedges Mills...... .4 B6
Wednesbury 41 D3
Wednesbury Oak ... 41 B1
Wednesfield 26 E6
Weeford 19 A4
Wellington Place ... 27 A4
Wells Green....... 89 B4
Weoley Castle 85 A1
Wergs 24 A6
West Bromwich ... 53 E3
West Chadsmoor ...1 F5
West Coseley...... 51 B7
Westcroft 12 B3
West Hagley 99 A5
West Heath 123 B7
West Hill......... 2 B6
Weston in Arden .. 79 A3
West Smethwick ... 64 C7
Westwood Gardens. 132 D8

Westwood Heath . 131 E6
Whateley .... .35 F3
Whiteheath Gate ... 63 D4
Whitehouse
  Common 46 E7
Whitemoor........ 148 B5
Whitemore Park.... 95 C1
White Stitch 92 C3
Whitestone 79 B7
Whitlock's End 125 E6
Whitnash 162 C3
Whittleford 72 C5
Whoberley 112 D2
Wightwick 23 E1
Wildmoor 120 F4
Willenhall Coventry . 134 D6
  Wolverhampton 27 B4
Wilncote .... .35 F8
Wilnecote .... .35 F8
Wimblebury 2 F3
Windmill End 62 E4
Windy Arbour 148 B3
Winson Green.....65 F5
Winyates 154 E2
Wirehill 159 B5
Wishaw 48 B2
Withybed Green .. 138 F6
Withymoor Village.. 81 C8
Witton 56 A3
Wollaston 80 D6
Wollescote 81 E4
Wolston 135 F3
Wolverhampton ... 25 A3
  163 B1
Wombourne 49 B6
Woodcock Hill ... 102 F8
Woodcross 40 A2
Wood End Coventry . 96 C1
  Tamworth 36 C1
  Tanworth-in-Arden ... 141 F3
  Wednesfield 26 D7

Woodgate Birmingham 84 A1
  Bromsgrove 151 B2
Woodgate Valley... 84 C3
Wood Green 42 A5
Woodloes Park.... 155 D2
Woodrow
  Kidderminster....... 118 D3
  Redditch 159 B7
Woods Bank 41 B5
Woodsetton 50 E6
Woodshires Green... 95 E5
Woodside 61 E6
Woodway Park 114 E8
Wootton Green ... 110 A1
Wordsley......... 60 E7
Worlds End 107 A6
World's End 84 D5
Worms Ash 136 C6
Wren's Nest...... 51 A4
Wroxall 145 E1
Wyken 114 D5
Wyken Green..... 114 C6
Wylde Green 46 C1
Wythall 125 B3
Wythall Green 124 E3

Y
Yardley 88 B5
Yardley Fields 68 D1
Yardley Wood 105 E5
Yew Tree
  Balsall Common 130 A6
  Wednesbury 43 B4
Yew Tree Hill 62 B4
Yieldingtree...... 118 F8

Index of streets, hospitals, industrial estates, railway stations, schools, shopping centres, universities and places of interest

3b B – Adm

3b Bsns Village B21.. 65 D7
10 Ctr The B98 ..... 154 C1

A

A1 Trad Est B66...... 65 A7
Aaron Ct B24 ....56 F3
Abberley B77 .... 22 C2
Abberley Cl
  Halesowen B63....... 82 F2
  Redditch B98 ...... 154 C5
Abberley Ind Ctr B66 65 D5
Abberley Rd
  Birmingham B68...... 84 B8
  Dudley DY3 .... 50 D4
Abberley St
  Dudley DY2 .... 62 C8
  Smethwick B66...... 65 D5
Abberton Cl B63 ..... 83 C3
Abberton Ct B23 ..... 56 C2
Abberton Gr B90.... 127 B7
Abberton Ho 4 B97. 153 A4
Abberton Way CV4 .. 132 E3
Abbess Gr B25 ...... 68 E1
Abbey CE Inf Sch
  CV11...........73 B5
Abbey Cl
  Bromsgrove B60..... 137 C2
  West Bromwich B71.. 53 C5
Abbey Cres
  Halesowen B63....... 82 D4
  Oldbury B68 .... 64 D1
Abbey Ct
  Coventry CV1 ...... 165 C3
  Coventry, Pinley CV3.. 134 B6
Abbeydale Cl CV3 .. 114 F2
Abbeydale Rd B31... 103 A2
Abbey Dr WS3 ..... 15 A5
Abbey End CV8..... 147 F4
Abbeyfield Rd
  Birmingham B23..... 56 E8
  Wolverhampton WV10.. 11 F4
Abbeyfields Dr B80.. 159 E6
Abbey Gate CV11.... 73 C4
Abbey Gate Sh Ctr
  CV11.............73 C4
Abbey Gdns B67 ..... 64 E1
Abbey Gn CV11..... 73 B5
Abbey Hill CV8 .... 147 F5

Abbey Ind Est CV2.. 114 F5
Abbey Inf Sch B67...64 E2
Abbey Jun Sch B67..64 E1
Abbey Mans 2 B24.. 57 B6
Abbey Prim Sch WS3 .13 E2
Abbey RC Jun & Inf Sch
  The B23 .... 57 A5
Abbey Rd
  Birmingham B17..... 85 D5
  Birmingham, Gravelly Hill
  B23 .... 56 D2
  Coventry CV3 ..... 134 A6
  Dudley, Gornalwood
  DY3............. 50 C3
  Dudley, Netherton DY2. 62 D6
  Halesowen B63...... 82 C4
  Kidderminster DY11 . 116 A6
  Redditch B97 ...... 153 E4
  Smethwick B67...... 64 E1
  Tamworth B77....... 21 D3
Abbey St N B18 ..... 66 A5
Abbey Sq WS3 ..... 13 E2
Abbey St
  Birmingham B18..... 66 A5
  Cannock WS12 ....2 B7
  Dudley DY3 .... 50 C3
  Nuneaton CV11..... 73 B5
Abbey The CV8 .... 147 F5
Abbey Trad Ind Area
  B97.............. 153 E5
Abbey Way CV3 .... 133 F6
Abbot Rd B63...... 100 C8
Abbotsbury Cl CV2.. 115 A4
Abbotsbury Way CV11 78 E7
Abbots Cl
  Dorridge B93 ...... 128 A7
  Walsall WS4 .... 29 C6
Abbots Field WS11....1 E5
Abbotsford Ave B43.. .43 F2
Abbotsford Dr DY1.. 61 E7
Abbotsford Rd
  Birmingham B11..... 87 C6
  Lichfield WS14 ......9 E7
  Nuneaton CV11...... 73 E1
Abbotsford Sch CV8 147 F6
Abbots Mews DY5... 61 D1
Abbots Rd B14..... 104 E7
Abbots Way
  Birmingham B18..... 66 B6
  Warwick CV34 ..... 160 D6
  Wolverhampton WV3 . 24 E1
Abbotts Gn LE10 ....75 F5

Abbotts La CV1 ..... 165 A3
Abbotts Pl WS3 .... 14 D1
Abbotts Rd B24 ......56 F1
Abbotts St
  4 Royal Leamington Spa
  CV31............ 161 F7
  Walsall WS3 ...... 14 D2
Abbotts Wlk CV3 ... 135 C7
Abdon Ave B29..... 103 C7
Abelia B77.......... 21 F3
Abercorn Rd CV5.... 112 E2
Aberdeen Cl CV5.... 112 A5
Aberdeen Rd CV11 .. 73 E1
Aberdeen St B18.... 65 E4
Aberford Cl WV12 ... 27 D4
Abergavenny Wlk
  CV3 .... 134 F6
Abigails Cl B26 ..... 89 B7
Abingdon Cl WV1 ... 26 B2
Abingdon Rd
  Birmingham B23..... 56 B7
  Dudley DY2 .... 62 D3
  Walsall WS3 ...... 13 F2
  Wolverhampton WV1 . 26 F2
Abingdon Way
  Birmingham B35..... 58 A3
  Nuneaton CV11..... 73 F7
  Walsall WS3 ...... 13 F2
Ablewell St WS1 .....28 F1
Ablow St WV2...... 163 B1
Abnalls La WS13 .....8 B8
Abney Dr WV14 .....39 F1
Abney Gr B44...... 45 B2
Aboyne Cl B5 ...... 86 D6
A B Row B4........66 F3
Acacia Ave
  Birmingham B37..... 69 F6
  Coventry CV1 ...... 113 E1
  Walsall WS5 ...... 43 A4
Acacia Cl
  Birmingham B37..... 69 F6
  Dudley DY1 .... 51 A3
  Tipton B69 .... 52 B2
Acacia Ct
  Coventry CV6 ..... 112 E5
  Stourbridge DY8.... 80 E6
Acacia Gr WS12 .....2 F3
Acacia Rd
  Birmingham B30.... 103 E8
  Nuneaton CV10..... 72 E5

Acacia Rd continued
  Royal Leamington Spa
  CV32............ 156 D1
Acanthus Rd B98.... 154 F6
Accord Mews WS10 .. 41 D7
Ace Bsns Pk B33 ... 69 D2
Acfold Rd B20 ..... 54 E5
Achal Cl CV6........95 F2
Acheson Rd B28, B90 105 F3
Achilees Cl WS6...... 4 F1
Achilles Cl CV34.... 161 F2
Achilles Rd CV6..... 114 A7
Ackleton Gdns WV3 .38 F7
Ackleton Gr B29 .....84 F1
Acocks Green Prim Sch
  B27............... 88 B4
Acocks Green Sta
  B27 .... 88 C4
Acorn Cl
  Bedworth CV12..... 95 C8
  Birmingham, Bournville
  B30............. 103 E8
  Birmingham, Stockfield
  B27............. 88 B5
  Cannock WS11 ....2 C2
  Great Wyrley WS6....5 A1
  Stoneleigh CV8..... 149 B7
  West Bromwich B70.. 53 B2
Acorn Ct
  Birmingham B45..... 122 D7
  Coventry CV2 ..... 114 C2
  1 Royal Leamington Spa
  CV32............ 157 A2
Acorn Ctr 1 WS1 ...28 F1
Acorn Gdns B30..... 104 A7
Acorn Gr
  Birmingham B1 ..... 66 B3
  Stourbridge DY8.... 60 E1
Acorn Rd Catshill B61 137 B8
  Halesowen B62..... 83 C8
  Wolverhampton WV13 . 13 A1
Acorn St
  Coventry CV3 ..... 134 B8
  Willenhall WV13 ... 27 C2
Acorn Starter Units
  WS7..............6 D7
Acorns The B61 .... 137 A8
Acorn View WS7.....7 C6
Acre Cl CV31...... 162 A4
Acre La B97....... 152 E2
Acres Rd DY5 ..... 81 E8

Acres The WV3....... 24 C1
Acton Cl B98....... 154 D5
Acton Dr DY3 ...... 50 B3
Acton Gr Bilston WV14. 40 B4
  Birmingham B44...... 45 A2
Acton Ho CV4....... 111 F3
Adam Ct Cannock WS11. 1 D1
  Halesowen B63..... 82 F4
Adam Rd 1 CV6 .... 113 F7
Adams Brook Dr B32. 84 B1
Adams Cl
  Smethwick B66..... 64 D7
  Tipton DY4 .... 40 F1
Adams Ct DY10..... 117 A7
Adams Hill B32 .... 84 B1
Adam's Hill DY9.... 99 E4
Adams Ho 3 DY11.. 116 C6
Adamson Cl WS11......1 B1
Adams Rd
  Brownhills WS8 .... 16 B5
  Wolverhampton WV3 . 38 C8
Adams St
  Birmingham B7 .... 66 F5
  Walsall WS2 ...... 28 D2
  West Bromwich B70.. 53 B3
Adam St DY11..... 116 C5
Ada Rd
  Birmingham B25..... 88 B6
  Smethwick B66..... 65 B3
Adare Dr CV3 ..... 133 C8
Ada Wrighton Cl
  WV12 .... 27 C7
Adcock Dr CV8..... 148 B5
Addenbrooke Cres
  DY11 .... 116 A1
Addenbrooke Dr B73. 46 B2
Addenbrooke Pl
  WS10 .... 41 D7
Addenbrooke Rd
  Keresley CV7 ..... 95 A6
  Smethwick B67..... 64 F3
Addenbrooke St
  Darlaston WS10 .... 41 D7
  Walsall WS3 ...... 28 C7
Addenbrook Ho
  3 Cradley Heath B64. 82 F8
  Sutton Coldfield B73.. 46 A3
Addenbrook Way DY4 52 D8
Adderley Gdns B8.... 67 D5
Adderley Park Cl B8.. 67 E4
Adderley Park Sta B8 67 D3

Adderley Prim Sch
  B8.................. 67 D4
Adderley Rd B8 .... 67 C4
Adderley Rd S B8 .... 67 C3
Adderley St
  Birmingham B9 .... 67 A1
  Coventry CV1 ..... 113 E4
Adderley Trad Est B8. 67 C4
Addingham Cl 2
  CV34 .... 155 E1
Addington Way B69 . 52 D3
Addison Cl
  Cannock WS11 ....1 E5
  Nuneaton CV10..... 72 A5
  Wednesbury WS10 .. 42 E2
Addison Croft DY3 .. 50 A5
Addison Gr WV11 .. 12 B1
Addison Pl
  Bilston WV14 ..... 41 A7
  Water Orton B46 .. 59 D1
Addison Rd
  Birmingham, King's Heath
  B14............... 104 F7
  Birmingham, Nechells
  B7................ 67 C8
  Brierley Hill DY5 ... 61 B2
  Coventry CV6 ..... 113 A8
  Wednesbury WS10 .. 42 F4
  Wolverhampton WV3 . 38 F8
Addison St WS10.....41 F2
Addison Terr WS10 ...41 F2
Adelaide Ave B70 ... 53 A7
Adelaide Ct 3 CV12. 78 A2
Adelaide Dr WS12.....2 F3
Adelaide Rd CV31,
  CV32............ 161 E8
Adelaide St
  Birmingham B12.... 86 F8
  Brierley Hill DY5 ... 61 D3
  Coventry CV1 ..... 165 D4
  Redditch B97 ..... 153 D4
Adelaide Tower B34.. 69 C8
Adelaide Wlk WV2 .. 163 D1
Adelphi Ct 3 DY5... 61 D2
Adey Rd WV11 .....26 F7
Adkins La B67...... 65 A1
Admington Rd B33.. 89 C8
Admiral Gdns CV8.. 148 C6
Admiral Parker Dr
  WS14..............17 C1
Admiral Pl B13.......86 F4

Admirals Way
Bramcote CV11 79 E6
Rowley Regis B65 63 B2
Admiral Wlk DY10 116 E8
Adonis Cl B79 21 C7
Adrian Croft B13 87 C1
Adrian Ct 1 B24 57 B6
Adria Rd B11 87 B4
Adshead Rd DY2 62 C7
Adstone Gr B31 103 A1
Advance Bsns Pk WS11 2 B3
Advanced Tech Unit CV4 132 C6
Advent Gdns B70 53 B3
Adwalton Rd WV6 23 F3
Aethelred Ct WV10 25 C6
Affleck Ave B78 20 D1
Agenoria Dr DY8 80 F5
Aggborough Cres DY10 116 E3
Aggborough Stadium (Kidderminster Harriers FC) DY10 116 F4
Agincourt Rd CV3 133 E7
Agmore La B60 138 B3
Agmore Rd B60 138 B4
Aiden Ct WS13 9 C7
Aimsbury Ct B26 89 C4
Ainsbury Rd CV5 132 E8
Ainsdale Cl
Coventry CV6 96 B4
Stourbridge DY8 80 F2
Ainsdale Gdns
Birmingham B24 57 C5
Halesowen B63 82 D2
Ainsworth Rd
5 Birmingham B31 103 D2
Wolverhampton WV10 11 E4
Aintree Cl
Bedworth CV12 78 B4
Cannock WS12 2 F6
Coventry CV6 113 E5
Kidderminster DY11 116 D8
Upper Catshill B61 121 A1
Aintree Dr CV32 157 C3
Aintree Gr B34 69 D6
Aintree Rd WV10 11 D4
Aintree Way DY1 50 F2
Aire Croft B31 103 B1
Airfield Dr WS4, WS9 29 E3
Airport Way B26 90 C3
Aitken Cl B78 21 A2
Aitken Wing B15 86 A6
Ajax Cl WS6 4 F1
Akon Ho CV6 94 F2
Akrill Cl B70 53 B5
Akrill Cottage Hos The B70 53 B5
Alamein Rd WV13 26 E1
Alan Bray Cl LE10 74 D7
Alandale Ave CV5 111 E4
Alandale Ct CV12 95 C8
Alan Higgs Way CV4 131 C8
Alasdair Ho 1 B17 85 B5
Albany Cl DY10 117 B6
Albany Cres WV14 40 C6
Albany Ct
1 Birmingham B62 84 A7
Coventry CV1 113 A2
Albany Dr WS12 2 E3
Albany Gdns B91 107 E4
Albany Gr
Kingswinford DY6 60 E7
Willenhall WV11 13 C1
Albany Ho B34 69 A7
Albany Mews WS10 41 E6
Albany Rd
Birmingham B17 85 C6
Coventry CV5 113 A1
Wolverhampton WV1 163 A3
Albany Terr CV32 156 E1
Albemarle Rd DY8 80 F2
Albermarle Rd DY6 61 A5
Albert Ave 1 B12 87 A6
Albert Bean Cl CV31 162 A4
Albert Bradbeer Inf Sch B31 122 F7
Albert Bradbeer Jun Sch B31 122 F7
Albert Cl B80 159 E4
Albert Clarke Dr WV12 27 C7
Albert Cres CV6 95 B3
Albert Davie Dr WS12 2 E4
Albert Dr B63 82 F2
Albert Fearn Gdns CV6 95 F1
Albert Ho 1 WS10 41 C6
Albert Pritchard Inf Sch WS10 42 A5
Albert Rd
Allesley CV5 111 A8
Birmingham, Aston B6 66 F8
Birmingham, Brandhall B68 84 C8
Birmingham, Gravelly Hill B23 56 D3
Birmingham, Handsworth B21 54 E1
Birmingham, Harborne B17 85 B5
Birmingham, King's Heath B14 104 F7
Birmingham, Stechford B33 68 D3
Bromsgrove B61 150 E8
Fazeley B78 35 A8
Halesowen B63 82 F3
Hinckley LE10 71 D1
Kidderminster DY10 116 F6
Tamworth B79 21 B5
Wolverhampton WV6 25 A3
Albert St E B69 64 B7
Albert Smith Pl B65 63 A4
Albert St
Birmingham B5 164 D3
Brierley Hill DY5 61 D7
Cannock, Broomhill WS11 1 E4
Cannock WS12 2 D5
Coventry CV1 113 E4
Kingswinford DY6 60 B8
Nuneaton CV10 72 E3
Oldbury B69 64 A8
Redditch B97 153 E5
Royal Leamington Spa CV32 156 C1
Stourbridge DY8 80 F5
Stourbridge, Lye DY9 81 E5
Tipton DY4 51 F8
Walsall WS1 28 E2
Warwick CV34 160 D7
Wednesbury WS10 41 F2
West Bromwich B70 53 C1
Albert Wlk 1 B17 85 C5
Albion Ave WV13 27 C2
Albion Bsns Pk B66 64 E8
Albion Cotts B46 59 B3
Albion Ct
Brierley Hill DY5 61 C6
Nuneaton CV11 73 D3
Albion Field Dr B71 53 D4
Albion Ind Est
Coventry CV6 113 D7
West Bromwich B70 52 F2
Albion Jun Sch B66 65 A7
Albion Par DY6 60 B8
Albion Pl WS11 1 E4
Albion Rd
Birmingham, Handsworth B21 54 E1
Birmingham, Sparkhill B11 87 D5
Brownhills WS8 15 E8
West Bromwich B70 53 A2
West Bromwich, Sandwell B71 65 B8
Willenhall WV13 27 B2
Albion Rdbt B70 53 B4
Albion St Bilston WV14 40 E6
Birmingham B1 66 C3
Brierley Hill DY5 61 D3
Kenilworth CV8 148 A5
Kingswinford DY6 60 B8
Oldbury B69 52 E1
Tamworth B79 21 C5
Tipton DY4 51 F5
Willenhall WV13 27 C2
Wolverhampton WV1 163 D3
Albion Terr B46 59 B3
Albion Works DY5 61 B3
Alborn Cres B38 123 D8
Albrighton Ho 4 B20 54 F3
Albrighton Rd B63 82 F3
Albrighton Wlk CV11 74 A2
Albright Rd B68 64 D4
Albury Rd B80 159 E4
Albury Wlk B11 87 A7
Albutts Rd WS11 6 B3
Alcester Dr
Sutton Coldfield B73 45 D3
Willenhall WV13 26 D1
Alcester Gdns B14 104 F7
Alcester Highway B98 158 F8
Alcester Rd
Birmingham B13 86 F3
Finstall B60 137 F1
Hollywood B47 124 F5
Lickey End B60 137 D5
Alcester Rd *continued*
Portway B47, B48 140 F7
Studley B80 159 E3
Tardebigge B60, B97 152 B7
Alcester Rd S
Birmingham, Billesley Common B14 104 E6
Birmingham, Highter's Heath B14 104 F2
Alcester St
Birmingham B12 86 F8
Redditch B98 153 E4
Alcombe Gr B33 68 E2
Alcott Cl B93 127 F2
Alcott Gr B33 69 E3
Alcott Hall Prim Sch B37 70 B1
Alcott La B37 89 F8
Alcove The WS3 14 D2
Aldborough La 4 B97 153 B5
Aldbourne Rd CV1 113 C5
Aldbourne Way B38 123 E7
Aldbury Rd B14 105 A3
Aldbury Rise CV5 112 C4
Aldeburgh Cl WS3 14 A3
Aldeford Dr DY5 81 D8
Alden Hurst WS7 6 F8
Alder Ave DY10 116 E8
Alderbrook Cl
Redditch B97 153 B5
Sedgley DY3 39 B1
Alderbrooke Dr CV11 74 A1
Alderbrook Rd B91 106 F3
Alderbrook Sch B91 106 F2
Alder Carr Cl B98 158 F8
Alder Cl
Hollywood B47 125 B6
Lichfield WS14 9 F7
Sutton Coldfield B76 57 E7
Alder Coppice DY3 39 C2
Alder Coppice Prim Sch DY3 39 C1
Alder Cres WS5 43 B4
Alder Ct B13 87 A3
Alder Dale WV3 24 E2
Alderdale Ave DY3 39 C3
Alderdale Cres B92 107 E7
Alder Dr B37 70 B1
Alderflat Pl B7 67 C5
Alderford Cl WV8 24 F8
Aldergate B79 21 B5
Alder Gr B62 83 E6
Alderham Cl B91 107 D4
Alderhithe Gr B74 31 B3
Alder Ho 12 CV34 161 D8
Alder La
Balsall Common CV7 130 C5
Birmingham B30 103 C6
Alderlea Cl DY8 81 A2
Alderley Cres WS3 28 E5
Alderley Rd B61 150 D8
Alderman Callow Sch & Com Coll CV4 132 A6
Alderman Gee Hall CV12 78 A4
Alderman's Green Com Prim Sch CV2 96 C3
Alderman's Green Ind Est CV2 96 D2
Alderman's Green Rd CV2 96 B3
Aldermans La B97 153 B6
Alderman Smith Sch CV10 72 D2
Alder Meadow Cl CV6 95 D4
Aldermere Rd DY11 116 C8
Alderminster Cl B97 158 E4
Alderminster Rd
Coventry CV5 112 A4
Solihull B91 107 C1
Aldermoor Farm Prim Sch CV3 134 B8
Aldermoor La CV3 114 A1
Aldermore Dr 1 B75 46 F6
Alderney Cl
Bramcote CV11 79 F6
Coventry CV6 95 B2
Alderney Gdns B38 103 D1
Alder Park Rd B91 106 F2
Alderpits Rd B34 69 D6
Alder Rd
Birmingham B12 87 A4
Coventry CV6 96 A2
Kingswinford DY6 60 F5
Wednesbury WS10 42 A5
Alders Cl B98 154 A3
Alders Dr B98 154 F4
Aldersea Dr B6 66 F7
Aldersgate CV11 73 C3
Alders Gr CV34 160 D4
Aldershaw Rd B26 88 E6
Aldershaws B90 126 A5
Alders La
Nuneaton CV10 72 A7
Tamworth B79 20 E6
Aldersley Ave WV6 24 E7
Aldersley Cl WV6 24 F7
Aldersley High Sch WV8 10 E1
Aldersley Rd WV6 24 F6
Aldersley Stadium WV6 24 F6
Aldersmead Rd B31 103 C1
Alderson Rd B8 67 F4
Alders The
Bedworth CV12 77 E2
Romsley B62 100 F4
Alderton Cl 3 B91 107 B1
Alderton Dr WV3 38 E8
Alderton Mews 16 CV31 162 C6
Alder Way
Bromsgrove B60 137 B2
Sutton Coldfield B74 44 E8
Alderwood Pl B91 107 C3
Alderwood Prec DY3 39 C1
Alderwood Rise DY3 50 D5
Aldgate Dr DY5 81 C7
Aldgate Gr B19 66 D5
Aldin Cl B78 20 E2
Aldington Cl B98 153 F1
Aldin Way LE10 71 A3
Aldis Cl
Birmingham B28 87 E1
Walsall WS2 42 A7
Aldis Rd WS2 42 A7
Aldrich Ave CV4 111 E2
Aldridge By-Pass WS9 30 A6
Aldridge Cl
Oldbury B68 64 C4
Polesworth B78 36 F8
2 Stourbridge DY8 80 E8
Aldridge Rd
Birmingham, Brandhall B68 84 B8
Birmingham, Perry Barr B42 55 E4
Hinckley LE10 75 D6
Sutton Coldfield B74 30 D1
Sutton Coldfield, Little Aston B74, WS9 31 B6
Sutton Coldfield, Streetly B74 44 E7
Walsall WS4 29 C3
Aldridge Sch & Science Coll WS9 30 A4
Aldridge St WS10 41 D7
Aldrin Way CV4 132 D5
Aldwick Cl CV32 157 A4
Aldwych Cl WS9 30 B8
Aldwyck Dr WV3 38 A8
Aldwyn Ave B13 86 F2
Alesmore Mdw WS13 8 F6
Alesworth Dr LE10 75 F4
Alexander Cl B61 121 A1
Alexander Ct 1 CV34 160 F7
Alexander Gdns
Birmingham B42 55 D3
Hinckley LE10 71 C2
Alexander Hill DY5 81 F8
Alexander Ind Pk WV14 40 C4
Alexander Rd
Bedworth CV12 78 C3
Birmingham B27 88 C4
Codsall WV8 10 C3
Smethwick B67 64 E2
Willenhall WS2 27 F2
Alexander Stad B42 55 C6
Alexander Terr B67 64 F6
Alexander Way B9 67 F3
Alexandra Ave B21 65 D7
Alexandra Cres B71 53 E8
Alexandra Ct
Dudley DY3 50 C3
Kenilworth CV8 148 A4
Oldbury B68 63 F3
Alexandra High Sch & Sixth Form Ctr DY4 52 B6
Alexandra Hospl The B98 159 C6
Alexandra Ind Est DY4 51 F5
Alexandra Mews B79 21 C5
Alexandra Pl
Bilston WV14 40 D6
Dudley DY1 51 C4
Alexandra Rd
Birmingham, Handsworth B21 65 D7
Birmingham, Highgate B5 86 E7
Birmingham, Stirchley B30 104 A7
Coventry CV1 113 F4
Darlaston WS10 41 E6
Halesowen B63 82 F4
Royal Leamington Spa CV31 162 B6
Tipton DY4 52 A6
Walsall WS1 42 E6
Wolverhampton WV4 39 A6
Alexandra St
2 Dudley DY1 51 B1
Nuneaton CV11 73 B4
Wolverhampton WV3 163 A2
Alexandra Terr CV6 95 E2
Alexandra Theatre* B5 164 B2
Alexandra Way
Aldridge WS9 30 B5
Tipton B69 52 A2
Alex Grierson Cl CV3 134 E7
Alex Stewart Ho CV11 73 E1
Alfall Rd CV2 114 B5
Alford Cl B45 122 C7
Alfreda Ave B47 125 A8
Alfred Ct B60 150 E2
Alfred Gunn Ho B68 64 B4
Alfred Rd
Birmingham, Handsworth B21 65 E8
Birmingham, Sparkhill B11 87 B5
Coventry CV1 113 F4
Alfred Squire Rd WV11 26 D5
Alfred St
Birmingham, Aston B6 67 B8
Birmingham, King's Heath B14 104 F7
Birmingham, Sparkbrook B12 87 B5
Darlaston WS10 41 C5
Smethwick B66 65 C7
Tamworth B79 21 A5
Walsall WS3 14 B1
West Bromwich B70 53 D3
Alfreds Well B61 136 C6
Alfreton Cl LE10 75 F5
Alfriston Rd CV3 133 C4
Alfryth Ct 4 B15 86 C8
Algate Cl CV6 95 C3
Algernon Rd B16 65 D4
Alhambra Rd B60 137 C1
Al Hira Sch B12 87 A6
Alice Arnold Ho 1 CV2 96 B1
Alice Cl CV12 77 F1
Alice St WV14 40 D6
Alice Stevens Sch CV3 134 A6
Alice Wlk WV14 40 D6
Alison Cl DY4 41 A2
Alison Dr DY8 80 E3
Alison Rd B62 83 F3
Alison Sq CV6 96 B4
Allan Cl
2 Smethwick B66 65 B5
7 Stourbridge DY8 80 F8
All Angels Wlk B68 64 B4
Allan Rd CV6 112 F4
Allard B77 21 E2
Allard Ho CV3 134 B6
Allard Way CV3 134 C7
Allbut St B64 62 D1
Allcock St
Birmingham B9 67 A1
Tipton DY4 52 C8
Allcroft Rd B11 87 F2
Allenby Cl DY6 61 A5
Allen Cl
Birmingham B43 54 E7
Studley B80 159 E3
Allendale Ave B80 159 E3
Allendale Cres B80 159 E3
Allendale Ct B80 159 E3
Allendale Gr B43 54 E8
Allendale Rd
Birmingham B25 88 B7
Sutton Coldfield B76 57 E8
Allen Dr
3 Darlaston WS10 41 C6
West Bromwich B70 53 F1
Allen Ho B43 54 E7
Allen Rd Tipton DY4 40 F1
Allen Rd *continued*
Wednesbury WS10 41 F5
Wolverhampton WV6 25 A3
Allens Ave
Birmingham B18 65 F6
West Bromwich B71 53 A7
Allens Cl WV12 27 B5
Allens Croft Prim Sch B14 104 C5
Allens Croft Rd B14 104 C6
Allens Farm Rd B31 102 E3
Allens La WS3 14 F2
Allensmead B77 21 C2
Allensmore Cl B98 154 F2
Allens Rd B18 65 F6
Allen St Tamworth B77 21 C1
West Bromwich B70 53 B3
Allerdale Rd WS8 15 E6
Allerton Cl CV2 114 E2
Allerton La B71 53 C8
Allerton Rd B25 88 B7
Allesley Cl B74 46 C7
Allesley Croft CV5 112 A6
Allesley Ct CV5 112 A6
Allesley Hall Dr CV5 112 C5
Allesley Hall Prim Sch CV5 112 B4
Allesley Old Rd CV5 112 D3
Allesley Prim Sch CV5 112 A7
Allesley Rd B92 106 D8
Allesley St B6 66 E5
Alleston Rd WV10 11 D1
Alleston Wlk WV10 11 D2
Alleyne Gr B24 57 A2
Alleyne Rd B24 57 A1
Alley The DY3 50 B3
Alliance Cl CV11 73 F3
Alliance Way CV2 114 A5
Allibone Cl CV31 162 A4
Allied Cl CV6 95 D2
Allingham Gr B43 44 D4
Allington Ave 5 WS13 8 F6
Allington Cl WS5 43 D8
Allison St B5 164 D2
Allitt Gr CV8 148 B5
Allman Rd B24 57 B4
Allmyn Dr B74 45 A6
Allport Mews WS11 1 E1
Allport Rd WS11 1 E1
Allport St WS11 1 E2
All Saints CE Inf Sch CV12 78 C2
All Saints' CE Jun Sch CV34 156 A1
All Saints CE Prim Sch
Coventry CV1 113 E1
Leek Wootton CV35 156 A5
Nuneaton CV10 73 C1
West Bromwich B71 53 C6
All Saints Dr B74 32 A2
All Saints Ind Est B18 66 A5
All Saints La CV1 113 F3
All Saints Pl B61 137 A4
All Saints Rd
Bedworth CV12 77 F1
Birmingham, King's Heath B14 104 E7
Warwick CV34 161 B8
Wolverhampton WV2 163 C1
All Saints' Rd
Birmingham, Hockley B18 66 B5
Bromsgrove B61 137 A3
Darlaston WS10 41 E6
All Saints Sq CV12 78 B3
All Saints' St B18 66 A5
All Saints Way B71 53 D5
Allsops Cl B65 62 F4
All Souls RC Prim Sch CV5 112 E2
Allton Ave B78 20 D1
Allton Ct B77 21 E3
Allwell Dr B14 104 F2
Allwood Gdns B32 84 A2
Allwood Ho B97 153 C3
Alma Ave DY4 52 A7
Alma Cres B7 67 B4
Alma Ct CV11 79 F6
Alma Ind Est WS10 41 C6
Alma Pl DY2 51 C1
Alma Rd LE10 71 D1
Alma St
Birmingham B19 66 E6
Coventry CV1 165 D3
Darlaston WS10 41 C6
Halesowen B63 82 C5
Smethwick B66 65 C6

Alma St *continued*
Walsall WS2 . . . . **28** D4
Wednesbury WS10 . . . . **42** B3
Willenhall WV13 . . . . . . **27** E2
Wolverhampton WV10 . . **25** F2
Alma Way B19 . . . . **66** D7
Alma Wks WS10 . . . . . . **41** D5
Almond Ave
Kidderminster DY11 . . **116** B8
Nuneaton CV10 . . . . . . **72** C6
Royal Leamington Spa
CV32 . . . . **156** F3
Walsall, Yew Tree WS5 . **43** A4
Willenhall WS2 . . . . . . **27** E4
Almond Cl
Birmingham B29 . . . . . **103** A6
Cannock WS11 . . . .**2** C2
Walsall WS3 . . . . **14** F2
Almond Croft B42 . . . **54** F7
Almond Gr
Warwick CV34 . . . . . . **156** A1
Wolverhampton WV6 . . **25** C4
Almond Rd
Huntington WS12 . . . .**1** D8
Kingswinford DY6 . . . . **60** E8
Almond Tree Ave CV2 . **96** C2
Almshouses
Rowington Green
CV35 . . . . **145** A1
Smethwick B67 . . . . . . **64** F5
Stoneleigh CV8 . . . . . . **149** C6
2 Warwick CV34 . . . . **160** E6
Alnwick Cl WS12 . . . .**2** E2
Alnwick Ho B23 . . . . . . **56** F6
Alnwick Rd WS3 . . . . . **14** A4
Alperton Dr DY9 . . . . . **81** E2
Alpha Bsns Pk CV2 . . **96** D1
Alpha Cl B12 . . . . **86** E6
Alpha Ho CV2 . . . . **114** A4
Alpha Way WS6 . . . . . . **14** A8
Alpine Cl CV8 . . . . **148** A6
Alpine Dr
Cannock WS12 . . . .**2** D4
Dudley DY2 . . . . **62** B4
Alpine Rise CV3 . . . . . **133** A5
Alpine Way WV3 . . . . . **24** C2
Alport Croft **4** B9 . . . **67** B2
Alspath La CV5 . . . . . . **111** F4
Alspath Rd CV7 . . . . . . **92** C1
Alston Cl Cannock WS12 . **2** E2
Solihull B91 . . . . **107** D6
Sutton Coldfield B74 . . . **32** A2
Alston Gr B9 . . . . **68** B2
Alston Ho B69 . . . . **63** D6
Alston Prim Sch B9 . . **68** B3
Alston Rd
Birmingham B9 . . . . **68** B3
Oldbury B69 . . . . **63** E7
Solihull B91 . . . . **107** D6
Alston St B16 . . . . **66** A2
Althorpe Dr B93 . . . . . **127** E3
Althorpe Ho CV31 . . . . **162** A6
Althorpe Ind Est **15**
CV31 . . . . **162** A7
Althorpe St CV31 . . . . **162** A7
Alton Ave WV12 . . . . . . **27** B5
Alton Cl Coventry CV2 . **96** D2
Redditch B97 . . . . **153** B1
Wolverhampton WV10 . **11** E3
Alton Gr Cannock WS11 . .**1** B1
Dudley DY2 . . . . **51** E1
West Bromwich B71 . . . **53** E7
Alton Rd B29 . . . .**85** F3
Alum Cl CV6 . . . . **113** D8
Alum Dr B9 . . . . **68** A3
Alumhurst Ave B8 . . . . **68** B4
Alum Rock Rd B8 . . . . **68** B4
Alumwell Bsns &
Enterprise Coll WS2 **28** A1
Alumwell Cl WS2 . . . . . **28** B1
Alumwell Jun & Inf Schs
WS2 . . . .**28** B2
Alum Well Rd WS2 . . **28** B1
Alvaston Cl WS3 . . . . . **14** C3
Alvechurch CE Mid Sch
B48 . . . . **139** B6
Alvechurch Crown
Meadow Fst Sch
B48 . . . . **139** B6
Alvechurch Highway
Lower Marlbrook
B60 . . . . **121** D2
Redditch B98, B97 . . . **153** F3
Alvechurch Ho B60 . **137** B3
Alvechurch Rd
Birmingham B31 . . . . **123** B7
Halesowen B63 . . . . . . **82** F2
Alvechurch Sta B48 . **139** A4

Alvecote Cotts B79 . . . **22** D6
Alvecote La B79 . . . . . . **22** D6
Alvecote Pools Nature
Reserve★ B79 . . . . . **22** E6
Alveley Cl B98 . . . . . . **154** D4
Alverley Cl DY6 . . . . . . **60** B8
Alverley Rd CV6 . . . . . **113** C6
Alverstoke Cl WV9 . . . **11** A2
Alverstone Rd CV2 . . . **114** A4
Alverton B77 . . . . **35** C4
Alveston Cl B98 . . . . . **154** C2
Alveston Gr
Birmingham B9 . . . . **68** B2
Knowle B93 . . . . **128** B7
Alveston Pl **19** CV32 . **156** F1
Alveston Rd B47 . . . . . **125** A7
Alvin Cl Coventry CV3 . **114** F1
Halesowen B62 . . . . **83** F8
Alvington Cl WV12 . . . **27** D4
Alvis Cl B79 . . . .**20** F7
Alvis Ho CV1 . . . . **165** B2
Alvis Ret Pk CV5 . . . **113** A3
Alvis Wlk B36 . . . . **58** F1
Alwen St DY8 . . . .**60** F2
Alwin Rd B65 . . . . **63** B2
Alwold Cl B29 . . . .**84** F2
Alwold Rd B29 . . . . **85** A2
Alwyn B77 . . . . **35** E7
Alwyn Cl WS6 . . . .**5** A3
Alwynne Freeman Ct
CV7 . . . . **95** A6
Alwynn Wlk B23 . . . . . **56** C3
Amal Way B6 . . . .**55** F2
Amanda Ave WV4 . . . . **38** F4
Amanda Dr B26 . . . . . . **68** F1
Ambassador Ct CV32 **156** F3
Ambassador Rd B26 . . **90** C4
Ambell Cl B65 . . . .**62** F5
Amber Bsns Village
B77 . . . .**22** B3
Amber Cl B77 . . . . **22** B3
Amber Ct B77 . . . . **22** B3
Amber Dr B69 . . . . **64** A5
Ambergate Cl
8 Redditch B97 . . . . . **153** B5
Walsall WS3 . . . . **14** C3
Ambergate Dr DY6 . . . **60** C8
Amber Gn WS11 . . . .**2** C2
Amber Gr WS11 . . . .**2** C2
Amberley Ave CV12 . . . **79** C2
Amberley Gn B43 . . . . . **54** E6
Amberley Gr B6 . . . . . . **56** A3
Amberley Ho CV8 . . . . **148** A3
Amberley Rd B92 . . . . **88** F4
Amberley Way B74 . . . **30** E1
Amber Terr DY10 . . . . **116** F5
Amber Way B62 . . . . . . **83** C6
Amberwood Cl WS2 . . **27** D3
Ambion Way LE10 . . . . **71** F1
Amblecote Ave B44 . . . **44** E2
Amblecote Prim Sch
DY8 . . . .**80** F8
Amblecote Rd
Brierley Hill DY5 . . . . . . **81** D8
Kidderminster DY10 . . **117** B5
Ambler Gr CV2 . . . . . . **114** C3
Ambleside
Birmingham B32 . . . . . . **84** C1
Coventry CV2 . . . . **96** E2
Ambleside Cl WV14 . . . **40** E3
Ambleside Dr DY5 . . . . **81** C8
Ambleside Gr WV11 . . **13** B1
Ambleside Rd CV12 . . **78** A2
Ambleside Way
Bromsgrove B60 . . . . . **137** B1
Kingswinford DY6 . . . . . **60** D6
Nuneaton CV11 . . . . **73** E6
Ambrose Cl WV13 . . . . **26** E2
Ambrose Cres DY6 . . . **60** D8
Amcombe B77 . . . . **22** C1
Amelas Cl **3** DY5 . . . . . **61** A1
Amelia Cl CV12 . . . . . . **79** C3
Amersham Cl
Birmingham B32 . . . . . . **84** E5
Coventry CV5 . . . . **112** B4
Ames Rd WS10 . . . . . . **41** C7
Amethyst Ct **2** B92 . . .**88** F1
Amherst Ave B20 . . . . . **55** A3
Amherst Rd CV8 . . . . . **147** E6
Amhurst Bsns Ctr
CV34 . . . . **160** B7
Amicombe B77 . . . . **22** C1
Amington Cl B75 . . . . . **32** D3
Amington Hall B79 . . . **22** A8
Amington Heath Com Sch
B77 . . . . **22** B3
Amington Ind Est B77 **22** B3
Amington Pk B77 . . . . . **22** A6

Amington Rd
Birmingham B25 . . . . . . **88** B6
Solihull B90 . . . . **126** A8
Tamworth B77 . . . . **21** D4
Amiss Gdns B10 . . . . . . **87** C8
Amity Cl B66 . . . . **65** B5
Amos Ave
Nuneaton CV10 . . . . **73** B2
Wolverhampton WV11 . **26** C7
Amos Jacques Rd
CV12 . . . . **78** A4
Amos La WV11 . . . . **26** C6
Amos Rd DY9 . . . .**81** F2
Amphlett Croft DY4 . . **52** B4
Amphlett Ct **2** B60 . . **137** A2
Amphletts Cl DY2 . . . . **62** E3
Ampton Rd B15 . . . . **86** B7
Amroth Cl B45 . . . . **122** B7
Amroth Mews CV31 . . **162** C6
Amwell Gr B14 . . . . . . **104** F3
Amy Cl CV6 . . . .**95** F4
Anchorage Rd
Birmingham B23 . . . . . . **56** D3
Sutton Coldfield B74 . . . **46** B6
Anchor Cl
Birmingham B16 . . . . . . **65** E1
Tamworth B77 . . . . **21** A4
Anchor Cres B18 . . . . . .**65** F5
Anchor Ct B77 . . . . **21** C4
Anchor Dr WS10 . . . . . . **42** A3
Anchorfields DY10 . . **116** F6
Anchor Hill DY5 . . . . . . **61** C1
Anchor La
Solihull B91 . . . . **107** D6
Wolverhampton WV14 . **40** B2
Anchor Par WS9 . . . . . **30** B6
Anchor Rd
Aldridge WS9 . . . . **30** B6
Dudley WV14 . . . . **40** C2
Anchorway Rd CV3 . . **133** B4
Anders B79 . . . . **21** A6
Andersleigh Dr WV14 . **51** A8
Anderson Cres B43 . . . **43** E2
Anderson Dr CV31 . . . **162** A2
Anderson Gdns DY4 . . **52** A4
Anderson Rd
Birmingham B23 . . . . . . **56** E6
Smethwick B66 . . . . **65** A1
Tipton DY4 . . . . **52** A4
Anders Sq WV6 . . . . . . **23** E4
Anderton Cl B74 . . . . . . **46** A7
Anderton Park Prim Sch
B12 . . . .**87** B4
Anderton Park Rd
B13 . . . . **87** A3
Anderton Rd
Bedworth CV12 . . . . **77** C1
Birmingham B11 . . . . . . **87** C6
Coventry CV6 . . . . **96** B4
Anderton St B1 . . . . **66** B3
Andover Cres **2** DY6 . .**60** F4
Andover Pl WS11 . . . .**2** A4
Andover St B5 . . . .**66** C4
Andressy Mews B61 . **137** A5
Andrew Cl WV12 . . . . . **27** D6
Andrew Ct B76 . . . .**46** F3
Andrew Dr WV12 . . . . . **27** D6
Andrew Gdns B21 . . . . **54** E1
Andrew Rd
Halesowen B63 . . . . **83** A3
Wednesbury DY4 . . . . . . **41** A1
West Bromwich B71 . . . **42** F2
Andrews Cl
Baginton CV8 . . . . **133** F2
Brierley Hill DY5 . . . . . . **81** E8
Andrews Ho WS13 . . . . . .**9** A7
Andrews Rd WS9 . . . . . **16** B4
Anerley Gr B44 . . . .**44** F4
Anerley Rd B44 . . . .**44** F4
Angela Ave
Coventry CV2 . . . . **96** E1
Rowley Regis B65 . . . . . **63** D4
Angela Pl WV14 . . . . . . **40** D6
Angelica B77 . . . .**21** F4
Angelica Cl **7** WS5 . . . **43** A3
Angelina St B12 . . . .**86** F7
Angel Mews **8** B46 . . .**70** F7
Angelo Ho B13 . . . . . . **105** D7
Angel Pas B5 . . . . **81** A5
Angel St Dudley DY1 . . **62** B8
Upper Bentley B97 . . . **152** B1
Anglesey Ave B36 . . . . **70** B6
Anglesey Bsns Pk
WS12 . . . .**2** E4
Anglesey Cl
Allesley CV5 . . . . **112** B7
Burntwood WS7 . . . .**6** F4
Anglesey Cres
Brownhills WS8 . . . .**6** C5
Cannock WS12 . . . .**2** C5

Anglesey Mews WS12 . .**2** C5
Anglesey Prim Sch
B19 . . . . **66** C7
Anglesey Rd
Brownhills WS8 . . . .**6** F2
Lichfield WS13 . . . .**3** D2
Anglesey St
Birmingham B19 . . . . . . **66** C7
Cannock WS12 . . . .**2** B5
Angless Way CV8 . . . . **147** F3
Anglian Rd WS9 . . . . . . **29** D6
Anglia Rd WS11 . . . .**1** D3
Anglo African Ind Pk
B69 . . . .**52** E2
Angorfa Cl WS13 . . . .**8** F7
Angus Cl
Coventry CV5 . . . . **112** A4
Kenilworth CV8 . . . . . . **148** C6
West Bromwich B71 . . . **53** C6
Anita Ave DY4 . . . . **52** A2
Anita Croft B23 . . . . . . **56** E2
Ankadine Rd DY8 . . . . **81** B6
Anker Cl WS7 . . . .**7** D6
Ankerdine Ct B63 . . . . **83** A3
Ankerdrive B79 . . . . . . **21** B4
Ankermoor Cl B34 . . . . **69** B6
Ankermoor Ct B77 . . . . **21** E5
Ankermoor Prim Sch
B77 . . . .**21** E5
Ankerside Sh Ctr B79 **21** B4
Anker St CV11 . . . . **73** D3
Anker View B77 . . . . . . **21** C3
Anley Way CV6 . . . . . . **113** C6
Annan Ave WV10 . . . . . **25** F7
Annandale B77 . . . . **22** B1
Ann Cres WS11 . . . .**1** E6
Ann Croft B26 . . . . **89** D4
Anne Cl B70 . . . . **52** E3
Anne Cres CV3 . . . . . . **134** C5
Anne Ct B76 . . . .**46** F3
Anne Gr DY4 . . . . **41** B1
Anne Rd
Birmingham B66 . . . . . . **65** D7
Brierley Hill DY5 . . . . . . **62** A1
Wolverhampton WV4 . . **39** B6
Annie Lennard Inf Sch
B67 . . . .**64** E3
Annie Osborn Prim Sch
CV2 . . . . **114** D7
Ann Rd B47 . . . . **125** A3
Annscroft B38 . . . . **103** D2
Ann St WV13 . . . . **27** B3
Ansbro Cl B18 . . . .**65** F5
Ansculf Rd DY5 . . . . . . **61** B1
Ansell Dr CV6 . . . . **96** A5
Ansell Rd
Birmingham, Gravelly Hill
B24 . . . . **56** F1
Birmingham, Sparkbrook
B11 . . . . **87** C6
Ansell Way CV34 . . . . **160** D7
Ansley Cl B98 . . . . **154** F1
Ansley Comm CV10 . . . **72** A7
Ansley Rd CV10 . . . . . . **72** B3
Ansley Way B92 . . . . . **107** D7
Anslow Gdns WV11 . . . .**12** F1
Anslow Rd B23 . . . . **56** C5
Anson Ave WS13 . . . .**3** A1
Anson Cl
Burntwood WS7 . . . .**7** C7
Great Wyrley WS6 . . . . . .**4** F1
Perton WV6 . . . . **23** E5
Anson Ct B78 . . . . **35** B8
Anson Gr B27 . . . . **88** D2
Anson Junc WS2 . . . . . **27** E1
Anson Rd
Great Wyrley WS6 . . . . . .**4** F1
Walsall WS2 . . . . **27** E1
West Bromwich B70 . . . **52** E7
Anson Way CV2 . . . . . . **114** F8
Anstey Croft B37 . . . . . **70** A4
Anstey Gr B27 . . . . **88** B1
Anstey Rd B44 . . . . **55** E6
Anston Way WV11 . . . . **26** D7
Anstree Cl WS6 . . . .**4** D1
Anstruther Rd B15 . . . . **85** E8
Ansty Dr WS12 . . . .**2** D1
Ansty Rd CV2 . . . . **114** C5
Antelope Gdns CV34 . **160** C8
Anthony Rd B8 . . . .**67** F4
Anthony Way CV2 . . . . **114** C2
Anton Dr B76 . . . . **58** A6
Antony Gardner Cres **5**
CV31 . . . . **162** A4
Antony Rd B90 . . . . . . **106** B1
Antrim Cl CV5 . . . . **112** B7
Antringham Gdns
B15 . . . .**85** D8

Antrobus Rd
Birmingham B21 . . . . . . **54** E1
Sutton Coldfield B73 . . . **45** F1
Anvil Cres WV14 . . . . . **40** C2
Anvil Dr B69 . . . . **63** E6
Anvil Wlk B70 . . . .**52** F4
Apex Bsns Pk WS11 . . . .**5** F4
Apex Rd WS8 . . . . **15** C7
Apley Rd DY8 . . . . **80** E7
Apollo B79 . . . .**20** F6
Apollo Cl WS11 . . . .**2** A5
Apollo Croft B24 . . . . . **57** D3
Apollo Rd Oldbury B68 **64** C6
Stourbridge DY9 . . . . . . **82** A5
Apollo Way
Birmingham B20 . . . . . . **55** D1
Royal Leamington Spa
CV32 . . . . **161** D5
12 Smethwick B66 . . . . **65** C5
Apperley Way B63 . . . . **82** B7
Appian Cl
Birmingham B14 . . . . . **104** E5
Tamworth B77 . . . . **35** D7
Appian Way B90 . . . . . **126** D4
Applebee Rd LE10 . . . . **75** D6
Applebees Mdw LE10 . **74** E6
Applebees Wlk LE10 . .**74** F6
Appleby Cl B14 . . . . . . **104** D5
Appleby Gdns WV11 . . **13** C2
Appleby Gr B90 . . . . . . **127** B6
Appleby Ho **1** LE10 . . **71** E1
Applecross B74 . . . . . . **31** F1
Applecross Cl CV4 . . . **131** C6
Appledore Cl
Cannock WS12 . . . .**2** E3
Great Wyrley WS6 . . . . . .**5** A3
Appledore Ct **3** WS3 . **28** B8
Appledore Dr CV5 . . . . **111** F5
Appledore Rd WS5 . . . . **43** D8
Appledore Terr WS5 . . **43** D8
Appledorne Gdns B34 **69** B6
Applesham Cl B11 . . . . **87** D6
Appleton Ave
Birmingham B43 . . . . . . **54** E8
Stourbridge DY8 . . . . . . **81** A2
Appleton Cl B30 . . . . . **103** E8
Appleton Cres WV4 . . . **39** A5
Appleton Ct **5** B15 . . . **86** B7
Appletree Cl
Birmingham B31 . . . . . **102** F1
Catherine de B B91 . . . **108** B5
Apple Tree Cl
Birmingham B23 . . . . . . **56** B4
Kidderminster DY10 . . **117** B7
Appletree Cotts
CV35 . . . . **144** F1
Appletree Gr
Aldridge WS9 . . . . **30** B5
Wolverhampton WV6 . . **25** C5
Appletree La B97 . . . . **153** B5
Appletrees Cres B61 **137** A5
Apple Wlk WS11 . . . .**2** C2
Applewood Gr **5** B64 .**62** F1
Appleyard Cl CV12 . . . . **78** B2
Approach The CV31 . . **161** E6
April Croft B13 . . . . **87** B3
Apsley Cl B68 . . . . **84** A7
Apsley Croft B38 . . . . **104** B2
Apsley Gr
Birmingham B24 . . . . . . **57** A2
Dorridge B93 . . . . **127** F2
Apsley Ho B64 . . . .**62** F2
Apsley Rd B68 . . . . **84** A7
Aqua Ho CV32 . . . . **157** A1
Aqueduct La B48 . . . . **138** F7
Aqueduct Rd B90 . . . . **105** E1
Aragon Dr
Royal Leamington Spa
CV34 . . . . **161** D6
Sutton Coldfield B73 . . . **46** B6
Aragon Ho CV3 . . . . . . **133** C8
Arbor Cl B77 . . . . **21** D4
Arbor Ct B71 . . . . **53** E6
Arbor Way B37 . . . . **70** C1
Arbour Cl CV8 . . . . **148** B3
Arbour Mews WS11 . . . . .**5** F6
Arbourtree Ct WV5 . . . . **49** B7
Arbour Tree La B93 . . **144** F7
Arbury Ave
Bedworth CV12 . . . . **78** A3
Coventry CV6 . . . . **95** F2
Arbury Cl CV32 . . . . . . **157** A4
Arbury Ct CV10 . . . . **72** C3
Arbury Dr DY8 . . . . **60** D3
Arbury Garth CV10 . . . **72** B3

Arbury Hall Park &
Gdns★ CV10 . . . . . . **77** D7
Arbury Hall Rd B90 . . **126** D8
Arbury Rd CV10 . . . . . . **72** D2
Arbury Wlk B76 . . . . . . **58** D5
Arcade WS1 . . . . **28** E1
Arcade The
Coventry CV3 . . . . **114** B2
Dudley DY3 . . . . **50** E7
Arcadian Sh Ctr B5 . **164** C1
Arcal St DY3 . . . . **50** E7
Archbishop Grimshaw RC
Sch The B37 . . . . . . **69** F3
Archbishop Ilsley RC Sch
B27 . . . .**88** C3
Archer Cl Oldbury B68 . **64** B4
Studley B80 . . . . **159** D4
Wednesbury WS10 . . . . **41** E3
Archer Ct DY9 . . . . **81** E2
Archer Gdns B64 . . . . . **62** C1
Archer Rd
Birmingham B14 . . . . . **105** C4
Kenilworth CV8 . . . . . . **147** E3
Redditch B98 . . . . **153** E4
Walsall WS3 . . . . **28** E6
Archers Cl B23 . . . . **56** D8
Archer Terr B97 . . . . . **153** C1
Archery Fields CV34 . **160** F6
Archery Rd
Meriden CV7 . . . . **92** B1
Royal Leamington Spa
CV31 . . . . **161** E8
Arches Ind Est The
CV5 . . . . **113** A3
Arch Hill St DY2 . . . . . . **62** C5
Archibald Rd B19 . . . . . **66** C8
Arch Rd CV2 . . . . **114** E5
Arch The B5 . . . . **67** A2
Archway The **2** WS4 . .**28** F3
Arcot Rd B28 . . . .**87** F2
Ardath Rd B38 . . . . **104** A2
Ardav Rd B70 . . . .**52** F8
Arden Bldgs B93 . . . . . **127** E3
Arden Cl
Balsall Common CV7 . . . **130** B7
Meriden CV7 . . . . **92** C1
Stourbridge DY8 . . . . . . **80** E7
Stourbridge, Wordsley
DY8 . . . . **60** C3
Tamworth B77 . . . . **21** E5
Warwick CV34 . . . . **156** A1
Whitnash CV31 . . . . . . **162** B5
Ardencote Rd B13 . . . . **105** A6
Arden Croft
Coleshill B46 . . . . **59** F1
Solihull B92 . . . . **89** C4
Arden Ct
Binley Woods CV3 . . . . **135** D6
Dudley DY3 . . . . **50** D3
Hampton-in-A B92 . . . . **109** A7
Sutton Coldfield B72 . . . **57** C8
Ardendale **6** B90 . . . **126** C8
Arden Dr
Birmingham B26 . . . . . . **88** F7
Dorridge B93 . . . . **128** A1
Sutton Coldfield, Falcon
Lodge B75 . . . . **47** B5
Sutton Coldfield, Wylde
Green B73 . . . . **57** B8
Arden Forest Inf Sch
CV12 . . . .**79** B3
Arden Gr
Birmingham, Ladywood
B16 . . . . **66** A1
8 Birmingham, Lozells
B19 . . . . **66** C8
Oldbury B69 . . . . **64** A5
Arden Jun & Inf Sch The
B11 . . . .**87** C5
Ardenleigh Way B24 . . **57** A2
Arden Leys B94 . . . . . . **141** D2
Arden Meads B94 . . . . **143** C6
Arden Oak Rd B26 . . . **89** D4
Arden Pl WV14 . . . . **41** B4
Arden Rd
Birmingham, Acock's Green
B27 . . . . **88** B4
Birmingham, Aston B6 . **66** D8
Birmingham, Rubery
B45 . . . . **102** A1
Birmingham, Saltley B8 **67** D3
Bulkington CV12 . . . . . . **79** C2
Dorridge B93 . . . . **127** F2
Hollywood B47 . . . . . . **125** A6
Kenilworth CV8 . . . . . . **148** B3
Nuneaton CV11 . . . . . . **74** A1
Smethwick B67 . . . . **65** A5
Tamworth B77 . . . . **35** F5
Arden Sch B93 . . . . . . **128** B5
Arden St CV5 . . . . **132** F8

Arden Vale Rd B93 . . 128 B7
Arderne Dr B37 . . . . . . 70 A1
Ardgay Dr WS12. . . . . . . .1 F7
Ardingley Wlk DY5 . . . 81 B7
Ardley Cl DY2 . . . . 62 D8
Ardley Rd B14. . . . . . . 105 A5
Arena Pk CV6 . . . . .95 F3
Arena Studios B73 . . . 57 A7
Arena Theatre★
WV1 . . . . 163 B3
Aretha Cl DY6. . . . . 61 A6
Argent Ctr The B1. . . . 66 C3
Argil Cl WV11 . . . . 26 D8
Arguile Pl LE10 . . . . . . 71 C1
Argus Cl B76. . . . . .46 F3
Argyle Ave B77. . . . . . . 21 D4
Argyle Cl
Stourbridge DY8 . . . . . . 60 E1
Walsall WS4 . . . . 29 B3
Argyle Rd Walsall WS4 29 B3
Wolverhampton WV2 . . 39 B6
Argyle St
Birmingham B7. . . . . . . 67 D8
Tamworth B77. . . . . 21 E4
Argyll Ct WV12 . . . . 13 C1
Argyll Ho 5 WV3 . . . . 25 C4
Argyll St CV2. . . . . 114 A3
Ariane B79. . . . . 20 E7
Arion Cl B77 . . . . 21 D5
Arkall Cl B79. . . . . 21 C7
Arkle B77. . . . . 35 D4
Arkle Croft
Birmingham B36 . . . . . . 68 C8
Rowley Regis B65. . . . . 62 F6
Arkle Dr CV2. . . . . 114 F7
Arklet Cl CV10 . . . . 72 C5
Arkley Gr B28. . . . . . . 106 B7
Arkley Rd B28. . . . . . . 106 B7
Arkwright Rd
Birmingham B32 . . . . . . 84 C5
Walsall WS2 . . . . 28 B5
Arlen Dr B43. . . . . 43 D1
Arlescote Cl B75 . . . . . 32 C2
Arlescote Rd B92 . . . . 89 C2
Arless Way B17 . . . . . . 85 B3
Arleston Way B90 . . . 126 E8
Arley Cl
Kidderminster DY11 . . 116 A2
Oldbury B69 . . . . 63 D5
Redditch B98 . . . . 154 D5
Arley Ct DY2 . . . . 62 C6
Arley Dr DY8. . . . . 80 E3
Arley Gr WV4 . . . . 38 D5
Arley Mews CV32. . . . 156 E1
Arley Rd
Birmingham B29 . . . . . . 85 F3
Birmingham, Saltley B8 67 D6
Solihull B91. . . . . 107 A4
Arley Villas 4 B18 . . . 65 D4
Arlidge Cl WV14. . . . . . 40 D4
Arlidge Cres CV8. . . . . 148 C5
Arlington Ave CV32. . 156 F2
Arlington Cl DY6 . . . . . 60 D4
Arlington Ct
2 Royal Leamington Spa
CV32. . . . . 156 F2
Stourbridge DY8 . . . . . . 81 B4
Arlington Gr B14. . . . 105 B2
Arlington Ho B15 . . . . 86 C7
Arlington Mews 5
CV32 . . . . 156 F2
Arlington Rd
Birmingham B14 . . . . . 105 B3
West Bromwich B71. . . 53 D6
Arlington Way CV11 . . .73 F2
Arlon Ave CV10 . . . . . . 72 D7
Armada Cl B23. . . . . . . 56 D1
Armadale Cl LE10 . . . . 71 A1
Armarna Dr CV5 . . . . 111 B8
Armfield St CV6. . . . . 114 A8
Armitage Ho WS13 . . . . . .3 E1
Armorial Rd CV3 . . . . 133 B7
Armour Cl LE10 . . . . . . 75 D5
Armoury Rd B11 . . . . . 87 D6
Armoury Trad Est
B11. . . . . .87 E6
Armscott Rd CV2. . . . 114 C6
Armside Cl WS3. . . . . . 15 B4
Armson Rd CV7 . . . . . . 78 A1
Armstead Rd WV9. . . . . 11 A3
Armstrong B79. . . . . . . .20 F6
Armstrong Ave CV3 . 114 B1
Armstrong Cl
Stourbridge DY8. . . . . . 81 B6
Whitnash CV31. . . . . . 162 A2
Armstrong Dr
Birmingham B36 . . . . . . 58 F1
Walsall WS2 . . . . 28 A4
Wolverhampton WV6 . . 25 A5
Armstrong Way WV13 41 B8
Arna Ho CV3. . . . . 134 B6
Arncliffe Cl CV11. . . . . 74 A2
Arncliffe Way 4
CV34 . . . . 155 F1
Arne Rd CV2 . . . . 115 A6
Arnhem Cl WV11 . . . . . 26 B8
Arnhem Cnr CV3 . . . . 134 D6
Arnhem Rd WV13 . . . . 40 E8
Arnhem Way DY4 . . . . 52 C5
Arnold Ave CV3 . . . . . 133 C5
Arnold Cl
Tamworth B79. . . . . 21 A6
Willenhall WS2 . . . . 27 F3
Arnold Gr
Birmingham B30. . . . . 103 D4
Solihull B90. . . . . 106 B4
Arnold Lodge Sch
CV32. . . . . 156 F2
Arnold Rd B90 . . . . . . 106 C4
Arnotdale Dr WS12. . . . .1 F7
Arnside Cl CV1. . . . . . 165 D4
Arnside Ct B23. . . . . . . 56 B4
Arnwood Cl WS2 . . . . . .27 F2
Arosa Dr B17 . . . . 85 B3
Arran Cl
Birmingham B43. . . . . . 43 E3
Cannock WS11 . . . . .2 A3
Nuneaton CV10. . . . . . . 73 A3
Arran Dr B77 . . . . .35 F7
Arran Rd B34 . . . . .68 F6
Arran Way
Birmingham B36. . . . . . 70 B7
Hinckley LE10 . . . . 71 B1
Arras Bvd CV35 . . . . . 160 A7
Arras Rd DY2 . . . . 51 E2
Arrow Cl B93 . . . . 128 A6
Arrowdale Rd B98. . . 154 A3
Arrowfield Gn B38 . . 123 D7
Arrow Ho 1 B68. . . . . 84 B8
Arrow Ind Est WV12. . 27 D6
Arrow Rd WS3 . . . . 28 E6
Arrow Rd N B98. . . . . 154 A4
Arrow Rd S B98. . . . . 154 A4
Arrow Vale Com High
Sch B98 . . . . 154 E2
Arrow Valley Park★
B98 . . . . 154 C4
Arrow Wlk B38. . . . . . 104 B1
Arsenal St B9. . . . . 67 C1
Artemis Dr CV34 . . . . 161 E5
Arthingworth Cl CV3 114 E1
Arthur Alford Ho
CV12 . . . . 77 D1
Arthur Dr (Road 2)
DY11 . . . . 116 E1
Arthur Greenwood Ct
WV14 . . . . 40 C6
Arthur Gunby Cl B75 . .46 F7
Arthur Harris Cl B66 . 65 C3
Arthur Pl B1. . . . . 66 B3
Arthur Rd
Birmingham, Edgbaston
B15. . . . . 86 B7
Birmingham, Erdington
B24. . . . . 57 B4
Birmingham, Handsworth
B21. . . . . 65 F8
Birmingham, Hay Mills
B25. . . . . 88 B6
Tipton DY4 . . . . 52 A7
Arthur St Bilston WV14 40 D6
Birmingham B10. . . . . . 67 B1
Cannock, Chadsmoor
WS11 . . . . .1 F4
Cannock WS12 . . . . .2 F3
Coventry CV1 . . . . 165 C4
Kenilworth CV8. . . . . . 148 A5
Redditch B98 . . . . 154 B3
West Bromwich B70. . . 53 D1
Wolverhampton WV2 . . 39 D7
Arthur Terry Sch The
B74. . . . . 32 A3
Artillery Rd CV11. . . . . .79 F6
Artillery St B9 . . . . 67 C2
Artingstall Ho B30 . . 104 B8
Arton Croft B24. . . . . . 57 A2
Arundel
Birmingham B17 . . . . . . 85 A6
Tamworth B77. . . . . 35 C7
Arundel Ave WS10. . . . .41 F3
Arundel Cl 2 CV34. . 160 F8
Arundel Cres B92 . . . . 89 A1
Arundel Ct 13 B29. . . 103 C7
Arundel Dr B69 . . . . . . .62 F8
Arundel Gr WV6. . . . . . .23 F3
Arundel Ho B23 . . . . . . .56 F6
Arundel Pl B11. . . . . . . 87 A6
Arundel Rd
Birmingham B14 . . . . . 105 A1
Bromsgrove B60. . . . . 137 B1
Arundel Rd *continued*
Bulkington CV12 . . . . . . 79 C3
Coventry CV3 . . . . 133 D6
Stourbridge DY8 . . . . . . 60 C2
Willenhall WV12 . . . . . . 27 C7
Wolverhampton WV10 . 11 B2
Arundel St WS1 . . . . . . 42 E7
Arun Way B76. . . . . 47 A1
Asbury Ct B43 . . . . 54 C8
Asbury Rd
Balsall Common CV7. . 130 B5
Wednesbury WS10 . . . . 42 E2
Ascot Cl
Bedworth CV12. . . . . . . 78 B4
Birmingham B16 . . . . . . 65 F2
Coventry CV3 . . . . 134 C6
Lichfield WS14 . . . . 9 D7
Oldbury B69 . . . . 63 E6
Ascot Ct 11 B29. . . . . 103 C7
Ascot Dr Cannock WS11. .4 C8
Dudley DY1 . . . . 50 F2
Tamworth B77. . . . . 35 D4
Wolverhampton WV4 . . 39 A4
Ascote La B90 . . . . . . 126 A5
Ascot Gdns DY8. . . . . . 60 D2
Ascot Rd B13 . . . . .86 F2
Ascot Ride CV32 . . . . 157 C3
Ascot Way B61. . . . . . 121 B1
Ascot Wlk B69 . . . . 63 E6
Asfare Bsns Pk LE10 . .75 E1
Ash Ave B12 . . . . 87 A5
Ashborough Dr B91 . 127 C8
Ashbourne Cl WS11 . . . .2 A4
Ashbourne Gr 3 B6. . 66 E8
Ashbourne Rd
Birmingham B16. . . . . . 65 D3
Walsall WS3 . . . . 14 C3
Wolverhampton, Heath Town
WV1 . . . . 26 A3
Wolverhampton, Lanesfield
WV4 . . . . 39 E3
Ashbourne Ridge B63 82 D5
Ashbourne Way B90. 126 E8
Ash Bridge Ct B45 . . 122 B6
Ashbridge Rd CV5. . . 112 C4
Ashbrook Cres B91. . 127 C8
Ashbrook Dr B45. . . . 122 B8
Ashbrook Gr B30. . . . 104 C8
Ashbrook Rd B30 . . . 104 C8
Ashburn Gr WV13 . . . . 27 C2
Ashburton Cl LE10 . . . 76 A6
Ashburton Rd
Birmingham B14. . . . . 104 D5
Coventry CV2 . . . . 114 E8
Ashbury Covert 3
B30 . . . . 104 C3
Ashby Cl
Birmingham B8. . . . . . . 68 C6
Coventry CV3 . . . . 134 F8
Ashby Ct
Nuneaton CV11. . . . . . . 73 D3
Solihull B91. . . . . 107 C1
Ashby Grange LE10. . . 71 E5
Ashby Rd
Hinckley LE9, LE10 . . . . 71 E5
Tamworth B79. . . . . 21 C8
Ash Cl WV8 . . . . 10 A3
Ashcombe Ave B20. . . 54 E3
Ashcombe Dr CV4. . . 111 F3
Ashcombe Gdns B24 . 57 D3
Ashcott Cl B38. . . . . . 103 D2
Ash Cres
Birmingham B37 . . . . . . 69 F6
Kingswinford DY6. . . . . 60 E6
Portway B47. . . . . 140 F8
Ashcroft
Birmingham B15 . . . . . . 85 E5
4 Smethwick B66 . . . . 65 C5
Tipton DY4 . . . . 52 A2
12 Wolverhampton
WV4 . . . . 39 F4
Ashcroft Cl CV2 . . . . . 115 A8
Ashcroft Gr B20. . . . . . 55 D2
Ashcroft Inf Sch B79. 21 C7
Ashcroft La
Lichfield WS14 . . . . .8 E1
Shenstone WS14. . . . . . 17 E7
Ashcroft Way CV2 . . . 115 B8
Ash Ct
Balsall Common CV7. . 130 C5
Oldbury B66 . . . . 64 C8
Stourbridge DY8 . . . . . . 81 A4
Ashdale Cl
Binley Woods CV3. . . . 135 E7
Huntington WS12 . . . . . . .1 C7
Kingswinford DY6. . . . . 60 D8
Ashdale Dr B14 . . . . . 105 A1
Ashdale Gr B26 . . . . . . 89 A8
Ashdale Rd B77 . . . . . . 21 D5
Ashdene Cl
Kidderminster DY10 . . 117 C5
Sutton Coldfield B73. . . 46 A3
Ashdene Gdns
Kenilworth CV8. . . . . . 148 B4
Stourbridge DY8 . . . . . . 60 C2
Ashdown Cl
Birmingham, Frankley
B45. . . . . 102 A2
Birmingham, Highgate
B13. . . . . 87 A1
Coventry CV3 . . . . 134 D8
Ashdown Dr
Nuneaton CV10. . . . . . . 72 F2
Stourbridge DY8 . . . . . . 60 E3
Ash Dr
Birmingham B31 . . . . . 102 C1
Hartshill CV10. . . . . 72 A8
Kenilworth CV8. . . . . . 148 A4
Lower Marlbrook B61. 121 B1
West Bromwich B71. . . 53 C6
Ashen Cl DY3 . . . . 39 C3
Ashenden Rise WV3 . . 38 A8
Ash End House Farm★
B78. . . . . 48 B8
Ashenhurst Rd DY1. . . .61 F8
Ashenhurst Wlk DY1 . 51 A1
Ashe Rd CV10 . . . . 72 B3
Ashes Rd B69 . . . . .63 F3
Ashes The Oldbury B69 .63 F3
Wolverhampton WV11 . 26 B6
Ashfern Dr B76 . . . . . . .57 F7
Ashfield Ave
Birmingham B14. . . . . . 86 F1
Coventry CV4 . . . . 111 D1
Ashfield Cl WS3. . . . . . .28 F4
Ashfield Cres
Dudley DY2. . . . . 62 C3
Stourbridge DY9 . . . . . . 82 A3
Ashfield Ct B38 . . . . . 103 E4
Ashfield Gdns B14 . . . .86 F1
Ashfield Gr
Halesowen B63. . . . . . . 82 E2
Wolverhampton WV10 . 11 C3
Ashfield Ho B28. . . . . 105 E3
Ashfield Rd
Bilston WV14 . . . . 41 A2
Birmingham B14 . . . . . . 86 F1
Kenilworth CV8. . . . . . 148 B4
Wolverhampton, Fordhouses
WV10 . . . . 11 C3
Wolverhampton WV3 . . 24 D2
Ashford Cl B24. . . . . . . 57 D4
Ashford Dr
Bedworth CV12. . . . . . . 78 A3
Sedgley DY3 . . . . 50 E7
Sutton Coldfield B76. . . 57 F5
Ashford Gdns CV31. . 161 F3
Ashford Ind Pk WV2 . 40 A7
Ashford La B94 . . . . . 143 B7
Ashford Rd
Hinckley LE10 . . . . 75 B7
Whitnash CV31. . . . . . 161 F2
Ashford Twr B12 . . . . . .86 F8
Ashfurlong Cl CV7 . . 130 B6
Ashfurlong Cres B75 . 46 E7
Ash Gn DY1. . . . . 51 A5
Ash Gr Ash Green CV7 . 95 C7
Birmingham, Balsall Heath
B12. . . . . 87 A5
11 Birmingham, Bordesley
B9. . . . . 67 B2
Cannock WS11 . . . . .1 F4
Dudley DY3 . . . . 50 C2
Kidderminster DY11 . . 116 B7
Lichfield WS14 . . . . .9 E8
Stourbridge DY9 . . . . . . 81 D3
Tamworth B77. . . . . 35 F5
Ash Green La CV7 . . . . 95 D6
Ash Green Mobile Home
Pk CV7 . . . . 95 C7
Ash Green Sch CV7 . . 95 D6
Ashgrove WS7 . . . . .6 F5
Ashgrove Cl B60 . . . . 121 D1
Ashgrove Rd B44. . . . . 44 C2
Ash Hill WV3. . . . . 24 D2
Ashill Rd B45 . . . . 122 B7
Ashington Gr CV3 . . . 134 A5
Ashington Rd CV12. . . 77 C1
Ash La
Alvechurch B48. . . . . . 123 D2
Great Wyrley WS6. . . . . . .5 A3
Ashlands Cl B79 . . . . . 21 C7
Ashland St
Wolverhampton WV3 . . 25 B1
Wolverhampton WV3 . . 39 B8
Ashlawn Cres B91. . . 106 D5
Ash Lawn Ho 8
CV31 . . . . 162 A7
Ashlea B78 . . . . .36 F5
Ashleigh Ct 8 DY2. . . 62 E8
Ashleigh Dr
Birmingham B20. . . . . . 55 B2
Nuneaton CV11. . . . . . . 73 F1
Tamworth B77. . . . . 35 E8
Ashleigh Gr B13 . . . . . 87 B1
Ashleigh Heights
B91 . . . . 107 A5
Ashleigh Ho B91 . . . . 107 C5
Ashleigh Mews Cotts
B76 . . . . 59 C6
Ashleigh Rd
Oldbury B69 . . . . 63 C8
Solihull B91. . . . . 107 B4
Ashley Cl
Birmingham B15 . . . . . . 86 C7
Kingswinford DY6. . . . . 60 C4
Stourbridge DY8. . . . . . 80 D2
Ashley Cres CV34. . . . 161 B6
Ashley Ct B45 . . . . 122 A1
Ashley Gdns B8 . . . . . . 67 D4
Ashley Ho DY2 . . . . 62 D4
Ashley Mount WV6 . . . 24 D5
Ashley Rd
Birmingham B23 . . . . . . 56 E3
Walsall WS3 . . . . 13 F1
Willenhall WS3 . . . . 27 F8
Wolverhampton WV4 . . 38 E5
Ashley St WV14 . . . . . . 40 E6
Ashley Way CV7 . . . . . 130 B7
Ashmall WS7. . . . . 7 D4
Ashmead Dr B45 . . . . 122 C4
Ashmead Gr B24 . . . . . 57 A2
Ashmead Rd WS7 . . . . . .7 A8
Ashmead Rise B45 . . 122 C4
Ash Mews 4 B27 . . . . 88 C5
Ashmole Ave WS7. . . . . .7 E8
Ashmole Cl WS14 . . . . . .9 E6
Ashmole Rd B70 . . . . . .52 F7
Ashmore Ave WV11. . . 13 A1
Ashmore Ind Est WS2 28 E3
Ashmore Lake Rd
WV12 . . . . 27 B4
Ashmore Lake Way
WV12 . . . . 27 B4
Ashmore Rd
Birmingham B30. . . . . 103 F5
Coventry CV6 . . . . 113 B4
Ashmores Cl B97. . . . 158 D5
Ashmore's Ind Est
DY1. . . . . .51 E3
Ashold Farm Rd B24 . 57 D2
Asholme Cl B36. . . . . . 68 C7
Ashorne Cl
Birmingham B28. . . . . 106 B7
Coventry CV2 . . . . 96 C2
Redditch B98 . . . . 159 D8
Ashover Gr 8 B18 . . . 65 E4
Ashover Rd B44. . . . . . 44 D3
Ashow Cl CV8. . . . . . . 148 B4
Ash Park Ind Est WS11 2 B3
Ashperton Cl B98 . . . 153 E1
Ash Priors Cl CV4 . . . 112 B1
Ash Rd Birmingham B8. 67 D4
Dudley DY1 . . . . 51 B3
Tipton DY4 . . . . 51 E4
Wednesbury WS10 . . . . 41 F5
Ashridge Cl CV11. . . . . .78 F8
Ash St Bilston WV14 . . . 40 E3
Cradley Heath B64 . . . . 62 F2
Walsall WS3 . . . . 14 D1
Wolverhampton WV3 . . 25 A1
Ashstead Cl B76 . . . . . 58 B6
Ashted Cir B7. . . . . 67 A4
Ashted Lock B7 . . . . . . .66 F4
Ashted Wlk B7. . . . . 67 B4
Ash Terr B69 . . . . 52 B1
Ashton Cl B97. . . . . . . 153 B1
Ashton Croft
Birmingham B16. . . . . . 66 A2
Solihull B91. . . . . 107 A1
Ashton Dr WS4. . . . . . . 15 C2
Ashton Park Dr DY5 . . 61 C1
Ashton Rd B25 . . . . 88 C7
Ash Tree Ave CV4. . . . 112 A2
Ashtree Cl DY5. . . . . . . 61 B1
Ashtree Ct WS11 . . . . . . 1 D4
Ash Tree Dr B26. . . . . . 88 D7
Ashtree Gr WV14 . . . . . 41 B3
Ash Tree Gr CV7 . . . . . . 97 E5
Ashtree Rd
Cradley Heath B64 . . . . 62 F2
Oldbury B69 . . . . 63 D8
Walsall WS3 . . . . 15 A3
Ash Tree Rd
Birmingham B30. . . . . 104 A6
Redditch B97 . . . . 153 B5
Ashurst Cl CV6. . . . . . . 96 B5
Ashurst Rd B76 . . . . . . .57 F7
Ash View WS12. . . . . 1 D8
Ashville Ave B34 . . . . . .68 F7
Ashville Dr B63 . . . . . . 83 A5
Ashwater Dr B14. . . . 104 D2
Ashway B11. . . . . 87 B5
Ash Way B23. . . . . 56 C7
Ashwell Dr B90 . . . . . 106 D4
Ashwells Gr WV9. . . . . 11 A2
Ashwin Rd B21. . . . . . . 66 A7
Ash Wlk B76 . . . . .46 F2
Ashwood Ave
Coventry CV6 . . . . 112 F5
Stourbridge DY8 . . . . . . 60 D2
Ashwood Cl
Oldbury B69 . . . . 63 F4
Sutton Coldfield B74. . . 44 E8
Ashwood Ct
Birmingham B13 . . . . . . 87 A3
Birmingham, Stechford
B34. . . . . 68 D5
Ashwood Dr B37 . . . . . 70 D3
Ashwood Gr WV4 . . . . 39 A5
Ashwoodhay DY8. . . . . .60 F3
Ashwood Park Prim Sch
DY8. . . . . 60 D1
Ashwood Rd CV10 . . . . 72 E5
Ashworth Ho
Cannock WS11 . . . . .2 A4
2 Lichfield WS13. . . . . . .9 B8
Ashworth Rd B42 . . . . 44 B1
Askew Bridge Rd DY3 50 B3
Askew Cl DY3 . . . . 50 E5
Aspbury Croft B36 . . . 58 D1
Aspects Park Gate
CV11 . . . . .73 F7
Aspen Cl
Birmingham B27 . . . . . . 88 B2
Coventry CV4 . . . . 111 D1
2 Lichfield WS13. . . . . . .9 E8
Sutton Coldfield B76. . . 46 F2
Aspen Dr
Bedworth CV6. . . . . 96 C6
Birmingham B37 . . . . . . 90 C8
Aspen Gdns B20 . . . . . . 55 B1
Aspen Gr
Birmingham B9. . . . . . . 68 A3
Burntwood WS7 . . . . .6 F8
Hollywood B47 . . . . . . 125 B5
Willenhall WV12 . . . . . . 27 E7
Aspen Ho B91. . . . . . . 106 F2
Aspens Way B61 . . . . 137 A6
Aspen Way WV3. . . . . . 25 A1
Asphodel B74. . . . . .31 F5
Asplen Ct CV8. . . . . . . 148 C4
Aspley Heath B94 . . . 141 D2
Aspley Heath La
B94 . . . . 141 D2
Asquith Dr
Cannock WS11 . . . . .2 C2
Oldbury B69 . . . . 52 D2
Asquith Rd B8 . . . . 68 B5
Asra Cl B66. . . . . 65 A8
Asra Ho B66 . . . . 65 A8
Astbury Ave B67 . . . . . .64 F3
Astbury Cl
Walsall WS3 . . . . 14 A4
Wolverhampton WV1 . . 26 A1
Astbury Ct 1 B68. . . . 84 B7
Aster Cl Hinckley LE10 . 75 E6
Nuneaton CV11. . . . . . . 74 A1
Aster Way
Hinckley LE10 . . . . 75 D6
Walsall WS5 . . . . 43 A3
Aster Wlk
Bedworth CV10. . . . . . . 78 A8
Wolverhampton WV9 . . 11 A3
Asthill Croft CV3 . . . . 133 C8
Asthill Gr CV3. . . . . . . 133 C8
Astley Ave
Coventry CV6 . . . . 95 E2
Halesowen B62. . . . . . . 83 F6
Astley Cl
Redditch B98 . . . . 159 A7
Royal Leamington Spa
CV32. . . . . 156 D2
Tipton DY4 . . . . 52 D6
Astley Cres B62 . . . . . . .83 F5
Astley La
Bedworth CV12. . . . . . . 77 C4
Nuneaton CV10. . . . . . . 72 B1
Astley Rd
Birmingham B21 . . . . . . 54 D1
Bromsgrove B60. . . . . 137 C1
Astley Wlk B90. . . . . . 106 B5
Aston Bridge B6 . . . . . .66 F6
Aston Brook Gn B6. . . .66 F5
Aston Brook St E B6 . .66 F5
Aston Brook St B6 . . . .66 F6
Aston Bury B15 . . . . . . 85 D7

Aston Church Rd B7,
B8 . . . . 67 D6
Aston Cl
Darlaston WV14 . . . . . . 41 A4
Shenstone WS14 . . . . . . 17 F6
Aston Cross Bsns Village
B6 . . . . 67 A6
Aston Ct B23 . . . . 56 C3
Aston Expressway B6 .66 F6
**Aston Expressway
(Elevated Rd)** B6 . . 67 A8
Aston Fields Mid Sch
B60 . . . . 151 C8
Aston Fields Trad Est ❷
B60 . . . . 150 F6
Aston Flamville Rd
LE10 . . . . 76 C7
Aston Hall* B6 . . . . . .66 F8
Aston Hall Rd B6 . . . . . 67 B8
Aston La
Aston Flamville LE10 . . 76 D7
Birmingham B20 . . . . . . 55 E2
Hinckley LE10 . . . . 76 A6
Aston Manor Cl B20... 55 E2
Aston Manor Sch B6..66 F4
Aston Manor Transport
Mus* B6 . . . . .55 F1
Aston Pk Ind Est CV11 73 B5
Aston Prim Est B74 . 31 C6
Aston Rd
Birmingham B6 . . . . 66 F5
Bromsgrove B60 . . . . . . 150 F6
Coventry CV5 . . . . 112 F1
Dudley DY2 . . . . 62 B8
Nuneaton CV11 . . . . 73 B5
Oldbury B69 . . . . 52 A1
Willenhall WV13 . . . . . . 26 E2
Aston Rd N B6 . . . . . . .66 F6
Aston Science Pk B7 .66 F4
Astons Cl DY5 . . . . 81 D7
Aston Seedbed Ctr
B7 . . . . 67 A6
Astons Fold DY5 . . . . . 81 D7
Aston St
Birmingham B4 . . . . . . .164 D4
Tipton DY4 . . . . 52 C7
Wolverhampton WV3 . . 39 A8
Aston Sta B6 . . . . .67 B8
Aston Tower Com Prim
Sch B6 . . . . .66 F7
Aston Univ B5...164 D4
Astor Dr B13 . . . . 87 C1
Astoria Cl WV12... 13 D1
Astoria Gdns WV12... 13 D1
Astor Rd
Kingswinford DY6 . . . . . 60 F5
Sutton Coldfield B74... 31 A1
Astwell Prep Sch B20 66 B8
Astwood Bank Fst Sch
B96 . . . . 158 E2
Astwood La B96... 158 C2
Atcham Cl B98 . . . . . 154 F3
Atcheson Cl B80 . . . 159 E4
Athelney Ct WS3 . . . 15 A3
Athelstan Gr WV6 . . .23 F5
Athelstan Way B79 . . .20 F7
Athena Dr CV34 . . . 161 E5
Athena Gdns CV6 . . . 96 A1
Atherstone Cl
Redditch B98 . . . . . . 154 F1
Solihull B90 . . . . 105 E2
Atherstone Rd WV1 . . 26 B2
Atherstone St B77,
B78 . . . . 35 B8
Atherston Pl CV4...132 D6
Athlone Rd WS5 . . . 43 C8
Athol Cl B32 . . . . 102 D8
Athole St B12 . . . . 87 A7
Atholl Cres CV10 . . . 72 E2
Atholl Ct CV10 . . . . . . 72 E2
Athol Rd CV2 . . . . 115 A6
Atkinson Dr WV10 . . . 25 D6
Atkins Way LE10 . . . . . 75 E7
Atlantic Ct ❹ WV13 . 27 A1
Atlantic Rd B44 . . . . . .44 F1
Atlantic Way WS10 . . . 41 E1
Atlas Croft WV10 . . . 25 C6
Atlas Est
Birmingham, Tyseley
B11 . . . . 88 A5
Birmingham, Witton B6.. 56 A2
Atlas Gr B70 . . . . .52 F3
Atlas Trad Est
Birmingham B11 . . . . . . 87 D5
Coseley WV14 . . . . 40 F2
Attenborough Cl B19.. 66 E5
Attingham Dr
Birmingham B43 . . . . . . 43 D2

Attingham Dr continued
Cannock WS11 . . . . .2 B2
Dudley DY1 . . . . 51 B2
Attleborough Fields Ind
Est CV11 . . . . .73 E3
Attleborough La B46. 59 A1
Attleborough Rd
CV11 . . . . 73 D3
Attlee Cl B69 . . . . 52 D2
Attlee Cres WV14... 40 E2
Attlee Gr WS11 . . . . .2 C2
Attlee Rd WS2 . . . . 27 E3
Attoxhall Rd CV2... 114 E4
Attwell Pk WV3 . . . . . . 38 D7
Attwell Rd DY4 . . . . .40 F1
Attwood Bsns Ctr ❷
DY9 . . . . .81 F5
Attwood Cl B8 . . . . . . 67 E6
Attwood Cres CV2... 114 C7
Attwood Gdns WV4... 39 E5
Attwood Rd WS7 . . . . . . .6 C7
Attwood St
Halesowen B63 . . . . 82 F5
Stourbridge DY9 . . . . . . 81 F5
Atworth Cl B98... 159 B5
Aubrey Rd
Birmingham B32 . . . . . . 84 E7
Birmingham, Small Heath
B10 . . . . 87 F8
Auchinleck Dr WS13... 3 E3
Auchinleck Sq ❺ B15 66 B1
Auckland Dr B36... 70 B7
Auckland Ho B32 . . . .84 F4
Auckland Rd
Birmingham B11 . . . . . . 87 A7
Kingswinford DY6 . . . . . 60 E4
Smethwick B67 . . . . 64 E5
Auden Ct WV6 . . . . . . .23 F4
Audleigh Ho ❶ B15.. 86 C8
Audlem Wlk WV10... 26 A5
Audley Dr DY11 . . . 116 A8
Audley Prim Sch B33 .68 F4
Audley Rd B33 . . . . . .68 F4
Audnam DY8 . . . . .60 F1
Augusta Pl CV32 . . . . 161 F8
Augusta Rd
Birmingham, Acock's Green
B27 . . . . 88 C5
Birmingham, Moseley
B13 . . . . 86 E4
Augusta Rd E B13...86 F4
Augusta St B18 . . . . . . 66 C4
Augustine Ave B80 159 D4
Augustine Gr
Birmingham B18 . . . . . . 65 F6
Sutton Coldfield B74... 31 F5
Augustines Wlk WS13 ..3 A3
Augustus Cl B46 . . . . .59 F1
Augustus Ct B15 . . . . .85 F8
Augustus Rd
Birmingham B15 . . . . . . 85 E8
Coventry CV1 . . . . 113 F4
Augustus St WS2... 28 D1
Aulton Cres LE10 . . . 71 B1
Aulton Rd B75 . . . . . . 32 E2
Aulton Way LE10 . . . 71 B1
Ault St B70 . . . . 53 D1
Austcliff Cl B97 . . . 158 D6
Austcliff Dr B91... 127 C8
Austen Ct CV32 . . . 157 E5
Austen Pl B15... 86 B8
Austen Wlk B71... 53 D6
Austin Cl
Birmingham B27 . . . . . . 88 D4
Dudley DY1 . . . . 50 F2
Austin Cote La WS14 ..9 F7
Austin Croft B36 . . . 58 E1
Austin Ct ❹ B74 . . . 31 E3
Austin Dr CV6 . . . . . . 114 A7
Austin Edwards Dr
CV34 . . . . 161 B8
Austin Ho WS4 . . . . . .28 F3
Austin Rd
Birmingham B21 . . . . . . 54 C1
Bromsgrove B60 . . . . . . 150 E7
Austin Rise B31 . . . 122 F7
Austin St WV6 . . . . . . 25 B4
Austin Way B42 . . . . . 55 A5
Austrey Cl B93 . . . 128 A6
Austrey Gr B29 . . . 103 A8
Austrey Rd DY6 . . . 61 A5
Austwick Cl CV34 . . . 155 E1
Austy Cl B36 . . . . 68 E8
Autobase Ind Est B69 52 C3
Auto Ctr B18 . . . . . . .65 E5
Autumn Berry Gr DY3 50 E6
Autumn Cl WS4 . . . 15 C1
Autumn Dr Dudley DY3 50 D4
Lichfield WS13 . . . . . . 3 D2
Walsall WS4 . . . . 15 C2

Autumn Gr B19 . . . . . . 66 C6
Auxerre Ave B98... 159 B8
Auxerre Ho B98 . . . 159 B8
Avalon Cl B24 . . . . 57 B4
Avalon Ho ❷ WS11...1 F4
Avalon Rd B60 . . . . . . 137 C2
Ave Maria Cl B64... 62 E1
Avebury Cl CV11 . . .73 F2
Avebury Gr B30 . . . 104 C7
Avebury Rd B30 . . . 104 C8
Ave Maria Cl B64... 62 E1
Avenbury Cl B98 . . . 154 F1
Avenbury Dr B91... 107 E4
Avenue Cl
Birmingham B7 . . . . 67 A6
Dorridge B93 . . . . 128 A3
Avenue Rd
Astwood Bank B96 . . . 158 E1
Birmingham, Aston B7,
B6 . . . . 67 A6
Birmingham, Erdington
B23 . . . . 56 F4
Birmingham, Handsworth
B21 . . . . 54 D2
Birmingham, King's Heath
B14 . . . . 104 D8
Cannock WS12 . . . . 2 E2
Darlaston WS10 . . . . . . 41 D6
Dorridge B93 . . . . 128 A3
Dudley, Woodside DY1,
DY2 . . . . 61 F6
Kenilworth CV8 . . . . . . 147 D6
Nuneaton CV11 . . . . 73 D2
Rowley Regis B65 . . . . . 63 D1
Royal Leamington Spa
CV31 . . . . 161 F7
Tipton WV14 . . . . 51 C8
Wolverhampton WV3 . . 24 E2
Avenue The
Birmingham, Acock's Green
B27 . . . . 88 D3
Birmingham B45 . . . . . 121 E7
❷ Birmingham, Lozells
B19 . . . . 66 C8
Blackwell B60 . . . . . . 138 A6
Blakedown DY10 . . . . . 98 B2
Coventry CV3 . . . . 134 A6
Featherstone WV10 . . . 12 C7
Rowington Green
CV35 . . . . 145 A1
Rowley Regis B65 . . . . . 63 A3
Sutton Coldfield B76... 46 F1
Wolverhampton, Castlecroft
WV3 . . . . 38 B8
Wolverhampton, Park Village
WV10 . . . . 25 F6
Wolverhampton, Penn
WV4 . . . . 38 E4
Averill Rd B26 . . . 69 A1
Avern Cl DY4 . . . . 52 B6
Aversley Rd B38... 123 E8
Avery Croft B35 . . .57 F2
Avery Ct ❻ CV34 . . . 160 F7
Avery Dell Ind Est
B30 . . . . 104 A6
Avery Dr B27 . . . . 88 C4
Avery Ho B16 . . . . . . 66 A1
Avery Myers Cl B68... 64 B5
Avery Rd
Smethwick B66 . . . . 65 D6
Sutton Coldfield B73... 45 C3
Aviary Ct B71 . . . . 53 C6
Aviemore Cl CV10 . . .73 A2
Aviemore Cres B43... 44 B4
Avill B77 . . . . 36 A5
Avill Gr DY11 . . . 116 C7
Avington Cl DY3 . . . 50 D7
Avion Cl WS1 . . . . . .42 F7
Avion Ctr WV6 . . . 25 A4
Avocet Cl
Birmingham B33 . . . . . . 68 E3
Coventry CV2 . . . . 96 B3
Avocet Dr DY10 . . . 117 A2
Avon B77 . . . . 36 A5
Avonbank Cl B97... 158 C6
Avon Bsns Pk WS11...4 C7
Avon Cl
Brierley Hill DY5 . . . . . 61 B7
Bromsgrove B60 . . . . . . 150 F6
Bulkington CV12 . . . . . . 79 B6
Perton WV6 . . . . 23 F4
Avon Cres WS3 . . . . . . 15 A1
Avoncroft ❽ WV4 . . .39 F4
Avoncroft Ho B37 . . . 70 A2
Avoncroft Mus of Historic
Buildings* B60 . . . 150 E5
Avoncroft Rd B60... 150 D6
Avon Ct
Kenilworth CV8 . . . . . . 147 F5
Sutton Coldfield B73... 46 B5
Avondale Cl DY6 . . . 60 E8

Avondale Rd
Birmingham B11 . . . . . . 87 D4
Brandon CV8 . . . . 135 F5
Coventry CV5 . . . . 133 A8
Royal Leamington Spa
CV32 . . . . 157 C4
Wolverhampton WV6 . . 24 F3
Avon Dr
Birmingham, Castle
Bromwich B36 . . . . 69 F7
Birmingham, Moseley
B13 . . . . 87 B2
Willenhall WV13 . . . . . . 27 C2
Wythall B47 . . . . 124 E2
Avon Gr WS5 . . . . 43 A4
Avon Ho
❸ Birmingham, Brandhall
B68 . . . . 84 B8
Birmingham, Lee Bank
B15 . . . . 86 D8
Coventry CV4 . . . . 132 C6
Dudley, Dibdale DY3 .. 50 E3
❷ Dudley, Russell's Hall
DY1 . . . . 61 E8
Avonlea Rise CV32 .. 156 D2
Avon Lodge CV11 . . . 73 A5
Avon Park Cvn Pk
B92 . . . . 90 D1
Avon Rd Burntwood WS7 .6 F5
Cannock WS11 . . . . 4 D8
Coventry CV4 . . . . 132 B6
Halesowen B63 . . . . 82 B5
Kenilworth CV8 . . . . . . 147 E3
Kidderminster DY11 . . . 116 B3
Solihull B90 . . . . 106 D1
Stourbridge DY8 . . . . . . 80 F3
Walsall WS3 . . . . 14 E1
Whitnash CV31 . . . . . . 162 A3
Avon St
Birmingham B11 . . . . . . 87 C5
Coventry CV2 . . . . 114 B5
Warwick CV34 . . . . 161 A7
Avon Wlk LE10 . . . 75 A8
Avro Way B35 . . . . . . 58 B2
Awbridge Rd DY2 . . . 62 C3
Awefields Cres B67 .. 64 E4
Awlmakers Gr WS3... 28 D7
Awson St CV6 . . . . . . 113 F6
Axcess 10 Bsns Pk
WS10 . . . . .41 E8
Axholme Rd CV2 . . . 114 E4
Axletree Way WS10... 42 B5
Axminster Cl CV11 . . .73 F2
Ayala Croft ❷ B36 . . . 68 E8
Aylesbury Cl B94 . . . 143 C6
Aylesbury Cres B44... 56 A8
Aylesbury Rd B94 . . . 143 D7
Aylesdene Ct CV5 . . . 132 F8
Aylesford Cl DY3 . . . 39 C2
Aylesford Ct ❼
CV31 . . . . 162 A6
Aylesford Dr
Birmingham B37 . . . . . . 90 A7
Sutton Coldfield B74... 31 E5
Aylesford Rd B21... 54 D1
Aylesford Sch &
Language Coll
CV34 . . . . 160 C4
Aylesford St
Coventry CV1 . . . . 113 E4
Royal Leamington Spa
CV31 . . . . 162 A6
Aylesmore Cl
Birmingham B32 . . . . . . 84 C1
Solihull B92 . . . . 106 C2
Aynho Cl CV5 . . . . . . 112 A3
Aynsley Ct B90 . . . 106 C2
Ayre Rd B24 . . . . 57 B4
Ayrshire Cl B36 . . . 68 D8
Ayrton Cl WV6 . . . . . . 24 A4
Aysgarth Cl CV11... 74 A2
Azalea Cl Codsall WV8.. 10 B3
Hinckley LE10 . . . . 75 E5
Azalea Dr LE10 . . . 75 E6
Azalea Gr B9 . . . . . . .67 F2
Azalea Wlk LE10 . . . 75 E5
Aziz Isaac Cl B68... 64 C6

B

Babbacombe Rd
CV3 . . . . 133 D5
Babington Rd B21... 65 E7
Bablake Cl CV6... 112 F8
Bablake Croft B92... 89 A1
Bablake Jun Sch
CV1 . . . . 165 A4
Bablake Sch CV1 . . . 113 B4
Babors Field WV14... 40 A3
Babworth Cl WV9 . . . 11 A2

Baccabox La B47... 124 E7
Bacchus Rd B18 . . .65 F6
Bache St B70 . . . . 53 D1
Bach Mill Dr B28... 105 D3
Backcester La WS13...9 B8
Backcrofts ❸ WS11...1 E1
Backhouse La WV11.. 26 C4
Back La Aldridge WS9 ..30 F8
Meriden CV7 . . . . 110 C5
Shenstone WS14 . . . . . . 17 E1
Solihull B90 . . . . 126 A5
Warwick CV34 . . . . 160 E6
Back Rd
Birmingham B38 . . . . . . 103 F2
Kingswinford DY6 . . . . . 60 D7
Back St CV11 . . . . 73 C5
Badbury Cl B80 . . . 159 D4
Badbury Gdns B80 .. 159 D4
Baddesley Cl CV31 .. 162 C5
Baddesley Clinton*
B93 . . . . 144 F4
Baddesley Rd B92... 88 E2
Bader Rd Perton WV6.. 23 E3
Willenhall WS2 . . . . . . 27 E2
Bader Wlk B35 . . .57 F2
Badger Brook La
B96 . . . . 158 D1
Badger Cl
Cheswick Green B90 . 126 D4
Huntington WS12 . . . 1 D6
Redditch B98 . . . . . . 154 D3
Badger Ct WV10 . . . 25 D4
Badger Dr WV10 . . . 25 D4
Badger Rd CV3 . . . 134 D8
Badgers Bank Rd B74 .31 F5
Badgers Cl WS3 . . . 15 A5
Badgers Croft B62 ... 83 B7
Badger St Dudley DY3. 50 E5
Stourbridge DY9 . . . . . . 81 E6
Badgers The B45 . . . 122 A2
Badgers Way
Birmingham B34 . . . . . . 69 A5
Cannock WS11 . . . . 2 D1
Badger Way B60 . . . 138 B5
Badminton Cl DY1...50 F3
Badon Covert B14... 104 D2
Badsey Cl B31 . . . 103 C4
Badsey Rd B69 . . . 63 D5
Baggeridge Cl DY3... 50 A8
Baggeridge Ctry Pk*
DY3 . . . . 49 E6
Baggeridge Ctry Pk
Visitor Ctr* DY3 . . .49 F7
Baggott St WV2 . . . 39 C7
Baginton Cl B91 . . . 107 B5
Baginton Fields Sch
CV3 . . . . 134 B4
Baginton Rd
Birmingham B35 . . . . . . 58 B4
Coventry CV3 . . . . 133 C5
Bagley's Rd DY5 . . . 81 D6
Bagley St DY9 . . . 81 C6
Bagnall Cl B25 . . . 88 D6
Bagnall Rd WV14 . . . 40 C5
Bagnall St
Walsall WS3 . . . . 28 C6
Wednesbury DY4 . . . . . 41 C1
West Bromwich B70... 53 E2
West Bromwich, Harvills
Hawthorn B70 . . . . 52 E7
Bagnall Wlk DY5 . . . 61 D1
Bagnell Rd B13 . . . 104 F7
Bagot St B4 . . . . 164 C4
Bagot Way CV34 . . . 161 E3
Bagridge Cl WV3 . . . 38 B8
Bagridge Rd WV3 . . . 38 B8
Bagshaw Cl CV8... 135 A1
Bagshawe Croft B23 . 56 D7
Bagshaw Rd B33 . . . 68 E3
Bailey Ave B77 . . .35 F5
Bailey Rd WV14 . . . 40 B7
Baileys Ct B65 . . . 63 B3
Bailey St
West Bromwich B70... 53 A4
Wolverhampton
WV10 . . . . 163 D3
Bailye Cl WS13 . . .3 F1
Baines' La ❶ LE10 . . . 71 D1
Bains Dr WS13 . . .9 A6
Baird Ho DY6 . . . 60 E8
Bakehouse La B93 . . . 145 B6
Bakeman Ho B26... 88 D6
Baker Ave
Royal Leamington Spa
CV31 . . . . 161 F6
Wolverhampton WV14... 39 F2
Baker Cl WS7 . . . . .6 F6

Baker House Gr B43.. 54 D7
Baker Rd WV14 . . . . . . 40 E3
Bakers La
Coventry CV5 . . . . 112 E2
Dorridge B93 . . . . 128 D1
Sutton Coldfield B73,
B74 . . . . 45 A5
Baker's La
Aldridge WS9 . . . . 30 B6
❺ Lichfield WS13 . . .9 B7
Bakers Mews B93 . . . 145 B6
Baker St Bedworth CV6 96 B6
Birmingham, Handsworth
B21 . . . . 65 F8
Birmingham, Small Heath
B10 . . . . 67 D1
Birmingham, Sparkhill
B11 . . . . 87 C5
Burntwood WS7 . . . . . . .6 F6
Tipton DY4 . . . . 51 E4
West Bromwich B70... 53 B3
Bakers Way WS12 . . . 2 B5
Bakers Wlk ❶ B77 . . .35 F2
Bakewell Cl
Coventry CV3 . . . . 134 F8
Walsall WS3 . . . . 14 C3
Balaams Wood Dr
B31 . . . . 102 B1
Balaclava Rd B14 . . . 104 E8
Balcaskie Cl B15 . . . 85 E7
Balden Rd B32 . . .84 F7
Baldmoor Lake Rd
B23 . . . . .56 F6
Bald's La DY9 . . .81 F5
Baldwin Cl B69 . . . 52 D2
Baldwin Croft CV6 . . . 96 B1
Baldwin Gr WS11 . . .2 C2
Baldwin Ho B19 . . . 66 E6
Baldwin Rd
Birmingham B30 . . . . . . 104 A3
Kidderminster DY10 .. 117 B7
Baldwins La B28 . . . 105 E4
Baldwin St
Bilston WV14 . . . . 40 F4
Smethwick B66 . . . . 65 B6
Balfour B79 . . . . 21 A4
Balfour Cl LE10 . . . 75 E7
Balfour Cres WV6 . . .24 F4
Balfour Ct
Sutton Coldfield B74... 32 A4
❷ Wolverhampton
WV6 . . . . 24 F4
Balfour Dr B69 . . . 52 D2
Balfour Ho ❷ B16...65 F1
Balfour Rd DY6 . . . 60 E8
Balfour St B12 . . . 86 E6
Balham Gr B44 . . . 45 A2
Balholm B62 . . . . 83 D5
Balking Cl WV14 . . . 40 B3
Ballantine Rd CV6 . . . 113 B6
Ballard Cres DY2 . . . 62 D3
Ballard Rd DY2 . . . 62 D3
Ballard Wlk B37 . . . 70 A6
Ball Fields DY4 . . . 52 D5
Ball Ho ❺ WS3 . . . 28 B8
Ballingham Cl CV4 .. 112 A3
Balliol Bsns Pk WV9 ..10 C1
Balliol Ho B37 . . .69 F2
Balliol Rd
Coventry CV2 . . . . 114 C4
Hinckley LE10 . . . . 75 F6
Ball La WV10 . . . . 11 C6
Ballot St B66 . . . . 65 B5
Balls Hill WS1 . . .28 F2
Balls St WS1 . . .28 F2
Balmain Cres WV11 .. 12 B1
Balmoral Cl
Coventry CV2 . . . . 114 E6
Halesowen B62 . . . . 83 D7
Lichfield WS14 . . . . . . 9 D6
Tamworth B79 . . . . 21 B7
Walsall WS4 . . . . 29 D1
Balmoral Ct
Birmingham B1 . . . . 66 C3
Cannock WS11 . . . . . . .2 A5
Kidderminster DY10 .. 117 A5
Nuneaton CV10 . . . . 72 E5
Balmoral Dr
Cannock WS12 . . . . . . .1 F7
Willenhall WV12 . . . . . . 27 C6
Wombourne WV5 . . . . . . 38 A1
Balmoral Ho WV3 . . . 163 A1
Balmoral Rd
Birmingham B36 . . . . . . 70 A7
Birmingham, Erdington
B23 . . . . 56 F5
Birmingham, Kitwell
B32 . . . . 102 B7
Stourbridge DY8 . . . . . . 60 C2

Balmoral Rd *continued*
Sutton Coldfield B74 . . . **31** F5
Wolverhampton WV4 . . **39** A5
Balmoral View DY1 . . **50** E2
Balmoral Way
Rowley Regis B65 . . . . . . **63** D4
Royal Leamington Spa
CV32 . . . . **157** C6
Walsall WS2 . . . . **28** B4
Balsall Common Prim
Sch CV7 . . . . **130** B5
Balsall Heath Rd B12. **86** E7
Balsall St E CV7. . . **130** B5
Balsall St B93, CV7. . **129** D7
Balthazar Cl CV34 . . **161** C4
Baltic Cl WS11 . . . . **1** E2
Baltimore Rd B42 . . . **55** A5
Balvenie Way DY1. . . . **50** F4
Bamber Cl WV3 . . . . . . **38** E8
Bamburgh B77 . . . . . . **35** C7
Bamburgh Gr CV32 . . **156** E3
Bamford Cl WS3 . . . . . **14** C3
Bamford Ho WS3 . . . . **14** C3
Bamford Rd
Walsall WS3 . . . . **14** C3
Wolverhampton WV3 . . **39** A8
Bamford St B77 . . . . . **21** D3
Bampfylde Pl B42 . . . . **55** C7
Bampton Ave 4 WS7. . **7** A8
Bamville Rd B8 . . . . . . **68** A5
Banbrook Cl B92 . . . **107** D8
Banbury Cl DY3 . . . . . **50** E6
Banbury Croft B37 . . . **69** F2
Banbury Ho B33 . . . . . **69** E2
Banbury Rd
Cannock WS11 . . . . **4** C8
Warwick CV34 . . . . . . **161** A3
Banbury St B5 . . . . **66** F2
Bancroft B77. . . . . **21** F3
Bancroft Cl WV14 . . . . **51** B7
Bandywood Cres B44. . **44** F3
Bandywood Rd B44 . . **44** F3
Baneberry Dr WV10 . . **12** B7
Banfield Ave WS10 . . . **41** C7
Banfield Rd WS10 . . . . **41** C4
Banford Ave B8 . . . . . . **68** A4
Banford Rd B8 . . . . . . **68** A4
Bangham Pit Rd B31 . **102** E6
Bangley La
Drayton Bassett B78 . . . **33** E6
Mile Oak B78 . . . . **34** A8
Bangor Ho B37 . . . . . . **70** B4
Bangor Rd B9 . . . . **67** D2
Bank Cres WS7 . . . . **6** F5
Bank Croft CV31 . . . **162** C5
Bankdale Rd B8 . . . . . **68** B4
Bankes Rd B10 . . . . . . **67** F1
Bank Farm Cl DY9 . . . **81** C1
Bankfield Dr CV32 . . **156** C1
Bankfield Rd
Bilston WV14 . . . . **40** D5
Tipton DY4 . . . . **52** C8
Bank Ho B27 . . . . **88** C3
Banklands Rd DY2 . . . **62** E6
Bank Rd
Dudley, Gornalwood
DY3 . . . . **50** C2
Dudley, Netherton DY2 . **62** D6
Banks Gn B97 . . . . . . **152** B2
Bankside
Birmingham, Great Barr
B43 . . . . **54** E7
Birmingham, Moseley
B13 . . . . **87** D2
Bankside Cl CV3 . . . . **134** A6
Bankside Cres B74 . . . **44** F7
Bankside Way WS9 . . . **16** B2
Banks Rd CV6 . . . . . . **113** A5
Banks St WV13 . . . . . . **27** A2
Bank St Bilston WV14. . **40** E3
Birmingham B14 . . . . . . **86** E1
Brierley Hill DY5 . . . . . **61** D3
Cannock WS12 . . . . **2** E1
Cradley Heath B64 . . . . **62** C1
Stourbridge DY9 . . . . . **81** F5
Tipton WV14 . . . . **51** C8
Walsall WS1 . . . . **28** F1
West Bromwich B71 . . . **53** D6
Wolverhampton WV10 . . **25** C5
Bank The CV8 . . . . . . **149** C6
Bankwell St DY5 . . . . . **61** D4
Banky Mdw LE10 . . . . . **76** A7
Banner La CV4 . . . . . . **111** D2
Bannerlea Rd B37. . . . . **69** F5
Bannerley Rd B33 . . . . **69** C1
Banners Ct B73 . . . . . . **45** B3
Banners Gate Inf Sch
B73 . . . . **45** A4
Banners Gate Jun Sch
B73 . . . . **45** A4

Banners Gate Rd B73. . **45** B3
Banners Gr B23 . . . . . . **57** A6
Banners La
Halesowen B63 . . . . . . **82** D6
Redditch B97 . . . . **158** E5
Banners St B63 . . . . . . **82** D6
Banners Wlk B44 . . . . . **45** B2
Bannington Ct WV12 . . **27** D4
Bannister Rd WS10 . . . **41** D2
Bannister St B64 . . . . . **62** D2
Banquo App CV34 . . . **161** F3
Banstead Cl WV2 . . . . . **39** E7
Bantam Gr CV6 . . . . . . **95** A3
Bantams Cl B33 . . . . . . **69** C2
Bant Mill Rd B60 . . . . **137** A1
Bantock Ave WV3 . . . . .**38** F8
Bantock Cl WV3 . . . . . . **38** E8
Bantock Gdns WV3 . . . **24** E1
Bantock House Mus *
WV3 . . . .**24** F1
Bantock Prim Sch
WV3 . . . . **39** A8
Bantock Rd CV4 . . . . . **111** E2
Bantocks The B70 . . . . **53** A6
Bantock Way 7 B17 . . **85** D5
Banton Cl B23 . . . . **56** D8
Bantry Cl B26 . . . . **89** C4
Baptist End Rd DY2 . . . **62** C6
Baptist Wlk LE10 . . . . . **71** D1
Barbara Rd B28 . . . . . **105** E4
Barbara St B79 . . . . . . **21** A5
Barbel Dr WV10 . . . . . . **26** B4
Barber Cl WS12 . . . .**2** E2
Barber Inst of Fine Arts
The * B15 . . . . **86** A3
Barberry Ho B38 . . . . **103** F1
Barbers La B91 . . . . . **108** C6
Barbican Rise CV2 . . . **114** E2
Barbourne Cl B91 . . . . **127** B7
Barbridge Cl CV12 . . . . **79** C2
Barbridge Rd CV12 . . . **79** C3
Barbrook Dr DY5 . . . . . **81** B7
Barcheston Rd
Birmingham B29 . . . . . . **85** A1
Dorridge B93 . . . . **128** A4
Barclay Ct WV3 . . . . . . **25** A2
Barclay Rd B67 . . . . . . **64** E1
Barcliff Ave B77 . . . . . . **21** E3
Barcroft WV13 . . . . **27** C2
Barcroft Prim Sch
WV13 . . . . **27** C2
Bardell Cl WS13 . . . .**8** E6
Bardenholme Gdns
DY9 . . . . **81** D3
Bardfield Cl 1 B42. . . **55** A8
Bardley Dr CV6 . . . . . . **113** C6
Bardon Dr B90 . . . . . . **106** D2
Bardsey Cl LE10 . . . . . . **71** B1
Bard St B11 . . . . **87** C5
Bardwell Cl WV8 . . . . . .**24** F8
Barford App CV31 . . . . **162** B2
Barford Cl
Coventry CV3 . . . . **134** D8
Darlaston WS10 . . . . . . **41** C8
Redditch B98 . . . . **154** F1
Sutton Coldfield B76. . . **46** F4
Barford Cres 5 B38. **104** C2
Barford Ho B5 . . . . **86** E8
Barford Prim Sch B16 **65** E3
Barford Rd
Birmingham B16 . . . . . . **65** F3
Kenilworth CV8 . . . . . . **148** B3
Solihull B90 . . . . **106** D2
Barford St B5 . . . . **86** E8
Bargate Dr WV6 . . . . . . **25** A4
Bargery Rd WV11. . . . . **13** A1
Barham Cl B90 . . . . . . **127** A5
Barker Rd B74 . . . . **46** B7
Barker's Butts La
CV6 . . . . **113** A4
Barkers' Butts La
CV6 . . . . **113** A5
Barkers La B47 . . . . . . **125** A1
Barker St
Birmingham B19 . . . . . . **66** B7
Oldbury B68 . . . . **64** C6
Bark Piece B32 . . . . . . **84** C3
Barlands Croft B34 . . . **69** C6
Barle Gr B36 . . . . **70** A7
Barleston Dr LE10 . . . . **71** A1
Barley Cl Cannock WS12 .**2** B5
Dudley DY3 . . . . **50** F7
Sutton Coldfield WS9 . . **30** C2
Wolverhampton WV8 . . . **10** E1
Barley Croft
Perton WV6 . . . . **23** D3
Stoke Heath B60 . . . . . **150** E6
Barley Ct CV32 . . . . . . **156** F2
Barleyfield LE10 . . . . . . **71** C3

Barleyfield Ho 3
WS1 . . . . **42** E8
Barleyfield Rise DY6. . **60** A8
Barleyfield Row WS1. . **42** E8
Barley Lea Ho CV3 . . **134** B8
Barley Lea The CV3. . **134** C8
Barley Mow La B61. . **137** B8
Barlich Way B98 . . . . **154** A2
Barling Way CV10 . . . . **73** B1
Barlow Cl
Birmingham B45 . . . . . **101** E2
Oldbury B68 . . . . **64** A3
Tamworth B77 . . . . **21** E4
Barlow Dr B70 . . . . **53** F1
Barlow Rd
Coventry CV2 . . . . **96** D2
Wednesbury WS10 . . . . **42** A5
Barlow's Rd B15 . . . . . **85** E5
Barmouth Cl WV12 . . . **27** C6
Barnabas Rd B23. . . . . **56** F4
Barnaby Sq WV10 . . . . .**11** F4
Barnack Ave CV3 . . . . **133** B5
Barnack Dr CV34 . . . . **155** E1
Barnacle La CV12 . . . . **79** C1
Barnard Cl
Birmingham B37 . . . . . . **70** D1
Royal Leamington Spa
CV32 . . . . **157** C3
Barnard Pl WV2 . . . . . . **39** E6
Barnard Rd
Sutton Coldfield B75. . . **46** E7
Wolverhampton WV11 . . **12** F1
Barnard Way WS11 . . . . .**1** F2
Barn Ave DY3 . . . . **50** C7
Barnbridge B77 . . . . . . **21** C2
Barnbrook Rd B93 . . . **128** A7
Barn Cl
Birmingham B30 . . . . . **104** B6
Coventry CV5 . . . . **112** C5
Cradley Heath B64 . . . . **82** E6
Dordon B78 . . . . **36** F6
Halesowen B63 . . . . . . **82** E2
Lichfield WS13 . . . .**3** B3
Stoke Heath B60 . . . . . **150** E6
Stourbridge DY9 . . . . . **81** C4
Whitnash CV31 . . . . . . **162** B3
Barn Croft
Birmingham B32 . . . . . . **84** E1
Burntwood WS7 . . . .**7** A4
Great Wyrley WS6. . . . . .**5** A3
Barncroft Rd B69 . . . . . **63** A8
Barncroft St B70 . . . . . **53** A8
Barne Cl CV11 . . . . **79** B7
Barnes Cl B37. . . . . **69** E2
Barnes Hill B29 . . . . . .**84** F2
Barnes Meadow Pl
WV14 . . . . **51** B8
Barnes Rd WS14 . . . . **18** A6
Barnesville Cl B10 . . . . **88** A8
Barnet Rd B23 . . . . **56** D5
Barnett Cl
Bilston WV14 . . . . **40** D4
Kingswinford DY6 . . . . . **60** D4
Barnett Gn DY6 . . . . . . **60** D4
Barnett La DY6, DY8. . . **60** D4
Barnett Rd WV13 . . . . . **26** E1
Barnetts Cl DY10 . . . . **117** B4
Barnetts Gr DY10 . . . . **117** A4
Barnetts La
Brownhills WS8 . . . .**6** F1
Kidderminster DY10 . . **117** A4
Barnett St
Stourbridge DY8 . . . . . . **60** D3
Tipton B69 . . . . **52** A2
Tipton DY4 . . . . **52** A4
Barney Cl DY4 . . . .**51** F7
Barn Farm Cl 4
WV14 . . . . **41** A7
Barnfield Ave CV5 . . . **112** B6
Barnfield Cl WS14. . . . . .**9** B6
Barnfield Dr B92 . . . . . **107** F6
Barnfield Gr B20 . . . . . **54** E5
Barnfield Rd
Bromsgrove B61 . . . . . **136** E1
Halesowen B62 . . . . . . **83** D7
Tipton DY4 . . . . **51** E6
Wolverhampton WV1 . . **26** A2
Barnfield Trad Est
DY4 . . . .**51** E7
Barnford Cl B10 . . . . . . **67** C1
Barnford Cres B68 . . . . **64** B3
Barnfordhill Cl B68. . . **64** B4
Barn Gn WV3 . . . .**38** F7
Barn Ho B8 . . . . **68** D4
Barnhurst La WV8. . . . . **10** E2
Barn La
Birmingham, Handsworth
B21 . . . . **65** E7
Birmingham, King's Heath
B13. . . . . **105** A7

Barn La *continued*
Solihull B92 . . . . **88** F3
Barn Leigh Dr CV4 . . **131** D6
Barn Mdw B25 . . . . **68** D1
Barnmoor Rise B91 . . . **107** C7
Barn Owl Dr WS3 . . . . . .**14** C7
Barn Owl Pl DY10 . . . . **117** A2
Barn Owl Wlk DY5. . . . **81** C6
Barnpark Covert 9
B14. . . . . **104** C2
Barn Piece B32 . . . . . . **84** B4
Barnsbury Ave B72. . . . **57** C6
Barns Cl WS9 . . . . **15** F4
Barns Croft B74. . . . . . **31** B4
Barns La WS4 . . . . **29** D7
Barnsley Cl CV7. . . . . . **118** D4
Barnsley Hall Dr B60 **137** B6
Barnsley Hall Rd
B61 . . . . **137** A6
Barnsley Rd
Birmingham B17 . . . . . . **65** A1
Bromsgrove B61 . . . . . **137** B4
Barn St B5 . . . .**66** F2
Barnstaple Cl CV5. . . . **111** F5
Barnstaple Rd B66 . . . . **65** B5
Barnswood Cl
Cannock WS11 . . . .**4** B8
Halesowen B63 . . . . . . **82** C5
Barnt Green Junc
B45. . . . . **138** D8
Barnt Green Rd B45. . **122** C3
Barn Way WS12 . . . .**2** F4
Barnwood Cl B98 . . . . **154** D5
Barnwood Rd
Birmingham B32 . . . . . . **84** F4
Wolverhampton WV8 . . **10** E1
Baron Bsns Ctr DY9. . .**81** E5
Barons Cl B17 . . . . **85** B6
Barons Court Trad Est
WS9 . . . .**15** E2
Barons Croft CV10. . . . **72** C4
Baron's Croft CV3 . . . **133** E7
Barons Ct B92 . . . . **89** C4
Baron's Field Rd
CV3 . . . . **133** E8
Barpool Rd CV10 . . . . .**72** F4
Barrack Cl B75. . . . . . . **47** A6
Barrack La B63 . . . . . . **82** B6
Barracks Cl WS3 . . . . . **28** E8
Barracks La
Beausale CV35 . . . . . . **146** C2
Brownhills WS9, WS14. . **16** C8
Walsall WS3 . . . . **28** E8
Barracks Pl WS3 . . . . . **28** E8
Barrack St
Birmingham B7 . . . . **67** A3
Warwick CV34 . . . . **160** E7
West Bromwich B70. . . . **53** A8
Barracks Way CV1. . . **165** B2
Barra Croft B35 . . . . . . **58** B4
Barrar Cl DY8 . . . . **80** E8
Barras Ct CV2 . . . . **114** A4
Barras Gn DY6 . . . . **60** D4
Barras Gn CV2 . . . . . . **114** A4
Barras La CV1. . . . . **113** B3
Barratts Croft DY5 . . . **50** C1
Barratts Ho B14 . . . . . **104** E2
Barratts Rd B38. . . . . . **104** A1
Barr Beacon Language
Coll WS9 . . . .**44** B5
Barr Common Cl WS9 . **30** B3
Barr Common Rd
WS9 . . . . **30** B3
Bar Rd CV3 . . . . **133** B3
Barrett Cl DY10 . . . . . **117** B6
Barretts La CV7 . . . . . **130** C6
Barrhill Cl B43 . . . . **43** E2
Barrie Ave DY10 . . . . . **117** C7
Barrie Rd LE10 . . . . **71** D3
Barrington Cl
Walsall WS5 . . . . **43** A3
Wolverhampton WV10 . **11** C1
Barrington Rd
Birmingham B45 . . . . . **121** E7
Solihull B92 . . . . **88** F2
Barr Lakes La
Birmingham WS9 . . . . . **44** A7
Walsall WS5, WS9 . . . . **43** F7
Barron Rd B31 . . . . . . **103** B3
Barrow Cl
Brownhills WS9 . . . . . . **15** F4
Coventry CV2 . . . . **115** B6
Redditch B98 . . . . **154** F3
Barrow Ho 1 B16. . . . **65** F1
Barrow Wlk B5 . . . . **86** E7
Barrows La B26 . . . . . . **89** A6
Barrows Rd B11. . . . . . . **87** C6

Barrow Wlk B5 . . . . . . **86** E7
Barrs Cres B64 . . . .**82** F8
Barr's Hill Sch & Com
Coll CV1 . . . . **165** A4
Barrs Rd B64 . . . . **82** E8
Barrs St B68 . . . . **64** A4
Barr St
Birmingham B19 . . . . . . **66** C5
Dudley DY3 . . . . **50** C3
Barry Ho CV2 . . . . **96** D1
Barry Jackson Twr
B6 . . . .**66** F7
Barry Rd WS5 . . . . **43** C7
Barsham Cl B5 . . . . **86** C6
Barsham Dr DY5 . . . . . **81** C8
Barston Cl CV6 . . . . **96** A2
Barston La
Balsall Common CV7. . . **129** D8
Barston B92 . . . . **109** C1
Catherine de B B91 . . . **108** B2
Eastcote B92 . . . . **108** D3
Solihull B91 . . . . **107** F2
Barston Rd B68 . . . . . . **84** B7
Bartestree Cl B98 . . . . **154** F1
Bartholemews La
B61 . . . . **136** F5
Bartholomew Ct
CV3 . . . . **134** A6
Bartholomew Row
B5 . . . . **164** D3
Bartholomew St B5 . **164** D2
Bartic Ave DY6 . . . .**60** F4
Bartleet Rd
Redditch B98 . . . . **159** E8
Smethwick B67 . . . . . . **64** D5
Bartlett Cl
Coventry CV6 . . . . **95** E2
3 Warwick CV34 . . . . **160** F7
Wednesbury WV14 . . . . **41** B1
Bartley Cl B92 . . . .**88** F2
Bartley Dr B31 . . . . . . **102** E8
Bartley Green Tech &
Sports Coll B32 . . . . **84** C1
Bartley Ho B32 . . . . . . **102** D8
Bartley Mews B31. . . . **102** E8
Bartley Woods B32 . . . **84** B2
Barton Cres CV31 . . . . **162** C6
Barton Ct B28 . . . . **105** F4
Barton Dr B93 . . . . **128** B4
Barton Ind Est WV14 . . .**40** E6
Barton La DY6 . . . . **60** C8
Barton Lodge Rd
B28 . . . . **105** E4
Barton Rd
Bedworth CV12 . . . . **78** A4
Coventry CV6 . . . . **95** F2
Nuneaton CV10 . . . . . . **73** C1
Wolverhampton WV4 . . **39** F4
Bartons Bank B6 . . . . . **66** E7
Barton's Mdw CV2 . . . **114** B6
Barton St B70 . . . . **53** C2
Barwell Cl
Dorridge B93 . . . . **127** E4
Royal Leamington Spa
CV32 . . . . **156** F3
Barwell Ct 8 B9 . . . . . **67** B2
Barwell La LE10 . . . . . . **71** E3
Barwell Rd B9 . . . . **67** B2
Barwick St B3 . . . . **164** B3
Basalt Cl WS2 . . . . **28** A3
Basant Cl CV34 . . . . . . **161** A4
Bascote Cl B97 . . . . . . **153** B1
Baseley Way CV6 . . . . .**95** D4
Basford Brook Dr CV6 .**95** F4
Basildon Wlk 3 CV2 **115** A7
Basil Gr B31 . . . . **102** E4
Basil Rd B31 . . . . **102** E4
Basin La B77 . . . . **21** D3
Baskerville Sch B17. . . **85** A5
Baskeyfield Cl WS14. . . **9** D7
Baslow Cl
Birmingham B33 . . . . . . **68** E4
Walsall WS3 . . . . **14** C3
Baslow Rd WS3 . . . . . . **14** B3
Basons La B68 . . . . **64** D5
Bassano Rd 1 B65 . . . **63** C1
Bassenthwaite Ct
DY6 . . . . **60** D6
Bassett Cl
Sutton Coldfield B76. . . **46** E4
Willenhall WV12 . . . . . . **27** D4
Wolverhampton WV4 . . **38** C6
Bassett Croft B10 . . . . **87** B8
Bassett Rd
Coventry CV6 . . . . **113** A5
Wednesbury WS10 . . . . **42** D3
Bassett St WS2 . . . . . . **28** C2

Bassnage Rd B63 . . . . **82** E2
Batchcroft
Bilston WV14 . . . . **40** D5
Darlaston WS10 . . . . . . **41** D8
Batchelor Cl DY8 . . . . .**80** F8
Batchley Fst Sch
B97 . . . . **153** B4
Batchley Rd B97 . . . . . **153** C4
Bateman Dr B73 . . . . . . **46** B1
Bateman Rd B46 . . . . . .**59** F1
Bateman's Acre S 1
CV6 . . . . **113** A4
Batemans La B47 . . . . **124** E5
Bates Cl B76 . . . . **58** B8
Bates Gr WV10 . . . . **26** A4
Bates Hill B97 . . . . **153** D4
Bates La B94 . . . . **141** F1
Bates Rd CV5 . . . . **132** E8
Bate St 3 Walsall WS2 **28** E3
Wolverhampton WV4 . . **40** A3
Batham Rd DY10 . . . . **117** A8
Bath Ave WV1 . . . . **163** A3
Bath Ct 4 B29 . . . . . . **103** B7
Batheaston Cl B38 . . . **123** D7
Bath Mdw B63 . . . . **82** E5
Bath Mews DY8 . . . .**80** F5
Bath Pas B5 . . . . **164** C1
Bath Pl 3 CV31 . . . . . **161** F7
Bath Rd
Brierley Hill DY5 . . . . . **62** A2
Cannock WS11 . . . .**1** E5
Nuneaton CV11. . . . . . . **73** C5
Stourbridge DY8 . . . . . **80** F5
Tipton DY4 . . . . **52** A5
Walsall WS1 . . . . **42** E8
Wolverhampton WV1 . . **163** A3
Bath Row
Birmingham B15 . . . . . . **66** C1
Oldbury B69 . . . . **63** D8
Bath St Bilston WV14. . . **40** E5
Birmingham B4 . . . . . . **164** C4
Coventry CV1 . . . . **165** C4
Dudley DY2 . . . . **62** C8
Royal Leamington Spa
CV31 . . . . **161** F7
Sedgley DY3 . . . . **39** E1
Walsall WS1 . . . . **42** E8
Willenhall WV13 . . . . . . **27** B1
Wolverhampton WV1 . **163** D2
Bathurst Rd CV6 . . . . . **113** A6
Bathway Rd CV3 . . . . . **133** A4
Bath Wlk Ind Est B12 .**86** E5
Bath Wlk B12 . . . . **86** E5
Batmans Hill Rd WV14,
DY4 . . . . **40** E1
Batsford Cl B98 . . . . . **159** B5
Batsford Rd CV6 . . . . . **112** F4
Batson Rise DY5 . . . . . **81** A8
Battalion Ct CV6 . . . . . **95** A1
Battenhall Rd B17. . . . . **85** A5
Battens Cl B98 . . . . . . **153** F3
Battens Dr B98. . . . . . . **154** D3
Battery Way B11 . . . . . . **87** E4
Battledown Cl LE10 . . **71** B2
Battlefield Hill WV5 . . **49** B7
Battlefield La WV5 . . . . **49** B6
Battlefield Terr WV5 . . **49** B6
Battling Brook Com Prim
Sch LE10 . . . .**71** B2
Battling Brook Sh Ctr
LE10 . . . .**71** B1
Baughan Ho B24 . . . . . **57** D3
Baulk La CV7 . . . . **110** D1
Bavaro Gdns DY5 . . . . . **62** A2
Baverstock Foundation
Sch and Specialist
Sports Coll B14 . . . **104** E2
Baverstock Rd B14. . . . **104** E2
Baxter Ave DY10 . . . . . **116** F7
Baxter Cl CV4 . . . . **112** A2
Baxter Coll DY11. . . . . **116** B6
Baxter Ct
Birmingham B13 . . . . . . **86** F2
10 Royal Leamington Spa
CV31 . . . . **162** A7
Baxter Gdns DY10 . . . **116** F7
Baxterley Gn
Solihull B91 . . . . **106** D4
Sutton Coldfield B76. . . **46** F1
Baxter Rd DY5 . . . . **61** C2
Baxters Gn B90 . . . . . . **126** B8
Baxters Rd B90 . . . . . . **126** B8
Bay Ave WV14 . . . .**51** C8
Bayer St WV14 . . . . **51** C8
Bayford Ave
Birmingham, Coft Common
B31 . . . . **122** E6

Bayford Ave continued
Birmingham, Sheldon
B26................ **89** C4
Bayley Cres WS10 .. **41** C8
Bayley La CV1...... **165** C2
Bayleys La DY4..... **52** C8
Bayley Tower 3 B36 .. **68** E8
Baylie St DY8.......**80** F5
Baylie St DY8.......**80** F4
Baylis Ave WV11......**26** F8
Bayliss Ave
Coventry CV6 .... **96** A4
Wolverhampton WV4 .. **40** A3
Bayliss Cl
Bilston WV14 ...... **40** C7
Birmingham B31 ... **103** B5
Bayliss Ct WV14 .... **40** C7
Bayliss Ct WV3 .... **24** E2
Baynton Rd WV12 .... **27** C8
Bayston Ave WV3... **38** E8
Bayston Rd B14.... **104** E3
Bayswater Rd
Birmingham B20...... **55** D1
Dudley DY3.......... **50** D2
Bayton Rd CV7...... **96** B7
Bayton Road Ind Est
CV7.................**96** B8
Bayton Way CV7 .... **96** C7
Baytree Cl WS3 ..... **14** A2
Bay Tree Cl
Birmingham B38..... **123** D8
Coventry CV2 .... **96** D1
Baytree Rd WS3..... **14** A2
Baywell Cl B90..... **127** A4
Bazzard Rd CV11....**79** F6
Beach Ave
Birmingham B12...... **87** B5
Wolverhampton WV4,
WV14 .... **40** A2
Beach Brook Cl B11.. **87** B5
Beachburn Way B20... **55** B3
Beach Cl B31....... **103** C1
Beachcroft Rd DY6... **49** C1
Beach Dr B63....... **83** A5
Beach Rd
Bilston WV14 ...... **40** D7
Birmingham B11..... **87** B5
Beach St B63....... **83** A5
Beach Trad Ctr B12...**87** B5
Beachwood Ave DY6 . **49** C1
Beacon Cl
Birmingham, Great Barr
B43.............. **43** F1
Birmingham, Rubery
B45............. **122** A6
Smethwick B66....... **65** A7
Beacon Ct
2 Birmingham B43 ... **43** F1
Sutton Coldfield B74... **44** F8
Beacon Ctr for the Blind
WV4................ **39** D4
Beacon Dr WS1 .... **43** A8
Beaconfields 1 WS13 ..9 A8
Beacon Gdns WS13....**3** A1
Beacon Hill
Aldridge WS9 ...... **30** C1
Birmingham, Aston B6 . **66** E8
Birmingham B45..... **121** F5
Beacon Hts WS9 .... **44** B6
Beacon La
Birmingham B60,
B45............. **121** E4
Sedgley DY3 .... **39** E1
Beacon Mews
1 Birmingham B43 ... **43** F1
5 Lichfield WS13.....**9** A8
Beacon Pas DY3 ... **39** D1
Beacon Prim Sch
WV12................ **27** D8
Beacon Rd
Aldridge WS9 .... **30** B1
Birmingham, Pheasey WS9,
B43.............. **44** C6
Coventry CV6 .... **95** D3
Sutton Coldfield, Banners
Gate B44 .... **45** A3
Sutton Coldfield, Boldmere
B73............. **46** A1
Walsall WS5 .... **43** D5
Willenhall WV12 ...... **27** C8
Beacon Rise
Aldridge WS9 ...... **30** B3
Sedgley DY3 .... **39** E1
Stourbridge DY9 ..... **81** D4
Beaconsfield Ave
WV4 .... **39** D5
Beaconsfield Cres 3
B12............. **86** E8

Beaconsfield Ct
Nuneaton CV11....... **73** D5
Walsall WS1 .... **43** B8
Beaconsfield Dr WV4. **39** D6
Beaconsfield Rd
Birmingham B12...... **86** E5
Coventry CV2 ...... **114** B2
Sutton Coldfield B74... **46** B7
Beaconsfield St W
CV31............... **162** B8
Beaconsfield St
Royal Leamington Spa
CV31............. **162** B7
West Bromwich B71... **53** C5
Beaconside Prim Sch
B45.............. **121** E6
Beacon Trad Est WS9 **30** A6
Beacon View
Birmingham B45..... **122** A6
Willenhall WS2 ...... **27** F2
Beaconview Dr B74...**44** F5
Beaconview Ho **4**
B71................**42** F1
Beacon View Rd B71 ..**42** F2
Beacon Way
Brownhills WS9 ...... **16** A3
Cannock WS12 ....**2** F3
Beake Ave CV6 .... **113** B7
Beakes Rd B67......**64** F3
Beaks Farm Gdns
B16................ **65** D2
Beaks Hill Rd B38... **103** E2
Beak St B1 .... **164** B2
Beale Cl B35....... **58** A2
Beale Ho B16.......**65** F1
Beales St B6....... **67** B8
Beale St DY8.......**80** F5
Bealeys Ave WV11.... **26** C8
Bealeys Cl WS3 .... **14** A3
Bealeys Ct WV11.... **26** C8
Bealeys La WS3 .... **14** A2
Beamans Cl B92.... **89** A4
Beaminster Rd B91.. **107** A4
Beamish Cl CV2.... **115** A6
Bean Croft B32.... **84** C2
Beanfield Ave CV3 . **132** F4
Bean Rd
Dudley, Dixon's Green
DY2.............. **62** D8
Dudley, Swan Village
DY4.............. **51** C6
Bean Road Ind Est
DY4.............. **51** C6
Beardmore Rd B72.. **57** C8
Bear Hill B48 ..... **139** B5
Bear Hill Dr B48 ... **139** B6
Bearing Dr WV11.... **26** E4
Bearley Croft B90 .. **126** D4
Bearmore Rd B64.... **62** E1
Bearnett Dr WV4.... **38** C2
Bearnett La WV4.... **38** B2
Bearsdon Cres LE10.. **71** B2
Bearwood Ho B66.... **65** A4
Bearwood Prim Sch
B66............... **65** A2
Bearwood Rd B66... **65** A3
Bearwood Sh Ctr B66 **65** A1
Beasley Gr B43...... **44** B1
Beaton Cl WV13..... **26** E2
Beaton Rd B74...... **32** A4
Beatrice St WS3.... **28** C6
Beatrice Wlk B69 ... **52** A2
Beattie Cl LE10..... **71** D3
Beatty Ho DY4...... **52** B8
Beaty's Gdns CV32 .. **157** A4
Beaubrook Gdns DY6. **60** E3
Beauchamp Ave
Birmingham B20...... **54** F5
Kidderminster DY11.. **116** D3
Royal Leamington Spa
CV32............. **156** D1
Beauchamp Cl
1 Birmingham B37 ... **70** B2
Sutton Coldfield B76... **58** B7
Beauchamp Ct
Kidderminster DY11.. **116** D3
1 Royal Leamington Spa
CV32............. **156** F1
Beauchamp Gdns
CV34............. **161** B6
Beauchamp Hill
CV32............. **156** D1
Beauchamp Hts
DY11............. **116** D3
Beauchamp Ind Pk
B77............... **35** D8

Beauchamp Rd
Birmingham B13..... **105** C5
Kenilworth CV8...... **147** F2
Royal Leamington Spa
CV32............. **156** F1
Solihull B91....... **107** B5
Tamworth B77...... **35** F5
Warwick CV34 ..... **161** B8
Beau Ct WS11.........**1** F1
Beaudesert Cl B47.. **125** A6
Beaudesert Rd
Birmingham B20...... **66** B8
Coventry CV5 ...... **113** A1
Hollywood B47...... **125** A6
Beaufell Cl CV34 ... **155** E1
Beaufort Ave
Birmingham B34..... **68** D5
Kidderminster DY11.. **116** A7
Royal Leamington Spa
CV32............. **157** C5
Beaufort Cl LE10.... **75** E4
Beaufort Dr CV3 ... **134** F7
Beaufort Pk B8 .... **68** C5
Beaufort Rd
Birmingham, Gravelly Hill
B23.............. **56** E2
Birmingham, Ladywood
B16.............. **66** A1
Beaufort Sch B34... **68** D5
Beaufort St B98... **153** E3
Beaufort Way WS9 ... **30** B4
Beaulieu Ave DY6 ...**60** F4
Beaulieu Cl DY11... **116** D8
Beaulieu Pk CV31... **162** D6
Beaumaris Cl
Coventry CV5 ..... **111** F5
Dudley DY1......... **50** F4
Beaumont Ave LE10.. **75** A7
Beaumont Cres CV6.. **113** A4
Beaumont Ct
9 Coventry CV6 .... **113** A4
8 Royal Leamington Spa
CV31............. **162** A6
Beaumont Dr
Birmingham B17...... **85** B4
Brierley Hill DY5..... **81** B7
Beaumont Gdns B18 ..**65** F6
Beaumont Gr B91.. **106** F5
Beaumont Lawns
B60............. **121** D1
Beaumont Pk B30.. **103** F4
Beaumont Pl CV11... **73** A4
Beaumont Rd
Birmingham B30.... **103** F6
Great Wyrley WS6.....**4** F2
Halesowen B62...... **83** E8
Keresley CV7 .... **95** A6
Nuneaton CV11..... **73** A4
Wednesbury WS10.... **41** F4
Beaumont Way WS11...**6** A4
Beaurevoir Way
CV34............. **161** A8
Beausale Croft CV5 . **112** A3
Beausale Dr B93 ... **128** C7
Beauty Bank B64.... **83** A8
Beauty Bank Cres
DY8................**80** F6
Beauty Bank Prim Sch
DY8................**80** F6
Beaver Cl WV11......**26** F5
Beaver Pk B63.......**82** F6
Bebington Cl WV8.....**24** F8
Beccles Dr WV13.....**40** F8
Beche Way CV5 .... **112** B5
Beckbury Ave WV4.... **38** C5
Beckbury Rd
Birmingham B29...... **85** A1
Coventry CV2 ...... **114** B2
Beck Cl B66......... **65** A4
Beckenham Ave B44.. **45** B1
Beckensall Cl DY1.... **51** B1
Becket Cl B74....... **31** F6
Beckett Cl B98..... **153** F5
Beckett St WV14.....**40** F6
Beckfield Cl
Birmingham B14.... **104** E2
Walsall WS4 .... **29** C8
Beckfoot Dr CV2.....**96** F1
Beckford Croft B93.. **127** F3
Beckford Ct B23 .... **56** C2
Beckman Rd DY9.... **81** C2
Beckminster Rd WV3..**38** F7
Becks La CV7....... **93** A5
Becks The B48 .... **139** A7
Beconsfield Cl B93... **127** F4
Becton Gr B42..... **55** D7
Bedale Ave LE10.....**71** F2

Bedcote Pl DY8 ..... **81** B5
Beddoe Cl DY4...... **52** D5
Beddow Ave WV14... **51** C7
Beddows Rd WS3 .... **28** E5
Bede Arc 2 CV12 ... **78** B3
Bede Rd
Bedworth CV12...... **78** A4
Coventry CV6 ...... **113** B6
Nuneaton CV10...... **72** D3
Bedford Cl LE10..... **71** E3
Bedford Dr B75...... **46** E6
Bedford Ho
Birmingham B36...... **70** B6
7 Birmingham, Erdington
B24.............. **56** F4
6 Wolverhampton
WV3.............. **25** C4
Bedford Pl
Cannock WS12 ....**2** B4
5 Royal Leamington Spa
CV32............. **161** F8
Bedford Rd
Birmingham B12...... **87** A8
Sutton Coldfield B75... **46** E7
West Bromwich B71... **53** B7
Bedford St
Coventry CV1 ...... **113** A2
Royal Leamington Spa
CV32............. **161** F8
Tipton DY4 .... **52** B5
Wolverhampton WV1... **40** B7
Bedford Terr 4 B19 .. **66** D8
Bedlam La CV6...... **95** E2
Bedlam Wood Rd
B31............. **102** C1
Bedworth Cl CV12.... **79** B2
Bedworth Croft DY4.. **52** B4
Bedworth Gr B9 .... **68** B2
Bedworth La CV12.... **77** D4
Bedworth Rd
Bedworth CV12...... **78** F2
Bulkington CV12..... **79** A2
Coventry CV6, CV7... **96** A5
Bedworth Sta CV12.. **78** C2
Beebee Rd WS10.....**41** F6
Beecham Bsns Pk
WS9.............. **30** A8
Beecham Cl WS9.... **30** A8
Beech Ave
Birmingham B32..... **84** D7
Birmingham, Chelmsley
Wood B37........ **70** B1
5 Birmingham, Showell
Green B12 .... **87** A5
Halesowen B62...... **83** C8
Tamworth B77...... **21** E3
Beech Cl
Hartshill CV10....... **72** A8
Rowington Green
CV35............ **145** A1
Sedgley DY3 .... **39** E1
Sutton Coldfield B75... **32** A4
Tamworth B79....... **21** A8
Wolverhampton WV10 . **25** B8
Beech Cliffe CV34 ... **160** F8
Beech Cres
Burntwood WS7 ......**6** F6
Tipton DY4 .... **52** C8
Wednesbury WS10.... **41** F5
Beechcroft
Bedworth CV12...... **77** F1
Birmingham B15..... **86** A7
Beechcroft Ave B28. **106** A6
Beechcroft Cres B74. **30** D1
Beechcroft Ct B74... **32** A1
Beechcroft Dr B61.. **137** B4
Beechcroft Est B63.. **82** C6
Beechcroft Pl WV10.. **25** C6
Beechcroft Rd
Birmingham B36...... **69** B8
Cradley Heath B64.... **62** F1
Kidderminster DY11.. **116** A8
Beech Ct
Birmingham, Bournville
B30............. **103** E4
Birmingham, Great Barr
B43.............. **43** D1
Birmingham, Longbridge
B45............. **122** D7
Birmingham, Short Heath
B73.............. **56** F8
Cannock WS12 ....**2** B7
Great Wyrley WS6.....**5** A4
Oldbury B66........ **64** C8
Stourbridge DY8 ..... **80** F3
Royal Leamington Spa
CV34............. **161** E2
Wednesbury WS10.... **41** F5
Beechdale B68...... **84** B7
Beechdale Ave B44... **44** E2
Beechdale Prim Sch
WS2.............. **28** C5

Beechdale Rd WS3 ...**27** F8
Beech Dene Gr B23.. **56** E5
Beech Dr CV8...... **148** B5
Beechen Gr WS7 ......**6** F1
Beecher Pl B63...... **82** D5
Beecher Rd B63..... **82** D5
Beecher Rd E B63.... **82** D5
Beecher's Keep CV8. **135** F5
Beecher St B63..... **82** C5
Beeches Ave B27.... **88** C4
Beeches Cl
Birmingham B45..... **121** D8
Kingswinford DY6..... **60** D5
Beeches Ct B45..... **122** B7
Beeches Dr B24..... **57** C5
Beeches Farm Dr
B31.............. **123** A7
Beeches Mews DY9 .. **98** F4
Beeches Pl WS3..... **28** D6
Beeches Rd
Birmingham B42..... **55** C7
Kidderminster DY11.. **116** A6
Oldbury B68 .... **64** C3
Rowley Regis B65..... **63** C1
Walsall WS3 .... **28** D6
West Bromwich B70... **53** E3
Beeches The
Bedworth CV12...... **77** E2
Birmingham B15..... **86** C8
Sutton Coldfield B74... **31** D4
Sutton Coldfield, Wylde
Green B73 .... **46** B1
Upton Warren B61 ... **150** A4
West Bromwich B70... **53** E2
Wolverhampton, Newbridge
WV1............. **25** A3
Wolverhampton WV11 . **26** B5
Beeches View Ave
B63.............. **82** C4
Beeches Way B31... **123** A7
Beeches Wlk B73.... **46** B3
Beechey Cl B43..... **44** D5
Beech Farm Croft
B31.............. **103** A3
Beechfield Ave 1
B11................ **87** B6
Beechfield Cl B62... **83** C8
Beechfield Dr DY11 . **116** C8
Beechfield Gr WV14.. **51** B7
Beechfield Rd
Birmingham B11..... **87** B6
Smethwick B67...... **64** F4
Beechfield Rise WS14 . **9** D8
Beech Gate B74...... **31** C5
Beech Gdns WS14......**9** C6
Beechglade B20..... **54** F4
Beech Gn DY1 ...... **51** A5
Beech Gr
Birmingham B14.... **105** A5
Huntington WS12 .....**1** D8
Warwick CV34 ..... **156** B1
Beech Hill Ct B72... **57** C8
Beech Hill Ho B32... **102** C8
Beech Hill Rd B72.... **57** C8
Beech Ho
Redditch B98 ...... **158** F8
Solihull B91....... **106** F2
Sutton Coldfield B74... **31** B5
6 Warwick CV34 ... **161** D8
Beechhouse La WV5.. **37** A1
Beech Hurst 1 B38. **123** E8
Beech Hurst Gdns
WV5............... **37** A2
Beech Mews B64..... **62** E2
Beechmore Rd B26... **89** A5
Beechmount Dr B23.. **57** A6
Beechnut Cl
Coventry CV4 ...... **111** D2
Solihull B91........ **107** C5
Beechnut La B91.... **107** E4
Beech Park Dr B45.. **138** C8
Beech Pine Cl WS12....**2** A8
Beech Rd
Birmingham, Bournville
B30............. **103** E6
Birmingham, Erdington
B23.............. **56** F8
Bromsgrove B61.... **136** F4
Coventry CV6 ...... **113** B6
Dudley DY1 .... **51** C4
Hollywood B47...... **125** B6
Kingswinford DY6..... **60** E5
Oldbury B69........ **63** A8
Stourbridge DY8 ..... **80** F3
Tamworth B79....... **21** A8
Wednesbury WS10.... **41** F5
Willenhall WV13 ..... **26** E2
Wolverhampton WV10 . **25** B8
Beech Tree Ave
Coventry CV4 ...... **112** B2

Beech Tree Ave continued
Wolverhampton WV11 . **26** C8
Beech Tree Cl
Kingswinford DY6..... **60** E8
Redditch B97 ...... **153** B4
Beech Tree La WS11 ...**4** D8
Beech Tree Rd WS9...**15** F3
Beech Way B66 ..... **65** B5
Beech Wlk B38 .... **123** F8
Beechwood B20...... **54** E3
Beechwood Ave
Coventry CV5 ...... **132** F8
Hinckley LE10....... **75** D3
Wolverhampton WV11 . **26** B8
Beechwood Bsns Pk
WS11...............**2** B3
Cheswick Green B90 . **126** D4
Walsall WS3 .... **14** B3
Beechwood Cres B77..**21** F5
Beechwood Croft
Kenilworth CV8...... **147** F2
Sutton Coldfield B74... **31** D5
Beechwood Ct
1 Birmingham B30 .. **104** C3
Coventry CV5 ...... **132** F8
Cradley Heath B64 ... **83** A7
Wolverhampton WV6 .. **24** C3
Beechwood Dr WV6... **24** C3
Beechwood Ho 10
WV3 .... **25** A2
Beechwood Park Rd
B91.............. **106** E5
Beechwood Rd
Bedworth CV12...... **78** D4
Birmingham B67..... **84** F8
Birmingham, Great Barr
B43.............. **43** F2
Birmingham, King's Heath
B14............. **104** F5
Dudley DY2......... **51** E1
Nuneaton CV10...... **72** C6
West Bromwich B70... **53** B3
Beecroft Ave WS13....**3** B1
Beecroft Ct WS11 .....**1** E2
Beecroft Rd WS11.....**1** E1
Beehive Cl B61...... **121** A1
Beehive Hill CV8.... **147** F4
Beehive La B76 ..... **59** C6
Beehive Wlk 4 DY4.. **51** E5
Beekes Croft B78 ... **35** A8
Bee La WV10........ **11** D3
Beeston Cl
Birmingham B6...... **67** A7
Brierley Hill DY5..... **81** D8
Coventry CV3 ...... **134** F8
Beeton Rd B18...... **65** E6
Beet St B65........ **63** C1
Beever Rd DY4...... **52** D7
Beggars Bush B73 ... **45** D2
Beggars Bush La WV5 **49** B5
Begonia Cl LE10..... **75** E5
Begonia Dr LE10..... **75** E5
Beighton Cl B74.....**31** F6
Beilby Rd B30...... **104** B5
Belbroughton CE Prim
Sch DY9 .... **119** E6
Belbroughton Cl
B98.............. **153** F2
Belbroughton Rd
Blakedown DY10...... **98** D1
Halesowen B63...... **82** F2
Holy Cross DY9...... **99** E2
Stourbridge DY8 ..... **80** E3
Belchers La B8, B9 ... **68** A3
Beldray Rd WV14.... **40** E6
Belfont Trad Est B62 . **83** C4
Belfry Cl Hinckley LE10 **75** D4
Walsall WS3 .... **14** A3
Belfry Dr DY8....... **80** E6
Belfry The WV6..... **23** D4
Belgrade Rd WV10 ... **11** B1
Belgrade Theatre
CV1.............. **165** B3
Belgrave Ct DY6......**60** F4
Belgrave High Sch
B77................**21** F1
Belgrave Middleway B5,
B12.............. **86** E7
Belgrave Rd
Birmingham B12..... **86** F6
Coventry CV2 ...... **114** E4
Halesowen B62...... **83** D8
Tamworth B77...... **35** E4
Belgrave Sq CV2 ... **114** E4
Belgrave Terr B21.... **66** A7
Belgrave Wlk WS2 ... **28** B3
Belgravia Cl B5...... **86** E7
Belgravia Ct B37.... **70** A5

Belgrove Cl B15 85 E6
Belgrove Ho WS11 1 D1
Belinda Cl WV13 26 F3
Bellairs Ave CV12 77 E1
Bellamy Cl B90 106 D1
Bellamy Farm Rd B90 106 D1
Bellamy La WV11 26 C7
Bell Barn Rd B15 86 C8
Bell Barn Sh Ctr 8 B15 86 C8
Bellbrooke Cl CV6 96 B1
Bell Cl Birmingham B36 70 B6
Birmingham, Bordesley Green B9 67 E3
Darlaston WS10 41 D7
Bellcroft 3 B16 66 B2
Bell Ct CV32 156 F2
Bell Dr Ash Green CV7 95 E7
Birmingham B9 67 F3
Cannock WS12 2 C7
Walsall WS5 43 A5
Belle Cotts B94 143 D5
Bellefield Ave 10 B18 65 E4
Bellefield Rd B18 65 E4
Belle Isle DY5 61 C3
Bellemere Rd B92 109 B6
Bellencroft Gdns WV3 38 C7
Bell End B65 63 C3
Belle Orch DY11 116 B5
Belle Vale B63 82 E5
Bellevue
Birmingham B5 86 D7
Dudley WV14 40 E2
Belle Vue
Nuneaton CV10 72 E3
Stourbridge DY8 60 D2
Belle Vue Ave B16 65 D4
Belle Vue Cl B61 121 C1
Belle Vue Ct DY8 60 D2
Belle Vue Dr B62 83 E6
Belle Vue Gdns B65 63 C3
Belle Vue Prim Sch DY8 60 C3
Bellevue Rd
Bilston WV14 41 A2
Birmingham B26 89 B7
Belle Vue Rd DY5 62 A1
Bellevue St WV14 39 F2
Belle Vue Terr B92 109 A6
Belle Wlk B13 87 B3
Bellfield
Birmingham B31 102 F4
Tanworth-In-A B94 142 A2
Bellfield Ho B14 104 D1
Bellfield Jun & Inf Schs B31 102 F4
Bellflower Cl WV10 12 A7
Bellflower Dr 1 WS5 42 F3
Bell Fold B68 64 C6
Bell Green La B38 124 B5
Bell Green Rd CV6 114 A8
Bell Heather Rd WS8 15 D6
Bell Heath Way B32 84 B2
Bell Hill
3 Birmingham B31 103 A4
Birmingham B31 103 A5
Bell Holloway B31 102 F5
Bellingham B77 22 D1
Bellington Croft 5 B90 127 A6
Bellis St B16 65 F1
Bell La
Birmingham, Kitt's Green B33 69 E1
Birmingham, Northfield B31 103 A4
Studley B80 159 E4
Walsall, Wallington Heath WS3 14 B1
Walsall, Yew Tree WS5 43 A5
Bellman Cl WS10 41 D7
Bell Mdw DY9 99 B8
Bell Mead B80 159 E4
Bell Meadow Way B14 104 E1
Bell Pl WV2 163 B1
Bell Rd Dudley DY2 62 C5
Trysull WV5 37 D1
Walsall WS5 43 D6
Bell St S DY5 61 D2
Bells Farm Cl B14 104 C2
Bells Farm Jun & Inf Sch B14 104 C2
Bell Sh Ctr The B31 103 A4
Bellsize Cl WS11 5 F5
Bells La
Birmingham B14 104 D2
Stourbridge DY8 60 D2
Bells Moor Rd B70 53 A6
Bell St Bilston WV14 40 C6
Brierley Hill, Barrow Hill DY5 61 D7
Brierley Hill, Silver End DY5 61 D2
Darlaston WS10 41 D7
Dudley WV14 40 C2
Stourbridge DY8 81 A5
Tipton DY4 51 E5
West Bromwich B70 53 D2
Wolverhampton WV1 163 B2
Bell Tower Mews CV32 156 F3
Bellview Way CV6 96 B1
Bell Vue Rd B65 63 C2
Bellwood Rd B31 102 F4
Belmont Ave WS11 1 C2
Belmont Cl
Aldridge WS9 30 A7
Great Wyrley WS11 5 A4
Redditch B97 153 B1
Tipton DY4 51 F6
Belmont Covert B31 103 B6
Belmont Cres B31 103 B6
Belmont Ct
Royal Leamington Spa CV32 157 A4
Sutton Coldfield B72 46 B4
Belmont Dr CV32 157 A4
Belmont Gdns WV14 41 A4
Belmont Mews CV8 147 F4
Belmont Pas B4 67 A3
Belmont Rd
Birmingham, Handsworth B21 65 C8
Birmingham, Rubery B45 122 A6
Brierley Hill DY5 61 D6
Coventry CV6 114 A7
Smethwick B66 65 A2
Stourbridge DY9 81 F4
Tamworth B77 35 E7
Wolverhampton WV4 39 A5
Belmont Rd E B21 65 C8
Belmont Row B4 67 A3
Belmont St WV14 41 A4
Belper DY1 51 B1
Belper Ent Pk B70 52 F4
Belper Rd Walsall WS3 14 C3
West Bromwich B70 52 F3
Belper Row DY2 62 E4
Belsize B77 21 E2
Belstone Cl B14 104 D6
Belton Ave WV11 12 B1
Belton Cl B94 143 C5
Belton Gr B45 122 C8
Belt Rd WS12, WS11 2 A5
Belvedere Ave WV4 39 B5
Belvedere Cl
Burntwood WS7 6 F5
Kidderminster DY10 117 A5
Kingswinford DY6 60 F4
Tamworth B79 21 C7
Belvedere Dr B61 137 A4
Belvedere Gdns WV6 24 E7
Belvedere Rd
Birmingham B24 57 B2
Coventry CV5 133 A8
Belvide Gr B29 103 B8
Belvidere Gdns B11 87 C4
Belvidere Rd WS1 42 F8
Belvoir B77 35 C7
Belvoir Cl DY1 50 E2
Belvoir Rd B60 137 C1
Belwell Dr B74 32 A2
Belwell Gdns B74 32 A2
Belwell La B74 32 A2
Bembridge Cl WV12 27 B8
Bembridge Rd B33 69 A3
Benacre Dr B5 66 F2
Benbeck Gr DY4 51 C6
Benbow Cl LE10 71 D4
Benches Cl WS7 6 D6
Bencroft WV8 10 B4
Bendall Rd B44 45 B2
Benedictine Ct CV1 165 C3
Benedictine Rd CV3 133 C8
Benedict Sq CV2 114 C8
Benedon Rd B26 89 B7
Bengrove Cl B98 159 A7
Benion Rd WS11 1 F5
Benjamin Gdns 4 B20 55 D1
Benmore Ave B5 86 D7
Bennett Ave DY1 51 B6
Bennett Ct CV8 135 F3
Bennett Dr CV34 161 C7
Bennett Rd B74 31 D3
Bennett's Hill
Birmingham B2 164 B2
Dudley DY2 62 E8
Bennetts Rd B8 67 D6
Bennett's Rd CV7 94 F4
Bennett's Road N CV7 94 E7
Bennett's Road S CV6 94 F2
Bennett St
Birmingham B19 66 D8
2 Kidderminster DY11 116 C6
Bennetts Well Jun & Inf Sch B37 69 F3
Ben Nevis Way DY8 81 A6
Bennick Trad Est WS11 4 E6
Bennitt Cl B70 53 C1
Benn Rd CV12 79 B2
Benson Ave WV4 39 D5
Benson Cl
Lichfield WS13 3 D1
Perton WV6 23 E5
Benson Com Sch B18 65 F6
Benson Ind Est B18 65 F6
Benson Rd
Birmingham, Highter's Heath B14 105 B1
Birmingham, Hockley B18 65 F6
Coventry CV6 95 A1
Benson View B79 21 C8
Bent Ave B32 84 D6
Benthall Rd CV6 95 F2
Bentham Ct B31 102 F5
Bentleybridge Island WV11 26 B4
Bentleybridge Way WV11 26 C4
Bentley Br L Pk WV11 26 B4
Bentley Cl
Redditch B97 153 D3
Royal Leamington Spa CV32 157 B3
Bentley Ct
Coventry CV6 95 C4
Nuneaton CV11 73 A4
Sutton Coldfield B76 57 F8
Bentley Dr WS2 28 B3
Bentley Drive JMI Sch WS2 28 B2
Bentley Farm Cl B93 127 E4
Bentley Gr B29 102 F8
Bentley Heath CE Prim Sch B93 127 F5
Bentley Heath Cotts B93 127 F5
Bentley La
Walsall, Birchills WS2 28 B3
Walsall, Leamore WS2 28 A5
Willenhall WV12 27 E5
Bentley Lane Bsns Pk WS2 28 B3
Bentley Mill Cl WS2 27 F1
Bentley Mill La WS2 27 F1
Bentley Mill Way WS2 27 F1
Bentley New Dr WS2 28 B3
Bentley Pl WS2 28 B2
Bentley Rd
Bedworth CV7 78 A1
Birmingham B36 69 D7
Nuneaton CV11 73 A4
Wolverhampton WV10 11 E2
Bentley Rd N WS2 27 E1
Bentley Rd S
Darlaston WS10 41 E8
Walsall WS10 27 E1
Bentley Way B79 20 F7
Bentley West Prim Sch WS2 27 E3
Bentley Wharf WV12 27 D5
Bentmead Gr B38 104 A1
Benton Ave B11 87 C6
Benton Cl WV12 27 D4
Benton Cres WS3 14 D2
Benton Green La CV7 110 F2
Benton Rd B11 87 C6
Benton's Ct DY11 116 C6
Benton's La WS6 5 A1
Bentons Mill Croft B7 67 C8
Bentree The CV3 134 B8
Bent St DY5 61 D4
Ben Willetts Wlk 3 B65 63 C1
Benyon Ctr The WS2 28 A7
Beoley Cl B72 46 C1
Beoley Fst Sch B98 154 E8
Beoley Gr B45 122 A7
Beoley Hall B98 140 C1
Beoley La Beoley B98 154 F8
Portway B98 141 B1
Beoley Rd E B98 154 A4
Beoley Rd W B98 153 F4
Berberry Cl B30 103 D6
Berenska Dr CV32 157 A2
Beresford Ave CV6 95 E1
Beresford Cres B70 53 B3
Beresford Dr B73 46 A1
Beresford Rd
Oldbury B69 64 C7
Walsall WS3 28 E8
Berets The B75 46 F6
Bericote Croft B27 88 D3
Bericote Rd CV32 156 E8
Berkeley Cl
Bromsgrove B60 151 B8
Nuneaton CV11 73 B3
Perton WV6 23 F3
Willenhall WS2 27 F3
Berkeley Dr DY6 60 C7
Berkeley Ho
Birmingham B23 56 F6
Sutton Coldfield B76 57 F8
Berkeley Mews B25 88 B7
Berkeley Prec B14 104 F2
Berkeley Rd
Birmingham B25 88 B7
Kenilworth CV8 147 E6
Solihull B90 105 F3
Berkeley Rd E B25 88 B7
Berkeley Rd N CV5 113 A1
Berkeley Rd S CV5 133 A8
Berkeley St WS2 42 B7
Berkeswell Cl B98 154 C7
Berkett Rd CV6 95 B2
Berkley Cres B13 87 C1
Berkley Ct B1 66 C1
Berkley St B1 66 C1
Berkshire Cl
Nuneaton CV10 72 E3
West Bromwich B71 53 B7
Berkshire Cres WS10 42 C4
Berkshire The WS3 14 A3
Berkswell CE Prim Sch CV7 110 C3
Berkswell Cl
Dudley DY1 50 E3
Solihull B91 107 B8
Sutton Coldfield B74 31 E4
Berkswell Hall CV7 110 C3
Berkswell Mus★ CV7 110 C3
Berkswell Rd
Birmingham B24 57 B4
Coventry CV6 96 B2
Meriden CV7 110 C7
Berkswell Sta CV7 130 C8
Berkswell Windmill★ CV7 130 D4
Bermuda Bsns Pk CV10 78 A7
Bermuda Cl DY1 51 B6
Bermuda Ind Est CV10 78 B8
Bermuda Rd CV10 73 A1
Bernard Pl B18 65 F5
Bernard Rd
Birmingham B17 65 B2
Oldbury B68 64 C2
Tipton DY4 52 B7
Bernard St
Walsall WS1 29 A1
West Bromwich B71 53 C4
Berners Cl CV4 111 E2
Berners St B19 66 D7
Bernhard Dr B21 65 E8
Bernie Crossland Wlk DY10 116 F3
Bernwall Cl DY8 80 F4
Berrandale Rd B36 57 F1
Berrington Cl B98 154 D2
Berrington Dr WV14 51 B8
Berrington Rd
Nuneaton CV10 72 D7
Royal Leamington Spa CV31 162 B6
Berrington Wlk B5 86 E7
Berrow Cottage Homes B93 128 C6
Berrow Dr B15 85 E7
Berrowside Rd B34 69 E6
Berrow View B61 150 D7
Berry Ave WS10 41 B5
Berrybush Gdns DY3 50 E7
Berry Cl B19 66 D6
Berry Cres WS5 43 C4
Berry Dr Aldridge WS9 29 E5
Barnt Green B45 122 A1
Smethwick B66 65 A6
Berryfield Rd B26 89 D6
Berryfields
Aldridge WS9 29 E5
Stonnall WS9 16 E5
Berryfields Rd B76 46 F3
Berry Hall La B91 108 B4
Berry Hill WS12 2 C4
Berrymound View B47 125 C7
Berry Rd
Birmingham B8 67 E5
Dudley DY1 51 C5
Berry St
Birmingham B18 65 F6
Coventry CV1 113 E4
Wolverhampton WV1 163 C3
Bertha Rd B11 87 D5
Bertie Rd CV8 148 A4
Bertie Terr CV32 156 E1
Bertram Cl DY4 41 C1
Bertram Rd
5 Birmingham B10 67 D1
Smethwick B67 64 E6
Berwick Cl
Coventry CV5 112 B4
Warwick CV34 155 E2
Berwick Dr WS11 4 B8
Berwick Gr
Birmingham, Frankley B31 102 D3
Birmingham, Pheasey B43 44 B4
Berwick Ho CV8 148 A3
Berwicks La B37 70 B1
Berwood Farm Rd B72 57 C6
Berwood Gdns B24 57 C6
Berwood Gr B92 89 B1
Berwood La B24 57 E3
Berwood Pk B35 58 A2
Berwood Rd B72 57 D6
Berwyn Ave CV6 95 A1
Berwyn Gr WS6 4 F3
Berwyn Way CV10 72 C4
Beryl Ave LE10 71 A2
Besant Gr B27 88 A1
Besbury Cl B93 127 E2
Bescot Cres WS1 42 D5
Bescot Croft B42 55 B6
Bescot Dr WS2 42 B6
Bescot Ind Est The WS10 41 D4
Bescot Rd WS2 42 B6
Bescot St WS1 42 E7
Bescot Stadium Sta WS1 42 D5
Besford Gr
Birmingham B31 102 D3
Solihull B90 127 B6
Besom Way WS6 4 C2
Bessborough Rd B25 88 D8
Best Ave CV8 148 C7
Best Rd WV14 40 D7
Best St B64 62 F2
Beswick Gr B33 69 A4
Beta Gr B14 105 C4
Bethany Mews 4 WS11 1 F4
Betjeman Ct DY10 117 B5
Betjeman Pl WV10 12 A1
Betley Gr B33 69 A5
Betony Cl WS5 43 A3
Betsham Cl B44 45 B1
Bettany Glade WV10 11 E4
Betteridge Dr B76 46 E4
Bettina Cl CV10 72 B5
Bettman Cl CV3 133 E6
Betton Rd B14 104 E5
Bett Rd B20 54 F3
Betty's La WS11 6 A4
Bevan Ave WV4 39 E4
Bevan Cl Bilston WV14 40 F6
Walsall WS4 15 C1
Bevan Ct CV3 133 D7
Bevan Lee Rd WS11 1 D3
Bevan Rd
Brierley Hill DY5 61 A2
Tipton DY4 52 B4
Bevan Way B66 64 F7
Beverley Ave CV10 72 B4
Beverley Cl
Astwood Bank B96 158 E2
Balsall Common CV7 130 C7
Sutton Coldfield B72 57 D7
Beverley Court Rd B32 84 C6
Beverley Cres WV4 39 F4
Beverley Croft B23 56 D2
Beverley Ct 1 B62 84 A6
Beverley Dr DY6 60 C7
Beverley Gr B26 89 B5
Beverley Hill WS12 2 D6
Beverley Rd
Birmingham B45 122 A7
Royal Leamington Spa CV32 156 D1
West Bromwich B71 42 D1
Beverly Dr CV4 132 D2
Beverston Rd
Perton WV6 24 A4
Wednesbury DY4 41 B2
Bevington Cres CV6 112 E5
Bevington Rd B6 66 F8
Bevin Rd WS2 27 E3
Bevis Gr B44 44 F3
Bewdley Ave 4 B12 87 A6
Bewdley Dr WV1 26 B2
Bewdley Grange DY11 116 A5
Bewdley Hill DY11 116 B5
Bewdley Rd
Birmingham B30 104 B8
Kidderminster DY11 116 C6
Bewdley Villas 3 B18 65 D4
Bewell Ct B61 136 F4
Bewell Gdns B61 136 F4
Bewell Head B61 136 F4
Bewick Ct WV6 24 C2
Bewlay Cl DY5 81 B7
Bewley Rd WV12 27 D4
Bewlys Ave B20 54 E4
Bexfield Cl CV5 112 A6
Bexhill Gr 3 B15 66 C1
Bexley Gr B71 53 E7
Bexley Rd B44 56 B8
Bexmore Dr WS13 3 F1
Beyer Cl B77 22 A2
Bhylls Acre Prim Sch WV3 38 B7
Bhylls Cres WV3 38 C7
Bhylls La WV3 38 C7
Bibbey's Gn WV10 11 F4
Bibsworth Ave B13 105 D8
Bibury Rd B28 105 E7
Bicester Sq B35 58 B4
Bickenhill Green Ct B92 90 D1
Bickenhill La
Birmingham B37 90 C6
Birmingham B40 90 D4
Catherine de B B92 108 C6
Bickenhill Park Rd B92 88 E1
Bickenhill Parkway B37 90 D6
Bickenhill Rd B37 90 B7
Bickford Rd
Birmingham B6 56 A1
Wolverhampton WV10 25 F5
Bickington Rd B32 84 D1
Bickley Ave
Birmingham B11 87 C6
Sutton Coldfield B74 31 E5
Bickley Gr B26 89 B5
Bickley Ho B74 31 E5
Bickley Rd
Bilston WV14 41 A7
Walsall WS4 29 C7
Bicknell Croft B14 104 E2
Bickton Cl B24 57 C5
Biddings La WV14 40 B2
Biddles Hill B94 141 C6
Biddlestone Pl WS10 41 B7
Biddleston Gr WS5 43 C3
Biddulph Ct 3 B73 46 A2
Bideford Dr B29 85 C1
Bideford Rd
Coventry CV2 114 C7
Smethwick B66 65 B5
Bideford Way WS11 4 B8
Bidford Cl B90 106 D2
Bidford Rd B31 102 E3
Bierton Rd B25 88 C8
Bigbury Cl CV3 133 E5
Biggin Cl
Birmingham B35 58 A3
Perton WV6 23 E5
Biggin Hall Cres CV3 114 B2
Bigwood Dr
Birmingham B32 84 D1
Sutton Coldfield B75 47 A5
Bilberry Bank WS11 1 E6
Bilberry Cres
Huntington WS12 1 C5
Sutton Coldfield B76 46 F3
Bilberry Dr B45 122 A6

Bilberry Rd
Birmingham B14 . . . . . **104** C6
Coventry CV2 . . . . **96** D2
Bilboe Rd WV14 . . . . . **41** A3
Bilbrook CE Mid Sch
WV8 . . . .**10** B3
Bilbrook Ct WV8 . . . . **10** B3
Bilbrook Gr
Birmingham B29 . . . . **84** F2
Codsall WV8 . . . . **10** B3
Bilbrook Rd WV8 . . . . **10** B4
Bilbrook Sta WV8 . . . . **10** A2
Bilbury Cl B97 . . . . . **158** C6
Bilhay La B70 . . . . **53** A5
Bilhay St B70 . . . . **53** B5
Billau Rd WV14 . . . . . **40** D2
Billesden Cl CV3 . . . . **134** E8
Billesley La
Birmingham B13 . . . . . **87** A1
Portway B48 . . . . . . **140** E6
Billesley Prim Sch
B13 . . . . **105** C6
Billingham Cl B91 . . **127** B8
Billing Rd CV5 . . . . . **112** D3
Billingsley Rd B26 . . . **89** A8
Billinton Cl CV2 . . . . **114** E2
Bills La B90 . . . . **106** A1
Billsmore Gn B92 . . . **107** C7
Bills St WS10 . . . . **41** E6
Billy Buns La WV5 . . . **49** B8
Billy La B45, B60 . . . . **138** A7
Billy Wright Cl WV4 . . **38** D6
Bilport La WS10 . . . . . **52** F8
Bilston Central Sta
WV14 . . . .**40** E5
Bilston CE Prim Sch
WV14 . . . .**40** B6
Bilston Ind Est WV14 . . **41** A4
Bilston Key Ind Est
WV14 . . . .**41** A5
Bilston La WV13 . . . . . **41** B8
Bilston Mus & Art Gall
WV14 . . . .**40** E6
Bilston Rd
Darlaston WV13 . . . . . **41** A8
Wednesbury, Church Hill
WS10 . . . . **41** E3
Wednesbury, Gospel Oak
DY4 . . . . **41** B2
Wolverhampton WV2 . . **39** F8
Bilston St
Darlaston WS10 . . . . . **41** D6
Sedgley DY3 . . . . **50** E8
Willenhall WV13 . . . . . **27** A1
Wolverhampton WV1 . **163** C2
Bilton Grange Rd B26 .**88** F8
Bilton Ind Est
Birmingham B38 . . . . **123** E8
Coventry CV3 . . . . . . **113** F1
Binbrook Rd WV12 . . . **27** D4
Bincomb Ave B26 . . . . **89** B6
Binfield St DY4 . . . . . . **52** A4
Bingley Ave B8 . . . . . . **68** B4
Bingley Ent Ctr WV3 . **39** A8
Bingley St WV3 . . . . . **39** A8
Binley Ave CV3 . . . . . **134** F7
Binley Ave CV3 . . . . . **134** F7
Binley Bsns Pk CV3 . **115** A1
Binley Cl
Birmingham B26 . . . . . **88** D6
Solihull B90 . . . . **126** A8
Binley Gr CV3 . . . . . . **134** F7
Binley Ind Est CV3 . . **135** A8
Binley Rd CV2, CV3 . . **114** D1
Binley Woods Prim Sch
CV3 . . . . **135** E7
Binns Cl CV4 . . . . **131** F8
Binstead Rd B44 . . . . . **45** A2
Binswood Ave CV32 . **156** F2
Binswood Cl CV2 . . . . . **96** D2
Binswood Ct 🗓
CV32 . . . . **156** F2
Binswood Mans 🗓
CV32 . . . . **156** F2
Binswood Rd B62 . . . . **84** A7
Binswood St CV32 . . **156** E1
Binton Cl B98 . . . . . . **154** F1
Binton Croft B13 . . . . **104** F8
Binton Rd
Coventry CV2 . . . . **96** D2
Solihull B90 . . . . **105** F1
Birbeck Ho B36 . . . . . . **70** B6
Birbeck Pl DY5 . . . . . . **61** B6
Birchall St B12 . . . . . .**66** F1
Birch Ave
Birmingham B31 . . . . **102** C1
Brierley Hill DY5 . . . . . **62** A2
Brownhills WS8 . . . . . **15** E8
Burntwood WS7 . . . .**6** F6

Birch Ave *continued*
Cannock WS11 . . . .**4** C8
Birchbrook Ind Pk
WS14 . . . .**17** E6
Birch Brook La WS14 . **17** E6
Birch Bsns Pk WS11 . . .**4** F6
Birch Cl
Bedworth CV12 . . . . . **78** D4
Birmingham B30 . . . . **103** E6
Coventry CV5 . . . . . . **111** F6
Sutton Coldfield B76 . . . **46** F2
Birch Coppice DY5 . . . **62** A1
Birch Coppice
Distribution Ctr B78 **36** E4
Birch Coppice Gdns
WV12 . . . . **27** E4
Birch Cres B69 . . . . . . **52** B1
Birchcroft 🗓 B66 . . . **65** C5
Birch Croft
Aldridge WS9 . . . . **30** C8
Birmingham B37 . . . . . **70** C1
Sutton Coldfield B24 . . . **57** D5
Birch Croft Rd B75 . . . **46** D7
Birch Ct
Birmingham B30 . . . . **103** E4
Oldbury B66 . . . . **64** D8
Royal Leamington Spa
CV34 . . . . **161** E2
Walsall WS4 . . . . **29** A4
🗓 Wolverhampton
WV3 . . . . **25** C4
Birchdale WV14 . . . . . **40** D7
Birchdale Ave B23 . . . **56** E3
Birchdale Rd B23 . . . . **56** D5
Birch Dr
Halesowen B62 . . . . . . **63** E1
Stourbridge DY8 . . . . . **80** E6
Sutton Coldfield, Little Aston
B74 . . . . **31** D5
Sutton Coldfield, Whitehouse
Common B75 . . . . **46** F7
Birchen Coppice Fst Sch
DY11 . . . . **116** B2
Birchen Coppice Mid Sch
DY11 . . . . **116** B2
Birch End CV34 . . . . . **161** B8
Birchensale Farm 🗓
B97 . . . . **153** B5
Birchensale Mid Sch
B97 . . . . **153** C4
Birchensale Rd B97 . **153** C5
Birches Ave WV8 . . . . . **10** C1
Birches Barn Ave
WV3 . . . .**38** F7
Birches Barn Rd WV3 . .**38** F7
Birches Cl B13 . . . .**86** F1
Birches Fst Sch WV8 . .**10** B1
Birches Green Inf Sch
B24 . . . .**57** B2
Birches Green Jun Sch
B24 . . . .**57** B3
Birches Green Rd B24 **57** B2
Birches Ho B97 . . . . . **153** B2
Birches La
Alvechurch B48 . . . . . **138** F6
Kenilworth CV8 . . . . . **148** B3
Birches Park Rd WV8 . **10** A2
Birches Rise WV13 . . . .**26** F1
Birches The CV12 . . . . **79** B4
Birchfield Ave WV6 . . . **24** B6
Birchfield Cl
Halesowen B63 . . . . . . **82** E2
Wood End CV9 . . . . **36** C1
Birchfield Com Sch
B20 . . . . **55** D1
Birchfield Cres DY9 . . .**81** F3
Birchfield Ct B97 . . . . **153** B2
Birchfield Gdns
🗓 Birmingham B6 . . . **66** D8
Walsall WS5 . . . . **43** C4
Birchfield La
Oldbury, Round's Green
B69 . . . . **63** F6
Oldbury, Whiteheath Gate
B69 . . . . **63** E4
Birchfield Rd
Birmingham B20 . . . . . **55** D2
Coventry CV6 . . . . **112** F8
Kidderminster DY11 . . **116** B5
Redditch B97 . . . . **153** B2
Stourbridge DY9 . . . . . **81** F3
Birchfields Dr WS12 . . . .**2** D1
Birchfields Rd WV12 . . **27** A5
Birchfield Twr 🗓 B20. **55** D1
Birchfield Way WS5 . . . **43** C4
Birchgate DY9 . . . .**81** F4
Birchglade WV3 . . . . . **24** D1
Birch Gr
Balsall Common CV7 . . **130** B8

Birch Gr *continued*
Birchmoor B78 . . . . . . **36** D7
Birmingham B68 . . . . . **84** D7
Lichfield WS14 . . . .**9** D8
Birchgrave Cl CV6 . . . **114** A7
Birch Ho
Redditch B98 . . . . . . **158** F8
Sutton Coldfield B74 . . . **31** B5
Birch Hollow B15 . . . .**85** F6
Birchills Canal Mus★
WS2 . . . . **28** C3
Birchills CE Prim Com
Sch WS2 . . . . **28** D2
Birchills St WS2 . . . . . **28** D2
Birch La Aldridge WS9 . **16** D1
Birmingham B68 . . . . . **84** D7
Walsall WS4 . . . . **15** C1
Birchley Ho
Oldbury B69 . . . . **63** D6
Redditch B97 . . . . **153** B1
Birchley Ind Est B69 . .**63** E5
Birchley Park Ave
B69 . . . . **63** E6
Birchley Rise B92 . . . .**88** F4
Birch Meadow Cl
CV34 . . . . **160** D7
Birchmoor Cl B28 . . . **106** B7
Birchmoor Rd B78 . . .**36** F8
Birchover Rd WS2 . . . **28** A4
Birch Rd
Birmingham, Rubery
B45 . . . . **121** E6
Birmingham, Warley Woods
B68 . . . . **84** D7
Birmingham, Witton B6. **56** A2
Sedgley DY3 . . . . **39** F1
Wednesfield WV11 . . . . **26** F8
Wolverhampton WV11 . **12** F1
Birch Rd E B6 . . . . **56** B2
Birch St Oldbury B68 . . **64** C5
Tipton DY4 . . . . **51** F5
Walsall WS2 . . . . **28** D3
Wolverhampton WV1 . **163** B3
Birch Terr DY2 . . . . . . **62** C4
Birch Tree Gdns DY5 . . **62** A1
Birch Tree Gdns WS9 . **30** B5
Birch Tree Gr B91 . . . **106** F4
Birchtree Hollow
WV12 . . . . **27** D5
Birchtree Rd CV10 . . . **72** C6
Birchtrees B24 . . . . . . **57** D4
Birchtrees Croft B26 . **88** D5
Birchtrees Dr B33 . . . . **69** D2
Birchway Cl CV32 . . . **156** C1
Birch Wlk B68 . . . . **84** D8
Birchwood Ave B78 . . .**36** F7
Birchwood Cl
Essington WV11 . . . . . . **13** A3
Kidderminster DY11 . . **116** A7
Birchwood Cres B12 . **87** B4
Birchwood Prim Sch
B78 . . . .**36** F7
Birchwood Rd
Binley Woods CV3 . . . . **135** C7
Birmingham B12 . . . . . **87** A4
Lichfield WS14 . . . .**9** F7
Wolverhampton WV4 . . **39** A5
Birchwoods B32 . . . . . **84** B2
Birchwood Wlk DY6 . . **60** E8
Birchy Cl B90 . . . . **125** E6
Birchy Leasowes La
B90 . . . . **125** E5
Birdbrook Rd B44 . . . . **55** E8
Birdcage Wlk 🗓 DY2 . **51** D1
Bird Cage Wlk B38 . . **103** F2
Bird End B71 . . . .**53** F8
Bird Grove Ct CV1 . . . **113** D5
Birdhope B77 . . . . **22** C1
Birdie Cl B38 . . . . **103** D1
Birdlip Gr B32 . . . . **84** C6
Bird Rd CV34 . . . . **161** D4
Birds Bush Prim Sch
B77 . . . . **35** E8
Birds Bush Rd B77 . . .**35** F8
Birds Mdw DY5 . . . . . . **61** B7
Bird St Coventry CV1 . **165** C3
Dudley DY3 . . . . **50** C3
Lichfield WS13 . . . .**9** B7
Birdwell Croft B13 . . **104** F6
Birkdale Ave
Birmingham B29 . . . . . **85** F1
Birkdale Cl
Coventry CV6 . . . . **95** B4
Nuneaton CV11 . . . . . . **74** A1
Stourbridge DY8 . . . . . **80** F2
Wolverhampton WV1 . . **26** A2
Birkdale Dr B69 . . . . . **63** A7
Birkdale Gr B29 . . . . . **104** A8
Birkdale Rd WS3 . . . . . **14** A3

Birkenshaw Rd B44 . . **55** E8
Birley Gr B63 . . . . **82** C1
Birlingham Ho B60 . . **137** B3
Birmingham Botanical
Gdns★ B15 . . . .**85** F7
Birmingham Bsns Pk
B37 . . . .**90** E8
Birmingham Children's
Hospl B4 . . . . **164** C3
Birmingham Christian
Coll B29 . . . . **85** C1
Birmingham Coll of Food,
Tourism & Creative
Studies B3 . . . . **164** A3
Birmingham
Conservatoire B1 . **164** B2
Birmingham Dental
Hospl The B4 . . . . . **164** C4
Birmingham Great Pk
B45 . . . . **122** B8
Birmingham Heartlands
Hospl B9 . . . . **68** B2
Birmingham Hippodrome
Theatre★ B5 . . . . . **164** C1
Birmingham Int Airport
B40 . . . . **90** B4
Birmingham Int
Convention Ctr★ B1 **66** C2
Birmingham Int Sta
B40 . . . . **90** D4
Birmingham & Midland
Mus of Transport★
B47 . . . . **124** E3
Birmingham Mus & Art
Gal★ B3 . . . . **164** B2
Birmingham Nature Ctr★
B5 . . . . **86** C3
Birmingham New Rd
Dudley DY1, DY4,
WV1 . . . . **51** C4
Wolverhampton WV4 . . **39** E4
Birmingham Nuffield
Hospl The B15 . . . . .**85** F2
Birmingham Rd
Aldridge WS9 . . . . **30** A4
Allesley CV5 . . . . **111** E7
Alvechurch B48 . . . . . **139** B7
Birmingham, Buckland End
B36 . . . . **69** A8
Birmingham, Rubery B45,
B61 . . . . **121** D5
Blakedown DY10 . . . . . **98** C2
Burton Green CV8 . . . **131** A1
Coleshill B46 . . . . **70** E5
Dudley DY1 . . . . **51** E2
Hagley DY9 . . . . **99** D7
Halesowen B63 . . . . . . **83** B4
Hopwood B31, B48 . . . **123** B4
Kenilworth CV8 . . . . . **147** C8
Kidderminster DY10 . . **117** D7
Lichfield WS14 . . . .**9** A4
Lickey End B60, B61 . . **137** B6
Little Packington CV7 . . **91** E3
Lower Marlbrook B61 . **121** B1
Oldbury B69 . . . . **64** B7
Redditch B97, B98 . . . **153** E8
Rowley Regis B65 . . . . **63** C2
Shenstone WS14 . . . . . **18** A4
Stoneleigh CV8 . . . . . **149** B6
Studley B80, B98 . . . . **159** E7
Sutton Coldfield B72,
B73 . . . . **46** B2
Walsall B43, WS1, WS5 **43** D5
Warwick CV34 . . . . . . **160** B8
Water Orton B46 . . . . . **59** A3
West Bromwich B71 . . . **54** A1
Wolverhampton WV2 . . **39** D7
Wroxall B93, CV35 . . . **145** D3
Birmingham Rly Mus★
B11 . . . .**87** F5
Birmingham Sch of
Acting B1 . . . . **164** B2
Birmingham Sch of
Speech & Drama
B15 . . . . **86** A7
Birmingham St
Darlaston WS10 . . . . . **41** E6
Dudley DY2 . . . . **51** D1
Halesowen B63 . . . . . . **83** B3
Oldbury B69 . . . . **64** A7
Stourbridge DY8 . . . . . **81** B5
Walsall WS1 . . . . **28** F1
Willenhall WV13 . . . . . **27** C2
Birmingham Women's
Hospl B15 . . . . **85** D4
Birnam B15 . . . . **86** A8
Birnham Cl DY4 . . . . . . **51** D5
Birstall Way B38 . . . . **123** C8
Birvell Ct CV12 . . . . . . **78** D3
Bisell Way DY5 . . . . . . **81** C6

Biset Ave DY10 . . . . . **117** B5
Bishbury Cl B15 . . . . . .**85** E8
Bishop Asbury Cres
B43 . . . . **54** C8
Bishop Asbury's
Cottage★ B43 . . . . . **54** C8
Bishop Challoner RC Sch
B14 . . . . **104** F8
Bishop Cl
Birmingham B45 . . . . **101** E1
Cannock WS11 . . . .**1** D2
Dudley DY2 . . . . **62** E8
Bishopgate Bsns Pk
CV1 . . . . **113** D5
Bishopgate Ind Est
CV1 . . . . **113** D5
Bishop Hall Cres
B60 . . . . **150** E7
Bishop Milner RC Sch
DY1 . . . . **51** A3
Bishop Rd WS10 . . . . . **42** C2
Bishops Cl B66 . . . . . . **65** C4
Bishop's Ct
Birmingham, Coleshill
Heath B37 . . . . **90** E8
Birmingham, Northfield
B31 . . . . **103** B3
Bishops Gate B31 . . . **103** A2
Bishopsgate St B15 . . **66** B1
Bishops Mdw B75 . . . . **32** E3
Bishops Rd B73 . . . . . . **46** B3
Bishops Walk B64 . . . . **83** A6
Bishops Way B74 . . . . .**31** F6
Bishops Wlk CV5 . . . **133** B8
Bishopstone Cl B98 . **154** F2
Bishopton Rd B67 . . . .**64** F1
Bishop Ullathorne RC Sch
CV3 . . . . **132** F4
Bishop Vesey's Gram Sch
B74 . . . . **46** C6
Bishop Walsh RC Sch
B72 . . . . **46** D1
Bishop Wilson CE Prim
Sch B37 . . . . **70** C3
Bishton Gr DY2 . . . . . . **62** D4
Bisley Gr B24 . . . . **57** B2
Bismillah Bldgs B19. **164** B4
Bissell Cl B28 . . . . . . **105** F6
Bissell Dr WS10 . . . . . **42** B3
Bissell St
Birmingham B32 . . . . . **84** A6
Birmingham, Highgate
B5 . . . . **86** E8
Bissel St WV14 . . . . . .**40** F5
Bisset Cres 🗓 CV31 . **162** C6
Bi Tec Ind Pk WV1 . . . **26** A1
Biton Cl B17 . . . .**85** B5
Bittell Cl
Birmingham B31 . . . . **122** F7
Wolverhampton WV10 . **11** E4
Bittell Ct B31 . . . . . . **122** F7
Bittell Farm Rd B48 . **123** A2
Bittell La B45 . . . . . . **138** E8
Bittell Rd
Alvechurch B48 . . . . . **139** A8
Barnt Green B45 . . . . **138** E8
Bitterne Dr WV6 . . . . . **25** A4
Bittern Wlk DY5 . . . . . **81** C6
Bittern Wood Rd
DY10 . . . . **117** B3
Bitterscote La B78 . . . **21** A2
Blackacre Rd DY2 . . . . **62** D8
Black-a-Tree Ct CV10 .**72** F5
Black-A-Tree Rd
CV10 . . . . **72** F5
Blackbades Bvd
CV34 . . . . **160** B4
Black Bank CV7 . . . . . . **78** B1
Blackberry Ave
Birmingham B9 . . . . . . **68** A3
Hockley Heath B94 . . . **143** C6
Blackberry Cl DY1 . . . **61** E8
Blackberry La
Brownhills WS9 . . . . . . **16** A1
Coventry, Neal's Green
CV7 . . . . **95** C5
Coventry, Wyken Green
CV2 . . . . **114** C2
Halesowen B63 . . . . . . **83** A4
Rowley Regis B65 . . . . **62** F5
Sutton Coldfield B74 . . . **31** E4
Blackbird Croft B36 . . **70** A7
Blackbrook Cl DY2 . . . **62** C5
Blackbrook Rd DY2 . . . **62** B5

Blackbrook Valley Ind Pk
DY2 . . . . **62** A5
Blackbrook Way
WV10 . . . . **11** E4
Blackburn Ave WV6 . . . **24** F7
Blackburne Rd B28. . **105** F6
Blackburn Rd CV6 . . . .**95** F3
Blackbushe Cl B17 . . .**84** F7
Blackcat Cl B37 . . . . . . **70** A3
Black Country Living
Mus★ DY1 . . . . **51** D3
Black Country New Rd
Darlaston WS10 . . . . . **41** C4
Tipton B70, WV14 . . . . **52** D6
Black Country Route
Bilston WV14 . . . . **40** E5
Darlaston WV13, WS10 **41** B7
Walsall WV14, WS10 . . **27** E1
Blackdown B77 . . . . . . **22** C1
Blackdown Cl B45 . . . **102** A2
Blackdown Hall
CV32 . . . . **156** F6
Blackdown Rd B93 . . **128** B6
Blackett Ct 🗓 B73 . . . **46** A2
Blackfirs La B37, B46 . **90** D7
Blackford Cl
Halesowen B63 . . . . . . **82** D2
Kidderminster DY11 . . **116** A1
Blackford Rd
Birmingham B11 . . . . . **87** C4
Solihull B90 . . . . **126** C8
Blackford St B18 . . . . . **65** E5
Blackfriars Cl B79 . . . . **20** E5
Blackgreaves La B76 . .**48** F1
Blackhalve La WV11 . . **12** D1
Blackham Dr B73 . . . . . **57** A7
Blackham Rd WV11 . . .**26** F8
Black Haynes Rd
B29 . . . . **103** A6
Blackheath Mkt B65 . . **63** C1
Blackheath Prim Sch
B65 . . . . **63** D2
Blackheath Trad Est
B65 . . . .**63** E2
Blackhorse La DY5 . . . **61** E1
Black Horse La 🗓
DY10 . . . . **116** F3
Black Horse Rd CV6,
CV7 . . . . **96** B6
Black La CV32 . . . . . . **157** C2
Black Lake B70 . . . . . . **53** A6
Black Lake La B60,
B97 . . . . **152** A2
Black Lake Sta B70 . . **53** A6
Blackley Ho B66 . . . . . **65** D6
Blacklow Rd CV34 . . . **156** A1
Blackmoor Croft B33 . **69** D2
Blackmore La B60 . . . **137** A3
Blackpit La WV4 . . . . . **37** C2
Black Prince Ave
CV3 . . . . **133** E6
Blackrock Rd B23 . . . . **56** B6
Blackroot Cl WS7 . . . . .**7** D4
Blackroot Ho B73 . . . . **45** C2
Blackroot Rd B74 . . . . **46** B7
Blackshaw Dr CV2 . . . **114** F6
Blacksmith Dr
Bromsgrove B60 . . . . . **151** A7
🗓 Sutton Coldfield B75 **32** E3
Blacksmiths La B94 . **143** C6
Blacksmith Way 🗓
B70 . . . . **53** C2
Black Soils Rd B98 . . **154** F5
Blackstitch La B97 . . **153** A1
Blackthorn Ave WS7 . . . .**6** F4
Blackthorn Cl
Birmingham B30 . . . . **103** C6
Coventry CV4 . . . . **132** D5
Blackthorn Ct B98 . . **154** E1
Blackthorne Cl
Dudley DY1 . . . . **50** F4
Solihull B91 . . . . **106** E4
Blackthorne Rd
Dudley DY1 . . . . **50** F5
Kenilworth CV8 . . . . . **148** A3
Lichfield WS14 . . . .**9** D7
Smethwick B67 . . . . . . **64** D4
Walsall WS5 . . . . **42** F5
Blackthorn Gr CV11 . . .**73** C2
Blackthorn Rd
Birmingham, Bournville
B30 . . . . **103** D6
Birmingham, Castle
Bromwich B36 . . . . . . **69** C8
Stourbridge DY8 . . . . . **61** A1
Blackwater Cl DY5 . . . **61** A6
Blackwell La 🗓 B97 . **153** B5

Blackwell Rd
  Barnt Green B45,
   B60.............**138** B5
  Coventry CV6 ......**113** E8
  Sutton Coldfield B72... **46** D1
Blackwell St DY10...**116** E6
Blackwood Ave WV11. **26** C8
Blackwood Dr B74 ... **44** E8
Blackwood Rd
  Bromsgrove B60.....**137** B2
  Sutton Coldfield B74... **30** E1
  Tamworth B77........ **35** C7
Blackwood Sch B74 ..**30** E1
Blades Rd B70 .... **52** D4
Bladon Cl CV11 ......**73** F8
Bladon Wlk **6** CV31. **162** C6
Blaenwern Dr B63 ... **82** B7
Blagdon Rd B63...... **83** A6
Blair Dr CV12 .... **77** D1
Blair Gr B37 .... **70** D1
Blakebrook DY11 ....**116** C6
Blakebrook Cl DY11 .**116** C6
Blakebrook Gdns
  DY11 ....**116** C6
Blakebrook Sch
  DY11 ....**116** C6
Blake Cl Cannock WS11 ..**2** A5
  Hinckley LE10 .... **71** D4
  Nuneaton CV10...... **72** A5
Blakedon Rd WS10 ... **41** E3
Blakedown CE Fst Sch
  DY10 .... **98** C1
Blakedown Rd B63...**82** F1
Blakedown Sta DY10. **98** C2
Blakedown Way **4**
  B69 .... **63** E4
Blake Hall Cl DY5 ... **81** C7
Blake Ho **2** WS2... **42** C8
Blake La B9........**67** F2
Blakeland Rd B44 ... **55** E6
Blakelands Ave
  CV31 ....**162** B6
Blakeland St B9.....**67** F2
Blakeley Ave WV6 ... **24** F7
Blakeley Ct B72 ..... **57** C8
Blakeley Hall Gdns
  B69 .... **64** B7
Blakeley Hall Rd B69. **64** B7
Blakeley Heath Dr
  WV5 .... **49** A5
Blakeley Heath Prim Sch
  WV5 .... **49** A5
Blakeley Rise WV6 ...**24** F7
Blakeley Wood Rd
  DY4 .... **52** D8
Blakemere Ave B25 .. **88** E8
Blakemere Cl B98 ...**154** F3
Blakemore Dr B75....**46** F6
Blakemore Rd
  Brownhills WS9 ..... **16** A3
  West Bromwich B70... **53** A1
Blakenall Heath WS3 . **28** D8
Blakenall Heath Jun Sch
  WS3 .... **28** C8
Blakenall La WS3.....**28** D8
Blakenall Row WS3...**28** C8
Blakeney Ave
  Birmingham B17...... **85** A7
  Stourbridge DY8 ..... **80** D6
Blakeney Cl DY3..... **50** C8
Blakenhale Jun & Inf
  Schs B33.........**69** B1
Blakenhale Rd B33... **69** B1
Blakenhall Gdns WV2. **39** D7
Blakenhall Ind Est
  WV2................**39** B7
Blake Pl B9...........**67** F2
Blake Rd B61 ....**137** B8
Blakes Field Dr B45 . **122** A1
Blakesley Cl B76.....**57** F5
Blakesley Gr B25 ....**68** D1
Blakesley Hall Mus★
  B25 ....**68** D1
Blakesley Hall Prim Sch
  B25..............**68** D1
Blakesley Mews B25.. **88** D8
Blakesley Rd B25..... **68** D1
Blakesley Way B33 .. **68** D2
Blake St B74 .... **31** E6
Blake Street Sta B74..**31** F6
Blake Valley Tech Coll
  WS12.............**1** F6
Blakewood Cl B34....**69** C5
Blandford Dr
  Coventry CV2 ......**114** F5
  Stourbridge DY8...... **60** E3
Blandford Gdns WS7 .**7** C6

Blandford Rd
  Birmingham B32......**84** F5
  Royal Leamington Spa
   CV32.............**156** C1
Blandford Way CV35. **160** A7
Blanefield WV8 ...... **10** E2
Blanford Mere Prim Sch
  DY6................**60** E8
Blanning Ct B93 ....**127** E3
Blay Ave WS2 .... **28** B2
Blaydon Ave B75..... **32** E2
Blaydon Ct **3** B17 ...**85** D4
Blaydon Rd WV9,
  WV10 .... **11** A1
Blaythorn Ave B92 ...**89** A3
Blaze Hill Rd DY6 ... **60** A8
Blaze La B96, B97....**158** A3
Blaze Pk DY6 .... **60** B8
Bleachfield La B98..**154** F8
Bleak Hill Rd B23 ... **56** C5
Bleak House Dr WS7 ..**6** D8
Bleakhouse Jun Sch
  B68..............**64** C1
Bleakhouse Rd B68 .. **64** C1
Bleak St B67 ....**64** F6
Blenheim **5** B17... **85** B6
Blenheim Ave CV6 .. **95** C2
Blenheim Cl
  Hinckley LE10 .... **71** F4
  Nuneaton CV11...... **73** F2
  Tamworth B77........ **21** C4
  Walsall WS4 .... **29** D7
Blenheim Cres
  Bromsgrove B60.....**151** A8
  Royal Leamington Spa
   CV31.............**162** C5
Blenheim Ct
  Birmingham B44..... **55** F8
  Solihull B91........**107** C4
Blenheim Dr
  Birmingham B43...... **54** D8
  Darlaston WS10 ..... **41** E5
Blenheim Rd
  Birmingham B13...... **86** F1
  Burntwood WS7 ....**7** A8
  Kingswinford DY6 .... **61** A6
  Norton Canes WS11 ...**6** B4
  Solihull B90.........**106** D2
  Willenhall WV12 ..... **27** B6
Blenheim Way
  Birmingham, Castle Vale
   B35............. **58** B2
  Birmingham, Old Oscott
   B44............. **55** F8
  Dudley DY1 .... **50** E2
Blenheim Wlk CV6 .. **95** B4
Bletchley Dr
  Coventry CV5 ......**112** B4
  Tamworth B77....... **35** C8
Bletchley Rd B24..... **57** E4
Blewitt Cl B36 ...... **58** D2
Blewitt St
  Brierley Hill DY5 .... **61** C6
  Cannock WS12 ....**2** B7
Blews St B6 .... **66** E5
Blick Rd CV34.......**161** C4
Blind La
  Berkswell CV7......**110** D4
  Kenilworth CV8......**131** F1
  Tanworth-In-A B94...**141** D1
Blindpit La B76 ..... **59** B8
Bliss Cl CV4..........**111** E3
Blithe Cl DY8 .... **81** A8
Blithe Cl DY8 .... **81** A8
Blithfield Dr DY5 .... **81** B7
Blithfield Gr B24 .... **57** C5
Blithfield Pl WS11....**2** B1
Blithfield Rd WS8 ....**6** C2
Blockall WS10.......**41** D6
Blockall Cl WS10.... **41** D7
Blockley Cl B97 ....**152** E2
Blockley Rd CV12 ... **78** C4
Blockley's Yd **4** LE10. **75** D8
Blondvil St CV3 .....**133** D7
Bloomfield Cres WS13. .**3** B2
Bloomfield Ct **3** B42. **55** A8
Bloomfield Dr WV12.. **13** D1
Bloomfield Pk DY4...**51** D6
Bloomfield Rd
  Birmingham B13...... **87** B3
  Tipton DY4 .... **51** E7
Bloomfield St N B63..**82** F5
Bloomfield St W B63..**82** F4
Bloomfield Terr DY4.. **51** E7
Bloomfield Way B79..**20** F8
Bloomsbury Gr B14 ..**104** C7
Bloomsbury St
  Birmingham B7...... **67** B5
  Wolverhampton WV2 ..**163** B1
Bloomsbury Way WS14 ..**9** E7

Bloomsbury Wlk **1**
  B7 .... **67** B5
Bloor Mill Cl WV13 ...**26** F1
Blossom Ave B29.....**85** F2
Blossom Dr B61......**137** A5
Blossomfield Cl
  Birmingham B38.....**123** D8
  Kingswinford DY6 .... **60** E8
Blossomfield Ct B38. **123** D8
Blossomfield Gdns
  B91 ....**107** A4
Blossomfield Inf Sch
  B90..............**106** D3
Blossomfield Rd B91 **106** F2
Blossom Gr
  Birmingham B36...... **68** E8
  Cradley Heath B64 ... **62** F1
Blossom Hill B24..... **57** A4
Blossom Rd B24 ..... **57** C4
Blossom's Fold WV1. **163** B3
Blossomville Way **9**
  B27 .... **88** C5
Blount Ho DY11 ....**116** B8
Blounts Rd B23 ..... **56** D5
Blount Terr DY11 ....**116** D3
Blowers Green Cres
  DY2 .... **62** B7
Blowers Green Pl
  DY2 .... **62** B7
Blowers Green Prim Sch
  DY2..............**62** B8
Blower's Green Rd
  DY2 .... **62** B8
Bloxcidge St B68.... **64** B4
Bloxwich Bsns Pk
  WS2 .... **28** A7
Bloxwich CE Prim Sch
  WS3.............**14** B1
Bloxwich Hospl WS3.. **28** B8
Bloxwich La WS2.... **28** A4
Bloxwich L Ctr WS3.. **28** C8
Bloxwich North Sta
  WS3.............**13** F2
Bloxwich Rd WS2,
  WS3 .... **28** D5
Bloxwich Rd N WV12 . **27** D6
Bloxwich Rd S WV13 . **27** A3
Bloxwich Sta WS3 ... **14** A1
Blucher St B1....... **164** B1
Blue Ball La B63 .... **82** C7
Bluebell Cl
  Cannock WS12 ....**2** B6
  Stourbridge DY8 ..... **60** C2
Bluebell Cres WV11 .. **26** D5
Bluebell Croft
  Birmingham, Northfield
   B31.............**102** F4
  Birmingham, Perry Common
   B23............. **56** C7
Bluebell Dr
  Bedworth CV12..... **77** E2
  Birmingham B37...... **70** E2
Bluebell La WS6 .....**5** A1
Bluebell Rd
  Brownhills WS9 ..... **16** B3
  Cradley Heath B64 ... **62** E3
  Dudley DY1 .... **51** B4
Bluebell Wlk CV4 ...**111** F1
Bluebellwood Cl B76. **47** A3
Bluebird Cl WS14 .....**9** D8
Blue Bird Pk B62 ...**101** B7
Bluebird Trad Est
  WV10.............**25** E5
Blue Cedar Dr B74 ...**44** F6
Blue Cedars DY8 .... **80** C6
Blue Coat CE Comp Sch
  WS1.............**28** F1
Blue Coat CE Inf Sch
  WS1.............**28** F1
Blue Coat CE Jun Sch
  WS1.............**28** F1
Blue Coat Sch The
  B17..............**85** E6
Blue La E WS2 ...... **28** E3
Blue Lake Rd B93 ...**128** B2
Blue La W WS2...... **28** D2
Blue Rock Pl B69 ... **63** C7
Bluestone Wlk B65... **63** C4
Blundell Rd B11...... **87** D5
Blundells The CV8...**148** A5
Blyth Ave CV7.......**130** C5
Blyth Cl CV12 .... **77** C1
Blyth Ct CV11 .... **73** C3
Blythe Cl
  Burntwood WS7 ......**7** D6
  Redditch B97 ....**158** D7
Blythe Ct Solihull B91. **106** F7
  Sutton Coldfield B73... **46** B5
Blythefield Ave B43 .. **43** C2
Blythe Gate B90.... **126** F3

Blythe Gr B44........**44** F3
Blythe Rd
  7 Coleshill B46..... **70** F7
  Coventry CV1 ......**113** E4
Blythe St B77 .... **21** C4
Blythesway B48 .....**139** A6
Blytheway B91 ......**107** C3
Blythewood Cl B91... **107** F1
Blythsford Rd B28....**106** A4
Blythswood Rd B11 .. **88** A4
Blyton Cl B16........**65** F3
Boar Croft CV4.......**111** F2
Board School Gdns
  DY3 .... **50** E6
Boar Hound Cl B18... **66** A4
Boat La WS14 ....**7** F1
Boatman's La WS9 ... **15** C2
Bobbington Way DY2. **62** E5
Bobs Coppice Wlk
  DY5 ....**81** F7
Bockendon Rd CV4..**131** C5
Boddington Cl CV32. **157** E5
Bodenham Cl B98...**154** D3
Bodenham Rd
  Birmingham, Brandhall
   B68............. **84** B8
  Birmingham, Frankley
   B31............. **102** E1
Boden Rd B28 ......**106** A7
Bodens La WS9 ..... **44** B7
Bodiam Ct WV6 ..... **24** A3
Bodicote Gr B75 .... **32** E3
Bodington Cl WS7....**7** C7
Bodington Rd B75... **32** B3
Bodmin Cl
  Hinckley LE10 .... **71** E4
  Walsall WS5 .... **43** D7
Bodmin Ct **16** DY5.. **61** D2
Bodmin Gr **2** B7... **67** B5
Bodmin Rd
  Coventry CV2 ......**114** F5
  Dudley DY2 .... **62** D2
Bodmin Rise WS5 ... **43** D7
Bodnant Way CV8...**148** C6
Bodymoor Heath Rd
  B76...............**48** F5
Bognop Rd WV11.... **12** D4
Bohun St CV4 .... **111** F1
Boldmere Cl B73..... **57** A7
Boldmere Ct B43..... **54** E7
Boldmere Dr B73 .... **57** A8
Boldmere Gdns B73.. **57** A8
Boldmere Inf Sch B73 **45** F1
Boldmere Jun Sch
  B73..............**45** F1
Boldmere Rd B73 ... **57** A8
Bolebridge Mews B79 **21** B5
Bolebridge St B79.... **21** C4
Bolehall Ho B77..... **21** C4
Boley Cl WS14 ....**9** D7
Boley Cottage La WS14.**9** E7
Boley La WS14 ......**9** D7
Boleyn Cl
  Cheslyn Hay WS6 ....**4** D2
  Warwick CV34 ......**161** C6
Boleyn Rd B45 ...... **121** C2
Boley Park Ctr WS14...**9** E7
Bolingbroke Dr
  CV34 ....**161** E3
Bolingbroke Rd CV3. **114** A1
Bolney Rd B32 ...... **84** E4
Bolton Cl CV3........**133** E5
Bolton Ct DY4....... **52** C8
Bolton Rd
  Birmingham B10...... **87** C8
  Wednesfield WV11... **26** D5
Bolton St B9........ **67** B2
Bolton Way WS3 .....**13** F3
Bolyfant Cres CV31.. **162** A2
Bomers Field B45...**122** C7
Bond Dr B35........ **58** A3
Bondfield Rd B13....**105** B6
Bond Gate CV11..... **73** C4
Bonds Hospl CV1....**165** A3
Bond Sq B18........ **66** A4
Bond St
  Birmingham, Ladywood
   B19............. **164** B4
  Birmingham, Stirchley
   B30............. **104** A7
  Coventry CV1 ......**165** B3
  Dudley WV14 .... **51** A8
  Nuneaton CV11...... **73** C5
  Rowley Regis B65.... **63** E3
  West Bromwich B70... **53** C2
  Wolverhampton WV2 . **163** B2
Bondway WS12.......**1** F7
Bonehill Ind Est B78..**20** F1
Bonehill Rd B78...... **20** E1

Bone Mill La WV1 ... **25** D4
Boney Hay Rd WS7 ...**7** B7
Bonfire Hill DY9 ....**120** E6
Bonham Dr B26...... **57** F5
Boningale Way B93 . **127** E3
Bonington Dr CV12... **78** A4
Bonner Dr B76.......**57** F5
Bonner Gr WS9 ..... **29** F5
Bonneville Dr CV5....**111** B8
Bonniksen Cl **7**
  CV31 ....**161** F5
Bonnington Way B43. **44** D4
Bonny Stile La WV11 . **26** B6
Bonsall Rd B23...... **57** A6
Bonville Gdns WV10.. **11** E4
Booth Cl
  Kingswinford DY6 .... **61** A6
  Lichfield WS13 ....**3** A2
  Walsall WS3 .... **28** D8
Booth Ct **17** DY5 ..... **61** D2
Booth Ho WS4 ...... **28** F3
Booth Rd WS10 ..... **42** C2
Booths Farm Rd B42. **55** B8
Booths Fields CV6... **95** E2
Booth's La B42....... **44** B1
Booth St
  Birmingham B21...... **65** D7
  Cannock WS12 ....**2** B6
  Darlaston WS10 ..... **41** D8
  Walsall WS3 .... **28** C8
Boot Piece La B97 .. **153** B5
Bordeaux Cl DY1 .... **50** E3
Borden Cl WV8.......**24** F8
Bordesley Abbey★
  B98 ....**153** F6
Bordesley Abbey Visitor
  Ctr★ B98 .... **153** F6
Bordesley Cir B10... **67** B1
Bordesley Cl B9...... **68** A2
Bordesley Cl CV32... **157** A3
Bordesley Gn B9..... **67** E2
Bordesley Gn E B9,
  B33 .... **68** C2
Bordesley Green Girls'
  Sch B9 .... **67** D2
Bordesley Green Prim
  Sch B9 .... **68** A2
Bordesley Green Rd
  B8 .... **67** D2
Bordesley Green Trad Est
  B9................ **67** D3
Bordesley La B98 ... **153** E6
Bordesley Middleway
  B12 .... **87** A8
Bordesley Park Rd
  B10 .... **67** B1
Bordesley St B5..... **164** D2
Bordesley Sta B10... **67** A1
Bordesley **7** B9..... **67** B2
Bore St WS13 ....**9** B7
Borman B79 ....**20** F5
Borneo St WS4......**28** F1
Borough Cres
  Oldbury B65 .... **63** E4
  Stourbridge DY8 ..... **80** E5
Borough Ct B63..... **83** B4
Borough Rd B45 .... **21** C7
Borough The LE10... **75** D8
Borrington Gdns
  DY10 ....**117** B4
Borrington Rd DY10 . **117** B5
Borrowcop Ho WS14...**9** C6
Borrowcop La WS14...**9** C5
Borrowdale Cl
  Brierley Hill DY5 .... **81** B8
  Coventry CV6 ......**113** A8
Borrowdale Dr CV32. **156** D2
Borrowdale Gr B31.. **102** D3
Borrowdale Rd B31.. **102** C3
Borrowell La CV8 ... **147** E4
Borrowell Terr CV8 .. **147** E4
Borrow St WV13..... **27** A3
Borwick Ave B70.... **53** A3
Bosbury Terr B30.... **104** B7
Boscobel Ave DY4...**51** F4
Boscobel Cl DY1.....**50** F3
Boscobel Cres WV1 . **25** C4
Boscobel Rd
  Birmingham B43..... **43** D2
  Cheswick Green B90. **126** D5
  Walsall WS1 .... **43** B8
Boscombe Ave B11... **87** C6
Boscombe Rd B11.... **87** E4
Bosmere Ct B31.....**102** C4
Boss Dr DY2 .... **62** C7
Boss Gate Cl WV5 .. **49** A5
Boston Cl WS12......**2** E1
Boston Gr B44.......**56** B8
Boston Pl CV6 ......**113** D8
Boston Way LE9.....**71** F6

Bla–Bou 177

Bosty La WS9 .... **29** E5
Boswell Cl
  Darlaston WS10 ..... **41** D5
  Wednesbury WS10... **41** C1
Boswell Dr CV2 .....**115** A7
Boswell Gr CV34 ... **155** D1
Boswell Rd
  Bilston WV14 .... **40** F7
  Birmingham B44..... **55** F6
  Cannock WS11 ....**1** D4
  Sutton Coldfield B74... **46** C6
Bosworth Cl
  Baginton CV8 ......**133** E2
  Dudley DY3 .... **51** A6
  Hinckley LE10 ...... **71** A1
  Sedgley DY3 .... **50** F7
Bosworth Dr B37.... **70** A2
Bosworth Ho **3** LE10. **71** E1
Bosworth Rd B26 ... **88** E4
Bosworth Wood Prim Sch
  B36..............**58** F1
Bosworth Wood Prim
  School B36 ....**69** F8
Botany Dr DY3 ...... **50** D6
Botany Rd WS5 ..... **43** A5
Botany Wlk **5** B16... **66** A2
Botham Ho CV11 .... **73** E1
Botha Rd B9.........**67** F2
Botoner Rd CV1......**113** F2
Botteley Rd B70..... **53** A6
Bottetourt Rd B29... **85** A2
Botteville Rd B27 ... **88** C2
Bott La
  Stourbridge DY9 ..... **81** E6
  Walsall WS1 .... **28** F1
Bottle Cotts B17 .... **85** D4
Bott Rd CV5.........**132** D8
Bottrill St CV11 ..... **73** B5
Boughton Rd B25 ... **88** C2
Boulevard The
  Brierley Hill DY5 .... **61** F2
  Sutton Coldfield B73... **57** B8
Boultbee Rd B72..... **57** C7
Boulters La CV9 ..... **36** D1
Boulton Cir B19...... **66** C6
Boulton Cl WS7 ....**7** C8
Boulton Ho **1** B70... **53** D1
Boulton Ind Ctr B18 ..**66** B5
Boulton Rd
  Birmingham B21...... **65** E7
  Smethwick B66....... **65** D6
  Solihull B91........**107** C2
  West Bromwich B70... **53** D1
Boulton Retreat B21 . **65** E7
Boultons La B97 ....**158** D6
Boulton Sq B70..... **53** D1
Boulton Wlk B23.... **56** B4
Boundary Ave B65... **63** C2
Boundary Cl WV13 .. **26** C1
Boundary Cres DY3.. **50** C3
Boundary Ct B37..... **69** E2
Boundary Dr B13.... **86** D2
Boundary Farm WV6. **23** F2
Boundary Hill DY3... **50** C4
Boundary Ho B5..... **86** C5
Boundary Ind Est
  WV10.............**11** C5
Boundary La B90.... **126** A6
Boundary Pl B21..... **54** B1
Boundary Rd
  Birmingham B23..... **56** E4
  Brownhills WS9 ..... **15** F3
  Sutton Coldfield B74... **44** F7
Boundary Way
  Wolverhampton, Penn
   WV4............. **38** C5
  Wolverhampton, Tettenhall
   Wood WV6......... **23** F2
Bourlay Cl B45......**101** E2
Bournbrook Ct B5....**86** A3
Bournbrook Rd B29.. **86** A2
Bourne Ave
  Fairfield B61 ....**120** F1
  Fazeley B78......... **20** E1
  Halesowen B62...... **83** F4
  Tipton DY4 .... **52** C7
Bourne Cl
  Birmingham B13.....**105** D6
  Cannock WS12 ....**2** E2
  Solihull B91........**107** E6
Bourne Gn B32 ..... **84** E6
Bourne Hill Cl DY2 .. **62** E3
Bourne Rd
  Birmingham B6...... **67** B7

Bourne Rd *continued*
Coventry CV3 114 C1
Bournes Cl B63 82 F3
Bournes Cres B63 82 E4
Bournes Hill B63 82 E4
Bourne St
Dudley, Bramford DY3, WV14 51 A7
Dudley DY2, DY3 51 D1
Bourne Vale WS9 30 D3
Bourne Way Gdns B29 104 A8
Bourne Wlk B65 62 F5
Bournheath Rd B61 120 D2
Bourn Mill Dr B6 66 E6
Bournville Coll of F Ed
Birmingham B30 103 E7
Birmingham B31 103 C7
Bournville Inf Sch B30 103 E7
Bournville Jun Sch B30 103 E7
Bournville La B30 103 E6
Bournville Mews B30 103 E5
Bournville Sch of Art B30 103 E7
Bournville Sch & Sixth Form Ctr B30 103 C6
Bournville Sta B30 104 A7
Bourton Cl 1 WS5 43 A3
Bourton Croft B92 106 F8
Bourton Dr CV31 162 B5
Bourton Rd B92 106 F8
Bovey Croft B76 58 A7
Bovingdon Rd B35 58 A3
Bowater Ave B33 68 D1
Bowater Ho
Birmingham B19 66 D5
2 West Bromwich B70 53 C2
Bowater St B70 53 C2
Bowbrook Ave B90 127 A5
Bowcroft Gr B24 57 C6
Bow Ct CV5 132 D8
Bowden Rd B67 64 E6
Bowden Way CV3 114 F1
Bowdler Rd WV2 163 D1
Bowen Ave WV4 40 A3
Bowen-Cooke Ave WV6 23 E6
Bowen Ct 4 B13 87 B2
Bowen St WV4 39 E5
Bower Cl WS13 3 D2
Bowercourt Cl B91 107 B2
Bower La DY5 82 A8
Bowers Croft CV32 157 A5
Bowes Dr WS11 1 F4
Bowes Rd B45 121 E7
Bowfell Cl CV5 112 B4
Bowker St WV13 26 C1
Bowlas Ave B74 46 B8
Bowling Green Ave B77 35 F7
Bowling Green Cl
Birmingham B23 56 E7
Darlaston WS10 41 D7
Bowling Green Dr B67 64 E2
Bowling Green La
Bedworth CV7, CV12 95 E8
Birmingham B20 66 A8
Bowling Green Rd
Dudley DY2 62 E2
Hinckley LE10 71 E1
Stourbridge DY8 80 E5
Bowling Green St CV34 160 D6
Bowls Ct CV5 112 F3
Bowman Gn LE10 75 F6
Bowman Rd B42 44 B1
Bowmans Harbour Island WV10 26 B4
Bowman's Rise WV1 26 B3
Bowmore Rd B60 137 B1
Bowness Cl CV6 113 A8
Bowness Gr WV11 13 B1
Bowness Ho B65 63 D4
Bowood Cres B31 103 B2
Bowood Ct B97 153 D4
Bowood Dr WV6 24 D6
Bowood End B76 46 E3
Bowshot Cl B36 58 D1
Bow St Bilston WV14 40 E6
Birmingham B1 164 B1
Willenhall WV13 27 A1
Bowstoke Rd B43 54 C8
Bowyer Rd B8 67 E4
Bowyer St B10 67 A1
Box Cl CV31 162 B3
Boxhill Cl B6 66 F6
Boxhill The CV3 114 B1
Boxnott Cl B97 153 A2
Box Rd B37 90 C8
Box St WS1 28 F1
Box Trees Rd B93, B94 127 C1
Boyd Cl CV2 115 A8
Boyden Cl WS11 1 B1
Boyd Gr B27 88 B2
Boydon Cl WV2 40 A6
Boyleston Rd B28 106 A6
Boyne Rd B26 89 B7
Boyslade Rd LE10 75 F6
Boyslade Road E LE10 75 F5
Boyton Gr B44 44 F3
Brabazon Gr B35 57 F3
Brabham Cres B74 44 F6
Bracadale Ave B24 57 A4
Bracadale Cl CV3 115 A2
Bracebridge Cl CV7 130 B6
Bracebridge Ct 2 B17 85 D5
Bracebridge Ho
Sutton Coldfield, New Oscott B73 45 C2
12 Sutton Coldfield, Streetly B74 31 F2
Bracebridge Rd
Birmingham B24 56 F1
Sutton Coldfield B74 46 A8
Bracebridge St
Birmingham B6 66 E6
Nuneaton CV11 73 B3
Braceby Ave B13 105 C6
Braces La B60 121 C1
Brace St WS1 42 E8
Brackenbury Rd B44 56 B8
Bracken Cl
Burntwood WS7 7 C7
Cannock WS12 2 D8
Lichfield WS14 9 E6
Wolverhampton WV8 10 E1
Bracken Croft 1 B37 70 C3
Brackendale Dr
Nuneaton CV10 72 F3
Walsall WS5 43 B3
Brackendale Sh Ctr WV12 27 D4
Brackendale Way DY9 81 D4
Bracken Dr B75 47 A5
Brackenfield Rd
Birmingham B44 44 D3
Halesowen B63 82 E3
Brackenfield View DY1 61 D8
Bracken Gr B61 121 A1
Brackenhill Rd WS7 7 A8
Brackenhurst Rd CV6 113 A7
Bracken Park Gdns DY8 60 F2
Bracken Rd
Birmingham B24 57 C2
Huntington WS12 1 C5
Bracken Way
Birmingham B38 123 D6
Sutton Coldfield B74 44 F8
Bracken Wood WS5 43 D5
Brackenwood Dr WV11 26 F5
Bracklesham Way B77 22 A6
Brackley Ave B20 55 C1
Brackley Cl CV6 112 F7
Brackleys Way B92 89 A2
Bracknell Wlk 1 CV2 115 A7
Bradbeer Ho B16 66 A1
Bradburne Way B7 67 A5
Bradburn Rd WV11 26 B8
Bradbury Cl WS8 15 F5
Bradbury Ct WS12 2 B7
Bradbury La WS12 2 B8
Bradbury Rd B92 107 A8
Braddock Cl CV3 115 A1
Brade Dr CV2 115 B7
Braden Rd WV4 38 D4
Brades Cl B63 82 B7
Brades Rd B69 63 E8
Brades Rise B69 63 D8
Bradestone Rd CV11 73 D1
Bradewell Rd B36 58 D1
Bradfield Cl CV5 112 C5
Bradfield Ho B26 89 D6
Bradfield Rd B42 55 D7
Bradford Cl B43 54 F7
Bradford Court Bsns Ctr B12 87 A8
Bradford La
Belbroughton DY9 119 D5
Walsall WS1 28 E1
Bradford Mall WS1 28 E1
Bradford Pl WS1 28 E1
Bradford Rd
Birmingham B36 69 B7
Brownhills WS8 15 E8
Dudley DY2 61 F6
Bradford St
Birmingham B12, B5 66 F1
Cannock WS11 2 A5
Tamworth B79 20 F5
Walsall WS1 28 E1
Bradgate Cl WV12 27 C6
Bradgate Dr B74 31 E5
Bradgate Pl 12 B12 87 A6
Bradgate Rd LE10 71 F2
Brading Rd CV10 73 D6
Bradley Croft CV7 130 B6
Bradley La WV14 41 A3
Bradley La Sta WV14 41 A3
Bradleymore Rd DY5 61 D3
Bradley Rd
Birmingham B34 69 D6
Stourbridge DY8 80 F6
Wolverhampton WV2 39 E7
Bradleys Cl B64 82 E7
Bradley's La DY4, WV14 51 E8
Bradley St
Bilston WV14 40 F4
Brierley Hill DY5 61 C7
Tipton DY4 51 F2
Bradley Thursfield Ct DY11 116 C7
Bradmore Cl 1 B91 107 A1
Bradmore Gr B29 103 A8
Bradmore Rd WV3 38 F8
Bradney Gn CV4 131 E7
Bradnick Pl CV4 111 F1
Bradnock Cl B13 105 C7
Bradnock's Marsh La B92 109 E2
Bradshaw Ave
Birmingham B38 103 D1
Darlaston WS10 41 C5
Bradshaw Cl
7 Birmingham B15 86 C8
Tipton DY4 52 A3
Bradshawe Cl B28 105 D3
Bradstock Rd B30 104 C4
Bradwell Croft B75 32 E3
Braeburn Cl WS13 3 D1
Braemar Ave DY8 60 C1
Braemar Cl
Coventry CV2 114 E6
Sedgley DY3 39 C1
Willenhall WV12 27 B5
Braemar Dr B23 56 B5
Braemar Gdns WS12 1 F7
Braemar Rd
Norton Canes WS11 6 B4
Royal Leamington Spa CV32 157 B4
Solihull B92 88 E1
Sutton Coldfield B73 46 A2
Braemar Way CV10 73 A2
Braeside Croft B37 70 D2
Braeside Way WS3 14 F3
Bragg Rd B20 55 D2
Braggs Farm La B90 126 A4
Braham B79 20 D6
Braid Cl B38 103 D1
Brailes Cl B92 107 E7
Brailes Dr B76 46 F3
Brailes Gr B9 68 B1
Brailsford Cl WV11 26 E8
Brailsford Dr B66 65 A5
Brain St B77 22 A2
Braithwaite Dr DY6 60 D6
Braithwaite Rd B11 87 B7
Brake La DY8 98 E6
Brakesmead CV31 161 F5
Brake The DY8 98 F6
Bramah Way DY4 52 C6
Bramber B77 21 D1
Bramber Dr WV5 49 A6
Bramber Way DY8 80 F2
Bramble Cl
Birmingham, Aston B6 66 E7
Birmingham, Shenley Fields B31 102 F6
Brownhills WS8 15 E5
6 Coleshill B46 70 F7
Cradley Heath B64 62 F4
Nuneaton CV11 73 F2
Willenhall WV12 27 C7
Bramble Dell B9 68 A3
Bramble Dr
Birmingham B26 89 A6
Cannock WS12 2 C7
Bramble Gn DY1 50 F5
Bramble Ho B98 158 F8
Bramble La WS7 7 B8
Brambleside DY8 60 F1
Bramble St CV1 113 E2
Brambles The
Catshill B61 137 A8
Lichfield WS14 9 D6
Norton Canes WS11 6 A5
Stourbridge DY9 81 D3
Sutton Coldfield B76 58 A8
Bramblewood WV5 49 A7
Bramblewood Dr WV3 38 E8
Bramblewoods B34 69 C5
Brambling B77 36 A7
Brambling Rise DY10 117 B1
Brambling Wlk
2 Birmingham B15 86 C7
Brierley Hill DY5 81 C6
Bramcote Cl
Bulkington CV12 79 D2
Hinckley LE10 71 F3
Bramcote Dr B91 107 C7
Bramcote Hospl CV11 79 E7
Bramcote Rd B32 84 C5
Bramcote Rise B75 46 C7
Bramdean Wlk WV4 38 C6
Bramdene Ave CV10 73 D8
Brame Rd LE10 71 C2
Bramerton Cl WV11 26 A6
Bramford Dr DY1 51 B6
Bramford Prim Sch DY1 51 B6
Bramley Cl
Birmingham B43 44 D3
Walsall WS5 43 D8
Bramley Croft B90 106 C2
Bramley Ct WV11 26 C6
Bramley Dr
Birmingham B20 55 B3
Hollywood B47 125 B6
Bramley Mews Ct B27 88 C4
Bramley Rd
Birmingham B27 88 C5
Walsall WS5 43 B4
Brampton Ave B28 106 A6
Brampton Cres B90 106 B6
Brampton Dr WS12 2 E2
Brampton Way CV12 79 B3
Bramshall Dr B93 127 E3
Bramshaw Cl B14 104 F2
Bramshill Ct B15 86 B8
Bramstead Ave WV6 24 B2
Bramston Cres CV4 111 F1
Bramwell Dr WS6 4 D1
Bramwell Gdns CV6 95 F5
Brancaster Cl B77 22 A5
Branchal Rd WS9 16 C1
Branch Rd B38 123 E8
Branden Rd B48 139 A5
Brandfield Rd CV6 112 F8
Brandhall Ct B68 64 A2
Brandhall La B68 64 B1
Brandhall Prim Sch B68 64 B1
Brandhall Rd B68 64 B2
Brandon Cl
Sedgley DY3 50 E7
Sutton Coldfield WS9 30 F3
West Bromwich B70 53 A2
Brandon Ct
Birmingham B31 103 B1
Coventry CV3 135 A7
Brandon Gr B31 122 F7
Brandon La CV3, CV8 135 C5
Brandon Marsh Nature Reserve* CV3 135 A4
Brandon Marsh Visitor Ctr* CV3 135 B4
Brandon Par CV32 162 A8
Brandon Pk WV3 38 E7
Brandon Pl B34 69 D7
Brandon Rd
Birmingham B28 87 E2
Coventry CV3 135 A8
Halesowen B62 63 E1
Hinckley LE10 75 B7
Solihull B91 107 C7
Brandon Thomas Ct B6 67 B8
Brandon Way
Brierley Hill DY5 81 E8
West Bromwich B70 53 A2
Brandon Way Ind Est B70 52 F3
Brandon Wood Farm* CV8 135 D5
Brandwood Cres B30 104 D3
Brandwood Gr B14 104 D5
Brandwood Ho B14 104 D7
Brandwood Park Rd B14 104 C4
Brandwood Rd B14 104 D5
Branfield Cl WV14 51 A8
Branksome Ave B21 65 F8
Branksome Rd CV6 112 E6
Branscombe Cl B14 104 D5
Bransdale Ave CV6 95 D3
Bransdale Cl WV6 25 A5
Bransdale Rd WS8 15 E6
Bransford Ave CV4 132 D5
Bransford Rise B91 108 B5
Bransford Twr B12 86 F8
Branston St B18 66 C4
Branstree Dr CV6 95 D2
Brantford Rd B25 88 C8
Branthill Croft 4 B91 107 B1
Brantley Ave WV3 24 C1
Brantley Rd B6 56 A2
Branton Hill La WS9 30 C5
Brantwood Ave WS7 7 A5
Brascote Rd LE10 74 F8
Brasshouse Inf Sch B66 65 A7
Brasshouse La B66 65 A7
Brassie Cl B38 103 D1
Brassington Ave B72, B73 46 B5
Bratch Cl DY2 62 C3
Bratch Hollow WV5 49 A8
Bratch La WV5 49 A8
Brathay Cl CV3 133 D6
Bratt St B70 53 C4
Braunston Cl B76 47 A2
Brawnes Hurst B26 69 A1
Brayford Ave
Brierley Hill DY5 81 B7
Coventry CV3 133 C6
Braymoor Rd B33 69 E1
Bray's La CV2 114 A3
Brays Rd B26 89 B6
Brays Sch B26 89 A6
Bray St WV13 27 B2
Braytoft Cl CV6 95 C2
Brazil St CV4 111 E2
Breaches La B98 159 D8
Breadmarket St WS13 9 B8
Breakback Rd B61 150 D8
Bream B77 35 D7
Bream Cl
Birmingham B37 70 C2
Wolverhampton WV10 26 B4
Breamore Cres DY1 50 F3
Brean Ave B92 88 F5
Brearley Cl B19 66 E5
Brearley St
Birmingham, Handsworth B21 65 D8
Birmingham, Hockley B19 66 E5
Brechin Cl LE10 75 A8
Brecknell Rise DY10 116 F8
Brecknock Rd B71 53 A6
Brecon Ave B61 137 A5
Brecon Dr DY8 81 B6
Brecon Rd B20 66 B8
Brecon Twr 1 B16 66 A2
Bredon Ave
Coventry CV3 134 F8
Kidderminster DY11 116 A1
Stourbridge DY9 81 C5
Bredon Croft B18 66 A5
Bredon Ct
Halesowen B63 83 A3
Sutton Coldfield B75 32 A4
Bredon Ho B98 159 B7
Bredon Rd
Bromsgrove B61 150 D7
Oldbury B69 63 D5
Stourbridge DY8 81 B6
Bredon Terr 4 B18 66 A5
Bredon View B97 158 D8
Breech Cl B74 44 E7
Bree Cl CV5 112 A7
Breeden Dr B76 59 B6
Breedon Ct B30 104 A5
Breedon Gdns B98 154 A3
Breedon Rd B30 104 A5
Breedon Way WS4 15 C1
Breener Ind Est DY5 61 B1
Breen Rydding Dr WV14 51 B8
Bree's La CV8 130 A1
Breeze Ave WS11 6 B5
Brelades Cl DY1 50 E3
Breme Lodge B60 151 A7
Brendon B77 22 B1
Brendon Way CV10 72 A3
Brenfield Dr LE10 75 A8
Brennand Cl B68 84 C8
Brennand Rd B68 84 B8
Brent B77 35 E7
Brentford Rd
Birmingham B14 105 A5
Solihull B91 106 E3
Brent Ho 3 DY1 61 E8
Brentmill Cl WV10 11 F4
Brentnall Dr B75 32 B3
Brenton Rd WV4 38 F3
Brent Rd B30 104 D8
Brentwood Ave CV3 133 C3
Brentwood Cl B91 106 E3
Brentwood Gdns CV3 133 C3
Brentwood Gr B44 55 E8
Brenwood Cl DY6 60 B7
Brereton Cl DY2 62 E8
Brereton Rd WV12 27 D7
Brese Ave CV34 155 F1
Bretby Gr B23 57 A6
Bretford Rd CV2 96 C1
Bretshall Cl B90 126 F5
Brett Dr B32 102 C8
Brettell La
Brierley Hill DY5, DY8 61 B1
Stourbridge DY8 80 F8
Brettell St 5 DY1 62 B8
Bretton Gdns WV10 25 F6
Bretton Rd B27 88 D2
Bretts Cl CV1 165 D4
Bretts Hall Est CV10 72 A7
Brett St B71 53 B5
Brett Young Cl DY10 117 B5
Brevitt Rd WV2 39 D6
Brewer Rd CV12 79 D2
Brewers Cl CV3 115 A1
Brewers Dr WS3 15 A1
Brewer St WS2 28 E4
Brewers Terr WS3 15 A2
Brewery St
Birmingham, Handsworth B21 65 D8
Birmingham, New Town Row B6 164 C5
Dudley DY2 51 E1
Smethwick B67 64 F6
Tipton DY4 51 F4
Brewins Way DY5 62 A4
Brewster Cl
Coventry CV2 114 E2
Fazeley B78 20 E1
Brewster St DY2 62 C5
Breydon Gr WV13 40 F8
Brian Rd B67 64 E6
Briansway CV6 95 E3
Briar B77 22 A3
Briar Ave B74 31 A1
Briarbeck WS4 29 C8
Briar Cl
Birmingham B24 57 A4
Cannock WS12 2 A8
Hinckley LE10 75 F6
Lickey End B60 137 C6
Royal Leamington Spa CV32 157 B2
Briar Coppice B90 126 D4
Briar Ct
14 Brierley Hill DY5 61 D2
Dudley DY2 62 C6
Briardene Ave CV12 78 B2
Briarfield Rd B11 88 A3
Briar Hill DY10 118 E1
Briar Hill Inf Sch CV31 162 B3
Briarley Ho 5 B71 42 F1
Briarmead LE10 75 E4
Briars Cl
Brierley Hill DY5 61 C4
Coventry CV2 114 C2
Nuneaton CV11 73 E5
Briars The
Aldridge WS9 30 A7
Birmingham B23 56 D6
West Hagley DY9 98 F4
Briarwood Cl B90 126 D4
Briar Wood Cl WV2 40 A7
Briarwood The WV2 40 A7
Brickfield Rd B25 88 B6
Brickheath Rd WV1 26 A3
Brickhill Dr B37 70 A2

Brick Hill La CV5 111 E8
Brickhouse Jun & Inf Sch B65 63 A3
Brickhouse La
Stoke Prior B60 150 C4
West Bromwich B70 52 E6
Brickhouse Lane S DY4 52 E6
Brickhouse Rd B65 63 A4
Brickiln Ct 2 DY5 61 D2
Brickiln St WS8 15 F7
Brick Kiln La
Birmingham B44 55 E6
Dudley DY3 50 B3
Middleton B78 48 D6
Solihull B91 126 F8
Wythall B47 124 F4
Brickkiln St WV13 26 F1
Brick Kiln St
Brierley Hill, Hart's Hill DY5 61 E5
Brierley Hill, Quarry Bank DY5 82 A8
Hinckley LE10 75 C8
Tipton DY4 51 F6
Brick Kiln Way CV12 78 D3
Brick St DY3 50 D8
Brickworks Rd WS12 2 E2
Brickyard Cl CV7 130 C7
Brickyard La B80 159 C4
Brickyard Rd
Aldridge, Leighswood WS9 30 A7
Aldridge, Leighswood WS9 30 A8
Aldridge, Vigo WS9 15 F1
Bridal Path The CV5 112 B6
Briddsland Rd B33 69 E2
Bridgeacre Gdns CV3 114 F2
Bridge Ave
Cheslyn Hay WS6 4 E4
Tipton DY4 52 C7
Bridgeburn Rd B31 102 E8
Bridge Cl
Birmingham B11 87 B3
Brownhills WS8 15 E6
Bridgecote CV3 134 E6
Bridge Croft B12 86 E6
Bridge Cross Rd WS7 7 A7
Bridge Ct DY8 60 E2
Bridge End CV34 160 F5
Bridgefield Wlk B65 62 F5
Bridgefoot Wlk WV8 10 F1
Bridgeford Rd B34 69 B6
Bridge Ho
Royal Leamington Spa CV31 162 A8
Smethwick B66 65 C6
Bridge Ind Est B91 107 C7
Bridgelands Way B20 55 D1
Bridgeman Croft B36 69 C8
Bridgeman Rd CV6 113 B4
Bridgeman St WS2 28 D1
Bridgemary Cl WV10 11 E4
Bridge Meadow Dr B93 127 F6
Bridgemeadow Ho 5 B36 68 E8
Bridgend Croft DY5 61 B6
Bridgenorth Ho B33 69 B2
Bridge Piece B31 103 B2
Bridge Rd
Birmingham B8 67 E3
Hinckley LE10 75 D7
Tipton DY4 52 C7
Walsall WS4 15 B1
Bridge St Ind Est WS10 41 F1
Bridge St N B66 65 B7
Bridge St S B66 65 B6
Bridge St W B19 66 D5
Bridge Sch The B23 56 E4
Bridges Cres WS11 5 F5
Bridgeside Trad Est B77 21 C3
Bridges Rd WS11 5 F5
Bridge St Bilston WV14 40 E5
Birmingham B1 164 A2
Brownhills WS8 15 E6
Cannock WS11 4 E5
Coventry CV6 114 A7
Halesowen B63 82 C7
Kenilworth CV8 147 F5
1 Kidderminster DY10 116 E5
Nuneaton, Chilvers Coton CV11 73 C2
Nuneaton CV11 73 C4
Oldbury B69 64 A8
Bridge St *continued*
Redditch B97 153 D4
Stourbridge DY8 60 E1
Tamworth B77 21 E5
Tipton WV14 51 C8
Walsall WS1 28 F2
Warwick CV34 161 C8
Wednesbury WS10 41 F1
West Bromwich B70 53 B4
Willenhall WV13 26 F1
Wolverhampton WV10 25 E5
Bridge The 3 WS1 28 E1
Bridge Trad Ctr The B64 82 D8
Bridge Trad Est The B66 65 B6
Bridge View
Baginton CV8 133 D3
3 Coleshill B46 70 F7
Bridgewater Ave B69 64 A4
Bridgewater Cres DY2 51 E1
Bridgewater Dr WV14 40 C2
Bridgewater St B77 21 D5
Bridge Way WS8 15 E6
Bridgnorth Gr WV12 27 B6
Bridgnorth Rd
Himley DY3 49 B3
Stourbridge DY7, DY8 80 C6
Trescott WV6 37 C7
Wolverhampton WV6 24 B2
Bridgtown Bsns Ctr WS11 4 E6
Bridgtown Prim Sch WS11 4 E6
Bridgwater Cl WS9 15 F3
Bridle Brook La CV5, CV7 94 A3
Bridle Gr B71 53 F7
Bridle La B74, WS9 44 E7
Bridle Mead B38 123 D8
Bridle Path The B90 106 B6
Bridle Rd DY8 80 D6
Bridlewood B74 44 F8
Bridley Moor Rd B97 153 C5
Bridport Cl CV2 115 A4
Bridport Ho B31 102 E7
Brierley Hill Prim Sch DY5 61 D2
Brierley Hill Rd DY8 60 F2
Brierley La WV14 40 E2
Brierley La Cvn Site WV14 40 E2
Brierley Rd
Bromsgrove B60 137 C1
Coventry CV2 114 C8
Brierley Trad Est The DY5 61 C3
Brier Mill Rd B63 83 C3
Brier Sch The DY6 60 F5
Brier Specl Sch The DY5 61 E2
Briery Cl B64 82 F7
Briery Rd B63 82 E3
Brigadoon Gdns DY9 81 C2
Brigfield Cres B13 105 B5
Brigfield Rd B13 105 B5
Bright Cres B77 21 C2
Brightmere Rd CV6 113 B4
Brighton Cl WS2 28 D3
Brighton Mews 8 WV3 25 A2
Brighton Rd B12 87 A5
Brighton St CV2 113 F3
Bright Rd B68 64 B5
Bright St
Coventry CV6 113 E6
Darlaston WS10 41 D5
Stourbridge DY8 80 D6
Wolverhampton WV1 163 A4
Brightstone Cl WV10 11 F4
Brightstone Rd B45 102 B2
Brightwalton Rd CV3 133 D7
Brightwell Cres B93 127 E3
Brill Cl CV4 132 C5
Brimfield Pl 1 WV6 24 F4
Brimstone La B61 136 D7
Brindle Ave CV3 114 C2
Brindle Cl B26 88 E5
Brindle Ct B23 56 B3
Brindlefields Way DY4 52 B2
Brindle Rd WS5 43 C4
Brindley Ave WV11 13 A1
Brindley Cl
1 Stourbridge DY8 60 E1
Willenhall WS2 27 F5
Brindley Cres WS12 2 C8
Brindley Ct 5 DY4 51 E5
Brindley Dr B1 164 A2
Brindley Heath Rd WS12 2 D8
Brindley Paddocks CV1 165 B4
Brindley Pl B1 66 B2
Brindley Point Apartments 7 B16 66 B2
Brindley Rd
Bedworth CV7 96 B8
Hinckley LE10 74 E8
West Bromwich B71 53 A8
Brindleys Bsns Pk WS11 2 B3
Brindley Way 10 B66 65 C5
Brineton Gr B29 85 A1
Brineton Ind Est 1 WS2 28 C1
Brineton St WS2 28 C1
Bringewood Gr B32 102 B8
Brinklow Cl B98 159 D8
Brinklow Croft B34 69 D7
Brinklow Rd
Birmingham B29 84 F2
Coventry CV3 115 A2
Brinklow Twr 4 B12 86 F7
Brinley Way DY6 60 C6
Brinsford La WV10 11 D7
Brinsford Rd WV10 11 C3
Brinsley Cl B91 107 B2
Brinsley Rd B26 89 B8
Brinton Cl DY11 116 C3
Brinton Cres DY11 116 C3
Brisbane Cl CV3 133 E6
Brisbane Ct 2 CV12 78 A2
Brisbane Rd B67 64 E5
Brisbane Way WS12 2 E3
Briscoe Rd CV6 95 D4
Briseley Cl DY5 81 D8
Bristam Cl B69 63 E6
Bristnall Hall Cres B68 64 C3
Bristnall Hall La B68 64 D3
Bristnall Hall Rd B68 64 C3
Bristnall Hall Tech Coll B68 64 D3
Bristol Cl WS11 2 B1
Bristol Ct 15 B29 103 C7
Bristol Rd
Birmingham, Balsall Heath B5 86 C5
Birmingham, Gravelly Hill B23 56 E3
Coventry CV5 112 F2
Dudley DY2 62 D2
Bristol Rd S
Birmingham B31 102 F2
Birmingham, Bournville B29, B30, B31 103 C7
Birmingham, Longbridge B31, B45 122 C8
Bristol St
Birmingham B15 86 D8
Wolverhampton WV3 39 B8
Briston Cl DY5 81 C8
Britannia Cl B98 153 F3
Britannia Gdns B65 63 C3
Britannia Gn DY3 50 E5
Britannia Rd
Bilston WV14 40 F3
Hinckley LE10 76 A5
Rowley Regis B65 63 C2
Britannia St
Coventry CV2 113 F3
Oldbury B69 52 C2
Britannia Way WS13 9 F8
Britannic Gdns B13 86 D2
Britannic Ho B13 86 D2
Britford Cl B14 104 F3
Briton Rd CV2 114 B4
Brittan Cl B34 69 E6
Brittania Pk WS10 41 D3
Brittania Rd WS1 42 D5
Brittania Sh Ctr 3 LE10 75 D8
Britten Cl CV11 79 A7
Britten St B97 153 D4
Britton Dr B72 57 C8
Britwell Rd B73 46 A2
Brixfield Way B90 126 B5
Brixham Cl CV11 73 F5
Brixham Dr CV2 114 C7
Brixham Rd B16 65 D4
Brixworth Cl CV3 134 E8
Broad Acres B31 102 E6
Broadbent Cl 1 WS13 8 F6
Broadcott Ind Est B64 83 A8
Broad Croft 1 DY4 52 C6
Broadfern Rd B93 128 B8
Broadfield Cl
Kingswinford DY6 60 D5
West Bromwich B71 42 F1
Broadfield House Glass Mus★ DY6 60 D5
Broadfields DY9 99 A6
Broadfields Rd B23 57 B7
Broadfield Wlk 1 B16 66 B1
Broadgate CV1 165 B3
Broad Ground Rd B98 154 B2
Broadhaven Cl CV31 162 C7
Broad Heath Cl B97 153 B5
Broad Heath Com Prim Sch CV6 113 E6
Broadheath Dr WS4 29 D8
Broadhidley Dr B32 84 B1
Broadhurst Gn WS12 2 A8
Broad La
Birmingham B14 104 E4
Burntwood WS7 8 B5
Coventry CV5 111 D4
Lichfield WS14 9 D6
Tanworth-In-A B98 141 E3
Walsall, Essington WS3 18 E4
Walsall WS4 15 C2
Wolverhampton WV3 38 E8
Broad La N WV12 27 B7
Broadlands WV10 11 D5
Broadlands Cl CV5 112 C2
Broadlands Dr DY5 61 E5
Broadlands Rise WS14 9 D7
Broad Lane Gdns WS3 14 A2
Broad Lanes WV14 40 C3
Broad La S WV11 27 A5
Broadlee B77 22 C1
Broad Mdw WS9 30 B8
Broadmead Ct CV5 112 C2
Broadmeadow DY6 60 E8
Broadmeadow Cl B30 104 B3
Broadmeadow Gn WV14 40 C7
Broadmeadow Ho B32 102 D8
Broadmeadow Inf Sch B30 104 B2
Broadmeadow Jun Sch B30 104 B2
Broad Meadow La
Birmingham B30 104 B3
Great Wyrley WS6 5 A2
Broadmeadows Cl WV12 27 E8
Broadmeadows Rd WV12 27 E8
Broadmede Ho B67 64 E2
Broadmere Rise CV5 112 A2
Broadmoor Ave B68 64 D2
Broadmoor Cl WV14 40 C4
Broadmoor Rd WV14 40 C3
Broad Oaks B76 47 A1
Broadoaks Cl WS11 5 F6
Broad Oaks Rd B91 107 A5
Broadoaks The B91 107 A4
Broad Park Rd CV2 114 D8
Broad Rd B27 88 B3
Broadsmeath B77 21 C1
Broad St Bilston WV14 40 D6
Birmingham B15, B1 66 C2
Brierley Hill DY5 61 C6
Bromsgrove B61 136 F4
Cannock WS11 4 E6
Coventry CV6 113 E7
Kidderminster DY10 116 E7
Kingswinford DY6 60 D5
Oldbury B69 64 A5
Tipton WV14 51 C8
Warwick CV34 160 F7
Wolverhampton WV1 163 C3
Broadstone Ave
Halesowen B63 82 B4
Walsall WS3 28 D7
Broadstone Cl WV4 39 D5
Broadstone Rd B26 69 A1
Broad Street Jetty CV6 113 E7
Broadsword Way LE10 75 D4
Broadwalk 5 B1 66 C1
Broadwalk Ret Pk WS1 42 D6
Broadwas Cl B98 154 C5
Broadwater CV5 133 A8
Broadwaters Ave WS10 41 C4
Broadwaters Dr
Kidderminster DY10 117 A8
Broadwaters Dr *continued*
West Hagley DY9 99 B4
Broadwaters Rd WS10 41 C4
Broadway
Cannock WS12 1 F6
Coventry CV5 113 A1
Cubbington CV32 157 E5
Oldbury B68 64 C1
Solihull B90 106 B4
Walsall WS5 43 A6
Wolverhampton, Bushbury WV10 11 E2
Wolverhampton WV3 24 C2
Broad Way WS4 15 C2
Broadway Ave
Birmingham B9 68 A3
Halesowen B63 83 A2
Broadway Croft
Birmingham B26 89 A6
Oldbury B68 64 C1
Broadway Gdns WV10 11 E2
Broadway Mans CV5 113 A1
Broadway N WS1 29 B2
Broadway Plaza B16 66 A1
Broadway Sch B20 55 E2
Broadway Sch The (Aston Campus) B6 66 E8
Broadway The
Birmingham B20 55 E2
Dudley DY1 51 B3
Stourbridge DY8 80 D3
West Bromwich B71 53 B7
Wombourne WV5 49 A5
Broadway W WS1 42 D6
Broadwell Ct CV4 131 F6
Broadwell Ind Pk B69 53 A1
Broadwell Rd
Oldbury B69 64 A8
Solihull B92 89 A2
Broadwells Cres CV4 132 A5
Broadyates Gr B25 88 C6
Broadyates Rd B25 88 C6
Brobury Croft B91 106 D4
Brockenhurst Ct B73 46 B1
Brockenhurst Way CV6 96 B6
Brockeridge Cl WV12 13 C1
Brockfield Ho WV10 25 F4
Brockhall Gr B37 69 F5
Brockhill Dr B97 153 A5
Brockhill La
Alvechurch B48 124 B2
Beoley B98 140 F2
Tardebigge B97 152 E8
Brockhurst Ave LE10 75 D4
Brockhurst Cres WS5 42 E4
Brockhurst Dr
Birmingham B28 106 A5
Coventry CV4 111 D2
Wolverhampton WV6 25 A4
Brockhurst Ho 4 WS2 28 D3
Brockhurst La
Solihull B90 126 B5
Weeford B75 33 B7
Brockhurst Pl WS5 42 F5
Brockhurst Rd
Birmingham B36 68 D6
Sutton Coldfield B75 32 D1
Brockhurst St WS1 42 E6
Brockley Cl DY5 61 D3
Brockley Gr B13 86 C1
Brockley Pl B7 67 C7
Brockmoor Cl DY9 81 C2
Brockmoor Prim Sch DY5 61 C3
Brock Rd DY4 52 C4
Brockton Rd B29 85 A1
Brockwell Gr B44 44 E4
Brockwell Rd B44 44 E4
Brockworth Rd B14 104 C2
Brocton Cl WV14 40 A3
Brodick Cl LE10 75 A8
Brodick Rd LE10 74 F8
Brodick Way CV10 72 F3
Brogden Cl 4 B71 53 F8
Brome Hall La B94 144 D2
Bromfield Cl B6 66 E7
Bromfield Cres WS10 42 C4
Bromfield Ct WV6 24 B3
Bromfield Rd B97 153 D2
Bromford Central B8 68 B8
Bromford Cl
Birmingham, Erdington B23 56 E5
Birmingham, Handsworth B20 55 A2
Bromford Cres B24 57 A2
Bromford Ct B8 68 B6
Bromford Dale 2 WV6 24 F3
Bromford Dell B31 103 C4
Bromford Dr B36 68 D8
Bromford Gdns B15 85 C8
Bromford Hill B20 55 C3
Bromford Ho B73 45 F2
Bromford La
Birmingham B8, B36 68 C6
West Bromwich B70 53 B2
Bromford Mere 4 B92 88 E1
Bromford Park Ho 3 B13 87 B2
Bromford Rd
Birmingham B36 68 D7
Dudley DY2 62 A6
West Bromwich B69, B70 53 A1
Bromford Rise WV3 163 A1
Bromford Road Ind Est B70 53 A1
Bromford Wlk B43 43 F1
Bromhurst Way CV34 160 B4
Bromleigh Dr CV2 114 C2
Bromleigh Villas CV8 133 F2
Bromley DY5 61 B5
Bromley Cl
Cannock WS12 2 C7
Kenilworth CV8 147 E6
Bromley Gdns WV8 10 A4
Bromley Hills Prim Sch DY6 60 F5
Bromley Ho WV4 39 A5
Bromley La DY6 60 E4
Bromley Lodge WV4 39 A5
Bromley-Pensnett Prim Sch The DY5 61 B5
Bromley Pl WV4 39 A5
Bromley St
Birmingham B9 67 A1
Stourbridge DY9 81 F6
Wolverhampton WV2 39 C7
Brompton Dr DY5 81 B7
Brompton Lawns WV6 24 A3
Brompton Pool Rd B28 105 E3
Brompton Rd B44 44 E4
Bromsgrove Highway
Bromsgrove B60 137 D1
Redditch B97 153 B2
Tardebigge B60, B97 152 C6
Bromsgrove Lower Sch B60 136 F1
Bromsgrove Mus★ B61 137 A3
Bromsgrove Private Hospl B60 138 B1
Bromsgrove Rd
Clent DY9 99 D4
Dodford B61 136 D6
Halesowen B63 83 C4
Mustow Green DY10 117 F2
Redditch B97 153 B3
Romsley B62 101 A5
Studley B80 159 D2
Bromsgrove Sch B61 136 F1
Bromsgrove St
Birmingham B5 164 C1
Halesowen B63 83 C4
Kidderminster DY10 116 E6
Bromsgrove Sta B60 151 B7
Bromwall Rd B13 105 B6
Bromwich Cl CV3 134 F8
Bromwich Dr B75 46 C7
Bromwich La DY9 99 B8
Bromwich Wlk B9 68 A3
Bromwynd Cl WV2 39 B6
Bromyard Ave B76 58 A8
Bromyard Rd B11 87 E3
Bronte Cl B90 106 D1
Bronte Ct
Solihull B90 106 D1
Tamworth B79 21 A6
Bronte Dr
Cannock WS11 2 C2
Kidderminster DY10 117 C6
Bronte Farm Rd B90 106 D1
Bronte Rd WV2 39 F6
Bronwen Ingham Ct DY10 116 E7
Bronwen Rd WV14 51 C7
Bronze Cl CV11 78 E8

Brook Ave B77 ... 36 A7
Brookbank Ave B34 ... 69 D6
Brookbank Gdns DY3 ... 50 B2
Brookbank Rd DY3 ... 50 B2
Brook Cl
Birmingham B33 ... 68 E4
Brownhills WS9 ... 16 A3
Coventry CV1 ... 113 E4
Lichfield WS13 ... 3 A1
Solihull B90 ... 105 F1
Brook Cotts B25 ... 88 A7
Brook Cres
Kingswinford DY6 ... 60 C7
Stourbridge DY9 ... 81 F3
West Hagley DY9 ... 99 B5
Brook Croft
Birmingham, Lyndon Green B26 ... 89 B7
Birmingham, Marston Green B37 ... 90 B7
Brook Ct B60 ... 137 B3
Brookdale Dudley DY3 ... 50 C3
Hinckley LE10 ... 75 B7
Kidderminster DY10 ... 116 F8
Brookdale Cl B45 ... 102 A1
Brookdale Dr WV4 ... 38 E6
Brookdale Rd CV10 ... 73 E7
Brook Dr B32 ... 84 D1
Brooke Cl CV34 ... 160 F5
Brooke Mews 8 CV34 ... 160 F7
Brook End
Burntwood WS7 ... 7 A4
Fazeley B78 ... 35 B8
Brookend Dr B45 ... 121 F7
Brooke Rd
Cannock WS12 ... 1 F6
Kenilworth CV8 ... 148 B4
Brookes Cl B69 ... 52 B1
Brookes Ho 3 WS1 ... 28 F1
Brooke St DY2 ... 62 C8
Brook Farm Ind Est B94 ... 126 B2
Brook Farm Wlk B37 ... 70 D2
Brookfield Cl
Aldridge WS9 ... 16 A1
Redditch B97 ... 158 D4
Brookfield Dr WS11 ... 4 E7
Brookfield Ho DY9 ... 119 C7
Brookfield Rd
Aldridge WS9 ... 16 A1
Birmingham B18 ... 66 A5
Birmingham, Brandwood End B30 ... 104 D3
Codsall WV8 ... 10 B3
Cubbington CV32 ... 157 E5
Hinckley LE10 ... 75 C6
Brook Fields Cl B60 ... 121 C1
Brookfields Prim Sch B18 ... 66 B4
Brookfields Rd B68 ... 64 C4
Brookfield Terr B18 ... 66 A5
Brookfield Way
Solihull B92 ... 106 D7
Tipton DY4 ... 52 B6
Brookford Ave CV6 ... 95 A3
Brook Gr WV8 ... 10 B2
Brook Green La B92 ... 109 A1
Brookhampton Cl B97 ... 158 E4
Brookhill Cl WV12 ... 13 D1
Brookhill Rd B8 ... 68 A4
Brookhill Way WV12 ... 13 D1
Brook Holloway DY9 ... 81 F4
Brookhouse Cl WV10 ... 12 B6
Brookhouse La
Featherstone WV10 ... 12 B7
Wolverhampton WV10 ... 11 F6
Brookhouse Rd
Blackwell B45 ... 137 F7
Walsall WS5 ... 43 B7
Brookhurst Ct CV32 ... 156 D1
Brookhurst Prim Sch CV32 ... 156 C1
Brookhus Farm Rd B76 ... 58 A8
Brooking Cl B43 ... 44 D4
Brook La
Birmingham B32 ... 84 F5
Birmingham, Billesley B13 ... 105 B7
Brownhills WS9 ... 15 F3
Cradley Heath B64 ... 62 E2
Great Wyrley WS6 ... 5 A3
Nuneaton CV10 ... 73 C6
Solihull B92 ... 106 D8
Brookland Gr WS9 ... 15 F3
Brookland Rd
Brownhills WS9 ... 15 F3
West Hagley DY9 ... 99 A4
Brooklands
Stourbridge DY8 ... 60 F1
Walsall WS5 ... 43 B3
Brooklands Ave WS6 ... 4 F4
Brooklands Cl B28 ... 87 F1
Brooklands Dr B14 ... 104 E5
Brooklands Ho 8 CV34 ... 161 D8
Brooklands La B98 ... 154 B5
Brooklands Par WV1 ... 26 B2
Brooklands Pk B98 ... 154 F5
Brooklands Rd
Birmingham B28 ... 87 F1
Cannock WS11 ... 2 A4
Brooklands Way B37 ... 90 A8
Brooklea CV12 ... 77 F2
Brooklea Gr B38 ... 104 A1
Brooklime Gdns WV10 ... 12 B7
Brooklyn Ave B6 ... 66 F7
Brooklyn Gr
Dudley WV14 ... 51 D8
Kingswinford DY6 ... 60 B8
Brooklyn Rd
Burntwood WS7 ... 7 A4
Cannock WS12 ... 2 D1
Coventry CV1 ... 113 D6
Brookmans Ave B32 ... 84 D4
Brook Mdws WV8 ... 10 B4
Brookmeadow Ct B28 ... 105 D6
Brook Meadow Rd
Birmingham B34 ... 69 B6
Walsall WS4 ... 29 D8
Brook Park Trad Est 4 DY9 ... 81 F5
Brookpiece Ho B14 ... 104 E2
Brook Piece Wlk B35 ... 58 B3
Brook Prim Sch DY8 ... 60 F1
Brook Rd
Birmingham, Chad Valley B15 ... 85 E7
Birmingham, Rubery B45 ... 121 E7
Bromsgrove B61 ... 136 E1
Cheslyn Hay WS6 ... 4 E4
Fairfield B61 ... 120 C2
Oldbury B68 ... 64 A2
Stourbridge DY8 ... 81 B3
Willenhall WV13 ... 26 E1
Brooksbank Dr B64 ... 62 F4
Brooksby Gr B93 ... 128 A2
Brooks Croft B35 ... 58 A2
Brookshaw Way CV2 ... 114 F8
Brookside
Birmingham, Great Barr B43 ... 54 D7
Birmingham, Northfield B31 ... 102 F5
Cheswick Green B90 ... 126 D3
Dudley DY3 ... 50 D2
Hinckley LE10 ... 75 E7
Wednesbury WS10 ... 42 B3
Brookside Ave
Birmingham B13 ... 105 B7
Coventry CV5 ... 112 C3
Kenilworth CV8 ... 147 E4
Brookside Cl
Alvechurch B48 ... 139 B6
Birmingham B23 ... 56 C7
Halesowen B63 ... 82 D3
Brookside Dr B61 ... 136 F8
Brookside Ind Est WS10 ... 42 B3
Brookside Rd B78 ... 20 D1
Brookside Way
Blakedown DY10 ... 98 B2
Kingswinford DY6 ... 60 C7
Tamworth B77 ... 36 A6
Brooks Rd B72 ... 57 C8
Brook St
Bedworth CV12 ... 78 B5
Bilston WV14 ... 40 E5
Birmingham B3 ... 164 A3
Brierley Hill DY5 ... 82 A8
Dudley DY3 ... 51 A7
Dudley, Gornalwood DY3 ... 50 C3
Kidderminster DY11 ... 116 C6
Kingswinford DY6 ... 49 B1
Redditch B98 ... 154 A4
Smethwick B66 ... 65 B6
Stourbridge, Amblecote DY8 ... 60 F1
Stourbridge DY8 ... 80 E5
Stourbridge, Lye DY9 ... 81 F5
Tipton DY4 ... 51 E6
Brook St *continued*
Walsall WS2 ... 28 D1
Warwick CV34 ... 160 E6
West Bromwich B70 ... 53 B3
Brookstray Flats CV5 ... 112 B3
Brook Street Bsns Ctr DY4 ... 51 E6
Brook Terr WV14 ... 40 E5
Brookthorpe Dr WV12 ... 27 C4
Brook Vale WS11 ... 4 F8
Brookvale Ave CV3 ... 114 E1
Brookvale Cl B61 ... 137 B4
Brookvale Gr B92 ... 88 D1
Brookvale Mews B29 ... 86 B2
Brookvale Park Rd B23 ... 56 B4
Brookvale Prim Sch B23 ... 56 B3
Brookvale Rd
Birmingham B23, B6 ... 56 A3
Solihull B92 ... 88 D1
Brookvale Trad Est B6 ... 56 A3
Brookview B67 ... 64 F3
Brook View Cl B19 ... 66 C6
Brookweed B77 ... 22 A3
Brookwillow Rd B63 ... 82 E1
Brook Wlk B32 ... 84 D2
Brookwood Ave B28 ... 105 D5
Brookwood Dr B45 ... 138 C8
Broom Cl B60 ... 137 B2
Broom Covert Rd WS14 ... 18 E8
Broom Cres DY10 ... 117 A6
Broomcroft Rd B37 ... 69 F5
Broomdene Ave B34 ... 69 A7
Broom Dr B14 ... 104 E4
Broome Ave B43 ... 54 C7
Broome Cl 5 B63 ... 83 A3
Broome Croft CV6 ... 95 B3
Broome Ct B36 ... 69 C8
Broome Gdns B75 ... 46 C5
Broomehill Cl DY5 ... 81 C7
Broome La DY9 ... 99 B2
Broome Rd WV10 ... 25 E7
Broomfield B67 ... 64 F5
Broomfield Ave B78 ... 35 A8
Broomfield Cl DY11 ... 116 C7
Broomfield Gn DY11 ... 116 C7
Broomfield Pl CV5 ... 113 A2
Broomfield Rd
Birmingham B23 ... 56 D2
Coventry CV5 ... 113 A1
Kidderminster DY11 ... 116 C7
Wednesbury WS10 ... 42 C3
Broomfield Rise CV10 ... 72 F2
Broomfields Ave B91 ... 107 D5
Broomfields Cl B91 ... 107 D5
Broomfields Farm Rd B91 ... 107 D5
Broomhall Ave WV11 ... 26 D6
Broom Hall Cres B27 ... 106 B8
Broom Hall Gr B27 ... 106 C8
Broomhill Bank WS11 ... 1 E3
Broomhill Cl
Birmingham B43 ... 54 D8
Cannock WS11 ... 1 E4
Broomhill La B43 ... 54 D8
Broomhill Rd B23 ... 56 B7
Broom Ho 3 B71 ... 42 F1
Broomhurst B15 ... 85 E8
Broomie Cl B75 ... 46 D4
Broom La B90 ... 126 A6
Broomlea Cl B74 ... 44 E8
Broom Rd Dudley DY1 ... 51 A5
Walsall WS5 ... 43 B3
Broom St B12 ... 87 A8
Broomybank CV8 ... 148 B6
Broomy Cl B34 ... 69 A5
Brosdale Dr LE10 ... 71 A1
Broseley Ave B31 ... 123 B8
Broseley Brook Cl 1 B9 ... 67 C1
Brosil Ave B20 ... 54 E3
Brotherton Ave B97 ... 152 F2
Brougham St B19 ... 66 B7
Brough Cl
Birmingham B7 ... 67 B6
Wolverhampton WV4, WV14 ... 39 F3
Broughton Cres B31 ... 122 D8
Broughton Ct
2 Birmingham, Edgbaston B15 ... 86 B7
Birmingham, Pheasey B43 ... 44 D4
Broughton Ct *continued*
Perton WV6 ... 24 A3
Broughton Rd
Birmingham B20 ... 66 A8
Stourbridge DY9 ... 81 D3
Wolverhampton WV3 ... 24 C1
Browett Rd CV6 ... 113 A5
Brown Ave B77 ... 35 C8
Brownfield Rd B34 ... 69 C7
Brownhills Com Tech Coll WS8 ... 6 F1
Brownhills Rd
Brownhills WS8 ... 16 A4
Norton Canes WS11 ... 6 B4
Brownhills West Prim Sch WS8 ... 6 C2
Brownhills West Sta* WS7 ... 6 C3
Browning Ave CV34 ... 160 C5
Browning Cl
Kidderminster DY10 ... 117 B6
Nuneaton CV10 ... 72 A5
Tamworth B79 ... 20 F8
Willenhall WV12 ... 27 E7
Browning Cres WV10 ... 11 C2
Browning Dr LE10 ... 71 C1
Browning Gr WV6 ... 23 E4
Browning Rd
Burntwood WS7 ... 7 C7
Coventry CV2 ... 114 C3
Dudley DY3 ... 50 A4
Browning St B16 ... 66 B2
Browning Twr B31 ... 103 C3
Brownley Rd B90 ... 126 E7
Brown Lion St DY4 ... 51 E7
Brownlow St 7 CV32 ... 157 A2
Brownmead Jun & Inf Sch B34 ... 69 B7
Brown Rd WS10 ... 41 C7
Brown's Coppice Ave B91 ... 106 E5
Brown's Ct 11 B13 ... 87 B2
Browns Dr B73 ... 56 F8
Brownsea Cl B45 ... 101 F1
Brownsea Dr B1 ... 164 B1
Brownsfield Rd WS13 ... 3 D1
Browns Gn B20 ... 54 F3
Brownshill Bsns Pk WS8 ... 15 F5
Brownshill Ct CV6 ... 112 F8
Brownshill Green Rd CV6 ... 94 E1
Brownshore La WV11 ... 13 A3
Browns La B93 ... 127 E6
Brown's La
Brownshill Green CV5 ... 94 C1
Dordon B78 ... 36 F5
Tamworth B79 ... 21 C8
Brownsover Cl B36 ... 58 B1
Brown St WV2 ... 39 D7
Brownswall Rd DY3 ... 50 C7
Browsholme B79 ... 20 D6
Broxell Cl CV34 ... 155 C1
Broxwood Pk WV6 ... 24 B3
Bruce Rd
Bedworth CV7 ... 95 F7
Coventry CV6 ... 113 B8
Kidderminster DY10 ... 117 B7
Brueton Ave
Bromsgrove B60 ... 151 A8
Solihull B91 ... 107 D3
Brueton Dr
Birmingham B24 ... 57 A3
Redditch B98 ... 154 A3
Brueton Rd WV14 ... 41 A7
Bruford Rd WV3 ... 39 A8
Brunel Cl
Birmingham B12 ... 87 A5
Burntwood WS7 ... 7 B8
Coventry CV2 ... 113 F3
Tamworth B79 ... 21 B6
Whitnash CV31 ... 162 B2
Brunel Ct
Darlaston WS10 ... 41 F6
Tipton WV14 ... 51 E8
Wombourne WV5 ... 49 A7
Brunel Dr DY4 ... 40 E1
Brunel Gr WV6 ... 23 E5
Brunel Rd
Hinckley LE10 ... 75 C8
Oldbury B69 ... 63 D6
Brunel St B1 ... 164 B2
Brunel Way WV2 ... 40 A7
Brunel Wlk WS10 ... 41 F6
Brunslow Cl
Willenhall WV13 ... 27 C1
Wolverhampton WV10 ... 11 C1
Brunswick Arc B1 ... 66 B2
Brunswick Ct
Wednesbury WS10 ... 42 C3
Whitnash CV31 ... 162 A5
Brunswick Gate DY8 ... 81 A1
Brunswick Gdns
Birmingham B21 ... 54 F1
Wednesbury WS10 ... 42 B4
Brunswick Ho
Birmingham, Buckland End B34 ... 69 A7
Birmingham, Marston Green B37 ... 89 F8
Brunswick Park Rd WS10 ... 42 B3
Brunswick Rd
Birmingham, Handsworth B21 ... 54 F1
Birmingham, Sparkbrook B12 ... 87 A5
Cannock WS11 ... 1 E2
Coventry CV1 ... 113 B2
Brunswick St
Birmingham B1 ... 66 B2
Royal Leamington Spa CV31 ... 162 A5
Walsall WS2 ... 42 C7
Brunswick Terr WS10 ... 41 F3
Bruntingthorpe Way CV3 ... 134 E8
Brunton Cl CV3 ... 115 B1
Brunton Rd B10 ... 87 F7
Brushfield Rd B42 ... 55 D8
Brutus Dr B46 ... 59 E1
Bryan Ave WV4 ... 38 D4
Bryan Rd WS2 ... 42 C6
Bryanston Cl CV2 ... 115 A4
Bryanston Ct B91 ... 106 F7
Bryanston Rd B91 ... 106 F6
Bryans Way WS12 ... 2 F4
Bryant Rd CV7 ... 96 A7
Bryant St B18 ... 65 E5
Bryce Rd DY5 ... 61 B5
Bryher Wlk B45 ... 101 E1
Brylan Croft B44 ... 55 F6
Brymill Ind Est DY4 ... 51 E7
Brympton Rd CV3 ... 114 C2
Bryn Arden Rd B26 ... 88 E5
Bryndale Ave B14 ... 104 C4
Bryn Jones Cl CV3 ... 134 F7
Brynmawr Rd WV4, WV14 ... 40 A3
Bryn Rd CV6 ... 113 F7
Brynside Cl B14 ... 104 D2
Bryony B74 ... 31 F5
Bryony Cl CV12 ... 77 E1
Bryony Croft B23 ... 56 B7
Bryony Gdns WS10 ... 41 D7
Bryony Rd B29 ... 103 B7
Bsns Ctr The B11 ... 87 F6
Bubbenhall Rd CV8 ... 133 F1
Buchanan Ave WS4 ... 29 A3
Buchanan Cl WS4 ... 29 A3
Buchanan Rd WS4 ... 29 A3
Buckbury Cl DY9 ... 81 D2
Buckbury Croft B90 ... 127 B6
Buckden B77 ... 22 C1
Buckden Cl 2 CV34 ... 155 F1
Buckfast Cl
Bromsgrove B61 ... 136 D1
Coventry CV3 ... 133 E5
Buckhold Dr CV5 ... 112 B5
Buckingham Cl
Hinckley LE10 ... 71 F4
Nuneaton CV10 ... 73 B1
Wednesbury WS10 ... 42 D4
Buckingham Ct
Birmingham B29 ... 85 D1
Birmingham, Griffin's Hill B29 ... 103 D8
Buckingham Dr WV12 ... 27 B7
Buckingham Gdns WS14 ... 9 B6
Buckingham Gr DY6 ... 60 C7
Buckingham Mews B73 ... 46 A3
Buckingham Pl 3 WS12 ... 2 C1
Buckingham Rd
Birmingham B36 ... 69 F7
Rowley Regis B65 ... 63 D4
Tamworth B79 ... 20 E7
Wolverhampton WV4 ... 39 A5
Buckingham Rise
Coventry CV5 ... 112 B4
Dudley DY1 ... 50 E2
Buckingham St B19 ... 164 B4
Buckland Cl WS12 ... 2 D1
Buckland End B34 ... 69 A6
Buckland Ho 3 B15 ... 86 C7
Buckland Rd CV6 ... 95 B2
Bucklands End La B34 ... 68 F6
Buckle Cl WS1 ... 42 E8
Buckler's Yd 5 CV12 ... 78 A2
Buckley Ct B14 ... 104 F8
Buckley Ho CV5 ... 112 F1
Buckley Rd
Royal Leamington Spa CV32 ... 157 C2
Wolverhampton WV4 ... 38 D5
Buckleys Gn B48 ... 139 A6
Buckleys The B48 ... 139 A6
Bucklow Wlk B33 ... 68 E4
Buckminster Dr B93 ... 127 E4
Bucknall Cres B32 ... 102 A8
Bucknall Ct 15 B13 ... 87 B2
Bucknall Ho B14 ... 104 E6
Bucknall Rd WV11 ... 13 B1
Bucknell Cl B91 ... 107 C5
Buckridge Cl B38 ... 123 D7
Buckridge La B90 ... 126 A5
Bucks Hill CV10 ... 72 C6
Buckthorn Cl WS12 ... 1 F8
Buckton Cl B75 ... 32 E2
Budbrooke Cl CV2 ... 96 D2
Budbrooke Ind Est CV34 ... 160 B7
Budbrooke Rd CV34 ... 160 B7
Budbrook Gr B34 ... 69 E6
Budden Rd WV14 ... 51 D7
Bude Rd WS5 ... 43 D7
Buffery Rd DY2 ... 62 D7
Bufferys Cl B91 ... 127 B8
Building Trade Ctr B92 ... 88 E2
Buildwas Cl WS3 ... 13 F2
Bulford Cl B14 ... 104 F2
Bulger Rd WV14 ... 40 C7
Bulkington La CV11 ... 79 A7
Bulkington Rd
Bedworth CV12 ... 78 D2
Shilton CV7 ... 97 E6
Bullace Croft 4 B15 ... 85 D3
Bulldog La WS13 ... 3 B1
Buller St WV4 ... 39 E6
Bullfield Ave CV4 ... 111 E1
Bullfields Cl B65 ... 62 F5
Bullfinch Ct DY1 ... 61 E8
Bullfurlong La LE10 ... 75 F4
Bullimore Gr CV8 ... 148 A2
Bullivents Cl B93 ... 127 F5
Bull La
Darlaston WV14, WS10 ... 41 B3
West Bromwich B70 ... 53 A3
Wombourne WV5 ... 49 B7
Bullmeadow La WV5 ... 49 A8
Bullmoor La
Muckley Corner WS14 ... 8 A1
Muckley Corner WS14 ... 8 B1
Bullock's Row WS1 ... 28 F1
Bullock St
Birmingham B7 ... 67 A5
4 West Bromwich B70 ... 53 D1
Bullows Rd WS8 ... 15 C6
Bullring B5 ... 164 C2
Bull Ring
4 Halesowen B63 ... 83 B3
Kidderminster DY10 ... 116 E6
Nuneaton CV10 ... 73 B2
Sedgley DY3 ... 50 D8
Willenhall WV13 ... 27 A3
Bull Ring Trad Est 2 B12 ... 66 F1
Bull's Head La CV3 ... 114 B2
Bull's La B76 ... 47 E1
Bull St Birmingham B17 ... 85 D5
Birmingham, Brookfields B4 ... 164 C3
Brierley Hill DY5 ... 61 B1
Darlaston WS10 ... 41 E6
Dudley, Gornalwood DY3 ... 50 C2
Dudley, Springs Mire DY1 ... 62 A8
Nuneaton CV11 ... 73 D2
West Bromwich B70 ... 53 D3
Bull Street Trad Est DY5 ... 61 B2
Bull Yd CV1 ... 165 B2
Bulrush Cl WS8 ... 15 E7
Bulwell Cl B6 ... 67 A7
Bulwer Rd CV6 ... 113 A6
Bulwick Cl CV3 ... 115 B1
Bumble Hole La B61 ... 136 E7
Bunbury Gdns B30 ... 103 D4
Bunbury Rd B30, B31 ... 103 C4
Bundle Hill B63 ... 83 A4
Bungalows The B70 ... 52 F6
Bunker's Hill La WV14 ... 40 E7

Bunneys Mdw LE10... 74 E6
Bunn's La DY2 ....51 F1
Buntsford Dr B60 ... 150 F6
Buntsford Gate Bsns Pk
B60................. 150 F6
Buntsford Hill B60 .. 150 F5
Buntsford Park Rd
B60 .... 150 F6
Bunyan Pl WS11.........1 E4
Burbage CE Inf Sch
LE10 .... 76 A5
Burbage Cl WV10 .... 25 E6
Burbage Jun Sch
LE10 ....75 F6
Burbage Rd LE10 .... 76 A7
Burbages La CV6..... 95 D4
Burberry Ct 3 DY4... 52 A8
Burberry Gr CV7 .. 130 A6
Burbidge Rd B9..... 67 E3
Burbury Cl
Bedworth CV12..... 78 C4
Royal Leamington Spa
CV32.............157 C2
Burbury Ct CV34 .... 161 B8
Burbury St S B19... 66 C6
Burbury St B19 ..... 66 C7
Burcher Gn DY10.. 117 B5
Burcombe Twr B23.. 57 B6
Burcot Ave
Bromsgrove B60..... 137 B4
Wolverhampton WV1 .. 26 A2
Burcot Ct 14 B74....31 F2
Burcot Ho B60 ..... 137 B3
Burcot La
Bromsgrove, Burcot
B60 ....137 B3
Bromsgrove, Stoney Hill
B60 ....137 C4
Burdock Cl
Cannock WS11 ....2 B3
Walsall WS5 .... 43 A3
Burdock Ho B38 ... 103 F1
Burdock Rd B29..... 103 A6
Burdons Cl B34 ..... 69 A5
Bure Gr WV13 ...... 27 D1
Burfield Rd B62 .... 83 C6
Burford Cl Solihull B92 89 A6
Walsall WS5 .... 43 A4
Burford Ct
18 Birmingham B13 ... 87 B2
Stourbridge DY8 ... 81 A4
Burford Mews 13
CV31 ....162 C6
Burford Park Rd
B38................ 123 E8
Burford Rd
Birmingham B44...... 55 F7
Hollywood B47 ... 125 A6
Burgage Pl CV11 ... 73 C4
Burgage Wlk CV11 ... 73 C4
Burges CV1 .... 165 B3
Burges Gr CV34 ... 155 F1
Burgess Croft B92... 107 F7
Burghley Cl CV11....73 F2
Burghley Dr
Kidderminster DY11 ..116 C5
West Bromwich B71... 42 F2
Burghley Wlk DY5... 81 B8
Burgh Way WS2..... 28 A4
Burhill Way B37..... 70 B5
Burke Ave B13 ..... 87 D1
Burland Ave WV6.... 24 E6
Burleigh Cl
Balsall Common CV7.. 130 B7
Cannock WS12 ....2 A8
Willenhall WV12 .... 27 B6
Burleigh Croft WS7....7 A4
Burleigh Rd
Hinckley LE10 .... 71 C2
Wolverhampton WV3 .. 39 A8
Burleigh St WS1 ... 29 A1
Burleton Rd B33 ... 69 E2
Burley Cl B90 ..... 105 F2
Burley Way B38 .... 123 C8
Burlington Arc 5
B2 ....164 B2
Burlington Ave B70.. 53 E1
Burlington Cl DY10.. 117 B4
Burlington Ct B78... 35 B8
Burlington Rd
Birmingham B10...... 67 F1
Coventry CV2 ..... 113 F4
Nuneaton CV10..... 78 B7
West Bromwich B70... 53 E1
Burlington St B6.... 66 E6
Burlish Ave 1 B92...88 F1

Burman Dr B46.......70 F5
Burman Inf Sch B90 106 A2
Burman Rd B90 .... 106 A1
Burmarsh Wlk WV8 ..24 F8
Burmese Way B65....62 F6
Burnaby Cl CV10 ... 72 B5
Burnaby Rd CV6..... 95 B1
Burnaston Cres B90. 127 C6
Burnaston Rd B28... 87 E1
Burnbank Gr B24.... 57 B4
Burn Cl B66......... 65 A4
Burncross Way WV10..25 F6
Burnell Gdns WV3.... 38 E8
Burnel Rd B29 ..... 85 B2
Burnet Gr WV10..... 12 B8
Burnett Ho 12 B69... 63 D5
Burnett Rd B74 .... 31 B2
Burney La B8 ...... 68 C4
Burnfields Way WS9.. 30 A7
Burnham Ave
Birmingham B25...... 88 C6
Wolverhampton WV10 .. 25 C8
Burnham Cl DY6 .....60 F4
Burnham Ct
Birmingham B23...... 56 C2
18 Brierley Hill DY5 .. 61 D2
Burnham Gn WS11.....4 B8
Burnham Mdw B28.. 106 A6
Burnham Rd
Birmingham B44..... 55 E7
Coventry CV3 ..... 134 A6
Burnham Rise CV11.. 74 A6
Burnhill Gr B29 .... 103 A8
Burnlea Gr B31..... 103 C1
Burnsall Cl
Birmingham B37...... 69 F2
Wolverhampton WV9 .. 11 A3
Burnsall Gr CV5.... 132 D8
Burnsall Rd CV5.... 132 D8
Burns Ave Tipton DY4.. 52 A7
Warwick CV34 ..... 160 C5
Wolverhampton WV10 .. 11 D2
Burns Cl
Kidderminster DY10 ..117 B6
Lichfield WS14 ....9 B6
Redditch B97 ..... 158 C8
Stourbridge DY8 ... 81 A8
Burns Dr WS7 ....7 C7
Burns Gr DY3 ...... 50 A4
Burnside CV3 ...... 115 A2
Burnside Ct B73 .... 46 A1
Burnside Gdns WS5.. 43 D6
Burnside Way B31... 122 F7
Burns Pl WS10 ...... 41 A5
Burns Rd
Coventry CV2 ..... 114 A4
Darlaston WS10 ..... 41 B5
Royal Leamington Spa
CV32..............157 B4
Tamworth B79....... 21 A6
Burns St WS11 ....2 A5
Burnsway LE10..... 71 C1
Burns Wlk CV12..... 78 C1
Burnthurst Cres B90 127 A7
Burnt Meadow Rd
B98 .... 154 F6
Burnt Oak Dr DY8... 81 B5
Burnt Tree DY4......51 F2
Burnt Tree Ind Est
B69................52 B2
Burnt Tree Island DY1,
DY4 ....51 F2
Burnt Tree Jun & Inf Sch
B69............... 52 A2
Burntwood Bsns Pk
WS7..................6 D7
Burntwood Rd
Hammerwich WS7 ..... 7 D4
Norton Canes WS11.....6 A7
Burntwood Town Sh Ctr
WS7..................6 F7
Burrelton Way 1
B43 .... 54 D8
Burrington Rd B32.. 102 A8
Burrowes St WS2... 28 D3
Burrow Hill Cl B36.. 69 C8
Burrow Hill La CV7.. 94 D7
Burrows Cl CV31.... 162 B3
Burrows Croft WV14.. 40 C6
Burrows Ho 7 WS2.. 28 D3
Burrows Rd DY6.....60 F4
Burrs Dr WS10 ..... 42 A1
Burslem Wlk WV1 .. 40 B8
Burslem Cl WS3.... 14 A3
Burton Ave WS4... 29 B8
Burton Cl
Brownshill Green CV5 .. 94 C3
Tamworth B79....... 21 C7
Burton Cres WV10... 163 D4

Burton Farm Rd WS4. 29 B3
Burton Gr B64 ..... 82 E8
Burton Green CE Prim
Sch CV8 .... 131 B3
Burton La
Bramcote CV11..... 79 F7
Redditch B98 ..... 153 F3
Burton Old Rd
Lichfield WS13 ....3 F1
Lichfield WS14 ....9 F8
Burton Old Rd E WS14..9 E8
Burton Old Rd W WS14 9 D8
Burton Rd Dudley DY1..50 F4
Lichfield WS13 ....3 F1
Wolverhampton WV10 .. 25 E3
Burton Wood Dr B20. 55 D2
Burwaye Cl WS13 .....9 A8
Buryfield Rd B91.... 107 B6
Bury Hill Rd B69.... 63 D8
Bury Ho CV4 .... 111 F3
Bury Mound Ct B90. 105 C2
Busby Cl CV3 ..... 134 F7
Bush Ave B66...... 65 C5
Bushbery Ave CV4... 111 F2
Bushbury Croft B37.. 70 C3
Bushbury Hill Prim Sch
WV10...............11 F1
Bushbury La
Wolverhampton, Bushbury
WV10 .... 11 E2
Wolverhampton, Elston Hall
WV10 .... 25 D7
Bushbury Rd
Birmingham B33...... 69 A5
Wolverhampton WV10 .. 26 A5
Bush Cl CV4 .... 111 F3
Bush Ct CV2 .... 114 B6
Bushell Dr B91..... 107 D4
Bushelton Cl CV1 ... 165 C1
Bushey Cl B74......30 F2
Bushey Fields Hospl
DY5................61 E8
Bushey Fields Rd DY1 61 E7
Bushfield Ct WV14 ...40 F5
Bush Gr
Birmingham B21..... 54 C1
Walsall WS3 ...... 15 A2
Bushley Cl B98..... 159 A7
Bushley Croft B91... 127 B8
Bushman Way B34 ... 69 E5
Bushmore Rd B28... 106 A7
Bush Rd Dudley DY2.. 62 C2
Tipton DY4 .... 51 E4
Bush St WS10 ...... 41 D7
Bushway Cl DY5..... 61 B2
Bushwood Ct B15... 86 C8
Bushwood Dr B93... 128 B3
Bushwood Rd B29... 85 B1
Bushy End CV34.... 161 E1
Busill Jones Prim Sch
WS3................27 F8
Bustleholme Ave B71..42 F1
Bustleholme Cres
B71 .... 42 E1
Bustleholme La B71.. 42 E1
Butchers La B63 ... 82 C7
Butcher's La CV5... 112 C6
Butchers Rd B92... 109 A6
Butcroft Gdns WS10. 41 E6
Bute Cl
Birmingham B45.... 101 E1
Hinckley LE10 ..... 71 C1
Willenhall WV12 ... 27 B6
Butler Cl CV8 ..... 148 C7
Butler Rd B92.......88 F3
Butlers Cl
Birmingham, Handsworth
B20................ 55 A3
Birmingham, Perry Common
B73.............. 45 D1
Butlers Cres CV7... 78 A1
Butlers End CV35... 146 C2
Butler's High La B97. 153 B5
Butlers La B74...... 32 A3
Butlers Lane Sta B74 32 A3
Butlers Prec 3 WS1. 28 E2
Butler's Rd B20..... 55 A3
Butler's St
Astwood Bank B96... 158 E1
West Bromwich B70.. 53 A4
Butlin St B7....... 67 C7
Buttercup Cl
Kidderminster DY10 .116 E8
6 Walsall WS5 ..... 43 A3
Buttercup Dr B60... 150 F5
Buttercup Way CV12..77 D2
Butterfield Cl WV6.. 23 D3

Butterfield Ct DY1... 51 A2
Butterfield Rd DY5... 61 B7
Butterfly Way 4 B64..62 F1
Buttermere B77...... 36 E3
Buttermere Ave CV11. 74 A6
Buttermere Cl
Brierley Hill DY5 .... 81 B7
Cannock WS11 ....2 A3
Coventry CV3 ..... 134 F7
Wolverhampton WV6 .. 24 D8
Buttermere Ct WV6 ..23 F4
Buttermere Dr
Birmingham B32..... 84 F3
Essington WV11 .... 13 A2
Buttermere Gr WV11. 13 B1
Butterworth Cl WV14. 40 A1
Butterworth Dr CV4. 132 A6
Buttery Rd B67..... 64 E6
Butt La Allesley CV5.. 112 B7
Hinckley LE10 ...... 71 F1
Butt Lane Cl LE10 ... 71 E1
Buttons Farm Rd
WV4................ 38 D3
Buttress Way B66... 65 A6
Butts Cl WS11 ....5 E4
Butts La
Norton Canes WS11.....5 E4
Stone DY10........ 117 D1
Tanworth-In-A B94 .. 142 B2
Butts Prim Sch WS4 ..28 F3
Butts Rd
Coventry CV1 ..... 113 B2
Walsall WS4 ...... 28 F3
Wolverhampton WV4 .. 38 F4
Butts St WS4........28 F3
Butts The
Lichfield WS14 ...... 8 D2
Walsall WS4 ...... 28 F3
Warwick CV34 ..... 160 E7
Butts Way WS11 .....5 E4
Buxton Ave B78.... 35 B8
Buxton Cl WS3..... 14 C3
Buxton Rd
Birmingham B23..... 56 B7
Dudley DY2........ 62 A6
Sutton Coldfield B73.. 57 A8
Walsall WS3 ...... 14 C3
Byfield Cl B33...... 69 E1
Byfield Pl CV7...... 130 D5
Byfield Rd CV6..... 112 E5
Byfleet Cl WV14 .... 40 A3
Byford Cl B98...... 153 E2
Byford Ct CV10......72 F4
Byford St B10.......72 F4
Byford Way B37..... 90 B8
Byland B77 .... 21 D3
Bylands Cl B61..... 136 E1
Byland Way WS3 ....13 F2
Bypass Link B91.... 107 F3
Byrchen Moor Gdns
DY5................ 61 B7
Byrne Rd WV2...... 39 D7
Byron Ave
Bedworth CV12..... 78 D2
Birmingham B23..... 56 B3
Lichfield WS14 ....9 B5
Warwick CV34 ..... 160 C4
Byron Cl
Birmingham B10..... 87 D7
Kidderminster DY10 ..117 B5
Byron Cres DY1.... 51 B6
Byron Croft
Dudley DY3 .... 50 A5
Sutton Coldfield B74.. 31 F6
Byron Ct
Dorridge B93 ..... 128 A6
Sutton Coldfield B74... 32 A5
Byron Gdns B71.... 53 B5
Byron Pl WS11 ......1 F5
Byron Rd
Birmingham B10..... 87 D7
Redditch B97 ..... 158 D8
Tamworth B79...... 21 A7
Willenhall WV12 .... 27 E7
Wolverhampton WV10 . 12 A1
Byron St
Brierley Hill DY5 .... 61 D7
Coventry CV1 ..... 165 C4
West Bromwich B71.. 53 B5
Byron Way B61..... 137 A8
Bywater Cl CV3.... 133 B5
Bywater Ho 5 WS1..28 F1
Byways WS3 ...... 14 C3

C

Caban Cl B31 ..... 102 E5

Cable Dr WS2...... 28 C5
Cable St WV2 ......39 F8
Cabot Gr WV6...... 23 E4
Cadbury Dr B35.... 58 A2
Cadbury Ho B19.... 66 D5
Cadbury Rd B13.... 87 B4
Cadbury Sixth Form Coll
B38............... 103 F1
Cadbury Way B17... 85 B5
Cadbury World*
B30............... 103 F7
Cadden Dr CV4.... 112 B2
Caddick Cres B71... 53 D7
Caddick Rd B42.... 44 B1
Caddick St WV14... 51 A8
Cadeby Cl LE10 ... 71 B3
Cadell Ct B13 ..... 87 A1
Cadet Dr B90 ..... 106 A3
Cadgwith Gdns WV14. 41 A2
Cadine Gdns B13... 86 C1
Cadleigh Gdns B17.. 85 C3
Cadle Rd WV10..... 25 E7
Cadman Cl CV12.... 78 C3
Cadman Cres WV10.. 26 A7
Cadman's La WS6,
WS3 .... 14 D6
Cadnam Cl
Birmingham B17..... 85 C3
Darlaston WV13 .... 41 B8
Cadogan Rd B77.... 35 D5
Caen Cl CV35..... 160 A7
Caernarfon Dr CV11.. 73 D3
Caernarvon Cl WV12. 27 C7
Caernarvon Way DY1. 50 F2
Caesar Rd CV8..... 147 E3
Caesar Way B46.... 59 E1
Cairndhu Dr DY10... 117 B7
Cairn Dr WS2.......27 F2
Cairns St WS2..... 28 C3
Caister B77....... 22 A6
Caister Dr WV13.....40 F8
Caistor Cl B78 .... 34 B8
Caithness Cl CV5... 112 A4
Cakemore Rd B65... 63 E2
Cala Dr B15....... 86 B7
Calcot Dr WV6..... 24 E7
Calcott Ho CV3.... 134 B5
Calcutt Way B90... 126 A6
Caldecote Cl CV10.. 73 C8
Caldecote Gr B9 ... 68 C1
Caldecote Rd CV6... 113 C5
Caldeford Ave B90.. 127 A7
Calder B77........ 22 B2
Calder Ave WS1.... 29 A2
Calder Cl
Bulkington CV12.... 79 B2
Coventry CV3 ..... 133 E7
Calder Dr B76...... 58 A7
Calder Gr B20...... 54 F2
Calder Rise DY3.....50 F6
Calder Twr 2 B20... 55 D1
Calder Wlk CV31... 162 C6
Caldmore Com Prim Sch
WS1...............42 E8
Caldmore Gn WS1... 42 E8
Caldmore Rd WS1... 42 E8
Caldon Cl LE10 .... 75 B8
Caldwall Cres DY11.. 116 D5
Caldwell Ct
Nuneaton CV11..... 73 D1
Solihull B91....... 107 C5
Caldwell Gr B91.... 107 C5
Caldwell Rd
Birmingham B9...... 68 B3
Nuneaton CV11..... 73 D1
Caldwell St B71.... 53 D8
Caldy Wlk 5 B45... 101 F1
Cale Cl B77....... 21 C2
Caledonian DY5.....81 D7
Caledonian Cl WS5.. 43 C3
Caledonia B77......21 F2
Caledonia Rd WV2.. 163 C4
Caledonia St WV14.. 40 E6
Caledon Pl WS2.... 42 C7
Caledon St 5 WS2.. 42 C7
Calewood Rd DY5... 81 D7
Calgary Cl CV3..... 115 A2
Caliban Mews CV34. 161 E3
California Ho B32... 84 E2
California Rd B69... 63 B8
California Way B32..84 F3
Callaghan Gr 3 WS11..2 C2
Callcott Dr DY5.... 81 D7
Callear Rd WS10... 41 D1
Callendar Cl CV11... 74 A7
Calley Cl DY4...... 52 A1
Callis Wlk 2 B77...35 F6

Callowbridge Rd
B45............... 121 F7
Callowbrook La B45.. 121 F7
Callow Hill La B97.. 158 B6
Callow Hill Rd B48.. 139 A6
Callows La 2 DY10.. 116 E6
Calmere Cl CV2.... 114 F8
Calpurnia Ave CV34. 161 E2
Calshot Prim Sch B42 55 B8
Calshot Rd B42..... 55 A8
Calstock Rd WV12... 27 D4
Calthorpe Cl WS5... 43 E6
Calthorpe Mans 4
B15............... 66 B1
Calthorpe Rd
Birmingham, Edgbaston
B15.............. 86 B8
Birmingham, Handsworth
Wood B20....... 55 C2
Walsall WS5 ...... 43 D6
Calthorpe Sch Sports
Coll B12 .... 87 A8
Caludon Castle Sch
CV2............. 114 E4
Caludon Lodge CV2. 114 E5
Caludon Park Ave
CV2.............. 114 E5
Caludon Rd CV2.... 114 A4
Calver Cres WV11.... 26 F5
Calver Gr B44...... 44 D3
Calverley Rd B38... 123 D8
Calvert Cl CV3..... 133 D6
Calverton Gr B43... 54 E8
Calves Croft WV13... 27 A3
Calvin Cl WV10..... 11 D3
Calving Hill WS11 ....1 E2
Camberley 6 B71...42 F1
Camberley Cres WV4. 39 E2
Camberley Dr WV4... 39 E2
Camberley Gr B23... 56 E6
Camberley Rd DY6... 61 A4
Camberwell Terr
CV31............. 162 A7
Camborne Cl B6.... 66 E7
Camborne Dr CV11...73 F5
Camborne Rd WS5... 43 D7
Cambourne Ct 4
WS5.............. 43 D7
Cambourne Rd
Hinckley LE10 ..... 76 A6
Rowley Regis B65... 63 C3
Cambrai Dr B28.... 105 F8
Cambria Cl B90.... 125 E7
Cambrian B77...... 22 A2
Cambria St WS11....1 D4
Cambridge Ave
Solihull B91....... 106 F3
Sutton Coldfield B73... 57 B8
Cambridge Cl WS9.. 30 B8
Cambridge Cres B15. 86 D7
Cambridge Dr
Birmingham B37..... 69 F1
Nuneaton CV10..... 72 E3
Cambridge Gdns
CV32............. 157 A1
Cambridge Rd
Birmingham B13..... 86 D7
Dudley DY2........ 62 A7
Smethwick B66..... 65 A7
Cambridge St
Birmingham B1..... 164 A2
Coventry CV1 ..... 113 E5
Walsall WS1 ...... 42 E1
West Bromwich B70.. 53 B2
Wolverhampton
WV10........... 163 C4
Cambridge Twr B1.. 164 A2
Cambridge Way B27.. 88 D4
Camden Cl
Birmingham B36..... 69 A8
Walsall WS5 ...... 43 A4
Camden Dr
Birmingham B1..... 66 C3
Tamworth B77...... 21 E3
Camden St
Birmingham B18, B1... 66 B4
Brownhills WS9 .... 15 F4
Coventry CV2 ..... 114 A4
Walsall WS1 ...... 42 E1
Camden Way DY6... 49 D1
Camel Cotts DY9.... 99 C2
Camellia Gdns
Stourbridge DY8.... 60 E2
Wolverhampton WV9 .. 10 F3
Camellia Rd 1 CV2.. 96 B2
Camelot Cl WS11.....1 F1
Camelot Gr CV8.... 148 C5
Camelot Way B10... 87 C8

Cameo Dr DY8 . . . . . . .80 F8
Cameron Cl
  Allesley CV5 . . . . 112 A7
  Royal Leamington Spa
  CV32 . . . . 157 A4
Cameron Rd WS4 . . . . . 29 B3
Camford Gr B14 . . . . 104 F3
Cam Gdns DY5 . . . . . . 61 B6
Cam Ho **7** DY1 . . . . . 61 E8
Camhouses B77 . . . . . 22 B1
Camino Rd B32 . . . . . .84 F3
Camomile Cl **5** WS5 . 43 A3
Campbell Cl
  Nuneaton CV10 . . . . . . 72 A4
  Tamworth B79 . . . . 20 F8
  Walsall WS4 . . . . 29 A3
Campbells Gn B26 . . . 89 B4
Campbell St DY5 . . . . 61 C4
Campden Cl B97 . . . . 158 D6
Campden Gn B92 . . . . 89 A3
Camp Hill
  Birmingham B12 . . . . . . 87 A8
  Stourbridge DY8 . . . . . 60 E1
Camp Hill Cir B12 . . . 87 A8
Camp Hill Dr CV10 . . 72 D7
Camp Hill Ind Est B12 87 A7
Camphill La WS10 . . . .41 F2
Camp Hill Middleway
  B12 . . . . 87 A7
Camp Hill Prim Sch
  CV10 . . . . .72 E6
Camp Hill Rd CV10 . . 72 C7
Campian's Ave WS6 . . 4 D2
Campion B74 . . . . .31 F5
Campion Cl
  3 Birmingham B38 . . 123 F8
  Coventry CV3 . . . . 133 D6
  Walsall WS5 . . . . 43 A3
Campion Ct **2** DY4 . . 51 E5
Campion Dr
  Featherstone WV10 . . . 12 A1
  Tamworth B77 . . . . 21 C3
Campion Gn CV32 . . . 157 A2
Campion Gr B63 . . . . 82 D3
Campion Ho
  2 Birmingham B38 . . 123 E8
  Wolverhampton WV10 . 25 F4
Campion Rd CV32 . . . 157 A2
Campion Sch & Com Coll
  CV31 . . . . 162 C5
Campion Terr CV32 . . 157 A1
Campion Way
  3 Bedworth CV12 . . . 77 D2
  Solihull B90 . . . . 126 A5
Camp La
  Birmingham, Handsworth
  B21 . . . . 54 C2
  Birmingham, King's Norton
  B38 . . . . 103 F3
Camplea Croft B37 . . 70 A2
Camplin Cres B20 . . . 54 E5
Campling Cl CV12 . . . 79 B2
Camp Rd B75 . . . . 32 D6
Campriano Dr CV34 . 161 A8
Camp St
  Birmingham B9 . . . . . . 67 C1
  Wednesbury WS10 . . . . 41 F2
  Wolverhampton WV1 . 163 B4
Campton Cl LE10 . . . . 75 E7
Campville Cres B71 . . 42 E1
Campville Gr B37 . . . .69 F5
Camp Wood Cl B30 . . 103 F8
Camrose Croft
  Birmingham, Balsall Heath
  B12 . . . . 86 F5
  Birmingham, Castle
  Bromwich B34 . . . . . . 69 B6
Camrose Gdns WV9 . . 11 A3
Camrose Twr B7 . . . . 67 B6
Camsey La WS7 . . . . . . .7 E8
Camville CV3 . . . . . . 115 A2
Canal La B24 . . . . 57 A1
Canal Rd CV6 . . . . . . 113 F8
Canalside
  Bedworth CV6 . . . . 96 B6
  Kingswood B94 . . . . . 144 D3
Canal Side Dudley DY2 62 E4
  Hopwood B48 . . . . . . 123 B2
Canalside Cl
  Walsall WS3 . . . . 14 F1
  Wednesbury WS10 . . . . 42 E2
Canal Side Ind Est
  DY5 . . . . 61 C1
Canal St
  Brierley Hill DY5 . . . . . 61 E5
  Dudley DY1 . . . . 51 D4
  Oldbury B69 . . . . 64 A7
  Stourbridge DY8 . . . . . 80 F6
Canal St continued
  Tipton WV14 . . . . 51 C8
Canal View Ind Est
  DY5 . . . . .61 B1
Canal Way LE10 . . . . .74 F7
Canary Gr B19 . . . . . . 66 C8
Canberra Ct **2** CV12 . .77 F2
Canberra Ho B34 . . . . 69 E6
Canberra Rd
  Coventry CV2 . . . . 96 C4
  Walsall WS5 . . . . 43 C6
Canberra Way
  4 Birmingham B12 . . 86 F8
  Hinckley LE10 . . . . 75 E4
Canford Cl
  Birmingham B12 . . . . . 86 F7
  Coventry CV3 . . . . 133 C3
Canley Ford CV4,
  CV5 . . . . 132 E7
Canley Rd CV5 . . . . . 132 D8
Canley Sta CV5 . . . . . 112 D1
Cannel Rd WS7 . . . . . . 6 D1
Cannes Ct CV4 . . . . . 132 D6
Canning Cl WS5 . . . . . 43 D6
Canning Gdns B18 . . . 65 E4
Canning Rd
  Tamworth B77 . . . . 21 F4
  Walsall WS5 . . . . 43 D6
Canning St LE10 . . . . 71 C1
Cannock Chase High Sch
  WS11 . . . . 1 E2
Cannock Chase Tech
  Coll
  Cannock, Blackfords
  WS11 . . . . 1 D1
  Cannock, Bridgtown
  WS11 . . . . .4 E7
Cannock Com Hospl
  WS11 . . . . .1 C2
Cannock Ind Ctr WS11 .4 D5
Cannock Motor Village
  WS11 . . . . .2 B3
Cannock Rd
  Burntwood, Chase Terrace
  WS7 . . . . 6 D7
  Burntwood, Gorstey Ley
  WS7 . . . . .7 B7
  Cannock, Heath Hayes
  WS12 . . . . .5 C8
  Cannock WS12, WS11 . .2 A5
  Featherstone WV10 . . . 12 C7
  Willenhall WV12 . . . . . 27 C7
Cannocks La CV4 . . . 132 D6
Cannock Sta WS11 . . . 4 F8
Cannon Cl CV4 . . . . . 132 F6
Cannon Dr WV14 . . . . 40 D2
Cannon Hill Gr **2**
  B12 . . . . 86 E5
Cannon Hill Pl **1** B12 86 E5
Cannon Hill Rd
  Birmingham B12 . . . . . 86 E5
  Coventry CV4 . . . . 132 D5
Cannon Park District Ctr
  CV4 . . . . 132 C6
Cannon Park Prim Sch
  CV4 . . . . 132 D5
Cannon Park Rd CV4 132 C6
Cannon Rd WV5 . . . . 49 A7
Cannon St N WS2 . . . 28 E4
Cannon St
  Birmingham B2 . . . . . 164 C2
  Walsall WS2 . . . . 28 E4
  Willenhall WV13 . . . . . 27 B2
Canon Bsns Pk WV14 . 40 C1
Canon Dr CV7 . . . . . . 95 D6
Canon Evans CE Inf Sch
  CV12 . . . . 78 A2
Canon Hudson Cl
  CV4 . . . . 134 C6
Canon Maggs CE Jun Sch
  CV12 . . . . .78 B2
Canon Young Rd
  CV31 . . . . 162 B3
Canterbury Ave WV13 27 D2
Canterbury Cl
  Birmingham B23 . . . . . 56 D2
  Kenilworth CV8 . . . . . 148 C3
  Lichfield WS13 . . . . . . .3 C3
  9 Rowley Regis B65 . 63 E4
  Studley B80 . . . . 159 C4
  Tamworth B77 . . . . 21 D3
  Walsall WS3 . . . . 15 A4
  West Bromwich B71 . . . 53 E8
Canterbury Cross Prim
  Sch B20 . . . . 55 D1
Canterbury Dr
  Birmingham B37 . . . . . 90 A7
  Burntwood WS7 . . . . . . .7 E7
Canterbury Dr continued
  Perton WV6 . . . . 23 E4
Canterbury Rd
  Birmingham B20 . . . . . 55 D1
  Kidderminster DY11 . . 116 A6
  West Bromwich B71 . . . 53 D8
  Wolverhampton WV4 . . 38 E5
Canterbury St CV1 . . 165 D3
Canterbury Twr **1** B1 66 B3
Canterbury Way
  Cannock WS12 . . . . . . .2 B1
  Nuneaton CV11 . . . . . . 74 A8
Cantlow Cl CV5 . . . . . 112 A3
Cantlow Ho **2** B12 . .86 F7
Cantlow Rd B13 . . . . 105 A6
Canton Ho LE10 . . . . . 71 C4
Canute Cl WS1 . . . . . .42 F7
Canvey Cl B45 . . . . . 101 E1
Canwell Ave B37 . . . .69 F5
Canwell Dr B75 . . . . . 33 B5
Canwell Gate B75 . . . 32 E4
Canwell Gdns WV14 . . 40 C4
Capcroft Rd B13 . . . . 105 B6
Cape Cl WS8 . . . . 16 A6
Cape Hill B66 . . . . . . 65 C4
Cape Hill Ret Ctr B66 65 C4
Cape Ind Est CV34 . . 160 E7
Capener Rd B43 . . . . . 44 A2
Cape Prim Sch B66 . . 65 C4
Cape Rd CV34 . . . . . 160 D8
Capern Gr B32 . . . . . .84 F5
Cape St
  Birmingham B18 . . . . . 65 D4
  West Bromwich B70 . . . 52 E4
Capethorn Rd B66 . . . 65 A3
Capilano Rd B23 . . . . 56 C7
Capmartin Rd CV6 . . 113 C7
Cappers La WS13, WS14 . .9 F8
Capponfield Cl WV14 . 40 B3
Capstone Ave
  Birmingham B18 . . . . . 66 A4
  Wolverhampton WV10 . 25 C8
Captain's Cl WV3 . . . . 24 D2
Captains Pool Rd
  DY10 . . . . 117 A1
Captain's Pool Rd
  DY10 . . . . 117 B2
Capulet Cl CV3 . . . . . 134 C6
Capulet Dr CV34 . . . 161 E3
Caradoc B77 . . . . 22 A2
Caradoc Cl CV2 . . . . 114 D7
Caradoc Hall CV2 . . . 114 D7
Carcroft Rd B25 . . . . 88 D8
Cardale Croft **1**
  CV3 . . . . 134 F8
Cardale St B65 . . . . . 63 D1
Carden Cl B70 . . . . . .52 F4
Carder Cres WV14 . . . 40 D4
Carder Dr DY5 . . . . . . 61 C2
Cardiff Cl CV3 . . . . . 134 D5
Cardiff St WV3 . . . . . 39 B8
Cardigan Cl B71 . . . . 53 C7
Cardigan Dr WV12 . . . 27 B6
Cardigan Ho WS12 . . . .2 C5
Cardigan Pl WS12 . . . .2 C5
Cardigan Rd CV12 . . . 77 C1
Cardigan St B4 . . . . . .66 F3
Cardinal Cres B61 . . 136 D1
Cardinal Dr DY10 . . . 117 B3
Cardinal Griffin RC High
  Sch WS11 . . . . .1 D1
Cardinal Newman RC Sch
  B17 . . . . 65 A2
Cardinal Newman RC Sch
  & Com Coll CV6 . . . . .94 F2
Cardinal Way WS11 . . . 1 D2
Cardinal Wiseman RC
  Sch CV2 . . . . .96 E1
Cardinal Wiseman Tech
  Coll B44 . . . . .44 F2
Carding Cl CV5 . . . . . 111 F4
Cardington Ave B42 . . 44 B1
Cardington Cl B98 . . 154 F3
Cardoness Pl DY1 . . . .50 F2
Cardy Cl B97 . . . . . . 153 B4
Careless Gn DY9 . . . . .81 F4
Carey B77 . . . . 36 A5
Carey St CV6 . . . . . . 114 B8
Carfax WS11 . . . . .4 E8
Cargill Cl CV6 . . . . . .95 F5
Carhampton Rd B75 . . 47 A5
Carillon Gdns B65 . . . 63 C3
Carisbrooke B77 . . . . 22 A2
Carisbrooke Ave B37 . 70 C2
Carisbrooke Cl WS10 . 42 E2
Carisbrooke Cres
  WS10 . . . . 42 E3
Carisbrooke Dr B62 . . 83 D3
Carisbrooke Gdns
  WV10 . . . . 11 E3
Carisbrooke Rd
  Birmingham B17 . . . . . 65 B1
  Perton WV6 . . . . 24 A3
  Wednesbury WS10 . . . . 42 E2
  Wolverhampton WV11 . 11 E3
Carisbrook Rd CV10 . . 73 D6
Carlcroft B77 . . . . 22 B2
Carless Ave B17 . . . . 85 B7
Carless St WS1 . . . . . 28 D5
Carl Eynon Ct **2** WS3 28 B8
Carlisle Rd WS11 . . . . .4 B7
Carlisle St B18 . . . . . .65 F5
Carlson Pk **2** B17 . . 85 B5
Carl St WS2 . . . . 28 D5
Carlton Ave
  Bilston WV14 . . . . 40 F7
  Birmingham B21 . . . . . 54 E1
  Stourbridge DY9 . . . . . 81 E3
  Sutton Coldfield B74 . . 31 A2
  Wolverhampton WV11 . 26 A7
Carlton Cl
  Bulkington CV12 . . . . . 79 B3
  Cannock WS12 . . . . 2 D1
  Dudley DY1 . . . . 51 C6
  Kidderminster DY11 . . 116 A8
  Redditch B97 . . . . 153 B1
  Sutton Coldfield B75 . . 46 E7
Carlton Cres
  Burntwood WS7 . . . . . . .7 A8
  Tamworth B79 . . . . 20 F8
Carlton Croft B74 . . . 31 A2
Carlton Ct CV5 . . . . . 112 F2
Carlton Gdns CV5 . . . 133 A8
Carlton Ho
  8 Royal Leamington Spa
  CV32 . . . . 161 F8
  Sutton Coldfield B75 . . 32 B2
Carlton Mews B36 . . . 69 D7
Carlton Mews Flats
  B36 . . . . 69 D7
Carlton Rd
  Birmingham B9 . . . . . . 67 D1
  Coventry CV6 . . . . 95 F1
  Smethwick B66 . . . . . . 65 B8
  Wolverhampton WV3 . . 39 A7
Carlyle Ave DY10 . . . 117 B6
Carlyle Bsns Pk B70 . .52 F5
Carlyle Gr WV10 . . . . 26 A8
Carlyle Rd
  Birmingham, Edgbaston
  B16 . . . . 65 E1
  Birmingham, Lozells
  B19 . . . . 66 C8
  Bromsgrove B60 . . . . . 151 B8
  Rowley Regis B65 . . . . 63 C2
  Wolverhampton WV10 . 26 A8
Carmel Cl WS12 . . . . .2 C5
Carmel Gr B32 . . . . . 84 B1
Carmelite Rd CV1 . . . 113 E2
Carmichael Cl WS14 . . 9 D7
Carmodale Ave B42 . . 55 B5
Carnation Way CV10 . 78 A8
Carnbroe Ave CV3 . . 134 F7
Carnegie Ave DY4 . . . 52 B4
Carnegie Cl CV3 . . . . 134 B5
Carnegie Dr WS10 . . . 42 A3
Carnegie Rd B65 . . . . 63 B2
Carnford Rd B26 . . . . 89 B6
Carnforth Cl DY6 . . . . 60 B7
Carnforth Rd B60 . . . 137 B1
Carnoustie B77 . . . . . 22 C5
Carnoustie Cl
  Bromsgrove B61 . . . . . 150 D8
  Nuneaton CV11 . . . . . . 79 C8
  Sutton Coldfield B75 . . 46 C8
  Walsall WS3 . . . . 14 A3
Carnwath Rd B73 . . . . 45 E2
Carol Ave B61 . . . . . . 136 D3
Carol Cres
  Halesowen B63 . . . . . . 82 F5
  Wednesfield WV11 . . . . 26 E6
Carol Gdns DY8 . . . . .80 F8
Caroline Cl CV11 . . . .78 F7
Caroline Pl B13 . . . . . .86 F3
Caroline Rd B13 . . . . .86 F4
Caroline St
  Birmingham B3 . . . . . 164 A4
  Dudley DY2 . . . . 51 E1
  West Bromwich B70 . . . 53 B2
Carousel Pk LE9 . . . . .71 F8
Carpathian Ct **4** B18 . 66 C4
Carpathian The **5**
  B18 . . . . 66 C4
Carpenter Glade B63 . 82 D5
Carpenter Pl **7** B12 . 87 A6
Carpenter Rd B15 . . . 86 B7
Carpenters Cl LE10 . . .75 F5
Carpenters Ct B12 . . .86 F7
Carpenter's Rd B19 . . 66 C7
Carisbrooke Rd
  Birmingham B17 . . . . . 65 B1
Carpet Trades Way
  DY11 . . . . 116 D7
Carrick Cl WS3 . . . . . 15 A5
Carrie Ho CV1 . . . . . 165 A2
Carriers Cl WS2 . . . . .27 F1
Carriers Fold WV5 . . . 49 B7
Carrington Rd WS10 . 42 D7
Carroll Wlk DY10 . . . 117 C5
Carroway Head Hill
  B78 . . . . 33 D4
Carrs La B4 . . . . 164 C2
Carsal Cl CV7 . . . . . . 95 D5
Carshalton Gr WV2 . . 39 E7
Carshalton Rd B44 . . . 45 A2
Cartbridge Cres WS3 . .28 F6
Cartbridge La WS4 . . . 29 A6
Cartbridge La S WS4 . 29 A5
Cartbridge Wlk WS3 . . 29 A6
Carter Ave
  Codsall WV8 . . . . 10 B3
  Kidderminster DY11 . . 116 B4
Carter Ct DY11 . . . . . 116 C4
Carter Rd
  Birmingham B43 . . . . . 43 F2
  Coventry CV3 . . . . 134 A8
  Wolverhampton WV6 . . 25 B5
Carters Cl
  Birmingham B37 . . . . . 90 A7
  Bromsgrove B61 . . . . . 150 D7
  Sutton Coldfield B76 . . 46 F3
Cartersfield La WS9 . . 16 E6
Carter's Gn B70 . . . . . 53 B4
Carters Hurst B33 . . . 69 B1
Carter's La
  Birmingham B62 . . . . . 84 A3
  Halesowen B62 . . . . . . 83 F4
Carthorse La B97 . . . 153 B5
Carthusian Rd CV3 . . 133 C7
Cartland Rd
  Birmingham, Sparkbrook
  B11 . . . . 87 C6
  Birmingham, Stirchley B14,
  B30 . . . . 104 C2
Cartmel Cl CV5 . . . . . 112 A4
Cartmel Ct B23 . . . . . 56 B4
Cartway The WV6 . . . . 23 D4
Cartwright Gdns B69 . 52 C2
Cartwright Ho WS3 . . 14 B1
Cartwright Rd
  Stoke Prior B60 . . . . . 150 D2
  Sutton Coldfield B75 . . 32 C3
Cartwright St WV2 . . 163 C1
Carvell Cl CV5 . . . . . . 94 B1
Carver Cl CV2 . . . . . . 114 E2
Carver Ct
  Sutton Coldfield B24 . . 57 C6
Carver Gdns DY8 . . . . 80 E2
Carver St B1 . . . . 66 B4
Casa Mia Ct WS12 . . . .2 C5
Cascade Cl CV3 . . . . 133 E6
Case La CV35 . . . . . . 145 E1
Casern View B74 . . . . 47 A6
Casewell Rd DY6 . . . . 60 C8
Casey Ave B23 . . . . . 56 D8
Cash Joynson Ave
  WS10 . . . . 41 C8
Cashmore Ave CV31 . 161 F5
Cashmore Rd
  Bedworth CV12 . . . . . . 77 E1
  Kenilworth CV8 . . . . . 148 C4
Cash's Bsns Ctr CV1 113 D5
Cash's La CV1 . . . . . . 113 D6
Casita Gr CV8 . . . . . . 148 C4
Caslon Cres DY8 . . . . 80 C4
Caslon Flats B63 . . . . 82 C4
Caslon Prim Sch B63 82 C4
Caslon Rd B63 . . . . . . 82 C6
Caspian Way CV2 . . . 115 A8
Cassandra Cl
  Coventry CV4 . . . . 132 D3
  Dudley DY5 . . . . 50 C1
Cassandra Gr CV34 . . 161 D4
Cassowary Rd **2** B20 . 54 F3
Castello Dr B36 . . . . . 58 D1
Castillo Ct B14 . . . . . 105 A5
Castings The WV14 . . 40 D2
Castlebridge Gdns
  WV11 . . . . .26 F7
Castlebridge Rd
  WV11 . . . . 27 A6
Castle Bromwich Bsns Pk
  B35 . . . . 58 A1
Castle Bromwich Hall
  Gdns* B36 . . . . 69 A8
Castle Bromwich Inf Sch
  B36 . . . . 69 E7
Castle Bromwich Jun Sch
  B36 . . . . 69 E7
Castle Cl Brownhills WS8 . 6 F2
Castle Cl continued
  Coventry CV3 . . . . 133 D6
  Cradley Heath B64 . . . . 63 B1
  Solihull B92 . . . . 89 B1
  Tamworth B77 . . . . 21 E4
  Warwick CV34 . . . . 160 E6
Castle Cres B36 . . . . . 69 C8
Castlecroft WS11 . . . .5 E5
Castle Croft B68 . . . . 84 D8
Castlecroft Ave WV3 . 38 A8
Castlecroft Gdns WV3 38 C8
Castlecroft Ho WV3 . . 38 A8
Castlecroft La WV6 . . 23 E7
Castlecroft Prim Sch
  WV3 . . . . .38 B8
Castlecroft Rd
  Bilston WV14 . . . . 40 F7
  Wolverhampton WV3 . . 38 B8
Castle Ct
  5 Darlaston WS10 . . 41 D6
  Hinckley LE10 . . . . 75 D6
  Kenilworth CV8 . . . . . 148 A6
Castleditch La B98 . . 158 E7
Castle Dr Coleshill B46 .70 F5
  Willenhall WV12 . . . . . 27 C5
Castle Dyke **6** WS13 . .9 B7
Castleford Gr B11 . . . 87 C4
Castleford Rd B11 . . . 87 C4
Castlefort Jun Mix & Inf
  Sch WS9 . . . . .16 B3
Castlefort Rd WS9 . . . 16 A3
Castlegate Dr DY1 . . . 51 E2
Castle Gate Island
  DY2 . . . . 51 E2
Castlegate Mews **5**
  CV34 . . . . 160 F7
Castlegate Way DY1 . . 51 E2
Castle Gn CV8 . . . . . 147 D5
Castle Gr
  Kenilworth CV8 . . . . . 147 E4
  Stourbridge DY8 . . . . . 81 B3
Castlehall B77 . . . . . . 22 A2
Castle High Sch DY1 . .51 B2
Castle Hill Dudley DY1 . 51 D2
  Kenilworth CV8 . . . . . 147 E5
  Warwick CV34 . . . . 160 E6
Castlehill Rd WS9 . . . 16 C3
Castlehills Dr B36 . . . 69 A8
Castle Ho B33 . . . . . . 69 D7
Castle Hts B64 . . . . . . 83 B8
Castle La Solihull B92 . 89 A2
  Warwick CV34 . . . . 160 E6
Castlemaine Dr LE10 . 71 E3
Castle Mews **6**
  CV34 . . . . 160 E6
Castle Mill DY1 . . . . . 51 D4
Castle Mill Rd DY1 . . . 51 C4
Castle Place Ind Est
  CV1 . . . . 165 D4
Castle Rd
  Birmingham B29 . . . . . 85 B1
  Birmingham, Kings Norton
  B30 . . . . 103 F4
  Brownhills WS9 . . . . . . 16 A2
  Kenilworth CV8 . . . . . 147 E5
  Kidderminster DY11 . . 116 A2
  Nuneaton CV10 . . . . . . 73 C7
  Studley B80 . . . . 159 F4
  Tamworth B77 . . . . 35 C4
  Tipton DY4 . . . . 51 D4
Castle Rd E B68 . . . . . 84 D8
Castle Rd W B68 . . . . 84 C8
Castlereagh Ct WV10 . 25 C6
Castle Specl Sch WS3 28 B7
Castle Sq B29 . . . . . . 85 A1
Castle St
  Astwood Bank B96 . . . 158 E2
  Brownhills WS8 . . . . . . .6 F2
  Coventry CV1 . . . . 165 D4
  Darlaston WS10 . . . . . 41 D8
  Dudley DY1 . . . . 51 D1
  Hinckley LE10 . . . . 75 D8
  Sedgley DY3 . . . . 50 D8
  Tipton DY4 . . . . 51 E5
  Warwick CV34 . . . . 160 E6
  West Bromwich B70 . . . 53 A8
  Wolverhampton WV1 . 163 C3
Castle The DY8 . . . . . 81 B3
Castleton Ct **1** B15 . 86 B7
Castleton Rd
  Birmingham B42 . . . . . 55 D7
  Walsall WS3 . . . . 14 C3
Castleton St DY2 . . . . 62 C4
Castle Vale Ent Pk
  B76 . . . . 58 C4
Castle Vale Ind Est
  B76 . . . . 58 A5
Castle Vale Ret Pk
  B35 . . . . .57 F2
Castle Vale Sch B35 . . .58 B3

Castle View
Dudley DY1 51 B2
Tamworth B77 21 C3
Castle View Cl WS10 41 A4
Castle View Rd WV14, WS10 41 B4
Castle Yd WV1 163 C3
Caswell Rd
Royal Leamington Spa CV31 162 B6
Sedgley DY3 50 C8
Cat And Kittens La WV10 11 E6
Caterbanck Way 2 WS13 8 F6
Cater Dr B76 46 F2
Caterham Dr DY6 60 F3
Catesby Dr DY6 60 D8
Catesby Ho B37 69 F4
Catesby La B94 144 B2
Catesby Pk
Birmingham B38 103 E3
Birmingham B38 103 E3
Catesby Rd
Coventry CV6 113 B8
Solihull B90 106 B1
Cateswell Rd B11, B28 87 F2
Cathcart Rd DY8 80 E5
Cathedral Ave DY11 116 A6
Cathedral Cl DY4 51 E5
Cathedral Ct 4 WS13 9 B8
Cathedral Lanes Sh Ctr CV1 165 B3
Cathedral Rise WS13 9 A8
Cathel Dr B42 55 A7
Catherine Cl B60 150 F8
Catherine Ct B24 57 C4
Catherine de Barnes La
Bickenhill B92 90 D1
Catherine de B B92 108 C7
Catherine Dr B73 46 A6
Catherine Rd WV14 40 A1
Catherines Cl B91 108 B4
Catherine St
Birmingham B6 67 A7
Coventry CV2 113 F3
Catherine Ward Hall CV12 78 B5
Catherton Cl DY4 41 C1
Catholic La DY3 50 D7
Catisfield Cres WV8 10 F1
Cat La B34 69 B7
Caton Gr B28 106 A7
Cato St N B7 67 C5
Cato St B7 67 B5
Catshill Fst Sch B61 137 A8
Catshill Mid Sch B61 136 F8
Catshill Rd WS8 16 A7
Cattell Dr B75 47 B5
Cattell Rd
Birmingham B9 67 C1
Warwick CV34 160 E7
Cattells Gr B7 67 C6
Cattermole Gr B43 44 C3
Cattock Hurst Dr B72 57 D7
Causeway B65 63 C2
Causeway Green Prim Sch B68 63 F3
Causeway Green Rd B68 64 A4
Causeway Rd WV14 51 D8
Causeway The B25 88 D7
Causey Farm Rd B63 100 C8
Cavalier Circus WV10 11 E4
Cavalier Cl CV11 73 E2
Cavalier Dr B63 83 A3
Cavandale Ave B44 44 E1
Cavans Cl CV3 135 A8
Cavan's Cl WS11 1 E4
Cavans Way CV3 135 A8
Cavans Wood Park Home Est WS12 1 D5
Cavell Cl 1 WS2 28 D2
Cavell Rd
Burntwood WS7 7 E8
Dudley DY2 51 F1
Cavendish B79 20 E7
Cavendish Cl
Birmingham B38 104 B1
Kingswinford DY6 60 D4
Lower Marlbrook B60 121 C1
Cavendish Ct
Birmingham B17 85 B8
Dorridge B93 128 A3
Cavendish Dr
Kidderminster DY10 117 B7
West Hagley DY9 98 F4
Cavendish Gdns
Walsall WS2 28 A4
Cavendish Gdns *continued*
Wolverhampton WV1 26 C1
Cavendish Rd
Birmingham B16 65 D4
Coventry CV4 111 E2
Halesowen B62 83 F4
Walsall WS2 28 B5
Wolverhampton WV1 26 B1
Cavendish Way WS9 30 B5
Cavendish Wlk CV11 79 C8
Caversham Cl CV11 74 A7
Caversham Pl B73 46 B4
Caversham Rd B44 45 A2
Cawdon Gr B93 127 F3
Cawdor Cres B16 65 F1
Cawnpore Rd CV6 95 B2
Cawthorne Cl 1 CV1 113 E4
Caxton Ct 4 WS11 4 E8
Caxton Gr B44 45 C1
Caxton St WS11 4 E8
Caynham Cl B98 154 D4
Caynham Rd B32 102 B8
Cayton Gr B23 56 F6
Cearl Ct B27 88 C2
Cecil Ct CV31 162 A8
Cecil Dr B69 52 D2
Cecil Leonard Knox Cres CV11 79 F6
Cecil Rd
Birmingham, Gravelly Hill B24 56 F3
Birmingham, Selly Park B13 86 C1
Cecil St
Birmingham B19 164 C4
Cannock WS11 1 F4
Stourbridge DY8 80 F5
Walsall WS4 28 F3
Cecily Rd CV3 133 E7
Cedar Ave
Birmingham B36 69 C8
Brownhills WS8 16 A8
Dudley WV14 51 B7
Ryton-on-D CV8 135 B1
Cedar Bridge Croft B74 46 B8
Cedar Cl
Birmingham, Bournville B30 103 E6
Birmingham, Brandhall B68 84 C8
Burntwood WS7 7 A6
Cannock WS12 2 A8
Lichfield WS14 9 F7
Royal Leamington Spa CV32 157 A4
Stourbridge DY8 80 D2
Walsall WS5 43 B4
Cedar Cres DY11 116 C6
Cedar Ct Allesley CV5 112 A6
Birmingham B43 54 B8
Hinckley LE10 76 A6
Tamworth B77 35 E6
Cedar Dr
Birmingham, Pype Hayes B24 57 C5
Birmingham, West Heath B31 123 B7
Bromsgrove B60 137 A1
Kidderminster DY11 116 C7
Sutton Coldfield B74 30 E1
Tamworth B79 21 A8
Cedar Gr Bilston WV14 40 F7
Codsall WV8 10 B3
Great Wyrley WS6 5 B4
Warwick CV34 156 A1
West Hagley DY9 99 A6
Wolverhampton WV3 38 F7
Cedarhill Dr WS11 1 F3
Cedar Ho
Birmingham B36 68 F8
7 Royal Leamington Spa CV32 161 E8
Solihull B91 106 F1
Sutton Coldfield B74 31 B5
Cedarhurst
Birmingham B32 85 A5
Solihull B91 107 C3
Cedar Park Rd
Redditch B97 153 D4
Willenhall WV12 13 C1
Cedar Rd
Birmingham B30 103 E6
Burntwood WS7 7 A7
Dudley DY1 51 B3
Nuneaton CV10 72 D6
Redditch B97 153 D4
Tipton DY4 51 D5
Wednesbury WS10 42 A2
Cedar Rd *continued*
Willenhall WV13 26 E2
Cedars Ave
Birmingham B27 88 C4
Coventry CV6 112 F5
Kingswinford DY6 60 D4
Wombourne WV5 49 A5
Cedars Bsns Ctr The WS11 4 C7
Cedars Hort Unit The WV3 24 D2
Cedars Mews The 3 CV32 161 D8
Cedars Rd CV7 78 B1
Cedars The
Birmingham B25 68 E1
Dorridge B93 128 A4
5 Wolverhampton, Newbridge WV6 24 F3
Wolverhampton, Tettenhall WV6 24 D5
Cedar Terr B60 137 A1
Cedar View B97 153 C4
Cedar Way
Birmingham B31 102 F1
Wolverhampton WV11 26 C7
Cedar Wlk 6 B37 70 B2
Cedarwood B74 46 B8
Cedarwood Croft B42 54 F8
Cedar Wood Dr CV7 130 B6
Cedar Wood Rd DY3 50 D5
Cedric Cl CV3 134 C5
Celandine
Sutton Coldfield B74 31 F5
Tamworth B77 21 C3
Celandine Cl DY6 60 C4
Celandine Rd
Coventry CV2 96 D2
Dudley DY1 51 A4
Celandine Way CV12 77 E2
Celbury Way B43 54 D8
Celeste Rd B60 137 C1
Celtic Rd WS11 1 E3
Celts Cl B65 63 C4
Cemetery La B18 66 B5
Cemetery Rd
Cannock WS11 1 E4
Darlaston WS10 41 F8
Oldbury B68 64 C6
Redditch B97 153 D3
Smethwick B67 64 F4
Stourbridge DY9 81 E5
Sutton Coldfield B75 46 D6
Willenhall WV13 27 A2
Cemetery St
Bilston WV14 40 C6
Cheslyn Hay WS6 4 C2
Cemetery Way WS3 14 B1
Centaur Rd CV5 112 F2
Centenary Bsns Ctr CV11 73 E3
Centenary Cl 1 B31 103 A1
Centenary Dr B21 54 E1
Centenary Plaza B1 164 A2
Centenary Rd CV4 132 D7
Centenary Sq B1 164 A2
Central Arc WV1 163 B2
Central Ave
Bilston WV14 40 E7
Birmingham B31 122 F8
Cannock WS11 1 F5
Coventry CV2 114 A2
Cradley Heath B64 82 D7
Nuneaton CV11 73 B5
Rowley Regis B65 63 C2
Royal Leamington Spa CV31 161 F6
Stourbridge DY9 81 E3
Tipton DY4 51 F7
13 Wolverhampton WV4 39 F4
Central Bldgs CV3 165 B1
Central Bsns Pk B33 69 D1
Central Bvd
Cheswick Green B90 127 A3
Coventry CV6, CV7 95 A5
Central City Ind Est CV6 113 F5
Central Cl WS3 14 A1
Central Dr
Dudley, Gornalwood DY3 50 D2
Dudley, West Coseley WV14 51 D7
Walsall WS3 14 A1
Central Gr B27 88 C2
Central Park Dr B18 65 F5
Central Park Ind Est DY2 62 E3
Central Rd B60 137 A2
Central Six Ret Pk CV1 165 A1
Central Sq B23 57 A4
Central Trad Est
Darlaston WS10 41 E6
Wolverhampton WV2 39 F8
Central Way DY5 61 F3
Centre Ct B63 83 B3
Centre La B63 83 B3
Centre Link Ind Est B7 67 B6
Centreway The B14 105 D4
Centrovell Ind Est CV11 73 C2
Centurion Cl B46 59 F1
Centurion Pk B77 36 B6
Centurion Way B77 36 B6
Century Ho B69 63 D6
Century Ind Est B44 44 E3
Century Mews B64 62 F2
Century Pk
Birmingham, Bordesley Green B9 67 C2
Birmingham, Marston Green B26 90 C6
Century Rd B69 64 A8
Century Twr B5 86 C5
Ceolmund Cres B37 70 B2
CE Prim Sch of St Edmund & St John The DY2 51 E1
Chace Ave CV3 134 C6
Chaceley Cl CV2 115 A8
Chaceley Ct B97 158 D8
Chaceley Gr B23 56 E7
Chace Prim Sch CV3 134 C6
Chadbrook Crest B15 85 E7
Chadbury Croft 1 B91 127 B8
Chadbury Rd B63 83 C3
Chadcote Way B61 120 F1
Chaddersley Cl 2 B45 101 F1
Chaddesley Cl
Oldbury B69 63 D5
Redditch B98 153 F1
Chaddesley Dr DY9 81 B1
Chaddesley Gdns 2 DY10 117 A5
Chaddesley Rd
Birmingham B31 103 D2
Halesowen B63 82 F2
Kidderminster DY10 117 A5
Chadley Cl B91 107 A6
Chad Rd
Birmingham B15 85 F8
Dudley DY1, WV14 51 B7
Chadsgrove Sch B61 136 F8
Chadshunt Cl B36 58 D2
Chadsmead Prim Sch WS13 3 A1
Chadsmoor CE Jun Sch WS11 2 A3
Chadsmoor Inf Sch WS11 2 A4
Chadsmoor Terr B7 67 B6
Chad Sq B15 85 E8
Chadstone Cl B90 127 B6
Chadswell Hts WS13 3 D2
Chad Vale Prim Sch B15 85 D7
Chad Valley Cl B17 85 D6
Chadwell Dr B90 106 B6
Chadwich La DY9 120 F7
Chadwick Ave B45 122 B6
Chadwick Cl
Coventry CV5 112 B3
Wolverhampton WV4 38 D6
Chadwick Ct B42 54 E8
Chadwick La
Chadwick End B93 145 B8
Temple Balsall B93 129 B2
Chadwick Manor B93 129 A1
Chadwick Mews
Chadwick End B93 145 B6
Redditch B98 159 A7
Chadwick Rd B75 46 F5
Chadworth Ave B93 127 E3
Chaffcombe Rd B26 89 C7
Chaffinch Cl
Cannock WS12 2 B4
Sedgley DY3 39 C3
Chaffinch Dr
Birmingham B36 70 B7
Kidderminster DY10 116 F2
Chaffinch Rd DY9 81 D3
Chainmakers Cl WV14 40 D2
Chainshop Mus★ DY2 62 B1
Chain Wlk B19 66 D7
Chalcot Dr WS12 2 A7
Chalcot Gr B20 54 E5
Chaldon Cl WV9 11 A1
Chale Gr B14 105 A3
Chalfield B79 20 D6
Chalfont Ave WS11 4 C7
Chalfont Cl
Bedworth CV12 78 A4
Coventry CV5 112 B4
Chalfont Ct WS11 4 C7
Chalfont Pl DY9 81 E2
Chalfont Rd B20 55 C1
Chalford Rd B23 56 C8
Chalford Way B90 106 C1
Chalgrove Ave B38 103 E1
Chalgrove Cres B91 107 B1
Challenge Bsns Pk CV1 113 D5
Challenge Cl CV1 165 C4
Challenge Way WV10 25 E5
Challenor Ave WV13 26 D1
Chalybeate Cl B45 101 F1
Chamberlain Cl
Cubbington CV32 157 E5
Oldbury B69 52 D2
Chamberlain Cres B90 106 A2
Chamberlain Ct
3 Birmingham, Hockley B18 66 C4
Birmingham, King's Heath B14 86 E1
Chamberlaine St CV12 78 B3
Chamberlain Ho B16 66 A1
Chamberlain Rd B13 105 A6
Chamberlain's Gn CV6 112 F7
Chamberlain's La WV4 38 E3
Chamberlain Sq B3 164 B2
Chamberlain Wlk
10 Coleshill B46 70 F7
1 Smethwick B66 65 B5
Champney DY10 116 E2
Chance Croft B68 84 B8
Chance Fields CV31 162 F6
Chancel Ct B91 107 C2
Chancel Ind Est
Darlaston WS10 41 D5
Kingswinford DY6 49 E1
Willenhall WV13 27 B2
Chancel Ind Est The WV1 26 A1
Chancellors Cl CV4 132 D4
Chancellor's Cl B15 85 E8
Chancel Way
Birmingham B6 55 F5
Halesowen B62 83 C6
Chancery Ct CV10 72 A7
Chancery Dr WS12 2 C7
Chancery La CV10 72 B7
Chancery Way DY5 61 F2
Chanders Rd CV34 155 D1
Chandler Dr WV4 38 D3
Chandler Ho B65 63 D4
Chandlers CV31 161 D7
Chandlers Cl
Birmingham B18 65 F5
Redditch B97 158 D7
Wolverhampton WV9 11 A1
Chandlers Dr B77 22 B5
Chandlers Keep WS8 16 A6
Chandlers Rd CV31 162 A2
Chandos Ave B13 86 F3
Chandos Ct 15 CV32 156 F1
Chandos Prim Sch B12 86 E8
Chandos St
Coventry CV2 114 A3
Nuneaton CV11 73 A4
Royal Leamington Spa CV32 156 F1
Change Brook Cl CV11 73 F8
Channel Way CV6 96 B6
Channon Dr DY5 81 D8
Chanston Ave B14 104 E4
Chanterelle Ct WV4 39 B4
Chanterelle Gdns WV4 39 B4
Chantrey Cres
Bilston WV14 40 F7
Birmingham B43 44 D4
Chantries The CV1 113 E5
Chantry Ave WS3 28 D8
Chantry Cl B47 125 A7
Chantry Ct B13 86 F3
Chantry Dr B62 84 A6
Chantry Heath Cres B93 128 C7
Chantry Ind Est B76 59 B7
Chantry Rd
Birmingham, Handsworth B21 65 F8
Birmingham, Moseley B13 86 E4
Stourbridge DY7 80 C7
Chantry The CV34 156 A1
Chapel Ash WV3 25 B2
Chapel Ash Island WV1 163 A3
Chapel Ave WS8 6 E2
Chapel Cl B64 83 B8
Chapel Ct
Astwood Bank B96 158 E1
Brierley Hill, Barrow Hill DY5 61 C7
4 Brierley Hill, Silver End DY5 61 D2
13 Royal Leamington Spa CV32 161 F8
Chapel Dr
Balsall Common CV7 130 B8
Brownhills WS8 6 E2
Mile Oak B78 20 C1
Wythall B47 124 F3
Chapel Farm Cl CV3 134 C6
Chapelfield Mews
Birmingham B45 121 F6
Stourbridge DY8 81 A4
Chapelfield Rd B45 122 A7
Chapel Fields Jun Sch B92 88 F3
Chapel Fields Rd B92 88 F2
Chapel Gn WV13 27 B2
Chapel House La B63 82 C6
Chapelhouse Rd B37 69 F1
Chapel House St 1 B12 66 F1
Chapel La
Barnacle CV7 97 B6
Beoley B98 154 F8
Birmingham B29 85 E2
Birmingham, Great Barr B43, WS9 44 A5
Kingswood B94 144 D7
Lichfield WS14 9 B6
Madeley Heath DY9 120 D7
Romsley B62 100 C6
Rowney Green B48 139 F4
Ryton-on-D CV8 135 B2
Walsall B43 43 F4
Wythall B47 124 E2
Chapel Mews B77 22 A5
Chapel Mill Apartments B62 83 C8
Chapelon B77 22 A2
Chapel Pl DY11 116 D6
Chapel Rd B96 158 E1
Chapel Row CV34 160 E7
Chapel Sq WS6 4 D3
Chapel St
Astwood Bank B96 158 E1
Bedworth CV12 78 C3
Bilston WV14 40 F4
Birmingham B5 164 D3
Birmingham, Handsworth B21 65 D7
Brierley Hill, Barrow Hill DY5 61 C6
Brierley Hill, Quarry Bank DY5 61 F1
Brierley Hill, Silver End DY5 61 D2
Bromsgrove B60 137 A2
Brownhills WS8 6 E2
Burntwood WS7 6 E8
Cannock WS12 2 E1
Coventry CV1 165 B3
Dudley DY2 62 D4
Halesowen B63 83 A3
Kidderminster DY11 116 D6
Kingswinford DY6 60 B8
Norton Canes WS11 5 F5
Nuneaton CV11 73 C4
Redditch B97 153 D1
5 Royal Leamington Spa CV31 162 A7
Stourbridge, Lye DY9 81 E5
Stourbridge, Wollaston DY8 81 A4
Stourbridge, Wordsley DY8 60 D3
Tipton DY4 51 E5

Chapel St continued
Walsall, Blakenall Heath
WS3 . . . . **28** D8
Walsall WS3 . . . . **15** A3
Warwick CV34 . . . . . . **160** E7
Wednesbury WS10 . . . . **41** E3
West Bromwich B70. . . **53** B5
West Hagley DY9 . . . . **99** A5
Wolverhampton WV2 . . **39** D7
Chapel Street Prec 1
B60 . . . . **137** A2
Chapel View B67 . . . . . **64** F4
Chapel Wlk
Birmingham B30 . . . . . **104** A2
Bromsgrove B60 . . . . . **137** A2
Dudley DY3 . . . . **50** C2
Chapelwood Gr B42 . . **55** D5
Chaplain Rd WS12 . . . . . .**2** E2
Chapman Cl CV31 . . . **162** E5
Chapman Ct CV34 . . . **161** C8
Chapman Rd B10 . . . . . **87** C8
Chapman's Hill B62 . **101** B1
Chapmans Pas B1 . . . **164** B1
Chapman St B70 . . . . . **53** B3
Chapter Ho B70 . . . . . . **53** A5
Chard Rd CV3 . . . . . . **134** D8
Charfield Cl B30 . . . **103** D7
Charford Fst Sch
B60 . . . . **150** F7
Charford Rd B60 . . . . **150** F8
Charingworth Rd B92 **89** C3
Charity Bick Way 7
B70 . . . . **53** C2
Charity Rd CV7 . . . . . . **95** A7
Charlbury Ave B37 . . . .**69** F2
Charlbury Cres B26 . . .**88** F8
Charlbury Mews
CV31 . . . . **162** C6
Charlbury Twr 2 B5. . **86** E8
Charlecote Cl B98 . . . **154** D2
Charlecote Croft
B90 . . . . **126** C8
Charlecote Dr
Birmingham B23 . . . . . **56** E7
Dudley DY1 . . . . **50** E3
Charlecote Gdns
Royal Leamington Spa
CV31 . . . . **162** D5
Sutton Coldfield B73 . . **57** A8
Charlecote Rd CV6 . . . **95** A2
Charlecote Rise 1
WV13 . . . .**40** F8
Charlecote Wlk CV11 . .**78** F4
Charlecott Cl B13 . . . **105** D7
Charlemont Ave B71 . **53** E8
Charlemont Cl WS5 . . . **43** C6
Charlemont Cres B71 **42** E1
Charlemonte Cl WS12 . **2** D3
Charlemont Gdns
WS5 . . . . **43** C6
Charlemont Jun & Inf
Sch B71 . . . .**53** E8
Charlemont Rd
Walsall WS5 . . . . **43** C6
West Bromwich B71 . . . **53** F8
Charles Ave
Essington WV11 . . . . . **12** F4
Rowley Regis B65 . . . . **63** C4
Wolverhampton WV4 . . **39** B5
Charles Burns Sch
B13 . . . .**86** E1
Charles Cl
Birmingham B8 . . . . . . **67** D4
Cheslyn Hay WS6 . . . . . . **4** D1
Charles Cres WS3 . . . . **15** A5
Charles Ct
8 Birmingham B13 . . . **87** B2
14 Royal Leamington Spa
CV31 . . . . **162** C6
Sutton Coldfield B76. . . **46** F3
Warwick CV34 . . . . . . **160** C7
1 Warwick, Emscote
CV34 . . . . **161** B8
Charlesdale Dr WS9 . . **30** B4
Charles Dr B7 . . . . **67** B6
Charles Eaton Rd
CV12 . . . .**77** F3
Charles Edward Rd
B26 . . . . **88** D6
Charles Foster St
WS10 . . . . **41** C4
Charles Gardner Rd 6
CV31 . . . . **161** F6
Charles Hayward Bglws
WV4 . . . . **39** D3
Charles Henry St B12 .**86** F4
Charles Holland St 2
WV13 . . . . **27** B2

Charles Lakin Cl CV7 . **97** C5
Charles Lane Trust
Homes The B28 . . . . **106** A8
Charles Pearson Ct
B66 . . . . **65** B5
Charles Rd
Birmingham, Aston
B6 . . . . **56** A1
Birmingham, Bordesley
Green B9, B10 . . . . . **67** E1
Birmingham, Handsworth
B20 . . . . **55** C1
Brierley Hill DY5 . . . . . **62** B1
Halesowen B63 . . . . . . **82** F4
Solihull B91 . . . . **106** E2
Stourbridge DY8 . . . . . **80** E4
Tipton DY4 . . . . **52** A7
Charles St
Coventry CV1 . . . . . . **165** D4
Hinckley LE10 . . . . **71** E1
Kidderminster DY10 . **116** F6
Nuneaton CV11 . . . . . . **73** A5
Redditch B97 . . . . . . **153** C1
Smethwick B66 . . . . . . **65** C7
Walsall WS2 . . . . **28** D2
Warwick CV34 . . . . . **161** A8
West Bromwich B70 . . . **52** E5
Willenhall WV13 . . . . . **27** C3
Charles Watson Ct 4
CV32 . . . . **157** A2
Charles Wesley Ct
WV3 . . . . **39** A7
Charles Wlk B65 . . . . . **63** C5
Charlesworth Ave
B90 . . . . **127** B6
Charleville Rd B19 . . . **66** B7
Charlewood Rd CV6 . . **95** B2
Charlock Gr WS11 . . . . . .**2** C3
Charlotte Cl
Nuneaton CV10 . . . . . . **72** C6
Tipton B69 . . . . **52** A2
Charlotte Rd
Birmingham, Edgbaston
B15 . . . . **86** C7
Birmingham, Stirchley
B30 . . . . **104** A6
Wednesbury WS10 . . . . **41** C2
Charlotte St
Birmingham B3 . . . . . **164** A3
15 Dudley DY1 . . . . . **51** B1
Royal Leamington Spa
CV31 . . . . **161** F6
Walsall WS1 . . . . **29** A2
Charlton Dr B64 . . . . . **82** D7
Charlton Pl B8 . . . . **67** D5
Charlton Rd B44 . . . . . **56** A4
Charlton St
Brierley Hill DY5 . . . . . **61** A1
4 Dudley DY1 . . . . . . **51** B1
Charminster Ave B25 . **88** D8
Charminster Dr CV3 . **133** D4
Charnley Dr B75 . . . . . **32** E2
Charnwood Ave
Nuneaton CV10 . . . . . . **72** C6
Sedgley DY3 . . . . **39** D2
Charnwood Bsns Pk
WV14 . . . .**40** C5
Charnwood Cl
Birmingham B45 . . . . **102** B3
Brierley Hill DY5 . . . . . **81** B8
Cannock WS12 . . . .**2** C4
Darlaston WV14 . . . . . **41** B3
Hinckley LE10 . . . . **71** E2
Lichfield WS13 . . . .**3** C1
Charnwood Ct DY9 . . . **81** E2
Charnwood Ho WS13 . . **3** B2
Charnwood Prim Sch
WS13 . . . .**3** C2
Charnwood Rd
Birmingham B42 . . . . . **54** F7
Hinckley LE10 . . . . **71** D2
Walsall WS5 . . . . **43** A4
Charnwood Way
CV32 . . . . **157** C3
Charter App CV34 . . . **160** D5
Charter Ave CV4 . . . . **132** C2
Charter Cl WS11 . . . .**5** E4
Charter Cres B64 . . . . **83** B8
Charterfield Dr
Cannock WS12 . . . .**2** C1
Kingswinford DY6 . . . . **60** D8
Charterfields Sh Ctr
DY6 . . . . **60** D8
Charter Ho CV4 . . . . . **132** A7
Charterhouse Dr
B91 . . . . **107** C1
Charterhouse Rd
CV1 . . . . **113** C3
Charter Prim Sch (Harris
Site) CV4 . . . . **131** F7

Charter Prim Sch (Parkes
Site) CV4 . . . . **132** C8
Charter Rd DY4 . . . . . **41** C1
Charters Ave WV8 . . . . **10** B1
Charter St DY5 . . . . **61** E5
Charters The WS13 . . . . .**3** B1
Chartist Rd B8 . . . . **67** D6
Chartley Cl
Dorridge B93 . . . . . . **127** E3
Perton WV6 . . . . **23** F4
Chartley Rd
Birmingham B23 . . . . . **56** D1
West Bromwich B71 . . . **53** D6
Chartway The WS3 . . . **15** B4
Chartwell B79 . . . . **20** D7
Chartwell Cl
Dudley DY1 . . . . **51** B6
Nuneaton CV11 . . . . . . **73** F1
Chartwell Ct B72 . . . . . **57** C8
Chartwell Dr
Cheswick Green B90 . **126** D5
Sutton Coldfield B74. . . **31** D4
Wolverhampton WV10 . **11** E1
Chartwell Grange
B64 . . . . **83** A7
Chase Acad WS11 . . . .**4** E4
Chase Ave WS6 . . . .**4** E3
Chase Cl CV11 . . . . **73** E6
Chase Gr B24 . . . . **57** D6
Chase La CV8 . . . . **147** B7
Chaselands WS7 . . . . **6** D7
Chase L Ctr WS11 . . . . . .**1** D2
Chaseley Ave WS11. . . . .**1** C2
Chaseley Croft WS11 . . . .**1** C2
Chaseley Gdns WS7 . . . . **7** C7
Chase Park Ind Est
WS7 . . . .**6** D7
Chase Rd
Brownhills WS8 . . . . **7** A1
Burntwood WS7 . . . . **7** B6
Dudley DY3, DY5 . . . . . **50** C1
Walsall WS3 . . . . **28** A8
Chaseside Dr WS11. . . . .**2** B3
Chaseside Ind Est
WS11 . . . .**2** B3
Chase Terrace Prim Sch
WS7 . . . .**6** F7
Chase Terrace Tech Coll
WS7 . . . .**7** A7
Chase The
Sutton Coldfield B76. . . **57** D7
Wolverhampton WV6 . . **25** B6
Chasetown Com Sch
WS7 . . . .**6** E5
Chasetown Ind Est
WS7 . . . .**6** E7
Chasetown Specialist
Sports Coll WS7. . . . . .**6** E4
Chasetown Sta* WS7 . **6** D5
Chase Vale WS7 . . . .**6** E6
Chase View WV4 . . . . . **39** E2
Chasewater* WS7 . . . . .**6** C4
Chasewater Country Pk*
WS7 . . . .**6** E6
Chasewater Heaths Sta*
WS7 . . . . **6** D6
Chasewater Rly*
WS11 . . . .**6** B5
Chasewater Way WS11 .**5** F5
Chase Wlk WS12 . . . . . .**1** C4
Chasewood Park Bsns Ctr
WS12 . . . .**2** E1
Chater Dr B76 . . . . **47** A1
Chaters Cl DY4 . . . . **51** E5
Chatham Cl CV3 . . . . . **134** C8
Chatham Rd B31 . . . . **103** A3
Chatillon Cl CV34 . . . **161** E3
Chatsworth B79 . . . . . . **20** C7
Chatsworth Ave B43 . . **43** C1
Chatsworth Cl
Cheswick Green B90 . **126** E5
Hinckley LE10 . . . . . . **75** F6
Sutton Coldfield B72. . . **57** D7
Willenhall WV12 . . . . . **27** B5
Chatsworth Cres WS4 **29** D7
Chatsworth Dr
Cannock WS11 . . . .**2** A4
Nuneaton CV11 . . . . . . **73** F2
Chatsworth Gdns
Royal Leamington Spa
CV31 . . . . **162** D6
Wolverhampton WV6 . . **24** A7
Chatsworth Gr CV8 . . **148** C5
Chatsworth Rd B62 . . . **83** A7
Chatsworth Rise
CV3 . . . . **133** E6
Chattaway Dr CV7 . . . **130** B6
Chattaway St B7 . . . . . **67** C7
Chatterton Ave WS13 . . **8** E6

Chatterton Wlk 4
DY10 . . . . **117** B6
Chattle Hill B46 . . . . . **59** E2
Chattock Ave B91 . . . **107** E3
Chattock Cl B36 . . . . . . **68** E7
Chatwell Gr B29 . . . . . **85** B2
Chatwin Pl WV14 . . . . . **40** E3
Chatwin St B66 . . . .**64** F7
Chatwins Wharf DY4 . .**51** F5
Chaucer Ave
Dudley DY3 . . . . **50** A5
Tipton DY4 . . . . **52** B8
Willenhall WV12 . . . . . **27** E8
Chaucer Cl
Birmingham B23 . . . . . **56** B3
Dudley DY14 . . . . **51** D8
Lichfield WS14 . . . .**9** B6
Stourbridge DY8 . . . . . **81** A8
Tamworth B79 . . . . **21** A6
Chaucer Cres DY10 . . **117** C5
Chaucer Dr CV10 . . . . . **72** A4
Chaucer Gr B27 . . . . . . **88** B2
Chaucer Ho B63 . . . . . . **82** B5
Chaucer Rd
Bromsgrove B60 . . . . **151** B8
Walsall WS3 . . . . **28** E8
Chauntry Pl CV1 . . . . **165** C3
Chauson Gr B91 . . . . . **127** A8
Chavasse Rd B72 . . . . . **46** D3
Chawn Hill DY9 . . . . . . **81** C3
Chawnhill Cl DY9 . . . . . **81** C3
Chawn Park Dr DY9 . . . **81** C3
Chaynes Gr B33 . . . . . . **69** D2
Chaytor Dr CV10 . . . . . **72** B6
Cheadle Cl CV2 . . . . **96** A4
Cheadle Dr B23 . . . . . . **56** D8
Cheam Cl CV6 . . . . **96** A1
Cheam Gdns WV6 . . . . . **24** E8
Cheapside
Birmingham B5, B12 . .**164** D1
3 Willenhall WV13 . . . **27** A1
Wolverhampton WV1 . **163** B3
Cheapside Ind Est **3**
B12 . . . .**66** F1
Cheatham St B7 . . . . . . **67** C6
Cheatle Ct B77 . . . . **35** D5
Checketts St WS2 . . . . . **28** C2
Checkley Cl B90 . . . . . **106** B4
Checkley Croft B76 . . .**57** F8
Cheddar Rd B12 . . . . . . **86** E6
Chedworth Cl
Birmingham B29 . . . . **103** B6
Redditch B98 . . . . . . **154** C5
Cheedon Cl B93 . . . . . **127** E2
Cheetah Rd CV1 . . . . . **165** C1
Chelford Cres DY6 . . . . **61** A3
Chells Gr B13 . . . . **105** B5
Chelmar Cl B36 . . . .**69** D6
Chelmar Dr DY5 . . . . . . **61** A6
Chelmarsh CV6 . . . . . . **113** C6
Chelmarsh Ave WV3 . . **38** B8
Chelmarsh Cl B98 . . . . **154** C7
Chelmorton Rd B42 . . . **55** D7
Chelmscote Rd B92 . . .**88** F2
Chelmsley Ave B46 . . . **70** F6
Chelmsley Circ B37 . . **70** B2
Chelmsley Gr B33 . . . . **69** E3
Chelmsley La B37 . . . . . **90** A8
Chelmsley Rd B37 . . . . **70** C2
Chelmsley Wood Ind Est
B37 . . . .**70** B4
Chelney Wlk CV3 . . . . **115** A1
Chelsea B37 . . . .**69** F5
Chelsea Cl
Birmingham B32 . . . . . **84** F4
Nuneaton CV11 . . . . . . **73** F7
Chelsea Ct 6 B29. . . . **103** B7
Chelsea Dr B74 . . . .**31** F4
Chelsea Trad Est B7 . . **67** A6
Chelsea Way DY6 . . . . . **60** C6
Chelsey Rd CV2 . . . . . . **114** E8
Chelston Dr WV6 . . . . . **24** E4
Chelston Rd B31 . . . . . **102** E2
Cheltenham Ave
B61 . . . . **121** B1
Cheltenham Cl
Bedworth CV12 . . . . . . **78** B4
Wolverhampton WV6 . . **25** B5
Cheltenham Croft
CV2 . . . . **114** F7
Cheltenham Dr
Birmingham B36 . . . . . **68** D2
Kingswinford DY6 . . . . **60** B6
Chelthorn Way B91 . . **107** C2
Cheltondale 3 B90 . . **126** C8
Cheltondale Rd B91 . . **106** F6
Chelveston Cres B91 **107** B1
Chelveston Rd CV6 . . . **112** C5
Chelwood Gdns WV14 **40** B5
Chelwood Gr CV2 . . . . . **96** F1

Chelworth Rd B38 . . . **104** B2
Chem Rd WV14. . . . . . . **40** C5
Chenet Way WS11 . . . . . .**1** E2
Chenies Cl CV5 . . . . . **112** B3
Cheniston Rd WV12 . . . **27** C7
Chepstow Cl
Coventry CV3 . . . . . . **134** C5
Perton WV6 . . . . **23** F4
Chepstow Dr B61 . . . . **121** B1
Chepstow Gr B45 . . . . **122** B6
Chepstow Rd
Walsall WS3 . . . . **13** F1
Wolverhampton WV10 . **11** D5
Chepstow Villas 5
B12 . . . .**87** B5
Chepstow Way WS3 . . .**13** F1
Chequers Ave WV5 . . . **38** C1
Chequers Ct WS11 . . . . .**6** A5
Chequer St
Bulkington CV12 . . . . . **79** C2
Wolverhampton WV3 . . **39** B6
Chequers The 3 WS13 .**9** C8
Cherhill Covert **7**
B14 . . . . **104** C2
Cherington Cl B98 . . . **154** F1
Cherington Rd B29 . . **104** A8
Cheriton Cl CV5 . . . . . **112** D4
Cheriton Gr WV6 . . . . . **23** E3
Cheriton Wlk B23 . . . . **56** B3
Cherrington Cl B31 . . **102** F7
Cherrington Dr WS6 . . . .**4** E4
Cherrington Gdns
Stourbridge DY9 . . . . . **99** C7
Wolverhampton WV6 . . **24** B2
Cherrington Way
B91 . . . . **107** B1
Cherry Bank WS12 . . . . .**2** C6
Cherry Blossom Gr
CV31 . . . . **162** B2
Cherrybrook Way
CV2 . . . . **96** C1
Cherry Cl
Burntwood WS7 . . . .**6** F6
Coventry CV6 . . . . **95** D2
Cherry Cres
Birmingham B24 . . . . . **56** F3
Bromsgrove B61 . . . . **136** E3
Cherrydale Ct DY1 . . . .**50** F2
Cherry Dr
Birmingham B9 . . . . . . **67** B1
1 Cradley Heath B64 . **62** F1
Cherry Gn DY1 . . . .**50** F4
Cherry Gr
Barnt Green B45 . . . . **138** C8
Smethwick B66 . . . . . . **65** C5
Stourbridge DY8 . . . . . **80** E4
Wolverhampton WV11 . **26** C7
Cherry Hill Ave B45 . . **138** C8
Cherry Hill Dr B45 . . . **138** C8
Cherry Hill Rd B45 . . . **138** C8
Cherry Hill Wlk DY1 . . **62** A8
Cherry La Himley DY3 . **49** C3
Sutton Coldfield B73 . . **57** A7
Wednesbury WS10 . . . . **42** A2
Cherry Lea B34 . . . . **69** B6
Cherryl Ho 3 B74. . . . . **31** E3
Cherry Oak Sch B29 . **85** D2
Cherry Orch
Cradley Heath B64 . . . . **62** F1
Kenilworth CV8 . . . . . **148** A5
Kidderminster DY10 . **116** F6
Lichfield WS14 . . . .**9** C7
Cherry Orchard Ave
B63 . . . . **82** F5
Cherry Orchard Cres
B63 . . . . **82** F6
Cherry Orchard Dr
B61 . . . . **136** E3
Cherry Orchard Prim Sch
B20 . . . . **55** A3
Cherry Orchard Rd
B20 . . . . **55** A4
Cherry Pit Cl B98 . . . . **141** A1
Cherry Rd DY4 . . . .**51** F7
Cherry St
Birmingham B2 . . . . . **164** C2
Halesowen B63 . . . . . . **82** F5
Stourbridge DY8 . . . . . **80** E4
Tamworth B79 . . . . **21** B5
Warwick CV34 . . . . . . **160** F7
Wolverhampton WV3 . . **25** B1
Cherry Tree Ave
Nuneaton CV10 . . . . . . **72** E6
Walsall WS5 . . . . **43** A5
Cherry Tree Croft 5
B27 . . . . **88** C5
Cherrytree Ct DY9 . . . . **81** E3
Cherry Tree Gdns
WV8 . . . . **10** B3

Cherry Tree La
Codsall WV8 . . . . **10** B3
Halesowen B63 . . . . . . **82** D1
Cherry Tree Rd
Huntington WS12 . . . . . .**1** D8
Kingswinford DY6 . . . . **60** E8
Norton Canes WS11 . . . .**6** B5
Cherry Tree Wlk
Redditch B97 . . . . **153** B4
Tamworth B79 . . . . **21** A8
Cherry Way CV8 . . . . . **148** A5
Cherry Wlk B47 . . . . . **125** B5
Cherrywood Cl WV14 . . **40** C1
Cherrywood Cres 3
B91 . . . . **127** C8
Cherrywood Ct B92 . . **89** C4
Cherrywood Gn WV14 . **40** D8
Cherrywood Gr CV5 . . **111** F5
Cherrywood Ind Est
B9 . . . . **67** D3
Cherrywood Rd
Birmingham B9 . . . . . . **67** E2
Sutton Coldfield B74. . . **30** D1
Sutton Coldfield B74. . . **44** D8
Cherrywood Way B74 . **31** D4
Chervil Cl B42 . . . . **55** C7
Chervil Rise WV10 . . . . **25** F3
Cherwell B77 . . . . **21** D1
Cherwell Cl LE10 . . . . . **75** A8
Cherwell Ct B73 . . . . . . **46** B5
Cherwell Dr
Birmingham B36 . . . . . **69** F8
Brownhills WS8 . . . .**6** C1
Cherwell Gdns 7 B6. . **66** D8
Chesford Cres
Coventry CV6 . . . . **96** B2
Warwick CV34 . . . . . **156** B2
Chesham St CV31 . . . . **162** B7
Cheshire Ave B90 . . . **106** A2
Cheshire Cl
Burntwood WS7 . . . .**7** F8
Stourbridge DY8 . . . . . **80** D8
Cheshire Cl
Kidderminster DY11 . . **116** A7
Perton WV6 . . . . **23** E4
Cheshire Ho 8 B66 . . **65** B5
Cheshire Rd
Birmingham B6 . . . . . . **56** A4
Smethwick B67 . . . . . . **65** A4
Willenhall WS2 . . . . . . **27** F2
Chesholme Rd CV6 . . . **95** B2
Cheshunt Ho 3 B37. . **70** B2
Cheshunt Sch CV1. . . **165** B1
Chesils The CV3 . . . . . **133** D6
Cheslyn Dr WS6 . . . . **4** D2
Cheslyn Gr B14 . . . . . . **105** A3
Cheslyn Hay High Sch
WS6 . . . .**4** C3
Cheslyn Hay Prim Sch
WS6 . . . .**4** C3
Chessetts Gr B13 . . . . **105** A6
Chessetts Wood Rd
B94 . . . . **144** C2
Chessher St LE10 . . . . . **71** C1
Chester Ave WV6 . . . . . **24** F7
Chester Cl
Birmingham B37 . . . . . **70** A2
Cannock WS11 . . . .**2** B1
Lichfield WS13 . . . .**3** C1
Willenhall WV13 . . . . . **27** D2
Chester Ct
4 Birmingham, Chelmsley
Wood B37. . . . . **70** D2
Birmingham, Chester Road
B73 . . . . **57** A7
5 Birmingham, Weoley
Castle B29 . . . . **103** B7
Chesterfield Cl B31 . **103** B2
Chesterfield Ct
Birmingham B38 . . . . **103** E4
Brownhills WS9 . . . . . . **15** F4
Chesterfield Rd WS14 . .**9** A5
Chestergate Croft
B24 . . . . **57** E4
Chester Gdns B73 . . . . **45** E1
Chester Hayes Ct B24 **57** C5
Chester Pl WS2 . . . . . . **28** C1
Chester Rd
Aldridge B74 . . . . **30** C4
Birmingham, Castle
Bromwich B36 . . . . . **69** E7
Birmingham, Chelmsley
Wood B37. . . . . **90** F8
Cradley Heath B64 . . . . **82** E4
Dudley DY2 . . . . **62** D2
Hampton-in-A B46, B92,
CV7 . . . . **91** B5
Stonnall WS9 . . . . **16** D3
Sutton Coldfield B23, B24,
B35, B73 . . . . **57** E4

Chester Rd continued
West Bromwich B71... **42** B1
Chester Rd N
Kidderminster DY10 .. **117** A7
Sutton Coldfield B73... **45** B4
Sutton Coldfield B74... **30** F2
Chester Rd S DY10 .. **116** F4
Chester Rise B68.... **84** B8
Chester Road N WS8 .. **6** D1
Chester Road Sta B73 **57** A7
Chester St
Birmingham B6....... **67** A6
Coventry CV1 ...... **113** B3
Wolverhampton WV6 .. **25** B4
Chesterton Ave B12 .. **87** B5
Chesterton Cl
Redditch B97 .... **158** D4
Solihull B91....... **106** E5
Chesterton Ct B13 ...**86** F1
Chesterton Dr
Nuneaton CV10...... **72** A5
Royal Leamington Spa
CV31............. **162** C5
Chesterton Rd
Birmingham B12..... **87** B5
Coventry CV6 .... **113** B3
Wolverhampton WV10 . **26** A8
Chesterton Way B79 . **21** A7
Chesterwood B47 ... **125** A6
Chester Wood WS9...**30** F2
Chesterwood Gdns
B20.............. **55** D2
Chesterwood Rd
B13............. **104** F6
Chestnut Ave
Dudley DY1....... **51** C3
Kenilworth CV8...... **147** F3
Tamworth B79....... **21** B7
Tipton DY4 .... **51** F7
Chestnut Cl
Birmingham B27..... **88** C4
Cannock WS11 ....**2** C2
Solihull B92....... **106** D8
Stourbridge DY8..... **80** D3
Sutton Coldfield B74... **31** A3
Chestnut Cres CV10 .. **72** E6
Chestnut Ct
Birmingham B36..... **69** E7
Burntwood WS7 ....**6** F4
Coventry CV3 ...... **134** B8
Kidderminster DY11 .. **116** B8
Royal Leamington Spa
CV34............. **161** E2
Chestnut Dr
Birmingham, Buckland End
B36.............. **69** B7
Birmingham, Erdington
B24............... **57** C4
Birmingham, Rednal
B45............. **122** D4
Cheslyn Hay WS6 .... **4** D3
Great Wyrley WS6......**4** F3
Nuneaton CV11....... **73** E3
Shenstone WS14...... **17** F5
Walsall WS4 .... **29** B8
West Hagley DY9 .... **98** F4
Wombourne WV5 .... **49** A5
Chestnut Gr
4 Birmingham B17... **85** D5
Coventry CV4 ...... **112** A2
Kidderminster DY11 . **116** B8
Kingswinford DY6..... **60** F6
Tamworth B77....... **21** C3
Wolverhampton WV11 . **26** C7
Chestnut Pl
Birmingham B14.... **104** E8
Walsall WS3 .... **28** D6
Chestnut Rd
Astwood Bank B96 ... **158** E1
Bedworth CV12...... **78** D4
Birmingham, Brandhall
B68.............. **84** C7
Birmingham, Showell Green
B13............. **87** A4
Bromsgrove B61..... **136** F4
Walsall WS3 .... **28** E6
Wednesbury WS10 ... **42** A2
Chestnuts Ave B26... **89** B7
Chestnut Sq CV32 ... **157** B2
Chestnuts The
Bedworth CV12...... **77** E2
Kidderminster DY11 .. **116** C3
Wolverhampton WV3 .. **26** B6
Chestnut Tree Ave
CV4 .... **112** A2
Chestnut Way WV3.. **38** D8
Chestnut Wlk 2 B37 . **70** D2
Cheston Ind Est B7 ..**67** B7
Cheston Rd B7...... **67** B6

Cheswell Cl WV6..... **24** B2
Cheswick Cl
Coventry CV6 .... **114** A7
Willenhall WV13 ..... **40** F8
Cheswick Green Prim
Sch B90.......... **126** E4
Cheswick Way B90... **126** D4
Cheswood Dr B76.... **58** B6
Chesworth Rd B60 .. **137** B1
Chetland Croft B92.. **107** F7
Chettle Rd WV14....**40** F2
Chetton Ave CV6 .... **113** C6
Chetton Gn WV10 ... **11** B3
Chetwode Cl CV5.... **112** B4
Chetwood Cl WV6.... **25** A5
Chetwynd Cl WS2.... **27** D3
Chetwynd Dr CV11 ... **79** B7
Chetwynd Gdns WS11 . **1** D3
Chetwynd Jun Sch
CV11............. **79** A7
Chetwynd Rd
Birmingham B8...... **68** B5
Wolverhampton WV2 .. **39** B6
Cheveley Ave B45 ... **122** B7
Chevening Cl DY3.... **50** E7
Cheveral Ave CV6.... **113** B6
Cheveral Rd CV12 ... **78** A3
Cheverel Pl CV11.... **73** B2
Cheverel St CV11.... **73** B2
Cheveridge Cl B91 .. **107** A2
Cheverton Rd B31.. **102** E4
Cheviot B77........ **22** C1
Cheviot Cl CV10.... **72** B3
Cheviot Ct B75...... **32** A4
Cheviot Rd
Stourbridge DY8..... **81** A6
Wolverhampton WV2 .. **39** F7
Cheviot Rise
Cannock WS12 ....**2** C5
Royal Leamington Spa
CV32............. **157** C3
Cheviot The CV4 ... **132** D6
Cheviot Way B63.... **82** D2
Cheylesmore CV1 ... **165** B2
Cheylesmore Cl B73.. **46** B4
Cheyne Ct 3 B17... **85** D5
Cheyne Gdns B28 ... **105** E3
Cheyne Pl B17...... **85** D5
Cheyne Wlk DY5.... **81** C7
Cheyney Cl WV6..... **25** A5
Chichester Ave CV2.. **62** D5
Chichester Cl CV11... **74** A7
Chichester Ct B73... **46** B5
Chichester Dr
Birmingham B32..... **84** A5
Cannock WS12 ....**2** C1
Chichester Gr B37... **70** B1
Chideock Hill CV3.. **133** A6
Chiel Cl CV5....... **111** F4
Chigwell Cl B35..... **58** A3
Chilcote Cl B28.... **105** F4
Chilcote Prim Sch
B28............. **105** F4
Childs Ave WV14 .... **40** A2
Childs Oak Cl CV7... **130** A6
Chilgrove Gdns WV6 . **24** C5
Chilham Dr B37..... **70** C2
Chillaton Rd CV6.... **95** B2
Chillenden Ct WV13 .. **27** C2
Chillingham B77.... **35** C7
Chillinghome Rd B36. **68** D8
Chillinghome Twr
B36.............**57** F1
Chillington Cl WS6....**4** F1
Chillington Dr
Codsall WV8 .... **10** A4
Dudley DY1........ **50** F3
Chillington Fields
WV1 .... **26** A1
Chillington Ho WV6 .. **24** C5
Chillington Pl WV14.. **40** C5
Chillington Rd DY4... **41** C1
Chillington St WV1... **25** F1
Chillington Wlk B65.. **63** D3
Chillington Works Ind Est
WV1.............**25** F1
Chiltern Cl
Cheslyn Hay WS6 .... **4** D1
Dudley DY3........ **50** D3
Halesowen B63...... **82** D1
Chiltern Ct
2 Coventry CV6 .... **113** A5
Sutton Coldfield B75... **32** A4
Chiltern Dr WV13.... **26** D1
Chiltern Ho
Coventry CV5 ...... **111** D4
Redditch B98 ...... **154** E1
Chiltern Leys 2 CV6 **113** A4
Chiltern Rd
Stourbridge DY8..... **81** B6

Chiltern Rd continued
Tamworth B77....... **22** C1
Chilterns The
Coventry CV5 ...... **112** B4
Oldbury B69....... **63** E5
Chilton Ct B23...... **56** C2
Chilton Rd B14..... **105** D4
Chilvers Coton Com Inf
Sch CV11..........**73** B3
Chilvers Coton Craft Ctr
CV11............. **73** C2
Chilvers Ct CV11 .... **73** C3
Chilvers Gr B37......**69** F5
Chilwell Cl B91 .... **107** B1
Chilwell Croft B19 ... **66** E6
Chilworth Ave WV11...**26** F7
Chilworth Cl
4 Birmingham B6... **66** F6
Nuneaton CV11...... **78** E8
Chimes Cl B33...... **69** E1
Chimney Rd DY4.... **52** D6
Chines The CV10 .... **73** D7
Chingford Cl DY8.... **60** C4
Chingford Rd
Birmingham B44...... **56** A8
Coventry CV6 ...... **96** A4
Chinley Gr B44...... **45** C1
Chinn Brook Ho B14 **105** B4
Chinn Brook Rd B13. **105** C5
Chip CI B38........ **103** D2
Chipperfield Rd B36.. **68** E8
Chipstead Rd B23.... **56** E7
Chipstone Cl B91.... **107** C1
Chirbury Gr B31..... **103** B1
Chirk Cl DY10 ...... **116** E2
Chirton Gr B14..... **104** D6
Chiseldon Croft B14. **105** A3
Chisholm Gr B27.... **106** C8
Chiswell Rd B18 .... **65** E4
Chiswick Ct 1 B23... **56** C2
Chiswick Ho 2 B15.. **86** C8
Chiswick Wlk B37.... **70** E2
Chivenor Ho B35.... **58** A2
Chivenor Jun & Inf Sch
B35.............. **58** A2
Chivington Cl B90... **127** B6
Chorley Ave B34.....**68** F6
Chorley Gdns WV14 .. **40** B5
Chorley Way CV6.... **113** C6
Christ Church CE Inf
Sch
Wolverhampton, Dunstall
Hill WV6 .... **25** B4
Wolverhampton WV6 .. **24** B3
Christ Church CE Jun Sch
WV6............. **24** C4
Christ Church CE Prim
Sch
Birmingham B11..... **87** B7
Dudley WV14 ...... **40** D1
Lichfield WS13 ....**8** F7
Oldbury B69 ...... **64** A8
Walsall WS3 .... **28** D7
Christchurch Cl
Birmingham B15..... **85** E8
Nuneaton CV10...... **72** F1
Christ Church Gdns
WS13 ....**8** F7
Christ Church Gr
WS1 .... **43** A7
Christchurch La WS13 .. **8** F7
Christchurch Rd
CV6 .... **113** A5
Christina Ct 5 B71.. **53** D4
Christine Cl DY4 .... **41** C2
Christine Ledger Sq 9
CV31............ **162** A6
Christopher Cadbury
Reserve The* B61 . **150** B3
Christopher Hooke Ho
CV6 .... **113** E8
Christopher Rd
Birmingham B29..... **85** C2
Halesowen B62...... **83** E3
Wolverhampton WV2 . **163** D1
Christopher Wlk WS13 .**3** A3
Christ the King RC Inf
Sch CV6 .... **112** F6
Christ the King RC Jun
Sch CV6 .... **112** F7
Christ The King RC Prim
Sch B44........... **56** A8
Chub B77......... **35** D7
Chubb St WV1..... **163** D3
Chuckery Prim Sch
WS1............. **29** A1
Chuckery Rd WS1.... **29** A1
Chudleigh Gr B43.... **54** D8

Chudleigh Rd
Birmingham B23..... **56** E4
Coventry CV2 ...... **114** E7
Churchacre B23..... **56** C8
Church Ave
Birmingham, Handsworth
B20.............. **55** C1
Birmingham, Moseley
B13.............. **86** F3
Clent DY9 .... **99** F3
Stourbridge DY8..... **81** A7
Water Orton B46..... **59** B3
Churchbridge B69....**63** F6
Churchbridge Pk WS11 **4** E5
Church Cl
Birmingham B37..... **70** A6
Drayton Bassett B78 .. **34** E5
Hartshill WV10..... **72** B8
Hinckley LE10 ..... **76** A5
Ryton-on-D CV8 .... **135** B2
Shenstone WS14..... **18** A5
Whitnash WS31..... **162** B4
Wood End CV9 ..... **36** C1
Wythall B47........ **124** F3
Church Cres WV11 ... **12** F3
Church Croft
Birmingham B17..... **85** B4
Halesowen B63...... **83** A4
Church Cross View
DY1 .... **61** D8
Church Ct
Astwood Bank B96 .. **158** E2
Coventry CV6 .... **94** F1
3 Cradley Heath B64 .. **62** E1
Stourbridge DY8..... **81** A5
Walsall WS1 .... **28** F1
Churchdale Cl CV10 .. **72** C4
Churchdale Rd B44... **44** D3
Church Down Cl
B97............. **158** D6
Churchdown Ct B23.. **56** C2
Church Dr
Birmingham B30..... **104** B7
Hopwas B78 .... **20** B7
Kenilworth CV8..... **147** F5
Church End CV31.... **162** E6
Church Farm Barn &
Cotts DY10 .... **98** B3
Churchfield Ave DY4 ..**51** F8
Churchfield Cl B7.... **67** C6
Churchfield Ind Est
DY2............. **62** C8
Churchfield Rd WV10. **25** B8
Churchfields
Birmingham B43..... **44** D4
Bromsgrove B61..... **136** F3
Kidderminster DY10 .. **116** E7
Churchfields Bsns Pk
DY10............ **116** E7
Churchfields Cl B61. **136** F3
Churchfields Gdns
B61............. **136** F3
Churchfields Rd
Bromsgrove B61..... **136** F3
Wednesbury WS10 ... **42** A4
Churchfield St DY2... **62** C8
Church Gdns
Smethwick B67..... **65** A4
Wolverhampton WV10 . **26** A4
Church Gn
Bilston WV14 ...... **40** D1
Birmingham B20..... **55** A2
Church Gn E B98.... **153** E4
Church Gn W B97... **153** E4
Church Gr B13..... **105** C5
Church Hill
Belbroughton DY9... **119** D6
Beoley B98 .... **154** D8
Birmingham, Northfield
B31............. **103** B3
Brierley Hill DY5.... **61** D2
Cannock WS12 .... **2** D4
Cubbington CV32.... **157** E5
Frankley B32....... **102** B6
Royal Leamington Spa
CV32............ **161** E8
8 Walsall WS1 .... **28** F1
6 Wednesbury WS10 . **41** F3
Wolverhampton WV4 .. **38** E4
Church Hill Cl B91.. **107** C2
Church Hill Ct 1
WS10 ....**41** F3
Church Hill Dr WV6.. **24** E5
Church Hill Mid Sch
B98............. **154** D6
Church Hill Rd
Birmingham B20..... **55** C1
Solihull B91....... **107** C3
Wolverhampton WV6.. **24** D5
Church Hill St B67...**64** F6

Church Hill Way
B98............. **154** D6
Church Ho
Brierley Hill DY5.... **61** C2
Walsall WS2 .... **42** C7
Churchill Ave
Coventry CV6 ...... **113** E8
Kenilworth CV8..... **148** A6
Churchill Cl B69.... **52** C2
Churchill Dr
Rowley Regis B65.... **63** B2
Stourbridge DY8..... **81** A7
Churchill Gdns DY3.. **50** C7
Churchill Ho 11
CV32............ **161** F8
Churchill La DY10 ... **98** B3
Churchill Par B75.... **47** A5
Churchill Pl B33.... **69** B1
Churchill Rd
Birmingham B9...... **67** F3
Halesowen B63...... **82** F2
Shenstone WS14..... **18** A5
Sutton Coldfield, Falcon
Lodge B75 .... **47** A5
Sutton Coldfield, New Oscott
B73............. **45** C3
Upper Catshill B61... **121** A1
Walsall WS2 .... **27** E3
Churchill Sh Ctr 3
DY2............. **51** D1
Churchill Wlk 5 DY4. **52** A8
Church La
Ash Green CV7..... **95** E7
Aston Flamville LE10 .. **76** F1
Berkswell CV7...... **110** C3
Bickenhill B92...... **90** E2
Birmingham, Aston B6 .. **67** A8
Birmingham, Handsworth
B20.............. **55** A2
Birmingham, Kitt's Green
B33............. **69** A3
Bromsgrove B61..... **136** F2
Corley CV7 .... **94** B7
Coventry, Middle Stoke
CV2............. **114** B3
Coventry, Upper Eastern
Green CV5 .... **111** C5
Cubbington CV32.... **157** E5
Curdworth B76..... **59** B6
Halesowen B63..... **83** B4
Hammerwich WS7 .... **7** D3
Lapworth B94...... **143** C5
Leek Wootton CV35.. **155** F6
Meriden CV7....... **110** E8
Middleton B78...... **34** C1
Nuneaton CV10..... **73** C7
Radford Semele CV31. **162** E6
Royal Leamington Spa
CV32............ **157** A3
Shuttington B79 .... **22** E7
Stoneleigh CV8..... **149** C6
Stonnall WS9 ...... **16** E4
Tamworth B79...... **21** B5
Trysull WV5........ **37** B2
West Bromwich B71... **53** C6
Whitnash CV31..... **162** B4
Wishaw B76 .... **48** A2
Wolverhampton WV2 . **163** D1
Church Lane Ind Est
B71............. **53** C6
Church Mews
Tipton DY4 .... **51** E8
Walsall WS3 .... **28** B8
Church Moat Way 1
WS3............. **28** B8
Church of the Ascension
CE Prim Sch DY6.. **60** C8
Churchover Cl B76... **57** D6
Church Park Cl CV6 ..**94** F1
Church Pl
Birmingham B12.... **86** F5
Walsall WS3 .... **28** D8
Church Rd
Astwood Bank B96 .. **158** E2
Baginton CV8 ..... **133** F2
Belbroughton DY9... **119** D6
Birmingham, Aston B6 . **67** B7
Birmingham, Edgbaston
B15.............. **86** A7
Birmingham, Erdington
B24............... **57** A4
Birmingham, Moseley
B13.............. **87** A3
Birmingham, Northfield
B31............. **103** A4
Birmingham, Perry Barr
B42............... **55** D5
Birmingham, Sheldon
B26.............. **89** C6

Church Rd continued
Birmingham, South Yardley
B25.............. **88** E8
Birmingham, Stechford
B33.............. **68** F2
Bromsgrove B61..... **136** F2
Brownhills WS8 .... **15** F7
Burntwood WS7 .... **7** D7
Catshill B61....... **136** F8
Coseley, Daisy Bank
WV14 .... **40** D1
Dodford B61....... **136** A7
Dudley, Netherton DY2. **62** C4
Halesowen B63...... **82** C7
Hartshill CV10...... **72** B8
Huntington WS11......**1** A2
Norton Canes WS11.....**5** E4
Nuneaton, Stockingford
CV10............. **72** C3
Perton WV6........ **23** C4
Redditch, St George's
B97............. **153** E4
Redditch, Webheath
B97............. **152** F2
Rowley Regis B65.... **63** C3
Ryton-on-D CV8 .... **135** B2
Shenstone WS14..... **17** F5
Shilton CV7 .... **97** E5
Smethwick B67..... **65** A4
Solihull B90....... **106** B2
Stonnall WS9 ...... **16** E3
Stourbridge DY8..... **60** E2
Stourbridge, Lye DY9 .. **81** E5
Stourbridge, Old Swinford
DY8.............. **81** B3
Sutton Coldfield B73... **56** F8
Sutton Coldfield, Maney B72,
B73............. **46** B3
Tamworth B77....... **35** C4
Walsall WS3 .... **15** A3
Willenhall WV12 .... **27** D6
Wolverhampton, Oxbarn
WV3 .... **38** F7
Wolverhampton, Oxley
WV10 .... **11** C1
Wolverhampton, Tettenhall
Wood WV6 .... **24** D5
Wolverhampton, Tettenhall
WV6............. **24** E5
Wombourne WV5 .... **49** B7
Church Row B78..... **34** B1
Church Row Cotts
DY9.............. **99** F3
Churchside Way WS9. **16** B2
Church Sq 4 B69... **64** A7
Church St
Bilston WV14 ...... **40** D5
Birmingham B3..... **164** B3
Birmingham, Lozells
B19.............. **66** C7
Brierley Hill, Barrow Hill
DY5.............. **61** D7
Brierley Hill, Quarry Bank
DY5.............. **61** F1
Brierley Hill, Silver End
DY5.............. **61** C2
Bromsgrove B61..... **136** F2
Brownhills WS8 .... **15** E6
Bulkington CV12 .... **79** C2
Burntwood WS7 .... **6** E5
Cannock, Bridgtown
WS11 .... **4** D6
Cannock, Chadsmoor
WS11.............. **2** A4
Cannock WS11 .... **1** E1
Coventry CV1 ...... **165** C4
Cradley Heath B64... **62** E1
Darlaston, Woods Bank
WS10............. **41** C4
Darlaston WS10 .... **41** D6
Dudley, Gornalwood
DY3.............. **50** D3
Dudley, Kate's Hill DY2. **62** C8
Halesowen B62...... **63** D1
Hinckley LE10 ..... **76** A5
Kidderminster DY10 .. **116** E6
Lichfield WS13, WS14....**9** C8
Nuneaton CV11..... **73** C4
Oldbury B69....... **64** A8
Royal Leamington Spa
CV31............ **162** A7
Stourbridge DY8..... **81** A5
Studley B80....... **159** E3
Tamworth B79...... **21** B5
Tipton DY4 .... **52** A2
Walsall, Blakenall Green
WS3............. **28** B8
Walsall WS1 .... **28** F1

Church St continued
Warwick CV34 . . . . . . **160** E6
Wednesfield WV11 . . . . **26** C5
West Bromwich B70 . . . **53** C4
West Hagley DY9 . . . . . **99** A5
Willenhall WV13 . . . . . **27** B2
Wolverhampton, Heath Town
 WV10 . . . . **26** A4
Wolverhampton WV2 . **163** B2
Churchstone Cl B61 . **136** F8
Church Terr
Cubbington CV32 . . . . **157** E7
1 Royal Leamington Spa
 CV31 . . . . **162** A7
Sutton Coldfield B75 . . . **32** C3
Church Vale
Birmingham B20 . . . . . . **55** B1
Norton Canes WS11 . . . . .**5** C4
West Bromwich B71 . . . **53** D5
Church Vale Mews
 B71 . . . . **53** D5
Church View
Aldridge WS9 . . . . **30** B6
Birmingham B11 . . . . . . **87** C6
Brownhills WS9 . . . . . . **15** F3
Dudley DY3 . . . . . **50** D3
Tamworth B77 . . . . **35** F7
Wythall B47 . . . . **124** E2
Church View Cl WS3 . . **28** D8
Church View Dr B64 . . **62** F1
Churchward Cl DY8 . . **81** B6
Churchward Gr WV5. . **49** A8
Church Way
Bedworth CV12 . . . . . . **78** B2
Walsall WS4 . . . . **15** C2
Churchwell Ct
Halesowen B63 . . . . . . **83** B4
Wombourne WV5 . . . . . **49** A6
Churchwell Gdns B71 **53** E6
Church Wlk
Allesley CV5 . . . . **112** C6
Birmingham B8 . . . . . . **68** A6
Hinckley LE10 . . . . **75** D8
Kidderminster DY11 . . **116** C6
Rowley Regis B65 . . . . . **63** C4
1 Royal Leamington Spa
 CV31 . . . . **161** F7
Wolverhampton, Oxbarn
 WV3 . . . . **38** F7
Wolverhampton, Tettenhall
 WV6 . . . . **24** E5
Churchyard Rd DY4 . . **52** B5
Churnet Gr WV6. . . . . . **23** F4
Churn Hill Rd WS9 . . . **30** B4
Churns Hill La DY3 . . . **49** B3
Churston Cl WS3 . . . . . **14** A3
Chylds Ct CV5. . . . . . . **112** A5
Cicero App CV34 . . . . **161** E2
Cider Ave DY5. . . . . . . **81** E8
Cinder Bank DY2 . . . . . **62** C6
Cinder Bank Island
 DY2 . . . . **62** B7
Cinder Rd
Burntwood WS7 . . . .**6** E7
Dudley DY3 . . . . **50** B2
Cinder Way 2 WS10 . **41** E3
Cinquefoil Leasow 5
 DY4 . . . . **52** C6
Circle The
Birmingham B17 . . . . . . **85** C6
Nuneaton CV10 . . . . . . **72** F4
Circuit Cl WV13 . . . . . **27** B3
Circular Rd B27 . . . . . **88** C2
Circus Ave B37 . . . . . . **70** C2
Cirencester Cl B60 . . **137** B2
City Arc
1 Birmingham B2 . . . **164** C2
Coventry CV1 . . . . . . **165** B2
1 Lichfield WS13 . . . . . .**9** B7
City Coll
Birmingham B33 . . . . . **89** B8
Birmingham, Sparkbrook
 B11 . . . . **87** A7
Birmingham, Sparkhill
 B11 . . . . **87** D5
City Coll Birmingham (St
 George's Sixth Form
 Ctr) B19 . . . . **164** B5
City Coll Coventry (Butts
 Ctr) CV1 . . . . **113** A2
City Coll Coventry
 (Maxwell Ctr) CV1. **113** B1
City College Coventry
 (Tile Hill Ctr) CV4 . **111** F1
City Coll (Handsworth
 Campus) B21 . . . .**65** F8
City Est B64 . . . . **82** D8
City Hospl B18 . . . . . .**65** F4

City of Wolverhampton
 Coll (Bilston Campus)
 WV14 . . . .**40** B7
City of Wolverhampton
 Coll (Metro One
 Campus) WV1 . . . . **163** C2
City Rd
Birmingham B16 . . . . . . **65** C2
Oldbury B69 . . . . **63** C8
City Road Prim Sch
 B16 . . . . **65** D3
City Tech Coll The
 B37 . . . . **70** A4
City Trad Est B16 . . . . **66** A3
City View
Birmingham, Saltley
 B8. . . . . **67** D4
Birmingham, Stockland
 Green B23 . . . . **56** D3
Civic Cl B1. . . . . **66** C2
Civic Hall★ WV1 . . . **163** B3
Cladsworth Ho 1
 B97 . . . . **153** A4
Claerwen Gr B31. . . . **102** E5
Claines Cres DY10 . . . **117** B5
Claines Rd
Birmingham B31 . . . . . **103** C4
Halesowen B63. . . . . . . **82** D5
Claire Ct B26 . . . . **89** C7
Clairvaux Gdns B91 . **106** D5
Clandon Cl B14 . . . . . **104** C2
Clanfield Ave WV11. .**26** F7
Clapgate Gdns WV14. **40** A3
Clapgate La B32 . . . . . **84** C2
Clapham Sq CV31 . . . **162** B7
Clapham St CV31 . . . **162** B6
Clapham Terr CV31 . . **162** B7
Clapham Terrace Com
 Prim Sch CV31 . . . **162** B7
Clapton Gr B44 . . . . . . **45** B1
Clarage Ho B62 . . . . . **83** D8
Clara St CV2 . . . . **114** A2
Clare Ave WV11 . . . . . .**12** F1
Clare Cl CV32 . . . . . . **157** C2
Clare Cres WV14 . . . .**39** F2
Clare Ct B90 . . . . **105** D2
Clare Dr B15. . . . .**85** F8
Claregate Prim Sch
 WV6. . . . .**24** F7
Clarel Ave B8 . . . . **67** C3
Claremont Cl CV12 . . . **79** B4
Claremont Cotts DY3. **50** E8
Claremont Ct 2 B64 . **62** E1
Claremont Mews
 WV3 . . . . **39** A7
Claremont Pl 1 B18 . **66** A5
Claremont Rd
Birmingham, Hockley
 B18. . . . . **66** B6
Birmingham, Sparkbrook
 B11 . . . . **87** B7
Royal Leamington Spa
 CV31 . . . . **161** F6
Sedgley DY3 . . . . **50** E8
Smethwick B66 . . . . . . **65** B4
Tamworth B79 . . . . **21** A8
Wolverhampton WV3 . . **39** B7
Claremont St
Bilston WV14 . . . . **40** C6
Cradley Heath B64 . . . . **62** E1
Claremont Way B63 . . **83** A3
Claremont Wlk CV5 . **112** C6
Clarence Ave B21 . . . . **65** C8
Clarence Ct
5 Hinckley LE10 . . . . **75** E8
Oldbury B68 . . . . **64** C2
Clarence Gdns B74. . . **31** F3
Clarence Ho 7 CV32 **156** F1
Clarence Mews 1
 B17 . . . . **85** D6
Clarence Rd
Bilston WV14 . . . . **40** F7
Birmingham B17 . . . . . . **85** D6
Birmingham, Gravelly Hill
 B23 . . . . **56** D3
Birmingham, Handsworth
 B21 . . . . **65** C8
Birmingham, King's Heath
 B13 . . . . **87** A1
Birmingham, Sparkhill
 B11 . . . . **87** D4
Dudley DY2 . . . . **62** D6
Hinckley LE10 . . . . **75** E8
Sutton Coldfield B74. . . **31** F4
Wolverhampton WV1 . **163** B3
Clarence St
5 Coventry CV1 . . . **113** C4
Dudley DY3 . . . . **50** E5
Kidderminster DY10 . . **116** F6
Nuneaton CV11 . . . . . . **73** A4

Clarence St continued
Royal Leamington Spa
 CV31 . . . . **162** A6
Wolverhampton WV1 . **163** B3
Clarence Terr 6
 CV32 . . . . **156** F1
Clarenden Pl B17 . . . . **85** C5
Clarendon Ave CV32. **156** F1
Clarendon Cl B97 . . . **153** B5
Clarendon Cres
 CV32 . . . . **156** E1
Clarendon Dr DY4 . . . . **52** D8
Clarendon Gdns 3
 B20 . . . . **55** D1
Clarendon Ho LE10 . . . **75** B7
Clarendon Pl
Birmingham B62 . . . . . . **84** A6
Royal Leamington Spa
 CV32 . . . . **156** E1
Walsall WS3 . . . . **14** F3
Clarendon Rd
Birmingham B16 . . . . . . **65** E1
Hinckley LE10 . . . . **75** C7
Kenilworth CV8 . . . . . **148** A3
Smethwick B67 . . . . . . **64** F4
Sutton Coldfield B75. . . **32** C3
Walsall WS4 . . . . **15** C2
Clarendon Sq CV32 . . **156** F1
Clarendon St
Coventry CV5 . . . . **112** F1
Royal Leamington Spa
 CV32 . . . . **157** A1
Walsall WS3 . . . . **14** B1
Wolverhampton WV3 . . **25** A2
Clare Rd Walsall WS3. . **29** A6
Wolverhampton WV10 . **25** A6
Clare's Ct DY11 . . . . **116** C6
Clarewell Ave B91. . . **127** B8
Clare Witnell Cl
 DY11 . . . . **116** B8
Clarion Way WS11. . . . . .**1** E5
Clarke Ho WS3 . . . . . . **14** B1
Clarke's Ave CV8 . . . . **148** A3
Clarkes Gr DY4 . . . . . . **52** C6
Clarkes La WV13 . . . . . **27** C3
Clarke's La B71 . . . . . . **53** C7
Clarke St 1 B97 . . . . **153** B1
Clark Rd WV3 . . . .**24** F2
Clarks La B90 . . . . . . **126** A6
Clarksland Gr B37. . . . **90** A8
Clarkson Dr CV31 . . . **162** A4
Clarkson Place Ind Est
 DY5. . . . .**81** E7
Clarkson Rd WS10 . . . . **42** A3
Clark St
Birmingham B16 . . . . . . **65** F2
Coventry CV6 . . . . **96** A1
Stourbridge DY8 . . . . . . **80** E4
Clarry Dr B74 . . . .**45** F8
Clary Gr WS5 . . . . **43** A3
Clatterbach La DY9. . **100** A4
Claughton Ct DY11 . . **116** C5
Claughton Rd DY2. . . . **51** D1
Claughton Road N 8
 DY2 . . . . **51** D1
Claughton St DY11 . . **116** C5
Clausen Cl B43. . . . . . . **44** E4
Clavedon Cl B31 . . . . **102** E7
Claverdon Cl
Brownhills WS8 . . . . . . **16** A8
Redditch B97 . . . . **158** D4
Solihull B91 . . . . **106** E3
Claverdon Dr
Birmingham B43. . . . . . **54** D7
Sutton Coldfield B74. . . **31** B4
Claverdon Gdns B27. . **88** B5
Claverdon Ho
Birmingham B13 . . . . . **105** A7
Warwick CV34 . . . . . . **161** B8
Claverdon Rd CV5. . . **112** B3
Claverley Ct 6 DY1 . . **51** B1
Claverley Dr WV4 . . . . **38** D5
Clay Ave CV11 . . . .**73** F7
Claybrook Dr B98 . . . **159** F7
Claybrook St B5 . . . . **164** C1
Claycroft Pl DY9 . . . . . **81** E5
Claycroft Terr DY1. . . **51** B6
Claydon Gr 3 B14 . . **105** A3
Claydon Rd DY6. . . . . . **49** C1
Clay Dr B32 . . . . **84** A5
Claygate Rd WS12. . . . . .**2** E3
Clayhanger La WS8 . . **15** D6
Clayhanger Rd WS8 . . .**15** F6
Clay La
Birmingham B26 . . . . . . **88** E5
Coventry CV2 . . . . **114** A4
Harvest Hill CV5 . . . . . **93** E3
Oldbury B69 . . . . **64** A4
Claymore B77 . . . . **35** E7

Claypit Cl B70 . . . . **53** A3
Claypit La
Fairfield B61 . . . . **120** E1
West Bromwich B70 . . . **53** A4
Clay Pit La
Lichfield WS14 . . . .**8** F3
Solihull B90 . . . . **126** A5
Clayton Cl WV2 . . . . . . **39** C7
Clayton Dr
Birmingham B36 . . . . . . **69** C7
Bromsgrove B60 . . . . . **151** B7
Clayton Gdns B45 . . . **122** A2
Clayton Ho 3 B16 . . .**65** F1
Clayton Rd
Birmingham B8 . . . . . . **67** D5
Coventry CV6 . . . . **112** E5
Dudley WV14 . . . . **51** B7
Clayton Wlk B35 . . . . . **58** A2
Clear View DY6. . . . . . **60** B6
Clearwater Ind Est
 WV2 . . . . **40** A7
Clearwell Gdns DY1. .**50** F3
Clearwell Rd B98 . . . **154** C3
Cleasby B77 . . . . **22** C1
Cleaveland Mews 2
 WS13 . . . .**3** A1
Cleaver Gdns CV10 . . **73** C6
Clee Ave DY11 . . . . . . **116** C2
Clee Hill Dr WV3 . . . . . **24** A1
Clee Hill Rd DY3 . . . . . **50** D4
Clee Rd
Birmingham B31 . . . . . **123** A8
Dudley DY2 . . . . **62** A7
Oldbury B69 . . . . **64** C4
Stourbridge DY8 . . . . . . **81** A6
Cleeton St WS12 . . . . . .**2** D1
Cleeve B77 . . . . **21** D3
Cleeve Cl B98 . . . . . . **154** D5
Cleeve Dr B74 . . . .**31** F6
Cleeve Ho B24 . . . . . . **57** A2
Cleeve Rd
Birmingham B14 . . . . . **105** C4
Walsall WS3 . . . . **13** F3
Cleeve Way WS3 . . . . .**13** F3
Clee View Mdw DY3 . . **39** D2
Clegg Rd WS7. . . . .**7** E7
Clematis B77 . . . . **21** F3
Clematis Dr WV9 . . . . .**10** F3
Clem Attlee Ct WV13 . **40** D8
Clemens St CV31. . . . **162** A7
Clement Ho CV8 . . . . **148** A5
Clement Pl WV14. . . . . **40** D7
Clement Rd
Bilston WV14 . . . . **40** D7
Halesowen B62 . . . . . . **63** D1
Clements Cl
Kenilworth CV8. . . . . . **148** A5
Oldbury B69 . . . . **63** F4
Clements Rd B25. . . . . **88** D8
Clements St CV2 . . . . **114** A3
Clement St
Birmingham B1 . . . . . . **66** B3
Nuneaton CV11 . . . . . . **73** B3
Walsall WS2 . . . . **28** D1
Clemson St WV13 . . . . **27** A2
Clennon Rise CV2 . . . **114** D8
Clensmore St DY10 . . **116** D7
Clent Ave
Kidderminster DY11 . . **116** B1
Redditch B97 . . . . **158** D7
Clent Cott DY9 . . . .**99** F3
Clent Ct 5 DY1 . . . . . **51** B1
Clent Dr Hagley DY9. . . **99** D6
Nuneaton CV10 . . . . . . **72** B3
Clent Hill Dr B65 . . . . . **63** A5
Clent Hills Ctry Pk★
 DY9 . . . . **100** A4
Clent Ho B63 . . . . **83** A2
Clent Prim Sch DY9. .**99** F2
Clent Rd
Birmingham B45 . . . . . **121** E8
Birmingham, Handsworth
 B21. . . . . **54** D1
Oldbury B68 . . . . **64** C1
Stourbridge DY8 . . . . . . **81** A6
Clent View B66 . . . . . . **65** B3
Clent View Rd
Birmingham B32 . . . . . . **84** A1
Halesowen B63. . . . . . . **82** C5
Stourbridge DY8 . . . . . . **80** C2
Clent Villas B12 . . . . . **87** B4
Clent Way B32 . . . . . . **102** A8
Cleobury Cl B97 . . . . **153** B5
Cleobury La B94 . . . . **126** A3
Cleopatra Gr CV34 . . **161** E4
Cleton St DY4 . . . . **52** B3
Cleton Street Bsns Pk
 DY4. . . . .**52** B3
Clevedon Ave B36. . . . **69** D8

Clevedon Rd B12. . . . . **86** E6
Cleveland Cl
Willenhall WV13 . . . . . **26** D1
Wolverhampton WV11 . **12** F1
Cleveland Ct
16 Birmingham B13 . . **87** B2
1 Royal Leamington Spa
 CV32 . . . . **156** F2
Wolverhampton WV2 . **163** B2
Cleveland Dr
Barnt Green B45 . . . . . **122** A2
Cannock WS11 . . . .**2** B4
Cleveland Pas WV1. . **163** B2
Cleveland Rd
Bulkington CV12 . . . . . **79** B3
Coventry CV2 . . . . **114** A4
Hinckley LE10 . . . . **75** C8
Wolverhampton WV2 . **163** C2
Cleveland St
14 Dudley, New Dock
 DY1. . . . . **51** B1
4 Dudley, Old Dock
 DY1. . . . . **62** B8
Stourbridge DY8 . . . . . . **80** E4
Wolverhampton WV1 . **163** B2
Cleveland Twr B1 . . . **164** B1
Cleveley Dr CV10 . . . . **72** D7
Cleves Cres WS6 . . . . . .**4** D1
Cleves Dr B45 . . . . . . **121** E7
Cleves Rd B45 . . . . . . **121** E8
Clewley Dr WV9 . . . . . **11** B3
Clewley Gr B32 . . . . . . **84** B5
Clews Cl WS1 . . . . **42** E7
Clewshaw La B38 . . . **124** C4
Clews Rd B98 . . . . . . **158** F7
Cley Cl B5 . . . . **86** D6
Clifden Gr CV8 . . . . . . **148** C6
Cliffe Ct CV32 . . . . . . **156** D1
Cliffe Dr B33 . . . . **69** C3
Cliffe Rd CV32 . . . . . . **156** D1
Cliffe Way CV34 . . . . . **161** A8
Cliff Hall La B78 . . . . . **35** C1
Clifford Bridge Prim Sch
 CV3. . . . . **115** A3
Clifford Bridge Rd
 CV3 . . . . **114** F4
Clifford Cl B77 . . . . . . **21** F3
Clifford Rd
Bentley Heath B93 . . . **127** F4
Smethwick B67 . . . . . . **64** F1
West Bromwich B70 . . . **53** B2
Clifford St
Birmingham B19 . . . . . . **66** D7
3 Dudley DY1 . . . . . . **62** B8
Tamworth B77 . . . . **21** E3
Wolverhampton WV6 . . **25** A3
Clifford Wlk B19 . . . . . **66** D7
Cliff Rock Rd B45 . . . **122** B7
Clift Cl WV12 . . . . **27** C6
Clifton Ave
Aldridge WS9 . . . . **16** C1
Brownhills WS8 . . . . . . **15** D7
Cannock WS11 . . . .**4** C7
Tamworth B79 . . . . **21** A7
Clifton Cl
Birmingham B6 . . . . . . **66** F7
Oldbury B69 . . . . **64** A4
Clifton Cres B91 . . . . **106** F1
Clifton Ct
Hinckley LE10 . . . . **71** B1
5 Royal Leamington Spa
 CV31 . . . . **162** B7
Clifton Dr B73 . . . . **46** B6
Clifton Gdns WV8 . . . . **10** C3
Clifton Gn B28 . . . . . . **106** A5
Clifton La B71 . . . . **53** E8
Clifton Prim Sch B12 **87** A5
Clifton Rd
Birmingham, Aston B6 . **66** F7
Birmingham, Balsall Heath
 B12. . . . . **87** A5
Birmingham, Castle
 Bromwich B36 . . . . . . **69** E8
Halesowen B62. . . . . . . **83** E8
Kidderminster DY11 . . **116** A1
Nuneaton CV10 . . . . . . **72** F4
Smethwick B67 . . . . . . **64** F4
Sutton Coldfield B73. . . **46** B5
Wolverhampton WV6 . . **24** D5
Clifton Road Ind Est
 B12. . . . .**86** F5
Clifton St
Coventry CV1 . . . . **165** D4
Cradley Heath B64 . . . . **62** F1
Dudley WV14 . . . . **51** A8
Sedgley DY3 . . . . **39** F1
Stourbridge DY8 . . . . . . **80** F4
Wolverhampton WV3 . . **25** B2
Clifton Terr B23 . . . . . . **56** F4

Clifton Way LE10 . . . . . **71** A1
Clinic Dr
Nuneaton CV11 . . . . . . **73** C3
Stourbridge DY9 . . . . . . **81** E5
Clinton Ave
Hampton Magna
 CV35. . . . . **160** A7
Kenilworth CV8. . . . . . **147** D6
Clinton Cres WS7 . . . . . .**7** B8
Clinton Gr B90 . . . . . . **106** E1
Clinton La CV8 . . . . . . **147** D6
Clinton Prim Sch
 CV8. . . . . **147** E3
Clinton Rd
Bilston WV14 . . . . **41** A7
Coleshill B46. . . . . **70** F6
Coventry CV6 . . . . **95** F2
Solihull B90 . . . . **106** C1
Clinton St
Birmingham B18 . . . . . . **65** E5
2 Royal Leamington Spa
 CV31 . . . . **162** A7
Clipper View B16. . . . . **65** E1
Clipstone Rd CV6 . . . **112** E6
Clipston Rd B8. . **67** F4
Clissold Cl B12. . . . . . . **86** E7
Clissold Pas B18 . . . . . **66** A4
Clissold St B18. . . . . . . **66** A4
Clive Cl B75 . . . . **32** D2
Cliveden Ave
Aldridge WS9 . . . . **16** B1
Birmingham B42 . . . . . . **55** D4
Cliveden Coppice B74 .**31** F1
Cliveden Wlk CV11 . . . **78** E8
Clivedon Way B62. . . . **83** B7
Cliveland St B19 . . . . **164** C4
Clive Rd
Balsall Common CV7. . **130** C5
Birmingham B32 . . . . . . **84** D7
Bromsgrove B60 . . . . . **151** B8
Burntwood WS7 . . . .**7** A7
Redditch B97 . . . . **153** D5
Clive St B71 . . . . **53** C5
Clivesway LE10 . . . . . . **71** C2
Clockfields Dr DY5 . . . **61** A1
Clock La B92 . . . . **90** C4
Clockmill Ave WS3 . . . **14** E3
Clockmill Pl WS3 . . . . .**14** F3
Clockmill Rd WS3 . . . . **14** E3
Clodeshall Rd B8 . . . . **67** E4
Cloister Croft CV2. . . **114** F6
Cloister Crofts CV32. **156** F3
Cloister Dr B62 . . . . . . **83** D3
Cloisters The
Royal Leamington Spa
 CV32 . . . . **156** F3
Studley B80. . . . . **159** D4
Walsall WS4 . . . . **28** C3
Cloister Way CV32. . . **156** F3
Clonmel Rd B30. . . . . **104** A6
Clopton Cres B37 . . . . **70** C4
Clopton Rd B33 . . . . . . **89** C8
Closers Bsns Ctr
 CV11. . . . . **73** D2
Close The
Birmingham B17 . . . . . . **84** F7
Birmingham, Griffin's Hill
 B29. . . . . **103** D8
Brandon CV8. . . . . **135** F5
Dudley DY3 . . . . **50** C4
Halesowen B63. . . . . . . **82** D6
Hollywood B47 . . . . . . **125** A5
Hunnington B62 . . . . . **101** A7
Kenilworth CV8. . . . . . **148** A6
Lichfield WS13 . . . .**9** A3
Solihull B92 . . . . **106** F8
Wednesbury WS10 . . . . **41** E3
Whitnash CV31 . . . . . . **162** A5
Clothier Gdns WV13 . . **27** A3
Clothier St WV13 . . . . **27** A3
Clothier Street Prim Sch
 WV13 . . . . **27** A3
Cloudbridge Dr B92. **107** F7
Cloud Gn CV4 . . . . . . **132** D5
Cloudsley Gr B92. . . . . .**88** F3
Clovelly Gdns CV2 . . . **114** C5
Clovelly Rd CV2 . . . . . **114** B5
Clovelly Way CV11 . . . **73** C6
Clover Ave B37 . . . . . . **70** C2
Clover Ct B38 . . . . **103** D2
Cloverdale
Perton WV6 . . . . **23** D4
Stoke Prior B60 . . . . . **150** C3
Cloverdale Cl CV6. . . . **95** B4
Clover Dr B32 . . . . **84** D2
Cloverfield LE10 . . . . . **71** C3
Clover Hill WS5 . . . . . . **43** E8
Clover La DY6. . . . . **60** B7
Clover Lea Sq B8 . . . . **68** A6
Clover Ley WV10 . . . . .**25** F3

Clover Mdws WS12.......2 C1
Clover Piece **6** DY4.. 52 C6
Clover Pk Trad Est
  LE10.............71 B3
Clover Rd B29....... 103 A7
Clover Ridge WS6.....4 C3
Clover Way CV12..... 77 D2
Cloweswood La B94. 141 F8
Club Cotts WV10.... 11 C6
Club La WV10........ 11 C6
Club Row DY3....... 50 E5
Club View B38....... 103 D2
Clunbury Croft B34.. 69 B5
Clunbury Rd B31... 123 A8
Clun Cl B69......... 52 A1
Clunes Ave CV11.... 73 E6
Clun Rd B31........ 102 F6
Clusters The DY9.... 81 E5
Clyde Ave B62...... 83 E8
Clyde Ct B73....... 46 B5
Clyde Mews DY5.... 61 B6
Clyde Rd
  Bulkington CV12...... 79 A2
  Dorridge B93........ 128 A2
Clydesdale B26...... 89 B5
Clydesdale Rd
  Birmingham B32...... 84 B6
  Brownhills WS8...... 15 E6
Clydesdale Twr B1.. 164 B1
Clyde St
  Birmingham B12...... 67 A1
  Cradley Heath B64.... 62 E1
Clyde Twr **3** B19.... 66 D7
Coach Cotts B45.... 138 D8
Coach House Mews **2**
  CV34............. 160 F7
Coach House Rise
  B77..............35 F7
Coalash La B60.... 151 C2
Coalbourne Gdns B63 82 C5
Coalbourn La DY8....80 F7
Coalbourn Way DY5.. 61 A3
Coal Haulage Rd WS12 .5 F8
Coalheath La WS4... 29 C6
Coalmeadow Cl WS3 .13 F3
Coalpit Fields Rd
  CV12............. 78 C1
Coal Pool La WS3...28 F5
Coalpool Pl WS3.....28 F6
Coalport Rd WV1.... 26 A1
Coalway Ave
  Birmingham B26...... 89 C4
  Wolverhampton WV3... 39 A6
Coalway Gdns WV3.. 38 D7
Coalway Rd
  Walsall WS3........ 28 A8
  Wolverhampton WV3.. 38 E6
Coates Rd DY10..... 117 B7
Coat Of Arms Bridge Rd
  CV3............. 133 A6
Coatsgate Wlk WV8...10 F1
Cobbett Rd WS7...... 6 D7
Cobbles The B72.... 57 C7
Cobble Wlk B18..... 66 A5
Cobbs Rd CV8...... 147 D6
Cobbs Wlk B65......62 F5
Cobden Ave CV31... 162 C5
Cobden Cl
  Cannock WS12.......2 C7
  Darlaston WS10..... 41 F6
  Tipton DY4.......... 51 F8
Cobden Gdns B12... 86 E6
Cobden St
  Coventry CV6....... 113 E5
  Darlaston WS10..... 41 F6
  Kidderminster DY11.. 116 C6
  Stourbridge DY8.... 80 E5
  Walsall WS1....... 42 D7
Cobham Bsns Ctr B9. 67 D2
Cobham Cl
  Birmingham B35..... 57 F3
  Bromsgrove B60.... 150 F7
Cobham Court Mews
  DY9.............. 99 D6
Cobham Gn **3** CV31. 162 A4
Cobham Rd
  Birmingham B9...... 67 D2
  Halesowen B63..... 83 B4
  Kidderminster DY10.. 116 E4
  Stourbridge DY8.... 81 B2
  Wednesbury WS10... 42 E2
Cobia B77........ 35 D7
Cob La B30....... 103 C6
Cobley Hill B48.... 138 E4
Cobnall Rd B61.... 121 A2
Cobs Field B30.... 103 C6
Coburg Croft **4** DY4. 52 C8
Coburn Dr B75.... 32 D2

Cochrane Cl
  Stourbridge DY9.... 99 C8
  2 Tipton DY4...... 52 C6
Cochrane Rd DY2....61 F5
Cockermouth Cl
  CV32............. 156 D2
Cock Hill La B45.... 121 F8
Cocksheds La B62... 83 C8
Cockshut Hill B26... 89 A8
Cockshut Hill Tech Coll
  B26............. 89 A8
Cockshutt La B61... 136 D7
Cockshutts La WV2.. 39 D7
Cocksmead Croft
  B14............. 104 D5
Cocksmoor Ho B14.. 104 D7
Cocksparrow La WS12,
  WS19.............1 B5
Cocksparrow St
  CV34............. 160 D7
Cockspur St B78.... 36 E7
Cockthorpe Cl B17...84 F7
Cocton Cl WV6..... 23 E5
Codsall Com High Sch
  WV8............. 10 A4
Codsall Mid Sch WV8 10 A3
Codsall Rd
  Codsall WV8........ 10 C1
  Cradley Heath B64... 82 E8
  Wolverhampton WV6.. 24 D7
Cofield Rd B73......45 F1
Cofton Church La
  B45............. 122 D3
Cofton Cl B97..... 153 B5
Cofton Ct B45..... 122 D2
Cofton Gr B31..... 122 E6
Cofton Lake Rd B45. 122 C3
Cofton Prim Sch
  B31............. 123 A6
Cofton Rd B31..... 123 B7
Cokeland Pl B64.... 82 D8
Colaton Cl WV10... 25 E4
Colbourne Ct B33... 68 D3
Colbourne Gr CV32.. 156 D2
Colbourne Rd
  Tamworth B78....... 21 A2
  Tipton DY4.......... 52 A4
Colbrand Gr B15.... 86 D8
Colbrook B77...... 21 D1
Coldbath Rd B13... 105 B8
Coldfield Dr B98... 158 E2
Coldridge Cl WV8....10 F1
Coldstream Cl LE10.. 71 A1
Coldstream Dr DY8.. 60 E3
Coldstream Rd B76.. 57 E8
Cole Bank Rd B28.. 105 E8
Colebourne Prim Sch
  B33.............. 68 E5
Colebourne Rd B13.. 105 D6
Colebridge Cres B46..70 F8
Colebrook Cl CV3... 114 F2
Colebrook Croft B90 105 F2
Colebrook Rd
  Birmingham B11..... 87 D5
  Solihull B90....... 105 F2
Coleby Cl CV4..... 131 D7
Cole Ct B37....... 70 B2
Coleford Cl
  Redditch B97...... 153 A2
  Stourbridge DY8.... 60 C2
Coleford Dr B37.... 70 A2
Cole Gn B90....... 105 F2
Cole Hall La B34... 69 A5
Coleman Rd WS10... 42 A5
Coleman St
  Coventry CV4...... 111 F3
  Wolverhampton WV6. 24 F4
Colemeadow Rd
  Birmingham B13.... 105 B6
  Coleshill B46...... 70 F7
  Redditch B98...... 154 F6
Colenso Rd B16.... 65 D4
Coleraine Rd B42... 55 A6
Coleridge Cl
  Redditch B97...... 158 C8
  Tamworth B79...... 21 A6
  Walsall WS3....... 15 A5
  Willenhall WV12.... 27 C8
Coleridge Dr WV6... 23 E4
Coleridge Pas B4... 164 C3
Coleridge Rd
  Birmingham B43.... 54 D4
  Coventry CV2...... 114 C3
Coleridge Rise DY3.. 50 A4
Colesbourne Ave
  B14............. 104 C2
Colesbourne Rd B92. 89 B3
Coles Cres B71..... 53 B7

Colesden Wlk WV4... 38 C6
Coleshill CE Prim Sch
  B46............. 70 F6
Coleshill Cl B97.... 158 C5
Coleshill Heath Rd
  Birmingham B37.... 90 C7
  Coleshill B37, B46.... 70 E2
Coleshill Heath Sch
  B37............. 70 C1
Coleshill Ind Est B46..59 F2
Coleshill Rd
  Birmingham, Hodgehill B34,
    B36............. 68 E6
  Birmingham, Marston Green
    B37............. 90 B8
  Curdworth B76..... 59 C5
  Fazeley B78....... 35 A7
  Hartshill CV10..... 72 A7
  Sutton Coldfield B75.. 46 D5
  Water Orton B46.... 59 B2
Coleshill St
  Birmingham B5..... 164 D3
  Fazeley B78....... 35 A8
  Sutton Coldfield B72.. 46 C5
Coleside Ave B13... 105 D7
Coles La
  Sutton Coldfield B72... 46 C3
  West Bromwich B71... 53 B7
Cole St DY2........ 62 E4
Cole Valley Rd B28.. 105 D6
Coleview Cres B33... 69 E3
Coleville Rd B76.... 58 B6
Coley Cl LE10...... 75 D7
Coleys La B31...... 103 A2
Colgreave Ave B13.. 87 D2
Colina Cl CV3..... 134 C5
Colindale Rd B44... 45 A3
Colinwood Cl WS6....4 F1
Colledge Rd CV6.... 95 D1
Colleen Ave B30.... 104 B3
College Cl WS10.... 42 A1
College Ct WV6.... 24 D4
College Dr
  Birmingham B20.... 54 F2
  Royal Leamington Spa
    CV32............. 156 F2
College Farm Dr B73. 45 D1
College Gate B8.... 67 E4
College High Sch The
  B44..............56 B6
College Hill B73.... 46 B4
College La
  Balsall Common CV8.. 129 E1
  Hinckley LE10...... 71 E1
  Tamworth B79...... 21 B5
College of Law The
  B18............. 164 A4
College Rd
  Birmingham, Alum Rock
    B8.............. 67 E4
  Birmingham B32.... 84 A6
  Birmingham, Handsworth
    B20............. 54 E2
  Birmingham, Moseley
    B13............. 87 C2
  Birmingham, Perry Common
    B44............. 56 B7
  Bromsgrove B60.... 137 A2
  Kidderminster DY10.. 116 E4
  Stourbridge DY8.... 81 A4
  Wolverhampton WV6. 24 D4
College St
  Birmingham B18.... 66 A4
  Nuneaton CV10..... 73 C1
College View WV6... 24 D3
College Wlk
  Birmingham B29.... 103 D8
  Bromsgrove B60.... 137 A2
  Kidderminster DY10.. 116 E4
Collet B77........ 23 E5
Collets Brook B75... 33 A2
Collett B77........ 22 A1
Collett Cl DY8..... 81 A6
Colletts Gr B37.....69 F4
Collett Wlk **2** CV1.. 113 B3
Colley Ave WV10....25 F7
Colley Gate B63.... 82 C6
Colley La B63...... 82 C6
Colley Lane Prim Sch
  B63.............. 82 C6
Colley Orch B63.... 82 C6
Colley St B70...... 53 D4
Collier Cl
  Cheslyn Hay WS6.... 4 D2
  Walsall WS8....... 15 C7
Colliers Cl WV12.... 27 B6
Colliers Fold DY5... 61 B6
Colliery Dr WS3.....13 F3
Colliery La CV7.... 78 B1
Colliery La N CV7... 78 B1

Colliery Rd
  Smethwick B71..... 65 A8
  West Bromwich B71... 54 A1
  Wolverhampton WV1. 25 F2
Collindale Ct DY6... 49 D1
Collingbourne Ave
  B36............. 68 E8
Collingdon Ave B26. 89 C6
Collings Ho B16.... 66 A1
Colling Wlk B37.... 70 A5
Collingwood Dr B43. 44 D3
Collingwood Ho B43. 44 D3
Collingwood Rd
  Birmingham, Brandwood
    End B30......... 104 D3
  Coventry CV5...... 113 A2
  Wolverhampton WV10. 11 C2
Collins Cl B32...... 84 A5
Collins Dr **3** WS13....8 F6
Collins Gr CV4.... 132 D5
Collins Hill WS13.....3 A2
Collinson Cl B98... 154 A1
Collins Rd
  Brownhills WS8..... 16 A5
  Royal Leamington Spa
    CV34............. 161 D5
  Wednesbury WS10... 42 C3
Collins St Walsall WS1. 42 E7
  West Bromwich B70... 52 E3
Collis Cl B60..... 150 E7
Collis St DY8.......80 F8
Collister Cl B90... 106 B4
Colly Croft B37.....69 F5
Collycroft Pl B27... 88 B5
Colman Ave WV11...26 F6
Colman Cres B68... 64 C2
Colman Hill B63.... 82 D5
Colman Hill Ave B63. 82 D6
Colmers Farm Inf Sch
  B45............. 122 B8
Colmers Farm Jun Sch
  B45............. 122 B8
Colmers Sch & Sports
  Coll B45.......... 122 B8
Colmers Wlk B31... 102 D1
Colmore Ave B14... 104 D7
Colmore Circus
  Queensway B4..... 164 C3
Colmore Cres B13... 87 B1
Colmore Dr B75.... 47 A5
Colmore Flats B19.. 164 B4
Colmore Gate B2... 164 C3
Colmore Inf Sch
  B14............. 104 D7
Colmore Jun Sch
  B14............. 104 D7
Colmore Rd B14.... 104 D7
Colmore Row B3.... 164 B3
Coln B31......... 102 F6
Colonial Ind Pk B64. 82 D7
Colonial Rd B9.....67 F2
Colshaw Rd DY8.... 80 E4
Colston Rd B24.... 57 B2
Colt Cl B74....... 44 E7
Coltham Rd WV12... 27 D7
Coltishall Cl B35....57 F2
Coltman Cl WS14.... 9 D7
Colton Hills Com Sch
  WV4.............39 B4
Colts Cl LE10...... 75 D4
Coltsfoot Cl WV11... 26 E5
Coltsfoot View WS6....4 E2
Colts La B98..... 154 D3
Columbia Cl B5..... 86 D7
Columbia Gdns CV12. 78 E2
Columbian Cres WS7...6 F8
Columbian Dr WS11...1 F3
Columbian Way WS11 .1 F3
Columbine Cl **4** WS5 .42 F3
Columbine Way CV12. 77 E1
Columbus Ave DY5...61 F3
Colville Cl DY4.... 52 D8
Colville Rd B12.... 87 B5
Colville Wlk B12.... 87 B5
Colwall Rd DY3.... 50 D4
Colwall Wlk B27.... 88 D4
Colworth Rd B31... 102 F4
Colyere Cl CV7.... 95 A6
Colyns Gr B33......68 F5
Combe Fields Rd
  CV3............. 115 F4
Comber Croft B13... 105 D8
Comber Dr DY5.... 61 B6
Comberford Ct **5**
  WS10............. 42 A3
Comberford Dr WS10. 42 A4
Comberford Rd B79.. 21 A7
Comberton Ave
  DY10............. 117 B5

Comberton Ct **5**
  DY10............. 117 A5
Comberton Fst Sch
  DY10............. 117 B4
Comberton Gdns
  DY10............. 117 B5
Comberton Hill
  DY10............. 116 F5
Comberton Mans **4**
  DY10............. 117 A5
Comberton Mid Sch
  DY10............. 117 B4
Comberton Park Rd
  DY10............. 117 B4
Comberton Pl DY10. 116 F5
Comberton Rd
  Birmingham B26.... 89 B8
  Kidderminster DY10.. 117 B4
Comberton Terr
  DY10............. 116 F5
Combine Cl B75.... 32 D4
Combrook Gn B34... 69 D6
Comet Rd B26..... 90 C4
Commainge Cl CV34. 160 D7
Commercial Rd
  Walsall WS2....... 28 A7
  Wolverhampton WV1. 25 E1
Commercial St B1.. 164 A1
Commissary Rd B26. 90 A3
Commonfield Croft
  B8.............. 67 D5
Common La
  Birmingham, Sheldon
    B26............. 89 B6
  Birmingham, Washwood
    Heath B8........ 67 F6
  Cannock WS11......2 A3
  Corley Moor CV7.... 93 E7
  Kenilworth CV8.... 148 B7
  Tamworth B79...... 21 B4
Common Rd WV5.... 49 A6
Commonside
  Brierley Hill DY5.... 61 C6
  Brownhills WS8..... 16 A6
  Walsall WS3....... 15 A2
Common View WS12....2 B7
Common Way CV2... 114 A6
Common Wlk WS12.. 1 C5
Communication Row
  B15............. 66 C1
Compass Ct **4** CV1. 113 B3
Compass Rd B60... 151 A7
Compton Cl
  Redditch B98...... 153 E2
  Royal Leamington Spa
    CV32............. 157 D2
  Solihull B91...... 106 D4
Compton Croft B37.. 70 D1
Compton Ct
  Coventry CV6...... 95 D2
  Dudley DY2........ 62 C6
  1 Sutton Coldfield B74. 31 F3
  7 Wolverhampton
    WV3............. 25 A2
Compton Dr
  Dudley DY2........ 62 F8
  Kingswinford DY6.... 60 D5
  Sutton Coldfield B74.. 44 C7
Compton Gr
  Halesowen B63..... 82 C4
  Kingswinford DY6.... 60 D5
Compton Grange B64. 82 C4
Compton Hill Dr WV3. 24 D2
Compton Ho B33.... 69 B2
Compton Pk WV6... 24 E3
Compton Rd
  Birmingham B24.... 56 E1
  Coventry CV6...... 95 D2
  Cradley Heath B64... 62 C1
  Halesowen B62..... 83 F5
  Stourbridge DY9.... 81 D2
  Tamworth B79...... 20 F7
  Wolverhampton WV3. 24 F2
Compton Rd W WV3.. 24 C2
Comrie Cl CV2..... 114 F6
Comsey Rd B43.... 44 B3
Comwall Cl WS3.... 28 C7
Comyn St CV32.... 157 B1
Conchar Cl B72.... 46 C2
Conchar Rd B72.... 46 C2
Concorde Dr B35....57 F2
Concorde Rd B26... 90 C4
Condor Gr WS12.....2 C1
Condover Cl WS2... 27 D3
Condover Rd B31... 123 B8
Conduit Rd WS11.....6 A4
Conduit St WS13.... 9 B8
Coneybury Wlk B76.. 58 D5
Coneyford Rd B34... 69 C6
Coneygre Ind Est DY4. 51 F2

Coneygre Bsns Pk
  DY4............. 51 F3
Coneygree Ind Est
  DY4............. 52 A3
Coney Green Dr B31. 122 F8
Coneygree Rd DY4.. 52 A3
Coneygre Ind Est DY4. 51 F2
Congleton Cl
  Coventry CV6...... 95 E2
  Redditch B97...... 153 B5
Congreve Cl CV34.. 155 F2
Congreve Wlk **3**
  CV12............. 78 B3
Conifer Cl
  Bedworth CV12..... 78 C4
  Brierley Hill DY5.... 81 C8
  Cannock WS12......2 A8
Conifer Ct B13..... 86 E2
Conifer Dr
  Birmingham, Handsworth
    B21............. 65 E7
  Birmingham, Northfield
    B31............. 103 B3
Conifer Gr B61.... 136 F3
  3 Royal Leamington Spa
    CV31............. 161 F5
Conifer Paddock
  Coventry CV3...... 114 E1
  Halesowen B62..... 83 E8
Conifer Rd B74.... 44 E8
Conifers The CV8... 148 B3
Coningsby Cl **3**
  CV31............. 162 C6
Coningsby Dr DY11. 116 A8
Conington Gr B17... 85 A5
Coniston B77...... 36 B7
Coniston Ave B92...88 F4
Coniston Cl
  Birmingham B28.... 105 F5
  Bromsgrove B60.... 137 B1
  Bulkington CV12.... 79 C3
Coniston Cres B43.. 54 F7
Coniston Ct
  Nuneaton CV11..... 73 F7
  2 Royal Leamington Spa
    CV32............. 156 D1
Coniston Dr
  Coventry CV5...... 111 D3
  Kingswinford DY6.... 60 B7
Coniston Grange
  CV8............. 147 F5
Coniston Ho
  10 Birmingham B17... 85 D5
  Kidderminster DY10.. 116 E7
  7 Oldbury B69..... 63 D5
Coniston Rd
  Birmingham B23.... 56 D4
  Coventry CV5...... 112 F1
  Royal Leamington Spa
    CV32............. 156 D1
  Sutton Coldfield B74.. 30 F3
  Wolverhampton WV6.. 24 D8
Coniston Way
  Cannock WS11......1 E1
  Nuneaton CV11..... 73 F7
Connaught Ave
  Kidderminster DY11.. 116 C4
  Wednesbury WS10... 42 C3
Connaught Cl WS5... 43 C7
Connaught Dr WV5... 38 A1
Connaught Gdns B5. 86 E6
Connaught Ho **1**
  WV3............. 25 A2
Connaught Rd
  Bilston WV14...... 40 F7
  Bromsgrove B60.... 137 C1
  Wolverhampton WV1. 25 A2
Connops Way DY9... 81 E5
Connor Rd B71..... 53 D6
Conolly Dr B45.... 102 B1
Conrad Cl B11..... 87 A7
Conrad Rd CV6.... 113 A7
Consort Cres DY5... 61 C6
Consort Dr WS10... 41 C8
Consort Pl B79.... 21 C5
Consort Rd B30.... 104 A3
Constable Cl
  Bedworth CV12..... 78 A5
  Birmingham B43.... 44 D3
Constables The B68.. 64 B2
Constance Ave B70.. 53 D1
Constance Cl CV12...95 F8
Constance Rd B5.... 86 D5
Constantine La B46..59 F2
Constantine Way
  WV14............. 41 A2

Constitution Hill
Birmingham B19..... **164** B4
1 Dudley DY2...... **62** D8
Constitution Hill E
DY2............... **62** D8
Consul Ho 6 LE10 .. **71** D1
Convent Cl
Cannock WS11 .... **4** D8
Kenilworth CV8...... **148** A7
Wolverhampton WV1 . **163** C2
Conway Ave
Birmingham B32.... **84** B6
Coventry CV4 ...... **131** D8
Oldbury B68 .... **64** B2
West Bromwich B71.. **42** B1
Conway Cl Dudley DY1. **51** C6
Kingswinford DY6.... **60** F4
Solihull B90........ **106** D1
Conway Cres WV12... **27** C7
Conway Gr B43 ..... **54** D7
Conway Ho WS3 .... **28** A4
Conway Prim Sch
B11.............. **87** C6
Conway Rd
Birmingham B37...... **70** B3
Birmingham, Sparkbrook
B11.............. **87** C6
Bromsgrove B60..... **136** F1
Cannock WS11 ....4 B8
Perton WV6......... **23** F3
Royal Leamington Spa
CV32............. **161** D8
Solihull B90........ **106** D1
Conwy Cl
Nuneaton CV11...... **73** D3
Walsall WS2 .... **28** A4
Conybere St B12....**86** F7
Conyworth Cl B27... **88** D4
Cook Ave DY2....... **62** D7
Cook Cl Knowle B93.. **128** C6
Perton WV6......... **23** E4
Cooke Cl Coventry CV6 **96** A4
Warwick CV34 ..... **155** F2
Cookes Croft B31... **103** B2
Cookesley Cl B43 ... **44** D4
Cooke St WV2....... **163** B1
Cookley Cl B63.....**82** F2
Cookley Way B69 ... **63** E5
Cookley Wharf Ind Est
DY5...............61 B4
Cooknell Dr DY8 .... **60** E2
Cook Rd WS3 ...... **14** D2
Cooksey La B44......44 F4
Cooksey Rd B10..... **87** C8
Cooks La B37 .... **70** A4
Cookspiece Wlk B33 .. **68** F3
Cook St Birmingham B7 **67** B5
Coventry CV1 ...... **165** B3
Darlaston WS10 ...... **41** F6
Coombe Abbey Ctry Pk★
CV3 .... **115** E3
Coombe Abbey Visitor
Ctr★ CV3 .... **115** E4
Coombe Ave CV3.... **134** F7
Coombe Croft WV9... **11** A3
Coombe Ct CV3 ..... **115** A2
Coombe Dr
Binley Woods CV3.... **135** E7
Nuneaton CV10...... **72** B4
Coombe Hill B64.... **83** B8
Coombe Park Rd
CV3 .... **114** F2
Coombe Pk B74......45 F7
Coombe Rd
Birmingham B20.... **55** E1
Solihull B90........ **106** C2
Coombes La B31.... **122** F7
Coombes Rd B62.... **83** B7
Coombe St CV3 .... **114** B2
Coombs Rd B62.... **83** B7
Coombswood Way
B65 .... **83** B8
Co-Operative St CV2.. **96** B3
Cooper Ave DY5..... **61** A2
Cooper Cl
Bromsgrove B60.... **150** E6
West Bromwich B70.. **53** D4
Cooper & Jordan CE
Prim Sch WS9...... **30** C6
Cooper's Bank Rd
DY5...............50 C1
Coopers Hill B48... **138** E6
Cooper's La B67.... **65** A5
Coopers Rd B20.... **55** A4
Cooper St
Nuneaton CV11...... **73** D4
West Bromwich B70.. **53** D3
Wolverhampton WV2 . **39** F8

Cope Arnolds Cl CV6 ..**95** F4
Copeley Hill B23 ..... **56** D1
Copenhagen Mews
B73.............**45** F1
Copes Cres WV10 ... **26** A7
Cope's Dr B79 ...... **21** B7
Cope St
Birmingham B18.... **66** A3
Coventry CV1 ...... **165** C3
Darlaston WS10 ..... **41** E6
Walsall WS3 .... **28** C6
Cophall St DY4...... **52** D5
Cophams Cl B92..... **89** C2
Copland Pl CV4 ..... **111** E1
Coplow Cl CV7..... **130** A6
Coplow Cotts B16....**65** F3
Coplow St B16.......**65** F3
Coplow Terr B16.....**65** F3
Copnor Gr B26..... **88** E6
Coppenhall Gr B33... **69** A3
Copperas St CV2 .... **96** B2
Copperbeach Dr 2
B12.............. **87** A5
Copperbeech Cl B32 ..**84** F5
Copper Beech Cl CV6 **95** E1
Copper Beech Dr
Kingswinford DY6.... **49** D1
Wombourne WV5 ..... **49** B6
Copper Beech Gdns
B20 .... **55** A2
Copperfield Rd CV2 . **114** B3
Copperfields WS14 .... **9** D7
Copperkins Rd WS12 ..2 E4
Coppermill Cl WS12 ...1 F7
Coppice Ash Croft
B19.............. **66** D8
Coppice Ave DY9....**81** F3
Coppice Cl
Birmingham B45 .... **121** F7
1 Birmingham, Erdington
B24............. **56** F3
Brierley Hill DY5...... **61** F1
Burntwood WS7 ....6 F8
Cheslyn Hay WS6 ..... **4** D4
Cheswick Green B90 . **126** C4
Hinckley LE10 .... **71** F3
Redditch B97 ...... **153** C3
Sedgley DY3 .... **50** C7
Wolverhampton WV11 . **13** A1
Coppice Cres WS8 ... **15** D7
Coppice Ct WS11.......4 B7
Coppice Dr
Birmingham B27.... **88** B2
Polesworth B78 ...... **36** F7
Coppice Farm Way
Walsall WV11 ...... **13** B1
Willenhall WV12 ..... **27** B8
Coppice Gdns B47 .. **125** A4
Coppice Gr WS14 ......9 C7
Coppice Ho
Birmingham, Acock's Green
B27............. **88** A2
Birmingham, Handsworth
B66............. **65** D6
Willenhall WV12 ..... **27** C7
Coppice Hollow B32.. **84** B1
Coppice Hts DY11... **116** B1
Coppice Jun Sch
B92.............. **107** E7
Coppice La
Aldridge WS9 .... **15** F1
Brierley Hill DY5..... **62** A2
Brownhills WS8 ..... **15** D8
Cheslyn Hay WS6 ..... **4** D4
Middleton B78....... **33** D2
Muckley Corner WS7,
WS14............. **8** A3
Willenhall WV12 ..... **27** C6
Wolverhampton WV6 .. **24** B6
Coppice Oaks B13... **87** A3
Coppice Performing Arts
Sch WV11 .... **27** A8
Coppice Prim Sch
B75.............**32** B1
Coppice Prim Sch The
B47.............**125** A6
Coppice Rd
Birmingham B13.... **87** A3
Brownhills WS8, WS9.. **15** F4
Cradley Heath B64... **82** E7
Dudley WV14....... **51** A8
Solihull B92........ **107** A8
Whitnash CV31..... **162** B2
Wolverhampton WV3 .. **38** D8
Coppice Rise DY5.... **62** A2
Coppice Side Ind Est
WS8.............. **15** C8
Coppice St Dudley DY1 **51** D4

Coppice St continued
Tipton DY4........ **51** E5
West Bromwich B70... **53** A4
Coppice The
Birmingham, Frankley
B31............. **102** C2
Birmingham, Handsworth
Wood B20......... **55** A2
Cannock WS12 ....2 C1
Coventry CV3 ...... **134** B8
Hinckley LE10 ...... **75** F8
Nuneaton CV10...... **73** C7
Wednesbury WV4 .... **41** C1
West Hagley DY8 .... **98** F5
Willenhall WV12 ..... **27** C6
Coppice View Rd B73. **45** A4
Coppice Way 7 B37 .. **70** B2
Coppice Wlk
Cheswick Green B90 . **126** D4
Hinckley LE10 ...... **71** F3
Copplestone Cl B34.. **69** B6
Copps Rd CV32..... **161** D8
Coppy Hall Gr WS9... **16** B1
Coppy Nook La WS7....7 C5
Copse Cl B31...... **103** A2
Copse Cres WS3 .... **15** A4
Copse Dr CV5 ...... **111** B8
Copse Rd DY2...... **62** B3
Copse The
Bedworth CV7 ...... **96** A8
Sutton Coldfield B74.. **31** F1
Copsewood Ave CV11 **79** B7
Copsewood Terr
CV3 .... **114** C2
Copson Cl B70..... **53** A3
Copstone Dr B93... **127** F3
Copston Gr B29.... **103** B8
Copthall Ho CV1 ... **165** B1
Copthall Rd B21.... **54** C2
Copt Heath Croft
B93............. **128** B8
Copt Heath Dr B93.. **128** A7
Copthorne Ave WS7...6 F4
Copthorne Lo CV6... **112** F8
Copthorne Rd
Birmingham B44..... **44** E3
Coventry CV6 ...... **112** F4
Wolverhampton WV3 .. **39** A7
Copt Oak Cl CV4 .... **131** C6
Copyholt La
Stoke Prior B60 .... **151** D3
Upper Bentley B60,
B97............. **152** A3
Coral Cl Coventry CV5 **112** C2
Hinckley LE10 ...... **75** F4
Coralin Cl B37 ..... **70** C2
Corbet Rd CV6 ..... **113** C7
Corbett Cl B60..... **151** B8
Corbett Cres DY8.... **81** A7
Corbett Dr B60..... **150** C1
Corbett Ho 8 DY8....**80** F7
Corbett Hospl DY8....**80** F7
Corbett Ind Est DY2.. **62** C6
Corbett Rd
Brierley Hill DY5..... **61** E1
Hollywood B47 ..... **125** A4
Kidderminster DY11 . **116** A8
Corbetts Cl B92.... **109** B7
Corbett St B66..... **65** B4
Corbin Rd B78......**36** F6
Corbison Cl CV34 .. **155** D1
Corbizum Ave B80.. **159** D4
Corbridge Ave B44....44 F1
Corbridge Rd B73....**45** F2
Corbyn Rd
Birmingham B9..... **68** B3
Dudley DY1 .... **61** F8
Corbyns Cl DY5 ..... **61** B7
Corbyns Hall La DY5.. **61** B7
Corbyns Hall Rd DY5.. **61** B7
Cordelia Gn CV34 .. **161** D4
Cordley St B70...... **53** B4
Corfe Cl
Birmingham B32.... **84** F1
Coventry CV2 ...... **114** F5
Perton WV6......... **23** F3
Corfe Dr B69....... **63** A8
Corfe Rd WV14...... **51** A8
Corfton Dr WV6..... **24** C3
Coriander Cl
Birmingham B45.... **102** B2
Stoke Prior B60 .... **150** C1
Corinne Cl B45..... **122** A6
Corinne Croft B37... **70** A4
Corinthian Pl CV2 .. **114** D6
Coriolanus Sq CV34 . **161** F3
Corisande Rd B29... **85** C2
Corley Ave B31..... **103** B3
Corley Cl B90...... **105** E1

Corley (Coventry) Sch
CV7...............**94** B6
Corley View CV7..... **95** C6
Cornbow Ctr B63.....**83** B3
Cornbrook Rd B29... **102** F7
Cornbury Gr B91.... **106** D4
Corncrake Cl B72.... **46** D2
Corncrake Dr B36.... **70** A7
Corncrake Rd DY1,
DY3............. **50** E3
Corndon Cl DY11.... **116** B2
Cornel B77.........**21** F4
Cornel Cl B37....... **90** C8
Cornelius St CV3.... **133** D8
Corner Ho B66..... **65** D6
Corner Ho The 9
CV32............. **156** F1
Corner La B97...... **152** E2
Corner Pl The 3 B17. **85** D6
Cornerstone B13.....**86** F3
Cornerstone Ho CV1 **165** C4
Cornerway B38 ..... **123** F7
Cornets End La CV7 . **109** E7
Cornet's End La CV7 . **110** B6
Corn Exchange The 5
WS13.............9 B8
Cornfield
Hinckley LE10 .... **71** C4
Wolverhampton WV8 .. **10** F2
Cornfield Ave B60... **150** D6
Cornfield Cl DY6 .... **60** A8
Cornfield Croft
Birmingham B37..... **70** D3
Sutton Coldfield B76.. **46** F3
Cornfield Dr WS14.....9 E7
Cornfield Pl B65......**62** F4
Cornfield Rd
Birmingham B31..... **103** B4
Rowley Regis B65..... **62** F4
Sutton Coldfield B76... **46** F2
Cornfield The CV3 ... **114** C1
Cornflower Cl WV10.. **12** A7
Cornflower Cres DY2.. **62** F8
Cornflower Rd WS8... **15** D6
Corngreaves Jun & Inf
Sch B64 .... **62** D1
Corngreaves Rd B64.. **82** E7
Corngreaves The B34. **69** B6
Corngreaves Trad Est
B64............. **82** D7
Corngreaves Wlk B64 **82** E7
Cornhampton Cl 7
B97............. **153** B5
Cornhill WS11........ **1** B8
Corn Hill Walsall WS5 . **43** E8
Wolverhampton
WV10........... **163** D3
Cornhill Gr
Birmingham B30.... **104** C7
Kenilworth CV8..... **148** C5
Cornish Cres CV10 .. **73** A2
Corn Mdws CV12.... **78** C2
Cornmill Cl WS1..... **42** D7
Corn Mill Cl
Birmingham B32.... **84** E1
Sutton Coldfield B76... **46** F1
Cornmill Gdns B60.. **138** A5
Cornmill Gr WV6.... **23** D3
Cornovian Cl WV6.... **23** E5
Corns Ho WS10 ..... **41** E6
Cornwall Ave
Birmingham B68.... **84** B8
Tamworth B78...... **21** A1
Cornwall Cl
Aldridge WS9 ...... **16** A1
Kingswinford DY6.... **60** D8
3 Warwick CV34 .... **160** F8
Wednesbury WS10.... **42** D3
Cornwall Gate WV12 . **27** B5
Cornwall Ho CV32... **156** D1
Cornwall Ind Est
Birmingham B8...... **67** C4
Smethwick B66...... **65** C7
Cornwallis Rd B70... **53** A1
Cornwall Pl
Royal Leamington Spa
CV32............ **156** D1
Walsall WS2 .... **27** E3
Cornwall Rd
Birmingham, Handsworth
B20............. **54** F7
Birmingham, Rubery
B45............. **101** E1
Cannock WS12 ....2 B5
Coventry CV1 ...... **113** C5
Smethwick B66...... **65** C7
Stourbridge DY8..... **80** D8
Walsall WS5 .... **43** B7
Wolverhampton WV6 .. **24** C1

Cornwall St B3...... **164** B3
Cornwall Twr B18.... **66** B5
Cornwall Way LE10.. **71** E4
Cornwell Cl
Redditch B98 ...... **159** B5
Tipton DY4 .... **52** A5
Cornyx La B91...... **107** D6
Coronation Ave
Mile Oak B78 ...... **20** D1
Willenhall WV13 ..... **27** C2
Coronation Cres B79 .**22** F2
Coronation Ct CV11 . **73** B4
Coronation Rd
Bilston WV14 .... **40** C6
Birmingham B29..... **85** F2
Birmingham, Great Barr
B43............. **43** E4
Birmingham, Washwood
Heath B8 .... **67** F6
Brownhills WS9 ..... **16** A3
Coventry CV1 ...... **113** F4
Tipton DY4 .... **52** B8
Walsall WS4 .... **15** B2
Wednesbury WS10.... **42** C4
Wolverhampton WV10 . **26** A5
Coronation St B79 ... **21** A5
Coronation Terr B60. **151** B7
Coronation Way
DY10............ **117** B5
Coronel Ave CV6 .... **95** E4
Corporation Rd DY2..**51** F1
Corporation St W
WS1 .... **42** D8
Corporation St
Birmingham B2..... **164** C3
Birmingham, New Town Row
B4.............. **164** D4
Coventry CV1 ...... **165** B3
Kidderminster DY10 . **116** E5
Nuneaton CV11...... **73** B5
Tamworth B79....... **21** B5
Walsall WS1 .... **42** E8
Wednesbury WS10.... **42** A2
Wolverhampton WV1 . **163** B3
Corpus Christi RC Prim
Sch
Birmingham B33..... **68** D2
Wednesfield WV11 ... **27** A8
Corpus Christi RC Sch
CV3............. **134** D7
Correen B77 .... **22** C1
Corrie Croft
Birmingham, Bartley Green
B32............. **102** B7
Birmingham, Lyndon Green
B26............. **89** B7
Corrie Roy Cotts B78. **21** A4
Corrin Gr DY6...... **60** C8
Corron Hill B63..... **83** B4
Corser St Dudley DY1. **51** A2
Stourbridge DY8..... **81** A3
Wolverhampton WV1 . **25** F1
Corsican Cl
Burntwood WS7 ....7 A8
Corsican Dr WS12....2 A8
Corston Mews CV31. **162** C6
Cort Dr WS7 ....7 B8
Corunna Rd CV34 ... **160** C7
Corvedale Rd B29... **103** A6
Corve Gdns WV6 .... **24** E5
Corve View DY3 .... **39** C1
Corville Gdns B26... **89** C4
Corville Rd B62......**83** F6
Corwen Croft B31... **102** E6
Cory Croft DY4...... **52** A5
Coseley Hall 1 WV14 **51** C8
Coseley Rd WV14.... **40** C4
Coseley Road Island
WV14............ **40** C4
Coseley Sch The
WV14.............40 B1
Coseley Sta WV14.... **40** C1
Cosford Cl
Redditch B98 ...... **154** F1
Royal Leamington Spa
CV32............ **157** B3
Cosford Cres B35 ... **58** A3
Cosford Ct WV6..... **23** E5
Cosford Dr DY2..... **62** C3
Cosgrove Wlk WV8...**10** F1
Cossington Rd B23... **56** F7
Costard Ave CV34 .. **161** E3
Costers La B98..... **154** F7
Costock Cl B37 ..... **90** B8
Coten End CV34 .... **160** F7
Coten End Prim Sch
CV34............ **160** F7
Cotes Rd LE10.......**75** F5
Cotford Rd B14..... **105** A2

Cotheridge Cl B90 .. **127** C6
Cot La DY6, DY8 ..... **60** C5
Cotleigh Gr B43..... **44** D3
Cotman Cl
Bedworth CV12..... **78** A4
Birmingham B43..... **44** C3
Cotman Dr LE10..... **71** A3
Coton Gr B90 ...... **105** E2
Coton Green Prec
B79..............**20** F7
Coton Green Prim Sch
B79..............**20** F8
Coton La
Birmingham B23..... **56** F4
Tamworth B79....... **20** E8
Coton Rd
Nuneaton CV11...... **73** C3
Wolverhampton WV4 .. **39** B5
Cotsdale Rd WV4.... **38** E3
Cotsford B91....... **107** A3
Cotswold Ave WS6....**4** F3
Cotswold Cl
Aldridge WS9 ...... **16** C1
Birmingham B45.... **102** B2
Cannock WS12 ....2 A8
Kidderminster DY11 . **116** C2
Oldbury B69........ **63** E5
Cotswold Cres CV10.. **72** B3
Cotswold Croft B63.. **82** C1
Cotswold Ct
Sutton Coldfield B75... **32** A4
Wolverhampton WV3 .. **39** B6
Cotswold Dr CV3.... **133** C3
Cotswold Gr WV12 .. **13** E1
Cotswold Rd
Cannock WS12 ....2 A8
Stourbridge DY8..... **81** B6
Wolverhampton WV2 . **39** F7
Cotswold Way B61 .. **137** A2
Cottage Cl
Burntwood WS7 ....6 F5
Cannock WS12 ..... **2** D5
Nuneaton CV11...... **73** D4
Royal Leamington Spa
CV31............ **162** C6
Wolverhampton WV11 . **26** C6
Cottage Ct WS7......**6** F5
Cottage Dr B60..... **121** D1
Cottage Farm La
B60............. **121** C1
Cottage Farm Lodge
CV6.............. **95** A1
Cottage Farm Rd
Coventry CV6 ...... **95** A2
Tamworth B77....... **35** D7
Cottage Gdns B45... **121** F6
Cottage La
Burntwood WS7 ....6 F5
Lower Marlbrook B60. **121** C1
Minworth B76....... **58** D6
Wolverhampton WV10 . **11** D3
Cottage Mews WS9 .. **30** E4
Cottage Sq CV31 ... **162** C6
Cottage St
Brierley Hill DY5..... **61** D3
Kingswinford DY6.... **60** D7
Cottages The
Birmingham B24..... **67** F8
Cradley Heath B63... **82** E6
Cottage View WV8... **10** B4
Cottage Wlk
4 Tamworth B77.... **35** F6
West Bromwich B70... **53** D2
Cottteridge Jun & Inf Sch
B30............. **104** A5
Cottteridge Rd B30... **104** A4
Cottterills Ave B8.... **68** C4
Cottterill's Cl CV31... **162** B4
Cottterills La B8..... **68** C4
Cottterills Rd DY4.... **52** B7
Cottesbrook Cl CV3 . **114** E1
Cottesbrook Inf Sch
B27.............. **88** D4
Cottesbrook Jun Sch
B27.............. **88** C4
Cottesbrook Rd B27.. **88** D4
Cottesfield Cl B8.... **68** B4
Cottesmore Cl B71....**53** F8
Cottesmore Ho 7
B20..............**54** F3
Cottle Cl WS2.......**27** F3
Cotton Dr CV8 ..... **148** C6
Cotton La B13 ...... **87** A2
Cotton Mill Spinney
CV32............ **157** C5
Cotton Pool Rd B61 . **136** E2
Cottrells Cl B14..... **105** C4
Cottrells Mews B46 .. **59** B2
Cottrell St B71...... **53** D4

Cottsmeadow Dr B8. . 68 C4
Cotwall End Countryside
& Craft Ctr* DY3 . . 50 C6
Cotwall End Ho DY3 . . 50 C7
Cotwall End Prim Sch
DY3. . . . . 50 D7
Cotwall End Rd DY3 . . 50 C5
Cotysmore Rd B75 . . 46 D7
Couchman Rd B8 . . . . 67 E4
Coughton Dr CV31 . . 162 D5
Coulter Gr WV6 . . . . . 23 D4
Coulter La WS7 . . . . . . .7 E8
Council Cres WV12 . . 27 C4
Council Hos CV5 . . . . 93 D1
Council House* B3. 164 B2
Council Rd 3 LE10 . . 71 D1
Coundon Court Sch &
Com Coll CV6 . . . . . 112 E7
Coundon Gn CV6. . . 112 E8
Coundon Prim Sch
CV6. . . . . 112 E5
Coundon Rd CV1 . . . 113 D3
Coundon St CV1 . . . 165 A4
Coundon Wedge Dr CV5,
CV6 . . . . 112 D7
Counterfield Dr B65. .62 F5
Countess Dr WS4 . . . 29 D7
Countess Rd CV11 . . 73 A4
Countess's Croft The
CV3 . . . . 133 D7
Countess St WS1 . . . 42 D7
Countinghouse Way 2
B60 . . . . 150 E6
County Bridge Prim Sch
WS2. . . . . .27 E1
County Cl
Birmingham B32 . . . . . 84 D3
Birmingham, Stirchley
B30. . . . . 104 C6
County Dr B78 . . . . . 21 A2
County La DY8 . . . . . 98 D8
County Park Ave B62. 83 D3
Courtaulds Way CV6. 113 D6
Court Cres DY6 . . . . . 60 C5
Court Dr WS14 . . . . . .17 F4
Courtenay Gdns B43 . 43 E2
Courtenay Rd B44. . . 55 E8
Court Farm Prim Sch
B23. . . . . .56 E6
Court Farm Rd B23. . 56 E6
Court Farm Way B29 102 F7
Courthouse Croft
CV8 . . . . 148 C4
Courthouse Green Prim
Sch CV6 . . . . 114 A8
Court La B23. . . . . . . 56 E7
Courtland Ave CV6 . . 112 F5
Courtland Rd DY6 . . . 60 E8
Courtlands Cl B5. . . . 86 C6
Courtlands The WV6. . 24 E4
Court Leet CV3. . . . . 135 D7
Court Leet Rd CV3 . . 133 E7
Courtney DY10 . . . . 116 E2
Courtney Cl CV11 . . . .73 F7
Court Oak Rd B17. . . 85 A6
Court of Lady Katherine
Leveson The B93. . 129 B5
Court Par WS9 . . . . . 30 B6
Court Pas DY1 . . . . . 51 C1
Court Rd
Birmingham, Balsall Heath
B12. . . . . 86 E6
Birmingham, Sparkhill
B11. . . . . 87 C4
Wolverhampton WV6 . . 24 F4
Woodcross WV4 . . . . . 40 A3
Court St
2 Cradley Heath B64. . 62 F1
Royal Leamington Spa
CV31. . . . . 162 A7
9 Stourbridge DY8 . . 81 A5
Court Way WS2 . . . . . 28 E2
Courtway Ave B14. . . 105 B1
Courtyard The
Coleshill B46. . . . . . 59 F2
Solihull B91. . . . . . . 107 C4
Stoke Prior B60 . . . . 150 D2
Warwick CV34 . . . . . 160 F5
West Bromwich B70. . . 53 A3
Cousins St WV2 . . . . 39 D7
Coveley Gr B18 . . . . . 66 A5
Coven Cl WS3. . . . . . 15 A5
Coven Gr B29 . . . . . . 85 B2
Coven St WV10 . . . . 25 D4
Coventry Airport
CV8. . . . . 134 B2
Coventry Blue Coat CE
Sch The CV1 . . . . . 113 F1
Coventry Bsns Pk
CV5. . . . . 112 D1

Coventry Canal Basin
Warehouse CV1 . . . 165 B4
Coventry Cath Church of
St Michael* CV1. . . 165 C3
Coventry Gram Sch
CV5. . . . . 112 F1
Coventry Highway
B98 . . . . 154 C4
Coventry Muslim Sch
CV6. . . . . 113 E8
Coventry Prep Sch
CV3. . . . . 133 B8
Coventry Railway Ctr
CV8. . . . . 134 A3
Coventry Rd
Aston Flamville LE10 . . 76 F1
Baginton CV8 . . . . . 133 F2
Barnacle CV7, CV12 . . 97 A8
Bedworth CV12. . . . . 78 B2
Bedworth, Hawkesbury
CV2. . . . . 96 E6
Berkswell CV7. . . . . 110 E3
Bickenhill B26, B92. . . 90 C2
Birmingham B10, B25,
B26. . . . . 88 C6
Bulkington CV12. . . . 79 B1
Coventry CV3 . . . . . 115 F3
Cubbington CV32 . . . 157 E7
Hampton-in-A B92 . . . 91 B3
Hinckley LE10 . . . . . 75 B7
Hinckley, Sketchley Hill
LE10 . . . . 75 F5
Kenilworth CV8. . . . 148 A7
Nuneaton CV10. . . . . 78 C7
Stoneleigh CV8, CV3. . 149 C7
Warwick CV34 . . . . 160 F8
Coventry Ret Mkt
CV1. . . . . 165 B2
Coventry Road Exhall
CV7 . . . . 96 A8
Coventry St
Birmingham B5. . . . . 164 D2
Coventry CV2 . . . . . 114 A4
Kidderminster DY10 . 116 F6
Nuneaton CV11. . . . . 73 C4
Stourbridge DY8 . . . . 81 A5
Wolverhampton WV1 . . 26 A2
Coventry Sta CV1 . . 165 B1
Coventry Toy Mus*
CV1. . . . . 165 C2
Coventry Univ CV1. . 165 C2
Coventry University Tech
Pk CV1. . . . . 165 C1
Coventry Walsgrave
Triangle Bsns Pk
CV2. . . . . 97 A1
Coventry & Warwickshire
Hospl CV1 . . . . . . 165 C4
Cove Pl CV2 . . . . . . 114 C7
Cover Croft B76. . . . . 47 A1
Coverdale Rd B92. . . 89 A4
Covers The B80 . . . . 159 E6
Covert La DY8. . . . . . 80 D2
Covert The WV8 . . . . 10 E1
Covey Cl WS13 . . . . . . 3 D1
Cowdray Cl CV31. . . 162 C7
Cow La B78. . . . . .35 F3
Cowles Croft B25 . . . 68 E1
Cowley B77 . . . . 21 E2
Cowley Cl B36 . . . . . .58 F1
Cowley Dr
Birmingham B27. . . . . 88 D4
Dudley DY1 . . . . 50 F2
Cowley Gn WS12 . . . . .1 F8
Cowley Gr B11 . . . . . 87 E5
Cowley Rd
Birmingham B11. . . . . 87 E5
Coventry CV2 . . . . . 114 D4
Cowper Cl
Warwick CV34 . . . . . 155 E1
Willenhall WV12 . . . . 27 E7
Cowper Rd LE10 . . . . 75 D6
Cowper Wlk DY10 . . 117 C6
Cowslip Cl
1 Birmingham, Hawkesley
B38. . . . . 123 D8
Birmingham, Selly Oak
B29. . . . . 103 A7
Cowslip Wlk DY5. . . . 81 C6
Coxcroft Ave DY5. . . .81 F8
Coxmoor Cl WS3. . . . .13 F3
Cox Rd WV14. . . . . . 40 E1
Cox's Cl CV10 . . . . . 73 B3
Cox's La B64. . . . . . . .62 F2
Cox's Orch 4 CV31. 162 A4
Cox St Birmingham B3 164 B4
Coventry CV1 . . . . . 165 C3
Coxwell Ave WV10. . . 25 C5
Coxwell Gdns B16. . . .65 F2
Coyne Cl DY4 . . . . . . 51 D5

Coyne Rd B70. . . . . . . 53 B2
Cozens Cl CV12 . . . . 78 A4
Crabbe St DY9 . . . . . .81 F5
Crabbs Cross La B97 158 E5
Crab La Cannock WS11 . .2 A3
Willenhall WV12 . . . . 13 D1
Crabmill Cl
Birmingham B38. . . . 123 E7
Knowle B93. . . . . . . 128 C7
Crabmill La
Birmingham B38. . . . 124 D8
Coventry CV6 . . . . . 113 F7
Crabourne Rd DY2 . . 62 B2
Crabtree Cl
Birmingham B31. . . . 103 C2
Redditch B98 . . . . . 154 A2
West Bromwich B71. . . 53 F8
West Hagley DY9 . . . . 99 B6
Crabtree Dr
Birmingham B37. . . . 69 F2
Bromsgrove B61. . . . 136 F3
Crabtree Gr CV31 . . 162 C6
Crab Tree Ho B33 . . . 68 E3
Crabtree La B61. . . . 136 E3
Crabtree Rd
Barwell LE9. . . . . . . 71 F5
Birmingham B18. . . . 66 A5
Walsall WS1 . . . . 29 A2
Crackley Cotts CV8. 148 B8
Crackley Cres CV8 . 148 B8
Crackley Hall Sch
CV8. . . . . 148 B7
Crackley La
Coventry CV4 . . . . . 131 F3
Kenilworth CV8. . . . 148 A7
Crackley Way DY2 . . 62 A6
Craddock Ct CV10 . . 72 C7
Craddock Dr CV10. . . 72 C7
Craddock Rd B67 . . . 64 E6
Craddock St WV6 . . . 25 B4
Cradley CE Prim Sch
B63. . . . . 82 C7
Cradley Cl B98. . . . . 154 F2
Cradley Croft B21 . . . 54 C3
Cradley Fields B63 . . 82 D5
Cradley Forge DY5 . . 82 B8
Cradley Heath Factory
Ctr B64 . . . . .82 B8
Cradley Heath Sta
B64. . . . . .82 B8
Cradley High Sch B63 82 B6
Cradley Park Rd DY2 . 62 D2
Cradley Rd
Cradley Heath B64 . . . 82 C8
Dudley DY2 . . . . 62 D3
Cradock Rd B8. . . . . . 67 E5
Craig Cl CV31 . . . . . 162 B6
Craig Croft B37 . . . . 70 D2
Craigends Ave CV3 . 134 E6
Crail Gr B43 . . . . 44 B4
Crakston Cl CV2. . . . 114 E2
Cramlington Rd B42. . 55 A8
Crammond Cl LE10. . 75 B8
Cramnore Cl DY4. . . . 52 A8
Cramper's Field CV6 113 A5
Cramp Hill WS10 . . . 41 D6
Cranborne Chase
CV2. . . . . 115 A5
Cranbourne Ave WV4. 39 E3
Cranbourne Cl B45. . 102 B2
Cranbourne Gr B44 . . 56 A8
Cranbourne Pl B71. . 53 D4
Cranbourne Rd
Birmingham B44. . . . . 45 A1
Stourbridge DY8 . . . . 81 B4
Cranbrook Ct WV13 . . 27 C2
Cranbrook Gr WV6 . . 23 F3
Cranbrook Rd B21. . . 54 C2
Cranby St B8 . . . . . . 67 C5
Craneberry Rd B37. . 69 E3
Cranebrook Hill B78. 33 E5
Cranebrook La WS14. .16 F7
Crane Cl CV34 . . . . . 155 D1
Crane Dr WS7. . . . . . .7 A4
Crane Field WS13 . . . .3 B1
Cranehouse Rd B44. . 45 A2
Cranemoor Cl B7 . . . 67 C6
Crane Rd WV14 . . . . .40 F3
Craner's Rd CV1 . . . 113 F4
Cranesbill Cl WV10. . 12 C7
Cranesbill Rd B29. . . 103 A6
Cranes Park Rd B26. . 89 C5
Crane St DY11 . . . . . 116 C6
Crane Terr WV6 . . . . . 24 E5
Cranfield Gr B26 . . . . .88 F8
Cranfield Pl WS5. . . . .42 F5
Cranfield Rd WS7 . . . .7 A7
Cranford Gr 6 B91. . 107 B1

Cranford Pl WS11 . . . . .1 F1
Cranford Rd
Coventry CV5 . . . . . 112 D4
Wolverhampton WV3 . . 38 D8
Cranford St B66. . . . . 65 C5
Cranford Way B66. . . 65 C5
Cranham Cl B97 . . . . 153 B1
Cranham Dr DY6 . . . . 60 E5
Cranhill Cl B92. . . . . 89 B1
Crankhall La WS10 . . 42 C3
Cranleigh Cl
Aldridge WS9 . . . . . . 30 B5
Willenhall WV12 . . . . 13 C1
Cranleigh Ho B23. . . .56 F6
Cranleigh Pl B44. . . . 55 E5
Cranleigh Way WS14. . .9 E7
Cranmer Ave WV12. . 27 D7
Cranmer Cl WS6 . . . . 4 D1
Cranmere Ave WV6. . 24 A6
Cranmere Ct WV6 . . . 24 A6
Cranmer Gr
Royal Leamington Spa
CV34. . . . . 161 D3
Sutton Coldfield B74. . 31 F6
Cranmoor Cres B63 . . 83 A5
Cranmore Ave
Birmingham B21. . . . . 65 D7
Solihull B90. . . . . . . 126 E8
Cranmore Bvd B90. . 126 D8
Cranmore Dr B90 . . . 106 E1
Cranmore Inf Sch
B91. . . . . 106 E1
Cranmore Rd
Birmingham B36. . . . . 58 E1
Solihull B90. . . . . . . 126 D8
Wolverhampton WV3 . . 24 F3
Cransley Gr B91. . . . 107 A1
Crantock Cl WV11 . . . 13 C1
Crantock Rd B42. . . . 55 C4
Crantock Way CV11. . .73 F4
Cranwell Gr B24 . . . . 57 D3
Cranwell Rise B78 . . 20 C1
Cranwell Way B35. . . 58 A3
Crathie Cl CV2 . . . . . 114 F6
Crathorne Ave WV10 . 11 C1
Craufurd Ct DY8 . . . . 81 A3
Craufurd St DY8. . . . 81 A3
Craven B77 . . . . 22 B1
Craven Ave CV3 . . . . 135 D7
Craven Ct CV3 . . . . . 114 F2
Craven St
Coventry CV5 . . . . . 112 F2
Wolverhampton WV2 . . 39 F6
Crawford Ave
Darlaston WS10 . . . . . 41 C7
Smethwick B67. . . . . 64 F4
Wolverhampton WV4 . . 39 F3
Crawford Cl CV32 . . 157 B5
Crawford Rd
Sutton Coldfield B76. . 57 F8
Wolverhampton WV3 . . 25 A8
Crawford St B8 . . . . . 67 C5
Crawley Wlk 1 B64 . 62 D1
Crawshaws Rd B36. . 58 C1
Crayford Rd B44. . . . 45 A1
Craythorne Ave B20. . 54 E4
Crecy Cl B76. . . . . . . 46 E4
Crecy Rd CV3 . . . . . . 133 E7
Credenda Rd B70. . . 53 A1
Crediton Cl CV11. . . .73 F5
Cregoe St B15. . . . . . 86 C8
Cremore Ave B8 . . . . 67 E5
Cremorne Rd B75. . . 32 B2
Cremorne Wlk B75. . 32 B2
Crendon Cl B80. . . . 159 E5
Crendon Rd B65 . . . . 63 A6
Crescent Arc 2 B91. 107 C3
Crescent Ave
Birmingham B18. . . . . 66 B6
Brierley Hill DY5. . . . 61 C1
Coventry CV3 . . . . . 114 C2
Crescent Grange Rd The
DY9 . . . . 81 C4
Crescent Ho B97 . . . 153 D2
Crescent Ind Pk DY2. .62 B7
Crescent Rd
Darlaston WS10 . . . . . 41 D6
Dudley DY2 . . . . 62 B5
Kidderminster DY11. . 116 C5
Willenhall WV13 . . . . 27 C2
Crescent Sta The
WV14. . . . . 40 D6
Crescent The
Bilston WV14 . . . . . . 40 D6
Birmingham, Coleshill Heath
B37. . . . . 90 E8
Birmingham, Great Barr
B43. . . . . 44 A1
Birmingham, Hockley
B18. . . . . 66 B6

Crescent The continued
Birmingham, Sparkbrook
B12. . . . . 87 B5
Bromsgrove B60. . . . 136 F1
Cradley Heath B64 . . . 83 A7
Dudley DY1 . . . . 51 E4
Great Wyrley WS6. . . . .5 A2
Hampton-in-A B92 . . 109 B7
Keresley CV7 . . . . . . 94 F6
Rowley Regis B65. . . 63 D3
Solihull, Lode Heath
B91. . . . . 107 B4
Solihull, Shirley B90 . 106 A4
Walsall WS1 . . . . 43 A8
Wednesbury WS10 . . . 42 A4
West Hagley DY8 . . . . 98 F5
Willenhall WS10, WV13 27 C1
Wolverhampton WV6 . . 24 B3
Crescent Twr B1 . . . . 66 C2
Cressage Ave B31. . . 103 A1
Cressage Rd CV2. . . 115 A6
Cressett Ave DY5. . . . 61 C4
Cressett La DY5. . . . . 61 C4
Cressida Cl CV34 . . . 161 F3
Cressington Dr B74. . 32 A1
Cresswell Cl CV10 . . .13 C8
Cresswell Cres WS3. . .13 F2
Cresswell Ct WV10 . . 11 A3
Cresswell Gr B24. . . . 57 D4
Cresswell Ho CV6 . . . 113 B7
Crest The
Birmingham B31. . . . 123 C7
Royal Leamington Spa
CV32. . . . . 157 D3
Crest View
Birmingham B14. . . . 105 B4
Sutton Coldfield B74. . 44 F8
Crestwood B77. . . . . 22 A5
Crestwood Ave DY11 116 A5
Crestwood Dr B44. . . 55 E7
Crestwood Glen WV6. 24 E7
Crestwood Park Prim Sch
DY6. . . . . 61 A5
Crestwood Sch The
DY6. . . . . 60 F5
Creswell Rd B28 . . . 106 B7
Creswick Gr B45. . . . 122 C1
Crewe Dr DY4. . . . . . 52 A2
Crew La CV8 . . . . 148 E6
Crew Rd WS10 . . . . . 42 A4
Creynolds Cl B90. . . 126 D3
Creynolds La B90. . . 126 E4
Cricket Cl
Coventry CV5 . . . . . 112 F3
Walsall WS1 . . . . 43 B7
Cricketers Mdw B64. .82 F7
Cricket La WS14. . . . . .9 C5
Cricket Mdw
Dudley DY3 . . . . 50 E5
Wolverhampton WV10 . 11 D4
Crick La B20 . . . . 66 A8
Cricklewood Dr B62. . 83 D3
Crigdon B77 . . . . 22 C1
Crimmond Rise B63. . 82 E5
Crimscote Cl B90 . . . 126 F6
Cringlebrook B77. . . . 21 D1
Cripps Rd WS2. . . . . . 27 E3
Crocketts Ave B21. . . 65 D7
Crockett's La B66 . . . 65 A6
Crocketts Lane Prim Sch
B66. . . . . .65 B5
Crocketts Rd B21. . . 65 D8
Crockett St DY1. . . . 51 A2
Crockford Dr B75. . . 32 B3
Crockford Rd B71. . . 42 C1
Crockington La WV5 . 37 A1
Crocus Cres WV9. . . 11 A3
Croft Apartments 2
WV13 . . . . 27 A2
Croft Ave B79 . . . . . . 21 B6
Croft Cl
Birmingham B25. . . . . 88 E8
Redditch B98 . . . . . 154 D3
Warwick CV34 . . . . . 161 C7
Croft Cres WS8. . . . . 15 D7
Croft Ct B36 . . . . 69 B8
Croftdown Rd B17. . . 85 A7
Croft Down Rd B92. . 89 D4
Crofters Cl DY8 . . . . . 81 B4
Crofters Ct B15. . . . . 85 E6
Crofters La B75. . . . . 32 E3
Crofters Wlk WS8 . . . 10 E1
Croft Fields CV12 . . . 78 B2
Croft Gdns WS7 . . . . .7 A8
Croft Ho 2 WS1 . . . . 28 F1
Croft Ind Est B37. . . . 70 D2
Croft Jun Sch CV10 . .72 F3
Croft La WV10. . . . . . 26 A7
Croftleigh Gdns B91. 106 E2
Croft Mews CV10. . . . 73 A4

Croft Par WS9. . . . . . 30 B6
Croft Pool CV12. . . . .77 F2
Croft Rd
Bedworth CV12. . . . . 77 F2
Birmingham B26. . . . . 88 E8
Coventry CV1 . . . . . 165 A2
Leek Wootton CV35 . 156 A4
Nuneaton CV10. . . . . 72 F3
Crofts La B96 . . . . . . 158 B2
Croft St Tamworth B79. 21 B6
Walsall WS2 . . . . 28 D3
Willenhall WV13 . . . . 27 A2
Crofts The B76 . . . . . 58 A8
Croft Street JMI Sch
WS2 . . . . 28 D3
Croft The
Birmingham B31. . . . 103 B2
Blakedown DY10. . . . 98 C2
Bulkington CV12 . . . . 79 B2
Cheslyn Hay WS6 . . . .4 E2
Coventry CV6 . . . . . . 95 F4
Dudley DY2 . . . . 61 F6
Kidderminster DY11. . 116 A4
Meriden CV7. . . . . . . 92 C1
Sedgley DY3 . . . . 39 E1
Walsall WS5 . . . . 43 E8
Croftway The B20 . . . 54 E6
Croftwood Rd DY9 . . 81 D4
Cromane Sq B43. . . . 54 E7
Cromarty Cl CV5 . . . 112 A5
Cromdale B77 . . . . . . 22 C1
Cromdale Cl CV10 . . 72 A3
Cromdale Dr B63. . . . 82 D3
Crome Rd B43 . . . . . 44 D3
Cromer Gdns WV6 . . .24 F1
Cromer Rd
Birmingham B12. . . . . 86 F5
Royal Leamington Spa
CV32. . . . . 157 B2
Cromes Wood CV4 . . 111 D1
Crompton Ave B20 . . 55 C1
Crompton Cl WS2 . . . 28 A5
Crompton Ct
Codsall WV8 . . . . . . 10 B4
Warwick CV34 . . . . . 160 D6
Crompton Rd
Birmingham, Handsworth
B20. . . . . 55 C1
Birmingham, Nechells
B7. . . . . 67 C8
Birmingham, Rubery
B45. . . . . 101 D1
Tipton DY4 . . . . 52 A4
Crompton St CV34. . . 160 D6
Cromwell Cl
Rowley Regis B65. . . . 63 A5
Willenhall WS4 . . . . . 27 E4
Cromwell Ct WS6 . . . .5 A1
Cromwell Dr DY2. . . .62 F8
Cromwell Jun & Inf Sch
B7. . . . . .67 B6
Cromwell La
Birmingham B31. . . . 102 E8
Coventry CV4, CV8 . . 131 C6
Cromwell Rd
Cannock WS12 . . . . . .2 E1
Tamworth B79. . . . . . 20 E8
Wolverhampton WV10 . 11 E4
Cromwells Mdw WS14. .9 C5
Cromwell St
Birmingham B7. . . . . 67 B5
Coventry CV6 . . . . . 113 F6
Dudley DY2 . . . . 62 E8
West Bromwich B71. . 53 C4
Crondal Pl B15. . . . . 86 B7
Crondal Rd CV7 . . . . 96 B7
Cronehills Jun & Inf Sch
B70. . . . . 53 D4
Cronehills Linkway
B70. . . . . 53 D3
Cronehills St B70 . . . 53 D3
Crookham Cl B17 . . . .84 F7
Crookhay La B71. . . . 53 B8
Crook La Aldridge WS9 30 B1
Birmingham WS9 . . . . 44 A3
Crooks La B80 . . . . . 159 D4
Croome Cl
Birmingham B11. . . . . 87 B3
Coventry CV6 . . . . . 112 F4
Redditch B98 . . . . . 154 F1
Cropredy Rd B31. . . . 123 B8
Cropthorne Cl B98 . . 159 B7
Cropthorne Dr B47. . 125 D2
Cropthorne Ho B60. . 137 B3
Cropthorne Rd B90. . 106 C3
Crosbie Rd
Birmingham B17. . . . . 85 B6
Coventry CV5 . . . . . 112 E3

Crosby Cl
Birmingham B1 . . . . . . 66 B3
Wolverhampton WV6 . . 24 F5
Cross Cheaping CV1. 165 B3
Cross Cl B64 . . . . .62 F2
Cross Farm Rd B17. . . 85 D4
Cross Farms La B45 . . 101 F1
Crossfell B77 . . . . 22 B1
Crossfield Rd
Birmingham B33 . . . . . 69 A3
Lichfield WS13 . . . . .9 E8
Crossfield Rd Ind Est
WS13 . . . . .9 E8
Cross Fields Rd ◆
CV34 . . . . 160 H8
Crossfield Way WV14 . 40 E5
Crossgate Rd
Dudley DY2 . . . . 61 F6
Redditch B98 . . . . 159 C7
Cross Ho WV2 . . . . 39 C7
Crossings Ind Est The ◆
WS3 . . . . .28 B8
Crossings The ◆ WS14 .9 E8
Crosskey Cl B33 . . . . . . 69 E2
Cross Keys WS13 . . . . . .9 B8
Cross Keys Island
WS12 . . . . .2 C3
Cross La
Birmingham B43 . . . . . . 43 E1
Cubbington CV32 . . . 157 E4
Lichfield WS14 . . . . 9 D6
Sedgley DY3 . . . . 39 E1
Crossland Cres WV6. . .24 F7
Crossland Row LE10. . 76 A6
Crossley Ct CV6 . . . . . 113 F7
Crossley Ret Pk
DY11 . . . . 116 D6
Crossley St DY2 . . . . . 62 D4
Crossley Wlk B60 . . . 150 E7
Cross Pl DY3 . . . . 39 E1
Cross Point Bsns Pk
CV2 . . . . 115 B8
Cross Rd
Coventry CV6 . . . . 113 F8
Keresley CV7 . . . . 94 F6
◆ Royal Leamington Spa
CV32 . . . . 156 D1
Cross Road Ind Est
CV6 . . . . 113 F7
Cross St N WV1 . . . . . 25 D4
Cross St S WV2 . . . . . 39 C7
Cross St Bilston WV14 .40 F2
Birmingham B21 . . . . . 65 C8
Burntwood WS7 . . . . . . .6 E8
Cannock, Bridgtown
WS11 . . . . .4 E5
Cannock WS11 . . . . .2 E1
Cheslyn Hay WS6 . . . . 4 D2
Coventry CV1 . . . . 165 C4
Dudley DY1 . . . . 51 C1
Halesowen B63 . . . . 83 A3
Kingswinford DY6 . . . . 60 D6
Kingswinford, Wall Heath
DY6 . . . . 60 B8
Nuneaton CV10 . . . . . . 72 D3
Oldbury B68 . . . . 64 A4
◆ Rowley Regis B65 . . 63 C1
Royal Leamington Spa
CV32 . . . . 157 A1
Smethwick B66 . . . . . . 65 A6
Stourbridge DY8 . . . . . 80 E5
◆ Stourbridge, Wordsley
DY6 . . . . 60 D3
Tamworth B79 . . . . . . 21 B5
Tamworth, Kettlebrook
B77 . . . . 21 C3
Walsall WS3 . . . . 15 A1
◆ Warwick CV34 . . . . 160 F7
Wednesbury WS10 . . . 41 E3
◆ Willenhall WV13 . . . 27 A1
Wolverhampton WV1 . . 25 F1
Cross The
Kingswinford DY6. . . . . 60 D6
Stourbridge DY9 . . . . . 81 E6
Crossway La B44. . . . .55 F6
Crossway Rd CV3 . . 133 B4
Crossways LE10 . . . . . .75 F5
Crossways Ct B44 . . . 56 B7
Crossways Gn B44 . . . 56 B7
Crossways Sh Ctr
WV10 . . . . 26 A3
Crosswells Rd B68. . . 64 B5
Cross Wlk B69 . . . . . . 63 C8
Cross Wlks DY9 . . . . . 81 E5
Crowberry Cl WS8. . . 15 D6
Crowberry La B78. . . . 48 C8
Crowden Rd B77 . . . . 22 A1

Crowesbridge Mews
WV14 . . . . 51 B8
Crowhill Rd CV11. . . . 74 A1
Crowhurst Rd B31. . . 122 E7
Crowland Ave WV6 . . . 23 E4
Crowle Dr DY9 . . . . . . 81 C5
Crowmere Rd CV2. . . 114 F7
Crown Cl
Bromsgrove B61 . . . . . 136 F2
Rowley Regis B65. . . . . 63 D4
Sedgley DY3 . . . . 39 D1
Crown Ct
Darlaston WS10 . . . . . 41 C8
⑩ Hinckley LE10 . . . . 71 D1
❶ Sutton Coldfield B74 31 E3
Crown Ctr The ❸
DY8 . . . . 81 A5
Crown Gn CV6 . . . . . . 95 E2
Crownhill Mdw B61. . 136 F7
Crownhill Rd LE10. . . 75 D4
Crown Ho CV5 . . . . . . 112 E3
Crown La Iverley DY8 . 98 C7
Kidderminster DY10 . . 116 E6
Stourbridge DY8 . . . . . 80 F5
Sutton Coldfield B74. . . 31 E3
Crown Mdw B48 . . . . 139 A7
Crownmeadow Dr
DY4 . . . . 52 D7
Crown Rd
Birmingham, Bordesley
Green B9 . . . . 67 D2
Birmingham, King's Norton
B30 . . . . 104 A4
Crown St WV1 . . . . . . 25 D4
Crown Terr CV31 . . . . 161 F7
Crown Way CV32 . . . . 157 B3
Crown Wharf Sh Pk
WS2 . . . . 28 D2
Crown Wlk DY4 . . . . . 52 A2
Crows Nest Cl B76. . .46 F3
Crowther Gdns B63 . . 82 C7
Crowther Gr WV6 . . . .24 F4
Crowther Rd
Birmingham B23 . . . . . 56 D5
Wolverhampton WV6 . . 24 F5
Crowther St
Kidderminster DY11 . . 116 C6
Wolverhampton WV10 . 25 E4
Croxall Way B66 . . . . . 65 B5
Croxdene Ave WS3 . . . 14 A1
Croxhall St CV12 . . . . 78 C3
Croxley Dr WS12 . . . . . .2 C3
Croxley Gdns WV13 . . .40 F8
Croxstalls Ave WS3. . . 28 A8
Croxstalls Cl WS3 . . . 14 A1
Croxstalls Pl WS3 . . . 28 A8
Croxstalls Rd WS3 . . . 28 A8
Croxton Gr B33 . . . . . 69 A4
Croyde Ave B42 . . . . . 55 A8
Croydon Cl CV3 . . . . . 133 E6
Croydon Ct ⑳ B29 . . 103 C7
Croydon Rd
Birmingham B29 . . . . . 85 F3
Birmingham, Erdington
B24 . . . . 57 A2
Croy Dr B35 . . . . 58 B4
Crucible The WV14 . . 40 D2
Crummock Cl CV6. . . . 95 D3
Crumpfields La B97. . 152 F1
Crump Ho WS1. . . . . . .28 F1
Crusader Cl B69 . . . . 63 E5
Crutchley Ave B78 . . . 21 A2
Crutchley Way CV31. 162 A2
Crychan Cl B45 . . . . . 102 B2
Cryersoak Cl B90 . . . 127 B7
Cryfield Grange Rd CV4,
CV8 . . . . 132 C2
Cryfield Hts CV4 . . . . 132 D2
Cryfield Village CV4 . 132 B4
Crystal Ave DY8 . . . . . 60 F1
Crystal Dr B66 . . . . . . 64 C8
Crystal Ho B66 . . . . . 65 C6
Cubbington CE Prim Sch
CV32 . . . . 157 F5
Cubbington Rd
Coventry CV6 . . . . 96 A2
Royal Leamington Spa
CV32 . . . . 157 B3
Cubley Rd B28 . . . . . . 87 E1
Cuckoo Cl WS11 . . . . . .2 C2
Cuckoo La CV1. . . . . . 165 C3
Cuckoo Rd B7 . . . . . . 67 D8
Cuin Rd B66 . . . . 65 C5
Cuin Wlk ❶ B66 . . . . . 65 C5
Culey Gr B33. . . . . 69 D2
Culey Wlk B37 . . . . . . 70 D2
Culford Dr B32. . . . . . 102 C8
Culham Cl B27 . . . . . . 88 D2
Cullwick St WV1 . . . . 40 A8
Cullington Rd B31 . . 122 F8

Culmore Cl WV12 . . . 27 D4
Culmore Rd B62 . . . . . 63 E1
Culpepper Cl CV10 . . 72 E4
Culverhouse Dr DY5. . 61 A1
Culverley Cres B93 . . 127 F6
Culvert Way B66 . . . . 64 D7
Culwell Ind Pk
WV10 . . . . 163 D4
Culwell St WV10 . . . . 163 C4
Culwell Trad Est
WV10 . . . . .25 F4
Culworth Cl CV31 . . . 161 F5
Culworth Ct
Coventry CV6 . . . . 113 E8
Whitnash CV31. . . . . . 162 A5
Culworth Row CV6 . . 113 E8
Cumberford Ave B33 . 69 E1
Cumberland Ave ❸
B5 . . . . 86 E7
Cumberland Cl DY6 . . 60 E4
Cumberland Cres
Burntwood WS7 . . . . . . .7 A8
Royal Leamington Spa
CV32 . . . . 157 C3
Cumberland Dr
Nuneaton CV10. . . . . . 72 E3
Tamworth B78. . . . . . . 21 A1
Cumberland Ho ❼
WV3 . . . . 25 C4
Cumberland Rd
Bilston WV14 . . . . 40 D7
Birmingham B68 . . . . . 84 D7
Cannock WS11 . . . . .2 A4
West Bromwich B71. . . 53 D7
Willenhall WV13 . . . . . 27 D2
Cumberland St B1 . . . 66 B2
Cumberland Wlk B75. 47 B5
Cumbernauld Wlk ❼
CV2 . . . . 115 A7
Cumbrae Dr LE10 . . . 71 B2
Cumbria Cl CV1 . . . . . 113 A3
Cumbrian Croft B63 . 82 D2
Cumbria Way B8 . . . . 67 D6
Cumming St ❶
CV31 . . . . 162 A7
Cundall Cl CV31 . . . . 162 B6
Cunnery The CV8 . . . 149 A3
Cunningham Rd
Perton WV6 . . . . 23 E4
Walsall WS2 . . . . 27 E2
Cupfields Ave DY4. . . 52 C8
Cupfields Cres DY4. . 52 C7
Curbar Rd B42. . . . . . 55 C6
Curborough Rd WS13 . .3 B2
Curdale Rd B32 . . . . . 102 B8
Curdworth La B76. . . . 59 A8
Curdworth Prim Sch
B76. . . . . 59 C6
Cur La B97. . . . . 152 D3
Curlew B77 . . . . 36 A7
Curlew Cl
Kidderminster DY10 . . 117 B2
Lichfield WS14 . . . . .9 E7
Curlew Dr WS8. . . . . . 15 E7
Curlew Hill WS11. . . . .2 A3
Curlews Cl B23 . . . . . 56 C8
Curlieu Cl CV35 . . . . 160 A7
Curral Rd B65. . . . . . . 63 C3
Curran Cl CV31 . . . . . 162 B4
Curriers Cl CV4 . . . . . 131 D7
Curslow La DY10 . . . . 117 F1
Curtin Dr WS10 . . . . . 41 B4
Curtis Cl Finstall B60. 151 F8
Smethwick B66. . . . . . 65 C4
Curtis Rd CV2 . . . . . . 114 D6
Curzon Ave CV6 . . . . 113 E8
Curzon Cl LE10. . . . . .75 F7
Curzon Gr CV31 . . . . 162 C6
Curzon St
Birmingham B4 . . . . . . 67 A3
Wolverhampton WV2 . . 39 D7
Cuthbert Rd B18. . . . . 65 E4
Cutlers Rough Cl
B31. . . . . 102 F5
Cutler St B66 . . . . 65 B6
Cutsdean Cl B31 . . . . 102 F6
Cutshill Cl B36. . . . . . 69 C8
Cut Throat La B94 . . 142 D7
Cutting The WS4 . . . . .28 F4
Cuttle Mill La B76. . . 48 D3
Cuttle Pool La B93 . . 128 F4
Cutworth Cl B76 . . . . 47 A3
Cwerne Ct DY3. . . . . . 50 C3
Cygnet Cl
Alvechurch B48. . . . . . 139 A7
Cannock WS12 . . . . . . .2 C7
Wolverhampton WV6 . . 24 C2
Cygnet Ct
Coventry CV1 . . . . 165 C4
Kidderminster DY10 . . 117 A1

Cygnet Dr
Brownhills WS8 . . . . . . 15 E7
Tamworth B79. . . . . . . 20 F5
Cygnet Gr B23 . . . . . . 56 B6
Cygnet La DY5 . . . . . . 61 C7
Cygnet Rd B70 . . . . . . 53 A5
Cygnus Way B70 . . . . .52 F5
Cymbeline Way
CV34 . . . . 161 E4
Cypress Ave DY3 . . . . 50 D5
Cypress Croft CV3. . . 134 F8
Cypress Ct DY10. . . . . 117 A4
Cypress Gdns
Kingswinford DY6 . . . . 60 D4
Sutton Coldfield B74. . . 46 A7
Walsall WS5 . . . . 43 C4
Cypress La CV31 . . . . 162 B3
Cypress Rd Dudley DY2 .51 F1
Walsall WS5 . . . . 43 C4
Cypress Sq ❷ B27 . . . 88 C5
Cypress Way
Birmingham B31 . . . . . 122 F8
Nuneaton CV10. . . . . . 72 D6
Cyprus Ave B96 . . . . . 158 D2
Cyprus Cl B29 . . . . . . 103 A7
Cyprus St Oldbury B69. 64 A8
Wolverhampton WV2 . . 39 C6
Cyril Gr ❺ B10. . . . . . 87 C8
Cyril Rd B10 . . . . 87 D8

D

Dace B77 . . . . 35 D7
Dacer Cl B30. . . . . 104 B5
Dace Rd WV10 . . . . . . 26 B4
Dadford View DY5 . . . 61 B2
Dad's La B13. . . . . 86 C1
Daffern Rd CV7 . . . . . 78 A1
Daffodil Cl DY3. . . . . . 50 E7
Daffodil Dr ❹ CV12 . . 77 D2
Daffodil Pl WS5 . . . . . 43 D8
Daffodil Rd WS5 . . . . 43 D8
Daffodil Way B31 . . . . 122 E8
Dagger La B71. . . . . . . 53 E4
Dagnall Rd B27 . . . . . 88 D3
Dagnell End Rd B98. . 154 B7
Dagtail La B97. . . . . . . 158 D3
Dahlia Cl Hinckley LE10 75 E6
Wolverhampton WV1 . . 26 C1
Dahlia Wlk CV10 . . . . 78 A8
Daimler Cl B36. . . . . . .58 F1
Daimler Rd
Birmingham B14. . . . . 105 D3
Coventry CV6 . . . . 113 C5
Dainton Gr B32 . . . . . 84 C1
Daintree Croft CV3. . 133 C7
Daintry Dr B78. . . . . . 20 B7
Dairy Cl DY4 . . . . 52 B5
Dairy Ct B68 . . . . 84 D7
Dairy La B97 . . . . 153 A5
Daisy Bank WS12. . . . . .1 F8
Daisy Bank Cl WS3 . . 15 B2
Daisy Bank Cres WS5. 43 D8
Daisy Croft CV12. . . . 77 D2
Daisy Dr B23 . . . . 56 A5
Daisy Farm Rd B14. . 105 B3
Daisy Mdw DY4 . . . . . 52 C6
Daisy Rd B16 . . . . .65 F2
Daisy St Dudley WV14 . 40 D2
Wolverhampton WV6 . . 25 A4
Daisy Wlk WV9 . . . . . . 11 A3
Dakota Apartments
B16 . . . . 66 B1
Dalbeg Cl WV8 . . . . . . 24 E8
Dalbury Rd B28 . . . . . 105 E5
Dalby Cl CV3. . . . . 134 E8
Dalby Rd WS3 . . . . . . .28 F6
Dale Cl
Birmingham B43 . . . . . 43 D1
Catshill B61. . . . . 136 F7
Smethwick B66. . . . . . 65 A3
Tipton DY4 . . . . 52 D5
Warwick CV34 . . . . . . 161 A8
Dale Ct WV1 . . . . 25 A3
Dale Dr WS7 . . . . .7 B7
Dale End
Birmingham B4. . . . . . 164 C3
Darlaston WS10 . . . . . 41 D6
Nuneaton CV10. . . . . . 72 E5
Dale End Cl LE10. . . . 75 A7
Dale Hill B60. . . . . 137 F6
Dalehouse Flats CV8 148 B6
Dalehouse La CV8. . . 148 D7
Dale Meadow Cl
CV7 . . . . 130 B6
Dale Rd
Birmingham B29 . . . . . 85 E3
Halesowen B62. . . . . . 83 F8

Dale Rd continued
Redditch B98 . . . . 153 F5
Stourbridge DY8 . . . . . 80 F2
Dales Cl WV6 . . . . 25 B6
Dales Com Jun Sch
B77. . . . . 36 B8
Dales Inf Sch The
B77. . . . . 36 B8
Dalesman Cl DY6. . . . 60 B7
Dale St Bilston WV14 . . 41 A5
Royal Leamington Spa
CV32. . . . . 161 E8
Smethwick B66 . . . . . . 65 A3
Walsall WS1 . . . . 42 E7
Wednesbury WS10 . . . 41 E4
Wolverhampton WV3 . . 163 A2
Daleswood Pk B62 . . . 100 F3
Dale Terr B69 . . . . 63 C8
Daleview Rd B14. . . . . 105 C4
Daleway Rd CV3 . . . . . 133 B4
Dalewood Croft B26. . .88 F6
Dalewood Rd B37. . . . .69 F5
Daley Cl B1. . . . . 66 B3
Daley Rd WV14 . . . . . .40 F2
Dalkeith Rd B73. . . . . . 45 E2
Dalkeith St WS2. . . . . 28 C3
Dallas Rd B23. . . . . . . 56 D5
Dallimore Cl B92. . . . 89 A3
Dallington Rd CV6 . . . 112 E6
Dalloway Cl B5 . . . . . . 86 D6
Dalmahoy Cl CV11. . . 79 C8
Dalmeny Rd CV4 . . . . 131 D7
Dalston Cl DY2 . . . . . . 62 D6
Dalston Rd B27 . . . . . 88 C4
Dalton Ct B23 . . . . 56 B3
Dalton Gdns CV2 . . . . 114 F4
Dalton Rd
Bedworth CV12 . . . . . . 78 A2
Coventry CV5 . . . . 113 B1
Walsall WS2 . . . . 28 A3
Dalton St
Birmingham B4 . . . . . . 164 C3
Wolverhampton WV3 . . 39 B8
Dalton Way B4 . . . . . . 164 C3
Dalvine Rd DY2 . . . . . 62 B2
Dalwood Cl WV14 . . . . 51 B7
Dalwood Way CV6 . . . 96 B4
Damar Croft B14. . . . . 104 D4
Dama Rd B78 . . . . .34 F8
Dame Agnes Gr CV6. . 114 B8
Dame Elizabeth Cadbury
Tech Coll B30 . . . . . 103 D7
Dame Ellen Pinsent Sch
B13. . . . . 105 A7
Damien Cl B67. . . . . . . .64 F5
Damson Cl
Redditch B97 . . . . 158 C6
Wednesfield WV12 . . . 27 A6
Damson La B91, B92 . 107 E7
Damson Parkway B91,
B92 . . . . 107 F7
Damson Wharf DY4 . . 52 A3
Damson Wood Inf Sch
B92. . . . . 107 D7
Dam St WS13 . . . . .9 B8
Danbury Cl B76. . . . . . 47 A2
Danbury Gdns WV10. . 11 C2
Danbury Rd B90 . . . . 106 B2
Danby Gr B24. . . . . . . 57 B2
Dando Rd DY2 . . . . . . 62 D8
Dandy Bank Rd DY6. . 61 A8
Dandy's Wlk WS1 . . . .42 F8
Dane Gr B13. . . . . 104 D8
Danehill Wlk WV8. . . .24 F8
Danehurst Ctr WV1. . 26 A3
Danelagh Cl B79 . . . . .20 F7
Dane Rd CV2. . . . . 114 B4
Danesbury Cres
Birmingham B44 . . . . . 56 A8
Royal Leamington Spa
CV31 . . . . 162 D6
Danes Cl WV11 . . . . . . 12 F4
Danescourt Rd WV6 . . 24 C6
Danesmoor Ho B26 . . 88 E7
Danesmore Park Jun &
Inf Sch WV11 . . . . . 13 A1
Daneswood Dr WS9 . . 15 F3
Daneswood Rd CV3 . . 135 C7
Daneways Cl B74 . . . . 45 A8
Danford Cl DY8 . . . . . 81 A4
Danford Gdns B10. . . 87 C8
Danford La B91 . . . . . 106 E3
Danford Rd B47. . . . . . 124 F6
Danford Way B43 . . . . 54 D8
Dangerfield Ho B70 . . 53 E1
Dangerfield La WS10. 41 C4
Daniel Ave CV10 . . . . 72 C3

Daniels La WS9 . . . . . . 30 C5
Daniels Rd B9 . . . . 68 A2
Danilo Rd WS11 . . . . . . 1 D1
Danks St DY4 . . . . 52 A2
Danzey Cl B98 . . . . . . 159 B5
Danzey Gr B14. . . . . . . 104 C3
Danzey Green La
B94 . . . . 142 B1
Danzey Green Rd B36 58 B1
Daphne Cl CV2. . . . . . 96 C3
Darby Cl WV14 . . . . . . 40 A2
Darby End Rd DY2. . . 62 E4
Darby Ho ❷ WS2 . . . . 42 C7
Darby Rd Oldbury B68 . 64 C5
Wednesbury WS10. . . . 42 B4
Darbys Hill Rd B69. . . 63 B7
Darby St B65. . . . . 63 C1
Darby Way DY4 . . . . . 52 B5
Darell Croft B76. . . . . . 46 E3
Daren Cl B36. . . . . .69 F8
Dare Rd B23 . . . . 56 E4
Dare's Wlk LE10. . . . . 71 D1
Darfield Wlk ❷ B12. . .86 F8
Darges La WS6. . . . . . . 4 F4
Dark La
Astwood Bank B96 . . . 158 D1
Bedworth CV12. . . . . . 77 D1
Belbroughton DY9. . . . 119 F8
Birchmoor B78 . . . . . . 36 E8
Brinsford WV10 . . . . . . 11 D8
Coventry CV1 . . . . 165 B4
Featherstone WV10 . . . 12 D7
Great Wyrley WS6. . . . . .5 C1
Hollywood B38, B47. . . 124 E7
Romsley B62 . . . . 100 F4
Stoke Heath B60. . . . . 150 D6
Darlaston Com Science
Coll WS10 . . . . .41 B6
Darlaston Ct CV7. . . . . 92 D1
Darlaston La WV14 . . . 41 A7
Darlaston Rd
Walsall WS2 . . . . 42 A8
Wednesbury WS10. . . . 41 E4
Darlaston Road Ind Est
WS10. . . . . 41 D5
Darley Ave B34. . . . . . .68 F6
Darleydale Ave B44 . . 44 E1
Darley Dr WV6 . . . . . . 25 B5
Darley Green Rd
B93 . . . . 128 B1
Darley Ho B69 . . . . . . 63 D6
Darley Mead Ct B91. . 107 E4
Darley Rd LE10. . . . . . 75 E6
Darley Way B74 . . . . . 45 A4
Darlington St
Darlaston WS10 . . . . . 41 D5
Wolverhampton WV1 . . 163 B3
Darlington Yd WV1. . . 163 B3
Darlston Row CV7. . . . 92 B1
Darnbrook B77. . . . . . . 22 C1
Darnel Croft ❸ B10. . 67 B1
Darnel Hurst Rd B75. 32 C3
Danford Cl
Birmingham B28. . . . . 106 A5
Coventry CV2 . . . . 114 F7
Sutton Coldfield B72. . . 57 D7
Danford La WS14. . . . .79 F8
Danford Moors WS14. .9 E6
Danford View WS13. . . 3 E1
Darnick Rd B73 . . . . . 45 D3
Darnley Rd ❸ B16 . . . 66 A2
Darrach Cl CV2 . . . . . 96 E1
Darris Rd B29. . . . . . . 104 A8
Dart B77. . . . . 36 A5
Dart Cl LE10 . . . . 75 A8
Dartford Rd WS3 . . . . .13 F1
Dartington Way CV11. .78 F8
Dartmoor Cl B45 . . . . 102 A2
Dartmouth Ave
Cannock WS11 . . . . . . .4 C8
Stourbridge DY8 . . . . . 60 D3
Walsall WS3 . . . . 28 E6
Willenhall WV13 . . . . . 27 A2
Dartmouth Cir B6 . . . 66 F5
Dartmouth Cl WS3 . . . 28 E5
Dartmouth Cres ❷
WV14 . . . . 41 A7
Dartmouth Dr WS9 . . . 30 A5
Dartmouth High Sch
B43. . . . . 43 D3
Dartmouth Ho ❷
WS3 . . . . .28 F4
Dartmouth Middleway
B7 . . . . .66 F4
Dartmouth Pl WS3 . . .28 F4
Dartmouth Rd
Birmingham B29 . . . . . 85 F2
Cannock WS11 . . . . 1 D1
Coventry CV2 . . . . 114 C5

Dartmouth Rd *continued*
Smethwick B66 . . . . 64 F8
Dartmouth Sch CV2. 114 D5
Dartmouth Sq B70 . . . 53 D2
Dartmouth St
West Bromwich B70 . . . 53 B3
Wolverhampton WV2 . 163 C1
Wolverhampton WV2 . 163 D1
Dartmouth Street Sta
B70. . . . . .53 B3
Dart St B9 . . . . 67 B1
Darvel Mews WV12 . . . 27 D4
Darvel Rd WV12 . . . . . . 27 D4
Darwall St WS1 . . . . . . 28 E2
Darwell Pk B77. . . . . . .22 B2
Darwin Cl
Burntwood WS7 . . . . .7 B7
Cannock WS12 . . . . .2 E2
Coventry CV2 . . . . 115 A6
Hinckley LE10 . . . . 71 E3
Lichfield WS13 . . . . .9 A8
Darwin Ct
1 Bedworth CV12 . . . . 78 A2
Perton WV6. . . . . 23 E4
Darwin Ho
3 Birmingham, Chelmsley Wood B37. . . . . 70 C1
3 Birmingham, Showell Green B13 . . . . 87 A2
Kingswinford DY6 . . . . . . 60 F7
Darwin Pl WS2 . . . . 28 B6
Darwin Rd WS2 . . . . . . 28 B6
Darwin St B12 . . . . .86 F8
Dassett Gr B9 . . . . 68 C2
Dassett Rd B93 . . . . . 127 F4
Datchet Cl CV5 . . . . . . 112 C4
Datteln Rd WS11 . . . . . . .2 A4
D'aubeny Rd CV4 . . . 132 C8
Dauntsey Covert
B14 . . . . 104 D2
Davena Dr B29 . . . . 84 E2
Davena Gr WV14 . . . . . 40 D3
Davenham Rd B60 . . 137 C1
Davenport Dr
Birmingham B35 . . . . . . 58 C3
Bromsgrove B60 . . . . . 137 B1
Davenport Lodge Sch
CV5. . . . . 133 B8
Davenport Rd
Coventry CV5 . . . . 133 B8
Wednesfield WV11 . . . . 26 E6
Wolverhampton WV6 . . 24 B5
Davenport Terr LE10 . . 75 E8
Daventry Gr B32 . . . . . 84 D6
Daventry Rd CV3 . . . . 133 D7
Davey Cl WS7 . . . . .6 F4
Davey Rd
Birmingham B20 . . . . . . 55 E1
West Bromwich B70 . . . 53 A5
David Cox Ct 1 B17 . . 85 D5
David Garrick Gdns
WS13 . . . . .3 B2
David Harman Dr B71 .53 F7
David Peacock Cl
DY4 . . . . 52 A5
David Rd
Bedworth CV7 . . . . 95 F8
Birmingham B20 . . . . . . 55 B2
Coventry CV1 . . . . 113 F2
Tipton DY4 . . . . 52 A7
Davidson Ave CV31 . . 162 A7
Davidson Rd WS14 . . . . .9 B7
Davids The B31 . . . . . 103 C5
Davies Ave WV14 . . . . . 40 D3
Davies Ho
7 Oldbury B69 . . . . . . 64 A7
Walsall WS3 . . . . 14 B1
Davies Rd CV7 . . . . .95 F7
Davis Ave DY4 . . . . 51 E4
Davis Cl CV32 . . . . 156 D2
Davis Gr B25 . . . . 88 D6
Davison Rd B67 . . . . . . .64 F3
Davis Rd
Tamworth B77 . . . . 21 F4
Willenhall WV12 . . . . . . 27 D8
Davy Rd WS2 . . . . 28 A5
Dawberry Cl B14 . . . . 104 D5
Dawberry Fields Rd
B14 . . . . 104 D5
Dawberry Rd B14 . . . 104 C6
Daw End WS4, WS9 . . . 29 C6
Daw End La WS4 . . . . . . 29 C6
Daw End Sch WS4 . . . 29 C6
Dawes Ave B70 . . . . . . 53 C1
Dawes Cl CV2 . . . . 114 A3
Dawes La WS8 . . . . .7 A1
Dawley Brook Prim Sch
DY6. . . . . 60 C7
Dawley Brook Rd DY6 60 D7
Dawley Cl 1 WS2 . . . . 42 B7
Dawley Cres B37 . . . . . 70 B1
Dawley Rd DY6 . . . . 60 C8
Dawley Trad Est DY6 . 60 D8
Dawley Wlk 9 CV2 . . 115 A7
Dawlish Cl CV11 . . . . . . 73 E5
Dawlish Dr CV3 . . . . . 133 D5
Dawlish Rd
Birmingham B29 . . . . . . 85 F2
Dudley DY1 . . . . 51 C5
Smethwick B66 . . . . 65 B5
Dawn Dr DY4 . . . . 41 C2
Dawney Dr B75 . . . . . . 32 A4
Dawn Rd B31 . . . . 102 E6
Dawson Ave WV14 . . . . .39 F2
Dawson Cl CV31 . . . . . 162 A2
Dawson Ct B24 . . . . . . .56 F4
Dawson Rd
Birmingham B21 . . . . . . 65 F8
Bromsgrove B61 . . . . . 136 E2
Coventry CV3 . . . . 114 A1
Dawson Sq WV14 . . . . . 40 C5
Dawson St
Smethwick B66 . . . . 65 A3
Walsall WS3 . . . . 28 D8
Day Ave WV11 . . . . 26 E7
Daybrook Cl B97 . . . . 153 B5
Day Ho DY4 . . . . 52 C8
Dayhouse Bank B62 . 101 B1
Daylesford Inf Sch
B92. . . . . 89 A3
Daylesford Rd B92 . . . 89 A3
Days Cl CV1 . . . . 113 E3
Day's La CV1 . . . . 113 F3
Day St WS2 . . . . 28 E3
Daytona Dr CV5 . . . . . 111 B8
Deacon St CV11 . . . . . . 73 C3
Deakin Ave WS8. . . . . . . .6 F1
Deakin Rd
Birmingham B24 . . . . . . 57 A3
Sutton Coldfield B75 . . . 46 E7
Deakins Rd B25 . . . . . . 88 B7
Deal Ave WS7 . . . . .7 A8
Deal Dr B69 . . . . 52 A1
Deal Gr B31 . . . . 103 A3
Deanbrook Cl B90 . . . 127 A6
Dean Cl
Birmingham B44 . . . . . . 56 B8
Hinckley LE10 . . . . 71 E2
Stourbridge DY8 . . . . . . 81 B6
Sutton Coldfield B72 . . . 57 B7
Dean Ct
5 Brierley Hill DY5 . . . 61 D2
Perton WV6. . . . . 23 E6
Deanery CE Prim Sch The
B76. . . . . .57 F8
Deanery Row WV1 . . 163 B4
Dean Rd
Birmingham B23 . . . . . . 56 F5
Hinckley LE10 . . . . 71 E2
Walsall WS4 . . . . 29 C7
Dean Rd W LE10 . . . . . 71 E2
Deans Cl B98 . . . . 154 D5
Deans Croft WS14 . . . . . .9 C8
Deanscroft Dr B60 . . 137 C6
Deansfield High Sch
WV1 . . . . 26 C2
Deansfield Rd WV1 . . . 26 A2
Deansford La DY10 . . 118 B6
Deans Pl WS3. . . . . . . .28 F6
Dean's Rd WV1 . . . . . . 26 B2
Deans Slade Dr WS14 . .9 A5
Dean St
Birmingham B5 . . . . . . 164 C1
Coventry CV2 . . . . 114 A3
Sedgley DY3 . . . . 50 D8
Deanston Croft CV2 . . .96 F1
Deansway
Bromsgrove B61 . . . . . 136 E2
Warwick CV34 . . . . . . 155 E1
Deans Way CV7 . . . . . . 95 D6
Deansway Ho DY10 . . 117 A7
Deansway The DY10 . 117 A7
Dearman Rd B11 . . . . . 87 B7
Dearmont Rd B31 . . . 122 E7
Dearne Ct DY3 . . . . 51 A6
Deasy Ho CV3 . . . . . . 134 B5
Deasy Rd CV1 . . . . . . 165 C1
Deavall Way WS11 . . . . . .2 B2
Debden Cl B93 . . . . . . 127 E2
Debenham Cres B25 . . 68 D1
Debenham Rd B25 . . . 68 D1
Deblen Dr B16 . . . . 65 D1
Deborah Cl WV4 . . . . . 39 C6
De-Compton Cl CV7 . . 95 A7
Deedmore Rd CV2 . . . 96 D1
Deedmore Sch CV2 . 114 C8
Deegan Cl CV2 . . . . . . 114 A5
Dee Gr
Birmingham B38 . . . . . 123 E8
Cannock WS11 . . . . 4 D8
Dee Ho 8 DY1 . . . . 61 E8
Deelands Rd B45 . . . . 121 F8
Deeley B77 . . . . 22 A1
Deeley Cl
Birmingham B15 . . . . . . 86 C7
Cradley Heath B64 . . . . 82 E7
Deeley Dr 3 DY4 . . . . 52 C6
Deeley Pl WS3 . . . . 28 B8
Deeley St
Brierley Hill DY5 . . . . . . 61 E1
Walsall WS3 . . . . 28 B8
Deepdale B77 . . . . 22 D2
Deepdale Ave B26 . . . . 89 B4
Deepdale La DY3 . . . . . 50 E3
Deeplow Cl 2 B72 . . . 46 C4
Deepmoor Rd B33 . . . .68 F3
Deepmore Ave WS2 . . 28 B2
Deepwood Cl WS4 . . . 29 B8
Deepwood Gr B32 . . . 102 B8
Deer Barn Hill B98 . . 154 A1
Deer Cl
Huntington WS12 . . . . . . .1 C6
Norton Canes WS11 . . . . .6 B7
Walsall WS3 . . . . 14 C1
Dee Rd WS3 . . . . 14 E1
Deerdale Terr 8
CV3 . . . . 134 F8
Deerdale Way CV3 . . 134 F8
Deerfold Cres WS7 . . . . .7 B7
Deerham Cl B23 . . . . . 56 D7
Deerhill B77 . . . . 22 C1
Deerhurst Cl B98 . . . . 154 C7
Deerhurst Ct B91 . . . 107 D4
Deerhurst Rd
Birmingham B20 . . . . . . 54 F5
Coventry CV6 . . . . 95 B2
Deerhurst Rise WS12 . . .2 F6
Deer Leap The CV8 . . 148 B6
Deerpark Dr CV34 . . . 160 E8
Deer Park Rd B78 . . . . 20 E1
Deer Park Way B91 . . 107 C1
Deer Wlk WV8 . . . . .10 F2
Dee Wlk
Birmingham B36 . . . . . . 70 A7
Birmingham B36 . . . . . . 70 A8
Defford Ave WS4 . . . . . 15 C1
Defford Cl B97 . . . . . . 152 E1
Defford Dr B68 . . . . 64 B4
Dehavilland Cl CV11 . . 73 B5
De Havilland Dr B35 . . 58 A2
De Havilland Way
LE10 . . . . 75 E4
Deighton Gr CV3 . . . . 134 C6
Deighton Rd WS5 . . . . 43 B4
De-La-Bere Cres
LE10 . . . . 76 A6
Delage Cl CV6 . . . . 96 B4
Delamere Cl B36 . . . . . 58 D1
Delamere Dr WS5 . . . . 43 C3
Delamere Rd
Bedworth CV12 . . . . 77 F2
Birmingham B28 . . . . . 105 F7
Willenhall WV12 . . . . . . 27 C7
Delamere Way CV32 . 157 C4
Delancey Keep B75 . . . 47 A5
Delaware Rd CV3 . . . 133 C5
Delf Ho CV2 . . . . 96 D1
Delhi Ave CV6 . . . . 95 D1
Delhurst Ave WV4 . . . . 39 E3
Delhurst Rd B44 . . . . . 44 D1
Delingpole Wlk 2
B64 . . . . 82 E8
Delius St CV4 . . . . 111 E3
Della Dr B32 . . . . 102 D8
Dell Cl CV3 . . . . 134 C5
Dell Farm Cl B93 . . . . 128 B6
Dellow Gr B48 . . . . . . 139 A5
Dellows Cl B38 . . . . . . 123 D7
Dell Rd
Birmingham B30 . . . . . 104 A5
Brierley Hill DY5 . . . . . . 61 B5
Dells Farm B47 . . . . . . 124 F6
Dell The
Birmingham, Edgbaston B16. . . . . 65 F2
Birmingham, Shenley Fields B31. . . . . 102 D6
Cannock WS12 . . . . .2 F4
Lichfield WS13 . . . . .8 F7
Solihull B92. . . . . 89 A1
Stourbridge DY8 . . . . . . 80 E6
Tamworth B79. . . . . 21 B6
Dellway Ct DY8 . . . . . . 80 E5
Delmore Way B76 . . . . 58 B6
Delph Dr DY5 . . . . 81 E7
Delphinium Cl B9 . . . . .67 F3
Delph La DY5 . . . . 81 D8
Delphi Cl CV34 . . . . . . 161 E4
Delph Rd DY5 . . . . 61 D1
Delph Road Ind Est
DY5. . . . . 61 C1
Delrene Rd B28, B90 . 105 F3
Delta Trad Est WV2 . . .39 F8
Delta Way WS11 . . . . 4 D7
Delta Way Bsns Ctr
WS11 . . . . .4 D6
Deltic B77 . . . . 22 A1
Deltic La B77 . . . . .35 F8
Delves Cres
Walsall WS5 . . . . 43 A5
Wood End CV9 . . . . 36 C1
Delves Green Rd WS5 43 A5
Delves Inf Sch WS5 . . 43 A5
Delves Jun Sch WS5 . 43 A5
Delves Rd WS1 . . . . .42 F7
Delville Cl WS10 . . . . . .41 F4
Delville Rd WS10 . . . . . .41 F4
Delville Terr WS10 . . . . .41 F3
De Marnham Cl B70 . . 53 E1
De Montfort Ho B37 . . .69 F5
De Montfort Rd
Hinckley LE10 . . . . 71 E1
Kenilworth CV8 . . . . . . 147 E6
De Montfort Way
CV4 . . . . 132 D5
De Moram Gr B92 . . . 107 F7
Dempster Ct CV11 . . . . 73 C4
Dempster Rd CV12 . . . 78 A4
Demuth Way B69 . . . . .63 F6
Denaby Gr B14 . . . . . . 105 D4
Denbigh Cl DY1 . . . . . . .50 F2
Denbigh Cnr B46 . . . . . 91 A6
Denbigh Cres B71 . . . . 53 B6
Denbigh Ct 3 B29 . . 103 C7
Denbigh Dr
Wednesbury WS10 . . . . 42 D4
West Bromwich B71 . . . 53 B6
Denbigh Rd
Coventry CV6 . . . . 112 E5
Tipton DY4 . . . . 52 C4
Denbigh St B9 . . . . 67 D2
Denbury Cl WS12 . . . . . . 2 D1
Denby Bldgs 17
CV32 . . . . 161 F8
Denby Cl
Birmingham B7 . . . . 67 B5
Royal Leamington Spa CV32. . . . . 157 C3
Denby Croft B90 . . . . 127 B6
Dencer Cl B45 . . . . . . 122 A8
Dencer Dr CV8 . . . . . . 148 C4
Dencil Cl B63 . . . . 82 D5
Dene Ave DY6 . . . . 60 C4
Dene Court Rd B92 . . . .88 F1
Dene Croft WS3 . . . . . . 14 A1
Denegate Cl B76 . . . . . 58 B6
Dene Hollow B13 . . . . 105 C7
Denehurst Cl B45 . . . 122 A1
Denehurst Way CV10 . .72 F3
Denemoor Ct CV8 . . . 148 B5
Dene Rd
Lower Penn WV4 . . . . . 37 F4
Stourbridge DY8 . . . . . . 80 F3
Denewood Ave B20 . . . 55 B2
Denewood Way CV8 . 148 C6
Denford Gr B14 . . . . . 104 D5
Dengate Dr CV7 . . . . . 130 B7
Denham Ave CV5 . . . . 112 C4
Denham Ct B23 . . . . . . 56 C2
Denham Gdns WV3 . . . 38 B8
Denham Rd B27 . . . . . . 88 C5
Denholme Gr B14 . . . 105 A3
Denholm Rd B73 . . . . . 45 D2
Denise Dr
Birmingham B17 . . . . . . 85 C4
Birmingham, Kingshurst B37. . . . . 69 F4
Dudley WV14 . . . . 51 B8
Denis Rd LE10 . . . . 75 D5
Denleigh Rd DY6 . . . . . .60 F4
Denmark Cl WV6 . . . . . 25 A4
Denmark Rise WS12 . . . 2 D7
Denmark Villas WS13 . . .8 C5
Denmead Dr WV11 . . . .26 F8
Denmore Gdns WV1 . . 26 C2
Dennett Cl CV34 . . . . 155 F2
Dennfield Dr WS6 . . . . . .4 C2
Dennis B77 . . . . 21 E2
Dennis Hall 9 DY8 . . . .80 F8
Dennis Hall Rd DY8 . . 81 A8
Dennis Rd
Birmingham B12 . . . . . . 87 B4
Coventry CV2 . . . . 114 B6
Dennis St DY8 . . . . .80 F8
Denshaw Croft CV2 . 115 A8
Denshaw Rd B14 . . . . 104 D6
Denston Ct 6 B74 . . . .31 F2
Denstone Gdns WV10 . .11 F3
Denton Cl CV8 . . . . . . 147 D6
Denton Croft B93 . . . 127 D3
Denton Gr
Birmingham, Great Barr B43. . . . . 54 D7
Birmingham, Stechford B33. . . . . 68 D2
Denton Rd DY9 . . . . 82 A4
Dent St B79 . . . . 21 C5
Denver Rd B14 . . . . . . 105 A2
Denville Cl WV14 . . . . . 40 E7
Denville Cres B9 . . . . . . 68 B3
Denville Rd CV32 . . . . 157 A3
Derby Ave WV6 . . . . . . .24 F7
Derby Dr B37 . . . . 70 B2
Derby Rd LE10 . . . . 71 D1
Derby St
Birmingham B9 . . . . 67 A2
Walsall WS2 . . . . 28 E4
Dereham Cl B8 . . . . . . 67 C4
Dereham Ct CV32 . . . 157 A2
Dereham Wlk WV14 . . . 40 E2
Dereton Cl DY1 . . . . . . 61 E8
Derick Burcher's Mall 5
DY10 . . . . 116 E6
Dering Cl CV2 . . . . 114 D8
Deronda Cl CV12 . . . . . 78 A3
Derron Ave B26 . . . . . . 88 E5
Derry Cl B17 . . . . 85 A3
Derrydown Cl B23 . . . . 56 E3
Derrydown Rd B42 . . . 55 B5
Derry St
Brierley Hill DY5 . . . . . . 61 D2
Wolverhampton WV2 . 163 C1
Dersingham Dr CV6 . . 96 B2
Derwent B77 . . . . 21 D1
Derwent Cl
Brierley Hill DY5 . . . . . . 61 B6
Coventry CV5 . . . . 111 E4
Royal Leamington Spa CV32. . . . . 156 D1
Sutton Coldfield WS9 . . 30 F3
Willenhall WV13 . . . . . . 27 C2
Derwent Ct B73 . . . . . . 46 B5
Derwent Gr
Birmingham B13 . . . . . . 86 C1
Burntwood WS7 . . . . 7 D6
Cannock WS11 . . . . 4 D8
Derwent Ho
8 Birmingham B17 . . . 85 D5
Kidderminster DY10 . . 116 F7
5 Oldbury B69 . . . . . . 63 D5
Derwent Rd
Bedworth CV12 . . . . 78 A2
Birmingham B30 . . . . . 104 C8
Coventry CV6 . . . . 95 A2
Wolverhampton WV6 . . 24 E8
Derwent Way
Bromsgrove B60 . . . . . 137 B1
Nuneaton CV11 . . . . 73 F6
Desdemona Ave
CV34 . . . . 161 E4
Desford Ave B42 . . . . . 55 C7
De Somerley Ho 1
B69 . . . . 64 A7
Despard Rd CV5 . . . . . 111 D4
Dettonford Rd B32 . . 102 B8
Devereux Cl
Birmingham B36 . . . . . . 69 C8
Coventry CV4 . . . . 111 C1
Devereux Ho B79 . . . . 21 A4
Devereux Rd
Sutton Coldfield B75 . . . 32 C1
West Bromwich B70 . . . 53 E1
Deveron Ct LE10 . . . . . 71 B1
Deveron Way LE10 . . . 71 B1
Devey Dr DY4 . . . . 52 D6
Devine Croft DY4 . . . . . 52 A5
Devitts Cl B90 . . . . 126 F7
Devon Cl
Birmingham B20 . . . . . . 54 F2
Nuneaton CV10 . . . . 72 F3
Devon Cres
Aldridge WS9 . . . . 16 A1
Dudley DY2 . . . . 61 F7
West Bromwich B71 . . . 53 C6
Devon Ct
3 Birmingham B29 . . 103 B7
Cannock WS11 . . . . .4 C8
Devon Gn WS11 . . . . .4 F8
Devon Gr CV2 . . . . 114 B6
Devon Ho 4 DY8 . . . . . .80 F8
Devonport Cl 3 B97 153 B5
Devon Rd
Birmingham B45 . . . . . 101 F1
Cannock WS11 . . . . .4 F8
Smethwick B67 . . . . 84 E7
Stourbridge DY8 . . . . . . 80 E7
Wednesbury WS10 . . . . 42 C4
Willenhall WV13 . . . . . . 27 D1
Wolverhampton WV1 . 163 A4
Devonshire Ave B18 . . .65 F6
Devonshire Ct B74 . . . 32 A2
Devonshire Dr
Tamworth B78 . . . . 21 A1
West Bromwich B71 . . . 53 E3
Devonshire Inf Sch
B67. . . . . .64 E5
Devonshire Jun Sch
B67. . . . . .64 E5
Devonshire Rd
Birmingham B20 . . . . . . 54 F2
Smethwick B67 . . . . 64 E6
Devonshire St B18 . . . 66 A6
Devonshire Villas
B10 . . . . 87 D8
Devon St B7 . . . . 67 C5
Devoran Cl
Bedworth CV7 . . . . 96 B8
Wolverhampton WV6 . . 25 B4
Dewberry Dr WS5 . . . . 43 A3
Dewberry Rd 3 DY8 . .60 F1
Dewhurst Croft B33 . . 69 B3
Dewis Ho 4 CV2 . . . . . 96 B1
Dewsbury Ave CV3 . . 133 B5
Dewsbury Cl
Astwood Bank B96 . . . 158 E1
Stourbridge DY8 . . . . . . 60 E3
Dewsbury Dr
Burntwood WS7 . . . . .7 C6
Wolverhampton WV4 . . 39 A4
Dewsbury Gr B42 . . . . 55 C5
Dexter Ho B67 . . . . .64 F6
Dexter Way B78 . . . . . . .36 F8
Dey Croft CV34 . . . . . . 160 B4
Deykin Ave B6 . . . . 56 B2
Deykin Avenue Jun & Inf Sch B6 . . . . .56 B2
Deykin Rd WS13. . . . . . . .9 A6
D'Eyncourt Prim Sch
WV11 . . . . .26 B7
D'Eyncourt Rd WV10 . . 26 A7
Dial Cl B14 . . . . 104 E2
Dial House La CV5 . . . 111 F4
Dial La Stourbridge DY8 80 E8
West Bromwich B70 . . . 52 F6
Diamond Ct 3 B64 . . . 62 D1
Diamond Gr WS11 . . . . . .2 C3
Diamond Park Dr 3
DY8 . . . . 60 E1
Diana Cl WS9 . . . . 16 B3
Diana Dr CV2 . . . . 96 E1
Diane Cl DY4 . . . . 41 B2
Dibble Cl WV12 . . . . . . 27 D5
Dibble Rd B67 . . . . .64 F6
Dibdale Ct DY3 . . . . 50 D3
Dibdale Rd DY1 . . . . . . .50 F3
Dibdale Rd W DY1 . . . . 50 E3
Dibdale St DY1 . . . . 51 A2
Dice Pleck B31 . . . . . 103 C2
Dickens Cl Dudley DY3 50 B5
Nuneaton CV10 . . . . 72 A4
Dickens Heath Prim Com Sch B90 . . . . 126 A6
Dickens Heath Rd
Solihull B90 . . . . 126 A5
Solihull B90 . . . . 126 A6
Solihull B90 . . . . 126 B6
Dickens Rd
Coventry CV6 . . . . 113 A8
Dudley WV14 . . . . 40 D2
Wolverhampton WV10 . 12 A1
Dickinson Ave WV10 . . .25 F8
Dickinson Dr
Sutton Coldfield B76 . . . 46 E4
Walsall WS2 . . . . 42 C6
Dickinson Rd WV5 . . . . 49 A4
Dickins Rd CV34 . . . . 156 B1
Dick Sheppard Ave
DY4 . . . . 52 B8
Didcot Cl B97 . . . . 158 C5
Diddington Ave B28 . 106 A5
Diddington La B92,
CV7 . . . . 91 C1
Didgley Gr B37 . . . . 70 A5
Didsbury Rd CV7 . . . . . 78 A1
Digbeth
Birmingham B5 . . . . . . 164 D1
Walsall WS1 . . . . 28 E1
Digbey Cl CV5 . . . . 112 B6
Digby Cres B46 . . . . . . 59 B3
Digby Ct 3 B27 . . . . . . 88 C3
Digby Dr B37 . . . . 90 B6
Digby Ho B37 . . . . .69 F4
Digby Pl CV7 . . . . 92 C1
Digby Rd Coleshill B46 . .70 F6
Kingswinford DY6 . . . . . . 60 D8
Sutton Coldfield B73 . . . 46 B4
Dilcock Way CV4 . . . . 131 F7

Dilke Rd WS9 ....29 F5
Dillam Cl CV6 .... 96 A4
Dilliars Wlk B70.... 53 A5
Dillington Ho 8 B37 . 70 B2
Dillon Ct CV11 .... 73 B5
Dillotford Ave CV3 .. 133 D6
Dilloways La WV13 ....40 F8
Dilwyn Cl B98.... 154 F1
Dimbles Hill WS13 ....3 B1
Dimbles La WS13....3 A2
Dimmingsdale Bank
B32 .... 84 C4
Dimmingsdale Rd
WV4 .... 37 E5
Dimminsdale WV13... 27 A1
Dimmocks Ave WV14 . 51 D8
Dimmock St WV4 .... 39 E5
Dimsdale Gr B31.... 102 E3
Dimsdale Rd B31.... 102 D3
Dinedor Cl B98 .... 154 D3
Dingle Ave B64 .... 82 E8
Dingle Cl
Birmingham B30.... 103 D7
Coventry CV6 .... 113 A6
Dudley DY2 .... 62 E7
Dingle Com Prim Sch
DY6.... 61 A4
Dingle Ct B91.... 106 F1
Dingle Hollow B69 ... 63 D8
Dingle La Solihull B91 106 F2
Willenhall WV13 .... 27 A4
Dingle Mead B14.... 104 C4
Dingle Rd
Brownhills WS8 .... 15 E6
Dudley DY2 .... 62 E7
Kingswinford DY6.... 61 A4
Stourbridge DY9.... 81 C2
Dingleside B98.... 153 E2
Dingleside Mid Sch
B98.... 159 B8
Dingle St B69.... 63 E8
Dingle The
Birmingham B29.... 85 E2
Cheswick Green B90 . 126 D5
Nuneaton CV10.... 72 E6
Oldbury B69 .... 63 D8
Wolverhampton WV3 .. 24 D1
Dingle View DY3 .... 50 C7
Dingley Rd
Bulkington CV12.... 79 B2
Wednesbury WS10.... 42 A5
Dinham Gdns DY1.... 50 E3
Dinmore Ave B31 ... 103 B4
Dinmore Cl B98.... 154 D3
Dinsdale Wlk WV6 ... 25 A5
Dippons Dr WV6 .... 24 A3
Dippons Ho WV6.... 24 A3
Dippons Mill Cl WV6 . 24 A3
Dirtyfoot La WV4.... 38 A5
Discovery Cl DY4.... 52 C5
Discovery Way CV3.. 135 B7
District Ctr WS12....2 C2
Ditchford Cl B97 .... 158 D4
Ditch The WS1 ....28 F1
Ditton Gr B31.... 122 F6
Dixon Cl
Birmingham B35.... 58 A2
Tipton DY4 .... 52 C6
Dixon Ct DY10.... 117 C8
Dixon Ho B16 .... 66 A1
Dixon Rd B10 .... 87 B8
Dixons Green Ct 7
DY2 .... 62 E8
Dixon's Green Rd DY2 62 E8
Dixon St
Kidderminster DY10 .. 116 E5
Wolverhampton WV2 .. 39 E7
Doal Trad Est B66....65 B6
Dobbins Oak Rd DY9 . 81 E1
Dobbs Mill Cl B29.... 86 B2
Dobbs St WV2.... 163 B1
Dobson La CV31.... 162 A4
Dockar Rd B31.... 102 E2
Dockers Cl CV7 .... 130 C7
Dock La 10 DY1 .... 51 B1
Dock Lane Ind Est 13
DY1....51 B1
Dock Mdw Dr Ind Est
WV4....40 B4
Dock Meadow Dr
WV4 .... 40 A4
Dock Rd DY8....60 F2
Dock The
Catshill B61.... 137 A8
Stourbridge DY9.... 81 F5
Doctors Cl B94.... 142 A2
Doctors Hill
Bournheath B61 .... 136 D8
Doctors Hill *continued*
Stourbridge DY9.... 81 C3
Tanworth-In-A B94... 142 A2
Doctors La
Kingswinford DY6.... 60 A4
Shenstone WS14.... 18 A6
Doctor's Piece WV13 . 27 B2
Dodd Ave CV34.... 161 C7
Doddington Gr B32 . 102 B8
Dodford Cl B45 .... 121 F7
Dodford Ct B61 .... 136 C6
Dodford Fst Sch
B61.... 136 A5
Dodford Ho B60.... 137 B3
Dodford Rd B61.... 120 D1
Dodgson Cl CV6.... 96 A4
Dodwells Bridge Ind Est
LE10....74 E8
Dodwells Rd LE10.... 74 E8
Doe Bank Ct B74.... 46 B8
Doe Bank La
Birmingham B43,
WS9.... 44 D5
Coventry CV1 .... 113 A3
Doe Bank Rd DY4.... 41 C1
Dogberry Cl CV3 .... 134 C6
Dogberry Way CV34 . 161 F2
Dogge Lane Croft
B27 .... 88 B2
Dogkennel La
Halesowen B63.... 83 B3
Oldbury B68 .... 64 C5
Dog Kennel La
Solihull B90.... 126 D7
3 Walsall WS1 .... 28 F2
Dog La Tamworth B77 . 22 B6
Weeford WS14 .... 19 A4
Doglands The CV31.. 162 B4
Dogpool La B30.... 86 B1
Doidge Rd B23.... 56 D3
Dolben La B98 .... 154 D3
Dollery Dr B5.... 86 C5
Dollis Gr B44 ....44 F3
Dollman St B7 .... 67 B4
Dolman Rd B6 .... 66 E8
Dolobran Rd B11.... 87 B7
Dolomite Ave CV4... 112 D1
Dolphin Cl WS3 ....14 F1
Dolphin Ct WV12.... 27 D8
Dolphin La B27 .... 88 C1
Dolphin Rd
Birmingham B11 .... 87 D5
Redditch B98 .... 154 A5
Dolton Way DY4.... 51 E6
Domar Rd DY11 .... 116 B7
Dominic Dr B30.... 103 D4
Donalbain Cl CV34 .. 161 F3
Doncaster Cl CV2 ... 114 D7
Doncaster Way B36 . 68 C8
Don Cl B15 .... 85 D8
Donegal Cl CV4 .... 132 A7
Donegal Rd B74....44 F5
Dongan Rd CV34 .... 160 E7
Don Gr WS11.... 4 D7
Donibristle Croft B35. 58 A4
Donnington Ave CV6 112 E5
Donnington Cl B98.. 154 C5
Donnington Ho B33 .. 69 B2
Donnithorne Ave CV10,
CV11 .... 73 D1
Donovan Dr B73 .... 46 A6
Dooley Cl WV13 .... 26 E2
Doone Cl CV2.... 114 E6
Dorado B77.... 35 D7
Dora Herbert Ct B12 . 86 E5
Doran Cl B63 .... 82 D1
Doranda Way B71....53 F1
Dora Rd
Birmingham B10.... 87 E8
Birmingham, Handsworth
B21.... 65 E7
West Bromwich B70... 53 C1
Dora St WS2 .... 42 B7
Dorcas Cl CV11 .... 79 C8
Dorchester Cl WV12.. 27 C8
Dorchester Ct B91 .. 107 A4
Dorchester Dr B17 ... 85 B4
Dorchester Rd
Cannock WS11 ....1 B1
Hinckley LE10 .... 76 B7
Solihull B91.... 107 A4
Stourbridge DY9.... 81 D2
Willenhall WV12 .... 13 C1
Dorchester Way
Coventry CV2 .... 115 A4
Nuneaton CV11.... 74 A7
Dordale Cl B31.... 102 C1
Dordale Rd DY9.... 119 E2
Dordon Cl B90 .... 105 E1
Dordon Rd B78 ....36 F8
Doreen Gr B24.... 57 B2
Doris Rd
Birmingham B11 .... 87 B4
Birmingham, Bordesley
Green B9 .... 67 D2
Coleshill B46.... 70 F8
Dorlcote Rd B8 .... 68 A4
Dorlecote Ct CV10 ... 73 C1
Dorlecote Pl CV10.... 78 C8
Dorlecote Rd CV10 ... 78 C8
Dormer Ave B77 .... 21 D5
Dormer Harris Ave
CV4 .... 111 F1
Dormer Ho 15 CV32 . 156 F2
Dormer Pl CV32.... 161 F8
Dormie Cl B38 .... 103 D1
Dormington Rd B44...44 F3
Dormston Cl
Redditch B98 .... 153 F1
Solihull B91.... 127 C8
Dormston Dr
Birmingham B29.... 84 F2
Sedgley DY3 .... 50 E8
Dormston Sch The
DY3....50 E8
Dormston Trad Est
DY1....50 F4
Dormy Dr B31 .... 123 A7
Dorncliffe Ave B33... 89 D7
Dorney Cl CV5 .... 132 E8
Dornie Dr B38 .... 103 F1
Dornton Rd B30.... 104 C8
Dorothy Adams Cl 3
B64 .... 82 E8
Dorothy Gdns B20.... 55 A2
Dorothy Goodman Specl
Sch LE10.... 71 D2
Dorothy Pattison Hospl
WS2....28 B1
Dorothy Powell Way
CV2 ....96 F1
Dorothy Rd
Birmingham B11.... 88 B5
Smethwick B67.... 65 A4
Dorothy St WS1 .... 42 D7
Dorridge Cl B97.... 153 B1
Dorridge Croft B93.. 127 F2
Dorridge Jun & Inf Schs
B93.... 128 A4
Dorridge Rd B93.... 128 A2
Dorridge Sta B93... 127 F2
Dorrington Gn B42... 55 A5
Dorrington Prim Sch
B42.... 55 A5
Dorrington Rd B42... 55 A5
Dorset Cl
Birmingham B45.... 101 F2
Nuneaton CV10.... 72 F3
Tamworth B78.... 21 A1
Dorset Cotts B30.... 104 A6
Dorset Ct 2 B29.... 103 B7
Dorset Dr WS9.... 16 B1
Dorset Pl WS3 .... 28 C7
Dorset Rd
Birmingham B8.... 67 C6
Cannock WS12 ....2 E1
Coventry CV1 .... 113 C5
Smethwick B17.... 65 B3
Stourbridge DY8.... 80 D8
Dorsett Rd
Darlaston WS10 .... 41 C6
Wednesbury WS10.... 42 D2
Dorsett Road Terr
WS10 .... 41 C6
Dorset Twr B18.... 66 B4
Dorsheath Gdns B23 ..56 F4
Dorsington Rd B27... 88 D1
Dorstone Covert
B14 .... 104 C2
Dorville Cl B38.... 123 D8
Dosthill Prim Sch
B77.... 35 D5
Dosthill Rd (Two Gates)
B77 .... 35 D7
Dotterel Pl DY10 ... 117 A1
Douay Rd B24.... 57 B6
Double Row DY2.... 62 E4
Doughty St DY4.... 52 C5
Douglas Ave
Birmingham B36.... 68 D6
Oldbury B68 .... 64 D5
Douglas Davies Cl
WV12 .... 27 C4
Douglas Ho CV1.... 165 D4
Douglas Pl WV10.... 25 C6
Douglas Rd
Birmingham B27.... 88 C4
Birmingham, Handsworth
B21.... 65 F8
Dudley WV14 .... 51 D8
Douglas Rd *continued*
Halesowen B62.... 63 E1
Hollywood B47 .... 125 A7
Oldbury B68 .... 64 D4
Sutton Coldfield B72... 46 C3
Douglass Rd DY2.... 62 D8
Doulton Cl
Birmingham B32.... 84 F3
Coventry CV2 .... 96 E1
Doulton Dr B66 .... 65 A6
Doulton Rd B64, B65...62 F4
Doulton Trad Est B65 .62 F4
Douper Hall B29 ....85 F3
Dovebridge Cl B76 ....46 F4
Dove Cl Bedworth CV12 77 E3
Birmingham B25.... 88 E8
Burntwood WS7 .... 7 D6
Hinckley LE10 .... 75 A8
Kidderminster DY10 .. 117 B2
Walsall WS1 .... 29 A1
Wednesbury WS10.... 42 B4
Dovecote Cl
Coventry CV6 .... 112 D5
Solihull B91.... 107 B8
Tipton DY4 .... 52 C5
Wolverhampton WV6 .. 24 C4
Dovecote Rd B61.... 136 E1
Dovecotes Prim Sch
WV8....10 F1
Dovecotes The
Coventry CV5 .... 112 B5
Sutton Coldfield B75... 32 B3
Dovedale WS11 ....2 A5
Dovedale Ave
Coventry CV6 .... 95 F2
Solihull B90.... 106 B1
Walsall WS3 .... 15 B5
Willenhall WV12 .... 27 B4
Dovedale Ct
19 Birmingham B29 .. 103 C7
Wolverhampton WV4 .. 39 F2
Dovedale Dr B28.... 105 F5
Dovedale Rd
Birmingham B23.... 56 C7
Kingswinford DY6.... 60 E8
Wolverhampton WV4 .. 39 E3
Dove Dr DY8 .... 81 A8
Dove Gdns B38 .... 104 B2
Dove Hollow
Cannock WS12 ....2 E4
Great Wyrley WS6....4 F1
Dove House Ct B91.. 106 F7
Dovehouse Fields
WS14 ....9 B6
Dovehouse La B91 .. 106 F7
Dove House La B91 . 107 A8
Dovehouse Pool Rd 1
B6 .... 66 E8
Dover Cl B32.... 102 A7
Dovercourt Rd B26... 89 C5
Doverdale Ave DY10 . 117 B5
Doverdale Cl
Halesowen B63.... 82 E5
Redditch B98 .... 159 B7
Dover Farm Cl B77... 36 B8
Dover Ho WS3 .... 28 C7
Dove Ridge DY8.... 81 A7
Doveridge Cl B91 ... 106 E6
Doveridge Pl WS1....42 F8
Doveridge Rd B28... 105 E5
Doversley Rd B14 .. 104 C5
Dover St Bilston WV14 . 40 D6
Birmingham B18.... 66 A6
Coventry CV1 .... 165 A3
Dovestone B77.... 22 D1
Doveton Ho DY8 .... 81 A3
Dove Way B36 ....69 F8
Dovey Dr B76 .... 58 A7
Dovey Rd
Birmingham B13.... 87 D2
Oldbury B69 .... 63 D8
Dowar Rd B45 .... 122 C7
Dowells Cl B13....86 F2
Dowells Gdns DY8.... 60 D3
Doweries The B45... 121 F8
Dower Rd B75 .... 32 B1
Dowler's Hill Cres
B98 .... 159 A8
Dowles Cl B29 .... 103 B6
Dowles Rd DY11.... 116 B2
Dowley Croft CV3 ... 115 B1
Downcroft Ave B38.. 103 E2
Downderry Way CV6 114 A6
Downend Cl WV10....11 F4
Downes Ct 7 DY4.... 51 E5
Downesway WS11 ....1 C2
Downey Cl B11.... 87 B7
Downfield Cl WS3.... 14 A4
Downfield Dr DY3.... 50 E6
Downham Cl WS5 .... 29 E1
Downham Pl WV3 ....38 F8
Downham Wood WS5 43 E8
Downie Rd WV8.... 10 C3
Downing Cl
Dorridge B93 .... 128 A4
6 Rowley Regis B65... 63 C1
Wednesfield WV11.... 27 A7
Downing Cres CV12 .. 78 C4
Downing Ct 2 B68... 84 B7
Downing Dr B79 .... 20 E5
Downing Ho B37.... 70 B1
Downing St
Halesowen B63.... 83 A5
Smethwick B66.... 65 C7
Downland Cl B38.... 103 F1
Downsell Ho B97.... 153 A2
Downsell Rd B97.... 153 A2
Downsfield Rd B26... 89 B7
Downside Rd B24.... 56 E1
Downs Rd WV13.... 41 C8
Downs The
Sutton Coldfield WS9 .. 30 E2
Wolverhampton WV10 . 25 C6
Downton Cl CV2 .... 115 A8
Downton Cres B33 ... 69 E3
Dowty Ave CV12.... 77 D1
Dowty Way WV9.... 11 A3
Doyle Dr CV6 ....95 F3
Dragoon Fields B60 . 151 B8
Drake Cl WS3 .... 14 B1
Drake Cres DY11 ... 116 A7
Drake Croft 4 WS13 ...9 C8
Drake Ct WS3.... 14 B1
Drake Rd
Birmingham B23.... 56 C3
Smethwick B66.... 64 E7
Walsall WS3 .... 14 C1
Drakes Cl
Redditch B97 .... 158 C6
Wythall B47.... 124 F4
Drakes Cross Par
B47 .... 125 A5
Drake's Gn WV14....40 F3
Drakes Hill Cl DY8.... 80 C4
Drake St
Coventry CV6 .... 113 D7
West Bromwich B71... 53 C5
Drake Way LE10.... 71 D4
Drancy Ave WV12 .... 27 D6
Draper Cl CV8 .... 148 C4
Drapers Ct CV1 .... 165 B4
Draper's Fields CV1 . 165 B4
Drawbridge Rd B90 . 125 E8
Draycote Cl B92.... 107 D6
Draycott Ave B23 .... 56 D4
Draycott Cl
9 Redditch B97.... 153 B5
Wolverhampton WV4 .. 38 C5
Draycott Cres B77.... 21 D1
Draycott Dr B31.... 102 E7
Draycott Rd
Coventry CV2 .... 114 C7
Smethwick B66.... 64 E7
Drayman Cl WS1 ....42 F8
Drayton Cl
Hartshill CV10.... 72 A8
Redditch B98 .... 159 D8
Sutton Coldfield B75... 32 B3
Drayton Cres CV5 ... 111 D5
Drayton Ct
Bromsgrove B60.... 151 B8
Warwick CV34 .... 155 E2
Drayton La B78 .... 34 C5
Drayton Manor Dr
Drayton Bassett B78 .. 34 F7
Fazeley B78.... 34 F8
Drayton Manor Pk*
B78 .... 34 E7
Drayton Rd
Bedworth CV12.... 78 D2
Belbroughton DY9.... 119 B5
Birmingham B14.... 104 F8
Smethwick B66.... 65 A1
Solihull B90.... 126 E8
Drayton St
Walsall WS2 .... 28 C2
Wolverhampton WV2 . 163 B1
Drayton Way CV10 ... 72 C7
Dreadnought Rd DY5 . 61 B8
Dreamwell Ind Est
B11.... 88 A6
Dreel The B15.... 85 E7
Dreghorn Rd B36 ....68 F8
Drem Croft B35.... 58 A2
Dresden Cl WV4.... 40 A4
Drew Cres
Kenilworth CV8.... 148 A4
Stourbridge DY9.... 81 D2
Drew Rd DY9.... 81 D3
Drews Ho B14 .... 104 D1
Drews Holloway B63 . 82 D5
Drews Holloway S
B63 .... 82 D5
Drews La B8 .... 68 A7
Drews Meadow Cl 1
B14 .... 104 C2
Driffield Cl B98 .... 154 D2
Driffold B73 .... 46 B3
Driftwood Cl B38.... 123 D7
Drinkwater Ho 7
CV1 .... 113 B2
Drive Fields WV4.... 38 B6
Drive Sch (Tettenhall
Coll) The WV6.... 24 D4
Drive The
Birmingham, Gravelly Hill
B23.... 56 E2
Birmingham, Handsworth
B20.... 55 B2
Brierley Hill DY5 .... 61 C5
Coventry CV2 .... 114 E3
Halesowen, Cradley
B63.... 82 D5
Halesowen, Hasbury
B63.... 83 A3
Hopwood B48.... 123 B3
Redditch B97 .... 152 C7
Shenstone WS14.... 18 E8
Walsall, Pelsall WS3... 14 E2
Walsall WS4 .... 15 C1
Wolverhampton WV6 .. 24 C5
Droicon Trad Est B65 63 C5
Dronfield Rd CV2 ... 114 B3
Drovers Way B60.... 150 E6
Drovers Wlk DY10... 116 F5
Droveway The WV9....10 F2
Droxford Wlk WV8 ... 10 E1
Droylsdon Park Rd
CV3 .... 133 B3
Dr Phillips Sh Ctr The
CV2.... 96 D1
Druid Park Rd WV12.. 13 C1
Druid Rd CV2 .... 114 B3
Druids Ave
Aldridge WS9 .... 30 C8
Rowley Regis B65.... 63 D4
Druids La B14.... 104 D1
Druid St LE10 .... 71 D1
Druids Wlk WS9.... 16 A3
Drummond Cl
Coventry CV6 .... 112 F7
Wolverhampton WV11 . 13 A2
Drummond Gr B43 ... 44 C3
Drummond Rd
Birmingham B9.... 68 A2
Bromsgrove B60.... 151 B8
Stourbridge DY9.... 81 F4
Drummond St WV1.. 163 B4
Drummond Way B37 . 70 C2
Drury La Solihull B91 . 107 C3
Stourbridge DY8 .... 81 A5
Drybrook Cl B38 .... 123 E8
Drybrooks Cl CV7 ... 130 B6
Dryden Cl
Kenilworth CV8.... 147 F3
Tipton DY4 .... 52 A7
Willenhall WV12 .... 27 E8
Dryden Gr B27 .... 88 B2
Dryden Pl WS3.... 28 E7
Dryden Rd
Tamworth B79.... 21 A6
Walsall WS3 .... 28 E7
Wolverhampton WV10 . 11 F1
Drylea Gr B36....68 F8
Dual Way WS12 .... 1 D8
Dubarry Ave DY6.... 60 C7
Duchess Pl B16 .... 66 A1
Duchess Rd
Birmingham B16.... 66 A1
Walsall WS1 .... 42 D5
Duckhouse Rd WV11 . 26 D7
Duck La WV8 .... 10 B3
Duddeston Dr B8 .... 67 D4
Duddeston Manor Rd
B7 .... 67 A4
Duddeston Mill Rd B7,
B8.... 67 C4
Duddeston Mill Trad Est
B8.... 67 C4
Duddeston Sta B7 ....67 B4
Dudding Rd WV4.... 39 D5
Dudhill Rd B65.... 63 A3
Dudhill Wlk B65 .... 63 A3
Dudley Castle* DY1.. 51 D2
Dudley Central Trad Est
DY2.... 62 C8
Dudley Cl B65.... 63 A5
Dudley Coll (Castle View
Campus) DY1 ....51 B2

Dudley Coll
(International Glass Ctr)
DY5............ **61** D3
Dudley Coll of Tech
(Broadway Campus)
DY1........... **51** C2
Dudley Coll of Tech
(Mons Hill Campus)
DY1...........**51** B5
Dudley Coll of Tech
(Wolverhampton St
Campus) DY1......**51** B1
Dudley Cres WV11... **26** E6
Dudley Gn CV32.... **157** B2
Dudley Gr 6 B18 .... **65** E4
Dudley Innovation Ctr
DY6..............**60** F7
Dudley L Ctr DY1 ...**51** B1
Dudley Museum & Art
Gall* DY1.......... **51** C1
Dudley Park Rd B27... **88** C3
Dudley Port DY4...... **52** A3
Dudley Port Sta DY4..**52** B4
Dudley Rd
Birmingham B18...... **65** E4
Brierley Hill DY5, DY6... **61** D4
Dudley DY3 .... **50** E6
Halesowen B63...... **83** B5
Himley DY3........ **49** D3
Kenilworth CV8..... **147** F2
Kingswinford DY6...... **60** F7
Kingswinford, Wall Heath
DY6........ **60** C8
Oldbury B69 .... **63** F8
Rowley Regis B65.... **63** A5
Stourbridge DY9...... **81** E6
Tipton DY4 .... **51** E5
Wolverhampton WV2 .. **39** B7
Dudley Rise LE10..... **75** D6
Dudley Road E B69... **52** D1
Dudley Road W B69... **52** B2
Dudley Row DY2 .... **51** D1
Dudley Southern Bypass
DY2.............. **62** C7
Dudley St
Bilston WV14 .... **40** D4
Birmingham B5...... **164** C2
Coventry CV6 .... **96** A1
Kidderminster DY10 .. **116** E7
Sedgley DY3 .... **50** D8
Walsall WS1 .... **28** E1
Wednesbury WS10 ... **41** E2
West Bromwich B70... **53** A5
Wolverhampton WV1 . **163** B3
Dudley Street, Guns
Village Sta B70....**53** B4
Dudley Terr CV8..... **149** B6
Dudley Wlk WV4 .... **39** C5
Dudley Wood Ave
DY2............... **62** C2
Dudley Wood Prim Sch
DY2................ **62** C2
Dudley Wood Rd DY2. **62** C2
Dudley Zoo* DY1... **51** D2
Dudmaston Way DY1. **50** E3
Dudnill Gr B32...... **102** A8
Duffield Cl WV8......**10** F1
Dufton Rd B32 ...... **84** E4
Dugdale Cl WS12......**2** F3
Dugdale Cres B75.... **32** C3
Dugdale 5 CV31 .. **162** A6
Dugdale Ho CV11 ... **73** C3
Dugdale Rd CV6.... **113** B6
Dugdale St
Nuneaton CV11...... **73** C4
Smethwick B66...... **65** D4
Duggins La CV4, CV7. **131** B8
Duke Barn Field
CV2............. **114** A5
Dukes Rd
Birmingham B30.... **104** A3
Dordon B78.......... **36** F6
Duke St Coventry CV5 **112** F2
Dudley DY3 .... **50** D5
Nuneaton CV11...... **73** B4
Rowley Regis B65.... **63** B2
Royal Leamington Spa
CV32...........**157** A1
Stourbridge DY8...... **81** A6
Sutton Coldfield B72... **46** B4
Wednesfield WV11 ... **26** D5
West Bromwich B70... **53** B4
Wolverhampton, Springfield
WV1...........**163** D2
Wolverhampton WV3 .. **39** A7
Dulais Cl B98 ...... **153** E1
Dulvern Gr B14 .... **104** D5
Dulverton Ave CV5 .. **112** C4
Dulverton Ct CV5.... **112** C4
Dulverton Rd B6 ..... **56** B1

Dulwich Gr B44...... **56** B8
Dulwich Rd B44...... **56** A8
Dumbleberry Ave
DY3 .... **50** C7
Dumbleberry Ct WS9 ..**29** F5
Dumblederry La
Aldridge WS9 .... **29** F6
Walsall WS9 .... **29** E7
Dumble Pit La B47,
B48............... **140** F7
Dumolo's La B77....**21** F3
Dumphouse La B48 . **140** C3
Dunard Rd B90..... **105** F3
Dunbar Cl
Birmingham B32...... **84** D1
Kidderminster DY10 . **117** C6
Dunbar Gr B43...... **44** B4
Dunblane Dr CV32... **157** C5
Dunblane Way LE10 .. **71** A2
Duncalfe Dr B75..... **32** B3
Duncan Edwards Cl
DY1 .... **62** A8
Duncan Ho B73 ..... **46** B1
Duncan St WV2 ..... **39** C7
Dunchurch Cl
Balsall Common CV7.. **130** B7
Redditch B98 ...... **154** F1
Dunchurch Cres B73 . **45** C3
Dunchurch Dr B31... **102** E7
Dunchurch Highway
CV5.............. **112** A4
Dunchurch Ho 4 B5 . **86** E8
Dunclent Cres DY10 . **117** B5
Dunclent La DY10 ... **117** B5
Duncombe Gn 12 B46 .**70** F7
Duncombe Gr B17 ... **85** A7
Duncombe St DY8.... **80** D5
Duncroft Ave CV6 ... **112** F7
Duncroft Rd B26..... **89** A8
Duncroft Wlk DY1... **51** B6
Duncumb Rd B75.... **47** A5
Dundalk La WS6 ..... **4** D2
Dundas Ave DY2 ....**62** F8
Dunedin B77........ **22** A1
Dunedin Dr B45..... **122** B1
Dunedin Ho B32 ....**84** F4
Dunedin Rd B44.....**44** F3
Dunham Croft B93 . **127** D3
Dunhill Ave CV4..... **111** E3
Dunkirk Ave B70 .... **52** E3
Dunkirk Pl CV3...... **134** F7
Dunkley St WV1..... **163** B4
Dunley Croft B90.... **126** F6
Dunley Ct B23 ...... **56** C2
Dunlin Cl
Birmingham B23..... **56** C2
Kingswinford DY6.... **61** A6
Dunlin Dr
Featherstone WV10 .. **12** B7
Kidderminster DY10 . **116** F2
Dunlop Rd B97..... **158** D5
Dunlop Way B35....**57** F2
Dunnerdale Rd WS8.. **15** D6
Dunnigan Rd B32 ....**84** F3
Dunnose Cl CV2 .... **114** E2
Dunns Bank DY5....**81** F7
Dunnose Cl CV6..... **113** E8
Dunrose Cl CV2 .... **114** E2
Dunsfold Cl WV14... **40** A3
Dunsfold Croft 3 B6..**66** F6
Dunsford Cl DY5.... **81** B7
Dunsford Rd B66.... **65** A2
Dunsink Rd B6...... **55** F1
Dunslade Cres DY5...**81** F8
Dunslade Rd B23.... **56** E7
Dunsley Dr DY8 .... **60** E3
Dunsley Gr WV4..... **39** A4
Dunsley Rd DY8..... **80** C4
Dunsmore Ave CV3.. **134** D2
Dunsmore Dr DY5...**81** F8
Dunsmore Gr B91... **106** F7
Dunsmore Rd B28... **87** E2
Dunstall Ave WV6 ... **25** C4
Dunstall Cl B97 .... **153** B2
Dunstall Gr B29.... **102** F8
Dunstall Hill WV6 ... **25** C5
Dunstall Hill Jun & Inf
Sch WV6........... **25** C4
Dunstall Hill Trad Est
WV6............. **25** C5
Dunstall La
Hopwas B78 .... **20** D4
Wolverhampton WV6 .. **25** B5
Dunstall Rd
Halesowen B63....... **82** D3
Wolverhampton WV6 .. **25** B4
Dunstan Croft B90.. **126** C8
Dunstan 3 B15.. **86** B7
Dunster B77 .... **35** C7
Dunster Cl B30..... **104** C4
Dunster Gr WV6....**23** C4

Dunster Pl CV6...... **95** D3
Dunster Rd B37..... **70** D2
Dunston Cl
Great Wyrley WS6.... **13** E8
Kingswinford DY6.... **60** D7
Dunston Dr WS7.....**7** A8
Dunsville Dr CV2.... **114** F8
Dunton Cl B75...... **32** A4
Dunton Hall Rd B90.. **106** A4
Dunton La B76...... **48** C1
Dunton Pk B76 ..... **59** C7
Dunton Rd B37......**69** F5
Dunton Trad Est B7... **67** D7
Dunvegan Cl
Coventry CV3 ..... **115** A2
Kenilworth CV8..... **148** C4
Dunvegan Rd B24... **57** A4
Duport Rd LE10.....**75** F7
Durant Cl B45...... **101** D1
Durban Rd B66..... **65** C4
Durbar Ave CV6.... **113** D8
D'Urberville Cl WV2..**39** F6
D'Urberville Rd WV2 ..**39** F6
D'Urberville Wlk 1
WS11.............**2** A2
Durham Ave WV13 ... **27** D3
Durham Cl
Bromsgrove B61..... **136** E4
Keresley CV7 .... **94** F4
Tamworth B78........ **21** A2
Durham Cres CV5... **112** B7
Durham Croft B37... **70** B2
Durham Dr B71..... **53** D7
Durham Ho 1 WV3 .. **25** C4
Durham Pl WS2..... **28** B1
Durham Rd
Birmingham B11...... **87** B4
Dudley DY2 .... **62** D2
Rowley Regis B65.... **63** E4
Walsall WS2 .... **42** B8
Wednesbury WS10 ... **42** D4
Durham Twr 3 B1 ... **66** B3
Durley Dean Rd B29.. **85** C2
Durley Dr B73...... **45** C3
Durley Rd B25...... **88** C6
Durlston Cl B77......**21** F1
Durlston Gr B28.... **106** A8
Durnford Croft B14.. **104** E1
Dursley Cl
Solihull B92........ **107** B8
Willenhall WV12 .... **27** D4
Dursley Dr WS11......**1** B2
Dursley Rd WS7......**7** A7
Dusthouse La B60... **151** D7
Dutton Rd CV2 ..... **96** D3
Dutton's La B75..... **32** E4
Duxford Cl B97..... **158** B8
Duxford Rd B42..... **55** B7
Dwarris Wlk CV34... **155** E2
Dwellings La B32.... **84** B5
Dyas Ave B42...... **55** A7
Dyas Rd
Birmingham B44...... **44** E1
Hollywood B47..... **125** A7
Dyce Cl B35........ **58** A4
Dyers La B94....... **142** D8
Dyers Rd CV11......**79** F6
Dymoke St B12......**86** F8
Dymond Rd CV6..... **95** D3
Dynes Wlk B67..... **65** A5
Dyott Rd B13....... **87** A1
Dysart Cl CV1 ..... **113** E4
Dyson Cl WS2.......**27** F3
Dysons Gdns B8 .... **67** E5
Dyson St CV4 ...... **111** E3

E

Eachelhurst Rd B24,
B76...............**57** F5
Eachus Rd WV14 ... **51** D8
Eachway B45 ...... **121** F6
Eachway Farm Cl
B45............. **122** A6
Eachway La B45.... **122** A6
Eacott Cl CV6 ..... **95** A3
Eadgar Ct B43...... **54** D7
Eadie Mews B97 ... **153** D1
Eadie St CV10...... **72** D4
Eagle Cl
Cheslyn Hay WS6.... **4** D2
Dudley DY1 .... **50** F1
Nuneaton CV11..... **79** B8
Rowley Regis B65.... **63** A4
Eagle Croft B14 .... **104** E2
Eagle Ct
Wolverhampton, Pendeford
WV10 .... **11** B3
Wolverhampton WV3 .. **39** A7

Eagle Dr B77........ **22** C4
Eagle Gdns B24.... **57** A2
Eagle Gr
Birmingham B36..... **70** A8
Cannock WS12 ....**2** C1
Eagle Ho CV1 ..... **113** D5
Eagle Ind Est DY4....**52** E7
Eagle La
Kenilworth CV8..... **147** F3
Tipton DY4 .... **52** D6
Eagle Rd B98 ...... **154** E5
Eagle St E CV1 ..... **113** D5
Eagle St
Coventry CV1 ..... **113** D5
Royal Leamington Spa
CV31........... **162** A6
Tipton DY4 .... **52** D6
Wolverhampton, Penn Fields
WV3 .... **39** A7
Wolverhampton WV2 .. **39** E8
Eagle Trad Est B63... **83** A4
Eales Yd 9 LE10 .... **71** D1
Ealing Gr B44...... **45** A1
Ealingham B77...... **22** B1
Eanwulf Ct B15.... **86** C8
Eardisley Cl B98 ... **154** F1
Earl Place Bsns Pk
CV4............. **112** B1
Earlsbury Gdns B20 . **55** D1
Earls Cl B97 ...... **152** F2
Earls Court Rd B17... **85** A6
Earl's Croft The CV3. **133** D7
Earlsdon Ave CV5... **133** A8
Earlsdon Ave N CV5. **112** F1
Earlsdon Ave S CV5.. **133** A8
Earlsdon Ho CV5... **133** A8
Earlsdon Prim Sch
CV5............. **113** A1
Earlsdon St CV5.... **132** F8
Earls Ferry Gdns
B32............. **102** B7
Earls High Sch The
B63............. **83** B4
Earlsmead Rd B21 .. **65** C7
Earlsmere B94..... **126** B1
Earls Rd
Nuneaton CV11..... **73** A5
Walsall WS4 .... **29** D7
Earls Rivers Ave
CV34............ **161** D3
Earl St Bedworth CV12 . **78** C2
Bilston WV14 .... **40** D5
Coventry CV1 ..... **165** C2
Dudley WV14 ...... **51** D8
Kingswinford DY6.... **60** D4
Royal Leamington Spa
CV32........... **157** A1
Walsall WS1 .... **42** D7
West Bromwich B70... **53** B4
Earlston Way B43.... **54** D8
Earls Way B63...... **83** B4
Earlswood Comm
B94............. **142** A6
Earlswood Cres WV9. **11** A3
Earlswood Ct B20... **55** A2
Earlswood Dr B74... **46** C7
Earlswood Ho 1 B5.. **86** E7
Earlswood Rd
Birmingham, Brandwood
End B30 .... **104** D3
Dorridge B93 ..... **127** D2
Kingswinford DY6.... **60** E8
Earlswood Sta B94.. **125** D1
Earlswood Trad Est
B94............. **141** C6
Easby Way
Birmingham B8...... **67** E5
Walsall WS3 .... **13** F2
Easedale Cl
Coventry CV3 ..... **133** B6
Nuneaton CV11..... **74** A6
Easemore Rd B98... **153** F5
Easenhall Cl B93... **128** A4
Easenhall La B98... **154** E1
Easmore Cl B14.... **104** D2
Eastacre WV13 ..... **27** A1
East Ave
Bedworth CV12..... **78** D2
Coventry CV2 ..... **114** A2
Oldbury B69 .... **63** C7
Wolverhampton WV11 . **26** C4
East Birmingham Coll
Bordesley Green
Campus B9 ...... **68** A2
Eastboro Ct CV11... **73** C4
Eastboro Fields CV11 **74** A4
Eastboro Way CV11...**73** F2
Eastbourne Ave B34.. **68** E6
Eastbourne Cl CV6... **112** E6

Eastbourne House Sch
B27............... **88** C4
Eastbourne St WS4...**28** F3
Eastbrook Cl B76.... **46** D4
Eastbury Dr B92 ... **89** A3
East Cannock Rd WS12 **2** C4
East Car Park Rd B40 .**90** F4
East Cl LE10 .... **75** D7
Eastcote Cl B90..... **106** D3
Eastcote Cres WS7....**7** A5
Eastcote La B92..... **108** F4
Eastcote Rd
Birmingham B27..... **88** A1
Wolverhampton WV10 . **25** F5
Eastcotes CV4 ..... **112** B1
East Croft Rd WV4... **38** C5
Eastdean Cl B23 .... **56** D6
East Dene CV32 .... **157** B2
East Dr B5......... **86** C4
Eastern Ave
Brierley Hill DY5 .... **61** B2
Lichfield WS13 ....**3** C2
Eastern Green Jun Sch
CV5............. **111** D5
Eastern Green Rd
CV5............. **111** F4
Eastern Hill B96.... **158** F2
Eastern Rd
Birmingham B29..... **86** B3
Sutton Coldfield B73... **46** B1
Eastern Way WS11....**2** A2
Easterton Croft B14.. **104** E2
East Farm Croft B10.. **87** D8
Eastfield Cl WS9 .... **30** A6
Eastfield Dr B92 ... **107** E8
Eastfield Gr WV1.....**25** F2
Eastfield Jun & Inf Sch
WV1............. **25** F2
Eastfield Rd
Birmingham B9..... **68** C3
Nuneaton CV10..... **73** D6
Royal Leamington Spa
CV32........... **162** A8
Tipton DY4 .... **52** A8
Wolverhampton WV1 . **25** F2
Eastfield Retreat WV1 .**25** F2
East Gate B16...... **65** E3
Eastgate Ct WS14 ....**9** C6
Eastgate Ho 4 CV34 **160** E6
Eastgate Mews 3
CV34............ **160** E6
Eastgate St WS7 ....**6** E8
East Gn WV4........ **38** D6
East Gr CV31....... **162** A6
Eastham Rd B13 ... **105** C6
East Holme B9..... **67** C2
Eastlake Cl B43 .... **44** D3
Eastlands Gr CV5... **112** E4
Eastlands Rd B13... **87** A1
Eastleigh DY3...... **50** C8
Eastleigh Ave CV5... **132** F7
Eastleigh Croft B76 .. **58** A2
Eastleigh Dr B62... **101** A4
Eastleigh Gr B25.... **88** D8
Eastley Cres CV34... **160** B8
East Meadway B33... **69** E3
East Mews B44...... **44** D2
East Moons Ho B98. **154** E4
Eastmoor Cl B74.... **31** B2
Eastney Cres WV8...**24** F8
Eastnor Cl
Kidderminster DY10 . **116** E2
Redditch B98 ...... **153** E1
Eastnor Gr CV31 ... **162** B7
Easton Gdns WV11 ...**26** F5
Easton Gr
Birmingham B27..... **88** C1
Hollywood B47..... **125** B7
East Park Inf Sch
WV1............. **26** B1
East Park Jun Sch
WV1............**40** B8
East Park Trad Est
WV1............. **40** B8
East Park Way WV1 .. **26** A1
East Pathway B17.... **85** C6
East Rd
Bromsgrove B60.... **137** A1
Featherstone WV10 .. **12** A7
Tipton DY4 .... **52** B8
Wolverhampton WV4 .. **39** F7
Eastridge Croft WS14. **18** A5
East Rise B75...... **46** D6
East St
Brierley Hill DY5.... **82** A8
Cannock WS11 ....**4** E6
Coventry CV1 ..... **113** E3
Dudley, Gornalwood
DY3........... **50** D3

East St continued
Dudley, Kate's Hill DY2.. **62** E8
Kidderminster DY10 . **116** F6
Tamworth B77....... **35** D5
Wolverhampton WV1 . **163** D2
East View
Shuttington B79 .... **22** F7
Tamworth B77...... **21** E3
East View Rd B72.... **46** D2
Eastville B31....... **103** B3
Eastward Glen WV8 .. **10** C1
Eastway
Birmingham B17..... **85** C6
Birmingham, Bickenhill
B40........... **90** F4
East Way B92 ...... **91** B3
Eastwood Ave WS7....**7** A8
Eastwood Cl CV31.. **162** D6
Eastwood Ct B96... **158** E1
Eastwood Dr DY10 . **117** B5
Eastwood Rd
Birmingham, Balsall Heath
B12........... **86** D5
Birmingham, Great Barr
B43........... **54** F8
Dudley DY2 .... **62** E6
Eastwoods Rd LE10...**71** F2
Eatesbrook Rd B33... **69** C3
Eathorpe Cl
Birmingham B34..... **69** D6
Coventry CV2 ..... **96** C5
Redditch B98 ..... **154** E1
Eaton Ave B70 ..... **53** A4
Eaton Cl CV32..... **156** D2
Eaton Cres DY3 .... **50** B3
Eaton Ct
Royal Leamington Spa
CV32........... **156** D1
Sutton Coldfield B74... **46** B7
Eaton Pl DY6...... **60** E5
Eaton Rd CV1 ..... **165** B3
Eaton Rise WV12.... **27** B6
Eaton Wood B24.... **57** D4
Eaton Wood Dr B26.. **88** D5
Eaves Court Dr DY3 .. **39** C1
Eaves Green Gdns
B27............... **88** B5
Eaves Green La CV7.. **92** E1
Eaves Green Mobile
Home Pk CV7......**92** F2
Ebbw Vale Terr CV3.. **133** D7
Ebenezer St
Cannock WS12 ....**2** A7
Tipton WV14 .... **51** C8
West Bromwich B70... **52** F6
Ebley Rd B20 ...... **55** A4
Ebmore Dr B14..... **104** D2
Eborall Cl CV34.... **155** E2
Eborne Croft CV7... **130** C8
Ebourne Cl CV8.... **148** A3
Ebrington Ave B92... **89** B3
Ebrington Cl B14... **104** D4
Ebrington Rd B71... **53** D6
Ebro Cres CV3 ..... **114** F1
Ebrook Rd B72...... **46** C4
Ebstree Mdw WV5... **37** A2
Ebstree Rd
Seisdon WV5....... **37** A2
Seisdon WV5....... **37** C4
Eburne Rd CV2..... **96** C3
Ebury Rd B30...... **104** B4
Eccles Cl CV2 ..... **114** C8
Eccleshall Ave WV10 . **25** C8
Eccleston Cl B75..... **46** F5
Ecclestone Rd WV11 . **27** A8
Eccleston Sch B17...**85** B5
Echells Cl B61..... **136** D2
Echo Way WV4 ..... **40** A4
Eckersall Rd B38.... **103** E3
Eckington Cl B98... **159** B8
Eckington Wlk B38... **123** E7
Eclipse Ind Est 1
DY4..............**51** E5
Edale B77 .... **22** B1
Edale Cl
Kingswinford DY6.... **60** B7
Wolverhampton WV4 .. **39** E3
Edale Gn LE10......**75** F6
Edale Rd B42...... **55** C7
Edale Way CV6..... **114** A7
Eddens Wood Cl B78.. **34** E5
Eddie Miller Ct CV12. **78** C2
Eddish Rd B33...... **69** B3
Eddy Rd DY10...... **116** F7
Edelweiss Cl WS5 ... **43** B3
Edenbridge Rd B28 . **106** B8
Edenbridge View DY1. **50** E3

Eden Cl
Birmingham B31.....**122** E8
Cannock WS12.........**2** E2
Oldbury B69.........**52** D2
Studley B80.......**159** D3
Edencroft B15.......**86** C8
Eden Croft CV8...**148** B3
Eden Ct
Featherstone WV10...**11** F8
Nuneaton CV10......**72** C7
Royal Leamington Spa
CV32.............**157** D3
Edendale Dr LE10...**71** E4
Edendale Rd B26......**89** B6
Edenfield Rd B97...**153** A5
Edenfield Pl B77...**22** B1
Eden Gdns
Rowley Regis B65......**63** B2
Sedgley DY3.......**50** E8
Eden Gr
Birmingham B37......**70** D1
West Bromwich B71......**53** D5
Edenhall Rd B32......**84** B6
Eden Ho 2 DY8....**81** A5
Edenhurst Rd B31...**122** F7
Eden Rd
Coventry CV2......**115** A8
Solihull B92.......**89** D3
Edensor Cl WV10......**25** E4
Eden St CV6......**113** F7
Edgar Cl B79......**20** F7
Edgar Stammers Jun &
Inf Schs WS3......**28** F6
Edgbaston High Sch for
Girls
Birmingham B15......**85** F7
Birmingham, Calthorpe
Fields B15......**86** B8
Edgbaston Park Rd
B15......**86** A5
Edgbaston Rd
Birmingham B12......**86** D5
Smethwick B66.......**65** A4
Edgbaston Rd E B12...**86** F5
Edgbaston Sh Ctr
B16......**86** A8
Edgbaston St B5....**164** C2
Edgbaston (Warwickshire
Cty Cricket Club)
B5......**86** D5
Edgcombe Rd B28....**87** F1
Edgefield Rd CV2...**115** A8
Edge Hill CV9......**36** B2
Edge Hill Ave WV10...**12** B1
Edge Hill Dr
Perton WV6......**23** E3
Sedgley DY3......**39** C2
Edgehill Pl CV4......**111** C1
Edgehill Rd B31.....**103** B1
Edge Hill Rd B74......**31** E4
Edgemond Ave B24...**57** F4
Edgemoor Mdw WS12...**2** C1
Edge St WV14......**51** D8
Edgewick Com Prim Sch
CV6......**113** E8
Edgewood Cl 2 B64...**82** F8
Edgewood Dr B45...**122** B1
Edgewood Rd
Birmingham, King's Norton
B38.............**123** F7
Birmingham, Rednal
B45..............**122** B6
Edgeworth Cl
Redditch B98......**154** C5
Willenhall WV12......**27** C4
Edgeworth Ho WS13...**3** A2
Edgmond Cl B98....**154** D4
Edgware Rd B23......**56** D5
Edgwick Park Ind Est
CV6.............**113** F8
Edgwick Rd CV6......**113** F7
Edgwood Ct 4 B16...**65** F1
Edinburgh Ave WS2...**27** F3
Edinburgh Cl DY10...**116** E8
Edinburgh Cres
Royal Leamington Spa
CV31.............**161** F6
Stourbridge DY8......**60** C1
Edinburgh Ct B24......**57** D4
Edinburgh Dr
Walsall WS4......**29** D7
Willenhall WV12......**27** B6
Edinburgh La WS2......**28** A4
Edinburgh Rd
Bilston WV14......**40** F3
Birmingham B68......**84** B8
Dudley DY2......**62** D6
Nuneaton CV10......**72** D6

Edinburgh Rd continued
Walsall WS5.........**43** B8
Edinburgh Villas
CV8.............**133** F2
Edingale Rd CV2.....**114** F8
Edison Cl WS12.........**2** C7
Edison Ct WV12......**27** D7
Edison Gr B32......**84** D5
Edison Rd
Curdworth B46, B76......**59** F4
Walsall WS2......**28** B5
Edison Wlk WS2......**28** B5
Edith Rd B66......**65** C3
Edith St B70......**53** B3
Edmondes Cl CV34....**155** F1
Edmonds Cl B33......**69** B2
Edmondscote Rd
CV32.............**161** D8
Edmonds Ct
Birmingham, Gilbertstone
B26..............**88** F7
Birmingham, Small Heath
B10.............**87** D7
Edmonds Rd B68.....**64** C2
Edmonton Ave B44......**45** B1
Edmonton Cl WS11......**2** B2
Edmonton Ho B5......**86** D7
Edmoor Cl WV12......**27** C6
Edmund Ho B3......**164** B3
Edmund Rd
Birmingham B8......**67** D4
Coventry CV1......**113** D5
Dudley DY3......**50** E6
West Bromwich B3......**164** B3
Ednall La B60......**136** F1
Ednam Cl 3 B71......**53** F8
Ednam Gr WV5......**38** A1
Ednam Rd Dudley DY1......**51** C2
Wolverhampton WV4......**39** C5
Edsome Way B36......**68** F8
Edstone Cl B93......**127** F4
Edstone Mews B36......**68** F8
Education Ctr The
DY5.............**61** D7
Edward Ave WS9......**30** A7
Edward Bailey Cl
CV3.............**134** E7
Edward Cl WV14......**40** E3
Edward Ct
Birmingham B16......**65** C1
Nuneaton CV11......**73** C3
Sutton Coldfield B76......**46** F3
Tamworth B77......**21** F4
Walsall WS1......**43** A8
Edward Fisher Dr
DY4......**52** A5
Edward Mews CV34.**160** E7
Edward Rd
Bedworth CV12......**78** C3
Birmingham B68......**84** C8
Birmingham, Balsall Heath
B12.............**86** E5
Birmingham, Highter's Heath
B14.............**105** A1
Coventry CV6......**95** A3
Halesowen B63......**82** F4
Perton WV6......**23** E5
Smethwick B67......**65** A4
Tipton DY4......**52** A7
Water Orton B46......**59** C3
Edwards Ctr 7 LE10..**75** D8
Edwards Rd CV8.....**148** C5
Edwards Rd
Birmingham B24......**57** A4
Burntwood WS7.........**6** F5
Dudley DY2......**62** C4
Sutton Coldfield B75......**32** D3
Edward St
Birmingham B1......**66** C3
Cannock WS11.........**1** E4
Coventry CV6......**113** E5
Darlaston WS10......**41** E6
7 Dudley DY1......**51** B1
Hinckley LE10......**71** C2
Nuneaton CV11......**73** D3
Oldbury B68......**64** A4
Redditch B97......**153** D4
Royal Leamington Spa
CV32.............**156** C1
Tamworth B79......**21** A5
Walsall WS2......**28** C3
Warwick CV34......**160** D7
West Bromwich B70......**53** D4
Wolverhampton WV4......**39** F5
Edward Street Hospl
B70......**53** C3
Edward Tyler Rd CV7...**78** A1
Edwin Ave (Road 4)
DY10.............**116** F1
Edwin Cres B60......**150** F7

Edwin Ct B9......**67** B3
Bromsgrove B60.....**150** F7
Bromsgrove B60.....**150** F8
Edwin Phillips Dr B71......**53** B8
Edwin Rd B30......**104** B7
Edyth Rd CV2......**114** E4
Edyvean Walker Ct
CV11......**73** B5
Eel St B69......**63** F7
Effingham Rd B13....**105** C7
Egbert Cl B6......**67** B8
Egelwin Cl WV6......**23** E5
Egerton Ct 4 B15......**86** B7
Egerton Rd
Birmingham B24......**57** E3
Sutton Coldfield B74......**30** F1
Wolverhampton WV11......**11** B3
Egghill La B31, B45....**102** B3
Eggington Rd DY8......**80** D6
Egginton Rd B28.....**105** E5
Egg La WV9, DY10......**119** A5
Eglamour Way CV34.**161** F3
Egmont Gdns WV11...**26** F5
Egret Ct DY10......**117** A1
Egret Wlk CV2......**96** B3
Eider Cl DY10......**117** B1
Eights Croft WS7.........**6** D8
Eileen Gdns B37......**69** F4
Eileen Rd B11......**87** C3
Elan Cl Dudley DY3......**50** D3
Royal Leamington Spa
CV32.............**157** C3
Elan Rd
Birmingham B31.....**102** C2
Sedgley DY3......**50** C8
Elbow St B64......**62** F2
Elbury Croft B93......**127** F5
Elcock Dr B42......**55** D5
Eldalade Way WS10......**42** D2
Elderberry Cl
Stourbridge DY8......**80** C3
3 Walsall WS5......**43** D7
Elderberry Way CV2...**114** B6
Elder Cl WS11.........**2** C2
Elderfield Rd B30....**104** B3
Elder La WS7.........**7** C7
Eldersfield Cl B98...**154** E7
Eldersfield Gr B91...**127** E7
Elderside Cl WS8......**15** F8
Elder Way B23......**56** E2
Eldon Ct WS1......**28** E1
Eldon Dr B76......**57** E1
Eldon Rd
Birmingham B32......**84** A3
Birmingham, Edgbaston
B16.............**65** F2
Halesowen B62......**83** F3
Eldon St
Darlaston WS10......**41** D7
Walsall WS1......**28** F1
Eldorado Cl B80.....**159** D4
Eld Rd CV6......**113** E7
Eldridge Cl WV9......**10** F2
Eleanor Rd WV14......**40** D6
Electra Park Ind Pk
B6......**56** B1
Electric Ave B6......**56** B1
Elford Cl
Birmingham B14......**104** E5
Sutton Coldfield B74......**31** A2
Elford Gr Bilston WV14......**40** C4
Birmingham B37......**70** B1
Elford Rd
Birmingham B17, B29......**85** B3
West Bromwich B71......**42** E2
Elgar Cl Cannock WS11......**1** E5
Lichfield WS13.........**3** B2
Nuneaton CV11......**79** A7
Redditch B97......**158** C8
Elgar Cres DY5......**61** D7
Elgar Ct B15......**86** A7
Elgar Mews 2 B60...**136** F2
3 Dudley DY1......**51** B1
Elgar Rd CV6......**114** B8
Elgin Cl Sedgley DY3......**39** E1
Stourbridge DY8......**81** A7
Elgin Ct WV6......**23** E4
Elgin Gr B25......**88** C7
Eliot Cl CV34......**160** D7
Elias Cl WS14.........**9** E6
Eliot Cl Tamworth B79......**21** A7
Warwick CV34......**155** E2
Eliot Croft WV14......**40** D2
Eliot St B7......**67** C8
Eliot Way CV10......**73** B2
Eliot Wlk DY10......**117** C6
Elisabeth Ct
Royal Leamington Spa
CV31.............**162** B8
Sutton Coldfield B74......**32** B3

Elizabeth Ave
Bilston WV14......**40** F3
Wednesbury WS10......**42** C3
Wolverhampton WV4......**39** B5
Elizabeth Cres B68......**64** D2
Elizabeth Ct
2 Birmingham, Acock's
Green B27......**88** C2
1 Birmingham B17......**85** D4
8 Coventry CV6......**113** A4
Warwick CV34......**161** B6
Elizabeth Dr B79......**21** A6
Elizabeth Gr
Dudley DY2......**62** F7
Solihull B90......**106** C2
Elizabeth Ho
Stourbridge DY9......**81** E5
Sutton Coldfield B76......**46** F3
1 Walsall WS5......**43** D7
Elizabeth Mews B69...**52** A2
Elizabeth Prout Gdns
B65......**63** B1
Elizabeth Rd
Birmingham, Moseley
B13.............**86** C2
Birmingham, New Oscott
B73.............**45** D1
Birmingham, Stechford
B33.............**68** D3
Cannock WS11.........**1** E6
Halesowen B63......**82** F3
Hinckley LE10......**71** D2
Royal Leamington Spa
CV31.............**161** F6
Walsall WS5......**43** C7
West Bromwich B70......**52** D4
Elizabeth Way
Coventry CV2......**114** F7
Kenilworth CV8......**147** E5
Redditch B97......**153** D5
Elizabeth Wlk DY4......**41** A2
Eliza Gdns B61......**121** B1
Elkington Croft B90...**127** A5
Elkington St
Birmingham B6......**66** E5
Coventry CV6......**113** F8
Elkstone Cl B92......**89** B3
Elkstone Covert B14....**104** C2
Ellacombe Rd CV2...**114** D8
Elland Gr B27......**88** D2
Ellards Dr WV11......**26** F5
Ellenbrook Cl 6
B97.............**153** B5
Ellen St B18......**66** B4
Ellenvale Cl WV14......**51** A8
Ellerbeck B77......**22** B1
Ellerby Gr B24......**57** E4
Ellerdene Cl B98.....**158** D8
Ellerman Gdns CV6......**95** F3
Ellerside Gr B31......**102** F2
Ellerslie Cl DY5......**81** D8
Ellerslie Rd B13.....**105** C7
Ellerton Rd B44......**45** B1
Ellerton Wlk WV10......**25** F5
Ellesboro' Rd B17......**85** B5
Ellesmere Rd
Bedworth CV12......**78** A2
Birmingham B8......**67** D4
Cannock WS11.........**4** B8
Ellice Dr B36......**70** B7
Elliot Ct 1 WV4......**39** F4
Elliot Gdns B45......**122** B5
Elliott Cl WS11.........**1** F5
Elliott Ct CV5......**112** C1
Elliott Rd B29......**85** E1
Elliotts La WV8......**10** A3
Elliott's Rd DY4......**51** E5
Elliott Way B6......**55** F3
Ellis Ave DY5......**61** A2
Ellison St B70......**53** C1
Ellis Park Dr CV3......**115** B1
Ellis St B1......**164** B1
Elliston Ave B44......**55** E8
Elliston Gr CV31......**162** C6
Ellis Wlk WS11.........**4** F8
Ellowes Hall Sch The
DY3......**50** C5
Ellowes Rd DY3......**50** C4
Ellsmore Mdw WS13......**9** A6
Ellys Rd CV1......**113** C5
Elm Ave Bilston WV14......**40** D6
Birmingham B12......**87** A5
Wednesbury WS10......**41** F4
Wolverhampton WV11......**26** B8
Elmay Rd B26......**89** A7
Elm Bank B13......**87** A3
Elm Bank Cl CV32......**157** A4
Elmbank Gr B20......**54** E5
Elmbank Rd
Kenilworth CV8......**147** E6

Elmbank Rd continued
Walsall WS5.........**43** C4
Elmbridge Cl B63......**82** D5
Elmbridge Dr B90....**127** B6
Elmbridge Rd B44......**55** E6
Elmbridge Way
7 Birmingham B31.....**103** D2
Sedgley DY3......**50** E6
Elm Cl
Binley Woods CV3....**135** C7
Dudley DY3......**50** D7
Stourbridge DY8......**80** D2
Elmcroft 5 B66......**65** C5
Elm Croft B68......**84** C7
Elmcroft Ave B32......**84** A1
Elmcroft Gdns WV10......**11** E3
Elmcroft Rd B26......**88** F7
Elm Ct Allesley CV5...**111** B8
Birmingham B13......**86** F4
Oldbury B66......**64** C8
Redditch B97......**153** D4
Walsall WS1......**43** A8
Elmdale B62......**84** A7
Elmdale Cres B31....**102** E4
Elmdale Dr
Aldridge WS9......**30** C8
Kidderminster DY10...**117** C5
Elmdale Gr B31......**102** E4
Elmdale Rd WV14......**51** A7
Elm Dale Rd WV4......**39** A5
Elmdene Rd CV8.....**148** B4
Elmdon Cl Solihull B92......**89** D2
Wolverhampton WV10......**11** A1
Elmdon Coppice
B92.............**107** F7
Elmdon Ct B37......**90** A7
Elmdon La
Birmingham B37......**90** A6
Solihull B26......**90** A3
Elmdon Park Rd B92...**89** D2
Elmdon Rd
Birmingham, Acock's Green
B27.............**88** D4
Birmingham, Marston Green
B37.............**90** A7
Birmingham, Selly Park
B29.............**86** A2
Wolverhampton WV10......**11** A1
Elmdon Trad Est B37...**90** C5
Elm Dr
Birmingham, Frankley
B31.............**102** C1
Birmingham, Grove Vale
B43.............**43** D1
Blakedown DY10......**98** B2
Halesowen B62......**63** B1
Elm Farm Ave B37......**89** F7
Elm Farm Rd WV2......**39** D7
Elmfield Ave B24......**57** F4
Elmfield Cres B13......**86** F2
Elmfield Rd
Birmingham B36......**69** F7
Nuneaton CV10......**73** C7
Elmfield Rudolf Steiner
Sch Ltd DY8......**81** A3
Elmfield View DY1......**51** A3
Elm Gdns WS14.........**9** C7
Elm Gn DY1......**51** A5
Elm Gr
Balsall Common CV7...**130** C6
Birmingham B37......**69** F6
Bromsgrove B61......**137** A4
Codsall WV8......**10** A3
Huntington WS12......**1** D8
Elmhurst B15......**85** D8
Elmhurst Ave B65......**63** C3
Elmhurst Cl B97......**158** D3
Elmhurst Dr
Burntwood WS7.........**7** A4
Kingswinford DY6......**60** F4
Elmhurst Rd
Birmingham B21......**54** E1
Coventry CV6......**96** A4
Elmhurst Sch B5......**86** B5
Elmley Cl Dudley WV14......**51** B7
Kidderminster DY11...**116** B3
Elmley Ct B23......**56** C2
Elmley Gr
Birmingham B30......**104** B2
Perton WV6......**23** F3
Elmley Ho 9 B97.....**153** A4
Elm Lodge B92......**109** A7
Elmore Cl
Birmingham B37......**70** A4
Coventry CV3......**134** D8
Elmore Green Cl WS3......**28** B1
Elmore Green Prim Sch
WS3......**14** B1
Elmore Green Rd
WS3......**14** B1

Elmore Rd B33......**69** A3
Elmore Row WS3......**14** B1
Elm Pl DY10......**118** B3
Elm Rd
Birmingham B15......**85** F5
Birmingham, Bournville
B30.............**103** F8
Dudley DY1......**51** C4
Kidderminster DY10...**117** A6
Kingswinford DY6......**60** E6
Norton Canes WS11.........**6** B5
Redditch B97......**153** D4
Royal Leamington Spa
CV32.............**157** B3
Sutton Coldfield B76......**46** F3
Walsall WS3......**28** D6
Elms Cl
Birmingham B38......**123** C8
Solihull B91......**107** D5
Elmsdale WV6......**24** A2
Elmsdale Ave CV6......**95** F2
Elmsdale Ct 6 WS1...**42** F8
Elms Dr WS11.........**1** C1
Elms Farm Prim Sch
B33.............**89** D7
Elms Rd B72......**46** C3
Elm St Willenhall WV13......**27** C2
Wolverhampton WV3......**25** A1
Elmstead Ave B33......**89** D7
Elmstead Cl WS5......**29** E1
Elmstead Twr 2 B5......**86** E7
Elmstead Wood WS5......**29** E1
Elms The
Bedworth CV12......**77** E2
Birmingham B16......**65** F3
Kingswood B94......**144** D3
Leek Wootton CV35...**155** F6
Wolverhampton WV11......**26** B3
Elmstone Cl
Dudley DY3......**50** F4
Redditch B97......**158** C5
Elm Terr B69......**52** B1
Elm Tree Ave CV4......**112** B2
Elm Tree Dr LE10......**75** F8
Elm Tree Gr B63......**82** D6
Elmtree Rd
Sutton Coldfield B74......**30** D1
Sutton Coldfield B74......**44** D8
Elm Tree Rd
Birmingham B17......**85** A4
Birmingham, Stirchley
B30.............**104** A6
Bulkington CV12......**79** D2
Elm Tree Rise B92...**109** B6
Elm Tree Way B64......**62** F1
Elm Tree Wlk B79......**20** F8
Elm Way CV10......**72** A8
Elmwood Ave
Coventry CV6......**112** F5
Essington WV11......**13** A3
Elmwood Cl
Balsall Common CV7...**130** C7
Cannock WS11.........**2** A2
Elmwood Ct
Birmingham B5......**86** D6
Coventry CV1......**165** B4
Sutton Coldfield B74......**45** A5
Elmwood Gdns B20......**55** B2
Elmwood Gr B47....**125** A6
Elmwood Rd
Birmingham B24......**57** C2
Stourbridge DY8......**60** C2
Sutton Coldfield B74......**45** A5
Elmwood Rise DY3......**39** B1
Elmwoods B32......**84** B2
Elphin Cl CV6......**95** A4
Elphinstone End B24...**57** C6
Elsma Rd B68......**84** C8
Elston Hall La WV10......**11** D1
Elston Hall Prim Sch
WV10......**11** D2
Elstree Rd B23......**56** D5
Elswick Gr B44......**56** B8
Elswick Rd B44......**45** B1
Elsworth Gr B25......**88** C6
Elsworth Rd 6 B31...**103** D2
Eltham Gr B44......**45** B1
Eltham Rd CV3......**133** E7
Elton Cl
Royal Leamington Spa
CV32.............**157** C2
Wolverhampton WV10......**11** A1
Elton Croft B93......**127** F4
Elton Gr B27......**88** A2
Eltonia Croft B26......**89** B6
Elunda Gr WV7.........**6** E5
Elva Croft B36......**58** F1
Elvers Green La B92,
B93.............**128** E7
Elvetham Rd B15......**86** C8

Elv–Fai 195

Elviron Dr WV6 24 B5
Elwell Cres DY1 50 F6
Elwells Cl WV14 40 A3
Elwell St
Wednesbury WS10 42 B3
West Bromwich B70 52 E5
Elwy Circ CV7 95 C6
Elwyn Rd B73 46 A3
Ely Cl Birmingham B37 70 B2
Cannock WS11 2 B1
Coventry CV2 115 A6
Kidderminster DY11 116 A6
Rowley Regis B65 63 E4
Ely Cres B71 53 B7
Ely Gr B32 84 F4
Ely Pl WS2 28 B1
Ely Rd WS2 28 B1
Emay Cl B70 52 F8
Embankment The DY5 61 E3
Embassy Dr
Birmingham B15 86 B8
Oldbury B69 63 E8
Embassy Ind Est 1 DY9 81 F5
Embassy Rd B69 63 E8
Embassy Wlk CV2 114 D8
Emberton Way B77 21 F5
Embleton Cl LE10 71 B1
Embleton Gr B34 69 A6
Emerald Ct
Birmingham B8 68 C5
5 Solihull B92 88 F1
Emerald Way CV31 161 F5
Emerson Cl DY3 50 A4
Emerson Gr WV10 25 F8
Emerson Rd
Birmingham B17 85 C6
Coventry CV2 114 C3
Wolverhampton WV10 25 E8
Emery Cl
Birmingham B23 56 D1
Coventry CV2 114 E7
Walsall WS1 42 F8
Emery Ct DY10 116 E7
Emery St WS1 42 F8
Emily Gdns B16 65 F3
Emily Rd B26 88 D6
Emily Smith Ho 2 CV2 96 B1
Emily St
Birmingham B12 86 F7
West Bromwich B70 53 B2
Emmanuel Rd
Burntwood WS7 7 B7
Sutton Coldfield B73 57 B8
Emmeline St B9 67 B1
Emmott Dr CV31 162 B5
Emperor Pl DY10 116 E8
Empire Cl WS9 29 F8
Empire Ind Est WS9 15 F1
Empire Ind Pk WS9 29 F8
Empire Rd CV4 111 E2
Empress Way WS10 41 D8
Emscote Dr B73 57 B7
Emscote Gn B91 106 E2
Emscote Inf Sch CV34 161 B8
Emscote Rd
Birmingham B6 55 F1
Coventry CV3 114 C2
Warwick CV34 161 B8
Emsworth Cres WV9 11 A2
Emsworth Gr B14 104 D6
Ena Rd CV1 113 D5
Endemere Rd CV6 113 D7
Enderby Cl B93 127 F4
Enderby Dr WV4 39 A5
Enderby Gr 9 B18 65 E4
Enderby Rd B23 56 C7
Enderley Cl WS3 14 B3
Enderley Dr WS3 14 B3
End Hall Rd WV6 24 A3
Endhill Rd B44 45 A3
Endicott Rd B6 55 F1
Endmoor Gr B23 56 D6
Endsleigh Gdns CV31 162 B6
Endsleigh Gr B28 106 A8
Endwood Court Rd B20 55 A2
Endwood Ct
Birmingham B11 87 D4
Birmingham, Handsworth Wood B20 55 A2
Endwood Dr
Solihull B91 106 F2
Sutton Coldfield B74 31 C4
Enfield Cl B23 56 F6
Enfield Ind Est B97 153 D5
Enfield Rd
Birmingham B15 86 B8
Coventry CV2 114 B3
Redditch B97 158 D5
Rowley Regis B65 63 D3
Enford Cl B34 69 D6
Engadine Rd B60 137 C1
Engine La
Brierley Hill DY5 61 F4
Darlaston WS10 41 A4
Stourbridge DY9 81 D6
Tamworth B77 22 A2
Walsall WS8 15 C8
Engine St Oldbury B69 64 B6
Smethwick B66 65 B6
England Cres CV31 161 E7
England Ho 10 CV32 156 F2
Englestede Cl B20 54 F3
Engleton Rd CV6 113 A6
Englewood Dr B28 106 A8
English Martyrs CE Prim Sch B11 87 C4
Ennerdale Cl
Brownhills WS8 15 E7
Royal Leamington Spa CV32 156 D2
Ennerdale Cres CV11 73 F6
Ennerdale Dr
Halesowen B63 82 D2
Perton WV6 23 F4
Ennerdale La CV2 114 F4
Ennerdale Rd
Birmingham B43 54 F6
Wolverhampton WV6 24 D8
Ennersdale Bglws B46 59 F1
Ennersdale Cl B46 59 F1
Ennersdale Rd B46 59 F1
Enright Cl CV32 156 E2
Ensall Dr DY8 60 E1
Ensbury Cl WV12 27 D4
Ensdale Row WV13 27 A1
Ensdon Gr B44 45 B1
Ensford Cl B74 31 E5
Ensign Bsns Ctr CV4 131 F6
Ensign Cl CV4 111 D1
Ensor Cl CV11 74 A6
Ensor Dr B78 22 F1
Enstone Rd
Birmingham B23 57 A7
Dudley DY1 61 F8
Enterprise Dr
Stourbridge DY9 81 F6
Sutton Coldfield B74 44 E7
Enterprise Gr WS3 15 B5
Enterprise Ho B92 109 A6
Enterprise Ind Pk WS13 9 F8
Enterprise Trad Est DY5 61 F3
Enterprise Way B7 164 D4
Enterprise Workshops DY6 61 A7
Enville Cl
Birmingham B37 70 B1
Walsall WS3 14 A3
Enville Gr B11 87 D5
Enville Pl DY8 80 E5
Enville Rd Dudley DY3 50 D4
Kingswinford DY6 60 B8
Wolverhampton WV4 38 C4
Enville St DY8 80 F5
Epperston Ct CV31 161 F7
Epping Cl
Birmingham B45 102 B2
Walsall WS3 28 F6
Epping Gr B44 56 A7
Epping Way CV32 157 C4
Epsom Cl
Bedworth CV12 78 B4
Lichfield WS14 9 D7
Perton WV6 23 F4
Redditch B97 158 C8
Tamworth B77 35 C4
Epsom Ct 16 B29 103 C7
Epsom Dr CV3 134 C6
Epsom Gr B44 56 B8
Epsom Rd
Royal Leamington Spa CV32 157 C4
Upper Catshill B61 121 A1
Epwell Gr B44 55 F6
Epwell Rd B44 55 F6
Epworth Ct DY5 61 B5
Erasmus Rd B11 87 A7
Erasmus Way WS13 9 A8
Ercall Cl B23 56 A6
Erdington Hall Prim Sch B24 56 F1
Erdington Hall Rd B24 56 F2
Erdington Ind Pk B24 57 F4
Erdington Rd WS9 30 C3
Erdington Sta B23 56 F5
Erica Ave CV12 77 F2
Erica Cl B29 103 A8
Erica Dr CV31 162 B2
Erica Rd WS5 43 B3
Eric Grey Cl CV2 114 A5
Eringden B77 22 B1
Erithway Rd CV3 133 B4
Ermington Cres B36 68 E7
Ermington Rd WV4 39 D4
Ernesford Grange Prim Sch CV3 114 E1
Ernesford Grange Sch & Com Coll CV3 134 D8
Ernest Clarke Cl WV12 27 C4
Ernest Ct B38 104 A1
Ernest Rd
Birmingham B12 87 B4
Dudley DY2 51 F1
Smethwick B67 64 E6
Ernest Richards Rd CV12 78 B4
Ernest St B1 164 B1
Ernsford Ave CV3 114 B1
Ernsford Cl B93 127 F2
Erskine Cl LE10 71 A2
Erskine St B7 67 B3
Erwood Cl B97 153 B2
Esher Dr CV3 133 E7
Esher Rd
Birmingham B44 44 F4
West Bromwich B71 53 D6
Eskdale Cl WV1 26 A2
Eskdale Rd LE10 75 A7
Eskdale Wlk
Brierley Hill DY5 81 B8
Coventry CV3 134 D7
Esk Ho 1 DY1 61 E8
Eskrett St WS12 2 C5
Esme Rd B11 87 B4
Esmond Cl B30 103 D5
Essendon Gr B8 68 B4
Essendon Rd B8 68 B4
Essendon Wlk B8 68 B4
Essex Ave
Kingswinford DY6 60 B5
Wednesbury WS10 42 C4
West Bromwich B71 53 D7
Essex Cl Coventry CV5 112 B3
Kenilworth CV8 147 E2
Essex Ct
5 Birmingham B29 103 C7
Warwick CV34 160 E8
Essex Dr WS12 2 B4
Essex Gdns DY8 80 D7
Essex Ho
2 Birmingham B2 164 B2
2 Wolverhampton WV3 25 C4
Essex Rd Dudley DY2 62 A6
Sutton Coldfield B75 32 D2
Essex St
Birmingham B5 164 C1
Walsall WS2 28 E5
Essington Cl
Lichfield WS14 9 A5
Shenstone WS14 18 A7
Stourbridge DY8 60 E1
Essington Ind Est WV11 12 F4
Essington Rd WV12 13 B1
Essington St B16 66 B1
Essington Way WV1 26 B1
Este Rd B26 69 A1
Esterton Cl CV6 95 C2
Estone Wlk B6 66 F7
Estria Rd B15 86 B7
Estridge La WS6 5 A2
Etchell Rd B78 20 F3
Ethelfield Rd CV2 114 B3
Ethelfleda Rd B77 35 F5
Ethelfleda Terr WS10 41 F3
Ethel Rd B17 85 D5
Ethelred Cl B74 32 A3
Ethel St
Birmingham B2 164 B2
Oldbury B68 64 A4
Smethwick B67 64 F2
Etheridge Rd WV14 40 D7
Eton Cl DY3 50 F6
Eton Ct Lichfield WS14 9 B6
1 Sutton Coldfield B74 31 F2
Eton Dr DY8 81 A3
Etone Com Sch CV11 73 D5
Etone Ct CV11 73 B5
Eton Rd B12 87 B4
Eton Wlk DY9 99 A6
Etruria Way WV14 40 E7
Etta Gr B44 44 F4
Ettingley Cl B98 159 B5
Ettingshall Park Farm La WV4 39 E4
Ettingshall Prim Sch WV14 40 B6
Ettingshall Rd
Bilston WV14 40 A2
Wolverhampton WV2 40 A7
Ettington Cl B93 127 D2
Ettington Rd
Birmingham B6 66 E8
Coventry CV5 112 A3
Ettymore Cl DY3 50 D8
Ettymore Rd DY3 50 D8
Ettymore Rd W DY3 50 C8
Etwall Rd B28 105 E6
Euan Cl B17 85 C8
Eunal Ct B97 158 E5
Euro Bsns Pk B69 52 D1
Euro Ct B13 87 B2
Europa Ave B70 53 F2
Europa Way
Lichfield WS13 9 F8
Royal Leamington Spa CV34 161 D5
European Bsns Pk B69 63 E7
Eustace Rd CV12 79 D1
Euston Cres CV3 134 C6
Euston Pl CV32 161 F8
Euston Sq 1 CV32 161 F8
Evans Cl
Bedworth CV12 78 C3
Dudley DY4 51 C5
Evans Croft B78 21 A1
Evans Gdns B29 85 D1
Evans Gr CV31 162 A2
Evans Pl WV14 40 E7
Evans St
Willenhall WV13 26 D1
Wolverhampton, Dunstall Hill WV6 25 B4
Wolverhampton WV4, WV14 39 F1
Eva Rd
Birmingham B18 65 D6
Oldbury B68 64 D3
Evason Ct B6 55 E1
Eve La DY1 50 F5
Evelyn Ave CV6 95 F2
Evelyn Croft B73 57 A8
Evelyn Rd B11 87 D4
Evenlode Cl
Redditch B98 153 F1
Solihull B92 89 B3
Evenlode Cres CV6 112 F5
Evenlode Gr WV13 27 D1
Evenlode Rd B92 89 B3
Everard Ct CV11 73 E2
Everdon Rd CV6 95 B2
Everene Ho 1 B27 88 C3
Everest Cl B66 64 F8
Everest Rd
Birmingham B20 55 A3
Willenhall WS2 27 F3
Everglade Rd CV9 36 C2
Evergreen Cl WV14 51 B8
Evergreen Hts WS12 2 A8
Evergreens The CV10 72 F6
Everitt Dr B93 128 A6
Eversfield Prep Sch B91 107 B4
Eversleigh Rd CV6 112 E7
Eversley Dale B24 57 A2
Eversley Gr
Sedgley DY3 39 C2
Wolverhampton WV11 26 C6
Eversley Rd 2 B9 67 D1
Evers St DY5 82 A8
Everton Rd B8 68 C4
Eves Croft B32 84 C1
Evesham Cres WS3 13 F3
Evesham Ct DY11 116 D5
Evesham Ho B60 137 B3
Evesham Mews 8 B97 153 E3
Evesham Rd B96, B97 158 E3
Evesham Rise DY2 62 D3
Evesham Sq 3 B97 153 E3
Evesham St B97 153 E3
Evesham Wlk
Coventry CV4 132 D5
2 Redditch B97 153 E4
Eveson Rd DY8 80 E2
Ewart Rd WS2 27 E3
Ewell Rd B24 57 B4
Ewhurst Ave B29 85 F1
Ewhurst Cl WV13 40 F8
Ewloe Cl DY10 116 E1
Exbury Cl WV9 10 F2
Exbury Way CV11 78 E8
Excelsior Gr WS3 15 B5
Exchange Ind Est The WS11 4 E5
Exchange St
Brierley Hill DY5 61 D4
Kidderminster DY10 116 E6
Wolverhampton WV1 163 B3
Exchange The WS3 14 B1
Exe Croft B31 123 B8
Exeter Cl
Coventry CV3 134 D8
Kidderminster DY11 116 A6
Exeter Dr
Birmingham B37 89 F8
Tamworth B79 20 E5
Exeter Ho 8 B24 56 F4
Exeter Pas B1 164 B1
Exeter Pl WS2 28 B1
Exeter Rd
Birmingham B29 85 F2
Cannock WS11 4 B8
Dudley DY2 62 D2
Smethwick B66 65 B5
Exeter St B1 164 B1
Exford Cl DY5 81 B7
Exhall Cedars Inf Sch CV7 96 A8
Exhall Cl
Redditch B98 154 D5
Solihull B91 106 E2
Exhall Ct B23 56 C2
Exhall Gn CV7 95 F7
Exhall Grange Sch & Science Coll CV7 95 C5
Exhall Rd CV7 95 A6
Exham Cl CV34 155 E1
Exhibition Way B40 90 D4
Exis Ct CV11 73 E2
Exley B77 21 D1
Exminster Rd CV3 133 E5
Exmoor Ct B61 137 A4
Exmoor Dr
Bromsgrove B61 137 A4
Royal Leamington Spa CV32 157 C4
Exmoor Gn WV11 26 C7
Exmouth Cl CV2 114 C7
Exonbury Wlk 5 WS11 1 F2
Exon Ct DY4 51 F6
Expressway The B70 53 C4
Exton Cl
Ash Green CV7 95 C6
Wednesfield WV11 26 F8
Exton Way B8 67 D5
Eyffler Cl CV34 160 D7
Eyland Gr WS1 28 F2
Eymore Cl B29 103 B6
Eynsham Ct WV6 24 E5
Eyre St B18 66 A3
Eyston Ave DY4 52 D8
Eyton Cl B98 154 D3
Eyton Croft B12 86 F7
Ezekiel La WV12 27 C6

F

Fabian Cl
Birmingham B45 102 A2
Coventry CV3 134 D7
Fabian Cres B90 106 B1
Fabius Cl LE10 75 C7
Facet Rd B38 104 A2
Factory La B61 136 F1
Factory Rd
Birmingham B18 66 A6
Hinckley LE10 71 D1
Tipton DY4 51 E6
Factory St WS10 41 C6
Fairbanks Cl CV2 115 A7
Fairbourne Ave
Birmingham B44 44 E2
Rowley Regis B65 63 E4
Fairbourne Gdns B97 158 C7
Fairbourne Twr B23 57 A6
Fairbourne Way CV6 112 E8
Fairburn Cres WS3 15 B5
Faircroft CV8 147 F3
Faircroft Ave B76 57 F6
Faircroft Rd B36 58 D1
Fairdene Way 3 B43 54 D8
Fairfax Ct 7 CV34 160 F7
Fairfax Rd
Birmingham B31 123 A8
Fairfax Rd *continued*
Sutton Coldfield B75 46 F5
Wolverhampton WV10 11 E3
Fairfax Sch B75 46 F5
Fairfax St CV1 165 C3
Fairfield Cl WS12 2 D1
Fairfield Ct CV3 134 A7
Fairfield Dr
Halesowen B62 63 E1
Walsall WS3 15 B4
Fairfield Fst Sch B61 120 D3
Fairfield Gr B62 63 E1
Fairfield Ho B60 137 B3
Fairfield Mount WS1 42 F8
Fairfield Park Ind Est B62 63 E1
Fairfield Rd
Birmingham B14 104 E8
Dudley DY2 62 D7
Fairfield B61 120 D1
Halesowen B63 83 A2
Halesowen, Hurst Green B62 63 E1
Stourbridge DY8 60 F2
Fairfield Rise
Meriden CV7 92 C1
Stourbridge DY8 80 D5
Fairfields Hill B78 36 F8
Fairford Cl
Redditch B98 154 E7
Solihull B91 106 D5
Fairford Gdns
Burntwood WS7 7 C6
Stourbridge DY8 60 E3
Fairford Rd B44 55 F6
Fairgreen Gdns DY5 61 C5
Fairgreen Way
Birmingham B29 85 F1
Sutton Coldfield B74 31 A1
Fairground Way WS1 42 D8
Fairhaven Croft B62 63 E1
Fairhaven Prim Sch DY8 60 D3
Fairhills DY3 50 D8
Fairhill Way B11 87 C7
Fairholme Rd B36 68 B7
Fairhurst Dr CV32 156 E3
Fair Isle Dr CV10 72 F2
Fair Lady Dr WS7 6 D8
Fairlands Pk CV4 132 E5
Fairlawn B15 86 A7
Fairlawn Cl
Royal Leamington Spa CV32 156 D1
Willenhall WV12 13 C1
Fairlawn Dr DY6 60 D4
Fairlawns
Birmingham B26 69 A1
Sutton Coldfield B76 58 A8
Fairlawn Way WV12 13 C1
Fairlie Cres B38 103 D1
Fairlight Dr B45 122 A1
Fairmead Rise B38 103 E1
Fairmile Cl CV3 134 C8
Fairmile Rd B63 83 A6
Fairmont Rd B60 151 B8
Fairmount Dr 5 WS11 4 E8
Fairoak Dr
Bromsgrove B60 150 F6
Wolverhampton WV6 24 B3
Fair Oaks Dr WS6 14 A8
Fairview Ave B42 55 B6
Fairview Cl
Cheslyn Hay WS6 4 D2
Tamworth B77 21 F5
Wolverhampton WV11 26 B7
Fairview Cres
Kingswinford DY6 60 F6
Wolverhampton WV11 26 B7
Fairview Ct WS2 27 D2
Fairview Gr WV11 26 B7
Fairview Ind Est B76 59 B7
Fairview Mews 9 B46 70 F7
Fairview Rd
Dudley DY1 51 A3
Wolverhampton, Scotlands WV11 26 B7
Wolverhampton, Spring Hill WV4 38 C4
Fairview Wlk CV6 95 E2
Fairway
Birmingham B31 102 E3
Cannock WS11 4 D6
Nuneaton CV11 79 B8
Tamworth B77 35 F5
Walsall WS4 15 D1

Fairway Ave B69 . . . . . 63 A8
Fairway Ct B77 . . . . . . 22 B3
Fairway Dr B45 . . . 121 F6
Fairway Gn WV14 . . 40 D8
Fairway Prim Sch
 B38 . . . . 103 D1
Fairway Rd B68 . . . . . .63 F2
Fairway Rise CV8 . . 148 C6
Fairways B93 . . . . . . 128 A8
Fairways Ave DY8 . . . 80 E2
Fairways
 Coventry CV5 . . . . . . 112 A6
 Stourbridge DY8 . . . . 80 E2
Fairways Dr B60 . . . . 138 B5
Fairways The CV32 . . 156 D2
Fairway The
 Birmingham B38 . . . . 103 D2
 Hinckley LE10 . . . . 75 F7
Fairyfield Ave B43 . . . 43 D1
Fairyfield Ct B43 . . . . 43 D1
Fakenham Croft B17 . .84 F7
Falcon B77 . . . . 36 A6
Falcon Ave CV3 . . . . 134 F8
Falcon Cl Cannock WS11 .1 C2
 Cheslyn Hay WS6 . . . . . .4 C2
 Kidderminster DY10 . 116 E2
 Nuneaton CV11 . . . . . . 79 B8
Falcon Cres WV14 . . . .39 F2
Falcondale Rd WV12 . 13 C1
Falconers Gn LE10 . . .75 F6
Falconhurst Rd B29 . . 85 C2
Falcon Lodge Cres
 B75 . . . . 47 A6
Falcon Pk B77 . . . . . .35 E7
Falcon Pl B69 . . . . . . 63 C7
Falcon Rd B68 . . . . . .63 F2
Falcon Rise DY8 . . . . . 80 C6
Falconry Ctr The★
 DY9 . . . . .98 F3
Falcons The B75 . . . . 47 B5
Falcon View B30 . . . 104 A4
Falcon Way DY1 . . . . .50 F1
Falfield Cl B65 . . . . . . 63 D6
Falfield Gr B31 . . . . . 122 E2
Falkener Ho CV6 . . . 113 E7
Falkland Cl CV4 . . . . 131 D7
Falkland Croft B30 . . 104 B6
Falkland Way B36 . . . 70 B5
Falkwood Gr B93 . . . 127 F6
Fallindale Rd B26 . . . 89 B6
Fallings Heath Cl
 WS10 . . . . .41 F7
Fallings Park Ind Est
 WV10 . . . . .25 F5
Fallings Park Prim Sch
 WV10 . . . . 26 A8
Fallowfield
 Birmingham B15 . . . . 85 E8
 Perton WV6 . . . . 23 D4
 Wolverhampton WV8 . . 10 E2
Fallow Field
 Cannock WS11 . . . . . . .1 E3
 Lichfield WS13 . . . . .3 C3
 Sutton Coldfield B74 . . 31 B3
Fallowfield Ave B28 . 105 F5
Fallowfield Rd
 Halesowen B63 . . . . . . 82 D3
 Rowley Regis B65 . . . . 63 A3
 Solihull B92 . . . . 89 D3
 Walsall WS5 . . . . 43 E8
Fallowfields CV6 . . . . 95 C4
Fallowfields Cl B61 . 136 E3
Fallow Hill CV31 . . . 162 C6
Fallow Rd B78 . . . . . .20 F1
Fallows Ho B19 . . . . . 66 E5
Fallows Rd B11 . . . . . 87 C6
Fallow Wlk B32 . . . . . 84 A2
Falmouth Cl CV11 . . . 74 A5
Falmouth Dr
 Hinckley LE10 . . . . 71 E4
 Tamworth B77 . . . . 21 F5
Falmouth Rd
 Birmingham B34 . . . . . 68 D4
 Walsall WS5 . . . . 43 D7
Falna Cres B79 . . . . . . .20 F7
Falstaff Ave B47 . . . 125 A6
Falstaff Cl
 Nuneaton CV11 . . . . . . 74 A1
 Sutton Coldfield B76 . . 58 B7
Falstaff Ct B75 . . . . . 47 C5
Falstaff Gr CV34 . . . . 161 E3
Falstaff Ho B13 . . . . 105 D7
Falstaff Rd
 Coventry CV4 . . . . . . 111 E1
 Solihull B90 . . . . 106 C4
Falstone Rd B73 . . . . 45 D2
Fanad Ho B23 . . . . . . 56 E5
Fancott Dr CV8 . . . . 147 F6

Fancott Rd B31 . . . . . 103 A5
Fancourt Ave WV4 . . . 38 D4
Fane Rd WV11 . . . . . . 13 B2
Fanshawe Rd B27 . . . . 88 C1
Faraday Ave
 Birmingham B32 . . . . . 84 D5
 Curdworth B46, B76 . . . 59 F5
Faraday Ct B32 . . . . . 84 D5
Faraday Ho 🄳 B15 . . . 86 C8
Faraday Rd
 Hinckley LE10 . . . . 74 E7
 Walsall WS2 . . . . 28 B6
Farber Rd CV2 . . . . . 115 A6
Farbrook Way WV12 . . 27 B6
Farclose Ho B15 . . . . . 86 C7
Farcroft Ave
 Birmingham B21 . . . . . 65 D8
 Coventry CV5 . . . . . . .111 D4
Farcroft Gr B21 . . . . . 54 D1
Farcroft Rd B21 . . . . . 54 D1
Fardon Way B23 . . . . . 56 D8
Fareham Cres WV4 . . . 38 C6
Farewell La WS7 . . . . . .7 E6
Farfield
 Kidderminster DY10 . . 116 F5
 Stoke Prior B60 . . . . . 150 F4
Farfield Cl B31 . . . . . 103 B2
Farfield Studios
 DY10 . . . . 116 F5
Far Gosford St CV1 . . 113 E2
Far High Dr 🄶 DY4 . . . 52 B5
Far Highfield B76 . . . 46 E4
Far Hill Cl B71 . . . . . .53 F8
Farlands Dr DY8 . . . . 81 A3
Farlands Gr B43 . . . . .54 F7
Farlands Rd DY8 . . . . 81 A3
Far Lash LE10 . . . . . .75 F7
Farleigh Dr WV3 . . . . 38 A8
Farleigh Rd WV6 . . . . 24 A3
Farley Ctr The B70 . . 53 D2
Farley La B62 . . . . . . 100 F1
Farley Rd B23 . . . . . . 56 B4
Farley St
 Royal Leamington Spa
 CV31 . . . . 162 B7
 Tipton DY4 . . . . 52 D5
Farlow Cl
 Coventry CV6 . . . . . . 114 A6
 Redditch B98 . . . . . . 154 D3
Farlow Croft B37 . . . .89 F8
Farlow Rd B31 . . . . . 103 C3
Farmacre B9 . . . . 67 B2
Farman Rd CV5 . . . . . 113 A2
Farm Ave B68 . . . . . . 64 A3
Farmbridge Cl WS2 . . 27 D3
Farmbridge Rd WS2 . . 27 D3
Farmbridge Way WS2 27 D3
Farmbrook Ave WV10 . 11 D3
Farm Cl
 Birmingham B33 . . . . . 68 F3
 Cannock WS12 . . . . . . .2 C3
 Codsall WV8 . . . . 10 B2
 Coventry CV6 . . . . 95 B3
 Kidderminster DY11 . . 116 B2
 Sedgley DY3 . . . . 50 B7
 Solihull B92 . . . . 89 C2
 Tamworth B79 . . . . 21 C7
Farmcote Cl B97 . . . . 158 D4
Farmcote Lodge CV2 . 96 B4
Farmcote Rd
 Birmingham B33 . . . . . 69 A4
 Coventry CV2 . . . . 96 B4
Farm Croft B19 . . . . . 66 C6
Farmcroft Rd DY9 . . . 81 E2
Farmdale Gr B45 . . . . 122 A6
Farmer Rd B10 . . . . . . 88 A7
Farmers Cl B76 . . . . . 46 E4
Farmers Ct B63 . . . . . .82 F4
Farmer's Fold WV1 . . 163 B3
Farmers Rd B60 . . . . 150 E7
Farmers Wlk B21 . . . . 65 D7
Farmer Ward Rd
 CV8 . . . . 148 A3
Farmer Way DY4 . . . . 41 C1
Farm House La 🄶
 B75 . . . . 32 E3
Farmhouse Rd WV12 . 27 D5
Farmhouse Way
 Solihull B90 . . . . 127 B7
 Willenhall WV12 . . . . . 27 D5
Farm House Way B43 . 43 E4
Farmoor Gr B34 . . . . . 69 E6
Far Moor La B98 . . . . 154 E6
Farmoor Way WV10 . . 11 E4
Farm Rd
 Birmingham B11 . . . . . 87 B7
 Brierley Hill DY5 . . . . . 61 E1
 Dudley DY2 . . . . 62 A4
 Hinckley LE10 . . . . 75 E6

Farm Rd continued
 Kenilworth CV8 . . . . . 147 E2
 Oldbury B68 . . . . 64 A3
 Redditch B98 . . . . . . 154 A3
 Rowley Regis B65 . . . . 63 A4
 Royal Leamington Spa
 CV32 . . . . 157 B3
 Smethwick B67 . . . . . . 64 E3
 Tipton DY4 . . . . 52 B7
 Wolverhampton WV3 . . 38 C8
Farmside CV3 . . . . . . 134 D5
Farmside Cl DY9 . . . . 82 A3
Farmside Gn WV9 . . . .10 F2
Farm St
 Birmingham B19 . . . . . 66 C6
 Walsall WS2 . . . . 28 E4
 West Bromwich B70 . . . 53 C1
Farmstead Cl WS1 . . . 42 E5
Farmstead Rd B92 . . . 89 C2
Farmstead The CV3 . 134 B8
Farnborough B98 . . . 154 F1
Farnborough Ct B75 . . 32 C2
Farnborough Dr B90 . 126 F6
Farnborough Rd B35 . 58 B3
Fanbury Croft B38 . . 104 B2
Farncote Dr B74 . . . . .31 F3
Farndale Ave
 Coventry CV6 . . . . 95 D3
 Wolverhampton WV6 . . 24 F5
Farndale Cl DY5 . . . . . 81 B6
Farndon Ave B37 . . . . 90 B7
Farndon Cl CV12 . . . . 79 B3
Farndon Rd B8 . . . . . .67 F4
Farneway LE10 . . . . . . 71 B1
Farnham Cl B43 . . . . .54 F8
Farnham Rd B21 . . . . 54 C2
Farnhurst Rd B36 . . . 68 B7
Farnol Rd B26 . . . . . .68 F1
Farnworth Gr B36 . . . 58 E1
Farquhar Rd
 Birmingham B15 . . . . . 85 F6
 Birmingham, Moseley
 B13 . . . . 86 F3
Farquhar Rd E B15 . . .85 F6
Farran Way B43 . . . . . 54 E7
Farr Dr CV4 . . . . 112 B2
Farren Rd
 Birmingham B31 . . . . 102 D1
 Coventry CV2 . . . . . . 114 E5
Farrier Cl
 Bromsgrove B60 . . . . . 150 E6
 Sutton Coldfield B76 . . 57 F8
Farrier Rd B43 . . . . . . 44 D3
Farriers Mill WS3 . . . . 14 E4
Farriers The B26 . . . . 89 B5
Farriers Way
 Hinckley LE10 . . . . 75 F6
 Nuneaton CV11 . . . . . . 73 F2
Farrier Way DY6 . . . . 60 A7
Farrington Ho 🄳
 WS2 . . . . 28 D3
Farringdon St WS2 . . 28 D3
Farrington Rd
 Birmingham B23 . . . . . 56 B5
 Wolverhampton WV4 . . 39 E3
Farrow Rd B44 . . . . . . 44 E3
Farthing Ct 🄶 B1 . . . 66 C3
Farthing La
 Curdworth B76 . . . . . . 59 C6
 Redditch B97 . . . . . . 153 B5
 Sutton Coldfield B72 . . 46 B4
Farthing Pools Cl 🄱
 B72 . . . . 46 C4
Farthings La DY2 . . . . 62 A7
Farthings Lodge 🄷
 DY1 . . . . 51 B1
Farthings The
 Birmingham B17 . . . . . 85 D6
 Shenstone WS14 . . . . . 17 F5
Farthing Wlk CV4 . . . 131 D6
Farvale Rd B76 . . . . . 58 C6
Far View WS9 . . . . . . 16 B2
Far Wood Rd B31 . . . 102 E8
Farzens Ave CV34 . . . 160 B3
Faseman Ave CV4 . . . 111 F3
Fashoda Rd B29 . . . . . 86 B1
Fasson Cl B77 . . . . . . 35 C8
Fastlea Rd B32 . . . . . . 84 D1
Fastmoor Oval B33 . . 69 E1
Fast Pits Rd B25 . . . . 88 C1
Fatherless Barn Cres
 B63 . . . . 82 D5
Faulconbridge Ave
 CV5 . . . . 111 E4
Faulconbridge Way
 CV34 . . . . 161 E3
Faulkland Cres WV1 . 163 C4
Faulkner Cl DY8 . . . . .80 F4
Faulkner Rd B92 . . . . 89 B1

Faulkners Farm Dr
 B23 . . . . 56 B6
Faulknor Dr DY5 . . . . 61 B7
Faultlands Cl CV11 . . .78 F8
Faversham Cl
 Willenhall WS2 . . . . . . 27 D3
 Wolverhampton WV8 . . 24 E8
Fawdry Cl B73 . . . . . . 46 B5
Fawdry St
 Birmingham B9 . . . . . . 67 A2
 Smethwick B66 . . . . . . 65 C5
 Wolverhampton WV1 . 163 A4
Fawley Cl
 Coventry CV3 . . . . . . 134 C6
 Willenhall WV13 . . . . . 26 F1
Fawley Gr B14 . . . . . 104 B5
Fawn CV12 . . . . .1 C6
Faygate Cl CV3 . . . . . 114 F3
Fazeley Cl B91 . . . . . 107 D4
Fazeley Ind Est B5 . . . 67 A2
Fazeley Rd
 Tamworth B78 . . . . 21 A4
 Tamworth, Fazeley B78 . 21 B2
Fazeley St B5 . . . . . . .66 F2
Fearings Cotts B97 . 158 D5
Fearon Pl 🄴 B66 . . . . 65 A5
Featherbed La
 Coventry CV4 . . . . . . 132 A5
 Redditch B97 . . . . . . 158 C5
Featherston Dr LE10 . 75 E6
Featherstone Cl
 Nuneaton CV10 . . . . . . 73 C2
 Solihull B90 . . . . 106 D2
Featherstone Cres
 B90 . . . . 106 D2
Featherstone La
 WV10 . . . . 12 B8
Featherstone Prim Sch
 B23 . . . . .56 E4
Featherstone Rd
 B14 . . . . 104 E6
Featherston Rd B74 . . 31 A2
Feckenham Ho B60 . 137 B3
Feckenham Rd
 Astwood Bank B96 . . . 158 E2
 Redditch, Headless Cross
 B97 . . . . 158 C5
 Redditch, Hunt End
 B97 . . . . 158 C4
Fecknam Way WS13 . . .3 C1
Feilding Cl CV2 . . . . . 115 A6
Feilding Way CV10 . . . 72 A5
Fein Bank CV4 . . . . . 111 C2
Felbrigg Cl DY5 . . . . . 81 D8
Feldings The B24 . . . . 57 C4
Feldon La B62 . . . . . . 83 E7
Felgate Cl B90 . . . . . 127 A6
Fell Gr Birmingham B21 54 C2
 Royal Leamington Spa
 CV32 . . . . 157 C3
Fellmeadow Rd B33 . . 69 A2
Fellmeadow Way DY3 . 50 D7
Fellmore Gr CV31 . . . 162 D7
Fellows Ave DY6 . . . . 60 C8
Fellows La B17 . . . . . 85 A5
Fellows Park Gdns
 WS2 . . . . 42 B6
Fellows Rd WV14 . . . . 40 D7
Fellows St WV2 . . . . . 163 B1
Felspar Rd B77 . . . . . 22 B3
Felstead Cl B77 . . . . . 35 C4
Felsted Way B7 . . . . . 67 A4
Felstone Rd B44 . . . . 44 E1
Feltham Cl B33 . . . . . 69 E1
Felton Cl Coventry CV2 96 E1
 Redditch B98 . . . . . . 154 E1
Felton Croft B33 . . . . 69 A3
Felton Gr B91 . . . . . . 107 C1
Fenbourne Cl WS4 . . . 29 C8
Fenchurch Cl WS2 . . . 28 D4
Fen Cl DY10 . . . . 116 E8
Fencote Ave B37 . . . . 70 A4
Fen End Rd CV8 . . . . 129 E4
Fenmere Cl WV4 . . . . 39 D5
Fennel Cl WS6 . . . . . . 4 D3
Fennel Croft B34 . . . . 69 B7
Fennell Ho 🄲 CV1 . . . 113 B2
Fennel Rd DY5 . . . . . . 81 C7
Fennis Cl B93 . . . . . . 127 F3
Fenn Rise
 Stourbridge DY8 . . . . . 60 D3
 Willenhall WV12 . . . . . 27 B5
Fenn St B77 . . . . 21 E1
Fennyland La CV8 . . . 148 B7
Fens Cres DY5 . . . . . . 61 C5
Fenside Ave CV3 . . . . 133 C4
Fens Pool Ave DY5 . . . 61 D5
Fensway The B34 . . . . 69 A5
Fenter Cl B13 . . . . . . .86 F5

Fentham Cl B92 . . . . 109 B6
Fentham Ct B92 . . . . 106 F8
Fentham Gn B92 . . . 109 A7
Fentham Rd
 Birmingham, Aston B6 . 66 E8
 Birmingham, Gravelly Hill
 B23 . . . . 56 E3
 Hampton-in-A B92 . . . 109 A6
Fenton Rd
 Birmingham B27 . . . . . 88 B5
 Hollywood B47 . . . . . 125 A7
Fenton St
 Brierley Hill DY5 . . . . . 61 D3
 Smethwick B66 . . . . . . 64 E7
Fenton Way B27 . . . . . 88 B5
Fenwick Cl B97 . . . . . 153 B1
Fereday Rd WS9 . . . . 16 B3
Fereday's Croft DY3 . . 50 D7
Fereday St DY4 . . . . . .51 F8
Ferguson Dr
 Kidderminster DY11 . . 116 A1
 Tipton DY4 . . . . 52 B6
Ferguson Rd B68 . . . . 64 D5
Ferguson St WV11 . . . 13 A1
Fern Ave DY4 . . . . . . .51 F7
Fernbank Cl B63 . . . . 82 E2
Fernbank Cres WS5 . . 43 C4
Fernbank Rd B8 . . . . . 68 A4
Fern Cl Coventry CV2 . 96 C2
 Dudley WV14 . . . . 51 B8
 Walsall WS4 . . . . 15 D1
Ferncliffe Rd B17 . . . . 85 B4
Ferndale Ave B43 . . . .54 F7
Ferndale Cl
 Burntwood WS7 . . . . . .7 B6
 Nuneaton CV11 . . . . . . 73 E5
 Upper Catshill B61 . . . 121 A1
 West Hagley DY9 . . . . . 99 A5
Ferndale Cres
 Birmingham B12 . . . . . 87 A8
 Kidderminster DY11 . . 116 B8
Ferndale Ct 🄱 B17 . . . 85 D4
Ferndale Dr CV8 . . . . 148 A2
Ferndale Gr LE10 . . . . 75 A7
Ferndale Pk DY9 . . . . 99 C8
Ferndale Prim Sch
 B43 . . . . .54 E8
Ferndale Rd
 Binley Woods CV3 . . . . 135 D7
 Birmingham B28 . . . . 105 F8
 Essington WV11 . . . . . 13 B3
 Oldbury B68 . . . . 64 A2
 Sutton Coldfield B74 . . 44 F8
Fern Dale Rd CV7 . . . 129 F6
Fern Dell Cl WS11 . . . . .1 C2
Ferndene Rd B11 . . . . 88 A3
Ferndown Ave DY3 . . . 50 C7
Ferndown Cl
 Birmingham B26 . . . . . 69 A1
 Coventry CV4 . . . . . . 112 A3
 Walsall WS3 . . . . 14 B4
Ferndown Gdns WV11 .26 F5
Ferndown Rd B91 . . . 107 C5
Fern Dr WS6 . . . . .5 A4
Ferneley Ave LE10 . . . 71 A3
Ferness Cl LE10 . . . . . 71 B2
Ferness Rd LE10 . . . . 71 B2
Ferney Hill Ave B97 . 153 C3
Fernhill Cl CV8 . . . . . 147 E6
Fernhill Ct B23 . . . . . 56 C2
Fernhill Dr CV32 . . . . 157 B1
Fernhill Gr B44 . . . . . .44 F3
Fernhill La CV7, CV8 . 129 F5
Fernhill Rd B92 . . . . . 88 E2
Fernhurst Dr DY5 . . . . 61 B7
Fernhurst Rd B8 . . . . . 68 A3
Fernleigh B60 . . . . . . 137 A1
Fernleigh Ave WS7 . . .7 A8
Fernleigh Ct B91 . . . 107 C5
Fernleigh Gdns DY8 . . 60 C3
Fernleigh Rd WS4 . . . 29 B3
Fernley Ave B29 . . . . 86 B2
Fernley Rd B11 . . . . . 87 C4
Fern Leys WV3 . . . . . 24 D1
Fern Rd
 Birmingham B24 . . . . . 57 A4
 Dudley DY1 . . . . 51 C4
 Huntington WS12 . . . . 1 D5
 Wolverhampton WV3 . 163 A1
Fernside Gdns B13 . . . 87 B3
Fernside Rd WV13 . . . 26 D3
Fernwood Cl
 Redditch B98 . . . . . . 159 B5
 Sutton Coldfield B73 . . 45 E1
Fernwood Croft
 Birmingham B14 . . . . 104 C6
 Tipton DY4 . . . . 51 F4
Fernwood Rd B73 . . . 56 E8
Fernwoods B32 . . . . . 84 B2

Ferrers Cl
 Coventry CV4 . . . . . . 111 F2
 Sutton Coldfield B75 . . 32 D2
Ferrers Rd B77 . . . . . 21 D4
Ferrie Gr WS8 . . . . . . 15 E8
Ferris Gr B27 . . . . . . 88 A1
Festival Ave WS10 . . . 41 C4
Festival Ct
 Cannock WS11 . . . . . . .1 E5
 Dudley DY2 . . . . 62 C5
 Lichfield WS13 . . . . . . .9 A7
Festival Mews WS12 . . .1 F6
Festival Way WV6 . . . 25 B5
Fetherston Cres CV8 . 135 B1
Fetherston Ct 🄴
 CV31 . . . . 161 B2
Fetherston Grange
 B94 . . . . 143 F5
Ffernfail Ct B23 . . . . . 56 E5
Fibbersley WV13,
 WV11 . . . . .26 E4
Fibbersley Bank
 WV13 . . . . .26 F4
Fiddlers Gn B92 . . . . 109 A7
Field Ave B31 . . . . . . 102 F5
Field Barn Rd CV35 . . 160 A1
Field Cl
 Birmingham B26 . . . . . 89 A6
 Bromsgrove B60 . . . . . 150 E6
 Hinckley LE10 . . . . 71 F3
 Kenilworth CV8 . . . . . 148 B5
 Stourbridge DY8 . . . . . 61 A2
 Tamworth B77 . . . . 21 C2
 Walsall, Blakenall Heath
 WS3 . . . . 28 C8
 Walsall WS4 . . . . 15 B2
Field Cottage Dr DY8 . 81 B3
Field Ct Coventry CV2 114 D7
 Walsall WS4 . . . . 15 B2
Fieldfare WS7 . . . . . . 7 D5
Fieldfare Cl B64 . . . . .62 F4
Fieldfare Croft B36 . . 70 A8
Fieldfare Ct DY10 . . . 117 A1
Fieldfare Rd DY9 . . . . 81 D4
Field Farm La B98 . . . 154 D2
Field Farm Rd B77 . . . 21 D1
Fieldgate La
 Kenilworth CV8 . . . . . 147 E5
 Whitnash CV31 . . . . . 162 B2
Fieldgate Lawn CV8 . 147 F6
Fieldgate Trad Est
 WS1 . . . . .28 F1
Field Head La CV34 . 161 B6
Field Head Pl WV6 . . . 24 B4
Fieldhead Rd B11 . . . . 88 A3
Field Ho CV8 . . . . . . 147 F5
Fieldhouse La B62 . . 100 E4
Fieldhouse Rd
 Birmingham B25 . . . . . 88 C8
 Burntwood WS7 . . . . . .7 A7
 Cannock WS12 . . . . . . 1 F7
 Wolverhampton WV4 . . 39 A4
Field La
 Birmingham B32 . . . . 102 B8
 Catherine de B B91 . . . 108 A5
 Clent DY9 . . . . 99 D4
 Great Wyrley WS6 . . . . .4 F3
 Stourbridge DY8 . . . . . 81 A3
 Walsall WS4 . . . . 15 B2
Field Maple Rd B74 . . .44 F6
Field March CV3 . . . . 134 E5
Field Mews DY2 . . . . . 62 E2
Fieldon Cl B90 . . . . . 106 C2
Field Rd Dudley DY2 . . 51 E2
 Lichfield WS13 . . . . . . .3 B3
 Tipton DY4 . . . . 52 A8
 Walsall WS3 . . . . 14 C1
Field Rd Ind Est WS3 . 28 C4
Fields Ct CV34 . . . . . 160 F8
Fieldside Cl CV3 . . . . 114 F3
Fieldside Wlk WV14 . . 40 D8
Field St Bilston WV14 . 40 E1
 Cannock WS11 . . . . . . 1 F3
 Willenhall WV13 . . . . . 27 A2
 Wolverhampton
 WV10 . . . . 163 D4
Fields The WV8 . . . . . .10 F6
Fieldstone View DY3 . . 50 D4
Field View CV31 . . . . 162 B3
Fieldview Cl WV14 . . . 40 E2
Field View Cl CV7 . . . 96 A8
Field View Dr B65 . . . .63 F3
Field Way B94 . . . . . . 143 C6
Fieldways Cl B47 . . . . 125 C7
Field Wlk WS9 . . . . . . 30 B7
Fiery Hill Dr B45 . . . . 138 C8
Fiery Hill Rd B45 . . . . 138 C8
Fife Rd CV5 . . . . 112 F2
Fife St CV11 . . . . 73 A4

Fifield Cl CV11 . . . . . . 73 D2
Fifield Gr B33 . . . . 68 F3
Fifth Ave
  Birmingham B9 . . . . . . 67 F2
  Wolverhampton WV10 . . 11 B2
Filey B77 . . . . .21 F6
Filey Cl WS11 . . . . .4 C8
Filey Rd WV10 . . . . 11 B2
Fillingham Cl B37 . . . . 70 D1
Fillongley Rd CV7 . . . . 92 E3
Filton Ave WS7 . . . . .7 A8
Filton Croft B35 . . . . . 58 A4
Fimbrell Cl DY5 . . . . . . 81 A8
Finbury Cl B92 . . . . .88 F1
Finchall Croft B92 . . . 107 E7
Fincham Cl WV9 . . . . . 11 A3
Finch Cl Coventry CV6 . . 95 C2
  Rowley Regis B65 . . . . . 62 F4
Finch Croft CV7 . . . . . 130 B7
Finchdene Gr WV3 . . . 24 D1
Finch Dr B74 . . . . 45 A5
Finches End B45 . . . . . 69 C5
Finchfield Cl DY8 . . . . 80 C4
Finchfield Gdns WV3 . . 24 E1
Finchfield Hill WV3 . . . 24 C1
Finchfield La WV3 . . . . 38 C8
Finchfield Rd WV3 . . . 24 E1
Finchfield Rd W WV3 . 24 D1
Finchley Ave ☑ B19 . . 66 C8
Finchley Cl DY3 . . . . . . 50 D2
Finchley Rd B44 . . . . . 45 B1
Finchmead Rd B33 . . . 69 E2
Finchpath Rd B70 . . . . 53 A6
Finch Rd B19 . . . . 66 C8
Findlay Rd B14 . . . . . . 86 E1
Findon Cl
  Bulkington CV12 . . . . . 79 C3
  Redditch B97 . . . . 153 A6
Findon Rd B8 . . . . 68 B6
Findon St DY10 . . . . . 116 F6
Finford Croft CV7 . . . 130 B6
Fingal Cl CV3 . . . . 134 C6
Finger Post Dr WS3 . . 15 A5
Fingest Cl CV5 . . . . . . 112 B4
Finham Cres CV8 . . . 148 B6
Finham Flats CV8 . . . 148 B6
Finham Gr CV3 . . . . . 133 C3
Finham Green Rd
  CV3 . . . . 133 B3
Finham Park Sch
  CV3 . . . . 133 A4
Finham Prim Sch
  CV3 . . . . 133 B3
Finham Rd CV8 . . . . . 148 B6
Finings Cl ☑ CV32 . . 156 F2
Finlarigg Dr B15 . . . . . .85 F6
Finlay Ct CV1 . . . . 165 C1
Finmere Rd B28 . . . . . 105 F8
Finmere Way B90 . . . 106 D3
Finnemore Cl CV3 . . . 133 B5
Finnemore Rd B9 . . . . 68 A2
Finney Well Cl WV14 . 40 B3
Finsbury Dr DY5 . . . . . 81 C7
Finsbury Gr B23 . . . . . 56 D6
Finstall Cl
  Birmingham B7 . . . . . . 67 A4
  Sutton Coldfield B72 . . . 46 C1
Finstall Fst Sch B60 137 B1
Finstall Rd
  Bromsgrove B60 . . . . . 151 C8
  Finstall B60 . . . . 137 D1
Finwood Cl B92 . . . . . 107 E8
Finwood Rd CV35 . . . 144 F1
Fir Ave B12 . . . . 87 A5
Firbank Cl B30 . . . . . . 103 E7
Firbank Way WS3 . . . .14 F2
Firbarn Cl B76 . . . . . . 46 D3
Firbeck Gr B44 . . . . . . 45 A1
Firbeck Rd B44 . . . . . . 45 A1
Fir Cl WS12 . . . . 1 D8
Fircroft
  Birmingham B31 . . . . . 102 F8
  Darlaston WV14 . . . . . . 41 A3
  Solihull B91 . . . . 106 F6
  ☑ Wolverhampton
    WV4 . . . . 39 F4
Fir Croft DY5 . . . . 81 C8
Fircroft Cl
  ☑ Cannock WS11 . . . . .2 A3
  Stoke Heath B60 . . . . 150 D6
Fircroft Coll B29 . . . 103 D8
Fircroft Ho B37 . . . . . 70 A2
Firecrest Cl
  Birmingham B23 . . . . . 56 B7
  Cannock WS11 . . . . . . .2 C2
Firecrest Way DY10 . . 117 B1
Firedrake Croft CV1 . 113 F2
Firenze Rd B60 . . . . . 137 C1
Fire Sta B44 . . . . 56 A7

Fire Station Flats
  B30 . . . . 103 F4
Firethorn Cres CV31 . 162 A2
Fir Gr
  Birmingham B14 . . . . . 104 F5
  Coventry CV4 . . . . 112 A2
  Stourbridge DY8 . . . . . 80 D6
  Wolverhampton WV3 . . 25 A1
Firhill Croft B14 . . . . . 104 D2
Firleigh Dr CV12 . . . . . 79 D2
Firmstone Ct DY8 . . . . 80 E7
Firmstone St DY8 . . . . 80 E7
Firsbrook Cl WV6 . . . . 25 A5
Firsbrook Ho WV6 . . . . 25 A5
Firsby Rd B32 . . . . 84 A5
Firs Cl
  Lower Marlbrook
    B60 . . . . 121 D1
  Smethwick B67 . . . . . . 65 A5
Firs Cl The DY10 . . . . 117 A5
Firs Dr B90 . . . . 106 A1
Firs Farm Dr B36 . . . . .68 F7
Firs Ho B36 . . . . .68 F8
Firsholm Cl B73 . . . . . 57 A7
Firs La B67 . . . . 65 A5
Firs Mobile Home Pk The
  ☑ WS11 . . . . .2 A2
Firs Prim Sch B36 . . . .68 F8
Firs Rd DY6 . . . . 60 E6
Firs St DY2 . . . . 51 D1
Fir St DY3 . . . . .49 F7
First Ave
  Birmingham, Bordesley
    Green B9 . . . . 67 E1
  Birmingham, Selly Oak
    B29 . . . . 86 B3
  Birmingham, Tyburn
    B35 . . . . 58 A5
  Birmingham, Witton B6 . 55 F2
  Brownhills WS8 . . . . . . 16 A1
  Coventry CV3 . . . . 114 C1
  Kingswinford DY6 . . . . 50 A1
  Wolverhampton WV10 . 25 E6
First Exhibition Ave
  B40 . . . . 90 D4
Firs The
  Bedworth CV12 . . . . . . 77 E2
  Birmingham B11 . . . . . 87 C6
  Coventry CV5 . . . . 133 B8
  Kidderminster DY10 . . 117 A5
  Meriden CV7 . . . . 92 B1
  Wolverhampton WV11 . 26 B5
First Meadow Piece
  B32 . . . . 84 E4
Firsvale Rd WV11 . . . .26 F5
Firsway WV6 . . . . 24 A2
Firswood Rd B33 . . . . 69 C1
Firth Dr
  Birmingham B14 . . . . . 105 B5
  Halesowen B62 . . . . . . 83 E8
Firth Park Cres B62 . . 83 E8
Fir Tree Ave CV4 . . . . 112 B2
Fir Tree Cl
  Birmingham B44 . . . . . 55 E7
  Redditch B97 . . . . 153 A6
  Tamworth B79 . . . . 20 E7
Fir Tree Dr Dudley DY3 . 50 E7
  Walsall WS5 . . . . 43 B4
Fir Tree Gr
  Nuneaton CV11 . . . . . . 78 D8
  Sutton Coldfield B73 . . . 45 F1
Fir Tree Prim Sch
  WS5 . . . . 43 A4
Firtree Rd B24 . . . . . . 57 B2
Fir Tree Rd WV3 . . . . . 38 D8
Fisher Cl B45 . . . . 101 E2
Fisher Rd
  Coventry CV6 . . . . 113 E8
  Oldbury B69 . . . . 64 C7
  Walsall WS3 . . . . 13 F2
Fisher's Ct CV34 . . . . 160 D4
Fishers Dr B90 . . . . . 125 F5
Fisher St
  Brierley Hill DY5 . . . . . 61 B2
  Cannock WS12 . . . . . . .1 F6
  Dudley DY2 . . . . 51 D1
  Tipton, Burnt Tree DY4 . 52 A3
  Tipton, Great Bridge
    DY4 . . . . 52 D5
  Willenhall WV13 . . . . . 27 C2
  Wolverhampton WV3 . . 39 B8
Fish Hill B97 . . . . 153 E4
Fish House La B60 . . . 150 E4
Fishing Line Rd B97 . 153 E6
Fishley Cl WS3 . . . . . . 14 C4
Fishley La WS3 . . . . . . 14 D5
Fishponds Cl CV8 . . . 147 E3
Fishpool Cl B36 . . . . . 68 C8
Fishpool La CV7 . . . . . 91 B5
Fistral Gdns WV3 . . . . .38 F7

Fitchet's Bank WS7 . . . .7 F6
Fithern Cl DY3 . . . . . . 50 E5
Fitters Mill Cl B5 . . . . 86 E6
Fitton Ave DY6 . . . . . . 61 A5
Fitton St CV11 . . . . . . 73 B3
Fitzgerald Pl DY5 . . . . 81 B6
Fitzguy Cl B70 . . . . . . 53 E1
Fitzmaurice Rd WV11 . 27 A7
Fitz Roy Ave B17 . . . . .84 F7
Fitzroy Cl CV2 . . . . . . 115 B6
Fitzroy Rd B31 . . . . . . 102 D3
Fivefield Rd CV7 . . . . . 94 E5
Five Fields Rd WV12 . . 27 A5
Five Oaks Rd WV13 . . . 40 E8
Fives Gr WS7 . . . . .6 C8
Five Ways
  Birmingham B33 . . . . . 68 D2
  Birmingham, Bordesley
    Green B9 . . . . 67 D2
  Birmingham, Ladywood
    B16 . . . . 66 B1
  Churchill DY10 . . . . . . 98 A5
  Cradley Heath B64 . . . . 82 C8
  Dudley DY3 . . . . 50 D3
  Wolverhampton, Dunstall Hill
    WV3 . . . . 25 C4
  Wolverhampton WV3 . . 38 C7
  Wroxall CV35 . . . . 145 F1
Five Ways Prim Sch
  WS12 . . . . .2 D2
Five Ways Rd CV35 . . 145 F1
Five Ways Sta B15 . . . .86 B8
Flackwell Rd B23 . . . . 56 E7
Fladbury Cl
  Dudley DY2 . . . . 62 D3
  Redditch B98 . . . . 159 B8
Fladbury Cres B29 . . . 85 D1
Fladbury Gdns B20 . . . 66 C5
Fladbury Pl ☑ B19 . . . 66 C7
Flamboro' Cl CV3 . . . 134 F8
Flamborough Cl B34 . 69 A7
Flamborough Way
  WV14 . . . . 51 B7
Flamville Rd LE10 . . . 76 B5
Flanders Cl B98 . . . . . 154 D5
Flanders Dr DY6 . . . . . 60 D8
Flash La WV4 . . . . 37 E2
Flash Rd B69 . . . . 64 A7
Flatlea B31 . . . . 102 F4
Flats La WS14 . . . . . . 19 A6
Flats The B61 . . . . . . 136 F3
Flatts The WS10 . . . . . 41 E7
Flaunden Cl CV5 . . . . 112 B4
Flavel Cres CV31 . . . . 161 F7
Flavell Ave WV14 . . . . 40 D1
Flavell Cl B32 . . . . . . 84 B1
Flavells La
  Birmingham B25 . . . . . 88 C8
  Dudley DY3 . . . . 50 B2
Flavell St DY1 . . . . . . 51 B6
Flavel Rd B60 . . . . . . 150 E7
Flax Cl B47 . . . . 125 A5
Flax Gdns B38 . . . . . . 123 F8
Flaxhall St WS2 . . . . . 42 B8
Flax Hill Jun Sch B79 21 B7
Flaxley Cl B33 . . . . . . .68 F3
Flaxley Parkway B33 . 68 E4
Flaxley Rd B33 . . . . . . 68 E4
Flaxton Gr B33 . . . . . . 69 A4
Flaxton Wlk WV6 . . . . 25 A5
Flecknoe Cl B36 . . . . . 58 C1
Flecknose St CV3 . . . 134 C6
Fledburgh Dr B76 . . . . 46 D4
Fleet St
  Birmingham B3 . . . . . . 164 A3
  Coventry CV1 . . . . 165 B3
Fleetwood Gr B26 . . . . 69 A1
Fleetwood Ho ☑ B13 .86 F4
Fleming Pl WS2 . . . . . . 28 A6
Fleming Rd
  Birmingham B32 . . . . . 84 D5
  Hinckley LE10 . . . . 74 F7
  Walsall WS2 . . . . 28 A6
Fletchamstead Highway
  CV5 . . . . 132 D7
Fletcher Gr B93 . . . . . 128 B4
Fletcher Rd
  Hinckley LE10 . . . . 75 E7
  Walsall WV12 . . . . 13 D1
  Willenhall WV12 . . . . . 27 D8
Fletcher's La WV13 . . . 27 C2
Fletcher St DY9 . . . . . .81 F5
Fletchers Wlk B3 . . . . 164 B2
Fletchworth Gate
  CV5 . . . . 132 D8
Fletchworth Gate Ind Est
  CV4 . . . . 132 D8
Fletton Gr B14 . . . . . . 105 A3
Fleur de-lys Ct CV34 161 B8
Flinkford Cl WS5 . . . . 43 D6

Flinn Cl WS14 . . . . 9 D7
Flint Cl DY10 . . . . 116 E2
Flint Green Rd B27 . . . 88 B3
Flintham Cl B92 . . . . . 88 E3
Flint Ho ☑ WV3 . . . . . 25 C4
Flintway The B33 . . . . 68 E4
Floodgate St B5 . . . . . .66 F1
Flood St DY2 . . . . 51 D1
Flood Street Island
  DY2 . . . . 62 D8
Flora Cl B79 . . . . 21 C7
Flora Rd B25 . . . . 88 B7
Florence Ave
  Birmingham B11 . . . . . 87 C5
  ☑ Sutton Coldfield B73 . 57 B7
  Wolverhampton WV4 . . 40 A4
Florence Bldgs ☑
  B29 . . . . .85 F2
Florence Cl CV12 . . . . .95 F8
Florence Dr ☑ B73 . . . 57 B7
Florence Gr
  ☑ Birmingham B18 . . . 65 E4
  West Bromwich B71 . . . 42 E1
Florence Pl ☑ B12 . . . 87 A6
Florence Rd
  Birmingham, Acock's Green
    B27 . . . . 88 D4
  Birmingham, Handsworth
    B21 . . . . 65 D8
  Birmingham, King's Heath
    B14 . . . . 104 F8
  Codsall WV8 . . . . 10 C3
  Coventry CV3 . . . . 115 A2
  Oldbury B69 . . . . 63 E7
  Smethwick B66 . . . . . . 65 B4
  Sutton Coldfield B73 . . . 57 B7
  Tipton DY4 . . . . 52 A7
  West Bromwich B70 . . . 53 E1
Florence St
  Birmingham B1 . . . . . . 164 B1
  Cannock WS12 . . . . . . .2 B7
  Walsall WS1 . . . . 29 A1
Florence Villas B11 . . 87 C7
Florendine St B77 . . . . 21 F5
Florendine Com Prim
  Sch B77 . . . . .21 F5
Florian Gr WS10 . . . . . 41 E7
Florian Way LE10 . . . . 71 A1
Florida Way DY6 . . . . . 61 A6
Florin Cl CV4 . . . . 131 E6
Flowerdale Cl WV14 . 51 B8
Flowerdale Dr CV2 . . . 114 B6
Floyd Gr CV7 . . . . 130 C7
Floyds La WS4 . . . . . . 29 C6
Floyer Rd B10 . . . . .67 F1
Flude Rd CV7 . . . . 95 C6
Flyford Cl B98 . . . . . . 153 F1
Flyford Croft B29 . . . .84 F2
Flynt Ave CV5 . . . . . . 112 B6
Fockbury Mill La
  B61 . . . . 136 E5
Fockbury Rd B61 . . . . 136 B5
Focus Pk B90 . . . . 126 E8
Foden Cl WS14 . . . . . . .17 F6
Foden Rd B42 . . . . 55 A7
Foinavon Cl B65 . . . . .62 F6
Fold St WV1 . . . . 163 B2
Fold The
  Birmingham B38 . . . . . 104 A1
  Darlaston WS10 . . . . . . 41 D6
  Wolverhampton WV4 . . 38 F4
Foldyard Cl B76 . . . . . 58 A8
Foleshill CE Prim Sch
  CV6 . . . . 96 A2
Foleshill Rd CV1,
  CV6 . . . . 113 D6
Foley Ave WV6 . . . . . . 24 C3
Foley Church Cl B74 . 31 A2
Foley Ct B74 . . . . .30 F1
Foley Dr WV6 . . . . 24 C3
Foley Gdns B60 . . . . . 150 E4
Foley Ind Est DY11 . . 116 D3
Foley Park Fst Sch
  DY11 . . . . 116 D3
Foley Rd
  Birmingham B8 . . . . . . 68 B5
  Stourbridge DY9 . . . . . 81 C2
Foley Rd E B74 . . . . . . 31 A2
Foley Rd W B74 . . . . . 30 E1
Foley St WS10 . . . . . . 42 A3
Foley Wood Cl B74 . . 30 E1
Foliot Fields B25 . . . . 88 D8
Folkes Rd DY9 . . . . . . 82 A6
Folkestone Croft B36 . 68 E8
Folkland Gn CV6 . . . . 113 A7
Folliott Rd B33 . . . . . . 69 B3
Follyhouse Cl WS1 . . .42 F7
Follyhouse La WS1 . . .42 F7
Folly The B97 . . . . 158 D8
Fontenaye Rd B79 . . . .20 F7

Fontley Cl B26 . . . . . . 69 A2
Fontmell Cl CV2 . . . . . 115 A4
Fontwell Rd WV10 . . . 11 D4
Footherley La WS14 . . 17 C4
Footherley Rd WS14 . . 17 C5
Fordbridge Cl B97 . . . 153 C1
Fordbridge Inf Sch
  B37 . . . . 70 A5
Fordbridge Rd B37 . . . 70 A5
Ford Brook La WS3 . . . 15 B2
Ford Cotts CV33 . . . . 157 F2
Forder Gr B14 . . . . . . 105 A2
Fore Way Gdns
  B38 . . . . 123 D7
Fordfield Rd B33 . . . . 69 C4
Fordham Gr WV9 . . . . 11 A3
Fordhouse La B30 . . . 104 B6
Fordhouse Rd
  Bromsgrove B60 . . . . . 137 B6
  Wolverhampton WV10 . 11 D1
Fordhouse Rd Ind Est
  WV10 . . . . 11 D1
Fordhouse Road Ind Est
  WV10 . . . . 25 D8
Fordraught La B62 . . . 101 B1
Ford Rd B61 . . . . 136 E1
Fordrift The B37 . . . . . 90 A6
Fordrough B25 . . . . . . .87 F7
Fordrough Ave B9 . . . . 67 E3
Fordrough La B9 . . . . . 67 E2
Fordrough The
  Birmingham B31 . . . . . 103 C1
  Hollywood B90 . . . . . . 125 C7
  Sutton Coldfield B74 . . . 32 A1
Fords Rd B90 . . . . 125 E6
Ford St
  Birmingham B18 . . . . . 66 B5
  Coventry CV1 . . . . 165 C3
  Nuneaton CV10 . . . . . . 72 E4
  Smethwick B67 . . . . . . 64 F6
  Walsall WS2 . . . . 42 C7
Fordwater Rd B44 . . . .44 F6
Fordwell Cl CV5 . . . . . 112 F3
Foredraft Cl B32 . . . . 84 C2
Foredraft St B63 . . . . 82 D5
Foredrought B80 . . . . 159 E4
Foredrift Cl B98 . . . . 153 E2
Foredrove La B92 . . . 107 A4
Foregate St B96 . . . . 158 E1
Forelands Gr B61 . . . 150 D8
Foreland Way CV6 . . . 95 A3
Fore St B2 . . . . 164 C2
Forest Ave WS3 . . . . . 28 D7
Forest Cl
  Lickey End B60 . . . . . . 137 B6
  Smethwick B66 . . . . . . 64 F4
  Sutton Coldfield B74 . . . 44 E7
Forest Ct
  Birmingham B13 . . . . . 87 A3
  Coventry CV5 . . . . 112 A4
  Dorridge B93 . . . . 127 F3
  Willenhall WV12 . . . . . 27 C8
Forest Dale B45 . . . . . 122 B6
Forest Dr
  Birmingham B17 . . . . . 85 D6
  Cradley Heath B64 . . . . 62 F3
Forester's Ct CV33 . . 133 E6
Forester Way DY10 . . 116 E3
Forest Gate WV12 . . . 27 D8
Forest Glade WS6 . . . . .4 F2
Forest Hill Rd B26 . . . 89 C5
Forest La WS2 . . . . . . 28 D5
Forest Lawns B74 . . . 31 C3
Forest Oak Sch B36 . .58 E1
Forest Pk B76 . . . . . . 46 E4
Forest Pl WS3 . . . . . . 28 E6
Forest Rd
  Birmingham B68 . . . . . 84 C7
  Birmingham, Moseley
    B13 . . . . 87 A3
  Birmingham, South Yardley
    B25 . . . . 88 C6
  Dorridge B93 . . . . 127 F3
  Dudley DY1 . . . . 51 C4
  Hinckley LE10 . . . . 75 F8
Forest View B97 . . . . 158 E6
Forest Way
  Great Wyrley WS6 . . . . .5 A1
  Hollywood B47 . . . . . . 125 B6
  Nuneaton CV10 . . . . . . 72 E4
Forfar Wlk B38 . . . . . 103 D2
Forfield Pl CV31 . . . . 162 A7
Forfield Rd CV6 . . . . . 112 C5
Forge Ave B60 . . . . . . 151 B2
Forge Cl
  Hammerwich WS7 . . . . 7 D5
  Wolverhampton WV8 . . 10 C1
Forge Croft B76 . . . . . 58 B6
Forge Dr B61 . . . . 136 F3

Forge La
  Aldridge, Leighswood
    WS9 . . . . 30 A5
  Aldridge, Mill Green
    WS9 . . . . 30 F7
  Belbroughton DY9 . . . . 119 D7
  Blakedown DY10 . . . . . 98 B1
  Burntwood WS7 . . . . . .7 F6
  Cradley Heath B64 . . . . 82 B8
  Halesowen B62 . . . . . . 83 C5
  Kingswinford DY6 . . . . 60 A8
  Lichfield WS13 . . . . . . .3 A1
  Shenstone B74, WS14 . . 31 C1
  Sutton Coldfield B76 . . . 58 B5
  West Bromwich B71 . . . 54 A6
Forge Mill Farm★
  B71 . . . . 54 B6
Forge Mill Needle Mus★
  B98 . . . . 153 F6
Forge Mill Rd B98 . . . 153 F6
Forge Rd
  Darlaston WS10 . . . . . . 41 C6
  Kenilworth CV8 . . . . . . 148 A5
  Stourbridge DY8 . . . . . 80 F6
  Walsall WS3 . . . . 14 C5
  Willenhall WV12 . . . . . 27 C4
Forge St Cannock WS12 . .2 C4
  Wednesbury WS10 . . . . 41 E4
Forge The B63 . . . . . . 82 B8
Forge Trad Est B62 . . 83 C5
Forge Way
  Coventry CV6 . . . . 95 C3
  Oldbury B69 . . . . 63 E6
Forhill Ho B38 . . . . . . 123 F3
Forknell Ave CV2 . . . . 114 C5
Formans Rd B11 . . . . . 87 E3
Formans Trad Est
  B11 . . . . 87 D3
Formby Ave WV6 . . . . 23 D4
Formby Way WS3 . . . . 14 A3
Forrell Gr B31 . . . . . . 123 B7
Forrest Ave
  Cannock WS11 . . . . . . .4 E8
  Essington WV11 . . . . . . 13 A4
Forrest Ct ☑ WS13 . . . .9 B7
Forresters Cl LE10 . . . .75 F6
Forresters Rd LE10 . . .75 F6
Forrester St WS2 . . . . 28 C2
Forrester Street Prec ☑
  WS2 . . . . 28 C2
Forrest Rd CV8 . . . . . 147 E4
Forryan Rd LE10 . . . . .75 F7
Forshaw Heath La
  B94 . . . . 141 A7
Forshaw Heath Rd
  B94 . . . . 125 C1
Forster St
  Birmingham B7 . . . . . . 67 A3
  Smethwick B67 . . . . . . 64 E7
Forsythia Cl B31 . . . . 102 F8
Forsythia Gr WV8 . . . . 10 A3
Fort Cres WS9 . . . . . . 16 A3
Forth Dr B37 . . . . 70 B4
Forth Gr B38 . . . . 123 E8
Forth Way B62 . . . . . . 83 E8
Forties B77 . . . . 35 E2
Fort Ind Pk The B35 . .57 F1
Fortnum Cl B33 . . . . . 69 D2
Forton Cl WV6 . . . . . . 24 B2
Fort Parkway B24, B35,
  B36 . . . . 57 D1
Fort Sh Pk The B24 . . 57 C1
Forum Rd B40 . . . . . . 90 E3
Forum The ☑ WS11 . . .1 E1
Forward Cotts B48 . . 138 F6
Forward Rd B26 . . . . . 90 A3
Fosberry Cl CV34 . . . 161 B8
Fosbrooke Rd B10 . . . 88 A8
Fossdale Rd B77 . . . . 36 A4
Fosse Cl LE10 . . . . . . 76 A5
Fosseway WS14 . . . . . .9 A5
Fosseway Dr B23 . . . . 56 E8
Fosseway La WS13,
  WS14 . . . . .8 E4
Fosseway Rd CV3 . . . 133 B4
Fossil Dr B45 . . . . 122 A7
Foster Ave
  Cannock WS12 . . . . . . .1 F6
  Studley B80 . . . . 159 E3
  Wolverhampton WV14 . 40 B1
Foster Gdns B18 . . . . .65 F6
Foster Gn WV6 . . . . . . 23 E3
Foster Pl DY8 . . . . 80 E6
Foster Rd
  Coventry CV6 . . . . 113 B7
  Wolverhampton WV10 . 25 D7
Foster St E DY8 . . . . . 81 A5

Foster St
Darlaston WS10 41 D7
8 Stourbridge DY8 81 A5
Walsall WS3 28 D8
Foster Way B5 86 C5
Fotherley Brook Rd
WS9 30 F5
Founder Cl CV4 131 F7
Foundry La
Smethwick B66 65 D6
Walsall WS3 14 E3
Foundry Prim Sch
B18 65 E6
Foundry Rd
Birmingham B18 65 E5
Kingswinford DY6 60 C8
Foundry St
Dudley WV14 40 C1
Kingswinford DY6 60 C8
Tipton DY4 51 E8
Fountain Arc 4 DY1 51 C1
Fountain Cl B31 122 E6
Fountain La
Tipton DY4, WV14 51 E8
West Bromwich B69 53 A1
Fountain Rd B17 65 C1
Fountains Rd WS3 13 E2
Fountains Way WS3 13 E2
Four Acres B32 84 C4
Four Ashes Rd B93 127 E4
Four Crosses Rd WS4 15 C1
Four Dwellings High Sch
B32 84 B5
Fourlands Ave B72 57 D7
Fourlands Rd B31 102 E6
Four Oaks Cl B98 158 D8
Four Oaks Common Rd
B74 31 F3
Four Oaks Ct B74 32 B1
Four Oaks Dr B61 121 B1
Four Oaks Inf Sch
B74 31 E4
Four Oaks Jun Sch
B74 31 E4
Four Oaks Rd B74 32 A1
Four Oaks Sta B74 46 B8
Four Pounds Ave
CV5 112 F3
Four Stones Cl B91 107 A1
Four Stones Gr B5 86 D6
Fourth Ave
Birmingham, Bordesley
Green B9 67 F2
Birmingham, Selly Oak
B29 86 C3
Brownhills WS8 7 A1
Wolverhampton WV10 25 E6
Four Winds Rd DY2 62 E6
Fowey Cl B76 58 A7
Fowey Rd B34 68 F6
Fowgay Dr B91 106 F1
Fowler Cl Perton WV6 23 E6
Smethwick B66 65 A8
Fowler Rd
Coventry CV6 113 B4
Sutton Coldfield B75 47 B5
Fowler St
Birmingham B7 67 B6
Wolverhampton WV2 39 C6
Fowlmere Rd B42 55 B8
Fownhope Cl B98 154 E3
Fow Oak CV4 111 C2
Fox Ave
Nuneaton CV10 73 D7
Willenhall WV13 27 A2
Foxbury Dr B93 128 B3
Fox Cl
Sutton Coldfield B75 46 F7
Tamworth B77 35 C8
Foxcote Ave B21 65 E7
Foxcote Cl
Redditch B98 154 F4
Solihull B90 126 D8
Foxcote Dr B90 126 D8
Foxcote La B63, DY9 82 B4
Fox Covert DY8 80 E5
Fox Cres B11 87 D4
Foxcroft Cl WS7 7 B5
Foxdale Dr DY5 61 B3
Foxdale Gr B33 69 C3
Foxdale Wlk 8
CV31 162 C6
Foxes Cl B60 138 B5
Foxes Mdw
Birmingham B30 103 F4
Sutton Coldfield B76 58 A8
Foxes Rake WS11 1 E3
Foxes Ridge B64 82 E8
Foxes Way
Balsall Common CV7 130 B6
Warwick CV34 160 D4
Foxfield B31 102 F4
Foxfield Dr DY8 81 A3
Foxfields Way WS12 1 C7
Fox Foot Dr DY5 61 C4
Foxford Cl
Birmingham B36 58 D1
Sutton Coldfield B72 57 D7
Foxford Cres CV2 96 B4
Foxford Sch & Com Arts
Coll CV6 96 A5
Foxglove B77 22 A4
Foxglove Cl
Bedworth CV12 77 E1
Birmingham B27 88 B1
Coventry CV6 95 C2
Featherstone WV10 12 B7
Lichfield WS14 9 A5
Walsall WS3 15 A5
Wednesfield WV11 26 E5
Foxglove Cres B37 69 E3
Foxglove Rd DY1 51 A4
Foxglove Way
Birmingham B21 65 D7
Lickey End B60 137 C6
Fox Glove Way B23 56 B7
Foxglove Wlk WS12 2 C7
Fox & Goose Sh Ctr
B8 68 C5
Fox Gr B27 88 A2
Fox Green Cres B27 88 A2
Fox Hill B29 103 C8
Foxhill Barns B48 138 E5
Foxhill Cl WS12 2 D2
Fox Hill Cl B29 103 C8
Foxhill La B48 138 E5
Fox Hill Rd B75 32 F2
Foxhills Cl CV11 74 C1
Foxhill's Cl WS7 7 A5
Foxhills Pk DY2 62 C4
Foxhills Rd
Stourbridge DY8 60 D1
Wolverhampton WV4 38 C4
Foxholes La B97 158 A6
Foxholes The DY10 116 F8
Foxhollies Dr B63 82 E4
Fox Hollies L Ctr B27 88 B1
Fox Hollies Rd
Birmingham B27, B28 88 A1
Sutton Coldfield B76 47 B2
Fox Hollies Sch
Birmingham, Acock's Green
B27 88 A1
Birmingham, Moseley
B13 86 E2
Foxhollow B61 150 D8
Fox Hollow WV6 24 C2
Fox Hollow Cl B45 122 C7
Foxhope Cl B38 104 B2
Foxhunt Rd B63 82 E2
Fox La
Bromsgrove B61 150 E8
Lichfield WS13 3 A5
Foxland Ave
Birmingham B45 122 C7
Great Wyrley WS6 5 A3
Foxland Cl
Birmingham B37 70 D2
Cheswick Green B90 126 D4
Foxlands Ave WV4 38 D3
Foxlands Cres WV4 38 C3
Foxlands Dr
Dudley DY3 50 D5
Gospel End Village
WV4 38 D3
Sutton Coldfield B72 57 D7
Foxlea Rd B63 82 D1
Foxley Dr B91 108 B5
Foxlydiate Cres B97 153 A4
Foxlydiate La B97 152 F3
Foxlydiate Mews 3
B97 153 A4
Foxmeadow Cl DY3 50 E7
Fox Mill Est B11 87 D3
Foxoak Ent Ctr B64 62 D1
Foxoak St B64 62 C1
Fox's La WV6 25 C4
Fox St Birmingham B5 164 D3
Dudley DY1 51 C6
Foxtail Way WS12 2 E4
Foxton Ct LE10 75 B7
Foxton Man B74 32 A1
Foxton Rd
Birmingham B8 67 F4
Coventry CV3 114 E1
Foxwalks Ave B61 150 D8
Foxwell Gr B9 68 C3
Foxwell Rd B9 68 C3
Fox Wlk WS9 16 B3
Foxwood Ave B43 44 B2
Foxwood Dr CV3 135 D7
Foxwood Gr B37 69 F5
Foxwood Rd B78 36 F8
Foxyards Cl DY4 51 D5
Foxyards Prim Sch
DY4 51 C5
Foxyards Rd DY4 51 D5
Foyle Rd B38 103 F1
Fozdar Cres WV14 40 B1
Fradley Cl B30 103 D4
Framefield Dr B91 107 F6
Framlingham Gr
Kenilworth CV8 148 C6
Perton WV6 24 A3
Frampton Cl
Birmingham, Bournville
B30 103 D7
Birmingham, Chelmsley
Wood B37 70 D3
Frampton Way B43 44 D5
Frampton Wlk CV2 114 F4
Frances Ave CV34 161 A7
Frances Cres CV12 78 A3
Frances Dr WS3 14 B2
Frances Havergal Cl 2
CV31 161 F6
Frances Rd
Baginton CV8 133 F3
Birmingham, King's Norton
B30 104 A5
Birmingham, Lozells
B19 66 C8
Birmingham, Stockland
Green B23 56 D3
Franche Fst Sch
DY11 116 B8
Franche Mid Sch
DY11 116 B8
Franche Rd DY11 116 C8
Franchise Gdns WS10 41 F6
Franchise St
Birmingham B42 55 E2
Darlaston WS10 41 F6
Kidderminster DY11 116 C5
Franciscan Rd CV3 133 D8
Francis Cl
1 Kingswinford DY6 60 D8
Sutton Coldfield B74 44 F8
Francis Gibbs Gdns 1
CV31 162 A4
Francis Rd
Birmingham, Acock's Green
B27 88 D5
Birmingham, Edgbaston
B16 66 A1
Birmingham, South Yardley
B25 88 A6
Birmingham, Stechford
B33 68 D2
Bromsgrove B60 150 F7
Lichfield WS13 3 A2
Smethwick B67 64 D4
Stourbridge DY8 80 C5
Francis St
Birmingham B7 67 A4
Coventry CV6 113 E7
West Bromwich B70 53 D1
Wolverhampton WV1 25 C4
Francis Ward Cl B71 53 A8
Francis Wlk B31 123 A7
Frankburn Rd B74 44 F8
Frank F Harrison Comp
Sch WS2 27 F7
Frank Fisher Way
B70 53 C2
Frankfort St B19 66 D6
Frank Freeman Ct
DY10 116 F8
Frankholmes Dr B90 127 A6
Frankland Rd CV6 96 A1
Frankley Ave B62 83 F5
Frankley Beeches Rd
B31 102 D3
Frankley Com High Sch
B45 101 F1
Frankley Gn B32 101 D5
Frankley Green La
B32 101 E5
Frankley Hill La B32 102 A4
Frankley Ind Pk B45 102 B1
Frankley La B31, B32 102 D6
Frankley Lodge Rd
B31 102 D4
Frankley Mid Sch
B45 102 B2
Frankley Rd B68 84 B8
Frankley Terr B17 85 B5
Franklin Ct CV11 73 D1
Franklin Dr WS7 7 B7
Franklin Gr CV4 111 E1
Franklin Rd
Birmingham B30 103 F5
Nuneaton CV11 73 D1
Whitnash CV31 162 A3
Franklins Gdns CV3 115 B1
Franklin St B18 65 E5
Franklin Way B30 103 F6
Franklyn Cl WV6 23 E5
Frankpledge Rd CV3 133 E7
Frank Rd B67 64 E6
Frank St
Birmingham B12 86 F7
Nuneaton CV11 73 B3
Franks Way B33 68 E2
Frank Tommey Cl 5
B65 63 C1
Frankton Ave CV3 133 C5
Frankton Cl
Redditch B98 159 E8
Solihull B92 89 B2
Frankton Gr B9 68 B2
Frank Walsh Ho CV1 165 C4
Frankwell Dr CV2 96 E1
Fraser Cl CV10 72 B6
Fraser Rd
Birmingham B11 87 D5
Coventry CV6 95 A1
Fraser St WV14 40 E6
Frayne Ave DY6 60 C7
Freasley Cl B90 106 D3
Freasley Rd B34 69 E6
Freda Eddy Ct 3
DY10 116 E6
Freda Rd B70 53 D1
Freda Rise B69 63 D8
Fredas Gr B17 85 A4
Frederick Ave LE10 71 B2
Frederick Bird Prim Sch
CV2 113 F5
Frederick Ct B77 21 E3
Frederick Eary Ho
B98 159 B7
Frederick Neal Ave
CV5 111 D4
Frederick Rd
Birmingham, Aston B6 66 F8
Birmingham, Beech Lanes
B68 84 D7
Birmingham, Edgbaston
B15 86 B8
Birmingham, Gravelly Hill
B23 56 E2
Birmingham, Selly Oak
B29 85 D2
Birmingham, Sparkhill
B11 87 C4
Birmingham, Stechford
B33 68 D3
Sutton Coldfield B73 46 A2
Wolverhampton WV11 26 C5
Frederick Rd (Road 1)
DY10 116 F1
Fredericks Cl DY8 80 E4
Frederick St
Birmingham B1 66 C4
Walsall WS2 28 D1
West Bromwich B70 53 C4
Wolverhampton WV2 163 B1
Frederick William St 1
WV13 27 B2
Fred Lee Gr CV3 133 D4
Fred Smith Cl WS10 42 B5
Freeburn Cswy CV4 132 C7
Freeford Gdns WS14 9 E6
Freehold St CV1 113 F4
Freeland Gr 3 DY6 60 F4
Freeman Cl CV10 72 D4
Freeman Ct DY11 116 B3
Freeman Dr B76 46 F4
Freeman Pl WV14 40 E8
Freeman Rd
Birmingham B7 67 B6
Wednesbury WS10 42 D3
Freemans Cl CV32 156 E2
Freeman's La LE10 76 A5
Freeman St
Birmingham B5 164 C2
Coventry CV6 113 F6
Wolverhampton WV10 25 F2
Freemantle Ct B37 69 F5
Freemantle Ho B24 57 D3
Freemount Sq B43 54 E7
Freer Dr WS7 7 E7
Freer Rd B6 66 E8
Freers Mews CV34 160 B4
Freer St
Nuneaton CV11 73 E2
Freer St *continued*
Walsall WS1 28 F2
Freesland Rise CV10 72 B6
Freeth Rd WS8 7 A1
Freeth St
Birmingham B16 65 F2
Oldbury B69 63 F8
Freezeland St WV14 40 B6
Fremantle Dr WS12 2 F2
Fremantle Ho B34 69 E6
Fremont Dr DY1 50 E3
French Ave B78 20 C1
French Rd DY2 51 F1
Frensham Cl
Birmingham B37 70 C2
Cheslyn Hay WS6 4 E4
Frensham Dr CV10 72 B5
Frensham Way B17 85 C6
Frenshaw Gr B44 55 F7
Freshfield Cl CV5 94 C1
Freshwater Dr DY5 81 B8
Freshwater Gr 1
CV31 162 C6
Fretton Cl CV6 113 F7
Freville Cl B79 21 A5
Frevill Rd CV6 114 B8
Friardale Cl WS10 42 D3
Friar Park Rd WS10 42 D3
Friar's Alley WS13 9 B7
Friars Cl
Binley Woods CV3 135 E7
Stourbridge DY8 60 C3
Friars Gate B90 126 E7
Friars Gorse DY7 80 C8
Friars' Rd CV1 165 B2
Friars St CV34 160 D6
Friar St WS10 42 B3
Friars Wlk
Birmingham B37 70 D2
Tamworth B77 21 C3
Friary Ave
Lichfield WS13 9 A6
Solihull B90 127 A6
Friary Cl
Birmingham B20 54 F3
Hinckley LE10 71 E1
Friary Cres WS4 29 C6
Friary Dr B74 31 F3
Friary Gdns
Birmingham B21 54 D2
Lichfield WS13 9 A7
Friary Rd
Birmingham B20 54 E3
Lichfield WS13 9 A7
Friary St CV11 73 B5
Friary The WS13 9 A7
Friday Acre WS13 3 A2
Friday Bridge 6 B1 66 C1
Friday La B92 108 D4
Friesland Dr WV1 26 B3
Friezeland Rd WS2 28 B2
Friezland La WS8 16 A5
Friezland Way WS8 16 A5
Frilsham Way CV5 112 B4
Fringe Green Cl B60 151 A7
Fringe Meadow Rd
B98 154 F6
Frinton Gr B21 65 C7
Frisby Ct CV11 73 E2
Frisby Rd CV4 111 E2
Friston Ave B16 66 B1
Friswell Dr CV6 113 F8
Friswell Ho 3 CV2 114 D8
Frith Way LE10 71 A3
Frobisher Cl
Great Wyrley WS6 4 F1
Hinckley LE10 71 D4
Frobisher Rd CV3 133 C5
Frobisher Way B66 64 D7
Frodesley Rd B26 89 B8
Froggatt Rd WV14 40 D7
Froggatts Ride B76 46 F3
Frog La
Balsall Common CV7 130 A5
Lichfield WS13 9 B7
Frogmere Cl CV5 112 C6
Frogmill Rd B45 102 B2
Frogmoor Ho B26 88 E7
Frogmore La CV8 129 F2
Frome Cl DY3 50 D2
Frome Dr WV11 26 C5
Frome Ho 4 DY1 61 E8
Frome Way B14 104 D6
Front Cotts B48 138 F6
Frost St WV2 40 A6
Froxmere Cl B91 127 C8
Froyle Cl WV6 24 C5
Froysell St WV13 27 B2
Fryer Ave CV32 156 E3
Fryer Rd B31 123 B7
Fryers Cl WS3 28 B7
Fryers Rd WS2, WS3 28 A7
Fryer St WV1 163 C3
Frythe Cl CV8 148 C6
Fuchsia Cl 3 CV2 96 B2
Fuchsia Dr WV9 10 F3
Fugelmere Cl B17 84 F7
Fulbrook Cl B98 154 C5
Fulbrook Gr B29 102 F8
Fulbrook Rd
Coventry CV2 96 C2
Dudley DY1 51 A1
Fulfen Prim Sch WS7 7 D7
Fulford Dr B76 58 B5
Fulford Gr B26 89 C6
Fulford Hall Rd B90,
B94 125 D3
Fulham Rd B11 87 B5
Fullbrook Cl B90 127 A5
Fullbrook Rd WS5 42 E5
Fullelove Rd WS8 16 A7
Fullers Cl CV6 112 F7
Fullerton Cl WV8 10 E1
Fullwood Cl CV2 96 E2
Fullwood Cres DY1,
DY2 61 F6
Fullwoods End WV14 40 C1
Fulmar Cres DY10 117 B2
Fulmer Wlk B18 66 A3
Fulton Cl B60 137 B1
Fulwell Gr B44 56 A8
Fulwell Mews B37 90 B8
Fulwood Ave B62 83 F8
Furber Pl DY6 60 F6
Furlong Ct B63 82 C6
Furlong La B63 82 D6
Furlong Mdw B31 103 C2
Furlong Rd CV1 165 C1
Furlongs Rd DY3 50 D6
Furlongs The
Stourbridge DY8 81 B3
Wolverhampton WV11 26 B5
Furlong The WS10 41 E5
Furlong Wlk DY3 50 D4
Furnace Cl CV12 78 D3
Furnace Hill B63 83 B5
Furnace La B63 83 B5
Furnace Par DY4 51 E6
Furnace Rd
Bedworth CV12 78 D4
Dudley DY2 62 C8
Furness B77 21 D3
Furness Cl WS3 13 F3
Furnivall Cres WS13 3 D1
Furr Marsh The
CV34 160 B4
Furrows The B60 150 D6
Furst St WS8 16 A8
Furzebank Way WV12 27 E4
Furze Way WS5 43 E8
Fylde Ho CV2 114 D4
Fynford Rd CV6 113 B5

G

Gable Croft WS14 9 F6
Gables The
Kingswinford DY6 60 B8
Sutton Coldfield B24 57 D4
Gaddesby Rd B14 104 F8
Gadds Dr B65 63 D4
Gadsby Ave WV11 27 A7
Gadsby Ct CV11 73 E3
Gadsby St CV11 73 E3
Gads Gn DY2 62 E5
Gads Green Cres DY2 62 E6
Gadshill CV34 161 E4
Gads La Dudley DY1 51 C1
West Bromwich B70 53 A3
Gadwall Croft B23 56 B3
Gaelic Rd WS11 1 D4
Gagarin B79 20 F5
Gaiafields Rd WS13 3 B1
Gaia La WS13 9 B8
Gaialands Cres WS13 3 B1
Gaia Stowe WS13 3 B1
Gail Cl WS9 16 B4
Gailey Croft B44 44 E3
Gail Pk WV3 38 D7
Gainford Cl WV8 10 F1
Gainford Rd B44 45 C1
Gainford Rise CV3 115 A3
Gainsborough Ave
LE10 71 A3
Gainsborough Cres
Birmingham B43 44 D4
Dorridge B93 128 A6
Gainsborough Dr
Bedworth CV12 78 A4
Mile Oak B78 34 B8

Gainsborough Dr continued
Perton WV6 . . . . 24 A4
Royal Leamington Spa CV31 . . . . 162 D6
Gainsborough Hill DY8 . . . . 81 A3
Gainsborough Mews DY11 . . . . 116 B5
Gainsborough Pl DY1. 50 E2
Gainsborough Rd B42 55 B6
Gainsborough Trad Est DY9 . . . . 81 C4
Gainsbrook Cres WS11 . 5 F5
Gainsford Dr B62 . . . . . 83 B6
Gains La WS3, WS11 . . . 5 D2
Gairloch Rd WV11 . . . . 13 B1
Gaitskell Terr B69 . . . . 52 D2
Gaitskell Way B66 . . . . . 64 F7
Galahad Way WS10 . . . 42 A2
Galbraith Cl WV14 . . . . 51 D8
Galena Cl B77 . . . . 22 B2
Galena Way B6 . . . . . . 66 E6
Gale Wlk B65 . . . . 62 F5
Galey's Rd CV3 . . . . . . 133 D8
Gallagher Bsns Pk CV6 . . . . 95 E5
Gallagher Ct 14 B13 . . 87 B2
Gallagher Rd CV12 . . . 78 A2
Gallagher Ret Pk CV6 . . . . 113 F8
Gallery Sq 1 WS1 . . . . 28 E2
Gallery The WV4 . . . . . 39 A6
Galliards The CV4 . . . 132 D4
Galliers Cl B77 . . . . 35 F5
Galloway Ave B34 . . . . . 68 F6
Galloway Cl LE9 . . . . 71 F7
Gallows Hill CV34 . . . 161 B4
Gallus Dr LE10 . . . . 71 A1
Galmington Dr CV3. . 133 B6
Galton Cl
Sutton Coldfield B24 . . . 57 F4
Tipton DY4 . . . . 52 C6
Galton Dr DY2 . . . . 62 B6
Galton Ho B67 . . . . 64 F2
Galton Rd B67 . . . . 64 F1
Galtons La DY9 . . . . . . 120 A7
Galton Twr B1 . . . . 66 C2
Galway Rd WS7 . . . . 7 A7
Gamesfield Gn WV3 . . . 24 F1
Gammage St DY2 . . . . 62 B8
Gamson Cl DY10 . . . . 116 E4
Ganborough Cl B98 . 154 E1
Gandy Rd WV12 . . . . . . 27 A7
Gannahs Farm Cl B76 . 46 F3
Gannaway B93 . . . . . . 128 A4
Gannow Green La B45 . . . . 101 D1
Gannow Manor Cres B45 . . . . 101 E2
Gannow Manor Gdns B45 . . . . 101 F1
Gannow Rd B45 . . . . . 121 E7
Gannow Wlk B45 . . . . 121 E7
Ganton Rd WS3 . . . . . . 14 A3
Ganton Wlk WV8 . . . . . . 24 F8
Garage Cl B77 . . . . 21 D5
Garden Cl
Birmingham, Frankley B45 . . . . 102 A2
Birmingham, Ward End B8 . . . . 68 A5
Hinckley LE10 . . . . 75 D6
Knowle B93 . . . . 127 F6
Garden Cres WS3 . . . . . 14 F3
Garden Croft WS9 . . . . 30 B7
Garden Ct
3 Birmingham B16 . . . 66 B1
Warwick, Emscote CV34 . . . . 161 C8
Warwick, Packmores CV34 . . . . 160 E7
Gardeners Cl DY11 . . 116 C8
Garden Flats CV5 . . . 111 D5
Garden Gr
Bedworth CV12 . . . . 95 F8
Birmingham B20 . . . . . . 54 E6
Gardenia Dr CV5 . . . . 112 B6
Garden Rd LE10 . . . . . . 71 D1
Garden St WS2 . . . . 28 E3
Gardens The
Birmingham, Chester Road B73 . . . . 57 B8
Birmingham, Stockland Green B23 . . . . 56 E3
Kenilworth CV8 . . . . . . 148 A3
Radford Semele CV31. 162 E5
Sutton Coldfield B72 . . . 46 B1
Garden Wlk
Bilston WV14 . . . . 40 F6
Dudley DY3 . . . . 50 C2
Gardner Ho 8 CV1 . . 113 B2
Gardner Way CV8 . . . 148 A2
Garfield Rd B26 . . . . . . 89 B8
Garganey Ct DY10 . . . 116 F1
Garibaldi Terr B60 . . . 137 A1
Garland Cres B62 . . . . 83 E8
Garlands Croft CV7 . . . 95 A6
Garland St B9 . . . . 67 C3
Garlands The WV11 . . . 26 C7
Garland Way B31 . . . . 103 C4
Garlick Dr CV8 . . . . . . 148 C6
Garman Cl B43 . . . . 43 E2
Garner Cl WV14 . . . . . . 40 D3
Garnet Ave B43 . . . . . . 44 B3
Garnet Cl WS9 . . . . 16 E4
Garnet Ct 4 B92 . . . . . . 88 F1
Garnett Dr B75 . . . . 46 E6
Garnette Cl CV10 . . . . . 72 B5
Garrard Gdns B73 . . . . 46 B5
Garrat St DY5 . . . . 61 E5
Garratt Cl B68 . . . . 64 C4
Garratt's La B65 . . . . . . 63 A2
Garratt St B71 . . . . 53 B5
Garratts Wlk B14 . . . . 104 E1
Garret Cl DY6 . . . . 60 D8
Garretts Green La B26, B33 . . . . 89 A8
Garrett St CV11 . . . . . . 73 E2
Garrick Cl
Coventry CV5 . . . . 111 C4
Dudley DY1 . . . . 50 F3
Garrick Rd
Bromsgrove B60 . . . . . 137 C1
Cannock WS11 . . . . 1 D4
Garrick Rise WS7 . . . . . . 7 B7
Garrick St WV1 . . . . . 163 C2
Garrigill B77 . . . . 22 B1
Garrington Rd B60 . . . 151 B7
Garrington St WS10 . . 41 C7
Garrison Ct 9 B9 . . . . 67 B2
Garrison La B9 . . . . 67 C2
Garrison St B9 . . . . 67 B3
Garston Way 4 B43 . . 54 D8
Garth Cres CV3 . . . . . 134 D8
Garth Ho CV3 . . . . 134 D8
Garth The
Birmingham B14 . . . . . 105 D4
Lichfield WS13 . . . . 3 B2
Garway Cl
Redditch B98 . . . . 154 E1
Royal Leamington Spa CV32 . . . . 156 F4
Garway Gr B25 . . . . 88 C6
Garwood Rd B26 . . . . . . 68 F2
Gas Sq B61 . . . . 136 F1
Gas St Birmingham B1 . 66 C2
Royal Leamington Spa CV31 . . . . 161 F7
Gas Street Basin* B1 . . . . 164 A2
Gatacre St DY3 . . . . 50 D3
Gatcombe Cl WV10 . . . . 11 F4
Gatcombe Rd DY1 . . . . 50 E2
Gatehouse CV31 . . . . 161 D7
Gatehouse Fold 5 DY2 . . . . 51 D1
Gatehouse La CV12 . . . 78 A2
Gate House La B60 . . 151 A7
Gatehouse Trad Est WS8 . . . . 7 B1
Gate La
Dorridge B93, B94 . . . 127 C3
Sutton Coldfield B73 . . . 45 F2
Gateley Rd B68 . . . . . . 84 D7
Gateside Rd CV6 . . . . . . 95 E2
Gate St Birmingham B8 67 D5
Sedgley DY3 . . . . 50 E7
Tipton DY4 . . . . 52 A2
Gateway The B26 . . . . . 89 F3
Gatis St WV6 . . . . 25 A5
Gatwick Rd B35 . . . . . . 58 B4
Gauden Rd DY9 . . . . . . 81 D2
Gaulby Wlk CV3 . . . . . 115 A1
Gaunts The B48 . . . . . 139 B6
Gaveston Cl 7 CV34 160 F8
Gaveston Rd
Coventry CV6 . . . . 112 F6
Royal Leamington Spa CV32 . . . . 156 E1
Gavin Way B6 . . . . 55 F4
Gawne La B64 . . . . 62 F3
Gawsworth B79 . . . . . . 20 D7
Gaydon Cl
Coventry CV6 . . . . 114 A8
Perton WV6 . . . . 23 E5
Redditch B98 . . . . 153 F1
Gaydon Gr B29 . . . . 85 A2
Gaydon Pl B73 . . . . 46 B4
Gaydon Rd
Aldridge WS9 . . . . 30 A4
Gaydon Rd continued
Solihull B92 . . . . 89 D3
Gayer St CV6 . . . . 96 A1
Gayfield Ave DY5 . . . . . 61 E1
Gay Hill La B38 . . . . . 124 B8
Gayhurst Cl CV3 . . . . . 134 E8
Gayhurst Dr B25 . . . . . 88 E8
Gayle B77 . . . . 22 A1
Gayle Gr B27 . . . . 106 C8
Gayton Rd B71 . . . . 53 D6
Gaywood Croft B15 . . 86 C8
Gaza Cl CV4 . . . . 112 A1
Gazelle Cl CV1 . . . . . . 165 D3
Geach St B19 . . . . 66 D6
Geach Twr B19 . . . . 66 D5
Gedney Cl B90 . . . . . . 105 C3
Geeson Cl B35 . . . . 58 B4
Gee St B19 . . . . 66 D6
Gemini Dr WS11 . . . . 4 F6
Gendle Ct B77 . . . . 21 D4
Geneva Rd DY4 . . . . . . 51 D5
Genge Ave WV4 . . . . . . 39 E4
Genners App B31 . . . 102 D8
Genners La B31 . . . . . 102 D7
Genthorn Cl 11 WV4 . . . 39 F4
Gentian B74 . . . . 31 F4
Gentian Cl B31 . . . . . . 102 F6
Geoffrey Cl
Coventry CV2 . . . . 114 B5
Sutton Coldfield B76 . . . 58 B7
Geoffrey Pl B11 . . . . . . 87 C3
Geoffrey Rd
Birmingham B11 . . . . . . 87 C3
Solihull B90 . . . . 105 F3
George Arthur Rd B8. 67 D5
George Ave
Mile Oak B78 . . . . 20 C1
Rowley Regis B65 . . . . . 63 D2
George Betts Prim Sch B66 . . . . 64 C7
George Bird Cl B66 . . . 65 A6
George Cl DY2 . . . . 62 E8
George Dance Cl 2 DY10 . . . . 117 B6
George Dixon Int Sch & Sixth Form Centre B17 . . . . 65 C2
George Dixon Jun & Inf Sch B17 . . . . 65 C2
George Eliot Ave CV12 . . . . 78 D2
George Eliot Com Sch
Nuneaton CV11 . . . . 73 D1
Nuneaton CV11 . . . . 78 D8
George Eliot Hospl CV10 . . . . 73 B2
George Eliot Rd CV1 113 D5
George Eliot St CV11 . 73 C2
George Fentham Endowed Sch B92. 109 B6
George Frederick Rd B73 . . . . 45 A4
George Henry Rd DY4 52 E6
George Hodgkinson Cl CV4 . . . . 111 F3
George La WS13 . . . . 9 C8
George Law Ct DY10. 116 F5
George Marston Rd CV3 . . . . 114 E1
George Park Cl CV2 . . 96 C1
George Poole Ho 6 CV1 . . . . 113 B2
George Rd
Alvechurch B48 . . . . . . 139 A5
Birmingham B29 . . . . . . 85 E3
Birmingham, Edgbaston B15 . . . . 86 B8
Birmingham, Great Barr B43 . . . . 43 F2
Birmingham, South Yardley B25 . . . . 88 A6
Birmingham, Stockland Green B23 . . . . 56 C3
Coseley, Daisy Bank WV14 . . . . 40 D1
Dudley, Tipton Green DY4 . . . . 51 D6
Halesowen B63 . . . . 82 F4
Oldbury B68 . . . . 64 C2
Solihull B91 . . . . 107 D3
Sutton Coldfield B73 . . . 45 D1
Warwick CV34 . . . . . . 161 A8
Water Orton B46 . . . . . . 59 C3
George Robertson Cl CV3 . . . . 134 E7
George Rose Gdns WS10 . . . . 41 C6
George St W B18 . . . . . 66 A4
George Salter High Sch B70 . . . . 53 A4
George St
Birmingham, Balsall Heath B12 . . . . 86 F5
Birmingham, Brookfields B3 . . . . 164 A3
Birmingham, Handsworth B21 . . . . 65 C8
Birmingham, Lozells B19 . . . . 66 B7
1 Bromsgrove B61 . . 136 F2
Cannock WS12 . . . . 2 C4
Coventry CV1 . . . . 113 E5
Dudley DY1 . . . . 51 B6
Hinckley LE10 . . . . 75 D8
Kidderminster DY10 . . 116 F6
Nuneaton CV11 . . . . 73 E2
Royal Leamington Spa CV31 . . . . 162 A7
Stourbridge DY8 . . . . . . 60 F1
Stow Heath WV2 . . . . . . 40 A7
Tamworth B79 . . . . 21 B4
Walsall WS1 . . . . 28 E1
West Bromwich B70 . . . 53 D2
Willenhall WV13 . . . . . . 27 A4
Wolverhampton WV2 . 163 C2
George Street Ringway CV12 . . . . 78 B3
George Wlk 5 B97 . . . 153 E3
Georgian Gdns 2 WS10 . . . . 41 F3
Georgian Pl WS11 . . . . . . 1 E2
Georgina Ave WV14 . . 40 D3
Geraghty Ct DY4 . . . . . 41 A2
Geraldine Rd B25 . . . . 88 B7
Gerald Rd DY8 . . . . 80 E7
Geranium Gr B9 . . . . . . 67 F3
Geranium Rd DY2 . . . . . 62 F8
Gerard B79 . . . . 20 E7
Gerard Ave CV4 . . . . . 132 B8
Gerardsfield Rd B33 . . 69 E2
Germander B74 . . . . 31 F5
Germander Dr WS5 . . 43 A3
Gerrard Cl B19 . . . . 66 D7
Gerrard Rd WV13 . . . . . 26 E1
Gerrard St
Birmingham B19 . . . . . . 66 C7
1 Warwick CV34 . . . . 160 E6
Gertrude Pl B18 . . . . . . 66 A5
Gervase Dr DY1 . . . . . . 51 C3
Geston Rd DY1 . . . . 61 F8
Gettings Cl WS7 . . . . 7 F7
Gheluvelt Ave DY10 . . 116 F7
Gibbet Hill Rd CV4 . . 132 B3
Gibbet La DY7 . . . . 80 B4
Gibbins Rd B29 . . . . . . 85 D2
Gibb La B61 . . . . 137 A8
Gibbons Cl CV4 . . . . . 111 F2
Gibbons Gr WV6 . . . . . . 24 F4
Gibbons Hill Rd DY3 . . 39 D2
Gibbons Ind Pk DY6 . . 61 A7
Gibbons La DY5 . . . . . . 61 A7
Gibbons Rd
Sutton Coldfield B75 . . . 32 B3
Wolverhampton WV6 . . 24 F4
Gibbs Cl CV2 . . . . 115 B6
Gibbs Hill Rd B31 . . . 123 C7
Gibb Sq B12 . . . . 67 A1
Gibbs Rd
Redditch B98 . . . . 154 A5
Stourbridge DY9 . . . . . . 82 A5
Gibbs St WV6 . . . . 25 A4
Gibb St B9 . . . . 66 F1
Gibson Cres CV12 . . . . 78 A1
Gibson Dr
Birmingham B20 . . . . . . 66 B8
Smethwick B66 . . . . 65 A6
Gibson Rd
Birmingham B20 . . . . . . 66 B8
Perton WV6 . . . . 23 E3
Gideon Cl B25 . . . . 88 C5
Gideons Cl DY3 . . . . . . 50 D5
Gielgud Way CV2 . . . . 115 B8
Giffard RC Prim Sch The WV6 . . . . 24 F5
Giffard Rd Bilston WV1 40 B7
Wolverhampton WV10 . 11 F3
Giffard Way CV34 . . . 155 E1
Gifford Ct 13 DY5 . . . . 61 D2
Giffords Croft WS13 . . . . 3 A1
Gigg La B76 . . . . 48 B3
Gig Mill Prim Sch DY8 . . . . 80 E4
Gigmill Way DY8 . . . . . 80 E4
Gilbanks Rd DY8 . . . . . 80 D7
Gilberry Cl B93 . . . . . . 128 A4
Gilbert Ave B69 . . . . . . 63 B7
Gilbert Cl
Bedworth CV12 . . . . 78 B2
3 Coventry CV1 . . . . . 113 E3
Wednesfield WV11 . . . . 27 A7
Gilbert Ent Pk WV12 . . 27 B4
Gilbert La WV5 . . . . 49 B7
Gilbert Rd
Bromsgrove B60 . . . . . 150 E7
Lichfield WS13 . . . . 3 C2
Smethwick B66 . . . . 65 B3
Gilbert Scott Way DY10 . . . . 116 F7
Gilberts Ct WS4 . . . . . . 29 A4
Gilbert St DY4 . . . . 52 A4
Gilbertstone Ave B26 . 88 E5
Gilbertstone Cl B98 . 153 E1
Gilbertstone Prim Sch B26 . . . . 88 E5
Gilbert Wlk WS13 . . . . . . 3 C2
Gilbeys Cl 5 DY8 . . . . 60 E1
Gilby Rd B16 . . . . 66 A1
Gilchrist Dr B15 . . . . . . 85 E8
Gildas Ave B38 . . . . . . 104 A1
Giles Cl
Birmingham B33 . . . . . . 68 E3
Coventry CV6 . . . . 95 C2
Solihull B92 . . . . 107 F7
Giles Close Ho B33 . . . 68 E3
Giles Rd Lichfield WS13 . . 3 A3
Oldbury B68 . . . . 64 B5
Gilfil Rd CV10 . . . . 73 B1
Gilldown Pl B15 . . . . . . 86 B7
Gillespie Croft B6 . . . . . 66 F7
Gillet Cl CV11 . . . . 73 B3
Gillhurst Rd B17 . . . . . . 85 C7
Gillians Wlk CV2 . . . . 115 A8
Gilling Gr B34 . . . . 69 A6
Gillingham Cl WS10 . . 42 D4
Gillity Ave WS5 . . . . . . 43 C8
Gillity Cl WS5 . . . . 43 C8
Gillity Ct 3 WS5 . . . . . 43 D7
Gilliver Rd B90 . . . . . . 106 B2
Gillman Cl B26 . . . . 89 D4
Gillott Cl B91 . . . . 107 E3
Gillott Rd B16 . . . . 65 D2
Gillows Croft B90 . . . 127 A7
Gillscroft Rd B33 . . . . . 69 A3
Gill St Dudley DY2 . . . . . 62 E4
West Bromwich B70 . . . 53 C1
Gillway B79 . . . . 21 B8
Gilmorton Cl
Birmingham B17 . . . . . . 85 B7
Solihull B91 . . . . 107 C1
Gilpin Cl B8 . . . . 68 C7
Gilpin Cres WS3 . . . . . . 15 A4
Gilpins Croft WS6 . . . . . 4 D1
Gilquart Way CV1 . . . 165 C1
Gilson Dr B46 . . . . 70 D8
Gilson Rd B46 . . . . 70 E8
Gilson St DY4 . . . . 52 C8
Gilson Way B37 . . . . . . 70 A5
Gilwell Rd B34 . . . . 69 E6
Gimble Wlk 2 B17 . . . . 84 F7
Ginkgo Wlk 2 CV31. 161 F5
Gipsy Cl CV7 . . . . 130 B5
Gipsy La
Balsall Common CV7 . . 130 C5
Birmingham B23 . . . . . . 56 B5
Nuneaton CV10, CV11 . 78 D7
Willenhall WV13 . . . . . . 27 B1
Girdlers Cl CV3 . . . . . 133 B5
Girtin Cl CV12 . . . . 78 A4
Girton Ho B36 . . . . 69 F8
Girton Rd WS11 . . . . 4 F8
Girvan Gr CV32 . . . . . . 157 C5
Gisborn Cl B10 . . . . 87 B8
Gisburn Cl
5 Redditch B97 . . . . . 153 B5
Warwick CV34 . . . . . . 155 F1
Givens Ho 9 CV1 . . . 113 B2
GK Davies Trad Est DY9 . . . . 82 A6
Gladeside Cl WS4 . . . . 29 D8
Glades The WS9 . . . . . . 30 B7
Glade The
Birmingham B26 . . . . . . 89 D4
Cannock WS11 . . . . 1 C2
Coventry CV5 . . . . 111 F3
Stourbridge DY9 . . . . . . 81 E5
Sutton Coldfield B74 . . . 30 E1
Wolverhampton WV8 . . 10 E1
Gladman Bsns Quarter WV9 . . . . 10 F3
Gladstone Cl LE10 . . . . 71 E4
Gladstone Ct 22 CV32 . . . . 156 F1
Gladstone Dr
Oldbury B69 . . . . 52 D3
Stourbridge DY8 . . . . . . 80 D6
Gladstone Gr 3 DY6 . 60 D8
Gladstone Rd
Birmingham, Gravelly Hill B23 . . . . 56 D3
Gladstone Rd continued
Birmingham, South Yardley B26 . . . . 88 D6
Birmingham, Sparkbrook B11 . . . . 87 B6
Cannock WS12 . . . . 2 E1
Dorridge B93 . . . . 128 A2
Stourbridge DY8 . . . . . . 80 D6
Gladstone St
Birmingham B6 . . . . 67 B8
Darlaston WS10 . . . . . . 41 E6
Walsall WS2 . . . . 28 D4
West Bromwich B71 . . . 53 C5
Gladstone Terr LE10 . . 75 E8
Gladys Rd
Birmingham B25 . . . . . . 88 B7
Smethwick B67 . . . . 64 F2
Gladys Terr B67 . . . . . . 65 A2
Glaisdale Ave CV6 . . . . 95 E3
Glaisdale Gdns WV6 . . 25 A5
Glaisdale Rd B28 . . . . 106 B8
Glaisedale Gr WV13 . . 27 C2
Glaisher Dr WV10 . . . . 25 C6
Glamis Rd WV12 . . . . . 27 B7
Glamorgan Cl CV3 . . . 134 D5
Glanville Dr B75 . . . . . 32 A4
Glasbury Croft B38 . . 123 E7
Glascote Cl B90 . . . . . 106 A4
Glascote Ct B77 . . . . . . 21 E4
Glascote Gr B34 . . . . . 69 C6
Glascote Heath Prim Sch B77 . . . . 22 A2
Glascote La B77 . . . . 35 F8
Glascote Rd
Tamworth B77 . . . . 22 B2
Tamworth, Glascote Heath B77 . . . . 21 E3
Glasscroft Cotts WS7 . . . 7 F7
Glassford Dr WV6 . . . . 24 E6
Glasshouse Coll DY8 . . 80 F7
Glasshouse Hill DY8 . . 81 B3
Glasshouse La
Hockley Heath B94 . . . 143 F6
Kenilworth CV8 . . . . . . 148 D4
Glastonbury Cl DY11 116 A6
Glastonbury Cres WS3 . . . . 13 E2
Glastonbury Rd
Birmingham B14 . . . . . 105 C5
West Bromwich B71 . . . 42 D1
Glastonbury Way WS3 . . . . 13 E1
Glaston Dr B91 . . . . . . 107 A1
Gleads Croft B62 . . . . . 84 A3
Gleason Wlk WV1 . . . . 26 C1
Gleave Rd
Birmingham B29 . . . . . . 85 E1
Whitnash CV31 . . . . . . 162 A3
Glebe Ave CV12 . . . . . . 77 E1
Glebe Cl
Coventry CV4 . . . . 132 A7
Redditch B98 . . . . 154 D2
Glebe Cres CV8 . . . . . 148 A3
Glebe Ct CV31 . . . . . . 162 A3
Glebe Dr B73 . . . . 56 F8
Glebefarm Gr CV3 . . . 114 F3
Glebe Farm Rd B33 . . . 69 A5
Glebe Fields B76 . . . . . 59 B6
Glebefields Prim Sch DY4 . . . . 52 A8
Glebefields Rd DY4 . . . 52 A7
Glebe La
Nuneaton CV11 . . . . 73 F6
Stourbridge DY8 . . . . . . 80 E4
Glebeland Cl B16 . . . . 66 B1
Glebe Pl
Darlaston WS10 . . . . . . 41 B6
Royal Leamington Spa CV31 . . . . 162 B7
Glebe Rd
Alvechurch B48 . . . . . . 139 A7
Hinckley LE10 . . . . 71 F1
Nuneaton CV11 . . . . 73 D4
Solihull B91 . . . . 107 D5
Willenhall WV13 . . . . . . 40 F8
Glebe St WS1 . . . . 42 E8
Glebe The
Belbroughton DY9 . . . . 119 E6
Beoley B98 . . . . 154 F7
Corley CV7 . . . . 94 C7
Glebe Way CV7 . . . . . . 130 A7
Gledhill Pk WS14 . . . . . . 9 C5
Gleeson Dr CV34 . . . . 155 E1
Glenavon Rd B14 . . . . 105 A3
Glen Bank LE10 . . . . . . 71 E1
Glenbarr Cl LE10 . . . . . 75 A8
Glenbarr Dr LE10 . . . . . 75 A8
Glen Cl Cannock WS11 . . . 1 E5

Glen Cl *continued*
Walsall WS4 . . . . 29 A3
Glencoe Dr WS11 . . . . . .2 A4
Glencoe Rd
Birmingham B16 . . . . . . 65 C4
Coventry CV3 . . . . 114 B1
Glencroft Rd B92 . . . . . 89 D4
Glen Ct Codsall WV8 . . . 10 A4
Wolverhampton WV6 . . 24 E2
Glendale Ave CV8 . . . 148 A6
Glendale Cl
Halesowen B63 . . . . 83 B4
Wolverhampton WV3 . . 38 C8
Glendale Ct B77 . . . . . . 36 B6
Glendale Dr
Birmingham B33 . . . . . . 68 F3
Wombourne WV5 . . . . . 49 A6
Glendale Gdns WS11 . . .2 A4
Glendale Inf Sch CV10 72 F2
Glendale Twr 5 B23. . 57 B6
Glendale Way CV4. . . 111 C2
Glendawn Cl 1 WS11 . .2 A3
Glendene Cres B38. . 123 C7
Glendene Dr 2 B43. . 54 D8
Glendene Rd WS12 . . . . 2 D6
Glen Devon Cl B45 . . 102 A2
Glendon Gdns CV12 . . 79 C3
Glendon Rd B23. . . . . . 56 D6
Glendon Way B93 . . . 127 E3
Glendower App
CV34 . . . . 161 E3
Glendower Ave CV5 . 112 D3
Glendower Rd
Aldridge WS9 . . . . 16 B1
Birmingham B42 . . . . . . 55 D4
Gleneagles B77 . . . . . . 22 B5
Gleneagles Cl
Hinckley LE10 . . . . 75 D4
Nuneaton CV11. . . . . . . 74 C1
Gleneagles Dr
Birmingham B43 . . . . . . 43 E3
Blackwell B60 . . . . 138 A5
Oldbury B69 . . . . 63 A7
Sutton Coldfield B75. . . 46 D8
Gleneagles Rd
Birmingham B26 . . . . . . 89 A8
Coventry CV2 . . . . 114 E6
Perton WV6. . . . . 23 D5
Walsall WS3 . . . . 13 F3
Glenelg Dr DY8 . . . . . . 81 B2
Glenelg Mews WS5. . . 43 D5
Glenfern Gdns CV8. . . 134 E2
Glenfern Rd WV14. . . . 51 A8
Glenfield
Tamworth B77. . . . . 21 C1
Wolverhampton WV8 . . 10 E2
Glenfield Ave CV10. . . 73 D7
Glenfield Cl
Redditch B97 . . . . 158 D6
2 Solihull B91 . . . . . . 127 C8
Sutton Coldfield B76. . . 46 E3
Glenfield Gr B29 . . . . . 86 A1
Glengarry Cl B32. . . . 102 B7
Glengarry Gdns WV3 . .24 F1
Glenhill Dr B38 . . . . . 124 A8
Glen Ho DY1 . . . . 61 D8
Glenhurst Cl WS2 . . . . 27 D3
Glenmead Prim Sch
B44. . . . . 55 D8
Glenmead Rd B44. . . . 55 D8
Glenmore Ave WS7. . . . .7 A6
Glenmore Cl WV3 . . . . 38 E7
Glenmore Dr
Birmingham B38 . . . . . 103 D2
Coventry CV6 . . . . 95 F5
Glenmount Ave CV6. . . 95 F5
Glenn St CV6 . . . . 95 D3
Glenpark Rd B8. . . . . . .67 F5
Glen Park Rd DY3 . . . . 50 D2
Glen Rd Dudley DY3 . . . 50 E6
Stourbridge DY8 . . . . . . 80 F3
Glenridding Cl CV6. . . .95 F5
Glen Rise B13. . . . . . . 105 C6
Glenrosa Wlk CV4 . . . 132 A7
Glenroy Cl CV2. . . . . . 114 E6
Glenroyde B38. . . . . . . 123 E7
Glen Side B32. . . . . 84 D2
Glenside Ave B92 . . . . 89 C3
Glen The B60 . . . . 138 A5
Glenthorne Dr WS6 . . . .4 E3
Glenthorne Ho WS6 . . . 4 D2
Glenthorne Prim Sch
WS6. . . . . .4 E3
Glenthorne Rd B24. . . 57 A2
Glentworth B76 . . . . . . 47 A2
Glentworth Ave CV6. . 95 A2
Glentworth Gdns
WV6 . . . . 25 B5
Glenville Ave CV9 . . . . 36 C1
Glenville Dr B23 . . . . . 56 E5
Glenwood Cl DY5 . . . . 81 D8
Glenwood Dr B90 . . . 126 D4
Glenwood Gdns
Bedworth CV12. . . . . . . 78 A5
Tamworth B77. . . . . 36 B6
Glenwood Rd B38 . . . 123 D8
Glenwood Rise WS9 . . 16 D3
Globe St WS10 . . . . .41 F1
Gloster Dr CV8. . . . . . 147 F6
Gloucester Cl
Lichfield WS13 . . . . .3 B3
Nuneaton CV11. . . . . . . 74 A7
Gloucester Ho
4 Birmingham B24 . . . 56 F4
4 Wolverhampton
WV3 . . . . 25 C4
Gloucester Pl WV13 . . 27 D2
Gloucester Rd
Dudley DY2 . . . . 62 D2
Walsall WS5 . . . . 43 C8
Wednesbury WS10 . . . . 42 C3
Gloucester St
Birmingham B5 . . . . . . 164 C1
Coventry CV1 . . . . 113 B3
3 Royal Leamington Spa
CV31. . . . . 162 A7
Wolverhampton WV6 . . 25 B4
Gloucester Way
Birmingham B37 . . . . . . 70 A1
Cannock WS11 . . . . .2 B1
Glover Cl
Birmingham B28. . . . . 105 F6
Warwick CV34 . . . . . . 160 B4
Glover Rd B75 . . . . 47 A5
Glovers Cl CV7 . . . . 92 C1
Glovers Croft B37 . . . . .69 F3
Glovers Field Dr B7 . . 67 C7
Glovers Rd B10 . . . . . . 87 D8
Glover St
Birmingham B9. . . . . . . 67 A2
Cannock WS12 . . . . .2 F3
Coventry CV3 . . . . 133 D8
Redditch B98 . . . . 153 E3
West Bromwich B70. . . 53 D1
Glover's Trust Homes
B73 . . . . .56 F7
Glyde Ct B27. . . . . 88 B2
Glyme Dr WV6 . . . . 24 E5
Glyn Ave WV14. . . . . . . 41 B3
Glyndebourne B79 . . . 20 D7
Glyn Dr WV14. . . . . 41 B3
Glyne Ct B73. . . . . 46 B5
Glyn Farm Rd B32. . . . 84 C6
Glynn Cres B63 . . . . . . 82 B7
Glynne Ave DY6 . . . . . . 60 D5
Glynne Prim Sch DY6 60 C4
Glyn Rd B32 . . . . 84 D6
Glynside Ave B32 . . . . 84 D6
Godfrey Cl CV31. . . . . 162 E5
Godiva Pl CV1. . . . . . . 165 D3
Godiva Trad Est CV6 113 F8
Godolphin B79. . . . . . . 20 D7
Godrich Ho B13. . . . . . . 87 B3
Godson Cres DY11. . . 116 C3
Godson Pl DY11 . . . . . 116 C3
Goffs Cl B32 . . . . .84 F3
Gofton B77 . . . . 36 A8
Goldacre Cl CV31 . . . 161 F4
Goldborough Cl
WV14 . . . . 40 D3
Goldby Dr WS10. . . . . . 41 E4
Gold Cl CV11. . . . . 78 E8
Goldcrest B77. . . . . 36 A6
Goldcrest Cl DY2 . . . . . 62 D2
Goldcrest Croft B36 . . 70 A8
Goldcrest Dr DY10. . . 117 B2
Golden Acres La
CV3 . . . . 134 F7
Goldencrest Dr B69 . . 63 E8
Golden Croft B20 . . . . .54 F1
Golden Cross La
B61 . . . . 121 B1
Goldencross Way DY5 61 B1
Golden End Dr B93. . 128 D6
Golden Hillock Rd
Birmingham B11. . . . . . 87 D6
Dudley DY2 . . . . 62 C3
Golden Hillock Sch &
Specialist Sports Coll
B11. . . . . 87 D5
Goldfinch Cl B30. . . . . 103 D8
Goldfinch Rd DY9 . . . . 81 C3
Goldicroft Rd WS10 . . 42 A4
Goldieslie Cl B73. . . . . 46 B2
Goldieslie Rd B73. . . . 46 B2
Goldsborough B77 . . . 22 A1
Golds Hill Gdns B21 . . .65 F7
Golds Hill Rd B21 . . . . .65 F8
Golds Hill Way DY4. . . 52 D7
Goldsmith Ave CV34. 160 C5
Goldsmith Pl B79 . . . . 21 A7
Goldsmith Rd
Birmingham B14 . . . . . 104 F8
Walsall WS3 . . . . 28 E7
Goldsmith Wlk DY10. 117 C5
Goldstar Way B33. . . . 69 C2
Goldtel Ind Est WV4 . 40 A5
Goldthorn Ave WV4 . . 39 B6
Goldthorn Cl CV5 . . . . 111 D4
Goldthorn Cres WV4. . 39 A6
Goldthorne Ave
Birmingham B26 . . . . . . 89 C4
Cannock WS11 . . . . .1 F2
Goldthorne Cl B97 . . 153 C1
Goldthorne Wlk DY5 . 81 D8
Goldthorn Hill WV2,
WV4 . . . . 39 C6
Goldthorn Mews
DY11 . . . . 116 C2
Goldthorn Park Prim Sch
WV4. . . . . 39 D5
Goldthorn Pl DY11 . . 116 C2
Goldthorn Rd
Kidderminster DY11 . . 116 C2
Wolverhampton WV2,
WV3 . . . . 39 B6
Golf Dr CV11 . . . . 74 B1
Golf La Bilston WV14 . . 40 D7
Whitnash CV31 . . . . . . 162 B2
Golson Cl B75. . . . . .46 F6
Gomeldon Ave B14. . 104 F3
Gomer St W WV13. . . . . 27 A2
Gomer St WV13 . . . . . . 27 A2
Gonville Ho B36. . . . . . .69 F8
Gooch Cl DY8 . . . . 81 B6
Gooch St N B5 . . . . 86 E8
Gooch St B5 . . . . 86 E8
Goodall Gr B43 . . . . . . 44 E5
Goodall St WS1 . . . . . . .28 F1
Goodby Rd B13 . . . . . . 86 D3
Goode Ave B18 . . . . . . 66 A5
Goode Cl Oldbury B68 . 64 C4
Warwick CV34 . . . . . . 160 C7
Goode Croft CV4 . . . . 111 F2
Goodeve Wlk B75 . . . . 47 B5
Goodfellow St CV32 . 156 C1
Good Hope Hospl
B75. . . . . 46 D6
Goodison Gdns B24 . . 57 B5
Goodleigh Ave B45 . . 122 E6
Goodman Cl B28 . . . . 105 F6
Goodman St B1 . . . . 66 B3
Goodman Way CV4 . . 111 C1
Goodrest Ave B62. . . . 84 A5
Goodrest Croft B14 . 105 C4
Goodrest La B38 . . . . 123 F6
Goodrich Ave WV6 . . . 24 A3
Goodrich Cl B98 . . . . 154 F2
Goodrich Covert 10
B14 . . . . 104 C2
Goodrick Way B7 . . . . 67 B6
Good Shepherd RC Sch
CV6. . . . . .95 F1
Goodway Ct 9 CV34 160 F7
Goodway Ho
Birmingham B4 . . . . . . 164 C4
Kenilworth CV8. . . . . . 148 A5
5 Royal Leamington Spa
CV32. . . . . 161 D8
Goodway Rd
Birmingham B44 . . . . . . 55 F8
Solihull B92. . . . . 89 E4
Goodwin Cl DY11. . . . 116 C7
Goodwood Cl
Birmingham B36 . . . . . . 68 D8
Coventry CV3 . . . . 134 C6
Lichfield WS14 . . . . 9 D7
Goodwood Dr B74 . . . .44 F7
Goodwood Rd B61 . . . 121 B1
Goodwyn Ave B68. . . . 84 C7
Goodyear Ave WV10. . . 25 E7
Goodyear Rd B67 . . . . 64 E2
Goodyers End La
CV12 . . . . 95 D8
Goodyers End Prim Sch
CV12. . . . . .95 E8
Goosehill Cl B98 . . . . 154 E1
Goosehills Rd LE10. . . 75 E5
Goosemoor La B23 . . . .56 F7
Goostry Cl B77 . . . . . . 21 D5
Goostry Rd B77 . . . . . . 21 D5
Gopsall Rd LE10. . . . . . 71 D2
Gopsal St B4. . . . . 67 A3
Gorcott La B90 . . . . . . 126 A5
Gordon Ave
Birmingham B19 . . . . . . 66 D7
West Bromwich B71. . . 53 C8
Wolverhampton WV4 . . 39 F3
Gordon Cl
Bedworth CV12. . . . . . . 78 C4
Oldbury B69 . . . . 52 D2
Gordon Cres DY5. . . . . 61 E5
Gordon Ct B33 . . . . 68 D3
Gordon Dr DY4. . . . . . . 52 C6
Gordon Pl WV14. . . . . . 40 C5
Gordon Rd
Birmingham B17 . . . . . . 85 D6
Birmingham, Lozells
B19. . . . . 66 C8
Gordon St
5 Birmingham B9 . . . . 67 B2
Coventry CV1 . . . . 113 B2
Darlaston WS10 . . . . . . 41 E6
Royal Leamington Spa
CV31. . . . . 162 A7
Wolverhampton WV2 . 163 C2
Gorey Cl WV12 . . . . 27 B8
Gorge Rd Sedgley DY3. 50 E8
Wolverhampton WV14,
DY3. . . . . 39 F1
Goring Rd CV2 . . . . . . 114 A4
Gorleston Gr B14 . . . 105 B2
Gorleston Rd B14 . . . 105 B2
Gorsebrook Rd WV6. . 25 B5
Gorse Cl
Birmingham, Fordbridge
B37. . . . . 69 F2
Birmingham, Selly Oak
B29. . . . . 103 A8
Gorse Dr WS12. . . . . 1 D5
Gorse Farm Rd
Birmingham B43 . . . . . . 54 E8
Nuneaton CV11. . . . . . . 79 B8
Gorsefield Rd B34. . . . 69 C5
Gorse Green La DY9. 120 C8
Gorse La WS14. . . . . .9 E6
Gorse Meadow Dr
B45 . . . . 138 B8
Gorsemoor Prim Sch
WS12. . . . . .2 D1
Gorsemoor Rd WS12 . . 2 D1
Gorsemoor Way
WV11 . . . . 13 B3
Gorse Rd Dudley DY1. . 51 A4
Wednesfield WV11 . . . . 27 A8
Gorseway
Burntwood WS7 . . . . .7 B5
Coventry CV5 . . . . 112 C3
Gorse Way WS12 . . . . . . .2 C8
Gorsey La
Cannock WS11 . . . . .1 C1
Coleshill B46. . . . . 59 F2
Great Wyrley WS6. . . . . . .4 F1
Norton Canes WS3 . . . . . .5 E1
Wythall B47. . . . . 125 A3
Gorsey Way
Aldridge WS9 . . . . 29 E5
Coleshill B46. . . . . 59 E2
Gorsly Piece B32. . . . . 84 C4
Gorstey Lea WS7 . . . . . . .7 C7
Gorstie Croft B43 . . . . 54 E8
Gorsty Ave DY5 . . . . . . 61 C3
Gorsty Bank WS14. . . . . . .9 E8
Gorsty Cl 2 B71 . . . . . .53 F8
Gorsty Hill Rd B65 . . . 83 B8
Gorsy Bank Rd B77. . . .35 F5
Gorsymead Gr B31 . . 102 C2
Gorsy Rd B32 . . . . 84 D5
Gorsy Way CV10. . . . . . 72 D5
Gorton Croft CV7. . . . 130 B7
Gorway Cl WS1 . . . . . . .42 F7
Gorway Gdns WS1. . . . 43 A7
Gorway Rd WS1 . . . . . . 43 A7
Goscote Cl
Redditch B97 . . . . 153 A5
Walsall WS3 . . . . 28 F7
Goscote Hospl WS3. . . .28 F8
Goscote Ind Est WS3. .14 E1
Goscote La WS3. . . . . . .28 F8
Goscote Lodge Cres
WS3 . . . . 29 A7
Goscote Pl WS3. . . . . . 29 A7
Goscote Rd WS3 . . . . . 15 A1
Gosford Dr LE10 . . . . . . 71 A1
Gosford Ind Est CV1 113 F2
Gosford Park Prim Sch
CV1. . . . . 113 F2
Gosford St
Birmingham B12 . . . . . . 86 F6
Coventry CV1 . . . . 165 D2
Gosford Wlk B92. . . . . 89 B1
Gosmoor Ho B26. . . . . 88 E7
Gospel End Rd DY3. . . 50 B8
Gospel End St DY3 . . . 50 D8
Gospel Farm Rd B27 106 B8
Gospel La B27 . . . . . . 106 C8
Gospel Oak Rd
Coventry CV6 . . . . 95 B4
Gospel Oak Rd *continued*
Wednesbury DY4 . . . . . 41 B1
Gosport Cl WV1 . . . . . . 40 B7
Gosport Rd CV6 . . . . . 113 E8
Goss Croft B29. . . . . . . 85 D1
Gossett La CV8. . . . . . 135 F7
Gossey La B33 . . . . 69 C2
Gossey Lane Jun & Inf
Sch B33 . . . . 69 C2
Goss The DY5 . . . . 61 D1
Gosta Gn B4 . . . . 164 D4
Gotham Rd B26 . . . . . . 88 E6
Goths Cl B65. . . . . 63 C4
Gough Ave WV11. . . . . 26 B8
Gough Rd
Birmingham, Edgbaston
B15. . . . . 86 C7
Birmingham, Sparkhill
B11. . . . . 87 D5
Dudley WV14 . . . . 40 C1
Gough St
Birmingham B1 . . . . . . 164 B1
Willenhall WV13 . . . . . . 27 C2
Wolverhampton WV1 . 163 C3
Gould Ave E DY11 . . . 116 A2
Gould Ave W DY11 . . . 116 A1
Gould Firm La WS9. . . 30 E6
Gould Rd CV35 . . . . . . 160 A7
Governor's Ct CV34 . 160 D8
Gowan Rd B8 . . . . 67 E4
Gower Ave DY6 . . . . . . .60 F4
Gower Ho B62 . . . . .83 F6
Gower Rd
Halesowen B62. . . . . . . 83 F6
Sedgley DY3 . . . . 50 B8
Gower St
Birmingham B19 . . . . . . 66 D7
Walsall WS2 . . . . 42 B7
Willenhall WV13 . . . . . . 27 A2
Wolverhampton WV2 . 163 D1
Gowland Dr WS11 . . . . . .1 B1
Gowrie Cl LE10. . . . . . . 71 B2
Goya Cl WS11 . . . . 2 D2
Gozzard St WV14. . . . . 40 E5
Gracechurch Sh Ctr
B72. . . . . .46 B5
Grace Mary Prim Sch
B69. . . . . 63 C7
Gracemere Cres B28 105 E3
Grace Moore Ct WS11 . . 1 F4
Grace Rd
Allesley CV5 . . . . 111 A8
Birmingham B11. . . . . . 87 C7
Oldbury B69 . . . . 63 C8
Tipton DY4 . . . . 52 A7
Gracewell Homes
B13 . . . . 105 D8
Gracewell Rd B13 . . . . 87 D1
Grafton Cl B98. . . . . . 159 B7
Grafton Cres B60. . . . 150 E8
Grafton Ct
Birmingham B23 . . . . . . 56 C2
Coventry CV4 . . . . 132 B7
4 Wolverhampton
WV6 . . . . 24 F4
Grafton Dr WV13 . . . . . 26 D1
Grafton Gdns DY3 . . . . 50 B3
Grafton Gr 1 B19. . . . 66 C7
Grafton Ho
Bromsgrove B60. . . . . 137 B3
Wolverhampton WV4 . . 39 E5
Grafton La B61. . . . . . 150 C7
Grafton Pl WV14 . . . . . 40 E7
Grafton Rd
Birmingham, Handsworth
B21. . . . . 54 D1
Birmingham, Sparkbrook
B11. . . . . 87 B7
Oldbury B68 . . . . 63 F2
Solihull B90. . . . . 105 C2
West Bromwich B71. . . 53 D4
Grafton St CV1. . . . . . 113 F2
Graham Cl
Coventry CV6 . . . . 96 B1
Wednesbury DY4 . . . . . 41 B1
Graham Cres B45 . . . 122 A7
Graham Ho B74. . . . . . .30 F2
Graham Rd
Birmingham, Saltley
B9. . . . . 67 F3
Birmingham, South Yardley
B25. . . . . 88 C6
Halesowen B62. . . . . . . 83 C8
Kingswinford DY6, DY8. 60 D4
West Bromwich B71. . . 53 D4
Graham St
Birmingham, Hockley
B1. . . . . 66 C3
Birmingham, Lozells
B19. . . . . 66 C7
Graham St *continued*
Nuneaton CV11. . . . . . . 73 C5
Grainger Cl DY4. . . . . . 52 D6
Grainger Ct WS11 . . . . . 1 D2
Grainger's La B64. . . . 82 D8
Grainger St DY2. . . . . . 62 D7
Graiseley Ct WV3. . . . 163 B2
Graiseley Hill WV2 . . 163 B1
Graiseley La WV11 . . . 26 C5
Graiseley Prim Sch
WV2. . . . . 163 B1
Graiseley Row WV2 . 163 B1
Graiseley St WV3. . . . 163 A2
Graith Cl B28 . . . . 105 E3
Grammar School La
B63 . . . . 83 A4
Grampian Rd DY8 . . . . 81 A6
Granada Trad Est B69 63 F6
Granary Cl
Cannock WS12 . . . . .2 B5
Kingswinford DY6. . . . . 60 A8
Granary La B76 . . . . . . .46 F3
Granary Rd
Stoke Heath B60. . . . . 150 E6
Wolverhampton WV8 . . 10 E1
Granary The WS9. . . . . 30 B6
Granborough Cl CV3 134 F8
Granborough Ct
CV32. . . . . 157 A3
Granbourne Rd WS2. . 27 D4
Granby Ave B33. . . . . . 69 C1
Granby Bsns Pk B33 . 69 D1
Granby Cl
Hinckley LE10 . . . . 75 C7
Redditch B98 . . . . 154 F4
Solihull B92. . . . . 106 E7
Granby Rd
Hinckley LE10 . . . . 75 C7
Nuneaton CV10. . . . . . . 72 F3
Grandborough Dr
B91 . . . . 107 A1
Grand Cl B66 . . . . 65 B3
Grand Depot Rd CV11 .79 F6
Grand Junction Way
WS1 . . . . 42 D5
Grand Theatre★
WV1 . . . . 163 C3
Grandys Croft B37 . . . .69 F2
Granefield Ct 4 B9 . . . 67 D1
Grange Ave
Aldridge WS9 . . . . 16 A1
Birmingham B8. . . . . . . 68 B6
Burntwood WS7 . . . . .7 B7
Coventry, Binley CV3. . 134 F7
Coventry, Finham CV3. 133 C3
Kenilworth CV8. . . . . . 147 E7
Sutton Coldfield B75. . . 32 C3
Grange Cl
Nuneaton CV10. . . . . . . 72 C7
Tamworth B77. . . . . 35 C8
Warwick CV34 . . . . . . 161 C8
Grange Cres
Birmingham B45 . . . . . 121 F8
Halesowen B63. . . . . . . 83 B3
Walsall WS4 . . . . 29 B8
Grange Ct
1 Dudley DY1 . . . . 51 B1
1 Redditch B98. . . . . . 153 F4
Stourbridge DY9 . . . . . . 81 C3
Willenhall WS2 . . . . 27 D2
Wolverhampton WV3 . 163 A2
Grange Dr
Cannock WS11 . . . . .1 F2
Hinckley LE10 . . . . 75 E5
Grange Education Unit
The CV6 . . . . .94 E1
Grange Farm Dr
B38 . . . . 123 D8
Grange Farm Prim Sch
CV3. . . . . 133 B5
Grangefield Cl WV8 . . .10 F1
Grange Hill B62 . . . . . . 83 C2
Grange Hill Rd B38. . 103 E1
Grangehurst Prim Sch
CV6. . . . . .96 B4
Grange La
Alvechurch B48. . . . . . 139 B3
4 Kingswinford DY6 . . 60 F4
Stourbridge DY9 . . . . . . 81 D4
Sutton Coldfield B75. . . 32 C3
Grange Mews The 1
CV32 . . . . 156 D1
Grangemouth Rd
CV6 . . . . 113 B7
Grange Pk DY1 . . . . 51 A1
Grange Rd
Balsall Common CV7. . 129 F7
Birmingham, Aston B6 . 66 E8
Birmingham B29 . . . . . . 85 F3

Grange Rd continued
Birmingham, Bordesley
  Green B10 .... 67 D1
Birmingham, Erdington
  B24 .... 57 C5
Birmingham, King's Heath
  B14 .... 104 E8
Burntwood WS7 ....7 A5
Coventry CV6 .... 96 B5
Cradley Heath B64 ... 83 B8
Dorridge B93 .... 127 E2
Dudley, New Dock DY1 . 51 B1
Dudley, Roseville WV14 51 B7
Halesowen B63........ 83 C3
Hockley Heath B94... 143 E8
Kidderminster DY11 . 116 B7
Norton Canes WS11....6 B6
2 Redditch B98........ 153 F4
Royal Leamington Spa
  CV32.............. 157 B3
Smethwick B66....... 65 A3
Solihull B91......... 106 E7
Stourbridge DY9 ..... 81 C4
West Bromwich B70... 53 B3
Wolverhampton, Blakenall
  WV2.............. 39 B6
Wolverhampton, Tettenhall
  Wood WV6 .... 24 C4
Grange Rise B38 .... 123 F7
Grangers La B98 ..... 158 F5
Grange St Dudley DY1 . 51 B1
Walsall WS1 .... 42 F7
Grange The
Birmingham B20 ...... 54 F4
Cubbington CV32 .... 157 F5
Halesowen B62....... 83 F6
Royal Leamington Spa
  CV32.............. 157 B1
Warwick CV34 .... 161 C7
Wombourne WV5 .... 49 A7
Grange Wlk CV6 ..... 96 B5
Grangewood Ct
Solihull B92......... 106 E7
Sutton Coldfield B73... 57 A7
Granhill Cl B98...... 159 A8
Granleigh Ct CV32... 157 E5
Granoe Cl CV3 ...... 134 E8
Granshaw Cl B38.... 103 F1
Grant Cl
Kingswinford DY6..... 60 D8
West Bromwich B71... 53 C5
Grant Ct B30........ 104 A5
Grantham Rd
Birmingham B11...... 87 B6
Smethwick B66....... 65 B3
Grantham St CV2... 113 F3
Grantley Cres DY6.... 60 C7
Grantley Dr B37...... 70 B3
Granton Cl B14 ..... 104 D5
Granton Rd B14..... 104 D5
Grantown Gr WS3.... 14 A4
Grant Rd
Bedworth CV7........ 78 A1
Coventry CV3 .... 114 B2
Grant St
Birmingham B15...... 86 D8
Walsall WS3 .... 28 B8
Granville B77 ....21 F1
Granville Cl
Bromsgrove B60..... 137 B1
Wolverhampton WV2 . 163 C1
Granville Crest DY10 117 B6
Granville Dr DY6 ....60 F5
Granville Gdns LE10 . 75 C8
Granville Rd
Cradley Heath B64 ... 83 B8
Dorridge B93 .... 128 A2
Hinckley LE10 .... 75 C8
Granville Sq B1 ..... 66 C1
Granville St
Birmingham B1...... 164 A1
Royal Leamington Spa
  CV32.............. 157 A2
Willenhall WV13 ..... 27 A3
Wolverhampton WV2 . 163 C1
Grapes Cl CV6 ..... 113 B5
Grasdene Gr B17..... 85 C4
Grasmere Ave
Coventry CV3 ...... 132 F6
Perton WV6.......... 23 F4
Sutton Coldfield B74... 31 A2
Grasmere Cl
Birmingham B43...... 54 F7
Kidderminster DY10 . 116 E7
Kingswinford DY6..... 60 B7
Wolverhampton, Palmers
  Cross WV6 .... 24 E8
Wolverhampton WV11 . 26 C7
Grasmere Cres CV11 . 73 F7
Grasmere Ho 13 B69 . 63 D5

Grasmere Pl WS11 .....1 E5
Grasmere Rd
Bedworth CV12....... 78 B2
Birmingham B21 ..... 65 F7
Grasscroft CV3... 133 E6
Grassholme B77 ...... 36 A8
Grassington Ave
CV34 .... 155 F1
Grassington Dr
Birmingham B37...... 69 F1
Nuneaton CV11....... 74 A2
Grassmere Ct WS6 .... 4 D3
Grassmere Dr DY8 ....80 F3
Grassmoor Rd B38.. 103 E2
Grassy La WV10, WV11 12 B1
Graston Cl B16...... 66 A2
Gratham Cl DY5...... 81 B7
Gratley Croft WS12.....1 C4
Grattidge Rd B27..... 88 D2
Gratton Ct CV3...... 132 F6
Gravel Bank B32..... 84 D2
Gravel Hill
Coventry CV4 .... 111 F1
Wombourne WV5 .... 49 B6
Gravel La WS12 ....1 C5
Gravelly Ct 4 B23 ... 56 E2
Gravelly Hill B23..... 56 E2
Gravelly Hill N B23... 56 E3
Gravelly Hill Sta B23..56 E2
Gravelly Ind Pk B24...67 F8
Gravelly La
Birmingham B23...... 56 F5
Stonnall WS9 .... 16 F3
Gravel Pit La B48 ... 139 E3
Gravel The B76....... 48 B2
Gray Cl DY10....... 117 B6
Graydon Ct B74...... 46 B7
Grayfield Ave B13.... 87 A3
Grayland Cl B27..... 88 B2
Graylands The CV3 .. 133 C4
Grayling B77......... 35 D6
Grayling Cl WS10.... 41 B3
Grayling Rd DY9 .... 81 C6
Grayling Wlk
Birmingham B37...... 70 C3
Wolverhampton WV10 . 26 B4
Gray Rd WS12........1 F6
Grayshott Cl
Birmingham B23...... 56 E5
Bromsgrove B61..... 136 E3
Grays Rd B17 .... 85 D6
Gray St B9........... 67 B2
Grayston Ave B77 .... 21 E4
Grayswood Ave CV5 . 112 D4
Grayswood Park Rd
B32 .... 84 C6
Grayswood Rd B31.. 122 F7
Grazebrook Croft
B32 .... 102 D8
Grazebrook Ind Pk
DY2................62 B6
Grazebrook Rd DY2 .. 62 C7
Grazewood Cl WV12.. 27 B7
Grazier Ave B77...... 35 C8
Grazing La B97 ..... 152 F2
Greadier St WV12.... 27 C5
Great Arthur St B66...64 F7
Great Barn La B97 .. 153 B1
Great Barr Bsna Pk
B42................. 55 A5
Great Barr Prim Sch
B44................. 44 B1
Great Barr Sch B44 . 44 D1
Great Barr St B9 .... 67 A2
Great Brickkiln St
WV3 .... 25 B1
Great Bridge DY4 .... 52 D5
Great Bridge Ind Est
DY4................. 52 C7
Great Bridge Prim Sch
DY4................. 52 C6
Great Bridge Rd
WV14 .... 41 B3
Great Bridge St B70.. 52 E5
Great Brook St B7... 67 A4
Great Charles St WS8 .15 F8
Great Charles Street
Queensway B3 .... 164 B3
Great Colmore St
B15 .... 86 D8
Great Cornbow 5
B63 .... 83 B3
Great Croft Ho 2
WS10 .... 41 D6
Great Farley Dr B31 . 102 C1
Greatfield Rd DY11 . 116 B4
Great Francis St B7 .. 67 A4
Great Hampton Row
B19 .... 164 A4

Great Hampton St
Birmingham B18..... 164 A4
Wolverhampton WV1 . 25 B4
Greatheed Rd CV32 . 156 E2
Great Hockings La
B97 .... 152 E2
Great King St N B19.. 66 C6
Great King St B19... 66 C5
Great Lister St B7..... 67 A4
Great Mdw DY4 ..... 52 B5
Greatmead B77 ...... 21 C1
Great Moor Rd WV6 .. 23 A3
Great Oaks B26 ..... 89 B5
Greatorex Ct B71.... 53 B8
Great Stone Rd B31.. 103 A3
Great Tindal St B16.. 66 A2
Great Western Arc
B2 .... 164 C3
Great Western Cl B18 65 E6
Great Western Ct B27 88 C4
Great Western Dr
B64 .... 63 A1
Great Western St
Wednesbury WS10.... 41 E2
Wolverhampton WV1 . 163 C4
Great Western Way
DY4 .... 52 D6
Great Wood Rd B10.. 67 C1
Great Wyrley High Sch
WS6................4 F3
Greaves Ave WS5..... 43 C8
Greaves Cl
Walsall WS5 .... 43 C8
Warwick CV34 ...... 161 C7
Greaves Cres WV12... 27 C8
Greaves Rd DY2..... 62 D5
Greaves Sq B38..... 104 B1
Greaves The B76.....58 F6
Grebe Cl B23 .... 56 B3
Greenacre Cl B77 ... 22 B5
Greenacre Dr WV8 .. 10 B2
Greenacre Rd DY4... 41 A1
Greenacres
Birmingham B32...... 84 E2
Sedgley DY3 .... 39 B1
Sutton Coldfield B76.. 58 A8
Wolverhampton WV6 .. 24 B5
Green Acres B27..... 88 B2
Greenacres Ave WV10 12 B2
Greenacres Cl WS9... 30 E2
Greenacres Prim Sch
B77................22 B5
Green Acres Prim Sch
WV14...............40 F6
Greenacres Rd B61.. 136 E3
Green Acres Rd B38. 123 D8
Greenaleigh Rd B14. 105 D3
Green Ave B28 ...... 87 E1
Greenaway Cl B43.... 44 E3
Greenaway Ct WV10.. 12 C7
Greenbank B45 ..... 138 D8
Green Bank Ave B28 . 87 E1
Greenbank Gdns DY8.. 60 E2
Greenbank Rd CV7 .. 129 F6
Green Barns La WS14 32 C8
Green Bower Dr B61 137 A5
Greenbush Dr B63 ... 83 A5
Green Cl Studley B80 . 159 E3
Whitnash CV31...... 162 B4
Wythall B47......... 125 A3
Greencroft
Bilston WV14 .... 40 D6
Kingswinford DY6..... 60 D4
Lichfield WS13 ....3 A2
Green Croft B9....... 68 A3
Green Ct
Birmingham, Gravelly Hill
  B23 .... 56 E2
Birmingham, Hall Green
  B28 .... 105 F8
8 Lichfield WS13......9 B7
Greendale Cl B61 .. 137 B8
Greendale Rd CV5... 112 D3
Green Dr
Birmingham B32..... 84 C1
Wolverhampton WV10 . 25 C7
Greenend Rd B13 .....86 F2
Greenfels Rise DY2...62 F8
Greenfield Ave
Balsall Common CV7. 130 A7
Cradley Heath B64 ... 62 B1
Lower Marlbrook B60. 121 D1
Stourbridge DY8...... 80 F5
Greenfield Bldgs
WV5 .... 49 A7
Greenfield Cotts
B48 .... 139 A5
Greenfield Cres B15. 86 A8
Greenfield Croft
WV14 .... 40 D2

Greenfield Ho B26 ... 89 D6
Greenfield La WV10 .. 11 E5
Greenfield Prim Sch
Stourbridge DY8...... 80 F5
Walsall WS4 .... 29 C8
Greenfield Rd
Birmingham B17...... 85 D5
Birmingham, Newton
  B43.............. 54 D7
Smethwick B67....... 64 E4
Greenfields
Aldridge WS9 .... 30 B7
Cannock WS11 ....1 C1
Redditch B98 .... 153 C1
Greenfields Rd
Kingswinford DY6..... 60 E6
Walsall WS4 .... 15 D2
Wombourne WV5 .... 49 A5
Green Field The CV3. 134 B8
Greenfield View DY3.. 50 B7
Greenfinch Cl
Birmingham B36...... 70 A7
Kidderminster DY10 . 117 B3
Greenfinch Rd
Birmingham B36...... 70 A7
Stourbridge DY9 ..... 81 D5
Greenford Cl B97 ... 153 B5
Greenford Ho
Birmingham B23...... 56 B6
7 West Bromwich B70 53 D1
Greenford Rd B14... 105 C3
Green Gables
Hollywood B47 ...... 125 A7
Sutton Coldfield B74... 46 B7
Greenheart B77 ...... 22 A4
Green Heath Rd WS12 ..2 C1
Greenhill
Blackwell B60....... 137 F4
Lichfield WS13 ....9 C8
Wombourne WV5 .... 49 B6
Greenhill Ave DY10 . 116 F7
Greenhill Cl
Tamworth B77........ 35 C5
Willenhall WV12 ..... 27 B5
Green Hill Cl B60 ... 137 D6
Greenhill Ct
Halesowen B62....... 83 E7
Sutton Coldfield B72.. 57 C8
Wombourne WV5 .... 49 B5
Greenhill Dr B29 .... 85 C1
Greenhill Gdns
Birmingham B43...... 43 E2
Halesowen B62....... 83 D6
Wombourne WV5 .... 49 B5
Greenhill Ind Est
DY10................ 117 A7
Greenhill Mews WS13 .9 C8
Greenhill Oak DY10. 116 F7
Greenhill Rd
Birmingham, Handsworth
  B21.............. 54 E2
Birmingham, Moseley
  B13.............. 87 A1
Dudley DY3 .... 50 E5
Halesowen B62....... 83 D7
Sutton Coldfield B72.. 57 C8
Whitnash CV31...... 162 B4
Greenhill Way WS9... 16 B1
Green Hill Way B90 . 106 B5
Greenholm Prim Sch
B44................55 E7
Greenholm Rd B44.. 55 E7
Greenhough Rd WS13 .9 A8
Greenhurst Dr B45 . 122 A1
Greening Dr B15..... 86 B7
Green La Aldridge WS9 30 E5
Balsall Common CV7. 130 B7
Birchmoor B77, B78.. 36 D7
Birmingham B32..... 84 C6
Birmingham, Bordesley
  Green B9........ 67 E1
Birmingham, Castle
  Bromwich B36..... 69 E8
Birmingham, Great Barr
  B43.............. 43 D1
Birmingham, Handsworth
  B21.............. 65 C8
Birmingham, Hawkesley
  B38............. 123 E8
Birmingham, Newton
  B43.............. 54 D8
Brownhills WS8 ....7 B2
Cannock WS11 ....4 E6
Coleshill B46......... 70 F5
Corley Moor CV7..... 93 D6
Coventry CV3 ...... 133 B4
Dudley DY3 .... 50 F5
Halesowen B62....... 63 D1
Kingswinford DY6..... 60 D7
Lichfield WS14 ....8 D2

Green La continued
Middleton B78........ 48 B6
Nuneaton CV10...... 72 C7
Redditch B97 .... 158 A7
Solihull B90......... 105 E1
Stourbridge DY9 ..... 81 E5
Studley B80......... 159 B5
Tamworth B77........ 36 C6
Upper Catshill B61 .. 121 A1
Walsall, Birchills WS2,
  WS3............. 28 C5
Walsall, High Heath WS4,
  WS9............. 15 D3
Walsall, Pelsall WS3.. 15 A4
Warwick CV34 ...... 160 F8
Wolverhampton WV6 . 24 F7
Greenland Ave CV5.. 111 F5
Greenland Cl DY6.... 60 E8
Greenland Ct
Birmingham B8....... 67 E6
Coventry CV5 ...... 111 F5
Greenland Rd B29... 86 B1
Greenland Rise B92. 107 D7
Greenlands Ave B98. 154 A1
Greenlands Bsns Ctr
B98................ 154 B2
Greenlands Dr B98.. 158 F8
Greenlands Rd B37.. 70 C1
Green Lane Ind Est
B9..................67 E1
Green Lanes
Bilston WV14 .... 40 C7
Sutton Coldfield B73... 57 B8
Green Lanes Prim Sch
B36.................69 F8
Green Lane Venture Ctr
WS11...............4 E6
Greenlawns DY4 .... 52 B8
Greenlea B77 .... 36 A8
Greenleaf Cl CV5.... 112 A3
Green Leigh B23 .....56 F8
Greenleas Gdns B63. 83 C3
Green Leighs DY3 ... 39 D3
Greenly Rd WV4..... 39 D5
Green Mdw
Stourbridge DY9 ..... 99 B7
Wednesfield WV11 ... 26 E5
Green Mdws 2 WS12 ..2 C1
Green Meadow Prim Sch
B29................ 102 F7
Green Meadow Rd
Birmingham B29..... 103 A7
Willenhall WV12 ..... 27 B7
Greenmoor Rd
Hinckley LE10 .... 75 D5
Nuneaton CV10...... 73 A3
Greenoak Cres
Birmingham B30..... 104 C8
Dudley WV14 .... 51 A7
Green Oak Rd WV8 .. 10 B2
Green Park Ave WV14 40 C8
Green Park Rd WV14 . 40 C8
Green Park Rd
Birmingham B31..... 102 E2
Bromsgrove B60..... 137 B2
Dudley DY2 .... 62 F8
Green Park Sch WV14 40 B8
Green Rd
Birmingham B28..... 87 E1
Dudley DY2 .... 62 D7
Greenridge Rd B20.. 54 E5
Green Rock La WS3 .. 14 D1
Green Rock Prim Sch
WS3................14 E1
Greenroyde DY9..... 81 B1
Greensand Dr WV14.. 40 D2
Greenside
Birmingham B17...... 85 C5
Cheswick Green B90. 126 D4
Stoke Prior B60 ..... 150 C2
Greenside Cl CV11... 74 C1
Greenside Rd B24... 57 C5
Greenside Way WS5.. 43 A4
Greensill Ave DY4....51 F8
Greens Ind Est WS12..2 C7
Green Slade Cres
B60................ 121 C2
Greenslade Croft
B31................ 103 A2
Green Slade Gr WS12..2 C7
Greenslade Rd
Sedgley DY3 .... 39 B2
Solihull B90......... 105 C2
Walsall WS5 .... 43 C7
Greensleeves B45.....31 F1
Greensleeves Cl CV6 . 95 B2
Greens Rd CV6...... 95 A1
Green St
Birmingham B12..... 66 F1

Green St continued
Kidderminster DY10 . 116 E5
Oldbury B69 .... 64 A7
Smethwick B67....... 64 F5
Stourbridge DY8 ..... 80 F5
Tipton WV14 .... 51 C8
Walsall WS2 .... 28 C3
West Bromwich B70.. 64 E8
Greenstead Rd B13.. 87 D1
Greens The WV6 .... 23 E3
Green Street Ind Est
DY10............... 116 E4
Greensward Cl CV8.. 148 B6
Green Sward La B98 154 D1
Greensward The
CV3................ 115 A2
Greensway WV11... 26 B8
Greens Yd CV12 ..... 78 C3
Green The
Aldridge WS9 .... 30 C6
Birmingham, Castle
  Bromwich B36..... 69 B7
Birmingham, Erdington
  B23.............. 57 A4
Birmingham, Frankley
  B31............. 102 C2
Birmingham, King's Norton
  B38............. 103 F2
4 Birmingham, Quinton
  B32.............. 84 A6
Bluntington DY10 ... 118 C1
Darlaston WS10...... 41 D7
Fazeley B78......... 20 E2
Freasley B78........ 36 C4
Meriden CV7........ 92 B1
Nuneaton CV11...... 73 E2
Oldbury B68 .... 64 B1
Solihull B91......... 107 D5
Stoneleigh CV8...... 149 C6
Stourbridge DY8 ..... 60 D2
Sutton Coldfield B72.. 46 D1
Tamworth B77........ 22 B5
Tanworth-In-A B94.. 142 A2
Walsall WS3 .... 14 B1
West Hagley DY9 .... 98 F4
Greenvale B31 ..... 102 F5
Greenvale Ave B26 .. 89 D6
Greenway
Birmingham B20..... 54 F6
Nuneaton CV11...... 79 B8
Sedgley DY3 .... 39 E1
Warwick CV34 ...... 155 E1
Green Way WS9 ..... 16 B2
Greenway Ave 2 DY8 60 E1
Greenway Dr B73 ... 45 C3
Greenway Gdns
Birmingham B38..... 123 E7
Sedgley DY3 .... 39 E1
Greenway Rd WV14 . 40 E4
Greenways
Birmingham B31..... 102 F8
Coventry CV4 ...... 111 C2
Halesowen B63...... 82 C6
Stourbridge DY8 ..... 60 C1
Greenway St B9 ..... 67 C2
Greenways The
CV32............... 157 B3
Greenway The
Birmingham, Marston
  Green B37........ 90 A6
Sutton Coldfield, New Oscott
  B73.............. 45 B3
West Hagley DY9 .... 98 F5
Greenway Wlk B33... 69 E1
Green Wickets B13.. 104 E6
Green Wlk 4 B17.....84 F7
Greenwood B25...... 88 D8
Greenwood Ave
Birmingham B27..... 88 B1
Oldbury B68 .... 64 C5
Rowley Regis B65.... 63 D3
Greenwood Cl B14.. 104 E5
Greenwood Cotts
DY1................. 51 A5
Greenwood Ct
Nuneaton CV11...... 73 E3
Royal Leamington Spa
  CV32............ 157 B1
Greenwood Dr WS14 ..9 B6
Greenwood Pk
Aldridge WS9 .... 16 C2
Cannock WS12 ....2 B8
Greenwood Pl B44... 45 B4
Greenwood Rd
Aldridge WS9 .... 16 B2
West Bromwich B71.. 53 B8
Wolverhampton WV10 . 25 C7

Greenwood Sq 5
B37 . . . . **70** B2
Greenwoods The DY8. **80** E5
Greenwoods Way B37 . **70** B2
Greethurst Dr B13 . . . **87** C2
Greet Prim Sch B11 . **87** D4
Greets Green Ind Est
B70. . . . .**52** F4
Greets Green Rd B70 . .**52** F3
Greetville Cl B34 . . . . . **69** A5
Gregory Ave
Birmingham B29 . . . . **103** A8
Coventry CV3 . . . . . . **133** A6
Gregory Cl 3 WS10 . .**41** F2
Gregory Ct WV11 . . . . **26** E5
Gregory Dr DY1 . . . . . **51** A2
Gregory Hood Rd
CV3 . . . . **133** E4
Gregory Rd
Burntwood WS7 . . . .**7** E4
Stourbridge DY8 . . . . . **80** D5
Gregston Ind Est B69 .**64** B8
Greig Cl WS11 . . . .**2** C2
Grendon Cl
Coventry CV4 . . . . . . **111** C1
Redditch B98 . . . . . . **154** D1
Grendon Dr B73. . . . . **45** D3
Grendon Gdns WV3 . . **38** D6
Grendon Jun & Inf Sch
B14. . . . . **105** A3
Grendon Rd
Birmingham B14 . . . . **105** A3
Solihull B92 . . . . **106** E8
Grenfell Cl CV31 . . . . **162** D6
Grenfell Ct B73 . . . . . . **46** B1
Grenfell Dr B15 . . . . . .**85** F8
Grenfell Rd WS3 . . . . . **14** D3
Grenville Ave CV2 . . . **114** B3
Grenville Cl WS2 . . . . . **27** D3
Grenville Dr
Birmingham B23 . . . . . **56** B4
Smethwick B66 . . . . . . **64** D8
Grenville Pl B70 . . . . . **52** E3
Grenville Rd
Dudley DY1 . . . . **50** E1
Solihull B90 . . . . **106** B2
Gresham Ave CV32 . . **157** B2
Gresham Pl CV32 . . . . **157** B2
Gresham Rd
Birmingham B28 . . . . **105** F6
Cannock WS11 . . . .**1** F3
Nuneaton CV10 . . . . . . **78** B8
Oldbury B68 . . . . **64** C6
Gresham St CV2 . . . . . **114** A2
Gresham Twr B12 . . . .**86** F8
Gresley B77 . . . .**21** F1
Gresley Cl B74 . . . . **32** A4
Gresley Gr B23 . . . . **56** C1
Gresley Rd CV2 . . . . . **114** D7
Gresley Row WS13 . . . . .**9** C8
Gressel La B33 . . . . **69** D3
Grestone Ave B20 . . . . **54** E3
Grestone Prim Sch
B20. . . . .**54** E4
Greswold Cl CV4 . . . . **111** F1
Greswolde Dr B24 . . . . **57** B4
Greswolde Park Rd
B27 . . . . **88** B4
Greswolde Rd
Birmingham B11 . . . . . **87** D4
Solihull B91 . . . . **106** E6
Greswoldes The
CV31 . . . . **162** F6
Greswold Gdns B34 . . **69** A5
Greswold Prim Sch
B91 . . . . **107** C6
Greswold St B71 . . . . . **53** B5
Gretna Rd CV3 . . . . . . **132** F4
Gretton Cres WS9 . . . . **29** E5
Gretton Rd
Aldridge WS9 . . . . **29** F5
Birmingham B23 . . . . . **56** D7
Greville Dr B15 . . . . . . **86** C6
Greville Ho 13 CV34 . **160** F7
Greville Rd
Kenilworth CV8 . . . . . **147** F4
Warwick CV34 . . . . . . **156** B1
Greville Smith Ave
CV31 . . . . **162** B4
Grevis Cl B13 . . . .**86** F4
Grevis Rd B25 . . . . **68** C1
Greycoat Rd CV6 . . . . . **95** A2
Greyfort Cres B92 . .**88** F1
Greyfriars Cl
Dudley DY1 . . . . **50** E3
Solihull B92 . . . . **106** D6
Greyfriars Ct CV6 . . . **113** A7

Greyfriars Dr
Bromsgrove B61 . . . **136** D2
Tamworth B79. . . . . . **20** E6
Greyfriars La CV1 . . . **165** B2
Greyfriars Rd CV1 . . . **165** B2
Greyhound La
Lower Penn WV4 . . . . . **37** E5
Stourbridge DY8 . . . . . **80** D2
Greyhurst Croft 5
B91 . . . . **127** B8
Grey Mill Cl B90. . . . . **126** F6
Greysbrooke WS14 . . . **18** A5
Greysbrooke Prim Sch
WS14 . . . . **18** A6
Grey's Rd B80. . . . . . . **159** E3
Greystoke Ave B36 . . **68** D7
Greystoke Dr DY6 . . . **60** D6
Greystone Cl B98. . . . **154** C5
Greystone Pas 16 DY1 **51** B1
Grice St B70 . . . . **64** D8
Griffin Ave DY10. . . . . **116** E4
Griffin Bsns Pk B37 . . **70** C3
Griffin Cl
Birmingham B31 . . . . **103** B6
Burntwood WS7 . . . .**6** E8
Griffin Ct B5 . . . . **86** C5
Griffin Gdns B17 . . . . **85** D4
Griffin Ho B16 . . . . **65** E1
Griffin Ind Est B65 . . .**63** F3
Griffin Rd
Birmingham B23 . . . . . **56** C5
Warwick CV34 . . . . . . **161** C7
Griffins Brook Cl
B30 . . . . **103** D7
Griffins Brook La
B30 . . . . **103** D6
Griffins La B90. . . . . . **126** A5
Griffin St Dudley DY2 . . **62** C4
West Bromwich B70 . . . **53** D3
Wolverhampton WV1 . . **25** F1
Griffiths Dr
Wolverhampton
WV11 . . . . **13** A1
Wombourne WV5 . . . . . **49** A5
Griffiths Rd
Dudley DY1 . . . . **51** A6
West Bromwich B71. . . . **42** C1
Willenhall WV12 . . . . . . **27** D8
Griffiths St DY4 . . . . . . **51** E5
Griff La Nuneaton CV10 **78** A6
Nuneaton CV10. . . . . . **78** B6
Grigg Gr B31. . . . . **102** E1
Grimley Cl B98. . . . . . **153** F1
Grimley La B60 . . . . . **151** E6
Grimley Rd 2 B31 . . . **103** D2
Grimley Way WS11 . . . .**1** F4
Grimpits La B38. . . . . **124** A7
Grimshaw Rd B27 . . . **88** A1
Grimshaw Villas
B93 . . . . **128** D8
Grimston Cl CV3 . . . . **115** A2
Grimstone St WV10. . **163** C4
Grindleford Rd B42 . . **55** D7
Grindle Rd CV6 . . . . . .**95** F4
Grindley Ho 5 CV1 . . **113** B2
Grindsbrook B77 . . . . **36** A8
Gristhorpe Rd B29 . . **104** A8
Grizebeck Dr CV5 . . . **112** A5
Grizedale Cl B45 . . . . **102** B2
Grocott Rd WS10 . . . . **41** B4
Grosmont Ave 8 B12 **87** A6
Grosvenor Ave
Birmingham B20. . . . . **55** C2
Kidderminster DY11 . . **117** A6
Sutton Coldfield B74 . . . **30** F1
Grosvenor Cl
Lichfield WS14 . . . . **9** D6
Sutton Coldfield B75 . . . **32** C1
Wolverhampton WV10 . . **11** D2
Grosvenor Cres
Hinckley LE10 . . . . **76** A6
Wolverhampton WV10 . . **11** D2
Grosvenor Ct
Birmingham, Handsworth
B20. . . . . **55** C2
Dudley DY3 . . . . **50** D2
2 Royal Leamington Spa
CV32. . . . . **156** F1
Shenstone WS14. . . . . . **17** F6
Stourbridge DY9 . . . . . . **81** B1
Wednesfield WV11 . . . . **26** E5
Wolverhampton, Tettenhall
Wood WV6 . . . . **24** A3
Wolverhampton WV3 . **163** B2
Grosvenor Gdns B61 **137** B5
Grosvenor Ho
Birmingham, Erdington
B23. . . . . **57** A5
Coventry CV1 . . . . . . **165** A2

Grosvenor Ho continued
Redditch B97 . . . . . . **153** E4
Grosvenor Pk WV4 . . . . .**38** F5
Grosvenor Rd
Birmingham, Aston B6 . **67** B8
Birmingham B17 . . . . . **85** A6
Birmingham, Handsworth
B20 . . . . **55** C2
Coventry CV1 . . . . . . **165** A1
Dudley DY3 . . . . **50** D2
Oldbury B68 . . . . **64** A3
Solihull B91 . . . . **106** F1
Whitnash CV31. . . . . . **162** A5
Wolverhampton, Bushbury
WV10 . . . . **11** D2
Wolverhampton WV4 . . **39** E3
Grosvenor Road S
DY3 . . . . **50** D2
Grosvenor St W B16. . **66** B1
Grosvenor Sh Ctr
B31. . . . . **103** A4
Grosvenor Sq B28. . . **105** F5
Grosvenor St
Birmingham B5 . . . . . **164** D3
Wolverhampton WV10 . **25** F3
Grosvenor Way DY5 . . **81** E7
Grotto La WV6 . . . . . . **24** C5
Groucutt Cl 6 WV14 . **51** C8
Grounds Dr B74 . . . . . .**31** F3
Grounds Rd B74 . . . . . .**31** F3
Grout St B70. . . . . **52** E4
Grove Ave
Birmingham B27 . . . . . **88** B3
Birmingham, Handsworth
B21. . . . . **65** F8
Birmingham, Moseley
B13. . . . . **87** A2
Halesowen B63. . . . . . **82** F3
Solihull B91 . . . . **107** C5
Grove Cl WS11 . . . .**5** F1
Grove Cottage Rd B9. **67** D2
Grove Cres
Brierley Hill DY5 . . . . . **61** C5
Walsall WS3 . . . . **14** F3
Grove Ct
Birmingham B43 . . . . . **54** F6
Coventry CV5 . . . . . . **133** B8
Nuneaton CV11 . . . . . . **73** E4
Grove Farm Dr B75. .**46** F5
Grovefield Cres CV7 . **130** C8
Grove Fields CV10. . . **73** D8
Grove Gdns
Birmingham B20 . . . . . **54** F2
Bromsgrove B61 . . . . **137** A6
Grove Hill WS5. . . . . . . **29** E1
Grove Hill Rd B21 . . . .**54** F1
Grovehurst Pk CV8 . . **149** B2
Grove La
Birmingham B17 . . . . . **85** C4
Birmingham, Handsworth
B20. . . . . **54** F1
Keresley CV7 . . . . **94** F7
Lapworth B94 . . . . **143** A4
Norton Canes WS3 . . . . . .**5** E1
Smethwick B66 . . . . . . **65** C5
Wishaw B76 . . . . **47** F2
Wolverhampton WV6 . . **24** B2
Groveland Rd DY4 . . . **52** B3
Grovelands Cres
WV10 . . . . **11** D3
Grovelands Ind Est
CV7. . . . . **96** A6
Groveley La B31, B45 **122** E5
Grove Mews B31 . . . . **123** B8
Grove Pk
Hinckley LE10 . . . . **76** A6
Kingswinford DY6 . . . . . **60** C8
Grove Pl
Nuneaton CV10. . . . . . **72** D3
2 Royal Leamington Spa
CV31. . . . . **162** A6
Grove Prim Sch
WV2. . . . . **163** D1
Grove Rd Ansty CV7 . .**97** D3
Birmingham, King's Heath
B14. . . . . **104** D6
Birmingham, Sparkhill
B11. . . . . **87** C2
Dorridge B93 . . . . . . **128** B3
Hinckley LE10 . . . . **76** A6
Nuneaton CV10. . . . . . **72** D3
Oldbury B68 . . . . **64** D1
Solihull B91 . . . . **107** C5
Stourbridge DY9 . . . . . . **81** F3
Grove Sch B21 . . . . . .**65** F8
Groveside Way WS3 . . **15** A5
Grove St
Coventry CV1 . . . . . . **165** C3
Dudley DY2 . . . . **62** E8
Redditch B98 . . . . . . **153** E4

Grove St continued
Royal Leamington Spa
CV32. . . . . **161** E8
Smethwick B66 . . . . . . **65** D4
Wolverhampton, Springfield
WV10 . . . . **25** F3
Wolverhampton WV2 . **163** C1
Grove Terr WS1 . . . . .**28** F1
Grove The
Bedworth CV12. . . . . . **78** C3
Birmingham, Edgbaston
B16. . . . . **65** F2
Birmingham, Great Barr
B43. . . . . **43** E4
Birmingham, Lozells
B19. . . . . **66** B7
Birmingham, Rednal
B45. . . . . **122** D4
Birmingham, Saltley B8 **67** C4
Birmingham, West Heath
B31. . . . . **123** B8
Brierley Hill DY5 . . . . . **61** C1
Burntwood WS7 . . . .**6** D8
Coleshill B46. . . . . **70** F4
Hampton-in-A B92 . . . . **91** A1
Hinckley LE10 . . . . **75** C8
Rowley Regis B65. . . . . **63** C2
Studley B80. . . . . **159** D3
Sutton Coldfield B74. . . **31** D6
Walsall WS5 . . . . **43** B3
Wolverhampton, New Cross
WV11 . . . . **26** B6
Wolverhampton, Parkfield
WV4 . . . . **39** E5
Grove Vale Ave B43. . **43** C1
Grove Vale Prim Sch
B43. . . . . **43** D1
Grove Villas B64. . . . . **82** D7
Grove Way B74. . . . . . .**44** F7
Grovewood Dr 2
B38 . . . . **103** E1
Guardhouse Rd CV6 . **113** B8
Guardian Angels RC Prim
Sch B34 . . . .**69** E6
Guardian Ct
Birmingham, Frankley
B31. . . . . **102** D3
Birmingham, Gilbertstone
B26. . . . . **88** F7
4 Bromsgrove B60 . . **137** A2
Solihull B91 . . . . **107** D3
Guardian Ho B68. . . . . **84** C7
Guardians Way B31 . **102** E6
Guernsey Dr B36. . . . . **70** B6
Guest Ave WV11. . . . . . **26** C8
Guest Gr B19 . . . . **66** C6
Guest Hospl DY1. . . . .**51** E3
Guild Ave WS3 . . . . **28** D3
Guild Cl B16 . . . . **66** A2
Guild Cotts The
CV34 . . . . **160** D6
Guild Croft B19 . . . . . . **66** D5
Guild Ct 4 B60 . . . . . **136** F2
Guildford Cl DY11 . . . . **116** A6
Guildford Croft B37 . .**89** F8
Guildford Ct
12 Birmingham B29 . . **103** C2
Coventry CV6 . . . . . . **113** C7
Guildford Dr B19 . . . . . **66** D6
Guildford St 4 B19 . . **66** D7
Guildhall Mews The **7**
WS1 . . . .**28** F1
Guild Rd
Bromsgrove B60 . . . . . **136** F1
Coventry CV6 . . . . . . **113** D7
Guillemard Ct B37 . . **70** B1
Guilsborough Rd
CV3 . . . . **134** E8
Guinea Cres CV4 . . . . **131** E6
Guinness Cl B98 . . . . **158** D8
Guiting Cl B97 . . . . . . **153** B1
Guiting Rd B29. . . . . . **103** A7
Gulistan Ct 6 CV32 . **156** E1
Gulistan Rd CV32. . . . **156** E1
Gullane Cl B38 . . . . . . **103** D1
Gullet The B78 . . . . . . **22** F1
Gullick Way WS7 . . . . . . **6** D8
Gulliman's Way
CV31 . . . . **162** D7
CV32 . . . . **157** B2
Gullswood Cl B14 . . . **104** D2
Gulson Hospl CV1 . . . **165** D2
Gulson Rd CV1. . . . . . **113** D2
Gumbleberrys Cl B8. . **68** C4
Gun Barrel Ind Ctr
B63. . . . .**82** F6
Gundry Cl CV31 . . . . . **162** A7
Gun La CV2 . . . . **114** A5
Gunmakers Wlk B19. **66** D7
Gunner Gr B75 . . . . . . **47** A6
Gunner La B45 . . . . . . **121** D7

Gunners La B80 . . . . . **159** E4
Gunnery Terr 3
CV32. . . . . **156** D1
Gunns Way B92 . . . . . **106** D7
Guns La B70 . . . . **53** B4
Gunstock Cl B74. . . . . **44** E7
Guns Village Prim Sch
B70. . . . . **53** A3
Gunter Prim Sch B24 .**57** E3
Gunter Rd B24 . . . . . . **57** E3
Gunton Ave CV3 . . . . . **134** C6
Guphill Ave CV5 . . . . . **112** D2
Guphill La CV5 . . . . . . **112** D3
Gurnard B77 . . . . **35** D6
Gurnard Cl WV12. . . . . **13** B1
Gurney Cl CV4 . . . . . . **111** E3
Gurney Pl WS2. . . . . . . **28** A5
Gurney Rd WS2 . . . . . . **28** A5
Guthrie Cl B19 . . . . . . **66** D6
Guthrum Cl
Birmingham B23 . . . . . **56** E8
Perton WV6 . . . . **23** F5
Gutteridge Ave CV6 . . **95** A2
Gutter The DY9. . . . . . **120** E7
Guy Ave WV10. . . . . . . **25** E6
Guy Pl E 13 CV32 . . . . **156** F1
Guy Pl W 12 CV32 . . . . **156** F1
Guy Rd CV8 . . . . **147** F2
Guy's Almshouses
B79 . . . . **21** B5
Guys Cl B79. . . . .**20** F7
Guys Cliffe Ave B76 . .**46** F1
Guy's Cliffe Ave
CV32. . . . . **156** D2
Guy's Cliffe Rd CV32 **161** E8
Guy's Cliffe Terr
CV34 . . . . **160** F7
Guy's Cross Park Rd
CV34 . . . . **160** F8
Guy's La DY3. . . . . **50** B2
Guys Motors Ind Pk
WV10 . . . .**25** F5
Guy St
Royal Leamington Spa
CV32. . . . . **156** F1
Warwick CV34 . . . . . . **160** F7
Guy's Wlk B61 . . . . . . **137** A5
Gwalia Gr B23 . . . .**56** F4
Gwendoline Ave LE10 **71** A2
Gwendoline Way WS9 **16** A4
GWS Ind Est WS10 . . . **41** D1
Gypsy La
Kenilworth CV8. . . . . . **147** F2
Redditch B97 . . . . . . **152** C5
Water Orton B46 . . . . . **59** D2

H

Habberley La DY11 . . . **116** A8
Habberley Rd
Kidderminster DY11 . . **116** B7
Rowley Regis B65. . . . . **63** D2
Habberley St 1
DY11 . . . . **116** C6
Habberley Croft 1
B91 . . . . **107** B1
Habitat Ct B76 . . . . . . **46** F3
Hackett Cl WV14 . . . . .**39** F1
Hackett Ct 2 B69 . . . . **64** A7
Hackett Dr B66 . . . . . . **64** D7
Hackett Rd B65 . . . . . . **63** E3
Hackett St DY4 . . . . . . **52** C7
Hackford Rd WV4 . . . . **39** F4
Hackmans Gate La
DY9 . . . . **119** B7
Hack St B9 . . . . **67** A1
Hackwood Ho 10 B69. **63** D5
Hackwood Rd WS10 . . **42** B2
Hadcroft Grange DY9. **81** D4
Hadcroft Rd DY9. . . . . **81** D4
Haddock Rd WV14. . . . **40** C7
Haddon Cres WV12. . . **27** C7
Haddon Croft B63. . . . **82** C1
Haddon End CV3 . . . . **133** E6
Haddon Rd
Birmingham B42 . . . . . **55** D4
Royal Leamington Spa
CV32. . . . . **157** B2
Haddon St CV6. . . . . . **114** A8
Haddon Twr 1 B15. . . **86** D8
Haden Arch Ct B64. . . **83** A7
Haden Cl
Cradley Heath B64 . . . . **83** A7
Stourbridge DY8 . . . . . **60** D2
Haden Cres WV11 . . . . **26** F6
Haden Cross Dr B64. . **83** A7
Haden Ct 5 WV3. . . . . **25** A2
Hadendale B64. . . . . . **83** A7

Haden Hill WV3 . . . . . **25** A2
Haden Hill Rd B63 . . . **83** B6
Haden Park Rd B64 . .**82** F7
Haden Rd
Cradley Heath B64 . . . . **62** E2
Wednesbury DY4 . . . . . **41** A1
Haden St B12 . . . .**86** F6
Haden Way B12 . . . . . .**86** F6
Haden Wlk 4 B65 . . . . **63** C3
Hadfield Cl B24 . . . . . . **57** E3
Hadfield Croft B19 . . . **66** C5
Hadfield Way B37 . . . . **70** A4
Hadland Rd B33 . . . . . **69** B1
Hadleigh Croft B76. . . **58** A6
Hadleigh Rd CV3 . . . . **133** C4
Hadley Cl Dudley DY2. . **62** E4
Hollywood B47 . . . . . . **125** A5
Hadley Croft B66. . . . . **65** A7
Hadley Ct B16. . . . . . . **65** D1
Hadley Mews CV11 . . . **73** D1
Hadley Pl WV14 . . . . . **40** C7
Hadley Rd
Bilston WV14 . . . . **40** C7
Willenhall WS2 . . . . . . **27** F6
Hadley St B68. . . . . . . **64** A4
Hadley Way WS2 . . . . . **28** A6
Hadlow Croft B33 . . . . **89** D7
Hadrian Cl CV32. . . . . **157** B4
Hadrian Dr B46 . . . . . .**59** F1
Hadrians Cl B77. . . . . . **35** D8
Hadyn Gr B26. . . . . **89** B6
Hadzor Ho 5 B97. . . **153** A4
Hadzor Rd B68. . . . . . . **84** D1
Hafren Cl B45. . . . . . . **102** B2
Hafton Gr B9. . . . . **67** D1
Haggar St WV2. . . . . . . **39** C6
Haglay Ct N DY5 . . . . . **61** E4
Haglay Ct S DY5. . . . . . **61** E4
Hagley Cl DY9. . . . . **99** C6
Hagley Cswy DY9. . . . **100** B8
Hagley Ct DY3 . . . . **50** D3
Hagley Hall★ DY9 . . . . **99** D6
Hagley Hall Gdns DY9 **99** E7
Hagley Hill DY9 . . . . . . **99** E7
Hagley Ho B60. . . . . . . **137** B3
Hagley Mews DY9 . . . . **99** D6
Hagley Park Dr B45 . . **122** A6
Hagley Prim Sch DY9 .**99** B5
Hagley RC High Sch
DY8. . . . .**98** F6
Hagley Rd
Birmingham B16 . . . . . **65** C1
Halesowen B63. . . . . . **82** E2
Stourbridge DY8 . . . . . **81** B3
Hagley Rd W B32, B68 **84** D7
Hagley St 3 B63. . . . . **83** B3
Hagley Sta DY9 . . . . . . **99** A6
Hagley View Rd DY2 . . **62** C8
Hagley Villas B12. . . . . **87** B4
Hagley Wood La DY9,
B62 . . . . **100** B8
Haig Cl Cannock WS11 . . **2** A5
Sutton Coldfield B75 . . . **46** C7
Haig Pl B13. . . . . **105** A7
Haig Rd DY2 . . . . **51** F1
Haig St B71 . . . . **53** C5
Hailes Park Cl WV2 . . **39** E6
Hailsham Rd B23 . . . . .**56** F5
Hailstone Cl B65 . . . . . **63** C4
Haines Cl DY4 . . . . **52** B4
Haines St B70. . . . . **53** D2
Hainfield Dr B91 . . . . . **107** E5
Hainge Rd B69. . . . . . . **52** C1
Hainult Cl DY8 . . . . **60** D4
Halas Ct B64. . . . . **62** E2
Halas Ind Est B63 . . . **83** C5
Halberd Cl LE10 . . . . . . **75** D5
Halberton St B66. . . . . **65** D4
Haldane Ct B33 . . . . . . **69** B2
Haldon Gr B31 . . . . . . **122** E7
Hale Gr B24. . . . . **57** D4
Halesbury Ct B63 . . .**82** F4
Halesbury Sch B62 . .**83** E7
Hales Cres B67. . . . . . . **64** E4
Hales Gdns B23 . . . . . .**56** C8
Hales La B67. . . . . **64** E4
Halesmere Way B63. . **83** C3
Halesowen CE Prim Sch
B63. . . . .**83** B4
Halesowen Coll (E-
Business Ctr) B62 . . **83** C8
Halesowen Coll
(Whittingham main
campus) B63. . . . . . .**83** B5
Halesowen Ind Pk
B62. . . . .**83** B6
Halesowen Rd
Dudley BY2, B64. . . . . **62** D4

Halesowen Rd *continued*
Halesowen B62....... **83** F6
Lower Marlbrook B61. **121** C3
Halesowen St
Oldbury B68 .... **63** F7
Rowley Regis B65..... **63** C1
Hales Park Ind Est
CV6.................**95** E4
Hales Rd
Halesowen B63....... **83** A4
Wednesbury WS10 .... **42** A5
Hales St CV1........ **165** C3
Hales Way B69.......**63** F7
Halesworth Rd WV9 .. **10** F2
Hale Trad Est DY4...**52** B6
Halewood Gr B28 ... **106** A7
Haley St WV12 ...... **27** C5
Halfcot Ave DY9...... **81** C3
Halford Cres WS3....**28** F5
Halford Gr B24...... **57** E4
Halford La CV6...... **95** A2
Halford Lodge CV6... **95** A2
Halford Rd B91 ..... **106** E6
Halford's La B66 .... **65** A8
Halfords Pk B66..... **65** A8
Halford St B71 ...... **21** A5
Halfpenny Field Wlk
B35 ....**58** A3
Halfshire La DY10 .... **98** B1
Halfway Cl B44...... **55** E6
Halifax Cl CV5 ...... **112** A7
Halifax Ct DY11 ..... **116** B8
Halifax Gr 7 B18 ... **65** E4
Halifax No B5....... **86** D7
Halifax Rd B90 ..... **106** B2
Haliscombe Gr 4 B6. **66** E8
Halkett Glade B33... **68** D3
Halladale B38....... **103** F1
Hallam Cl B71 ...... **53** E5
Hallam Cres WV10.... **25** E6
Hallam Ct B71 ...... **53** E5
Hallam Dr B71....... **53** E5
Hallam Rd CV6...... **95** B2
Hallams Cl CV8 ..... **135** F5
Hallam St
Birmingham B12...... **86** E5
West Bromwich B71... **53** D5
Hallbridge Cl WS3....**14** F2
Hallbridge Way B69.. **52** B2
Hall Brook Rd CV6 ... **95** A4
Hallchurch Rd DY2 ... **61** F6
Hall Cl CV8 .... **149** B6
Hallcourt Cl 3 WS11...**4** E8
Hallcourt Cres 2
WS11...............**4** E8
Hallcourt La WS11 ... **4** E8
Hall Cres B71 .... **53** C6
Hallcroft Cl B72...... **57** C7
Hallcroft Way
Aldridge WS9 .... **30** C5
Dorridge B93 .... **128** A6
Hall Dale Cl B28 .... **105** F5
Hall Dr Baginton CV8 . **133** E3
Birmingham B37...... **90** A4
Hagley DY9 .... **99** D6
Hall End
Nuneaton CV11....... **73** D2
Wednesbury WS10 .... **41** F3
Hall End Pl CV11 .... **73** D2
Hallens Dr WS10 ..... **41** D2
Hallet Dr WV3........ **163** A2
Hallewell Rd B16..... **65** D3
Hallfields CV31....... **162** E5
Hallfield Sch B15... **86** A7
Hall Gr WV14........ **51** C8
Hall Green Inf Sch
B28................**105** F7
Hall Green Jun Sch
B28................**105** F7
Hall Green Prim Sch
B71................**42** D1
Hall Green Rd
Coventry CV2, CV6 ... **96** B2
West Bromwich B71... **42** D1
Hall Green Sch B28. **105** E8
Hallgreen St WV14 ... **40** E2
Hall Green Sta B28..**87** F1
Hall Hays Rd B34.... **69** F7
Hall La Brownhills WS9. **15** E3
Coventry CV2 .... **114** F6
Dudley DY2 .... **62** C6
Great Wyrley WS6....**5** A3
Hagley DY9 .... **99** D6
Hammerwich WS7....**7** E4
Muckley Corner WS7,
WS14 ....**7** F2
Tipton DY4 .... **52** B8
Walsall WS3 .... **14** F3
Wolverhampton WV14 . **39** F1
Hall Mdw Hagley DY9.. **99** D7

Hall Mdw *continued*
Wedges Mills WS11 ....**4** B6
Hallmoor Rd B33.... **69** B3
Hallmoor Sch B33...**69** B3
Hallot Cl B23 .... **56** D8
Halloughton Rd B74.. **46** A7
Hallow Cl 3 B31.... **103** D2
Hallowfields Cl B98 . **153** E1
Hall Park St WV14.... **40** B7
Hall Rd
Birmingham, Castle
Bromwich B36 ...... **69** A8
Birmingham, Handsworth
B20................**66** A8
Birmingham, Saltley B8. **67** D4
Hinckley LE10 .... **75** D5
Royal Leamington Spa
CV32...............**156** F1
Smethwick B67....... **64** E4
Hall St E WS10 ...... **41** C7
Hall St S B70........ **64** D8
Hall's Cl CV31....... **162** B3
Hall St Bilston WV14... **40** E5
Birmingham B18...... **164** A4
Cradley Heath B64 ... **62** F2
Darlaston WS10 ..... **41** B7
Dudley DY2 .... **51** D1
Oldbury B68 .... **64** B5
Sedgley DY3 .... **50** D8
Stourbridge DY8 ..... **81** A3
Tipton DY4 .... **51** E5
Walsall WS2 .... **28** D3
West Bromwich B70... **53** C2
Willenhall WV13 ..... **27** B1
Wolverhampton WV11 . **26** C5
Hallstead Rd B13.... **105** B5
Hallswelle Gr B43.... **44** E4
Hallway Dr CV7 ...... **97** E6
Hall Wlk B46........ **70** F4
Halsbury Gr B44..... **56** B8
Halstead Gr B91..... **127** A8
Halston Rd WS7......**7** B8
Haltonlea B77....... **36** A8
Halton Rd B73....... **45** E2
Halton St DY2....... **62** C5
Hamar Way B37...... **70** B1
Hamberley Ct B18.... **65** D5
Hamble B77......... **21** D2
Hamble Cl DY5...... **61** A6
Hamble Ct B73...... **46** B5
Hambledon Cl WV9... **11** A2
Hamble Gr WV6...... **23** E4
Hamble Rd
Birmingham B42...... **43** F1
Wolverhampton WV4 .. **38** C6
Hambleton Rd B63.... **82** D2
Hambletts Rd B70.... **53** A3
Hambrook Cl WV6.... **25** A5
Hambury Cl B14..... **104** D7
Ham Dingle Prim Sch
DY9................**81** C2
Hamelin St WS11......**1** E3
Hamilton Ave
Birmingham B17...... **85** A7
Halesowen B62....... **83** C3
Stourbridge DY8 ..... **80** D6
Hamilton Cl
Bedworth CV12...... **77** C1
Cannock WS12 ....**2** F4
Hinckley LE10 .... **71** A2
Lickey End B60 ...... **137** C6
Sedgley DY3 .... **50** C8
Stourbridge DY8 ..... **60** C2
Hamilton Ct
1 Birmingham, Moseley
B13................**86** F4
Birmingham, Showell Green
B13................**87** B3
Coventry CV1 .... **165** B4
Nuneaton CV10....... **72** D4
Hamilton Dr
Birmingham B29...... **103** D8
Oldbury B69 .... **52** C2
Stourbridge DY8 ..... **60** C2
Studley B80......... **159** D3
Hamilton Gdns WV10..**11** F3
Hamilton Ho WS3 .... **14** C1
Hamilton Lea WS11 ...**6** A6
Hamilton Rd
Birmingham B21...... **65** D8
Coventry CV2 .... **114** A3
Kidderminster DY11 .. **116** B3
Radford Semele CV31. **162** E5
Redditch B97 .... **158** C8
Smethwick B67....... **64** E2
Tipton DY4 .... **52** C6
Hamilton Sch B21.. **65** D8
Hamilton St WS3..... **14** D1
Hamilton Terr CV32.. **161** F8

Ham La
Kingswinford DY6..... **49** E1
Stourbridge DY9 ..... **81** C2
Hamlet Cl CV11 ..... **74** B1
Hamlet Gdns B28 ... **105** F8
Hamlet Rd B28 ..... **105** F8
Hamlet The
Leek Wootton CV35 .. **156** A7
Norton Canes WS11 ..**5** D8
Hammer Bank DY5.... **82** A8
Hammersley Cl B63... **82** C7
Hammersley St CV12.. **77** E1
Hammerwich Hospl
WS7................**7** B5
Hammerwich La WS7...**7** F3
Hammerwich Rd WS7 . **7** D5
Hammond Ave WV10.. **25** E8
Hammond Bsns Ctr
CV11...............**73** E3
Hammond Cl CV11 ... **73** E3
Hammond Dr B23.... **56** F5
Hammond Rd CV2.... **113** F4
Hammonds Terr
CV8................**147** D5
Hammond Way DY8... **81** A7
Hampden Cl 3 DY5.. **82** A8
Hampden Retreat
B12................**86** E6
Hamps Cl WS7...... **7** D7
Hampshire Cl
Coventry CV3 .... **134** F8
Tamworth B78........ **20** F2
Hampshire Ct 1
B29................**103** B7
Hampshire Dr B15 ... **85** E8
Hampshire Rd B71... **42** A1
Hampson Cl B11 .... **87** B6
Hampstead Glade
B63................**83** C2
Hampton Ave
Bromsgrove B60..... **151** A8
Nuneaton CV10....... **72** B4
Hampton Cl
Coventry CV6 .... **113** F6
Redditch B98 .... **159** B7
Sutton Coldfield B73.. **45** C2
Tamworth B79........ **21** C7
Hampton Court Rd
B17................**85** A6
Hampton Ct
Birmingham B15...... **86** B8
Hampton-in-A B92 ... **109** B6
Solihull B91......... **107** D4
Wednesbury B71 ..... **42** C1
Wolverhampton WV10 . **12** B2
Hampton Dr B74..... **46** B8
Hampton Gdns DY9 .. **81** D3
Hampton Gn WS11....**4** E7
Hampton Gr
Royal Leamington Spa
CV32...............**157** B1
Walsall WS3 .... **15** A4
Hampton Grange CV7 **92** B1
Hampton-in-Arden Sta
B92................**109** B7
Hampton La
Catherine de B B91 .. **108** B5
Meriden CV7........ **109** E4
Hampton Pl WS10.... **41** C8
Hampton Rd
Birmingham, Aston
B6.................**66** D8
Birmingham, Stockland
Green B23 .... **56** D4
Coventry CV6 .... **113** F6
Knowle B93......... **128** C8
Warwick CV34 ...... **160** B5
Wolverhampton WV10 . **11** B1
Hampton St
Birmingham B19...... **164** B4
Cannock WS11 ....**4** D7
Dudley, Netherton DY2. **62** C5
Dudley WV14 .... **51** B8
Warwick CV34 ...... **160** D6
Hampton View WV10..**25** F3
Hampton Wlk WV1... **163** B3
Hams La B76........ **59** F6
Hams Rd B8........ **67** D4
Hamstead Cl WV11... **26** D6
Hamstead Ct B19 ... **66** B7
Hamstead Hall Ave
B20................**54** E5
Hamstead Hall Rd
B20................**54** F4
Hamstead Hall Sch
B20................**54** E6
Hamstead Hill B20... **54** F4
Hamstead Ho B43... **54** F7
Hamstead Jun & Inf Sch
B43................**54** D7

Hamstead Rd
Birmingham, Hamstead
B43................**54** D7
Birmingham, Lozells B19,
B20................**66** B7
Hamstead Sta B42..**54** F6
Hamstead Terr WS10 . **42** A2
Hanam Cl B75.......**46** F6
Hanbury Cl
Bromsgrove B60..... **151** A8
Halesowen B63....... **82** F2
Hanbury Cres WV4... **38** E6
Hanbury Croft B27... **88** E3
Hanbury Ct DY8..... **81** A4
Hanbury Hill DY8.... **81** A4
Hanbury Ho B97..... **153** B4
Hanbury Rd
Bedworth CV12...... **78** C4
Brownhills WS8......**6** F2
Dorridge B93 .... **127** F4
Norton Canes WS11 ..**5** F5
Stoke Heath B60..... **150** D4
Tamworth B77........ **21** A4
West Bromwich B70... **53** A3
Hanbury's Farm Com
Prim Sch B77 ..... **21** D1
Hanch Pl WS1........**42** F8
Hancock Gn CV4..... **131** F8
Hancock Rd B8...... **67** F4
Hancox St B68 ..... **64** B2
Handcross Gr CV3... **133** A5
Handel Ct WS11......**2** C2
Handel Wlk WS13 .....**3** C2
Handley Gr
Birmingham B31...... **102** C2
Warwick CV34 ...... **155** D1
Handley's Cl CV8.... **135** A1
Handley St WS10..... **42** A4
Handsworth, Booth
Street Sta B21 .... **65** C7
Handsworth Cl B21.. **65** D7
Handsworth Coll B6 .**66** E8
Handsworth Cres
CV5................**111** E4
Handsworth Dr B43 .. **44** A3
Handsworth Gram Sch
B21................**65** F8
Handsworth New Rd
B18................**65** E6
Handsworth Wood Girls'
Sch B20 .... **54** F2
Handsworth Wood Rd
B20................**55** A2
Hanford Cl CV6 ..... **113** E6
Hanford Close Ind Est
CV6................**113** E6
Hanger Rd B26...... **90** A3
Hanging La B31...... **102** E2
Hangleton Dr B11.... **87** D6
Hangman's La LE10 .. **71** E3
Hanley Cl B63....... **82** E4
Hanley Ct B23....... **56** C2
Hanley St B19....... **164** C4
Hanley Villas 1 B12.. **87** B5
Hanlith B77......... **36** A8
Hannaford Way WS11..**1** F2
Hannafore Rd B16.... **65** D3
Hannah Rd WV14..... **41** A4
Hanney Hay Rd WS7,
WS8................**7** B3
Hannon Rd B14...... **104** E5
Hanover Cl B6....... **66** E7
Hanover Ct
Hinckley LE10 .... **75** E6
Redditch B97 .... **158** D8
Tamworth B79........ **20** F7
Walsall WS2 .... **27** E1
Wolverhampton WV6 .. **24** C4
Hanover Dr B24......**67** F8
Hanover Gdns 8
CV32...............**157** A1
Hanover Glebe CV11 . **73** C2
Hanover Ho 6 DY8...**80** F8
Hanover Pl
Bromsgrove B60..... **136** F1
Cannock WS11 ....**1** E2
Hanover Rd B65..... **63** C4
Hanover St B61...... **136** F1
Hans Cl CV2 .... **113** F4
Hansell Dr B93...... **127** E2
Hansom Ct 2 LE10... **75** D8
Hansom Rd
Birmingham B32...... **84** C5
Hinckley LE10 .... **71** D4
Hanson Gr B92...... **.88** F5
Hanson Man B74..... **32** A4
Hanson's Bridge Rd
B24................**57** F5
Hanson Way CV6..... **96** A4
Hanwell Cl B76...... **58** B7

Hanwood Cl
Birmingham B12...... **86** F8
Coventry CV5 .... **111** D4
Hanwood Ho 1 B12... **86** F8
Hanworth Cl CV32... **157** C2
Hanworth Rd CV34 .. **160** D8
Harald Cl WV6...... **23** E5
Harbeck Ave B44..... **55** F8
Harberrow Cl DY9.... **99** A6
Harbet Dr B40...... **90** E4
Harbinger Rd B38.... **104** B2
Harborne Ct B17..... **85** C4
Harborne Hill Sch
B15................**85** E6
Harborne Ho B17 ... **85** A4
Harborne La B17..... **85** D3
Harborne Park Rd
B17................**85** C4
Harborne Prim Sch
B17................**85** C6
Harborne Rd
Birmingham, Chad Valley
B15................**85** E7
Birmingham, Warley Woods
B68................**84** E8
Harborough Cotts
B94................**144** D3
Harborough Ct B74... **32** A2
Harborough Dr
Aldridge WS9 .... **30** B5
Birmingham B36...... **58** D1
Harborough Rd CV6... **95** B2
Harborough Wlk DY9. **81** B2
Harbourne Ct CV8... **148** A5
Harbours Cl B61..... **150** D7
Harbours Hill DY9... **120** E6
Harbury Cl
Redditch B98 .... **154** D1
Sutton Coldfield B76.. **58** B6
Harbury La CV33,
CV34...............**161** E2
Harbury Rd B12..... **86** D5
Harby Cl B37........ **90** B8
Harcourt CV3 .... **134** E5
Harcourt Dr
Dudley DY3 .... **50** D2
Sutton Coldfield B74.. **31** F4
Harcourt Gdns CV11.. **73** C3
Harcourt Ho B79..... **21** A4
Harcourt Rd
Birmingham B23...... **56** E6
Cradley Heath B64 ... **82** F8
Wednesbury WS10 .... **41** F4
Harden Cl WS3...... **28** E7
Harden Ct B31....... **102** E1
Harden Gr WS3...... **28** E7
Harden Keep B66.... **65** A4
Harden Manor Ct B63 **83** C3
Harden Prim Sch
WS3................**28** E7
Harden Rd WS3 ..... **28** E7
Harden Vale B63..... **82** E5
Hardie Ct 2 WV4.... **39** F4
Hardie Gn WS11......**1** F3
Harding St WV14..... **40** D2
Hardon Rd WV4...... **39** F5
Hardware St B70.... **53** D4
Hardwick Cl CV5..... **112** A4
Hardwick Ct
Stourbridge DY9 ..... **81** D5
Sutton Coldfield B74.. **30** F2
Tamworth B79........ **21** C5
Hardwick Dr B62..... **83** A7
Hardwicke Way DY9.. **81** D5
Hardwick La B80..... **159** F4
Hardwick Rd
Solihull B92......... **88** E4
Sutton Coldfield B74.. **31** A2
Hardwick Wlk B14 .. **104** D2
Hardwyn Cl CV3..... **115** A1
Hardy Ave DY10..... **117** A6
Hardy Cl Hinckley LE10 **71** D4
Nuneaton CV10....... **72** A4
Hardy Ct 4 B13......**86** F4
Hardy Rd
Coventry CV6 .... **113** A8
Walsall WS3 .... **28** E8
Wednesbury WS10 .... **42** A3
Hardy Sq WV2........**39** F7
Hare And Hounds La
CV10...............**73** A2
Harebell B77........ **22** A4
Harebell Cl
Cannock WS12 ......**2** D2
Featherstone WV10 .. **12** A7
Walsall WS5 .... **43** A3
Harebell Cres DY1.... **51** A4
Harebell Gdns B38 .. **123** F8
Harebell Wlk 1 B37.. **70** D2

Harefield La CV12......**77** F8
Harefield Rd
Coventry CV2 .... **114** B3
Nuneaton CV11....... **73** C4
Hare Gr B31 .... **102** D3
Haresfield B90 ...... **126** A5
Haresfield Cl B97 ... **153** D3
Hare St WV14........**40** F5
Harewell Dr B75..... **32** C1
Harewood 6 B17..... **85** B6
Harewood Ave
Birmingham B43...... **43** C2
Wednesbury WS10 .... **42** C3
Harewood Cl B28 ... **105** E5
Harewood Rd CV5.... **112** C2
Harford St B18, B19.. **164** A5
Hargate La B71 ..... **53** D4
Hargate Prim Sch
B71................**53** C4
Harger Ct CV8 ...... **147** F4
Harger Mews CV8... **147** F4
Hargrave Cl
Coventry CV3 .... **115** A1
Water Orton B46 .... **59** B3
Hargrave Rd B90..... **105** D1
Hargreave Cl B76.... **57** F8
Hargreaves Ct DY11 . **116** C3
Hargreaves St WV1... **40** A7
Harington Rd CV6.... **113** A5
Harland Cl B61...... **136** D3
Harland Rd B74..... **32** A3
Harlech Cl
Birmingham B32...... **102** A7
Kenilworth CV8...... **148** C5
Oldbury B69 .... **52** A1
Harlech Ho 2 WS3... **28** C6
Harlech Rd WV12.... **27** C6
Harlech Twr B23 .... **57** A6
Harlech Way
Dudley DY1 .... **50** F2
Kidderminster DY10 .. **116** E2
Harlequin Dr B13.... **86** E2
Harlestones Ho DY8..**80** F7
Harleston Rd B44..... **55** F8
Harley Cl WS8....... **16** A6
Harley Dr WV14...... **40** B4
Harley Grange 6 DY2 **62** E4
Harley St CV2....... **114** A3
Harlow Gr B28 ..... **106** A6
Harlow Wlk 8 CV2.. **115** A7
Harlstones Cl DY8.... **81** A8
Harlyn Cl WV11 ..... **41** A2
Harman Dr WS13......**8** F6
Harman Rd B72...... **57** B6
Harmar Cl CV34..... **155** D1
Harmer Cl CV2...... **115** A4
Harmer St B18...... **66** A5
Harmon Rd DY8..... **80** C5
Harmony Ct CV10 ... **73** B2
Harmony Ho 3 B12.. **67** C1
Harnall Cl B90...... **126** E7
Harnall Ind Est CV1. **165** C4
Harnall La CV1...... **165** C4
Harnall La E CV1.... **113** E4
Harnall La W CV1.... **165** C4
Harnall Row
Coventry CV1 .... **113** E2
Coventry CV1 .... **113** E3
Harness Cl WS5......**42** F4
Harold Evers Way
DY10...............**116** F7
Harold Rd
Birmingham B16...... **65** F1
Coventry CV2 .... **114** D2
Smethwick B67....... **64** E3
Harold St CV11...... **73** C3
Harpenden Dr CV5... **112** A5
Harper Ave WV11 ... **26** C7
Harper Bell Sch The
B12................**87** A8
Harper Rd
Bilston WV14 .... **40** D6
Coventry CV1 .... **113** E2
Harpers Rd
Birmingham, Highter's
Heath B14 .... **105** A1
Birmingham, Northfield
B31................**103** A2
Harper St WV13..... **27** A2
Harport Rd B98 ..... **154** A1
Harpur Cl WS4...... **29** A4
Harpur Rd WS4..... **29** A4
Harrier Rd B27...... **88** D2
Harriers Gn DY10.... **117** B8
Harriers Ind Est
DY10...............**116** F5
Harriet Cl DY5 ...... **61** B5
Harringay Dr DY8.... **80** E3

Harringay Rd B44 45 A2
Harrington Croft B71 53 F7
Harrington Ct CV3 114 F2
Harrington Way CV10 78 A7
Harrington Wlk WS13 8 F8
Harringworth Ct WS4 29 C8
Harriott Dr CV34 161 D4
Harris Bsns Pk B60 150 E2
Harris Cl B98 158 F8
Harris Ct B18 66 A6
Harris Dr
[2] Birmingham B42 55 A8
Smethwick B66 65 B3
Harrison Cl
Cheslyn Hay WS6 4 D1
Walsall WS3 14 C1
Harrison Cres CV12 78 A2
Harrison Ct DY8 61 A1
Harrison Ho B14 104 F3
Harrison Rd
Birmingham B24 56 F4
Cannock WS11 4 E7
Redditch B97 158 C8
Stourbridge DY8 61 A1
Sutton Coldfield B74 31 E5
Walsall WS4 15 C2
Harrison's Fold DY2 62 C5
Harrisons Gn B15 85 E6
Harrisons Pleck B13 86 F3
Harrison's Rd B15 85 E6
Harrison St WS3 14 C1
Harrison Way CV31 161 F5
Harris Rd
Coventry CV3 114 B2
Warwick CV34 160 C8
Harrold Ave B65 63 E3
Harrold Rd B65 63 E3
Harrold St DY4 52 C7
Harrold Terr B19 66 C8
Harrop Way DY8 80 E8
Harrowbrook Ind Est
LE10 74 E7
Harrowbrook Rd LE10 74 E7
Harrowby Ct WV10 11 B3
Harrowby Dr DY4 52 A4
Harrowby Pl WV13 27 D1
Harrowby Rd
Darlaston WV14 41 A4
Wolverhampton WV10 11 C2
Harrow Cl
Coventry CV6 96 A4
Stoke Heath B60 150 E6
West Hagley DY9 99 A6
Harrow Ct [5] B74 31 F2
Harrowfield Rd B33 68 E4
Harrow Rd
Birmingham B29 85 F3
Kingswinford DY6 49 D1
Whitnash CV31 162 B3
Harrow St WV1 25 B4
Harry Caplan Ho
CV5 112 B6
Harry Edwards Ho [2]
CV2 114 D8
Harry Perks St WV13 27 A3
Harry Price Ho [9]
B69 63 D5
Harry Rose Rd CV2 114 E3
Harry Salt Ho CV1 165 D3
Harry Stanley Ho
CV6 114 A8
Harry Taylor Fst Sch The
B97 158 E6
Harry Taylor Ho B98 154 A4
Harry Truslove Cl
CV6 113 A7
Harry Weston Rd
CV3 115 A1
Hart Dr B73 57 A8
Hartfield Cres B27 88 B2
Hartfields Way B65 62 F5
Hartford Cl B17 85 A7
Hartford Rd B60 137 B1
Hartill Rd WV4 38 D3
Hartill St WV13 41 B8
Hartington Cl B93 127 E3
Hartington Cres CV5 112 F1
Hartington Gn LE10 75 E6
Hartington Rd B19 66 D7
Hartland Ave
Coventry CV2 114 B5
Dudley WV14 51 A8
Hartland Rd
Birmingham B31 122 E6
Tipton DY4 51 D5
West Bromwich B71 53 F8
Hartland St DY5 61 D7
Hartlebury Cl
Cannock WS11 2 C2
Dorridge B93 127 F3
Redditch B98 154 E7
Hartlebury Rd
Halesowen B63 82 F2
Oldbury B69 63 D5
Hartledon Rd B17 85 B5
Hartle La DY9 119 F6
Hartlepool Rd CV1 165 D4
Hartleyburn B77 36 A8
Hartley Dr WS9 30 B4
Hartley Gr B44 45 B3
Hartley Pl B15 85 F8
Hartley Rd B44 45 B3
Hartley St WV3 25 A2
Harton Way B14 104 C5
Hartopp Rd
Birmingham B8 67 E4
Sutton Coldfield B74 45 F8
Hart Rd
Birmingham B24 57 A5
Willenhall WV11 26 D4
Hartridge Wlk CV5 112 B4
Hartsbourne Dr B62 83 D4
Harts Cl B17 85 D6
Harts Green Rd B17 85 A5
Hartshill Cl B34 69 A6
Hartshill Ho B27 88 E2
Hartshill Rd
Birmingham B34 69 A6
Solihull B27 88 D2
Hartshill Sch CV10 72 B8
Hartshorn St WV14 40 D5
Hartside Cl B63 82 D2
Hartslade WS14 9 E6
Harts Rd B8 67 E5
Hart St WS1 42 E8
Hartswell Dr B13 104 F6
Hartwell Cl B91 107 B1
Hartwell La WS6 5 A3
Hartwell Rd B24 57 B2
Hartwood Cres WV3 38 F5
Harvard Cl DY1 50 F4
Harvard Rd B92 89 B4
Harvest Cl
Birmingham B30 104 B6
Dudley DY3 50 E5
Stoke Heath B60 150 E6
Harvesters Cl
Coventry CV3 115 A2
Sutton Coldfield WS9 30 E2
Harvesters Rd WV12 27 D5
Harvesters Way WV12 27 D5
Harvesters Wlk WV8 10 E1
Harvester Way DY6 60 A8
Harvest Fields Way
Sutton Coldfield B75 32 D4
Sutton Coldfield B75 32 E3
Harvest Gdns B68 64 A4
Harvest Hill Cl [7]
CV31 162 C6
Harvest Hill Cotts
CV5 93 D1
Harvest Hill La CV5,
CV7 93 C4
Harvest Hill Pk CV5 93 D1
Harvest Rd
Rowley Regis B65 63 A3
Smethwick B67 64 D3
Harvest Wlk B65 63 A3
Harvey Cl CV5 112 A7
Harvey Ct B33 69 D3
Harvey Dr B75 32 C2
Harvey Mews B30 103 D7
Harvey Rd
Birmingham B26 88 D7
Walsall WS2 28 B5
Harveys Terr DY2 62 D4
Harvey Works Ind Est
B63 82 F6
Harvills Hawthorn
B70 52 F7
Harvills Hawthorn Prim
Sch B70 52 F7
Harvine Wlk DY8 80 E3
Harvington Cl
Kidderminster DY11 116 A8
Redditch B97 153 B5
Harvington Dr B90 127 B6
Harvington Hall★
DY10 118 B1
Harvington Hall La
DY10 118 B1
Harvington Rd
Birmingham, Brandhall
B68 84 A8
Birmingham, Weoley Castle
B29 103 A8
Bromsgrove B60 151 A8
Harvington Rd *continued*
Dudley WV14 40 B1
Halesowen B63 82 F2
Harvington Way B76 58 A8
Harvington Wlk [5]
B65 63 C3
Harwell Cl B79 21 C7
Harwin Cl WV6 24 F7
Harwood Dr
Hinckley LE10 71 F4
Tamworth B77 35 D4
Harwood Gr [1] B90 126 C8
Harwood Rd WS13 3 B3
Harwood St B70 53 B3
Hasbury CE Prim Sch
B63 82 F2
Hasbury Cl B63 82 E2
Hasbury Rd B32 102 B8
Haselbech Rd CV3 114 F1
Haselbury Cnr CV10 72 F1
Haseley Cl
Redditch B98 154 E1
Whitnash CV31 162 B5
Haseley Rd
Birmingham B21 65 E7
Coventry CV2 96 C1
Solihull B91 106 E6
Haselor Rd B73 45 E1
Haselour Rd B37 69 F5
Haselwell Dr B30 104 D3
Hasilwood Sq CV3 114 B2
Haskell St WS1 42 F7
Haslucks Croft B90 106 A3
Haslucks Green Rd
Solihull, Major's Green
B90 125 E7
Solihull, Shirley B90 106 B4
Haslucks Green Sch
B90 106 A3
Hassop Rd B42 55 D7
Hastang Fields CV31 162 C5
Hastings Cl B77 35 F6
Hastings Ct DY1 50 E2
Hastings High Sch
LE10 75 F7
Hastings Rd
Birmingham B23 56 B7
Bromsgrove B60 150 E7
Coventry CV2 114 A4
Hastingwood Ind Pk
B24 57 B1
Haswell Rd B63 82 D4
Hatcham Rd B44 45 C2
Hatchford Ave B92 89 C3
Hatchford Brook Inf Sch
B92 89 C3
Hatchford Brook Jun Sch
B92 89 C3
Hatchford Brook Rd
B92 89 C3
Hatchford Com Prim Sch
B37 69 F2
Hatchford Ct B92 89 C3
Hatchford Wlk B37 70 B1
Hateley Dr WV4 39 E4
Hateley Heath Prim Sch
B71 53 B7
Hatfield Cl
Birmingham B23 56 D8
Redditch B98 154 E1
Hatfield Rd
Birmingham B19 66 D8
Stourbridge DY9 81 C4
Hathaway Cl
Balsall Common CV7 130 B7
Willenhall WV13 40 F8
Hathaway Dr
Nuneaton CV11 74 A1
Warwick CV34 155 E2
Hathaway Mews DY8 60 C3
Hathaway Rd
Coventry CV4 111 D1
Solihull B90 106 B1
Sutton Coldfield B74 32 A4
Hatherden Dr B76 47 A2
Hatherell Rd CV31 162 E5
Hathersage Rd B42 55 D7
Hatherton Croft WS11 1 C1
Hatherton Gdns WV10 11 E2
Hatherton Gr B29 84 F1
Hatherton Pl WS9 30 A7
Hatherton Prim Sch
WS2 28 A6
Hatherton Rd
Bilston WV14 40 F6
Cannock WS11 1 C1
Walsall WS1 28 E2
Hatherton St
Cheslyn Hay WS6 4 C2
Walsall WS1, WS4 28 E3
Hatters Ct CV12 78 D2
Hattersley Gr B11 88 A3
Hatton Cres WV10 26 A7
Hatton Gdns B42 55 B7
Hatton Rd
Cannock WS11 1 A1
Wolverhampton WV6 24 F3
Hattons Gr WV8 10 B2
Hatton St WV14 40 E4
Haughton Rd B20 55 D1
Haunch La B13 105 A5
Haunchwood Dr B76 57 F7
Haunchwood Rd
CV10 72 D4
Havacre La WV14 40 C1
Havefield Ave WS14 9 E7
Havelock Cl WV3 38 F8
Havelock Rd
Birmingham, Handsworth
B20 55 C1
Birmingham, Saltley B8 67 D5
Birmingham, Sparkhill
B11 87 E4
Haven Croft B43 54 D8
Havendale Cl CV6 113 B5
Haven Dr B27 88 B3
Haven The
Barnt Green B45 138 A8
Birmingham B14 105 D4
Stourbridge DY8 60 D2
Wolverhampton WV2 163 B1
Haverford Dr B45 122 B6
Havergal Wlk B63 82 B4
Haverhill Cl WS3 14 A3
Hawbridge Cl B90 127 B6
Hawbush Gdns DY5 61 A1
Hawbush Prim Sch
DY5 61 B2
Hawbush Rd
Brierley Hill DY5 61 A2
Walsall WS3 28 E6
Hawcroft Gr B34 69 C6
Hawes Cl WS1 42 F6
Hawes La B65 63 B3
Hawes Rd WS1 42 F6
Haweswater Dr DY6 60 D6
Hawfield Cl B69 63 C7
Hawfield Gr B72 57 C7
Hawfield Rd B69 63 C7
Hawfinch B77 36 A6
Hawfinch Rise DY10 117 A2
Hawford Ave DY10 117 B6
Hawk Cl CV11 79 B8
Hawker Dr B35 57 F2
Hawkesbury Fields Sch
CV2 96 C3
Hawkesbury La CV2 96 D5
Hawkesbury Rd B90 105 F1
Hawkes Cl B30 104 A7
Hawkes Dr CV34 161 D4
Hawkesford Cl
Birmingham B36 69 A8
Sutton Coldfield B74 32 B1
Hawkesford Rd B33 69 D3
Hawkes La B70 53 A7
Hawkesley CE &
Methodist Prim Sch
B38 123 E7
Hawkesley Cres B31 103 A1
Hawkesley Dr B31 122 F8
Hawkesley End B38 123 E7
Hawkesley Mill La
B31 102 F2
Hawkesley Rd DY1 61 F8
Hawkesley Sq B38 123 E7
Hawkes Mill La CV5 94 B2
Hawkesmoor Dr WS14 9 D8
Hawkes St B10 87 D8
Hawkestone Cres B70 53 A6
Hawkestone Rd B29 103 A7
Hawkesville Dr [7]
WS11 1 F2
Hawkeswell Cl B92 106 E8
Hawkeswell Dr [4]
DY6 60 D8
Hawkesworth Dr
CV8 148 A6
Hawkesyard Rd B24 56 E1
Hawkhurst Rd B14 104 F2
Hawkinge Dr B35 58 A4
Hawkins Cl
Birmingham B5 86 E6
Hinckley LE10 71 D4
Lichfield WS13 3 B2
Hawkins Croft DY4 52 A3
Hawkins Dr WS11 4 C4
Hawkin's Pl WV14 40 F3
Hawkins Rd CV5 113 A2
Hawkins St B70 53 A8
Hawkley Cl WV1 26 B2
Hawkley Rd WV1 26 B2
Hawkmoor Gdns
B38 124 A8
Hawksbury Cl B98 154 D5
Hawks Cl WS6 4 D2
Hawksford Cres
WV10 25 E7
Hawks Green La WS11 2 A1
Hawkshead Dr B93 127 F6
Hawkside B77 36 B8
Hawksmill Ind Est B9 67 C1
Hawksmoor Dr WV6 23 D3
Hawkstone Cl DY11 116 D8
Hawkstone Ct WV6 23 D5
Hawkswell Ave WV5 49 A5
Hawkswell Dr WV13 40 F8
Hawkswood Dr
Balsall Common CV7 130 B7
Darlaston WS10 41 B3
Hawkswood Gr B14 105 B3
Hawksworth B77 21 F2
Hawksworth Cres
B37 70 D3
Hawksworth Dr [1]
CV1 113 B3
Hawkyard Ct WS11 2 A4
Hawley Cl WS4 28 F4
Hawley Ct B43 43 E1
Hawley Rd LE10 75 D7
Hawnby Gr B76 47 A2
Hawne Cl B63 82 E6
Hawne La B63 82 F6
Hawnelands The B63 82 F5
Hawskford Cres
WV10 25 D7
Hawthorn Ave WS6 5 A1
Hawthorn Brook Way
B23 56 E8
Hawthorn Cl
Birmingham, Erdington
B23 56 F7
Birmingham, Spring Vale
B9 67 B1
Lichfield WS14 9 D8
Hawthorn Coppice
DY9 99 A6
Hawthorn Cres LE10 75 E4
Hawthorn Croft B68 84 D7
Hawthorn Ct CV4 111 E1
Hawthornden Ct B76 57 D7
Hawthorn Dr
Balsall Common CV7 130 B8
Birmingham B29 85 C1
Hawthorne Ave B79 21 B8
Hawthorne Cres WS7 7 A6
Hawthorne Croft
B30 103 D5
Hawthorne Dr B47 125 B6
Hawthorne Gr DY3 50 D2
Hawthorne Ho WV10 25 F3
Hawthorne Rd
Birmingham B15 85 E7
Birmingham, Castle
Bromwich B36 69 F7
Birmingham, King's Norton
B30 103 D5
Cannock WS12 2 F3
Cheslyn Hay WS6 4 E4
Dudley DY1 51 C4
Essington WV11 13 A3
Halesowen B63 82 E2
Huntington WS12 1 D8
Wednesfield WV11 27 A5
Willenhall WV12 27 D7
Wolverhampton WV2 39 D6
Hawthorne Terr CV10 72 F5
Hawthorn Gr
[9] Birmingham B19 66 C8
Kidderminster DY11 116 A6
Hawthorn La CV4 111 E1
Hawthorn Park Dr [1]
B20 54 F3
Hawthorn Pk B20 54 E3
Hawthorn Pl WS2 27 E3
Hawthorn Prim Sch
B44 56 A7
Hawthorn Rd
Bilston WV1 40 B8
Birmingham B44 56 A7
Brierley Hill DY5 81 E8
Bromsgrove B61 137 B4
Redditch B97 153 A4
Royal Leamington Spa
CV31 161 F6
Sutton Coldfield, Streetly
B74 31 A1
Sutton Coldfield, Wylde
Green B72 46 C1
Tipton DY4 52 B8
Walsall, Bescot WS5 42 F5
Hawthorn Rd *continued*
Walsall, Shelfield WS4 29 B8
Walsall WS4 15 B1
Wednesbury WS10 41 F4
Hawthorns Sta The
B71 65 A8
Hawthorns The
Birmingham, Showell Green
B13 86 F3
Birmingham, Warley Woods
B68 84 D7
[1] Kidderminster
DY10 117 A5
West Hagley DY9 98 F4
Wolverhampton WV11 26 B6
Hawthorns The (West
Bromwich Albion FC)
B21 54 B1
Hawthorn Terr WS10 41 F4
Hawthorn Way CV10 72 A8
Haxby Ave B34 69 A6
Haybarn The B76 58 A8
Haybridge Ave DY8 98 F5
Haybridge High Sch &
Sixth Form DY8 98 F6
Hay Brook Dr B11 87 F4
Hay Cl DY11 116 C7
Haycock Pl WS10 41 C8
Haycroft Ave B8 67 E5
Haycroft Dr B74 32 A4
Haydn Sanders Sq [7]
WS1 42 E8
Haydock Cl
Birmingham B36 68 C8
Coventry CV6 96 B4
Tamworth B77 35 D4
Wolverhampton WV6 25 B5
Haydock Rd B61 121 B1
Haydon Cl B93 127 F2
Haydon Croft B33 69 A3
Haydon Way B49 159 F1
Haye House Gr B36 68 E7
Hayes Cres B68 64 D5
Hayes Croft B38 123 F7
Hayes Dr B24 57 D5
Hayes Gr B24 57 D6
Hayes Green Rd CV12 95 F8
Hayes La
Bedworth CV7 96 A8
Stourbridge DY9 82 A6
Hayes Mdw B72 57 D7
Hayes Rd
Hartshill CV10 72 A8
Oldbury B68 64 D5
Hayes St B70 53 A4
Hayes The
Birmingham B31 123 C7
Leek Wootton CV35 155 F5
Stourbridge DY9 82 A5
Willenhall WV12 27 B6
Hayes Trad Est DY9 82 A6
Hayes View Dr WS6 4 E4
Hayes Way WS12 2 C1
Hayfield Ct B13 87 B2
Hayfield Gdns B13 87 C2
Hayfield Rd B13 87 B2
Hayford Cl B98 154 A5
Hay Gn DY9 81 D5
Hay Gr WS8 15 F8
Hay Green Cl B30 103 D6
Hay Green La B30 103 D6
Hay Hall Rd B11 87 F5
Hayhead Wood Nature
Reserve★ WS4 29 E2
Hay Hill WS5 43 E8
Hay La Coventry CV1 165 C2
Solihull B90 127 A6
Hayland Rd B23 56 E6
Hayle B77 21 D2
Hayle Ave CV34 155 F1
Hayle Cl
Birmingham B38 104 B2
Nuneaton CV11 74 A5
Hayley Ct
Kingswinford DY6 60 D6
Sutton Coldfield B24 57 C6
Hayley Green Rd
B32 102 B8
Hayley Park Rd B63 100 C8
Hayling Cl B45 101 F1
Hayling Ct WS4 15 D1
Hayling Gr WV2 39 B6
Hayloft Cl B60 150 E6
Haylofts The B63 82 C1
Haymaker Way WS12 2 F4
Haymarket The WV8 10 E1
Haymoor WS14 9 E7
Haynes Cl B61 137 B8
Haynes Ho B97 153 D2
Haynes La WS5 43 B4

Haynestone Rd CV6 112 E6
Haypits Cl B71 53 E7
Hay Pk B5 86 D6
Hay Rd B25 88 A7
Hayrick Dr DY6 60 B7
Hayseech B64 83 A7
Hayseech Rd B63 82 F6
Hays Kent's Moat The B26 69 A1
Hays La LE10 75 B7
Hayton Gn CV4 131 F8
Haytor Ave B14 104 D5
Haytor Rise CV2 114 C7
Haywain Cl WV9 10 F2
Hayward Rd B75 46 C7
Haywards Cl
Birmingham B23 56 E5
Walsall WS3 14 F3
Hayward's Gn CV6 113 A7
Hayward St WV14 51 B8
Haywharf Rd DY5 61 B5
Haywood Dr
Halesowen B62 83 C8
Wolverhampton WV6 24 D4
Hay Wood La B93, CV35 145 A3
Haywood Rd B33 69 E2
Haywood's Farm B71 42 F2
Hayworth Cl B79 20 F8
Hayworth Rd WS13 3 C2
Hazel Ave
Birmingham B73 45 C1
Wednesbury WS10 42 A4
Hazelbank B38 103 E2
Hazelbeach Rd B8 67 F5
Hazelbeech Rd B70 53 B3
Hazel Cl Hartshill CV10 72 A8
Royal Leamington Spa CV32 157 A2
Hazel Croft
Birmingham, Chelmsley Wood B37 70 B1
Birmingham, Northfield B31 103 A3
Hazeldene Gr 5 B6 66 E8
Hazeldene Rd
Birmingham B33 89 D7
Halesowen B63 82 E2
Hazel Dr B47 125 B5
Hazeley Cl B17 85 A7
Hazelgarth B77 36 B8
Hazel Gdns
Birmingham B27 88 C5
Codsall WV8 10 A4
Hazel Gr
Bedworth CV12 78 D3
Bilston WV14 40 E7
Hockley Heath B94 143 C6
Lichfield WS14 9 C7
Stourbridge DY8 80 C3
West Bromwich B70 53 C1
Wolverhampton WV11 26 C7
Wombourne WV5 49 A7
Hazelhurst Rd
Birmingham, Castle Bromwich B36 69 E7
Birmingham, King's Heath B14 104 E7
Hazel La WS6 5 B2
Hazell Way CV10 73 A1
Hazelmead Ct B73 57 A7
Hazelmere Dr
Burntwood WS7 6 F4
Wolverhampton WV3 24 A1
Hazelmere Rd B28 105 F8
Hazeloak Rd B90 106 A2
Hazel Oak Sch B90 106 A2
Hazel Rd
Birmingham B45 121 F6
Coventry CV6 96 B1
Dudley DY1 51 C2
Kingswinford DY6 60 E5
Nuneaton CV10 72 D5
Redditch B97 153 C5
Wednesbury DY4 41 D1
Wolverhampton WV3 38 E7
Hazelslade Ho WS12 2 F6
Hazels The DY9 98 F5
Hazelton Cl
Catshill B61 137 C8
2 Solihull B91 107 B1
Hazelton Rd B61 121 C1
Hazeltree Croft B27 88 B2
Hazeltree Gr B93 127 E3
Hazelville Gr B28 106 A6
Hazelville Rd B28 106 A7
Hazelwell Cres B30 104 B6
Hazelwell Dr B14 104 D6
Hazelwell Fordrough B30 104 B6
Hazelwell La B30 104 B7
Hazelwell Rd B30 104 A6
Hazelwell St B30 104 A7
Hazelwood Cl
Cheslyn Hay WS6 4 D2
Kidderminster DY11 116 B4
Hazelwood Dr WV11 26 A5
Hazelwood Gr
Cannock WS11 4 C8
Willenhall WV12 27 D5
Hazelwood Rd
Birmingham B27 88 B2
Dudley DY1 50 F5
Sutton Coldfield B74 30 D1
Hazlemere Cl CV5 112 B4
Hazlemere Dr B74 32 B1
Hazlemere Gr WS11 4 B8
Hazlitt Gr B30 103 D4
Headborough Rd CV2 114 A5
Headborough Wlk WS9 16 B1
Headingley Rd B21 54 E2
Headington Ave CV6 95 A2
Headland Dr B8 67 D5
Headland Rd WV3 24 A1
Headlands The
Coventry CV5 112 D4
Sutton Coldfield B74 31 C3
Headless Cross Dr B97 153 D1
Headley Croft B38 123 D8
Headley Ct B97 158 D8
Headley Heath La B38 124 B6
Headley Rise B90 106 D2
Headway Rd WV10 11 C3
Heale Cl B63 82 A7
Healey B77 21 E2
Healey Ct CV34 160 F7
Health Centre Rd CV4 132 C4
Heanor Croft B6 67 B8
Heantun Croft WV10 26 A5
Heantun Ct WV3 25 B1
Heantun Ho WV3 163 B2
Heantun Lodge WV14 40 C6
Heantun Mill Ct WS10 41 D1
Heantun Rise WV3 25 C4
Heantun Row WV11 13 B2
Hearsall Comm CV5 112 F2
Hearsall Com Prim Sch CV5 112 F2
Hearsall Ct CV4 112 D2
Hearsall La CV5 112 F2
Heartland Mews B65 63 B2
Heartlands High Sch B7 67 B4
Heartlands Parkway B7 67 D7
Heartlands Pl B8 67 E4
Heart of England Sch CV7 130 C6
Heart of England Way CV11 73 F3
Heart Of The Country Ctr* WS14 18 E8
Heath Acres WS10 41 C4
Heath Ave CV12 77 E1
Heathbank Dr WS12 1 C6
Heath Bridge Cl WS4 29 A8
Heathbrook Ave DY6 60 B7
Heath Cl
Birmingham B30 103 D5
Bromsgrove B60 150 E6
Stonnall WS14 16 E5
Sutton Coldfield B75 46 F7
Tipton DY4 52 B5
Heathcliff Rd
Birmingham B11 87 F4
Dudley DY2 62 F7
Heathcote Ave B91 106 E3
Heathcote Cl B77 36 F7
Heathcote Ct CV6 113 A7
Heathcote Dr B78 20 C1
Heathcote Ho B17 85 C5
Heathcote Ind Est CV34 161 D4
Heathcote La
Royal Leamington Spa CV34 161 D4
Warwick CV34 161 A5
Heathcote Rd
Birmingham B30 104 A5
Whitnash CV31 162 A4
Heathcote St CV6 113 A7
Heathcote Way CV34 161 D4
Heathcot Pl WS13 8 F5
Heath Cres CV2 114 A6
Heath Croft B31 123 A7
Heath Croft Rd B75 32 D1
Heath Ct 2 B12 86 F5
Heath Cvn Pk WV10 11 C6
Heath End Rd
Madeley Heath DY9 120 D7
Nuneaton CV10 72 F2
Heather Ave WS5 43 B4
Heather Cl
Birmingham B36 70 A8
Lichfield WS13 3 D1
Nuneaton CV10 72 F3
Walsall WS3 28 A8
Wednesfield WV11 26 E5
Heather Court Gdns B74 46 A8
Heather Croft B44 44 F1
Heather Ct B13 86 D3
Heather Dale B13 86 C2
Heather Dr
Bedworth CV12 77 E2
Birmingham B45 121 F6
Huntington WS12 1 D5
Heather Gr
Solihull B91 107 E6
Willenhall WV12 27 E4
Heather Ho B38 103 F1
Heatherleigh Rd B36 69 F8
Heather Mews WS12 2 A8
Heather Rd
Binley Woods CV3 135 D7
Birmingham, Great Barr B43 54 D8
Birmingham, Small Heath B10 87 F8
Cannock WS12 2 A8
Coventry CV2 96 C2
Dudley DY1 51 C4
Smethwick B67 64 E6
Walsall WS3 28 A8
Heather Valley WS12 2 D6
Heath Farm Rd
Codsall WV8 10 B2
Stourbridge DY8 80 E3
Heathfield Ave B20 66 B8
Heathfield Cl
Cradley Heath B64 62 F2
Dorridge B93 128 A5
Heathfield Cres DY11 116 B4
Heathfield Ct 1 B19 66 B7
Heathfield Dr WS3 14 B2
Heathfield Foundation Technology Coll The B64 62 F2
Heathfield Gdns DY8 80 F4
Heathfield La WS10 41 C6
Heathfield La W WS10 41 B6
Heathfield Prim Sch B19 66 C8
Heathfield Rd
Birmingham, King's Heath B14 104 F8
Birmingham, Lozells B19 66 C8
Coventry CV5 112 C2
Halesowen B63 82 E3
Redditch B97 153 A1
Sutton Coldfield B74 31 F3
Heathfields WV8 23 E8
Heathfields Inf Sch B77 35 F6
Heathfield Way B64 62 F1
Heath Gap Rd WS11 1 F3
Heath Gdns B91 107 D6
Heath Gn DY1 50 F5
Heath Gr WV8 10 B3
Heathgreen Cl B37 70 D3
Heath Green Gr 4 B18 65 E4
Heath Green Rd B18 65 E4
Heath Green Way CV4 131 F6
Heath Hayes Prim Sch WS12 2 F2
Heath Hill Rd WV6 23 E1
Heath Ho B14 104 F2
Heath House La WV8 23 E8
Heath La
Kidderminster DY10 117 C1
Stourbridge DY8 81 A4
West Bromwich B71 53 D7
Heathland Ave B34 69 A7
Heathland Cl WS12 2 D2
Heathlands Cl DY6 60 E8
Heathlands Cres B73 45 F1
Heathlands Gr B31 103 A1
Heathlands Prim Sch B34 68 F7
Heathlands Rd B73 45 F1
Heathlands The
2 Rowley Regis B65 63 C1
Stourbridge DY8 81 B4
Heath Lane Hospl B71 53 D7
Heathleigh Rd B38 123 C8
Heathley La B78 34 E5
Heathmere Ave B25 88 D8
Heathmere Dr B37 69 F2
Heath Mill La B9 67 A1
Heath Mount Prim Sch B12 86 F6
Heath Park Bsns & Ent Coll WV11 26 A5
Heath Rd
Bedworth CV12 77 F1
Birmingham B30 103 D5
Coventry CV2 114 A4
Darlaston WS10 41 E8
Dudley DY2 62 C2
Hollywood B47 125 A7
Solihull B91 107 D6
Willenhall WV12 13 D1
Heath Rd S B31 103 B4
Heath Rise B14 105 A1
Heath St S B18 65 F4
Heathside Dr
Birmingham B38 104 B2
Walsall WS3 15 A4
Heath St
Birmingham B18 65 E4
Cannock WS12 2 B7
Rowley Regis B65 63 C1
Tamworth B79 21 C5
Heath Terr
Beausale CV35 146 C2
Royal Leamington Spa CV32 156 E1
Heath Trad Pk B66 65 D5
Heath View
Cannock WS12 5 E8
Willenhall WS2 27 F3
Heath Way
Birmingham B34 69 B6
Cannock WS11 2 B2
Heathway Cl B34 69 A7
Heathy Farm Cl B32 84 B1
Heathy Rise B32 84 A2
Heaton Cl WV10 11 E5
Heaton Dr
Birmingham B15 85 E8
Sutton Coldfield B73 45 F8
Heaton Rd B91 107 A7
Heaton St B18 66 B5
Hebden B77 36 B8
Hebden Ave CV34 155 F1
Hebden Gr
Birmingham B28 105 E3
Willenhall WV11 13 B1
Hebden Way CV11 74 A2
Heckley Rd CV7 96 A7
Heddle Gr CV6 114 B8
Heddon Pl B7 67 A3
Hedera Cl WS5 43 B3
Hedera Rd B98 154 F6
Hedgefield Gr B63 82 C4
Hedgefield Way CV4 131 F8
Hedgerow Cl WS12 1 F7
Hedgerow Dr DY6 49 D1
Hedgerows The
Lichfield WS14 9 B5
Nuneaton CV10 72 F6
Romsley B62 100 F4
Tamworth B77 35 F8
Hedgerow Wlk
Coventry CV6 95 B4
Wolverhampton WV8 10 E1
Hedges Way B60 137 B1
Hedgetree Croft B37 70 C2
Hedge Way CV10 72 C7
Hedging La B77 35 E5
Hedging Lane Ind Est B77 35 E5
Hedgings The B34 69 B6
Hedgley Gr B33 69 A4
Hedingham Gr B37 70 D2
Hedley Croft B35 58 B4
Hednesford Hills Common Nature Reserve* WS12 2 E5
Hednesford Rd
Brownhills WS8 6 C2
Cannock, Blackfords WS11 1 F2
Cannock WS12 2 E1
Norton Canes WS11 5 F6
Hednesford St WS11 1 E1
Hednesford Sta WS12 2 B5
Heeley Rd B29 85 F1
Heemstede La CV32 157 A2
Heera Cl CV6 113 D8
Hefford Dr B66 65 A6
Helena Cl CV10 72 F3
Helena St 2 B1 66 C3
Helen Dixon Ct 8 B13 86 F4
Helenny Cl WV11 26 A5
Helen St CV6 113 F6
Hele Rd CV3 133 D6
Helford Cl DY4 51 D4
Heligan Pl WS12 2 E2
Hellaby Cl 3 B72 46 C4
Hellaby Ct B73 57 A7
Hellaby Ho B74 31 F3
Hellidon Cl 6 CV32 157 A2
Hellier Ave DY4 52 B4
Hellier Rd WV10 11 E2
Hellier St DY2 62 C8
Helming Dr WV1 26 B3
Helmingham B79 20 D7
Helmsdale Rd CV32 157 B5
Helmsdale Way DY3 51 A7
Helmsley Cl DY5 81 C8
Helmsley Rd WV11 26 C8
Helmswood Dr B37 90 C8
Helston Cl
Nuneaton CV11 74 A5
Stourbridge DY8 60 C2
Tamworth B79 21 C8
Walsall WS5 43 D7
Helstone Gr B11 88 A3
Helston Rd WS5 43 D7
Hembs Cres B43 54 C8
Hemdale CV11 74 A4
Hemdale Bsns Pk CV11 74 A4
Hemingford Rd CV2 115 A8
Heming Rd B98 159 E8
Hemlingford Croft B37 90 A7
Hemlingford Rd
Birmingham B37 69 F6
Sutton Coldfield B76 58 A6
Hemlock Bsns Ctr WS11 2 B2
Hemlock Pk WS11 2 B2
Hemlock Way WS11 2 B3
Hemmings Cl
Radford Semele CV31 162 E5
Stourbridge DY8 80 F5
Wolverhampton WV10 25 E3
Hemmings St WS10 41 C8
Hemming St DY11 116 C4
Hemmings Yard DY6 61 A8
Hemplands Rd DY8 80 F5
Hempole La DY4 52 D6
Hemsby Cl CV4 132 A7
Hemsworth Dr CV12 79 B2
Hemyock Rd B29 103 B8
Henbury Rd B27 88 D3
Henderson Cl
Allesley CV5 112 C7
Lichfield WS14 9 D7
Henderson Ct 7 B68 84 B8
Henderson Way B65 63 C1
Henderson Wlk DY4 52 B8
Hendon Cl Dudley DY3 50 D2
Wolverhampton WV10 25 E7
Hendon Rd B11 87 B5
Hendre Cl CV5 112 D2
Heneage Pl 6 B7 67 A4
Heneage St W B7 66 F4
Heneage St B7 67 A4
Henfield Cl WV11 26 D7
Hengham Rd B26 69 A1
Hen La CV6 95 D3
Henley Cl
Burntwood WS7 7 B5
Nuneaton CV11 73 F8
Sutton Coldfield B73 57 B8
Tamworth B79 21 C6
Tipton DY4 52 D5
Walsall WS3 14 E1
Henley Coll CV2 114 C8
Henley Cres B91 107 B7
Henley Ct
Coventry CV2 114 D7
Lichfield WS14 9 B6
Henleydale 4 B90 126 C8
Henley Dr B74 32 A3
Henley Mill La CV2 114 C7
Henley Park Ind Est CV2 114 E7
Henley Rd
Coventry CV2 114 D7
Whitnash CV31 162 B5
Henley Rd *continued*
Wolverhampton WV10 11 B1
Henley St B11 87 B7
Henley Wlk CV2 114 D8
Henlow Cl DY4 51 D5
Henlow Rd B14 105 A2
Hennalls The B36 68 F7
Hennals Ave B97 152 F2
Henn Dr DY4 40 E1
Henne Dr WV14 40 C1
Henn St DY4 52 A8
Henrietta St
Birmingham B19 164 B4
Coventry CV6 113 E5
Henry Boteler Rd CV4 132 B7
Henry Boys' Almshouses WS1 42 D8
Henry Ct DY1 51 B1
Henry Lloyd Ind Est WS10 41 C7
Henry Rd B25 88 C7
Henry St
Coventry CV1 165 B3
Hinckley LE10 71 A2
Kenilworth CV8 148 A5
Nuneaton CV11 73 C2
Walsall WS2 28 D1
Henry Tandey Ct 4 CV32 156 E1
Henry Wlk B60 150 E7
Hensborough B90 126 A5
Hensel Dr WV3 38 C8
Henshaw Gr
6 Birmingham, Small Heath B10 87 C8
Birmingham, Yardley B25 88 C7
Henshaw Rd B10 87 D8
Henson Rd CV12 77 E1
Henstead St B5 86 D8
Hentland Cl B98 154 D4
Henwood Cl WV6 24 C3
Henwood La B91 108 B4
Henwood Rd WV6 24 D3
Hepburn Cl WS9 30 A4
Hepburn Edge B24 57 B4
Hepworth Cl WV6 23 F4
Hepworth Rd CV3 115 B1
Herald Ave CV5 112 D1
Herald Bsns Pk CV3 134 F7
Herald Ct 2 DY1 51 C1
Herald Rd B26 90 C4
Heralds Ct 6 CV34 161 B8
Herald Way
Coventry CV3 135 A7
Hinckley LE10 75 D4
Herbert Art Gall & Mus* CV1 165 C2
Herbert Austin Dr B60 121 E1
Herbert Rd
Aldridge WS9 16 A1
Birmingham, Handsworth B21 54 F1
Birmingham, Small Heath B10 87 C8
Smethwick B67 65 A1
Solihull B91 107 B4
Herbert's La CV8 148 A5
Herberts Park Rd WS10 41 B6
Herbert St
Bilston WV14 40 B6
Nuneaton CV10 72 E3
Redditch B98 153 E4
West Bromwich B70 53 D3
Wolverhampton WV1 163 C4
Herbhill Cl WV4 39 D4
Hereford Ave 5 B12 87 A6
Hereford Cl
Aldridge WS9 30 A8
Barwell LE9 71 F6
Birmingham B45 102 A2
Kidderminster DY11 116 A5
Nuneaton CV10 72 E4
Hereford Ho WV1 163 B4
Hereford Pl B71 53 B7
Hereford Rd
Birmingham B68 84 B7
Bramcote CV11 79 F6
Cannock WS12 2 B4
Dudley DY2 62 E3
Hereford Sq B8 67 C5
Hereford St WS2 28 E4
Hereford Way B78 21 A2
Hereford Wlk B37 69 F1
Hereward Coll CV4 111 F1

Hereward Rise B62... **83** C5
Herford Way LE10...**75** F6
Heritage Cl B68..... **64** C4
Heritage Ct
　Birmingham B18...... **66** C4
　Coventry CV4 ...**132** D3
　Kenilworth CV8..... **148** B7
　Lichfield WS14 ...... **9** D6
Heritage Dr CV6 ... **96** C6
Heritage The **7** WS1.. **28** E1
Heritage Way
　Birmingham B33...... **69** D3
　Tipton DY4 .... **52** B5
Hermes Cl CV34..... **161** E5
Hermes Cres CV2 ... **114** E6
Hermes Ct
　Royal Leamington Spa
　　CV34............ **161** E5
　Sutton Coldfield B74... **31** F3
Hermes Rd
　Birmingham B26...... **90** C4
　Lichfield WS13 .... **3** D1
Hermione Cl CV34... **161** F3
Hermitage Cl B78 ....**22** F1
Hermitage Dr B76... **47** A4
Hermitage Rd
　Birmingham B15...... **85** C8
　Birmingham, Gravelly Hill
　　B23............... **56** E3
　Coventry CV2 ...... **114** D4
　Solihull B91........ **107** C6
Hermitage The B91.. **107** C6
Hermitage Way CV8. **148** A3
Hermit's Croft CV3 .. **133** D8
Hermit St DY3 .... **50** D5
Hernall Croft B26 .... **89** A7
Herne Cl B18 .... **66** A4
Hernefield Rd B34 ... **69** A7
Hern Rd DY5 .... **81** C6
Heronbank CV4 ..... **111** C2
Heron Cl
　Alvechurch B48...... **139** A7
　Brownhills WS8 ..... **15** E7
　Cheswick Green B90 . **126** D4
Heron Ct **3** B73 ... **57** B7
Herondale WS12 ......**2** B4
Herondale Cres DY8.. **80** C4
Herondale Rd
　Birmingham B26...... **88** F6
　Stourbridge DY8 .... **80** C4
Heronfield Cl B98 ... **154** C5
Heronfield Dr B31... **122** F6
Heronfield Way B91. **107** E5
Heron Ho CV3........ **114** B2
Heron Mill WS3 ..... **14** E3
Heron Rd B68....... **64** A2
Heronry The WV6 .....**23** F7
Herons Ct LE10...... **75** A7
Heronsville Ho DY4.. **52** B3
Herons Way B29 .... **85** C3
Heronswood Dr DY5.. **61** D1
Heronswood Rd
　Birmingham B45..... **122** B6
　Kidderminster DY10 . **117** A2
Heronville Dr B70... **53** A7
Heronville Rd B70... **53** A6
Heron Way B45 ..... **121** F7
Herrick Rd
　Birmingham B8...... **67** E5
　Coventry CV2 ...... **114** D3
Herrick St WV3 ..... **163** A2
Herringshaw Croft
　B76................. **46** E3
Hertford Pl CV1 ..... **165** A2
Hertford St
　Birmingham B12...... **87** A5
　Coventry CV1 ...... **165** B2
Hertford Way B93... **128** B4
Hervey Gr B24 ...... **57** D6
Hesket Ave B68 ..... **64** C1
Hesketh Cres B23 ... **56** C5
Hesketh Pl B37 ......**89** F8
Hesleden B77 .... **36** B8
Heslop Cl CV3...... **134** F8
Hessian Cl WV14 .... **40** B2
Hestia Dr B29...... **103** E8
Heston Ave B42 ..... **55** B8
Hetton Cl **1** CV34... **155** F1
Hever Ave B44 ...... **45** A1
Hever Cl DY1........ **50** E3
Hewell Ave B60 .... **150** F7
Hewell Cl
　Birmingham B31..... **122** F7
　Kingswinford DY6.... **49** D1
　Redditch B97 ...... **152** C6
Hewell La
　Barnt Green B45..... **138** D1

Hewell La continued
　Redditch B60, B97 ...**152** D6
Hewell Rd
　Barnt Green B45..... **138** D8
　Redditch B97 ...... **153** D4
Hewitson Gdns B67.. **64** F2
Hewitt Ave CV6 .... **113** B4
Hewitt Cl WS13 .... **3** A2
Hewitt St WS10 ..... **41** C5
Hewston Croft WS12.. **2** D4
Hexby Cl CV2 ...... **115** A6
Hexham Way DY1....**50** F2
Hexton Cl B90 ...... **105** D2
Hexworthy Ave CV3.. **133** B5
Heybarnes Cir B10 ...**87** F7
Heybarnes Rd B10 ... **88** A8
Heybrook Cl CV2 ... **114** C7
Heycott Gr B38...... **104** C2
Heycroft CV4........ **132** D4
Heydon Rd
　Brierley Hill DY5..... **61** B6
　Finstall B60........ **137** D1
Heyford Cl CV2...... **96** D3
Heyford Gr B91..... **127** C8
Heyford Way B35.... **58** B5
Heygate Way WS9.... **16** B1
Heyland Cnr B10..... **67** F1
Heynesfield Rd B33 .. **69** C3
Heythrop Gr B13 ... **105** D8
Heyville Croft CV8... **148** C3
Heywood Cl CV6 .... **114** A7
Hibberd Ct CV8 .... **147** F4
Hickman Ave WV1,
　WV2 .... **40** A8
Hickman Gdns B16... **65** F1
Hickman Rd
　Bilston WV14 .... **40** C5
　Birmingham B11..... **87** B6
　Brierley Hill DY5..... **61** C4
　Tipton DY4 .... **51** F8
Hickman's Ave B64... **62** E2
Hickmans Cl **2** B62.. **84** A6
Hickman St WS3 ..... **81** C6
Hickmerelands La
　DY3 .... **39** C1
Hickory Cl WS11 ......**2** C2
Hickory Dr B17...... **65** A2
Hicks Cl CV34...... **155** E2
Hidcote Ave B76 .... **58** A8
Hidcote Cl
　Nuneaton CV11...... **78** F8
　Royal Leamington Spa
　　CV31............ **162** C5
Hidcote Gr
　Birmingham, Garret's
　　Green B33......... **89** C8
　Birmingham, Marston Green
　　B37.............. **90** A7
Hidcote Gr CV8 .... **148** C6
Hidson Rd B23...... **56** C5
Higgins Ave WV14... **40** D2
Higgins La B32...... **84** C5
Higgins Wlk B66 ..... **64** F8
Higgs Field Cres B64. **63** B1
Higgs Rd WV11..... **13** A1
Higham La CV11 .... **73** E7
Higham Lane Sch
　CV10............... **73** D6
Higham's Cl B65 .... **63** B3
Higham Way
　Hinckley LE10 ...... **75** E7
　Wolverhampton WV10. **25** E6
Higham Way Ho LE10. **75** E7
High Arcal Dr DY3....**50** F7
High Arcal Rd DY3... **49** F4
High Arcal Sch The
　DY3................ **50** F6
High Ash Cl CV7 .....**95** F7
High Ave B64 ....**82** F8
High Bank WS11 ...... **4** E8
High Beech CV5..... **112** A6
High Beeches B43 ... **43** D1
Highbridge Rd
　Dudley DY2 .... **62** B3
　Sutton Coldfield B73... **46** A1
High Brink Rd B46... **70** F7
Highbrook Cl WV9 ... **11** A2
High Broome Ct B78.. **21** A3
High Brow B17...... **85** B7
High Bullen WS10 ....**41** F3
Highbury Ave
　Birmingham B21..... **65** F8
　Rowley Regis B65.... **63** D3
Highbury Cl B65 .... **63** D3
Highbury Ct B13 ... **104** E7
Highbury Gn CV10... **72** C7
Highbury Rd
　Birmingham B14... **104** D8
　Oldbury B68........ **64** B5
　Smethwick B66...... **64** D7

Highbury Rd continued
　Sutton Coldfield B74... **31** C3
Highclare Sch B23... **57** A5
Highclare Sch St Paul's
　B74................ **46** C1
Highclare Woodfield Sch
　B72................ **46** C1
High Clere B64...... **83** A7
Highcliffe Rd B77 .... **35** D8
Highcrest Cl B31.... **123** A4
Highcroft WS3 ...... **15** B6
High Croft
　Aldridge WS9 .... **16** B2
　Birmingham B43..... **43** C1
Highcroft Ave DY8... **60** C3
Highcroft Cl B92..... **89** C2
Highcroft Cres CV32. **156** C1
High Croft Cres WS14 ..**9** C7
Highcroft Dr B74..... **31** E3
Highcroft Hospl B23. **56** D3
Highcroft Rd B23 ... **56** E3
Highdown Cres **3**
　B90.............. **127** A6
Highdown Rd CV31.. **162** B6
High Elms La B60 ... **151** E1
High Ercal Ave DY5... **61** C2
High Farm Rd
　Halesowen, Hasbury
　　B63.............. **82** F3
　Halesowen, Hurst Green
　　B62.............. **83** F8
Highfield CV7 ...... **92** C1
Highfield Ave
　Bilston WV14 .... **40** E4
　Burntwood WS7 ......**7** B4
　Redditch B97 ...... **158** D8
　Tamworth B77...... **22** A5
　Walsall WS4 .... **29** C8
　Wolverhampton WV10. **12** A2
Highfield Cl
　Birmingham B28..... **105** D5
　Burntwood WS7 ......**7** B7
　Kenilworth CV8..... **147** E4
Highfield Cres
　Halesowen B63...... **82** D6
　Rowley Regis B65.... **63** B1
　Wolverhampton WV11 . **26** B6
Highfield Ct
　Cannock WS11 ....**2** B5
　Sutton Coldfield B73... **46** B1
Highfield Dr B73..... **56** F7
Highfield Gdns WS14...**9** A4
Highfield Inf & Jun Sch
　B8.................. **67** E5
Highfield La
　Birmingham B32..... **84** B4
　Clent DY9 .... **100** A3
　Corley CV7 .... **94** D8
　1 Halesowen B63.... **83** A3
Highfield Mews B63.. **82** D6
Highfield Pl B14 ... **105** D5
Highfield Rd
　Birmingham, Edgbaston
　　B15.............. **86** A8
　Birmingham, Moseley
　　B13.............. **87** B3
　Birmingham, Newton
　　B43.............. **54** C7
　Birmingham, Saltley B8. **67** E5
　Birmingham, Yardley Wood
　　B14, B28......... **105** D5
　Bromsgrove B61..... **150** E8
　Burntwood WS7 ......**7** C7
　Cannock WS12 ....**2** E1
　Coventry CV2 ...... **113** F4
　Dudley DY2 .... **51** E1
　Halesowen B63...... **82** D5
　Kidderminster DY10 . **117** A8
　Nuneaton CV11...... **73** E2
　Redditch B97 ...... **158** D8
　Rowley Regis B65.... **63** B1
　Sedgley DY3 .... **39** D1
　Smethwick B67...... **65** A5
　Stourbridge DY8 ..... **61** A2
　Studley B80........ **159** D4
　Tipton DY4 .... **52** B8
　Walsall WS3 .... **15** A4
Highfield Rd N WS3 ...**14** F5
Highfields
　Bromsgrove B61.... **136** E1
　Burntwood WS7 ......**7** B7
Highfields Cl WS4.... **38** D6
Highfields Dr
　Dudley WV14 .... **40** D3
　Wombourne WV5 .... **49** A5
Highfields Grange
　WS6................ **4** D1
Highfields Pk WS6 ... **4** D1
Highfields Prim Sch
　Burntwood WS7 ......**7** C7

Highfields Prim Sch
continued
　Cradley Heath B65 ... **83** C8
　Dudley WV14 .... **40** C2
Highfields Rd
　Burntwood WS7 ....**6** F4
　Dudley WV14 .... **40** D3
　Hinckley LE10 ...... **71** E1
Highfields Science
　Specialist Sch WV4. **38** C5
Highfields The WV6 .. **24** A3
Highfield Terr
　Birmingham B18...... **66** A5
　Royal Leamington Spa
　　CV32............ **156** D1
Highfield Way WS9... **16** B2
Highgate Dudley DY3.. **50** E5
Highgate Ave
　Walsall WS1 .... **42** F8
　Wolverhampton WV4 .. **38** D6
Highgate Bsns Ctr
　B12................**87** B6
Highgate Cl
　Birmingham B12..... **86** F7
　Kidderminster DY11 . **116** A4
　Walsall WS1 .... **42** F8
Highgate Ct **4** WS1..**42** F8
Highgate Dr WS1.....**42** F8
Highgate Ho **1** B5... **86** E8
Highgate Middleway
　B12................**86** F7
Highgate Pl B12 .... **87** A7
Highgate Prim Sch
　DY2................**61** F6
Highgate Rd
　Birmingham B12..... **87** A6
　Dudley DY1, DY2..... **61** F6
　Walsall WS1 .... **42** F7
Highgate Ret Pk B11. **87** A7
Highgate Sq B12.....**86** F7
Highgate Sq Craft Ctr **9**
　B12................**86** F7
Highgate St
　Birmingham B12..... **86** F7
　Cradley Heath B64 ... **62** F2
Highgrove
　Coventry CV4 ...... **131** F5
　Wolverhampton WV6 .. **24** C3
Highgrove Cl
　Tamworth B79....... **21** B7
　Willenhall WV12 ..... **27** B7
Highgrove Pl DY1....**50** F2
High Haden Cres B64. **83** A8
High Haden Rd B64 .. **83** A8
High Heath Cl B30 .. **103** D5
High Hill WV11...... **13** A2
High Holborn DY3.... **50** D7
High House Dr B45.. **121** F3
High House La B60.. **152** A6
Highland Ho B62.... **83** C8
Highland Mews WV14. **40** D1
Highland Rd
　Birmingham, Erdington
　　B23.............. **56** F5
　Birmingham, Great Barr
　　B43.............. **43** E3
　Cannock WS12 ....**1** C4
　Coventry CV5 ...... **112** F1
　Cradley Heath B64 ... **62** E2
　Dudley DY1 .... **51** A3
　Kenilworth CV8...... **148** C7
　Royal Leamington Spa
　　CV32............ **157** B4
High Land Rd WS9 ... **16** B3
Highland Ridge B62.. **83** E5
Highlands Cl
　Kidderminster DY11 . **116** A5
　Warwick CV34...... **161** A8
Highlands Ct B90 .. **126** E8
Highlands Rd
　Solihull B90........ **126** F6
　Wolverhampton WV3 .. **38** D8
Highland Way B98 .. **159** A7
High Leasowes B63 .. **83** A4
Highley Cl
　Kidderminster DY11 . **116** B2
　Redditch B98 ...... **154** E4
High Mdws
　Bromsgrove B60.... **150** D7
　Wolverhampton WV6 .. **24** C3
　Wombourne WV5 .... **49** B6
High Meadow Inf Sch
　B46................ **70** F8
High Meadow Rd
　B38.............. **104** A2

Highmoor Cl
　Dudley WV14 .... **40** D3
　Willenhall WV12 ..... **27** B7
Highmoor Rd B65.... **63** B3
Highmore Dr B32 ... **102** C8
High Mount St WS12 ...**2** B6
High Oak DY5 ...... **61** C7
Highover Dr B75.... **32** A4
Highpark Ave DY8.... **80** D5
High Park Cl
　Coventry CV5 ...... **111** F3
　Sedgley DY3 .... **50** D8
High Park Cnr B7 ... **67** B6
High Park Cres DY3.. **39** D1
High Park Rd B63.... **82** C5
High Park St B7...... **67** B6
High Point B15...... **85** E6
High Rd WV12....... **27** E6
High Ridge WS9.....**29** F5
High Ridge Cl
　Aldridge WS9 ....**29** E5
　Darlaston WS10 ..... **41** A4
High St Duchess Par
　B70................ **53** D3
High St Princess Par
　B70................ **53** D3
High St Aldridge WS9.. **30** B6
　Astwood Bank B96 ... **158** E1
　Bedworth CV12....... **78** B2
　Belbroughton DY9.... **119** E7
　Bilston WV14 .... **40** D5
　Birmingham, Aston B6,
　　B19.............. **66** C7
　Birmingham B4...... **164** C2
　Birmingham, Castle Vale
　　B35.............. **58** B4
　Birmingham, Erdington
　　B23.............. **56** F4
　Birmingham, Harborne
　　B17.............. **85** D6
　Birmingham, King's Heath
　　B14.............. **104** E8
　Birmingham, Quinton
　　B32.............. **84** A6
　Birmingham, Saltley B8. **67** D5
　Brierley Hill, Barrow Hill
　　DY5.............. **61** C7
　Brierley Hill, Brockmoor
　　DY5.............. **61** C4
　Brierley Hill, Quarry Bank
　　DY5.............. **82** A8
　Bromsgrove B61.... **137** A2
　Brownhills, Clayhanger
　　WS8.............. **15** E6
　Brownhills, Vigo WS9 .. **15** F5
　Brownhills WS8 ..... **15** F8
　Burntwood, Chasetown
　　WS7............... **6** F6
　Cheslyn Hay WS6 .... **4** D1
　Coleshill B46........ **70** F7
　Coventry CV1 ...... **165** C2
　Coventry, Keresley CV6. **94** F1
　Cradley Heath B64 ... **62** D1
　Cubbington CV32 ... **157** E5
　Darlaston WS10 ..... **41** A4
　7 Dudley, Old Dock
　　DY1.............. **62** B8
　1 Halesowen B63.... **83** B3
　Hampton-in-A B92 ... **109** A2
　Kenilworth CV8..... **147** E5
　Kidderminster DY10 . **116** E6
　Kingswinford DY6.... **60** E6
　Kingswinford, Wall Heath
　　DY6.............. **60** C8
　Knowle B93........ **128** C6
　Norton Canes WS11 ...**6** B5
　Nuneaton CV11...... **73** B4
　Rowley Regis B65.... **63** C1
　Royal Leamington Spa
　　CV31............ **162** A7
　Ryton-on-D CV8 .... **135** B1
　Sedgley DY3 .... **50** D8
　Smethwick B66...... **65** A5
　Solihull B91........ **107** C3
　Solihull, Shirley B90 .. **105** D2
　Stourbridge, Amblecote
　　DY8.............. **80** F7
　Stourbridge DY8 ..... **81** A5
　Stourbridge, Lye DY9 .. **81** E5
　Stourbridge, Wollaston
　　DY8.............. **80** E7
　Stourbridge, Wordsley
　　DY8.............. **60** E2
　Studley B80........ **159** E4
　Sutton Coldfield B72... **46** C5
　Tamworth B77....... **35** C5
　Tipton, Princes End DY4. **51** E8

High St continued
　Tipton, Tipton Green
　　DY4.............. **51** E5
　Walsall, Pelsall WS3... **15** A4
　Walsall, Wallington Heath
　　WS3.............. **14** B1
　Walsall WS1 .... **28** E1
　Warwick CV34 ...... **160** E6
　Wednesfield WV11.... **26** D5
　West Bromwich B70... **53** C3
　Wolverhampton WV6 .. **24** D4
　Wombourne WV5 .... **49** B7
High Street Bordesley
　B12................ **67** A1
High Street Deritend
　B12................**66** F1
Highters Cl B14 .... **105** B2
Highter's Heath La
　B14.............. **105** A2
Highters Heath Prim Sch
　B14.............. **105** B3
Highters Rd B14 ... **105** A3
High Timbers B45... **101** F1
Hightown B63....... **82** C6
Hightree Cl B32..... **84** B1
High Trees B20......**54** F3
High Trees Cl B98 .. **158** E7
High Trees Ho B69 ... **63** F3
High Trees Rd B93.. **128** A7
Highview **9** WS1....**42** F8
High View B46...... **89** F1
High View Dr CV7 ... **95** C7
High View Rd CV32.. **157** C5
Highview St DY2 .... **51** F8
Highwaymans Croft
　CV4.............. **132** D5
Highwood Ave B92... **89** A1
High Wood Cl DY6 ... **60** C6
Highwood Croft B38. **103** D1
Hiker Gr **3** B37..... **70** D2
Hilary Cres DY1...... **51** B6
Hilary Dr Aldridge WS9. **30** A5
　Sutton Coldfield B76... **47** A3
　Wolverhampton WV3 .. **38** D7
Hilary Gr B31 ...... **102** F3
Hilary Rd
　Coventry CV4 ...... **132** E6
　Nuneaton CV10...... **72** F5
Hilden Rd B7 .... **67** B4
Hilderic Cres DY1.... **61** C7
Hilderstone Rd B25... **88** C6
Hildicks Cres WS3....**28** F7
Hildicks Pl WS3 ..... **29** A1
Hilditch Way CV11... **73** E2
Hillaire Cl B38...... **104** C2
Hillaries Rd B23..... **56** D2
Hillary Ave WS10.... **42** C3
Hillary Crest DY3.... **50** C5
Hillary Prim Sch WS2. **42** C7
Hillary St WS2....... **42** C7
Hill Ave WV4........**39** F3
Hill Avenue Prim Sch
　WV4................**39** F3
Hillbank B69........ **63** D8
Hill Bank DY9.......**81** F5
Hill Bank Dr B33 ... **68** D4
Hill Bank Rd
　Birmingham B38.... **104** A2
　Halesowen B63...... **82** D6
Hillborough Rd B27 .. **88** D2
Hillbrook Gr B33..... **68** F3
Hillbrow Cres B62....**83** F8
Hillbury Dr WV12.... **27** B8
Hill Cl
　Birmingham B31.... **103** C1
　Royal Leamington Spa
　　CV32............ **157** A3
　Sedgley DY3 .... **39** D1
Hill Crest
　Cubbington CV32 ... **157** E5
　Dudley DY3 .... **50** C4
Hillcrest Ave
　Birmingham B43..... **43** E2
　Halesowen B63...... **82** B7
　Wolverhampton WV10. **11** E1
Hill Crest Ave DY5... **61** C2
Hillcrest Bsns Pk DY2. **62** C2
Hillcrest Cl
　Dudley DY2 .... **62** C5
　Tamworth B79....... **21** B6
Hill Crest Dr WS13 ....**3** A1
Hillcrest Gdns WV12.. **27** D5
Hill Crest Gr B44..... **56** F2
Hill Crest Hosp B98. **159** D4
Hillcrest Ind Est B64. **82** D6
Hillcrest Pk B47.... **140** F8
Hillcrest Rd
　Birmingham B43..... **43** E2
　Dudley DY2 .... **51** E1

Hillcrest Rd *continued*
Nuneaton CV10 72 E5
Polesworth B78 36 F7
Romsley B62 101 A4
Sutton Coldfield B72 46 C1
Hill Crest Rd B13 86 E2
Hillcrest Rise WS7 7 B4
Hillcrest Sch & Com Coll The DY2 62 C5
Hillcrest Sch & Sixth Form Ctr B32 84 E3
Hillcroft Ho B14 104 F2
Hillcroft Ho DY6 60 E7
Hill Croft Rd B14 104 C6
Hillcross Wlk B36 68 F8
Hilldene Rd DY6 60 C4
Hilldrop Gr 1 B17 85 D3
Hilleys Croft B37 69 F2
Hill Farm Ave CV11 74 B1
Hill Farm Prim Sch CV6 113 B7
Hillfield Hall Ct 1 B91 107 C1
Hillfield Mews 3 B91 127 B8
Hillfield Rd
Birmingham B11 87 D3
Solihull B91 107 C2
Solihull, Hillfield B91 107 B1
Hillfields B67 64 D3
Hillfields Ho 1 CV1 113 E3
Hillfields Rd DY5 81 B7
Hillfield Wlk B65 62 F5
Hill Fray Dr CV3 134 A5
Hill Gr B20 55 C2
Hill Grove Cres DY10 117 A4
Hillgrove Gdns DY10 117 A4
Hillhampton Cl B92 89 C1
Hill Ho B66 65 C6
Hill Hook Ho B74 31 E5
Hill Hook Rd B74 31 F5
Hill House La B33 68 F3
Hillhurst Gr B36 58 D1
Hillhurst Rd B73 45 C3
Hilliard Cl CV12 78 B4
Hilliards Croft B42 55 A8
Hillingford Ave B43 44 D3
Hill La
Alvechurch B47, B48 124 D1
Birmingham B43 43 E2
Bromsgrove B60 136 F1
Clent DY9 99 E4
Middleton B75 33 B2
Hillman B77 21 E2
Hillman Dr DY2 62 E7
Hillman Gr B36 58 F1
Hillman Ho CV1 165 B3
Hillmeads Dr DY2 62 F7
Hillmeads Rd B38 104 A1
Hillmorton B74 31 F3
Hillmorton Cl B98 154 E6
Hillmorton Rd
Coventry CV2 96 C1
Dorridge B93 128 A5
Sutton Coldfield B74 31 F4
Hillmount Cl B28 87 E2
Hill Pas B64 62 E2
Hill Pk WS9 16 A4
Hill Pl WV11 13 A1
Hill Rd Keresley CV7 94 F6
Tipton B69 52 A2
Willenhall WV13 26 E1
Hillrise LE10 75 F8
Hill Rise View B60 137 C6
Hillsborough Ho B27 88 E2
Hillside
Brownhills WS8 16 A6
Hartshill CV10 72 A8
Lichfield WS14 9 D6
Redditch B98 153 D2
Hill Side
Coventry CV2 114 A6
Dudley DY3 50 C4
Hillside Ave
Brierley Hill DY5 82 A8
Cradley Heath B65 83 B8
Halesowen B63 82 D6
Hillside Cl
Birmingham B32 102 A8
Brownhills WS8 16 A6
Burntwood WS7 6 E5
Cannock WS12 2 A7
Kidderminster DY11 116 A7
Hillside Cres WS3 14 F3
Hillside Croft B92 89 E4
Hillside Ct B43 43 E2
Hillside Dr
Birmingham, Great Barr B42 55 A6
Hillside Dr *continued*
Birmingham, Kingshurst B37 69 F4
Kidderminster DY11 116 A7
Lickey End B61 137 B6
Nuneaton CV10 72 C7
Sutton Coldfield B74 44 F7
Hillside Gdns
Birmingham B37 69 F4
Wolverhampton WV1 26 A3
Hillside N CV2 114 A6
Hillside Rd
Birmingham, Gravelly Hill B23 56 D2
Birmingham, Great Barr B43 43 D2
Dudley DY1 51 A5
Hinckley LE10 75 D6
Sutton Coldfield B74 32 A4
Hill St Bedworth CV12 78 B5
Bilston WV14 40 E3
Birmingham B5 164 B2
Brierley Hill, Quarry Bank DY5 82 A8
Brierley Hill, Silver End DY5 61 D2
Burntwood WS7 6 E5
Cannock WS12 2 C3
Cheslyn Hay WS6 4 C2
Coventry CV1 165 B3
Darlaston WS10 41 E6
Dudley, Netherton DY2 62 C5
Dudley, Upper Gornal DY3 50 D5
Essington WV11 12 F3
Halesowen B63 83 A3
Hinckley LE10 75 E8
Kidderminster DY11 116 D6
Norton Canes WS11 5 F6
Nuneaton CV10 72 D4
Royal Leamington Spa CV32 157 A1
Smethwick B66 65 A6
Stourbridge, Amblecote DY8 80 F8
Stourbridge DY8 80 F4
Stourbridge, Lye DY9 81 F5
Tipton DY4 51 F4
Walsall WS1 28 F1
Warwick CV34 161 B8
Hillstone Gdns WV10 25 F8
Hillstone Prim Sch B34 69 D5
Hillstone Rd B34 69 D5
Hill The B32 84 E2
Hilltop DY9 81 F3
Hill Top Coventry CV1 165 C3
Redditch B97 152 F1
West Bromwich B70 53 A7
Hill Top Ave
Halesowen B62 83 E7
Tamworth B79 21 B8
Hilltop Cl CV8 145 E8
Hill Top Cl B44 55 E6
Hill Top Ct DY3 50 E3
Hilltop Dr B36 68 D7
Hill Top Ind Est B70 52 F8
Hilltop Rd DY2 62 E8
Hill Top Rd
Birmingham B31 102 F3
Oldbury B68 64 C2
Hill Top Wlk WS9 16 C1
Hill View WS9 16 B2
Hillview Cl
Halesowen B63 82 E6
Lickey End B60 137 C6
Hillview Rd
Birmingham B45 121 E8
Lickey End B60 137 C6
Hill Village Rd B75 32 A4
Hillville Gdns DY8 81 B3
Hill West Prim Sch B74 31 F4
Hill Wood WS3 14 F2
Hillwood Ave B90 127 A6
Hillwood Cl DY6 60 C4
Hillwood Common Rd B75 32 B6
Hillwood Rd
Birmingham B31 102 E7
Halesowen B62 83 C7
Sutton Coldfield B75 32 C5
Hill Wootton Rd CV32, CV35 156 C6
Hillyfields Rd B23 56 C4
Hilly Rd WV14 40 E2
Hilmore Way B77 35 E8
Hilsea Cl WV8 10 F1
Hilston Ave
Halesowen B63 82 F4
Hilston Ave *continued*
Wolverhampton WV4 38 C4
Hilton Ave
Birmingham B28 105 F4
Nuneaton CV10 72 B6
Hilton Cl WS3 14 A2
Hilton Cross WV10 12 B5
Hilton Cross Bsns Pk WV10 12 B5
Hilton Ct
Coventry CV5 112 F2
Sutton Coldfield B72 57 C8
Hilton Dr B72 57 C8
Hilton La
Featherstone WV10, WV11 12 E8
Great Wyrley, Warstone WV11 13 B7
Great Wyrley WS6 5 A2
Hilton Main Ind Est WV11 12 C5
Hilton Park Service Area WV11 13 B7
Hilton Pl WV14 40 F5
Hilton Rd
Burntwood WS7 6 C8
Featherstone WV10 12 C7
Oldbury B69 63 C8
Willenhall WV12 13 C1
Wolverhampton WV4 39 F4
Hilton St
West Bromwich B70 53 A3
Wolverhampton WV10 163 D4
Hilton Trad Est WV4 39 F4
Hilton Way WV12 27 C8
Himbleton Cl B98 153 F1
Himbleton Croft 1 B90 127 A6
Himley Ave DY1 50 F2
Himley Cl
Birmingham B43 43 C2
Willenhall WV12 27 B5
Himley Cres WV4 39 B5
Himley Ct DY3 50 E3
Himley Gdns DY3 49 F4
Himley Gr B45 122 B6
Himley Hall* DY3 49 D4
Himley Rd
2 Bedworth CV12 77 D2
Dudley DY1, DY3 50 C2
Himley Rise B90 126 E4
Himley St DY1 51 A1
Hinbrook Rd DY1 50 E1
Hinchliffe Ave WV14 40 B2
Hinchwick Ct B93 127 F3
Hinckes Rd WV6 24 B5
Hinckley Bsns Pk LE10 74 F8
Hinckley Coll LE10 71 F1
Hinckley & District Hospl LE10 75 D8
Hinckley & District Mus* LE10 71 D1
Hinckley Rd
Ansty CV2, CV7 97 C2
Aston Flamville LE10 76 E6
Barwell LE9 71 E5
Burbage LE9 76 D8
Burton Hastings CV11 75 A1
Burton Hastings CV11, LE10 75 D1
Burton Hastings LE10 75 E1
Coventry CV2 115 A8
Hinckley LE10 76 A6
Nuneaton CV11 73 E5
Hinckley St B5 164 C2
Hinckley Sta LE10 75 D7
Hincks St WV2 40 A7
Hind Cl CV34 155 F2
Hindhead Rd B14 105 C4
Hindlip Cl B63 82 F2
Hindlow Cl B7 67 B4
Hindon Gr B27 106 C7
Hindon Sq B15 85 E8
Hindon Wlk B32 84 C2
Hingeston St B18 66 B4
Hingley Croft WS9 30 F3
Hingley Ind Pk B64 62 C1
Hingley Rd DY9 82 A6
Hingley St B64 62 D1
Hinsford Cl DY6 60 E8
Hinstock Cl WV4 39 A4
Hinstock Rd B20 54 F1
Hintlesham Ave B15 85 D5
Hinton Ave B48 139 A6
Hinton Fields B61 136 E7
Hinton Gr WV11 26 F5
Hintons Coppice B93 127 E6
Hints Ct B78 19 D2
Hints La Hopwas B78 20 B5
Weeford B78 19 F4
Hints Rd Hopwas B78 20 B6
Mile Oak B78 20 C2
Hipkins St DY4 51 E7
Hiplands Rd B62 83 F4
Hipsley Cl B36 58 C1
Hipsmoor Cl B37 69 F3
Hipswell Highway CV2 114 D3
Hirdemonsway B90 126 A5
Hiron Croft CV3 133 C8
Hiron The CV3 133 C8
Hiron Way CV34 160 B7
Histons Hill WV8 10 A3
Hitchcock Cl B67 64 D5
Hitches La B15 86 B7
Hitchman Ct CV31 162 A5
Hitchman Rd CV31 162 A5
Hither Green La B98 153 F7
Hitherside B90 126 B5
Hive Ind Ctr The B18 66 A6
HM Young Offender Inst (Swinfen Hall) WS14 9 E1
Hoarestone Ave CV11 79 A7
Hoarstone DY8 98 F5
Hobacre Cl B45 122 A8
Hobart Croft 1 B7 67 A4
Hobart Ct B74 32 A3
Hobart Dr WS5 43 C6
Hobart Rd
Cannock WS12 2 E2
Tipton DY4 40 E1
Hobbis Ho B38 123 C7
Hobble End La WS6 14 B7
Hobden Hall Farm Ind Units B60 150 B3
Hobgate Cl WV10 25 F4
Hobgate Rd WV10 25 F4
Hob Green Prim Sch DY9 81 E2
Hob Green Rd DY9 81 E2
Hobhouse Cl B43 54 F7
Hob La
Balsall Common CV7 130 E4
Burton Green CV8 131 A3
Temple Balsall B92 129 A8
Hobley St WV13 27 C2
Hobmoor Croft B25 88 D7
Hobmoor Prim Sch B25 88 D8
Hob Moor Rd B10, B25 88 C8
Hobnock Rd WV11 13 B5
Hobs Hole La WS9 30 D7
Hob's Mdw B92 89 B2
Hob's Moat Rd B92 89 B3
Hobson Cl B18 66 A5
Hobson Rd B29 86 B1
Hobs Rd WS10 42 A4
Hob's Rd WS13 3 E1
Hockett St CV3 133 D8
Hocking Rd CV2 114 E4
Hockley Brook Cl B18 66 A5
Hockley Brook La DY9 119 F3
Hockley Brook Trad Est B18 66 A6
Hockley Cir B18 66 B6
Hockley Cl B19 66 D6
Hockley Ct B94 143 C7
Hockley Ctr 1 B18 66 C4
Hockley Heath Prim Sch B94 143 C6
Hockley Hill B18 66 B5
Hockley La
Coventry CV5 111 C5
Dudley DY2 62 C4
Hockley Pool Cl B18 66 B5
Hockley Rd
Birmingham B23 56 D4
Dudley WV14 51 A7
Tamworth B77 35 F5
Hockley St B19 66 C5
Hodder Gr B71 53 F7
Hodge Hill Ave DY9 81 F3
Hodge Hill Comm B36 68 E7
Hodge Hill Cotts DY10 117 C7
Hodgehill Ct B36 68 E7
Hodge Hill Girls Sch B36 68 C7
Hodge Hill Prim Sch B36 68 D7
Hodge Hill Rd B34 68 E6
Hodge Hill Sch B36 68 C7
Hodge La B77 22 B6
Hodges Dr B69 63 B8
Hodgetts Cl B67 64 D3
Hodgetts Dr B63 100 C8
Hodgett's La
Balsall Common CV7 130 F7
Coventry CV7, CV8 131 A6
Hodgkins Cl WS8 16 A6
Hodgkiss Cl WS10 41 E4
Hodgson Twr B19 66 D6
Hodnell Cl B36 58 C1
Hodnet Cl
Bilston WV14 40 B5
Kenilworth CV8 148 B5
Hodnet Dr DY5 61 C6
Hodnet Gr B5 86 E8
Hodnet Pl WS11 2 B2
Hodson Ave WV13 27 C1
Hodson Cl WV11 26 F8
Hodson Way WS11 2 B2
Hoff Beck Ct 6 B9 67 B2
Hogarth Cl
Bedworth CV12 78 A4
Birmingham B43 44 D5
Hinckley LE10 71 A3
Willenhall WV13 26 E2
Hogarth Dr LE10 71 A3
Hogarth Ho 6 B15 86 C8
Hoggs La B31 102 E4
Holbeache La DY6 49 D1
Holbeache Rd DY6 60 C8
Holbeach Rd B33 69 B2
Holbeche Rd
Dorridge B93 128 A7
Sutton Coldfield B75 47 B5
Holbein Cl CV12 78 A4
Holberg Gr WV11 26 F5
Holborn Ave CV6 95 C2
Holborn Hill B6, B7 67 C7
Holborn Sh Ctr The DY3 50 D7
Holbrook Gr B37 70 A1
Holbrook La CV6 95 D2
Holbrook Park Est CV6 113 D8
Holbrook Prim Sch CV6 95 E1
Holbrook Tower B36 68 D8
Holbrook Way CV6 95 D1
Holbury Cl WV9 11 A2
Holcombe Rd B11 88 A3
Holcroft Rd
Halesowen B63 82 C5
Kingswinford DY6 49 C1
Stourbridge DY9 81 C4
Holcroft St Tipton DY4 52 A2
Wolverhampton WV2 40 A7
Holden Cl B23 56 E2
Holden Cres WS3 28 F5
Holden Croft DY4 52 A3
Holden Pl WS3 28 E5
Holden Rd
Wednesbury WS10 42 A2
Wolverhampton WV4 38 D3
Holdens The B28 105 E6
Holder Dr WS11 1 B2
Holder Rd
Birmingham, South Yardley B25 88 C7
Birmingham, Sparkbrook B11 87 C6
Holders Gdns B13 86 C2
Holders La B13 86 C2
Holdford Rd B6 55 F2
Holdgate Rd B29 103 C7
Hole Farm Rd B31 103 C5
Hole Farm Way B38 123 F7
Hole House La B94 143 F1
Hole La B31 103 C5
Holford Ave WS2 42 C6
Holford Dr B42, B6 55 F4
Holford Way B6 55 F3
Holifast Rd B72 57 C7
Holioak Dr CV34 161 B6
Holland Ave
Knowle B93 128 B8
Oldbury B68 64 D4
Holland Ho B19 66 D5
Holland House Inf Sch B72 46 C4
Holland Ind Pk WS10 41 D8
Holland Rd
Bilston WV14 40 E7
Birmingham B43 54 D7
Coventry CV6 113 A6
Sutton Coldfield B72 46 C4
Holland Rd W 6 B6 66 F6
Hollands Pl WS3 14 D1
Hollands Rd WS3 14 D1
Holland St
Birmingham B3 164 A3
1 Dudley DY1 62 B8
Holland St *continued*
Sutton Coldfield B72 46 C4
Tipton DY4 52 C7
Holland's Way WS3 14 F4
Hollaway Ct B63 82 D5
Hollemeadow Ave WS3 28 D7
Holliars Gr B37 69 F5
Hollicombe Terr CV2 114 D8
Holliday Rd
Birmingham, Erdington B24 57 A4
Birmingham, Handsworth B21 65 F7
Holliday St
Birmingham B1 66 C1
Birmingham B1 164 A2
Holliday Wharf B1 164 A1
Hollie Lucas Rd B13 104 F7
Holliers Walk Prim Sch LE10 71 D1
Hollier's Wlk LE10 71 D1
Hollies Ave WS11 1 F1
Hollies Croft B5 86 C5
Hollies Ct WS11 1 F1
Hollies Dr
Halesowen B62 83 E6
Wednesbury WS10 41 F3
Hollies Ind Est WV2 163 B1
Hollies La WV6 23 A4
Hollies Park Rd WS11 1 F1
Hollies Rd B69 63 B8
Hollies Rise B64 82 F8
Hollies St DY5 61 D7
Hollies The
Barnt Green B45 122 A1
Birmingham, Aston B6 67 B8
Birmingham, Winson Green B16 65 F3
Smethwick B66 65 C4
Wolverhampton, New Cross WV11 26 B5
Wolverhampton WV2 163 B1
Hollin Brow Cl B93 128 B3
Hollingberry La B76 46 F3
Hollings Gr B91 127 B8
Hollington Cres B33 69 A4
Hollington Rd WV1 26 B1
Hollington Way B90 127 C7
Hollinwell Cl
Nuneaton CV11 79 C8
Walsall WS3 14 A3
Hollis La CV8 147 E8
Hollis Rd CV3 114 A2
Hollister Dr B32 84 F3
Holloway
Birmingham B31 102 E5
Tamworth B79 21 B4
Holloway Bank
Wednesbury WS10 41 F1
West Bromwich B70, B71 53 A8
Holloway Bank Trad Est WS10 41 F1
Holloway Circus Queensway B1 164 B1
Holloway Dr B98 154 B3
Holloway Field CV6 113 A6
Holloway Head B1 164 B1
Holloway La B98 153 F3
Holloway Pk B98 154 A3
Holloway St W DY3 50 D4
Holloway St
Dudley DY3 50 D4
Wolverhampton WV1 40 A7
Holloway The
Alvechurch B48 139 D3
Bluntington DY10 118 E2
Seisdon WV5 37 A3
Stourbridge DY8 80 F7
Warwick CV34 160 D6
Wolverhampton WV6 24 C2
Hollow Cres CV6 113 B5
Hollow Croft B31 103 B3
Hollow Croft Rd WV12 27 B7
Hollowmeadow Ho B36 68 D8
Hollows The CV11 73 F1
Hollow The B13 86 E4
Hollowtree La B60 138 A3
Holly Ave
Birmingham, Balsall Heath B12 87 A5
Birmingham, Selly Oak B29 86 B1
Holly Bank CV5 133 A8

Hollybank Ave WV11.. **13** A3
Hollybank Cl WS3 .... **14** A2
Hollybank Gr B63 .... **82** D1
Hollybank Rd B13 ... **105** A6
Hollyberry Ave B91.. **127** A8
Hollyberry Cl **8** B63 . **83** A3
Hollyberry Croft B34 . **69** C6
Hollybrow B29 ...... **103** B7
Holly Bush Gr B32.... **84** D7
Hollybush La
　Coventry CV6 .... **96** A4
　Stourbridge DY8 .... **80** F7
　Wolverhampton WV4 . **38** D4
Hollybush Wlk **2** B64 **62** D1
Holly Cl Hinckley LE10 . **75** E5
　Sutton Coldfield B76.. **46** F2
　Tamworth B79........ **21** B7
　Willenhall WV12 ..... **27** C6
Hollycot Gdns B12 ...**86** F6
Hollycroft LE10...... **71** C1
Hollycroft Cres LE10.. **71** C1
Hollycroft Gdns WV6 . **24** B6
Hollycroft Rd B21 .... **54** D1
Holly Ct
　Balsall Common CV7. . **130** B3
　Birmingham B23 ...... **57** A5
　Kidderminster DY10 . **116** D8
　Walsall WS5 .... **43** A4
Hollydale Rd
　Birmingham B24...... **57** C3
　Rowley Regis B65..... **63** D2
Holly Dell B38 ...... **104** B2
Holly Dr
　Birmingham B27...... **88** B2
　Hollywood B47 ...... **125** B7
　Ryton-on-D CV8 ..... **135** B1
Holly Farm Bsns Pk
　CV8............... **146** B7
Hollyfaste Rd B33.... **69** B1
Hollyfast La CV7 ..... **94** C4
Hollyfast Prim Sch
　CV6............... **112** E7
Hollyfast Rd CV6 .... **112** E6
Hollyfield Ave B91 ... **106** A3
Hollyfield Cres B75... **46** E4
Hollyfield Ct B75..... **46** E5
Hollyfield Dr
　Barnt Green B45...... **122** A1
　Sutton Coldfield B75... **46** E5
Hollyfield Prim Sch
　B75...............**46** F5
Hollyfield Rd B75 .... **46** E5
Hollyfield Rd S B76 ..**46** F4
Holly Gr
　4 Birmingham B29 ... **85** F2
　Birmingham, Bournville
　　B30............... **103** F8
　Birmingham, Lozells
　　B19............... **66** B8
　Bromsgrove B61..... **136** F3
　Coventry CV4 ...... **112** B2
　Stourbridge DY8.... **80** F5
　Wolverhampton WV3 . . **38** F7
Holly Grange B66 .... **64** D7
Holly Hall Maths &
　Computing Coll DY1 **61** F8
Holly Hall Rd DY2 ... **62** A7
Hollyhedge Cl
　Birmingham B31..... **102** D6
　Walsall WS2 .... **28** C2
Hollyhedge La WS2 . . **28** C2
Hollyhedge Prim Sch
　B71.............. **53** E8
Hollyhedge Rd B71.. **53** E7
Holly Hill
　4 Birmingham B45.. **101** F1
　Great Wyrley WS6..... **13** E8
Hollyhill La WS14 .... **17** F5
Holly Hill Meth & CE Inf
　Sch B45 .... **101** F2
Holly Hill Rd
　Birmingham B45...... **102** A2
　Shenstone WS14...... **17** F5
Hollyhock Rd
　Birmingham B27...... **88** A2
　Dudley DY2 .... **51** F1
Hollyhurst
　Bedworth CV12....... **77** F1
　Water Orton B46 ..... **59** C2
Hollyhurst Dr B73.... **60** E3
Hollyhurst Farm Cvn Site
　B62............... **101** B6
Hollyhurst Gr
　Birmingham B26...... **88** E6
　Solihull B90........ **126** B8
Hollyhurst Rd B73... **45** B3
Holly La Aldridge WS9 . .**30** F8
　Balsall Common CV7. . **130** B3

Holly La continued
　Birmingham, Erdington
　　B24............... **57** C4
　Birmingham, Marston Green
　　B37.............. **89** F8
　Brownhills WS9 ...... **16** A4
　Great Wyrley WS6..... **13** F8
　Huntington WS12 .....**1** C7
　Portway B48........ **140** F5
　Smethwick B66....... **64** E6
　Sutton Coldfield B74... **32** A3
　Wishaw B76 .... **47** D4
Holly Lodge High Sch
　Coll of Science B67 **64** D6
Holly Lodge Wlk B37..**69** F2
Hollymoor Way
　Birmingham B31..... **102** B1
　Birmingham B31..... **102** D1
Hollymount B62...... **84** A7
Holly Mount **7** B15 .. **65** B3
Hollyoak Croft B31.. **123** B8
Hollyoake Cl B68..... **64** A2
Hollyoak Gr B91 .... **107** A1
Hollyoak Rd B74......**44** F6
Hollyoak St B71..... **53** D4
Hollyoak Way WS11 ....**1** F1
Holly Park Dr B24.... **57** C4
Holly Park Ind Est
　B24............... **57** C2
Hollypiece Ho B27.... **88** A2
Holly Pl B29 .... **86** B2
Holly Rd
　Birmingham B68..... **84** C8
　Birmingham, Edgbaston
　　B16............... **65** D1
　Birmingham, Handsworth
　　B20............... **66** A8
　Birmingham, King's Norton
　　B30............... **104** A4
　Bromsgrove B61..... **136** F4
　Dudley DY1 .... **51** A3
　Rowley Regis B65..... **63** B1
　Wednesbury WS10 .... **41** F5
　West Bromwich B71... **53** E8
Holly St Cannock WS12 . .**1** F6
　Dudley DY1 .... **61** G6
　Royal Leamington Spa
　　CV32.............. **157** B1
　Smethwick B67...... **64** F5
Hollystitches Rd CV10 **72** E6
Holly View WV11 .... **13** A3
Hollywell Rd
　Birmingham B26..... **89** B6
　Dorridge B93 ...... **128** A5
Hollywell St WV14.... **40** A1
Holly Wlk
　Baginton CV8 ...... **133** E2
　Nuneaton CV11...... **73** F2
　Royal Leamington Spa
　　CV32.............. **157** A1
Holly Wood B43...... **44** A1
Hollywood By-Pass
　Birmingham B47..... **104** F1
　Hollywood B38, B47... **124** E6
Hollywood Croft B42 ..**54** F8
Hollywood Gdns
　B47............... **125** A6
Hollywood La B47... **125** B7
Hollywood Motor Pk
　B47............... **125** A6
Hollywood Prim Sch
　B14.............. **105** A1
Hollyword Dr B47 ... **125** A8
Holman Cl WV13 ..... **26** E2
Holman Rd WV13 ..... **26** E2
Holman St DY11..... **116** C5
Holman Way
　Nuneaton CV11...... **73** D3
　Willenhall WV13 ..... **26** E2
Holmbridge Gr WS4 . . **15** D2
Holmcroft
　Coventry CV2 ...... **114** F8
　10 Wolverhampton
　　WV4.............. **39** F4
Holmcroft Rd DY10.. **117** A5
Holme Mill WV10..... **11** D4
Holmes Ct CV8..... **147** F5
Holmes Dr
　Birmingham B45..... **121** F6
　Coventry CV5 ...... **111** D5
Holmesfield Rd B42... **55** E7
Holmes La B60...... **151** B1
Holmes Rd
　Whitnash CV31..... **162** B3
　Willenhall WV12 ..... **27** D6
Holmes The WV10 .... **11** D3
Holme Way WS4 ..... **29** B7
Holmewood Cl CV8.. **148** B5
Holmewood Ct CV8 . **148** B5

Holmfield Rd CV2 .... **114** B3
Holmsdale Rd CV6 ... **113** E7
Holm View Cl WS14....**17** F6
Holmwood Ave
　DY11 .... **116** A6
Holmwood Dr B97 ... **153** C3
Holmwood Ho B97 ... **153** C3
Holmwood Rd **3** B10 **67** D1
Holroyd Ho CV4 ..... **111** F2
Holston Cl WS12 ......**2** C1
Holsworth Cl B77 .... **21** D1
Holsworthy Cl CV11 .. **73** E5
Holt & Bracebridge
　Almshouses B24..... **57** A4
Holt Cres WS11 ....**2** B2
Holt Ct B7 ....**66** F4
Holte Dr B75......... **32** D2
Holte Rd
　Birmingham, Aston
　　B6................. **56** A1
　Birmingham, Sparkhill
　　B11................ **87** D5
Holte Sch B19 ...... **66** D7
Holtes Wlk B6 .... **67** B8
Holt Farm Prim Sch
　B62................**63** E1
Holt Gdns B80 ..... **159** E2
Holt Hill B98....... **154** F8
Holt Ho B61 .... **137** A3
Holt La B62 .... **100** D4
Holton Ct WV13 ..... **27** C2
Holt Rd Halesowen B62 **63** E1
　Hinckley LE10 .... **75** E6
　Studley B80........ **159** E2
Holtshill La WS1 .....**28** F2
Holt St B7 .... **164** D4
Holwick B67 .... **36** B8
Holy Cross Ct CV2 .. **114** E4
Holy Cross Gn DY9 ... **99** E2
Holy Cross La DY9... **119** E8
Holy Cross RC Prim Sch
　B76............... **47** A3
Holy Family RC Prim
　Sch
　Birmingham B10..... **87** F7
　Coventry CV6 .... **95** B3
Holyhead L Ctr B21.. **65** D8
Holyhead Prim Sch
　WS10 ....**41** E3
Holyhead Rd
　Birmingham B21..... **65** D8
　Codsall WV8 .... **23** E7
　Coventry CV5 ...... **112** E5
　Darlaston WS10 ..... **41** C4
　Wednesbury WS10 .... **41** F3
Holyhead Road Ind Est
　WS10 .... **41** D3
Holyhead Sch B21... **65** D8
Holyhead Way B21... **65** D8
Holy Name RC Prim Sch
　B43................**43** E1
Holyoak Cl
　Bedworth CV12...... **77** F1
　3 Birmingham B6... **55** F1
Holyoakes Field Fst Sch
　B97.............. **153** D4
Holyoakes La B97 ... **152** C5
Holy Oaks Cl B98... **154** E4
Holyoke Gr CV31 ... **162** B2
Holyrood Ct CV10 ... **72** D5
Holyrood Gr **2** B6 .. **66** E8
Holy Rosary RC Prim Sch
　WV1 .... **26** A1
Holy Souls RC Prim Sch
　B27............... **88** C3
Holy Trinity CE Prim
　Sch
　Birmingham B20..... **55** C2
　Brownhills WS8 ...... **15** E6
　West Bromwich B70... **53** D1
Holy Trinity RC Prim Sch
　WV14..............**40** E6
Holy Trinity RC Sch
　B10............... **87** C8
Holy Trinity Sch
　DY10.............. **116** F6
Holywell Cl CV4 ..... **111** A1
Holy Well Cl B16..... **66** A2
Holywell La B45..... **121** D6
Holywell Prim Sch
　B45.............. **121** D7
Holywell Rise WS14 ...**9** D6
Home Cl B28........ **105** E6
Homecroft Rd B26.... **88** E8
Homedene Rd B31.. **102** E7
Home Farm
　Leek Wootton CV35.. **155** F6
　Stoneleigh CV8..... **149** A3

Home Farm Cres
　CV31 .... **162** B4
Homefield Rd WV8 ... **10** C3
Homelands B42 ..... **55** B7
Homelands Park The
　WV10 .... **11** C6
Homelea Rd B25..... **88** D8
Homelodge Ho **7**
　WS3................**9** B7
Homemead Gr B45... **121** F7
Home Meadow Ct
　B13 .... **105** A5
Home Meadow Ho
　B27 .... **88** A2
Home Meadow La
　B98 .... **154** E6
Home Park Rd CV11... **73** C3
Home Peal Ho B14.. **104** E6
Homer Cl CV34...... **161** E5
Homer Hill Rd B63 .. **82** C7
Homer Rd
　Solihull B91........ **107** B3
　Sutton Coldfield B75... **32** D2
Homers Fold WV14... **40** D5
Homer St B12........**86** F5
Homerton Rd B44.... **45** B1
Homestead Cl DY3 ... **50** E5
Homestead Dr B75... **32** C3
Homestead Rd B33... **69** B1
Homeward Way CV3. **115** A1
Homewood Cl B76.... **46** E3
Honesty Cl WS8 ..... **15** D6
Honeswode Cl B20... **66** A8
Honeybone Rd B75.. **46** D7
Honeybourne B77.... **21** D2
Honeybourne Cl
　Coventry CV5 ...... **112** B3
　3 Halesowen B63... **83** A3
Honeybourne Rd
　Birmingham B33..... **89** C8
　Halesowen B63...... **83** C3
Honeybourne Sch
　B28 .... **105** F8
Honeybourne Way
　WV13 .... **27** C2
Honeychurch Cl B98 **153** F3
Honeycomb Way
　B31 .... **102** E3
Honeyfield Rd CV1 .. **113** D5
Honeysuckle Ave DY6 **60** E7
Honeysuckle Cl B32.. **84** B5
Honeysuckle Dr
　Coventry CV2 .... **96** B2
　Featherstone WV10 ... **12** C7
　Walsall WS5 .... **43** A3
Honeysuckle Gr **8**
　B27 .... **88** C5
Honeysuckle Way WS6 .**5** B4
Honeytree Cl DY6 .... **60** F3
Honiley Ct CV2....... **96** D1
Honiley Dr B73....... **45** C2
Honiley Rd
　Birmingham B33..... **69** A2
　Honiley CV8 .... **146** B6
　Meer End CV8..... **130** A1
Honiley Way CV2 .... **96** D1
Honister Cl DY5......**61** F1
Honiton Cl B31...... **102** E4
Honiton Cres B31... **102** E4
Honiton Rd CV2 .... **114** C5
Honiton Way WS9 .... **29** F5
Honiton Wlk **7** B66.. **65** B5
Honnington Ct **2** B29.**84** F1
Honor Ave WV4 ..... **39** C5
Hoobrook Ent Ctr
　DY10.............. **116** E2
Hoobrook Ind Est
　DY10.............. **116** E2
Hoo Farm Ind Est
　DY10.............. **116** F1
Hood Gr B30........ **103** D4
Hood St CV1 .... **113** E3
Hoo Rd DY10....... **116** E4
Hoosen Cl B62....... **84** A6
Hope Aldridge Bsns Ctr
　CV10.............. **73** C6
Hope Cl CV7 .... **95** A7
Hopedale Cl CV2 ... **114** E3
Hopedale Rd B32.... **84** C5
Hope Pl **10** B29......**85** F2
Hope Rd DY4........ **52** C6
Hope St Birmingham B5 **86** E8
　Coventry CV1 ...... **113** B2
　Dudley DY2 .... **62** C8
　Halesowen B62...... **83** D8
　Stourbridge DY8..... **60** D3

Hope St continued
　Walsall WS1 .... **42** E8
　West Bromwich B70... **53** E2
Hope Terr DY2 .... **62** C5
Hopgardens Ave
　B60 .... **137** B2
Hopkins Ct **4** WS10. **42** E8
Hopkins Dr B71...... **53** E7
Hopkins Rd CV6 .... **113** A4
Hopkins St DY4...... **52** A2
Hopleys Cl B77...... **21** E4
Hopstone Gdns WV4 .**38** F4
Hopstone Rd B29.... **85** A1
Hopton Cl
　Coventry CV5 ...... **112** A4
　Perton WV6......... **23** F3
　Wednesbury WV14 .... **41** C2
Hopton Cres WV11 ... **26** E6
Hopton Crofts CV32. **156** C2
Hopton Dr DY10..... **116** E1
Hopton Gdns DY1 ... **51** A3
Hopton Gr B13...... **105** C5
Hopton Mdw WS12.....**2** C1
Hopwas Gr B37 ......**69** F5
Hopwas Hill B78 .... **20** A6
Hopwood Cl B63 .... **83** A2
Hopwood Gr B31.... **122** E6
Hopyard Cl DY3 ..... **50** B3
Hopyard Gdns WV14.. **40** B3
Hopyard La
　Dudley DY3 .... **50** B3
　Redditch B98 ...... **154** D4
Hopyard Rd WS2 .... **27** E2
Horace Partridge Rd
　WS10 .... **41** A5
Horace St WV14..... **51** A4
Horatio Dr B13......**86** F4
Hordern Cl WV6..... **24** F5
Hordern Cres DY5.... **81** D8
Hordern Gr WV6..... **24** F5
Hordern Rd WV6..... **24** F5
Horeston Grange Sh Ctr
　CV11.............. **74** A5
Hornbeam B77....... **22** A4
Hornbeam Cl B29 ... **103** B7
Hornbeam Dr CV4.... **111** D1
Hornbeam Gr CV31.. **162** C6
Hornbeam Wlk WV3.. **25** A1
Hornbrook Gr B92 .. **106** C7
Hornby Gr B14...... **105** C4
Hornby Rd WV4 ..... **39** C5
Hornchuch Close Ind Est
　CV1.............. **165** B1
Hornchurch Cl CV1.. **165** B1
Horndean Cl CV6.... **113** E8
Horner Way B62..... **63** C1
Horne Way B34 ..... **69** E5
Horning Dr WV14.... **40** C3
Horninghold Cl CV3 . **134** E8
Hornsey Cl CV2..... **114** E7
Hornsey Gr B44..... **45** A2
Hornsey Rd B44..... **45** A2
Hornton Cl B74..... **31** D5
Horrell Rd
　Birmingham B26..... **89** B7
　Solihull B90........ **105** F2
Horsecroft Dr B71... **54** A8
Horse Fair
　Birmingham B1...... **164** B1
　Kidderminster DY10 . **116** E7
Horsefair The **8**
　LE10 .... **75** D8
Horsehills Dr WV3... **24** E2
Horselea Croft B8... **68** C4
Horseley Fields
　WV1 .... **163** D3
Horseley Heath DY4.. **52** C5
Horseley Rd
　Tipton DY4......... **52** C5
　Tipton DY4......... **52** C6
Horsepool LE10 ..... **76** A5
Horsepool Hollow
　CV31 .... **162** C5
Horseshoe Cl **2** WS2. **42** B7
Horseshoe Dr WS12....**2** F4
Horse Shoe Rd CV6 .. **96** A4
Horse Shoes La B26.. **89** B5
Horseshoe The B68... **64** C2
Horseshoe Wlk **6**
　DY4 .... **51** E5
Horsfall Rd B75..... **47** A5
Horsford Rd CV3.... **133** E6
Horsham Ave DY8 ... **60** C3
Horsley La WS14..... **17** D8
Horsley Rd
　Birmingham B43..... **44** D4
　Sutton Coldfield B74... **31** B2
Horton Cl
　Bedworth CV7....... **95** F7
　3 Cannock WS11 ....**1** F4

Horton Cl continued
　Darlaston WS10 ..... **41** D7
　Sedgley DY3 .... **50** C8
Horton Gr B90..... **127** A5
Horton Pl WS10..... **41** D7
Horton Sq B12...... **86** E7
Horton St
　Darlaston WS10 ..... **41** D7
　Tipton DY4.......... **52** D5
　West Bromwich B70... **53** C2
Hosiery St CV12..... **78** C2
Hospital Dr B15..... **85** E4
Hospital La
　Bedworth CV12...... **77** B1
　Cheslyn Hay WS6 .....**4** C1
　Dudley WV14 .... **51** D7
Hospital Rd WS7 ......**7** C1
Hospital St
　Birmingham B19.... **164** B4
　Birmingham, Newtown
　　B19................ **66** D6
　Birmingham, Stockland
　　Green B23 .... **56** E4
　Tamworth B79....... **21** B5
　Walsall WS2 .... **28** D4
　Wolverhampton WV2 . **163** D4
Hossil La
　Belbroughton DY9... **119** C8
　Clent DY9 .... **99** D1
Hotchkiss Way CV3.. **135** A7
Hotel Bldgs WS14.....**8** A2
Hothersall Dr B73...**56** F8
Hothorpe Cl CV3.... **114** F1
Hotspur Rd B44......**44** F1
Hough Pl WS2 ...... **42** B7
Hough Rd
　Birmingham B14..... **104** D6
　Walsall WS2 .... **42** A7
Houghton Ct B28... **105** D4
Houghton St
　Oldbury B69 .... **63** F6
　West Bromwich B70... **64** D4
Houlbrooke Ho **1**
　WS14...............**9** C8
Houldey Rd B31..... **103** B1
Houldsworth Cres
　CV6............... **95** C4
Houliston Cl WS10 .. **42** B5
Houndsfield Cl B47.. **125** C6
Houndsfield Farm
　B47 .... **125** B5
Houndsfield Gr B47. **125** A5
Houndsfield La B47 . **125** C6
Housman Cl B60.... **150** E8
Housman Ct B60.... **137** A3
Housman Pk B60.... **137** A2
Housman Wlk DY10 . **117** C6
Houting B77........ **35** F7
Houx The DY8 ...... **80** E8
Hove Ave CV5....... **111** E4
Hovelands Cl CV2 .. **114** C8
Hove Rd B27........ **88** C1
Hoveton Cl B98 .... **154** B2
Howard Ave B61..... **136** E3
Howard Cl CV5...... **111** E4
Howard Cres WS12....**2** C7
Howard Ct B16...... **65** E1
Howard Rd
　Bilston WV14 .... **40** F3
　Birmingham, Handsworth
　　B20................ **55** B2
　Birmingham, King's Heath
　　B14................ **104** E7
　Birmingham, Newton
　　B43................ **54** C8
　Birmingham, South Yardley
　　B25................ **88** C7
　Nuneaton CV10....... **73** A3
　Redditch B98 ...... **159** C4
　Solihull B92........ **88** E3
　Wednesfield WV11 ... **26** F8
Howard Rd E B13 ... **104** F7
Howard St
　Birmingham B19.... **164** B4
　Coventry CV1 ...... **165** C4
　Tipton DY4 .... **52** B5
　West Bromwich B70... **52** F7
　Wolverhampton WV2 . **163** C1
Howard Street Ind Est
　B70................**52** F8
Howard Wlk CV31 .. **161** D2
Howarth Way B6..... **67** A7
Howat Rd CV7 ....**94** F7
Howcotte Gn CV4... **131** E8
Howden Pl B33...... **69** A5
Howdle's La WS8..... **6** F2
Howe Cres WV12..... **27** C6
Howell Rd WV2 ..... **39** E7
Howells Cl CV12..... **77** D1

Howes Com Prim Sch
CV3. . . . . 133 E5
Howes Croft B35 . . . . . 58 A2
Howes La CV3 . . . . . . 133 D3
Howe St B4 . . . . 66 F3
Howfield Ct B16 . . . . . . 65 C1
Howford Gr B7 . . . . 67 B4
Howland Cl WV9 . . . . . .10 F2
Howlette Rd CV4 . . . . . 111 E2
Howley Ave B44 . . . . . . 44 E1
Howley Grange Prim Sch
B62 . . . . .83 F5
Howley Grange Rd
B62 . . . . 84 A4
Howl Pl DY4 . . . . .51 F5
Hoylake B77 . . . . 22 B4
Hoylake Cl
Nuneaton CV11 . . . . . 74 B1
Walsall WS3 . . . . 14 B4
Hoylake Dr B69 . . . . . . 63 A7
Hoylake Rd WV6 . . . . . 23 D5
Hoyland Way B30 . . . . 103 E8
HRS Bsns Pk B33 . . . . . 69 C1
Huband Cl B98 . . . . . . 154 A5
Hubert Croft B29 . . . . .85 F2
Hubert Rd B29 . . . . . . .85 F2
Hubert St B6 . . . . .66 F5
Hucker Cl WS2 . . . . . . 42 A7
Hucker Rd WS2 . . . . . . 42 A7
Huddesford Dr CV7 . . 130 C8
Huddisdon Cl **5**
CV34 . . . . 155 F1
Huddlestone Cl WV10 . 12 B6
Huddleston Way B29 . 85 C1
Huddocks View WS3 . . .14 F5
Hudson Ave B46 . . . . . .70 F6
Hudson Cl WS11 . . . . . .2 B2
Hudson Dr WS7 . . . . . . .7 C6
Hudson Gr WV6 . . . . . 23 E5
Hudson Rd
Birmingham B20 . . . . 55 A4
Tipton DY4 . . . . 52 C4
Hudson's Dr B30 . . . . 104 A4
Hudswell Dr DY5 . . . . . 81 D8
Huggins Cl CV7 . . . . . 130 C7
Hughes Ave WV3 . . . . .38 F8
Hughes Cl
Warwick CV34 . . . . . 155 D2
Whitnash CV31 . . . . . 162 A2
Hughes Pl WV14 . . . . . 40 D7
Hughes Rd
Bilston WV14 . . . . . . 40 D7
Darlaston WS10 . . . . . 41 A5
Hughes The CV34 . . . . 160 E6
Hugh Gaitskill Ct
WV14 . . . . 40 C8
Hugh Porter Way
WV6 . . . . .24 F6
Hugh Rd
Birmingham B10 . . . . . 67 E1
Coventry CV3 . . . . . . 114 A2
Smethwick B67 . . . . . 64 E5
Hugh Villas B10 . . . . . . 67 E1
Huins Cl B98 . . . . 154 A4
Hulbert Dr DY2 . . . . . . 62 B6
Hulbert Ind Est DY2 . . .62 B6
Hulland Pl DY5 . . . . 61 C3
Hullbrook Rd B13 . . . . 105 C6
Hulme Cl CV3 . . . . 115 B1
Humara Ghar **9** WS1. 42 E8
Humber Ave
Coventry CV1 . . . . . . 113 F1
Sutton Coldfield B76 . . 58 A7
Humber Gdns B63 . . . . 82 C5
Humber Gr B36 . . . . . .58 F1
Humber Ho DY1 . . . . . 61 D8
Humber Rd
Coventry CV3 . . . . . . 134 A8
Wolverhampton WV3 . . 25 A1
Humberstone Rd
4 Coventry CV6 . . . 113 A5
Sutton Coldfield B24 . . 57 E4
Humber Twr **2** B7 . . 67 A4
Hume St
Kidderminster DY11 . . 116 C5
Smethwick B66 . . . . . 65 B4
Humpage Rd B9 . . . . . 67 E2
Humphrey Ave B60 . . 150 F7
Humphrey Burton's Rd
CV3 . . . . 133 C8
Humphrey-Davy Rd
CV12 . . . . 95 D8
Humphrey Middlemore
Dr B17 . . . . 85 D4
Humphrey St DY3 . . . . 50 D3
Humphries Cres
WV14 . . . . .40 F2
Humphries Dr DY10 . 116 F2
Humphries Ho WS8 . . .15 F7
Humphries Rd WV10 . 25 D6

Humphris St CV34 . . . 161 B8
Hundred Acre Rd B74 .44 F7
Hungary Cl DY9 . . . . . . 81 C5
Hungary Hill DY9 . . . . . 81 C5
Hungerfield Rd B36 . . . 58 C1
Hungerford Rd DY8 . . . 80 E2
Hungry La WS14 . . . . . .18 F5
Hunningham Gr **6**
B91 . . . . 127 B8
Hunnington Cl B32 . . . 84 A1
Hunnington Cres B63 . 83 B2
Hunscote Cl B90 . . . . 105 F1
Hunscote Ho B90 . . . . 105 F1
Hunslet Cl B32 . . . . . . .84 F4
Hunslet Rd
Birmingham B32 . . . . . 84 F4
Burntwood WS7 . . . . . .7 B8
Hunstanton Ave B17 . .84 F8
Hunstanton Cl DY5 . . . 81 C7
Hunt End Ind Est
B97 . . . . 158 C5
Hunt End La B97 . . . . 158 C5
Hunter Ave WS7 . . . . . .7 B7
Hunter Cl WS14 . . . . . . 9 D6
Hunter Cres WS3 . . . . .28 F7
Hunter Ct B5 . . . . 86 D5
Hunter Rd WS11 . . . . . .4 E8
Hunters Cl
Bilston WV14 . . . . . . 41 A7
Coventry CV5 . . . . . . 115 A2
Hunters Hill Sch B60 137 F6
Hunter's Ride DY7 . . . . 60 B2
Hunters Rise B63 . . . . 82 D1
Hunter St WV6 . . . . . . 25 A4
Hunters Vale B19 . . . . 66 C6
Hunters Wlk B23 . . . . . 56 C8
Hunter Terr CV5 . . . . . 132 D8
Huntingdon Cl
Redditch B98 . . . . . . 154 F2
Tamworth B78 . . . . . . 20 F2
Huntingdon Rd
Coventry CV5 . . . . . . 133 A8
West Bromwich B71 . . 53 B7
Huntingdon Way
CV10 . . . . 72 E3
Huntington Ho B23 . . 56 B6
Huntington Ind Est
WS12 . . . . .1 B6
Huntington Prim Sch
WS12 . . . . .1 C8
Huntington Rd WV12 . 27 D8
Huntington Terrace Rd
WS11 . . . . .1 F4
Huntingtree Prim Sch
B63 . . . . .82 E3
Huntingtree Rd B63 . . 82 E3
Huntlands Rd B63 . . . .82 F2
Huntley Dr B91 . . . . . . 107 B2
Huntly Rd B16 . . . . 66 A1
Hunton Ct **2** B23 . . . 56 E2
Hunton Hill B23 . . . . . 56 E2
Hunton Rd B23 . . . . . . 56 E3
Hunt Paddocks CV8 . . 147 E1
Hunt's La WV12 . . . . . . 27 D6
Huntsman Cl WV14 . . . 40 D2
Huntsmans Gate WS7 . .7 B8
Huntsmans Rise WS12. .1 C8
Hunts Mill Dr DY5 . . . . 50 C1
Hunts Rd B30 . . . . 104 A4
Hunt Terr CV4 . . . . . . 132 B7
Hurcott Ct DY10 . . . . . 117 A8
Hurcott La DY10 . . . . . 117 C8
Hurcott Rd DY10 . . . . . 117 B8
Hurdis Rd B90 . . . . . . 106 A2
Hurdlow Ave B18 . . . . 66 B5
Hurlbutt Rd CV34 . . . 161 C4
Hurley Cl
Royal Leamington Spa
CV32 . . . . 157 A2
Sutton Coldfield B72 . . 46 C2
Walsall WS5 . . . . 43 D6
Hurley Gr B37 . . . . . . .69 F5
Hurleys Fold DY2 . . . . 62 C5
Hurlingham Rd B44 . . 45 A1
Hurn Way CV6 . . . . . . 96 A4
Huron Cl WS11 . . . . . . .2 B2
Hurricane Pk B24 . . . . 68 A8
Hurricane Way B35 . . 58 A2
Hursey Dr DY4 . . . . . . 52 A6
Hurstbourne Cres
WV1 . . . . 26 B1
Hurst Bsns Pk DY6 . . . 62 A4
Hurst Cl B36 . . . . 69 E7
Hurstcroft Rd B33 . . . . 69 B3
Hurst Ct DY9 . . . . .81 F5
Hurst Green Prim Sch
B62 . . . . .83 E8
Hurst Green Rd
Bentley Heath B93 . . . 127 F4

Hurst Green Rd continued
Halesowen B62 . . . . . . 83 F8
Minworth B76 . . . . . . 58 D6
Hurst Hill Ct WV14 . . . 51 A8
Hurst Hill Prim Sch
WV14 . . . . 51 A8
Hurst La
Birmingham B34 . . . . 69 E6
Brierley Hill DY5 . . . . 61 F3
Tipton DY4 . . . . 51 D6
Hurst Lane N B36 . . . . 69 E7
Hurst Rd
Bedworth CV12 . . . . . 78 B3
Coventry CV6 . . . . . . 96 A4
Dudley WV14 . . . . . . 40 A1
Hinckley LE10 . . . . . . 75 D8
Sedgley WV14 . . . . . . 39 F1
Smethwick B67 . . . . . 64 D2
Hurst St B5 . . . . 164 C1
Hurst The
Birmingham B13 . . . . 105 D7
Hollywood B47 . . . . . 125 A6
Hurstway The B23 . . . 56 C8
Hurst Wlk CV6 . . . . . . 96 A4
Hurstwood Rd B23 . . . 56 C8
Huskison Cl B69 . . . . . 52 B1
Huskisson Ct WV10 . . . 25 C6
Hussey Rd
Brownhills WS8 . . . . . 15 E8
Norton Canes WS11 . . . 5 F8
Husum Way DY10 . . . 117 C7
Hutchings La B90 . . . 126 B5
Hut Hill La WS6 . . . . . . .5 A4
Hutton Ave B8 . . . . . . 67 D5
Hutton Rd
Birmingham, Handsworth
B20 . . . . 55 C1
Birmingham, Saltley B8 67 D5
Huxbey Dr B92 . . . . . 107 F8
Huxley Cl WV9 . . . . . . 11 A3
Hyacinth Cl **9** WS5 . . 43 A3
Hyacinth Way LE10 . . . 75 D5
Hyatt Sq DY5 . . . . 81 C7
Hyatts Wlk B65 . . . . . .62 F5
Hyde Cl B60 . . . . 137 B2
Hyde Pl CV32 . . . . 161 E8
Hyde Rd
Coventry CV2 . . . . . . 114 E4
Kenilworth CV8 . . . . . 148 A5
Wednesfield WV11 . . . 26 E6
Hydes La LE10 . . . . . . 74 E4
Hydes Rd
Wednesbury WS10 . . . 42 B2
West Bromwich B71 . . 42 C1
Hydesville Tower Sch
WS1 . . . . 29 A2
Hyde The DY9 . . . . 81 D2
Hyett Way WV14 . . . . . 41 B2
Hylda Rd B20 . . . . 55 B1
Hylstone Cres WV11 . . 26 D6
Hylton St B18 . . . . 66 C5
Hypericum Gdns
CV2 . . . . 114 C4
Hyperion Dr WV4 . . . . 39 A3
Hyperion Rd
Stourbridge DY7 . . . . . 80 C7
Sutton Coldfield B36 . . 57 F1
Hyron Hall Rd B27 . . . 88 C2
Hyssop Cl
Birmingham B7 . . . . . 67 A5
Cannock WS11 . . . . . . 2 B3

I

Ibberton Rd B14 . . . . 105 B3
Ibex Cl CV3 . . . . 114 F1
Ibis Cl DY10 . . . . 117 B3
Ibis Gdns DY6 . . . . . . 61 A6
Ibstock Cl B98 . . . . . . 154 E4
Ibstock Dr DY8 . . . . . . 81 A4
Ibstock Ho B98 . . . . . 154 E4
Ibstock Rd CV6 . . . . . . 96 A5
Icknield Cl B74 . . . . . . 31 A1
Icknield Fst Sch B98 154 D1
Icknield Port Rd B16 . .65 F3
Icknield Sq B16 . . . . . 66 A3
Icknield St
Alvechurch B38 . . . . . 124 B2
Beoley B48, B98 . . . . . 140 C2
Birmingham B18 . . . . 66 B4
Redditch, Church Hill
B98 . . . . 154 C7
Redditch, Ipsley B98. . 154 D2
Rowney Green B48 . . . 140 B6
Icknield Street Dr
B98 . . . . 159 D7
Ida Rd Walsall WS2 . . . 28 C1
West Bromwich B70 . . 53 D1

Idbury Rd B44 . . . . . . 56 A7
Ideal Bldgs **7** DY11 . 116 D6
Ideal Wks DY9 . . . . . . 82 A6
Iden Rd CV1 . . . . 113 E4
Idmiston Croft B14 . . 104 F2
Idonia Rd WV6 . . . . . . .23 F5
Ilam Pk CV8 . . . . 148 C5
Ilex Ct CV34 . . . . 161 A7
Ilford Cl CV12 . . . . . . 78 A3
Ilford Ct CV3 . . . . 135 D7
Ilford Dr CV3 . . . . 133 B5
Ilford Rd B23 . . . . 56 D6
Ilfracombe Gr CV3 . . 133 A5
Iliffe Ho LE10 . . . . 75 B7
Iliffe Way B17 . . . . . . 85 D4
Ilkley Gr B37 . . . . .69 F2
Illeybrook Sq B32 . . . 84 D2
Illey Cl B31 . . . . 102 C1
Illey La
Birmingham B32 . . . . 102 A7
Halesowen B62 . . . . . 101 E8
Illshaw WV9 . . . . 11 A3
Illshaw Heath Rd B90,
B94 . . . . 126 D2
Ilmington Cl
Coventry CV3 . . . . . . 133 B5
Redditch B98 . . . . . . 154 D1
Ilmington Dr B73 . . . . 45 C3
Ilmington Rd B29 . . . .84 F1
Ilminster Cl LE10 . . . . 76 B7
Ilsham Gr B31 . . . . . . 122 E6
Ilsley Rd B23 . . . . 56 E4
Image Bsns Pk WS11. . 2 B3
I-Max Bsns Pk B11 . . 88 A6
Imber Rd DY10 . . . . . . 117 A1
Imex Auto Ctr DY4 . . . 52 A3
Imex Bsns Ctr
Bilston WV14 . . . . . . 40 E4
Redditch B98 . . . . . . 154 E4
Wolverhampton WV13 . 26 C3
Imex Bsns Pk
Birmingham, Bordesley
Green B9 . . . . 67 D2
Birmingham, Stechford
B33 . . . . 68 E4
Tipton DY4 . . . . 52 A3
Wolverhampton WV2 . . 39 C7
Imex Ho WV2 . . . . 39 B7
Imogen Gdns CV34 . . 161 E8
Imperial Ave DY10 . . . 116 F8
Imperial Ct DY10 . . . . 116 F8
Imperial Gr DY10 . . . . 116 F8
Imperial Rd B9 . . . . . . 67 E1
Imperial Rise B46 . . . . 59 E2
Impey Rd B31 . . . . . . 102 F1
Impney Cl B98 . . . . . . 154 E6
Impsley Cl B36 . . . . . . 69 B8
Inca Cl CV3 . . . . 134 F8
Ince Rd WS10 . . . . 41 C7
Incestre Dr B43 . . . . . 43 D1
Inchbrook Rd CV8 . . . 148 C7
Inchcape Ave B20 . . . 55 A3
Inchford Ave CV34 . . 155 E2
Inchford Cl CV11 . . . . .73 F1
Inchford Rd B92 . . . . . 107 E7
Inchlaggan Rd WV10 . 25 F6
Infantry Pl B75 . . . . . 47 A6
Ingatestone Dr DY8 . . 60 C3
Inge St B5 . . . . 164 C1
Ingestre Cl
Cannock WS11 . . . . . . .2 B1
Walsall WS3 . . . . 13 F3
Ingestre Dr B43 . . . . . 43 C1
Ingestre Ho WV6 . . . . 24 E5
Ingestre Rd
Birmingham B28 . . . . 106 A2
Wolverhampton WV10 . 11 C1
Ingeva Dr B45 . . . . . . 122 A1
Ingham Way B17 . . . . 85 A8
Ingleby Gdns WV6 . . . 25 A5
Ingle Ct CV31 . . . . . . 161 E7
Ingledew Cl WS2 . . . . 27 D3
Inglefield Rd B33 . . . .68 F3
Inglemere Gr B29 . . . 102 F7
Inglenook Dr B20 . . . . 55 B2
Ingleside Villas **3**
B11 . . . . 87 C5
Ingleton Cl CV11 . . . . 74 A2
Ingleton Rd B8 . . . . . . 68 A7
Inglewood Ave WV3 . .38 F4
Inglewood Cl
Kingswinford DY6 . . . . 60 D5
Royal Leamington Spa
CV32 . . . . 157 A3
Inglewood Gr B74 . . . .30 F2
Inglewood Rd B11 . . . 87 C5
Ingoldsby Ct **17** B13. . 87 B2
Ingoldsby Rd B31 . . . 103 C3
Ingot Cl WS2 . . . . 28 B6
Ingram Gr B27 . . . . . . 88 A2

Ingram Pit La B77 . . . . 22 A5
Ingram Pl WS3 . . . . . . 14 D1
Ingram Rd
Coventry CV5 . . . . . . 132 D8
Walsall WS3 . . . . 14 D1
Inhedge St DY3 . . . . . 50 E5
Inhedge The DY1 . . . . 51 C1
Inkberrow Cl **1** B65. . 63 E4
Inkberrow Rd B63 . . . .82 F2
Inkerman Gr WV10 . . .25 F2
Inkerman Ho B19 . . . . 66 E6
Inkerman St
Birmingham B7 . . . . . 67 B4
Wolverhampton WV10 . 25 F3
Inland Rd B24 . . . . 57 B2
Innage Cl CV31 . . . . . 162 B8
Innage Rd B31 . . . . . . 103 B4
Innage The B47 . . . . . 125 A5
Innis Rd CV5 . . . . 132 E8
Innsworth Dr B35 . . . . 58 A4
Insetton Cl B98 . . . . . 154 D4
Instow Cl WV12 . . . . . 27 B8
Insull Ave B14 . . . . . . 105 B1
Intended St B63 . . . . . 82 C7
International Ho B43 . .54 F6
Intersection Ho B70. . 53 F1
Instone Rd
Coventry CV6 . . . . . . 95 A1
Halesowen B63 . . . . . 83 A3
Intown WS1 . . . . .28 F2
Intown Row WS1 . . . . .28 F2
Int Sch and Com Coll The
B33 . . . . 69 D3
Inveraray Cl CV8 . . . . 148 C4
Inverclyde Rd B20 . . . 55 A3
Inverness Cl CV5 . . . . 112 A4
Inverness Ho WV1 . . . 163 B4
Inverness Rd B31 . . . . 102 F3
Invicta Rd CV3 . . . . . . 134 F8
Inworth WV9 . . . . 11 B3
Io Ctr The B98 . . . . . . 159 C8
Ipsley Alders Marsh
Nature Reserve*
B98 . . . . 154 F4
Ipsley CE Mid Sch
B98 . . . . 154 E3
Ipsley Church La
B98 . . . . 154 C1
Ipsley Gr B23 . . . . 56 A5
Ipsley La B98 . . . . 154 D2
Ipsley St B98 . . . . 153 E3
Ipstones Ave B33 . . . .68 F4
Ipswich Cres B42 . . . . 55 B7
Ipswich Wlk B37 . . . . 70 B2
Ireland Green Rd B70 53 B2
Ireton Cl CV4 . . . . 111 C1
Ireton Rd
Birmingham B20 . . . . 55 A4
Wolverhampton WV10 . 11 E3
Iris Cl
Birmingham B29 . . . . 103 B8
Dudley DY2 . . . . 51 F1
Hinckley LE10 . . . . . . 75 E5
Tamworth B79 . . . . . . 21 C6
Iris Dr B14 . . . . 104 D3
Iron Bridge Wlk DY9 . . 99 B8
Iron La B33 . . . . 68 D4
Ironmonger Row
CV1 . . . . 165 B3
Ironstone Rd WS7 . . . . .6 E8
Iron Way B60 . . . . 151 B7
Irvan Ave B70 . . . . . . .52 F5
Irvine Cl WS3 . . . . 28 B7
Irvine Rd WS3 . . . . . . 28 B7
Irving Cl DY3 . . . . 50 A7
Irving Rd
Coventry CV1 . . . . . . 113 E4
Solihull B92 . . . . 89 E3
Wednesbury DY4 . . . . 41 A1
Irving St B1 . . . . 66 D1
Irwell B77 . . . . 21 E2
Irwin Ave B45 . . . . . . 122 C7
Isaac Walton Pl B70 . . 52 E7
Isambard Dr CV6 . . . . .95 F5
Isbourne Way **1** B9 . . 67 B2
Isis Ct B73 . . . . 46 B5
Isis Gr Birmingham B36 .69 F8
Willenhall WV13 . . . . . 27 C2
Isis Ho CV1 . . . . 61 D8
Island Cl LE10 . . . . . . 71 E2
Island Dr DY10 . . . . . . 116 A4
Island Rd B21 . . . . 54 C1
Island The B70 . . . . . . 20 C1
Islington B63 . . . . 83 A4
Islington Cres CV9 . . . 36 C1
Islington Gates B3 . . 164 A3

Islington Row B15 . . . 66 B1
Islington Row Middleway
B15 . . . . 86 C8
Ismere Rd B24 . . . . . . 57 B2
Itchen Gr WV6 . . . . . . 23 E4
Ithon Gr B38 . . . . 123 E8
Ivanhoe Ave CV11 . . . 73 E1
Ivanhoe Rd
Birmingham B43 . . . . 44 C3
Lichfield WS14 . . . . . . .9 B6
Wolverhampton WV2 . . 40 A6
Ivanhoe St DY2 . . . . . 62 A7
Ivatt B77 . . . . .21 F2
Ivatt Cl WS4 . . . . 29 B7
Iverley La DY10, DY8 . . 98 C5
Iverley Rd B63 . . . . . . 83 C4
Iverley Wlk DY9 . . . . . 81 C4
Ivor Rd
Birmingham B11 . . . . 87 B4
Coventry CV6 . . . . . . 95 F2
Redditch B97 . . . . . . 153 D2
Ivy Ave
Birmingham B12 . . . . 87 A5
3 Birmingham B12 . . 87 B5
Ivybridge Gr B42 . . . . 55 C3
Ivybridge Rd CV3 . . . 133 D6
Ivy Cl WS11 . . . . 4 D8
Ivy Croft WV9 . . . . . . .10 F3
Ivydale Ave B26 . . . . . 89 C5
Ivy Farm La CV4 . . . . . 132 C5
Ivyfield Rd B23 . . . . . . 56 B5
Ivy Gr Brownhills WS8. . 16 A4
Nuneaton CV10 . . . . . 72 D6
Ivy Ho WS9 . . . . 16 A4
Ivyhouse La WV14 . . . 51 B8
Ivyhouse Rd B38 . . . . 123 C8
Ivy House Rd B69 . . . 63 D6
Ivyhouse Wlk **6** B77 . .35 F6
Ivy La Birmingham B9 . . 67 A2
Romsley B62 . . . . 100 D5
Ivy Lodge Cl B37 . . . . 90 A7
Ivy Rd
Birmingham, Handsworth
B21 . . . . 66 A7
Birmingham, Stirchley
B30 . . . . 104 A6
Dudley DY1 . . . . 51 A4
Sutton Coldfield B73 . . 45 F1
Tipton DY4 . . . . 51 F7
Ivy Way B90 . . . . 126 A6
Izod St B97 . . . . 153 D4
Izons La B70 . . . . 53 A1
Izons Lane Ind Est
B70 . . . . 53 A1
Izons Rd B70 . . . . 53 C3

J

Jacey Rd
Birmingham B16 . . . . 65 D2
Solihull B90 . . . . 106 B4
Jack Cade Way CV34 161 E4
Jack David Ho CV4 . . . 52 D5
Jackdaw Cl DY3 . . . . . 39 C2
Jackdaw Dr B36 . . . . . 70 A8
Jacker's Rd CV2 . . . . . 96 B4
Jackfield Cl B98 . . . . . 154 E1
Jack Hayward Way
WV1 . . . . 163 B4
Jack Holden Ave
WV14 . . . . 40 A2
Jacklin Dr CV3 . . . . . . 133 C4
Jacknell Rd LE10 . . . . 74 D8
Jack Newell Ct **3**
WV14 . . . . 51 C8
Jack O'Watton Bsns Pk
B46 . . . . 59 D3
Jackson Ave B8 . . . . . .67 F4
Jackson Cl
Birmingham B11 . . . . 87 B7
Featherstone WV10 . . 12 A6
Keresley CV7 . . . . . . 95 A7
Norton Canes WS11 . . .5 E4
Oldbury B68 . . . . 64 B5
Wednesbury DY4 . . . . 41 B1
Jackson Ct
Brierley Hill DY5 . . . . 61 F1
Oldbury B69 . . . . 63 F4
Jackson Dr B67 . . . . . 64 D5
Jackson Gr CV8 . . . . . 148 C4
Jackson Ho **9** B69 . . 64 A7
Jackson Rd
Birmingham B8 . . . . . 67 F4
Coventry CV6 . . . . . . 95 D1
Lichfield WS13 . . . . . .3 B3

Jackson St
Oldbury B68 . . . . **64** B4
Stourbridge DY9 . . . . . . **81** E6
Wolverhampton WV6 . . **25** B4
Jackson Way B32 . . . **84** A5
Jackson Wlk B35. . . . . **58** A2
Jackwood Gn CV12. . **95** C8
Jacmar Cres B67. . . . . **64** E6
Jacob Dr CV4 . . . . . . **132** D6
Jacobean La B93. . . . . **108** B1
Jacob's Hall La WS6. . . . **5** B1
Jacoby Pl B5 . . . . **86** C5
Jacox Cres CV8 . . . . . **148** C5
Jacquard Cl CV3. . . . . **133** D4
Jacquard Ho 3 CV1. **113** E4
Jade Cl CV1. . . . . **165** C4
Jade Gr WS11. . . . . **2** C2
Jaffray Cres B24 . . . . . .**56** F3
Jaffray Ct B23 . . . . . . **56** E3
Jaffray Rd B24. . . . .**56** F3
Jaguar B77 . . . . **21** E2
Jakeman Cl B98. . . . . **154** E4
Jakeman Rd B12. . . . . **86** E5
James Beattie Ho
WV6 . . . . **24** C4
James Bridge Cl WS2 **42** B7
James Brindley Sch
(Parkway Ctr) B15 . **86** C8
James Brindley Sch
(Willow Ctr) B13 . . . .**86** E1
James Cl
Darlaston WS10 . . . . . . **41** F7
Smethwick B67. . . . . . **65** A5
James Clift Ho 3
B69. . . . . **63** D5
Jamescroft CV3. . . . . **134** E6
James Ct
Birmingham, King's Norton
B38. . . . . **103** F2
13 Birmingham, Moseley
B13. . . . . **87** B2
Warwick CV34 . . . . . . **160** F7
James Dawson Dr
CV5. . . . . **111** B8
James Dee Cl DY5. . . . **62** A1
James Diskin Ct CV11 **73** E2
James Eaton Cl B71. . **53** C5
James Galloway Cl
CV3. . . . . **134** E7
James Green Rd
CV4. . . . . **111** F2
James Greenway WS13. .**3** A2
James Ho
Birmingham B19. . . . . **66** C6
Coventry CV2 . . . . **114** C8
James Hutchens Ct
WS7. . . . .**6** F5
James Lloyd Trust Flats
B30. . . . . **103** C5
James Meml Homes The
4 B7. . . . . **67** C7
Jameson Rd B6. . . . . . **67** C8
Jameson St WV6. . . . . **25** B4
James Rd
Birmingham, Great Barr
B43. . . . . **54** E7
Birmingham, Tyseley
B11. . . . . **87** F6
Coleshill B46. . . . . **70** F8
Kidderminster DY10. . **117** A8
James Samuel Pl 7
B12 . . . .**86** F7
James Scott Rd B63. . **82** A6
James St Bilston WV14 **40** E6
Birmingham B3. . . . . . **164** A3
Cannock WS11 . . . .**1** F5
Nuneaton CV11. . . . . . **73** A5
Willenhall WV13 . . . . . **27** A3
James Turner St B18. . **65** E6
James Watt Dr B19. . . **66** C8
James Watt Ho B66 . . **65** B6
James Watt Prim Sch
B21. . . . .**65** E7
James Watt Queensway
B4 . . . . **164** C3
James Watt St
Birmingham B4. . . . . . **164** C3
West Bromwich B71. . . **53** B8
Jane Lane Cl WS2. . . . .**27** F4
Jane Lane Sch WS2. . . .**27** F3
Janice Gr B14. . . . . . . **105** B4
Janie Ct B13. . . . . **87** C2
Janine Ave WV11. . . . . **26** E7
Jaques Cl B46 . . . . **59** B2
Jardine Cres CV4. . . . . **111** F2
Jardine Rd B6. . . . .**55** F1
Jarvis Cl LE10. . . . .**71** D4
Jarvis Cres B69. . . . . . **64** A4

Jarvis Rd B23 . . . .**56** F6
Jarvis Way B24 . . . . . **67** E8
JAS Ind Pk B65. . . . . . .**63** E4
Jasmin Croft B14 . . . . **104** E3
Jasmine Cl WV9. . . . . . **11** A3
Jasmine Gr
Bromsgrove B61. . . . . **136** F4
Codsall WV8 . . . . **10** B3
Coventry CV4 . . . . **134** C8
Royal Leamington Spa
CV32. . . . . **157** A2
Jasmine Rd
Dudley DY2 . . . . **51** F1
Tamworth B77. . . . . . . **22** A4
Jasmine Way WS10. . . **41** D7
Jason Cl B77. . . . . **21** D5
Jason Rd DY9. . . . .**81** F4
Javelin Ave B35. . . . . . **58** B2
Javelin Way WS10. . . . **41** D2
Jayne Cl
Wednesfield WV11. . . . **26** D7
West Bromwich B71. . . **42** E1
Jay Park Cres DY10 . . **117** B2
Jay Rd DY6 . . . . **60** D8
Jays Ave DY4 . . . . **52** B4
Jays Cres B48. . . . . . . **123** B1
Jayshaw Ave B43. . . . . **54** E8
Jeal Cl B47. . . . . **124** E2
Jean Dr DY4 . . . . **52** D6
Jeavons Pl WV14. . . . . **40** C5
Jedburgh Ave WV6. . . **23** E4
Jedburgh Gr CV3. . . . . **133** A4
Jeddo St WV2. . . . . . . **163** B1
Jeffcock Rd WV3. . . . . **39** A7
Jefferies LE10. . . . . **71** E2
Jefferson Cl B71. . . . . . **53** B8
Jeffrey Ave WV4. . . . . .**39** F5
Jeffrey Cl CV12 . . . . . . **95** D8
Jeffrey Rd B65. . . . . . . **63** E3
Jeffrey Woods Cross
CV1. . . . . **113** F4
Jeffries Ho 3 B69 . . . . **64** A7
Jeffs Ave WV2 . . . . **163** C1
Jeliff St CV4. . . . . **111** F2
Jelleyman Cl DY11. . . . **116** C6
Jellicoe Ho 9 DY4. . . . **52** A8
Jellicoe Way LE10. . . . **71** D3
Jenkins Ave CV5 . . . . . **111** F4
Jenkins Cl WV14. . . . . **40** C5
Jenkinson Rd WS10. . . **41** D1
Jenkins St B10. . . . . . . **87** C8
Jenks Ave WV10. . . . . . **25** E8
Jennens Rd B4. . . . . . . **66** F3
Jenner Cl WS2. . . . . . . **28** A6
Jenner Ho WS2. . . . .**27** F6
Jenner Rd WS2. . . . . . . **28** A6
Jenner St
Coventry CV1 . . . . **165** C4
Wolverhampton WV2. . **163** D2
Jennifer Wlk B25. . . . . **88** E8
Jennings St B64. . . . . . .**62** F2
Jenny Cl WV14. . . . . . . **40** E1
Jennyns Ct 3 WS10. . . **42** A3
Jenny Walkers La
WV6 . . . . **23** D1
Jensen B77. . . . . **21** E2
Jenton Rd CV31. . . . . . **162** B6
Jephcott Gr B8. . . . . . . **68** A4
Jephcott Ho 2 CV1. . . **113** E3
Jephcott Rd B8. . . . . . . **68** A4
Jephson Cl CV2. . . . . . . **96** C4
Jephson Dr B26. . . . . . .**88** F7
Jephson Pl 3 CV31. . . **162** B7
Jeremy Gr B92. . . . . . . **89** B3
Jeremy Rd WV4 . . . . . . **39** C5
Jerome Ct B74. . . . .**30** F1
Jerome Dr WS11 . . . .**6** A5
Jerome K Jerome Mus*
WS1 . . . . **28** E1
Jerome Prim Sch
WS11. . . . .**5** F5
Jerome Rd
Norton Canes WS11. . . .**6** A5
Sutton Coldfield B72. . . **46** B4
Walsall WS2. . . . . **28** B1
Jerome Way WS7 . . . . . .**7** C7
Jerrard Dr B75. . . . . . . **46** C6
Jerrard Mews B75. . . . **46** C5
Jerry's La
Birmingham B23. . . . . **56** E6
Weeford WS14 . . . . . . **19** B8
Jersey Gr B38. . . . . **154** D7
Jersey Croft B36. . . . . **70** B6
Jersey Rd B8. . . . . **67** D4
Jerusalem Wlk DY10. **116** E7
Jervis Cl DY5 . . . . **61** C7
Jervis Cres B74. . . . . . **31** D3
Jervis Ct 2 WS1. . . . . . .**28** F2
Jervis Pk B74. . . . . **31** C4
Jervis Rd B77. . . . .**35** F5

Jervis Terr B21. . . . . . **65** D8
Jervoise Dr B31. . . . . . **103** B5
Jervoise Jun & Inf Sch
B29. . . . . **85** A1
Jervoise La B71. . . . . . **42** E1
Jervoise Rd B29. . . . . . **85** A2
Jervoise St B70. . . . . . **53** A4
Jesmond Gr B24. . . . . . **57** E4
Jesmond Rd CV1. . . . . **113** F4
Jessel Rd WS2 . . . . **28** C2
Jessie Rd WS9. . . . . . . **16** B1
Jesson Cl WS1. . . . . . . **43** A7
Jesson Ct WS1. . . . . . . **43** A7
Jesson Rd Dudley DY3. **51** A6
Sutton Coldfield B75. . **47** A6
Walsall WS1 . . . . **43** A8
Jesson's CE Prim Sch
DY1. . . . .**51** B1
Jesson St B70. . . . . **53** E2
Jessop Dr B77 . . . . **21** E5
Jevons Dr 7 DY4 . . . . . **52** B5
Jevons Rd B73. . . . . . . **45** C3
Jevon St WV14 . . . . **51** B8
Jewellery Quarter Sta
B18. . . . .**66** B4
Jew's La DY3 . . . . **50** E4
Jiggins La B32. . . . . . . **84** D1
Jill Ave B43 . . . . **43** C1
Jillcot Rd B92. . . . . **89** B3
Jill La B96. . . . . **159** B2
Jim Forrest Cl 4
CV3. . . . . **134** F8
Jinnah Cl B12. . . . .**86** F8
Jinnah Rd B98. . . . . . . **153** E2
Joanna Dr CV3. . . . . . . **133** C3
Joan of Arc Ho CV3. **133** E6
Joan's Cl CV31. . . . . . . **162** C6
Joan St WV2 . . . . **39** E6
Joan Ward St CV3. . . **133** D8
Job's La CV4. . . . . **112** A2
Jockey Field DY3. . . . . **50** E6
Jockey La WS10. . . . . . **42** A4
Jockey Rd B73. . . . . . . **46** A2
Jodrell St CV11. . . . . . **73** B6
Joe Jones Ct DY3 . . . . . **39** D1
Joe O'Brien Ct CV3 . . **134** C6
Joe Williams Cl 7
CV3. . . . . **134** F8
Joeys La WV8 . . . . **10** C3
John Black Day Hospl
B37. . . . .**90** C8
John Bosco Cl B71. . . . **53** B7
John Bright Cl DY4. . . .**51** F8
John Bright St B1. . . . **164** B2
John Cleveland Coll
LE10. . . . . **71** F1
Johndory B77. . . . . **35** D6
John F Kennedy Wlk 4
DY4 . . . . **52** A8
John Fletcher Cl
WS10. . . . . **42** B4
John Grace St CV3. . . **133** D8
John Gulson Prim Sch
CV1. . . . .**113** D5
John Harper St WV13 **27** B2
John Haynes Ct CV7. . **96** A7
John Ho DY1. . . . . **61** D8
John Howell Dr DY4. . **52** A5
John Kempe Way
B12. . . . . **87** A7
John Knight Rd CV12. **78** B5
John McGuire Cres
CV3. . . . . **134** E7
John Nash Sq CV8 . . . **147** F3
John Nichols St LE10. **75** B7
John of Gaunt Ho
CV3. . . . . **133** E6
John O'Gaunt Rd
CV8. . . . . **147** E3
John Rd B62. . . . .**83** F3
John Riley Dr WV12. . **27** C8
John Rous Ave CV4. . . **132** B7
Johns Cl B80. . . . . **159** C4
John's Cl LE10. . . . . . . **75** D5
Johns Gr B43. . . . . **54** C8
John Shelton Com Prim
Sch CV6. . . . . **95** D4
John Shelton Dr CV6. **95** D4
John Sinclair Ho
CV1. . . . . **165** B4
Johns La WS6. . . . .**5** A3
John's La Oldbury B69. **52** C3
Tipton DY4 . . . . **52** B4
John Smith Ho 3 B1. **66** C3
Johnson Ave WV11. . . .**26** F7
Johnson Cl
Birmingham, Sparkhill
B11. . . . . **87** C5
Birmingham, Ward End
B8. . . . . **68** C6

Johnson Cl continued
Darlaston WS10 . . . . . **41** D5
Lichfield WS13 . . . .**3** C1
Redditch B98 . . . . **154** A5
Johnson Dr B35. . . . . . .**57** F3
Johnson Pl 3 WV14. . **41** A7
Johnson Rd
Bedworth CV12. . . . . . **78** C3
Birmingham B23 . . . . . **57** A6
Burntwood WS7 . . . .**6** F8
Cannock WS11 . . . .**1** D4
Coventry CV6 . . . . **114** A8
Darlaston WS10 . . . . . **41** D5
Wednesbury WS10 . . . . **42** C2
Willenhall WV12 . . . . . **27** D7
Johnsons Bridge Rd
B71. . . . . **53** C6
Johnsons Gr B68. . . . . **84** D8
Johnson St
Birmingham B7. . . . . . **67** C6
Wolverhampton, Cinder Hill
WV14 . . . . **39** F1
Wolverhampton WV2. . **39** D7
Wood End CV9 . . . . **36** C1
John St Bedworth CV12 **78** A2
Birmingham B19. . . . . **66** B7
Brierley Hill DY5. . . . . **61** D4
Cannock, Chadsmoor
WS11. . . . .**2** A4
Cannock, Wimblebury
WS12. . . . .**2** F3
Hinckley LE10. . . . . . . **71** E1
Nuneaton, Coton CV11. **73** C2
Nuneaton, Stockingford
CV10. . . . . **72** E3
Oldbury B69 . . . . **64** A7
Rowley Regis B65. . . . . **63** C1
Royal Leamington Spa
CV32. . . . . **161** F8
Stourbridge DY8 . . . . . **60** F1
Tamworth B77. . . . . . . **21** E4
West Bromwich, Great
Bridge B70 . . . . **52** F5
West Bromwich, Guns Village
B70. . . . . **53** B4
Willenhall WV13 . . . . . **27** A1
Wolverhampton WV2. . **40** A6
Johnstone St B19. . . . **66** D8
John Street N B71. . . . **53** B5
John Tofts Ho CV1. . . **165** B4
John Wesley Way
WS10. . . . . **42** A1
John Willmott Sch
B76. . . . .**46** F4
John Wooton Ho 3
WS10. . . . . **41** D6
Joiners Croft B92. . . . **107** E8
Joinings Bank B68. . . . **64** B4
Jonathan Rd CV2. . . . **114** F8
Jon Baker Ct LE10. . . . **75** E8
Jonesfield Cres WV1. **26** B2
Jones Ho WS2 . . . . **28** D3
Jones La
Burntwood WS7 . . . .**7** F7
Great Wyrley WS6. . . . . .**5** B1
Jones Wood Cl B76. . . **58** A7
Jonfield Gdns B43 . . . .**43** F1
Jonkel Ave B77. . . . . . . **36** A5
Jonquil Cl B23 . . . . **56** C7
Jordan Cl
Kenilworth CV8. . . . . . **148** B2
Kidderminster DY11 . . **116** A6
4 Lichfield WS13. . . . . . .**9** A8
Smethwick B66. . . . . . **65** B5
Sutton Coldfield B75. . . **32** B1
Jordan Ho B36. . . . . . . **68** E8
Jordan Leys 2 DY4. . . **52** B5
Jordan Pl WV14. . . . . . **40** E3
Jordan Rd B75. . . . . . . **32** C2
Jordans Cl B97. . . . . . . **158** D6
Jordans The CV5. . . . . **112** C4
Jordan Way WS9. . . . . **16** B1
Jordan Well CV1. . . . . **165** C2
Joseph Cash Prim Sch
CV6. . . . .**113** C7
Joseph Chamberlain Coll
B12. . . . .**86** F6
Joseph Creighton Cl
CV3. . . . . **134** E7
Joseph Dewsbury Cl
WS7. . . . .**6** F8
Joseph Halpin Ho 3
CV1. . . . . **165** C4

Joseph Latham Ho 3
CV2. . . . . **96** B1
Joseph Leckie Com Tech
Coll WS5. . . . . **42** E5
Joseph Luckman Rd
CV12. . . . . **78** B5
Joseph St B69 . . . .**63** E6
Joseph Turner Prim Sch
DY4. . . . .**52** B7
Josiah Mason Coll
B23. . . . . **56** C4
Josiah Rd B31 . . . . **102** D2
Jourdain Pk CV34 . . . **161** E3
Jovian Dr LE10. . . . . . . **71** A1
Jowett B77. . . . . **21** E2
Jowett's La B71. . . . . . **53** B8
Joyberry Dr DY8 . . . . . **81** A3
Joyce Pool CV34 . . . . . **160** E7
Joynson St WS10. . . . . **41** E5
Jubilee Ave
Redditch B97 . . . . **158** D2
West Bromwich B71. . . **53** B7
Jubilee Bldgs WS10. . **41** D5
Jubilee Bsns Pk DY9. **82** A5
Jubilee Cl
Great Wyrley WS6. . . . . .**4** C1
Stoke Prior B60 . . . . . **150** C1
Walsall WS3 . . . . **28** E6
Jubilee Cres CV6. . . . . **113** B7
Jubilee Ct
Birmingham, Acock's Green
B27. . . . . **88** C2
Birmingham, Turves Green
B31. . . . . **103** B1
Jubilee Dr N DY11. . . . **116** B2
Jubilee Dr S DY11. . . . **116** B2
Jubilee Gdns B23 . . . . **56** B7
Jubilee Ho B98 . . . . . . **153** E2
Jubilee Park Prim Sch
DY4. . . . .**52** B8
Jubilee Rd
Birmingham B45. . . . . **101** C2
Darlaston WV14 . . . . . **41** A4
Tipton DY4 . . . . **52** B8
Jubilee St B71. . . . . **53** D8
Jubilee Terr
Bedworth CV12. . . . . . **78** B4
Stoke Prior B60 . . . . . **150** C1
Jubilee Trad Ctr B5. .**66** E1
Judd Cl CV12 . . . .**77** F3
Judds La CV6 . . . . **95** E4
Judge Cl B69. . . . . **64** A7
Judge Rd DY5. . . . .**81** F7
Juggins La B94. . . . . . . **141** B7
Julia Ave B24. . . . .**57** F4
Julia Gdns B71. . . . .**53** F8
Julian Cl Catshill B61. **137** A8
Coventry CV2 . . . . **114** F8
Great Wyrley WS6. . . . . .**5** A3
Wolverhampton WV1 . . **26** B2
Julian Rd WV1 . . . . **26** B2
Juliet Cl CV11. . . . . **74** A1
Juliet Dr CV34 . . . . **161** F3
Juliet Rd B62. . . . .**83** F3
Julius Dr B46. . . . . **59** F1
Junction 2 Ind Est
B69. . . . .**63** F6
Junction 6 Ind Pk B6 .**56** B2
Junction Rd
Birmingham B21. . . . . **65** C8
Bromsgrove B61. . . . . **136** D4
Stourbridge, Amblecote
DY8. . . . . **60** E1
Stourbridge DY8 . . . . . **81** B4
Wolverhampton WV2. . **40** B7
Junction St S B69. . . . **64** C8
Junction St
Coventry CV1 . . . . **165** A2
Dudley DY2 . . . . **62** B8
Oldbury B69. . . . . **52** E1
Walsall WS1 . . . . **42** D7
Junction The 1 DY8 . **80** E8
June Cres B77. . . . . **21** E5
June Croft B26. . . . . . . **89** D5
Juniper B77 . . . . **22** A4
Juniper Cl
Bedworth CV12. . . . . . .**77** E2
Birmingham B27. . . . . **88** B5
Burntwood WS7 . . . .**7** A6
Sutton Coldfield B76. . . **46** F3
Juniper Ct DY10. . . . . . **117** A4
Juniper Dr
Coventry CV5 . . . . **111** C4
Sutton Coldfield B76. . . **58** A7
Walsall WS5 . . . . **43** B4
Juniper Ho B36. . . . . . .**68** F7
Juniper Rise B63. . . . . **82** C5
Juno Dr CV31. . . . . **161** F5
Jurist Ho 5 LE10. . . . . **71** D1

Jury Rd DY5 . . . .**81** F7
Jury St CV34 . . . . **160** E6
Justice Cl CV31. . . . . . **162** A4
Jutland Rd B13 . . . . . . **105** B8

K

Kanzan Rd CV2. . . . . . . **96** B4
Kareen Gr CV3 . . . . **135** C2
Karen Cl CV10. . . . . **72** E7
Karen Way DY5. . . . . . . **81** D8
Karlingford Cl CV5 . . **132** D8
Kate's Hill Prim Sch
DY2. . . . .**62** E8
Katherine Ho 3 B17. **85** B5
Katherine Rd B67 . . . .**64** C7
Kathleen Ave CV12 . . **77** E1
Kathleen Rd
Birmingham B25. . . . . **88** C7
Sutton Coldfield B72. . . **46** C4
Katie Rd B29. . . . . **85** E1
Katmandu Rd B60. . . **137** C1
Katrine Cl CV10. . . . . . **72** C5
Kayne Cl DY6. . . . . **60** C7
Keanscott Dr B68 . . . . **64** C4
Keasden Gr WV13. . . . . **27** C3
Keating Gdns B75. . . . . **32** A4
Keatley Ave B33. . . . . . **69** E2
Keats Ave
Birmingham B10. . . . . **87** D7
Cannock WS11 . . . .**1** E5
Keats Cl Dudley DY3. . . **50** A5
Nuneaton CV10. . . . . . **72** A4
Stourbridge DY8 . . . . . **81** A8
Sutton Coldfield B74. . . **31** F6
Tamworth B79. . . . . . . **20** F8
Keats Dr WV14. . . . . . . **40** D2
Keats Gr
Birmingham B27. . . . . **88** B1
Wolverhampton WV10 . **26** A8
Keats Ho
2 Oldbury B68. . . . . . **64** C4
Redditch B97 . . . . **158** C8
Keats Pl DY10. . . . . **117** B6
Keats Rd
Coventry CV2 . . . . **114** D2
Walsall WS3 . . . . **28** E7
Willenhall WV12 . . . . . **27** E7
Wolverhampton WV10 . **12** A1
Keble Cl
Burntwood WS7 . . . .**7** C7
Cannock WS11 . . . .**4** E8
Keble Gr
Birmingham B26. . . . . **89** B6
Walsall WS1 . . . . **43** A7
Keble Ho B37. . . . . **70** A2
Keble Wlk B79. . . . . **21** A6
Kebull Gn CV4 . . . . **131** E8
Kedleston Cl WS3 . . . . **14** A3
Kedleston Ct B28. . . . . **105** F4
Kedleston Rd B28. . . . . **105** F5
Keegan Wlk WS2. . . . . .**27** F4
Keel Dr B13. . . . . **87** D1
Keele Cl B98. . . . . **154** E6
Keele Ho B37. . . . . **70** B4
Keeley St B9. . . . . **67** B2
Keeling Dr WS11 . . . .**1** B1
Keelinge St DY4. . . . . . **52** B5
Keeling Rd CV8 . . . . . . **148** B5
Keenan Dr CV12. . . . . . **77** D1
Keen St B66. . . . . **65** D6
Keepers Cl
Birmingham B18. . . . . **65** F5
Brownhills WS9 . . . . . . **15** F3
Kingswinford DY6. . . . . **60** B8
Lichfield WS14 . . . .**9** E7
Keeper's Cl WS7 . . . .**7** A6
Keepers Gate Cl B74. **46** C7
Keepers Ho B73. . . . . . **45** C2
Keepers La WV6, WV8. **10** A5
Keepers Rd B74. . . . . . . **31** C5
Keepers Wlk CV12. . . . **77** D1
Keer Ct B9. . . . . **67** B2
Kegworth Cl CV6. . . . . **96** A4
Kegworth Rd B23. . . . . **56** C2
Keir Cl CV32. . . . . **157** A2
Keir Hardie Wlk B69. **52** D2
Keir Pl DY8. . . . . **80** E8
Keir Rd WS10. . . . . **42** D2
Keith Rd CV32. . . . . . . **157** B4
Keith Winter Cl B61. **136** F6
Kelby Cl B31. . . . . **102** E4
Kelby Rd B31. . . . . **102** F4
Keldy Cl WV6. . . . . **24** F5
Kele Rd CV4. . . . . **132** A2
Kelfield Ave B17. . . . . . **85** B4
Kelham Pl B92. . . . . **89** B1
Kelia Dr B67. . . . .**64** F6
Kellett Rd B7. . . . . **67** A4
Kelling Cl DY5 . . . . **81** C8

Kellington Cl B8 67 F4
Kelmarsh Dr B91 107 B1
Kelmscote Rd CV6 112 F8
Kelmscott Rd B17 85 B7
Kelsall Cl WV1 26 B2
Kelsall Croft B1 66 B3
Kelsey Cl
Birmingham B7 67 B4
Nuneaton CV11 73 E3
Kelsey La CV7 130 D5
Kelsey's Cl CV8 135 F3
Kelso Gdns WV6 23 D4
Kelsull Croft B37 70 A2
Kelton Ct B15 86 A7
Kelvedon Gr B91 107 C4
Kelverdale Gr B14 104 C4
Kelverley Gr B71 43 A1
Kelvestone Ho WS11 1 D1
Kelvin Ave CV2 114 D5
Kelvin Cl DY11 116 A8
Kelvin Dr WS11 2 A3
Kelvin Pl WS2 28 B6
Kelvin Rd
Birmingham B31 103 B1
Royal Leamington Spa CV32 157 C5
Walsall WS2 28 B6
Kelvin Way B70 53 C1
Kelvin Way Trad Est B70 53 B1
Kelway CV3 115 A2
Kelway Ave B43 44 B3
Kelwood Dr B63 83 A5
Kelynmead Rd B33 69 A2
Kemberton Cl WV3 24 C1
Kemberton Rd
Birmingham B29 85 B2
Wolverhampton WV3 24 C1
Kemble Cl WV12 27 D3
Kemble Croft B5 86 E7
Kemble Dr B35 58 A3
Kemelstowe Cres B63 100 C8
Kemerton Ho B97 153 B4
Kemerton Way B90 126 F6
Kemp Cl CV34 161 A7
Kempe Rd B33 69 A4
Kempley Ave CV2 114 C2
Kempsey Cl
Halesowen B63 82 E4
Oldbury B69 63 E4
Redditch B98 159 B7
Solihull B92 89 A3
Kempsey Covert B38 123 E7
Kempsey Ho B32 102 A8
Kempsford Cl B98 158 F6
Kemps Green Rd
Balsall Common CV7 130 B6
Kemps Green B94 143 A1
Kempson Ave
Sutton Coldfield B72 46 C1
West Bromwich B71 53 B5
Kempson Rd B36 68 F8
Kempsons Gr WV14 40 B3
Kempthorne Ave
Wolverhampton WV10 11 E1
Wolverhampton WV10 25 E8
Kempthorne Gdns WS3 14 A2
Kempthorne Rd WV14 40 F6
Kempton Cres CV32 157 C4
Kempton Ct B61 121 A1
Kempton Dr
Great Wyrley WS6 4 F2
Tamworth B77 35 D4
Kempton Park Rd B36 68 D8
Kempton Way DY8 80 E3
Kemsey Dr WV14 40 F3
Kemshead Ave B31 122 E8
Kemsley Rd B14 104 F2
Kem St CV11 73 E2
Kenchester Cl B98 154 F2
Kendal Ave
Birmingham B45 122 B7
Coleshill B46 70 F7
Royal Leamington Spa CV32 156 C2
Kendal Cl
Bromsgrove B60 137 B1
Nuneaton CV11 74 A6
Wolverhampton WV6 24 F6
Kendal Ct
14 Birmingham, Selly Oak B29 103 C7
Birmingham, Stockland Green B23 56 B3
Brownhills WS9 15 F4
Cannock WS11 4 B8
Kendal Dr B45 122 D1
Kendal End Rd B45 122 D1
Kendal Gr B92 107 F8
Kendall Ho 15 B69 63 D5
Kendall Rise DY6 60 F5
Kendal Rd B11 87 B7
Kendal Rise
Coventry CV5 112 C4
Oldbury B68 64 B3
Wolverhampton WV6 24 F6
Kendal Rise Rd B45 122 B7
Kendal Tower 5 B17 85 D5
Kenderdine Montessori Sch CV5 133 A8
Kendon Ave CV6 112 E6
Kendrick Ave B34 69 E5
Kendrick Cl
Coventry CV6 96 A4
Solihull B92 107 F6
Kendrick Pl WV14 41 A4
Kendrick Rd
Darlaston WV14 41 A4
Sutton Coldfield B76 57 F5
Wolverhampton WV10 25 E6
Kendricks Rd WS10 41 F7
Kendrick St WS10 42 A3
Kenelm Ct
Coventry CV3 134 C5
Romsley B62 101 A4
Sutton Coldfield B73 46 B4
Kenelm Rd
Birmingham B10 87 E8
Dudley WV14 40 C1
Oldbury B68 64 A3
Sutton Coldfield B73 46 B4
Kenilcourt CV8 147 D6
Kenilworth Castle* CV8 147 D5
Kenilworth Cl
Balsall Common CV7 130 A6
Redditch B97 158 D6
Stourbridge DY8 60 D2
Sutton Coldfield B74 46 A8
Tipton DY4 51 D4
Kenilworth Cres
Walsall WS2 28 A4
Wolverhampton WV4 39 E4
Kenilworth Ct
Birmingham B15 85 F8
Birmingham, Gravelly Hill B24 56 E2
2 Cannock WS11 1 E1
Coventry CV3 133 C8
Dudley DY1 61 F8
Kenilworth Dr
Cannock WS11 1 D4
Kidderminster DY10 116 E2
Nuneaton CV11 73 B3
Kenilworth Hall Mews CV8 147 F5
Kenilworth Ho
Birmingham B13 105 A6
3 Walsall WS3 28 C6
Kenilworth Rd
Balsall Common CV7, CV8 130 D4
Birmingham, Birchfield B20 55 E2
Birmingham, Warley Woods B68 84 D7
Blackdown CV32 156 E5
Bradnock's Marsh B92 109 E5
Coventry CV4 132 E3
Kenilworth CV8 148 C8
Knowle B93 128 E5
Lichfield WS14 9 B6
Meriden CV7 91 D1
Perton WV6 23 F4
Royal Leamington Spa CV32 157 C6
Tamworth B77 21 E4
Kenilworth Sch CV8 148 C5
Kenilworth Sch Castle Hall Sixth Form CV8 147 F2
Kenilworth St 20 CV32 156 F1
Kenley Gr B30 104 B3
Kenley Way B91 106 D4
Kenmare Way WV11 26 C4
Kenmore Ave WS12 1 F7
Kenmore Dr LE10 71 B2
Kenmure Rd B33 89 C8
Kennan Ave CV31 161 F6
Kennedy Cl
Kidderminster DY10 116 F3
Sutton Coldfield B72 46 C4
Tamworth B77 21 C1
Kennedy Cres
Darlaston WS10 41 C7
Dudley DY3 50 D4
Kennedy Croft B26 89 A7
Kennedy Ct DY8 80 F5
Kennedy Gr B30 104 B6
Kennedy Rd WV10 163 D4
Kennedy Sq 3 CV32 157 A1
Kenneggy Mews B29 85 F2
Kennerley Rd B25 88 D6
Kennet B77 21 D1
Kennet Cl
Brownhills WS8 6 C2
Coventry CV2 114 C8
Kennet Gr B36 69 F8
Kenneth Gr B23 56 B5
Kennet Ho 5 DY1 61 E8
Kenneth Vincent Cl B97 158 E4
Kennford Cl B65 63 C6
Kennington Rd WV10 25 F5
Kenpas Highway CV3 133 A5
Kenrick Croft B35 57 F2
Kenrick Ho
Birmingham B16 66 A1
West Bromwich B70 53 E1
Kenrick Park Sta B70 53 E1
Kenrick Way B70 64 E8
Kensington Ave B12 87 A4
Kensington Ct
Coventry CV5 113 A1
Nuneaton CV10 72 C6
Kensington Dr
Sutton Coldfield B74 31 F5
Tamworth B79 21 B7
Kensington Gdns
Cannock WS11 1 C2
Stourbridge DY8 60 C1
Kensington Pl
Birmingham B8 67 E5
Cannock WS12 5 C8
Kensington Rd
Birmingham B29 86 B2
Coventry CV5 113 A1
Willenhall WV12 27 B7
Kensington St B19 66 D6
Kenswick Dr B63 83 A2
Kent Ave Fazeley B78 20 F2
Walsall WS2 28 B3
Kent Cl Aldridge WS9 16 B1
Coventry CV3 133 E6
Kidderminster DY10 116 E3
Walsall WS2 28 E5
West Bromwich B71 53 C7
Kent Close Jun & Inf Sch B71 53 B7
Kent Dr LE10 71 F4
Kenthurst Cl CV5 111 C4
Kentish Rd B21 65 C8
Kentmere Cl CV2 96 E2
Kentmere Rd B60 137 C1
Kentmere Twr 4 B23 57 B6
Kenton Ave WV6 24 F4
Kenton Wlk 7 B29 85 F2
Kent Pl Cannock WS12 2 F1
Dudley DY2 62 A6
Kent Rd
Birmingham B45 101 F1
Halesowen B62 83 F5
Stourbridge DY8 80 D7
Wednesbury WS10 42 D4
Willenhall WS2 27 F3
Wolverhampton WV2 39 E7
Kent St N B18 65 F5
Kent's Cl B92 88 F3
Kents Ho B33 69 B2
Kent St Birmingham B5 66 E1
Dudley DY3 50 E5
Walsall WS2 28 E5
Kentwell B79 20 D7
Kenward Croft B17 84 F7
Kenway B47 125 A7
Kenwick Rd B17 85 B4
Kenwood Rd B9 68 B3
Kenwyn Gn CV7 96 B8
Kenyon Cl
Bromsgrove B60 137 A1
Stourbridge DY8 81 A7
Kenyon St B18 164 A4
Kepler B79 20 E7
Keppel St CV1 113 E5
Kerby Rd B23 56 D4
Kererwin Cl B64 63 A1
Keresley Brook Rd CV6 95 A2
Keresley Cl
Coventry CV6 95 A2
Solihull B91 107 C5
Keresley Gr B29 84 F2
Keresley Grange Prim Sch CV6 94 F1
Keresley Green Rd CV6 94 F1
Keresley Newland Prim Sch CV7 94 F7
Keresley Rd CV6 113 A8
Kernthorpe Rd B14 104 D4
Kerr Dr DY4 51 E8
Kerria Ct 3 B15 86 D8
Kerria Ctr B77 22 A4
Kerria Rd B77 22 B4
Kerridge Cl WV9 11 A2
Kerris Way CV3 115 A1
Kerr La B90 126 A6
Kerry Cl Barwell LE9 71 F7
Birmingham B31 102 F6
Brierley Hill DY5 61 C4
Kerry Croft Cl B97 158 E5
Kerry Ct WS1 43 A8
Kerry Hill 3 B60 150 E6
Kerry's Ho 4 CV1 113 B2
Kersley Gdns WV11 26 F5
Kerswell Cl 2 B97 153 B5
Kerswell Dr B90 127 A5
Kesterton Rd B74 31 E5
Kesteven Cl B15 86 B6
Kesteven Rd B71 53 C7
Keston Rd B44 44 F4
Kestrel B77 36 A6
Kestrel Ave B25 88 C8
Kestrel Cl
Birmingham, Castle Vale B35 58 B3
Birmingham, Short Heath B23 56 D6
Hinckley LE10 75 F6
Kidderminster DY10 116 E3
Kestrel Croft 2 CV3 134 F8
Kestrel Ct WS7 7 F8
Kestrel Dr B74 31 F5
Kestrel Gr
Birmingham B30 103 D8
Cannock WS12 2 C1
Willenhall WV12 27 C8
Kestrel Rd Dudley DY1 51 A1
Halesowen B63 82 B7
Oldbury B68 63 F2
Kestrel Rise WV6 24 F7
Kestrel View B60 137 C7
Kestrel Way WS6 4 C2
Keswick Cl CV11 74 A6
Keswick Dr DY6 60 D6
Keswick Gn CV32 156 D1
Keswick Gr B74 30 F8
Keswick Ho 14 B69 63 D5
Keswick Rd B92 89 A4
Keswick Wlk CV2 114 F4
Ketley Croft B12 86 F7
Ketley Fields DY6 61 A5
Ketley Hill Rd DY1 61 F8
Ketley Rd
Kingswinford DY6 60 F6
Kingswinford DY6 60 F7
Kettlebrook Rd
Solihull B90 127 C6
Tamworth B77 21 C3
Kettlehouse Rd B44 44 F3
Kettlesbank Rd DY3 50 B2
Kettles Wood Dr B32 84 C2
Kettlewell Cl CV34 155 E1
Kettlewell Way B37 69 F1
Ketton Gr B33 89 D7
Keviliok St CV3 133 D6
Kew Cl Birmingham B37 69 F3
Kenilworth CV8 148 C5
Kew Dr DY1 51 A2
Kew Gdns B33 68 E1
Kew Ho CV4 111 F3
Kewstoke Cl WV12 13 B1
Kewstoke Croft B31 102 E6
Kewstoke Rd WV12 13 C1
Key Bsns Pk B24 57 D3
Keyes Dr DY6 49 D1
Key Hill B18 66 B5
Key Hill Dr B18 66 B5
Key Ind Pk WV13 26 D3
Keynell Covert B30 104 C2
Keynes Dr WV14 40 E6
Keys Cl WS12 2 C3
Keys Cres B71 53 C6
Keyse Rd B75 46 F7
Keysmith Cl WV13 27 C1
Keys Park Rd WS12 2 E3
Keyte Cl DY4 52 A5
Keyway Jct WV13 41 B8
Keyway Ret Pk WV13 41 B8
Keyway The WV13 41 A8
Keyworth Cl DY4 52 B5
Khyber Cl WS10 41 C8
Kidd Croft DY4 41 C2
Kidderminster Coll DY10 116 E5
Kidderminster General Hospl DY11 116 C5
Kidderminster Railway Mus* DY10 116 F5
Kidderminster Rd
Bromsgrove B61 136 C3
Iverley DY8 98 C7
Kingswinford DY6 60 B7
West Hagley DY9 99 B5
Kidderminster Rd S DY9 98 F3
Kidderminster Sta DY10 116 F5
Kidderminster Town Sta* DY10 116 F5
Kidson Eventide Homes WV6 24 F5
Kielder Cl
Cannock WS12 2 E2
Walsall WS5 43 C3
Kielder Dr CV10 72 E2
Kielder Gdns DY9 81 B1
Kier's Bridge Cl DY4 52 B3
Kilberry Cl LE10 71 A1
Kilburn Dr
Coventry CV5 112 F3
Kingswinford DY6 49 E1
Kilburn Gr B44 44 F3
Kilburn Pl DY2 62 D6
Kilburn Rd B44 44 F3
Kilby Ave B16 66 A2
Kilby Ct CV31 162 A6
Kilbye Cl B77 35 F5
Kilby Gn LE10 75 F6
Kilby Gr CV31 162 C5
Kilbys Gr B20 54 F2
Kilcote Rd B90 105 C2
Kildale Cl CV1 165 D3
Kilderkin Ct CV1 165 C1
Kildwick Way 5 CV34 155 E1
Kilmarie Cl LE10 71 A1
Kilmet Wlk 1 B67 65 A5
Kilmore Croft B36 68 E8
Kilmorie Rd
Birmingham B27 88 C5
Cannock WS11 1 C2
Kiln Cl Nuneaton CV10 72 E3
Royal Leamington Spa CV32 157 A1
Studley B80 159 C4
Kiln Croft B65 63 A4
Kiln La Birmingham B11 88 B6
Solihull B90 126 A5
Kilnsey Gr CV34 155 E1
Kiln Way B78 22 F1
Kilpeck Cl B98 154 F2
Kilsall Ct 12 WV3 25 C4
Kilsby Gr B91 127 C8
Kilvert Rd WS10 42 B2
Kilworth Ho 8 CV32 156 F1
Kimberley B77 35 F7
Kimberley Ave B8 67 E5
Kimberley Cl
Coventry CV5 111 F4
Redditch B98 154 B7
Sutton Coldfield B74 31 A2
Kimberley Pl WV14 51 B7
Kimberley Rd
Baginton CV8 133 F2
Bedworth CV12 78 C4
Smethwick B66 65 A7
Solihull B92 89 A1
Kimberley St WV3 25 A1
Kimberley Wlk B76 58 D6
Kimble Cl CV5 112 B4
Kimble Gr B24 57 D3
Kimbley Rise B71 53 A7
Kimbolton Dr B60 138 A5
Kimmond Ct 21 CV32 156 F1
Kimpton Cl B14 104 E2
Kimsan Croft B74 45 A7
Kinchford Cl B91 127 B8
Kineton Cl B98 154 D1
Kineton Croft B32 102 D8
Kineton Green Prim Sch B92 88 D1
Kineton Green Rd B92 106 D8
Kineton Ho B13 105 A6
Kineton La B90, B94 127 A1
Kineton Rd
Birmingham B45 121 E7
Coventry CV2 114 C6
Kenilworth CV8 148 C4
Sutton Coldfield B73 45 E1
Kineton Rise DY3 39 C2
Kinfare Dr WV6 24 B4
Kinfare Rise DY3 50 E4
King Charles Ave WS2 27 E2
King Charles Cl DY11 116 C6
King Charles Ct B44 45 B2
King Charles I Sch DY10 117 A5
King Charles Prim Sch WS2 27 F2
King Charles Rd B62 83 F4
King Charles Sq 4 DY10 116 E6
King David Jun & Inf Sch B13 86 F2
King Edmund St 1 DY1 51 B2
King Edward Ave B61 136 F5
King Edward Rd
Birmingham B13 86 F3
Bromsgrove B61 136 F5
Coventry CV1 113 F4
Nuneaton CV11 73 D4
King Edwards Cl B20 66 B8
King Edwards Gdns B20 66 B7
King Edwards Rd B1 66 B2
King Edward's Row WV2 163 B1
King Edward's Sch B15 86 A4
King Edward's Sq B73 46 B5
King Edward St WS10 41 D6
King Edwards Wharf B16 66 B2
King Edward VI Aston Sch B6 66 F8
King Edward VI Camp Hill Sch For Boys B14 104 D7
King Edward VI Camp Hill Sch For Girls B14 104 D7
King Edward VI Coll
Nuneaton CV11 73 D4
Stourbridge DY8 81 A6
King Edward VI Five Ways Sch B32 102 C8
King Edward VI Handsworth Sch B21 66 A7
King Edward VI High Sch for Girls B15 86 A4
King Edward VI Sch WS14 9 C6
Kingfield Ind Est CV1 113 C6
Kingfield Rd
Coventry CV1, CV6 113 D7
Solihull B90 105 C2
Kingfisher B77 36 A6
Kingfisher Ave CV10 72 C5
Kingfisher Cl
Birmingham B26 89 A6
Brownhills WS8 15 E7
Sedgley DY3 39 C2
Kingfisher Ct
Alvechurch B48 139 A7
Burntwood WS7 7 F8
Hinckley LE10 74 F6
Kingfisher Dr
Birmingham B36 70 A8
Cannock WS12 2 C5
Stourbridge DY8 80 C4
Kingfisher Ent Pk B98 154 A3
Kingfisher Gr
Kidderminster DY10 117 B3
Willenhall WV12 27 C8
Kingfisher Ind Est B70 52 F4
Kingfisher Prim Sch B36 70 A8
Kingfisher Rd B23 56 C7
Kingfisher Sh Ctr 2 B97 153 E3
Kingfisher Sq B97 153 D4
Kingfisher View B34 69 A5
Kingfisher Way B30 103 D8
Kingfisher Wlk B97 153 D4
King George Ave B61 136 F4
King George Cl B61 136 F4
King George Cres WS4 29 B6
King George Pl WS4 29 B6

King George's Ave
Bedworth CV12........ **78** B5
Coventry CV6 ...... **95** F2
King George's Way
LE10 .... **75** B7
King George VI Ave
WS5 .... **29** C1
King George V Prim Sch
B70............. **53** D3
Kingham Cl
Dudley DY3 .... **50** C2
Redditch B98 ...... **154** F4
Kingham Covert
B14 .... **104** D2
King Henry VIII Sch
CV3............. **165** A1
Kingland Dr CV32 ... **156** C1
Kingmead Ho B14.... **104** D4
King Richard Rd LE10 **71** C2
King Richard St CV2. **113** F3
Kings Ave WS12.....**2** C4
King's Ave B69...... **52** B2
Kingsbridge Ho B23.. **56** B6
Kingsbridge Rd
Birmingham B32...... **84** D1
Nuneaton CV10...... **73** D6
Kingsbridge Wlk 6
B66 .... **65** B5
Kingsbrook Dr B91.. **127** B8
Kings Bsns Pk B44....**44** E3
Kingsbury Ave B24 ... **57** D3
Kingsbury Bsns Pk
B76............**58** E6
Kingsbury Cl
Minworth B76........ **58** D5
Walsall WS4 .... **29** B4
Kingsbury Rd
Birmingham B35, B76.. **58** B5
Birmingham, Birches Green
B24........... **57** B3
Birmingham, Tyburn B24,
B35............ **57** E3
Coventry CV6 ...... **112** E5
Curdworth B76 ..... **59** B6
Minworth B76....... **58** D5
2 Tipton DY4 .... **52** A8
Kingsbury Sch & Sports
Coll B24 .... **57** A2
Kings Centre B23....**56** E3
King's CE Sch The
WV6............**24** B5
Kings Cl B14 ...... **104** C6
Kingsclere Wlk WV4.. **38** C6
Kingscliff Rd B10.. **88** A8
Kingscote Cl B98... **154** D7
Kingscote Gr CV3... **133** A4
Kingscote Rd
Birmingham B15...... **85** E6
Dorridge B93 ...... **127** E2
Kings Croft
Birmingham, Castle
Bromwich B36 ...... **69** F7
Birmingham, Sheldon
B26............. **89** A5
Cannock WS12 ....**2** E4
Kingscroft Cl B74.. **45** A8
Kingscroft Rd B74.. **45** A8
Kings Ct
Stourbridge DY8..... **80** E5
Sutton Coldfield B75... **32** B3
Tipton DY4 .... **52** A4
King's Ct CV11 ..... **73** B4
Kingsdene Ave DY6... **60** C4
Kingsdown Ave B42.. **55** A6
Kingsdown Rd B31... **84** F1
Kingsfield Cl B36... **58** D1
Kingsford Ct B92... **89** B3
Kingsford Nouveau
DY6 .... **61** A5
Kingsford Rd CV6 ... **113** C7
Kingsgate Ho B37... **70** A2
Kings Gdn B30 ..... **103** E4
Kings Gdns CV12.... **78** C2
Kings Gr CV2 ...... **114** B3
Kings Green Ave
B38 .... **103** F2
Kings Hall 2 B13 ... **87** A2
Kingshayes Rd WS9 .. **16** B1
Kings Heath Boys
Mathematics and
Computing Coll
B13............. **105** A6
Kings Heath Jun Sch
B14............**86** E1
King's High Sch for Girls
The CV34 .... **160** E7
Kings Hill Cl WS10... **41** E5

King's Hill Day Hospl
WS10..............**41** E5
Kingshill Dr B38 .... **103** F2
King's Hill Field WS10 **41** E5
King's Hill La CV3 ... **133** B2
Kings Hill Mews
WS10 .... **41** D5
Kings Hill Pk Ind Est
WS10..............**41** E5
King's Hill Prim Sch
WS10..............**41** E5
Kings Ho B24 ...... **57** A4
Kingsholm Cl CV3... **115** B1
Kingshurst CV31 .... **162** E6
Kingshurst Ho B37...**69** F5
Kingshurst Inf Sch
B37.............. **70** A6
Kingshurst Jun Sch
B37.............. **70** A6
Kingshurst Rd
Birmingham B31...... **103** A3
Solihull B90...... **105** F1
Kingshurst Way B37...**69** F5
Kingsland Ave CV5... **112** F2
Kingsland Dr B93... **127** E4
Kingsland Prim Sch
B44..............**44** F4
Kingsland Rd
Birmingham B44...... **44** F4
Wolverhampton WV1... **25** B3
Kingslea B73.........**45** F1
Kingslea Rd B91 .... **106** E2
Kingsleigh Croft B75 . **32** B2
Kingsleigh Dr B36... **69** A8
Kingsleigh Rd B20 ... **55** B2
Kingsley Ave
Cannock WS12 ....**2** C7
Redditch B98 ...... **154** A3
Wolverhampton WV6 ... **24** B4
Kingsley Bank Way
B26 .... **89** B7
Kingsley Cl B79...... **21** A6
Kingsley Coll B98... **159** C6
Kingsley Cres CV12... **79** B3
Kingsley Ct
Binley Woods CV3.... **135** D6
Birmingham B25...... **88** E8
Kingsley Gr DY3..... **50** A5
Kingsley Prep Sch
B93............. **128** A4
Kingsley Rd
Birmingham, Balsall Heath
B12........... **87** A4
Birmingham, King's Norton
B30............ **103** D4
Kingswinford DY6..... **60** C5
Kingsley Sch The
CV32............. **156** F1
Kingsley St
Dudley DY2 .... **62** C5
Walsall WS2 .... **42** B7
Kingsley Terr CV2 ... **114** E8
Kingsley Wlk CV2 ... **114** F7
Kingslow Ave WV4... **38** D6
Kings Mdw CV10 .... **72** A3
King's Mdw DY9 ..... **99** E3
Kingsmead Mews
CV3 .... **134** D6
Kingsmead Tech Coll
WS12............**2** C4
Kingsmere Cl B24....**56** F2
Kings Mews WS14......**9** B5
King's Norton Boys Sch
B30............. **103** C4
Kings Norton Bsns Ctr
B30............. **104** A4
King's Norton Girls Sch
B30............. **103** F5
Kings Norton High Sch
B38............. **123** F8
King's Norton Prim Sch
B30............. **104** A2
King's Norton Sta
B30............. **103** F4
Kingsoak Gdns DY2 .. **62** E7
Kings Par B4 ...... **164** C2
Kings Park Dr CV3 .. **115** B1
Kingspiece Ho 6 B36 **68** E8
Kings Rd
Birmingham, Stirchley
B14........... **104** C6
Birmingham, Stockland
Green B23 .... **56** D4
Birmingham, Tyseley
B11........... **88** A6
Sedgley DY3 .... **50** E8
Sutton Coldfield B44,
B73........... **45** B2
Walsall WS4 ...... **29** C7

King's Rd
Birmingham B44...... **44** E3
Kidderminster DY11 .. **116** C6
King's Rise Com Prim
Sch B44 .... **45** A2
Kings Road Ind Est
B25............. **88** A6
Kings Sq WV14...... **51** A8
King St Bedworth CV12 **78** C2
Bilston WV14 .... **40** E3
Birmingham B11...... **87** A7
Brierley Hill DY5..... **82** A8
Brownhills WS9 ..... **15** F2
Burntwood WS7 ......**6** C5
Cradley Heath B64 ... **62** F1
Darlaston WS10 ..... **41** D6
Dudley DY2 .... **51** C1
Dudley, The Coppice
WV14.......... **51** A8
Halesowen B63....... **83** A4
2 Hinckley LE10 .... **71** D1
Royal Leamington Spa
CV32.......... **157** A1
Smethwick B66...... **65** B7
Stourbridge DY8 .... **80** E6
Stourbridge, Lye DY9 .. **81** F5
Tamworth B79...... **21** B5
Walsall WS1 ...... **42** D7
Wednesbury WS10 ... **41** E3
6 Willenhall WV13 ... **27** B2
Wolverhampton WV1 . **163** C3
Kingstanding Ctr B44 **44** F3
Kingstanding Rd B44. **55** F7
Kingstanding Sch
B44..............**44** E1
Kings Terr B14 ..... **104** D6
Kingsthorne Prim Sch
B44.............. **45** A1
Kingsthorpe Rd B14. **105** A3
Kingston Arc WS11.....**1** E1
Kingston Cl B79...... **21** C7
Kingston Ct
17 Birmingham, Selly Oak
B29............. **103** C7
Sutton Coldfield B74... **46** B7
Kingston Ctr PRU
WV6..............**24** F5
Kingston Dr LE10..... **71** E4
Kingston Ho CV12.... **95** C8
Kingston Ind Est B9 ..**67** B1
Kingston Mews
CV31 .... **162** C6
Kingston Rd
Birmingham B9........ **67** B1
Coventry CV5 ...... **112** F2
Sutton Coldfield B75... **46** F6
Kingston Row B1 .... **66** C2
Kingston Way DY6.... **60** C7
King Street Pas
Brierley Hill DY5..... **82** A8
2 Dudley DY2 ...... **51** D1
Kingsway
Birmingham B68...... **84** B7
Cannock WS11 ....**2** A4
Coventry CV2 ...... **114** A3
Essington WV11 .... **13** A4
Nuneaton CV11..... **73** B4
Royal Leamington Spa
CV31............. **161** F6
Kingsway Ave 8 DY4. **52** A8
Kingsway Com Prim Sch
CV31............. **161** F6
Kingsway Dr B38... **103** F2
Kingsway Ho CV12 ... **78** C2
Kingsway Rd WV10... **26** A6
Kingswear Ave WV6...**23** F3
Kingswinford Rd DY1..**61** F7
Kingswinford Sch The
DY6.............. **60** D7
Kingswood Ave
Cannock WS11 ....**4** C7
Corley CV7 ...... **94** B8
Kingswood Cl
Coventry CV6 ...... **95** D1
Kingswood B94...... **144** E5
Solihull B90...... **106** D1
Kingswood Colliery Cvn
Site WS6 ....**5** A4
Kingswood Cotts
B94............. **144** D3
Kingswood Croft B7...**67** C7
Kingswood Dr
Birmingham B30..... **104** C3
Great Wyrley WS6......**5** A4
Norton Canes WS11.....**5** F5
Sutton Coldfield B74... **44** F5
Kingswood Gdns
Nuneaton CV10...... **72** B4

Kingswood Gdns continued
Wolverhampton WV4 .. **38** F6
Kingswood Ho B14.. **104** E2
Kingswood Rd
Birmingham, Coft Common
B31........... **122** F7
Birmingham, Moseley
B13........... **87** A4
Kingswinford DY6..... **60** C4
Nuneaton CV10...... **72** B4
Kingswood Sch B90 **106** B2
Kington Cl WV12..... **27** B8
Kington Gdns B37.....**69** F2
Kington Way B33..... **68** E1
King William St
Coventry CV1 ...... **113** E4
Stourbridge DY8 ..... **80** F8
Kiniths Cres B71..... **53** E5
Kiniths Way
Halesowen B62...... **63** E1
West Bromwich B71... **53** E4
Kinlet Cl
Redditch B98 ...... **154** E3
Wolverhampton WV3 .. **38** A8
Kinlet Gr B31...... **103** C2
Kinloch Dr DY1......**50** F3
Kinnerley St WS1 .... **29** A1
Kinnersley Cl B98... **154** E3
Kinnersley Cres B69.. **63** D5
Kinnerton Cres B29...**84** F2
Kinross Ave WS12......**1** F7
Kinross Cl CV10.....**72** F2
Kinross Cres B43..... **44** B4
Kinross Rd CV32.... **157** B4
Kinross Way LE10 ... **71** A1
Kinsall Gn B77...... **36** C6
Kinsey Gr B14...... **104** F4
Kinsham Dr B91..... **127** B8
Kintore Croft B32... **102** A7
Kintyre Cl
Birmingham B45...... **101** E1
Hinckley LE10 ...... **71** B1
Kintyre The CV2 .... **115** B7
Kinver Ave
Kidderminster DY11 .. **116** A1
Willenhall WV12 ..... **27** B5
Kinver Cl CV2 ...... **96** E1
Kinver Cres WS9 .... **16** C1
Kinver Croft
Birmingham B12...... **86** E7
Sutton Coldfield B76... **58** A8
Kinver Ct B11...... **87** D4
Kinver Dr Hagley DY9 . **99** C7
Wolverhampton WV4 .. **38** C5
Kinver Rd B31...... **103** D2
Kinver St DY8...... **60** E1
Kinwalsey La CV7 ....**92** F6
Kinwarton Cl B26.... **88** D6
Kipling Ave
Dudley WV14 .... **40** B1
Warwick CV34 ...... **160** C4
Kipling Cl
Nuneaton CV10...... **72** A5
Tipton DY4 .... **52** A8
Kipling Rd
Birmingham B30..... **103** C4
Coventry CV6 ...... **113** A8
Dudley DY3 .... **50** A5
Willenhall WV12 ..... **27** E8
Wolverhampton WV10 . **11** D2
Kipling Rise B79..... **20** D8
Kipling Wlk 3 DY10. **117** B6
Kirby Ave CV34..... **155** F1
Kirby Cl Bilston WV14.. **40** E3
Brandon CV8........ **135** F5
Coventry CV1 ...... **113** D6
Kirby Cnr CV4...... **132** B5
Kirby Corner Rd CV4 **132** B6
Kirby Dr DY1...... **50** E3
Kirby Rd
Birmingham B18...... **65** E6
Coventry CV5 ...... **112** F2
Kirfield Dr LE10......**71** F3
Kirkby Gn B73...... **46** B3
Kirkdale Ave CV6..... **95** D3
Kirkham Gdns DY5... **61** C6
Kirkham Gr B33......**68** F4
Kirkham Way DY4.... **52** A5
Kirkland Way B78.... **34** B8
Kirkside Gr WS8..... **15** F7
Kirkstall Cl WS3..... **13** F2
Kirkstall Cres WS3 ... **13** F2
Kirkstone Cres
Birmingham B43...... **54** F6
Wombourne WV5 ..... **49** A6
Kirkstone Ct DY5..... **81** B8
Kirkstone Rd CV12 ... **78** A2
Kirkstone Way DY5... **81** B8
Kirkstone Wlk CV11 .. **74** A6
Kirkwall Rd B32..... **84** D1

Kirkwood Ave B23....**56** F7
Kirmond Wlk WV6.... **25** C5
Kirstead Gdns WV6... **24** E3
Kirtley B77......... **21** E2
Kirton Cl Coventry CV6 .**94** F1
Whitnash CV31 ..... **162** B3
Kirton Gr
Birmingham B33..... **69** A4
Solihull B91...... **107** A1
Wolverhampton WV6 .. **24** C4
Kitchener Rd
Birmingham B29..... **86** B1
Coventry CV6 ...... **113** E8
Dudley DY2 .... **51** F1
Kitchener St B66..... **65** D6
Kitchen La
Wednesfield WV11 ... **26** F8
Wolverhampton WV11 . **12** F1
Kitebrook Cl
Redditch B98 ...... **154** E4
Solihull B90...... **127** A7
Kite La B97 ...... **153** A5
Kites Cl CV34 ..... **155** E2
Kites Nest La CV35.. **146** C1
Kitsland Rd B34..... **69** E6
Kitswell Gdns B32... **102** A8
Kittermaster Rd CV7 . **92** C1
Kittiwake Dr
Brierley Hill DY5..... **81** D7
Kidderminster DY10 .. **117** B3
Kittoe Rd B74....... **32** A3
Kitt's Green Rd B33 .. **69** B3
Kitwell La B32...... **102** A8
Kitwell Prim Sch
B32............. **102** A7
Kitwood Ave B78......**36** F6
Kitwood Dr B92..... **107** D7
Kixley La B93...... **128** C6
Klaxon Ind Est B11....**87** F4
Klevedon Cl CV11 .... **74** A1
Knapton Cl LE10 .... **71** A3
Knaresdale Cl DY5 ... **81** B8
Knaves Castle Ave WS8.**6** F2
Knebley Cres CV10 ... **73** C1
Knebworth Cl B44.... **55** E8
Knibbs The CV34.... **160** E7
Knight Ave CV1 ..... **113** E1
Knightcote Dr
Royal Leamington Spa
CV32.......... **161** E8
Solihull B91...... **127** B8
Knight Ct B75...... **47** C5
Knight Ho B13 ..... **105** D7
Knightley Cl CV32... **157** E5
Knightley Rd B91 ... **106** F2
Knightlow Ave CV3.. **134** C6
Knightlow Cl CV8 ... **148** C3
Knightlow Rd B17.... **85** B8
Knighton Cl B74..... **31** F3
Knighton Ct B23 .... **56** C2
Knighton Dr B74..... **31** F3
Knighton Rd
Birmingham B31...... **103** C4
Cannock WS12 ....**2** E3
Dudley DY2 .... **62** D4
Sutton Coldfield B74... **31** D5
Knights Ave WV6..... **24** E6
Knightsbridge Ave
CV12 .... **78** C4
Knightsbridge Cl B74. **31** F4
Knightsbridge Ct B37 .**69** F5
Knightsbridge La
WV12 .... **27** C6
Knightsbridge Rd
B92 .... **89** A1
Knights Cl
Birmingham B23..... **56** E2
Hinckley LE10 ...... **75** D4
3 Willenhall WV13 ... **27** B2
Knights Cres WV6.... **24** E7
Knights Ct
Birmingham B37...... **90** E8
Hinckley LE10 ...... **74** E8
Norton Canes WS11.....**6** A4
Warwick CV34 ...... **160** D6
Knightsfield Cl B73... **45** C3
Knightsford Cl B97.. **152** F2
Knights Hill WS9 .... **30** B3
Knights Rd B11...... **88** A4
Knights Templar Way
CV4 .... **112** A1
Knightstone Ave B18.. **66** A4
Knights Wood Cl B75. **46** D7
Knightwick Cres B23. **56** C5
Knipersley Rd B73.... **57** A7
Knoll Cl WS7.........**7** A5
Knollcroft 4 B16.... **66** A2
Knoll Croft
Aldridge WS9 .... **16** C1
Cheswick Green B90 . **126** D4

Knoll Croft continued
Coventry CV3 ...... **133** C6
Knoll Dr
Coventry CV3 ...... **133** C6
Warwick CV34 ...... **155** E1
Knoll Sch The DY11 . **116** A7
Knoll The
Birmingham B32...... **84** C1
Kingswinford DY6..... **60** C5
Knott Ct 11 DY5 .... **61** D2
Knottesford Cl B80.. **159** C3
Knotting Way CV3... **114** C1
Knottsall La B68..... **64** A4
Knotts Farm Rd DY6.. **61** A4
Knowesley Cl B60... **137** E6
Knowlands Rd B90 .. **127** A6
Knowle CE Prim Sch
B93............. **128** C6
Knowle Cl
Birmingham B45..... **122** D7
Redditch B98 ...... **154** C6
Knowle Hill CV8..... **148** C6
Knowle Hill Rd DY2... **62** B4
Knowle La WS14.......**9** B3
Knowle Rd
Birmingham B11...... **87** D3
Eastcote B92....... **108** E2
Rowley Regis B65.... **63** A4
Knowles Ave CV10.... **72** C4
Knowles Dr B74...... **46** A7
Knowles Rd WV1.....**25** F1
Knowles St WS10.... **42** A3
Knowle Wood Rd
B93............. **128** B3
Knox Cres CV11......**73** F8
Knox Rd WV2....... **39** D6
Knox's Grave La WS14,
B78............. **19** D7
Knoyle Ct 1 DY8.....**80** F6
Knutswood Cl B13 .. **105** D7
Kohima Dr DY8...... **80** E5
Kossuth Rd WV14 .... **40** A1
Kurtus B77 .... **35** D6
Kwikform Bldg CV6...**95** E4
Kyle Cl WV10........ **11** B1
Kyles Way B32...... **102** B7
Kynaston Cres WV8 .. **10** B2
Kynaston Ho B71.... **53** C8
Kyngsford Rd B33.... **69** C8
Kynner Way CV3 ... **135** B8
Kynoch Wks B6 .....**55** F3
Kyotts Lake Rd B11.. **87** B7
Kyotts Lake Unit Factory
B11...............**87** B7
Kyrwicks La B11..... **87** A7
Kyter La B36........ **69** B8

L

Laburnham Ct WS14....**9** C5
Laburnham Rd DY6... **60** E6
Laburnum Ave
Birmingham B37...... **69** F6
Cannock WS11 ....**4** E7
Coventry CV6 ...... **112** F5
Kenilworth CV8...... **148** C4
Smethwick B67...... **64** E4
Tamworth B79...... **21** B8
Laburnum Cl
Bedworth CV12...... **77** B3
Birmingham B37...... **69** F6
Cannock WS11 ....**4** E7
Hollywood B47...... **125** A5
Redditch B98 ...... **153** C4
Stourbridge DY8 .... **80** E7
Walsall WS3 .... **15** A2
Laburnum Cotts B21.. **65** E8
Laburnum Croft B69 .. **52** B2
Laburnum Dr
Sutton Coldfield B76... **47** A3
Whitnash CV31 ..... **162** B3
Laburnum Gr
Birmingham B13...... **86** F3
Bromsgrove B61..... **136** F4
Burntwood WS7 ......**6** F6
Kidderminster DY11 .. **116** B8
Nuneaton CV10...... **72** B5
Warwick CV34 ...... **156** B1
Willenhall WS2 ..... **27** F3
Laburnum Ho WS4 ... **15** D1
Laburnum Rd
Bilston WV1 .... **40** B8
Birmingham B30..... **103** F8
Brownhills WS9 ..... **16** A3
Dudley DY1 .... **51** C4
Tipton DY4 .... **51** F7
Walsall WS5 .... **43** C4
Wednesbury WS10 ... **42** B4
Wolverhampton WV4 .. **39** F3

Laburnum St
  Stourbridge DY8 ...... 80 E7
  Wolverhampton WV3 .. 25 B1
Laburnum Trees B47 124 F7
Laburnum Villas **2**
  B11 .... 87 C5
Laburnum Way B31 . 103 A1
Laceby Gr B13 ...... 87 D1
Lacell Cl CV34 ..... 155 E1
Ladbroke Dr B76 ..... 46 F2
Ladbroke Gr B27 .. 106 C8
Ladbroke Pk CV34 .. 155 E1
Ladbrook Cl B98 ... 158 E7
Ladbrook Gr DY3 .... 50 B3
Ladbrook Rd
  Coventry CV5 ...... 112 A4
  Solihull B91 ...... 107 C2
Ladbury Gr WS5 ..... 43 A4
Ladbury Rd WS5 .... 43 A3
Ladeler Gr B33 ..... 69 E2
Ladies Wlk DY3 ..... 50 D8
Lady Bank
  Birmingham B32 ... 102 B7
  Tamworth B79 .... 21 B4
Lady Bracknell Mews
  B31 .... 103 C4
Lady Brades Ho **5**
  B69 .... 64 A7
Lady Byron La B93 . 127 F8
Ladycroft
  5 Birmingham B16 ... 66 B2
  Cubbington CV32 .... 157 E5
Ladyfields Way CV6 . 95 B4
Lady Grey Ave CV34 . 161 E3
Lady Grey's Wlk DY8 . 80 D5
Ladygrove Cl B98 .. 159 A8
Lady Harriet's La
  B98 .... 153 F4
Lady Katherine Leveson
  CE Sch B93 .... 129 B5
Lady La Coventry CV6 . 95 F4
  Earlswood B90, B94 . 126 B3
  Kenilworth CV8 ..... 147 F4
Lady Lane Mobile Home
  Pk CV6 .... 95 F4
Lady Meadow Dr CV6 . 95 B2
Lady Moor Rd WV14 . 40 C3
Ladymoor Rd WV14 . 40 C3
Ladypool Ave **3** B11 . 87 B6
Ladypool Cl
  Halesowen B62 ..... 83 C4
  Walsall WS4 .... 29 A5
Ladypool Rd B11, B12 . 87 A5
Ladypool Sch B11 ... 87 B6
Ladysmith Rd B63 .. 82 C6
Lady Warwick Ave
  CV12 .... 78 D2
Ladywell Cl WV5 .... 49 A8
Ladywell Wlk B5 ... 164 C1
Ladywood Cl DY5 ... 61 F2
Ladywood Middleway
  B16 .... 66 A2
Ladywood Rd
  Birmingham B16 .... 66 A1
  Sutton Coldfield B74 . 46 A8
Laertes Gr CV34 ... 161 F2
Laggan Cl CV10 ..... 72 C5
Lagonda B77 .... 21 E3
Lagrange B79 ...... 20 E6
Laing Ho **2** B69 ..... 63 D5
Lair The B78 .... 36 F8
Lake Ave WS5 ...... 43 C7
Lake Cl WS5 .... 43 C7
Lakedown Cl B14 ... 104 E1
Lakefield B31 ...... 102 F4
Lakefield Cl B28 ... 106 B7
Lakefield Rd WV11 .. 26 E5
Lakehouse Ct B23 .. 56 E8
Lakehouse Gr B38 .. 103 D3
Lakehouse Rd B73 .. 56 F8
Lakeland Dr B77 ... 36 B7
Lakeland Ho CV34 .. 161 A7
Lakenheath B79 .... 21 C7
Laker Cl DY5 .... 81 A7
Lakes Cl DY11 ..... 116 C7
Lakeside
  Bedworth CV12 ..... 78 A2
  Redditch B97 ..... 152 D7
  Sutton Coldfield B74 . 31 B5
Lakeside Cl WV13 .. 26 E3
Lakeside Ct
  Birmingham B20 .... 55 A4
  Brierley Hill DY5 ... 81 B8
Lakeside Dr
  Birmingham B23 ... 56 B6
  Norton Canes WS11 .. 6 B6
  Solihull B90 ...... 126 F7
Lakeside Ind Est
  B98 .... 154 B3
Lakeside Pk B78 ... 20 F1

Lakeside Prim Sch
  Tamworth B77 ...... 21 E2
  Willenhall WV13 .... 26 E3
Lakeside Rd B70 .... 53 A6
Lakeside Wlk B23 ... 56 C3
Lakes Rd B23 ...... 56 A6
Lake St DY3 .... 50 D3
Lakes The B94 .... 141 F8
Lakeview B43 ...... 44 B2
Lake View Rd CV5 . 112 F4
Lakewood Dr B45 .. 102 B1
Lakey La B28 ...... 106 B7
Lakey Lane Jun & Inf Sch
  B28 .... 106 B7
Lakin Ct CV34 ..... 160 F8
Lakin Ho CV34 .... 160 F8
Lakin Rd CV34 ..... 160 F8
Lambah Cl WV14 .... 40 F7
Lamb Cl B34 .... 69 E5
Lambert Cl B23 .... 56 D6
Lambert Ct
  Kingswinford DY6 ... 60 D8
  Warwick CV34 ..... 160 D6
Lambert Dr WS7 ..... 7 A8
Lambert End B70 ... 53 B3
Lambert Fold **4** DY2 . 62 E8
Lambert Rd WV10 ... 25 F6
Lambert St B70 .... 53 B3
Lambeth Cl
  Birmingham B37 .... 70 B4
  Coventry CV2 ..... 114 E7
Lambeth Rd
  Bilston WV14 ...... 40 B7
  Birmingham B44 .... 44 E3
Lambourn Cl WS3 ... 14 C2
Lambourn Cres
  CV31 .... 162 C6
Lambourne Cl
  Coventry CV5 ..... 112 A4
  Great Wyrley WS6 ... 4 F3
  4 Lichfield WS14 ..... 9 E8
Lambourne Gr B37 .. 69 E2
Lambourne Way
  Brierley Hill DY5 ... 81 B8
  Norton Canes WS11 .. 6 A5
Lambourn Rd
  Birmingham B23 .... 56 D4
  Willenhall WV13 .... 27 D1
Lambscote Cl B90 . 105 C2
Lamb St CV1 ...... 165 B3
Lamerton Cl CV2 .. 114 C6
Lamford Cl LE10 .... 71 B1
Lamintone Dr CV32 . 156 F2
Lammas Cl B92 ..... 89 C1
Lammas Croft CV31 . 162 A3
Lammas Ct CV34 ... 160 D6
Lammas Ho **6** CV6 . 113 A4
Lammas Rd
  Coventry CV6 ..... 112 F4
  Stourbridge DY8 ... 60 C3
Lammas Wlk CV34 . 160 D7
Lammermoor Ave
  B43 .... 43 F2
Lamont Ave B32 .... 84 F3
Lamorna Cl
  Nuneaton CV11 ..... 73 F4
  Wolverhampton WV3 . 38 B8
Lamprey B77 .... 35 D6
Lanark Cl DY6 ...... 60 F5
Lanark Croft B35 ... 57 F3
Lancaster Ave
  Aldridge WS9 ...... 30 B8
  Birmingham B45 ... 122 A8
  Wednesbury WS10 ... 42 C3
Lancaster Circus
  Queensway B4 .... 164 C4
Lancaster Cl B30 .. 104 A6
Lancaster Dr B35 ... 58 B2
Lancaster Gdns WV4 . 38 E5
Lancaster Ho
  Cannock WS12 ...... 2 D1
  7 Rowley Regis B65 . 63 E4
  5 Stourbridge DY8 ... 80 F8
Lancaster Pl
  Kenilworth CV8 .... 147 E2
  Walsall WS3 .... 14 C2
Lancaster Rd
  Brierley Hill DY5 ... 61 C2
  Hinckley LE10 ...... 75 D8
Lancaster St B4 ... 164 C4
Lance Cl LE10 ...... 75 D5
Lancelot Cl B8 ..... 67 E3
Lancelot Ho DY10 . 117 C8
Lancelot Pl B70 .... 52 E4
Lanchester Cl B79 .. 20 E7
Lanchester Rd
  Birmingham B38 .. 104 A1
  Coventry CV6 ..... 113 B6
Lanchester Way B36 . 58 F1
Lancia Cl CV6 ...... 96 B4

Lancing Rd CV12 ... 79 C2
Lander Cl B45 ..... 122 A6
Landgate Rd B21 ... 54 C2
Land La B37 .... 90 A7
Land Oak Dr DY10 . 117 B7
Landor Ho CV31 ... 162 A2
Landor Rd
  Dorridge B93 ..... 128 A6
  Redditch B98 ..... 154 A1
  Warwick CV34 ..... 160 D8
  Whitnash CV31 .... 162 A3
Landor St B8 .... 67 B3
Landport Rd WV2 ... 39 F8
Landrail Wlk B36 ... 70 A8
Landrake Rd DY6 ... 61 A5
Landsberg B79 ..... 20 F6
Landsdown Pl **2** B18 . 66 A5
Landseer Dr LE10 ... 71 B3
Landseer Gr B43 .... 44 D4
Landsgate DY8 ..... 81 A1
Landswood Cl B44 .. 45 A1
Landswood Rd B68 . 64 C4
Landywood Ent Pk
  WS6 .... 13 F8
Landywood Gn WS6 .. 4 E2
Landywood La WS6 .. 4 E2
Landywood Prim Sch
  WS6 .... 13 F8
Landywood Sta WS6 . 4 F2
Lane Ave WS2 ...... 28 B3
Lane Cl WS2 .... 28 B3
Lane Croft B76 ..... 58 A8
Lane Ct **8** WV3 .... 25 C4
Lane Green Ave WV8 . 10 C1
Lane Green Ct WV8 . 10 B3
Lane Green Fst Sch
  WV8 .... 10 B4
Lane Green Rd WV8 . 10 C2
Lane Green Rd
  Maisonettes WV8 ... 10 B3
Lane Green Sh Par
  WV8 .... 10 B3
Lane Rd WV4 ...... 40 A3
Lanesfield Dr WV4 .. 40 A4
Lanesfield Drive Ind Est
  WV4 .... 40 A4
Lanesfield Jun & Inf Sch
  WV4 .... 40 A4
Laneside CV3 ..... 134 E6
Laneside Ave B74 .. 44 F7
Laneside Dr LE10 ... 71 F3
Laneside Gdns WS2 . 28 B2
Lanfear Ct LE10 .... 75 C7
Langbank Ave CV3 . 134 D7
Langbay Ct CV2 ... 114 F6
Langcliffe Ave CV34 . 156 F1
Langcomb Rd B90 . 126 A8
Langdale Ave CV6 .. 95 D3
Langdale Cl
  Brownhills WS8 ..... 15 E6
  Royal Leamington Spa
  CV32 .... 157 D3
Langdale Croft B21 . 65 E7
Langdale Ct B77 ... 22 A6
Langdale Dr
  Bilston WV14 ...... 40 D7
  Cannock WS11 .... 4 C7
  Nuneaton CV11 ..... 74 A6
Langdale Gn WS11 .. 4 C7
Langdale Rd
  Birmingham B43 .... 54 F7
  Hinckley LE10 ...... 75 A8
Langdale Way DY9 .. 81 D4
Langdon St B9 ..... 67 B2
Langdon Wlk B27 ... 88 E4
Langfield Rd B93 .. 128 A7
Langford Ave B43 ... 54 E8
Langford Cl WS1 ... 29 A1
Langford Croft B91 . 107 C2
Langford Gr B17 ... 85 C3
Langham Cl B26 .... 89 A7
Langham Gn WV2 ... 30 F1
Langholm Dr
  Birmingham B44 .... 45 D1
  Cannock WS12 ...... 2 C1
Langland Dr DY3 ... 50 C8
Langley Ave WV14 .. 51 C8
Langley Cl
  Brownhills WS9 ..... 16 A3
  Redditch B98 ..... 154 D1
Langley Cres B68 ... 64 B4
Langley Croft CV4 . 112 A2
Langley Dr B35 ..... 58 A1
Langley Gdns
  Oldbury B68 .... 64 B4
  Wolverhampton WV3 . 38 D7
Langley Gr B10 .... 87 D8

Langley Green Rd
  B69 .... 64 A4
Langley Green Sta
  B68 .... 64 B5
Langley Hall Dr B75 . 47 B5
Langley Hall Rd
  Solihull B92 ...... 106 C7
  Sutton Coldfield B75 . 47 A5
Langley Heath Dr B76 47 A3
Langley High Sch B68 64 C4
Langley High St B69 . 64 A5
Langley Mede B68 .. 64 B5
Langley Park Way
  B75 .... 46 F6
Langley Prim Sch
  Oldbury B69 .... 64 A4
  Solihull B92 ...... 106 D6
Langley Rd
  Birmingham B10 .... 87 D8
  Oldbury B68 .... 64 B4
  Whitnash CV31 .... 162 A4
  Wolverhampton WV3,
  WV4 .... 38 B7
Langley Rise B92 ... 89 D3
Langley Sch B92 .. 106 D7
Langley Specl Sch
  B75 .... 47 A6
Langleys Rd B29 ... 85 E1
Langley Wlk B37 ... 70 D2
Langlodge Rd CV6 .. 95 B2
Langmead Cl WS2 .. 27 D3
Langnor Rd CV2 ... 114 C6
Langsett Rd WV10 .. 25 E4
Langstone Rd
  Birmingham B14 .. 105 A3
  Dudley DY1 .... 50 F1
Langton Cl
  Birmingham B36 .... 70 B6
  Coventry CV3 ..... 134 E8
Langton Ct **1** WS13 .. 3 A1
Langton Pl WV14 ... 41 A6
Langton Rd B8 ..... 67 E4
Langtree Ave B91 . 107 B1
Langtree Cl WS12 ... 2 D1
Langwood Cl CV4 . 132 B7
Langwood Ct B36 ... 69 B8
Langworth Ave B27 . 88 C5
Lannacombe Rd B31 122 E6
Lansbury Ave WS10 . 41 C4
Lansbury Cl CV2 .. 114 E7
Lansbury Dr WS11 ... 1 E4
Lansbury Gn B64 ... 83 B8
Lansbury Rd B64 ... 83 B8
Lansbury Wlk **6** DY4 . 52 A8
Lansdale Ave B92 . 107 F8
Lansdowne Cir CV32 157 A1
Lansdowne Cl
  Bedworth CV12 ..... 78 A3
  Dudley, West Coseley
  WV14 .... 51 A7
  Rowley Regis DY2 ... 62 F6
Lansdowne Cres
  6 Royal Leamington Spa
  CV32 .... 157 A1
  Studley B80 ...... 159 D3
  Tamworth B77 ...... 35 D8
Lansdowne Ct DY9 . 81 C1
Lansdowne Rd
  Bilston WV14 ...... 40 E7
  Birmingham, Erdington
  B24 .... 56 F3
  Birmingham, Handsworth
  B21 .... 66 A8
  Halesowen, Hasbury
  B63 .... 82 D2
  Halesowen, Hurst Green
  B62 .... 63 F1
  2 Royal Leamington Spa
  CV32 .... 157 A1
  Studley B80 ...... 159 D3
  Wolverhampton WV1 . 163 A4
Lansdowne St
  Birmingham B18 .... 65 F4
  Coventry CV2 ..... 113 F3
  Royal Leamington Spa
  CV32 .... 157 A1
Lansdown Gn DY11 . 116 C5
Lansdown Ho B15 .. 86 D8
Lant Cl CV7 .... 131 B7
Lantern Rd DY2 .... 62 C2
Lanthorn Cl WS13 ... 9 A7
Lapal Cl B62 .... 84 A2
Lapal La N B62 ..... 83 E3
Lapal La S B32, B62 . 83 F2
Lapal Prim Sch B62 . 83 F4
Lapley Cl WV1 ..... 26 B2
Lappath Ho B32 ... 102 D8
Lapper Ave WV4 ... 39 F2
Lapwing B77 ...... 36 A6

Lapwing Cl
  Brownhills WS8 .... 15 E7
  Cheslyn Hay WS6 .... 4 C1
  Kidderminster DY10 . 117 B1
Lapwing Croft B23 .. 56 C2
Lapwing Dr B92 ... 109 B7
Lapwood Ave DY6 .. 61 A5
Lapworth CE Prim Sch
  B94 .... 144 D3
Lapworth Cl B98 .. 158 F7
Lapworth Dr B73 ... 45 C3
Lapworth Gr B12 ... 86 F6
Lapworth Oaks B94 144 D3
Lapworth Rd CV2 .. 96 C1
Lapworth St B94 .. 144 B2
Lapworth Sta B94 . 144 D4
Lara Cl B17 .... 85 B8
Lara Gr DY4 .... 52 A2
Larch Ave B21 ..... 54 D2
Larch Cl WS14 .... 9 E7
Larch Croft
  Birmingham B37 .... 70 B2
  Tipton B69 .... 52 B2
Larch Dr B31 ...... 102 C1
Larches Cottage Gdns
  DY11 .... 116 C3
Larches La WV3 .... 25 A2
Larches Rd DY11 .. 116 D4
Larches St B11 ..... 87 B6
Larches The
  Bedworth CV7 ..... 96 B8
  Wolverhampton WV11 . 26 B5
Larchfield Cl B20 ... 55 B3
Larch Gdns WV14 ... 40 F4
Larch Gr Sedgley DY3 . 50 E7
  Warwick CV34 ..... 156 A1
Larch Ho
  Birmingham B36 .... 68 F8
  Stourbridge DY8 ... 80 C6
Larchmere Dr
  Birmingham B28 .. 105 F8
  Bromsgrove B61 .. 136 E3
  Essington WV11 .... 13 B3
Larch Rd DY6 ...... 60 E7
Larch Tree Ave CV4 . 112 A2
Larch Wlk B25 ..... 88 B8
Larchwood Cres B74 . 44 E8
Larchwood Dr WS11 . 2 A4
Larchwood Gn WS5 . 43 B4
Larchwood Rd
  Bedworth CV7 ..... 78 B1
  Walsall WS5 .... 43 A4
Larcombe Dr WV4 .. 39 D5
Large Ave WS10 .... 41 C4
Lark Cl B14 .... 105 A2
Larkfield Ave B36 .. 69 B8
Larkfield Rd B98 .. 154 A1
Larkfield Way CV5 . 112 A6
Lark Hall Com Inf Sch
  B79 .... 21 A8
Larkhill DY10 ..... 116 E7
Larkhill Rd DY8 .... 80 C4
Larkhill Wlk B14 .. 104 D1
Larkin Cl
  Bulkington CV12 ... 79 B3
  Wolverhampton WV10 . 12 A1
Larkin Gr CV2 ..... 114 E1
Lark Meadow Dr B37 . 69 F3
Larksfield B66 ..... 65 B4
Larksfield Mews DY5 . 81 C7
Larks Mill WS3 .... 14 E4
Larkspur B77 ...... 35 D4
Larkspur Ave WS7 ... 7 A5
Larkspur Croft B36 . 68 D8
Larkspur Ct
  Bedworth CV12 ..... 95 C8
  Halesowen B62 .... 83 F7
Larkspur Dr WV10 .. 12 B7
Larkspur Gr **5** CV12 . 77 D2
Larkspur Rd DY2 ... 62 F8
Larkspur Way WS8 . 15 D6
Larkswood Dr
  Sedgley DY3 .... 50 D7
  Wolverhampton WV4 . 38 C3
Larne Rd B26 ...... 89 A7
Lashbrooke Ho B45 . 121 F7
Lassington Cl B98 . 154 E4
Latches Cl WS10 ... 41 E6
Latchford Cl B98 . 154 E6
Latelow Rd B33 .... 69 A2
Latham Ave B43 .... 54 E7
Latham Cres DY4 ... 52 A3
Latham Rd CV5 .... 113 A2
Lath La B66 .... 64 D8
Lathom Gr B33 ..... 68 F5
Latimer Cl CV8 .... 147 F2
Latimer Gdns B15 .. 86 D7
Latimer Pl B18 ..... 65 E6
Latimer Rd B48 ... 139 A5
Latimer St WV13 ... 27 B3

Latymer Cl B76 ..... 58 A7
Lauder Cl Sedgley DY3 . 39 C1
  Willenhall WV13 .... 26 D1
Lauderdale Ave CV6 . 95 D3
Lauderdale Cl WS8 . 15 E6
Lauderdale Gdns
  WV10 .... 11 E3
Laughton Cl B31 .. 123 B7
Launce Gr CV34 ... 161 F2
Launceston Cl
  Tamworth B77 ..... 21 D2
  Walsall WS5 .... 43 D7
Launceston Dr CV11 . 73 F4
Launceston Rd WS5 . 43 D7
Launde The B28 ... 105 E3
Laundry Cotts CV35 . 145 E4
Laundry Rd B66 .... 65 C3
Laureates Wlk B74 . 46 A8
Laurel Ave B12 .... 87 A5
Laurel Bank B79 ... 21 B6
Laurel Bank Mews
  B60 .... 137 F4
Laurel Cl Coventry CV2 . 96 E2
  Dudley DY1 .... 51 A3
  Lichfield WS14 ...... 9 D8
  Redditch B98 ..... 153 E2
Laurel Ct
  Birmingham B13 .... 87 A2
  Coventry CV5 ..... 112 F1
Laurel Dr
  Burntwood WS7 ...... 7 C7
  Cannock WS12 ...... 2 E4
  Hartshill CV10 ..... 72 A7
  Smethwick B66 .... 65 A8
  Sutton Coldfield B74 . 44 E8
Laurel Gdns
  Barnt Green B45 .. 138 E8
  Birmingham B21 .... 54 E1
  3 Birmingham, Stockfield
  B27 .... 88 C5
Laurel Gr
  Birmingham B30 ... 103 E6
  Bromsgrove B61 .. 136 F4
  Darlaston WV14 .... 41 A4
  Wolverhampton WV4 . 38 E6
Laurel La B63 ..... 83 B3
Laurel Rd
  Birmingham, Handsworth
  B21 .... 54 F1
  Birmingham, King's Norton
  B30 .... 104 A4
  Dudley DY1 .... 51 A3
  Tipton DY4 .... 51 F7
  Walsall WS5 .... 43 B4
Laurels Cres CV7 . 130 C6
Laurels The
  Bedworth CV12 ..... 77 E2
  Birmingham B68 ... 84 B6
  Birmingham, Ladywood
  B16 .... 65 F3
  Birmingham, Sheldon
  B26 .... 89 C5
  Coventry CV4 ..... 132 F6
  Portway B47 ...... 140 F8
  Smethwick B66 .... 65 C4
  Sutton Coldfield B73 . 46 B1
Laurence Ct B31 .. 103 B5
Laurence Gr WV6 .. 24 E7
Lauriston Cl DY1 ... 50 F3
Lavender Ave CV6 . 112 F5
Lavender Cl
  Bedworth CV12 ..... 77 E1
  2 Walsall WS5 ...... 42 F3
  Wolverhampton WV9 . 10 F3
Lavender Gdns **1**
  B23 .... 56 B7
Lavender Gr
  Bilston WV14 ...... 40 F6
  Walsall WS3 .... 28 E5
Lavender Hall La
  CV7 .... 110 C2
Lavender Ho B38 .. 123 F8
Lavender La DY8 ... 80 D3
Lavender Rd
  Dudley DY1 .... 51 B3
  Tamworth B77 ..... 21 F4
Lavendon Rd B42 .. 55 B5
Lavenham Cl CV11 . 79 C8
Lavinia Rd B62 .... 83 E3
Law Cl B69 .... 52 D2
Law Cliff Rd B42 ... 55 B6
Lawden Rd B10 .... 87 B8
Lawford Ave WS14 ... 9 D8
Lawford Cl
  Birmingham B7 .... 67 A3
  Coventry CV3 ..... 114 E1
Lawford Gr
  Birmingham B5 .... 86 E8

Lawford Gr continued
Solihull B90......... 105 D2
Lawford Rd CV31... 162 B5
Lawfred Ave WV11... 26 D5
Lawley Cl
Coventry CV4....... 112 A2
Walsall WS4......... 15 B1
Lawley Middleway B4 67 A3
Lawley Rd WV14..... 40 B6
Lawley St Dudley DY1. 51 A1
West Bromwich B70.... 52 F3
Lawley The B63....... 82 D1
Lawn Ave DY8......... 80 E4
Lawn La WV9......... 11 A7
Lawnoaks Cl WS8..... 6 D2
Lawn Rd WV2.........39 F6
Lawns Bsns Ctr The
LE10................75 E8
Lawnsdale Cl B46.....70 F7
Lawnsdown Rd DY5...81 F6
Lawnsfield Gr B23... 56 D7
Lawnside Gn WV14... 40 D8
Lawn St DY8........ 80 E4
Lawns The
Bedworth CV12....... 77 C2
Hinckley LE10....... 75 E8
Portway B47........ 140 F7
Lawnswood
Hinckley LE10....... 75 A8
Stourbridge DY7...... 60 A2
Sutton Coldfield B76... 58 A8
Lawnswood Ave
Burntwood WS7........6 F5
Solihull B90....... 106 D3
Stourbridge DY8...... 60 C3
Wolverhampton, Parkfield
WV4............... 39 E4
Wolverhampton WV6.. 24 E8
Lawnswood Cl 2
WS12............... 2 D1
Lawnswood Dr
Brownhills WS9...... 16 A3
Stourbridge DY7...... 60 A4
Lawnswood Gr B21... 54 C1
Lawnswood Rd
Dudley DY3........ 50 D5
Stourbridge DY8...... 60 D3
Lawnswood Rise WV6.24 F8
Lawnwood Rd DY2... 62 C2
Lawrence Ave
Wednesfield WV11.... 26 F6
Wolverhampton WV10. 26 A4
Lawrence Ct
6 Birmingham B68... 84 B8
Tamworth B79........ 21 A6
Lawrence Dr B76..... 58 D6
Lawrence Gdns CV8. 148 A6
Lawrence La B64..... 62 E1
Lawrence Rd CV7... 96 A8
Lawrence Saunders Rd
CV6............... 113 B5
Lawrence St
Stourbridge DY9...... 81 C6
Willenhall WV13..... 27 A3
Lawrence Way WS13...8 F5
Lawrence Wlk B43.... 44 D4
Lawson Cl WS9...... 30 B4
Lawson St B4...... 164 C4
Law St B71......... 53 C5
Lawton Ave B29..... 86 B2
Lawton Cl
Hinckley LE10....... 74 F8
Rowley Regis B65..... 63 D6
Lawton Ct WV3..... 25 B1
Laxey Rd B16...... 65 D3
Laxford Cl B12...... 86 E6
Laxton Cl DY6....... 61 A5
Laxton Gr
Birmingham B25..... 68 D1
Solihull B91....... 107 C7
Lay Gdns CV31...... 162 E5
Lazy Hill
Birmingham B38..... 104 B2
Stonnall WS9....... 16 D2
Lazy Hill Rd WS9..... 16 C1
Lea Ave WS10....... 41 D1
Lea Bank Ave DY11... 116 B5
Lea Bank Rd DY2... 62 C3
Leabon Gr B17...... 85 C4
Leabrook B26........88 F8
Leabrook Rd DY4,
WS14............ 41 D1
Leabrook Rd N WS10. 41 D2
Leach Green La B45. 122 B6
Leach Heath La B45. 122 A4
Leacliffe Way WS9...30 F3
Leacote Dr WV6..... 24 C4
Leacrest Rd CV6..... 95 A2

Leacroft WV12....... 27 C7
Leacroft Ave WV10... 25 E8
Leacroft Cl WS9...... 16 B1
Leacroft Gr B71..... 53 B7
Leacroft Rd DY6..... 60 E8
Lea Croft Rd B97... 158 D5
Lea Cswy The DY11. 116 A4
Leadbeater Ho 6
WS3............... 28 B8
Leadbetter Dr B61... 136 D2
Lea Dr B26........ 89 A6
Lea End La B48..... 123 D3
Leaf Cl CV3........ 133 D4
Leafdown Cl WS12.... 2 D3
Leafenden Ave WS7....7 A6
Leafield Cl CV2..... 114 F8
Leafield Cres B33..... 69 A5
Leafield Gdns B62.... 83 D8
Leafield Rd B92..... 89 C1
Leaf La CV3........ 133 E5
Lea Ford Rd B33..... 69 C4
Leaford Way DY6.....60 F5
Leafy Glade B74..... 31 A3
Leafy Rise DY3...... 50 D4
Lea Gdns WV3...... 163 A1
Leagh Cl CV8...... 148 B7
Lea Green Ave DY4... 51 D5
Lea Green Dr B47... 125 C4
Lea Green La B47... 125 C5
Lea Hall Rd B33..... 69 A2
Leahill Croft B37.....69 F2
Lea Hall Sta B33.....69 B2
Lea Ho 6 DY1..... 61 E8
Leaholme Gdns DY9.. 81 B2
Leahouse Gdns B68.. 64 A3
Leahouse Rd B68... 64 A3
Lea House Rd B30... 104 A7
Leahurst Cres B17... 85 C4
Lea La WS6.........5 A3
Lealholme Ct CV5... 132 F8
Lea Manor Dr WV4... 38 E4
Leam Cl CV11.......73 F1
Leam Cres B92...... 89 B1
Leam Dr WS7........ 7 D7
Leam Gn CV4...... 132 D5
Leamington Cl WS11...4 C7
Leamington Rd
Birmingham B12..... 87 B5
Coventry CV3...... 133 C6
Kenilworth CV8.... 148 B2
Ryton-on-D CV8.... 135 B1
**Leamington Spa Art
Gallery & Mus★**
CV32............. 161 F8
Leamington Spa Sta
CV31............. 161 F7
Leamore Cl WS2..... 28 A7
Leamore Ind Est WS2 28 C6
Leamore La WS2..... 28 B6
Leamore Prim Sch
WS3............... 28 C7
Leamount Dr B44.... 45 C2
Leam Rd CV31...... 161 D1
Leam Side Ho 9
CV34............. 161 D8
Leam St CV31...... 162 B7
Leam Terr CV31.... 162 B8
Leander Cl WS6.......4 F1
Leander Gdns B14.. 104 F5
Leander Rd DY9......81 F4
Leandor Dr B74..... 45 A7
Lea Park Rise B61.. 136 F5
Lea Rd
Birmingham B11..... 87 D4
Wolverhampton WV3.. 39 B8
Lear Gr CV34...... 161 E4
Lear Rd WV5........ 49 B8
Leas Cl CV12....... 78 A3
Leason La WV10..... 26 A7
Leasow Dr B15...... 85 D3
Leasowe Rd
Birmingham B45.... 121 F8
Tipton DY4......... 51 E4
Leasowe's Ave CV3.. 132 F4
Leasowes Com Coll
B62................83 E6
Leasowes Ct B63.....82 F3
Leasowes Dr
Perton WV6......... 23 D4
Wolverhampton WV4.. 38 D6
Leasowes La B62.... 83 D4
Leasowes Rd B14....86 F1
Leasowes The DY4... 52 C5
Leasow The WS13.....3 A1
Leasow The WS9.... 29 E5
Lea St DY10...... 116 F6
Leas The WV10..... 12 C7

Lea Street Fst Sch
DY10............. 116 F6
Lea The
Birmingham B33..... 69 A2
Kidderminster DY11.. 116 A5
Leatherhead Cl 5 B6 .66 F6
Lea Vale Rd DY8.....80 F3
Lea View Aldridge WS9. 29 E5
Wednesfield WV12.... 27 A5
Lea Village B33..... 69 B3
Leaward Cl CV10.... 72 E2
Lea Wlk
Birmingham B45.... 121 F8
Ryton-on-D CV8.... 135 B1
Lea Wood Gr DY11.. 116 A5
Lea Yield Cl B30.... 104 A7
Lebanon Gr WS7......6 F8
Lechlade Cl B98.... 154 B7
Lechlade Rd B43.... 54 C8
Leckie Rd WS2...... 28 E4
Ledbrook Rd CV32... 157 E5
Ledbury Cl
Aldridge WS9....... 16 C1
Birmingham B16..... 66 A2
Redditch B97...... 154 F2
Ledbury Dr WV1..... 26 B1
Ledbury Ho
Birmingham B33..... 69 E2
Redditch B97...... 153 B4
Ledbury Rd CV31... 162 C6
Ledbury Way B76.... 58 A8
Ledsam Gr B32 ....84 F6
Ledsam St B16...... 66 A2
Ledwell B90....... 126 A5
Lee Bank Ho B1.... 164 B1
Lee Bank Middleway
B15............... 86 C8
Leebank Rd B63..... 82 E2
Leech St DY4....... 52 C5
Lee Cl CV34...... 155 E2
Lee Cres B15...... 86 C8
Lee Ct WS9.........15 F3
Leeder Cl CV6...... 95 C2
Leedham Ave B77... 21 D5
Lee Gdns B67...... 64 E5
Lee Meadow CV34.. 160 B4
Leeming Cl CV4... 132 C6
Lee Mount B15...... 86 C8
Lee Rd
Cradley Heath B64.... 82 F8
Hollywood B47..... 125 A7
Royal Leamington Spa
CV31............. 161 E6
Leeson Wlk 9 B17... 85 D5
Lees Rd WV14.......40 F3
Lees St B18.........65 F6
Lees Terr WV14......40 F3
Lee The CV5....... 112 C4
Lee Wlk WS11........2 B4
Legg Bros Ind Est
WV4.............. 40 A5
Legge La
Birmingham B1..... 66 C3
Dudley WV14....... 40 D1
Legge St
Birmingham B4.... 164 D4
West Bromwich B70.... 53 E3
Wolverhampton WV2.. 39 E6
Legion Cl WS11........6 A6
Legion Rd B45..... 121 E7
Legs La WV10.......11 F3
Le Hanche Cl CV7... 95 A7
Leicester Cl B67..... 64 E1
Leicester Cswy CV1. 113 D5
Leicester La CV32... 79 C2
Cubbington CV32.... 149 E1
Royal Leamington Spa
CV32............. 157 C6
Leicester Pl B71.... 53 C7
Leicester Rd
Bedworth CV12...... 78 B4
Hinckley LE10....... 71 F2
Nuneaton CV11...... 73 D5
Shilton CV7........ 97 F6
Leicester Row CV1.. 165 B4
Leicester St
Bedworth CV12...... 78 B3
Bulkington CV12..... 79 C2
Royal Leamington Spa
CV32............. 157 A1
Walsall WS1....... 28 E2
Wolverhampton WV6.. 25 B4
Leigham Dr B17..... 85 A7
Leigh Ave
Burntwood WS7.......7 B7
Coventry CV3...... 133 C3

Leigh CE Prim Sch
CV4.............. 131 D8
Leigh Cl WS4....... 29 A4
Leigh Ct
Birmingham B23..... 56 C2
Walsall WS4........ 29 A3
Leigh Jun &Inf Sch
B8................67 E6
Leigh Rd
Birmingham B8..... 67 E6
Sutton Coldfield B75... 47 B5
Walsall WS4........ 29 A4
Leighs Cl WS4...... 15 C1
Leighs Rd WS4...... 15 C1
Leigh St 4 CV1..... 113 E4
Leighswood Ave WS9. 30 B7
Leighswood Cl WS11...5 F5
Leighswood Gr WS9... 30 B6
Leighswood Gr WS9... 30 A7
Leighswood Ind Est
WS9............... 30 A8
Leighswood Rd WS9.. 30 A4
Leighswood Sch WS9. 30 B8
Leighton Cl
Birmingham B43..... 44 C3
Coventry CV4..... 132 D2
Dudley DY1......... 50 E2
Royal Leamington Spa
CV32............. 157 C4
Leighton Rd
Birmingham B13..... 86 F2
Darlaston WV14..... 41 A4
Wolverhampton WV4.. 38 F6
Leisure Wlk 7 B77...35 F6
Lelant Gr B17...... 85 A5
Lellow St B71...... 53 C8
Le More B74....... 32 A2
Lemox Rd B70...... 53 A8
Lench Cl
Halesowen B62...... 63 C1
Redditch B97...... 153 A5
Lench's Cl B13...... 87 A3
Lench St B4...... 164 C4
Lenchs Gn B5....... 86 E7
Lench St B32...... 84 E6
**Lench's Trust
Almshouses**
3 Birmingham, Edgbaston
B12................ 87 A8
3 Birmingham, Highgate
B12................ 86 F7
Len Davis Rd WV12... 27 B7
Lennox Cl CV3..... 134 E6
Lennox Gdns WV3... 39 A8
Lennox Gr B73...... 57 A7
Lennox St B19...... 66 D6
Lenton Croft B26... 88 E4
Lenton's La CV2..... 96 E4
Lenwade Rd B68.... 84 D8
Leofric Ct 3 B15.... 86 C8
Leofric St CV6..... 113 A5
Leomansley Cl WS13...8 F7
Leomansley Ct WS13...8 E7
Leomansley Rd WS13...8 F7
Leomansley View
WS13...............8 E7
Leominster Ct B45.. 121 F8
Leominster Ho B33... 69 E2
Leominster Rd B11... 87 E3
Leominster Wlk B45. 121 F8
Leona Ind Est B62... 63 D1
Leonard Ave 5 B19.. 66 D8
Leonard Gr 6 B19... 66 D8
Leonard Parkins Ho
CV12............. 79 D2
Leonard Rd
Birmingham B19..... 66 D8
Stourbridge DY8.... 80 C5
Leontes Mdws CV34. 161 D4
Leopold Ave B20....54 F5
Leopold Rd CV1.... 113 F4
Leopold St B12......86 F8
Lepid Gr B29....... 85 D2
Lerryn Cl DY6.......60 F5
Lerwick Cl DY6......60 F5
Lesingham Dr CV4... 111 E1
Lesley Bentley Ho 4
B1................ 66 C3
Lesley Dr DY6...... 60 E4
Leslie Dr DY4....... 41 B1
Leslie Rd
Birmingham, Edgbaston
B16................ 65 F2
Birmingham, Handsworth
B20............... 55 D2
Sutton Coldfield B74... 31 B2

Leslie Rd continued
Wolverhampton WV10. 25 F4
Leslie Rise B69..... 63 C8
Lesscroft Cl WV9.... 11 A3
Lester Gr WS9...... 30 E2
Lester St WV14......40 F5
Leswell Gr DY10.... 116 F6
Leswell La DY10.... 116 F6
Leswell St DY10.... 116 F6
Letchlade Cl CV2.... 114 C8
Levante Gdns B33... 68 D2
Leve La WV13...... 27 B1
Level St DY5....... 61 E3
Leven Cl LE10...... 75 B8
Leven Croft B76..... 58 A7
Leven Dr WV11..... 13 B1
Leven Way CV2.... 115 A8
Levenwick Way B38.. 124 A8
Leverretts The B21... 54 C3
Lever St WV2...... 163 C1
Leverton Rise WV10.. 25 C6
Leveson Ave WS6.....4 E2
Leveson Cl DY2..... 62 E8
Leveson Cres CV7... 130 B6
Leveson Ct
1 Willenhall WV13.... 27 A2
Wolverhampton WV6.. 25 A4
Leveson Dr DY4..... 51 E6
Leveson Rd
Wednesfield WV11.... 26 F8
Wolverhampton WV11. 12 F1
Leveson St WV13.... 27 A2
Leveson Wlk 5 DY2.. 62 E8
Levett Rd B77...... 22 B5
Levetts Fields WS14...9 C7
Levetts Hollow WS12.. 2 D3
Levetts Sq 4 WS13...9 B7
Levington Cl WV6.....23 F5
Leviss Trad Est B33.. 68 D4
Lewis Ave WV1...... 26 B2
Lewis Cl Lichfield WS14...9 E7
Willenhall WV12.... 27 D5
Lewis Gr WV11..... 26 D6
Lewisham Ind Est
B66............... 65 A7
Lewisham Rd
Smethwick B66...... 65 A7
Wolverhampton WV10. 11 B2
Lewisham St B71.... 53 D4
Lewis Rd
Birmingham, Brandhall
B68............... 84 B7
Birmingham, Stirchley
B30.............. 104 C7
Coventry CV1..... 113 D5
Radford Semele CV31. 162 F5
Stourbridge DY9..... 81 D5
Lewis St Bilston WV14. 40 E6
Tipton DY4......... 52 D5
Walsall WS2........ 28 E4
Lewkner Almshouses The
B48.............. 139 A5
Lewthorn Rise WV4.. 39 D4
Lexington Ct CV11... 73 B5
Lexington Gn DY5.... 81 C7
Leybourne Cres WV9 ..10 F2
Leybourne Gr B25... 88 C6
Leybrook Rd B45.... 122 B8
Leyburn Cl
Coventry CV6...... 95 E2
Nuneaton CV11...... 74 A2
3 Warwick CV34.... 155 F1
Willenhall WS2..... 27 D3
Leyburn Rd B16..... 66 A1
Leycester Cl B31... 123 A7
Leycester Ct 13
CV34............. 160 E6
Leycester Pl 12 CV34 160 E6
Leycester Rd CV8... 148 A2
Leycroft Ave B33.... 69 D3
Leydon Croft B38... 104 B2
Leyes La CV8...... 148 C5
Leyfields WS13.........3 B2
Leyfields Cres CV34. 160 D4
Ley Hill Farm Rd
B31.............. 102 E5
Ley Hill Jun & Inf Sch
B31.............. 102 E5
Ley Hill Rd B75..... 32 C1
Leylan Croft B13... 105 D7
Leyland Ave WV3....24 F1
Leyland Croft WS3... 14 F4
Leyland Rd
Bulkington CV12..... 79 B2
Coventry CV5...... 112 D4
Nuneaton CV11...... 73 E1
Tamworth B77...... 21 E3
Leylands Way CV34.. 160 B4
Leyman Cl B14..... 105 C4
Leymere Cl CV7..... 92 C1

Ley Rise DY3........ 39 C1
Leys Cl DY9........ 81 C2
Leys Cres DY5...... 61 B3
Leysdown Gr B27... 106 C8
Leysdown Rd B27... 106 C8
Leyside CV3....... 134 C5
Leys Ind Est DY5... 61 A3
Leys La CV7........ 92 C1
Leys Rd DY5....... 61 B3
Leysters Cl B98... 154 C7
Leys The
Birmingham B31.... 103 B5
1 Darlaston WS10... 41 D6
Hinckley LE10...... 76 A6
Leys Wood Croft B26. 89 B6
Leyton Cl DY5...... 81 D8
Leyton Gr B44...... 45 A1
Leyton Rd B21......65 F4
Libbards Gate 4
B91.............. 127 C8
Libbards Way B91.. 127 B8
Liberty Ct WS6....... 4 D3
Liberty Pl 1 B16.... 66 B2
Liberty Rd B77.......35 F5
Liberty Way CV11...73 F3
Libra Cl B79........20 F7
Library Cl LE10..... 76 A5
Library Rd CV4..... 132 B5
Library Sq 3 B91... 107 C3
Library Way B45... 121 F7
Lich Ave WV11...... 26 E7
Lichen Cl WS12........1 C6
Lichen Gdns B38... 123 D7
Lichen Gn CV4..... 132 D5
Lichfield Bsns Ctr
WS13................3 D1
Lichfield Cath★ WS13.9 B8
Lichfield Cathedral Sch
WS13................9 B8
Lichfield City Sta WS14 9 B7
Lichfield Cl CV11.... 74 A7
Lichfield Cres B78.... 20 E5
Lichfield Ct
Solihull B90........ 105 D2
Sutton Coldfield B75... 46 C5
Walsall WS4......... 29 A4
Lichfield Pas WV1... 163 C3
Lichfield Rd
Birmingham B6...... 67 C3
Brownhills, Shireoak Hill
WS8, WS9...... 16 B5
Brownhills WS8, WS14. 16 A8
Burntwood WS7...... 7 D6
Cannock WS11........5 B8
Coventry CV3...... 133 C3
Lichfield SW7, SW13....8 B6
Sutton Coldfield B74... 32 A3
Tamworth B78, B79... 20 E6
Walsall, Highbridge
WS3............... 15 B5
Walsall, New Invention WS3,
WS4, WS8, WS9... 13 A1
Walsall, Rushall WS4.. 29 B6
Walsall, Shelfield WS4.. 15 C1
Walsall, Wallington Heath
WS3............... 14 C2
Water Orton B46, B76.. 59 C4
Wednesfield WV11.... 26 C6
Willenhall WV12..... 27 B5
Wishaw B76, B78..... 48 B3
Lichfield Road Ind Est
B79................20 E6
Lichfield St
Bilston WV14....... 40 E5
Fazeley B78........ 20 F1
Tamworth B79....... 21 A5
Tipton DY4......... 51 F8
Walsall WS1....... 28 F2
Wolverhampton WV1. 163 C3
Lichfield Trent Valley Sta
WS13................9 B8
Lichwood Rd WV11...26 F7
Lickey Coppice B45. 122 C4
Lickey End Fst Sch
B60.............. 137 C6
Lickey Gr DY11.... 116 B2
Lickey Grange Dr
B60.............. 121 E1
**Lickey Hills Country Pk &
Visitor Ctr★** B45... 122 B3
Lickey Hills Prim Sch
B45.............. 121 F3
Lickey Rd
Birmingham B45.... 122 C6
Stourbridge DY8..... 81 B6
Lickey Rock B60.... 121 D1
Lickey Sq B45..... 122 A2
Liddard Gr B27.... 106 C8
Liddon Gr B27..... 106 C8
Liddon Rd B27..... 106 C8

Lifford Cl B14 104 C4
Lifford La B30 104 B4
Lifford Way CV3 135 A7
Lifton Croft DY6 60 F5
Lightfields Wlk B65 63 A5
Light Hall Sch B90 126 B8
Lighthorne Ave B16 66 B2
Lighthorne Rd B91 107 C6
Light La CV1 165 B4
Lightning Way B31 123 B7
Lightoak Cl B97 158 C6
Lightwood Cl B93 128 B8
Lightwood Rd DY1 51 A3
Lightwoods Hill B67 84 E8
Lightwoods Jun & Inf Sch B68 84 D8
Lightwoods Rd
Smethwick B67 65 A1
Stourbridge DY9 81 C1
Lilac Ave
1 Birmingham, Balsall Heath B12 87 A5
Birmingham, Perry B44 55 E7
Cannock WS11 4 D7
Coventry CV6 112 F5
Sutton Coldfield B74 44 E8
Tipton DY4 51 E7
Walsall WS5 43 A4
Lilac Cl Hinckley LE10 75 E6
Redditch B98 153 E2
Lilac Gr Burntwood WS7 6 F7
Walsall WS2 27 E3
Warwick CV34 156 A1
Wednesbury WS10 42 A2
Lilac Ho WS4 15 D1
Lilac La WS6 14 A8
Lilac Rd
Bedworth CV12 78 D5
Bilston WV1 40 B8
Dudley DY1 51 C4
Tamworth B79 21 A8
Willenhall WV12 27 E7
Lilacvale Way CV4 132 D5
Lilac Way B62 83 F8
Lilian Gr WV14 40 E1
Lilleburne Dr CV10 72 B7
Lilleshall Cl B98 154 E3
Lilleshall Cres WV2 39 D7
Lilleshall Rd B26 89 B7
Lilley Cl CV6 95 C2
Lilley Green Rd B48 140 D5
Lilley La B31 123 B8
Lillington Ave CV32 156 F2
Lillington Cl
2 Lichfield WS13 9 A8
Royal Leamington Spa CV32 157 A3
Sutton Coldfield B75 47 A4
Lillington Gr B34 69 D5
Lillington Prim Sch CV32 157 B3
Lillington Rd
Coventry CV2 96 D1
Royal Leamington Spa CV32 157 A3
Solihull B90 126 B8
Lilycroft La B38 124 A7
Lily Green La B97 153 A4
Lily Rd B26 88 D7
Lily St B71 53 C5
Limberlost Cl B20 55 A3
Limbrick Ave CV4 112 A1
Limbrick Cl B90 105 F2
Limbrick Wood Prim Sch CV4 111 F3
Limbury Gr B92 107 F8
Lime Ave
8 Birmingham B29 85 F2
Royal Leamington Spa CV32 157 A4
Walsall WS2 27 E3
Lime Cl
Great Wyrley WS6 4 F4
Hollywood B47 125 A5
Tipton DY4 51 E5
Walsall WS2 27 E3
West Bromwich B70 53 A4
Lime Ct
Birmingham B11 87 C4
Kidderminster DY10 117 A4
Lime Gr Bilston WV14 40 C7
Birmingham B25, B26 88 D6
Birmingham, Balsall Heath B12 86 F5
Birmingham, Chemsley Wood B37 70 B1
Birmingham, Lozells B19 66 C8
Birmingham, Small Heath B10 87 D8
Lime Gr *continued*
Bromsgrove B61 136 F4
Burntwood WS7 7 C6
Coventry CV4 112 B2
Kenilworth CV8 148 A4
Lichfield WS14 9 D8
Nuneaton CV10 72 E5
Smethwick B66 65 B3
Smethwick B66 65 B4
Sutton Coldfield B73 57 B7
Walsall WS4 29 C6
Limehurst Ave WV3 24 C1
Limehurst Rd WS4 29 C6
Lime Kiln Cl B38 123 D7
Limekiln La
Birmingham B14 105 A4
Earlswood B94 126 D1
Lime La
Norton Canes WS3 6 A1
Walsall WS3 15 A7
Limepit La Dudley DY1 51 A3
Huntington WS11, WS12 1 D6
Lime Rd
Huntington WS12 1 D8
Sedgley DY3 39 F1
Wednesbury WS10 41 F4
Limes Ave
Brierley Hill DY5 61 C5
Rowley Regis B65 63 C2
Limescroft Cl WS4 29 B7
Limes Ct WV6 24 D5
Limes Rd Dudley DY1 51 B3
Wolverhampton WV6 24 D4
Lime St Dudley WV14 51 A8
Walsall WS1 29 A1
Wolverhampton WV3 39 B8
Limes The
Bedworth CV12 77 E2
Birmingham, Gravelly Hill B24 56 F3
Birmingham, Ladywood B16 65 F2
Birmingham, Rotton Park B16 65 F3
Birmingham, Sparkbrook B11 87 C6
Coventry CV6 112 E5
Himley DY3 49 B3
Walsall WS1 29 A2
Wolverhampton WV11 26 B5
Limes View DY3 50 D7
Lime Tree Ave
Coventry CV4 112 A2
Wolverhampton WV6 24 A3
Lime Tree Cres B97 153 B4
Lime Tree Gdns WV8 10 B3
Lime Tree Gr B31 103 C2
Limetree Rd B74 30 D1
Lime Tree Rd
Birmingham, Acock's Green B27 88 C5
Birmingham, Saltley B8 67 F6
Codsall WV8 10 B4
Walsall WS5 43 A4
Linacre Ho B37 69 F2
Linaker Rd CV3 134 C5
Linchmere Rd B21 54 C2
Lincoln Ave
Nuneaton CV10 72 B7
Tamworth B79 20 E6
Willenhall WV13 27 D2
Lincoln Cl
Birmingham B27 88 E3
Lichfield WS13 3 C3
Warwick CV34 155 E1
Lincoln Croft WS14 17 F6
Lincoln Ct
9 Birmingham B29 103 C7
Royal Leamington Spa CV32 162 A8
Lincoln Dr WS11 4 F8
Lincoln Gn WV10 11 D2
Lincoln Gr B37 70 A1
Lincoln Ho WV10 25 E3
Lincoln Rd
Birmingham B27 88 D2
Bromsgrove B61 136 E4
Dudley DY2 62 D2
Smethwick B67 64 E2
Walsall WS1 29 A1
West Bromwich B71 42 D1
Lincoln Rd N B27 88 E3
Lincoln St
Birmingham B12 86 E6
Coventry CV1 165 C4
Wolverhampton WV10 25 E3
Lincoln Twr B16 66 A1
Lincroft Cres CV5 112 E4
Lindale Ave B36 68 C6
Lindale Cres DY5 81 B6
Linden Ave
Birmingham B43 54 D8
Burntwood WS7 7 A8
Halesowen B62 83 E7
Kidderminster DY10 117 A7
Oldbury B69 63 D8
Linden Cl
Tamworth B77 21 F4
Warwick CV34 155 E2
Willenhall WS2 27 D2
Linden Ct B91 107 E4
Linden Dr DY8 81 A3
Linden Gdns DY10 117 A6
Linden Glade B63 83 A4
Linden Gr DY10 117 A7
Linden Ho WV3 163 A1
Linden La WV12 27 E6
Linden Lea
Bedworth CV12 78 B3
Wolverhampton WV3 24 D1
Linden Rd
Birmingham B30 103 E7
Dudley DY1 51 B3
Hinckley LE10 71 C1
Smethwick B66 65 A2
Lindens Dr B74 44 F5
Lindens Prim Sch B74 44 F6
Lindens The
Birmingham B32 84 E7
Birmingham, Edgbaston B16 65 D1
Wolverhampton WV6 24 E3
Linden View WS12 2 B4
Lindenwood B73 46 B6
Lindera B77 22 A4
Lindfield The CV3 134 C8
Lindford Way B38 104 B2
Lindhurst Dr B94 143 C6
Lindisfarne B77 21 D3
Lindisfarne Dr CV8 148 C4
Lindley Ave DY4 51 F4
Lindley Rd
Bedworth CV12 77 D2
Coventry CV3 114 B2
Lindon Cl WS8 16 A6
Lindon Dr WS8 15 F7
Lindon Rd WS8 15 F5
Lindon View WS8 16 A5
Lindop Cl CV32 157 D5
Lindrick Cl WS3 13 F3
Lindridge Dr B76 58 D6
Lindridge Rd
Birmingham B23 56 C5
Solihull B90 105 F1
Sutton Coldfield B75, B76 47 B6
Lindrosa Rd B74 30 F3
Lindsay Rd B42 44 B1
Lindsey Ave B31 103 C4
Lindsey Cres CV8 148 A1
Lindsey Pl DY5 61 C3
Lindsey Rd B71 53 C7
Lindsworth App B30 104 C3
Lindsworth Ct 2 B30 104 C3
Lindsworth Rd B30 104 C3
Lindsworth Sch (North) B23 57 A6
Lindsworth Sch (South) B30 104 C3
Lineholt Cl B98 159 A6
Linehouse La
Catshill B60 137 D8
Lower Marlbrook B60 121 D1
Linen St CV34 160 D6
Linfield Gdns DY3 39 C1
Linford Gr B25 68 D1
Linford Wlk CV2 96 F1
Linforth Dr B74 45 A7
Lingard Cl B7 67 B5
Lingard Ho B76 57 F8
Lingard Rd B75 47 A5
Lingen Cl B98 154 E3
Lingfield Ave
Birmingham B44 44 F1
Wolverhampton WV10 11 D5
Lingfield Cl WS6 4 F2
Lingfield Ct
Birmingham B43 54 D7
Coventry CV6 96 B4
Lingfield Dr WS6 4 F2
Lingfield Gdns B34 69 B6
Lingfield Gr WV6 23 F4
Lingfield Rd WS11 6 A5
Lingfield Way DY6 61 A5
Lingfield Wlk B61 121 B1
Lingham Cl B92 107 D7
Ling Ho WV10 25 F3
Lingmoor Gr WS9 30 A7
Ling Rd WS12 1 C5
Lingwood Dr CV10 72 F3
Linhope Dr DY6 61 A5
Link One Ind Pk DY4 52 E6
Link Rd
Birmingham B16 65 E3
Brownhills WS9 16 B3
Wombourne WV5 49 A7
Links Ave WV6 24 D7
Links Cres B68 84 B8
Links Dr
Birmingham B45 122 A5
Solihull B91 107 B6
Stourbridge DY8 80 E2
Links Rd
Birmingham, Brandhall B68 84 B8
Birmingham, Highter's Heath B14 105 A1
Coventry CV6 113 B8
Wolverhampton WV4 39 A3
Links Side Way WS9 30 C8
Links The DY10 117 A4
Links View
Halesowen B62 83 D4
Sutton Coldfield B74 31 B1
Linkswood Cl B13 87 B1
Link The B27 88 A1
Linkway CV31 161 E6
Linkway Ret Pk WS11 4 B6
Linkwood Ind Est DY8 80 F6
Linley Cl WS9 29 E5
Linley Dr WV10 11 E1
Linley Gr
Birmingham B14 104 C6
Dudley DY3 50 B2
Linley Lodge Ind Est WS9 29 E6
Linley Rd WS4 29 D7
Linley Wood Rd WS9 29 E5
Linnet Cl
Birmingham B30 103 E8
Coventry CV3 134 D5
Halesowen B62 83 B6
Huntington WS12 1 D7
Linnet Gr
Birmingham B23 56 B6
Willenhall WV12 27 C8
Linnet Rise DY10 116 F1
Linpole Wlk B14 104 D2
Linsey Rd B92 89 C2
Linslade Cl WV4 39 D4
Linstock Way CV6 96 B4
Linthouse La WV11 26 E8
Linthouse Wlk 3 B77 35 F6
Linthurst Fst Sch B60 138 A6
Linthurst Newtown B60 138 B5
Linthurst Rd B45, B60 138 A7
Lintly B77 22 B1
Linton Ave B91 107 A1
Linton Cl
Halesowen B63 82 D5
Redditch B98 154 F2
Linton Croft WV14 40 D5
Linton Mews B98 154 F2
Linton Rd
Birmingham, Acock's Green B11 88 A4
Birmingham, Great Barr B43 44 C3
Cradley Heath B64 62 F3
Wolverhampton WV4 38 E5
Linton Wlk B23 56 C3
Linwood Cl LE10 71 B2
Linwood Ct B15 86 D7
Linwood Dr
Cannock WS12 1 F7
Coventry CV2 96 F1
Linwood Rd
Birmingham B21 65 E8
Dudley DY1 51 B5
Solihull B91 106 D5
Lionel St B3 164 B3
Lion Fields Ave CV5 112 B6
Lion Ind Est WS9 30 A8
Lion Pas DY8 80 F5
Lion's Den WS7, WS14 7 E2
Lion Sq DY10 116 E6
Lion St
Kidderminster DY10 116 E6
Stourbridge DY8 80 F5
Liskeard Cl CV11 74 A5
Liskeard Rd WS5 43 D7
Lisko Cl DY5 81 A8
Lisle Ave DY11 116 D3
Lisle Ct 4 CV31 162 A6
Lismore Cl B45 101 E1
Lismore Croft CV2 115 B7
Lismore Dr
Birmingham B17 85 A3
Hinckley LE10 71 C1
Lissimore Dr DY4 52 B2
Lisson Gr B44 44 F4
Listelow Cl B36 69 B8
Lister Cl Tipton DY4 52 A4
Walsall WS2 28 B5
Lister Rd Dudley DY2 62 D7
Kidderminster DY11 116 B4
Walsall WS2 28 B5
Lister St
Birmingham B7 66 F4
Nuneaton CV11 73 D3
Willenhall WV13 27 B1
Listowel Rd B14 104 D6
Lisures Dr B76 46 D4
Little Acre B97 158 D6
Little Albert St WS2 28 E2
Little Ann St B5 66 F2
Little Aston Hall B74 31 B5
Little Aston Hall Dr B74 31 B5
Little Aston Hospl B74 31 B5
Little Aston La B74 31 D6
Little Aston Park Rd B74 31 A3
Little Aston Rd WS9 30 D6
Little Barrow Wlk 3 WS13 3 A1
Little Barr St B9 67 A2
Little Birches WV3 38 F8
Little Bloxwich CE Prim Sch WS3 14 D3
Little Brickiln St WV3 163 B2
Little Bromwich Rd B9 68 C2
Little Broom St B12 87 A8
Little Caldmore 6 WS1 42 E8
Little Church La B79 21 B5
Little Church St 1 CV1 165 C4
Little Clothier St WV13 27 A3
Little Clover Cl 3 B7 67 C7
Little Comm WS3 15 A4
Little Cornbow B63 83 B3
Littlecote B79 20 D7
Littlecote Croft 1 B14 105 A3
Littlecote Dr B23 56 F2
Little Cottage St DY5 61 D2
Little Croft B43 43 C1
Little Cross St WS10 41 D7
Little Cryfield CV4 132 C2
Little Duke St CV11 73 B4
Little Edward St B9 67 A2
Little Farm CV3 134 D5
Little Field CV2 114 A5
Little Fields Way B69 63 F7
Little Forge Rd B98 159 C8
Little Francis Gr 3 B7 67 B5
Little Gorway WS1 42 F7
Little Grebe Rd DY10 117 B3
Little Green La B9 67 C1
Little Green Lanes B73 57 B7
Little Hall Rd B7 67 B5
Little Hardwick Rd WS9 30 D2
Little Hay La WS14 18 C3
Little Heath Croft B34 69 B7
Little Heath Ind Est CV6 96 A2
Little Heath La B60 137 D6
Little Heath Prim Sch CV6 95 F1
Little Hill WS10 41 F3
Little Hill Gr B38 104 A1
Little Hill Way B32 84 D2
Little Johnson's La
Aldridge WS9 30 B1
Walsall WS9 44 B8
Little John St DY5 61 D4
Little La
West Bromwich B71 53 D5
Willenhall WV12 27 D7
Little Lawns Cl WS9 16 A4
Little London WS1 42 F8
Little London Ho 1 WS1 42 F7
Little London JMI Sch WV13 27 A2
Littlemead Ave B31 103 C1
Little Meadow Croft B31 102 F4
Little Meadow Wlk B33 68 F3
Littlemead Rd B90 125 E8
Little Moor Hill B67 64 F5
Little Newport St 5 WS1 28 E1
Little Oaks Dr DY7 60 A2
Little Oaks Rd B6 66 E8
Littleover Ave B28 105 F6
Little Park St
Coventry CV1 165 C2
Wolverhampton WV1 163 C3
Little Pitts Cl B24 57 D5
Little Pk B32 84 B4
Little Potter St DY5 61 D2
Little Pountney St WV2 163 B1
Little Shadwell St B4 164 C4
Littleshaw Croft B47 125 C4
Littleshaw La B47 125 C4
Little's La WV1 163 C4
Little South St CV1 113 E3
Little St DY2 51 D1
Little Station St WS2 28 E2
Little Sutton La B75 46 C8
Little Sutton Prim Sch B75 32 D3
Little Sutton Rd B75 32 D2
Littlethorpe CV3 134 D6
Littleton Bsns Pk WS12 1 C7
Littleton Cl
Kenilworth CV8 148 A7
Sutton Coldfield B76 47 A2
Littleton Croft 6 B91 127 C8
Littleton Dr WS12 1 C7
Littleton Rd WV12 27 D7
Littleton St E WS1 28 F3
Littleton St W WS1 28 E2
Littlewood Cl 2 B91 127 B8
Littlewood Gn B80 159 D3
Littlewood La WS6 4 E4
Littlewood Rd WS6 4 E4
Little Woods B97 158 E6
Little Wood St WV13 27 A2
Littleworth Ave DY1 51 B6
Littleworth Croft CV31 162 C5
Littleworth Gr B76 46 F4
Littleworth Hill WS12 2 D4
Littleworth Rd WS12 2 E4
Litton B77 22 C1
Liveridge Cl B93 127 F6
Liverpool Croft B37 89 F8
Liverpool St B9 67 A2
Livery St
Birmingham B3 164 B3
Birmingham B3 164 B4
Royal Leamington Spa CV32 161 F8
Livingstone Ave WV6 23 E5
Livingstone Rd
Bilston WV14 40 B5
Birmingham, Handsworth B20 55 D1
Birmingham, King's Heath B14 104 E6
Coventry CV6 113 E7
Walsall WS3 14 E2
West Bromwich B70 53 B1
Lizafield Ct B66 64 E7
Llewellyn Rd CV31 162 A6
Lloyd Cl CV11 73 D2
Lloyd Cres CV2 114 E3
Lloyd Dr WV4 38 C2
Lloyd George Gr WS11 2 C2
Lloyd Hill WV4 38 C3
Lloyd Ho B19 66 C6
Lloyd Rd
Birmingham B20 55 A4
Wolverhampton WV6 24 D5
Lloyd Roberts Bldgs WV4 38 F1
Lloyds Rd B62 83 C8
Lloyd St
Birmingham B10 87 D8
Cannock WS11 1 D1
Dudley DY2 62 D8
Wednesbury WS10 41 E3
West Bromwich B71 53 E4
Wolverhampton WV6 24 F4
Loach Dr CV2 96 B4
Lobelia Cl LE10 75 E5
Locarno Rd DY4 52 A6
Lochalsh Gr WV11 13 B1
Lochmore Cl LE10 75 A8
Lochmore Dr LE10 75 A8

Lochmore Way LE10... **75** A8
Lochranza Croft B43 . **43** E2
Lochsong Cl B77...... **35** D4
Loch St CV3........ **114** C1
Lock Cl B97........ **153** A4
Lock Dr B33 ..... **68** D3
Locke Cl CV6....... **95** A1
Locket Cl WS2........ **27** F4
Locketts Ct WS11.......**1** F5
Lockfield Cl DY8 ..... .**60** F2
Lockhart Cl CV8.... **148** A4
Lockhart Dr B75 .... **32** C1
Lockheed Cl **8** CV31 **161** F5
Lockhurst La CV6.... **113** D7
Locking Croft B35.... **58** B3
Lockington Croft B62 .**83** F6
Lock Keepers Cl WS11..**5** F4
Lock Keepers Reach
 B48............. **138** F6
Lock La CV34...... **160** D8
Lock Mus The*
 WV13............. **27** A1
Lockside WS9.......**29** F7
Lockside Cl DY5... **61** D1
Locksmith Cl WV13... **27** B2
Lock St WV1....... **163** C4
Locks The CV31.... **161** D7
Locks View DY8..... **60** E1
Lockton Rd B30..... **104** C8
Lockwood Rd B31... **102** F4
Lode Heath Sch B91 **107** C6
Lode La B91....... **107** C6
Loder Cl CV4....... **111** F3
Lodge Cl
 Halesowen B62..... **83** E3
 Hinckley LE10..... **76** A5
 Walsall WS5....... **43** D6
Lodge Cres
 Dudley DY2....... **62** A4
 Warwick CV34..... **160** D4
 West Hagley DY9... **99** B5
Lodge Croft
 Birmingham B31..... **102** E6
 Knowle B93....... **128** B6
Lodge Dr B26........**88** F8
Lodge Farm Cl B76....**46** F3
Lodge Farm JMI Sch
 WV12...........**27** E4
Lodgefield Rd B62... **83** B7
Lodge Forge Trad Est
 B64............. **82** C7
Lodge Gr WS9..... **30** A5
Lodge Green La CV7..**92** F2
Lodge Green La N
 CV7............. **92** E3
Lodge Hill Rd B29... **85** D1
Lodge La
 Cheslyn Hay WS11.....**4** C5
 Kingswinford DY6.... **60** B6
Lodgepool Cl B44.... **55** E6
Lodge Pool Dr B98.. **153** F1
Lodge Prim Sch B70 .**53** B3
Lodge Rd Bilston WV14 .**40** F4
 Birmingham B18..... **65** F5
 Coventry CV3..... **114** B1
 Darlaston WS10..... **41** D5
 Knowle B93........ **128** B6
 Redditch B98..... **153** E3
 Smethwick B67..... **64** E7
 Walsall, The Chuckery
 WS5............. **43** D6
 Walsall WS4....... **15** B1
 West Bromwich B70.. **53** C3
 Wolverhampton WV10 . **25** B8
Lodge Rd/ West
 Bromwich TH Sta
 B70............. **53** C3
Lodge St Oldbury B69 . **64** A7
 Willenhall WV12...... **27** C5
Lodge The B15..... **65** D1
Lodge View WS6.....**4** C3
Loeless Rd B33 ..... **69** A3
Lofthouse Cres B31. **102** F3
Lofthouse Gr B31... **102** F3
Lofthouse Rd B20... **54** F3
Loftus Cl B29..... **102** F8
Loftus Ct WS7.......**7** A5
Logan Cl WV10..... **25** C6
Logan Rd CV2..... **114** E2
Lole Cl CV6....... **96** A4
Lollard Croft CV3... **133** D8
Lomaine Dr B30.... **103** E4
Lomas Dr B31..... **102** E3
Lomas St WV1..... **25** C4
Lomax Cl WS13......**3** A1
Lomax Rd WS12......**2** B7
Lombard Ave DY2... **62** D3

Lombard Gdns **1**
 WS13............**9** B8
Lombard St W B70... **53** C3
Lombard St
 Birmingham B12..... **86** F8
 Lichfield WS13......**9** B8
 West Bromwich B70... **53** C3
Lombardy Croft **3**
 B62............. **84** A6
Lombardy Gdns WV12 **27** E7
Lombardy Gr WS7.....**6** F8
Lomita Cres B77..... **35** D8
Lomond Cl
 Birmingham B34..... **69** E6
 Hinckley LE10..... **75** B8
 Tamworth B79..... **20** F8
Lomond Rd DY3 .... **39** C1
Lomond Way CV10... **72** C5
Lomsey Cl CV4..... **112** A1
Londonderry Gr B67..**64** F5
Londonderry La B67.. **64** E4
Londonderry Rd B68.. **64** D4
London Hts DY1..... **51** A2
London La
 Bromsgrove B60.... **151** F7
 Tardebigge B60.... **152** A6
London Pl WV2.... **163** B2
London Rd
 Birmingham B20..... **55** E2
 Coventry, Cheylesmore
 CV3............. **133** E8
 Coventry, Willenhall
 CV3............. **134** D5
 Hinckley LE10..... **75** E8
 Lichfield WS14......**9** C5
 Middleton B75, B78... **47** D7
 Ryton-on-D CV8.... **135** B1
 Shenstone B75, WS14 . **32** F7
 Sutton Coldfield B75.. **33** A4
 Weeford WS14..... **18** F3
London St B66..... **65** C5
Lones Rd B71...... **65** B8
Longacre WS10..... **41** A8
Long Acre
 Birmingham B7...... **67** C7
 Kidderminster DY10 . **116** F7
Longacre Ind Est B7. **67** C7
Longacres
 Cannock WS12 ....**2** F5
 Sutton Coldfield B74... **31** C4
Long Acre St WS2... **28** D3
Long Acre Trad Est
 B7.............**67** B7
Longbank Rd B69... **63** C8
Longboat La DY8.... **60** E1
Longboat Quay DY2.. **62** D4
Longborough Cl B97 **158** B6
Longbow Rd B29.... **102** F7
Longbridge La B31.. **122** E8
Long Bridge Rd WS14 ..**9** C5
Longbridge Sta B31. **122** E8
Long Brook La CV7,
 CV8............. **129** E5
Long Cl DY9....... **99** A4
Long Close Ave CV5. **112** B6
Long Close Wlk B35. **58** A3
Long Compton Dr
 DY9............. **99** A6
Long Croft WS12......**1** C4
Longcroft Ave **1**
 WS10............. **42** A3
Longcroft Cl B35.... **58** A3
Longcroft The
 Halesowen B63...... **82** E4
 Walsall WS4....... **29** C7
Longdales Rd B38... **123** E7
Longdon Ave WV4... **39** D5
Longdon Cl B98.... **159** B7
Longdon Croft B93.. **128** A8
Longdon Dr B74.... **31** E4
Longdon Rd B93.... **128** A6
Longfellow Ave
 CV34............. **160** C4
Longfellow Cl B97.. **158** C7
Longfellow Gn DY10. **117** C6
Longfellow Pl WS11....**1** E4
Longfellow Rd
 Birmingham B30.... **103** D4
 Coventry CV2..... **114** C3
 Dudley DY3....... **50** B5
Longfellow Wlk B79..**20** F8
Longfield Cl
 Birmingham B28.... **105** F6
 Tamworth B77...... **21** E4
Longfield Ho
 Coventry CV6..... **114** A8
 Wolverhampton WV10 . **25** F3
Longfield Rd
 Birmingham B31..... **102** E8

Longfield Rd *continued*
 Royal Leamington Spa
 CV31............. **162** B6
 Stourbridge DY9..... **81** D5
Longford Cl
 Birmingham B32.... **102** A7
 Dorridge B93..... **128** B3
Longford Ct WS11......**4** B8
Longford Gn WS11......**4** C7
Longford Gr B44.... **45** A3
Longford Rd
 Bedworth CV7..... **96** A6
 Birmingham B44.... **45** A2
 Cannock WS11 .... **4** D7
 Coventry CV6..... **96** A4
 Wolverhampton WV10 . **26** A4
Longford Sq CV6.... **96** A4
Long Furrow WV8.... **10** E1
Longham Croft B32 .**84** F4
Longhurst Croft B31 **123** B7
Long Hyde Rd B67...**64** F1
Long Innage B63.... **82** B6
Long Knowle La
 WV11............. **26** B8
Long Knowle Prim Sch
 WV11............. **26** C8
Long La
 Brownshill Green CV5,
 CV7............. **94** D2
 Great Wyrley WS6... **13** E6
 Halesowen B62..... **83** E8
Longlake Ave WV6... **24** B3
Longlands B38 .... **123** C8
Longlands Dr B77.....**21** F4
Longlands Rd B62... **83** E3
Longlands The
 Barnt Green B45.... **138** D7
 Wombourne WV5.... **49** A6
Long La Trad Est B62 **83** D8
Long Leasow B29 .. **103** B7
Longleat
 Birmingham B43.... **43** C2
 Tamworth B79........ **20** D7
Longleat Ave **2** B15. **66** C1
Longleat Dr
 Cheswick Green B90. **126** E5
 Dudley DY1....... **50** E2
Longleat Gr **17** CV31. **162** C6
Longleat Rd WS9.... **16** A1
Long Ley WV10......**25** F3
Longley Ave B76.... **58** D5
Longley Cres B26... **88** E4
Long Leys Croft B46.. **59** B2
Long Leys Ct B46.... **59** B2
Longley Wlk B37.... **70** C2
Long Mdw B65...... **63** C3
Longmeadow Cl B75 .**46** F5
Longmeadow Cres
 B34............. **69** E6
Long Meadow Dr
 Hinckley LE10..... **74** F7
 Sedgley DY3....... **39** B2
Longmeadow Gr
 B31............. **123** A6
Longmeadow Rd WS5 **43** E8
Long Meadow Rd
 B60............. **137** C6
Long Mill Ave WV11.. **26** B7
Long Mill N WV11... **26** B7
Long Mill S WV11... **26** B7
Longmoor Cl
 Redditch B97..... **153** B5
 Wednesfield WV11... **26** F5
Longmoor Ho **13** B74. .**31** F2
Longmoor Rd
 Halesowen B63..... **82** E3
 Sutton Coldfield B73.. **45** B3
Longmoor Sch B73.. **45** A4
Longmore Ave WS2 ..**27** F1
Longmore Ct B73.... **45** A5
Longmore Ho B73... **45** C3
Longmore Rd B90... **106** D2
Longmore St
 Birmingham B12.... **86** E7
 Wednesbury WS10... **41** F3
Long Mynd B63..... **82** D1
Long Mynd Cl WV11.. **13** C8
Long Mynd Rd B31.. **102** F6
Long Nuke Rd B31.. **102** E7
Long Saw Dr B31... **102** D1
Longshaw Gr B34... **69** D6
Long Shoot The CV11. **74** C6
Long St
 Birmingham B11..... **87** A6
 Bulkington CV12.... **79** D2

Long St *continued*
 Walsall WS2........ **28** D1
 Wolverhampton WV1 . **163** C3
Longstone B90 .... **127** B6
Longstone Rd B42... **55** C7
Longville Ct CV3.... **134** A6
Longwill Prim Sch For
 Deaf Children B31. **103** A5
Long Wood B30..... **103** E5
Longwood Cl CV4... **131** F6
Longwood La WS5,
 WS4............. **29** E2
Longwood Path B78.. **20** D1
Longwood Prim Sch
 B78............. **20** D1
Longwood Rd
 Aldridge WS9...... **30** B2
 Birmingham B45.... **122** A7
Longwood Rise WV12 **27** D5
Lonicera Cl WS5.... **43** B3
Lonscale Dr CV3.... **133** B5
Lonsdale Cl
 Birmingham B33.... **68** D2
 Willenhall WV12.... **27** B5
Lonsdale Ct B17.... **85** C6
Lonsdale Rd
 Bilston WV14...... **40** F6
 Birmingham B17.... **85** B6
 Royal Leamington Spa
 CV32............. **157** B4
 Smethwick B66..... **64** D7
 Walsall WS5....... **43** C6
 Wolverhampton WV3 . **39** B7
Lord Austin Dr B60.. **121** E1
Lord Cromwell Ct
 WS11.............**2** A5
Lord Leycester Hospl &
 Knot Gdn* CV34... **160** E6
Lord Lytton Ave CV2. **114** D2
Lord St W WV14.... **40** E3
Lord's Dr WS2..... **28** E3
Lords La B80...... **159** E2
Lordsmore Cl WV14.. **40** D1
Lord St Bilston WV14.. **40** E3
 Birmingham B7...... **66** F5
 Coventry CV5..... **112** F2
 Walsall WS1....... **42** E6
 Wolverhampton WV3 . **25** B1
Lordswood Boys Sch
 B17.............**65** A1
Lordswood Cl B97... **152** F2
Lordswood Girls Sch &
 Sixth Form Ctr B17. **85** A8
Lordswood Rd B17... **85** A7
Lordswood Sq B17 .. **85** B7
Lorenzo Cl CV3.... **134** D6
Lorimer Way B43.... **44** D5
Loriners Gr WS1.... **29** B1
Lorne Gr DY10..... **117** A5
Lorne St Burntwood WS7.**6** E8
 Kidderminster DY10 . **117** A5
Lorrainer Ave DY5... **81** A8
Lorton B79....... **20** D7
Lothersdale B77.... **36** C8
Lothians Rd
 Walsall WS3....... **15** A5
 Wolverhampton WV6 . **24** E6
Lottie Rd B29...... **85** E1
Lotus B77......... **21** E3
Lotus Croft B67.....**64** F4
Lotus Ct B16...... **65** E1
Lotus Dr Cannock WS11..**1** E5
 Cradley Heath B64.... **62** F2
Lotus Way B65..... **63** A4
Loudon Ave CV6.... **113** A5
Loudon Gate CV11...**73** F1
Loughshaw B77..... **22** C1
Loughton Gr B63.....**82** F4
Louisa Pl **3** B18.... **66** A5
Louisa St **1** B1..... **66** C3
Louis Ct B67........**64** F5
Louise Croft B14.... **104** E2
Louise Ct
 2 Birmingham B27... **88** C3
 Solihull B91..... **106** E1
Louise Ho DY5..... **61** D7
Louise Lorne Rd B13 .**86** F4
Louise Rd B21......**65** F7
Louise St DY3..... **50** C3
Lount Wlk B19..... **66** E5
Lovage Rd B98.... **154** F6
Lovatt Cl DY4...... **41** C1
Lovatt Pl WS11......**1** E5
Lovatt St WV1..... **163** A3
Loveday Cl CV32... **156** E2
Loveday Ho B70.... **53** D3
Loveday St B4..... **164** C4
Love La
 Birmingham B7.... **164** D4

Love La *continued*
 Great Wyrley WS6......**5** B3
 Hinckley LE10...... **76** A6
 Hollywood B47..... **124** F7
 Stourbridge, Lye DY9 . **81** F5
 Stourbridge, Old Swinford
 DY8............. **81** A3
 Walsall WS1....... **42** E7
 Wolverhampton WV6 . **24** D6
Lovelace Ave B91... **127** D8
Lovell B79.........**20** F6
Lovell Cl Bedworth CV7 **96** A8
 Birmingham B29.... **103** B6
Lovell Rd CV12..... **78** A3
Love Lyne B97..... **158** A5
Lover's Wlk **5** WS10 .**41** F3
Lovett Ave B69..... **63** D5
Lovetts Cl LE10.....**74** F8
Lovett B79......... **20** D7
Lowans Hill Cotts
 B97............. **153** C5
Lowans Hill View
 B97............. **153** C4
Low Ave B43........**43** F2
Lowbridge Cl WV12.. **27** C5
Lowbrook La B90... **125** D4
Lowcroft Gdns WV10 . **25** E8
Lowden Croft B26.... **88** E4
Lowdham B77...... **22** C1
Lowe Ave WS10..... **41** C7
Lowe Dr
 Kingswinford DY6.... **60** E4
 Sutton Coldfield B73.. **45** C3
Lower Ave CV31.... **161** F7
Lower Beeches Rd
 B31............. **102** C2
Lower Bentley La
 B60............. **151** F1
Lower Bond St LE10.. **71** D1
Lower Cape CV34... **160** D8
Lower Chapel St B69. **52** C2
Lower Church La DY4 **52** B5
Lower City Rd B69... **52** D1
Lower Common La
 B97............. **153** B2
Lowercroft Way B74. **31** E6
Lower Dartmouth St
 B9.............. **67** B2
Lower Darwin St B12. .**86** F8
Lower Derry St DY5.. **61** D2
Lower Eastern Green La
 CV5............. **111** F4
Lower Essex St B5... **66** E1
Lower Farm WS9.... **16** E4
Lower Farm Prim Sch
 WS3............. **14** C3
Lower Ford St CV1.. **165** D3
Lower Forster St WS1.**28** F2
Lower Gambolds La
 B60............. **151** B6
Lower Gn Tipton DY4.. **51** F8
 Wolverhampton WV6 . **24** E5
Lower Grinsty La
 B97............. **158** A8
Lower Ground Cl **1**
 B6.............. **55** F1
Lower Gungate B79.. **21** B5
Lower Hall La WS1... **28** E1
Lower Hall St WV13.. **27** B1
Lower High St
 Cradley Heath B64... **82** C8
 Stourbridge DY8..... **80** F6
 Wednesbury WS10... **41** F2
Lower Higley Cl B32. **84** E4
Lower Holyhead Rd
 CV1............. **165** A3
Lower Horseley Fields
 WV1............. **25** F2
Lower House La CV9 ..**36** F2
Lower Keys Bsns Pk
 WS12.............**2** D3
Lower Ladyes Hills
 CV8............. **148** A6
Lower Leam St CV31 **162** B7
Lower Lichfield St
 WV13............. **27** B2
Lower Loveday St
 B19............. **164** C4
Lower Mill St DY11.. **116** D6
Lower Moor B30.... **103** E8
Lower North St WS4.. **28** E3
Lowerpark B77..... **21** C1
Lower Parklands
 DY11............. **116** C5
Lower Par The B72.. **46** C5
Lower Prec CV1.... **165** B3
Lower Prestwood Rd
 WV11............. **26** C7
Lower Queen St B72. **46** C4

Lower Rd
 Barnacle CV7..... **97** C6
 Cannock WS12.......**2** C3
Lower Reddicroft B73 **46** C5
Lower Rushall St WS1.**28** F2
Lower Sandford St
 WS13............**9** A7
Lower Severn St B1. **164** B2
 B60............. **137** E6
Lower Shepley La
 B60............. **137** E6
Lower St WV6..... **24** E5
Lowerstack Croft B37 .**69** F3
Lower Temple St **4**
 B2.............. **164** B2
Lower Tower St B19. **164** C5
Lower Trinity St B9... **67** A1
Lower Valley Rd DY5. **61** A2
Lower Vauxhall WV1.. **25** A3
Lower Villiers St
 1 Royal Leamington Spa
 CV32............. **157** A1
 Wolverhampton WV2 . **39** C7
Lower Walsall St WV1.**25** F1
Lower White Rd B32. **84** D5
Lowes Ave CV34.... **155** E1
Lowesmoor Rd B26.. **89** C7
Lowe St
 Birmingham B12.... **87** A8
 Wolverhampton WV6 . **25** B4
Loweswater CV11... **74** A6
Loweswater Dr DY3.. **50** D3
Loweswater Ho B38. **104** B1
Loweswater Rd CV3. **114** E1
Lowfield Cl B62..... **84** A3
Lowfield La B97.... **153** B5
Lowfield Rd CV3.... **114** C1
Lowforce B77....... **22** C1
Low Hill Cres WV10 .. **25** E8
Lowhill La B45..... **122** D6
Lowland Cl B64......**62** F1
Lowland Rd WS12......**1** C5
Lowlands Ave
 Sutton Coldfield B74... **44** E8
 Wolverhampton WV6 . **24** E6
Lowlands Ct WV6.... **24** E6
Lowlands La B98.... **154** D3
Lowndes Rd DY8.... **80** E6
Lowrey Ct B68..... **64** C3
Lowry Cl
 Bedworth CV12..... **78** A4
 Perton WV6....... **23** F4
 Smethwick B67..... **64** F6
 Willenhall WV13.... **26** E2
Low St WS6........ **4** D3
Low Thatch B38.... **123** E7
Lowther Ct **10** DY5.. **61** D2
Lowther St CV2.... **113** F4
Low Town **6** B69.... **64** A7
Low Wood Rd B23... **56** E5
Loxbrook Park Ind Est
 WV14............**40** E4
Loxdale Prim Sch
 WV14............**40** E4
Loxdale Sidings WV14 .**40** F4
Loxdale St
 Bilston WV14........ **40** F4
 Wednesbury WS10... **41** E2
Loxdale Sta WV14....**40** F4
Loxley Ave
 Birmingham B14.... **105** C3
 Solihull B90..... **105** F1
Loxley Cl
 Birmingham B31.... **102** E8
 Coventry CV2..... **96** D2
 Redditch B98..... **154** D6
Loxley Ct CV2...... **96** D2
Loxley Rd
 Smethwick B67..... **64** F1
 Sutton Coldfield B75.. **32** C1
Loxley Sq B92..... **106** D8
Loxley Way CV32... **157** A2
Loxton Cl B74...... **31** D5
Loynells Rd B45.... **122** A6
Loyns Cl B37....... **69** E3
Lozells Inf & Jun Sch
 B19............. **66** D7
Lozells Rd B19..... **66** C7
Lozells St B19..... **66** C7
Lozells Wood Cl **2**
 B19............. **66** B7
Luanne Cl B64..... **63** A1
Lucas Cl CV32..... **161** D8
Lucas Ho CV32.... **156** F2
Lucas Rd LE10..... **75** D6
Luce Cl B35....... **58** B4
Luce Rd WV10..... **25** E6
Lucerne Cl CV2..... **96** C3
Lucerne Ct B23.... **56** D6
Lucian Cl CV2..... **115** C7
Lucknow Rd WV12... **27** B5

Lucy Edwards Ct DY11 116 C5
Luddington Rd B92 107 E8
Ludford Cl B75 46 E7
Ludford Rd
Birmingham B32 84 A1
Nuneaton CV10 72 C6
Ludgate B79 21 A5
Ludgate Ave DY11 116 A4
Ludgate Cl
Oldbury B69 63 B8
Water Orton B46 59 B3
Ludgate Ct 2 WS5 43 D7
Ludgate Hill B3 164 B3
Ludgate Ho B13 86 F4
Ludgate St 11 DY1 51 B1
Lud La B79 21 A5
Ludlow Cl
Birmingham B37 70 C2
Cannock WS11 2 C2
Willenhall WV12 27 B6
Ludlow Ct B11 87 B6
Ludlow Ho
Birmingham B13 105 A6
1 Walsall WS3 28 C6
Ludlow La WS2 28 A4
Ludlow Rd
Birmingham B8 67 F4
Coventry CV5 113 A2
Kidderminster DY10 116 E3
Redditch B97 153 E3
Ludlow Way DY1 50 E2
Ludmer Way B20 55 C2
Ludstone Ave WV4 38 D5
Ludstone Rd B29 84 F1
Ludworth Ave B37 90 B8
Luff Cl CV3 134 B8
Lugtrout La
Catherine de B B91 108 A6
Solihull B91 107 F6
Lukes The B64 62 C1
Lukes Wlk WS13 3 A2
Lulworth Cl B63 82 C6
Lulworth Pk CV8 148 C6
Lulworth Rd
Birmingham B28 88 A1
Burntwood WS7 7 A7
Lulworth Wlk WV4 38 C6
Lumley Gr B37 70 D2
Lumley Rd WS1 29 A1
Lumsden Cl CV2 114 F8
Lunar Cl CV4 132 D5
Lundy Cl LE10 71 B1
Lundy View B36 70 B6
Lunn Ave CV8 147 E3
Lunn Poly Ho 3 CV32 156 F1
Lunns Croft WS13 9 C8
Lunt Gr B32 84 D5
Lunt Jct The WV14 41 A6
Lunt Pl WV14 41 A6
Lunt Rd WV14 40 F6
Lunt The* CV8 133 E3
Lupin Cl LE10 75 D5
Lupin Gr
Birmingham B9 67 F3
Walsall WS5 43 B4
Lupin Rd DY2 51 F1
Lupton Ave CV3 133 C7
Lupton Ct B60 137 A1
Lusbridge Cl B63 82 B4
Luscombe Rd CV2 114 E8
Luther Way CV5 111 F4
Lutley Ave B63 82 E4
Lutley Cl WV3 38 E7
Lutley Dr DY9 81 C3
Lutley Gr B32 84 B1
Lutley La B63 82 C2
Lutley Mill Rd B63 82 E4
Lutley Prim Sch B63 82 D1
Luton Rd B29 85 F3
Lutterworth Rd
Coventry CV2 114 C5
Hinckley LE10 76 C3
Nuneaton CV11 79 C8
Luttrell Rd B74 32 A1
Luxor La CV5 111 B8
Lyall Gdns B45 101 E1
Lyall Gr B27 88 A2
Lychgate Ave DY9 81 C1
Lychgate Cl LE10 76 A5
Lychgate La LE10 76 C5
Lydate Rd B62 83 F4
Lydbrook Covert 5 B38 123 E8
Lydbury Gr B33 69 A4
Lyd Cl WV11 26 B5
Lydd Croft B35 58 B4
Lyddington Dr B62 83 B7
Lyde Gn B63 82 B7
Lydford Cl CV2 114 C7
Lydford Gr B24 57 A1
Lydford Rd WS3 14 B3
Lydgate Ct
Bedworth CV12 78 A4
Nuneaton CV11 73 C3
Lydgate Rd
Coventry CV6 113 B5
Kingswinford DY6 60 F6
Lydget Gr B23 56 D7
Lydham Cl
Bilston WV14 40 B4
Birmingham B44 56 A6
Redditch B98 153 E5
Lydia Croft B74 31 E6
Lydian Cl WV6 25 B4
Lydiate Ash Rd B60 121 C3
Lydiate Ave B31 102 D1
Lydiates Cl DY3 50 B7
Lydney Cl
Redditch B98 154 D7
Willenhall WV12 27 D4
Lydney Gr B31 102 F3
Lydstep Gr CV31 162 C7
Lye Ave B32 84 A2
Lye Bsns Ctr DY9 81 F6
Lye By-Pass DY9 81 E6
Lye Close La B32 84 A2
Lyecroft Ave B37 70 D2
Lye Cross Rd B69 63 B7
Lye Sta DY9 81 E6
Lye Valley Ind Est DY9 81 F6
Lygon Cl B98 154 A5
Lygon Gr B32 84 E4
Lymedene Rd B42 55 B5
Lyme Green Rd B33 68 F4
Lymer Rd WV10 11 C1
Lymesy St CV3 133 D7
Lymington Cl CV6 113 D8
Lymington Ct B73 46 B1
Lymington Dr CV6 96 B6
Lymington Rd WV13 27 D2
Lymore Croft CV2 115 A8
Lynbrook Cl
Dudley DY2 62 D5
Hollywood B47 125 A7
Lynbrook Rd CV5 132 D8
Lynchgate Ct CV4 132 C6
Lynchgate Ho CV4 132 C6
Lynchgate Rd CV4 132 C6
Lynch The
Nuneaton CV11 73 D2
Polesworth B78 22 F1
Lyncourt Gr B32 84 B6
Lyncroft Rd B11 87 F2
Lyndale B77 35 F6
Lyndale Cl CV5 112 C3
Lyndale Dr WV11 26 E6
Lyndale Rd
Coventry CV5 112 C3
Dudley DY2 62 E6
Sedgley DY3 39 B2
Lynden Cl B61 136 E3
Lynden Ho CV5 133 B8
Lyndenwood B97 153 A2
Lyndholm Rd DY10 117 A6
Lyndhurst Cl
Bedworth CV6 96 B6
Hinckley LE10 76 A7
Lyndhurst Croft CV5 111 C4
Lyndhurst Dr
Kidderminster DY10 116 E8
Stourbridge DY8 60 F1
Lyndhurst Rd
Birmingham B24 56 F2
Cannock WS12 2 E1
West Bromwich B71 53 E7
Wolverhampton WV3 39 A7
Lyndon B71 53 D5
Lyndon Cl
Birmingham, Castle Bromwich B36 69 C8
Birmingham, Handsworth B20 55 C2
Halesowen B63 82 F4
Sedgley DY3 39 E1
Lyndon Croft B37 90 B7
Lyndon Ct CV32 161 E8
Lyndon Gr
Kingswinford DY6 60 B8
West Bromwich B71 53 D4
Lyndon Green Inf Sch B26 89 A6
Lyndon Green Jun Sch B26 89 A6
Lyndon Ho B31 103 B3
Lyndon Rd
Birmingham, Rubery B45 121 E7
Birmingham, Stechford B33 68 E3
Solihull B92 88 F2
Sutton Coldfield B73 46 B5
Lyndon Sch B92 89 A3
Lyndworth Rd B30 104 C8
Lyneham Cl
Hinckley LE10 71 A1
Tamworth B79 21 C8
Lyneham Gdns B76 58 B6
Lyneham Way B35 57 F3
Lyne Ho 1 CV2 114 D8
Lynfield Cl B38 123 F7
Lyng Cl CV5 112 A4
Lyng Hall Sch CV2 114 C6
Lyng La B70 53 C2
Lyng Prim Sch B70 53 C1
Lynmouth Cl
Aldridge WS9 30 A5
Nuneaton CV11 73 E5
Lynmouth Rd CV2 114 E8
Lynn Gr B29 85 C3
Lynn La WS14 17 D6
Lynnon Field CV34 160 B4
Lynton Ave
Smethwick B66 65 A6
West Bromwich B71 53 C7
Wolverhampton WV6 24 F6
Lynton Cl CV34 155 E1
Lynton Ho B23 56 B6
Lynton Rd
Birmingham B6 67 B7
Coventry CV6 95 F1
Lynval Rd DY5 81 F7
Lynwood Ave DY6 60 B7
Lynwood Cl
Walsall WV12 13 E1
Willenhall WV12 27 E8
Lynwood Dr DY10 98 C2
Lynwood Way B45 122 A3
Lynwood Wlk
Birmingham B17 85 D4
10 Royal Leamington Spa CV31 162 C6
Lyon Ct B72 46 C5
Lyons Gr B11 87 C3
Lysander Cl LE10 75 E4
Lysander Rd B45 102 A2
Lysander Way
Birmingham B35 58 B2
Cannock WS11 1 E3
Lyster Cl CV34 160 B8
Lysway Ct 3 WS1 42 F8
Lysways St WS1 42 F8
Lythall Cl CV31 162 F5
Lythalls La CV6 95 E2
Lythalls Lane Ind Est CV6 95 E1
Lytham B77 22 C5
Lytham Cl
Stourbridge DY8 80 F2
Sutton Coldfield B76 58 B6
Lytham Croft B15 86 D8
Lytham Gr WS3 14 A4
Lytham Rd WV6 23 D4
Lythwood Dr DY5 81 C8
Lyttelton Pl DY9 99 C6
Lyttelton Rd
Birmingham, Edgbaston B16 65 D1
Birmingham, Stechford B33 68 D3
Stourbridge DY8 80 D5
Warwick CV34 160 E8
Lyttleton Ave
Bromsgrove B60 150 E7
Halesowen B62 83 E7
Lyttleton Cl
Coventry CV3 115 A1
Dudley DY2 62 C4
Lyttleton Ho B63 83 A2
Lyttleton St B70 53 C2
Lytton Ave WV4 38 E4
Lytton Gr B27 88 B1
Lytton La B32 84 F3

M

Maas Rd B31 103 A4
Mabey Ave B98 153 F5
MacAdam Cl WS7 7 B8
MacArthur Rd B64 82 C8
MacAulay Ho 5 B70 53 D1
MacAulay Rd CV2 114 D4
McBean Rd WV6 24 F4
Macbeth App CV34 161 D4
McCalla Ho WV3 25 B1
McConnell Cl B60 151 B7
MacDonald Cl B69 52 D2
MacDonald Rd CV2 114 D3
MacDonald St B5 86 E8
McDonnell Dr CV6, CV7 95 F6
McDougall Rd WS10 42 C3
Macefield Cl CV2 96 D2
Mace St B64 62 E1
McGeough Wlk WS11 2 B5
McGhie St WS12 2 B6
McGregor Cl 4 B6 55 F1
MacGregor Cres B77 21 F3
MacGregor Tithe B79 21 B5
Machin Rd B23 56 F4
Mackadown B33 69 D2
Mackay Rd WS3 14 D2
McKean Rd
Oldbury B69 64 A8
West Bromwich B70 53 C1
Mcken Ct B70 53 C1
Mackenzie Cl CV5 112 A7
Mackenzie Rd B11 87 C2
Mackmillan Rd B65 63 C2
McLean Rd WV10 11 C1
McMahon Rd CV12 95 E8
Macmillan Cl B69 52 C2
Macrome Rd WV6 24 E8
Madam's Hill Rd B90 126 D7
Maddocke Wlk 4 WS13 8 F6
Maddocks Hill B72 46 C2
Madehurst Rd B23 56 E6
Madeira Ave WV8 10 A2
Madeira Croft CV5 112 E2
Madeira Ct DY8 60 F1
Madeley Rd
Birmingham B11 87 C5
Kingswinford DY6 61 A4
Madeley Heath DY9 120 D6
Redditch B98 154 F5
Madinatul Uloom Al Islamiya Sch DY10 117 D1
Madin Rd DY4 51 E4
Madison Ave
Birmingham B36 68 D6
Brierley Hill DY5 61 F3
Walsall WS2 28 B2
Madley Cl B45 121 E8
Madox Cl B79 20 E8
Madresfield Dr B63 83 B2
Madrona B77 22 B4
Maer Cl B65 63 C3
Mafeking Rd B66 65 A7
Mafeking Villas B62 83 B7
Magdala St B18 65 E5
Magdalen Cl DY1 51 A2
Magdalen Ct B16 65 E1
Magdalene Rd WS1 43 A7
Magee Cl LE10 71 C2
Magna Cl WS6 4 E3
Magness Cres WV12 27 C5
Magnet Wlk B23 56 C3
Magnolia B77 22 A4
Magnolia Cl
Birmingham B29 103 A7
Coventry CV3 133 B5
Magnolia Dr 1 WS5 42 F4
Magnolia Gr
Codsall WV8 10 B3
Willenhall WV12 27 B4
Magnolia Way 1 DY8 60 F1
Magnum Cl B74 44 F7
Magnus B77 35 E6
Magpie Cl DY2 62 E3
Magpie Ho CV5 111 D5
Magpie La CV7 129 E6
Magpie Way DY10 117 B2
Maguire Ind Est CV4 131 F8
Magyar Cres CV11 79 A8
Maidavale Cres CV3 133 C4
Maiden Cl WV13 27 C2
Maidendale Rd DY6 60 B7
Maidensbridge Dr DY6 60 C8
Maidensbridge Gdns DY6 49 B1
Maidensbridge Prim Sch DY6 49 B1
Maidensbridge Rd DY6 49 B1
Maiden Way B60 151 A6
Maidstone Dr
Burntwood WS7 7 D6
Stourbridge DY8 60 E3
Maidstone Rd B20 55 E1
Maidwell Dr B90 126 E8
Mailbox The B1 164 B1
Main Rd Ansty CV7 97 D3
Main Rd *continued*
Meriden CV7 110 D8
Tamworth B79 21 B8
Main St
Birmingham B11 87 A7
Brandon CV8 135 F4
Shenstone WS14 17 F6
Stonnall WS9 16 D4
Mainstone Cl B98 154 E3
Mainstream Forty Seven Ind Pk B7 67 C5
Mainstream Way B7 67 C5
Main Terr B11 87 A7
Mainwaring Dr B75 32 E2
Maisemore Cl B98 154 D6
Maitland B77 21 F2
Maitland Rd
Birmingham B8 67 F4
Dudley DY1 50 E1
Maizefield LE10 71 C4
Majestic Way B65 63 D4
Major Ct 6 B13 87 B2
Major St WV2 39 E7
Majuba Rd B16 65 C4
Makepeace Ave CV34 155 F1
Malam Cl CV4 112 A1
Malcolm Ave
Birmingham B24 57 C5
Bromsgrove B61 136 E3
Malcolm Ct WV1 25 A3
Malcolm Gr B45 122 A7
Malcolm Rd B90 106 B1
Malcolmson Cl B15 85 F8
Maldale B77 22 C1
Malfield Ave B97 152 F3
Malfield Dr B27 88 E3
Malham Cl CV11 74 A2
Malham Rd
Tamworth B77 36 C8
Warwick CV34 155 F1
Malhay Gdns 4 B42 55 A8
Malin Ct B23 56 B8
Malins Rd
Birmingham B17 85 D5
Wolverhampton WV4 39 E5
Malins The CV34 161 B6
Malkit Cl WS2 27 F4
Mallaby Cl B90 126 A8
Mallard Ave
Kidderminster DY10 117 B3
Nuneaton CV10 72 C6
Mallard Cl
Birmingham B27 88 C3
Brierley Hill DY5 81 C7
Redditch B98 153 F5
Walsall WS3 15 A5
Mallard Croft 5 WS13 9 C8
Mallard Dr
Birmingham B23 56 B3
Hinckley LE10 75 A7
Oldbury B69 63 F4
Mallard Rd B80 159 F4
Mallards Reach B92 106 E8
Mallender Dr B93 127 F6
Mallen Dr B69 52 B1
Mallerin Croft CV10 72 B5
Mallicot Cl WS13 3 D1
Mallin Gdns DY1 61 E8
Mallin St B66 64 D7
Mallory Cres WS3 14 D2
Mallory Dr
Kidderminster DY11 116 D8
Warwick CV34 160 D7
Mallory Rd WV6 23 E3
Mallory Rise B13 87 C1
Mallory Way CV6 95 E4
Mallow Cl 8 WS5 43 A3
Mallow Cres DY10 116 F4
Mallow Croft CV12 77 E2
Mallow Ct WV6 25 B5
Mallow Dr B61 136 F6
Mallow Rise 2 B23 56 B7
Mallows Cl WS10 41 D6
Malmesbury Pk B15 85 E7
Malmesbury Rd
Birmingham B10 87 E7
Coventry CV6 95 A3
Malpas Dr B32 102 C8
Malpass Rd DY5 81 F7
Malpas Wlk WV10 26 A4
Malt Cl B17 85 D6
Malthouse Croft B6 66 E8
Malthouse Dr DY1 51 A2
Malthouse Gdns B19 66 D7
Malthouse Gr B25 68 E1
Malthouse La
Birmingham B8 67 E6
Birmingham, Great Barr B42 55 D8
Malthouse La *continued*
Earlswood B94 141 E7
Kenilworth CV8 147 E6
Wolverhampton WV6 24 E6
Malthouse Mdw 2 B91 107 C1
Malthouse Rd DY4 51 E5
Malthouse Row B37 90 A8
Maltings Ct B17 65 A1
Maltings The
Aldridge WS9 30 C6
Nuneaton CV11 73 E5
Royal Leamington Spa CV32 156 F2
Studley B80 159 D4
Wolverhampton WV1 163 C4
Malt Mill La B62 83 D8
Malt Mill Lane Trad Est B62 83 D8
Malton Ave B65 63 D6
Malton Gr B13 105 B7
Malvern Ave
Nuneaton CV10 72 B3
Stourbridge DY9 81 C5
Malvern Cl
Birmingham B15 85 C8
West Bromwich B71 53 D5
Willenhall WV12 27 B4
Malvern Cres DY2 61 F6
Malvern Ct
Birmingham, Stockfield B27 88 C4
Birmingham, Stockland Green B23 56 C2
8 Sutton Coldfield B74 31 F2
Wolverhampton WV10 25 D8
Malvern Dr
Aldridge WS9 30 C8
Kidderminster DY10 116 E3
Sutton Coldfield B76 58 A8
Wolverhampton WV1 26 B1
Malvern Hill Rd B7 67 C7
Malvern Ho
Coventry CV5 111 D4
7 Halesowen B63 83 A3
Redditch B97 153 C1
Malvern Park Ave B91 107 D3
Malvern Rd
Balsall Common CV7 130 C6
Barnt Green B45 122 A2
Birmingham, Acock's Green B27 88 D4
Birmingham B68 84 B8
Birmingham, Handsworth B21 54 C1
Bromsgrove B61 150 D7
Coventry CV5 112 F4
Redditch B97 158 D8
Malvern St B12 87 A5
Malvern View
Bluntington DY10 118 E1
Kidderminster DY11 116 B1
Malvern View Rd DY3 50 D4
Mamble Rd DY8 80 E5
Mammoth Dr WV10 25 D6
Manby Cl WV6 25 A4
Manby Rd B35 58 A4
Manby St DY4 51 F8
Mancetter Rd
Nuneaton CV10 72 D7
Solihull B90 106 C3
Manchester St
Birmingham B6 164 C5
Oldbury B69 64 B7
Mancroft Cl DY6 60 B7
Mancroft Gdns WV6 24 C5
Mancroft Rd WV6 24 C5
Mandale Rd WV10 25 F6
Mandarin Ave DY10 117 B3
Mandarin Cl LE10 75 A6
Mander Ctr WV1 163 B3
Mander Gallery WV1 163 B3
Mander Gr CV34 160 C4
Manderley Cl
Coventry CV5 111 C5
Sedgley DY3 39 C2
Manders Ind Est WV1 26 A3
Mander Sq WV1 163 B3
Mander St WV3 163 A1
Manderston Cl DY1 50 E3
Manderville Gdns DY6 60 C6
Mandeville Gdns WS1 42 F8
Mandeville Way B61 136 F5
Mandrake Cl CV6 95 D4
Maney Cnr B72 46 B4

Maney Hill Prim Sch
B72 .... 46 D2
Maney Hill Rd B72 .. 46 C2
Manfield Ave CV2 ... 115 A7
Manfield Rd WV13.... 26 C3
Manifold Cl WS7 .... 7 D6
Manifoldia Grange
B70 .... 53 B2
Manifold Way WS10 .. 42 E3
Manilla Rd B29 ..... 86 B1
Manitoba Croft [2]
B38 .... 123 F8
Manley Cl B70 ..... 53 A3
Manley Rd WS13 .... 3 D1
Manningford Ct B14. 104 F3
Manningford Rd B14 104 E3
Manor Abbey Rd B62. 83 E4
Manor Ave
Cannock WS11 ...... 1 D1
Great Wyrley WS6....5 A4
Kidderminster DY11 . 116 A7
Manor Ave S DY11... 116 A6
Manor Cl
Birmingham B16..... 65 D1
Codsall WV8 .... 10 B4
Hinckley LE10 .... 75 C5
Kidderminster DY11 . 116 A6
Willenhall WV13 .... 26 F3
Wolverhampton WV4 .. 38 F4
Manor Cotts WS14 ....8 E2
Manor Court Ave
CV11 .... 73 B5
Manor Court Mews
CV11 .... 73 A5
Manor Court Rd
Bromsgrove B60..... 150 F8
Nuneaton CV11....... 73 A5
Manor Ct
[5] Birmingham, Hurst
Green B62 .... 84 A7
Birmingham, King's Norton
B30.............. 104 A2
Dorridge B93 ...... 127 F2
Dudley DY2 .... 62 C5
Kenilworth CV8..... 148 A6
Mile Oak B78 .... 20 D1
Royal Leamington Spa
CV31.............. 161 F7
Walsall WS2 .... 28 C1
Manor Dr Dudley DY3 . 50 B3
Sutton Coldfield B73... 46 B4
Manor Est CV8...... 135 F3
Manor Farm Craft Ctr★
B94 .... 125 F2
Manor Farm Dr WV12 27 D5
Manor Farm Rd B11.. 87 E4
Manor Flats B13 .... 50 D8
Manorford Ave B71 .. 43 A1
Manor Gdns
Birmingham B33...... 68 D2
Wednesbury WS10.... 41 F4
Wombourne WV5 .... 49 B7
Manor Hall Mews
CV3 .... 134 D6
Manor High Sch
WS10.............. 42 D3
Manor Hill B73...... 46 B4
Manor Ho WV6...... 24 D5
Manor Hospl WS2 .... 28 C1
Manor Ho The CV31 . 161 F7
Manor House Cl
Aston Flamville LE10 .. 76 E6
Birmingham B29..... 84 F1
Manor House Dr
Birmingham B29..... 103 B7
Coventry CV1 .... 165 B2
Manor House La
Astwood Bank B96... 158 E3
Birmingham B26..... 88 F6
Water Orton B46..... 59 B3
Manor House Pk WV8 10 B4
Manor House Rd
WS10.............. 41 F4
Manorial Rd B75.... 32 E3
Manor Ind Est WS2 . 28 C1
Manor Jun & Inf Sch
WV4...............40 B2
Manor La
Halesowen B62...... 83 E4
Honiley CV8, CV35 ... 146 A5
Lower Marlbrook B61. 121 C4
Stourbridge DY8..... 80 D3
Wroxall CV35 ...... 145 F4
Manor Mews B80 ... 159 E4
Manor Park Cl B13... 87 A2
Manor Park Com Sch
CV11.............. 73 A5

Manor Park Gr B31.. 102 C1
Manor Park Prim Sch
Birmingham B6...... 67 A8
Coventry CV3 ......133 D7
Manor Park Rd
Birmingham B36..... 69 D8
Nuneaton CV11...... 73 A5
Manor Pl LE10 ...... 71 D1
Manor Prim Sch
Drayton Bassett B78 .. 34 E5
Sutton Coldfield B74... 31 A1
Manor Rd
Birmingham, Birchfield
B6................ 55 F1
Birmingham, Edgbaston
B16.............. 65 D1
Birmingham, Stechford
B33.............. 68 A3
Coventry CV1 ...... 165 B1
Dorridge B93 ...... 127 F3
Ettingshall WV4 .... 40 A5
Kenilworth CV8..... 147 F6
Mile Oak B78 .... 20 D1
Royal Leamington Spa
CV32............. 157 B3
Smethwick B67..... 64 E4
Solihull B91....... 107 C5
Stourbridge DY8..... 60 E2
Studley B80........ 159 E4
Sutton Coldfield B74... 31 A1
Sutton Coldfield, Maney
B73.............. 46 B4
Sutton Coldfield, Streetly
B74.............. 45 A8
Tamworth B77...... 21 D4
Tipton DY4 .... 51 F4
Upper Bentley B97... 152 B1
Walsall WS2 .... 28 C2
Wednesbury WS10.... 42 C2
Wolverhampton, Oxley
WV10 .... 25 C7
Wolverhampton WV4 .. 38 F4
Wythall B47........ 125 A3
Manor Rd N B16 .... 65 D1
Manor Rise
Burntwood WS7 .....7 A5
Lichfield WS14 ..... 9 C7
Manor Road Prec [2]
WS2 .... 28 C2
Manor Side Ind Est
B98............... 154 E6
Manor Sq B91....... 107 C3
Manor St
Hinckley LE10 ...... 71 C1
Wolverhampton WV6 .. 24 D5
Manor Terr CV8..... 148 A6
Manor View CV8 .... 135 F3
Manor Way
Halesowen B62, B63 .. 83 D3
Hinckley LE10 ...... 75 D5
Manor Wlk
[4] Solihull B91...... 107 C3
Sutton Coldfield B73... 46 B4
Mansard Cl
Wolverhampton, Bradmore
WV3.............. 38 F8
Wolverhampton, Scotlands
WV10 .... 26 B8
Mansard Rd B90.... 106 A3
Manse Cl CV7 ...... 78 A1
Manse Gdns B80.... 159 E3
Mansell Cl B63...... 82 B7
Mansell Rd
Redditch B97 ......158 D7
Tipton DY4 .... 52 A8
Mansel Rd B10...... 87 E8
Mansel St CV6 ..... 113 E8
Mansfield Cl B79.... 20 E6
Mansfield Green Com
Sch B6 ....66 E8
Mansfield Ho B37 ... 70 D3
Mansfield Rd
Birmingham, Aston B6.. 66 E8
Birmingham, South Yardley
B25.............. 88 C5
Mansion Cl DY1..... 51 A3
Mansion Cres B67... 64 E4
Mansion Ct B62..... 83 E7
Mansion Dr
Hammerwich WS7 ... 7 D4
Tipton DY4 .... 52 C5
Mansion St [1] LE10 . 75 D8
Manson Ct WV4..... 38 D5
Manson Dr B64 ..... 63 A1
Manston Dr WV6.... 23 E5
Manston Rd B26.... 89 B7
Manston View B79 .. 21 C8

Manta Rd B77........ 35 D6
Mantilla Dr CV3......133 A5
Manton Croft B93... 127 E3
Manton Ho B19 ..... 66 E7
Manway CV1 B20 .....54 F4
Manwoods Cl B20... 55 B2
Maple Ave
Bedworth CV7....... 78 B1
Wednesbury WS10 .. 42 C4
Maple Bank B15 .... 86 A7
Maplebeck Cl CV5... 113 A3
Maple Bsns Pk B7 ...67 B6
Maple Cl
Birmingham B21..... 54 E1
Burntwood WS7 ......6 F7
Dudley WV14 .... 51 A7
Hinckley LE10 ...... 75 E5
Kidderminster DY11 .. 116 B8
Stourbridge DY8 .... 80 D2
Maple Cres WS11 .....1 C1
Maple Croft B13 .... 104 F5
Maple Ct Bilston WV14 .40 F7
[2] Birmingham, Erdington
B24............... 56 F3
[1] Birmingham, Harborne
B17............... 85 B6
Lichfield WS14 ....9 C5
Oldbury B66 .... 64 D8
Maple Ctr The WS10 ..41 B3
Mapledene B13 ..... 87 B2
Mapledene Inf Sch
B26............... 89 D6
Mapledene Jun Sch
B26............... 89 D6
Mapledene Rd B26... 89 D6
Maple Dr
Birmingham B44...... 56 C8
Dudley DY3 .... 50 B2
Huntington WS12 .... 1 D8
Walsall, Shelfield WS4 . 29 B8
Walsall, Yew Tree WS5 . 43 B4
Maple Gn DY1....... 51 A5
Maple Gr Bilston WV14 .40 F4
Birmingham, Aston B19 66 D8
Birmingham, Kingshurst
B37............... 69 F6
Kingswinford DY6 .... 60 E6
Lichfield WS14 ....9 F7
Warwick CV34 ..... 156 A1
Wolverhampton WV3 . 24 C2
Maple Hayes Hall Sch
WS13 ....8 D8
Maple Ho
Redditch, Greenlands
B98............... 158 F8
Redditch, Webheath
B97............... 153 B2
Sutton Coldfield B74... 31 B5
Walsall WS4 .... 15 D1
Maple Leaf Dr B37 .. 90 B8
Maple Leaf Ind Est
WS2 .... 28 A3
Maple Leaf Rd WS10 . 41 C1
Maple Rd
Birmingham B45..... 121 F6
Birmingham, Selly Oak
B30............... 103 E8
Dudley DY1 .... 51 C3
Halesowen B62...... 83 D8
Nuneaton CV10...... 72 E5
Royal Leamington Spa
CV31............. 161 F6
Sutton Coldfield B72.. 46 C3
Walsall WS3 .... 14 F2
Wolverhampton WV3 . 38 E8
Maple Rise
Oldbury B68 .... 64 C2
Tamworth B77....... 22 A4
Maple Row [1] DY5... 61 D2
Maple St WS3 ...... 14 D2
Maples The
Bedworth CV12...... 77 E2
Wolverhampton WV11 . 26 B5
Mapledon B28...... 106 B7
Mapleton Rd
Birmingham B28..... 106 B7
Coventry CV6 ...... 112 F8
Maple Tree La B63 .. 82 C6
Maple Way B31...... 102 F1
Maple Wlk
[4] Birmingham B37... 70 B2
Coventry CV6 ...... 95 F5
Maplewood B76...... 58 A8
Mapperley Cl CV2... 115 A8
Mapperley Gdns B13. 86 C3
Mappleborough Cl
B97............... 153 B6
Mappleborough Rd
B90............... 105 E1

Mapps Cl B63........ 82 C6
Marans Croft B38... 123 D7
Marble Alley B80.... 159 E4
Marbury Cl B38..... 103 D2
Marbury Dr WV14 ... 41 A6
Marbury Mews DY5 .. 61 D1
Marchant Rd
Bilston WV14 .... 40 D7
Hinckley LE10 ...... 75 C8
Wolverhampton WV6 . 24 F2
March Cl WS6....... 4 D1
March End Rd WV11.. 26 D5
Marchfont Cl CV11... 74 A1
Marchmont Rd B9 ... 68 A2
Marchmount Rd B72. 57 C8
March Way
Aldridge WS9 .... 16 C1
Coventry CV3 ...... 134 D7
Marchwood Cl B97... 153 A5
Marcliff Cres B90... 105 C2
Marconi Pl WS12.....2 C7
Marcos Dr B36......58 F1
Marcot Rd B92......88 F5
Marcroft Pl CV31... 162 D6
Marden Cl WV13 .....26 F1
Marden Gr B31..... 123 A7
Marden Wlk B23 .... 56 C3
Mardol Cl CV2 ..... 114 D7
Mardon Rd B26..... 89 C5
Maree Gr WV11 ..... 13 B1
Maret Ct [2] WS1 ....42 F8
Marfield Cl B76..... 58 A6
Margam Cres WS3 ...13 F2
Margam Terr WS3 ...13 F2
Margam Way WS3 ...13 F2
Margaret Ave
Bedworth CV12...... 78 B3
Halesowen B63...... 82 F4
Margaret Cl DY5 .... 81 E8
Margaret Dr
Cannock WS11 ....1 E6
Stourbridge DY8..... 81 B4
Margaret Gdns B67 .. 64 E5
Margaret Gr B17 .... 85 C7
Margaret Ho B76....46 F3
Margaret Rd
Birmingham, Harborne
B17............... 85 C5
Birmingham, New Oscott
B73.............. 45 D1
Darlaston WS10 ..... 41 C4
Walsall WS2 .... 27 E3
Margaret St
Birmingham B3...... 164 B3
West Bromwich B70.. 53 B2
Margaret Vale DY4 .. 41 C1
Margaret Vine Ct B62. .63 F1
Margeson Cl CV2.... 114 E2
Margesson Dr B45 .. 122 D1
Margetts Cl CV8..... 147 F4
Margreal Ind Est B16 .65 F3
Marholm Cl WV9.....10 F2
Marian Croft B26.... 89 D5
Maria St B70........ 53 B2
Marie Brock Cl CV4 . 112 B1
Marie Dr B27 ...... 106 B8
Marigold Cl WS11 ....2 C3
Marigold Cres DY1 .. 51 A4
Marigold Dr LE10 ... 75 C5
Marigold Wlk CV10 .. 78 A8
Marina Cl CV4 ..... 131 E7
Marina Cres WS12.....2 A5
Marine Cres DY8 .... 60 E1
Marine Dr B44...... 55 E6
Marine Gdns DY8 ... 60 E1
Mariner B79 .... 20 E6
Mariner Ave B16 .... 65 E1
Marion Cl DY5 ......61 F2
Marion Rd
Coventry CV6 ...... 113 D7
Smethwick B67..... 64 E5
Marion Way B28 .... 105 E7
Marita Cl DY2 ...... 62 E3
Marjoram Cl B38.... 123 F8
Marjorie Ave B30 ... 104 B3
Mark Antony Dr
CV34 .... 161 D4
Mark Ave WS10 ..... 41 E3
Markby Rd B18 ..... 65 E6
Mark Cl B98 .... 153 E2
Mark Ct WS1........ 29 A3
Market Cnr
Baginton CV8 ...... 133 D2
[7] Royal Leamington Spa
CV31............. 161 F6
Market End Cl CV12 . 77 C2
Market Hall St WS11 . 1 C1
Market La
Lichfield WS14 ......8 E2
Lower Penn WV4 .... 37 F5

Market Pl
Bromsgrove B61..... 136 F2
[4] Cannock WS11 ....1 E1
Dudley DY1 .... 51 D1
Hinckley LE10 ...... 75 D8
Redditch B98 ...... 153 E4
Rowley Regis B65.... 63 C1
Tamworth B79...... 21 B4
Tipton DY4 .... 52 D5
Walsall WS3 .... 14 B1
Warwick CV34 ..... 160 E6
Wednesbury WS10.... 41 F2
Willenhall WV13 .... 27 A1
Market Sq
Cradley Heath B64 ... 82 C8
Wolverhampton WV3 . 163 B2
Market St
Bromsgrove B61..... 136 F2
Cannock WS12 ......2 C5
Kidderminster DY10 . 116 E5
Kingswinford DY6 ... 60 D6
Lichfield WS13 ....9 B8
Oldbury B69 .... 64 A8
Stourbridge DY8..... 81 A5
Tamworth B79...... 21 B4
Warwick CV34 ..... 160 D6
Wolverhampton WV1 . 163 C3
Market Way
Bilston WV14 .... 40 D5
Coventry CV1 ...... 165 B2
Hagley DY9 .... 99 C6
Market Wlk [4] B97.. 153 E4
Markfield Rd B26.... 89 B8
Markford Wlk B19... 66 D6
Markham Cres B92...89 F1
Markham Croft WV9.. 11 A2
Markham Dr
Kingswinford DY6.... 60 E4
Whitnash CV31..... 162 B3
Markham Rd B73.... 45 C3
Mark Ho B13........ 87 A2
Marklew Cl WS8 .... 16 A5
Marklin Ave WV10... 11 D1
Mark Rd WS10 ..... 41 E3
Marksbury Cl WV6 .. 25 A5
Marks Mews [7]
CV34 .... 160 E6
Marks Wlk WS13 .....3 A2
Marlbank Rd DY8 ... 61 A1
Marlborough Ave
B60 .... 151 B8
Marlborough Cl
Hinckley LE10 ...... 76 B7
Sutton Coldfield B74... 31 E6
Marlborough Ct
Bromsgrove B60..... 151 B8
Lichfield WS13 ....9 B7
[3] Sutton Coldfield B74 31 F2
Sutton Coldfield, Falcon
Lodge B75 .... 47 A6
Marlborough Dr
Royal Leamington Spa
CV31............. 162 D5
Stourbridge DY8..... 81 A3
Marlborough Gdns
Stourbridge DY8..... 60 D2
Wolverhampton WV6 . 24 E4
Marlborough Gr B25. 88 D1
Marlborough Ind Est
WV2.............. 39 D7
Marlborough Inf Sch
B10................67 E1
Marlborough Jun Sch
B10................67 E1
Marlborough Mews
B80 .... 159 E4
Marlborough Rd
Birmingham, Castle
Bromwich B36...... 69 D8
Birmingham, Small Heath
B10............... 67 E1
Coventry CV2 ...... 114 A3
Dudley DY3 .... 50 F6
Nuneaton CV10...... 73 B3
Smethwick B66..... 65 A3
Marlborough St
[2] Kidderminster
DY10.............. 116 E5
Walsall WS3 .... 14 B1
Marlborough Way
B77...............21 F2
Marlbrook Cl B92.... 89 C4
Marlbrook Dr WV4 .. 39 B6
Marlbrook Gdns B61. 121 B1
Marlbrook La B60... 121 D2
Marlcliff Gr B13..... 105 A6
Marlcroft CV3....... 134 C5
Marldon Rd B14.... 104 E6

Marlene Croft B37 ... 70 C1
Marler Rd CV4 ..... 131 F7
Marley Hts B27 ..... 88 D4
Marley Rd DY6 ..... 61 A4
Marlfield Farm Fst Sch
B98............... 154 C6
Marlfield La
Redditch, Abbeydale
B98............... 154 B4
Redditch, Church Hill
B98............... 154 B5
Marlgrove Ct B61 ... 137 B8
Marlin B77......... 35 D6
Marling Croft B92... 107 F7
Marlissa Dr CV6..... 95 E2
Marloes Wlk CV31... 162 C6
Marlow Cl
Coventry CV5 ...... 112 B4
Dudley DY2 .... 62 E3
Marlowe Cl DY10 ... 117 B6
Marlowe Dr WV12.... 27 A7
Marlow Rd
Birmingham B23..... 56 D5
Tamworth B77...... 21 D5
Marlow St
Rowley Regis B65.... 63 B1
Walsall WS2 .... 28 E3
Marlpit La
Redditch B97 ...... 153 C1
Sutton Coldfield B75.. 32 E3
Marlpit Rise [1] B75 .. 32 E3
Marlpool Ct DY11 ... 116 C8
Marlpool Dr
Redditch B97 ...... 153 C3
Walsall WS3 .... 15 A1
Marlpool Fst Sch
DY11.............. 116 C8
Marlpool La DY11 ... 116 C8
Marlpool Pl DY11 ... 116 C8
Marl Rd DY2 .... 62 B4
Marlston Wlk CV5... 112 B4
Marl Top B38........ 103 F8
Marlwood Cl CV6 ... 95 F4
Marmion Dr B43 .....43 F2
Marmion Gr DY1 ... 62 A8
Marmion Ho B70....52 F6
Marmion Pk B79 ... 21 B6
Marmion St B79 ... 21 B5
Marmion Way B70...52 F6
Marne Cl CV34 ..... 161 A1
Marnel Dr WV3 ..... 38 E7
Marner Cres CV6.... 113 B3
Marner Rd
Bedworth CV12...... 78 A3
Nuneaton CV10...... 73 B1
Marnhull Cl CV2 .... 114 F4
Marquis Dr B62..... 83 A7
Marrick B77........ 22 C1
Marriners La CV5 ... 112 A5
Marriott Rd
Bedworth CV12...... 77 D2
Coventry CV6 ...... 113 A4
Dudley DY2 .... 62 C4
Smethwick B66..... 64 D7
Marroway St B16....65 F3
Marrowfat La B21....65 F7
Mars Cl WV14 ..... 40 A1
Marsdale Dr WS10 .. 72 E3
Marsden Cl B92..... 88 E1
Marsden Rd B98.... 153 E3
Marsett B77........ 36 C3
Marshall Cl WS9 .... 30 B4
Marshall Gr B44.....55 F7
Marshall Ho [4] WS2.. 42 C8
Marshall Lake Rd
B90............... 106 D1
Marshall Rd
Bedworth CV7...... 95 F8
Oldbury B68 .... 64 C1
Willenhall WV13 .... 26 A6
Marshalls Ind Est
WV2.............. 39 C7
Marshall St
Birmingham B1...... 164 B1
Smethwick B67..... 64 D7
Tamworth B77...... 21 E5
Marsham Cl CV34 ... 161 B8
Marsham Court Rd
B91............... 106 F7
Marsham Rd B14.... 104 F3
Marshbrook Cl
Coventry CV2 ...... 96 E3
Sutton Coldfield B24.. 57 B8
Marshbrook Rd B24.. 57 D4
Marsh Cl B23....... 56 F5
Marsh Cres DY8 .... 60 D3
Marshdale Ave CV6 . 95 E3
Marsh End B38 ..... 124 A8
Marshfield B90..... 126 B5
Marshfield Cl B98... 154 B1

Marshfield Dr CV4 .. 132 D2
Marshfield Gdns B24 .. 56 F2
Marsh Gr DY10 .... 116 E8
Marsh Hill B23 .... 56 C4
Marsh Hill Jun & Inf Sch B23 .... 56 C4
Marsh Ho CV2 .... 115 A7
Marsh House Farm La B92 .... 109 D3
Marsh La
Birmingham B23 ...... 56 E5
Bradnock's Marsh B92 .... 109 D5
Curdworth B76 .... 59 D5
Hampton-in-A B92 ... 109 B6
Lichfield WS14 .... 9 C5
Solihull B91 .... 107 E3
Walsall WS2 .... 28 E2
Water Orton B46 ..... 59 C3
West Bromwich B71 ... 53 D8
Wolverhampton WV10 . 11 B2
Marshland Way WS2 . 27 E1
Marsh Lane Par WV10 .... 11 C2
Marshmont Way B23 . 56 D8
Marsh St WS2 .... 28 E2
Marsh The WS10 ...... 41 E3
Marsh Way B61 ..... 120 F1
Marshwood Cl 2 WS11 .... 2 A2
Marshwood Croft B62 84 A3
Marsland Cl B17 ..... 65 C1
Marsland Rd B92 .... 106 E8
Marston Ave WS10 ... 41 C6
Marston Cl
Royal Leamington Spa CV32 .... 157 B2
Stourbridge DY8 ...... 80 D4
Marston Croft B37 .... 89 F7
Marston Dr B37 ...... 70 A5
Marston Gr B43 ...... 54 C8
Marston Green Inf Sch B37 .... 90 A7
Marston Green Jun Sch B37 .... 90 A7
Marston Green Sta B37 .... 89 F7
Marston Ind Est WV2 39 C7
Marston La
Bedworth CV12 .... 78 D5
Nuneaton CV11 .... 78 E8
Wishaw B76 .... 48 E1
Marston Pk B78 .... 20 F4
Marston Rd
Birmingham B29 ..... 102 F8
Cannock WS12 .... 1 F6
Dudley DY1 .... 61 E8
Sutton Coldfield B73 ... 57 A7
Wolverhampton WV2 .. 39 C7
Marston St WV13 ..... 27 C2
Marten Cl CV35 ..... 160 A7
Martham Dr WV6 ...... 24 B2
Martin Cl
Birmingham B26 ...... 88 D6
Bromsgrove B61 ..... 136 E1
Coventry CV5 .... 111 E4
Dudley WV14 .... 51 D7
Martin Croft WS13 ..... 3 A1
Martindale WS11 .... 2 A2
Martindale Rd CV7 ... 96 C8
Martindale Trad Est WS11 .... 2 A2
Martindale Wlk DY5 .. 81 B6
Martin Dr WV12 ...... 27 C5
Martineau Pl B2 .... 164 C2
Martineau Twr B19 ... 66 D5
Martingale Cl
4 Bromsgrove B60 .. 150 E6
Walsall WS5 .... 42 F4
Martin Hill St DY2 .... 62 C8
Martinique Sq CV34 . 160 D6
Martin Rd
Bilston WV14 .... 40 F3
Tipton DY4 .... 52 A4
Walsall WS5 .... 43 C8
Martin Rise B37 .... 89 F8
Martins Rd CV12 ..... 77 E1
Martin St WV4 .... 39 F5
Martlesham Sq B35 .. 58 A4
Martley Cl B98 ...... 159 B7
Martley Croft
Birmingham B32 ...... 84 E4
Solihull B91 .... 127 B8
Martley Dr DY9 .... 81 C4
Martley Rd
Oldbury B69 .... 63 D5
Walsall WS4 .... 15 C2
Marton Ave WS7 .... 7 A8
Marton Cl B7 .... 67 B6
Martyrs' Cl The CV3 . 133 D8
Marwood Cl CV11 .... 78 E7
Marwood Croft B74 .. 31 A2
Mary Ann St
Birmingham B3 ...... 164 B4
Wolverhampton WV1 . 163 D2
Mary Elliot Specl Sch WS2 .... 28 E4
Mary Herbert St CV3 .... 133 D7
Maryland Ave B34 ..... 68 F5
Maryland Cl LE9 ...... 71 F6
Maryland Dr B31 .... 103 B5
Maryland Rd DY5 ...... 81 F7
Marylebone Cl DY8 ... 81 A7
Mary Macarthur Dr B64 .... 62 C1
Mary Rd
Birmingham, Handsworth B21 .... 65 E7
Birmingham, Stechford B33 .... 68 D3
Oldbury B69 .... 63 C8
West Bromwich B70 ... 53 D1
Mary Rose Cl WS6 ..... 4 D1
Mary Slessor St CV3 . 134 D7
Mary St
Birmingham, Balsall Heath B12 .... 86 E5
Birmingham, Brookfields B3 .... 164 A4
Cannock WS12 .... 2 B7
Walsall WS2 .... 28 D3
Marystow Cl CV5 .... 112 B8
Maryvale Ct
Lichfield WS14 .... 9 D7
2 Walsall WS1 ...... 42 E8
Maryvale RC Prim Sch B44 .... 44 E1
Mary Vale Rd B30 ... 103 F6
Marywell Cl B32 .... 102 B7
Masefield Ave
Dudley DY1 .... 51 C7
Warwick CV34 ...... 160 C4
Masefield Cl
Bilston WV14 .... 40 F2
Lichfield WS14 .... 9 B6
Masefield Dr B79 ..... 21 A7
Masefield Gdns 1 DY10 .... 117 B6
Masefield Gr WS11 ..... 1 E4
Masefield Mews WV10 .... 12 A1
Masefield Rd
Dudley DY3 .... 50 A4
Walsall WS3 .... 28 E7
Wolverhampton WV10 . 12 A1
Masefield Rise B62 ... 83 D3
Masefield Sq B31 ... 103 C4
Masham Cl B33 ...... 68 E3
Mashie Gdns B38 ... 103 D1
Maslen Pl B63 .... 83 B3
Maslin Dr WV14 ...... 40 A1
Mason Ave CV32 .... 157 C3
Mason Cl B97 .... 158 D7
Mason Cotts B24 ..... 57 B5
Mason Cres WV4 ..... 38 E5
Mason Ct LE10 .... 75 B8
Mason Gr CV8 ...... 148 B5
Mason La B94 .... 125 F1
Masonleys Rd B31 .. 102 D3
Mason Rd
Birmingham B24 ...... 57 A4
Coventry CV6 .... 95 F1
Kidderminster DY11 .. 116 C6
Redditch B97 .... 158 D8
Walsall WS2 .... 28 B5
Masons Cl B63 .... 82 C6
Mason St Dudley WV14 51 B7
West Bromwich B70 ... 53 B4
Wolverhampton WV2 .. 39 C7
Masons View B24 ..... 57 A2
Mason's Way B92 .... 88 E2
Masons Yd DY11 .... 116 D6
Massbrook Gr WV10 .. 25 F6
Massbrook Rd WV10 .. 25 F6
Masser Rd CV6 .... 95 D4
Masshouse La
Birmingham, Digbeth B5 .... 164 D3
Birmingham, King's Norton B38 .... 103 F1
Masters La B62 ...... 63 E1
Masters Rd CV31 .... 162 A4
Matchborough Ctr B98 .... 154 E1
Matchborough Fst Sch B98 .... 154 E1
Matchborough Way B98 .... 154 E1
Matchlock Cl B74 .... 44 E7
Matfen Ave B73 .... 45 F2
Mathe Croft CV31 ... 162 C5
Math Mdw B32 .... 84 F5
Matlock Cl Dudley DY2 62 D3
Walsall WS3 .... 14 C3
Matlock Dr WS11 .... 2 A4
Matlock Rd
Birmingham B11 ...... 87 F3
Coventry CV1 .... 113 D6
Walsall WS3 .... 14 C3
Matlock Villas 2 B12 . 87 B5
Matterson Rd CV6 ... 113 A5
Matthew Boulton Coll
Birmingham B5 ..... 164 D3
Birmingham, Lee Bank B15 .... 86 D8
Matthew Boulton Com Prim Sch B21 .... 65 E7
Matthew La (Road 3) DY10 .... 116 F1
Matthews Cl B65 ..... 63 B1
Matthews Wlk WS13 ... 3 A2
Mattox Rd WV11 ..... 26 D6
Matty Rd B68 .... 64 C4
Maud Rd
Water Orton B46 ..... 59 D3
West Bromwich B70 ... 53 C1
Maudslay Rd CV5 ... 112 E2
Maughan St
Brierley Hill DY5 ...... 82 A8
Dudley DY1 .... 51 B1
Maund Cl B60 .... 150 E7
Maureen Cl CV4 ..... 111 C1
Maurice Gr WV10 .... 26 A6
Maurice Mead Ct 12 CV31 .... 162 A6
Maurice Rd
Birmingham B14 ..... 104 E5
Smethwick B67 .... 64 E2
Mavis Gdns B68 ...... 84 B8
Mavis Rd
Birmingham B31 ..... 102 E1
Cannock WS12 .... 2 B7
Mavor Dr CV12 .... 77 D1
Mawgan Dr WS14 ..... 9 D6
Mawnan Cl CV7 ...... 96 B8
Maw St WS1 .... 42 F6
Maxholm Rd B74 ..... 44 E8
Max Rd
Birmingham B32 ...... 84 D5
Coventry CV6 .... 112 F5
Maxstoke Cl
Birmingham B32 ..... 102 A7
Meriden CV7 .... 92 B1
Redditch B98 .... 154 D1
Sutton Coldfield B73 ... 45 E2
Tamworth B77 .... 35 C4
Walsall WS3 .... 14 A3
Maxstoke Croft B90 . 126 C8
Maxstoke Gdns CV31 161 F6
Maxstoke La
Meriden CV7 .... 92 B2
White Stitch CV7 ...... 92 B3
Maxstoke Rd B73 .... 45 E1
Maxstoke St B9 ...... 67 B2
Maxted Rd B23 .... 56 C7
Maxtock Ave WS13 .... 9 A6
Maxwell Ave B20 ..... 55 B1
Maxwell Cl WS14 .... 9 C7
Maxwell Ct B33 ...... 68 F3
Maxwell Rd WV2 .... 163 C1
Mayall Dr B75 .... 32 D4
Mayama Rd B78 .... 34 F8
May Ave 3 B12 ...... 87 A5
Maybank B9 .... 67 F3
Maybank Cl WS14 ...... 9 E8
Maybank Pl B44 ...... 55 E6
Maybank Rd DY2 ..... 62 C3
Mayberry Cl B14 .... 105 B2
Maybridge Dr B91 ... 127 B8
Maybrook Ind Est WS8 .... 15 F5
Maybrook Rd
Brownhills WS8 ...... 15 F5
Sutton Coldfield B76 ... 58 A5
Maybush Gdns WV10 . 11 C1
Maycock Rd CV6 .... 113 D7
Maycroft Cl WS12 ...... 1 F7
Maydene Croft B12 .... 86 F6
Mayfair
Birmingham B37 ...... 69 F5
Stourbridge DY9 ...... 81 D2
Mayfair Cl
Birmingham B44 ...... 56 B7
Dudley DY1 .... 51 A2
Mayfair Dr
Fazeley B78 .... 35 A7
Kingswinford DY6 ..... 60 C7
Mayfair Gdns
Tipton DY4 .... 52 A4
Mayfair Gdns continued
Wolverhampton WV3 .. 24 D2
May Farm Cl B47 .... 125 A6
Mayfield B77 .... 36 C8
Mayfield Ave B29 .... 86 B2
Mayfield Cl
Bedworth CV12 .... 78 B3
Fairfield B61 .... 120 F1
Kidderminster DY11 .. 116 A8
9 Royal Leamington Spa CV31 .... 162 C6
Solihull B91 .... 107 C1
Mayfield Cres B65 .... 63 A3
Mayfield Ct
Birmingham B13 ...... 87 A2
Kidderminster DY11 .. 116 C7
Mayfield Dr CV8 ..... 148 C4
Mayfield Prep Sch WS1 .... 43 A8
Mayfield Rd
Birmingham, Acock's Green B11 .... 88 A3
Birmingham, Lozells B19 .... 66 C8
Birmingham, Moseley B13 .... 87 A3
Birmingham, Stirchley B30 .... 104 A6
Coventry CV5 .... 113 A1
Dudley DY1 .... 51 C4
Halesowen B62 .... 63 F1
Halesowen, Hasbury B63 .... 82 E2
Nuneaton CV11 .... 73 E2
Sutton Coldfield, Boldmere B73 .... 46 A2
Sutton Coldfield, Streetly B74 .... 44 F8
Wolverhampton WV1 .. 26 B1
Mayfields B98 .... 153 E2
Mayfield Sch B19 .... 66 C8
Mayfields Dr WS8 ...... 6 B2
Mayfield The WV1 ..... 26 B1
Mayflower Cl B19 .... 66 D6
Mayflower Dr
Brierley Hill DY5 ...... 61 A7
Coventry CV2 .... 114 E2
Mayford Gr B13 ..... 105 B6
Maygrove Rd DY6 .... 60 C7
Mayhurst Cl
Hollywood B47 ...... 125 C6
Tipton DY4 .... 52 A8
Mayhurst Rd B47 .... 125 B6
May La
Birmingham B14 ..... 104 F5
Hollywood B47 ...... 125 A7
Mayland Dr B74 ...... 45 A5
Mayland Rd B16 ..... 65 C2
Maynard Ave
Bedworth CV12 .... 95 D8
Stourbridge DY8 ...... 80 D3
Warwick CV34 ...... 161 A7
Mayo Dr CV8 .... 148 A4
Mayor's Croft CV4 ... 132 B7
Mayou Ct WS3 .... 15 A4
Maypole Cl B64 ...... 82 B8
Maypole Ct WV5 ..... 49 A6
Maypole Dr DY8 ...... 80 E5
Maypole Fields B63 .. 82 A7
Maypole Gr B14 ..... 105 B2
Maypole Hill B63 ..... 82 A7
Maypole La B14 ..... 105 A2
Maypole Rd B68 ..... 64 B1
Maypole St WV5 ..... 49 B7
May St Coventry CV6 . 113 E8
Walsall WS3 .... 28 D6
Mayswood Dr WV6 .... 23 F1
Mayswood Gr B32 .... 84 D4
Mayswood Rd B92 ... 89 C2
Maythorn Ave B76 .... 58 A6
Maythorn Gdns
Codsall WV8 .... 10 A4
Wolverhampton WV6 .. 24 C3
Maythorn Gr 4 B91 . 127 B8
Maytree Cl B37 ...... 70 A2
May Tree Gr B20 ...... 54 F3
May Trees B47 ...... 124 F6
Maywell Dr B92 ..... 107 F8
Maywood Cl DY6 ..... 60 B6
Meaburn Cl B29 ..... 103 A7
Mead Cl WS9 .... 30 B6
Mead Cres B9 .... 68 B3
Meadfoot Ave B14 .. 104 F3
Meadfoot Dr DY6 ..... 60 B7
Meadfoot Rd CV3 .. 134 E6
Meadow Ave B71 ...... 53 F8
Meadow Bank B78 ... 21 B1
Meadowbank Dr B46 . 59 D1
Meadowbank Grange WS6 .... 4 E4
Meadowbrook Gdns WV8 .... 10 B4
Meadowbrook Rd
Halesowen B63 .... 82 E3
Lichfield WS13 .... 3 B3
Meadow Brook Rd B31 .... 102 F5
Meadow Cl Ansty CV7 . 97 D3
Birmingham B17 ...... 65 B1
Hockley Heath B94 ... 143 C6
Royal Leamington Spa CV32 .... 157 C4
Solihull B90 .... 126 D8
Sutton Coldfield B74 ... 30 F2
Sutton Coldfield B76 ... 46 F1
Walsall WS4 .... 29 C8
Meadow Croft
Cannock WS12 .... 1 C4
Perton WV6 .... 23 D3
West Hagley DY9 ..... 98 F4
Wythall B47 .... 125 A3
Meadowcroft Cl CV4 131 F8
Meadow Ct
Birmingham B17 ...... 65 B1
Nuneaton CV11 .... 73 B4
Meadow Dr
Hampton-in-A B92 ... 109 B7
Hinckley LE10 .... 76 A7
Meadowfield Rd B45 .... 122 A6
Meadowfields Cl DY8 . 60 E2
Meadow Gr
Great Wyrley WS6 .... 5 A2
Solihull B92 .... 88 D1
Meadow Grange Dr WV12 .... 27 B7
Meadow Green Prim Sch B47 .... 125 A3
Meadow Hill Cl DY11 .... 116 A5
Meadowhill Cres B98 .... 153 F5
Meadowhill Dr DY8 ... 60 E2
Meadow Hill Dr 5 WS11 .... 2 A3
Meadowhill Rd B98 . 153 F5
Meadow Hill Rd B38 103 E2
Meadow Ho 5 CV1 . 113 B3
Meadow La
Alvechurch B48 ...... 139 B6
Coven Heath WV10 .... 11 C6
Kingswood B94 ...... 144 D3
Wednesfield WV12 .... 27 A5
Wolverhampton WV14 . 40 B2
Wombourne WV5 ..... 49 B8
Meadowlands Dr WS4 .... 15 D1
Meadow Lark Cl WS12 .. 2 B4
Meadow Mills Ind Est DY10 .... 116 E5
Meadowpark Rd DY8 . 80 D8
Meadow Pk B79 .... 20 F5
Meadow Pleck La B90 .... 126 A6
Meadow Rd
Aldridge WS9 .... 30 A4
Birmingham B32 ...... 84 A6
Birmingham, Harborne B17 .... 65 B1
Catshill B61 .... 136 F8
Coventry CV6 .... 95 B4
Dudley DY1 .... 51 B3
Halesowen B62 .... 83 C8
Hartshill CV10 .... 72 A8
Oldbury B68 .... 64 B3
Smethwick B67 .... 65 A4
Tamworth B78 .... 20 E3
Warwick CV34 ...... 161 A7
Wolverhampton WV3 .. 38 D8
Wythall B47 .... 125 A3
Meadow Rise
Balsall Common CV7 .. 130 C7
Birmingham B30 ..... 103 E7
Meadows Fst Sch B61 .... 137 A3
Meadows Gr WV8 .... 10 A4
Meadowside CV11 .... 79 B8
Meadowside Cl B43 .. 43 E1
Meadowside Rd B74 .. 31 F3
Meadows Prim Sch The B31 .... 102 E1
Meadows Sch The
Coventry CV4 .... 111 E3
Oldbury B69 .... 52 E1
Meadow St
Coventry CV1 .... 165 A2
5 Cradley Heath B64 . 82 F8
Nuneaton CV11 .... 73 B5
Tamworth B77 .... 21 C3
Walsall WS1 .... 42 D8
Meadow St continued
1 Wolverhampton WV1 .... 25 B2
Meadows The
Aldridge WS9 .... 29 E5
Catshill B61 .... 136 F8
Hinckley LE10 .... 76 A7
Leek Wootton CV35 .. 156 A7
Stourbridge DY9 ...... 99 B7
Meadowsweet Ave B38 .... 123 F8
Meadowsweet Pl DY10 .... 116 D8
Meadowsweet Way
Cannock WS12 .... 2 E4
Kingswinford DY6 ..... 61 A6
Meadow Vale WV8 .... 10 B2
Meadowvale Rd B60 137 C6
Meadow View
Birmingham B13 ..... 105 C8
Burntwood WS7 .... 7 D6
Sedgley DY3 .... 39 C1
Meadow View Cvn Pk WV10 .... 11 C6
Meadow View JMI Sch B43 .... 44 D5
Meadow View Terr WV6 .... 24 E4
Meadow Way
Cannock WS12 .... 2 C1
Stourbridge DY8 ...... 60 C2
Meadow Wlk
Birmingham B14 ..... 104 E1
Cradley Heath B64 .... 82 D8
Mead Rise B15 .... 85 F6
Mead The DY3 .... 50 B8
Meadthorpe Rd B44 .. 55 D8
Meadvale Rd B45 ... 122 B6
Meadway
Birmingham B33 ...... 69 B2
Coventry CV2 .... 114 B6
Meadway Cl WS12 ..... 2 C3
Meadway N CV2 ..... 114 B6
Meadway St WS7 ...... 7 A5
Meadway The
Hinckley LE10 .... 75 F7
Redditch B97 .... 153 C1
Wolverhampton WV6 .. 24 A5
Meadwood Ind Est WV14 .... 40 E5
Meakins Cl CV34 .... 160 B4
Mears Cl B23 .... 56 D8
Mears Coppice DY5 .. 81 E6
Mears Dr B33 .... 68 D4
Mearse Cl B18 .... 66 A5
Mearse La
Barnt Green B45 ..... 122 A1
Madeley Heath DY9 .. 120 B6
Mease Ave WS7 .... 7 D6
Mease Croft 2 B9 .... 67 B2
Measham Gr B26 ..... 88 E5
Measham Way WV11 . 26 E7
Meaton Gr B32 ...... 102 B8
Medcroft Ave B20 .... 54 E4
Medici Rd B60 ...... 137 C2
Medina B77 .... 21 E1
Medina Cl WV10 ...... 11 F4
Medina Rd
Birmingham B11 ...... 87 E4
Coventry CV6 .... 95 E1
Medina Way DY6 ..... 60 C6
Medland Ave CV3 ... 132 F5
Medley Gdns DY4 .... 52 E4
Medley Gr CV31 .... 161 F3
Medley Rd B11 .... 87 D5
Medlicott Rd B11 .... 87 C6
Medway B77 .... 21 E1
Medway Cl DY5 ...... 61 A6
Medway Croft B36 .... 69 F7
Medway Ct B73 ...... 46 B5
Medway Gr B38 ..... 123 E8
Medway Rd WS8 .... 6 C2
Medway Twr B7 ...... 67 B5
Medway Wlk WS8 ...... 6 C2
Medwin Gr B23 ...... 56 D7
Meerash La WS7 .... 7 C3
Meer End B38 .... 123 D7
Meer End Rd CV8 ... 130 D1
Meerhill Ave B90 .... 127 A6
Meeting Ho The 3 WS10 .... 41 E3
Meeting House La
Balsall Common CV7 .. 130 C6
Birmingham B31 ..... 103 A4
Meeting La DY5 ...... 61 B1
Meeting Lane Ind Est DY5 .... 61 B1
Meeting St Dudley DY2 62 C5

Meeting St *continued*
Tipton DY4 .... 52 D5
Wednesbury WS10 .... 41 E3
Meg La WS7 ....7 C8
Meir Rd B98 .... 159 C8

Melbourne Ave
Birmingham, Newtown
B19............... 66 C6
Birmingham, Selly Oak
B66............... 65 B7
Bromsgrove B61.... 136 E4

Melbourne Cl
Bromsgrove B61..... 136 E3
Kingswinford DY6..... 60 E4
Nuneaton CV11...... 78 E8
West Bromwich B70... 53 A7
Melbourne Cres WS12..2 F2
Melbourne Ct **3**
CV12...............77 F2
Melbourne Gdns WS5 43 B6

Melbourne Rd
Bromsgrove B61..... 136 E3
Cannock WS12 ....2 F2
Coventry CV5 ...... 113 A2
Halesowen B63..... 83 B5
Smethwick B66..... 65 B7
Melbourne St WV2.. 163 C2
Melbury Cl WV3...... 25 A1
Melbury Gr B14.... 104 E5
Melbury Way **1** WS11..1 F2

Melchester Wlk **2**
WS11...............1 F2
Melchett Rd B30 .. 104 A4
Melcote Gr B44 .... 55 E8
Meldon Dr WV14.... 41 A2
Meldrum Rd CV10.... 72 D4
Melen St B97 ...... 153 D4
Melford B79 .... 20 E6
Melford Cl DY3....... 39 C2
Melford Hall Rd B91. 106 F7

Melfort Cl
Coventry CV3 ...... 114 F2
Nuneaton CV10...... 72 C5
Melfort Gr B14..... 105 A3
Melksham Sq B35.... 58 A3
Mellis Gr B23 ..... 56 A5
Mellish Ct WS4..... 29 A3
Mellish Dr WS4..... 29 B3
Mellish Rd WS4 ..... 29 B3
Mellor Dr B74....... 31 E4
Mellors Cl B17..... 85 B3

Mellowdew Rd
Coventry CV2 ...... 114 C4
Stourbridge DY8 .... 60 C5
Mellowship Rd CV5 . 111 D5
Mell Sq B91....... 107 C4
Mellwaters B77...... 36 C8
Mere Croft WS11......5 F4
Melmerby B77....... 36 C8
Melplash Ave B91... 107 A4

Melrose Ave
Bedworth CV12..... 95 D8
Birmingham, Sparkbrook
B12............... 87 A6
Birmingham, Sparkhill
B11............... 87 C6
Stourbridge DY8 .... 81 A2
Sutton Coldfield B73... 45 E2
West Bromwich B71... 42 D1

Melrose Cl
Birmingham B38.... 103 F1
Hinckley LE10 ...... 75 B8
Melrose Ct WS4..... 29 A3

Melrose Dr
Cannock WS12 ....1 F7
Perton WV6.......... 23 E4
Melrose Gr B19...... 66 B7
Melrose Pl B66..... 64 D8
Melrose Rd B20..... 55 E1
Melstock Cl DY4.... 51 D5
Melstock Rd B14.... 104 D7
Melton Ave B92..... 89 B4
Melton Dr B15 ...... 86 B7

Melton Rd
Birmingham B14..... 104 F8
Royal Leamington Spa
CV32............. 157 B4
Melverley Gr B44....55 F7
Melverton Ave WV10 . 25 E8
Melville Cl CV7...... 96 A8
Melville Hall **1** B16.. 65 D1

Melville Rd
Birmingham B16.... 65 D1
Coventry CV1 ...... 113 A3
Melvina Rd B7...... 67 B5
Melzer Ho DY10.... 116 F2
Membury Rd B8..... 67 D6
Memorial Cl WV13.. 27 A4

Memory La
Darlaston WS10 ..... 41 D8
Wolverhampton WV11 . 26 B5

Menai Cl WV12...... 27 C6
Menai Wlk B37...... 70 B4
Mendip Ave B8 ..... 67 E5

Mendip Cl
Bromsgrove B61....137 A5
Dudley DY3 .... 50 D3
Wolverhampton WV2 . 39 F7
Mendip Dr CV10..... 72 B3
Mendip Ho B98 ... 154 D6

Mendip Rd
Birmingham B8..... 67 E5
Halesowen B63..... 82 D1
Stourbridge DY8..... 81 B6
Mendip Way B77.... 22 C1
Menin Cres B13.... 105 B7

Menin Rd
Birmingham B13.... 105 B8
Tipton DY4 .... 51 D5
Mentone Ct B20.... 54 E3

Menzies High Sch
B71................ 53 C8

Meon Gr
Birmingham B33.... 89 B8
Perton WV6......... 23 F4
Meon Rise DY9.... 81 C3
Meon Way WV11 ...26 F7
Meranti Cl WV12.... 27 C8

Mercer Ave
Coventry CV2 ...... 114 A5
Water Orton B46 .... 59 A3
Mercer Gr WV11..... 26 D7
Mercers Mdw CV7... 95 A6

Merchants Ct 5
CV32............. 157 A1
Merchants Pk WS9 . 30 A7
Merchants Way WS9 . 30 A7

Mercia Bsns Village
CV4.............. 131 F6

Mercia Cl
Bromsgrove B60.... 150 F7
Tamworth B79....... 20 E7

Mercia Dr
Birmingham B14.... 104 D6
Perton WV6......... 23 E5
Mercia Ho CV1.... 165 B3
Mercian Ct WS14......9 C7
Mercian Pk B77.... 22 A3
Mercian Way B77.... 22 B3
Mercia Way CV34 .. 161 B7
Mercot Cl B98..... 159 A6
Mercury Pk B77..... 22 B3
Mercury Rd WS11......2 A5
Merecote Rd B92... 106 D7
Mere Croft WS11.......5 F4

Meredith Gn DY11... 116 A1
Meredith Pool Cl B18.65 F6

Meredith Rd
Coventry CV2 ...... 114 D2
Dudley DY3 .... 50 A5
Wolverhampton WV11 . 26 C8
Meredith St B64..... 62 D1
Mere Dr B75........ 32 B2
Mere Green Cl B75.. 32 C2

Mere Green Comb Sch
B75................32 B2
Mere Green Rd B75 . 32 C2
Mere Oak Rd WV6... 23 E5
Mere Pool Rd B75... 32 E2

Mere Rd
Birmingham B23.... 56 D3
Stourbridge DY8..... 80 E3
Mereside Way B92 . 106 E8
Meres Rd B63....... 82 C5
Mere View WS4..... 29 C8

Mereways B90..... 126 A5

Merevale Ave
Hinckley LE10 ...... 75 C7
Nuneaton CV11..... 73 A4

Merevale Cl
Hinckley LE10 ...... 75 C7
Redditch B98...... 159 D8
Merevale Ct CV11... 73 A4
Merevale Rd B92... 89 B2
Mere View WS4..... 29 C8
Mereworth Dr WV4 . 38 D4

Merganser B77..... 36 A6
Merganser Way
DY10............. 117 B3
Meriden Ave DY8.... 80 D6

Meriden Bsns Pk
CV5............. 111 B8
Meriden CE Prim Sch
CV7.............. 92 C1

Meriden Cl
Birmingham B25.... 88 B7

Meriden Cl *continued*
Cannock WS11 ....4 B8
Stourbridge DY8..... 80 D6
Meriden Cross CV7. 92 B1
Meriden Ct 3 WV4...39 F4
Meriden Dr B37..... 70 A6
Meriden Hill CV7... 110 E8

Meriden Park Homes
CV7............. 110 C8

Meriden Rd
Berkswell CV7...... 110 C4
Chapel Green CV7.... 93 B7
Hampton-in-A B92 .. 109 C7
Wolverhampton WV10 . 25 A8
Meriden Rise B92... 89 D3

Meriden St
Birmingham B5.... 164 D2
Coventry CV1 ...... 113 B3
Meridian Pl B60... 137 A1
Merino Ave B31.... 123 A8
Merlin Ave CV10 .... 72 B6

Merlin Cl
Birmingham B35.... 58 A3
Cannock WS11 ....1 C2
Dudley DY1 .... 61 F8
Tamworth B77....... 36 A6
Merlin Ct WS7........7 F8
Merlin Dr DY10.... 117 B3
Merlin Gr B26...... 89 B5

Merrick Cl B63..... 82 D2
Merrick Ct LE10....75 F5
Merrick Rd WV11.... 27 A6
Merridale Ave WV3..24 F2
Merridale Cres WV3.. 25 A2
Merridale Ct WV3... 24 F1
Merridale Gdns WV3. 25 A1
Merridale Gr WV3... 24 E1

Merridale Jun & Inf Sch
WV3............. 25 A1
Merridale La WV3... 25 A1
Merridale Rd WV3... 25 A1
Merridale St W WV3.. 39 A8
Merridale St WV3... 163 A2
Merriemont Dr B45 . 122 A1
Merrifield Gdns LE10. 75 E5
Merrill Cl WS6 ....4 E2
Merrill Gdns B60.. 121 D2

Merrills Hall Island
WV11 .... 26 D4
Merrills Hall La WV11 26 E4
Merrington Cl 5
B91.............. 127 C8
Merrion's Cl B43.... 43 E4
Merrishaw Rd B31.. 123 A8

Merritts Brook Cl
B29.............. 103 A5

Merritts Brook La
B31.............. 102 E5
Merritts Hill B31... 102 E6

Merrivale Rd
Coventry CV5 ...... 112 E3
Halesowen B62..... 83 F8
Smethwick B66..... 65 A2
Merryfield Cl B92.. 107 D7
Merryfield Gr B17... 85 C4
Merryfield Rd DY1... 50 E1
Merryhills Way CV2 . 96 F1
Merry Hill DY5......61 F2
Merry Hill Ctr DY5..61 F3
Merryhill Dr B18....65 F6
Merryhills Ent Pk
WV10........... 25 F5
Merry Husrt Pl LE10.. 74 E7
Merse Rd B98...... 154 E1
Mersey Gr B38..... 123 E8

Mersey Rd
Bulkington CV12..... 79 A3
Walsall WS3 .... 14 E1
Merstal Dr B92...... 107 F7
Merstone Cl WV14... 40 C6
Merstone Sch B37... 70 A1
Merstowe Cl B27.... 88 B3

Merton Cl
Kidderminster DY10.. 117 B7
Oldbury B68......... 64 B2
Merton Ct WS7.......6 F5
Merton Ho B37......69 F2
Merton Rd B13...... 87 B3
Mervyn Pl WV14..... 41 A3

Mervyn Rd
Bilston WV14....... 41 A3
Birmingham B21..... 54 E1
Meryhurst Rd WS10.. 42 B5
Merynton Ave CV4 . 132 C3
Meschines St CV3.. 133 D6
Messenger La B70,
B71.............. 53 D3
Messenger Rd B66... 65 B6

Mesty Croft Prim Sch
WS10............ 42 B3
Metalloys Ind Est B76 58 B5
Metcalf Cl WS7.......7 C8
Metchley Abbey 11
B17.............. 85 D5
Metchley Croft B90 . 126 F6
Metchley Ct B17..... 85 D4
Metchley Dr B17..... 85 D4
Metchley Ho 6 B17.. 85 D5
Metchley La B17.... 85 D5

Metchley Park Rd
B15.............. 85 E4
Metfield Cl B79..... 21 C8
Metfield Croft
Birmingham B17..... 85 D4
Kingswinford DY6.... 60 F6
Metlin Gr B33....... 69 E3
Metric Wlk 2 B67... 65 A5
Metro Way B66..... 65 C7
Mews Rd CV32..... 161 D8

Mews The
Bedworth CV12..... 78 B2
Birmingham B27..... 88 B3
Cannock WS11 ..... 1 D1
Kenilworth CV8..... 147 E3
Rowley Regis B65.... 63 B2
Mey Coppice B36....69 F7
Meynell Ho 5 B20... 54 F3
Meyrick Rd B70..... 53 A6
Meyrick Wlk B16....65 F1
Miall Park Rd B91... 106 E5
Miall Rd B28...... 106 A8
Mica Cl B77........ 22 B2

Michael Banning Pl
CV7............. 130 B7
Michael Blanning Gdns
B93............. 127 E3
Michael Blanning Ho 10
B13.............. 87 B2
Michael Ct B5 ..... 86 D6
Michael Dr B15..... 86 C6

Michael Drayton Jun Sch
CV10............72 B8
Michaelmas Rd CV3 . 165 B1

Michael Rd
Darlaston WS10 ..... 41 B7
Smethwick B67..... 64 E6
Michaelwood Cl B97 152 F2
Michel Ho CV1..... 165 C4
Michell Cl CV3..... 134 B8
Michelle Cl B13.... 105 A5
Michigan Cl WS11......2 B2
Micklehill Dr B90 .. 126 B8
Mickle Mdw B46.... 59 B3
Mickleover Rd B8.... 68 C5
Mickleton Ave B33.. 89 C8
Mickleton Cl B98... 158 E7

Mickleton Rd
Coventry CV5 ...... 133 A8
Solihull B92....... 106 D8
Mickley Ave WV10... 25 E5
Midacre WV13...... 27 A1
Middelburg Cl CV11.. 74 A1
Middle Acre Rd B32.. 84 C2
Middle Ave WV13.... 40 E8

Middle Bickenhill La
B92.............. 91 A4

Middleborough Rd
CV1............. 165 A4
Middlecotes CV4.... 112 B1
Middle Cres WS3.... 29 A7
Middle Cross WV1.. 163 D3
Middle Dr B45..... 122 D4
Middle Entry B79.... 21 B4
Middlefield WV8 .... 10 E2

Middlefield Ave
Dorridge B93...... 128 B4
Halesowen B62...... 63 F1

Middlefield Cl
Halesowen B62...... 63 F1
Hinckley LE10 ...... 71 D2
Middlefield Ct LE10 .. 71 D2
Middlefield Dr CV3.. 115 B1
Middlefield Gdns B62 .83 F8
Middlefield Ho B14 . 104 F4

Middlefield La
Hinckley LE10 ...... 71 D3
West Hagley DY9 .... 99 B6
Middlefield Pl LE10 .. 71 D3

Middlefield Rd
Bromsgrove B60..... 151 B7
Oldbury B69........ 63 A8
Middle Field Rd B31 103 D2
Middlefield Rd CV3.. 115 A1
Middle Gdns WV13.. 27 B2
Middlehill Rise B32.. 84 D3

Middle House Dr
B60............. 121 D1
Middlehouse La B97 153 E6
Middle La
Wolverhampton WV9 . 11 A5
Wythall B38....... 124 D5
Middle Leaford B34.. 69 A5
Middle Leasowe B32.. 84 D4

Middlemarch Bsns Pk
CV3............. 134 C2
Middlemarch Rd
Coventry CV6 ...... 113 C7
Nuneaton CV10..... 73 C1

Middlemarch Sch
CV10............73 B1
Middle Mdw DY4.... 52 B5
Middle Meadow Ave
B32.............. 84 C5
Middlemist Gr B43...54 F6

Middlemore Bsns Pk
WS9............. 29 E6
Middlemore Cl B80 . 159 D3
Middlemore Ind Est
B66.............65 B8
Middlemore La WS9. 30 A6
Middlemore La W
WS9............. 29 E6

Middlemore Rd
Birmingham B31..... 103 B3
Smethwick B66..... 65 B8
Middle Park Cl B29.. 103 B8
Middlepark Dr B31.. 103 B6
Middlepark Rd DY1...61 F8
Middle Park Rd B29.. 103 C8
Middle Piece Dr B97 153 B1

Middle Rd
Fairfield B61....... 120 F4
Upper Bentley B60 ... 152 A2
Middle Ride CV3.... 134 C5
Middlesmoor B77.... 36 C8

Middleton Cl
Hammerwich WS7 ..... 7 D4
Redditch B98...... 154 F2
Walsall WS5 .... 42 F5
Middleton Gdns B30 103 D4

Middleton Grange
B31.............. 103 C4
Middleton Hall
Birmingham B30..... 103 E4
Middleton B78........ 34 E1
Middleton Hall Rd
B30.............. 103 E4

Middleton La B78....47 F6
Middleton Mews
B98.............. 154 F2

Middleton Rd
Birmingham B14..... 104 F7
Bromsgrove B61..... 136 F4
Brownhills WS8 ....7 A1
Solihull B90........ 106 A2
Sutton Coldfield B74... 31 A1

Middleton Trad Est
WV13............26 E1
Middletown B80... 159 D1

Middletown La B96,
B80.............. 159 D1
Middletree Rd B63... 82 C7
Middle Vauxhall 4
WV1.............. 25 A2

Midland Air Mus
CV8............. 134 B3
Midland Cl B21..... 66 A7
Midland Croft B33... 69 D3
Midland Ct 3 ..... 164 A4
Midland Dr B72..... 46 C5

Midland Oak Trad Est
CV6..............95 E2

Midland Rd
Birmingham B30..... 103 F5
Coventry CV6 ...... 113 E5
Darlaston WS10 ..... 41 C8
Huntington WS12 ......1 C5
Nuneaton CV11..... 73 A5
Sutton Coldfield B74.... 46 A6
Walsall WS1 .... 28 E1
Midland St B9...... 67 C3
Midpoint Ctr WV6....24 F7
Midpoint Park Ind Est
B76.............. 58 C5
Midvale Dr B14.... 104 D2

Mikado Rd B60 .... 137 D1
Milburn B77 .... 36 C8
Milburn Hill Rd CV4 . 132 B6
Milburn Rd B44..... 45 A3
Milby Ct CV11...... 73 C2
Milby Dr CV11...... 74 A7
Milby Prim Sch CV11 .73 F8
Milcote Cl B98..... 159 A7

Milcote Dr
Sutton Coldfield B73... 45 C3
Willenhall WV13..... 26 D1

Milcote Rd
Birmingham B29..... 103 A8
Smethwick B67..... 64 F1
Solihull B91........ 107 B4
Milcote Way DY6.... 60 B7
Mildenhall B79...... 21 C8
Mildenhall Rd B42... 44 A1
Mildred Rd B63..... 62 E2
Mildred Way B65.... 63 C6
Milebrook Gr B32... 102 B8
Mile End B94...... 142 A2
Mile Flat DY6....... 60 A7
Mile La CV1....... 165 C1

Mile Oak Cross Rds
B78............... 20 C2
Milesbush Ave B36... 58 D1
Miles Gr DY2........62 F7
Miles Mdw CV6..... 96 B1

Miles Meadow Cl
WV12............ 27 C8
Milestone Ct WV6... 24 A3
Milestone Dr DY9.... 98 F4
Milestone Ho 2 CV1 113 B2
Milestone La B21 ... 65 C6
Milestone Way WV12. 27 C8
Mile Tree La CV2 ... 96 F7
Milfoil Cl LE10......74 F7

Milford Ave
3 Birmingham B12... 87 A6
Willenhall WV12..... 27 A5

Milford Cl
Allesley CV5 ...... 112 B6
Redditch B97...... 158 C6
Stourbridge DY8..... 60 E3
Milford Copse B17 . 85 B5
Milford Croft B65... 62 F4

Milford Ct
Birmingham B19.... 164 B5
Royal Leamington Spa
CV31............ 162 A8
Milford Gr B90..... 127 C7
Milford Pl B14..... 104 E8

Milford Rd
Birmingham B17..... 85 B5
Wolverhampton WV2 . 39 C7
Milford St CV10..... 73 B2
Milhill Rd B98..... 154 E1
Milholme Gn B92... 107 D8
Milking Bank DY1... 50 E2

Milking Bank Prim Sch
DY1..............50 E2
Milk St B5..........66 F1
Millais Cl CV12..... 78 A4
Millais Rd LE10..... 71 A3
Millard Ind Est B70.. 53 A1
Millard Rd WV14.... 40 B1
Millbank CV34 .... 156 B1

Mill Bank DY3....... 50 D8
Mill Bank Cotts
DY11............. 116 D6
Millbank B23 ...... 56 B6
Mill Bank Mews CV8 148 B6
Millbank St WV11.....12 F1
Millbrook Cl 4 WS11...1 F2
Millbrook Ct B62.... 83 A7
Millbrook Dr WS14....17 F6
Mill Brook Dr B31... 122 E8
Millbrook Rd B14 ... 104 C6
Millbrook Way B31... 81 B8
Mill Burn Way 3 B9 . 67 B2

Mill Cl Blakedown DY10 98 B2
Bromsgrove B60..... 150 F6
Coventry CV2 .... 96 B3
Dudley DY3......... 50 D6
Hollywood B47..... 125 A7
Nuneaton CV11..... 73 F1
Wolston CV8....... 135 F3
Mill Cres WS11........2 C7
Mill Croft WV14.... 40 E6
Millcroft Cl B32..... 84 C2
Millcroft Rd B74.... 45 A8
Mill Ct WS14....... 18 A6
Milldale Cl DY10... 116 E6
Milldale Cres WV10.. 11 D3
Milldale Rd WV10... 11 D4
Mill Dr B66......... 65 B5
Mill End CV8...... 148 A6
Millenium Pk B70... 53 C6
Millennium Cl WS3... 15 A4

Millennium Forge DY4 51 D5
Millennium Gdns B64 62 F2
Millennium Way
Codsall WV8 10 B4
Wolston CV8 135 F3
Miller Cl
Bromsgrove B60 150 E6
Lichfield WS13 3 B2
Miller Cres WV14 40 A1
Millers Cl WS2 27 F1
Millers Ct
[1] Kidderminster DY11 116 D6
Solihull B90 105 F2
Millersdale Dr B71 42 F2
Millers Gn LE10 75 F6
Millers Green Dr DY6 60 A8
Millers Rd CV34 160 E8
Miller St B6 66 E5
Millers Vale WS12 2 D1
Millers Wharf B78 22 F1
Millers Wlk WS3 14 E3
Mill Farm Pk CV12 79 B6
Mill Farm Rd B17 85 C3
Millfield
Birmingham B31 103 A4
Royal Leamington Spa CV31 162 A8
Millfield Ave
Walsall, Little Bloxwich WS3 14 D3
Walsall WS4 15 B1
Millfield Gdns [2] DY11 116 D6
Millfield Prim Sch
Brownhills WS8 16 A7
Fazeley B78 35 A8
Millfield Rd
Birmingham B20 54 F5
Bromsgrove B61 136 E1
Brownhills WS8 16 A7
Millfields B33 69 E3
Millfields Cl B71 42 B1
Millfields Fst Sch B61 136 E1
Millfields Rd
Bilston WV14, WV4 40 B5
West Bromwich B71 42 B1
Millfield View B63 82 E4
Millford Cl B28 106 A5
Mill Gdns
Birmingham B14 105 D5
Smethwick B67 64 F3
Mill Gn WV10 11 D4
Mill Gr WV8 10 C3
Mill Green Nature Pk* WS11 1 F1
Millhaven Ave B30 104 B6
Mill Hill Baginton CV8 133 D3
Smethwick B67 64 F3
Mill Hill Rd LE10 71 C1
Mill Ho B8 68 D4
Mill House Cl CV32 161 C8
Millhouse Ct CV6 113 F7
Mill House Dr CV32 161 C8
Millhouse Rd B25 88 C8
Mill House Terr CV32 161 C8
Millicent Cl WS12 2 B6
Millicent Pl [11] B12 87 A6
Millichip Rd WV13 26 E1
Millington Rd
Birmingham B36 68 E7
Tipton DY4 40 F1
Wolverhampton WV10 25 E6
Millison Gr B90 127 A7
Mill La Aldridge WS9 31 A7
Bentley Heath B93 127 F4
Birmingham B32 84 E2
Birmingham, Digbeth B5 164 D1
Birmingham, Northfield B31 103 A2
Blakedown DY10 98 B2
Bramcote CV11 79 F8
Bromsgrove B61 136 F2
Bulkington CV12 79 A3
Coventry CV3 114 F2
Cubbington CV32 157 F5
Earlswood B94 141 B8
Fairfield B61 120 F3
Fazeley B78 35 A8
Halesowen B63 83 C4
Hammerwich WS7 7 D3
Kidderminster, Blakebrook DY11 116 D6
Kidderminster, Hoobrook DY10 116 F2
Kingswood B94 144 C4
Mill La *continued*
Oldbury B69 64 A5
Shenstone WS14 18 A6
Solihull B91 107 C4
Stonnall WS9, WS14 17 A4
Tamworth B79 21 C5
Walsall WS3, WS4 28 F4
Willenhall WV12 27 C5
Wolverhampton, Scotlands WV11 26 B7
Wolverhampton, Tettenhall Wood WV6 24 A3
Wombourne WV5 49 B6
Wythall B47, B94 125 B1
Mill La Arc B91 107 C3
Mill Lodge Prim Sch B90 105 E2
Millmead Lodge B13 105 D8
Millmead Rd B32 84 E1
Mill Park Ind Est WS11 2 A1
Mill Pk WS11 2 A2
Mill Pl WS3 28 E4
Mill Pleck B80 159 E3
Mill Pond The WS13 3 C2
Mill Pool Cl DY9 99 A4
Millpool Gdns B14 104 F3
Millpool Hill B14 104 F4
Mill Pool La B93 144 A8
Mill Pool Rd WS12 2 B6
Millpool Way B66 65 A4
Mill Race La
Coventry CV6 96 B3
Stourbridge DY8 81 A6
Millrace Rd B98 153 E5
Mill Rd Brownhills WS8 16 A7
Cradley Heath B64 82 E7
Royal Leamington Spa CV31 162 A8
Walsall WS4 15 C1
Mills Ave B76 46 E4
Millsborough Rd B98 153 F3
Mills Cl WV11 26 B8
Mills Cres WV2 163 D1
Millside B28 105 E3
Mills Rd WV2 163 D1
Mill St Barwell LE9 71 F5
Bedworth CV12 78 B3
Bilston WV14 40 C5
Birmingham B6 164 D5
Brierley Hill DY5 61 E2
Cannock WS11 1 E1
Coventry CV1 165 A3
Darlaston WS10 41 C6
Halesowen B63 82 C7
Kidderminster DY11 116 D6
Nuneaton CV11 73 C4
Redditch B97 153 D4
Royal Leamington Spa CV31 162 A7
Stourbridge DY8 60 F2
Sutton Coldfield B72 46 C5
Tipton DY4 52 D5
Walsall WS2 28 E3
Warwick CV34 160 E6
West Bromwich B70 53 C4
Willenhall WV13 27 C2
Millstone Cl B76 46 F1
Mill Stream Cl WV8 10 B4
Millsum Ho [6] WS1 28 F1
Mills Wlk DY4 51 F7
Mill Terr CV12 78 B5
Mill The WV1 163 D3
Millthorpe Cl B8 67 F5
Mill View
Birmingham B33 69 C4
Hinckley LE10 71 E1
Millwalk Dr WV9 11 A3
Millward St
Birmingham B9 67 C1
West Bromwich B70 53 A3
Mill Wlk CV11 73 C4
Mill Wlk The B31 102 F1
Millwright Cl [4] DY4 52 B5
Milner Cl CV12 79 D2
Milner Cres CV2 96 E1
Milner Dr B79 22 E7
Milner Rd B29 86 A1
Milner Way B13 105 D8
Milnes Walker Ct B44 44 E1
Milo Cres B78 21 A2
Milrose Way CV4 131 F8
Milsom Gr B34 69 D6
Milstead Rd B26 69 A1
Milston Cl B14 104 E1
Milton Ave
[2] Birmingham B12 87 A6
Tamworth B79 21 A7
Warwick CV34 160 C5
Milton Cl
Bedworth CV12 78 D1
Bentley Heath B93 127 F4
Hinckley LE10 71 C1
Kidderminster DY11 116 A6
Redditch B97 158 C8
Stourbridge DY8 81 A7
Walsall WS1 42 D6
Willenhall WV12 27 E7
Milton Cres
Birmingham B25 88 D7
Dudley DY3 50 A5
Milton Ct WV6 23 E4
Milton Dr DY9 99 D7
Milton Gr
Birmingham, Edgbaston B29 85 F3
Birmingham, Handsworth B21 65 C8
Milton Ho B63 82 B5
Milton Pl WS1 42 D6
Milton Rd
Bentley Heath B93 127 F4
Cannock WS11 1 E4
Catshill B61 137 A8
Dudley WV14 51 D8
Smethwick B67 64 E5
Wolverhampton WV10 26 A5
Milton St
Birmingham B19 66 E6
Brierley Hill DY5 61 D7
Coventry CV2 114 A4
Walsall WS1 42 D7
West Bromwich B71 53 B5
Milverton Cl
Halesowen B63 83 A6
Sutton Coldfield B76 57 F7
Milverton Cres [1] CV32 156 E1
Milverton Cres W [3] CV32 156 E1
Milverton Ct
[3] Birmingham B62 84 A7
Royal Leamington Spa CV32 161 E8
Milverton Hill CV32 161 E8
Milverton House Prep Sch CV11 73 D3
Milverton Lodge [2] CV32 156 E1
Milverton Prim Sch CV32 156 E1
Milverton Rd
Birmingham B23 56 E4
Coventry CV2 96 D2
Knowle B93 128 C5
Milverton Terr CV32 161 E8
Milward Sq [7] B97 153 E3
Mimosa Cl B29 103 B7
Mimosa Wlk DY6 60 E8
Mincing La B65 63 D3
Mindelsohn Way B15 85 D4
Minden Gr B29 85 B1
Minehead Rd
Dudley DY1 61 D8
Wolverhampton WV10 11 B2
Miner St WS2 28 C3
Miners Way WS7 6 C7
Miners Wlk B78 22 F1
Minerva Cl
Tamworth B77 21 D5
Willenhall WV12 27 E4
Minerva La WV1 25 E1
Minewood Cl WS3 13 F3
Minith Rd WV14 51 D8
Miniva Dr B76 47 A2
Minivet Dr B12 86 E6
Minley Ave B17 84 F7
Minories B4 164 C3
Minories The [1] DY2 51 D1
Minors Hill WS14 9 D6
Minstead Rd B24 56 D1
Minster Cl
Knowle B93 128 B8
Rowley Regis B65 63 E3
Minster Dr B10 87 D7
Minsterley Cl WV3 38 E8
Minsterpool Wlk WS13 9 B8
Minster Rd CV1 113 B3
Minster The WV3 39 A7
Minster Wlk B61 136 F8
Mintern Rd B25 88 C8
Minton Cl WV1 26 A1
Minton Ho [3] B12 86 F5
Minton Mews B60 151 B8
Minton Rd
Birmingham B32 84 F4
Coventry CV2 96 E1
Minworth Cl B97 153 B2
Minworth Ind Pk B76 58 B5
Minworth Jun & Inf Sch B76 58 D5
Minworth Rd B46 59 A3
Miranda Cl
Birmingham B45 102 A2
Coventry CV3 134 D7
Miranda Dr CV34 161 E2
Miras Bsns Est WS12 2 D3
Mirfield Cl WV9 11 A3
Mirfield Rd
Birmingham B33 69 B2
Solihull B91 107 A6
Mission Cl B64 63 A1
Mission Dr DY4 52 A3
Mistletoe Dr WS5 43 B3
Mistral Cl LE10 75 F8
Mitcham Cl WS12 1 F7
Mitcham Gr B44 45 B1
Mitcheldean Cl B98 158 E7
Mitcheldean Covert B14 104 D2
Mitchell Ave
Coventry CV4 132 A7
Dudley WV14 40 B1
Mitchell Ho
Coventry CV4 132 A7
Warwick CV34 160 E7
Mitchell Rd CV12 78 C2
Mitchell's Ct B79 21 B5
Mitchel Rd DY6 60 F4
Mitford Dr B92 107 D7
Mitre Cl
Essington WV11 13 A3
Willenhall WV12 27 D7
Mitre Ct
Bromsgrove B61 137 A3
Sutton Coldfield B74 46 C6
Mitre Fold WV1 163 B3
Mitre Rd
Cheslyn Hay WS6 4 D2
Stourbridge DY9 81 E5
Mitten Ave B45 102 A1
Mitton Rd B20 54 E2
Moat Ave CV3 132 F5
Moat Coppice B62 84 A1
Moat Croft
Birmingham B37 70 A2
Sutton Coldfield B76 58 B7
Moat Dr
Drayton Bassett B78 34 E5
Halesowen B62 63 F1
Moat Farm Dr
Bedworth CV12 95 C8
Birmingham B32 84 A1
Moat Farm Inf Sch B68 64 C3
Moat Farm Jun Sch B68 64 C3
Moat Farm Way WS3 15 A5
Moatfield Terr [2] WS10 42 A3
Moat Gn CV35 160 A1
Moat Green Ave WV11 26 E7
Moat Hall Prim Sch WS6 4 F3
Moat House La CV4 132 C7
Moathouse La E WV11 26 E7
Moathouse La W WV11 26 D7
Moat House Prim Sch
Coventry CV2 96 D1
Wednesfield WV11 26 E7
Moat House Rd B8 68 A4
Moat La
Birmingham, Digbeth B5 164 C1
Birmingham, South Yardley B26 88 E7
Great Wyrley WS6 5 A2
Solihull B91 107 C6
Moat Mdws B32 84 E4
Moatmead Wlk B36 68 E8
Moat Rd Oldbury B68 64 B3
Tipton DY4 52 A7
Walsall WS2 28 C2
Moatside Cl WS3 15 A5
Moat St WV13 27 A2
Moat Way LE9 71 F6
Moatway The B38 123 E7
Mobberley Rd WV14 40 A1
Mob La WS4 15 C3
Mockley Wood Rd B93 128 B7
Modbury Ave B32 84 D1
Modbury Cl CV3 133 D5
Moden Cl DY3 50 D6
Moden Hill DY3 50 D6
Mogul La B63 82 A7
Moillett St B18 65 D4
Moilliett Ct B66 65 C6
Moira Cres B14 105 C4
Moises Hall Rd WV5 49 B7
Moland St B4 164 C4
Mole St B11 87 B6
Molesworth Ave CV3 114 A1
Molineux Grounds (Wolverhampton Wanderers FC) WV1 163 B4
Molineux St WV1 163 B4
Mollington Cres B90 106 C3
Mollington Rd CV31 162 A3
Molyneux Rd DY2 62 E2
Momus Bvd CV2 114 C2
Monarch Dr DY4 52 C6
Monarch Ho B68 64 B2
Monarch Ind Est B11 88 A5
Monarch Way DY2 62 C4
Monarch Works [7] DY9 81 F5
Mona Rd B23 56 F5
Monastery Dr B91 106 E6
Monckton Rd B68 84 A7
Moncrieff Dr CV31 162 C5
Moncrieffe Cl DY2 62 E8
Moncrieffe St WS1 29 A1
Mondrian Rd B60 137 C1
Money La B61 121 A7
Monica Rd B10 87 F8
Monins Ave DY4 52 A2
Monk Cl DY4 52 B3
Monkgate Dr B71 53 C6
Monk Rd B8 68 B5
Monk's Croft The CV3 133 C7
Monks Dr B80 159 D4
Monkseaton Rd B72 46 B2
Monksfield Ave B43 43 D1
Monks Field Cl CV4 112 A1
Monkshood Mews B23 56 B7
Monkshood Retreat B38 123 F8
Monks Kirby Rd B76 46 F3
Monkspath
Solihull B90 127 A6
Sutton Coldfield B76 46 F1
Monks Path B97 152 F4
Monkspath Bsns Pk B90 126 F8
Monkspath Cl B90 126 D7
Monkspath Hall Rd B90, B91 127 B7
Monkspath Jun & Inf Sch B90 127 B6
Monks Rd
Binley Woods CV3 135 C7
Coventry CV1 113 F2
Monksway B38 104 B1
Monks Way
Tamworth B77 21 F5
Warwick CV34 160 D6
Monkswell Cl
Birmingham B10 87 D7
Brierley Hill DY5 61 D1
Monkswood Cres CV2 114 D8
Monkswood Rd B31 103 C2
Monkton Rd B29 85 A2
Monmer Cl WV13 27 B3
Monmer Close Ind Est WV13 27 B3
Monmer Ct WV12 27 B5
Monmer La WV12, WV13 27 B4
Monmore Bsns Pk WV2 39 F7
Monmore Park Ind Est WV2 40 A6
Monmore Rd WV1 40 A7
Monmouth Cl
Coventry CV5 112 B3
Kenilworth CV8 147 F6
Monmouth Dr
Sutton Coldfield B73 45 D3
West Bromwich B71 53 B7
Monmouth Gdns CV10 72 E3
Monmouth Ho B33 69 E2
Monmouth Rd
Birmingham, Bartley Green B32 102 D8
Birmingham, Warley Woods B67 84 E8
Walsall WS2 27 E3
Monnington Ho CV8 148 B7
Monsal Ave WV10 25 E4
Monsaldale Cl WS8 15 D7
Monsal Rd B42 55 C7
Monsieurs Hall La B61 136 B3
Mons Rd DY2 51 F1
Montague Ho
Birmingham B16 65 E1
Warwick CV34 161 A8
Montague Rd
Birmingham, Birches Green B24 57 A1
Birmingham, Edgbaston B16 65 E1
Birmingham, Handsworth B21 65 F8
Smethwick B66 65 C3
Warwick CV34 161 A8
Montague St
Birmingham, Aston B6 67 B8
Birmingham, Bordesley B9 67 A2
Montalt Rd CV3 133 E7
Montana Ave B42 55 A5
Montana Wlk CV10 72 E3
Monteagle Dr DY6 49 D1
Montford Gr DY3 50 D7
Montfort Rd
Coleshill B46 70 F5
Walsall WS2 42 B6
Montfort Wlk B32 84 A2
Montgomery Cl
Coventry CV3 134 C4
Upper Catshill B61 121 A1
Montgomery Cres DY5 81 F7
Montgomery Croft B11 87 C7
Montgomery Prim Sch B11 87 C7
Montgomery Rd
Walsall WS2 27 E2
Whitnash CV31 161 F4
Montgomery St Bsns Ctr B11 87 D7
Montgomery St B11 87 C7
Montgomery Way B8 68 A4
Montgomery Wlk [1] B71 53 D4
Montjoy Cl CV3 134 D7
Montley B77 36 C8
Montpelier Ho CV8 147 F5
Montpelier Rd B24 57 A1
Montpellier Cl CV3 133 C6
Montpellier Gdns DY1 50 E2
Montpellier St B12 87 A6
Montreal Ho B5 86 D7
Montrose Ave CV32 157 B5
Montrose Cl WS11 1 F5
Montrose Dr
Birmingham B35 58 A4
Dudley DY1 62 A8
Nuneaton CV10 72 F3
Montsford Cl B93 127 F6
Monument Ave DY9 81 E4
Monument Dr WV10 12 C8
Monument Ho [6] B16 65 F1
Monument La
Birmingham B45 121 F4
Hagley DY9 99 D7
Sedgley DY3 39 E1
Monument Rd B16 65 F2
Monway Bldgs [1] WS10 41 E3
Monway Ind Est WS10 41 E3
Monway Terr WS10 41 E3
Monwood Gr B91 106 F2
Monyhull Hall Rd B30 104 C3
Moodyscroft Rd B33 69 C3
Moon's La WS6 4 D1
Moons Moat Dr B98 154 E5
Moons Moat Fst Sch B98 154 D5
Moons Pk B98 154 E6
Moorbrooke CV10 72 A7
Moor Cl WS7 7 B7
Moorcroft Cl
Nuneaton CV11 74 B1
Redditch B97 158 B6
Moorcroft Dr WS10 41 C2
Moorcroft Gdns B97 158 B6
Moorcroft Pl [5] B7 67 A4
Moorcroft Rd B13 86 E3
Moorcroft Wood Prim Sch WV14 41 B3
Moor Ct B24 56 F3
Moor Ctr The DY5 61 D3
Moordown Ave B92 89 A2

Moore Cl Coventry CV6 **96** A5
Perton WV6. . . . . . . **23** F4
Sutton Coldfield B74. . . **31** F6
Warwick CV34 . . . . . **155** F2
Moore Cres B68. . . . . **64** C3
Moorend Ave B37 . . . . **70** B2
Moor End Ct B24. . . . . **57** B4
Moor End La B24. . . . . **57** B4
Moore Rd WV12. . . . . **27** D8
Moore's Row B5. . . . . . **66** F1
Moore St Cannock WS12 . .**2** C7
Wolverhampton WV1 . . **25** F1
Moore Wlk CV34 . . . . **161** C7
Moorfield Ave B93 . . **127** F6
Moorfield Dr
Bromsgrove B61. . . . **136** F3
Halesowen B63. . . . . . **83** A5
Sutton Coldfield B73. . .**57** A8
Moorfield Rd
Birmingham B34 . . . . **69** B6
Wolverhampton WV2 . . **39** C7
Moorfields Cl WS9 . . . **30** A7
Moorfield The CV3 . . **134** B8
Moorfoot Ave B63. . . . **82** C1
Moorgate B79 . . . . . . **21** A5
Moorgate Cl B98. . . . **154** E6
Moorgate Com Prim Sch
B79. . . . . **21** A5
Moorgate Rd B60. . . . **151** A2
Moor Green Inf Sch
B13. . . . . **86** C1
Moor Green Jun Sch
B13. . . . . **86** C1
Moor Green La B13 . . **86** D2
Moor Hall Dr
Clent DY9 . . . . **100** A1
Sutton Coldfield B75. . .**32** D1
Moor Hall Prim Sch
B75. . . . . **32** D2
Moorhen Cl WS8 . . . . . **15** E7
Moorhill Prim Sch
Cannock WS11 . . . .**1** E4
Cannock WS11 . . . .**1** E5
Moorhill Rd CV31 . . **162** A3
Moorhills Croft B90 . **126** B8
Moor Ho B14 . . . . . . **104** C2
Moorings Bsns Pk The
CV6. . . . . **96** A6
Moorings The
Birmingham B18. . . . . **65** F5
Brierley Hill DY5 . . . . **62** A4
Oldbury B69. . . . . **63** E8
Royal Leamington Spa
CV31. . . . . **161** A2
Wolverhampton WV9 . . **10** F2
Moor La
Birmingham B6. . . . . . **56** A4
Rowley Regis B65. . . . . **63** B3
Shenstone WS14. . . . . . **17** E2
Tamworth B77. . . . . . . **22** A6
Tamworth, Bolehall
B77. . . . . **21** D5
Moorland Ave WV10 . . **25** C6
Moorland Ct B16. . . . . **65** D1
Moorland Rd
Birmingham B16. . . . . **65** D1
Cannock WS11 . . . .**1** E5
Walsall WS3 . . . . **28** A8
Moorlands Ave CV8 . . **147** F3
Moorlands Ct **6** B75 . .**46** F6
Moorlands Cl B65. . . . . **63** D4
Moorlands Dr B90. . . **106** C2
Moorlands Lodge
CV8 . . . . **147** F3
Moorlands Prim Sch
B71. . . . .**53** B8
Moorlands Rd B71 . . . **42** C1
Moorlands The B71 . . . **45** F8
Moor Lane Ind Est B6 **55** F5
Moor Leasow B31. . . **103** C2
Moor Meadow Rd
B75. . . . . **46** D7
Moorpark Cl CV11. . . . **79** C8
Moorpark Rd B31. . . **103** A1
Moor Pk Perton WV6 . .**23** D5
Walsall WS3 . . . . **14** B3
Moor Pool Ave B17. . . **85** C6
Moor Rd CV10 . . . . . . **72** A8
Moor St S WV2. . . . . . **39** C7
Moors Croft B32 . . . . . **84** B1
Moorside Gdns WS2. . **28** B3
Moorside Rd B14 . . . **105** D3
Moors La B31. . . . . . . **102** E7
Moors Mill La DY4 . . . **52** D7
Moorsom St B6 . . . . . . **66** E5
Moorsom Way B60. . . **151** B7
Moor St
Brierley Hill DY5 . . . . **61** C3

Moor St continued
Coventry CV5 . . . . . . **112** F1
Tamworth B79. . . . . . . **21** A5
Wednesbury WS10 . . . **42** B2
West Bromwich B70. . . **53** C2
Moors The B36 . . . .**68** F8
Moor Street Ind Est
DY5. . . . . **61** C3
Moor Street Queensway
B5. . . . . **164** C2
Moor Street Sta B5. **164** C2
Moor The B76. . . . . . . **58** A8
Moorville Wlk B11 . . . **87** A7
Moorwood Cres CV10 **72** A8
Moorwood La
Hartshill CV10. . . . . . . **72** A7
Hartshill CV10. . . . . . . **72** A8
Morar Cl B35. . . . . **58** C4
Moray Cl
Halesowen B62. . . . . . **83** E8
Hinckley LE10 . . . . **75** A8
Morcom Rd B11. . . . . . **87** E5
Morcroft WV14. . . . . . **41** A3
Mordaunt Dr B75. . . . . **32** E2
Morden B33 . . . . **68** D3
Mordern Mobile Home
Pk WV10. . . . . **11** C6
Mordiford Cl B98. . . **154** E4
Moreall Mdws CV4 . . **132** D3
Morecroft Dr CV34 . . **160** B4
Moreland Croft B76. . **58** B6
Moreland Pl B31. . . . **102** F1
Morelands The B31. . **103** B1
Morestead Ave B26 . . **89** C5
Moreton Ave
Birmingham B43. . . . . **44** C3
Wolverhampton WV4 . . **39** E4
Moreton Cl
Birmingham, Queen's Park
B32. . . . . **84** F5
Birmingham, Yardley
B25. . . . . **88** B7
Wednesbury DY4 . . . . . **41** B8
Moreton Com Sch
WV10 . . . .**11** F1
Moreton Rd
Solihull B90. . . . . **106** C2
Wolverhampton WV10 . **11** D1
Moreton St
Birmingham B1. . . . . . **66** B4
Cannock WS11 . . . .**1** F4
Morfa Gdns CV6 . . . . **112** D5
Morford Rd WS9 . . . . . **30** A7
Morgan Cl
1 Cradley Heath B64 . . **82** E8
Oldbury B69. . . . . **63** D8
Studley B80. . . . . **159** F2
Willenhall WV12 . . . . . **27** B4
Morgan Ct B24. . . . . . **57** C6
Morgan Gr B36. . . . . . **58** F1
Morgan Rd B78 . . . . . . **21** A2
Morgans Rd CV5 . . . **111** C4
Morgrove Ave B93 . . **127** F6
Morillon Ct DY10 . . . **117** A1
Morjon Dr B43. . . . .**43** F2
Morland Cl CV12 . . . . **79** D2
Morland Dr LE10 . . . . **71** B3
Morland Rd
Birmingham B43. . . . . **44** C4
Coventry CV6 . . . . **95** C2
Morley Gr WV6. . . . . . **25** C4
Morley Rd
Birmingham B8. . . . . . **68** B6
Burntwood WS7 . . . .**7** B7
Morley Road Sh Ctr
WS7. . . . .**7** B7
Morlich Rise DY5. . . . . **81** B8
Morlings Dr WS7. . . . . .**7** B8
Morning Pines DY8. . . **80** E4
Morningside
Coventry CV5 . . . . . . **133** B8
Sutton Coldfield B73. . **46** B6
Mornington Rd B66 . . **65** B7
Morpeth B77. . . . . **35** C7
Morrell St CV32 . . . . **156** F1
Morris Ave
Coventry CV2 . . . . . . **114** D4
Walsall WS2 . . . . **27** E2
Morris Cl B27. . . . . **88** D4
Morris Croft B36. . . . . .**58** F1
Morris Ct
Brierley Hill DY5 . . . . **61** B1
4 Wolverhampton
WV4 . . . . **39** F4
Morris Dr
Nuneaton CV11. . . . . . **73** D1
Whitnash CV31. . . . . . **162** B3
Morris Field Croft
B28 . . . . **105** E4
Morris Hill B78. . . . . . .**36** F7

Morrison Ave WV10 . . **25** D8
Morrison Rd DY4. . . . . **52** C4
Morris Rd B8 . . . . **68** C6
Morris St B70. . . . . **53** C1
Morris Wlk B60 . . . . . **150** E8
Morsefield La B98. . . **154** D1
Morse Rd CV31. . . . . . **162** B3
Morston B77. . . . . **35** D4
Mortimer Rd CV8 . . . **147** F2
Mortimers Cl B14 . . . **105** B1
Morton Cl CV6. . . . . . . **95** A1
Morton Ho B97. . . . . . **153** A3
Morton La B97. . . . . . **158** B7
Morton Rd
Brierley Hill DY5. . . . . **81** D7
Harvington DY10. . . . . **118** B2
Morton St CV32 . . . . **156** F1
Morvale Ct DY9 . . . . . . **81** E5
Morvale Gdns DY9 . . . **81** E5
Morvale St DY9 . . . . . . **81** E5
Morven Rd B73 . . . . . . **46** A3
Morville Cl B93 . . . . . **127** D3
Morville Croft WV14. . **40** B5
Morville Rd DY2. . . . . . **62** E4
Morville St B16. . . . . . **66** B2
Mosborough Cres
B19. . . . . **66** C5
Mosedale Dr WV11 . . .**26** F5
Moseley Ave CV6. . . . **113** A4
Moseley CE Prim Sch
B13. . . . .**86** F2
Moseley Ct
19 Birmingham B13. . . **87** B2
Essington WV11 . . . . . **12** F3
Willenhall WV13 . . . . . **26** D1
Moseley Dr B37. . . . . . .**89** F8
Moseley Gate B13. . . .**86** F3
Moseley Hall Hospl
B13. . . . .**86** E3
Moseley Old Hall*
WV10 . . . . **12** A5
Moseley Old Hall La
WV10 . . . . **12** A5
Moseley Park Sch
WV14. . . . .**40** E8
Moseley Prim Sch
CV6. . . . . **113** A4
Moseley Rd
Bilston WV14 . . . . **40** E8
Birmingham B12. . . . . **86** F6
Kenilworth CV8. . . . . **148** B3
Willenhall WV14, WV13 **26** D1
Wolverhampton WV10 . **12** A4
Moseley Sch B13 . . . . **87** C2
Moseley St
Birmingham B12. . . . . **86** F8
Tipton DY4 . . . . **52** C7
Wolverhampton WV6 . . **25** C4
Mossbank Rd WS7 . . . .**7** A6
Moss Cl Aldridge WS9 . **30** A5
Walsall WS4 . . . . **29** A3
Moss Cres WS12 . . . .**1** C5
Mossdale B77. . . . . **36** C8
Mossdale Cl CV6 . . . . **113** B6
Mossdale Cres CV10. .**72** F2
Mossdale Way DY3. . . **50** E7
Moss Dr B72. . . . . **46** C3
Mossfield Rd B14 . . . **104** F7
Moss Gdns WV14. . . . . **40** B3
Moss Gr
Birmingham B14. . . . **104** D6
Kenilworth CV8. . . . . **148** B7
Kingswinford DY6 . . . . **60** D7
Moss House Cl B15. . . **66** B1
Moss La B98 . . . . **154** F8
Moss Lane Cl B98. . . . **154** F8
Mossley Cl WS3. . . . . . **13** F1
Mossley La WS3. . . . . . **13** F2
Mossley Prim Sch
WS3. . . . . **13** F2
Mosspaul Cl CV32 . . . **156** D2
Moss Rd WS11 . . . .**2** A3
Moss St Cannock WS11 . .**2** A4
12 Royal Leamington Spa
CV31. . . . . **162** A7
Mossvale Cl B64. . . . . .**62** F1
Mossvale Gr B8. . . . . . .**67** F5
Moss Way B74. . . . . . .**44** F7
Mosswood St WS11 . . . **4** D7
Mostyn Cres B71. . . . . **53** A7
Mostyn Rd
Birmingham, Edgbaston
B16. . . . . **65** F2
Birmingham, Handsworth
B21. . . . . **65** F8
Mostyn St WV1. . . . . . **25** B4
Mother Teresa Ho
B70. . . . . **53** D2
Mott Cl DY4. . . . . **52** C8
Mottistone Cl CV3. . . **133** D6

Mottram Cl B70. . . . . . **53** B2
Mottrams Cl B72. . . . . **46** C2
Mott St B19. . . . . **164** B4
Moule Cl DY11 . . . . . . **116** C6
Moundsley Gr B14 . . **105** A3
Moundsley Ho B14 . . **104** F2
Mounds The B38 . . . . **123** E8
Mountain Ash Dr DY9 **81** C2
Mountain Ash Rd
WS8 . . . . **15** E5
Mountain Pine Cl
WS12 . . . .**2** A8
Mount Ave
Brierley Hill DY5 . . . . **61** C4
Cannock WS12 . . . .**2** B7
Mountbatten Ave
CV8 . . . . **148** C3
Mountbatten Cl B70. .**53** F2
Mountbatten Rd WS2. .**27** F2
Mount Cl
Birmingham B13. . . . . **86** F4
Cheslyn Hay WS6 . . . . . .**4** E2
Dudley DY3 . . . . **50** C2
Wombourne WV5 . . . . **49** A7
Mount Ct WV6 . . . . . . **24** B2
Mount Dr
Bedworth CV12. . . . . . **78** A3
Wombourne WV5. . . . . **49** A7
Mountfield Cl B14. . . **105** A2
Mount Field Ct CV1 . **165** D4
Mountford Cl **1** B65 . **63** C3
Mountford Cres WS9 . **30** C8
Mountford Dr B75. . . . **46** B8
Mountford Ho B71. . . **53** C1
Mountford La WV14 . . **40** D6
Mountford Rd B90. . . **105** D1
Mountford St B11. . . . **87** D5
Mount Gdns CV5 . . . . **133** B8
Mount Grace High Sch
LE10 . . . . **71** E1
Mountjoy Cres B92. . . **89** C3
Mount La Clent DY9 . . **99** E4
Dudley DY3 . . . . **50** C2
Mount Nod Prim Sch
CV5. . . . . **112** A3
Mount Nod Way CV5 **112** B3
Mount Pleasant
Bilston WV14 . . . . **40** E6
Birmingham, King's Heath
B14. . . . . **86** F1
Birmingham, Small Heath
B10. . . . . **67** B1
Brierley Hill DY5. . . . . **61** E1
Cheslyn Hay WS6 . . . . . .**4** E2
Kingswinford DY6. . . . . **60** C4
Redditch B97 . . . . **153** D2
Tamworth B77. . . . . . . **35** C8
Mount Pleasant Ave
B21 . . . . **54** E1
Mount Pleasant Cotts
CV2 . . . . **115** A7
Mount Pleasant Ct **1**
B10 . . . . **67** B1
Mount Pleasant Mobile
Home Pk B77. . . . . . **21** C1
Mount Pleasant Prim Sch
DY5. . . . .**61** E1
Mount Pleasant Rd
CV12 . . . . **78** A3
Mount Pleasant St
Dudley WV14 . . . . **51** B8
West Bromwich B70. . . **53** C2
Mount Pleasant Terr
CV10 . . . .**72** F6
Mountrath St WS1 . . . **28** E1
Mount Rd
Birmingham B21. . . . . **65** D7
Burntwood WS7 . . . .**7** B6
Fairfield B61. . . . . . . **120** E2
Hinckley LE10 . . . . **75** D8
Oldbury B69. . . . . **63** C8
Rowley Regis B65. . . . . **63** E3
Stourbridge, Stambermill
DY8. . . . . **81** B5
Stourbridge, Wordsley
DY8. . . . . **60** E2
Walsall WS3 . . . . **15** A4
Willenhall WV13 . . . . . **40** E8
Wolverhampton, Goldthorn
Hill WV4 . . . . **39** A4
Wolverhampton, Tettenhall
Wood WV6 . . . . **24** E5
Wolverhampton, Woodcross
WV4 . . . . **39** F2
Wombourne WV5 . . . . **49** A7
Mount Road Ind Est
WS7. . . . .**7** B6
Mountserrat Rd B60. **137** B1
Mount Side St WS12. . .**2** C7
Mounts Rd WS10. . . . . **41** F2

Mount St
Birmingham B7. . . . . . **67** C7
Cannock WS12 . . . .**2** B7
Coventry CV5 . . . . . . **112** F2
Halesowen B63. . . . . . **83** A3
Nuneaton CV11. . . . . . **73** B4
Redditch B98 . . . . **153** E3
Stourbridge DY8 . . . . . **81** B5
Tipton DY4 . . . . **52** C6
Walsall WS1 . . . . **42** E8
Mount Street Bsns Ctr
B7. . . . . **67** C6
Mount Street Ind Est
B7. . . . . **67** D7
Mount Street Pas
CV11 . . . . **73** B4
Mounts Way B7. . . . . . **67** C7
Mount The
Birmingham B23. . . . . **56** D1
Coventry CV3 . . . . . . **133** E8
Cradley Heath B64 . . . **63** A1
Curdworth B76. . . . . . . **59** C6
Mount Vernon Dr
B61 . . . . **137** A5
Mount View B75. . . . . **46** E4
Mountwood Covert
WV6 . . . . **24** B3
Mousehall Farm Rd
DY5. . . . . **81** D7
Mouse Hill WS3. . . . . . **14** F3
Mouse La DY11. . . . . . **116** B8
Mousesweet Cl DY2 . . **62** E4
Mousesweet La DY2. . **62** E3
Mousesweet Wlk B64 **82** B8
Mowbray Cl B45. . . . . **102** A2
Mowbray St
Birmingham B5. . . . . . **86** E8
Coventry CV2 . . . . . . **113** F3
Mowe Croft B37. . . . . . **90** B7
Mows Hill Rd B94. . . **143** A1
Moxhull Cl WV12 . . . . **13** C1
Moxhull Dr B76. . . . . . **57** E7
Moxhull Gdns WV12 . . **13** C1
Moxhull Rd B37. . . . . . **70** A5
Moxley Ind Ctr WS10. **41** C4
Moxley Jct WS10. . . . . **41** B4
Moxley Rd WS10. . . . . **41** C5
Moyle Cres CV5 . . . . . **111** D4
Moyle Dr B63 . . . . **82** B7
Moyses Croft B66. . . . **65** A8
Mozart Ct WS11. . . . .**2** C1
Muchall Rd WV4 . . . . . **39** A5
Much Park St CV1. . . **165** C2
Mucklow Hill B62. . . . **83** D5
Mucklow Hill Trad Est
B62. . . . . **83** C5
Muirfield B77. . . . . **22** C5
Muirfield Cl WS3 . . . . **14** A3
Muirfield Cres B69 . . . **63** B7
Muirfield Gdns B38 . . **103** D1
Muirfields Cl CV11 . . . **79** C8
Muirville Cl **1** DY8. . . **60** D3
Mulberry Cl CV32 . . . **157** A2
Mulberry Ct CV8 . . . . **147** F4
Mulberry Dr
Birmingham B13. . . . . **87** B1
3 Lichfield WS13. . . . . .**9** B8
5 Warwick CV34. . . . **160** F8
Mulberry Gn DY1. . . . .**50** F5
Mulberry Pl WS3 . . . . .**13** F1
Mulberry Rd
Birmingham B30. . . . **103** C5
Cannock WS11 . . . .**1** E3
Coventry CV6 . . . . . . **114** A7
Walsall WS3 . . . . **14** A1
Mulberry Way WV10 . **72** A8
Mulberry Wlk B74. . . . **44** E8
Muldoon Cl WS11 . . . . .**2** B7
Mullard Dr CV31 . . . . **162** B3
Mull Cl B45. . . . . **101** C1
Mull Croft B36. . . . . . . **70** B7
Mullein B74. . . . .**31** F5
Mullensgrove Rd B37 **70** A5
Mullett Rd WV11 . . . . **26** B7
Mullett St DY5 . . . . . . **61** B5
Mulliners Cl **2** B37. . **70** D2
Mulliner St CV6. . . . . **113** F5
Mullion Croft B38. . . **103** E1
Mulroy Rd B74 . . . . . . **46** B6
Mulwych Rd B33. . . . . **69** C3
Munches La B62. . . . . **120** C8
Munnings Dr LE10. . . **71** A3
Munro Cl DY10. . . . . . **117** C6
Munsley Cl B98. . . . . **154** F1
Munslow Gr B31. . . . . **122** F6
Muntz Cres B94. . . . . **143** C6
Muntz Ho B16. . . . . . . **66** A1
Muntz St B10. . . . . **87** D8
Murcott Ct CV31 . . . . **162** A3
Murcott Rd E CV31 . . **162** A3

Murcott Rd W CV31 . **162** A3
Murcroft Rd DY9 . . . . **81** E1
Murdoch Dr DY6 . . . . . **60** C7
Murdoch Rd WV14 . . . **41** A6
Murdock Ct WV12 . . . **27** D7
Murdock Gr B21. . . . . . **65** E7
Murdock Rd
Birmingham B21. . . . . **65** E8
Smethwick B66. . . . . . **65** D6
Murdock Way **1** WS2 **28** A5
Murray Ct
Birmingham B20. . . . . **55** A2
Sutton Coldfield B73. . **46** A3
Murrayfield Way
CV3 . . . . **115** B1
Murray Ho WV14 . . . . **40** D5
Murray Rd CV6. . . . . . **113** A7
Murrell Cl B5. . . . . **86** D7
Murton B77. . . . . **36** C8
Musborough Cl B36. . **58** C1
Muscott Gr B17 . . . . . . **85** B5
Muscovy Rd B23 . . . . . **56** C3
Musgrave Cl B76. . . . . **46** E3
Musgrave Rd B18 . . . .**65** F6
Mushroom Hall Rd
B68. . . . . **64** B5
Musketts Ct B97. . . . . **153** B2
Musk La DY3. . . . . **50** B3
Musk La W DY3 . . . . . . **50** B3
Mus of British Road
Transport* CV1. . . . **165** B3
Mus of Cannock Chase*
WS12 . . . . 2 D6
Mus of the Jewellery
Quarter* B19. . . . . . **66** C5
Muswell Cl B91. . . . . **107** D5
Muxloe Cl WS3 . . . . . . **14** A3
Myatt Ave
Aldridge WS9 . . . . **29** F5
Burntwood WS7 . . . .**7** A7
Wolverhampton WV2 . . **39** E6
Myatt Cl WV2 . . . . **39** E6
Myatt Way WS9 . . . . . .**29** F5
Myddleton St B18. . . . **66** A4
Myles Ct DY5 . . . . **61** D4
Mylgrove CV3. . . . . . . **133** D3
Mynors Cres B47. . . . **125** A6
Myring Dr B75. . . . . . .**46** F5
Myrtle Ave
4 Birmingham, Balsall
Heath B12 . . . . **87** A5
Birmingham, Highter's Heath
B14. . . . . **104** F2
Redditch B98 . . . . **153** E2
Myrtle Cl WV12 . . . . . . **27** C6
Myrtle Gr
10 Birmingham B19 . . **66** C8
Coventry CV5 . . . . . . **112** F1
Wolverhampton WV3 . . **38** E6
Myrtle Pl B29 . . . . **86** B2
Myrtle Rd DY1 . . . . **51** B3
Myrtle St WV2 . . . .**39** F6
Myrtle Terr DY4 . . . . . **41** B2
Myton Cres CV34 . . . **161** C6
Myton Crofts CV31 . . **161** D7
Myton Dr B90. . . . . . . **105** D1
Myton Gdns CV34 . . . **161** A6
Myton La CV34. . . . . . **161** C6
Myton Rd CV31, CV34 **161** B6
Myton Sch CV34. . . . . **161** B6
Mytton Cl DY2 . . . . . . **51** E1
Mytton Gr DY4 . . . . . . **51** E1
Mytton Rd
Birmingham B30. . . . **103** C5
Water Orton B46. . . . . **58** F3
Myvod Rd WS10. . . . . **42** A5

N

Naden Ho WS12. . . . .**1** C5
Naden Rd B19. . . . . . . **66** B6
Nadin Rd B73 . . . . **57** A8
Naesby Rd WV6 . . . . . .**23** F3
Nafford Gr B14. . . . . . **104** F1
Nagersfield Rd DY5 . . **61** A2
Nailcote Ave CV4. . . . **131** C8
Nailcote La CV7. . . . . **131** A7
Nailers Cl
Birmingham B32. . . . . **83** F2
Stoke Heath B60. . . . **150** E6
Nailers Ct **3** B60 . . **136** F2
Nailers Dr WS7. . . . .**7** D6
Nailors Fold WV14 . . . **40** D2
Nailstone Cres B27. . **106** C8
Nailsworth Rd
Dorridge B93 . . . . **127** D2
Redditch B98 . . . . **153** F2
Nairn Cl
Birmingham B28. . . . . **105** F5
Nuneaton CV10. . . . . . **73** B4

Nairn Cl *continued*
Redditch B98 154 E4
Nairn Rd WS3 14 A4
Nally Dr WV14 40 A2
Nanaimo Way DY6 61 A4
Nansen Prim Sch B8 67 F5
Nansen Rd
Birmingham B8 67 F5
Birmingham, Sparkhill B11 87 C3
Nantmel Gr B32 102 C8
Naomi Way WS9 16 B4
Napier B77 21 E3
Napier Dr DY4 52 C6
Napier Rd
Walsall WS2 28 A5
Wolverhampton WV2 39 D7
Napier St CV1 113 E3
Napton Cl B98 154 D1
Napton Dr CV32 157 A2
Napton Gn CV5 112 A3
Napton Gr B29 84 F2
Narberth Way CV2 114 F8
Narraway Gr DY4 52 D8
Narrowboat Cl CV6 96 B6
Narrowboat Way DY5, DY2 62 A5
Narrow Hall Mdw CV34 160 B4
Narrow La
Brownhills WS8 15 F8
Halesowen B62 83 E8
Walsall WS2 42 B7
Narrows The 1 LE10 75 E8
Naseby Cl
Coventry CV3 134 F8
Redditch B98 154 D6
Naseby Dr B63 82 D2
Naseby Rd
Birmingham B8 67 F5
Solihull B91 107 B6
Nash Ave WV6 23 E3
Nash Cl B65 63 C1
Nash Croft B37 90 B8
Nashe Cl DY10 117 C5
Nash Ho B15 86 D8
Nash La
Belbroughton DY9 119 D7
Lichfield WS13 3 A5
Nash Rd B98 154 B1
Nash Sq B42 55 D4
Nash Wlk 8 B66 65 C5
Nately Gr B29 85 C3
Nathan Cl B75 46 C8
Nathaniel Newton Inf Sch CV10 72 B8
National Ex Ctr B40 90 E4
National Indoor Arena* B1 66 B2
National Motorcycle Mus The* B92 91 A2
National Sea Life Ctr* B1 66 B2
Naul's Mill Ho CV1 165 B4
Naunton Cl B29 103 A7
Naunton Rd WS2 28 A3
Navenby Cl B90 105 C3
Navigation Dr DY5 62 A4
Navigation La B71 42 F2
Navigation Rdbt DY4 52 E6
Navigation St
Birmingham B2 164 B2
Walsall WS2 28 D1
Wolverhampton WV1 25 E1
Navigation Way
Birmingham B18 65 F5
Cannock WS11 2 A2
Coventry CV6 114 A8
West Bromwich B70 52 F2
Nayland Croft B28 106 A5
Naylor Cl DY11 116 B3
Naylors Gr DY3 50 E4
Neachells Ct WV13 26 E1
Neachells La
Wednesfield WV11 26 D5
Willenhall WV13 26 D3
Neachells Lane Ind Est WV11 26 D4
Neachells Lane Island WV11 26 D4
Neachless Ave WV5 49 A5
Neachley Gr B33 68 F4
Neal Ct CV2 115 A8
Neale Ave CV5 112 A6
Neale Cl CV12 79 C1
Neale Ho
6 West Bromwich B70 53 D1
Wolverhampton WV2 39 C7
Neale St WS2 28 C2
Neander B79 20 F6
Near High Dr 5 DY4 52 B5
Nearhill Rd B38 123 C8
Near Lands Cl B32 84 B4
Nearmoor Rd B34 69 D6
Near Oak Ho B32 102 D8
Neasden Gr B44 56 B8
Neath Rd WS3 13 F2
Neath Way Dudley DY3 51 A6
Walsall WS3 13 F2
Nebsworth Cl B90 106 D5
Nechells Jun & Inf Sch B7 67 C8
Nechells Park Rd B7 67 C7
Nechells Parkway B7 67 A5
Nechells Pl B7 67 C5
Needham St B7 67 C7
Needhill Cl B93 127 F6
Needle Cl B80 159 E4
Needle Mill La B98 153 E6
Needlers End La CV7 130 A7
Needless Alley B2 164 B2
Needwood Cl WV2 39 B6
Needwood Dr WV4 39 F4
Needwood Gr B71 42 E1
Needwood Hill WS13 3 A2
Needwood Ho B27 88 D3
Neighbrook Cl B97 152 F2
Neilston St 13 CV31 162 A7
Nelson Ave
Bilston WV14 40 C7
Warwick CV34 161 A8
Nelson Ct 5 B13 86 F4
Nelson Dr
Cannock WS12 2 F4
Hinckley LE10 71 D4
Nelson Ho DY4 52 A7
Nelson La CV34 161 A8
Nelson Mandela Sch B12 87 B5
Nelson Prim Sch B1 66 B3
Nelson Rd
Birmingham B6 55 F1
Dudley DY1 51 B1
Nelson St
Birmingham B1 66 B3
7 Coventry CV1 113 E4
Oldbury B69 64 B6
West Bromwich B71 53 C5
Willenhall WV13 27 B3
Nemesia B77 22 B4
Nene Cl Coventry CV3 134 D7
Stourbridge DY8 81 A5
Nene Way B36 69 F8
Neptune Ind Est WV13 41 B8
Neptune St DY4 51 E5
Nesbit Gr B9 68 B3
Nesfield Cl B38 103 C1
Nesfield Gr B92 109 B7
Nesscliffe Gr B23 56 D7
Nest Comm WS3 14 F5
Neston Gr B33 68 C2
Nestor Ho B13 105 D7
Netheravon Cl B14 104 D1
Nether Beacon WS13 3 A1
Netherbridge Ave WS14 9 E7
Netherbrook Prim Sch DY2 62 D2
Netherby Rd DY3 50 C8
Nethercote Gdns B90 105 E3
Netherdale Cl B72 57 C7
Netherdale Rd B14 105 A1
Netherend Cl B63 82 A7
Netherend La B63 82 B7
Netherend Sq B63 82 A7
Netherfield B98 159 A8
Netherfield Gdns B27 88 B3
Nethergate DY3 50 F5
Nether La WS7 7 D8
Netherley Ct LE10 71 D3
Netherley Rd LE10 71 D3
Nethermill Rd 1 CV6 113 A5
Netherstone Gr B74 31 F5
Netherstowe WS13 3 C2
Nether Stowe High Sch WS13 3 B1
Netherstowe La WS13 3 D2
Netherton Bsns Pk DY2 62 E3
Netherton CE Prim Sch DY2 62 B4
Netherton Gr B33 69 C3
Netherwood Cl B91 106 E6
Netherwood La B93 145 A7
Nethy Dr WV6 24 B5
Netley Gr B11 87 F3
Netley Ho B32 84 F5
Netley Rd WS3 13 E2
Netley Way WS3 13 E2
Network Pk B7 67 C4
Nevada Way B37 70 C1
Neve Ave WV10 25 F8
Nevill Cl CV31 161 F6
Neville Ave
Kidderminster DY11 116 D3
Wolverhampton WV4 39 D5
Neville Cl B98 154 A5
Neville Ct
Birmingham B13 104 F6
Kidderminster DY11 116 D3
5 Warwick CV34 160 E6
Neville Gr CV34 155 F1
Neville Ho DY3 50 D7
Neville Rd
Birmingham, Castle Bromwich B36 58 E1
Birmingham, Stockland Green B23 56 C3
Solihull B90 105 F1
Neville St B77 21 E3
Neville Wlk B35 58 A2
Nevill St B79 21 A5
Nevin Gr B42 55 C5
Nevis Ct WV6 24 E2
Nevis Gr WV12 13 B1
Nevison Gr B43 44 B4
Newall Ho B97 153 D2
Newark Croft B26 89 B6
Newark Rd
Dudley DY2 62 D2
Willenhall WV12 27 C7
New Art Gall The* WS2 28 E2
New Ash Dr CV5 111 F5
Newbank Gr B9 68 A3
New Barns La WS14 17 B3
New Bartholomew St B5 164 D2
New Birmingham Rd B69, DY2 52 B1
New Bldgs
Coventry CV1 165 C3
Darlaston WS10 41 E6
Hinckley LE10 71 D1
Newbold Cl
Bentley Heath B93 127 F5
Coventry CV3 114 F1
Lichfield WS13 9 A5
Newbold Comyn Pk* CV32 162 D8
Newbold Croft B7 67 B5
Newbold Ct B63 83 B3
Newbold Lawn CV32 162 A8
Newbold Pl CV32 162 A8
Newbolds Rd WV10 26 A6
Newbold St CV32 162 A8
Newbold Terr CV32 162 A8
Newbold Terr E CV32 162 B8
Newbolt Rd WV14 40 E6
Newbolt St WS5 42 E5
New Bond St
Birmingham B9 67 B1
2 Dudley DY2 62 D8
Newborough Gr B28, B90 105 F3
Newborough Rd
Birmingham B28 105 F4
Solihull B90 106 A3
Newbourne Hill B48 139 E4
Newbridge Ave WV6 24 E3
Newbridge Cres WV6 24 E4
Newbridge Dr WV6 24 E4
Newbridge Gdns WV6 24 E4
Newbridge Mews 3 WV6 24 F4
Newbridge Prep Sch WV6 24 E4
Newbridge Rd
Birmingham B9 68 B1
Kingswinford DY6 60 C8
Newbridge St WV6 24 F4
Newbrook Farm* B32 101 D4
New Brook St 3 CV32 161 E8
Newburgh Cres CV34 160 E8
Newburgh Prim Sch CV34 160 C4
Newburn Croft B32 84 B5
Newbury Cl
Great Wyrley WS6 4 F2
Halesowen B62 83 D3
Lower Marlbrook B61 121 B1
Newbury Cl *continued*
4 Royal Leamington Spa CV31 162 C6
Newbury Ho 1 B69 63 D5
Newbury La B69 63 D6
Newbury Rd
Birmingham B19 66 E7
Norton Canes WS11 6 A5
Stourbridge DY8 60 D1
Wolverhampton WV10 11 C2
Newbury Wlk B65 63 C6
Newby Cl CV3 133 E6
Newby Gr B37 70 B5
New Canal St B5 164 D2
Newcastle Croft B35 58 C3
New Century Pk CV3 114 C2
New Century Way CV11 73 B4
Newchurch Gdns 6 B24 56 E2
New Church Rd B73 57 A8
New Cole Hall La B33, B34 69 B5
New College Cl WS1 43 A7
Newcombe Rd
Birmingham B21 54 D2
Coventry CV5 113 A1
Newcome Ct B24 57 D4
Newcomen Cl
Bedworth CV12 95 D8
Burntwood WS7 7 C8
Newcomen Ct WS4 29 B7
Newcomen Dr DY4 51 F3
Newcomen Rd CV12 77 D1
New Coppice Ct B97 158 E6
Newcott Cl WV9 10 F2
New Coventry Rd B26 89 A5
New Croft B19 66 E7
Newcroft Gr B26 88 E7
New Cross Ave WV10 26 B4
New Cross Hospl WV11 26 B5
New Cross Ind Est WV1 26 A3
New Cross Junc WV10 26 B4
New Cross St
Darlaston WS10 41 D5
Tipton DY4 51 E5
New Ct 7 DY5 61 D2
Newdegate Cl CV12 78 A4
Newdegate Pl CV11 73 C4
Newdegate Rd CV12 78 A3
Newdegate St CV11 73 C4
Newdigate CV31 162 C5
Newdigate Prim Sch CV12 77 C1
Newdigate Rd
Coventry CV6 113 F6
Sutton Coldfield B75 47 A5
New Dudley Rd DY6 60 C8
Newells Dr DY4 52 D7
Newells Rd B26 89 B8
New England B62 83 E7
New England Cl B69 52 E1
Newent Cl WV12 27 D3
Newent Rd B31 103 C4
New Ent Workshops B18 66 A5
Newey Ave CV12 95 D8
Newey Cl B45 122 A6
Newey Dr CV8 148 A2
Newey Rd
Birmingham B28 105 F6
Coventry CV2 114 D4
Wednesfield WV11 27 A8
Newey St DY1 51 A2
New Farm Rd DY9 81 C4
Newfield Ave CV8 148 B3
Newfield Cl
Solihull B91 107 D6
Walsall WS2 28 C5
Newfield Cres B63 83 A5
Newfield Dr DY6 60 E4
Newfield Gdns DY9 99 A4
Newfield La B63 83 B5
Newfield Park Prim Sch B63 83 A5
Newfield Pl DY9 99 A4
Newfield Rd
Coventry CV1 113 C5
Oldbury B69 63 F8
West Hagley DY9 99 A4
New Forest Rd WS3 28 F6
Newgale Wlk CV31 162 C7
New Gas St B70 53 A5
New Gate Ct CV1 165 C2
Newgate St WS7 7 A5
New Gdns WS7 6 F5
New Green Pk CV2 114 D7
Newhall Cres WS11 2 B3
Newhall Ct 9 B3 66 C3
New Hall Dr
Sutton Coldfield, Maney B75 46 D4
Sutton Coldfield, Wylde Green B76 46 E2
Newhall Farm Cl B76 46 D4
Newhall Gdns WS11 1 F2
Newhall Hill B1 66 C3
Newhall Ho 5 WS1 42 E8
New Hall Inf Sch B75 47 B5
New Hall Jun Sch B75 47 B5
Newhall Pl B1 66 C3
New Hall Pl WS10 42 A3
Newhall Rd
Coventry CV2 114 D7
Rowley Regis B65 63 C3
Newhall St
Birmingham B3 164 B3
Cannock WS11 1 D1
Tipton DY4 51 E8
Walsall WS1 42 E8
West Bromwich B70 53 C2
New Hall St WV13 27 B2
Newhall Wlk B72 46 C4
Newham Gn CV10 72 C7
Newhampton Rd E WV1 163 A4
New Hampton Rd W WV6 24 F4
Newhaven Cl
Birmingham B7 67 A5
Coventry CV6 112 E6
Newhay Croft B19 66 C7
New Heath Cl WV11 26 B5
New Henry St B68 64 B4
Newhope Cl 2 B15 86 D8
New Hope Rd B66 65 C4
New Horse Rd WS6 4 E3
Newhouse Croft CV7 130 B6
Newhouse Farm Cl B76 46 F3
New House Farm Dr B31 103 C6
Newick Ave B74 31 B3
Newick Gr B14 104 C4
Newick St DY2 62 C4
Newington Cl CV6 112 D6
Newington Rd B37 90 B8
New Inn Rd 2 B19 66 D8
New Inns Cl B21 65 D8
New Inns La B45 101 E1
New Invention Inf & Jun Schs WV12 27 C7
New John St W B19 66 D5
New John St
Birmingham B6 66 E5
Halesowen B62 83 C8
New King St 7 DY1 51 C1
Newland Cl
Redditch B98 159 B7
Walsall WS4 15 C2
Newland Ct B23 56 C3
Newland Gdns B64 82 E7
Newland Gr DY2 61 F7
Newland La CV7 95 B7
Newland Rd
Birmingham B9 67 F1
Coventry CV1 113 D5
Royal Leamington Spa CV32 157 C3
Newlands Cl
Kidderminster DY11 116 C7
Willenhall WV13 27 A1
Newlands Ct
Cannock WS12 5 E8
Coventry CV3 113 F2
Newlands Dr B62 83 E7
Newlands Gn B66 65 A4
Newlands La
Birmingham B37 90 A6
Norton Canes WS12 5 D8
Newlands Rd
Bentley Heath B93 127 F4
Birmingham B30 104 C7
Newlands The
Birmingham B34 69 C7
Studley B80 159 D3
New Landywood La WS6 13 E7
New Leasow B76 58 A7
Newlyn Cl
Lichfield WS14 9 D7
Nuneaton CV11 73 F4
Newlyn Rd
Birmingham B31 102 F3
Cradley Heath B64 82 D8
Newman Ave WV4 39 F4
Newman Cl CV12 78 B4
Newman College Cl B32 102 C8
Newman Coll of Higher Ed B32 102 C8
Newman Pl WV14 40 F7
Newman Rd
Birmingham B24 56 F4
Wednesbury DY4 41 C1
Wolverhampton WV10 12 A1
Newmans Cl B66 65 C4
Newman Way B45 122 A6
Newmarket Cl
Coventry CV6 96 B4
Wolverhampton WV6 25 A5
Newmarket Rd WS11 6 B4
New Market St B3 164 B3
Newmarket Way B36 68 B7
Newmarsh Rd B76 58 A6
New Meadow Cl B31 103 B2
New Meadow Rd B98 154 B3
New Meeting St B69 64 A8
New Mill La B78 35 A7
New Mills St WS1 42 D7
New Mill St DY2 51 C1
Newmore Gdns WS5 43 C5
New Moseley Rd B12 87 A8
Newnham Gr B23 56 E6
Newnham Ho B36 70 B5
Newnham Rd
Birmingham B16 65 C2
Coventry CV1 113 F5
Royal Leamington Spa CV32 157 B3
Newnham Rise B90 106 D3
New Oscott Prim Sch B73 45 C3
New Park Sch WV6 24 F5
New Penkridge Rd WS11 1 C1
New Plant La WS7 6 C8
New Pool Rd B64 82 B8
Newport B77 21 F5
Newport Cl B97 158 B6
Newport Rd
Birmingham, Balsall Heath B12 87 A4
Birmingham, Buckland End B36 68 F8
Coventry CV6 95 D1
Newport St
4 Walsall WS1 28 E1
Wolverhampton WV10 25 E4
Newquay Cl
Hinckley LE10 71 E4
Nuneaton CV11 73 F5
Walsall WS5 43 E7
Newquay Rd WS5 43 D7
New Railway St WV13 27 B2
New Rd Aldridge WS9 30 A5
Ash Green CV7 95 B6
Astwood Bank B96 158 E1
Birmingham B45 121 F7
Bromsgrove B60 137 A1
Bromsgrove, Sidemoor B61 136 E3
Brownhills WS8 15 F7
Burntwood WS7 7 B6
Coventry CV6 94 F1
Dudley DY2 62 C7
Fairfield B61 120 E2
Halesowen B63 83 B4
Hinckley LE10 76 A6
Hollywood B47 125 A8
Kidderminster DY10 116 E5
Shenstone WS14 17 F6
Shuttington B79 22 E8
Solihull B91 107 D3
Stourbridge DY8 81 A5
Studley B80 159 E3
Tamworth B77 35 F7
Tipton DY4 52 D6
Water Orton B46 59 B3
Willenhall WV13 27 A1
Wolverhampton, Newbridge WV6 24 E4
Wolverhampton, Scotlands WV10 26 B8
New Row B78 34 E5
New Rowley Rd DY2 62 E7
New Shipton Cl B76 46 F1
Newshire Ind Est B11 87 D6
Newsholme Cl 1 CV34 155 E1
New Spring St N B18 66 A4
New Spring St B18 66 A4
New St Bedworth CV12 78 C2

New St *continued*
Birchmoor B78 . . . . **36** E7
Birmingham B23 . . . . . . **57** A4
Birmingham, Castle
Bromwich B36 . . . . . . **69** B8
Birmingham, Digbeth
B2 . . . . **164** C2
Birmingham, Erdington
B23 . . . . **56** F5
Birmingham, Frankley
B45 . . . . **102** A1
Brierley Hill DY5 . . . . . **82** A8
Bulkington CV12 . . . . . **79** D2
Burntwood, Chase Terrace
WS7 . . . . **6** E8
Burntwood, Chasetown
WS7 . . . . **6** E5
Cannock, Bridgtown
WS11 . . . . **4** D6
6 Cannock, Mill Green
WS11 . . . . **4** E8
Cannock WS12 . . . .**2** C4
Cubbington CV32 . . . . **157** E5
Darlaston WS10 . . . . . **41** D6
Dudley, Eve Hill DY1 . . **51** D1
Dudley, Gornalwood
DY3 . . . . **50** C3
Essington WV11 . . . . . . **13** A3
Ettingshall WV2 . . . . . . **40** A6
Fazeley B78 . . . . **35** B8
Great Wyrley WS6 . . . . . .**5** A1
Hinckley LE10 . . . . **71** D1
Kenilworth CV8 . . . . . **147** F6
Kingswinford DY6 . . . . **60** D4
Kingswinford, Wall Heath
DY6 . . . . **60** C8
Royal Leamington Spa
CV31 . . . . **162** A7
Smethwick B66 . . . . **65** B6
Stourbridge DY8 . . . . . **80** F5
Stourbridge, Wordsley
DY8 . . . . **60** D2
Tamworth, Bolehall B77 **21** E4
Tamworth, Mount Pleasant
B77 . . . . **21** C1
Tipton DY4 . . . . **51** F2
Walsall, Rushall WS4 . . **29** B7
Walsall, The Chuckery
WS1 . . . . **28** F1
Walsall, Wallington Heath
WS3 . . . . **14** B1
Walsall WS4 . . . . **15** D1
Warwick CV34 . . . . . . **160** E6
Wednesbury WS10 . . . **41** F1
West Bromwich, Hill Top
B70 . . . . **53** A7
West Bromwich, Mayer's
Green B70 . . . . **53** D3
Willenhall WV13 . . . . . **26** E1
Wolverhampton, Merry Hill
WV3 . . . . **38** D7
Wolverhampton, Parkfield
WV4 . . . . **39** E6
Newstead B79 . . . . **20** D6
Newstead Ave LE10 . . **75** D4
Newstead Cl CV11 . . . .**73** F2
Newstead Rd B44 . . . . **45** B3
Newstead Way CV3 . . **115** B1
New Street N B71 . . . **53** D3
New Street Sta B2 . . **164** B2
New Summer St B19 **164** B4
New Swan La B70 . . . **53** A5
New Swinford Hall
DY9 . . . . **81** C4
Newton Chambers **1**
B2 . . . . **164** B2
Newton Cl
Birmingham B43 . . . . . **43** C1
Coventry CV2 . . . . . . **114** F7
Redditch B98 . . . . . . **159** A6
Newton Gdns B43 . . . **54** B8
Newton Gr **5** B29 . . . .**85** F2
Newton Ind Est B9. . . **67** D2
Newton Manor Cl
B43 . . . . **54** D8
Newton Pl
Birmingham B18 . . . . . **66** A7
Walsall WS2 . . . . **28** B6
Newton Rd
Birmingham, Balsall Heath
B11 . . . . **87** B5
Birmingham, Newton
B43 . . . . **54** B8
Bromsgrove B60 . . . . **151** A7
Hinckley LE10 . . . . . . **74** E7
Knowle B93 . . . . **128** D3
Walsall WS2 . . . . **28** B5
West Bromwich B71 . . **53** F6

Newton's Coll WS13 . . . .**9** B8
Newton Sq
Birmingham B43 . . . . . **43** E1
Bromsgrove B60 . . . . **151** A7
Newton St
Birmingham B4 . . . . . **164** C3
West Bromwich B71 . . **53** C2
Newton Works B60 . **151** A6
New Town
Brierley Hill DY5 . . . . . **61** C4
Dudley DY2 . . . . **62** D1
Newtown Bldgs CV12. **78** B3
Newtown Dr B19 . . . . **66** C6
Newtown La
Cradley Heath B64 . . . . **62** D1
Madeley Heath B62 . . **120** D8
Romsley B62 . . . . **101** D2
Newtown Middleway
B6 . . . . **66** E5
Newtown Prim Sch
B70 . . . . **52** D3
Newtown Rd
Bedworth CV12 . . . . . . **78** A2
Nuneaton CV11 . . . . . . **73** C5
New Town Row B6 . . . **66** E5
Newtown Sh Ctr B19. .**66** E6
Newtown St B64 . . . . . **62** D2
New Union St CV1 . . **165** B2
New Village DY2 . . . . . **62** C6
New Wharf Cotts
B60 . . . . **152** B7
New Wlk **3** B97 . . . . **153** E4
New Wood Cl DY7. . . . **80** C8
New Wood Dr B31 . . . **102** D1
New Wood Gr WS9 . . . **16** A3
New Wood La DY10 . . **118** B8
Ney Ct DY4 . . . .**51** F2
Niall Cl B15 . . . . **85** E8
Nibletts Hill B61 . . . **136** B7
Nicholas Chamberlaine
Tec Coll CV12 . . . . . . **78** D3
Nicholas Cl CV12 . . . . . **78** C3
Nicholas Rd B74 . . . . . **44** E8
Nicholds Cl WV14 . . . . **40** B1
Nicholds Cl DY4 . . . . . **40** E1
Nicholls St
Coventry CV2 . . . . . . **113** F4
West Bromwich B70 . . **53** E2
Nicholls Way WS12 . . . . .**2** F1
Nichols Cl B92 . . . . . . **107** F7
Nicholson Cl CV34 . . **155** F1
Nickson Rd CV4 . . . . . **111** E1
Nigel Ave B31 . . . . . . **103** A5
Nigel Cl B16 . . . . **65** C1
Nigel Rd
Birmingham B8 . . . . . . **67** E6
Dudley DY1 . . . . **51** A2
Nightingale B77 . . . . . **36** A6
Nightingale Ave B36 . **70** A8
Nightingale Cl
Birmingham B23 . . . . . **56** C7
Huntington WS12 . . . . . .**1** C7
Nightingale Cres
Brierley Hill DY5 . . . . . **81** D2
Willenhall WV12 . . . . . **27** C8
Nightingale Ct
Burntwood WS7 . . . .**7** F8
Royal Leamington Spa
CV31 . . . . **162** B8
Solihull B91 . . . . **107** C4
Nightingale Dr
Kidderminster DY10 . . **117** B2
Tipton DY4 . . . . **52** C5
Nightingale La CV5. . . **132** E7
Nightingale Pl WV14 . **40** D7
Nightingale Wlk
1 Birmingham B15 . . . **86** C7
Burntwood WS7 . . . .**7** F8
Nightjar Gr B23 . . . . . . **56** C6
Nighwood Dr B74 . . . . .**44** F7
Nijon Cl B21 . . . . **54** D1
Nimbus B77 . . . . **35** D4
Nimmings Cl B31 . . . . **122** F6
Nimmings Rd B62 . . . . **63** D1
Nimmings Visitor Ctr*
B62 . . . . **100** B6
Nineacres Dr B37 . . . . **70** A3
Nine Days La B98 . . . . **159** B6
Nine Elms La WV10 . . . **25** E4
Ninefoot La
Tamworth, Belgrave
B77 . . . . **35** E8
Tamworth, Wilnecote
B77 . . . . **35** F7
Nine Leasowes B66 . **64** E7
Nine Locks Ridge
DY5 . . . . **61** D2
Nine Pails Wlk **2**
B70 . . . . **53** D1

Ninestiles Sch (Tech
Coll) B27 . . . . **88** B1
Nineveh Ave B21 . . . . . **65** F7
Nineveh Rd B21 . . . . . . **65** F7
Ninfield Rd B27 . . . . . . **88** A4
Ninian Pk B77 . . . . **35** D6
Ninian Way B77 . . . . . . **35** E6
Nirvana Cl WS11 . . . .**1** C2
Nith Pl DY1 . . . . **51** B3
Niton Rd CV10 . . . . **73** D6
Niven Cl CV5 . . . . **112** A6
Noakes Ct WS10 . . . . . .**41** F7
Noble Cl CV34 . . . . . . **160** D5
Nocke Rd WV11 . . . .**12** C1
Nock St DY4 . . . . **52** C7
Noddy Park Rd WS9 . . **30** B7
Noddy Pk WS9 . . . . . . **30** B7
Node Hill B80 . . . . **159** D3
Node Hill Cl B80 . . . . **159** D3
Nod Rise CV5 . . . . . . **112** B3
Noel Ave B12 . . . . **87** A6
Noel Ct B97 . . . . **153** B2
Noele Gordon Gdns **10**
WS1 . . . . **42** E8
Noel Rd B16 . . . .**65** F1
Nolan Cl CV6 . . . . **95** D4
Nolton Cl B43 . . . . **54** D8
No Name Rd WS7 . . . .**6** E7
Nonsuch Prim Sch
B32 . . . . **84** D2
Nooklands Croft B33 . **69** A2
Nook The
Brierley Hill DY5 . . . . . **61** B5
Cheslyn Hay WS6 . . . . . .**4** C1
Nuneaton CV11 . . . . . . **73** E2
Noonan Cl B97 . . . . . **153** B2
Noose Cres WV13 . . . . **26** E2
Noose La WV13 . . . . . . **26** E3
Nora Rd B11 . . . . **87** C3
Norbiton Rd B44 . . . . . **56** A8
Norbreck Cl B43 . . . . . **43** D1
Norbury Ave WS3 . . . . **15** A3
Norbury Cl B98 . . . . . **154** B7
Norbury Cres WV4 . . . . **40** A4
Norbury Dr DY5 . . . . . . **61** D1
Norbury Gr B92 . . . . . . **89** A3
Norbury Rd
Bilston WV14 . . . . **40** F6
Birmingham B44 . . . . . **44** F3
West Bromwich B70 . . **53** A7
Wolverhampton B29 . . **53** A7
Norcombe Gr B90 . . . **127** A5
Nordic Drift CV2 . . . . **115** A6
Nordley Rd WV11 . . . . **26** C5
Norfolk Ave B71 . . . . . . **53** D7
Norfolk Cl
Birmingham B30 . . . . **104** B6
Hinckley LE10 . . . . **75** D4
Norfolk Cres
Aldridge WS9 . . . . **30** B8
Nuneaton CV10 . . . . . . **72** E4
Norfolk Ct
Birmingham B16 . . . . . **65** D1
6 Birmingham, Selly Oak
B29 . . . . **103** C7
Norfolk Dr
Tamworth B78 . . . . **21** A1
Wednesbury WS10 . . . **42** D4
Norfolk Gdns B75 . . . **46** B7
Norfolk Gr WS6 . . . .**4** F1
Norfolk Ho
Birmingham, Short Heath
B23 . . . . **56** F5
Birmingham, Walker's Heath
B30 . . . . **104** A3
Norfolk House Sch
B15 . . . . **85** D8
Norfolk New Rd WS2 . **28** A4
Norfolk Pl WS2 . . . . . . **28** D5
Norfolk Rd
Birmingham, Brandhall
B68 . . . . **84** B7
Birmingham, Chad Valley
B15 . . . . **85** D8
Birmingham, Erdington
B23 . . . . **56** F5
Birmingham, Frankley
B45 . . . . **101** F2
Dudley DY2 . . . . **62** A7
Stourbridge DY8 . . . . . **80** D8
Sutton Coldfield B75 . . **46** C7
Wolverhampton WV3 . . **39** A8
Norfolk St
Coventry CV1 . . . . . . **113** B3
Royal Leamington Spa
CV32 . . . . **157** A1
Norfolk Twr B18 . . . . . **66** B5
Norgrave Rd B92 . . . . **89** C2
Norlan Dr B14 . . . . . . **104** F3
Norland Rd B27 . . . . . . **88** C1

Norley Gr B13 . . . . . . **105** C7
Norman Ashman Coppice
CV3 . . . . **135** C7
Norman Ave
Birmingham B32 . . . . . **84** E7
Coventry CV2 . . . . **96** F1
Nuneaton CV11 . . . . . . **73** B4
Normanby Mdws
CV31 . . . . **162** A2
Norman Cl B79 . . . . . . **20** E7
Normandy Cl CV35 . . **160** A7
Normandy Rd B20 . . . . **55** E1
Normandy Way LE10 . **71** C3
Norman Place Rd
CV6 . . . . **112** F7
Norman Rd
Birmingham B31 . . . . **103** B8
Smethwick B67 . . . . . . **64** E2
Walsall WS5 . . . . **43** D7
Normansell Twr B6 . . . **67** B8
Norman St
Birmingham B18 . . . . . **65** E5
Dudley DY2 . . . . **62** E7
Norman Terr B65 . . . . **63** C4
Normanton Ave B26 . . **89** D5
Normanton Twr B23 . . **57** A6
Normid Ct B13 . . . . . . **87** A4
Norrington Gr B31 . . **102** C3
Norrington Rd B31 . . **102** D3
Norris Dr B33 . . . . **68** E3
Norris Rd B6 . . . .**55** F1
Norris Way B75 . . . . . . **46** D5
Northampton St B18 . . **66** C4
Northam Wlk WV6 . . . . **25** B4
Northanger Rd B27 . . **88** B2
North Ave
Bedworth CV12 . . . . . . **78** D2
Birmingham B40 . . . . . **90** F5
Coventry CV2 . . . . . . **114** A3
Wolverhampton WV11 . **26** C6
Northbourne Dr CV11 .**78** F7
North Bromsgrove High
Sch B60 . . . . **137** B3
Northbrook Ct B90 . . **106** C5
Northbrook Rd B90 . **106** D5
North Brook Rd CV6. **112** D8
Northbrook St B16 . . .**65** F7
North Cl
Cubbington CV32 . . . . **157** E5
Hinckley LE10 . . . . **75** E6
Northcliffe Hts DY11 **116** C7
Northcote Rd B33 . . . . **68** D4
Northcote St
7 Royal Leamington Spa
CV31 . . . . **162** B7
Walsall WS2 . . . . **28** C4
Northcott Rd
Bilston WV14 . . . . **40** F4
Dudley DY2 . . . . **62** D4
North Cres WV10 . . . . . **12** C7
Northdale WV6 . . . . . . **24** B4
Northdown Rd B91 . . **106** F1
North Dr
Birmingham, Balsall Heath
B5 . . . . **86** C5
Birmingham, Lozells
B20 . . . . **66** B8
Sutton Coldfield B75 . . **46** C6
North East
Worcestershire Coll
(Bromsgrove Campus)
B60 . . . . **137** B3
North East
Worcestershire Coll
(Redditch Campus)
B98 . . . . **153** E4
Northey Rd CV6 . . . . . **113** D8
Northfield Children's
Farm* B31 . . . . **102** C4
Northfield Cl B98 . . . **154** D6
Northfield Gr WV3 . . . **38** C7
Northfield Manor Prim
Sch B29 . . . . **103** B7
Northfield Rd
Birmingham B17, B32 . . **85** A3
Birmingham, King's Norton
B30 . . . . **103** E4
Coventry CV1 . . . . . . **113** F2
Dudley DY2 . . . . **62** A4
Hinckley LE10 . . . . **75** C7
Northfield Road Prim Sch
DY2 . . . . **62** D5
Northfield Sta B31 . . **103** A2
Northfields Way WS8 . **15** D7
Northfolk Terr CV4 . . **132** B7
Northgate
Aldridge WS9 . . . . **30** A7
Cradley Heath B64 . . . **82** D8
Warwick CV34 . . . . . . **160** D7
North Gate B17 . . . . . . **85** C7

Northgate Cl
2 Dudley DY1 . . . . . . **51** B2
Kidderminster DY11 . **116** A4
Northgate St CV34 . . **160** E7
Northgate Way WS9 . . **30** A8
North Gn WV4 . . . . **38** D6
North Holme B9 . . . . . **67** C2
Northicote Recn Ctr
WV10 . . . .**11** E3
Northicote Sch The
WV10 . . . .**11** E3
Northland Rd B90 . . . **106** E1
Northlands Rd B13 . . . **87** A1
Northleach Ave B14 . **104** C2
Northleach Cl B98 . . **154** B5
North Leamington Com
Sch & Arts Coll
CV32 . . . . **156** F4
North Leamington Com
Sch & Arts Coll (Sixth
Form) CV32 . . . . **156** F2
Northleigh Rd B8 . . . . **68** A6
Northmead B33 . . . . . . **69** A2
Northolt Dr B35 . . . . . . **58** A4
Northolt Gr B42 . . . . . .**43** F1
North Oval DY3 . . . . . . **50** E5
Northover Cl WV9 . . . . **11** A2
North Park Rd B23 . . . **56** B3
North Pathway B17 . . . **85** B7
North Rd
Birmingham, Edgbaston
B29 . . . . **85** F3
Birmingham, Handsworth
B20 . . . . **55** E2
Birmingham, Harborne
B17 . . . . **85** D6
Bromsgrove B60 . . . . **137** A2
Tipton DY4 . . . . **52** B8
Wolverhampton, Dunstall Hill
WV1 . . . . **25** C2
Wolverhampton, Parkfield
WV4 . . . . **39** F5
North Roundhay B33 . **69** A4
Northside Cl B98 . . . . **158** E2
Northside Dr B74 . . . .**44** F8
North Springfield
DY3 . . . . **39** E1
North St
Brierley Hill DY5 . . . . . **61** C2
Cannock WS11 . . . .**4** E6
Coventry CV2 . . . . . . **114** B5
Dudley DY2 . . . . **51** D1
Nuneaton CV10 . . . . . . **72** F3
Smethwick B67 . . . . . . **64** F5
Walsall WS2, WS4 . . . . **28** C3
Wednesbury WS10 . . . **41** F3
Wolverhampton WV1 . **163** B3
North Street Ind Est
DY5 . . . . **61** C2
Northumberland Ave
Kidderminster DY11 . **116** D3
Nuneaton CV10 . . . . . . **72** F3
Northumberland Cl
B78 . . . . **21** A1
Northumberland Lodge
CV32 . . . . **156** F3
Northumberland Mews
CV32 . . . . **156** F3
Northumberland Pk
CV32 . . . . **156** F3
Northumberland Rd
Coventry CV1 . . . . . . **113** A3
Royal Leamington Spa
CV32 . . . . **156** E2
Northumberland St
B7 . . . . **67** A3
Northvale Cl CV8 . . . . **148** B6
North View CV2 . . . . . . **97** A5
North View Dr DY5 . . . **61** E5
North Villiers St
CV32 . . . . **157** A1
North Walsall Prim Sch
WS2 . . . .**28** E4
North Warwickshire &
Hinckley Coll LE10 . .**71** C4
North Warwickshire &
Hinkley Coll
Hinckley LE10 . . . . **75** F8
Nuneaton CV11 . . . . . . **73** E6
North Warwick St **1**
B9 . . . . **67** D1
Northway
Birmingham B40 . . . . . **90** F5
Sedgley DY3 . . . . **39** C2
Whitnash CV31 . . . . . **162** A5
North Western Arc
B2 . . . . **164** C3
North Western Rd
B66 . . . . **65** A6

North Western Terr
B18 . . . .**65** F7
Northwick Cres B91 . **107** B1
North Wlk B31 . . . . . . **103** C1
Northwood Ct **9** DY5 **61** D2
Northwood Park Cl
WV10 . . . . **11** E3
Northwood Park Prim
Sch WV10 . . . .**11** E1
Northwood Park Rd
WV10 . . . . **11** E3
Northwood St B3 . . . **164** A4
Northwood Way DY5 . **81** B2
Northycote Farm & Ctry
Pk* WV10 . . . .**11** F3
Northycote La WV10. . .**11** F3
Norton Canes High Sch
WS11 . . . .**6** A7
Norton Canes Prim Sch
WS11 . . . .**6** A6
Norton Cl
Birmingham B31 . . . . **103** A3
Redditch B98 . . . . . . **154** F2
Smethwick B66 . . . . . . **65** C5
Tamworth B79 . . . . **21** C3
Wolverhampton WV4 . . **38** C3
Norton Cres
Bilston WV14 . . . . **40** D1
Birmingham B9 . . . . . . **68** B3
Dudley DY2 . . . . **62** E3
Norton Dr
Warwick CV34 . . . . . . **155** E2
Wythall B47 . . . . **125** C4
Norton East Rd WS11. . .**6** B6
Norton Gate B38 . . . . **103** F1
Norton Grange
Allesley CV5 . . . . **112** C6
Norton Canes WS11 . . . .**5** F4
Norton Grange Cres
WS11 . . . .**5** F4
Norton Green La
Dorridge B93 . . . . **128** C2
Norton Canes WS11 . . . .**5** D4
Norton Hall La WS11 . .**5** D4
Norton Hill Dr CV2 . . **114** E6
Norton La
Burntwood WS7 . . . .**7** C6
Great Wyrley WS6 . . . . . .**5** A4
Norton Canes WS12 . . . .**5** F4
Tidbury Green B47, B90,
B94 . . . . **125** C3
Norton Lakeside Sta*
WS11 . . . .**6** C6
Norton Mews B61 . . **137** C2
Norton Rd
Coleshill B46 . . . . **70** F8
Kidderminster DY10 . . **117** B6
Norton Canes WS11,
WS12 . . . .**5** F8
Stourbridge DY8 . . . . . **80** E2
Walsall WS3 . . . . **15** A5
Norton Springs WS11. . .**5** F5
Norton St
Birmingham B18 . . . . . **66** A6
Coventry CV1 . . . . . . **165** C3
Norton Terr
Birmingham B30 . . . . **104** B6
Norton Canes WS11 . . . .**5** F6
Norton Twr B1 . . . . . . **66** C2
Norton View B14 . . . . **104** D7
Norton Wlk B23 . . . . . . **56** C3
Nortune Cl B38 . . . . . **103** D2
Norwich Cl
Lichfield WS13 . . . .**3** C3
Nuneaton CV11 . . . . . . **74** A4
Norwich Croft B37 . . .**69** C1
Norwich Dr
Birmingham B17 . . . . . **84** F8
Coventry CV3 . . . . . . **133** B5
Norwich Rd
Dudley DY2 . . . . **62** D2
Walsall WS2 . . . . **28** B1
Norwood Ave B64 . . . **82** C4
Norwood Cl LE10 . . . . **71** C4
Norwood Gr
Birmingham B19 . . . . . **66** B7
Coventry CV2 . . . . **96** E2
Norwood Ho **13**
CV32 . . . . **156** F2
Norwood Rd
Birmingham B9 . . . . . . **67** C2
Brierley Hill DY5 . . . . . **61** C3
Norwood Villas B16 . . .**65** F1
Nottingham Dr WV12 . **27** C7
Nottingham New Rd
WS2 . . . . **28** A5
Nottingham Way DY5. .**61** F2
Nova Croft CV5 . . . . . **111** C4
Nova Ct B43 . . . . **44** B1
Nova Lodge CV32 . . . **156** E3

Nov–Old 225

Nova Scotia St B4 164 D3
Nowell St WS10 41 E5
Nuffield Ho B36 70 A8
Nuffield Hospl WV6 24 C4
Nuffield Rd
Coventry CV6 114 A7
Hinckley LE10 74 E7
Nugent Cl B6 66 E7
Nugent Gr B90 126 D3
Nuneaton Borough Football Club CV11 73 A4
Nuneaton Mus & Art Gal* CV11 73 C3
Nuneaton Rd
Bedworth CV12 78 B4
Bulkington CV12 79 B4
Nuneaton CV10 72 D8
Nuneaton Trant Valley Sta CV11 73 C5
Nunts La CV6 95 B3
Nunts Park Ave CV6 95 B4
Nursery Ave
Aldridge WS9 30 B5
Birmingham B12 86 F5
Nursery Cl
Birmingham B30 103 F5
Kidderminster DY11 116 B8
West Hagley DY9 99 A4
Nursery Dr B30 103 F5
Nursery Gdns
Solihull B90 125 E8
Stourbridge DY8 60 F1
Nursery Gr DY11 116 B8
Nursery La
Hopwas B78 20 B6
Sutton Coldfield B74 32 A2
Whitnash CV31 162 A5
Nursery Rd
Birmingham, Cotteridge B30 103 E5
Birmingham, Harborne B15 85 D7
Birmingham, Lozells B19 66 C6
Walsall WS3 28 B7
Nursery St WV1 163 B4
Nursery View Cl WS9 30 E2
Nursery Wlk WV6 24 D4
Nurton Bank WV6 23 A3
Nutbrook Ave CV4 111 E2
Nutbush Dr B31 102 D6
Nutfield Wlk B32 84 F5
Nutgrove Cl B14 104 F7
Nuthatch Dr DY5 81 C7
Nuthurst B75 47 B4
Nuthurst Dr WS11 4 F4
Nuthurst Gr
Birmingham B14 104 F2
Dorridge B93 128 A4
Nuthurst Grange Rd B94 143 C4
Nuthurst Rd
Birmingham B31 122 F6
Kemps Green B94 143 A2
Nutley Dr DY4 52 D8
Nutmeg Gr WS1 29 A2
Nuttall Gr B21 65 C7
Nutt's La LE10 75 A7
Nymet B77 35 E8

O

Oakalls Ave B60 137 B2
Oak Apple Rd B61 137 B8
Oak Ave
Birmingham B12 87 A5
Great Wyrley WS6 5 A1
Huntington WS12 1 D8
Walsall WS2 27 E3
West Bromwich B70 53 B3
Oak Bank B18 66 A6
Oak Barn Rd B62 83 E8
Oak Cl Baginton CV8 133 F2
Bedworth CV12 78 C4
Birmingham B17 85 A6
Hinckley LE10 75 E5
Wednesbury DY4 41 A1
Oak Cottage Prim Sch B91 106 F6
Oak Cotts B14 105 C2
Oak Cres Oldbury B69 52 B1
Walsall WS3 28 D6
Oak Croft B37 69 E3
Oakcroft Rd B13 105 C7
Oak Ct Coventry CV3 133 F7
Halesowen B63 82 F2
Oldbury B66 64 C8
Royal Leamington Spa CV34 161 E2
Stourbridge DY8 81 A4
Oak Ct *continued*
Sutton Coldfield B74 31 E5
Walsall WS5 43 A4
Oakdale B74 31 A1
Oakdale Cl
Brierley Hill DY5 61 A7
Oldbury B68 64 A2
Oakdale Rd
Binley Woods CV3 135 C7
Birmingham B36 68 E7
Oldbury B68 64 A2
Oakdale Trad Est DY6 49 E1
Oakdene Cl WS6 4 D2
Oakdene Cres CV10 73 D7
Oakdene Dr B45 138 C8
Oakdene Rd WS7 7 A6
Oakden Pl DY11 116 C7
Oak Dr
Birmingham B23 56 C7
Hartshill CV10 72 A8
Mile Oak B78 20 C1
Oaken Dr Solihull B91 106 F5
Willenhall WV12 27 E7
Oakenfield WS13 3 A2
Oaken Gdns WS7 7 A8
Oaken Grange WS6 4 F1
Oakenhayes Cres
Brownhills WS8 6 F1
Minworth B76 58 C5
Oakenhayes Dr WS8 6 F1
Oaken Pk WV8 10 A2
Oakenshaw Rd
Redditch B98 154 A1
Solihull B90 106 D1
Oakeswell St WS10 42 A3
Oakey Cl CV6 95 F4
Oakeywell St DY2 51 D1
Oak Farm Cl B76 58 A7
Oak Farm Craft Ctr* B78 34 B5
Oak Farm Rd B30 103 E5
Oakfield Ave
9 Birmingham, Balsall Heath B12 87 A6
Birmingham, Sparkbrook B11 87 C6
Dudley DY1 51 B6
Kingswinford DY6 60 E5
Oakfield Cl
Smethwick B66 65 C6
Stourbridge DY8 60 F1
Oakfield Ct 6 DY5 61 D2
Oakfield Dr
Birmingham B45 122 D4
Walsall WS3 15 B5
Oakfield Ho
Coventry CV3 115 A1
12 Royal Leamington Spa CV32 156 F2
Oakfield Rd
Birmingham, Balsall Heath B12 86 E5
Birmingham, Erdington B24 56 F3
Birmingham, Selly Oak B29 86 B3
Codsall WV8 10 C2
Coventry CV6 112 F5
Kidderminster DY11 116 B5
Smethwick B66 65 C6
Stourbridge DY8 61 A1
Stourbridge, Wollescote DY9 81 F2
Oakfields Way B91 108 B5
Oakford Dr CV5 111 F6
Oak Gn Dudley DY1 51 A5
Wolverhampton WV6 24 B3
Oak Gr
Birmingham B31 102 E1
Kidderminster DY10 117 A5
Wolverhampton WV11 26 B7
Oak Green Way B68 64 A4
Oakhall Dr B93 127 F4
Oakham Ave DY2 62 E7
Oakham Cl B98 159 A5
Oakham Cres
Bulkington CV12 79 D2
Dudley DY2 62 E7
Oakham Ct 9 DY2 62 E8
Oakham Dr DY2 62 F8
Oakham Prim Sch B69 63 B7
Oakham Rd
Birmingham B17 85 B7
Dudley DY2 62 F7
Oldbury B69 63 A7
Oakham Way B92 89 A1
Oak Hill WV3 24 C1
Oakhill Ave DY10 116 E4
Oakhill Cl B17 85 B8
Oakhill Cres B27 106 B8
Oakhill Dr DY5 81 B7
Oak Hill Dr B15 85 E7
Oak Hill Fst Sch B98 154 A2
Oakhill Prim Sch B77 21 F2
Oakhill Rd WS11 1 F2
Oak Ho
Great Wyrley WS6 5 A1
Sutton Coldfield B74 31 B5
7 Warwick CV34 161 D8
Oak House Mus* B70 53 B2
Oakhurst WS14 9 C7
Oakhurst Ct B72 57 C8
Oakhurst Dr B60 137 A3
Oakhurst Rd
Birmingham B27 106 B8
Sutton Coldfield B72 57 C8
Oak Ind Pk The DY6 49 E1
Oakington Dr B35 58 A3
Oak La Barston B92 109 B2
Harvest Hill CV5 93 E1
Kingswinford DY6 50 A1
West Bromwich B70 53 B3
Oakland Cl B91 107 E4
Oakland Ct B79 21 A5
Oakland Dr DY3 50 B2
Oakland Gr B61 137 B4
Oakland Ho B74 32 A4
Oakland Rd
Birmingham, Handsworth B21 65 E8
Birmingham, Moseley B13 87 A3
Walsall WS3 28 E7
Oaklands
Birmingham B62 84 A4
Birmingham, Moseley B13 87 A3
Birmingham, Northfield B31 102 F4
Curdworth B76 59 B6
Wolverhampton WV3 39 B8
Oaklands Ave B17 85 B5
Oaklands Cl WS12 1 C6
Oaklands Croft B76 58 B7
Oaklands Ct
Bromsgrove B61 150 D6
Kenilworth CV8 148 A2
Oaklands Dr B20 54 F2
Oaklands Gn WV14 40 D8
Oaklands Ind Est WS12 2 B3
Oaklands Prim Sch The B27 88 C2
Oaklands Rd
Sutton Coldfield B74 46 B8
Wolverhampton WV3 39 B8
Oaklands The
Birmingham B37 90 A7
Coventry CV4 112 A2
Halesowen B62 83 F6
Kidderminster DY10 117 A7
Oaklands Way
Birmingham B31 102 C1
Walsall WS3 15 B3
Oaklea Dr B64 62 F2
Oakleaf Cl B32 84 C2
Oak Leaf Dr B13 87 A3
Oak Leasow B32 84 B4
Oakleigh B31 103 C2
Oakleigh Ct 3 WV3 25 B2
Oakleigh Dr
Codsall WV8 10 A3
Sedgley DY3 50 C7
Oakleigh Rd DY8 81 B2
Oakleighs DY8 60 C1
Oakleigh Trad Est WV14 40 B2
Oakleigh Wlk DY6 60 E8
Oakley CV8 129 F1
Oakley Ave
Aldridge WS9 30 A5
Tipton DY4 52 A6
Oakley Cl WS13 3 B2
Oakley Ct
Bedworth CV12 77 D1
Birmingham B15 85 E5
Oakley Gr WV4 38 D5
Oakley Ho
Bromsgrove B60 137 A1
Smethwick B66 65 C6
Oakley Rd
Birmingham, Sparkbrook B10 87 C7
Birmingham, Stirchley B30 104 B5
Wolverhampton WV4 38 D5
Oak Leys WV3 24 C1
Oakley Wood Dr B91 107 E4
Oakley Wood Rd CV33 161 F1
Oakly Rd B97 153 D3
Oakmeadow Ave B24 57 D3
Oakmeadow Cl
Birmingham, Acock's Green B26, B27 88 D4
Birmingham, Tile Cross B33 69 D3
Oak Meadow Jun & Inf Sch WV11 27 A7
Oakmeadow Way B24 57 D3
Oakmoor Pl WS9 30 F2
Oakmoor Rd CV6 96 A4
Oakmount Cl WS3 14 F3
Oakmount Rd B74 45 A7
Oak Park Ct
Stourbridge DY8 60 F1
5 Sutton Coldfield B74 31 E3
Oak Park Rd DY8 60 F1
Oak Rd
Birmingham B68 84 C7
Brownhills WS9 16 A3
Catshill B61 137 B8
Dudley DY1 51 C3
Tipton DY4 51 E6
Walsall, Pelsall Wood WS3 14 F5
Walsall WS4 15 C1
West Bromwich B70 53 B2
Willenhall WV13 26 E2
Oakridge Cl
Redditch B98 154 C7
Willenhall WV12 27 C4
Oakridge Dr
Cheslyn Hay WS6 4 E2
Willenhall WV12 27 C4
Oakridge Rd
Birmingham B31 103 D2
Royal Leamington Spa CV32 157 C4
Oak Rise B46 70 F5
Oakroyd Cres CV10 72 D7
Oaks Cres WV3 25 A1
Oaks Dr Cannock WS11 1 C1
Featherstone WV10 11 F8
Wolverhampton WV3 25 B2
Wombourne WV5 49 A5
Oakslade Dr B92 107 E8
Oaks Pl CV6 96 A3
Oaks Prec CV8 147 E3
Oaks Prim Sch The B14 104 D2
Oaks Rd CV8 147 E2
Oak St Brierley Hill DY5 61 F1
Cradley Heath B64 62 D1
Dudley, Darby End DY2 62 E4
Dudley, West Coseley DY1, WV14 51 B7
Kingswinford DY6 60 D6
Wolverhampton WV3 25 A1
Oaks The
Bedworth CV12 77 F2
Birmingham B34 69 B7
Birmingham, Hawkesley B38 123 F7
Portway B47 140 F8
Redditch B98 158 F7
Royal Leamington Spa CV32 161 D8
Smethwick B67 64 F5
Sutton Coldfield B76 47 A3
Walsall WS3 14 A1
Wolverhampton, Merridale WV3 25 A2
Wolverhampton WV11 26 B5
Oakstreet Ent Ctr B64 62 D1
Oak Street Trad Est DY5 61 F1
Oakthorpe Dr B37 69 F5
Oakthorpe Gdns B69 52 A2
Oak Tree Ave
Coventry CV3 133 A6
Redditch B97 153 B4
Oaktree Cl B48 139 A7
Oak Tree Cl
Bentley Heath B93 127 E4
Royal Leamington Spa CV32 157 A2
Oak Tree Cres B62 83 F6
Oak Tree Ct
Birmingham B28 106 A5
Royal Leamington Spa CV32 157 A2
Oaktree Farm Mobile Homes Pk B94 141 B7
Oak Tree Gdns
Birmingham B28 105 E3
2 Stourbridge DY8 61 A1
Oak Tree Ho B30 103 E7
Oak Tree La
Birmingham B29 85 E1
Hollywood B47 125 B6
Sambourne B96 159 B2
Oak Tree Pk B98 154 F6
Oaktree Rd WS10 42 B3
Oak Tree Rd
Birmingham B8 67 D6
Coventry CV3 135 A7
Oak Trees B47 125 A7
Oak Tree Wlk B79 20 F7
Oak View WS2 27 E3
Oak Way
Coventry CV4 111 D2
Sutton Coldfield B76 46 F2
Oak Wlk The B31 103 A1
Oakwood Cl
Brownhills WS9 15 E4
Essington WV11 13 B3
Shenstone WS14 18 A6
Oakwood Cres DY2 61 F6
Oakwood Croft B91 107 C1
Oakwood Ct B63 83 A4
Oakwood Dr
Birmingham B14 104 D4
Sutton Coldfield B74 44 E8
Oakwood Gr CV34 156 A1
Oakwood Rd
Birmingham B11 87 C3
Hollywood B47 125 A6
Smethwick B67 64 F4
Sutton Coldfield B73 45 E1
Walsall WS3 28 E7
Oakwoods WS11 4 D8
Oakwood Specl Sch WS9 16 A3
Oakwood St B70 53 B5
Oakworth Cl CV2 114 F8
Oasis The DY9 98 F5
Oast Ho B8 68 D4
Oasthouse Cl
Kingswinford DY6 60 A7
Stoke Heath B60 150 D6
Oaston Rd
Birmingham B36 69 D8
Nuneaton CV11 73 D4
Oatfield Cl WS7 7 A4
Oatlands Cl CV6 95 C4
Oatlands Way WV6 23 D3
Oatlands Wlk 3 B14 104 C2
Oatmill Cl WS10 41 E5
Oban Dr CV10 73 A2
Oban Rd Coventry CV6 95 F5
Hinckley LE10 75 A7
Solihull B92 88 F1
Oberon Cl
Birmingham B45 102 A2
Nuneaton CV11 74 A1
Royal Leamington Spa CV34 161 E4
Oberon Dr B90 106 B1
Occupation Rd
Brownhills WS8 16 A4
Coventry CV2 114 C3
Occupation St DY1 51 A2
Ocean Dr WS10 41 E1
Ockam Croft B31 103 C2
Ocker Hill Inf Sch DY4 52 C8
Ocker Hill Jun Sch DY4 41 C1
Ocker Hill Rd DY4 52 C8
O'Connor Dr DY4 41 C1
Oddicombe Croft CV3 133 D5
Oddingley Ct B23 56 C3
Oddingley Rd B31 103 C2
Odell Cres WS3 28 C7
Odell Pl B5 86 C5
Odell Rd WS3 28 B7
Odell Way WS3 28 B7
Odensil Gn B92 89 B2
Odiham Cl B79 21 C7
Odin Cl WS11 2 A5
Odnall La DY9 99 F3
Odstone Dr LE10 74 F8
Offa Dr CV8 148 A4
Offadrive B79 21 B5
Offa Rd CV31 162 B5
Offa's Dr WV6 23 E5
Offa St B79 21 B5
Offchurch La CV31 162 F6
Offchurch Rd CV32 157 E4
Offenham Cl B98 154 B6
Offenham Covert B38 123 E8
Offini Cl B70 53 F2
Offmoor Rd B32 102 B8
Offmore Ct DY10 117 C6
Offmore Farm Cl DY10 117 C6
Offmore Fst Sch The DY10 117 B6
Offmore La DY10 117 A6
Offmore Rd DY10 116 F6
Offwell Rd B98 154 D1
Ogbury Cl B14 104 C2
Ogley Cres WS8 16 A7
Ogley Dr B75 47 A5
Ogley Hay Rd
Burntwood, Gorstey Ley WS7 7 B8
Burntwood, Triangle WS7, WS8 7 A3
Ogley Rd WS8 16 A7
Ogley Vale WS7 7 B8
O'Hare Ho WS4 28 F3
O'keeffe Cl B11 87 B6
Okeford Way CV10 73 A1
Okehampton Dr B71 53 C6
Okehampton Rd CV3 133 E5
Okement Dr WV11 26 C5
Oken Ct CV34 160 D7
Oken Rd CV34 160 D8
Olaf Pl CV2 115 A7
Old Abbey Gdns B17 85 D4
Oldacre Cl B76 57 D6
Old Acre Dr B21 65 E7
Oldacre Rd B68 84 A7
Oldany Way CV10 72 F2
Old Bakery Ct DY9 99 A5
Old Bank Pl B72 46 C5
Old Bank Top B31 103 B2
Old Barn Rd
Birmingham B30 103 D6
Stourbridge DY8 61 A1
Old Beeches B23 56 C8
Old Bell Rd B23 57 B6
Oldberrow Cl 4 B90 127 A6
Old Birchills WS2 28 C3
Old Birmingham Rd
Alvechurch B48 139 B8
Catshill B60 137 C8
Lower Marlbrook B60, B45 121 E1
Old Bridge St B19 66 C6
Old Bridge Wlk B65 62 F5
Old Bromford La B8 68 C6
Old Brookside B33 68 E2
Old Budbrooke Rd CV35 160 A8
Oldbury Bsns Ctr B68 64 A2
Oldbury Cl B98 154 B6
Oldbury Ct B79 21 B5
Oldbury Green Ret Pk B69 63 F8
Oldbury Rd
Hartshill CV10 72 A8
Rowley Regis B65 63 D2
Smethwick B66 64 D7
West Bromwich B70 52 F2
Oldbury Ringway B69 63 F8
Oldbury Road Ind Est
Smethwick B66 64 D7
West Bromwich B70 52 F2
Oldbury St WS10 42 B3
Old Bush St DY5 61 E3
Old Bush Trad Est DY5 61 E3
Old Camp Hill B12 87 A8
Old Canal Wlk 1 DY4 52 B5
Old Castle Gr WS8 6 F2
Old Chapel Rd B67 64 F3
Old Chapel Wlk B68 64 A4
Old Chester Rd S DY10 116 E2
Old Church CE Prim Sch WS10 41 C6
Old Church Ct 4 B17 85 B5
Old Church Gn B33 68 E2
Old Church Rd
Birmingham B17 85 B4
Coventry CV6 96 A1
Water Orton B46 59 B3
Old Crescent Ct 8 B68 84 B8
Old Crest Ave B98 153 E2
Old Croft La
Birmingham B34 69 C7
Birmingham, Castle Bromwich B36 69 B7
Old Cross St DY4 51 E5
Old Crown Cl B32 84 B1
Old Crown Mews CV2 96 D5
Old Damson La B92 90 A2

Old Dickens Heath Rd
B90 . . . . **126** A5
Old Dominion Wks
WV1 . . . . **40** A7
Olde Hall La WS6. . . . . . **4** F3
Olde Hall Rd WV10 . . . **12** C7
Old End La WV14 . . . . **51** C7
Old Fallings Cres
WV10 . . . .**25** F6
Old Fallings La WV10. .**25** F8
Old Fallow Ave WS11 . . .**1** E3
Old Fallow Rd WS11. . . .**1** E3
Old Falls Cl WS6 . . . . **4** D3
Old Farm Dr WV8 . . . . **10** A4
Old Farm Cl B14 . . . . **105** D5
Old Farm Mdw WV3 . . . **38** C8
Old Farm Rd B33 . . . . **68** E4
Oldfield Dr DY8 . . . . . **81** A3
Oldfield Rd
Birmingham B12 . . . . . **87** A6
Coventry CV5 . . . . **112** E3
Dudley WV14 . . . . **51** A8
Oldfields
Cradley Heath B64 . . . . **82** D8
West Hagley DY9 . . . . . **99** B6
Oldfield Trad Est B64 **82** D8
Old Fire Sta The B17 . . **85** D6
Old Flour Mills **6**
B70 . . . . **53** C2
Old Fordrove B76 . . . . **46** D3
Old Forest Way B34 . . **69** B6
Old Forge Bsns Ctr
B98. . . . . **159** C8
Old Forge Cl WS1 . . . . .**42** F8
Old Forge Dr B98 . . . . **159** C8
Old Forge Trad Est
DY9. . . . .**81** E6
Old Grange Rd B11. . . **87** C4
Old Green La CV8 . . . **129** C1
Old Grove Gdns DY9. . **81** D3
Old Hall Cl DY8 . . . . **81** A8
Old Hall Ct WS9 . . . . **44** A5
Old Hall Ind Est WS3. **28** C8
Old Hall La
Norton Canes WS11,
WS12 . . . .**5** B7
Walsall WS9 . . . . **44** B5
Old Hall Sch WS2. . . . .**27** E5
Old Hall St WV1. . . . **163** C2
Oldham Ave CV2 . . . . **114** E4
Old Ham La DY9 . . . . . **81** D2
Old Hampton La
WV11 . . . . **12** C2
Old Hawne La B63 . . . **83** A5
Old Heath Cres WV1. . **26** A1
Old Heath Rd WV1 . . . **26** A2
Old Hedging La B77. . . **35** D5
Old Hednesford Rd
WS11 . . . .**2** A3
Old High St DY5. . . . . .**61** F1
Old Hill WV6 . . . . **24** D5
Old Hill Prim Sch B64 **62** F1
Old Hill Sta B64. . . . . **83** A8
Old Hinckley Rd CV10 **73** D5
Old Hobicus La B68 . . **64** B5
Old Horns Cres B43,
B44. . . . . **44** C2
Oldhouse Farm Cl
B28 . . . . **105** F6
Old House La
Hawkes End CV7. . . . . **94** A7
Romsley B62. . . . . **101** B1
Oldington Gr B91 . . . **127** B8
Oldington Trad Est
DY11. . . . . **116** B1
Old Kingsbury Rd B76 **58** C5
Old Know Ct B10. . . . . **87** E7
Oldknow Jun Sch B10 **87** E7
Oldknow Rd B10 . . . . . **87** E7
Old La
Featherstone WV10 . . . **12** C7
Rowney Green B48. . . . **140** D4
Walsall WS3 . . . . **28** C8
Wolverhampton WV6 . . **23** F2
Old Landywood La
WS6 . . . . **13** D7
Old Langley Hall B75. **47** C4
Old Level Way DY2 . . . **62** D4
Old Lime Gdns B38. . **123** E8
Old Lindens CI B74. . . **44** E2
Old Lode La B92 . . . . . **89** C3
Old London Rd WS14. . . . **9** D1
Old Manor CI B78 . . . . **34** E5
Old Manor Flats WV6. **24** D5
Old Masters Cl WS1 . . **29** A1
Old Meadow Rd B31 **123** C7
Old Meeting Rd WV14 **51** C8
Old Meeting St B70 . . **53** B5

Old Meeting Yd **1**
CV12 . . . . **78** B3
Old Mill Ave CV4 . . . . **132** D5
Old Mill Cl B90. . . . . **105** D2
Old Mill Gdns
Birmingham B33 . . . . . **68** E2
Walsall WS4 . . . . **15** C2
Old Mill Gr B20 . . . . . **55** C2
Old Mill House Cl
WS4 . . . . **15** B1
Old Mill Rd B46. . . . . .**70** F7
Old Milverton CV32. . **156** C3
Old Milverton La
CV32 . . . . **156** E5
Old Milverton Rd
CV32 . . . . **156** C2
Old Moat Dr B31 . . . **103** B3
Old Moat Way B8 . . . . **68** B6
Oldnall Cl DY9 . . . . . .**81** F4
Oldnall Rd
Kidderminster DY10 . . **117** A4
Stourbridge B63, DY9. . **82** A4
Old Oak Cl WS9 . . . . . **30** B8
Old Oak Rd B38. . . . . **104** A2
Old Oscott Hill B44. . . .**44** F2
Old Oscott La B44. . . . **55** E8
Old Park Cl B6. . . . . . **66** E7
Old Park La B69. . . . . **64** A5
Old Park Prim Sch
WS10. . . . .**41** E5
Old Park Rd
Darlaston WS10 . . . . . **41** E5
Dudley DY1 . . . . **51** A5
Old Park Special Sch
DY1. . . . .**61** F8
Old Park Trad Est
WS10. . . . .**41** E4
Old Park Wlk B6 . . . . **66** E7
Old Penkridge Mews
WS11 . . . . **1** D1
Old Penkridge Rd
WS11 . . . .**1** C2
Old Penns La B46. . . . .**70** F7
Old Penn's Yd **4**
CV12 . . . . **78** A2
Old Pk B29 . . . . **103** A5
Old Pl WS3 . . . . **28** C8
Old Pleck Rd WS2. . . . **42** C7
Old Port Cl DY4 . . . . . **52** B2
Old Portway B38 . . . **123** E7
Old Postway B19. . . . **66** D7
Old Quarry Cl B45. . . **121** F8
Old Quarry Dr DY3 . . . **50** D5
Old Rd CV7 . . . . **92** E1
Old Rectory Gdns
WS9 . . . . **30** C6
Old Rectory La B48. . **139** B7
Old School Cl WV13 . . **27** A2
Old School Dr **2** B65 **63** C3
Old School Mews
CV32 . . . . **157** B3
Old School Wlk B79 . . **21** B6
Old School Yd The
B77. . . . . **22** A5
Old Scott Cl B33 . . . . **69** C2
Old Smithy Pl B18. . . **66** A5
Old Snow Hill B3. . . . **164** B4
Old Sq CV34 . . . . **160** E6
Old Sq The **1** WS1 . . **28** E1
Old Square B4 . . . . . **164** C3
Old Stables Wlk **2**
B7. . . . . **67** C7
Old Stafford Rd WV10 **11** C8
Old Station Rd
Birmingham B33. . . . . **68** D4
Bromsgrove B60. . . . . **137** A1
Hampton-in-A B92 . . . **109** A8
Old Stone Cl B45. . . **101** F1
Old Stone Yd CV32 . . **156** E1
Old Stowheath La
WV1 . . . . **26** C1
Old Stratford Rd
B60 . . . . **137** C2
Oldswinford CE Prim Sch
DY8. . . . .**81** A4
Old Swinford Hospital
DY8. . . . .**81** A4
Old Tokengate **2**
B17. . . . . **85** D6
Old Town Cl B38 . . . . **103** F2
Old Town La WS3. . . . .**14** F3
Old Union Mill B16. . . **66** B2
Old Vicarage Cl
Walsall WS3 . . . . **15** A2
Wombourne WV5 . . . . . **49** B7
Old Vicarage Gdns
B80. . . . . **159** E4
Old Walsall Rd B42. . .**54** F7
Old Warstone La
WV11 . . . . **13** B8

Old Warwick Ct **1**
B92 . . . . **88** E1
Old Warwick Rd
Kingswood B94,
CV35. . . . . **144** D3
Royal Leamington Spa
CV31 . . . . **161** E7
Solihull B92. . . . . **88** E1
Old Waste La CV7 . . **130** E6
Oldway Dr B91. . . . . **107** E2
O ld Well Cl WS4 . . . . **29** B7
Old Wharf Rd DY8. . . .**80** F6
Oldwich La E
Balsall Common CV8. . **129** D1
Honiley CV8 . . . . **145** E8
Oldwich La W B93 . . **145** C8
Old Winnings Rd CV7. **94** F6
Old Woodyard The
DY9 . . . . **99** D6
Old Yd The CV2. . . . . **114** F7
Olga Dr DY4 . . . . **41** B1
Olinthus Ave WV11 . . **26** E7
Olive Ave
Coventry CV2 . . . . . . **114** D5
Wolverhampton WV4 . . **39** E5
Olive Dr B62 . . . . **83** C8
Olive Hill Prim Sch
B62. . . . . **83** D7
Olive Hill Rd B62. . . . **83** D8
Olive La B62 . . . . **83** D8
Olive Mount B69 . . . . **63** D8
Olive Pl B14 . . . . **104** E7
Oliver Cl **1** DY2. . . . **62** E8
Oliver Cres WV14. . . . .**40** F2
Oliver Ct B65 . . . . . . **63** B2
Oliver Rd
Birmingham, Erdington
B23. . . . . **56** F6
Birmingham, Ladywood
B16. . . . . **65** F2
Smethwick B66. . . . . . **65** C3
Oliver St
Birmingham B7 . . . . . . **67** B5
Coventry CV6 . . . . **113** F6
Olivier Way CV2. . . . **115** B8
Ollerton Rd B26. . . . . .**88** F7
Ollison Dr B74. . . . . . .**30** F2
Olliver Cl B62. . . . . . . **84** A3
Olton Ave CV5 . . . . . **111** E4
Olton Bridge B92 . . . **106** F8
Olton Bvd E B27 . . . . **88** C2
Olton Bvd W B11. . . . .**87** F3
Olton Croft B27 . . . . . **88** D2
Olton Mere B92. . . . . **88** E1
Olton Pl CV11 . . . .**72** F4
Olton Rd B90 . . . . . . **106** B5
Olton Sta B92. . . . . . . **88** E1
Olton Wharf B92. . . . **88** E2
Olympus Ave CV34 . . **161** D5
Olympus Cl CV5. . . . **111** B8
Olympus Dr DY4 . . . . **52** D6
Omar Rd CV2 . . . . . . **114** D2
Ombersley Cl
Oldbury B69 . . . . **63** D5
Redditch B98 . . . . **159** C7
Ombersley Rd
Birmingham B12. . . . . **87** A6
Halesowen B63. . . . . . **82** F2
Ombersley Way **4**
B31 . . . . **103** D2
One Stop Sh Ctr B42. **55** D3
Onibury Rd B21. . . . . . **54** D1
Onley Terr CV4 . . . . . **132** C7
Onslow Cres B92. . . . **89** A1
Onslow Croft CV32 . . **156** F2
Onslow Rd B11. . . . . . **88** A4
Ontario Cl B38 . . . . . **124** A8
Oozells St N B1 . . . . . **66** B2
Oozells Sq B1. . . . . . . **66** B2
Oozells St B1. . . . . . . **66** B2
Open Field Cl B31. . . **103** C2
Openfield Croft B46. . **59** C2
Ophelia Dr CV34 . . . . **161** E3
Orangery The DY9. . . **99** D7
Oratory Dr CV3. . . . . **134** C6
Oratory RC Prim Sch The
B16. . . . .**65** F2
Orbital Way WS11 . . . . . **4** F6
Orchard Ave
Cannock WS11 . . . . **1** C2
Solihull B91. . . . . **107** D5
Orchard Cl
Birmingham B21. . . . . **54** F1
Cheslyn Hay WS6. . . . . .**4** E3
Coleshill B46. . . . .**70** F7
Curdworth B76. . . . . . **59** B7
Halesowen B63. . . . . . **82** C6
Hartshill CV10. . . . . . . **72** B7

Orchard Cl continued
Rowley Regis B65. . . . **63** A3
Sutton Coldfield B73. . **57** A8
Tamworth B77. . . . . . . **35** C5
Walsall WS4 . . . . **29** C5
West Hagley DY9 . . . . **99** B4
Willenhall WV13 . . . . . **27** B1
Orchard Cres
Coventry CV3 . . . . . . **133** C8
Stoke Prior B60 . . . . **150** C3
Wolverhampton WV3 . . **38** B7
Orchard Croft B45. . . **138** D8
Orchard Ct
Birmingham, Erdington
B23. . . . . **57** A5
Birmingham, Stockland
Green B23 . . . . **56** B4
Coventry CV3 . . . . . . **115** A1
Kingswinford DY6 . . . . **60** D6
Rowley Regis B65. . . . **63** B3
Solihull B91. . . . . **107** C6
Orchard Dr
Birmingham B31. . . . . **122** F7
Coventry CV5 . . . . . . **111** C4
Orchard Gdns WS12 . . .**1** F6
Orchard Gr
Aldridge WS9 . . . . **30** B4
Dudley DY3 . . . . **50** B3
Sutton Coldfield B74. . **31** F3
Wolverhampton WV4 . . **39** A4
Orchard Ho CV6 . . . . . **96** A4
Orchard La
Codsall WV8 . . . . **10** B3
Kenilworth CV8. . . . . **148** C3
Orchard Leigh B13 . . **87** A3
Orchard Meadow Wlk
B35 . . . . **58** B3
Orchard Pl B80 . . . . . **159** F8
Orchard Rd
Birmingham B24. . . . . **57** B5
Bromsgrove B61. . . . . **136** F4
Dudley DY2 . . . . **62** C2
Hockley Heath B94. . . **143** C6
Walsall WS5 . . . . **43** B3
Willenhall WV13 . . . . . **27** B1
Wolverhampton WV11 . . **26** C7
Orchard Ret Pk CV3 **134** D4
Orchard Rise B26 . . . . .**88** F7
Orchard Sch The B67 **65** A5
Orchard St
Bedworth CV12 . . . . . **78** B4
Brierley Hill DY5 . . . . . **61** D4
Hinckley LE10 . . . . **75** E8
Kidderminster DY10 . . **116** E6
Nuneaton CV11. . . . . . **73** D4
Redditch B98 . . . . **153** E3
Tamworth, Kettlebrook
B77. . . . . **21** C3
Tamworth, The Leys
B79. . . . . **21** B5
Tipton DY4 . . . . **51** F2
Orchards The
Astwood Bank B96. . . **158** D1
Cheswick Green B90. **126** D4
Hollywood B47 . . . . . **125** A7
Sutton Coldfield B74. . **46** A8
Orchard The
Bilston WV14 . . . . **40** E5
Birmingham B37. . . . . **89** F8
Bromsgrove B61. . . . . **136** E4
Burntwood WS7 . . . .**7** B7
Oldbury B68 . . . . **64** C4
Wolverhampton WV6 . . **24** E6
Orchard Villas
Fairfield B61. . . . . **120** D2
Wythall B47. . . . . **124** D4
Orchard Way
Birmingham, Acock's Green
B27. . . . . **88** B4
Birmingham, Balsall
B12. . . . . **86** E6
Birmingham, Great Barr
B43. . . . . **43** F1
Hollywood B47 . . . . . **125** A8
Nuneaton CV10. . . . . . **72** C6
Studley B80. . . . . **159** E2
Orcheston Wlk B14. . **104** D2
Orchid Cl
Bedworth CV12. . . . . . **77** C2
Smethwick B66. . . . . . **64** D7
Orchid Dr B19 . . . . . . **66** D6
Ordnance Rd CV6. . . **113** E5
Oregon Cl DY6 . . . . . . **60** F6
Oregon Dr WV12 . . . . **27** E7
Oregon Gdns WS7. . . . . . **6** F8
Orford Gr B21. . . . . . . **65** C8
Oriel Cl Cannock WS11. . . **4** E8

Oriel Cl continued
Dudley DY1 . . . . **50** E2
Oriel Dr WV10. . . . . . . **11** D3
Oriel Ho B37. . . . . **70** A3
Oriel Villas **4** B11. . . **87** C5
Oriole Gr DY10 . . . . . **117** B2
Orion Cl
Birmingham B8 . . . . . . **68** B4
Great Wyrley WS6. . . . . .**4** F1
Orion Cres CV2 . . . . . **96** E2
Orion Way WS11 . . . .**1** F5
Orkney Ave B34 . . . . . .**68** F7
Orkney Cl
Hinckley LE10 . . . . **71** C1
Nuneaton CV10. . . . . . **73** C1
Orkney Croft B36. . . . **70** B7
Orkney Dr B77 . . . .**35** F7
Orlando Cl WS1 . . . . . **42** E8
Orlando Ho **4** WS1 . . **42** E8
Orlescote Rd CV4 . . . **132** E6
Ormande Cl B63 . . . . .**82** F7
Orme Cl DY5 . . . . **81** B8
Ormes La WV6 . . . . . . **24** C3
Ormond Pl WV14. . . . .**40** F6
Ormond Rd B45. . . . . **101** F1
Ormonds Cl WS13 . . . . .**8** E6
Ormsby Gr B27. . . . . . **106** D3
Ormscliffe Rd B45. . . **122** B6
Orphanage Rd B24 . . **57** B6
Orpington Dr CV6. . . . **95** D4
Orpington Rd B44. . . . **44** E3
Orpwood Rd B33. . . . . **69** B2
Orsino Cl CV34. . . . . **161** E2
Orslow Wlk WV10 . . . **26** A5
Orton Ave B76 . . . . . . **58** A6
Orton Cl B46. . . . . **59** A3
Orton Gr WV4 . . . . . . **38** D4
Orton La WV4, WV5. . **38** A2
Orton Rd CV6 . . . . **95** D4
Orton Way B35. . . . . . **58** A1
Orwell Cl
Nuneaton CV10. . . . . . **72** A5
Stourbridge DY8 . . . . . **80** D4
Wednesfield WV11 . . . **26** F5
Orwell Ct CV1. . . . . . **165** C4
Orwell Dr
Birmingham B38. . . . . **123** C8
West Bromwich B71. . . **53** D6
Orwell Pas B5 . . . . . . **164** C2
Orwell Rd
Coventry CV1 . . . . . . **113** F1
Walsall WS1 . . . . **43** B8
Osbaston Cl
Coventry CV3 . . . . . . **111** E4
Hinckley LE10 . . . . **71** F3
Osberton Dr DY1. . . . . **50** F2
Osborn Ct B73 . . . . . . **46** B1
Osborne B79. . . . . **20** D7
Osborne Cl
Birmingham B6 . . . . . . **67** A7
Brierley Hill DY5 . . . . . **81** F8
Kidderminster DY10 . . **117** B6
Osborne Ct **7** CV31. **162** A4
Osborne Dr WS10 . . . **41** D8
Osborne Gr B19. . . . . **66** C7
Osborne Prim Sch
B23. . . . . **57** A5
Osborne Rd
Birmingham, Erdington
B23. . . . . **56** F5
Birmingham, Handsworth
B21. . . . . **65** B8
Bromsgrove B60. . . . . **137** C1
Coventry CV5 . . . . . . **133** A8
West Bromwich B70. . . **53** C3
Wolverhampton WV4 . . **38** F5
Osborne Rd S **1** B23. .**56** F4
Osborne Twr B6. . . . . **67** A8
Osborn Rd B11. . . . . . **87** C6
Osbourne Croft B90. **126** D5
Osbourne Ho CV1. . . **165** A2
Oscott Cir B6. . . . . **55** F3
Oscott Coll B73. . . . . **45** D1
Oscott Gdns B42. . . . . **55** E3
Oscott Rd B6, B42. . . **55** C5
Oscott School La B44 **44** E2
Osier Gr B23. . . . . **56** B6
Osier Pl WV1. . . . .**25** F2
Osier St WV1. . . . .**25** F2
Osler St B16. . . . .**65** F2
Oslo Gdns CV2 . . . . . **115** A7
Osmaston Rd
Birmingham B17. . . . . **85** B3
Stourbridge DY8 . . . . . **80** D4
Osmington Gr B63. . . **82** D6
Osnor Ct B60 . . . . **151** B1
Osprey
Coventry CV2 . . . . . . **115** B6
Nuneaton CV11. . . . . . **79** B4

Osprey Ct WS7 . . . .**7** F8
Osprey Dr DY1 . . . .**50** F1
Osprey Gr WS12. . . . .**2** C1
Osprey Ho B80 . . . . . **159** D4
Osprey Park Dr
DY10 . . . . **117** B3
Osprey Rd
Birmingham, Acock's Green
B27. . . . . **88** D2
Birmingham, Perry Common
B23. . . . . **56** C6
Ostler Cl DY6 . . . . **60** B7
Oswald Rd CV32. . . . . **161** D8
Oswald St B98 . . . . . **153** E3
Oswestry Cl B97 . . . . **158** C7
Oswestry Ct B11. . . . . **87** B6
Oswin Gr CV2 . . . . **114** C4
Oswin Pl WS3. . . . .**28** F5
Oswin Rd WS3. . . . . . .**28** F5
Othello Ave CV34. . . . **161** F3
Other Rd B98 . . . . . . **153** E4
Otley Gr B9 . . . . **68** C3
Ottawa Twr **2** B5 . . . . **86** D7
Otterburn Cl WS12 . . . . .**2** E2
Otter Croft B34 . . . . . **69** D5
Otters Rest CV31 . . . **162** C5
Otterstone Cl DY3 . . . **39** C2
Ottery B77 . . . . **36** B5
Ottilie Hild Sch B60. **150** C5
Oughton Rd B12 . . . . . **87** A7
Oulsnam Ct **12** B13. . **87** B2
Oulton Cl DY11 . . . . . **116** D8
Oundle Ct **7** B74 . . . **31** F2
Oundle Rd B44. . . . . . .**55** F7
Ounsdale Cres WV5 . . **49** A7
Ounsdale Dr DY2 . . . . **62** C4
Ounty John La DY8. . . **81** A1
Our Lady & Kenelm RC
Sch B63 . . . . **83** A4
Our Lady of Compassion
RC Prim Sch B92. . **106** D7
Our Lady of Fatima RC
Prim Sch B17 . . . . .**84** F7
Our Lady of Lourdes RC
Prim Sch B13 . . . . **105** D5
Our Lady of Mount
Carmel RC Fst Sch
B97. . . . . **153** A2
Our Lady of the Angels
RC Inf Sch CV11. . . **73** C3
Our Lady of the
Assumption RC Prim
Sch CV4 . . . . **111** E1
Our Lady Of the Wayside
RC Prim Sch B90. . **126** C8
Our Lady & St Chad's RC
Sch WV10 . . . .**25** F7
Our Lady & St Rose of
Lima RC Prim Sch
B29. . . . .**85** B1
Our Lady & St Teresa's
RC Prim Sch CV32. **157** C1
Our Lady's RC Prim Sch
B33. . . . . **69** D2
Outermarch Rd CV6. **113** C7
Outfields B13 . . . . . . **104** E6
Outlands Dr LE10. . . . **71** B2
Outmore Rd B33. . . . . **69** B1
Outwood Cl B98. . . . . **158** E7
Outwoods The LE10 . . .**75** F4
Oval Prim Sch The
B33. . . . . **68** F2
Oval Rd
Birmingham B24. . . . . **56** E1
Tipton DY4 . . . . **51** F6
Oval The Dudley DY1. . **61** E8
Smethwick B67. . . . . . **64** D2
Wednesbury WS10 . . . **41** F4
Ovarbare Cl B94 . . . . **142** A1
Overberry Cl CV2. . . . **96** D2
Overbrook Cl DY3 . . . **50** C2
Over Brunton Cl B31 **103** B2
Overbury Cl
Birmingham B31. . . . . **103** C3
Halesowen B63. . . . . . **83** B2
Overbury Rd B31. . . . **103** C3
Overdale B96 . . . . . . **158** E1
Overdale Ave B76. . . . **57** F5
Overdale Cl WS2 . . . . **27** C3
Overdale Ct B13. . . . . .**86** F4
Overdale Dr WS2. . . . . **27** C3
Overdale Rd
Birmingham B32. . . . . **84** E5
Coventry CV5 . . . . **112** C3
Overell Gr CV32 . . . . **156** D3
Overend Rd B63, B64. **82** D7
Overend St B70 . . . . . **53** D2
Overfield Dr WV14 . . . **40** A3

Overfield Rd
Birmingham B32 ... 84 F1
Dudley DY1 ... 61 E8
Over Green Dr B37 ... 69 F5
Overhill Rd WS7 ... 7 B5
Overlea Ave B27 ... 88 B3
Over Mill Dr B29 ... 86 B2
Overmoor Cl B19 ... 66 C7
Over Pool Rd B8 ... 68 A6
Overseal Rd WV11 ... 26 E8
Overslade Cres CV6 ... 112 E8
Overslade Rd B91 ... 106 F2
Oversley Cl B97 ... 153 C5
Oversley Rd B76 ... 58 A6
Over St CV6 ... 114 A8
Overstrand WV9 ... 10 F3
Overton Cl B28 ... 106 A6
Overton Dr B46 ... 59 C3
Overton Gr B27 ... 106 C8
Overton La WS7 ... 7 C4
Overton Pl
Birmingham B7 ... 67 A3
West Bromwich B71 ... 53 D6
Overton Rd B27 ... 106 C8
Overtons Cl CV31 ... 162 F5
Overton Wlk WV4 ... 38 C6
Overwood Croft B8 ... 67 E3
Overwoods Rd B77 ... 36 A4
Owenford Rd CV6 ... 113 C7
Owen Pl WV14 ... 40 D6
Owen Rd Bilston WV14 ... 40 D6
Darlaston WV13 ... 41 C8
Wolverhampton WV3 ... 39 A8
Owen Road Ind Est
WV13 ... 27 C1
Owens Croft B38 ... 104 A1
Owen St
Darlaston WS10 ... 41 D7
Dudley DY2 ... 62 E8
Tipton DY4 ... 51 E5
Owens Way B64 ... 63 A1
Ownall Rd B34 ... 69 C6
Oxbarn Ave WV3 ... 38 E7
Ox Bow Way DY10 ... 116 E8
Oxbridge Way B79 ... 20 E6
Ox Cl CV2 ... 114 A6
Oxendon Way CV3 ... 134 E8
Oxenton Croft B63 ... 82 D2
Oxford Cl
Birmingham B8 ... 68 B5
Great Wyrley WS6 ... 4 F3
Nuneaton CV11 ... 73 F8
Oxford Ct 8 B29 ... 103 C7
Oxford Dr
Birmingham B27 ... 88 D4
Stourbridge DY8 ... 80 F4
Oxford Gn WS11 ... 4 F8
Oxford Pl 14 CV32 ... 156 F1
Oxford Rd
Birmingham, Acock's Green
B27 ... 88 C3
Birmingham, Erdington
B23 ... 56 F4
Birmingham, Moseley
B13 ... 87 A2
Cannock WS11 ... 4 F8
Ryton-on-D CV8 ... 134 F1
Smethwick B66 ... 65 A7
West Bromwich B70 ... 53 B3
Oxford Row 16 CV32 ... 156 F1
Oxford St Bilston WV14 ... 40 F5
Birmingham, Digbeth
B5 ... 164 D2
Birmingham, Stirchley
B30 ... 104 A8
Coventry CV1 ... 113 E3
Dudley DY1 ... 51 B1
Kidderminster DY10 ... 116 E5
Royal Leamington Spa
CV32 ... 156 F1
Walsall WS2 ... 42 C7
Wednesbury WS10 ... 42 B3
Wolverhampton WV1 ... 163 D2
Oxford Street Ind Pk
WV14 ... 40 F5
Oxford Street Island
WV14 ... 40 E5
Oxford Terr WS10 ... 42 B2
Oxford Trad Est B5 ... 164 D1
Oxford Way DY4 ... 51 D5
Oxhayes Cl CV7 ... 130 C6
Oxhill Cl B98 ... 154 E1
Oxhill Rd
Birmingham B21 ... 54 E2
Solihull B90 ... 105 C2
Ox Leasow B32 ... 84 C2
Oxleasow Rd B98 ... 154 E4
Oxley Ave WV10 ... 25 C6
Oxley Cl Dudley DY2 ... 62 B2
Great Wyrley WS6 ... 4 F1
Oxley Court Cvn Pk
WV10 ... 25 A8
Oxley Dr CV3 ... 133 C3
Oxley Gr B29 ... 103 A8
Oxley La WV1 ... 163 B4
Oxley Links Rd WV10 ... 25 B8
Oxley Moor Rd WV9,
WV10 ... 25 A8
Oxley Prim Sch WV10 ... 25 C7
Ox Leys Rd B75, B76 ... 47 D3
Oxley St WV1 ... 25 C4
Oxlip Cl WS5 ... 43 A3
Oxpiece Dr B36 ... 68 D8
Ox St DY3 ... 50 D5
Oxstall Cl B76 ... 58 D5
Oxted Cl WV11 ... 26 F8
Oxted Croft B23 ... 56 E3
Oxwood La B32 ... 101 D4

P

Pace Cres WV14 ... 41 A2
Pacific Ave WS10 ... 41 D1
Packenham Dr B76 ... 57 F8
Packhorse La B38,
B47 ... 124 E6
Packington Ave
Allesley CV5 ... 112 B6
Birmingham B34 ... 69 D5
Packington Ct B74 ... 31 E4
Packington La
Little Packington CV7 ... 91 C6
Outwoods B46, CV7 ... 92 B8
Weeford B78 ... 19 F5
Packington Pl 6
CV31 ... 162 A7
Packmores B90 ... 126 A5
Packmore St CV34 ... 160 F8
Packwood Cl
Bentley Heath B93 ... 127 E4
Birmingham B20 ... 55 A2
Nuneaton CV11 ... 78 F8
Redditch B97 ... 152 F1
Royal Leamington Spa
CV31 ... 162 C5
Willenhall WV13 ... 40 F8
Packwood Cotts B93 ... 127 F1
Packwood Ct
1 Birmingham B29 ... 84 F1
Solihull B91 ... 107 C5
Packwood Dr B43 ... 43 D1
Packwood Gn CV5 ... 112 A3
Packwood Ho
Birmingham B15 ... 86 C8
Sutton Coldfield B73 ... 46 A3
Packwood House*
B94 ... 144 A5
Packwood La B94 ... 144 A4
Packwood Mews 5
CV34 ... 161 B8
Packwood Rd
Birmingham B26 ... 89 B8
Lapworth B94 ... 144 A7
Oldbury B69 ... 52 A1
Padarn Cl DY3 ... 39 C1
Padbury WV9 ... 11 B3
Padbury Ho B31 ... 102 D5
Paddiford Pl CV10 ... 72 C3
Paddington Rd B21 ... 54 C1
Paddington Wlk WS2 ... 27 F4
Paddock Dr
Birmingham B26 ... 89 A7
Dorridge B93 ... 128 A2
Paddock La
Aldridge WS9 ... 30 A5
Great Wyrley WS6 ... 5 A3
Redditch B98 ... 158 E7
Walsall WS1 ... 28 F1
Paddocks Cl B78 ... 22 F1
Paddocks Gn B18 ... 66 A5
Paddocks Rd B47 ... 124 F6
Paddocks The
Bulkington CV12 ... 79 B3
Kenilworth CV8 ... 148 B5
Warwick CV34 ... 160 F7
Paddock The
Bilston WV14 ... 40 D1
Birmingham B31 ... 103 C4
Dudley DY3 ... 50 E5
Lichfield WS14 ... 9 C5
Perton WV6 ... 23 D4
Stoke Heath B60 ... 150 D6
Stourbridge DY9 ... 99 C8
Sutton Coldfield B76 ... 47 A4
Paddock View WV6 ... 25 B5
Paddock Way LE10 ... 74 E6
Paddys Wide Water Est
DY5 ... 61 C5
Padgate Cl B35 ... 58 B3
Padgets La B98 ... 154 D4
Padmore Ct CV31 ... 162 B6
Padstow B77 ... 21 F5
Padstow Cl CV11 ... 73 F5
Padstow Rd
Birmingham B24 ... 57 D4
Coventry CV4 ... 131 E8
Padua Rd B60 ... 137 C1
Paganal Dr B70 ... 53 E1
Paganel Dr DY1 ... 51 C3
Paganel Prim Sch
B29 ... 85 A2
Paganel Rd B29 ... 85 A2
Pageant Ct B12 ... 86 E5
Page Rd CV4 ... 131 E7
Pages Cl B75 ... 46 C5
Pages Ct B43 ... 43 E1
Pages La B43 ... 43 E1
Paget Cl
Bromsgrove B61 ... 136 E2
Dudley WV14 ... 51 B8
Lichfield WS13 ... 3 B2
Paget Ct CV2 ... 96 B3
Paget Ho DY4 ... 52 B3
Paget Mews B76 ... 46 F2
Paget Prim Sch B24 ... 57 C4
Paget Rd
Birmingham B24 ... 57 D4
Wolverhampton WV3,
WV6 ... 24 F3
Paget St WV1 ... 163 A4
Pagham Cl WV9 ... 10 F2
Pagnell Gr B13 ... 105 C6
Paignton Rd B16 ... 65 D3
Pailton Cl CV2 ... 96 C2
Pailton Gr B29 ... 85 B1
Pailton Rd B90 ... 106 B5
Painswick Cl
Redditch B98 ... 158 E6
Walsall WS5 ... 43 B3
Painswick Rd B28 ... 105 F7
Paint Cup Row DY2 ... 62 E5
Painters Cnr 7 B66 ... 65 C5
Painters Croft WV14 ... 40 E1
Pakefield Rd B30 ... 104 C3
Pakenham Cl B76 ... 57 F8
Pakenham Ho B76 ... 57 F8
Pakenham Rd B15 ... 86 C7
Pakenham Village
B15 ... 86 C7
Pake's Croft 3 CV6 ... 113 A5
Pakfield Wlk B6 ... 66 F8
Palace Cl B65 ... 63 D4
Palace Dr B66 ... 64 D8
Palace Rd B9 ... 67 E1
Palefield Rd B90 ... 126 F6
Pale La B17 ... 84 F8
Palermo Ave CV3 ... 133 E6
Pale St DY3 ... 50 E5
Palethorpe Rd DY4 ... 52 A8
Palfrey Inf Sch WS1 ... 42 D7
Palfrey Jun Sch WS1 ... 42 D7
Palfrey Rd DY8 ... 80 D5
Pallasades Sh Ctr The
B2 ... 164 B2
Pallett Dr CV11 ... 73 F7
Palmcourt Ave B28 ... 105 E7
Palm Croft DY5 ... 81 C8
Palmer Cl WV11 ... 12 F1
Palmer La CV1 ... 165 B3
Palmer Rd
Hinckley LE10 ... 71 B2
Whitnash CV31 ... 162 B4
Palmers Cl
Codsall WV8 ... 10 C1
Solihull B90 ... 106 B5
Palmers Cross Prim Sch
WV6 ... 24 D8
Palmers Gr B36 ... 68 E8
Palmers Rd B98 ... 154 F5
Palmer St B9 ... 67 A2
Palmerston Ave B77 ... 35 E6
Palmerston Ct B77 ... 35 F6
Palmerston Dr B69 ... 52 D2
Palmerston Rd
Birmingham B11 ... 87 B6
Coventry CV5 ... 132 F8
Palmers Way WV8 ... 10 C1
Palm Tree Ave CV2 ... 96 C2
Palmvale Croft B26 ... 89 A6
Palmyra Rd B60 ... 137 C2
Palomino Pl B16 ... 65 F2
Pamela Rd B31 ... 103 A3
Pancras Cl CV2 ... 96 E1
Pan Croft B36 ... 68 C7
Pandora Rd CV2 ... 114 E7
Pangbourne Cl CV11 ... 73 F8
Pangbourne Rd CV2 ... 114 C8
Pangfield Pk CV5 ... 112 C4
Panjab Gdns B67 ... 64 F6
Pannel Croft B19 ... 66 D6
Panther Croft B34 ... 69 D5
Papenham Gn CV4 ... 132 A8
Paper Mill Cotts B97 ... 152 E5
Paper Mill Dr B98 ... 154 B5
Paper Mill End B44 ... 55 D6
Paper Mill End Ind Est
B42 ... 55 D6
Papworth Dr B61 ... 136 F5
Papyrus Way B36 ... 57 F1
Parade
Birmingham B1 ... 164 A3
Royal Leamington Spa
CV32 ... 161 F8
Parade The
Birmingham B37 ... 70 A5
Brownhills WS8 ... 6 E1
Cradley Heath B64 ... 82 E8
Dudley DY1 ... 51 B2
6 Hinckley LE10 ... 75 D8
Kingswinford DY6 ... 60 B7
Nuneaton CV11 ... 73 C3
Sutton Coldfield B72 ... 46 C5
Parade View WS8 ... 15 E8
Paradise DY2 ... 62 D8
Paradise Circus
Queensway B1, B3 ... 164 A2
Paradise Ct B28 ... 105 D6
Paradise Gr WS3 ... 14 F3
Paradise Ho 4 CV6 ... 113 F7
Paradise La
Birmingham B28 ... 105 E6
Walsall WS3 ... 14 F3
Wolverhampton WV10 ... 11 E8
Paradise Row B60 ... 136 F2
Paradise St
Birmingham B3 ... 164 B2
Coventry CV1 ... 165 C1
Warwick CV34 ... 160 F8
Paradise Way CV2 ... 97 B1
Paradise Works CV6 ... 113 F7
Paragon Pk CV1 ... 113 D6
Paragon Way CV7 ... 96 B8
Parbrook Cl CV4 ... 131 E8
Parbury B77 ... 35 D5
Parchments The WS13 ... 3 B1
Pardington Cl B92 ... 107 E8
Pargeter Ct 1 WS2 ... 28 C2
Pargeter Rd B67 ... 64 F2
Pargeter St
Stourbridge DY8 ... 80 F4
Walsall WS2 ... 28 C3
Par Gn B38 ... 103 D1
Parish End CV31 ... 162 C4
Parish Gdns DY9 ... 81 C1
Parish Hill B61 ... 120 D1
Parisienne Ho CV5 ... 112 E2
Park App B23 ... 56 C2
Park Ave
1 Birmingham, Balsall
Heath B12 ... 86 F5
Birmingham, Hockley
B18 ... 66 A6
Birmingham, King's Norton
B30 ... 104 A5
Burntwood WS7 ... 7 B5
Coleshill B46 ... 70 F6
Coventry CV6 ... 95 C3
Norton Canes WS11 ... 6 A5
Nuneaton CV11 ... 73 E3
Oldbury B68 ... 64 B3
Rowley Regis B65 ... 63 C3
Smethwick B67 ... 64 F4
Solihull B91 ... 107 D3
Studley B80 ... 159 E3
Tipton DY4 ... 51 E5
Willenhall WV13 ... 26 F2
Wolverhampton, Goldthorn
Park WV4 ... 39 C5
Wolverhampton WV1 ... 163 A4
Wombourne WV5 ... 49 A5
Park Bldgs DY3 ... 50 C4
Parkbrook Ind Est 5
DY9 ... 81 F5
Park Butts Ringway
DY11 ... 116 D6
Park Cir B6 ... 66 F7
Park Cl Brownhills WS8 ... 15 F8
Cheslyn Hay WS6 ... 4 E3
Dudley DY1 ... 51 B7
Kenilworth CV8 ... 148 B5
Oldbury B69 ... 63 C7
Solihull B92 ... 89 D2
Sutton Coldfield B24 ... 57 D5
Park Cres
West Bromwich B71 ... 53 D4
Wolverhampton WV1 ... 163 A3
Park Croft
Burntwood WS7 ... 6 C8
Hollywood B47 ... 125 A5
Park Ct Allesley CV5 ... 112 B6
Park Ct *continued*
Kidderminster DY11 ... 116 D5
Redditch B98 ... 154 A3
Rowley Regis B65 ... 63 C3
Sutton Coldfield B73 ... 45 F1
Parkdale DY3 ... 50 D8
Parkdale Ave WS10 ... 42 A4
Parkdale Cl B24 ... 56 F2
Parkdale Ct WS10 ... 42 A4
Park Dale Ct WV1 ... 25 A3
Parkdale Dr B31 ... 123 A7
Park Dale E WV1 ... 25 A3
Parkdale Rd B26 ... 89 D6
Park Dale W WV1 ... 25 A3
Park Dr
Royal Leamington Spa
CV31 ... 161 E7
17 Sutton Coldfield, Four
Oaks B74 ... 31 F2
Sutton Coldfield, Streetly
B74 ... 31 C4
Wolverhampton WV4 ... 39 C5
Park Edge B17 ... 85 C7
Park End WS14 ... 9 E7
Park End Dr B32 ... 84 D1
Parker Ho B14 ... 104 F3
Parker Paul Ind Est
WV2 ... 39 C7
Parker Rd WV11 ... 12 F1
Parker St
Birmingham B16 ... 65 F1
Walsall WS3 ... 14 A1
Parkes Ave WV8 ... 10 B2
Parkes Ct CV34 ... 160 D7
Parkes Fold DY4 ... 51 F8
Parkes Hall Rd DY1 ... 51 A6
Parkes Ho 8 B69 ... 64 A7
Parkes La Dudley DY3 ... 51 A7
Tipton DY4 ... 51 F8
Parkes St
Brierley Hill DY5 ... 61 D3
Smethwick B67 ... 64 F4
Warwick CV34 ... 160 D7
Willenhall WV13 ... 27 B1
Parkeston Cres B44 ... 45 C1
Park Farm Ind Est
B98 ... 159 C7
Park Farm Rd
Birmingham B43 ... 44 B3
Tamworth B77 ... 21 C1
Parkfield
Birmingham B32 ... 84 A2
Dorridge B93 ... 128 A1
Parkfield Ave B77 ... 21 C1
Parkfield Chalet Pk
WV2 ... 39 D6
Parkfield Cl
Birmingham, Lee Bank
B15 ... 86 C7
Birmingham, Quinton
B62 ... 84 A5
Redditch B98 ... 154 B6
Tamworth B77 ... 35 C8
Parkfield Colliery
WV4 ... 39 F5
Parkfield Cres
Tamworth B77 ... 35 C8
Wolverhampton WV2 ... 39 E6
Parkfield Ct 11 B46 ... 70 F7
Parkfield Dr
Birmingham B36 ... 58 C1
Kenilworth CV8 ... 148 B5
Parkfield Gr WV2 ... 39 E6
Parkfield High Sch
WV4 ... 39 E5
Parkfield Jun & Inf Sch
B8 ... 67 E3
Parkfield Prim Sch
WV4 ... 39 E5
Parkfield Rd
Birmingham B8 ... 67 E4
Coleshill B46 ... 70 F6
Dudley DY2 ... 62 E6
Keresley CV7 ... 95 A6
Oldbury B68 ... 64 A3
Stourbridge DY8 ... 81 B5
Wolverhampton WV2,
WV4 ... 39 E6
Parkgate Prim Sch
CV6 ... 95 B3
Parkgate Rd CV6 ... 95 C3
Park Gr
Birmingham B10 ... 87 D8
Water Orton B46 ... 59 C2
Park Hall Cl WS5 ... 43 C6
Park Hall Cres B36 ... 69 C8
Parkhall Croft B34 ... 69 C7
Park Hall Inf Sch
WS5 ... 43 C7
Park Hall Jun Sch
WS5 ... 43 C7
Park Hall Rd
Walsall WS5 ... 43 D6
Wolverhampton WV4 ... 39 D5
Park Hall Sch B36 ... 58 E1
Park Head Cres DY2 ... 62 B8
Park Head Rd DY2 ... 62 B8
Park Hill
Birmingham B13 ... 86 E4
Kenilworth CV8 ... 148 B5
Rowley Regis B65 ... 63 B1
Wednesbury WS10 ... 42 C4
Parkhill Dr CV5 ... 112 A5
Park Hill Dr B20 ... 54 F4
Park Hill Jun Sch
CV8 ... 148 C5
Park Hill La
Allesley CV5 ... 112 A6
Coventry CV5 ... 112 A5
Park Hill Prim Sch
Birmingham B13 ... 86 F4
Coventry CV5 ... 112 A4
Wednesbury WS10 ... 42 C4
Parkhill Rd
Burntwood WS7 ... 7 A8
Sutton Coldfield B76 ... 57 F6
Park Hill Rd
Birmingham B17 ... 85 C6
Smethwick B67 ... 65 A5
Park Hill St DY2 ... 62 E8
Park Ho
Essington WV11 ... 13 A3
Kidderminster DY11 ... 116 C3
1 Smethwick B66 ... 65 C5
Parkhouse Ave WV11 ... 26 B6
Parkhouse Dr B23 ... 56 B5
Parkhouse Gdns DY3 ... 50 C4
Park Inn DY4 ... 52 A4
Park La
Berkswell CV7 ... 110 B2
Birmingham, Aston B6 ... 66 F7
Birmingham, Castle Vale
B35 ... 58 C4
Birmingham, Handsworth
B21 ... 54 B3
Fazeley B78 ... 20 E2
Great Wyrley WS6 ... 5 A3
Halesowen B63 ... 82 B6
Harvington DY10 ... 118 A2
Kidderminster DY11 ... 116 D6
Kingswinford DY6 ... 60 E7
Nuneaton CV10 ... 72 A3
Oldbury B69 ... 64 A6
Shenstone WS14 ... 18 B4
Wednesbury WS10 ... 42 A5
Wolverhampton WV10 ... 25 E6
Parkland Ave DY11 ... 116 B5
Parkland Cl CV6 ... 95 C3
Parklands B91 ... 107 A3
Parklands Ave CV32 ... 157 C4
Parklands Cl B97 ... 153 A5
Parklands Ct B17 ... 85 A6
Parklands Dr B74 ... 45 F8
Parklands Gdns WS1 ... 43 A8
Parklands Rd
Bilston WV14 ... 40 D3
Darlaston WS10 ... 41 E5
Wolverhampton WV1 ... 26 A1
Parklands The
Birmingham B23 ... 56 D6
Kingswinford DY6 ... 60 D6
Stourbridge DY9 ... 81 D3
Wolverhampton WV3 ... 24 D1
Park Lane E DY4 ... 52 B4
Park Lane Ind Est
West Bromwich B21 ... 54 B1
Wolverhampton WV10 ... 25 E5
Park Lane Trad Est
B69 ... 64 A6
Park La W DY4 ... 51 F4
Park Lime Dr WS4 ... 29 B4
Park Lime Pits Ctry Pk*
WS4 ... 29 C4
Park Mall WS1 ... 28 E2
Park Meadow Ave
WV14 ... 40 C8
Park Mews B29 ... 85 B1
Park Paling The CV3 ... 133 E7
Park Pl B7 ... 67 C7
Park Rd
Bedworth CV12 ... 78 B2
Bilston WV14 ... 40 C5
Birmingham, Aston B6 ... 67 A7
Birmingham, Hockley
B18 ... 66 A6
Birmingham, Moseley
B13 ... 86 F4

Park Rd continued
Birmingham, Sparkhill
B11. . . . . **87** C3
Birmingham, Stockland
Green B23 . . . . **56** C2
Brierley Hill DY5 . . . . . **81** F8
Burntwood, Chase Terrace
WS7. . . . .**6** F8
Burntwood, Triangle
WS7 . . . .**7** B5
Cannock WS11 . . . . **1** D1
Coleshill B46. . . . . **70** F6
Coventry CV1 . . . . **165** B1
Darlaston WS10 . . . . . **41** C6
Dudley, Lower Gornal
DY3. . . . . **50** C4
Dudley, Netherton DY2 . **62** C6
Dudley, West Coseley
DY1. . . . . **51** B7
Featherstone WV10 . . . **12** D8
Halesowen B63. . . . . . **82** B5
Hinckley LE10 . . . . **75** E8
Kenilworth CV8. . . . . **148** A6
Norton Canes WS11 . . . . .**6** A5
Oldbury B69. . . . . **63** C8
Royal Leamington Spa
CV32. . . . . **157** A4
Smethwick B67. . . . . . **64** F1
Solihull B91. . . . . **107** D3
Stourbridge DY8 . . . . . **80** D5
Sutton Coldfield B73 . . **46** B5
Tamworth B77. . . . . . . **35** C5
Walsall, Daw End WS4 . **29** C5
Walsall, The Chuckery
WS5 . . . . **43** D5
Walsall, Wallington Heath
WS3 . . . . **14** B1
West Hagley DY9 . . . . . **99** B6
Willenhall WV13 . . . . . **26** F3
Park Rd E WV1. . . . . **163** A4
Park Rd N B6. . . . . . . **67** A7
Park Rd S B18 . . . . . . **66** B5
Park Rd W
Stourbridge DY8 . . . . . **80** D5
Wolverhampton WV1 . . **25** A3
Park Retreat B66. . . . . **65** B5
Park Ridge B74 . . . . . . **46** A7
Park Ridge Dr B63 . . **82** B6
Park Rise
Kidderminster DY11 . . **116** D5
Wolverhampton WV3 . . **24** E2
Parkrose Ind Est B66 .**65** B7
Park St Arc ◢ WS1. . . **28** E2
Park St S WV2 . . . . . . **39** C6
Park St Sch B79. . . . . . **21** A7
Parks Cres WV11 . . . . **13** A3
Parkside
Birmingham B32. . . . . . **84** C2
Coventry CV1 . . . . **165** C2
Tamworth B77. . . . . . . **21** E1
Parkside Ave WV13 . . . **26** E2
Parkside Cl WS10 . . . . **42** B3
Parkside Ct LE10 . . . . **75** E8
Parkside La WS11 . . . . . .**1** A2
Parkside Mid Sch
B61. . . . . **137** A3
Parkside Rd
Birmingham B20 . . . . . **54** E6
Halesowen B63. . . . . . **82** D5
Parkside Way
Birmingham B31. . . . . **102** C1
Sutton Coldfield B74. . . **31** A1
Park Sq B37 . . . . **90** D8
Park St
Birmingham, Aston
B6. . . . . **67** A7
Birmingham, Digbeth
B5. . . . . **164** D2
Cannock WS11 . . . .**4** E6
Cheslyn Hay WS6 . . . .**4** E3
Coventry CV6 . . . . **113** E7
Cradley Heath B64 . . . . **62** E2
Darlaston WS10 . . . . . . **41** C5
Kidderminster DY11 . . **116** D5
Kingswinford DY6. . . . . **60** D6
Nuneaton CV11. . . . . . **73** D8
Oldbury B69 . . . . **63** F6
Rowley Regis B65. . . . . **63** D1
Royal Leamington Spa
CV32. . . . . **156** F1
Stourbridge DY8 . . . . . **80** F8
Stourbridge, Lye DY9 . . **81** F5
Stourbridge, Stambermill
DY8. . . . . **81** A5
Tamworth B79. . . . . . . **21** A5
Tipton DY4 . . . . **52** A5
Walsall WS1 . . . . **28** E2

Park St continued
Wednesbury WS10 . . . . **41** F3
West Bromwich B70. . . **53** D3
Parkstone Ave B61. . . **150** D8
Parkstone Cl WS4 . . . . **15** C1
Parkstone Rd CV6. . . . .**95** F2
Park Street Gdns
DY11 . . . . **116** D6
Park Terr
Birmingham B21. . . . . . **65** E8
Darlaston WS10 . . . . . **41** B6
Park The B97 . . . . . . **152** C7
Park Trad Est B18. . . . . **66** A6
Parktree Wlk B24 . . . . **57** D4
Park Venture Ctr WS11 **4** E6
Park View
Birmingham, Rotton Park
B18. . . . . **65** E4
Birmingham, Small Heath
B10. . . . . **87** D7
Burntwood WS7 . . . .**6** E8
Coventry CV3 . . . . **114** A2
Darlaston WS10 . . . . . . **41** C6
Hockley Heath B94. . . . **143** C6
Sutton Coldfield B73. . . **46** A6
Park View Cl CV7. . . . . **96** A8
Parkview Cres WS2 . . . **28** A4
Parkview Ct DY6 . . . . . **60** B8
Park View Ct WS11 . . . . **1** D1
Parkview Dr
Birmingham B8. . . . . . . **68** A6
Brownhills WS8 . . . .**6** F2
Parkview Rd WV14 . . . **40** C8
Park View Rd
Birmingham B31. . . . . **102** F3
Stourbridge DY9 . . . . . **81** F4
Sutton Coldfield B74. . . **31** D3
Park View Sch B8. . . . . .**67** F5
Parkview Trad Est
B38. . . . . **103** F3
Park Villas 🔟 B9. . . . . **67** B2
Parkville Ave B17 . . . . **85** B3
Parkville Cl CV6. . . . . . **95** C3
Parkville Highway
CV6 . . . . **95** B3
Parkway
Birmingham B8. . . . . . . **68** A5
Coventry CV2 . . . . **115** B8
Park Way
Birmingham B45. . . . . **122** B8
Redditch B98 . . . . **154** A5
Wolverhampton WV11 . . **13** A1
Parkway Ind Ctr B7. .**67** A4
Parkway Rd DY1 . . . . . **51** A2
Parkway Rdbt WS10 . . **41** E1
Parkway The
Perton WV6. . . . . **23** F4
Walsall WS4 . . . . **29** C8
Park Wlk
Brierley Hill DY5 . . . . . **81** F8
◢ Redditch B97. . . . . **153** E3
Parkwood Cl WS8. . . . . **16** A5
Parkwood Croft B43. . **44** B1
Parkwood Ct CV8 . . . **148** B5
Park Wood Ct 🔢 B74. .**31** F2
Parkwood Dr B73. . . . . **45** C2
Park Wood La CV4 . . **131** D7
Parkwood Rd B61. . . **136** E3
Parkyn St WV2. . . . . . **163** D1
Parliament St
Birmingham, Aston B6 . **66** F4
Birmingham, Small Heath
B10. . . . . **87** C8
West Bromwich B70. . . **53** D1
Parlows End B38. . . . **123** D7
Parmington Cl B97. . . **158** B6
Parmiter Ho CV32. . . **156** F2
Parnell Ave WS13 . . . . . .**9** A6
Parolles Cl CV34 . . . . **161** E3
Parr Cl CV34 . . . . **161** D6
Parrotts Gr CV2 . . . . . **96** D5
Parry Rd
Coventry CV2 . . . . **114** C7
Kidderminster DY11 . . **116** B3
Wednesfield WV11 . . . . **27** A8
Parsonage Dr
Birmingham B45. . . . . **122** D4
Halesowen B63. . . . . . **82** A7
Parsonage St
Oldbury B69 . . . . **64** B7
West Bromwich B71. . . **53** D6
Parsons Hill B68 . . . . **64** B2
Parson's Hill B30 . . . **104** B2
Parsons Hollow B77. . **35** E7
Parson's La LE10 . . . . .**75** F8
Parson's Nook CV2. . **114** A5
Parsons Rd B98 . . . . **153** E2
Parsons St DY1 . . . . . . **51** C1
Parson St B77 . . . . . . **35** E7

Parsons Way WS2 . . . .**27** F6
Partons Rd B14 . . . . **104** D6
Partridge Ave WS10 . . **41** B6
Partridge Cl
Birmingham B37. . . . . . **70** D3
Cannock WS11 . . . .**2** A1
Huntington WS12 . . . . . .**1** D7
Partridge Croft
Coventry CV6 . . . . **96** A1
Lichfield WS13 . . . .**9** C8
Partridge Ct
Birmingham B4. . . . . . **164** C4
◢ Wednesbury WS10 . **41** F3
Partridge Gr DY10. . . **117** A2
Partridge Ho B97 . . . **153** D2
Partridge La B97. . . . **158** A7
Partridge Mill WS3 . . **14** E3
Partridge Rd
Birmingham B26. . . . . . **69** A1
Stourbridge DY8. . . . . . **80** C4
Passey Rd B13 . . . . . . **87** D2
Passfield Ave WS12 . . .**2** C7
Passfield Rd B33. . . . . **69** A3
Pastorale Rd B60 . . . **137** C1
Pasture Gate WS11 . . . .**1** C2
Pastures The WV6 . . . **23** D4
Pastures Wlk B38 . . . **123** D7
Pasture View WS3 . . . .**14** F2
Pasture Way CV34 . . **160** B4
Patch La B98 . . . . **158** F6
Pat Davis Ct DY10 . . **116** E7
Patent Dr WS10 . . . . . **41** D3
Patent Shaft Rdbt
WS10 . . . . **41** D3
Paternoster Row
◢ Kidderminster
DY11. . . . . **116** D6
Wolverhampton WV1 . **163** B3
Paterson Ct B93 . . . . **128** C6
Paterson Pl WS8 . . . . **16** B5
Pathlow Cres B90 . . . **106** A1
Pathway The B14. . . . **104** C5
Patience Gr CV34 . . . **161** F3
Patios The DY11. . . . **116** C7
Paton Gr B13 . . . .**86** F2
Patricia Ave
Birmingham B14. . . . . **105** C4
Wolverhampton WV4 . . **39** D5
Patricia Cl CV4. . . . . . **111** C1
Patricia Cres DY1 . . . . **51** B7
Patricia Dr DY4 . . . . . **52** A2
Patrick Gregory Rd
WV11 . . . .**26** F7
Patrick Ho ◢ WS11 . . . .**2** A3
Patrick Rd B26. . . . . . . **88** E7
Patriot Cl WS1 . . . . . . **42** D5
Patshull Ave WV10 . . . **11** B3
Patshull Cl B43 . . . . . **43** D1
Patshull Ct WV10 . . . . **11** B3
Patshull Gr WV10 . . . . **11** B3
Patshull Ho WV6. . . . . **24** E5
Patshull Pl 🔽 B19. . . . **66** C7
Pattens Rd CV34 . . . . **156** B1
Patterdale Rd
Birmingham B23. . . . . . **56** D4
Cannock WS11 . . . .**2** A4
Patterdale Way DY5. . **81** B8
Patterton Dr B76. . . . . **58** A7
Pattingham Rd WV6. . **23** C2
Pattison Coll CV3. . . . **114** A2
Pattison Gdns B23 . . . **56** D2
Pattison St WS5. . . . . **42** E4
Paul Byrne Ct B20. . . . **55** B1
Pauline Ave CV6 . . . . . **96** B2
Paul Pursehouse Rd
WV14 . . . . **40** D3
Pauls Coppice WS8 . . **16** A5
Paul St Dudley WV14 . . **40** A1
Wednesbury WS10 . . . . **42** B2
Wolverhampton WV2 . **163** B2
Paul Stacy Ho CV1. . . **165** D4
Pauls Wlk WS13. . . . . . .**3** A3
Paul Vale DY4 . . . . **52** B5
Pavenham Dr B5. . . . . **86** C4
Pavilion Ave B67. . . . . **64** D3
Pavilion Dr B6. . . . .**55** F3
Pavilion Gdns
Bromsgrove B61. . . . . **136** F5
Dudley DY2 . . . . **62** C2
Pavilions Sh Ctr B4. **164** C2
Pavilions The B37. . . . . **90** E8
Pavilion The B77. . . . . **22** B3
Pavilion Way CV5 . . . **112** F3
Pavillion Cl WS9 . . . . . **30** C7
Pavior's Rd WS7 . . . . . .**6** E4
Paxford Cl B98. . . . . . **154** A5
Paxford Way B31. . . . **102** F6
Paxmead Cl CV6. . . . . **95** A2
Paxton Ave WV6. . . . . **23** E3

Paxton Cl B60. . . . . . **137** B1
Paxton Rd
Birmingham B18. . . . . . **66** A5
Coventry CV6 . . . . **113** A4
Stourbridge DY9 . . . . . . **82** A4
Payne Cl CV32 . . . . . . **157** A2
Paynell Cl CV6 . . . . . . **95** B2
Payne's La CV1 . . . . . **113** F3
Payne St B65 . . . . **63** C1
Payton Cl B69. . . . . . . **52** E1
Payton Rd B21. . . . . . . **65** D8
PDH Ind Est
Wednesbury WS10 . . . . **41** C3
Willenhall WV13 . . . . . **26** D3
Peace Cl WS6. . . . .**4** E3
Peace Wlk B37. . . . . . . **70** B1
Peach Ave WS10 . . . . . **41** C6
Peachley Cl 🔳 B63. . . **83** B3
Peach Ley Rd B29. . . **102** F7
Peach Rd WV12 . . . . . **27** A6
Peacock Ave
Coventry CV2 . . . . **96** F1
Wednesfield WV11 . . . . **27** A7
Peacock Cl DY4 . . . . . . **52** B4
Peacock Mews DY10 **116** E8
Peacock Rd
Birmingham B13. . . . . **104** C5
Darlaston WS10 . . . . . . **41** B7
Peacocks The CV34 . . **160** B2
Peacocks Est B64. . . . . **62** C1
Peak Croft B36. . . . . . . **68** D8
Peak Dr DY3 . . . . **50** C4
Peake Ave CV11. . . . . . **73** E7
Peake Cres WS8. . . . . . **15** F5
Peake Dr DY4 . . . . **52** B4
Peake Rd WS8 . . . . **16** A5
Peak House Rd B43 . . **43** E4
Peakman Cl B45 . . . . **122** A6
Peakman St B98. . . . **153** E4
Peak Rd DY8 . . . . **81** B6
Peaks L Ctr B79. . . . . .**21** B3
Peal St WS1 . . . . **28** F1
Pearce Cl DY1 . . . . . . **61** E8
Pearl Gr
Birmingham, Acock's Green
B27 . . . . **88** B3
🔢 Birmingham, Rotton Park
B18. . . . . **65** E4
Pearl Hyde Com Prim
Sch CV2 . . . . **115** A5
Pearl Hyde Ho 🔳
CV1 . . . . **165** C4
Pearman Rd
Birmingham B45. . . . . **101** C1
Smethwick B66. . . . . . . **65** A3
Pearmans Croft B47. **125** A6
Pearsall Dr B69. . . . . . **63** E8
Pears Cl CV8 . . . . **147** F5
Pearson Ave CV6 . . . . **96** B2
Pearson Ct WV12. . . . . **27** D4
Pearson St
Brierley Hill DY5 . . . . . **61** D3
Cradley Heath B64 . . . . **62** E1
Stourbridge DY9 . . . . . . **81** F4
West Bromwich B70. . . **53** B4
Wolverhampton WV2 . **163** B1
Peart Dr B80. . . . . **159** C4
Peartree Ave WV13 . . **27** B1
Pear Tree Ave
Nuneaton CV10. . . . . . **72** E6
Tipton DY4 . . . . **51** F5
Pear Tree Cl
Birmingham, Grove Vale
B43. . . . . **43** B1
Birmingham, Stechford
B33. . . . . **68** D2
🔳 Coventry CV2. . . . . **96** B2
Huntington WS12 . . . . . .**1** C7
Kidderminster DY10 . . **117** B7
Shuttington B79 . . . . . . **22** E7
Solihull B90. . . . . **105** D2
Pear Tree Cres B90. . **105** C2
Pear Tree Ct
Birmingham B43 . . . . . . **54** C8
Rowley Regis B65. . . . . **63** D3
Pear Tree Dr
Birmingham B43 . . . . . . **43** C1
Rowley Regis B65. . . . . **63** D3
Pear Tree Gr B90. . . . **105** D2
Peartree Ind Est DY2. **62** A6
Peartree La
Cradley Heath B64 . . . . **62** E1
Dudley DY2 . . . . **62** A6
Pear Tree La
Brownhills WS8 . . . .**6** C2
Dudley WV14 . . . . **51** D8
Wolverhampton WV11 . **26** B8
Pear Tree Rd
Birmingham B34. . . . . . **69** C6

Pear Tree Rd continued
Birmingham, Grove Vale
B43. . . . . **43** B1
Smethwick B67. . . . . . . **64** E4
Peascroft La WV14 . . . **40** E6
Peasefield Cl B21. . . . . **65** C8
Pebblebrook Way
CV12 . . . . **78** C1
Pebble Cl
Stourbridge DY8 . . . . . . **81** B5
Pebble Island Way
CV31. . . . . **162** C5
Pebble Mill Cl WS11. . .**1** F2
Pebble Mill Dr WS11 . .**2** B1
Pebble Mill Rd B5. . . . **86** C4
Pebworth Ave B90 . . . **127** B6
Pebworth Cl
Birmingham B29. . . . . . **86** B2
Coventry CV5 . . . . **112** B3
Redditch B98 . . . . **154** C7
Pebworth Gr
Birmingham B33. . . . . . **89** C8
Dudley DY1 . . . . **51** B3
Peckham Rd B44. . . . . **45** A2
Peckingham St 🔢
B63. . . . . **83** B3
Peckover Cl B65. . . . . **63** C1
Peckstone Cl CV1 . . . **165** C1
Peddimore La B76 . . . **58** C7
Pedmore CE Prim Sch
DY9. . . . . **81** C1
Pedmore Cl B98 . . . . **159** B7
Pedmore Court Rd
DY8 . . . . **81** B1
Pedmore Gr B44 . . . . .**44** F2
Pedmore Hall La DY9. **99** C8
Pedmore La
Hagley DY9 . . . . **99** F8
Stourbridge DY9 . . . . . . **81** E1
Pedmore Rd
Brierley Hill DY5, DY2. . **61** F4
Stourbridge DY9 . . . . . . **81** E5
Pedmore Road Ind Est
DY5. . . . .**61** F4
Pedmore Tech Coll &
Com Sch DY9 . . . . . **81** D4
Pedmore Wlk B69. . . . **63** D5
Peel Cl Coventry CV6 . . **113** E6
Darlaston WS10 . . . . . . **41** D8
Drayton Bassett B78 . . **34** E5
Hampton-in-A B92 . . . **109** B6
Willenhall WV13 . . . . . **27** A1
Peel Ct Fazeley B78 . . . **35** B8
Tamworth B77. . . . . . . **35** F6
Peel Dr Cannock WS12. . .**1** F8
Tamworth B77. . . . . . . **35** F6
Peelers Way B77. . . . . **21** C1
Peel Ho B79 . . . . **21** A4
Peel La CV6. . . . . **113** F5
Peel Rd CV34 . . . . . . **160** E8
Peel St
Birmingham B18. . . . . . **65** E5
Coventry CV6 . . . . **113** E6
Dudley DY2 . . . . **62** E8
Kidderminster DY11 . . **116** D5
Tipton DY4 . . . . **52** A4
West Bromwich B71. . . **53** C5
Willenhall WV13 . . . . . **27** A1
Wolverhampton WV3 . **163** B2
Peel Way B69 . . . . **52** D2
Peel Wlk 🔢 B17 . . . . . **84** F7
Pegasus Ct
Halesowen B62. . . . . . . **83** F5
Sutton Coldfield B74. . . **32** A3
Pegasus Prim Sch
B35. . . . .**58** B3
Pegasus Wlk
Birmingham B29. . . . . . **85** D1
Tamworth B79. . . . . . . **20** F7
Pegleg Wlk 🔢 B14. . . **104** C2
Pegmill Cl CV3. . . . . . **133** F8
Pelham Dr DY1. . . . . . **51** A2
Pelham Lodge DY10 . **117** A5
Pelham Rd B8 . . . . **68** B4
Pelham St WV3 . . . . . . **25** B1
Pelsall La
Walsall, Little Bloxwich
WS3 . . . . **14** D3
Walsall, Shelfield WS4 . **29** B8
Walsall WS3, WS4 . . . . . **15** A1
Pelsall Rd WS8. . . . . . **15** D7
Pelsall Village Sch
WS3. . . . .**14** F4
Peltland Trad Ctr
B98. . . . . **154** D4
Pemberley Rd B27 . . . **88** A2
Pemberton Cl B66 . . . **65** B3
Pemberton Cres
WS10 . . . . **42** D5

Pemberton Rd
Dudley WV14 . . . . **40** D1
West Bromwich B70. . . **53** A6
Pemberton St B18 . . . **66** B4
Pembridge Cl
Birmingham B32. . . . . **102** A7
Brierley Hill DY5 . . . . . **61** F1
Redditch B98 . . . . **154** D2
Pembridge Rd B93 . . **127** E3
Pembroke Ave WV2 . . **40** A7
Pembroke Cl
Bedworth CV12. . . . . . **77** C1
Tamworth B79. . . . . . . **20** C6
🔳 Warwick CV34 . . . . **160** F8
West Bromwich B71. . . **42** A1
Willenhall WV12 . . . . . **27** C8
Pembroke Croft B28 **106** A6
Pembroke Ct 🔳
CV32 . . . . **156** F2
Pembroke Gdns DY8 . **60** C2
Pembroke Ho 🔳 WS3 . **28** C6
Pembroke Rd
Birmingham B12. . . . . . **87** A4
West Bromwich B71. . . **42** B1
Pembroke Way
Birmingham, Vauxhall
B8. . . . . **67** C5
Birmingham, Yardley Wood
B28. . . . . **106** A5
Nuneaton CV11. . . . . . **73** D3
West Bromwich B71. . . **53** B7
Pembrook Rd CV6. . . . **95** C2
Pembury Ave CV6 . . . . **96** A3
Pembury Cl B74. . . . . .**44** F6
Pembury Croft B44. . . **45** A1
Penarth Gr CV3 . . . . . **134** F7
Pencombe Dr WV4 . . . **39** D5
Pencraig Cl CV8 . . . . **148** C5
Pencroft Rd B34. . . . . **69** C7
Penda Ct B20. . . . . . . **66** A8
Penda Gr WV6 . . . .**23** F5
Pendeen Rd B14. . . . . **105** C4
Pendeford Ave WV6 . . **24** D4
Pendeford Bsns Pk
WV9 . . . .**10** F3
Pendeford Cl WV6. . . . **24** D4
Pendeford Hall La
WV9 . . . . **10** D5
Pendeford High Sch
WV10 . . . .**11** B2
Pendeford La WV9 . . . **11** A3
Pendeford Mill La
WV8 . . . . **10** C3
Pendeford Mill Nature
Reserve* WV9. . . . . . **10** E4
Pendene Ct WV4 . . . . **39** A5
Pendenis Cl CV6 . . . . **114** A8
Pendennis Cl B30 . . . **103** C4
Pendennis Dr B69. . . . **63** A8
Penderel Ct CV6 . . . . . **95** C3
Penderell Cl WV10 . . . **12** A6
Penderel St WS3 . . . . **14** C1
Pendigo Way
Birmingham B40. . . . . . **90** E3
Pendine Ct 🔢 CV32 . **161** D8
Pendle Hill WV10 . . . . .**2** C4
Pendleton Gr B27 . . . **106** B8
Pendragon Rd B42. . . **55** C4
Pendrel Cl WS6 . . . . . . **13** C4
Pendrell Cl
Birmingham B37. . . . . . **70** A3
Codsall WV8 . . . . **10** A3
Pendrill Rd WV10 . . . . **11** E3
Penfields Rd DY8. . . . . **81** B6
Penge Gr B44. . . . . **44** E3
Penhallow Dr WV4 . . . **39** E5
Penhurst Ave B20 . . . . **55** D1
Penk Dr WS7. . . . . **7** D6
Penkridge Cl WS2. . . . **28** D3
Penkridge Ct WS11. . . **1** D1
Penkridge Gr B33. . . . .**68** F4
Penkridge St WS2. . . . **28** D3
Penk Rise WV6. . . . . . **24** B4
Penley Gr B8. . . . . **68** B6
Penmakers Ct B67 . . . **65** B4
Penmanor B60. . . . . . **151** D8
Pennant Ct
Rowley Regis B65. . . . . **63** B4
Wolverhampton WV3 . **163** A1
Pennant Gr B29. . . . . . **85** A2
Pennant Rd
Cradley Heath B64 . . . . **62** C1
Hinckley LE10 . . . . **75** D5
Rowley Regis B65. . . . . **63** B3
Pennard Gr B32. . . . . . .**84** F4
Penn Cl WS3. . . . . **14** C1

Penn Common Rd
WV4 . . . . 38 F1
Penncricket Ct B68 . . . . 63 F3
Penncricket La B65,
B68 . . . . 63 E3
Penncroft WV4 . . . . 38 E4
Penn Croft La WV4 . . . . 39 A1
Penndale Cl B24 . . . . . 57 C6
Penn Fields Sch WV3 .38 F7
Penn Gr B29 . . . . 85 B2
Penn Hall Sch WV4 . . . .38 E3
Penn Ho CV4 . . . . 111 F1
Penn Hospl WV4 . . . . .38 E4
Pennhouse Ave WV4 . .38 F5
Penn Ind Est B64 . . . . 62 D1
Pennine Dr
Cannock WS11 . . . . .1 E2
Dudley DY3 . . . . 50 D3
Pennine Rd B61 . . . . . 137 A5
Pennine Way
Birmingham B8 . . . . . . 67 D6
Nuneaton CV10 . . . . 72 B3
Stourbridge DY8 . . . . . 81 A6
Tamworth B77 . . . . 36 C8
Willenhall WV12 . . . . . 27 D4
Pennington Cl B70 . . . 53 A2
Pennington Way
CV6 . . . . 113 E8
Penn La B94 . . . . 141 C4
Penn Rd
Gospel End Village
DY3 . . . . 49 F8
Rowley Regis B65 . . . . . 63 E3
Wolverhampton WV2, WV3,
WV4 . . . . 39 A6
Penn Road Island
WV2 . . . . 163 B2
Penns Cl CV32 . . . . . 157 E5
Penns Ct B76 . . . . . . .57 F7
Penns La B72, B76 . . . 57 D7
Penns Lake Rd B76 . . . 57 E7
Penns Prim Sch B72 . 57 D6
Penn St Birmingham B4 67 A3
[6] Cradley Heath B64 . . 82 F8
Wolverhampton WV3 . 163 A1
Penns Wood Cl DY3 . . 39 C2
Penns Wood Dr B76 . .57 F7
Pennwood Ct WV4 . . . 38 D6
Pennwood La WV4 . . .38 F3
Pennyacre Rd B14 . . 104 D2
Pennycress Gdns
WV10 . . . . 12 C7
Penny Cress Gn WS11 . .5 F4
Pennycroft Ho B33 . . 68 E3
Penny Ct
Great Wyrley WS6 . . . . . 13 F8
Tamworth B79 . . . . 21 B5
Penny Farthing Arc
DY3 . . . . 50 D8
Pennyfield Croft B33 . 68 E3
Pennyford Cl B97 . . . 153 A5
Pennyhill La B71 . . . . .53 F7
Pennymoor Rd B77 . . 36 B7
Penny Park La CV6 . . . 95 A3
Pennyroyal Cl WS5 . . 43 B3
Penny Royal Cl DY3 . . 50 D2
Pennystone Cl CV31 . 162 D6
Penrice Dr B69 . . . . . 52 A1
Penrith Cl
Brierley Hill DY5 . . . . . 81 B8
Coventry CV6 . . . . 95 C2
Royal Leamington Spa
CV32 . . . . 156 C2
Penrith Croft B32 . . 102 D8
Penrith Gr B37 . . . . . 70 C2
Penrose Cl CV4 . . . . 132 A7
Penrhyn Cl CV8 . . . . 148 C5
Penryn Cl
Nuneaton CV11 . . . . . . 74 A4
Walsall WS5 . . . . 43 D7
Penryn Rd WS5 . . . . 43 D7
Pensby Cl B13 . . . . . 105 D8
Pensett Trad Est The
DY6 . . . . 50 A1
Pensford Rd B31 . . . 103 C3
Pensham Croft B90 . 127 A6
Penshaw Cl WV9 . . . . 11 A2
Penshaw Gr B13 . . . . 87 D1
Penshurst Rd B60 . . 137 C1
Penshurst Way CV11 .78 F8
Pensilva Way [2] CV1 113 E4
Pens Meadow Sch
DY8 . . . . .60 E3
Pensnett Rd
Brierley Hill DY5 . . . . 61 C4
Dudley DY1 . . . . 61 F7
Pensnett Sch of Tech
DY5 . . . . .61 B6

Pensnett Trad Est The
DY6 . . . . .60 F8
Penstock Ct DY10 . . 117 C8
Penstock Dr B69 . . . . 64 A4
Penstone La WV4 . . . 37 E4
Pentire Cl CV11 . . . . .73 F5
Pentire Rd WS14 . . . . . 9 D6
Pentland Cl LE10 . . . 71 B1
Pentland Croft B12 . .86 F7
Pentland Gdns WV6 . . 24 E2
Pentos Dr B11 . . . . . 87 D3
Pentridge Cl B76 . . . .57 F5
Penwood Gdns WV14 . 51 C8
Penzance Cl LE10 . . . 71 E4
Penzance Way CV11 . . 74 A5
Penzer Dr B45 . . . . . 138 D8
Penzer St DY6 . . . . . . 60 D7
Peolsford Rd WS3 . . . 15 A4
Peony Wlk B23 . . . . . . 56 B3
Peplins Way B30 . . . 104 B3
Peplow Rd B33 . . . . . 69 A4
Pepperbox Dr DY4 . . 52 A5
Peppercorn Pl B70 . . 53 C4
Pepper Hill DY8 . . . . 81 A4
Pepper La CV1 . . . . . 165 B2
Pepperwood Cl B61 . 120 C3
Pepper Wood Dr
B31 . . . . 102 C1
Pepys Cnr CV4 . . . . . 111 E3
Pepys Ct B43 . . . . . . .54 F7
Perch Ave B37 . . . . . 70 A3
Perch Cl WV10 . . . . . 26 B4
Perchfoot Cl CV1 . . . 165 C1
Perch Rd WS2 . . . . . . 28 A4
Percival Rd B16 . . . . 65 C1
Percy Bsns Pk B69 . . .63 F7
Percy Cres CV8 . . . . 147 E2
Percy Rd
Birmingham B11 . . . . . 87 D4
Kenilworth CV8 . . . . . 147 E2
Warwick CV34 . . . . . . 160 E8
Percy Shurmer Prim Sch
B12 . . . . .86 E7
Percy St CV1 . . . . . . 165 A3
Percy Terr [5] CV32 . 156 D1
Peregrine Cl DY1 . . . .50 F1
Peregrine Dr CV5 . . . 112 A5
Peregrine Gr DY10 . . 117 A2
Pereira Rd B17 . . . . . 85 C7
Pericles Cl CV34 . . . 161 E3
Perimeter Rd
Birmingham B40 . . . . . 90 A4
Birmingham B40 . . . . . 90 E4
Perivale Gr
Bilston WV14 . . . . 40 D1
Dudley WV14 . . . . 51 D8
Perivale Way DY8 . . . 81 A8
Periwinkle Cl WS8 . . . 15 D6
Perkins Cl DY1 . . . . . 51 C6
Perks Rd WV11 . . . . . 13 A1
Perott Dr B75 . . . . . . 32 D2
Perrett Wlk [5] DY11 . 116 D6
Perrin Ave DY11 . . . . 116 B4
Perrins Gr B8 . . . . . . 68 A6
Perrins La DY9 . . . . . .81 F4
Perrins Rise DY9 . . . .81 F4
Perrott Gdns DY5 . . . 61 B1
Perrott St B18 . . . . . 65 E6
Perry Ave
Birmingham B42 . . . . . 55 C5
Wolverhampton WV10 . 25 F8
Perry Barr Sta B20 . . 55 D2
Perry Barr Stad
(Greyhound) B42 . . . 55 D3
Perry Beeches Inf Sch
B42 . . . . 55 C8
Perry Beeches Jun Sch
B42 . . . . 55 C8
Perry Beeches Sch
B42 . . . . 55 C8
Perry Cl Dudley DY2 . . 62 D8
Tamworth B79 . . . . . . 21 B6
Perry Common Jun & Inf
Sch B23 . . . . .56 B7
Perry Common Rd
B23 . . . . 56 C6
Perrycrofts Cres B79 . 21 C7
Perryfields Cl B98 . . 158 F6
Perryfields Cres B61 136 F5
Perryfields High Sch
B68 . . . . 84 A8
Perryfields Prim Sch
B68 . . . . 84 A7
Perryfields Rd B61 . 136 D4
Perryford Dr B91 . . . 127 C8
Perry Green Ho B42 . 55 C5
Perry Hall Dr WV12 . . 27 B5
Perry Hall Prim Sch
WV11 . . . . .26 F6

Perry Hall Rd WV11 . .26 F6
Perry Hill Cres B68 . . 84 B7
Perry Hill Ho B68 . . . 84 C8
Perry Hill La B68 . . . 84 B7
Perry Hill Rd B68 . . . 84 B7
Perry La B61 . . . . . . 136 F2
Perrymill La B96 . . . 159 B1
Perry Park Cres B42 . . 55 C6
Perry Park Rd B64 . . . 63 B1
Perry St Bilston WV14 . 40 E3
Darlaston WS10 . . . . . 41 D8
Smethwick B66 . . . . . 65 A7
Tipton DY4 . . . . 52 A4
Wednesbury WS10 . . . 41 F2
Perry Trad Est WV14 . .40 E3
Perry Villa Dr B42 . . . 55 D5
Perrywell Rd A4 . . . . 56 A4
Perry Wood Rd B42 . . 55 A8
Persehouse St WS1 . .28 F2
Pershore Ave B29 . . . 86 B2
Pershore Cl WS3 . . . .13 F2
Pershore Ct WS11 . . 116 D5
Pershore Pl CV4 . . . 132 E6
Pershore Rd
Birmingham, Balsall Heath
B5 . . . . 86 C4
Birmingham, Breedon Cross
B30 . . . . 104 A5
Birmingham, Ten Acres
B30 . . . . 104 B8
Halesowen B63 . . . . . 83 A2
Kidderminster DY11 . . 116 A6
Walsall WS3 . . . . 13 F2
Pershore Rd S B30 . . 103 F3
Pershore St B5 . . . . 164 C1
Pershore Way WS3 . . .13 F2
Perth Rd WV12 . . . . . 27 B6
Perth Rise CV5 . . . . 112 A4
Perton Brook Vale
WV6 . . . . .23 F2
Perton Fst Sch WV6 . .23 E5
Perton Gr
Birmingham B29 . . . . 103 A8
Wolverhampton WV6 . . 23 F2
Perton Mid Sch WV6 . 24 A5
Perton Rd WV6 . . . . . .23 F2
Perton Sandown Fst Sch
WV6 . . . . .23 F4
Pestilence La
Alvechurch, Arrowfield Top
B48 . . . . 139 C8
Alvechurch B48 . . . . . 139 D8
Petard Cl B77 . . . . . . 35 C8
Petchells Cl DY5 . . . 61 B5
Peter Ave WV14 . . . . .40 F2
Peterborough Dr WS12 .2 C1
Peterbrook Cl B98 . . 158 F7
Peterbrook Prim Sch
B90 . . . . 105 D2
Peterbrook Rd B90 . 105 D1
Peterbrook Rise
B90 . . . . 105 D1
Peterdale Dr WV4 . . .38 F3
Peter Hall La CV7 . . . 115 F6
Peterhead B77 . . . . . .21 F5
Peterhouse Mews [1]
B13 . . . . 87 A2
Peterlee Wlk [6] CV2 115 A7
Peters Ave B31 . . . . 102 F2
Petersbourne Ct
B28 . . . . 105 F8
Petersfield Dr B65 . . 63 E3
Petersfield Ct B28 . . 105 E8
Petersfield Rd B28 . 105 E7
Peter's Finger B60 . 136 F1
Peter's Hill Prim Sch
DY5 . . . . 81 C7
Peter's Hill Rd DY5 . 81 C6
Petershouse Dr B74 . .31 F5
Peter's La WS7 . . . . . .8 A5
Peters St B70 . . . . . 53 A7
Peters Wlk
Coventry CV6 . . . . 96 A4
Lichfield WS13 . . . . . . .3 A2
Petford St B64 . . . . . 62 E1
Petitor Cres CV2 . . . . 96 C1
Peto Gr CV34 . . . . . . 161 F2
Pettitt Cl B14 . . . . . . 104 E2
Petton Cl B98 . . . . . 154 F3
Pettyfield Cl B26 . . . . 89 A6
Pettyfields Cl B93 . . 128 A5
Petunia Cl CV10 . . . . 78 A8
Petworth Cl [3] WV13 .40 F8
Petworth Gr B26 . . . 88 E6
Pevensey Cl B69 . . . .62 F8
Pevensey Rd B60 . . 137 C1
Peverell Dr B28 . . . . 105 F7

Peveril Dr CV3 . . . . . 133 B5
Peveril Gr B76 . . . . . 46 E4
Peverill Rd
Perton WV6 . . . . 23 F4
Wolverhampton WV4 . . 39 E3
Pevril Way B43 . . . . .43 F7
Peyto Cl CV6 . . . . . . 95 C2
Pheasant Cl
Bedworth CV12 . . . . . 77 D1
Kidderminster DY10 . . 117 A2
Pheasant Croft B36 . . 70 A8
Pheasant La B98 . . . 158 F7
Pheasant Oak CV4 . . 111 C2
Pheasant Rd B67 . . . 64 D1
Pheasant St DY5 . . . 61 C3
Pheasant Way WS11 . .2 A1
Pheasey Park Farm Prim
Sch B43 . . . . 44 C4
Philip Ct
[1] Royal Leamington Spa
CV31 . . . . 161 F6
Sutton Coldfield B76 . . 46 F3
Philip Gr WS11 . . . . . . .1 E6
Philip Rd
Halesowen B63 . . . . . 82 F3
Tipton DY4 . . . . 52 D5
Philip Sidney Rd B11 . 87 C3
Philip St WV14 . . . . . 40 D1
Philip Victor Rd B20 . .54 F1
Phillimore Rd B8 . . . . 67 D5
Phillip Docker Ct
CV12 . . . . 79 B2
Phillippes Rd [6]
CV34 . . . . 155 F1
Phillip Rd WS2 . . . . . 42 C6
Phillips Ave WV11 . . .12 F1
Phillips St B6 . . . . . . 66 E6
Phillips Street Ind Est
B6 . . . . .66 F6
Phillips Terr B98 . . . 153 F4
Phipson Rd B11 . . . . 87 B3
Phoebe Cl CV34 . . . . 161 E3
Phoenix Bsns Pk
Birmingham B7 . . . . . 67 A6
Hinckley LE10 . . . . . . 74 E8
Phoenix Ct
Birmingham, Castle Vale
B35 . . . . 58 A3
Birmingham, Edgbaston
B5 . . . . 86 C5
Phoenix Ctr WS11 . . . .4 E6
Phoenix Gn B15 . . . . 85 E7
Phoenix Ind Est
Bilston WV14 . . . . 40 F4
Willenhall WV11 . . . . . 26 D3
Phoenix International Ind
Est B70 . . . . .52 F5
Phoenix Pk B62 . . . . .63 E2
Phoenix Pk Ind Est
CV7 . . . . .96 B7
Phoenix Rd
Cannock WS11 . . . . . . .2 A2
Tipton DY4 . . . . 51 F6
Willenhall WV11 . . . . . 26 D3
Phoenix Rise
Birmingham B23 . . . . . 56 B7
Wednesbury WS10 . . . 41 E4
Wolverhampton WV2 . . 39 C6
Phoenix St
West Bromwich B70 . . . 52 F4
Wolverhampton WV2 . . 39 D6
Phoenix Way CV6 . . . 95 E3
Picasso Cl WS11 . . . . 2 D2
Piccadilly B78 . . . . . .35 F1
Piccadilly Arc [3] B2 . 164 B2
Piccadilly Cl B37 . . . 70 C1
Piccadilly Cres B78 . .35 F1
Pickard St CV34 . . . . 161 A7
Pickenham Rd B14 . . 105 A1
Pickering Croft B32 . 84 D1
Pickering Rd WV11 . . 26 D5
Pickersleigh Cl [6]
B63 . . . . 83 A3
Pickford Cl CV11 . . . 74 A1
Pickford Grange La
CV5 . . . . 111 C7
Pickford Green La
CV5 . . . . 111 C7
Pickford St B5 . . . . . .66 F2
Pickford Way CV5 . . . 112 B6
Pickrell Rd WV14 . . . 40 B1
Pickwick Cl B13 . . . . 87 B2
Pickwick Gr B13 . . . . 87 C2
Pickwick Pl WV14 . . . 40 E4
Picton Croft [6] B37 . 70 D2
Picton Gr B13 . . . . . 105 B6
Picturedrome Way [4]
WS10 . . . . 41 D6
Piddock Rd B66 . . . . 65 A5
Pierce Ave B92 . . . . . 88 C3

Piercy St B70 . . . . . . 53 A3
Piers Cl CV34 . . . . . 160 F8
Piers Rd B21 . . . . . . 66 A7
Pier St WS8 . . . . .15 F7
Piggots Croft B37 . . .69 F3
Pike Cl
Birmingham B20 . . . . . 54 F1
Hinckley LE10 . . . . . . 75 D5
Pike Dr B37 . . . . 70 C3
Pikehelve St B70 . . . 52 E7
Pike Hill B60 . . . . . . 138 A7
Pikehorne Croft B36 . 58 D2
Pike Rd WS2 . . . . . . 28 A4
Pikers La CV7 . . . . . . 94 A3
Pikes Pool La B60 . . 137 E2
Pikes The B45 . . . . . 121 F8
Pikewater Rd B9 . . . . 67 D2
Pilgrims Gate LE10 . . 76 A6
Pilgrims Wlk CV6, CV7 95 B6
Pilkington Ave B72 . . 46 C2
Pilkington Rd CV5 . . 132 D8
Pillaton Dr WS12 . . . . .1 C6
Pilling Cl CV2 . . . . . . 114 F8
Pilson Cl B36 . . . . . . .68 F8
Pimbury Rd WV12 . . . 27 D7
Pimlico Ct DY3 . . . . . 50 D3
Pimpernel Dr WS5 . . 43 A3
Pinbury Croft B37 . . . 70 B1
Pinchers Cl DY9 . . . 119 E7
Pineapple Cl B14 . . . 104 C6
Pineapple Gr B30 . . 104 C8
Pineapple Pl B14 . . . 104 D6
Pineapple Rd B30 . . 104 C7
Pine Ave
Smethwick B66 . . . . . 64 E7
Wednesbury WS10 . . . 41 F4
Pine Cl
Great Wyrley WS6 . . . . .4 F4
Kingswinford DY6 . . . . 60 D5
Solihull B91 . . . . 106 F2
Tamworth B79 . . . . . . 21 B8
Wolverhampton WV3 . . 25 A1
Pine Ct Coventry CV5 . 111 C4
Royal Leamington Spa
CV32 . . . . 157 B3
Stourbridge DY9 . . . . 81 B1
Wolverhampton WV11 . 26 C6
Pine Gn DY1 . . . . 51 A5
Pine Gr
Birmingham B14 . . . . 105 A5
Burntwood WS7 . . . . . .6 F8
Lower Marlbrook B45 . 121 F2
Pine Ho B36 . . . . .68 F8
Pine Leigh B74 . . . . . 32 B1
Pineneedle Croft
WV12 . . . . 27 E4
Pine Rd Dudley DY1 . . 51 C4
Oldbury B69 . . . . 63 A8
Pineridge Dr DY11 . . 116 B5
Pines Park Home Est The
WS12 . . . . 1 D5
Pine Sq B37 . . . . 70 B2
Pines Specl Sch The
B36 . . . . .68 F8
Pine St WS3 . . . . 14 D2
Pines The
Bedworth CV12 . . . . . 77 E2
Birmingham B45 . . . . 102 A1
Cheswick Green B90 . 126 D5
Coventry CV4 . . . . . . 131 D7
Lichfield WS14 . . . . . . .9 F7
Walsall WS1 . . . . 42 F8
Wolverhampton WV3 . . 24 D1
Pine Tree Ave CV4 . . 112 A2
Pine Tree Cl B97 . . . 152 F3
Pine Tree Ct CV12 . . 78 C4
Pine Tree Rd CV12 . . 78 D4
Pinetree Dr B74 . . . . 30 D1
Pineview B31 . . . . . . 102 F2
Pinewall Ave B38 . . . 104 A1
Pineways
Stourbridge DY8 . . . . . 60 C2
Sutton Coldfield B74 . . 31 C3
Pineways Dr WV6 . . . 24 E4
Pineways The B69 . . . 63 C5
Pine Wlk
Birmingham B31 . . . . 103 B3
Stourbridge DY9 . . . . 81 D3
Pinewood Ave
Cannock WS11 . . . . . . 1 D4
Wood End DY9 . . . . . . 36 C4
Pinewood Bsns Pk
B37 . . . . .90 B8
Pinewood Cl
Birmingham B45 . . . . 121 D8
Birmingham, Great Barr
B44 . . . . 55 E7
Brownhills WS8 . . . . . .6 E2

Pinewood Cl continued
Walsall WS5 . . . . 43 B4
Willenhall WV12 . . . . . 27 E7
Wolverhampton WV3 . . 38 A8
Wombourne WV5 . . 49 A6
Pinewood Dr
Binley Woods CV3 . . . 135 C7
Birmingham B32 . . . . 84 A1
Pinewood Gr CV5 . . . 133 B8
Pinewoods
Birmingham, Hurst Green
B62 . . . . 84 A7
Birmingham, Woodcock Hill
B31 . . . . 102 F8
Pine Woods B32 . . . . 84 A2
Pinewoods Ave DY9 . .98 F4
Pinewoods Cl DY9 . . .98 F4
Pinewoods Ct DY9 . . .98 F4
Pinewood Wlk DY6 . . 60 E8
Pinfield Dr B45 . . . . 122 B1
Pinfold WS3 . . . . 28 C8
Pinfold Cl LE10 . . . . .74 F7
Pinfold Cres WV4 . . . 38 D6
Pinfold Ct WS10 . . . . 41 C5
Pinfold Gdns WV11 . . 26 D5
Pinfold Gr WV4 . . . . . 38 D6
Pinfold Hill WS14 . . . .17 F6
Pinfold Ind Est WS3 . . 28 C8
Pinfold La
Cheslyn Hay WS6 . . . . .4 C2
Norton Canes WS11 . . . .5 E4
Walsall WS9 . . . . 44 B6
Wolverhampton WV4 . . 38 E5
Pinfold Rd B91 . . . . . 107 E5
Pinfold St
Bilston WV14 . . . . 40 D1
Birmingham B2 . . . . . 164 B2
Darlaston WS10 . . . . . 41 D5
Oldbury B69 . . . . 64 A8
Pinfold Street Extension
WS10 . . . . 41 C5
Pinfold Street JMI Sch
WS10 . . . . 41 C5
Pingle Cl B71 . . . . . . .42 F1
Pingle Ct CV11 . . . . . 73 D2
Pingle La WS7 . . . . . . 7 D5
Pink Green La B97 . . 153 C5
Pinkney Pl B68 . . . . . 64 C3
Pinley Fields CV3 . . . 134 B8
Pinley Gr B43 . . . . . . 44 C3
Pinley Way [2] B91 . . 107 A1
Pinnacle Ho B97 . . . 158 E5
Pinner Ct B17 . . . . . . 85 C6
Pinner Gr B32 . . . . . 84 E4
Pinner's Croft CV2 . . 114 A5
Pinnock Pl CV4 . . . . 111 F1
Pinson Gdns WV13 . . .26 F1
Pinson Rd WV13 . . . .26 F2
Pintail Dr B23 . . . . . 56 C2
Pintail Gr DY10 . . . . 117 B3
Pinto Cl B16 . . . . . . .65 F2
Pinvin Ho B97 . . . . . 153 A3
Pinza Croft B36 . . . . 68 D8
Pioli Pl WS2 . . . . 28 D5
Pioneer Cl B97 . . . . 153 D4
Pioneer Ho CV1 . . . . 165 D4
Pioneer Way B35 . . . 58 B2
Pipe Hall Farm Nature
Reserve* WS13 . . . . . .8 A8
Piper Cl WV6 . . . . . . .23 F4
Piper Pl DY8 . . . . . . .80 F8
Piper Rd WV3 . . . . . . 38 C8
Pipers Cl B61 . . . . . . 150 D7
Pipers Croft WS13 . . . .3 A2
Pipers Ct CV3 . . . . . 132 F4
Pipers Gn B28 . . . . . 105 F5
Piper's La CV8 . . . . . 148 A5
Pipers Rd B98 . . . . . 159 D7
Piper's Row WV1 . . . 163 C3
Pipes Mdw WV14 . . . 40 E5
Pipit Ct DY10 . . . . . . 117 A2
Pipkin Ct CV1 . . . . . 165 D1
Pippin Ave B63 . . . . . 82 B7
Pirbright Cl WV14 . . . 40 E3
Pirrey Cl WV14 . . . . . 40 E1
Pitcairn Cl B30 . . . . 104 B6
Pitcairn Dr B62 . . . . 83 B5
Pitcairn Ho B67 . . . . 64 E2
Pitcairn Rd B67 . . . . 64 D2
Pitchcombe Cl B98 . . 154 A2
Pitcheroak Cotts
B97 . . . . 153 A3
Pitcheroak Sch B97 . 153 B4
Pitclose Rd B31 . . . . 103 B1
Pitfield Rd B33 . . . . . 69 E1
Pitfield Row [17] DY1 . 51 B1
Pitfields Cl B68 . . . . 84 A8
Pitfields Rd B68 . . . . 84 A8

Pitfield St **5** DY1 .... 51 C1
Pithall Rd B34 .... 69 D5
Pit Leasow Cl B30... 104 B8
Pitman Rd B32....... 84 C5
Pitmaston Ct B13 ... 86 D3
Pitmaston Rd B28... 106 B6
Pitmeadow Ho B14.. 104 C2
Pitsford St B18...... 66 B4
Pitt La B92........... 90 D2
Pitts Farm Rd B24... 57 C6
Pitt St Birmingham B4.. 67 A3
Wolverhampton WV3 . 163 B2
Pixall Dr B15........ 86 B6
Pixhall Wlk B35.... 58 B3
Plainview Cl WS9... 30 E2
Plaistow Ave B36 .... 68 C7
Plane Cl CV10 .... 72 E7
Plane Gr B37 .... 70 B1
Planetary Ind Est
WV13.............. 26 C4
Planetary Rd WV13.. 26 C3
Planet Rd DY5 .... 61 D4
Planetree Cl B60.... 137 B2
Plane Tree Cl DY10 .. 116 F7
Planetree Rd B74 ... 44 D8
Plane Tree Rd WS5 ... 43 C4
Plank La B46......... 59 A2
Planks La WV5...... 49 A7
Plantagenet Pk
CV34............... 161 E3
Plantation Dr B75....46 F6
Plantation La
Himley DY3 .... 49 B3
Hopwas B78 .... 20 B4
Plantation Rd WS5 .. 43 A4
Plantation The DY5.. 61 B7
Plant Ct **19** DY5 ...... 61 D2
Plant La WS7 ....6 E7
Plants Brook Rd B76 ..57 F6
Plantsbrook Sch B72 46 C4
Plants Cl
Great Wyrley WS6... 14 A8
Sutton Coldfield B73... 45 D1
Plants Gr B24........ 57 D5
Plants Hill Cres CV4. 111 E1
Plants Hollow DY5... 61 D1
Plant St
Cradley Heath B64 ... 62 D1
Stourbridge DY8...... 60 E2
Plant Way WS3.......14 F4
Plascom Rd WV1.... 26 A1
Plato Cl CV34 .... 161 E5
Platts Cres DY8 ...... 80 E8
Platts Dr DY8 ....80 F8
Platts Rd DY8........ 80 E8
Platt St Cannock WS11....2 A5
Darlaston WS10 ...... 41 D5
Playdon Gr B14..... 105 A3
Pleasant Cl DY6..... 60 C4
Pleasant St
Kidderminster DY10.. 116 E7
West Bromwich, Hill Top
B70 .... 53 A8
West Bromwich, Lambert's
End B70 .... 53 C2
Pleasant View DY3.. 50 D2
Pleasant Way CV32.. 157 A2
Pleck Bsns Pk WS2 .. 28 C1
Pleck Ho B14 .... 104 C1
Pleck Ind Est WS2 ... 42 C8
Pleck Rd WS2....... 28 C1
Pleck Wlk B38 ...... 104 A1
Plestowes Cl B90... 106 B5
Pleydell Cl CV3 .... 134 C5
Plimsoll Gr B32..... 84 C5
Plimsoll St DY11 ... 116 D5
Plough And Harrow Rd
B16.................65 F1
Plough Ave B32...... 84 C2
Plough Hill Rd CV10.. 72 A6
Ploughmans Pl B75.. 32 D4
Ploughmans Wlk
Kingswinford DY6..... 60 A7
Lichfield WS13 ....3 C3
Stoke Heath B60..... 150 D6
Wolverhampton WV8 .. 10 F1
Plover Cl WV10 ...... 12 B7
Ploverdale Cres DY6 . 61 A6
Plover Gr DY10 ..... 117 B1
Plowden Rd B33....68 F4
Plume St B6......... 67 C8
Plumstead Cl B97... 153 C6
Plumstead Rd B44... 56 B8
Plym Cl WV11....... 26 C5
Plymouth Cl
Birmingham B31..... 123 A7
Coventry CV2 .... 114 C7
Redditch B97 .... 153 C1

Plymouth Ct B97.... 153 C1
Plymouth Dr B45.... 138 A8
Plymouth Ho B60 ... 152 B7
Plymouth Pl CV31 .. 162 A7
Plymouth Rd
Barnt Green B45..... 138 A8
Birmingham B30..... 104 B7
Redditch B97 .... 153 D2
Plympton Mews B71. 53 C6
Pochard Cl DY10 ... 116 F1
Poets Cnr B10 .... 87 D7
Poins Cl CV34....... 161 F3
Pointon Cl WV14.... 40 A2
Poitiers Rd CV3 .... 133 D6
Polden Cl B63....... 82 C1
Polesworth Cl B98.. 154 D1
Polesworth Gr B34... 69 B6
Polesworth High Sch
B78.................36 F7
Pollard Rd B27...... 88 C1
Pollards The B23.... 56 E8
Polly Brooks Yd DY9.. 81 E5
Polo Fields DY9..... 81 B1
Polperro Dr CV5 .... 112 A5
Pomeroy Cl CV4.... 131 D7
Pomeroy Rd
Birmingham B32...... 84 C1
Birmingham, Pheasey
B43 .... 44 D4
Pommel Cl WS5......42 F4
Pond Cres WV2 ...... 39 E7
Pond Farm Mews
CV5 .... 111 E5
Pond Gr WV2 .... 39 E7
Pond La WV2 .... 39 D7
Pondthorpe CV3 .... 134 E6
Ponesfield Rd WS13...3 B2
Ponesgreen WS13.....3 B2
Pontypool Ave CV3 . 134 F6
Pool Ave WS11.........6 B5
Pool Bank B98...... 153 E2
Pool Bank St CV11 .. 73 B4
Poole Cres
Birmingham B17..... 85 C3
Brownhills WS8 .... 6 D2
Dudley WV14 .... 40 D2
Poolehouse Rd B43 .. 43 E3
Pool End Cl B93..... 127 F6
Pool Rd CV6........ 113 A6
Pooles Ct DY10..... 116 E7
Pooles La WV12..... 27 D8
Poole St
Stourbridge DY8...... 80 E4
Wolverhampton WV10 . 25 E4
Poole's Way WS7 .....7 C7
Pooley La B78 ....22 F2
Pool Farm Rd B27... 88 C1
Pool Field Ave B31.. 102 E7
Poolfield Dr B91.... 106 F3
Poolfield Rd WS13 ....8 E6
Pool Furlong DY9... 99 E1
Pool Gn WS9........ 30 A5
Pool Green Terr WS9. 30 A5
Pool Hall Cres WV3 .. 38 A8
Pool Hall Rd WV3 ... 38 A8
Pool Hayes Com Sch
WV12...............27 B5
Pool Hayes La WV12.. 27 B5
Pool Hayes Prim Sch
WV12...............27 B6
Poolhead La
Earlswood B94 ...... 141 C7
Tanworth-In-A B94... 141 E5
Pool La B69.........63 F3
Pool Mdw
Cheslyn Hay WS6...... 4 D1
Sutton Coldfield B76... 58 A8
Pool Meadow Cl
Birmingham B13...... 87 C1
Solihull B91......... 107 F2
Pool Rd Brownhills WS7...6 E3
Burntwood WS7 ....6 E4
Halesowen B63....... 83 B3
Nuneaton CV10...... 72 F5
Smethwick B66....... 65 B5
Studley B80......... 159 E4
Wednesfield WV11.... 27 A6
Pool Road Bsns Ctr
WV10...............72 F5
Poolside Gdns CV3.. 133 A5
Pool St Birmingham B6..66 F6
Dudley DY1 .... 51 A6
Walsall WS1 .... 28 F1
Wolverhampton WV2 . 163 B1
Pooltail Wlk B31... 102 D1
Pool View
Great Wyrley WS6......5 A4
Walsall WS4 .... 29 D7
Pool Way B33....... 69 A1
Pope Gr WS12 ....1 F6

Pope Rd WV10 .... 12 B1
Popes La
Astwood Bank B96 ... 158 E2
Birmingham B30, B31,
B38............... 103 D3
Wolverhampton WV6 . 24 A6
Pope's La B69 .... 64 B7
Pope St Birmingham B1 66 B3
Smethwick B66....... 65 B7
Poplar Arc B91...... 107 C4
Poplar Ave
Bedworth CV12....... 78 D2
Birmingham, Balsall Heath
B12............... 87 A5
Birmingham, Coleshill Heath
B37 .... 90 C8
Birmingham, Edgbaston
B17............... 65 B2
2 Birmingham, Erdington
B23.............. 56 F4
Birmingham, King's Heath
B14............... 104 F8
6 Birmingham, Lozells
B19.............. 66 C8
Brownhills WS8 ...... 16 A8
Burntwood WS7 ....6 F6
Cannock WS11 ....1 F4
Oldbury, Grace Mary Estate
B69.............. 63 C8
Oldbury, Langley B69.. 64 A4
Sutton Coldfield B75... 46 F7
Tipton DY4 .... 51 D5
Walsall, Yew Tree WS5. 43 A4
West Bromwich B70... 53 E2
Willenhall WS2 ...... 27 E4
Wolverhampton WV11 . 26 B7
Poplar Cl Catshill B61 136 F8
Oldbury B69 .... 52 C1
Willenhall WS2 ...... 27 E4
Wombourne WV5 ..... 49 B6
Poplar Cres
Dudley DY1 .... 51 B3
Stourbridge DY8...... 80 D3
Poplar Dr
Barnt Green B45..... 138 D8
Birmingham, Washwood
Heath B8 .... 67 D6
Birmingham, Witton B6. 55 F5
Poplar Gn DY1 ...... 51 A6
Poplar Gr
7 Birmingham B19.. 66 C8
Ryton-on-D CV8 ..... 135 B1
Smethwick B66....... 65 B3
West Bromwich B70... 53 E1
Poplar Ho CV12 ..... 78 D2
Poplar La
Cannock WS11 ....1 B1
Romsley B62........ 101 A4
Poplar Rd
Bilston WV14 .... 40 F7
Birmingham, Moseley
B14............... 86 E1
Birmingham, Sparkhill
B11............... 87 C5
Brownhills WS8 ...... 16 A8
Coventry CV5 .... 112 F1
Dorridge B93 .... 127 F3
Great Wyrley WS6......5 A1
Kidderminster DY11.. 116 C4
Kingswinford DY6.... 60 E5
Oldbury B69 .... 64 A8
Redditch B97 .... 153 A3
Smethwick B66....... 65 A1
Solihull B91......... 107 C1
Stourbridge DY8..... 80 E3
Wednesbury WS10.... 42 A5
Wolverhampton WV3 . 39 A6
Poplar Rise
Birmingham B42...... 55 B7
Oldbury B69 .... 63 C8
Sutton Coldfield B74... 31 D6
Poplar Row DY11... 116 C4
Poplars Dr B36 ...... 69 B8
Poplars La B96..... 158 A1
Poplar St
Norton Canes WS11....6 A6
Smethwick B66....... 65 C5
Wolverhampton WV2 . 39 D6
Poplars The
Birmingham, Rotton Park
B16............... 65 F3
Birmingham, Sparkhill
B11............... 87 C6
Brierley Hill DY5..... 61 B7
Cannock WS11 ....1 E4
Nuneaton CV10...... 72 D3
Smethwick B66....... 65 C4
Stourbridge DY8...... 60 F2
Poplars Trad Est
B80................ 159 D6

Poplar Trad Est B6...55 F5
Poplar Trees B47 ... 125 A6
Poplar Way B91..... 107 C4
Poplarwoods B32 ... 84 B2
Poppy Cl CV10 ...... 78 A8
Poppy Ct CV3 ...... 134 C6
Poppy Dr **3** WS5... 43 A3
Poppy Gr B8.........67 F4
Poppy La B24....... 57 C5
Poppymead B23 .... 56 B8
Porchester Cl
Brownhills WS9 ..... 16 A2
Coventry CV3 .... 115 A2
Porchester Dr B19... 66 D6
Porchester St B19... 66 D6
Porlock Cl CV3 ..... 133 E5
Porlock Cres B31... 102 D3
Porlock Rd DY8..... 81 A6
Portal Rd WS2.......27 F2
Portchester Dr WV11. 26 D5
Porter Cl
Coventry CV4 ...... 131 E8
Sutton Coldfield B72... 57 B7
Porters Croft B17 ... 85 A8
Porters Field **6** DY2. 51 D1
Portersfield Ind Est
B64................ 82 D8
Portersfield Rd B64. 82 C8
Portershill Dr B90.. 106 C1
Porter St DY2....... 51 D1
Porter Street S **9**
DY2............... 51 D1
Porters Way B9...... 67 E2
Portfield Dr DY4.... 52 A3
Portfield Gr B23.... 57 A6
Porthkerry Gr DY3... 50 B7
Port Hope Rd B11... 87 A7
Porthouse Gr WV14 .. 40 B3
Portia Ave B90...... 106 B1
Portia Cl CV11...... 74 A1
Portia Way CV34.... 161 E3
Portland Ave
Aldridge WS9 .... 30 B5
Tamworth B79....... 20 F8
Portland Cres DY9... 81 B1
Portland Ct
Aldridge WS9 .... 30 B6
9 Royal Leamington Spa
CV32............. 161 F8
Portland Dr
Hinckley LE10 ...... 71 E4
Nuneaton CV10...... 72 C4
Oldbury B69 .... 52 D3
Stourbridge DY9..... 81 B1
Portland Mews **10**
CV32............... 161 F8
Portland Pl
Cannock WS11 ....4 C7
Dudley WV14 .... 51 B7
Portland Pl E CV32.. 161 F8
Portland Pl W **5**
CV32............... 161 E8
Portland Rd
Aldridge WS9 .... 30 B6
Birmingham B16..... 65 D1
Portland St
Birmingham B6...... 67 A7
Royal Leamington Spa
CV32............. 161 F8
Walsall WS2 .... 28 E3
Portland Terr **6** B18. 66 A5
Portleys La B78 ..... 34 D4
Portman Rd B13 ... 104 F7
Portmanteau Mews
B94................ 143 C6
Portobello Cl WV13 . 26 D1
Portobello Rd B70... 53 A8
Portreath Dr CV11... 74 A5
Portree Ave CV3 ... 114 F2
Portrush Ave B38 ... 103 C5
Portrush Rd WV6.... 23 D4
Portsdown Cl WV10..25 F7
Portsdown Rd B63.. 82 D2
Portsea Cl CV3..... 133 D6
Portsea St WS3..... 28 C6
Portswood Cl WV9 ...10 F1
Portway Cl
Coventry CV4 ...... 131 E8
Kingswinford DY6.... 60 E5
Royal Leamington Spa
CV31............. 162 D6
Solihull B91......... 106 E1
Portway Hill B65.... 63 C6
Portway Rd
Bilston WV14 .... 40 E7
Oldbury B69 .... 63 F7
Rowley Regis B65.... 63 B5
Wednesbury WS10.... 41 E2
Portway The DY6.... 60 E5

Portway Wlk B65.... 63 C6
Portwrinkle Ave CV6 114 A6
Poseidon Way CV34 . 161 F4
Posey Cl B21........ 54 C3
Post Box B1 .... 164 B1
Postbridge Rd CV3 . 133 D5
Post Office Wlk B96. 158 E1
Poston Croft B14... 104 D3
Potter Cl CV3....... 134 C6
Potter Ct **8** DY5 ..... 61 D2
Potters Brook **8** DY4 52 B5
Potters Green Prim Sch
CV2...............96 E2
Potters Green Rd CV2 96 E1
Potters La
Birmingham B6 ...... 66 E7
Wednesbury WS10.... 41 F2
Potters Rd CV12..... 77 E1
Potterton Way B66...64 F8
Pottery Rd B68...... 64 D1
Potton Cl CV3...... 134 E6
Potts Cl CV8........ 148 C4
Pouk Hill Cl WS2.... 28 A3
Pouk La WS14.......16 F7
Poultney Rd CV6.... 113 A6
Poultney St B70......52 F7
Poulton Cl B13...... 87 A2
Pound Cl
Berkswell CV7....... 110 D3
Lapworth B94 ...... 144 B3
Oldbury B68 .... 63 F3
Pound Gn B8........67 F6
Pound House La
Nuthurst B94 ...... 143 A4
Tanworth-in-A B94 ... 142 F4
Pound La
Birmingham B32..... 101 F3
Royal Leamington Spa
CV32............. 157 A3
Poundley Cl B36.... 69 C8
Pound Rd
Birmingham B14.... 104 E2
Oldbury B68 .... 64 A2
Wednesbury WS10.... 42 A3
Pountney St WV2.... 163 B2
Pourbaix Ho WS13 ....9 B6
Poverty B96......... 158 E2
Powell Ave B32..... 84 A6
Powell Pl
Bilston WV14 .... 40 E3
Tipton DY4 .... 52 C5
Powell Rd CV2...... 114 A4
Powells Cl B72...... 46 C2
Powells Ho B73..... 45 C2
Powell St
Birmingham B1...... 66 B3
7 Halesowen B63... 83 B3
Wolverhampton WV10 . 25 F4
Powell Way CV11.... 73 C4
Power Cres B16..... 66 A2
Powers Ct **4** CV32.. 156 F1
Powers Rd LE9....... 71 F5
Power Way DY4..... 52 D8
Powick Rd B23...... 56 D1
Powis Ave DY4...... 52 B7
Powis Gr CV8....... 148 C5
Powke La B65....... 63 A2
Powke Lane Ind Est
B65................ 63 A2
Powlers Cl DY9 ..... 81 E2
Powlett St WV2..... 163 C2
Poxon Rd WS9...... 16 A3
Poynings The WV6.. 24 C5
Poyser Rd CV10..... 78 C8
Praetor Ho **8** LE10.. 71 D1
Pratts La B80...... 159 F7
Precinct The
Tamworth B79....... 21 B5
Willenhall WV12 .... 27 B5
Premier Bsns Ctr **3**
DY9...............81 E5
Premier Bsns Pk WS2 28 D1
Premier Ct B30 .... 104 C3
Premier Partnership Ind
Est DY5............ 61 A3
Premier St B7....... 67 D8
Premier Trad Est B7 ..66 F5
Prescelly Cl CV10... 72 B3
Prescelly Cl CV8 ... 147 F5
Prescot Rd DY9..... 81 C3
President Kennedy Sch &
Com Coll CV6.....95 B4
Prestbury Rd B6.... 66 E8
Presthope Rd B29.. 103 B7
Prestley Smith Sch
B42................ 55 C8
Preston Ave B76.... 46 E3
Preston Cl
Coventry CV4 ...... 131 F7
Redditch B98 ...... 154 B6

Preston Ho **4** WS1...28 F1
Preston Rd
Birmingham, Hockley
B18............... 65 E6
Birmingham, South Yardley
B26.............. 88 D7
Hinckley LE10 ...... 71 B2
Prestons Row WV14 . 40 A3
Prestwick Cl B75.... 46 C7
Prestwick Rd
Birmingham B35..... 58 B4
Kingswinford DY6.... 60 C6
Prestwood Ave WV11. 26 D7
Prestwood Dr DY7 .. 80 B7
Prestwood Rd
Birmingham B29..... 103 B8
Wolverhampton WV11 . 26 A5
Prestwood Rd W
WV11.............. 26 B7
Pretoria Rd B9...... 67 E3
Priam Cir CV34..... 161 E5
Priam Gr WV3....... 15 B5
Price Ave B78....... 20 D1
Price Cl E CV34..... 160 B4
Price Cl W CV34.... 160 B4
Price Cres WV14.... 40 D7
Price Rd
Cubbington CV32... 157 E5
Stourbridge DY9..... 82 A6
Wednesbury WS10.... 42 C3
Prices Rd DY3....... 50 C3
Price St Bilston WV14 .40 F5
Birmingham B4...... 164 C4
Cannock WS11 ....1 E1
Dudley DY2......... 51 E1
Smethwick B66...... 65 B5
West Bromwich B70... 53 C3
Pridmore Rd CV6 ... 113 D7
Priestbrook Cl B44.. 44 D2
Priestfield Rd B97.. 158 E5
Priestfield St WV14.. 40 B6
Priestfield Sta WV14.. 40 A7
Priesthills Rd LE10... 75 D8
Priestland Rd B34... 69 B7
Priestley Cl
Birmingham B20..... 55 A2
Halesowen B63...... 82 B6
Priestley Rd
Birmingham B11..... 87 A7
Walsall WS2 .... 28 A5
Priest Meadow Cl
B96................ 158 D1
Priest St B64.........62 F1
Primley Ave
Birmingham B36..... 68 D7
Tamworth B77....... 35 F5
Walsall WS2 .... 28 B2
Primley Cl WS2..... 28 B2
Primrose Ave
Birmingham B11..... 87 C5
Tipton DY4 .... 52 C8
Wolverhampton WV10 . 11 D3
Primrose Bank B68 . 64 C4
Primrose Cl
Cradley Heath B64 ... 82 B8
Lickey End B60 ..... 137 C6
Walsall WS3 .... 15 A5
Primrose Cres DY1... 51 C4
Primrose Croft
Birmingham, Perry
Common B23 ...... 56 C7
Birmingham, Yardley Wood
B28.............. 105 F5
Primrose Dr
Bedworth CV12...... 77 E1
Hinckley LE10 ...... 75 E4
Primrose Gdns
Birmingham B38..... 123 F8
Codsall WV8 .... 10 A3
Featherstone WV10 .. 12 B7
Primrose Hill
Birmingham B38..... 124 A8
Smethwick B67...... 64 D4
Stourbridge DY8..... 60 E1
Warwick CV34 ...... 155 E2
Primrose Hill Com Sch
B38............... 123 F8
Primrose Hill St CV1 165 C4
Primrose Hill Trad Est
DY2............... 62 D4
Primrose La
Birmingham B28..... 105 F5
Solihull B90........ 126 A5
Wolverhampton WV10 . 26 A8
Primrose Mdw **1**
WS11................2 C2
Primrose Pk DY5.... 61 C2
Primrose Rd DY2.... 62 C4
Primroses The WS5.. 43 B4
Primrose Way DY10 . 116 F4

Primrose Woods B32. . 84 B2
Primsland Cl B90 . . . 127 C7
Prince Albert Inf & Jun
 Sch B6 . . . . .66 E8
Prince Albert St B9 . . 67 D1
Prince Andrew Cres
 B45 . . . . 101 E2
Prince Charles Cl
 B45 . . . . 101 E2
Prince Charles Rd
 WV14 . . . . .40 F3
Prince Edward Dr
 B45 . . . . 101 E2
Prince George Rd
 WS10 . . . . 42 A5
Prince Of Wales La
 B14 . . . . 105 C3
Prince Of Wales Rd
 CV5 . . . . 112 E3
Prince of Wales Wlk 3
 B66 . . . . 65 C5
Princep Cl B43. . . . . 44 D4
Prince Philip Cl B45. 101 E2
Prince Rd B30 . . . . . 104 A3
Prince Regent Ct 3
 CV31 . . . . 161 F6
Prince Rupert Mews
 WS13 . . . . .9 A8
Prince Rupert's Way
 WS13 . . . . .9 A8
Princes Ave WS1 . . . . 43 A8
Prince's Ave
 Nuneaton CV11 . . . . 73 B3
 Walsall WS1 . . . . 29 B1
Princes Cl CV3 . . . . 134 B8
Princes Dr
 Codsall WV8 . . . . 10 A2
 Coventry CV6 . . . . . . 96 B1
 Kenilworth CV8. . . . . . 148 B7
Prince's Dr CV31 . . . 161 D7
Princes End Ind Pk
 DY4. . . . . .40 E1
Princes Gate
 Solihull B91 . . . . 107 B4
 West Bromwich B70 . . . 53 E2
Princes Gdns WV8 . . . 10 A2
Princes Rd DY8 . . . . . 80 D3
Prince's Rd B69 . . . . . 52 B2
Princess Alice Dr B73 45 D2
Princess Alley WV1. . 163 C3
Princess Anne Dr
 B45 . . . . 101 E2
Princess Anne Rd
 Bilston WV14 . . . . . . 40 F3
 Willenhall WS2 . . . . . . 27 F3
Princess Cl WS7 . . . . .6 E7
Princess Cres B63. . . 82 E6
Princess Ct WV10 . . . 26 A6
Princess Gr B71. . . . 53 D8
Princess of Wales Com
 Hospl The B61. . . . . 137 A4
Princess Sq WV1 . . . . 163 C3
Princess Rd
 Birmingham B5 . . . . . . 86 E7
 Hinckley LE10 . . . . . 75 E8
 Oldbury B68 . . . . 64 D2
Princess Sq WV14 . . . .40 F3
Princess St
 Burntwood WS7 . . . . . .6 E8
 Cannock WS11 . . . . . .1 F5
 Coventry CV6 . . . . . . 113 F7
 Wolverhampton WV1 . 163 C3
Prince's St
 Nuneaton CV11. . . . . . 73 C3
 Royal Leamington Spa
 CV32. . . . . 157 B1
Princess Way WS10 . 41 C8
Prince St
 Brownhills WS9 . . . . . 15 F2
 Cannock WS12 . . . . . . 1 E6
 Cradley Heath B64 . . . 82 D8
 Dudley DY2 . . . . 62 C6
 Walsall WS2 . . . . 42 C8
Prince's Way B91 . . 107 B3
Princethorpe Cl
 Birmingham B34. . . . . 69 D7
 Solihull B90. . . . . 106 A2
Princethorpe Inf Sch
 B29. . . . . 85 A1
Princethorpe Jun Sch
 B29. . . . . 85 A1
Princethorpe Rd B29. 85 A1
Prince Thorpe Rd
 WV13 . . . . 41 B8
Princethorpe Way
 CV3. . . . . 134 E8
Princeton Gdns WV9 .10 F2
Prince William Cl
 Birmingham B23. . . . . 56 D2
 Coventry CV6 . . . . . . 112 E6

Principal Ct B67 . . . . . 65 A5
Princip St B4 . . . . . . 164 C4
Printing House St
 B4 . . . . 164 C3
Prior Ave B60 . . . . . . 150 C3
Prior Cl DY10 . . . . . . 117 C5
Prior Deram Wlk
 CV4 . . . . 132 C7
Priors Cl CV7 . . . . . 130 B6
Priors Field Prim Sch
 CV8. . . . . 147 D7
Priorsfield Rd
 4 Coventry CV6 . . . . 113 A4
 Kenilworth CV8. . . . . 147 D6
Priorsfield Rd N 3
 CV6. . . . . 113 A4
Priorsfield Rd S CV6 113 A4
Priors Harnall CV1 . . 165 D4
Priors Mill DY3. . . . . 50 E5
Priors Oak B97. . . . . 153 B4
Priors Way B23 . . . . . 56 C8
Priory Ave B29. . . . . . 86 B2
Priory Cl Dudley DY1 . . 51 B3
 Kingswood B94. . . . . 144 D5
 Smethwick B66 . . . . . 65 C4
 Stourbridge DY8 . . . . 81 B3
 Tamworth B79. . . . . . 20 F7
 West Bromwich B70 . . . 53 F2
Priory Croft CV8 . . . 148 A4
Priory Ct
 Brownhills WS9 . . . . . 16 A4
 Coventry CV5 . . . . . . 113 A1
 3 Dudley DY1 . . . . . 51 C1
 Nuneaton CV11. . . . . . 73 A4
 Stourbridge DY8 . . . . 81 B3
 Studley B80. . . . . . . 159 E5
 Wolverhampton WV1 . 163 B4
Priory Cts The B2. . . 164 C3
Priory Dr B68 . . . . . . 64 C5
Priory Field CV11 . . 39 F1
Priorygate Way B9 . . 67 E3
Priory Gdns B28 . . . 105 D4
Priory Green Prim Sch
 WV9. . . . . 11 A2
Priory Ho
 Halesowen B63. . . . . 82 F5
 Kenilworth CV8. . . . . 147 F4
Priory La DY3 . . . . . . 50 D7
Priory Mews CV34. . . 160 E7
Priory New Way Ind Est
 B6. . . . . .66 F5
Priory Pl CV1 . . . . . 165 C3
Priory Prim Sch DY1 .51 B3
Priory Prim Sch The
 WS10 . . . . 42 D2
Priory Queensway The
 B4 . . . . 164 C3
Priory Rd
 Birmingham, Aston B6 . 67 B8
 Birmingham, Edgbaston B5,
 B15. . . . . 86 B5
 Birmingham, Stirchley
 B14. . . . . 104 C7
 Birmingham, Warstock
 B28. . . . . 105 D3
 Cannock WS12 . . . . . . 2 D4
 Dodford B61. . . . . . . 136 A6
 Dudley DY1 . . . . 51 C3
 Halesowen B62. . . . . . 83 F4
 Kenilworth CV8. . . . . 148 A4
 Stourbridge DY8 . . . . 81 B3
 Warwick CV34 . . . . . . 160 E7
Priory Row CV1 . . . . 165 C3
Priory Sch B15 . . . . . .86 B6
Priory Sq
 Birmingham B4. . . . . 164 C3
 Studley B80. . . . . . . 159 E5
Priory St
 Coventry CV1 . . . . . . 165 C3
 Dudley DY1 . . . . 51 C1
 Nuneaton CV10. . . . . . 72 D3
 Royal Leamington Spa
 CV31. . . . . 161 F6
Priory Terr CV31. . . . 162 A7
Priory The DY3 . . . . . 50 D8
Priory Visitors Ctr*
 CV1 . . . . 165 C3
Priory Wlk
 Birmingham B4. . . . . 164 C3
 Hinckley LE10 . . . . . 71 E1
 Sutton Coldfield B72. . 57 C7
 10 Warwick CV34 . . . 160 F7
Pritchard Ave WV11 . 26 E6
Pritchard Cl B66 . . . . 65 B5
Pritchard St
 Brierley Hill DY5. . . . 61 B3
 Wednesbury WS10 . . . 42 A3

Pritchatts Rd B15 . . . .85 F5
Pritchett Ave WV4. . . .39 F3
Pritchett Rd B31 . . . . 123 B7
Pritchett St B6. . . . . 66 E5
Pritchett Twr 4 B10. . 67 B5
Private Way B45 . . . . 122 C4
Privet Cl B44. . . . . 44 E3
Privet Rd CV2 . . . . . . 96 B2
Probert Rd WV10. . . . . 11 B1
Proctors Barn La
 B98 . . . . 154 B4
Proctor St B7. . . . . . 67 A5
Proffitt Ave CV6. . . . . 96 A1
Proffitt Cl
 Brownhills WS8 . . . . 16 A5
 Walsall WS2 . . . . 28 E4
Proffitt St WS2. . . . . . 28 E4
Progress Dr CV3. . . . 135 A7
Progress Dr WS11. . . . .4 F6
Progress Ind Ctr WS11 4 F7
Progress Way CV3. . . 135 A8
Prole St WV10. . . . . . 25 E4
Prologis Pk CV6. . . . . .95 B5
Promenade The DY5. . 61 D2
Prophets Cl B97. . . . 153 D3
Prospect Dr WV13. . . . .9 F8
Prospect Gdns B5. . . 81 A4
Prospect Hill
 Kidderminster DY10 . . 116 E6
 Redditch B97 . . . . . . 153 E4
 Stourbridge DY8 . . . . 81 A4
Prospect La
 Kidderminster DY10 . . 116 E6
 Solihull B91. . . . . . . 106 D4
Prospect Manor Ct
 WS12 . . . . .2 C3
Prospect Pk WS11 . . . .4 D7
Prospect Pl B12. . . . .86 F5
Prospect Rd
 Birmingham B13. . . . . 86 F1
 Burntwood WS7 . . . . . .7 B6
 Dudley DY3 . . . . 50 C2
 Halesowen B62. . . . . . 83 C5
 Whitnash CV31. . . . . 162 B5
Prospect Rd N B98. . . 154 A4
Prospect Rd S B98. . . 154 A4
Prospect Row
 Dudley DY2 . . . . 62 D8
 Stourbridge DY8 . . . . 81 A3
Prospect St
 Bilston WV14 . . . . . . 40 E6
 Tamworth B79. . . . . . 21 A5
 Wednesbury DY4 . . . . 41 C1
Prosper Mdw DY6. . . .60 F7
Prospero Cl B45 . . . . 102 A2
Prospero Dr CV34 . . . 161 E3
Prosser St
 Bilston WV14 . . . . . . 40 D5
 Wolverhampton WV10 . 25 E5
Prossers Wlk B46. . . .70 F7
Proud Cross Ringway
 DY11 . . . . 116 C6
Proud's La WV14 . . . . 40 D7
Provence Cl WV10. . . .25 F4
Providence Cl WS3. . . 28 C7
Providence Ct B64 . . . 82 C8
Providence Dr DY9. . . 81 E6
Providence Ind Est
 DY9. . . . . .81 E6
Providence La WS3. . . 28 C6
Providence Rd B61. . . 136 F3
Providence Row
 WV14 . . . . 51 B8
Providence St
 Coventry CV5 . . . . . . 132 F8
 Cradley Heath B64 . . . 62 D1
 Stourbridge DY9 . . . . 81 F6
 Tipton DY4 . . . . 52 C5
Providence Terr
 WS10 . . . . 41 E6
Provost Williams CE Prim
 Sch CV8 . . . . 135 A1
Pruden Ave WV4 . . . . .39 F3
Pryor Rd B68 . . . . . . 64 C4
Ptarmigan Pl CV11 . . .73 F3
Puckering's La 11
 CV34 . . . . 160 E6
Pudsey Dr B75. . . . . . 32 C3
Pugh Cres WS2 . . . . . 27 E2
Pughe's Cl LE10. . . . . 76 A6
Pugh Rd Bilston WV14. 40 E3
 Birmingham B6. . . . . . 67 A8
 Wolverhampton WV4,
 WV14 . . . . 39 F2
Pugin Cl WV6 . . . . . . 23 D3
Pugin Gdns B23. . . . . 56 D8
Pullman Cl B77 . . . . . 22 A2
Pulman Cl B97. . . . . 153 C4
Puma Way CV1. . . . . . 165 C1
Pumphouse Cl CV6. . . 96 B6

Pumphouse La
 Blackwell B45, B60. . . 137 F7
 Redditch B97 . . . . . . 152 D1
Pumphouse Way 2
 B69 . . . . .63 F4
Pump St
 Kidderminster DY10 . . 116 E4
 Wolverhampton WV2 . . 40 A7
Puppy Gn DY4 . . . . . 52 B5
Purbeck Cl B63. . . . . 82 D1
Purbeck Croft B32 . . .84 F4
Purbrook B77. . . . . . . 35 E8
Purbrook Rd WV1 . . . 40 A8
Purcell Ave
 Lichfield WS13 . . . . . . .3 C2
 Nuneaton CV11. . . . . . 79 A7
Purcell Cl CV32 . . . . 162 A8
Purcell Rd
 Coventry CV6 . . . . . . 114 B8
 Wolverhampton WV10 . 25 D8
Purdy Rd WV14 . . . . . 40 E1
Purefoy Rd
 Birmingham B13. . . . . 105 C5
 Coventry CV3 . . . . . . 133 D8
Purley Gr B23. . . . . . 56 A5
Purlieu La CV8. . . . . 147 D5
Purnells Way B93 . . . 128 A5
Purser Dr CV34 . . . . 160 B4
Pursall Cl B97. . . . . 153 C3
Purslet Rd WV1 . . . . . 26 A2
Purslow Gr B31. . . . . 103 A1
Purton Mews CV31. . . 162 C6
Putney Ave B20. . . . . 55 C1
Putney La B62. . . . . . 101 B1
Putney Rd B20. . . . . . 55 C1
Putney Wlk B37. . . . . 70 B3
Puxton Dr DY11 . . . . 116 D8
Puxton La DY11 . . . . 116 C7
Pye Green Rd WS11 . . .1 E4
Pye Green Valley Prim
 Sch WS12. . . . . .2 A7
Pyeharps Rd LE10. . . 75 E5
Pype Hayes Cl B24 . . . 57 D4
Pype Hayes Rd B24 . . . 57 D4
Pyree Sq CV34 . . . . . 160 B4
Pytchley Ho 6 B20 . . .54 F3
Pytman Dr B76. . . . . . 58 A7
Pyt Pk CV5. . . . . 112 D4

Q
Quadrangle The B90. 126 E8
Quadrant Ho B32 . . . 84 E7
Quadrant The
 Coventry CV1 . . . . . . 165 B2
 Nuneaton CV11. . . . . . 73 E3
 Sedgley DY3 . . . . 39 D1
Quadrille Lawns WV9. .10 F2
Quail Gn WV6 . . . . . . 23 F2
Quail Park Dr DY10. . . 117 A2
Qualcast Rd WV1,
 WV10 . . . . .25 F2
Quantock Cl
 Birmingham B45. . . . . 102 B2
 Brownhills WS8 . . . . 16 A4
 Halesowen B63. . . . . 82 D2
Quantock Dr
 Kidderminster DY10 . . 117 A6
 Nuneaton CV10. . . . . . 72 B3
Quantock Rd DY8 . . . 81 B6
Quantry La DY9 . . . . 120 F8
Quarrington Gr B14 . 105 A3
Quarry Bank Prim Sch
 DY5. . . . . 62 A1
Quarry Brow DY3. . . . 50 E6
Quarry Cl
 Cheslyn Hay WS6. . . . .4 E3
 Leek Wootton CV35 . . 155 F7
Quarryfield La CV1. . . 165 D1
Quarry Fields CV35. . 155 F7
Quarry Hill B63 . . . . .82 F2
Quarry Hills La WS14. 9 D6
Quarry House Cl B45 101 F1
Quarry La
 Birmingham B31. . . . . 103 A2
 Bromsgrove B61. . . . . 150 D8
 Halesowen B63. . . . . . 83 A4
 Nuneaton CV11. . . . . . 73 F1
 Rowington Green
 CV35. . . . . 145 C1
Quarry Lodge WS14 . . . 9 D5
Quarry Park Rd DY8. . 99 A8
Quarry Rd
 Birmingham B29. . . . . 103 A2
 Dudley DY2 . . . . 62 B1
 Kenilworth CV8. . . . . 147 E6
Quarry Rise B69. . . . . 63 B8
Quarry St CV32. . . . . 161 C8
Quarry The DY10 . . . . 116 F8
Quarry Wlk B45 . . . . 122 A7

Quarrywood Gr CV2. 114 A4
Quarry Yd CV10 . . . . . 72 C4
Quasar Ctr 2 WS1 . . . 28 E2
Quatford Gdns WV10 . 25 E5
Quayle Gr 2 DY8 . . . 60 D3
Quayside B18. . . . . . . 66 A5
Quayside Cl B69. . . . . 63 E8
Quayside Dr WS2. . . . 42 C8
Queen Alexandra Coll
 B17. . . . . 85 A6
Queen Eleanors Dr
 B93 . . . . 128 B8
Queen Elizabeth Ave
 WS2 . . . . .27 F2
Queen Elizabeth Ct
 B19 . . . . 66 B6
Queen Elizabeth Hospl
 B15. . . . . .85 E4
Queen Elizabeth
 Psychiatric Hospl
 B15. . . . . .85 E4
Queen Elizabeth Rd
 Birmingham B45. . . . . 101 E2
 Kidderminster DY10 . . 117 B5
 Nuneaton CV10. . . . . . 72 D5
Queen Isabel's Ave
 CV3 . . . . 133 D8
Queen Margaret's Rd
 CV4 . . . . 132 C8
Queen Mary's Gram Sch
 WS1 . . . . 43 A8
Queen Mary's High Sch
 WS4 . . . . .28 F3
Queen Mary's Rd
 Bedworth CV12. . . . . 78 C5
 Coventry CV6 . . . . . . 113 F7
Queen Mary St WS1 . . 42 D6
Queen Philippa St
 CV3 . . . . 133 D6
Queens Arc CV11. . . . 73 C4
Queen's Ave WV1. . . . 163 B3
Queens Ave
 Birmingham B14. . . . . 104 E8
 Solihull B90. . . . . . . 106 B1
Queen's Ave B69 . . . . 52 A1
Queensbridge Rd B13 86 E2
Queensbridge Sch
 B13. . . . . .86 E2
Queensbury Sch B24. .56 F2
Queens CE Jun Sch
 CV11. . . . . 73 A4
Queens Cl
 Birmingham B24. . . . . 56 F2
 Smethwick B67. . . . . . 65 A5
Queen's Cl CV8 . . . . 147 F3
Queen's Coll The B15 .85 F5
Queen's Cotts B97 . . 153 B4
Queens Court Trad Est
 B70. . . . . .52 F3
Queens Cres WV14 . . 40 A1
Queen's Cres B81. . . . 81 A7
Queen's Croft Com Sch
 WS13. . . . . .9 B7
Queen's Cross DY1. . . 62 B8
Queens Ct
 Birmingham B3. . . . . 164 B6
 Brierley Hill DY5. . . . 61 C6
 Nuneaton CV11. . . . . . 73 A4
Queens Dr
 Birmingham B5. . . . . 164 C2
 Birmingham, Lifford
 B30. . . . . 104 A4
 Burntwood WS7 . . . . . .6 F5
 Rowley Regis B65. . . . 63 D4
Queen's Dr CV35 . . . 145 A1
Queens Dr The B62. . 83 C5
Queens Gdns
 Bilston WV14 . . . . . . 40 D7
 4 Birmingham B23. . 56 B7
 Dudley DY2 . . . . 62 C4
Queens Head Rd B21. 65 E7
Queens Hill DY9. . . . 119 D7
Queens Hospital Cl
 B15. . . . . 66 C1
Queensland Ave CV5 112 F2
Queensland Gdns 4
 CV12 . . . . .77 F2
Queen's Lea WV12. . . 27 C5
Queen's Own Hussars
 Mus The* CV34. . . . 160 E6
Queens Par WS3 . . . . 14 B1
Queen's Park Ct 3
 LE10 . . . . 75 E8
Queen's Park Flats 2
 LE10 . . . . 75 E8
Queen's Park Rd B32. .84 F6

Pri–Que 231

Queen's Park Terr 4
 LE10 . . . . 75 E8
Queen Sq WV1 . . . . . 163 B3
Queens Rd
 Birmingham, Aston
 B6. . . . . 67 A8
 Birmingham, Yardley
 B26. . . . . 68 F1
 Sedgley DY3 . . . . 50 E8
 Walsall WS4 . . . . 29 C7
Queen's Rd
 Birmingham B23 . . . . . 56 C3
 Coventry CV1 . . . . . . 165 A2
 Hinckley LE10 . . . . . 75 E8
 Kenilworth CV8. . . . . 147 E3
 Nuneaton CV11 . . . . . 73 B4
 Oldbury B68 . . . . 64 D5
 Smethwick B67. . . . . . 64 D4
 Stourbridge DY8 . . . . 80 F6
 Tipton DY4 . . . . 51 F5
 Walsall WS5 . . . . . . 43 B6
Queen's Ride B12 . . . . 86 D4
Queens Sq WS11 . . . . .1 E1
Queen's Sq CV34 . . . 160 D5
Queen St
 Astwood Bank B96. . . 158 E1
 Bedworth CV12. . . . . 78 C2
 Bilston, Bunker's Hill
 WV14 . . . . 40 E5
 Birmingham B12 . . . . . 87 B5
 Brierley Hill, Pensnett
 DY5. . . . . 61 C6
 Brierley Hill, Quarry Bank
 DY5. . . . . 82 A8
 Brownhills WS9 . . . . 15 F2
 Burntwood WS7 . . . . .6 F5
 Cannock, Blackfords
 WS11 . . . . 1 D1
 Cannock WS11 . . . . . . .2 A5
 Cheslyn Hay WS6 . . . 4 D3
 Coventry CV1 . . . . . . 165 C4
 Cradley Heath B64 . . . 62 D1
 Cubbington CV32 . . . 157 E5
 Darlaston, Darlaston Green
 WS10 . . . . 41 C8
 Darlaston, Moxley
 WS10 . . . . 41 B4
 Halesowen B63. . . . . 83 A4
 Kidderminster DY10 . . 116 E7
 Kingswinford DY6. . . . 60 D7
 Lichfield WS13 . . . . . . .9 A7
 Oldbury B69 . . . . 64 A8
 Redditch B98 . . . . . . 153 E4
 Royal Leamington Spa
 CV32. . . . . 157 A1
 Stourbridge DY8 . . . . 80 F6
 Stourbridge, Wordsley
 DY8. . . . . 60 E3
 Sutton Coldfield B72. . 46 C4
 Tipton DY4 . . . . 51 F8
 Walsall WS2 . . . . 28 D1
 Wednesbury WS10 . . . 41 E3
 West Bromwich B70 . . . 53 D3
 Wolverhampton WV1 . 163 C3
Queen Street Pas 1
 DY5. . . . . 82 A8
Queensway
 Birmingham B6. . . . . . 55 F2
 Halesowen B63. . . . . 83 B3
 Nuneaton CV10. . . . . . 73 E6
 Oldbury B68 . . . . 64 B1
 Royal Leamington Spa
 CV31. . . . . 161 E6
 Stourbridge DY8 . . . . 81 E2
 Sutton Coldfield B74. . 45 A8
 Tamworth B79. . . . . . 21 A8
Queens Way B78. . . . .36 F6
Queensway Cl B68 . . . 64 B1
Queensway Trad Est
 Birmingham B5. . . . . 164 D3
 Royal Leamington Spa
 CV31. . . . . 161 E6
Queensway (Tunnel)
 B3. . . . . 164 B3
Queenswood Ct CV7. . 94 D4
Queens Wood Ho
 B14 . . . . 104 D4
Queenswood Rd
 Birmingham B13. . . . . 87 A4
 Sutton Coldfield B75. . 32 B1
Queen Victoria Ct 4
 LE10 . . . . 71 D1
Queen Victoria Prim Sch
 DY3. . . . . .50 E8
Queen Victoria Rd
 Coventry CV1 . . . . . . 165 B2
 Coventry CV1 . . . . . . 165 B3
Quenby Dr DY1 . . . . . 51 A3

Quentin Dr DY1 . . . . . .61 F8
Queslade Cl B43 . . . . . 44 A1
Queslett Rd B43 . . . . . 44 C2
Queslett Rd E B74,
B43. . . . . .44 F5
Quibery Cl B98. . . . . 154 F3
Quicksand La WS9 . . .29 F4
Quigley Ave B9 . . . . . 67 B2
Quillets Rd DY8 . . . . . 60 C1
Quilletts Cl CV6 . . . . . 96 A1
Quilter Cl
  Dudley WV14 . . . . . . 51 A8
  Willenhall WS2 . . . . . . 27 F3
Quilter Rd B24 . . . . . 57 B2
Quince B77 . . . . 22 B3
Quince Tree Sch B77. 22 A3
Quincey Dr B24 . . . . . 57 C3
Quincy Rise DY5 . . . . 81 C7
Quinn Cl CV3 . . . . . . 134 B7
Quinneys La B98 . . . 159 B6
Quinton Ave WS6. . . . . .4 F3
Quinton Bsns Pk B32 84 A4
Quinton Church Prim Sch
  B32. . . . . 84 A6
Quinton Cl
  Redditch B98 . . . . . 154 D1
  Solihull B92. . . . . 89 D3
Quintondale 5 B90. 126 C8
Quinton Expressway
  B32 . . . . 84 B4
Quinton Flats CV3 . . 133 D7
Quinton La B32 . . . . . 84 D6
Quinton Par CV3 . . . 133 D7
Quinton Pk CV3 . . . . 133 D7
Quinton Pl WS11 . . . . .6 A4
Quinton Rd
  Birmingham B17 . . . . 85 C3
  Coventry CV1 . . . . . 165 C1
Quinton Rd W B32 . . 84 D4
Quonians La WS13 . . . .9 B8
Quorn Cres DY8 . . . . 60 C3
Quorn Gr B24 . . . . . . 57 C3
Quorn Ho 3 B20. . . .54 F3
Quorn Way CV3 . . . . 134 E7

R

Rabbit La WV10 . . . . . 12 A8
Rabone La B66. . . . . . 65 C6
Raby Cl B69. . . . . . . .62 F8
Raby St WV2 . . . . . . 163 C2
Racecourse La DY8. . .80 F1
Racecourse Rd WV6 . 25 A5
Race Leys Inf Sch
  CV12. . . . . .78 B3
Race Leys Jun Sch
  CV12. . . . . .78 B4
Racemeadow Cres
  B64 . . . . 62 C1
Rachael Gdns WS10 . 42 C4
Rachel Cl DY4. . . . . . 41 C1
Rachel Gdns B29. . . . 85 D2
Radbourn Dr B74 . . . . 46 C6
Radbourne Dr B63 . . . 82 A7
Radbourne Rd B90 . . 106 D3
Radbrook Way CV31. 162 D6
Radcliffe Dr B62 . . . . 83 E6
Radcliffe Gdns 6
  CV31 . . . . 162 A6
Radcliffe Rd CV5 . . . 132 F8
Radcliffe Twr 3 B12 .86 F8
Radclyffe Ho B16 . . . 86 A8
Raddens Rd B62 . . . . .83 F3
Raddington Dr B92. . 106 E8
Raddlebarn Ct B29. . . 86 A1
Raddlebarn Farm Dr
  B29 . . . . 103 F8
Raddlebarn Prim Sch
  B29. . . . . .85 F1
Raddlebarn Rd B29 . 103 F8
Radford Ave DY10 . . 116 E7
Radford Circ 5 CV6. 113 A4
Radford Cl WS5. . . . . 43 A3
Radford Ct DY10 . . . 116 E7
Radford Dr WS4. . . . . 15 C2
Radford Hall CV31. . 162 E6
Radford Ho
  Coventry CV6 . . . . . 113 A7
  2 Redditch B97. . . 153 A4
Radford La WV3, WV4 . .37 F2
Radford Prim Sch
  CV6. . . . . 113 B5
Radford Rd
  Alvechurch B48. . . . 139 D7
  Birmingham B29 . . . 103 A6
  Coventry CV1, CV6 . 113 B5
  Royal Leamington Spa
  CV31. . . . . 162 C7

Radford Rise B91 . . . 107 E5
Radford Semele CE Prim
  Sch CV31 . . . . 162 E5
Radley Ct B26. . . . . . 89 C7
Radley Dr CV10 . . . . . 73 A1
Radley Gr B29 . . . . . . 85 A2
Radley Rd
  Stourbridge DY9 . . . . 81 F4
  Walsall WS4 . . . . 29 C7
Radleys Prim Sch The
  WS4 . . . . 29 D7
Radleys The B33 . . . . 89 D8
Radleys Wlk B33 . . . . 89 D8
Radlow Cres B37. . . . 90 B8
Radmore Cl WS7 . . . . . .6 D8
Radmore Rd LE10 . . . 71 D3
Radnor Cl B45. . . . . . 102 B2
Radnor Croft WS5 . . . 43 C3
Radnor Ct WS9. . . . . .15 F4
Radnor Dr CV10 . . . . . 72 E2
Radnor Gn B71. . . . . . 53 C7
Radnor Rd
  Birmingham, Brandhall
  B68. . . . . 84 B7
  Birmingham, Lozells
  B20. . . . . 66 B8
  Sedgley DY3 . . . . 50 C8
Radnor Rise WS12. . . . .2 B4
Radnor St B18 . . . . . . 66 A6
Radnor Wlk CV4 . . . . 114 F8
Radstock Ave B36. . . 68 C7
Radstock Rd WV12 . . 13 C1
Radway Cl B98. . . . . 154 B6
Radway Ind Est B90. 126 E2
Radway Rd B90 . . . . 126 E8
Raeburn Rd B43 . . . . 44 C4
RAF Cotts B35. . . . . .57 F2
Raford Rd B23 . . . . . 56 D6
Ragees Rd DY6. . . . . .60 F4
Raglan Ave
  Perton WV6. . . . . 23 F3
  Smethwick B66. . . . . 65 C4
Raglan Cl
  Nuneaton CV11. . . . . 73 D4
  Sedgley DY3 . . . . 50 B7
  Sutton Coldfield WS9 . 30 F3
Raglan Ct
  Bromsgrove B60. . . 137 A1
  7 Coventry CV1. . . 113 E3
Raglan Gr CV8 . . . . . 148 B5
Raglan Ho B33. . . . . . 69 A2
Raglan Rd
  Birmingham, Balsall Heath
  B5. . . . . 86 D5
  Birmingham, Handsworth
  B21. . . . . 65 C8
  Smethwick B66. . . . . 65 C4
Raglan St
  Brierley Hill DY5 . . . . 61 C4
  Coventry CV1 . . . . . 165 D3
  Wolverhampton WV3 . 163 A2
Raglan Way B37. . . . . 70 D1
Ragley Cl Knowle B93 128 B2
  Walsall WS3 . . . . 14 A1
Ragley Cres B60 . . . . 151 A8
Ragley Dr
  Birmingham, Grove Vale
  B43. . . . . 43 D2
  Birmingham, Sheldon
  B26. . . . . 89 C6
  2 Birmingham WV13 . 40 F8
Ragley Ho 8 B97 . . . 153 A4
Ragley Way CV11. . . .73 F2
Ragley Wlk 3 B65 . . . 63 C3
Raglis Cl B97 . . . . . . 153 A1
Ragnall Ave B33 . . . . 89 D7
Raikes La WS14 . . . . . 17 C7
Rail Bridge Est B70. . 53 A1
Railswood Dr WS3 . . . 15 B3
Railway Cl B80. . . . . 159 D4
Railway Dr
  Bilston WV14 . . . . 40 E5
  Wolverhampton WV1 . 163 C3
Railway Rd
  Birmingham B20. . . . . 55 F2
  Sutton Coldfield B73. . 46 B5
Railway Side Cl B66. . 64 E7
Railway Terr
  Bedworth CV12. . . . . 78 C2
  Birmingham, Aston B7 . 67 B6
  Birmingham, Hamstead
  B42. . . . . 54 F6

Railway Terr continued
  4 Wednesbury WS10 . 41 F2
Railway View B10 . . . . 87 C7
Railway Wlk B60 . . . . 151 A6
Railwharf Sidings
  DY2. . . . . 62 D4
Rainbow St
  Dudley WV14 . . . . . . 40 D2
  Wolverhampton WV2 . 163 C1
Rainford Way B38. . . 123 C8
Rainham Cl DY4. . . . . 51 D5
Rainsbrook Dr
  Nuneaton CV11. . . . . 74 A1
  Solihull B90. . . . . . . 126 F6
Rainscar B77 . . . . . . 36 B7
Raison Ave CV11 . . . .73 F8
Rakegate Prim Sch
  WV10. . . . . .11 B1
Rake Hill WS7. . . . . . .7 B8
Rake Way B15. . . . . . 66 B1
Raleigh Cl
  Birmingham B21. . . . . 54 B1
  Hinckley LE10 . . . . . 71 D4
Raleigh Croft B43 . . . 43 E3
Raleigh Ind Est B21. . .54 B1
Raleigh Rd
  Bilston WV14 . . . . 41 A3
  Birmingham B9 . . . . . 67 D2
  Coventry CV2 . . . . . 114 B2
Raleigh St
  Walsall WS2 . . . . 28 C2
  West Bromwich B71. . 53 C4
Ralph Barlow Gdns
  B44 . . . . 56 B8
Ralph Rd
  Birmingham B8. . . . . . 67 D4
  Coventry CV6 . . . . . 112 F5
  Solihull B90. . . . . . . 106 C4
Ralphs Mdw B32 . . . . 84 D2
Ralston Cl WS3 . . . . . 14 A4
Rambures Cl CV34 . . 161 F3
Ramillies Cres WS6 . . .4 F1
Ramp Rd B26. . . . . . . 90 C5
Ramsay Cl B71. . . . . .53 F8
Ramsay Cres CV5 . . . 112 B7
Ramsay Rd
  Oldbury B68 . . . . 64 C1
  Tipton DY4 . . . . 51 E7
  Walsall WS2 . . . . 28 A5
Ramsden Ave CV10. . . 72 D6
Ramsden Cl B29 . . . . 103 B7
Ramsden Ct CV10 . . . 72 C7
Ramsey Cl
  Birmingham B45. . . . 101 F1
  Hinckley LE10 . . . . . 71 B1
Ramsey Rd
  1 Birmingham B7 . . . 67 C7
  Royal Leamington Spa
  CV31. . . . . 162 B7
Ranby Rd CV2. . . . . . 113 F4
Randall Ave B48. . . . 139 A6
Randall Cl DY6. . . . . .60 F4
Randall Rd CV8 . . . . . 147 F3
Randle Dr B75. . . . . . 32 C3
Randle Rd
  Nuneaton CV10. . . . . 72 D4
  Stourbridge DY9 . . . . 81 C4
Randle St CV6 . . . . . 113 B5
Randolph Cl 11
  CV31 . . . . 162 C6
  2 CV31 . . . . 162 A6
Randwick Dr B44 . . . . 44 E1
Ranelagh Ho WV2 . . . 39 D7
Ranelagh Rd WV2. . . . 39 D6
Ranelagh St CV31 . . 162 A6
Ranelagh Terr CV31 . 161 F6
Range Meadow Cl
  CV32 . . . . 156 C3
Rangemoor CV3. . . . 134 D6
Rangeview Cl B74. . . .44 F6
Rangeways Rd
  Kidderminster DY11 . 116 A8
  Kingswinford DY6. . . . 60 F4
Rangeworthy Cl B97 158 C7
Rangifer Rd B78 . . . . .20 F1
Rangoon Rd B92. . . . 89 E4
Ranleigh Ave DY6. . . .60 F4
Rann Cl B16. . . . . 66 A1
Rannoch Cl
  Brierley Hill DY5. . . . . 81 B8
  Hinckley LE10. . . . . . 75 B8
Rannoch Dr CV10 . . . 72 C5
Rannock Cl CV3. . . . . 114 F2
Ranscombe Dr DY3. . 50 D2
Ransom Rd
  Birmingham B23. . . . . 56 C4
  Coventry CV6 . . . . . 113 E8
Ran-tan The B97. . . . 158 E5
Ranton Park Area 3
  WS11 . . . . .2 A2
Ranulf Croft CV3 . . . 133 C7

Ranulf St CV3 . . . . . . 133 C7
Ranworth Rise WV4 . . 39 D4
Raphael Cl CV5 . . . . . 112 C3
Rashwood Cl B94 . . . 143 B6
Ratcliffe Ave B30. . . 104 D3
Ratcliffe Cl DY3. . . . . .50 F6
Ratcliffe Ct CV10 . . . 72 C4
Ratcliffe Dr WV13 . . . 41 B8
Ratcliffe Rd
  Hinckley LE10 . . . . . 75 F6
  Solihull B91. . . . . . . 107 C7
  Wednesfield WV11 . . 27 A6
Ratcliffe Way DY4 . . . 52 D6
Ratcliff Wlk 3 B69. . . 64 A7
Rathbone Cl
  Bilston WV14 . . . . . . 40 D5
  Birmingham B5. . . . . . 86 F7
  Keresley CV7 . . . . . . 94 F6
  Keresley CV7 . . . . . . 95 A6
Rathbone Rd B67. . . .64 F2
Rathlin Cl WV9 . . . . . 11 A3
Rathlin Croft B36 . . . 70 B6
Rathmore Cl DY8. . . . 80 E2
Rathvilly Sch B31. . . 103 B3
Rathwell Cl WV9 . . . . 11 A1
Rattle Croft B33. . . . . 68 E3
Raveloe Dr CV11 . . . . 73 D1
Ravenall Cl B34. . . . . 69 B7
Raven Cl Cannock WS12 . .2 E4
  Cheslyn Hay WS6. . . . 4 D2
  Huntington WS12 . . . . .1 C7
Raven Cres WV11 . . . .26 F8
Raven Ct
  21 Brierley Hill DY5 . . 61 D2
  Wolverhampton WV10 . 11 B3
Ravenfield Cl B8. . . . . 68 A5
Ravenhayes La B32. . 102 A6
Raven Hays Rd B31. . 102 B1
Ravenhill Dr WV8 . . . 10 A4
Ravenhurst Dr B43 . . 43 E3
Ravenhurst Mews
  B23. . . . . 56 E3
Ravenhurst Rd B17. . 85 C6
Ravenhurst St B12 . . 87 A8
Raven Rd WS5 . . . . . 43 B6
Ravens Bank B98. . . 154 E7
Ravens Bank Fst Sch
  B98. . . . . 154 D6
Ravensbourne Gr
  WV13 . . . . 27 C2
Ravenscroft DY8 . . . . 80 C6
Ravenscroft Rd
  Solihull B92. . . . . . . 107 A8
  Willenhall WV12 . . . . 27 B5
Ravens Ct WS8. . . . . .15 F7
Ravensdale Ave
  CV32 . . . . 156 C2
Ravensdale Cl WS5. . 43 B7
Ravensdale Gdns
  WS5 . . . . 43 B7
Ravensdale Prim Sch
  CV2. . . . . 114 D4
Ravensdale Rd
  Birmingham B10. . . . . 87 F7
  Coventry CV2 . . . . . 114 D3
Ravenshaw La B91 . . 108 A4
Ravenshaw Rd B16. . 65 C2
Ravenshaw Way B91 108 A3
Ravenshill Rd B14. . . 105 D4
Ravensholme WV6. . .23 F2
Ravenshout CV4 . . . . 132 D6
Ravensitch Wlk DY5. . 61 E1
Ravensmere Rd B98. 154 B1
Ravensthorpe Cl
  CV3. . . . . 134 E8
Ravenstone B77. . . . . 36 B8
Ravenswood B15. . . . 85 E8
Ravenswood Cl B74 . . 46 B8
Ravenswood Dr B91. 106 F1
Ravenswood Dr S
  B91 . . . . 106 E1
Ravenswood Hill B46. .70 F7
Raven Way CV11 . . . .73 F2
Raven Wlk 4 B15. . . . 86 C7
Rawdon Gr B44 . . . . . 56 B8
Rawlett Sch B79. . . . 21 A8
Rawlings Rd B67. . . . 65 A2
Rawlins Croft B35. . . 58 C3
Rawlinson Rd CV32. . 157 B2
Rawlins St B16. . . . . . 66 A1
Rawnsley Dr CV8. . . . 148 C6
Rawnsley Rd WS12 . . . .2 E5
Raybolds Bridge Rd
  WS2 . . . . 28 C4
Raybon Croft B45 . . . 122 A6
Raybould's Fold DY2 . 62 C5
Rayford Dr B71. . . . . . 43 A2
Raygill B77 . . . . 36 B8

Ray Hall La
  Birmingham B43 . . . . 54 B8
  West Bromwich B43,
  B71. . . . . 43 A1
Rayleigh Ho B27 . . . . 88 D3
Rayleigh Rd WV3 . . . . 39 A8
Ray Mercer Way
  DY10 . . . . 116 F5
Raymond Ave B42. . . 55 B6
Raymond Cl
  Coventry CV6 . . . . . . 95 F5
  Walsall WS2 . . . . 28 D5
Raymond Gdns WV11. 26 E6
Raymond Rd B8. . . . . 67 E4
Raymont Gr B43 . . . . 44 A8
Raynor Cres CV12 . . . 77 D1
Raynor Rd WV10 . . . .25 F4
Raynsford Wlk CV34. 155 D1
Rayswood Cl CV10. . .72 F3
Rea Ave B45 . . . . 121 E8
Reabrook Rd B31. . . . 122 F8
Rea Bsns Pk B7 . . . . . 67 C4
Rea Cl B31. . . . . 123 A7
Readers Wlk B43. . . . .43 F1
Reading Ave CV11. . . .73 F7
Reading Cl CV2 . . . . . 96 B3
Read St CV1 . . . . 113 E3
Rea Fordway B45 . . . 101 F1
Reansway Sq WV6. . . 25 A4
Reapers Cl WV12. . . . 27 D5
Reapers Wlk WV8 . . . .10 F1
Rear Cotts B48. . . . . 138 F6
Rea Rd B31. . . . . 102 F1
Reardon Ct CV34 . . . 155 E1
Reaside Cres B14 . . . 104 B5
Reaside Croft B12. . . 86 E6
Reaside Dr B45 . . . . . 102 B1
Reaside Jun Sch
  B45. . . . . 101 E1
Rea St B5. . . . . 164 D1
Rea Terr B5 . . . . .66 F2
Rea Twr B19 . . . . 66 F2
Rea Valley Dr B31. . . 103 B2
Reaview Dr B29. . . . . 86 B2
Reay Nadin Dr B73. . 45 B4
Rebecca Dr B29. . . . . 85 E2
Rebecca Gdns WV4 . .38 F4
Recreation Rd
  Bromsgrove B61. . . . 136 F3
  Coventry CV6 . . . . . . 96 A3
Recreation St DY2. . . 62 D5
Rectory Ave WS10. . . 41 D6
Rectory Cl
  Allesley CV5 . . . . . . 112 C6
  Bedworth CV7. . . . . . 78 A1
  Drayton Bassett B78 . 34 E5
  Stourbridge DY8. . . . . 81 B3
  Whitnash CV31. . . . . 162 B4
Rectory Ct B97. . . . . 153 D1
Rectory Dr CV7 . . . . . 78 A1
Rectory Fields DY8. . . 60 E2
Rectory Gdns
  Birmingham B36. . . . . 69 A8
  Oldbury B68 . . . . 64 C5
  Solihull B91. . . . . . . 107 D3
  Stourbridge DY8 . . . . 81 B3
Rectory Gr B18 . . . . . 65 E6
Rectory La
  Allesley CV5 . . . . . . 112 C6
  Birmingham B36. . . . . 69 A8
  Upton Warren B61 . . 150 A4
Rectory Park Ave B75 46 E4
Rectory Park Cl B75. . 46 F6
Rectory Park Ct 7
  B75 . . . . 46 F6
Rectory Park Rd B26. 89 C5
Rectory Rd
  Birmingham B31. . . . 103 B3
  Solihull B91. . . . . . . 107 C3
  Stourbridge DY8. . . . . 81 B3
  Sutton Coldfield B75. . 46 E6
Rectory St DY8. . . . . . 60 E3
Redacre Rd B73. . . . .45 F2
Redacres WV6 . . . . . . 24 E6
Redbank Ave B23 . . . 56 C3
Redbourn Rd WS3. . . 14 A4
Red Brick Cl B64. . . . 82 D7
Redbrook Cl WS12 . . . 2 D2
Redbrook Covert 7
  B38. . . . . 123 E8

Redcar Cl
  Lower Marlbrook
  B61. . . . . 121 B1
  Royal Leamington Spa
  CV32. . . . . 157 C4
Redcar Croft B36. . . . 68 C8
Redcar Rd
  Coventry CV1 . . . . . . 113 E5
  Wolverhampton WV10 . 11 E4
Redcliff B77 . . . . .21 F5
Redcliffe Dr WV5. . . . 49 B6
Redcotts Cl WV10 . . . 26 A8
Redcroft Dr B24. . . . . 57 C5
Redcroft Rd DY2 . . . . 62 E6
Reddal Hill Prim Sch
  B64. . . . . .62 E1
Reddal Hill Rd B64 . . 62 E2
Red Deeps CV11 . . . . 78 D8
Reddicap Heath Rd
  B75. . . . . .46 F4
Reddicap Hill B75. . . 46 E4
Reddicap Trad Est
  B76. . . . . 46 D4
Reddicroft B73. . . . . . 46 C5
Reddings Ct B13. . . . 86 D3
Reddings La B11, B28. 87 E3
Reddings Rd B13. . . . 86 E2
Reddings The B47. . . 125 A5
Redditch Ho B33. . . . 69 E2
Redditch Rd
  Alvechurch, Arrowfield Top
  B48. . . . . 139 B8
  Alvechurch, Rowney Green
  B48. . . . . 139 C3
  Birmingham B31, B38. 123 C8
  Hopwood B48. . . . . . 123 B1
  Stoke Heath B60. . . 150 D5
  Studley B80. . . . . . . 159 D5
Redditch Ringway B97,
  B98. . . . . 153 D4
Redditch Sta B97. . . 153 D4
Redditch Wlk 4
  CV2. . . . . 115 A7
Redesdale Ave CV6. . 112 F5
Redfern Ave CV8. . . . 148 A6
Redfern Cl B92. . . . . . 89 B1
Redfern Dr WS7. . . . . .7 B5
Redfern Park Way
  B11. . . . . 88 A8
Redfern Rd B11. . . . . 88 A5
Redfly La DY5. . . . . . 61 C6
Redford Cl B13. . . . . . 87 B2
Redgate Cl B38. . . . . 103 D2
Redgrave Cl CV2 . . . . 115 A8
Red Hall Prim Sch
  DY3. . . . . 50 C3
Redhall Rd
  Birmingham B32. . . . . 84 E7
  Dudley DY3 . . . . 50 F2
Red Hill Redditch B98. 153 F2
  Stourbridge DY8. . . . . 81 B4
Redhill Ave WV5 . . . . 49 A6
Redhill Cl
  Stourbridge DY8. . . . . 81 B4
  Tamworth B79. . . . . . 21 A7
Red Hill Cl B80. . . . . 159 E6
Redhill Cl DY8 . . . . . . 81 B4
Redhill Furrows
  CV31 . . . . 162 C5
Red Hill Gr B38. . . . . 123 F7
Redhill Jun & Inf Sch
  B25. . . . . 88 A6
Redhill La B45, B61. . 121 C5
Red Hill Pl B62. . . . . 101 A7
Redhill Prim Sch WS11 1 F4
Redhill Rd
  Birmingham, King's Norton
  B38. . . . . 123 D7
  Birmingham, Tyseley
  B25. . . . . 88 A6
  Cannock WS11 . . . . . .1 F4
Redhill Sch DY8. . . . .81 B4
Red Hill St WV1 . . . . 163 B4
Red House Ave WS10. 41 E5
Redhouse B93. . . . . . 127 E4
Redhouse Cone & Mus*
  DY8. . . . . 60 E1
Redhouse Ind Est
  WS9. . . . . .29 F6
Red House Ind Est
  WS9. . . . . 30 A6
Redhouse JMI Sch
  WS9. . . . . .29 E5
Red House La WS9 . . .29 F5
Red House Park Rd
  B43. . . . . 43 E2
Redhouse Rd WV6 . . 24 D5
Red House Rd B33. . . 68 E2
Redhouse St WS1 . . . 42 E7
Redhurst Dr WV10. . . 11 B3

Red La
Burton Green CV8.... **131** C2
Coventry CV6 .... **113** F5
Essington WV11 ..... **13** C3
Gospel End Village DY3 **50** B8
Kenilworth CV8...... **147** D8
Redlake B77 .... **35** E8
Redlake Dr DY9.... **99** B8
Redlake Rd DY9..... **81** B1
Redland Cl
Coventry CV2 .... **96** E2
Lower Marlbrook B60. **121** C1
Redland La CV8 ..... **135** A2
Redland Rd CV31.... **162** B5
Redlands Cl B91 .... **107** D5
Redlands Rd B91.... **107** D5
Redlands Way B74 ... **31** A1
Red Leasowes Rd
B63 .... **83** A3
Redliff Ave B36 ..... **58** D1
Red Lion Cl WS11..... **6** A4
Red Lion Cl B69...... **52** A1
Red Lion Cres WS11....**6** A4
Red Lion La WS11....**6** B4
Red Lion St
Alvechurch B48...... **139** B6
Redditch B98 ...... **153** E4
Wolverhampton WV1 . **163** B3
Redlock Field WS14....**9** A5
Redmead Cl B30 .... **103** C4
Redmoor Gdns WV4.. **39** A5
Redmoor High Sch
LE10.............. **71** B3
Redmoor Way B76 .. **58** D6
Rednal Hill Jun & Inf
Schs B45 .... **122** C7
Rednal Hill La B45.. **122** A6
Rednall Dr B75...... **32** C3
Rednal Mill Dr B45.. **122** C7
Rednal Park Ct B38 . **103** F2
Rednal Rd B38...... **103** E1
Rednell Ho B69 ...... **63** D6
Redoak Ho WV10.....**25** F3
Redpine Crest WV12.. **27** D5
Red River Rd WS2.... **28** A5
Redruth Cl
Coventry CV6 ...... **114** A8
Kingswinford DY6.... **60** D8
Nuneaton CV11....... **74** A4
Walsall WS5 .... **43** D7
Redruth Rd WS5.... **43** D7
Red Sands Rd DY10 . **116** E8
Redstart Ave DY10.. **117** B2
Redstone Cl B98 .... **154** C6
Redstone Dr WV11...**26** F5
Redstone Farm Rd
B28 .... **106** B6
Redstone Way DY3... **50** D4
Redthorne Gr CV8.. **148** B8
Redthorn Gr B33.... **68** D3
Redvers Rd B9....... **67** E1
Redway Ct B75....... **46** E4
Redwell Cl B77 ..... **21** D5
Redwing B77 .... **36** A6
Redwing Cl WS7 ..... **7** D5
Redwing Ct DY10.... **117** A1
Redwing Dr WS12.....**1** C1
Redwing Gr B23 .... **56** B7
Red Wing Wlk B36 .. **70** A8
Redwood Ave DY1....**50** F5
Redwood Bsns Pk
B66............... **64** C7
Redwood Cl
Birmingham B30..... **103** E4
Sutton Coldfield B74... **30** F2
Redwood Croft
Birmingham B14..... **104** E7
Nuneaton CV10....... **73** A1
Redwood Dr
Burntwood WS7 ......**6** F4
Cannock WS11 ....**2** A3
Tipton B69 .... **52** B2
Redwood Gdns B27.. **88** B5
Redwood Ho B37 ....**69** F5
Redwood Rd
Birmingham B30..... **103** E4
Dudley WV14 .... **40** D2
Walsall WS5 .... **43** B4
Redwood Way WV12.. **27** B8
Reedham Gdns WV4.. **38** D5
Reedly Rd WV12...... **13** C1
Redmace B77........ **21** C2
Reedmace Cl B38 ... **123** F4
Reed Mace Dr B61.. **137** A5
Reedswood Cl WS2.... **28** C3
Reedswood Gdns
WS2 .... **28** C3
Reedswood La WS2 .. **28** C3
Reedswood Way WS2 **28** B4
Rees Dr Coventry CV3 **133** D4

Rees Dr *continued*
Wombourne WV5 .... **49** B7
Reeve Ct DY10 ..... **117** A1
Reeve Dr CV8 ...... **148** A4
Reeve La WS13.......**9** B8
Reeves Cl DY4 ...... **52** B2
Reeves Gdns WV8 ... **10** A4
Reeves Rd
Birmingham B14..... **104** C6
Hinckley LE10 .... **75** F6
Reeves St WS3 ...... **28** B8
Reflex Ind Pk WV13.. **27** A3
Reform St B70 ...... **53** D3
Regal Cl B77........ **35** C8
Regal Croft B36..... **68** B8
Regal Dr WS2 ...... **42** C8
Regal Ho CV11 ...... **73** D3
Regan Ave B90...... **106** A1
Regan Cres B23..... **56** E6
Regan Ct B75 .... **47** C5
Regan Dr B69 ...... **63** D8
Regan Ho B13 ...... **105** D7
Regency Arc 🄶
CV32 .... **161** F8
Regency Cl
🄶 Birmingham B9 .... **67** D1
Nuneaton CV10 ..... **73** D6
Regency Ct
Coventry CV5 ...... **132** F8
Hinckley LE10 .... **76** A7
Walsall WS1 .... **43** A7
Wolverhampton WV1 . **163** B4
Regency Dr
Birmingham B38 .... **103** F2
Coventry CV3 ...... **132** F5
Kenilworth CV8...... **147** F3
Regency Gdns B14 .. **105** C3
Regency Ho
Birmingham B16 .... **66** A1
Royal Leamington Spa
CV32 .... **162** A8
Regency Mews CV32 **162** A8
Regency Wlk B74 ... **31** D5
Regent Ave B69 .... **52** A1
Regent Cl
Birmingham B5...... **86** D6
Halesowen B63....... **83** A4
Kingswinford DY6.... **60** C6
Oldbury B69 .... **63** A8
Regent Ct
🄸 Birmingham B62 .... **84** A7
🄶 Darlaston WS10 ... **41** D6
🄵 Hinckley LE10 ..... **75** D8
🄷 Smethwick B66 .... **65** A5
Regent Dr B69 ...... **52** A1
Regent Gr CV32 ..... **161** F8
Regent Ho
Oldbury B68 .... **64** B2
🄶 Walsall WS2 .... **28** D3
Regent Mews B61... **150** E8
Regent Par B1 ...... **66** C4
Regent Park Rd B10.. **67** C1
Regent Pl
Birmingham B1 ..... **66** C4
🄸 Royal Leamington Spa
CV31.............. **162** A7
Tipton B69 .... **52** B2
Regent Rd
Birmingham B17..... **85** D6
Birmingham, Handsworth
B21............... **65** D8
Oldbury B69 .... **63** A8
Wolverhampton WV4 . **38** E5
Regents Park Com Prim
Sch B10 ....**87** B8
Regents Park Rd
B60 .... **137** C2
Regent St
Bedworth CV12...... **78** C4
Bilston WV14 ...... **40** D6
Birmingham, Hockley
B1................ **66** C4
Birmingham, Stirchley
B30.............. **104** A7
Coventry CV1 ...... **165** A2
Cradley Heath B64 ... **62** F2
Dudley DY1.......... **51** C6
Hinckley LE10 ...... **75** D8
Nuneaton CV11....... **73** D3
Royal Leamington Spa
CV32 .... **161** F8
Smethwick B66...... **65** A6
Tipton DY4 .... **51** E8
Willenhall WV13 .... **27** A3
Regents The B15 .... **85** D8
Regents Way B75 ...**46** F6
Regent Wlk B8...... **68** B7
Reg Hadden Ct CV10 **73** D6
Regiment Ct CV6.... **95** A1
Regina Ave B44...... **55** E8

Regina Cl B45...... **101** E2
Regina Cres
Coventry CV2 ...... **115** A7
Wolverhampton WV6 . **24** B4
Regina Dr
Birmingham B42..... **55** D3
Walsall WS4 .... **29** B4
Reginald Rd
Birmingham B8...... **67** D4
Smethwick B67...... **64** F2
Regis Beeches WV6 . **24** C5
Regis Gdns B65..... **63** C2
Regis Heath Rd B65.. **63** E2
Regis Rd
Rowley Regis B65..... **63** C2
Wolverhampton WV6 . **24** C5
Reid Ave WV12...... **27** D6
Reid Cl WS7 ....**7** F7
Reid Rd B68........ **64** D1
Reigate Ave B8 ..... **68** B4
Reignier Pl CV34.... **161** F2
Reindeer Rd B78.... **20** E1
Relay Dr B77........ **36** C7
Reliance Trad Est
WV14............. **40** B5
Relko Dr B36 .... **68** C7
Relton Mews CV6 ... **113** F6
Rembrandt Cl
Cannock WS11 ......**2** D2
Coventry CV5 ...... **112** C3
Remburn Gdns CV34 **160** F8
Remembrance Rd
Coventry CV3 ...... **134** D6
Wednesbury WS10 ... **42** C3
Remington Dr WS11....**4** F8
Remington Pl WS2 .. **28** C5
Remington Rd WS2 .. **28** B5
Renaissance Ct 🄸
B12 .... **67** A1
Rene Rd B77........ **21** E5
Renfrew Cl DY8 .... **60** C3
Renfrew Gdns DY11 . **116** C5
Renfrew Sq B35..... **58** B4
Renfrew Wlk CV4 ... **132** A8
Renison Rd CV2 .... **77** E1
Rennie Gr B32 ..... **84** D5
Rennison Dr WV5 ... **49** A6
Renolds Cl CV4 .... **112** C2
Renown Ave CV5 ... **112** C1
Renown Cl DY5 ..... **61** B7
Renshaw B91 ...... **108** A3
Renshaw Ind Est
B80............... **159** B4
Renton Gr WV10 ... **11** A1
Renton Rd WV10 ... **11** A1
Repington Rd N B77.. **22** A5
Repington Rd S B77.. **22** A5
Repington Way B75 .. **47** B5
Repton Ave WV6 ... **23** E3
Repton Cl WS11......**4** B8
Repton Dr CV6 ..... **96** B2
Repton Gr B9 ...... **68** B3
Repton Ho B23......**56** F6
Repton Rd B9....... **68** B3
Reservoir Cl WS2 ... **42** B8
Reservoir Pas WS10...**41** F3
Reservoir Pl WS2 ... **42** B8
Reservoir Rd
Birmingham B29..... **85** C3
Birmingham, Edgbaston
B16.............. **65** F2
Birmingham, Rednal
B45.............. **122** C3
Birmingham, Stockland
Green B23 .... **56** E4
Cannock WS12 ......**2** D4
Kidderminster DY11 . **116** C3
Oldbury B68 .... **64** C4
Rowley Regis B65..... **63** D3
Solihull B92........ **106** C4
Reservoir Retreat B16. **65** F1
Reservoir St WS2 ... **42** B8
Reswood Cl 🄷 B24...**56** F3
Retallack Cl B66 .... **65** B8
Retford Dr B76...... **46** E4
Retford Gr B25...... **88** C6
Retreat Gdns DY3 ... **50** E7
Retreat St
Astwood Bank B96 .. **158** E1
Wolverhampton WV3 . **163** A1
Retreat The B64..... **82** E7
Reuben Ave CV10 ... **72** B6
Revesby Wlk 🄸 B7... **67** A4
Revival St WS3...... **14** B1
Rex Cl CV4.......... **131** D8
Reyde Cl B97 ...... **153** A2
Reynalds Cross Sch
B92............... **106** D7
Reynard Cl B97 .... **152** F3

Reynards Cl DY3 .... **51** A7
Reynolds Cl
Hinckley LE10 .... **71** A3
Lichfield WS13 ....**3** B2
Reynolds Gr WV6... **23** F5
Reynolds Ho B19.... **66** E7
Reynolds Rd
Bedworth CV12...... **78** A4
Birmingham B21..... **65** E7
Reynolds Wlk WV11 . **27** B8
Rhayader Rd B31.... **102** E5
Rhodes Alms Houses The
B21................**65** F7
Rhodes Cl DY3 ..... **50** A4
Rhone Cl B11....... **87** C3
Rhoose Croft B35.... **58** B3
Rhuddlan Way DY10 . **116** E1
Rhyl Rd CV11........**79** F6
Rhys Thomas Cl
WV12 .... **27** D4
Rian Ct B64......... **82** D8
Ribbesford Ave WV10. **25** B8
Ribbesford Cl B63... **82** D6
Ribbesford Cres
WV14 .... **40** D1
Ribble Cl CV12 ..... **79** B2
Ribble Ct B73 ...... **46** B5
Ribble Rd CV3 ...... **113** F2
Ribblesdale B77 .... **36** B7
Ribblesdale Ave LE10. **71** E3
Ribblesdale Rd B29,
B30 .... **104** A8
Ribble Wlk B36 .....**69** F8
Ribbonbrook CV11... **73** D3
Ribbonfields CV11... **73** D3
Richard Cooper Rd
WS14 .... **17** F5
Richard Joy Cl CV6... **95** C2
Richard Lee Prim Sch
CV2.............. **114** E3
Richard Lighton Ho 🄵
B1................ **66** C3
Richard Pl WS5 .... **43** C8
Richard Rd WS5..... **43** C8
Richard Rd S B70 ... **53** C2
Richards Cl
Birmingham B31..... **122** F6
Kenilworth CV8...... **147** C6
Rowley Regis B65.... **63** E4
Richards Ct WS11 ....**5** F6
Richards Gr CV31 ... **162** A5
Richards Ho
🄷 Oldbury B69 ...... **63** E4
🄸 Walsall WS2 .... **28** D3
Richardson Cl CV34 . **155** F1
Richardson Ct WS7....**6** E8
Richardson Dr DY8.. **80** E8
Richardson Ho DY4... **52** C8
Richardson Way CV2 **115** B8
Richards Rd DY4.....**40** F1
Richards St WS10 ... **41** D7
Richard St
Birmingham B7...... **66** F5
West Bromwich B70... **53** B3
Richard Street W 🄸
B70 .... **53** C2
Richard Williams Rd
WS10 .... **42** B2
Richborough Dr DY1..**50** F4
Rich Cl CV34....... **161** B7
Riches St WV6......**24** F3
Richford Gr B33..... **69** D2
Richmere Ct WV6 ... **24** B3
Richmond Aston Dr
DY4 .... **52** A5
Richmond Ave
Birmingham B12..... **86** F5
Wolverhampton WV3 . **24** F1
Richmond Cl
Birmingham B20..... **55** A3
Cannock WS11 ....**2** A5
Hollywood B47 ..... **125** C7
Tamworth B79....... **21** A5
Richmond Croft B42 ..**54** F7
Richmond Ct
Birmingham, Calthorpe
Fields B15 .... **86** B8
🄸 Birmingham, Weoley
Castle B29 .... **103** C7
Halesowen B63....... **82** E3
Oldbury B68 .... **64** C5
🄶 Royal Leamington Spa
CV31.............. **162** B7
Stourbridge DY9..... **81** B1
🄸 Sutton Coldfield B72 **57** B7
Richmond Dr
Lichfield WS14 ......**9** D7
Perton WV6......... **23** D4
Sutton Coldfield B75... **46** F6

Richmond Dr *continued*
Wolverhampton WV3 .. **24** E1
Richmond Gdns
Stourbridge DY8..... **80** F7
Wombourne WV5 .... **49** A5
Richmond Gr DY8 ... **80** E8
Richmond Hill B68... **64** C5
Richmond Hill Gdns
B15............... **85** E7
Richmond Hill Rd B15.**85** F6
Richmond Ho 🄿 B37. **70** C1
Richmond Mews WV3 **25** A1
Richmond Pk DY6.... **60** C8
Richmond Pl B14 ... **104** C8
Richmond Prim Sch
LE10.............. **71** C3
Richmond Rd
Birmingham B45..... **121** E7
Birmingham, Hockley
B18............... **66** B6
Birmingham, Yardley
B33............... **68** D2
Dudley DY2......... **62** C8
Hinckley LE10 .... **71** C3
Nuneaton CV11....... **73** A4
Sedgley DY3 .... **50** E7
Smethwick B66...... **65** A2
Solihull B92........ **88** F2
Wolverhampton WV3 . **24** E1
Richmond St S B70... **52** E5
Richmond St
Coventry CV2 ...... **114** A3
Halesowen B63....... **83** A4
Walsall WS1 .... **29** A1
West Bromwich B70... **52** F6
Richmond Way 🄿
B37............... **70** C3
Rickard Cl B93 ..... **127** E6
Rickman Dr B15 ..... **86** D8
Rickyard Cl
Birmingham, Northfield
B29............... **103** A6
Birmingham, Yardley
B25............... **68** D1
Rickyard La B98..... **154** D5
Rickyard Piece B32 .. **84** E4
Ricoh Arena (Coventry
City FC) CV6.......**95** E3
Riddfield Rd B36.... **68** E8
Ridding La WS10 .....**41** F2
Riddings Cres WS3... **14** F4
Riddings Hill CV7 ... **130** C8
Riddings The
Birmingham B33..... **68** F4
Coventry CV5 ...... **132** E7
Stourbridge DY9..... **81** D2
Sutton Coldfield B76... **58** B8
Tamworth B77....... **21** E5
Wolverhampton WV10 . **26** A7
Riddon Dr LE10 ..... **75** B8
Ridesdale Gr CV31 .. **162** A1
Ridgacre Ent Pk B71..**53** B6
Ridgacre La B32 .... **84** C6
Ridgacre Rd
Birmingham B32..... **84** C6
West Bromwich B71... **53** B6
Ridgacre Rd W B32 .. **84** A6
Ridge Cl
Birmingham B13..... **105** C6
Willenhall WS2 ..... **27** D3
Ridge Ct CV5 ...... **112** A6
Ridgefield Rd B62... **83** C7
Ridge Gr DY9 ...... **81** C5
Ridge La WV11...... **26** D7
Ridgeley Cl CV34.... **155** E2
Ridgemount Dr B38 . **123** D8
Ridge Prim Sch The
DY8............... **80** C5
Ridge Rd DY6 ...... **60** C5
Ridge St DY8....... **80** C6
Ridgethorpe CV3.... **134** E6
Ridgewater Cl B45 .. **122** B6
Ridgeway
Birmingham B17..... **65** B2
Sedgley DY3 .... **50** D7
Ridgeway Ave
Birmingham B62..... **84** A6
Coventry CV3 ...... **133** C6
Ridgeway Cl B80... **159** E2
Ridgeway Ct WS2.....**27** F2
Ridgeway Dr WV4....**38** F2
Ridgeway Prim Sch
WS7...............**7** A5
Ridgeway Rd
Stourbridge DY8..... **60** F2
🄸 Tipton DY4......... **52** A8
Ridgeway Sch The
CV34.............. **156** A1

Ridgeway The
Birmingham, Quinton
B32............... **84** A4
Birmingham, Upper Witton
B23............... **56** A5
Burntwood WS7 .....**7** A4
Hinckley LE10 ...... **75** D6
Warwick CV34 ...... **156** A1
Ridgeway Trad Est
B96.............. **158** E1
Ridgewood B34..... **69** B6
Ridgewood Ave DY8.. **80** C7
Ridgewood Cl
Royal Leamington Spa
CV32 .... **156** C1
🄷 Walsall WS1 ...... **42** F8
Ridgewood Dr B75 ... **32** B1
Ridgewood Gdns B44 ..**55** F7
Ridgewood High Sch
DY8............... **80** C5
Ridgewood Rise B77 . **22** A5
Ridgley Rd CV4 ..... **131** E8
Ridgmont Croft B32.. **84** E5
Riding Cl B71.......**53** F7
Ridings Brook Dr 🄴
WS11 ....**2** A2
Ridings La B98..... **154** B6
Ridings Park Trad Est
WS11 ....**2** A3
Ridings The WS11 .....**4** F8
Riding Way WV12 ... **27** D6
Ridley St B1 .... **164** A1
Ridpool Prim Sch B33 **69** B3
Ridpool Rd B33..... **69** B3
Ridware Ho WS13 .....**3** E1
Rifle Range Rd DY11 **116** B3
Rifle St WV14 ...... **51** A8
Rigby Cl CV34...... **161** D4
Rigby Dr WS11...... **1** F4
Rigby Hall B60 .... **151** C8
Rigby Hall Day Specl Sch
B60.............. **151** C8
Rigby La B60....... **151** C8
Rigby St WS10 ..... **42** A1
Rigdale Cl CV2...... **114** E2
Righton Ho B77..... **21** D1
Riland Ave B75..... **46** D5
Riland Ct B72....... **57** C7
Riland Gr B75....... **46** C5
Riland Ind Est B75... **46** D5
Riland Rd B75...... **46** D5
Riley B77 .... **21** E3
Riley Cl CV8 .... **148** D4
Riley Cres WV4...... **39** A6
Riley Ho CV1....... **165** B2
Riley Rd B14....... **105** D3
Riley Sq CV2....... **96** B1
Riley St WV13...... **27** B2
Rills The LE10 ...... **71** E2
Rilstone Rd B32......**84** F5
Rindleford Ave WV4.. **38** C6
Ringhills Rd WV8.... **10** B2
Ringinglow Rd B44... **44** D2
Ringmere Ave B36 .. **69** B7
Ring Rd WS7........**6** E7
Ring Rd N B15......**85** F4
Ring Rd S B15 .....**85** F3
Ring Road St Andrews
WV1 .... **163** A3
Ring Road St Davids
WV1 .... **163** C3
Ring Road St Georges
WV2 .... **163** C2
Ring Road St Johns
WV2 .... **163** B2
Ring Road St Marks
WV3 .... **163** B2
Ring Road St Patricks
WV1 .... **163** C4
Ring Road St Peters
WV1 .... **163** B3
Ringswood Rd B92... **88** E4
Ring The B25....... **88** C8
Ringway WS11.......**1** E1
Ringway Hill Cross
CV1 .... **165** A3
Ringway Ind Est WS13 **.3** C3
Ringway Queens
CV1 .... **165** A2
Ringway Rudge CV1. **165** A2
Ringway St Johns
CV1 .... **165** C2
Ringway St Nicholas
CV1 .... **165** A2
Ringway St Patricks
CV1 .... **165** B1

Ringway Swanswell
 CV1 . . . . 165 C3
Ringway The DY10 . . 116 F5
Ringway Whitefriars
 CV1 . . . . 165 C3
Ringwood Ave WS9 . . . . 30 B5
Ringwood Dr B45 . . . . 102 A1
Ringwood Highway
 CV2 . . . . 96 E2
Ringwood Rd WV10 . . . 11 D1
Rinhill Gr CV31 . . . . . 162 D6
Ripley Cl B69 . . . . 62 F8
Ripley Gr B23 . . . . 56 B5
Riplingham 🖪 CV32 . . 156 F2
Ripon Cl CV5 . . . . 112 B8
Ripon Dr B71 . . . . 42 D1
Ripon Rd
 Birmingham B14 . . . . . 105 C4
 Walsall WS2 . . . . 28 B2
 Wolverhampton WV10 . . 25 C7
Rippingille Rd B43 . . . 44 C4
Ripple Rd B30 . . . . . . 104 B7
Risborough Cl CV5 . . 112 C3
Rischale Way WS4 . . . 29 D8
Risdale Cl CV32 . . . . . 156 C1
Rise Ave B45 . . . . 122 A7
Riseley Cres B5 . . . . . 86 D7
Rise The
 Birmingham, Great Barr
  B42 . . . . 55 A8
 Birmingham, Marston Green
  B37 . . . . 90 A7
 Hopwood B48 . . . . 123 B4
 Kingswinford DY6 . . . . . 60 E5
 Lichfield WS13 . . . . 8 F7
Rising Brook WV6 . . . . 24 B4
Rising La
 Chadwick End B93 . . . 145 B5
 Kingswood B94, B93 . . . 144 F5
Rising Rd B94 . . . . . . 144 C5
Rissington Ave B29 . . 104 A8
Ritchie Cl B13 . . . . . . 87 A1
Rivendell Ct B28 . . . . 87 E1
Rivendell Gdns WV6 . . 24 B5
Riverbank Rd WV13 . . . 27 C2
River Brook Dr B30 . . 104 B8
River Cl Bedworth CV12 . 77 F1
 Royal Leamington Spa
  CV32 . . . . 161 D8
River Ct 🖪 CV1 . . . . . 113 B3
Riverdrive B78, B79 . . . 21 B3
Riverfield Gr B77 . . . . . 21 D5
Riverford Croft CV4 . . 132 D4
River Lee Rd B11 . . . . . 87 E5
Rivermead CV11 . . . . . 73 A4
Rivermead Pk B34 . . . . 69 A6
Riversdale 🖪 CV32 . . 161 E8
Riversdale Rd B14 . . . 105 D3
Riverside
 Royal Leamington Spa
  CV32 . . . . 161 E8
 Studley B80 . . . . 159 F5
Riverside Cl
 Coventry CV3 . . . . 134 A7
 Lickey End B60 . . . . . . 137 C6
Riverside Cres B28 . . 105 D4
Riverside Ct
 Birmingham B38 . . . . . 103 D3
 🖪 Coleshill B46 . . . . . . 70 F7
Riverside Dr
 Birmingham, Cannon Hill
  B29 . . . . 86 C3
 Birmingham, Stechford
  B33 . . . . 68 D4
 Solihull B91 . . . . 107 C4
Riverside Gdns WV8 . . 10 B5
Riverside Ind Est B78 . 21 B1
Riverslea Rd CV3 . . . . 114 C1
Riversleigh Dr DY8 . . . 80 E8
Riversleigh Rd CV32 . 156 C1
Riversley Rd CV11 . . . 73 C3
River St B5 . . . . 67 A2
Riverway WS10 . . . . . . 42 B2
River Wlk CV2 . . . . 96 C2
Rivington Cl DY8 . . . . . 80 E4
Rivington Cres B44 . . . 45 C1
Roach B77 . . . . 35 D6
Roach Cl
 Birmingham B37 . . . . . . 70 C3
 Brierley Hill DY5 . . . . . . 61 D6
Roach Cres WV11 . . . . 26 F8
Roach Pool Croft B16 65 C2
Road No 1 DY10 . . . . 116 E2
Road No 2 DY10 . . . . 116 E2
Road No 3 DY10 . . . . 116 E2
Roadway Cl CV12 . . . . 78 B2
Roanne Ringway
 CV11 . . . . 73 B4

Robert Ave B23 . . . . . . 56 E6
Robert Cl
 Coventry CV3 . . . . 134 C4
 Tamworth B79 . . . . 20 F7
Robert Cramb Ave
 CV4 . . . . 131 F8
Robert Ct
 Birmingham, Pheasey
  B44 . . . . 44 D4
 🖪 Birmingham, Wake Green
  B13 . . . . 87 B2
Robert Rd
 Bedworth CV7 . . . . 95 F8
 Birmingham B20 . . . . . . 55 B1
 Tipton DY4 . . . . 51 F6
Roberts Cl
 Brownhills WS9 . . . . . . 15 C2
 Darlaston WS10 . . . . . . 41 B4
Roberts Ct B24 . . . . . . 57 C6
Roberts Green Rd
 DY3 . . . . 50 A4
Roberts La DY9 . . . . . . 99 B8
Robertson Knoll B36 . . 68 F7
Robertsons Gdns 🖪
 B7 . . . . 67 C7
Roberts Prim Sch
 DY3 . . . . 50 D4
Roberts Rd
 Birmingham B27 . . . . . . 88 D3
 Walsall WS5 . . . . 28 F5
 Wednesbury WS10 . . . . 42 E2
Robert St DY3 . . . . 50 D4
Robert Wynd WV14 . . . 40 A1
Robeson Cl DY4 . . . . . 51 D5
Robey's La B78 . . . . . . 22 D3
Robin Cl
 Birmingham B36 . . . . . . 70 A8
 Huntington WS12 . . . . . . 1 C7
 Kingswinford DY6 . . . . . 61 A6
 Tamworth B77 . . . . 35 C8
Robin Ct DY10 . . . . . . 117 A2
Robin Gr WV11 . . . . . . 26 C7
Robin Hood Cres
 B28 . . . . 105 E7
Robin Hood Croft
 B28 . . . . 105 F6
Robin Hood La B28 . . 105 E7
Robin Hood Rd
 Brierley Hill DY5 . . . . . . 61 F2
 Coventry CV3 . . . . 134 C6
Robin Hood Sch B28 106 B6
Robinia B77 . . . . 22 A4
Robinia Cl CV32 . . . . 157 B2
Robin Rd B23 . . . . 56 E5
Robins Bsns Pk B70 . . 52 E7
Robins Cl WS6 . . . . 4 D1
Robin's Cl DY8 . . . . . . 81 A3
Robins Croft WS11 . . . . 2 A1
Robins Ct B14 . . . . 86 F1
Robinsfield Dr B31 . . . 123 A7
Robins Gr CV34 . . . . . 160 C4
Robins Hill Dr B48 . . . 139 A5
Robins La B97 . . . . . . 153 C6
Robinson Cl B79 . . . . . 20 E7
Robinson Rd
 Bedworth CV12 . . . . . . 95 D8
 Burntwood WS7 . . . . 6 F8
Robinson's Way B76 . . 58 D5
Robinson Way LE10 . . . 75 F4
Robins Rd WS7 . . . . 6 E7
Robins Way CV10 . . . . 72 A3
Robin Wlk WS2 . . . . . . 27 F3
Robottom Cl WS2 . . . . 28 B6
Robson Cl WS8 . . . . . . 15 F5
Rocester Ave WV11 . . . 26 E7
Rochdale Wlk B10 . . . . 87 C7
Roche Rd WS3 . . . . . . 13 F1
Robey's La B78 . . . . . . 22 D3
Rochester Ave WS7 . . . . 7 A7
Rochester Cl
 Nuneaton CV11 . . . . . . 73 B3
 Redditch B97 . . . . 158 C8
Rochester Croft WS2 . . 28 A4
Rochester Rd
 Birmingham B31 . . . . . 103 A4
 Coventry CV5 . . . . 132 E8
Rochester Way WS12 . . . 2 C1
Rochester Wlk DY10 . . 117 C5
Roche The WS13 . . . . . 8 A8
Roche Way WS3 . . . . . 13 F1
Rochford Cl
 Birmingham B45 . . . . . 121 E7
 Halesowen B63 . . . . . . 82 F2
 Sutton Coldfield B76 . . . 58 A8
 🖪 Walsall WS2 . . . . . . 42 C7
Rochford Ct
 Royal Leamington Spa
  CV31 . . . . 161 E7
 Solihull B90 . . . . 127 A6
Rochford Gr WV4 . . . . 38 D5
Rock Ave B45 . . . . . . 122 C7

Rock Cl CV6 . . . . 96 B1
Rock Cotts 🖪 DY11 . . 116 D6
Rocken End CV6 . . . . . 113 D8
Rocket Pool Dr WV14 . . 41 A2
Rockford Cl B98 . . . . . 158 F5
Rockford Rd B42 . . . . . 55 A7
Rock Gr B92 . . . . 88 E3
Rock Hill
 Bromsgrove B61 . . . . . 150 D7
 Weeford B78, WS14 . . . 19 C4
Rockingham Cl
 Dorridge B93 . . . . 127 D2
 Dudley DY3 . . . . 50 B3
 Walsall WS3 . . . . 14 B1
Rockingham Dr
 Nuneaton CV11 . . . . . . 78 F7
 Perton WV6 . . . . 23 F3
Rockingham Gdns
 B74 . . . . 46 B6
Rockingham Hall Gdns
 DY9 . . . . 99 D7
Rockingham Rd B25 . . 88 D8
Rock La CV7 . . . . 94 C7
Rockland Dr B33 . . . . . 68 E4
Rockland Gdns WV13 . 40 F8
Rocklands Cres WS13 . . 3 D1
Rocklands Dr B75 . . . . 46 B8
Rocklands Sch WS13 . . . 9 D8
Rockmead Ave B44 . . . 44 F2
Rock Mill CV32 . . . . . . 156 C1
Rock Mill La CV32 . . . 161 C8
Rockmoor Cl B37 . . . . 69 E3
Rock Rd Sedgley WV14 . 50 F8
 Solihull B92 . . . . 88 E3
Rockrose Gdns WV10 . . 12 A7
Rock St DY3 . . . . 50 E5
Rock The WV6 . . . . . . 24 D5
Rockville Rd B8 . . . . . . 68 A4
Rockwell La B48 . . . . 139 E4
Rockwood Rd B27 . . . . 88 B4
Rocky La
 Birmingham, Aston
  B6 . . . . 67 A6
 Birmingham, Great Barr
  B42 . . . . 55 B5
 Birmingham, Nechells Green
  B7 . . . . 67 B6
 Catshill B61 . . . . 136 E7
 Kenilworth CV8 . . . . . . 148 D2
Rodborough Rd
 Birmingham B26 . . . . . . 89 B7
 Dorridge B93 . . . . 127 E3
Rodbourne Rd B17 . . . 85 C3
Roddis Cl B23 . . . . 56 D8
Roden Ave DY10 . . . . . 117 A7
Roderick Dr WV11 . . . . 26 D7
Roderick Rd B11 . . . . . 87 C5
Rodhouse Cl CV4 . . . . 111 D1
Rodlington Ave B44 . . . 44 F1
Rodman Cl B15 . . . . . . 85 D8
Rodney Cl
 Birmingham B16 . . . . . . 66 A2
 Hinckley LE10 . . . . 71 D4
 Solihull B92 . . . . 89 B1
Rodney Rd B92 . . . . . . 89 B1
Rodway Cl
 Birmingham B19 . . . . . . 66 E7
 Brierley Hill DY5 . . . . . . 81 D7
 Wolverhampton WV4 . . . 39 D3
Rodway Dr CV5 . . . . . 111 D4
Rodwell Gr B44 . . . . . . 56 A8
Rodyard Way CV1 . . . 165 C1
Roebuck Cl B34 . . . . . . 69 E5
Roebuck Glade WV12 . 27 E4
Roebuck La
 Smethwick B66 . . . . . . 64 F8
 West Bromwich B70 . . . 53 E1
Roebuck Pl WS3 . . . . . 28 E6
Roebuck Rd WS3 . . . . 28 E6
Roebuck St B70 . . . . . 53 F1
Roe Cl CV34 . . . . 160 F8
Roedean Cl B44 . . . . . 56 B7
Roford Ct DY3 . . . . . . 50 E5
Rogerfield Rd B23 . . . . 57 A6
Rogers Cl WV11 . . . . . 13 A2
Rogers Rd B8 . . . . 68 B5
Rogers Way CV34 . . . . 160 B4
Rogue's La LE9, LE10 . 71 C6
Rokeby Cl B76 . . . . . . 46 E4
Rokeby Rd B43 . . . . . . 43 F2
Rokeby Wlk B34 . . . . . 69 A6
Rokewood Cl DY6 . . . . 49 D1
Rokholt Cres WS11 . . . . 1 C1
Roland Ave CV6 . . . . . 95 C3
Roland Gdns 🖪 B19 . . 66 C8
Roland Gr 🖪 B19 . . . . 66 C8
Roland Mount CV6 . . . 95 C3
Rolan Dr B90 . . . . 125 E8

Roland Rd B19 . . . . . . 66 C8
Roland Terr 🖪 B19 . . . 66 C8
Roland Vernon Way
 DY4 . . . . 52 C7
Rolfe St B66 . . . . 65 A6
Rollason Cl CV6 . . . . . 113 C8
Rollason Rd
 Birmingham B24 . . . . . . 57 A3
 Coventry CV6 . . . . 113 B8
 🖪 Dudley DY2 . . . . 62 D8
Rollason's Yd CV6 . . . . 96 A3
Rollesby Dr WV13 . . . . 40 F8
Rolling Mill Cl B5 . . . . 86 D7
Rolling Mill Rd WS11 . . 5 F4
Rollingmill St WS2 . . . 28 C1
Rollswood Dr B91 . . . 107 A4
Rolvenden CV13 . . . . . 27 C2
Roman Cl WS8 . . . . 6 E2
Roman Ct
 Birmingham B38 . . . . . 124 B8
 Cannock WS11 . . . . 4 E5
 Tamworth B77 . . . . 35 E7
Roman La B74 . . . . 31 B4
Romani Cl CV34 . . . . . 160 D7
Roman La B74 . . . . 31 B4
Roman Pk
 Coleshill B46 . . . . 59 F1
 Sutton Coldfield B74 . . . 31 B4
Roman Pl B74 . . . . 31 B2
Roman Rd
 Coventry CV2 . . . . 114 B3
 Sutton Coldfield B74 . . . 31 C4
Roman Rd (Sandy La)
 DY8 . . . . 80 C3
Romans Grange B74 . . 31 C5
Roman View WS11 . . . . 4 F5
Roman Way
 Birmingham B15 . . . . . . 85 D3
 Bromsgrove B61 . . . . . 137 B4
 Coleshill B46 . . . . 59 F2
 Coventry CV3 . . . . 133 D3
 Lichfield WS14 . . . . 9 D7
 Rowley Regis B65 . . . . 63 C3
 Tamworth B77 . . . . 20 F7
Roman Way Fst Sch
 B98 . . . . 154 E3
Roman Wlk WS14 . . . . . 8 D2
Romany Rd B45 . . . . . 101 D1
Romany Way DY8 . . . . 80 C3
Roma Rd B11 . . . . 87 E5
Romeo Arbour CV34 . 161 E3
Romford Cl B26 . . . . . . 89 B6
Romford Rd CV6 . . . . . 95 B2
Romilly Ave B20 . . . . . 55 B3
Romilly Cl
 Lichfield WS14 . . . . 9 E7
 Stourbridge DY8 . . . . . . 80 E6
 Sutton Coldfield B76 . . . 47 A4
Romney B77 . . . . 35 F8
Romney Cl
 Birmingham B28 . . . . . 105 F4
 Hinckley LE10 . . . . 71 A3
Romney House Ind Est
 WS10 . . . . 41 B7
Romney Way B43 . . . . 44 D4
Romsey Ave CV10 . . . . 73 D8
Romsey Gr WV10 . . . . 11 C3
Romsey Ho WS2 . . . . . 42 C7
Romsey Rd WV10 . . . . 11 C3
Romsey Way WS3 . . . . 13 F3
Romsley Cl
 Birmingham B45 . . . . . 121 E8
 Halesowen B63 . . . . . . 83 B2
 Redditch B98 . . . . 154 F3
 Walsall WS4 . . . . 15 C2
Romsley Hill Grange
 B62 . . . . 100 F1
Romsley Rd
 Birmingham B32 . . . . . 102 B8
 Coventry CV6 . . . . 113 C6
 Oldbury B68 . . . . 64 B2
 Stourbridge DY9 . . . . . . 81 C5
Romsley, St Kenelm's CE
 Fst Sch B62 . . . . 101 A4
Romulus Cl B20 . . . . . . 55 B3
Ronald Gr B36 . . . . 58 D1
Ronald Pl B9 . . . . 67 E2
Ronald Rd B9 . . . . 67 D2
Ron Davis Cl B66 . . . . 65 B5
Ro-Oak Rd CV6 . . . . . 112 F5
Rood End Prim Sch
 B68 . . . . 64 C6
Rood End Rd B69 . . . . 64 C7
Rooker Ave WV2 . . . . . 39 F6
Rooker Cres WV2 . . . . 39 F6
Rookery Ave
 Brierley Hill DY5 . . . . . . 61 A2
 Wolverhampton WV4 . . . 40 A3
Rookery Cl B97 . . . . . . 153 D1
Rookery Ct WS13 . . . . . 8 E7

Rookery La
 Aldridge WS9 . . . . 30 B6
 Coventry CV6 . . . . 95 B4
 Weeford B75, B78 . . . . 19 C2
 Wolverhampton WV2 . . . 39 B6
Rookery Par WS9 . . . . 30 B6
Rookery Pk DY5 . . . . . 61 B5
Rookery Rd
 Birmingham B29 . . . . . . 85 F2
 Birmingham, Handsworth
  B21 . . . . 54 E1
 Wolverhampton WV14,
  WV4 . . . . 40 A3
 Wombourne WV5 . . . . . 49 B6
Rookery Rise WV5 . . . . 49 B6
Rookery Sch B21 . . . . 54 E1
Rookery St WV11 . . . . 26 C5
Rookery The B62 . . . . . 84 A2
Rooks Mdw DY9 . . . . . 99 B6
Rookwood Dr WV6 . . . 23 F2
Roosevelt Dr CV4 . . . . 111 E2
Rooth St WS10 . . . . . . 42 B4
Roper Way DY3 . . . . . . 50 F6
Roper Wlk DY3 . . . . . . 50 F6
Rosafield Ave B62 . . . . 83 F6
Rosalind Ave DY1 . . . . 51 B6
Rosalind Gr WV11 . . . . 27 A5
Rosamond St WS1 . . . . 42 D7
Rosary RC Prim Sch
 B8 . . . . 67 E3
Rosary Rd B23 . . . . . . 56 D3
Rosary Villas 🖪 B11 . . 87 C5
Rosaville Cres CV5 . . . 112 A6
Rose Ave
 Alvechurch B48 . . . . . . 139 A5
 Birmingham B68 . . . . . . 84 C7
 Coventry CV6 . . . . 112 F5
 Kingswinford DY6 . . . . . 60 F5
Rosebank Dr WS3 . . . . 28 E4
Rosebay Ave B38 . . . . 123 E4
Rose Bay Mdw 🖪
 WS11 . . . . 2 C2
Roseberry Ave CV2 . . . 96 C1
Rosebery Rd
 Smethwick B66 . . . . . . 65 C4
 Tamworth B77 . . . . 35 D4
Rosebery St
 Birmingham B18 . . . . . . 66 A4
 Wolverhampton WV3 . . . 25 B1
Rosebriars B90 . . . . . . 125 E7
Rose Cl B66 . . . . 65 C5
Rose Cottage Dr 🖪
 DY8 . . . . 60 D3
Rose Cottage Flats
 CV5 . . . . 111 D5
Rose Cotts
 🖪 Birmingham B29 . . . . 85 F2
 Birmingham, Stirchley
  B30 . . . . 104 A6
Rose Croft CV8 . . . . . 147 E6
Rosecroft Rd B26 . . . . 89 C6
Rose Ct
 Balsall Common CV7 . . 130 B8
 Dudley DY2 . . . . 51 F4
Rosedale Ave
 Birmingham B23 . . . . . . 56 E3
 Smethwick B66 . . . . . . 65 C5
Rosedale CE Inf Sch
 WV12 . . . . 27 D5
Rosedale Cl B97 . . . . . 153 A4
Rosedale Gr B25 . . . . . 88 C8
Rosedale Pl WV13 . . . . 41 A8
Rosedale Rd B25 . . . . . 88 C8
Rosedale Wlk DY6 . . . . 60 E8
Rosedene Dr B20 . . . . 54 F2
Rose Dr WS8 . . . . 15 E5
Rosefield Croft B6 . . . . 66 F7
Rosefield Ct B67 . . . . . 65 A4
Rosefield Pl 🖪 CV32 . 161 F8
Rosefield Rd B67 . . . . . 65 A4
Rosefield St CV32 . . . 162 A8
Rosefield Wlk 🖪
 CV32 . . . . 161 F8
Rosegardens The B63 . 82 E2
Rosegreen Cl CV3 . . . 133 E6
Rosehall Cl
 Redditch B98 . . . . 158 E6
Rosehill B91 . . . . 106 F1
Rosehill WS12 . . . . 1 F8
Rose Hill
 Barnt Green B45 . . . . . 122 B4
 Brierley Hill DY5 . . . . . . 62 A1
 Darlaston WV13 . . . . . . 41 A8
Rose Hill Cl B36 . . . . . 69 B8
Rose Hill Gdns WV13 . 27 B1
Rose Hill Rd B21 . . . . . 66 A7
Rosehip Dr CV2 . . . . . 114 B6
Rose La Burntwood WS7 . 7 C7
 Dodford B61 . . . . 136 A6

Rose La continued
 Nuneaton CV11 . . . . . . 73 C3
 Oldbury B69 . . . . 52 C2
Roseland Ave DY2 . . . . 51 F1
Roseland Rd CV8 . . . . 147 F3
Roselands Ave CV2 . . . 114 D8
Roseland Way 🖪 B15 . 66 B1
Roseleigh Rd B45 . . . . 122 B6
Rosemary Ave
 Bilston WV14 . . . . 40 F6
 Cheslyn Hay WS6 . . . . . 4 D3
 Wolverhampton WV4 . . . 39 C6
Rosemary Cl
 Brownhills WS8 . . . . . . 15 D6
 Coventry CV4 . . . . 111 E3
Rosemary Cres
 Dudley DY1 . . . . 51 A6
 Wolverhampton WV4 . . . 39 C5
Rosemary Cres W
 WV4 . . . . 39 B5
Rosemary Ct B74 . . . . 31 D4
Rosemary Dr
 Huntington WS12 . . . . . . 1 D5
 Stoke Prior B60 . . . . . 150 C1
 Sutton Coldfield B74 . . . 31 D4
Rosemary Hill CV8 . . . 147 F5
Rosemary Hill Rd B74 31 D4
Rosemary La DY8 . . . . 80 D3
Rosemary Mews CV8 147 F5
Rosemary Nook B74 . . 31 D4
Rosemary Rd
 Birmingham B33 . . . . . . 68 F2
 Cheslyn Hay WS6 . . . . . 4 D3
 Halesowen B63 . . . . . . 82 C2
 Kidderminster DY10 . . . 117 B7
 Tamworth B77 . . . . 21 F4
 Tipton DY4 . . . . 52 A6
Rosemary Way LE10 . . 75 B7
Rosemont Ho B93 . . . 127 F3
Rosemoor Dr DY5 . . . . 81 B7
Rosemount
 Birmingham B32 . . . . . . 84 D5
 Wolverhampton WV6 . . . 24 D5
Rosemount Cl CV2 . . . 114 E7
Rosemullion Cl CV7 . . 96 B8
Rose Rd
 Birmingham B17 . . . . . . 85 D6
 Coleshill B46 . . . . 70 F5
Rose St WV14 . . . . 40 F4
Rose Terr B45 . . . . . . 138 D8
Rosetti Cl DY10 . . . . . 117 C6
Roseville Ct 🖪 WV14 . 51 C8
Roseville Gdns WV8 . . 10 A4
Roseville Prec 🖪
 WV14 . . . . 51 C8
Rosewood CV11 . . . . . 73 F1
Rosewood Cl
 Hinckley LE10 . . . . 75 F6
 Tamworth B77 . . . . 21 D4
Rosewood Cres
 CV32 . . . . 157 B2
Rosewood Ct B77 . . . . 21 D4
Rosewood Dr
 Barnt Green B45 . . . . . 138 C7
 Birmingham B23 . . . . . . 56 D2
 Willenhall WV12 . . . . . . 27 B8
Rosewood Gdns
 WV11 . . . . 13 B3
Rosewood Pk WS6 . . . . 4 D2
Rosewood Rd DY1 . . . . 51 B5
Rosewood Sch DY1 . . . 50 E1
Roshven Rd B12 . . . . . 87 A4
Roslin B60 . . . . 137 B1
Roslin Gr B19 . . . . 66 C6
Roslyn Cl B66 . . . . 65 A6
Ross B65 . . . . 63 B2
Ross Cl Coventry CV5 . 112 A5
 Wolverhampton WV6 . . . 24 E2
Ross Dr DY6 . . . . 60 C7
Rosse Ct B92 . . . . 107 F8
Rossendale Cl B63 . . . 82 D6
Rossendale Way CV10 . 72 C2
Ross Hts B65 . . . . 63 B3
Rosslyn Ave CV6 . . . . 112 E6
Rosslyn Rd B76 . . . . . . 57 F6
Ross Rd WS3 . . . . 28 F6
Roston Dr LE10 . . . . . . 71 A4
Rostrevor Rd B10 . . . . 67 F1
Rosy Cross B79 . . . . . . 21 B5
Rotary Ct 🖪 WV3 . . . . 25 B2
Rotary Ho DY1 . . . . . . 50 F1
Rothay B77 . . . . 35 F8
Rotherby Gr B37 . . . . . 90 B4
Rotherfield Cl CV31 . . 162 B7
Rotherfield Rd B26 . . . 89 B8
Rotherham Rd CV6 . . . 95 C3
Rotherhams Oak La
 B94 . . . . 142 F7

Rothesay Ave CV4 ... 112 B2
Rothesay Cl CV10 ... 73 A2
Rothesay Croft B32 . 102 B7
Rothesay Dr DY8 ..... 60 C3
Rothesay Way WV12 . . 27 B6
Rothley Wlk B38 ... 123 C8
Rothwell Dr B91 .... 106 D4
Rothwell Rd CV34 ... 155 C1
Rotten Row WS14 ......9 C7
Rotten Row Barns
　B93 .... 128 C4
Rotton Park Rd B16 . . 65 D2
Rotton Park St B16 ...65 F3
Rough Coppice Wlk
　B35 .... 58 A2
Rough Hay Pl WS10 . . 41 C7
Rough Hay Prim Sch
　WS10 .... 41 C7
Rough Hay Rd WS10 . 41 C7
Rough Hill Dr
　Redditch B98 .... 158 F6
　Rowley Regis B65 ..... 62 F6
Rough Hills Cl WV2 ...39 F6
Rough Hills Rd WV2 ..39 F6
Roughknowles Rd
　CV4 .... 131 D6
Roughlea Ave B36 .....68 F7
Roughley Dr B75 ... 32 C2
Roughley Farm Rd
　B75 .... 32 E3
Rough Rd B44 ..... 45 A3
Rough The B97 .... 158 D8
Rough Wood Ctry Pk
　WV12 ....27 E6
Rouncil Cl B92 ..... 107 D7
Rouncil La CV8 ..... 155 C8
Roundabout The
　B31 .... 102 D1
Round Cl B90 ...... 126 A6
Round Croft WV13 ... 27 A2
Round Hill DY3 ...... 39 D2
Round Hill Ave DY9 .. 81 C1
Roundhill Cl B76 ..... 46 E4
Roundhills Rd B62 ....83 F8
Roundhill Terr B62 ... 63 E1
Roundhill Way WS8 ...7 A2
Round Hill Wharf
　DY11 .... 116 D5
Round House Rd
　Coventry CV3 ...... 134 B8
　Dudley DY3 .... 50 E4
Roundlea Cl WV12 ... 27 B7
Roundlea Rd B31 ... 102 E7
Round Moor Wlk B35 58 A3
Round Oak Sch The
　CV32 .... 157 A3
Round Rd B24 ...... 57 B2
Round Saw Croft
　B45 .... 121 F8
Rounds Green Prim Sch
　B69 ....63 E7
Rounds Green Rd B69 .63 F7
Rounds Hill CV8 ..... 147 E2
Rounds Hill Rd WV14 . 51 D8
Rounds Rd WV14 ... 40 D3
Round St DY2 ...... 62 C6
Roundway Down WV6 .23 F3
Rounton Cl B74 ...... 31 D4
Rousay Cl B45 ..... 101 F1
Rousdon Gr B43 ..... 54 D8
Rover Dr
　Birmingham, Acock's Green
　B27 ....88 D4
　Birmingham, Castle
　Bromwich B36 ...... 58 F1
Rover Rd CV1 ...... 165 B2
Rovex Bsns Pk B11 ...87 F5
Rowallan Rd B75 ..... 32 C2
Rowan Cl
　Binley Woods CV3 .... 135 D7
　Bromsgrove B61...... 136 E2
　Hollywood B47 ..... 125 B5
　Lichfield WS14 ...... 9 D8
　Sutton Coldfield B76 ... 46 F2
Rowan Cres
　Dudley WV14 ..... 40 B1
　Redditch B97 .... 153 A4
　Wolverhampton WV3 ... 38 E7
Rowan Ct
　Birmingham B30 .... 104 A2
　Oldbury B66 .... 64 D8
Rowan Dr
　Birmingham B28 .... 106 A5
　Essington WV11 .... 13 B3
　[6] Warwick CV34 .... 160 F8
Rowan Gr
　Burntwood WS7 ....6 F7
　Coventry CV2 ...... 96 E2
Rowan Rd
　Cannock WS11 ....1 C2

Rowan Rd continued
　Nuneaton CV10....... 72 C6
　Redditch B97 .... 153 A4
　Sedgley DY3 .... 39 F1
　Sutton Coldfield B72.... 46 C3
　Walsall WS5 .... 42 F4
Rowan Rise DY6........ 60 E6
Rowans The CV12 .... 77 E2
Rowantrees B45 .... 122 B5
Rowan Way
　Birmingham, Chelmsley
　Wood B37.......... 70 C1
　Birmingham, Longbridge
　B31................ 122 F8
　Hartshill CV10....... 72 A8
Roway La B69........ 52 F1
Rowborough Cl B96. 158 E2
Rowbrook Cl B90 ... 125 E8
Rowcroft Covert
　B14 .... 104 C2
Rowcroft Rd CV2 ... 115 A6
Rowdale Rd B42 .... 55 C6
Rowden Dr
　Birmingham B23 ..... 57 A6
　Solihull B91 .... 106 E2
Rowena Gdns DY3 ... 39 C2
Rowheath Ho B30 ... 103 E5
Rowheath Rd B30 ... 103 E5
Rowington Ave B65 . . 63 D3
Rowington Cl CV6 ... 112 D5
Rowington Gn CV35 . 144 F1
Rowington Rd B34 .. 69 E6
Rowington Terr B25 . . 88 B7
Rowland Ave B80 ... 159 E3
Rowland Gdns WS2 .. 28 C3
Rowland Hill Ave
　DY11 .... 116 B5
Rowland Hill Ctr [9]
　DY10............... 116 E6
Rowland Hill Dr DY4 . 52 C5
Rowlands Ave
　Walsall WS2 .... 27 E3
　Wolverhampton WV1 .. 26 B2
Rowlands Cl WS2 .... 27 E4
Rowlands Cres B91.. 107 C4
Rowlands Rd B26 .... 88 E7
Rowland St WS2 .... 28 C3
Rowland Way (Road 1a)
　DY11 .... 116 E1
Rowley Cl WS12 ....2 B8
Rowley Dr CV3 ..... 134 B4
Rowley Gr B33 ..... 69 D3
Rowley Hall Ave B65 . 63 C4
Rowley Hall Prim Sch
　B65................ 63 C4
Rowley Hill View B64 ..82 F8
Rowley La CV3 ..... 134 D3
Rowley Pl WS4 ...... 29 B7
Rowley Rd
　Coventry CV3, CV8 ... 134 B3
　Whitnash CV31 ..... 162 A2
Rowley Regis Com Hospl
　B65.................. 63 B2
Rowley Regis Sta B65 63 C2
Rowley's Green La
　CV6 .... 95 E4
Rowleys Green Lane Ind
　Est CV6 ....95 E4
Rowley St WS1 ...... 29 A2
Rowley View
　Bilston WV14 .... 41 A3
　Darlaston WS10 ..... 41 C4
　West Bromwich B70 . . . 53 B3
Rowley Village B65 ... 63 C3
Rowney Croft B28 .. 105 E4
Rowney Green La
　B48 .... 139 F5
Rowood Dr B91, B92.. 107 D7
Row The CV7........ 97 D3
Rowthorn Cl B74 .... 45 A7
Rowthorn Dr B90 ... 127 A6
Rowton Ave WV6 .... 23 E3
Rowton Dr B74......44 F5
Roxall Cl DY10 ...... 98 C2
Roxboro Ho B97 ... 153 D2
Roxburgh Croft
　CV32 .... 157 C6
Roxburgh Gr B43.... 44 C4
Roxburgh Rd
　Nuneaton CV11....... 73 D3
　Sutton Coldfield B73... 46 A3
Roxby Gdns WV6.... 25 A5
Royal Brierley
　Glassworks* DY5... 61 C2
Royal Cl
　Brierley Hill DY5 ..... 81 C8
　Rowley Regis B65..... 63 C5
Royal Cres CV3...... 134 C5
Royal Ct Hinckley LE10. 75 D7
　Sutton Coldfield B73... 46 B2

Royal Gr [3] B23 ...... 56 B7
Royal Leamington Spa
Rehabilitation Hospl
　CV34 .... 161 E4
Royal London Bldgs
　WV1 .... 163 C3
Royal Mail St B1 ... 164 B2
Royal Oak La CV7,
　CV12 .... 95 C7
Royal Oak Rd
　Halesowen B62...... 83 F5
　Rowley Regis B65..... 62 F5
Royal Oak Yd CV12 ... 78 B4
Royal Orthopaedic Hospl
The B31 .... 103 B5
Royal Priors [18] CV32 156 F1
Royal Rd B72 ..... 46 C4
Royal Scot Gr WS1 .. 42 D5
Royal Star Cl B33 ... 69 C2
Royal Sta The WV1.. 163 D2
Royal Way DY4 ..... 52 A2
Royal Wolverhampton
Sch The WV3.......39 B7
Royal Worcester Cres
　B60 .... 137 C1
Roy Carver Ctr The (St
John Ambulance HQ)
　WV1 .... 163 D2
Roydon Rd B27 .... 106 C8
Roylesden Cres B73 .. 45 C2
Royston Chase B74... 31 A3
Royston Cl CV3 .... 115 A3
Royston Croft B12....86 F6
Royston Ct [7] B13... 87 B2
Royston Way DY3 ... 50 C8
Rubens Cl
　Coventry CV5 ...... 112 C3
　Dudley DY3 .... 50 D5
Rubery Cl WS10 ..... 41 C7
Rubery Farm Gr B45 121 F7
Rubery Field Cl B45. 102 B1
Rubery La B45 ..... 102 A1
Rubery La S B45 .... 121 F8
Rubery St WS10 .... 41 D8
Ruckleigh Sch B91 . 107 C4
Ruckley Ave [4] B19 ... 66 C7
Ruckley Rd B29 .... 103 B8
Rudd Gdns WV10.... 26 B4
Rudgard Rd CV6 .... 96 A4
Rudge Ave WV1 .... 26 B3
Rudge Cl WV12 ..... 27 C4
Rudge Croft B33 .... 69 A4
Rudgewick Croft [1]
　B6 ....66 F6
Rudge Wlk B18 ..... 66 A3
Rudyard Cl WV10.... 11 E4
Rudyard Gr B33 .... 69 B3
Rudyngfield Dr B33 ...68 F4
Rufford B79............ 20 E6
Rufford Cl
　Birmingham B23 ..... 56 D8
　Hinckley LE10 ...... 75 D3
Rufford Prim Sch
　DY9................ 81 C5
Rufford Rd DY9 ..... 81 C4
Rufford St DY9 ..... 81 D5
Rufford Way WS9 ... 29 E7
Rugby Rd
　Binley Woods CV3... 135 D8
　Bulkington CV12 .... 79 D2
　Cubbington CV32 .... 157 E6
　Hinckley LE10 ...... 75 D5
　Royal Leamington Spa
　CV32.............. 156 D1
　Stourbridge DY8 .... 80 D7
Rugby St WV1....... 25 B4
Rugeley Ave WV12 ... 27 D6
Rugeley Cl DY4 ..... 51 E5
Rugeley Rd
　Burntwood, Gorstey Ley
　WS7 ....7 C7
　Cannock, Hednesford
　WS12 ....2 F6
　Cannock, West Hill
　WS12 ....2 D7
Ruislip Cl B35........ 58 A4
Ruiton St DY3........ 50 D4
Rumbow B63 ..... 83 B4
Rumbow La B62..... 100 D3
Rumbush La
　Earlswood B90, B94... 125 F3
　Solihull B90........ 126 A5
Rumer Hill Bsns Est
　WS11................4 E7
Rumer Hill Rd WS11....4 F8
Runcorn Cl
　Birmingham B37..... 70 C4
　Redditch B98 .... 158 F8
Runcorn Rd B12..... 87 A5
Runcorn Wlk [10] CV2 115 A7

Runnymede Gdns
　CV10 ....72 F3
Runnymede Dr CV7 . 130 C5
Runnymede Rd B11 .. 87 E3
Rupert Rd CV6 ..... 113 B8
Rupert St
　Birmingham B7....... 67 A4
　Wolverhampton WV3 .. 25 A2
Rushall Cl
　Stourbridge DY8 .... 80 E8
　Walsall WS4 .... 29 B4
Rushall Com Coll
　WS4 ....29 B6
Rushall Ct B43 .... 54 E7
Rushall JMI Sch WS4 .15 B1
Rushall Manor Cl
　WS4 .... 29 B4
Rushall Manor Rd
　WS4 .... 29 B4
Rushall Rd WV10 ... 11 E2
Rushbrook Cl
　Brownhills WS8 ..... 15 D6
　Solihull B92........ 88 E2
Rushbrooke Cl B13....86 F4
Rushbrooke Dr B73 .. 45 C3
Rushbrook Gr B14 .. 104 C4
Rushbrook La B94... 141 D3
Rushbury Cl
　Bilston WV14 .... 40 B5
　Solihull B90........ 106 D4
Rushden Croft B44....44 F1
Rushes Mill WS3 .... 14 E3
Rushey La B11 ..... 88 A4
Rushford Ave WV5 ... 49 A6
Rushford Cl B90 ... 127 A7
Rush Gn B32........ 84 E2
Rush La Redditch B98. 154 B6
　Tamworth B77, B78 ... 35 D4
Rushlake Gn B34.... 69 B5
Rushleigh Rd B90 ... 125 E8
Rushmead Gr B45 .. 122 A7
Rushmere Rd DY4 ... 52 A8
Rushmoor Cl B74.... 46 B6
Rushmoor Dr CV5... 112 F3
Rushmore St CV31 . 162 B7
Rushmore Terr [9]
　CV31............... 162 B7
Rushock Cl B98..... 159 C7
Rushton Cl CV7 .... 130 C7
Rushton Hall Sch CV7 95 D5
Rushwick Croft B34 .. 69 D6
Rushwick Ct B23.... 56 B3
Rushwick Gr B90.... 127 A6
Rushwood Cl WS4.... 29 A3
Rushy Piece B32 .... 84 D3
Rusina Ct CV31...... 161 F6
Ruskin Ave
　Dudley DY3 .... 50 A5
　Kidderminster DY10 .. 117 C6
　Rowley Regis B65..... 63 D2
　Wolverhampton WV4 .. 39 F2
Ruskin Cl
　Birmingham B6....... 66 F7
　Coventry CV6 ...... 112 D6
　Nuneaton CV10...... 72 A5
Ruskin Ct [5] B68.... 84 B8
Ruskin Glass Ctr*
　DY8.................80 F7
Ruskin Gr B27 ..... 88 B2
Ruskin Hall Gr B6....66 F7
Ruskin Rd WV10.... 12 A1
Ruskin St B71....... 53 C5
Russel Croft B60 ... 151 A7
Russell Bank Rd B74 . 31 C4
Russell Cl Oldbury B69 52 D2
　Tamworth B77....... 35 E6
　Wednesbury WV4 .... 41 C1
　Wolverhampton WV11 . 12 F1
Russell Ct
　[7] Royal Leamington Spa
　CV31.............. 162 A7
　Sutton Coldfield B74... 31 D3
　Wolverhampton WV3 . 163 A2
Russell Ho
　Tamworth B77....... 21 F2
　Wednesbury WS10 ... 41 F2
Russell Rd
　Bilston WV14 .... 40 F7
　Birmingham, Hall Green
　B28 .... 87 E1
　Birmingham, Moseley
　B13................ 86 D3
　Kidderminster DY10 .. 116 F4
Russell St N [2] CV1 . 165 C4
Russells Hall Hospl
　DY5..................61 E7
Russells Hall Prim Sch
　DY1..................50 E8
Russell's Hall Rd DY1..50 F1

Russell St
　Coventry CV1 ...... 165 C4
　Dudley DY1 .... 51 B1
　Royal Leamington Spa
　CV32.............. 156 F1
　Wednesbury WS10 ... 41 F2
　Willenhall WV13 .... 27 B2
　Wolverhampton WV3 . 163 A2
Russells The B13.... 86 D3
Russell Terr CV31 ... 162 A7
Russet Gr CV4 ..... 132 D3
Russett Cl
　Burntwood WS7 ......7 A6
　Walsall WS5 .... 43 D8
Russett Way DY5 ... 61 B7
Russet Way B31 ... 102 E6
Russet Wlk WV8 ... 10 E1
Ruston St B16 ..... 66 B1
Ruthall Cl B29 ..... 103 C7
Ruth Chamberlain Ct [3]
　DY11 .... 116 D6
Ruth Cl DY4......... 41 C2
Rutherford Glen CV11 .73 F1
Rutherford Rd
　Birmingham B23 ..... 56 E7
　Bromsgrove B60..... 151 B7
　Walsall WS2 .... 28 A5
Rutherglen Ave CV3 . 134 A6
Rutland B17 .... 85 A6
Rutland Ave
　Hinckley LE10 ...... 75 C7
　Nuneaton CV10...... 72 F4
　Wolverhampton WV4 .. 38 D4
Rutland Cres
　Aldridge WS9 ...... 16 B1
　Bilston WV14 ...... 40 E7
Rutland Croft [3]
　CV3 .... 134 F8
Rutland Ct [2] B29... 103 C7
Rutland Dr
　Birmingham B26 ..... 88 E7
　Bromsgrove B60..... 151 B8
　Tamworth B78....... 21 A1
Rutland Pas [8] DY1 . 51 C1
Rutland Pl DY8 ..... 80 D8
Rutland Rd
　Cannock WS12 ....2 E1
　Smethwick B66...... 65 A1
　Wednesbury WS10 ... 42 D4
　West Bromwich B71... 53 C7
Rutland St WS3 ..... 28 E5
Rutland Terr [5] B18 . 66 A5
Rutley Gr B32........84 F4
Rutter St WS1........ 42 E8
Ryan Ave WV11..... 27 A7
Ryan Pl DY2 .... 62 C6
Rycroft Gr B33 ..... 69 C2
Rydal B77 .... 36 A7
Rydal Ave CV11 .... 74 A6
Rydal Cl Allesley CV5 . 112 B8
　Cannock WS12 ....2 A8
　Hinckley LE10 ...... 75 C7
　Sutton Coldfield B74... 30 F2
　Wolverhampton WV11 . 26 C7
Rydal Dr WV6....... 23 F4
Rydal Ho [6] B69 ... 63 D5
Rydal Way B28 ..... 105 F2
Rydding La B71..... 53 B8
Rydding Sq B71..... 53 B8
Ryde Ave CV10 ..... 73 D7
Ryde Gr B27 .... 88 A1
Ryde Park Rd B45... 122 C7
Ryders Green Prim Sch
　B70................ 53 A4
Ryders Green Rd B70. .52 F4
Ryders Hayes Com Sch
　WS3 .... 15 A5
Ryders Hayes La WS3 . 15 B4
Ryders Hill Cres CV10 72 C1
Ryder St
　Birmingham B4...... 164 C3
　Stourbridge DY8 .... 60 D2
　West Bromwich B70... 52 F5
Ryebank Cl B30 .... 103 C5
Ryeclose Croft B37... 70 D3
Rye Croft
　[7] Birmingham B27 ... 88 C5
　Hollywood B47 ..... 125 A5
　Stourbridge DY9 .... 81 E2
Ryecroft Ave WV4 ... 39 B5
Ryecroft Cl DY3 .... 50 C8
Ryecroft Cotts WV4 .. 39 B5
Ryecroft Dr [3] WS7 ...7 A8
Ryecroft Pk [1] WS2... 28 E3
Ryecroft Pl WS3...... 28 F6
Ryecroft Sh Ctr WS7 ..7 A8
Ryecroft St [2] WS2... 28 E3
Ryefield WV8 ...... 10 E1

Ryefield Cl
　Solihull B91........ 106 E5
　West Hagley DY9 .... 99 A4
Ryefield La B76 .... 48 B2
Ryefields Rd B60 ... 150 C3
Rye Gr B11 .... 87 F4
Ryegrass La B97 ... 158 C6
Rye Grass Wlk B35... 58 B3
Rye Hill CV5 .... 112 A6
Rye Hill Office Pk
　CV5................ 112 A7
Ryemarket Sh Ctr [7]
　DY8................ 81 A5
Rye Piece Ringway
　CV12 .... 78 C3
Ryhope Cl CV12 .... 77 C1
Ryhope Wlk WV9.... 11 A3
Ryknild Cl B74 ......31 F6
Ryknild Dr B74...... 45 A7
Ryknild St WS14.......9 E6
Ryland Cl
　Halesowen B63...... 82 E2
　Royal Leamington Spa
　CV32.............. 162 C6
　[3] Tipton DY4 ..... 52 B5
Ryland Ho B19 ..... 66 D5
Ryland Rd
　Birmingham, Edgbaston
　B15................ 86 C8
　Birmingham, Gravelly Hill
　B24................ 56 F1
Rylands Dr WV4 .... 39 A4
Ryland St B16....... 66 B1
Rylcroft [7] WV4.....39 F4
Ryle St WS3........ 14 D1
Ryley St CV1 ...... 165 A3
Rylston Ave CV6..... 95 A1
Rylstone Way [4]
　CV34 .... 155 E1
Rymond Rd B34..... 68 E6
Ryton B77 .... 35 F8
Ryton Cl
　Coventry CV4 ...... 132 B8
　Redditch B98 .... 154 D1
　Sutton Coldfield B73... 46 B5
　Wolverhampton WV10 . 26 A5
Ryton Gr B34 ...... 69 D7
Ryton Organic Gdns*
　CV8 .... 135 E1

S

Sabell Rd B67..........64 F6
Sabrina Rd WV6...... 23 E1
Sackville Ho [1] CV1. 165 D4
Sacred Heart Prim Sch
　DY4................ 52 A4
Sacred Heart RC Prim
　Sch CV2 .... 114 A3
Sacred Heart Sch
　B20................ 55 D1
Saddington Rd CV3 . 134 E8
Saddlers Cl
　Halesowen B63...... 82 B5
　Hinckley LE10 ...... 75 F6
　Lichfield WS14 ....9 F8
Saddlers Court Ind Est
　WS2 .... 28 A7
Saddlers Ctr WS1 ... 28 E1
Saddlers Mews B91 . 107 C1
Saddlestones The
　WV6 .... 23 D4
Saddleworth Rd WS3. 14 A4
Sadler Cres B11..... 87 D4
Sadler Ctr WS8...... 16 A8
Sadler Gdns CV12 ... 78 C2
Sadler Ho B19 ..... 66 C6
Sadler Rd
　Brownhills WS8 ..... 16 A8
　Coventry CV6 ...... 113 A8
　Sutton Coldfield B75... 46 F7
Sadlers Ct WS2 .... 42 B7
Sadlers Mill WS8.... 16 A7
Sadlerswell La B94.. 143 B6
Sadlers Wlk B16 ... 66 A1
Saffron B77.......... 22 B4
Saffron Gdns WV4... 39 A4
Saffron Ho [3] B38... 123 E8
Sagebury Dr B60.... 150 C1
Sage Croft B31..... 102 F5
St Agatha's Rd
　Birmingham B8...... 68 B5
　Coventry CV2 ...... 114 A3
St Agnes Cl
　Birmingham B13..... 87 B2
　Studley B80........ 159 C4
St Agnes Rd B13.... 87 B1
St Agnes Way CV11 ...73 F4

St Aidan's Ct WV4.... **39** A5
St Aidan's Rd WS11 ....**1** E5
St Aidans Wlk **3** B10 **87** C8
St Alban's Ave DY11 **116** A7
St Alban's CE Prim Sch
WV11..............**27** B8
St Alban's CE Sch
B12..............**86** F7
St Albans Cl
  Royal Leamington Spa
  CV32..............**156** C2
  Smethwick B67......**64** E6
  Wednesfield WV11 ....**27** A8
  Wolverhampton WV11 . **13** A1
St Albans Dr WV13 .... **26** E1
St Albans Ho B32......**84** F5
St Alban's RC Prim Sch
B14..............**104** F4
St Albans Rd
  Birmingham B13...... **87** A4
  Smethwick B67......**64** E6
St Alphege CE Inf Sch
B91..............**107** C3
St Alphege Jun Sch
B91..............**107** C2
St Alphege Cl B91... **107** C3
St Ambrose Barlow RC
  Prim Sch B28 ...... **106** A6
St Ambrose Cl B62,
  B65..............**83** C8
St Ambrose RC Prim Sch
DY10..............**116** F6
St Andrews B77....... **22** B4
St Andrews Ave WS3 . **15** B4
St Andrew's CE Fst Sch
B45..............**138** D8
St Andrew's CE Inf Sch
CV5..............**111** C5
St Andrews CE Prim Sch
WV6..............**24** F4
St Andrews Cl
  Birmingham B32...... **85** A3
  Stourbridge DY8...... **80** F2
  Wolverhampton WV6 .. **25** A4
St Andrew's Cl DY3... **50** A3
St Andrews Ct **2** B10 **67** B1
St Andrews Dr
  Nuneaton CV11....... **74** B1
  Oldbury B69 .... **63** B7
  Perton WV6......... **23** D5
St Andrew's Gd
  (Birmingham City FC)
  B9..............**67** C1
St Andrews Gn DY10 **116** E4
St Andrews Ho WV6 .. **25** B4
St Andrews Ind Est
  B9..............**67** C2
St Andrew's Jun & Inf
  Sch B9..............**67** B2
St Andrew's RC Prim Sch
B92..............**89** A2
St Andrews Rd B75... **46** D7
St Andrew's Rd
  Birmingham B9....... **67** B2
  Coventry CV5 ...... **132** F8
  Royal Leamington Spa
  CV32..............**157** B5
St Andrew's St
  Birmingham B9....... **67** B2
  Dudley DY2......... **62** C5
St Andrews Way
  B61..............**150** D8
St Annes Cl B20......**54** F4
St Anne's Cl WS7......**6** E4
St Annes Cl B44......**56** A7
St Anne's Ct
  Birmingham B13...... **86** E4
  Willenhall WV13 ..... **27** B1
St Annes Gr B93 ... **128** A6
St Annes Ind Est
  WV13..............**27** B3
St Anne's RC Prim Sch
  B37..............**70** A2
St Anne's RC Prim Sch
  B12..............**87** A8
St Anne's RC Prim Sch
  Coventry CV3 ...... **134** C6
  Nuneaton CV10...... **72** D7
  Sutton Coldfield B74.... **44** E8
St Annes Rd WS13......**3** B3
St Anne's Rd
  Cradley Heath B64 .... **62** C1
  Willenhall WV13 ..... **27** B3
  Wolverhampton WV10 . **11** B1
St Annes Way B44... **56** A7
St Ann's Cl CV31 .... **162** C1
St Ann's Rd CV2.... **114** A3
St Anthonys Dr WS3.. **15** B5

St Anthony's RC Prim
  Sch
  Royal Leamington Spa
  CV31..............**162** C7
  Wolverhampton WV10 . **11** D3
St Antony's RC Prim Sch
  B37..............**70** A5
St Asaphs Ave B80 .. **159** D4
St Athan Croft B35 ... **58** B3
St Audries Ct B91.... **106** F2
St Augustine's RC High
  Sch B97 .... **158** D5
St Augustine's RC Prim
  Sch
  Birmingham B21...... **54** D2
  Coventry CV6 ...... **113** A7
St Augustine's RC Prim
  Sch CV8 .... **147** E7
St Augustine's RC Prim
  Sch B91 .... **107** A2
St Augustine's Rd
  B16..............**65** D1
St Augustine's Wlk
  CV6..............**113** A7
St Augustus Cl B70...**53** F2
St Austell Cl
  Nuneaton CV11....... **74** A5
  Tamworth B79....... **21** A6
St Austell Rd
  Coventry CV2 ...... **114** E3
  Walsall WS5 .... **43** E7
St Barnabas CE Prim Sch
  B24..............**57** A3
St Bartholemews Cl
  CV3..............**115** A2
St Bartholomew's CE
  Prim Sch
  Coventry CV3 ...... **134** E7
  Wolverhampton WV4 .. **38** E3
St Bartholomew Terr **3**
  WS10..............**41** F3
St Bede's RC Mid Sch
  B98..............**153** F3
St Benedict Bishop CE
  Prim Sch WV5......**49** B7
St Benedict's Cl B70 ..**53** F2
St Benedict's Inf Sch
  B10..............**87** F7
St Benedicts Rd
  Birmingham B10...... **87** F8
  Wombourne WV5 ..... **49** A6
St Benedict's Rd WS7 . .**7** B6
St Bernadette's RC Prim
  Sch
  Birmingham B25...... **88** B8
  Brownhills WS8 ..... **15** F8
St Bernard's Rd B72 .. **46** C2
St Bernard's Rd B92. **106** E7
St Bernard's Wlk
  CV3..............**134** D6
St Blaise Ave B46 .... **59** C2
St Blaise Rd B75...... **32** D3
St Brades Cl B69...... **63** C7
St Brides Cl DY3 ..... **50** C8
St Bride's Cl CV31.... **162** C6
St Brigid's RC Prim Sch
  B31..............**102** F3
St Buryan Cl CV11.... **74** A5
Saintbury Dr B91.... **127** C8
St Caroline Cl B70 ... **53** F2
St Catharines Cl WS1. **43** A7
St Catherine of Siena RC
  Prim Sch B1 .... **66** D1
St Catherines Cl
  Blackwell B60...... **138** A5
  Oldbury DY2 .... **52** A1
  Sutton Coldfield B75... **46** F7
St Catherine's Cl
  Coventry CV3 ...... **134** B8
  Hinckley LE10 ...... **75** F7
St Catherine's Cres
  Whitnash CV34...... **161** F3
  Wolverhampton WV4 .. **38** F4
St Catherine's Ct
  B91..............**107** B3
St Catherine's Lodge **7**
  CV6..............**113** A4
St Catherines Rd WS13 .**3** B3
St Catherine's Rd
  B60..............**138** A5
St Cecilia Cl DY10 ... **116** E2
St Cecilia's WV11.... **26** C5
St Chad Ct B77......**21** F2
St Chad's Cath* B4. **164** B4
St Chad's CE Prim Sch
  WS13..............**9** C8

St Chad's Circus
  Queensway B3 ..... **164** B3
St Chads Cl WS13 .....**3** B1
St Chad's Cl
  Cannock WS11 ....**2** A4
  Dudley DY3......... **50** D3
St Chads Ct **3** WS13 .....**9** B8
St Chads Ind Est B19..**66** E5
St Chads Mews B94 . **144** D3
St Chads Queensway
  B4..............**164** C4
St Chads RC Prim Sch
  DY3..............**50** D7
St Chad's RC Prim Sch
  B19..............**66** D5
St Chads Rd B80 .... **159** C4
St Chad's Rd
  Bilston WV14 .... **40** F7
  Birmingham B45..... **121** F7
  Lichfield WS13 ....**3** C1
  Sutton Coldfield B75... **46** F5
  Wolverhampton WV10 . **25** F8
St Christian's Croft
  CV3..............**133** E8
St Christian's Rd
  CV3..............**133** E8
St Christopher Cl B70 **53** E2
St Christopher Dr
  WS10..............**42** E3
St Christopher Prim Sch
  CV5..............**112** D4
St Christophers B20...**54** F4
St Christopher's Cl
  CV34..............**160** D8
St Christopher's Dr
  B77..............**21** C1
St Christophers RC Prim
  Sch WV8............**10** A3
St Clare's RC Prim Sch
  B20..............**55** B1
St Clement's Ave
  WS3..............**28** D7
St Clement's CE Prim Sch
  B7..............**67** C7
St Clements Ct CV2 . **114** D8
St Clements Ho **3**
  B71..............**53** D4
St Clement's La B71.. **53** D4
St Clements Rd B7... **67** C6
St Columba's Cl CV1 **165** B4
St Columbas Dr B45. **122** D7
St Columba's RC Prim
  Sch B45 .... **122** D7
St Cuthbert's Cl B70 ..**53** F2
St Cuthberts RC Prim Sch
  B8..............**68** C4
St David Dr WS10 .... **42** E3
St Davids Cl WS3.... **15** B5
St David's Cl
  Royal Leamington Spa
  CV31..............**162** C7
  West Bromwich B70... **53** F2
St Davids Dr B32..... **84** B5
St Davids Gr B20..... **54** F4
St Davids Orch CV3 . **134** F4
St Davids Pl WS3..... **14** D2
St Davids Way CV10 . **78** A6
St Denis B29........ **103** B7
St Dennis Ho **5** B15 . **65** D1
St Dominic's Rd B24 . **56** E1
St Dunstan's RC Prim Sch
  B14..............**104** F8
St Edburghs Rd B25.. **68** E1
St Editha's Cl B79.... **21** B5
St Editha's Ct B79.... **21** B7
St Edith's Gn **3**
  CV34..............**161** B8
St Edith's Ho **2**
  CV34..............**161** B8
St Edmund Campion RC
  Lower Sch B24...... **57** C6
St Edmund Campion RC
  Sch B23 ....**57** B5
St Edmund's Cl
  West Bromwich B70... **53** F2
  Wolverhampton WV6 .. **24** F3
St Edmund's RC Prim Sch
  B18..............**66** A4
St Edmunds RC Sch
  WV3..............**24** E3
St Edward's RC Prim Sch
  B29..............**86** B1
St Edward's Rd B29 .. **85** F2
Sainte Foy Ave WS13 ..**9** A6
SS John & Monica RC
  Prim Sch B13 ......**86** E4
St Eleanor Cl B70 ....**53** F3
St Elizabeth's RC Prim
  Sch
  Coventry CV6 ...... **113** E7

St Elizabeth's RC Prim
  Sch continued
  Tamworth B79....... **20** F8
St Elizabeth's Rd
  CV6..............**113** E7
St Foy Ave WS13 ......**8** F5
St Francis Ave B91.. **106** E6
St Francis CE Prim Sch
  B30..............**103** D6
St Francis Cl
  Hinckley LE10 ...... **71** C3
  Walsall WS3 .... **15** B5
St Francis Factory Est
  B70..............**53** D2
St Francis of Assisi Tech
  Coll WS9........... **30** C5
St Francis RC Prim Sch
  Bedworth CV12...... **78** C3
  Birmingham B19...... **66** B6
  Walsall WS4 .... **15** C1
St Francis Xavier RC Sch
  B69..............**64** A8
St Fremund Way
  CV31..............**162** C5
St Gabriel's RC Prim Sch
  B77..............**21** E1
St George Cl WS10 ... **42** E3
St George Dr B66 .... **65** A7
St George & St Teresa RC
  Prim Sch B93 ..... **128** A4
St Georges Ave B23 .. **57** A5
St George's Ave LE10 . **71** C1
St George's CE Fst Sch
  DY10..............**116** F7
St George's CE Fst Sch
  B98..............**153** F3
St George's CE Prim Sch
  B19..............**164** B5
St George's CE Prim Sch
  B16..............**65** F1
St Georges Cl B15.... **86** A7
St George's Cl
  Darlaston WS10 ..... **41** D7
  Sutton Coldfield B75... **46** F6
St Georges Ct
  10 Kidderminster
  DY10..............**116** E6
  Sutton Coldfield B74... **31** E5
  5 Walsall WS1 ..... **28** F2
St George's Ct
  Birmingham B30..... **103** C4
  Darlaston WS10 ..... **41** D7
St George's Gdns **3**
  B98..............**153** F4
St George's Par
  WV1..............**163** C2
St Georges Pl B70.... **53** C4
St George's Pl
  Kidderminster DY10 .. **116** E7
  4 Walsall WS1 ..... **28** F2
St Georges Rd
  Dudley DY2......... **62** E6
  Redditch B98 ...... **153** F4
St George's Rd
  Coventry CV1 ...... **113** C2
  Royal Leamington Spa
  CV31..............**161** F6
  Solihull B90....... **126** D8
  Stourbridge DY8...... **80** D2
St George's St
  Birmingham B19..... **164** B5
  Darlaston WS10 ..... **41** D7
St George's Sta WV1 **163** C2
St George's Terr
  DY10..............**116** F6
St Georges Way CV10 **78** B8
St George's Way B77 ..**21** F4
St Gerards Ct B91... **106** E2
St Gerards RC Prim Sch
  B35..............**58** B4
St Gerards Rd B91... **106** E2
St Giles Ave B65 .... **63** B4
St Giles' CE Prim Sch
  WV13..............**27** B1
St Giles Cl B65...... **63** C4
St Giles Cres WV1 ... **26** A2
St Giles Ct B65...... **63** D3
St Gile's Cl WV13.... **27** B1
St Giles Jun Sch CV7 .**95** F8
St Giles Rd
  Birmingham B33..... **69** D2
  Burntwood WS7 ......**7** B6
  Coventry CV7 ...... **95** D6
  Willenhall WV13 ..... **27** B1
  Wolverhampton WV1 . **26** A2
St Giles Row DY8..... **81** A6
St Giles St DY2...... **62** C5
St Godwald's Cres
  B60..............**151** B8

St Godwald's Rd
  B60..............**151** C7
St Govan's Cl **2**
  CV31..............**162** C6
St Gregory's RC Prim
  Sch
  Coventry CV2 ...... **114** E4
  Smethwick B67...... **64** F2
St Helens Ave DY4 ... **52** C5
St Helens Pas B1 .... **66** C3
St Helens Rd WS13... **3** B1
St Helen's Rd
  Solihull B91........ **107** A6
  Whitnash CV31...... **162** A5
St Helen's Way CV5 . **112** B8
St Heliers Rd B31.... **102** F4
St Hellier Ho **4** B15.. **65** D1
St Hubert's RC Prim Sch
  B68..............**84** C8
St Ives Cl B79...... **21** B6
St Ives Rd
  Coventry CV2 ...... **114** E3
  Walsall WS5 .... **43** D7
St Ives Way CV11.....**73** F5
St James Ave B65.... **63** B4
St James CE Jun Sch
  Bulkington CV12 ..... **79** C2
  Solihull B90....... **106** D3
St James CE Prim Sch
  Birmingham B21...... **54** D1
  Oldbury B69 .... **63** D5
  Stourbridge DY8...... **80** D7
St James Cl
  Walsall WS3 .... **15** B5
  West Bromwich B70... **53** F2
St James Ct
  Bromsgrove B60..... **137** A3
  Coventry CV3 ...... **134** E6
St James Gdns
  Brownhills WS8 ..... **15** F7
St James' La CV3... **134** D6
St James Meadow Rd
  CV32..............**156** C2
St James Pl
  Birmingham, Edgbaston
  B15..............**86** B8
  Solihull B90....... **106** B8
St James' Pl B7...... **67** A3
St James Prim Sch
  WS8..............**15** F8
St James' RC Jun & Inf
  Sch B45 .... **122** A7
St James Rd
  Birmingham, Edgbaston
  B15..............**86** B8
  Cannock WS11 ....**1** C1
  Norton Canes WS11.....**6** B5
  Oldbury B69 .... **63** E8
  Sutton Coldfield B75... **32** C2
St James's Cl LE10 ... **75** D5
St James's Rd DY1 ... **51** B2
St James St
  Wednesbury WS10 ... **41** E2
  Wolverhampton WV1 . **163** D3
St James' St DY3..... **50** D3
St James's Terr DY1 .. **51** A2
St James Wlk WS8 ...**15** F7
St John Bosco RC Jun &
  Inf Sch B71 ....**53** B7
St John Cl B75....... **32** D4
St John Fisher RC Prim
  Sch
  Birmingham B31..... **123** B7
  Coventry CV2 ...... **114** D5
St Johns Hinckley LE10 **71** E1
  Warwick CV34...... **160** F7
St John's Ave
  Kenilworth CV8...... **148** A3
  Kidderminster DY11 .. **116** B6
St John's CE Foundation
  Mid Sch B61 ...... **136** F1
St John's CE Fst Sch
  DY11..............**116** B6
St John's CE Mid Sch
  DY11..............**116** B6
St John's CE Prim Sch
  B11..............**87** C4
St John's CE Prim Sch
  Brownhills WS9 ..... **16** A3
  Coventry CV5 ...... **112** C4
  Essington WV11 ..... **13** A4
  Wednesbury WS10 ... **41** F2
St Johns Cl B93..... **128** B6
St John's Cl
  Brownhills WS9 ..... **15** F3
  Cannock WS11 ....**4** D8

St John's Cl continued
  6 Kidderminster
  DY11..............**116** C6
  Lichfield WS13 ....**9** B6
  West Bromwich B70... **53** F3
St Johns Ct
  2 Birmingham, Harborne
  B17..............**85** B6
  Birmingham, Turves Green
  B31..............**103** B8
  20 Brierley Hill DY5 ... **61** D2
  5 Wednesbury WS10 . **41** F2
St John's Ct
  Cannock WS12 ....**2** E1
  Walsall WS3 .... **14** B1
  4 Warwick CV34... **160** F7
St John's Dr WS14 ... **17** F5
St John's Flats CV8 . **148** A3
St Johns Gr B37......**69** F3
St John's Hill WS14 ... **17** F5
St Johns Ho **2** B74 .. **31** E3
St John's House Mus*
  CV34..............**160** F7
St John's Ladywood CE
  Prim Sch B16...... **66** A2
St John's Prim Sch
  CV8..............**147** F2
St Johns Rd
  Birmingham B11...... **87** C5
  Brownhills WS8 ..... **16** A5
  Essington WV11 ..... **13** A3
  Oldbury B68 .... **64** C5
  Walsall, Pleck WS2... **42** B8
  Walsall WS3 .... **15** B5
St John's Rd
  Birmingham B17...... **85** D6
  Cannock WS11 ....**4** E7
  Darlaston WS10 ..... **41** C5
  Dudley DY2......... **51** E1
  Halesowen B63...... **82** E4
  Royal Leamington Spa
  CV31..............**162** A6
  Stourbridge DY8...... **81** A5
  Tipton DY4 .... **51** F8
St Johns Ret Pk
  WV2..............**163** B1
St Johns Sch WS13 ...**9** B7
St John's Sq WV2 ... **163** B2
St John's St
  Coventry CV1 ...... **165** C2
  Dudley DY2 .... **62** C5
  Kenilworth CV8...... **148** A3
  5 Kidderminster
  DY11..............**116** C6
  Tamworth B79....... **21** B5
  Wolverhampton WV1 . **163** B2
St John St
  Bromsgrove B61..... **136** F2
  Lichfield WS13 ....**9** B7
St John's Terr **13**
  CV31..............**162** A6
St Johns Way B93... **128** C6
St Johns Wlk B42.... **55** D4
St Johns Wood
  Birmingham B45..... **122** B5
  Shenstone WS14...... **18** A5
St John the Baptist RC
  Prim Sch B36......**70** B7
St John the Divine CE
  Prim Sch CV3 ...... **134** C5
St John Vianney RC Prim
  Sch CV5 .... **112** D3
St John Wall RC Sch
  B21..............**54** C2
St Joseph & St Theresa
  RC Prim Sch WS7 ...**6** E6
St Josephs Ave B31 . **103** B5
St Josephs Cl WS3... **15** A4
St Joseph's Convent Sch
  WV6..............**24** E6
St Josephs Cl WV4 .. **38** D3
St Joseph's RC Jun Sch
  CV11..............**73** C3
St Josephs RC Prim Sch
  B30..............**103** F5
St Joseph's RC Prim
  Sch
  Birmingham B7....... **67** B6
  Cannock WS12 ....**2** C4
  Darlaston WS10 ..... **41** D7
  Dudley DY2......... **51** E1
  Lichfield WS14 ....**9** C7
  Sutton Coldfield B75... **46** C7
  Whitnash CV31...... **162** A3
St Josephs Rd B8.... **68** C5
St Joseph St **7** DY2.. **51** E1
St Judes Ave B80 ... **159** C4
St Jude's CE Prim Sch
  WV3..............**24** F3

St Judes Cl
Birmingham B14..... **104** F2
4 Sutton Coldfield B75 **46** F6
St Jude's Cres CV3.. **134** D7
St Judes Ct B14...... **104** F2
St Jude's Ct **4** WV6...**24** F3
St Jude's Pas B5.... **164** B1
St Judes RC Prim Sch
B14............. **104** F2
St Jude's Rd WV6.....**24** F3
St Jude's Rd W WV6 ..**24** F3
St Katherine's Rd B68 **64** B2
St Kenelms Ave B63.. **82** E1
St Kenelm's Cl B70...**53** F2
St Kenelm's Rd B62. **100** E5
St Kilda's Rd B8 ..... **67** E5
St Laurence Ave
CV34 .... **160** D5
St Laurence CE Inf Sch
B31............. **103** B4
St Laurence CE Jun Sch
B31............. **103** B4
St Laurence Cl B48... **139** B6
St Laurence Rd B31. **103** B5
St Lawrence Cl
1 Birmingham B5 ... **86** D7
Knowle B93......... **128** B5
St Lawrence Dr WS11 ..**2** B2
St Lawrence Ho **6**
B15............... **65** D1
St Lawrence Mews
B31............. **103** A3
St Lawrence's Rd CV6 .**95** F1
St Lawrence Way
WS10 .... **41** D6
St Leonards Cl B37... **90** A7
St Leonards View B78 .**36** F8
St Leonard's Wlk
CV8............. **135** A1
St Loye's Cl B62...... **83** D8
St Luke's CE Fst Sch
B97.............**153** D1
St Luke's CE Prim Sch
WV2.............**39** B7
St Lukes Cl B65 ...... **63** B4
St Luke's Cl WS11 ..... **4** D8
St Luke's Cotts B97 .**153** D1
St Lukes Prim Sch (Inf
Site) WV2.......... **39** C7
St Luke's Rd
Birmingham B5 ..... **86** E7
Burntwood WS7 ....**7** C6
Coventry CV6 .... **95** D3
Wednesbury WS10.... **42** A3
St Lukes St B64 ...... **62** D1
St Luke's Terr DY1... **62** A8
St Lukes Way CV10 ... **72** C4
St Margaret Mary RC Jun
& Inf Sch B36 ...... **56** C6
St Margaret Rd CV1 . **113** C2
St Margaret's B74.... **31** C3
St Margarets Ave B8 . **68** B6
St Margaret's CE Jun Sch
CV31.............**162** B3
St Margaret's CE Prim
Sch
Birmingham B43 ..... **43** E4
Solihull B92......... **88** F2
St Margaret's Ct **3**
B92.............. **88** E1
St Margarets Dr B63 .**82** F2
St Margaret's Ho
CV31.............**162** B4
St Margarets Rd
Birmingham B8....... **68** B6
Lichfield WS13 ....**3** B3
Walsall WS3 .... **15** A4
St Margaret's Rd
Birmingham B43...... **43** F2
2 Solihull B92...... **88** E1
Tamworth B79........ **21** B7
Whitnash CV31...... **162** B5
St Mark's Annexe
(Coventry &
Warwickshire Hospl)
CV1.............**165** C4
St Mark's CE Prim Sch
DY5............. **61** C7
St Marks Cl
Great Wyrley WS6.....**4** F4
Nuneaton CV10...... **72** C4
St Marks Cres B11... **66** B3
St Mark's Ct DY5 .... **61** D7
St Mark's Mews
CV32.............**156** E1
St Mark's RC Prim Sch
B42.............**54** F6
St Marks Rd
Brownhills WS8 ..... **16** A5
Walsall WS3 .... **15** A4

St Mark's Rd
Burntwood WS7 ....**7** C6
Dudley DY2......... **51** F1
Royal Leamington Spa
CV32.............**156** D1
Smethwick B67....... **64** D3
Stourbridge DY9 ..... **81** D5
Tipton DY4 .... **52** A8
Wolverhampton WV3 .. **25** B1
St Marks St B1........ **66** B3
St Mark's St WV3 ... **163** A2
St Martin De Porres RC
Prim Sch B13...... **87** A3
St Martins Ave B80.. **159** D4
St Martin's CE Prim Sch
Bilston WV14 .... **41** A2
Tipton DY4 .... **52** B5
St Martin's Cl
West Bromwich B70... **53** F2
Wolverhampton WV2 .. **39** A6
St Martin's Dr DY4 ... **52** A5
St Martins Ind Est
B69................ **64** A6
St Martin's Mkt B5 . **164** C1
St Martin's Queensway B2,
B4, B5........... **164** C2
St Martins Rd B75....**46** F5
St Martin's Rd CV3 . **133** C2
St Martin's Sch B91 **107** D3
St Martin's St **6** B15. **66** B1
St Martin's Terr WV14 **40** E4
St Mary Magdalene CE
Jun & Inf Sch B71 .. **53** D6
St Mary of the Angels RC
Prim Sch WS9......**30** B5
St Mary & St Benedict RC
Prim Sch CV1......**113** E4
St Mary & St John RC
Jun & Inf Sch WV2 **163** C1
St Mary & St Jun & Inf
Sch B23 .... **56** E3
St Mary & St Margaret's
CE Prim Sch B36 ...**69** B8
St Mary's Ave LE9.....**71** F5
St Mary's CE Fst Sch
DY10............. **116** E2
St Mary's CE Jun & Inf
Sch B20 .... **55** B1
St Mary's CE Prim Sch
B29.............. **85** D1
St Mary's CE Prim Sch
Hinckley LE10........ **75** D8
Kingswinford DY6..... **60** D7
St Marys Cl B27...... **88** B3
St Mary's Cl
Sedgley DY3 .... **50** F8
Sutton Coldfield B24... **57** D4
Warwick CV34 .... **160** D8
St Mary's Cres CV31. **162** B7
St Marys Ct **12** DY5... **61** D2
St Mary's Ct
Kenilworth CV8....... **147** F2
Nuneaton CV11....... **73** B5
3 Willenhall WV13 ... **27** A2
St Mary's Hall WV1.. **163** C2
St Mary's Ho **4** B71.. **53** D4
St Mary's Immaculate RC
Prim Sch CV34 .... **160** E8
St Mary's La DY8 .... **81** B3
St Marys Park Cvn Pk
B47.............. **124** E2
St Mary's RC Prim Sch
B17.............. **85** C5
St Mary's RC Prim Sch
DY5..............**61** D2
St Mary's RC Prim Sch
WS11............**4** E8
St Mary's RC Prim Sch
Studley B80....... **159** E4
Wednesbury WS10.... **41** F4
Wolverhampton WV10 . **26** A7
St Marys Rd B17..... **85** C5
St Mary's Rd
Hinckley LE10........ **75** D8
Lichfield WS13 ....**3** B3
Nuneaton CV11....... **73** B5
Royal Leamington Spa
CV31.............**162** B7
Smethwick B67....... **64** F1
Wednesbury WS10.... **41** F3
St Marys Ringway
DY10............. **116** E6
St Mary's Row
Birmingham, Moseley
B13............. **86** F4
Birmingham, New Town Row
B4..............**164** C4
St Mary's St WV1.... **163** B1
St Mary St CV1...... **165** C2

St Mary's Terr CV31 . **162** B7
St Mary's The Mount RC
Prim Sch WS1......**42** F8
St Marys View B23 ... **56** D8
St Mary's Way
Aldridge WS9 .... **30** B5
Tamworth B77....... **21** E4
St Matthew's Ave WS7..**7** F7
St Matthews CE Prim Sch
B7................ **67** A4
St Matthew's CE Prim
Sch B66 .... **65** C5
St Matthews Cl
Nuneaton CV10....... **72** C4
Walsall WS3 .... **15** B5
St Matthew's Cl WS1..**28** F1
St Matthews Rd
Oldbury B68......... **64** A2
Smethwick B66....... **65** C5
St Matthew's Rd WS7 ..**7** F7
St Matthew St WV1....**25** F1
St Mawes Rd WV6.....**24** A3
St Mawgen Cl B35 .... **58** C4
St Michael Ho **3** B15 **65** D1
St Michael Rd WS13...**9** C8
St Michael's CE High Sch
B65................ **63** C5
St Michaels CE Inf & Jun
Sch B21 .... **66** A7
St Michael's CE Jun & Inf
Sch WV6..........**24** E5
St Michaels CE Prim
Sch
Walsall WS3 .... **14** F2
Walsall WS3 .... **15** A3
St Michael's CE Prim Sch
CV12.............. **78** D3
St Michael's CE Prim
Sch
Birmingham B32..... **102** C8
Lichfield WS14 ....**9** C7
Lichfield WS14 ....**9** C8
St Michaels Cl CV9.... **36** C1
St Michael's Cl WS3... **15** A2
St Michael's Cres B69 **64** A4
St Michaels Ct
Birmingham B18...... **66** B4
West Bromwich B70... **53** C3
St Michael's Ct B68 .. **64** A4
St Michael's Ct
5 Smethwick B66..... **65** A5
Wolverhampton WV6 .. **24** E5
St Michaels Dr WS12 ..**2** F5
St Michael's Gr DY2... **52** A1
St Michael's Hill B18.. **66** A7
St Michael's Hospl
Lichfield WS13 ...... **9** D8
Warwick CV34 ...... **160** D8
St Michael's Mews
B69.............. **52** A2
St Michael's RC Prim Sch
WV3.............. **38** D7
St Michaels Rd DY3 ...**49** F5
St Michael's Rd
Birmingham B18...... **66** A7
Coventry CV2 .... **114** A3
Sutton Coldfield B73... **56** F8
Warwick CV34 ...... **160** D8
St Michael St
Walsall WS1 .... **42** E8
West Bromwich B70... **53** C3
St Michaels Way DY4. **52** A3
St Michael's Way
CV10 .... **72** C4
St Nicholas Ave CV8. **147** F3
St Nicholas CE Com Prim
Sch CV8 .... **147** F5
St Nicholas Church St
CV34 .... **160** F6
St Nicholas Cl
Coventry CV1 .... **113** C5
Walsall WS3 .... **15** A4
St Nicholas Ct
3 Coventry, Edgwick
CV6............. **113** F7
Coventry, Radford
CV6............. **113** B6
St Nicholas Pk CV34 . **160** F6
St Nicholas RC Prim Sch
B73.............**45** F2
St Nicholas Rd CV31. **162** F5
St Nicholas St CV1 .. **165** B4
St Nicholas Terr
CV31............ **162** E4
St Nicholas Wlk B76 . **59** B6
St Nicolas CE Prim Sch
CV11.............**73** F6
St Nicolas Gdns B38. **103** F2
St Nicolas Park Dr
CV11.............**73** F7

St Nicolas Rd CV11... **73** D5
St Osburg's RC Prim Sch
CV1.............**165** A3
St Osburg's Rd CV2 . **114** A3
St Oswalds Cl DY10.. **116** F8
St Oswald's Ct B10... **87** E8
St Oswalds Rd B10... **87** E8
St Patrick's CE Jun & Inf
Sch B94 .... **126** C2
St Patricks Cl B14.... **104** C5
St Patrick's Ct DY11. **116** B1
St Patricks RC Prim Sch
Birmingham B18...... **65** F4
Royal Leamington Spa
CV31.............**161** F6
St Patrick's RC Prim
Sch
Birmingham B37..... **70** C2
Coventry CV2 .... **96** D1
Walsall WS2 .... **28** E3
Wolverhampton WV11 . **26** C5
St Patrick's Rd CV1 . **165** A4
St Paul's Ave
Birmingham B12..... **87** A5
Kidderminster DY11 . **116** A6
St Pauls CE Prim Sch
WV9.............. **11** A2
St Paul's CE Prim Sch
Nuneaton CV10....... **72** C3
Royal Leamington Spa
CV32.............**157** B1
Tipton DY4 .... **51** F6
St Paul's Cl
Cannock WS11.......**2** B1
5 Walsall WS1 ... **28** E2
Warwick CV34 ...... **160** D6
St Pauls Com Foundation
Sch B12 .... **87** A5
St Pauls Cres WS3 ... **15** B5
St Paul's Cres
5 Coleshill B46...... **70** F7
West Bromwich B70... **52** E7
St Pauls Ct
Halesowen B62....... **63** D1
Water Orton B46 ..... **59** B3
St Paul's Ct B77...... **35** C4
St Pauls Dr B62...... **63** D1
St Paul's Dr DY4 ..... **52** B4
St Pauls Gdns LE10... **71** E1
St Paul's RC Prim Sch
B38.............**104** A1
St Paul's Rd
Birmingham B12..... **87** A5
Burntwood WS7 ....**7** C6
Cannock WS12 ....**2** F3
Coventry CV6 .... **113** E6
Dudley DY2 .... **62** D5
Nuneaton CV10....... **72** D3
Smethwick B66....... **64** E7
Wednesbury WS10.... **42** C5
St Paul's Sch for Girls
B16.............**65** E1
St Paul's Sq
Birmingham B3 ..... **164** A4
4 Royal Leamington Spa
CV32.............**157** A1
St Paul's St WS1..... **28** E2
St Paul's Sta B19 ... **164** B4
St Pauls Terr B3..... **164** A4
St Paul's Terr CV34 . **160** D6
St Peter & St Paul RC
Prim Sch
Birmingham B24..... **57** C3
Lichfield WS13 ....**3** B1
St Peter's CE Prim Sch
Birmingham B17..... **85** B5
Cannock WS12 .... **2** D4
St Peter's CE Prim Sch
WS9..............**16** E4
St Peters Cl
Birmingham B28..... **105** D6
Bromsgrove B61..... **136** E1
Sutton Coldfield B72... **46** B3
St Peter's Cl
Redditch B97....... **158** E5
Stonnall WS9 .... **16** E4
Tamworth B77....... **21** D1
Water Orton B46 ..... **59** B2
West Bromwich DY4... **52** B4
St Peter's Collegiate CE
Sch WV3..........**24** E3
St Peter's Croft B73.. **46** B3
St Peters Ct
2 Hinckley LE10...... **71** E1
Lichfield WS13 ....**3** B1
Walsall WS3 .... **14** B1
St Peter's Ct CV1.... **165** D4
St Peters Dr WS3 .... **15** A4

St Peters La B92 ..... **90** D1
St Peter's RC Fst Sch
B61............. **150** E8
St Peters RC Prim Sch
B32.............. **84** C1
St Peter's RC Prim Sch
Royal Leamington Spa
CV32.............**161** F8
Walsall WS3 .... **14** B2
St Peter's RC Sch
Hinckley LE10........ **71** E1
Solihull B91........ **107** B2
St Peters Rd B17..... **85** B5
St Peter's Rd
Birmingham B20..... **66** C8
Burntwood WS7 ....**7** C6
Cannock WS12 .... **2** D4
Dudley DY2 .... **62** D5
7 Royal Leamington Spa
CV32.............**161** F8
Stourbridge DY9 ..... **81** C1
St Peters Terr WS2 ... **28** E4
St Philip's Cath* B3 **164** B3
St Philip's Pl B2 .... **164** C3
St Philip's RC Prim Sch
B66...............**65** B6
St Phillips Ave WV3...**38** F8
St Phillip's Ave WV3...**38** F7
St Phillip's Gr WV3...**38** F7
St Quentin St WV2 ... **42** C7
St Saviour's CE Prim Sch
B8................ **67** D5
St Saviour's Cl WV2 ...**39** F6
St Saviour's Ct DY9 .. **99** A6
St Saviour's Rd B8 ... **67** D4
St Silas' Sq B19 ..... **66** B7
St Simons Cl **3** B75...**46** F6
Saint's Peter & Paul RC
Prim Sch CV2 ..... **114** F7
St Stephan's Ho B97 **153** E4
St Stephen's Ave
WV13 ....**26** F2
St Stephen's CE Fst Sch
B98.............. **153** F5
St Stephen's CE Prim Sch
WV10.............**25** F4
St Stephens Ct WS12 ...**2** C4
St Stephens Gdns
B98.............. **153** F5
St Stephen's Gdns **1**
WV13 .... **27** A1
St Stephens Rd
Birmingham B29.... **104** B8
West Bromwich B71... **65** B8
St Stephen's Rd WS7 ..**7** C6
St Stephens St B6.... **66** E6
Saints Way CV10 ..... **73** D5
St Teresa's RC Prim Sch
B20............. **55** A3
St Teresa's RC Prim Sch
WV4.............**39** E5
St Thomas Aquinas RC
Sch B38 .... **103** D3
St Thomas CE Prim Sch
WV11 .... **26** D7
St Thomas' CE Prim Sch
B15.............. **86** D8
St Thomas Cl
Sutton Coldfield B75... **46** F5
Walsall WS3 .... **28** E6
St Thomas' Cl WS9 ... **16** B1
St Thomas More RC Fst
Sch B98 .... **159** B7
St Thomas More RC
Prim Sch
Coventry CV3 .... **133** D5
Great Wyrley WS6......**5** A4
St Thomas More RC Sch
Bilston WV14 .... **41** A7
Nuneaton CV10....... **73** A3
St Thomas More's RC
Prim Sch B26 ......**89** B5
St Thomas of Canterbury
RC Prim Sch WS3 ...**28** F4
St Thomas' Rd
Birmingham B23..... **56** D3
Coventry CV6 .... **96** A3
St Thomas's Cl CV10.. **72** C3
St Thomas's Ct **13**
CV1.............. **113** B2
St Thomas's Ho **12**
CV1.............. **113** B2
St Thomas St DY2 .... **62** C5
St Valentines Cl B70...**53** F2
St Vincent Cres B70...**52** F6
St Vincent St W B16... **66** A2
St Vincent's RC Prim Sch
B7................**67** B3

St J–Sam **237**

St Vincent St B16..... **66** B2
St Wilfrid's RC Prim Sch
B36................**68** F8
Saladin Ave B69...... **63** E5
Salcombe Ave B26 ... **89** C5
Salcombe Cl
Cannock WS11 ....**4** C7
Coventry CV3 .... **134** D6
Nuneaton CV11....... **73** F5
Salcombe Dr DY5 .... **81** C7
Salcombe Gr WV14 ... **40** D1
Salcombe Rd **3** B66.. **65** B5
Saldavian Ct WS2 .... **42** B6
Salem Rd LE10....... **75** F5
Salem St DY4 .... **52** D5
Salford Cir B23 ...... **56** D1
Salford Cl
Coventry CV2 .... **114** A5
Redditch B98 .... **159** B6
Salford St B6........ **67** C8
Salford Trad Est B6... **67** C8
Salisbury Ave CV3... **133** C6
Salisbury Cl
Birmingham B13..... **86** E3
Dudley DY1 .... **50** F3
Lichfield WS13 ....**3** C3
Wolston CV8........ **135** F3
Salisbury Dr
Cannock WS11 ....**2** B1
Kidderminster DY11 . **116** A6
Nuneaton CV10..... **72** B7
Water Orton B46 ..... **59** C3
Salisbury Gr B72..... **57** C7
Salisbury Ho
3 Birmingham B24... **56** F4
Hinckley LE10........ **71** C4
Salisbury Pl WV3..... **25** B1
Salisbury Prim Sch
WS10.............**41** F7
Salisbury Rd
Birmingham, Lozells
B19............. **66** D8
Birmingham, Moseley
B13............. **86** E3
Birmingham, Saltley B8 **67** E5
Hinckley LE10........ **76** B7
Smethwick B66....... **65** B4
West Bromwich B70... **53** E1
Salisbury St
Darlaston WS10 ..... **41** E7
Wolverhampton WV3 .. **25** B1
Salisbury Twr B18.... **66** A3
Sallow Gr WS8........**7** A1
Sally Ward Dr WS9 ... **16** A4
Salop Cl B71......... **53** B6
Salop Dr Cannock WS11..**4** F8
Oldbury B68......... **64** C2
Salop Rd Oldbury B68.. **64** C2
Redditch B97 .... **153** D3
Salop St Bilston WV14. **40** E4
Birmingham B12..... **86** F8
Dudley DY1 .... **51** B2
Oldbury B69......... **52** E1
Wolverhampton WV3 . **163** B2
Salstar Cl B6........ **66** E6
Saltash Gr B25....... **68** C1
Saltbrook Rd B63.... **82** A7
Saltbrook Trad Est
B63............. **82** A7
Salter Rd DY4........**51** F7
Salters La B79 ...... **21** B6
Salter's La
Redditch B97....... **153** B6
West Bromwich B71... **53** E4
Salter's Rd WS9..... **16** A3
Salter St B94....... **126** C2
Salters Vale B70...... **53** E1
Saltisford CV34 ..... **160** D7
Saltisford Canal Ctr*
CV34 .... **160** C8
Saltisford Gdns
CV34 .... **160** C8
Salt La CV1 .... **165** B2
Saltley Ind Ctr B8.... **67** C3
Saltley Rd B7....... **67** C5
Saltley Sch B8....... **68** A3
Saltley Trad Est B8... **67** D6
Saltley Viaduct B8.... **67** C4
Saltney Cl B24 ...... **57** D5
Salts La B78 .... **34** E5
Saltwells La DY2 .... **62** B2
Saltwells Nature
Reserve* DY5,
DY2.............. **62** A3
Saltwells Rd DY2.... **62** C2
Salwarpe Gr B29..... **84** C2
Salwarpe Rd B60.... **150** F8
Sam Barber Ct WS12 ...**2** E1

Sambar Rd B78 . . . .**20** F1
Sambourn Cl B91 . . . **107** E6
Sambourne Dr B34. . . **69** D7
Sambourne La
  Astwood Bank B96 . . . **158** F1
  Sambourne B96 . . . . . **159** A1
Sambourne Park La
  B96 . . . . **159** A1
Sambrook Rd WV10 . . **26** A6
Sam Gault Cl CV3 . . . **134** E7
Sammons Way CV4. . **111** D1
Sampson Cl
  Birmingham B21 . . . . . . **54** C1
  Coventry CV2 . . . . **114** C8
  Oldbury B69 . . . . **63** C7
Sampson Ho B11 . . . . **87** B8
Sampson Rd B11 . . . . **87** B7
Sampson Rd N B11. . . **87** B8
Sampson St WS10 . . . . **42** B3
Samsara Rd B60 . . . . **137** C1
Sams La B70 . . . . **53** C1
Sam Spencer Ct
  DY10 . . . . **118** A2
Samuel Cl WS13 . . . .**3** C2
Samuel Hayward Ho [5]
  CV2 . . . . **96** B1
Samuel Ho WS3 . . . . . . **14** B1
Samuel Johnson's
  Birthplace Mus★
  WS13 . . . .**9** B8
Samuels Rd B32 . . . . . **84** A5
Samuel St WS3 . . . . . . **14** B1
Samuel Vale Ho CV1. **165** B4
Sanby Cl CV12 . . . . . . **78** A4
Sanda Croft B36 . . . . . **70** B6
Sandalls Cl B31 . . . . **102** D1
Sandal Rise B91 . . . . **107** E3
Sandals Rise B62. . . . **83** D3
Sandalwood Cl WV12. **27** B8
Sand Bank WS3 . . . . . **14** A1
Sandbarn Cl B90 . . . **126** F6
Sandbeds Rd WV12. . . **27** C4
Sandbourne Rd B8. . **68** A4
Sanderling Cl WV10 . . **12** B7
Sanderling Ct DY10 . **117** A1
Sanderling Rise
  Burntwood WS7 . . . .**7** B8
  Kingswinford DY6. . . . . **61** A6
Sanders Cl Dudley DY2 **62** E7
  Redditch B97 . . . . **153** B4
Sanders Ct CV34 . . . . **161** C8
Sanders Ind Est **[1]**
  B61. . . . . **136** E1
Sanderson Ct DY11. . **116** C5
Sanders Rd
  Bedworth CV6. . . . . **96** B6
  Bromsgrove B61. . . . . **136** E1
Sandfield Bridge DY5 **50** D1
Sandfield Cl B90 . . . **126** B8
Sandfield Gr DY3 . . . . **50** B2
Sandfield Mdw WS13 . . .**9** A6
Sandfield Rd
  Stourbridge DY8 . . . . . **60** F2
  West Bromwich B71. . . . **42** E2
Sandfields Ave B10. . **87** B8
Sandfields Rd B68 . . **64** C2
Sandford Ave B65 . . . **63** C3
Sandford Cl
  Coventry CV2 . . . . **96** E3
  Hinckley LE10 . . . . **71** F1
Sandford Ho WS13 . . . . .**9** A7
Sandford Rd
  Birmingham B13. . . . . . **87** A3
  Dudley DY1 . . . . **50** E1
Sandford Rise WV6. . . **24** E6
Sandford St WS13 . . . . . .**9** B7
Sandgate Cres CV2. . **114** E2
Sandgate Rd
  Birmingham B28. . . . . **106** A4
  Tipton DY4 . . . . **52** A8
Sandhill Farm Cl [1]
  B19. . . . . **66** D7
Sandhills Cres B91. . **127** B8
Sandhills Gn B48. . . **138** E7
Sandhills La B45. . . . **138** D7
Sandhills Rd B45. . . . **138** D8
Sandhill St WS3. . . . . **14** A1
Sandhurst Ave
  Birmingham B36. . . . . . **68** D6
  Stourbridge DY9 . . . . . **81** D2
Sandhurst Cl B98 . . . **154** C6
Sandhurst Dr WV4 . . **39** A4
Sandhurst Gr
  Coventry CV6 . . . . **113** C6
  Stourbridge DY8. . . . . . **60** E3
Sandhurst Ho B38. . . **104** B1
Sandhurst Rd
  Birmingham B13. . . . . . **86** F2

Sandhurst Rd *continued*
  Kingswinford DY6. . . . . **61** A4
  Sutton Coldfield B74. . . **31** F5
Sandicliffe Cl DY11. . **116** C8
Sandilands Cl CV2. . . **114** E4
Sandland Cl WV14. . . . **40** F6
Sandland Rd WV12. . . **27** D8
Sandmartin Cl DY2 . . **62** D2
Sandmartin Way
  DY10 . . . . **117** A2
Sandmeadow Pl DY6 . **60** C5
Sandmere Gr B14 . . . **105** D3
Sandmere Rd B14. . . **105** D3
Sandmere Rise WV10. **11** E1
Sandon Cl B98 . . . . . **154** A3
Sandon Gr B24. . . . . . . **57** B4
Sandon Ho WV6. . . . . . **24** E5
Sandon Rd
  Birmingham B17. . . . . . **65** B1
  Nuneaton CV11. . . . . . . **73** B5
  Stourbridge DY9 . . . . . **81** F4
  Wolverhampton WV10 . **11** B1
Sandown B77 . . . . **21** F5
Sandown Ave
  Cheslyn Hay WS6 . . . .**4** E3
  Coventry CV6 . . . . **95** F2
Sandown Cl CV32 . . . **157** C4
Sandown Ct [18] B29 . **103** C7
Sandown Dr
  Lower Marlbrook
    B61. . . . . **121** B1
  Perton WV6. . . . . **23** F4
Sandown Rd B36. . . . . **68** D8
Sandown Tower [3]
  B31. . . . . **103** A1
Sandpiper B77 . . . . **36** A5
Sandpiper Cl
  Cannock WS12 . . . .**2** C7
  Kidderminster DY10 . . . **117** B2
  Stourbridge DY9 . . . . . . **81** F5
Sandpiper Gdns B38 **123** F7
Sandpiper Rd CV2. . . . **96** B3
Sandpiper Way B23 . . **56** C6
Sandpit Cl WS10 . . . . . **42** E2
Sandpits Cl B76 . . . . . **59** C6
Sandpits Ind Est **[4]**
  B1. . . . . **66** B3
Sandpits La CV6 . . . . . **94** F2
Sandpits The
  Birmingham B30. . . . . **103** E8
  Bulkington CV12 . . . . . . **79** C2
Sandra Cl WS9 . . . . . . **30** B5
Sandringham Ave
  WV12 . . . . **27** B6
Sandringham Cl CV4 **131** F5
Sandringham Ct
  [3] Birmingham B43 . . . **43** F1
  Nuneaton CV10. . . . . . . **72** F6
Sandringham Dr
  Aldridge WS9 . . . . **16** B1
  Rowley Regis B65. . . . . **63** C4
Sandringham Ho
  WV3 . . . . **163** A1
Sandringham Pl DY8 . **60** D1
Sandringham Rd
  Birmingham B42. . . . . . **55** B6
  Halesowen B62. . . . . . . **83** B7
  Stourbridge DY8. . . . . . **60** D1
  Wolverhampton WV4 . . **39** A4
Sandringham Way
  DY5 . . . . **81** C8
Sand St B70 . . . . **52** E4
Sandstone Ave B45. . **122** A8
Sandstone Cl DY3 . . . **50** D4
Sandstone Cl B77 . . . **36** A7
Sandway Gdns B8. . . **67** D6
Sandway Gr B13 . . . . **105** C7
Sandwell Ave WS10 . . **41** B5
Sandwell Bsns
  Development Ctr
  B66. . . . . **64** C7
Sandwell Bsns Pk
  B66. . . . . **64** C8
Sandwell Coll Oldbury
  Campus B68 . . . . **64** A3
Sandwell Coll
  (Smethwick Campus)
  B66. . . . . **65** A5
Sandwell Coll (West
  Bromwich Campus)
  B70. . . . . **53** C3
Sandwell Ct B21 . . . . **65** D8
Sandwell Ctr B70. . . . **53** D3
Sandwell & Dudley Sta
  B70. . . . . **53** A1
Sandwell General Hospl
  B71. . . . . **53** D5
Sandwell Ho [1] WS1 .**42** F8

Sandwell Park Farm★
  B71 . . . . **53** F3
Sandwell Pl WV12. . . . **27** D7
Sandwell Rd
  Birmingham B21. . . . . . **54** D1
  West Bromwich B70. . . . **53** C4
  Wolverhampton WV10 . **11** B1
Sandwell Rd N B71. . . **53** D4
Sandwell Road Pas
  B70 . . . . **53** C4
Sandwell St WS1 . . . .**42** F8
Sandwell Valley Country
  Pk★ B70, B71. . . . . . .**53** F5
Sandwell Valley Ctry Pk
  B71. . . . . **54** A5
Sandwell Valley Nature
  Ctr★ B43 . . . . **54** C6
Sandwell Wlk [8] WS1 .**42** F8
Sandwick Cl CV3 . . . **134** F8
Sandwood Dr B44. . . . .**55** F8
Sandyacre Way DY8 . . **81** B5
Sandy Cres
  Hinckley LE10 . . . . **71** C1
  Wednesfield WV11 . . . . **27** A8
  Wolverhampton WV11 . **13** A1
Sandy Croft
  Birmingham B13. . . . . **105** C7
  Sutton Coldfield B72. . . **46** C3
Sandyfields Rd DY3 . . **50** B6
Sandygate Cl B97 . . . **152** F2
Sandy Gr WS8. . . . .**6** F1
Sandy Hill Rd B90 . . **106** A4
Sandy Hill Rise B90 . **106** A4
Sandy Hollow WV6 . . **24** C2
Sandy La
  Birmingham, Aston B6 . **67** B7
  Birmingham, Great Barr
    B42. . . . . **55** D8
  Blackdown CV32 . . . . . **156** F6
  Blakedown DY10. . . . . **118** C3
  Cannock WS11 . . . .**1** B1
  Codsall WV8 . . . . **10** A4
  Coventry CV1 . . . . **113** C5
  Madeley Heath B61,
    B62. . . . . **120** E5
  Royal Leamington Spa
    CV32. . . . . **156** D4
  Wednesbury WS10 . . . . **42** F3
  Wolverhampton, Bushbury
    WV10 . . . . **11** E1
  Wolverhampton WV6 . . **24** E6
Sandy Lane Bsns Pk
  CV1. . . . . **113** C5
Sandy Mount WV5. . . **49** B7
Sandymount Rd WS1 .**42** F8
Sandy Rd DY8 . . . . **80** D1
Sandys Gr DY4 . . . . . . **51** E5
Sandythorpe CV3 . . . **134** E6
Sandy Way
  Birmingham B15. . . . . . **66** B1
  Tamworth B77. . . . . **22** B3
Sandy Wlk LE10 . . . . . **71** B2
Sangwin Rd WV14. . . . **51** C7
Sankey Rd WS11 . . . .**1** F3
Sankey's Cnr WS7. . . . . .**6** F7
Sannders Cres DY4. . . **52** B5
Sansome Rd B90. . . . **105** F2
Sansome Rise B90 . . **105** F2
Sanstone Cl WS3. . . . . **14** C3
Sanstone Rd WS3 . . . . **14** C3
Santolina Dr WS5 . . . . **43** A3
Santos Cl CV3. . . . . . . **134** F8
Sant Rd B31. . . . . **123** B7
Santridge Ct B61. . . . **137** A4
Santridge La B61. . . . **137** A4
Sapcote Bsns Ctr B10 **87** E6
Sapcote Gr CV2. . . . . . **96** B4
Sapcote Ind Est B64. .**62** F3
Sapcote Rd LE10 . . . . **76** B7
Saplings The B76. . . . **58** A8
Sapphire Ct
  Birmingham B3. . . . . . **164** A4
  [3] Solihull B92. . . . . . . **88** F1
Sapphire Dr
  Cannock WS11 . . . .**2** C3
  Royal Leamington Spa
    CV31. . . . . **161** F5
Sapphire Gate CV2. . **114** C2
Sapphire Hts B1 . . . . . **66** B4
Sapphire Twr [2] B6 . .**66** F6
Saracen Dr
  Balsall Common CV7. . **129** C6
  Sutton Coldfield B75. . . **47** A6
Sara Cl B74. . . . . **32** A3
Sarah Cl WV14 . . . . . . **40** E1
Sarah Ct B73. . . . . **45** D1
Sarah Gdns WS5 . . . .**42** F4
Sarah Siddons Ho [2]
  WS13 . . . .**9** B7
Sarah St B9. . . . . **67** B2

Saredon Cl WS3. . . . . . **15** A1
Saredon Rd WS6, WS11,
  WV10 . . . .**4** B3
Sarehole Mill Mus★
  B13. . . . . **105** D8
Sarehole Rd B28 . . . . . **87** E1
Sargeaunt St CV31. . . **161** F7
Sargent Cl B43. . . . . . . **44** D4
Sargent Turner Trad Est
  DY9. . . . .**81** F6
Sark Dr B36. . . . . **70** B6
Satchwell Ct [15]
  CV32 . . . . **161** F8
Satchwell Wlk [16]
  CV32 . . . . **161** F8
Satellite Ind Pk WV11 **26** D4
Saturday Bridge [7]
  B1 . . . . **66** C1
Saturn Rd WS11. . . . . . .**2** A5
Saumur Way CV34. . . **161** C6
Saunders Ave CV12. . . **78** B2
Saunders Ho [11]
  CV32 . . . . **156** F2
Saunton Cl CV5 . . . . . **112** B8
Saunton Way B29 . . . **85** C2
Saveker Dr B76 . . . . . . **46** E4
Savernake Cl B45. . . . **102** A2
Saville Cl
  Birmingham B45. . . . . **122** B7
  Hinckley LE10 . . . . **71** E2
Saville Gr CV8 . . . . . . **148** C5
Savoy Cl B32. . . . . **85** A5
Saw Mill Cl WS4 . . . . . **28** E3
Saxelby Cl B14 . . . . . **104** E2
Saxelby Ho B14 . . . . **104** E2
Saxifrage Pl DY10 . . . **116** F4
Saxon Bsns Pk B60 . **150** E2
Saxon Cl
  Binley Woods CV3. . . . **135** D7
  Great Wyrley WS6. . . . . . .**5** A2
  Polesworth B78 . . . . . . **22** F1
  Studley B80. . . . . **159** E5
  Tamworth B77. . . . . **35** F6
Saxoncourt WV6 . . . . **24** C5
Saxondale Ave B26. . . **88** F6
Saxon Dr B65 . . . . **63** C4
Saxondrive B79 . . . . . **21** C5
Saxonfields WV6 . . . . **24** C5
Saxon Hill Sch WS14. . .**9** C6
Saxon Mdws CV32. . . **156** C2
Saxon Mill La B79. . . . **21** C4
Saxon Rd CV2. . . . . . . **114** B4
Saxons Way B14 . . . . **105** A2
Saxon Way B37 . . . .**69** F3
Saxon Wlk WS13 . . . . . .**8** E7
Saxon Wood Cl [2]
  B31. . . . . **103** A4
Saxon Wood Rd B90. **126** B8
Saxton Dr B74. . . . .**31** F6
Scafell Cl CV5. . . . . . . **112** A4
Scafell Dr
  Bilston WV14 . . . . **40** F7
  Birmingham B23. . . . . . **56** D5
Scafell Rd DY8 . . . . **81** B6
Scaife Rd B60. . . . . . . **151** B7
Scammerton B77 . . . . **36** B7
Scampton Cl WV6. . . . **23** E5
Scampton Way B79 . . **21** C8
Scar Bank CV34 . . . . **155** E1
Scarborough Cl [2]
  WS2 . . . . **42** B8
Scarborough Rd WS2. **42** B8
Scarborough Way
  CV4 . . . . **131** F7
Scarecrow La B75. . . . **32** E4
Scarfield Hill B48. . . **138** E5
Scarman Rd CV4 . . . . **132** B5
Scarsdale Rd B42. . . . **55** D8
Schofield Ave B71. . . . **53** B8
Schofield Bsns Pk
  B60. . . . . **151** A7
Schofield Rd B37 . . . . **70** A5
Scholars Cl B21. . . . . . **66** A7
Scholars Ct DY10. . . . **116** E4
Scholars Gate
  Birmingham B33. . . . . . **69** B2
  Burntwood WV3 . . . . . . **7** B7
Scholars Wlk WS4. . . . **29** B7
Scholfield Rd CV7. . . . **95** A6
Schoolacre Rd B34. . . **69** B6
Schoolacre Rise B74 . **30** E1
School Ave WS8. . . . . . **15** F8
School Bell Mews
  CV8 . . . . **149** B6
School Cl
  Birmingham, Castle Vale
    B35. . . . . **58** B3

School Cl *continued*
  Birmingham, Kingshurst
    B37. . . . . **70** A6
  Burntwood WS7 . . . .**6** D8
  Codsall WV8 . . . . **10** A4
  Coventry CV3 . . . . **113** F2
  Hinckley LE10 . . . . **76** A6
  Norton Canes WS11 . . . . .**6** B6
  Oldbury B69 . . . . **63** C7
  Wolverhampton WV3 . . **38** B7
School Cotts CV35 . . **145** F3
School Cres WS11. . . . . .**6** A6
School Croft CV35. . . **146** C2
School Ct WS12 . . . .**2** C6
School Dr
  Bilston WV14 . . . . **41** A2
  Bromsgrove B60. . . . . **137** A3
  Stourbridge DY8 . . . . . **80** F8
  Wythall B47. . . . . **125** A3
School Dr The DY2 . . . **62** D7
Schoolfields Rd WS14 **18** A5
Schoolgate Cl
  Birmingham B8. . . . . . . **68** A6
  Walsall WS4 . . . . **15** D1
School Gn WV14 . . . . . **40** C8
School Hill CV10 . . . . . **72** A8
School Ho The WS7 . . .**7** D7
Schoolhouse Cl B38. **104** B2
School House La
  CV2 . . . . **115** A6
School La
  Alvechurch B48. . . . . . **139** B5
  Bedworth CV7. . . . . **95** F7
  Birmingham, Buckland End
    B34. . . . . **69** B7
  Birmingham, Kitt's Green
    B33. . . . . **68** F1
  Brierley Hill DY5 . . . . . . **61** B4
  Burntwood WS7 . . . .**6** D8
  Hagley DY9 . . . . **99** D6
  Halesowen B63. . . . . . . **82** F2
  Hopwas B78 . . . . **20** B7
  Kenilworth CV8. . . . . . **147** F5
  Lickey End B60 . . . . . . **137** B6
  Little Packington CV7. . . **91** D7
  Norton Canes WS3 . . . . . .**5** C2
  Radford Semele CV31. . **162** E5
  Shuttington B79 . . . . . . **22** F7
  Solihull B91. . . . . **107** D4
  Tamworth B77. . . . . **35** D5
  Walsall WS3 . . . . **14** F4
  Weeford B78. . . . . **19** D2
  Wolverhampton WV10 . **11** E2
  Wroxall CV35. . . . . **145** E4
School Rd
  Birmingham B45. . . . . **121** E6
  Birmingham, Hall Green
    B28. . . . . **106** A8
  Birmingham, Moseley
    B13. . . . . **86** F7
  Birmingham, Yardley Wood
    B14. . . . . **105** C4
  Brierley Hill DY5 . . . . . . **62** A4
  Bulkington CV12 . . . . . . **79** C2
  Himley DY3 . . . . **49** B3
  Hockley Heath B94. . . . **143** B7
  Norton Canes WS11 . . . . .**6** A6
  Solihull B90. . . . . **106** B2
  Trysull WV5. . . . . **37** C1
  Wednesbury WS10 . . . . **42** D2
  Wolverhampton, Nordley Hill
    WV11 . . . . **26** C6
  Wolverhampton, Tettenhall
    Wood WV6 . . . . **24** B3
  Wombourne WV5 . . . . . **49** B7
School St W [2] WV14. **51** C8
School St
  Brierley Hill DY5 . . . . . . **61** D7
  Cradley Heath B64. . . . . **62** D1
  Darlaston WS10 . . . . . . **41** E5
  Dudley, Eve Hill DY1 . . . **51** B1
  Sedgley DY3 . . . . **50** E8
  Stourbridge DY8 . . . . . **80** F6
  Tamworth B77. . . . . **21** D8
  Tipton WV14 . . . . **51** C8
  Walsall WS4 . . . . **15** D1
  Willenhall WV13 . . . . . . **26** F1
  Wolverhampton WV3 . . **163** B2
School Terr [1] B29 . .**85** F2
School Wlk
  Bilston WV14 . . . . **40** C8
  Burntwood WS7 . . . .**6** D8
  Nuneaton CV11. . . . . . . **73** E2
  Tamworth B79. . . . . **21** B6
Scimitar Cl B79 . . . . . . **20** E7
Scorers Cl B90. . . . . . **106** B6
Scotchill The CV6 . . . . **95** A1
Scotch Orch WS13 . . . **3** D1

Scotch Orchard Prim Sch
  WS13 . . . .**3** D1
Scotia Rd WS11 . . . .**1** D3
Scotland La B32 . . . . . **102** C7
Scotland St B1. . . . . . . **66** C3
Scots Cnr B14 . . . . . . **104** E8
Scots La CV6. . . . . **112** F6
Scott Arms Sh Ctr
  B43. . . . . **43** F1
Scott Ave
  Nuneaton CV10. . . . . . . **73** D8
  Wednesbury WS10. . . . **42** B2
  Wolverhampton WV4 . . **38** E4
Scott Cl Lichfield WS14 . .**9** B6
  West Bromwich B71. . . . **53** D5
Scott Gr B92 . . . . **88** E3
Scott Ho B43 . . . . **54** F7
Scott Rd
  Birmingham B43 . . . . . **43** F2
  Kenilworth CV8. . . . . . **147** E2
  Redditch B97 . . . . **158** C8
  Royal Leamington Spa
    CV31. . . . . **162** B6
  Solihull B92. . . . . **88** E2
  Tamworth B77. . . . . **21** E4
  Walsall WS5 . . . . **43** D6
Scott's Green Cl DY1 . **62** A8
Scotts Green Island
  DY1 . . . .**61** F7
Scott's Rd DY8 . . . .**80** F5
Scott St WS12. . . . . **2** F3
Scotwell Cl B65 . . . . . . **63** B3
Scout Cl B33. . . . . **69** C2
Scribban Cl B66. . . . . . **65** B4
Scribers La B28. . . . . **105** E4
Scribers Mdw B28 . . **105** E4
Scrimshaw Ho [1]
  WS2 . . . . **42** C7
Sculthorpe Rd DY10 . **98** B2
Seacole Ho B97 . . . . . **153** B2
Seacroft Ave B25. . . . . **68** E1
Seafield B77 . . . .**21** F5
Seafield Cl DY6 . . . . . . **60** E4
Seafield La
  Beoley B98 . . . . **141** A2
  Portway B48, B98. . . . . **140** E4
Seaford Cl CV6. . . . . . . **96** B4
Seaforth Dr LE10 . . . . **71** A1
Seaforth Gr WV11 . . . **13** B1
Seagar St B71 . . . . **53** E4
Seager's La DY5. . . . . . **61** D2
Seagrave Rd CV1. . . . **165** D1
Seagull Bay Dr WV14. **40** D1
Sealand Dr CV12 . . . . . **78** A3
Seal Cl B76. . . . . **46** E3
Seals Gn B38 . . . . **123** D7
Seamless Dr WV11 . . . **26** D4
Sear Hills Cl CV7. . . . **130** D6
Seaton B77 . . . . **35** F4
Seaton Cl
  Hinckley LE10 . . . . **76** B7
  Nuneaton CV11. . . . . . . **73** F5
  Wednesfield WV11 . . . . **26** F5
Seaton Gr B13 . . . . **86** D1
Seaton Pl DY8 . . . . **60** C2
Seaton Rd B66. . . . . . . **65** B5
Sebastian Cl CV3 . . . **134** B5
Seckham Rd [3] WS13 . .**9** A8
Second Ave
  Birmingham B29. . . . . . **86** A3
  Birmingham, Bordesley
    Green B9 . . . . **67** F1
  Birmingham, Witton B6. **55** F3
  Brownhills WS8 . . . .**7** A1
  Coventry CV3 . . . . **114** C4
  Kingswinford, Barrow Hill
    DY6. . . . . **61** A7
  Kingswinford, Wall Heath
    DY6. . . . . **60** F8
  Wolverhampton WV10 . **25** E7
Second Exhibition Ave
  B40. . . . . **90** D4
Securehold Bsns Ctr
  B98. . . . . **154** B2
Sedge Ave B38. . . . . . **103** F3
Sedgeberrow Covert [4]
  B38. . . . . **123** E8
Sedgeberrow Rd B63. **83** A2
Sedgebourne Way
  B31. . . . . **102** C1
Sedge Dr B61. . . . . **137** A6
Sedgefield Cl DY1 . . . **50** E3
Sedgefield Gr WV6. . . .**23** F4
Sedgefield Wlk B61. . **121** B1
Sedgeford Cl DY5 . . . . **81** D8
Sedgehill Ave B17. . . . **85** B4
Sedgemere Gr
  Balsall Common CV7. . **130** C5
  Walsall WS4 . . . . **29** C1
Sedgemere Rd B26. . .**68** C7

Sedgemoor Ave WS7 . . . 7 B5
Sedgemoor Rd CV3 . 134 B5
Sedgfield Way WS11 . . . 6 B4
Sedgley Cl B98. . . . . . 153 F4
Sedgley Gr B20 . . . . . . 54 E4
Sedgley Hall Ave DY3. 50 C8
Sedgley Rd
Dudley DY1 . . . . 51 B6
Gospel End Village WV4 38 F2
Sedgley Rd W DY4 . . . 51 D5
Sedgley Road E DY4. . 52 A3
Sedgley St WV2 . . . . . . 39 C7
Seed Field Croft
CV3 . . . . 133 E7
Seedhouse Ct B64 . . . 83 B8
Seeds La WS8. . . . . 15 B8
Seekings Dr CV8 . . . . . 148 B4
Seekings The CV31 . . 162 B3
Seeleys Rd B11 . . . . . . 87 E5
Seeswood Cl CV10 . . . 72 C2
Sefton Dr B65. . . . . 62 F6
Sefton Gr DY4. . . . . 41 C2
Sefton Rd
Birmingham B16. . . . . . 65 F2
Coventry CV4 . . . . 132 E6
Tamworth B77. . . . . 35 D4
Segbourne Rd B45 . . 121 F8
Segundo Cl WS5 . . . . . . 42 F4
Segundo Rd WS5. . . . . . 42 F4
Seisdon Rd WV5 . . . . . 37 A1
Selba Dr DY11 . . . . 116 A6
Selborne Cl WS1 . . . . . 29 A1
Selborne Gr B13 . . . . 105 C5
Selborne Rd
Birmingham B20. . . . . . 55 A2
Dudley DY2. . . . . 62 D7
Selborne St WS1 . . . . . 29 A1
Selbourne Cres WV1 . 26 B1
Selby Cl B26 . . . . 68 F1
Selby Gr B13. . . . . 105 C6
Selby Ho B69 . . . . 63 D6
Selby Way
Nuneaton CV10. . . . . . . 72 B5
Walsall WS3 . . . . 13 E2
Selcombe Way B38. . 123 F7
Selco Way B76. . . . . . . 58 A5
Selcroft Ave B32 . . . . . . 84 F5
Selecta Ave B44. . . . . . 44 D2
Selina Dix Ho CV1. . . 165 C4
Selker Dr B77. . . . . 21 F5
Selkirk Cl B71 . . . . 53 C6
Selly Ave B29 . . . . 86 A2
Selly Cl B29. . . . . 86 B2
Selly Hall Croft B30 . 104 A6
Selly Hill Rd B29 . . . . . . 85 F2
Selly Manor Mus★
B30 . . . . 103 F7
Selly Oak Colls B29. 103 D8
Selly Oak Hospl B29 . . 85 F1
Selly Oak Ind Est B29 .85 E1
Selly Oak Rd B30. . . . 103 E5
Selly Oak Specl Sch
B29. . . . . 103 E8
Selly Oak Sta B29. . . . . 85 E2
Selly Park Rd B29 . . . . 86 A2
Selly Park Tech Coll For
Girls B29. . . . . 86 B1
Selly Wharf B29. . . . . . 85 E2
Selly Wick Dr B29. . . . 86 B2
Selly Wick Rd B29. . . . 86 B2
Sellywood Rd B29,
B30 . . . . 103 E8
Selma Gr B14 . . . . 105 D5
Selmans Hill WS3 . . . . 14 C2
Selman's Par WS3. . . . 14 C2
Selsdon Cl
Kidderminster DY11 . . 116 B5
Wythall B47. . . . . 125 C5
Selsdon Rd WS3 . . . . . . 13 F3
Selsey Ave B66. . . . . . . 65 B3
Selsey Cl CV3 . . . . 134 C4
Selsey Rd B17 . . . . 65 B3
Selston Rd B6 . . . . 66 E7
Selvey Ave B43. . . . . . . 44 C3
Selworthy Rd
Birmingham B36 . . . . . . 69 F8
Coventry CV6 . . . . 95 E3
Selwyn Cl WV2. . . . . . . 39 C7
Selwyn Ho B37. . . . . . . 70 D3
Selwyn Rd
Bilston WV14 . . . . 40 F7
Birmingham B16 . . . . . . 65 D2
Burntwood WS7 . . . . 7 F8
Selwyn Wlk B74. . . . . . 31 C4
Semele Cl CV31 . . . . . 162 E5
Seneschal Rd CV3. . . 133 E7
Senior Cl WV11 . . . . . . 13 A3
Senneleys Park Rd
B31 . . . . 84 E1
Sennen Cl
Nuneaton CV11. . . . . . . 74 A5
Willenhall WV13 . . . . . . 26 F1
Sensall Rd DY9. . . . . 81 F3
Sentry Way B75 . . . . 46 F6
Sephton Dr CV6. . . . . . 96 C6
Serin Cl DY10 . . . . 117 A1
Serpentine Rd
Birmingham, Aston
B6. . . . . 56 A1
Birmingham B17. . . . . . . 85 C6
Birmingham, Selly Oak
B29. . . . . 86 A2
Serpentine The
DY11 . . . . 116 C4
Servite Ct B14 . . . . . . 105 A2
Servite Ho
2 Coleshill B46 . . . . . . 70 F7
Kenilworth CV8. . . . . . 147 F3
Seton Ho B74 . . . . 31 E2
Settle Ave B34 . . . . 68 F6
Settle Croft B37. . . . . . 69 F1
Setton Dr DY3 . . . . 50 E7
Seven Acres WS9 . . . . 30 B5
Seven Acres La B98 . 154 C5
Seven Acres Rd
Birmingham, Quinton
B62. . . . . 84 A5
Birmingham, Turves Green
B31. . . . . 103 C1
Sevendwellings View
DY5 . . . . 61 C1
Seven Star Rd B91 . . 107 B5
Seven Stars Ind Est
CV3. . . . . 134 A7
Seven Stars Rd B69 . . 64 A7
Severn Ave LE10 . . . . . 75 A8
Severn Cl
Birmingham B36. . . . . . 69 F7
Catshill B61. . . . . 137 A8
Royal Leamington Spa
CV32. . . . . 157 C3
Tipton DY4 . . . . 51 F5
Wednesfield WV12 . . . . 27 A7
Severn Ct
Birmingham B23. . . . . . 56 B3
Sutton Coldfield B73. . . 46 B5
Severn Dr
Brierley Hill DY5 . . . . . . 61 B7
Burntwood WS7 . . . . 7 D6
Perton WV6. . . . . 23 E4
Severne Gr B27 . . . . . . 88 C1
Severne Jun & Inf Sch
B27. . . . . 106 C8
Severne Rd B27. . . . . 106 C8
Severn Gr
5 Birmingham B19 . . . 66 C7
8 Birmingham B19 . . . 66 C7
Kidderminster DY11 . . 116 B3
Severn Ho
4 Birmingham B68 . . . 84 B8
Dudley DY3 . . . . 50 D3
Severn Rd
Brownhills WS8 . . . . 6 C2
Bulkington CV12 . . . . . . 79 A3
Coventry CV1 . . . . 113 F1
Halesowen B63. . . . . . . 82 B5
Stourbridge DY8 . . . . . . 80 F3
Walsall WS3 . . . . 14 E1
Severn St B1. . . . . 164 B1
Severn Twr B7 . . . . 67 B5
Severn Valley Rly★ DY10,
DY11 . . . . 116 D2
Severn Way B47. . . . . . 124 E2
Sevilla Cl CV3. . . . . . . 115 A2
Sevington Cl B91. . . . 127 C8
Sewall Ct CV6. . . . . . . 114 A8
Sewall Highway CV2 114 B6
Seward Cl WS14. . . . . . . 9 D6
Seymour Cl
Birmingham B29. . . . . . 86 A2
Cheslyn Hay WS6 . . . . . . 4 D1
Coventry CV3 . . . . 134 C5
Seymour Dr B98 . . . . 154 A5
Seymour Gdns B74. . . 31 E3
Seymour Gr CV34 . . . 161 D6
Seymour Ho CV3. . . . 133 C8
Seymour Rd
Kidderminster DY11 . . 116 B8
Nuneaton CV11. . . . . . . 73 D3
Oldbury B69 . . . . 64 C7
Stourbridge DY9. . . . . . 82 A4
Wednesbury DY4 . . . . . 41 C1
Shackleton Dr
Hinckley LE10 . . . . 75 E4
Perton WV6. . . . . 23 E5
Shackleton Rd WS3 . . 14 D2
Shadowbrook La
B92 . . . . 108 E7
Shadowbrook Rd
CV6 . . . . 113 A5
Shadwell Dr DY3 . . . . . 50 D3
Shadwell St B4 . . . . . 164 C4
Shady La B44 . . . . 44 E2
Shadymoor Dr DY5 . . . 81 C8
Shaftesbury Ave
Keresley CV7 . . . . 95 A7
Stourbridge DY9 . . . . . . 81 C2
Shaftesbury Cl B60. . 137 B2
Shaftesbury Dr WS12. . . 2 C7
Shaftesbury Rd
Coventry CV5 . . . . 132 F8
Wednesbury WS10 . . . . 42 B2
Shaftesbury Sq B71 . . 53 C5
Shaftesbury St B70,
B71 . . . . 53 C4
Shaft La CV7. . . . . 93 A4
Shaftmoor Ind Est
B28. . . . . 87 F2
Shaftmoor La B27,
B28 . . . . 87 F2
Shaftsbury Ave B63 . . 82 B7
Shaftsbury Cl WV14 . . . 40 F7
Shaftsbury Dr WS7 . . . . . 7 F7
Shaftsbury Rd B26 . . . 89 C5
Shahjalal Rd B8. . . . . . 67 D5
Shakels Cl B97 . . . . . . 158 E4
Shakespeare Ave
Bedworth CV12. . . . . . . 78 D2
Lichfield WS14 . . . . 9 B6
Redditch B98 . . . . 154 A2
Warwick CV34 . . . . . . 160 C4
Shakespeare Cl
Dudley WV14 . . . . 40 D2
Tamworth B79. . . . . 21 A6
Shakespeare Cres
WS3 . . . . 28 F7
Shakespeare Dr
Hinckley LE10 . . . . 71 C1
Kidderminster DY10 . . 117 B6
Nuneaton CV11. . . . . . . 74 A1
Solihull B90. . . . . 106 B1
Shakespeare Gr WS11 . 1 D4
Shakespeare Ho
B31 . . . . 123 A8
Shakespeare Pl WS3 . . 28 F7
Shakespeare Rd
Birmingham B23. . . . . . 56 B3
Burntwood WS7 . . . . 6 F8
Dudley DY3. . . . . 50 A4
Smethwick B67. . . . . . . 64 E4
Solihull B90. . . . . 126 D8
Tipton DY4 . . . . 52 A8
Shakespeare St
Birmingham B11. . . . . . 87 C5
Coventry CV2 . . . . 114 B4
Wolverhampton WV1 . 163 D2
Shakleton Rd CV5. . . 113 A2
Shaldon Wlk 4 B66. . . 65 B5
Shale St WV14 . . . . 40 C5
Shalford Rd B92 . . . . . 88 E4
Shallcross La DY3. . . . 50 D3
Shalnecote Gr B14 . . 104 C5
Shambles 2 WS10 . . . . 41 F2
Shandon Cl B32. . . . . . . 84 F3
Shanklin Cl WS6 . . . . 5 A3
Shanklin Dr CV10 . . . . 73 D6
Shanklin Rd CV3 . . . . 134 B4
Shannon B77 . . . . 35 F8
Shannon Dr WS8. . . . . . . 6 C2
Shannon Rd B38 . . . . 123 E7
Shannon's Mill B79 . . 21 A5
Shannon Wlk WS8 . . . . . 6 C2
Shanti Niketan WV2 . . 39 D7
Shapinsay Dr B45 . . . 101 F1
Shard End Cres B34. . 69 C6
Shardlow Rd WV11. . . 26 E8
Shardway The B34 . . . 69 C5
Sharesacre St WV13. . 27 B3
Sharington Cl 3 DY2. 62 E8
Sharman Rd WV10 . . . 25 E6
Sharmans Cross Jun Sch
B91. . . . . 106 E4
Sharmans Cross Rd
B91 . . . . 106 F4
Sharnford Rd LE10 . . . . 76 F6
Sharon Cl WV4. . . . . . . 39 E5
Sharon Ct B27 . . . . 88 C3
Sharon Way WS12. . . . . 2 D3
Sharp Cl CV6 . . . . 95 C2
Sharpe Cl CV34 . . . . . 160 E8
Sharpe St B77 . . . . 22 A5
Sharpless Rd LE10 . . . . 75 F7
Sharpley Ct CV2. . . . . 115 A8
Sharps Cl B45. . . . . . . 122 A7
Sharrat Field B75 . . . . 32 D2
Sharratt Rd CV12. . . . . 78 A2
Sharrocks St WV1. . . 163 D2
Shaw Ave DY10. . . . . . 117 B6
Shawbank Rd B98. . . 154 B3
Shawberry Ave B35 . . 58 B4
Shawberry Rd B37 . . . . 69 F5
Shawbrook Gr 4
B14 . . . . 105 A3
Shawbury Cl B98. . . . 154 E3
Shawbury Gr
Birmingham B12. . . . . . 86 F8
Perton WV6. . . . . 23 E5
Shawbury Rd WV10 . . . 25 F5
Shaw Ct WS11 . . . . 6 A5
Shaw Dr B33. . . . . 68 E2
Shawe Ave CV10 . . . . . 73 C7
Shawfield B47 . . . . . . 125 A5
Shaw Hall La WV9. . . . 11 C7
Shaw Hellier Ave DY5 61 E2
Shaw Hill Gr B8. . . . . . 68 A4
Shaw Hill Prim Sch
B8. . . . . 67 F4
Shaw Hill Rd B8 . . . . . 68 A4
Shawhurst Croft
B47 . . . . 125 A7
Shawhurst Gdns B47 125 B7
Shawhurst La B47. . . 125 A6
Shaw La Lichfield WS13 . . 9 A8
Stoke Prior B60 . . . . . 150 C3
Wolverhampton WV6 . . 24 B3
Shaw Lane Ind Est
B60. . . . . 150 C2
Shawley Croft B27 . . . 88 E4
Shaw Park Bsns Village
WV10. . . . . 25 D6
Shaw Rd
Dudley, Netherton
DY2. . . . . 62 C7
Hurst Hill WV14 . . . . . . 40 B1
Tipton DY4 . . . . 52 C4
Wolverhampton WV4 . . 39 C6
Shaws Cl B97 . . . . 152 F2
Shawsdale Rd B36 . . . . 68 F7
Shaw's La WS6. . . . . 5 A2
Shaw's Pas B5 . . . . . . 164 D2
Shaw St B70 . . . . 52 E7
Shayler Gr WV2 . . . . . . 39 D7
Sheaf La B26 . . . . 89 B4
Sheapecoate Ho 1
B71 . . . . 42 F1
Shearers Pl 4 B75. . . . 32 E3
Shearwater Cl
Birmingham B45 . . . . . 121 F6
Kidderminster DY10. . 117 B1
Shearwater Ct WV10 . . 11 B3
Shearwater Wlk B23 . 56 B7
Sheaves Cl WV14. . . . . 40 B3
Shedden St 3 DY2. . . 62 D8
Sheddington Rd B23 . 56 D7
Sheen Ho CV2 . . . . . . 114 D8
Sheen Rd B44. . . . . 44 E4
Sheepclose Dr B37. . . . 70 A3
Sheepcote Cl CV32 . . 157 A1
Sheepcote Grange
B61 . . . . 136 F5
Sheepcote La B77. . . . . 21 F4
Sheepcote St B16 . . . . 66 B2
Sheepcroft Cl B97. . . 152 F2
Sheepfold Cl B65 . . . . 63 A4
Sheepmoor Cl B17 . . . 84 F8
Sheepwash La DY4 . . . 52 D5
Sheepy Cl LE10 . . . . 71 F1
Sheerwater Dr DY5. . . 81 D7
Sheffield Rd B73 . . . . . 57 A7
Sheffield St DY5 . . . . . 62 A1
Shefford Rd B6 . . . . 66 F5
Sheila Ave WV11 . . . . . 26 E7
Shelah Rd B63 . . . . 83 A6
Shelbourne Cl B69 . . . 52 D2
Sheldon Ave WS10 . . . 42 A4
Sheldon Cl WV14. . . . . 40 D4
Sheldon Ctry Pk★
B26 . . . . 89 E5
Sheldon Dr B31 . . . . 102 D2
Sheldonfield Rd B26 . 89 D5
Sheldon Gr
Birmingham B26. . . . . . 89 B5
Warwick CV34 . . . . . . 155 F2
Sheldon Hall Ave B33 69 D3
Sheldon Heath Com Arts
Coll B26 . . . . 89 C8
Sheldon Heath Rd
B26 . . . . 89 B8
Sheldon Rd
Redditch B98 . . . . 159 A8
West Bromwich B71. . . 53 E8
Wolverhampton WV10 . 11 A1
Sheldon Wlk B33. . . . . 69 C1
Sheldrake Cl CV3 . . . 115 A1
Shelduck Cl DY10 . . . 117 B3
Shelfield Cl
Coventry CV5 . . . . 112 B3
Hockley Heath B94. . . 143 C6
Shelfield Rd B14 . . . . 104 C3
Shelfield Sports & Com
Coll WS4. . . . . 15 C2
Shell Corner Trad Est
B62. . . . . 83 D8
Shelley Ave
Kidderminster DY10 . . 116 E7
Tipton DY4 . . . . 52 B8
Warwick CV34 . . . . . . 160 C4
Shelley Cl
Bedworth CV12. . . . . . . 78 D1
Catshill B61. . . . . 137 A8
Dudley DY3 . . . . 50 A5
Redditch B97 . . . . 158 C8
Stourbridge DY8 . . . . . . 81 A8
Shelley Dr
Birmingham B23 . . . . . . 56 B3
Sutton Coldfield B74. . . 31 F6
Shelley Gdns LE10. . . . 71 E3
Shelley Ho
Halesowen B63. . . . . . . 82 B5
1 Oldbury B68 . . . . . . 64 C4
Shelley Rd
2 Burntwood WS7 . . . . . 7 A8
Cannock WS11 . . . . 1 E5
Coventry CV2 . . . . 114 C3
Tamworth B79. . . . . 21 A7
Willenhall WV12 . . . . . . 27 E7
Wolverhampton WV10 . 11 D2
Shellon Cl CV3. . . . . . 134 F8
Shelly Cl B37 . . . . 69 F2
Shelly Cres B90 . . . . . 127 B6
Shelly Croft B33 . . . . . 69 A3
Shelly La B90 . . . . 127 B6
Shelly Twr B31 . . . . . . 103 C3
Shelsley Ave B69. . . . . 63 D5
Shelsley Dr B13 . . . . . . 87 B2
Shelsley Way B91 . . . 107 B1
Shelton Cl WS10 . . . . . 42 C5
Shelton La B63. . . . . . . 82 E5
Shelton Sq CV1 . . . . . 165 B2
Shelton St B77 . . . . 35 F7
Sheltwood Cl B97 . . . 153 A2
Sheltwood La B60,
B97 . . . . 152 A3
Shelwick Gr B93 . . . . 127 F4
Shenley Ave DY1 . . . . 51 C6
Shenley Court Sch
B29. . . . . 102 F7
Shenley Fields Dr
B31 . . . . 102 F8
Shenley Fields Rd
B29 . . . . 103 B8
Shenley Gn B29. . . . . 102 F6
Shenley Hill B31 . . . . 102 F6
Shenley La B29 . . . . . 102 F7
Shenstone Ave
Halesowen B62. . . . . . . 83 E5
Stourbridge DY8 . . . . . . 80 D3
Shenstone Cl
Bromsgrove B60. . . . . 137 B3
Sutton Coldfield B74. . . 31 E6
Shenstone Ct
Bromsgrove B60. . . . . 137 B3
Solihull B90. . . . . 105 D2
Wolverhampton WV3 . . 39 A6
Shenstone Dr
Aldridge WS9 . . . . 30 A8
Balsall Common CV7. . 130 A6
Shenstone Flats B62 . . 83 F5
Shenstone Ho WS13. . . . 3 E1
Shenstone Lodge Sch
WS14. . . . . 18 A3
Shenstone Rd
Birmingham, Edgbaston
B16. . . . . 65 C3
Birmingham, Great Barr
B43. . . . . 54 E8
Birmingham, Highter's Heath
B14. . . . . 105 A1
Shenstone Sta WS14 . . 17 F6
Shenstone Trad Est
B63. . . . . 83 C4
Shenstone Valley Rd
B62 . . . . 83 F6
Shenton Wlk B37 . . . . . 69 F5
Shepheard Rd B26 . . . 89 D5
Shepheards La CV7 . . 92 A3
Shepherd Cl
Coventry CV4 . . . . 111 F3
Lichfield WS13 . . . . 3 C3
Shepherd Dr WV12 . . . 27 C5
Shepherds Brook Rd
DY9 . . . . 81 D5
Shepherds Fold B65. . 63 B2
Shepherds Gdns 8
B15 . . . . 66 B1
Shepherds Green Rd
B24 . . . . 56 F1
Shepherds Pool Rd
B75 . . . . 32 E2
Shepherds Standing
B34 . . . . 69 B6
Shepherds Way B23 . . 56 C8
Shepherds Wlk
Bromsgrove B60. . . . . 150 E7
Wolverhampton WV8 . . 10 F2
Shepley Mdw B45 . . . 138 B8
Shepley Rd
Barnt Green B45. . . . . 138 A7
Birmingham B45 . . . . . 122 B6
Shepperton Bsns Pk
CV11. . . . . 73 C1
Shepperton Ct CV11. . 73 C1
Shepperton St CV11. . 73 C2
Sheppey Dr B36. . . . . . 70 B5
Shepwell Gdns WV10. 12 C7
Shepwell Gn WV13 . . . 27 C1
Sherard Croft B36. . . . 70 B6
Sheraton Cl
Aldridge WS9 . . . . 30 B6
Cannock WS12 . . . . 2 A7
Sheraton Dr DY10. . . 117 B6
Sheraton Grange DY8 . 80 F2
Sheraton Rd B60. . . . 137 C1
Sherborne Cl WS3. . . . 28 C7
Sherborne Ct WV10 . . 11 E1
Sherborne Gdns WV8. 10 A3
Sherborne Gr B1. . . . . 66 A3
Sherborne Rd
Hinckley LE10 . . . . 76 B7
Wolverhampton WV10 . 11 D1
Sherborne St B16 . . . . 66 B2
Sherbourne Arc CV1 165 B2
Sherbourne Ave
Cannock WS12 . . . . 2 E4
Nuneaton CV10. . . . . . . 72 B4
Sherbourne Cl B98. . 154 D2
Sherbourne Cres
CV5 . . . . 112 E4
Sherbourne Ct CV1. . 165 B1
Sherbourne Dr B27 . . 88 C4
Sherbourne Fields Sch
CV6. . . . . 112 D5
Sherbourne Rd
Birmingham, Acock's Green
B27. . . . . 88 C4
Birmingham, Balsall Heath
B12. . . . . 86 F7
Cradley Heath B64 . . . . 83 B8
Stourbridge DY8 . . . . . . 81 B4
Sherbourne St CV1. . 113 A2
Sherbrooke Ave B77. . 35 E6
Sherbrook Rd WS11 . . . . 1 C1
Sherdmore Croft
B90 . . . . 126 F6
Sheridan Cl 3 WS2 . . 42 B7
Sheridan Gdns DY3. . . 49 F5
Sheridan St
Walsall WS2 . . . . 42 B7
West Bromwich B71. . . 53 D4
Sheridan Wlk B35. . . . 58 A3
Sheriff Ave CV4 . . . . . 132 B7
Sheriff Dr DY5 . . . . 61 F2
Sheriffs Cl WS14 . . . . . . 9 E6
Sheriffs Orch CV1 . . . 165 B2
Sherifoot La B75 . . . . . 32 B4
Sheringham B15 . . . . . 85 E8
Sheringham Cl CV11 . . 73 F2
Sheringham Rd B30. . 104 B3
Sherington Ave CV5. 112 C4
Sherington Dr WV4. . . 39 D5
Sherlock Cl WV12 . . . . 27 D5
Sherlock Rd CV5. . . . 112 D3
Sherlock St B5. . . . . . . 86 E8
Sherrans Dell WV4 . . . 39 D4
Sherratt Cl B76 . . . . 57 F8
Sherringham Dr
WV11 . . . . 13 C1
Sherron Gdns B12. . . . . 86 F5
Sherston Covert 11
B30 . . . . 104 C2
Shervale Cl WV4 . . . . . 39 A6
Sherwin Ave WV14 . . . 40 A2
Sherwood Ave DY4 . . . . 51 F4
Sherwood Cl
Birmingham B28 . . . . . 105 F5
Solihull B92. . . . . 106 F7
Wood End CV9 . . . . 36 C1
Sherwood Dr
Brierley Hill DY5 . . . . . . 61 F2
Cannock WS11 . . . . 2 A3
Sherwood Ho 1 B64 . . 82 F8
Sherwood Jones Cl
CV6 . . . . 113 B6
Sherwood Mews
B28 . . . . 105 E6

Sherwood Rd
Birmingham B28..... **105** E7
Bromsgrove B60.....**151** A6
Smethwick B67...... **65** A1
Stourbridge DY8...... **80** E7
Sherwood St WV1.. **163** B4
Sherwood Wlk
Birmingham B45..... **102** B2
Royal Leamington Spa
CV32..............**157** C4
Walsall WS9 .... **29** E2
Shetland Ave B77 ....**35** F7
Shetland Cl
Birmingham B16...... **65** F2
Coventry CV5 ....**112** A4
Wolverhampton WV6 .. **25** B5
Shetland Dr
Nuneaton CV10....... **73** A2
Smethwick B66...... **64** D8
Shetland Wlk B36... **70** B6
Shevlock Way CV6 .. **114** A6
Shidas La B69........ **63** E7
Shifnal Wlk B31..... **122** F8
Shifrall Way B75.....**46** F7
Shillcock Gr B19.... **66** E5
Shillingstone Cl CV2 **115** A4
Shillingstone Dr CV10 **73** A1
Shilton & Ansty CE Fst
Sch CV7...........**97** E7
Shilton Cl B90 ...... **126** F6
Shilton Gr B29 ...... **102** F8
Shilton Ind Est CV7 ...**97** E7
Shilton La
Barnacle CV2, CV7 .... **97** B4
Bulkington CV12...... **79** D1
Coventry CV2 .... **96** F3
Shilton CV7, CV12..... **97** D8
Shinwell Cres B69.... **52** D2
Shipbourne Cl B32....**84** F5
Shipley Fields B24 ... **57** A3
Shipley Gr B29......**103** A8
Shipston Rd
Birmingham B31..... **103** B1
Coventry CV2 ....**114** C6
Shipton Cl Dudley DY1..**50** F3
Redditch B97 ....**153** A6
Shipton Rd B72 ...... **46** C3
Shipway Rd B25...... **88** A7
Shirebrook Cl CV2 ... **96** D2
Shire Brook Cl B6... **66** E8
Shire Brook Ct 2
B19 .... **66** D7
Shire Cl
Birmingham B16...... **65** F2
Coventry CV6 .... **96** B1
Oldbury B68........ **64** B2
Shirehall Pl WS11 .....**2** B2
Shirehampton Cl
B97 ....**152** F2
Shireland Brook Gdns 1
B18 ....**65** D4
Shireland Cl B20....**54** F1
Shireland Hall Jun & Inf
Sch B66 ....**65** C3
Shireland La B97.....**153** A4
Shireland Language Coll
B66...............**65** B3
Shireland Rd B66.... **65** B3
Shire Lea WS8 ...... **16** B6
Shirelea Cl WS7.......**7** B8
Shire Oak Sch WS9 .. **16** A5
Shire Ridge WS9..... **16** B4
Shires Gate Ret Pk
CV31..............**161** E6
Shires Gate Trad Est
CV31..............**161** E6
Shires Ind Est WS14 ...**9** A6
Shires Ret Pk CV34 .**161** D6
Shirestone Com Prim Sch
B33...............**69** D2
Shirestone Rd B33.... **69** E2
Shireview Gdns WS3 .. **15** B4
Shireview Rd WS3.... **15** B4
Shirewood WS11 ......**1** B2
Shirland Rd B37 ..... **70** A1
Shirlett Cl CV2 ...... **96** B4
Shirleydale 2 B90 .. **126** C8
Shirley Dr B72 ...... **46** C4
Shirley Heath Jun Sch
B90...............**106** C1
Shirley La CV7 ....**111** A5
Shirley Park Rd B90. **106** B2
Shirley Rd
Birmingham, Hall Green
B27, B28...........**106** A7
Birmingham, King's Norton
B30..............**104** A5
Coventry CV2 ....**115** A7

Shirley Rd *continued*
Dudley DY2.......... **62** E8
Oldbury B68 .... **64** C6
Shirley Sta B90...... **105** F1
Shirley Wlk B79.......**20** F7
Shirral Gr B37.......**69** F5
Shirrall Dr B78....... **33** E4
Shoal Hill Cl WS11 .....**1** B2
Sholing CV8 ....**10** F1
Shooters Cl B5....... **86** D6
Shooters Hill B72 .... **46** D2
Shop La WV6 .... **37** B7
Shopping Ctr The
CV31..............**162** B5
Shopping Prec The
CV34...............**156** A1
Shops The DY6 ...... **60** D4
Shopton Rd B34...... **69** A7
Shoreham Cl WV13... **26** D1
Shorncliffe Rd CV6.. **112** E6
Short Acre St WS2 ... **28** D3
Shortbutts La WS14 ....**9** B5
Shorters Ave B14 ... **105** B4
Shortfield Cl CV7.... **130** B7
Short Heath Ct B23 ...**56** F5
Short Heath Jun Sch
WV12.............. **27** D5
Short Heath Prim Sch
B23............... **56** D6
Short Heath Rd B23 .. **56** E6
Short La WS6........**4** E3
Shortland Cl B93.... **128** A7
Shortlands CV7 ...... **95** D6
Shortlands Cl B30.... **104** A2
Shortlands La WS3....**14** F3
Shortley Rd CV3..... **133** F8
Short Rd
Smethwick B67...... **64** D3
Wolverhampton WV10 .. **11** E1
Short St Bilston WV14.. **40** D6
Brownhills WS8 ..... **15** F7
Cannock WS11 ....**1** F3
Coventry CV1 ......**165** C2
Darlaston WS10 ..... **41** F7
Dudley DY1......... **51** A2
Halesowen B63...... **82** F5
Nuneaton CV10...... **72** D4
Rowley Regis B65.... **63** C2
Solihull B90........ **126** A5
Stourbridge DY8..... **80** F5
Tipton DY4......... **51** E8
Walsall WS2 .... **28** D1
Wednesbury WS10 ... **41** E3
Willenhall WV12.... **27** C5
Wolverhampton WV1 . **163** C3
Shorwell Pl DY5....... **61** B1
Shottery Cl
Coventry CV5 ....**112** B3
Sutton Coldfield B76... **46** F1
Shottery Gr B76.......**46** F1
Shottery Rd B90 .... **106** B1
Shotteswell Rd B90 . **126** B8
Showell Cir WV10 .... **25** E7
Showell Green La
B11................ **87** C3
Showell Ho 10 B69... **64** A7
Showell La
Eaves Green CV7 ..... **93** A1
Wombourne WV4 .... **38** B3
Showell Rd WV10 .... **25** D6
Showell Road Ind Est
WV10.............. **25** D6
Showells Gdns B7.... **67** C7
Showmans Cvn Site
WS3 .... **14** E2
Shrawley Ave DY11.. **116** B3
Shrawley Cl
Birmingham B45..... **121** F7
Halesowen B63...... **83** A2
Shrawley Rd B31..... **123** A8
Shreres Dyche CV34. **160** C4
Shrewley Cres B33... **69** E1
Shrewsbury Cl WS3...**13** F1
Shrewsbury Rd
DY11..............**116** B3
Shrewton Ave B14 .. **104** D2
Shrubberies The
CV4 ....**132** E4
Shrubbery Ave DY4.. **51** D5
Shrubbery Cl
Sutton Coldfield B76... **57** D6
Walsall WS1 .... **29** B1
Shrubbery Ct DY10.. **116** F1
Shrubbery Rd B61... **136** E1
Shrubbery Sch The
B76................**57** F7
Shrubbery St DY10 .. **116** F1
Shrubbery The
Birmingham B16..... **65** F3
4 Dudley DY1...... **51** B2

Shrub La B24 .... **57** B4
Shrublands Ave B68.. **84** B7
Shrubland St CV31.. **162** A6
Shrubland Street Com
Prim Sch CV31..... **162** A6
Shuckburgh Gr 5
CV32..............**157** A2
Shugborough Cl WS3. **14** B1
Shugborough Dr DY1. **50** E2
Shugborough Way
WS11...............**2** C1
Shulman's Wlk CV2 ..**114** D7
Shultern La CV4......**132** D6
Shuna Croft CV2 .... **115** B7
Shustoke La WS5..... **43** B4
Shustoke Rd
Birmingham B34...... **69** C6
Solihull B91........**107** D5
Shutlock La B13 ...... **86** D1
Shut Mill La B62 .... **100** D2
Shuttington Rd B79,
B79 .... **22** B6
Shutt La B94......... **126** B1
Shuttle St CV6 ......**114** B8
Shylock Gr CV34 .... **161** E2
Shyltons Croft B16.... **66** A2
Sibdon Gr B31...... **123** A8
Sibree Rd CV3 ...... **134** B4
Sibton Cl CV2 .... **96** C1
Sidaway Cl B65...... **63** C6
Sidaway St B64...... **62** E1
Sidbury Gr B93...... **127** E3
Sidbury Rd CV6 ..... **113** C6
Sidcup Cl WV14...... **40** B3
Sidcup Rd B44....... **45** A1
Siddeley Ave
Coventry CV3 ......**114** B1
Kenilworth CV8..... **147** E3
Siddons Factory Est
B70.................**52** F8
Siddons Rd WV14 .... **40** D2
Siddons Way B70 .... **53** A7
Sidemoor Fst Sch
B61................**136** E3
Sidenhill Cl B90.... **126** B8
Sidestrand WV9......**10** F3
Sidford Gdns B24 .... **57** C3
Sidford Gr B23 ...... **56** E7
Sidings The
Birmingham, Gravely Hill
B23............... **56** E3
Birmingham, Lozells
B20.............. **66** C8
Cannock WS12 ....**2** C7
5 West Bromwich B70 **53** C2
Sidlaw Cl
Halesowen B63...... **82** D2
Wolverhampton WV10 . **25** C6
Sidmouth Cl
Coventry CV2 ......**114** C7
Nuneaton CV11..... **73** F5
Sidney St WV2 .....**163** B1
Sidney Stringer Com
Tech Coll CV1 .....**165** C3
Sidon Hill Way WS11 ...**2** C2
Sidwick Cres WV2... **40** B6
Sigmund Cl WV1..... **26** B3
Signal Gr WS3 .... **14** A1
Signal Hayes Rd B76. **47** A2
Signal Wlk B77...... **22** A2
Silesbourne Cl B36... **69** C8
Silhill Hall Rd B91.. **107** A5
Silica Rd B77 .... **22** B2
Silken Ct CV11 ...... **73** B4
Silksby St CV3...... **133** D8
Sillins Ave B98...... **154** A3
Silva Ave DY6 ....**60** F4
Silver Birch Ave CV12 **77** E2
Silverbirch Cl CV10.. **72** A7
Silver Birch Cl
Binley Woods CV3... **135** D7
Birmingham B8..... **67** D6
Silver Birch Coppice
B74............... **31** D5
Silverbirch Ct B24.... **57** B6
Silver Birch Ct DY10. **117** A4
Silver Birch Dr
Hollywood B47 ..... **125** B6
Kidderminster DY10 .. **117** C5
Silver Birches Bsns Pk 3
B60................**150** F6
Silver Birch Gr 5
CV31..............**161** F5
Silverbirch Rd B91.. **107** E3
Silver Birch Rd
Birmingham, Erdington
B24............... **57** B6
Birmingham, Kingshurst
B37............... **69** F6
Huntington WS12 ....**1** D8

Silver Birch Rd *continued*
Norton Canes WS11.....**6** B5
Sutton Coldfield B74... **30** F1
Wolverhampton WV2 . **39** E7
Silver Court Gdns
WS8 ....**15** F7
Silvercroft Ave B21... **54** D3
Silver Ct WS8 ....**15** F7
Silverdale B61 ...... **136** F4
Silverdale Cl CV2.... **96** B4
Silverdale Dr
Burntwood WS7 ......**6** D7
Wolverhampton WV10 . **25** E5
Silverdale Gdns DY8.. **60** C3
Silverdale Rd B24.... **57** D5
Silver End Ind Est & Bsns
Pk DY5............. **61** C1
Silverfield Cl B14.... **104** E8
Silver Fir Cl WS12 ....**2** A8
Silver Innage B63.... **82** C7
Silverlands Ave B68.. **64** B3
Silverlands Cl B28....**87** F1
Silver Link Rd B77....**21** F1
Silvermead Ct B47 .. **124** F5
Silvermead Rd B73.. **46** A1
Silvermere Rd B26 .. **89** D6
Silver's Cl WS3.......**14** F7
Silver St
Birmingham B14.... **104** E8
Brierley Hill DY5.... **61** C1
Brownhills WS8 ..... **15** F7
Coventry CV1 ......**165** B3
Hollywood B47 .... **124** E5
Kidderminster DY10 . **116** F7
Redditch B97, B98 .. **153** E4
Tamworth B79....... **21** B5
Silverstone Ave
DY11..............**116** D8
Silverstone Cl WS2... **27** D3
Silverstone Ct B30 . **104** B8
Silverstone Dr
Coventry CV6 ...... **95** E5
Sutton Coldfield B74... **44** F6
Silverthorne Ave DY4. **51** D5
Silverthorne La B64.. **82** B8
Silverton Cres B13 ... **87** D1
Silverton Hts B67 ....**64** F6
Silverton Rd
Coventry CV6 ...... **113** F7
Smethwick B67...... **64** E6
Silverton Way WV11...**26** F5
Silver Trees Dr CV12.. **79** B4
Silvertrees Rd DY4... **51** E5
Silver Wlk CV10......**72** F4
Silvester Ct B70...... **53** E3
Silvester Rd WV14....**40** F7
Silvester Way DY5.... **81** B8
Silvington Cl B29 ... **103** C2
Simcox Gdns B32 .... **84** D2
Simcox Rd WS10 .....**41** F5
Simcox St WS12...... **2** D4
Simeon Bissell Cl
DY4................ **52** A5
Simeon's Wlk DY5.....**81** F7
Simmonds Cl WS3....**14** D3
Simmonds Pl WS10...**41** F7
Simmonds Rd WS3 ... **14** D3
Simmonds Way WS8 .. **16** A6
Simmons Cl B78 ..... **34** B1
Simmons Dr B32 ..... **84** D4
Simmons Leasow B32 **84** E2
Simmons Rd WV11 ... **13** B1
Simms La Dudley DY2.. **62** C5
Hollywood B47 ..... **125** A5
Simon Cl
Nuneaton CV11..... **73** D2
West Bromwich B71... **42** E1
Simon Ct CV7 .... **96** A8
Simon Rd B47 ...... **125** A7
Simon Stone St CV6. **113** F8
Simpkins Cl WS9..... **16** A3
Simpson Gr
Coventry CV3 ...... **134** C6
Wolverhampton WV10 . **25** E6
Simpson Rd
Lichfield WS13 ....**3** B2
Sutton Coldfield B72... **46** C1
Walsall WS2 .... **28** B5
Wolverhampton WV10 . **25** E6
Simpson St B69...... **64** A8
Sinclair Ct B13....... **86** E4
Sinclair Dr CV6 ...... **96** C6
Singer Cl CV6 ...... **114** B8
Singer Croft B36......**58** F1
Singh Cl B21........ **54** E1
Sion Cl DY5......... **61** D3
Sir Alfreds Way B76... **46** E1
Sir Frank Whittle Prim
Sch CV2 .... **114** F8

Sir George's Mall **6**
DY10..............**116** E6
Sir Harrys Rd B5..... **86** C6
Sir Henry Parkes Rd
CV5 ....**132** D7
Sir Hilton's Rd B31.. **123** C7
Sir John's Rd B29.... **86** C3
Sir Richards Dr B17...**84** F7
Sir Robert Peel Hospl
B78................ **20** D2
Sir Thomas White's Rd
CV5 ....**112** F2
Sir Toby Belch Dr
CV34 ....**161** F3
Sir Walter's Mall **8**
DY10..............**116** E6
Sir William Lyons Rd
CV4 ....**132** C2
Sir Winston Churchill Pl
CV3 ....**135** C7
Sisefield Rd B38 .... **104** A1
Siskin Cl
Hammerwich WS7 ....**7** D5
Oldbury B68 .... **64** C2
Siskin Dr
Birmingham B12..... **86** E6
Coventry CV3 ...... **134** C4
Siskin Parkway E
CV3 ....**134** C1
Siskin Parkway W
CV3 ....**134** C2
Siskin Rd DY9....... **81** C3
Sisley Way LE10 ..... **71** A3
Siskin Way DY10 ... **117** B1
Sister Dora Ave WS7....**7** F7
Sister Dora Bldgs **2**
WS1 .... **28** E1
Sister Dora Gdns **1**
WS1 .... **42** E8
Siviter's Cl B65...... **63** B3
Siviter's La B65...... **63** B3
Siviter St B63 .... **83** B4
Six Acres B32....... **84** C4
Sixth Form Coll Solihull
The B91 ....**107** D2
Six Towers Rd WS2... **28** C4
Six Ways B23 ....**56** F4
Six Ways Ho B23 ....**56** F4
Skelcher Rd B90 .... **106** A3
Skelwith Rise CV11... **74** A6
Skemp Cl WV14 ..... **40** D4
Sketchley Cl B66.... **65** A6
Sketchley Hall Gdns
LE10 .... **75** C5
Sketchley Hill Prim Sch
LE10...............**75** E5
Sketchley La LE10 ... **75** C5
Sketchley La Ind Est
LE10...............**75** B5
Sketchley Manor La
LE10 .... **75** D5
Sketchley Mdws LE10 **75** C5
Sketchley Meadows Bsns
Pk LE10 .... **75** C4
Sketchley Old Village
LE10 .... **75** C5
Sketchley Rd LE10... **75** E5
Skey Dr CV10 .... **72** B6
Skidmore Ave
Tamworth B77....... **35** C5
Wolverhampton WV3 .. **38** F8
Skidmore Dr B70..... **53** A4
Skidmore Rd WV14... **40** D2
Skilts Ave B98 ...... **153** F1
Skinner La B5....... **66** E1
Skinner St WV1 ..... **163** B3
Skip La WS5 .... **43** E6
Skipness B77 .... **21** E5
Skipton Gdns CV2... **114** B6
Skipton Gn WV6..... **25** A5
Skipton Lodge CV2.. **114** B6
Skipton Pl WS11 ......**4** B7
Skipton Rd B16...... **66** A1
Skipworth Rd CV3... **115** A1
Skomer Cl B45...... **101** E1
Sky Blue Way CV1... **113** E3
Skydome The CV1 .. **165** A2
Skye Cl
Birmingham B36..... **70** B6
Nuneaton CV10..... **72** F4
Tamworth B77....... **35** F7
Skye Wlk 5 B64 .... **62** E1
Skylark Cl
Birmingham B23..... **56** C7
Dudley DY5......... **50** C1
Huntington WS12 .....**1** C7
Skylark Way DY10 .. **117** A2
Slack La B20....... **54** E2
Slacky La WS3 ...... **14** F1
Slade Ave WS7........**7** A8

Slade Cl
Nuneaton CV11...... **79** C8
West Bromwich B71... **42** F2
Sladefield Inf Sch B8 **68** A5
Sladefield Rd B8..... **68** A5
Slade Gdns WV8 ..... **10** A4
Slade Gr B93........ **127** F6
Slade Hill 3 WV6...**24** F3
Slade Jun & Inf Sch
B23............... **56** D2
Slade La
Birmingham B28..... **105** E3
Sutton Coldfield B75... **33** A3
Tamworth B77....... **35** C4
Slade Lanker B34 ... **69** A5
Slade Mdw CV31 ... **162** A6
Sladen CE Mid Sch The
DY10..............**116** F7
Sladepool Farm Rd
B14 ....**105** A2
Slade Rd
Birmingham B23..... **56** D3
Halesowen B63...... **82** C6
Sutton Coldfield B75... **32** E3
Wolverhampton WV10 . **11** C3
Slaithwaite Rd B71... **53** E4
Slaney Ct WS2 ...... **42** C7
Slaney Rd WS2...... **42** B6
Slatch House Rd B67. **64** E2
Slateley Cres B90 ... **126** F6
Slater Cl B64........**62** F1
Slater Rd B93....... **127** F4
Slaters La WS2...... **42** B7
Slaters Pl WS2...... **42** B7
Slater St Bilston WV14. **40** E3
Darlaston WS10 ..... **41** D6
Tipton, Dudley Port DY4 **52** A4
Tipton, Great Bridge
DY4.............. **52** D5
Willenhall WV13 .... **27** C3
Sleaford Gr B28..... **106** A7
Sleaford Rd B28..... **106** B7
Sleath's Yd CV12 .... **78** B3
Sledmere Cl CV2 .... **96** B3
Sledmere Prim Sch
DY2................ **62** D6
Sledmore Rd DY2 ... **62** E7
Sleets Yd CV12...... **78** A2
Slideslow Ave B60 .. **137** D2
Slideslow Dr B60.... **137** B3
Slieve The B20 ...... **55** A3
Slim Ave WV14...... **40** E3
Slimbridge Cl
Redditch B97 ...... **158** E5
2 Solihull B90...... **127** A6
Slim Rd WS2........ **27** E2
Slims Gate B63 ..... **83** A4
Slingfield Rd B31.... **103** C1
Slingsby B77........ **35** C7
Slingsby Cl CV11.....**73** F2
Sling The Dudley DY2.. **62** C6
Kidderminster DY10 .. **116** A6
Slitting Mill Cl B21... **65** C8
Sloane Ho 6 B1..... **66** C3
Sloane St B1........ **66** C3
Slough The B97, B80. **159** B4
Smallbrook La WV5 .. **49** B7
Smallbrook Queensway
B5 ....**164** C1
Small Cl B67........ **64** D5
Smalldale Rd B42 .... **55** D7
Smalley Cl WS11 ......**2** A5
Smalley Pl CV8...... **147** F4
Small Heath Bridge B10,
B11................ **87** B3
Small Heath Bsns Pk
B10................**87** F7
Small Heath Highway B10,
B11................ **87** D6
Small Heath Sch
Birmingham B10..... **87** D7
Birmingham B10..... **87** D8
Small Heath Sta B10. **87** D7
Small Heath Trad Est
B11................ **87** D6
Small La B94........ **141** E6
Smallman Rd CV10... **72** A4
Smallshire Cl WV11...**26** F5
Smallshire Way DY8.. **80** E8
Small St Walsall WS1.. **42** E8
West Bromwich B71... **53** A5
Smallwood Almshouses
B98 ....**153** E3
Smallwood Arch 5
B98 ....**153** E4
Smallwood Cl
Birmingham B24..... **57** D3
Sutton Coldfield B76... **46** E3
Smallwood Rd WV8 .. **10** D2
Smallwood St B98 .. **153** E3

Smarts Ave WS14 ... 32 A7
Smarts Rd CV12 ... 77 F1
Smeaton Gdns B18 ... 65 E4
Smedley Crooke Pl B48 ... 123 C2
Smeed Gr B24 ... 57 B3
Smercote Cl CV12 ... 77 D1
Smestow Ho B68 ... 64 B1
Smestow Sch WV3 ... 24 B1
Smestow St WV10 ... 25 D4
Smethwick Galton Bridge Sta B66 ... 64 E7
Smethwick Rolfe Street Sta B66 ... 65 A6
Smillie Pl WS11 ... 1 F3
Smirrells Rd B28 ... 105 E5
Smith Ave WS10 ... 41 D4
Smith Cl
Smethwick B67 ... 64 D3
Wolverhampton WV14 ... 40 A1
Smithfield Rd WS3 ... 14 D1
Smithfield Rise WS13 ... 9 C8
Smithfields 4 DY8 ... 81 A5
Smithford Way CV1 ... 165 B3
Smith Ho WS3 ... 14 C3
Smithmoor Cres B71 ... 53 F8
Smith Pl DY4 ... 52 B4
Smith Rd Walsall WS2 ... 42 C6
Wednesbury WS10 ... 41 F1
Smiths Cl B32 ... 84 B1
Smith's Cl WS7 ... 6 D6
Smiths La B93 ... 127 E7
Smith St
Bedworth CV12 ... 77 E1
Bilston WV14 ... 40 D5
Birmingham B19 ... 66 C5
Coventry CV6 ... 113 F5
Dudley DY2 ... 62 D7
2 Royal Leamington Spa CV31 ... 161 F7
Warwick CV34 ... 160 F7
Wood End CV9 ... 36 C1
Smiths Way B46 ... 59 A3
Smiths Wood Sch B36 ... 70 A6
Smithy Dr WS3 ... 15 A4
Smithy La
Aston Flamville LE9 ... 76 C8
Aston Flamville LE9 ... 76 D8
Dudley DY5 ... 50 B1
Lichfield WS13 ... 3 A1
Tamworth B77 ... 35 F7
Smithy The B26 ... 89 C6
Smorrall La CV12 ... 77 C2
Smout Cres WV14 ... 39 F2
Smythe Gr CV34 ... 155 E1
Snake La B48 ... 139 A6
Snakes Lake La B61 ... 136 D6
Snake Terr B48 ... 139 A6
Snapdragon Dr WS5 ... 43 A3
Snape Rd
Coventry CV2 ... 114 F5
Wolverhampton WV11 ... 13 B1
Sneyd Com Sch WS3 ... 13 E2
Sneyd Hall Cl WS3 ... 28 A8
Sneyd Hall Rd WS3 ... 14 A1
Sneyd Ho WS3 ... 13 F1
Sneyd La Walsall WS3 ... 13 F1
Willenhall WV11 ... 13 C1
Snipe Cl WV10 ... 12 B7
Snowberry Dr DY5 ... 50 C1
Snowberry Gdns 6 B27 ... 88 C5
Snowdon Cl CV10 ... 72 B3
Snowdon Gr B63 ... 82 D1
Snowdon Rd
Cannock WS11 ... 1 E6
Stourbridge DY8 ... 81 B6
Snowdon Rise DY3 ... 50 D6
Snowdon Way
Willenhall WV12 ... 13 B1
Wolverhampton WV10 ... 25 B6
Snowdrop Cl
Bedworth CV12 ... 77 E1
Brownhills WS8 ... 15 D6
Snowford Cl B90 ... 105 F1
Snow Hill WV2 ... 163 C2
Snow Hill Queensway B4 ... 164 C3
Snow Hill Sta B3 ... 164 B3
Snows Drive Hill B90 ... 126 D5
Snowshill Cl
Nuneaton CV11 ... 78 F8
Redditch B98 ... 154 B6
Snowshill Gdns DY1 ... 50 F4
Soar Way LE10 ... 75 A8
Soberton Cl WV11 ... 26 F7
Soden Cl CV3 ... 134 D6
Soden's Ave CV8 ... 135 A1
Soho Ave B18 ... 66 A7
Soho, Benson Road Sta B18 ... 65 F6
Soho Cl B66 ... 65 C6
Soho Hill B19 ... 66 B7
Soho Ho B66 ... 65 C6
Soho House Mus* B18 ... 66 A7
Soho Pool Way B18 ... 66 A6
Soho Rd B21 ... 65 F8
Soho St B66 ... 65 C6
Soho Way B66 ... 65 B6
Solari Cl DY4 ... 52 C8
Solent Cl WV9 ... 10 F2
Solent Ct B73 ... 46 B5
Solent Dr CV2 ... 96 F1
Solihull By-Pass B91 ... 107 E4
Solihull Coll B91 ... 107 A3
Solihull Coll (Chelmsley Campus) B37 ... 70 C4
Solihull Hospl B91 ... 107 C4
Solihull La B28 ... 106 A6
Solihull Parkway B37 ... 90 E8
Solihull Parkway Hospl B91 ... 107 E5
Solihull Rd
Birmingham B11 ... 87 D3
Hampton-in-A B92 ... 108 E6
Solihull B90 ... 106 D3
Solihull Ret Pk B90 ... 126 C8
Solihull Sch B91 ... 107 D4
Solihull Sta B91 ... 107 A4
Solly Gr DY4 ... 52 D7
Solva Cl WV1 ... 26 B1
Solway Cl
Royal Leamington Spa CV31 ... 162 C6
Tamworth B79 ... 21 A7
Wednesbury WS10 ... 41 C4
Somerby Dr B91 ... 127 A8
Somercotes Rd B42 ... 55 D8
Somerdale Rd B31 ... 103 C4
Somerfield Cl WS4 ... 15 C1
Somerfield Rd WS3 ... 28 C7
Somerford Cl WS6 ... 4 E1
Somerford Gdns WV10 ... 11 E2
Somerford Pl WV13 ... 26 F1
Somerford Rd B29 ... 102 F8
Somerford Way WV14 ... 51 B8
Somerland Rd B26 ... 69 A1
Somerleyton Ave DY10 ... 117 A5
Somerleyton Ct 3 DY10 ... 117 A5
Somerly Cl CV3 ... 134 F8
Somerset Cl B78 ... 21 A1
Somerset Cres WS10 ... 42 D4
Somerset Dr
Birmingham B31 ... 122 F7
Nuneaton CV10 ... 72 E4
Stourbridge DY8 ... 80 D7
Somerset Ho B33 ... 69 A2
Somerset Pl WS11 ... 1 F3
Somerset Rd
Birmingham B15 ... 85 F5
Birmingham, Erdington B23 ... 56 F6
Birmingham, Handsworth B20 ... 54 F2
Coventry CV1 ... 113 C5
Walsall WS4 ... 29 A4
West Bromwich B71 ... 53 D6
Willenhall WV13 ... 27 D2
Somers Pl 4 CV32 ... 161 E8
Somers Rd
Halesowen B62 ... 83 C5
Keresley CV7 ... 95 A6
Meriden CV7 ... 91 F1
Walsall WS2 ... 42 A7
Somers Sq 9 B63 ... 83 B3
Somerton Dr
Birmingham, Erdington B23 ... 57 A6
Birmingham, Marston Green B37 ... 90 B7
Somerville Ct
2 Sutton Coldfield B73 ... 46 A2
Tamworth B79 ... 20 D6
Somerville Ho B37 ... 70 D3
Somerville Prim Sch B10 ... 87 D8
Somerville Rd
Birmingham B10 ... 87 E8
Sutton Coldfield B73 ... 46 A3
Somery Rd
Birmingham B29 ... 85 A2
Dudley DY1 ... 51 C3
Sommerfield Rd B32 ... 84 D3
Sommerville Dr B73 ... 46 A4
Sommerville Rd CV2 ... 114 C4
Sonata Rd B60 ... 137 C1
Sonning Dr WV9 ... 10 F2
Sopwith Croft B35 ... 58 A2
Sorbus B77 ... 22 B4
Soredale Croft CV3 ... 115 A1
Sorrel B77 ... 22 B5
Sorrel Cl
Coventry CV4 ... 131 E8
Featherstone WV10 ... 12 B7
Lichfield WS13 ... 8 E6
Tipton B69 ... 52 B2
Sorrel Dr
Birmingham B27 ... 88 B2
Walsall WS5 ... 43 A3
Sorrel Gr B24 ... 57 D3
Sorrel Ho B24 ... 57 D3
Sorrell Pl CV10 ... 78 D8
Sorrell Rd CV10 ... 78 D8
Sorrell Wlk DY5 ... 81 B6
Sorrento Ct B13 ... 87 A3
Soudan B97 ... 153 D2
Souters Ho B32 ... 102 D8
Southacre Ave B5 ... 86 E8
Southall Cres WV14 ... 40 C1
Southall Rd WV11 ... 27 A8
Southall's La DY1 ... 51 B1
Southam Cl
Birmingham B28 ... 105 E8
Coventry CV4 ... 131 E7
Southam Dr B73 ... 46 B1
Southampton St WV1 ... 163 C4
Southam Rd
Birmingham B28 ... 105 E8
Radford Semele CV31 ... 162 E6
South Ave
Coventry CV2 ... 114 A2
Stourbridge DY8 ... 80 F4
Wolverhampton WV11 ... 26 C5
Southbank Ct CV8 ... 147 F4
Southbank Ho 10 CV34 ... 161 D8
Southbank Rd
Coventry CV6 ... 112 E5
Cradley Heath B64 ... 82 F8
Kenilworth CV8 ... 147 F4
South Bank Rd B64 ... 82 E8
Southbank View DY6 ... 60 E4
South Birmingham Coll (Digbeth Ctr for Arts &Digital Media) B5 ... 66 F1
South Birmingham Coll (Hall Green Campus) B28 ... 105 E8
Southborough Terr 1 CV31 ... 162 A6
Southbourne Ave
Birmingham B34 ... 68 D6
Walsall WS2 ... 28 B1
Southbourne Cl B29 ... 86 A2
Southbourne Pl WS11 ... 1 D2
Southbourne Rd WV10 ... 11 C3
South Bromsgrove Com High Sch (Tech Coll) B60 ... 150 F8
South Car Park Rd B40 ... 90 E3
South Cl WS11 ... 4 C8
Southcote Gr B38 ... 103 D1
Southcott Ave DY5 ... 81 D8
Southcott Way CV2 ... 96 F1
South Cres
Bromsgrove B60 ... 137 A1
Featherstone WV10 ... 12 C6
Southcrest Gdns B97 ... 153 D1
Southcrest Rd B98 ... 154 A2
Southcroft Rd B23 ... 56 E3
South Dene B67 ... 64 F5
Southdown Ave B18 ... 66 A6
Southdown Ct DY6 ... 60 D6
South Dr
Birmingham B5 ... 86 C4
Coleshill B46 ... 70 E6
Sutton Coldfield B75 ... 46 C6
South East Quadrant 8 B98 ... 153 E4
Southern Cl DY6 ... 60 F3
Southern Cross WS14 ... 9 C7
Southerndown Rd DY3 ... 50 B7
Southern Dr B30 ... 104 D3
Southern Ho B13 ... 105 A7
Southern Rd B8 ... 68 C6
Southern Way WS10 ... 41 C3
Southey Cl
Solihull B91 ... 127 B8
Willenhall WV12 ... 27 E8
Southfield Ave
Birmingham, Castle Bromwich B36 ... 69 B8
Birmingham, Edgbaston B16 ... 65 D3
Southfield Cl
Aldridge WS9 ... 30 A6
Nuneaton CV10 ... 73 D5
Southfield Dr
Birmingham B28 ... 106 A5
Kenilworth CV8 ... 148 A6
Southfield Gr WV3 ... 38 C7
Southfield Rd
Birmingham B16 ... 65 D3
Hinckley LE10 ... 75 E7
Wednesfield WV11 ... 26 F5
Southfields CV32 ... 157 A3
Southfields Prim Sch CV1 ... 113 E3
Southfields Rd B91 ... 106 F1
Southfield Way WS6 ... 4 F2
Southgate
Cannock WS11 ... 4 B7
Cradley Heath B64 ... 82 D8
Wolverhampton WV1 ... 163 A3
Southgate Cl DY11 ... 116 A4
Southgate End WS11 ... 4 B7
Southgate Rd B44 ... 44 E2
Southgate Way 3 DY1 ... 51 B2
South Gdns DY9 ... 99 A4
South Gn WV4 ... 38 D5
South Gr
Birmingham, Aston B6 ... 66 D8
Birmingham, Erdington B23 ... 56 F5
Birmingham, Lozells B19 ... 66 B8
South Holme B9 ... 67 C2
Southlands 8 CV31 ... 162 B7
Southlands Ct B97 ... 153 C1
Southlands Rd B13 ... 87 A1
Southlea Ave CV31 ... 161 E6
Southlea Cl CV31 ... 161 E6
Southleigh Ave CV5 ... 132 F7
Southmead Cres B98 ... 153 F3
Southmead Dr B60 ... 137 B6
Southmead Gdns B80 ... 159 E3
Southminster Dr B14 ... 104 E6
South Moons Moat Ind Est B98 ... 154 D4
South Oval DY3 ... 50 E5
South Par B72 ... 46 C4
South Park Mews DY5 ... 61 C2
Southport Cl CV3 ... 134 B5
South Range 4 B11 ... 87 B6
South Rd
Birmingham, Erdington B23 ... 56 F4
Birmingham, Hockley B18 ... 66 A6
Birmingham, King's Heath B14 ... 104 E8
Birmingham, Northfield B31 ... 102 F2
Birmingham, Sparkbrook B11 ... 87 B7
Bromsgrove B60 ... 151 B7
Smethwick B67 ... 64 F5
Stourbridge DY8 ... 80 E4
Tipton DY4 ... 52 B8
West Hagley DY9 ... 99 A4
Wolverhampton WV4 ... 39 F4
South Ridge CV5 ... 112 B4
South Road Ave B18 ... 66 A6
South Roundhay B33 ... 69 A3
Southside Bsns Ctr B12 ... 87 A5
South St
Birmingham B17 ... 85 D5
Brierley Hill DY5 ... 61 C2
Coventry CV1 ... 113 E3
3 Kidderminster DY10 ... 116 F6
Redditch B98 ... 153 E3
Walsall WS1 ... 42 D8
Willenhall WV13 ... 26 F1
Wolverhampton WV10 ... 25 C6
South Staffordshire Bsns Pk WS11 ... 4 C4
South Street Gdns WS1 ... 42 D8
South Terr CV31 ... 162 B3
South View
Birmingham B43 ... 54 E7
Hampton Magna CV35 ... 160 A6
South View Cl
Codsall WV8 ... 10 B2
Featherstone WV10 ... 12 B6
South View Rd
Royal Leamington Spa CV32 ... 157 C5
Sedgley DY3 ... 50 C8
Southview Ridge DY5 ... 81 D7
Southville Bglws For Old People B14 ... 105 B4
Southwark Cl WS13 ... 3 C3
Southway CV31 ... 162 A5
South Way B40 ... 90 F3
Southway Ct DY6 ... 60 F4
Southwick Dr B77 ... 21 C3
Southwick Pl WV14 ... 40 D7
Southwick Rd B62 ... 83 D8
South Wlk B31 ... 103 C1
Southwold Ave B30 ... 104 C3
Southwood Ave B34 ... 69 B7
Southwood Cl DY6 ... 60 E5
Southwood Covert B14 ... 104 C2
Sovereign Cl CV8 ... 147 F1
Sovereign Ct 7 B1 ... 66 C3
Sovereign Dr DY1 ... 50 E2
Sovereign Hts B31 ... 102 C1
Sovereign Rd
Birmingham B30 ... 104 A4
Coventry CV5 ... 113 A2
Sovereign Row CV5 ... 113 A2
Sovereign Way B13 ... 86 F4
Sovereign Wlk 7 WS1 ... 28 F2
Sovereign Works DY1 ... 50 E4
Sowerby March B24 ... 57 D4
Sowers Cl WV12 ... 27 D5
Sowers Ct B75 ... 32 D4
Sowers Gdns WV12 ... 27 D5
Sowe Valley Prim Sch CV3 ... 134 D7
Spa Cl LE10 ... 71 E1
Spadesbourne Rd B60 ... 137 C6
Spa Gr B30 ... 104 C8
Spa La LE10 ... 71 E1
Sparkbrook St CV1 ... 113 F3
Sparkbrook Workshops CV1 ... 113 F3
Spark St B11 ... 87 A7
Sparrey Dr B30 ... 104 A8
Sparrow Cl WS10 ... 42 B5
Sparrow Cock La B93 ... 129 C1
Spartan Cl CV34 ... 161 E4
Spartan Ind Ctr B70 ... 52 E6
Spa View CV31 ... 162 B4
Speakers Cl B69 ... 63 B7
Spearhill WS14 ... 9 E8
Speed Rd DY4 ... 51 E7
Speedway La CV8 ... 135 F7
Speedwell Cl
Aldridge WS9 ... 30 A5
6 Bedworth CV12 ... 77 D2
Birmingham B25 ... 88 A6
Wednesfield WV11 ... 26 E5
Speedwell Dr CV7 ... 130 A6
Speedwell Gdns
Brierley Hill DY5 ... 81 B6
Featherstone WV10 ... 12 B8
Speedwell Ho B38 ... 104 A1
Speedwell Rd
Birmingham, Balsall Heath B5 ... 86 D6
Birmingham, Tyseley B25 ... 88 A6
Speedwell Trad Est B11 ... 88 A6
Speedy Cl WS11 ... 1 E5
Spencer Ave
Coventry CV5 ... 113 A1
Tipton WV14 ... 51 C8
Spencer Cl
Birmingham B24 ... 57 D4
Dudley DY3 ... 50 A4
Oldbury B69 ... 63 B8
5 West Bromwich B71 ... 53 F8
Spencer Dr WS7 ... 6 E8
Spencer Rd
Coventry CV5 ... 165 A1
Lichfield WS14 ... 9 B6
Spencer's La CV7 ... 110 E1
Spencer St
Birmingham B18 ... 66 C4
Hinckley LE10 ... 71 D1
Kidderminster DY11 ... 116 C4
Spencer St *continued*
Royal Leamington Spa CV31 ... 161 F7
Spencer Yd CV31 ... 161 F7
Spennells Fst Sch DY10 ... 117 A2
Spennells Valley Nature Reserve* DY10 ... 117 A3
Spennells Valley Rd DY10 ... 117 A3
Spenser Ave WV6 ... 23 F4
Spenser Cl B79 ... 21 A6
Spenser Wlk B61 ... 137 A8
Spernal Ash B80 ... 159 F1
Spernal La B80 ... 159 F1
Spernall Gr B29 ... 85 A1
Spetchley Cl B97 ... 158 C6
Spey Cl B5 ... 86 D6
Sphinx Dr CV3 ... 114 B1
Spiceland Rd B31 ... 102 F6
Spiers Cl B93 ... 128 A6
Spies Cl B62 ... 83 F6
Spies La B62 ... 83 F5
Spills Mdw DY3 ... 50 E5
Spilsbury Cl CV32 ... 156 E2
Spilsbury Croft B91 ... 127 A8
Spindle La B90 ... 126 A6
Spindle St CV1 ... 113 D6
Spindles The LE10 ... 75 F5
Spindlewood Cl 1 WS12 ... 2 D1
Spinners End Dr B64 ... 62 D1
Spinners End Ind Est B64 ... 82 D8
Spinney Cl
Binley Woods CV3 ... 135 E7
Birmingham B31 ... 103 B3
Kidderminster DY11 ... 116 A7
Norton Canes WS11 ... 5 F5
Polesworth B78 ... 36 F8
Stourbridge DY8 ... 60 C3
Walsall WS3 ... 15 A2
Spinney Dr B90 ... 126 D4
Spinney Farm Rd WS11 ... 4 B7
Spinney Hill CV34 ... 156 A1
Spinney La CV10 ... 72 C4
Spinney Mews B97 ... 153 C1
Spinney Rd LE10 ... 75 C6
Spinney The
Birmingham B15 ... 85 E5
Birmingham, Brown's Green B20 ... 54 E4
Coventry CV4 ... 132 D3
Dudley DY3 ... 50 C2
Royal Leamington Spa CV32 ... 156 D1
Solihull B91 ... 127 C8
Sutton Coldfield B74 ... 31 B6
Wolverhampton WV3 ... 24 D1
Wythall B47 ... 125 B4
Spinning School La B79 ... 21 B5
Spiral Cl B62 ... 83 E8
Spiral Ct
Birmingham B24 ... 56 E2
Dudley DY3 ... 50 D3
Stourbridge DY8 ... 81 A4
Sutton Coldfield B76 ... 46 F3
Wednesfield WV11 ... 26 E7
Spiral Gn B24 ... 57 C4
Spirehouse La B60 ... 137 E5
Spires The
Lichfield WS14 ... 9 E6
Nuneaton CV10 ... 72 C4
Spires View B61 ... 136 F3
Spitfire Cl CV5 ... 112 C1
Spitfire Pk B24 ... 57 C2
Spitfire Rd B24 ... 57 D2
Spitfire Way B35 ... 58 A2
Splash La WS12 ... 2 C3
Spode Pl WS11 ... 2 B2
Spondon Gr B34 ... 69 C5
Spondon Rd WV11 ... 26 E8
Spon End CV1, CV5 ... 113 A3
Spon Gate Ho CV1 ... 113 A2
Spon Gate Prim Sch CV1 ... 113 A3
Spon La B70 ... 53 D1
Spon Lane Ind Est B66 ... 64 D8
Spon Lane S B70 ... 53 D1
Spon Lane Trad Est B70 ... 53 D2
Spon La S B66 ... 64 D8
Spon St CV1 ... 165 A3
Spoon Dr B38 ... 103 D2
Spooner Croft B5 ... 86 E8
Spooners Cl B92 ... 107 F7

Spouthouse La B43 ...54 F7
Spout La Walsall WS1 . 42 E7
  Walsall WS1 .... 42 E8
Spreadbury Cl B17 ..84 F8
Sprig Croft B36 ...... 68 C8
Spring Ave B65 ...... 63 D2
Springavon Croft B17 85 B6
Springbank B9 .... 68 A3
Springbank Rd B15 .. 86 D7
Springbrook Cl B36 .. 58 D1
Springdale La B94 .142 A7
Spring Cl
  6 Coventry CV1 .... 113 E3
  Solihull B91 .... 106 F3
  Walsall WS1 .... 15 C2
  West Hagley DY9 ... 98 F4
Spring Coppice Dr
  B93 ....128 A3
Spring Cres B64 .....82 F7
Springcroft Rd B11...87 F2
Spring Ct Walsall WS1. 43 A8
  West Bromwich B70.. 53 D2
Springdale Ct CV1 .. 73 D3
Springdale Jun & Inf
  Schs WV4 .... 38 D5
Springfield B23 ...... 56 E3
Springfield Ave
  6 Birmingham B12 ... 87 A6
  Bromsgrove B60.....151 A8
  Sedgley DY3 .... 39 E1
  Stourbridge DY9 ..... 81 E4
Springfield Cl B65 ... 63 A5
Springfield Cres
  Bedworth CV12....... 78 B2
  Dudley DY2 .... 62 F8
  Solihull B92 .... 89 C3
  Sutton Coldfield B76.. 47 A4
  West Bromwich B70... 53 E1
Springfield Ct
  Birmingham B28 .... 105 F8
  Sutton Coldfield B75.. 47 C5
  Wolverhampton WV10 . 11 D4
Springfield Dr
  Birmingham B14..... 86 E1
  Halesowen B62......83 D7
Springfield Gn DY3... 39 E1
Springfield Gr DY3.. 39 D1
Springfield Ho DY10.. 116 F8
Springfield House Com
  Specl Sch B93 .... 129 A5
Springfield Ind Est
  B69................64 B7
Springfield La
  Kidderminster DY10 .. 116 F8
  Rowley Regis B65, DY2. 62 F5
  Wolverhampton WV10 . 11 D4
Springfield Mill Ct
  WS10 .... 41 E6
Springfield Pk LE10 .. 71 A3
Springfield Pl CV1 .. 165 C4
Springfield Prim Sch
  Birmingham B13..... 87 D2
  Rowley Regis B65.... 63 A4
Springfield Rd
  Bilston WV14 .... 40 E7
  Birmingham, Castle
    Bromwich B36 ..... 69 D8
  Birmingham, King's Heath
    B14............... 104 F8
  Birmingham, Moseley
    B13............... 87 D2
  Coventry CV1 ...... 165 C4
  Halesowen B62...... 83 D7
  Hinckley LE10 .... 75 D7
  Nuneaton CV11..... 73 E2
  Oldbury B68 .... 64 C4
  Sutton Coldfield B75,
    B76............... 47 A4
  Tamworth B77....... 35 D8
  Wolverhampton WV10 . 25 E3
Springfield Rise WS12....2 C6
Springfields
  Coleshill B46........ 70 F5
  Walsall WS4 .... 29 C6
Springfields Rd DY5.. 61 B2
Springfield St B18 ... 66 A3
Springfield Terr B65..62 F5
Spring Gdns
  Birmingham B21...... 65 F7
  4 Dudley DY2 ...... 62 D8
  Smethwick B66....... 65 B3
Spring Gr B19........ 66 B6
Spring Grove Cres
  DY11...............116 B3
Spring Grove Gdns
  B18.................65 F6
Spring Grove Rd
  DY11..............116 B3

Spring Head WS10 ...41 F2
Springhill CV10 ......72 A8
Spring Hill
  Birmingham, Erdington
    B24............... 56 F3
  Birmingham, Hockley
    B18............... 66 A4
Springhill Ave WV4... 38 C4
Springhill Cl
  Walsall WS4 .... 15 D1
  Willenhall WV12 ..... 27 D7
Springhill Ct **5** WS1 .42 F8
Springhill Gdns B97. 152 F2
Springhill Gr WV4.... 38 C4
Spring Hill Ind Est
  B18................ 66 A4
Spring Hill Pas B18 .. 66 A3
Springhill Pk WV4.... 38 B3
Springhill Prim Sch
  WS7................7 B6
Springhill Rd
  Brownhills WS8 ...... 16 A7
  Burntwood WS7 ......7 A6
  Walsall WS1 .... 28 F1
  Wednesfield WV11 ... 26 E7
Spring Hill Rd CV10 . 72 C6
Spring La
  Birmingham B24...... 57 A3
  Hockley Heath B94...143 B5
  Kenilworth CV8......148 A5
  Lapworth B94.......143 D3
  Radford Semele CV31. 162 E5
  Romsley B62........100 D4
  Walsall WS4 .... 15 C2
  Willenhall WV12 ..... 27 C4
Spring Mdw
  Cheslyn Hay WS6 ..... 4 D1
  3 Cradley Heath B64. 62 F1
  Halesowen B63...... 82 F2
  Tipton DY4 .... 52 C6
Springmeadow Gr
  B19................ 66 D6
Springmeadow Rd
  B15................ 86 D7
Spring Meadow Rd
  DY2................ 62 C2
Spring Meadows Cl
  WV8................ 10 B4
Spring Parklands DY1 62 A8
Spring Pool CV34 ... 160 E7
Spring Rd
  Barnacle CV7 .... 97 B6
  Birmingham, Balsall Heath
    B15............... 86 D7
  Birmingham, Tyseley
    B11............... 87 F3
  Coventry CV6 .... 95 F1
  Dudley DY2 .... 62 D6
  Lichfield WS13 .... 3 D2
  Smethwick B66....... 64 D8
  Walsall WS4 .... 15 D1
  Wolverhampton WV4 .. 40 A4
Spring Road Ind Est
  WV4................ 40 A4
Spring Road Sta B28. 88 A2
Springs Ave B61 .... 121 A1
Springside B98 ......159 C8
Springslade B32 .....84 F5
Springslade Dr B24 .. 57 D3
Spring St
  Birmingham B15..... 86 D8
  Cannock WS11 .....4 E8
  Halesowen B63...... 82 D6
  Stourbridge DY9 ..... 81 E4
  Tipton DY4 .... 52 C8
Springs The B64 ..... 63 A1
Spring Terr WS7.......6 E5
Springthorpe Gn B24. 57 C4
Springthorpe Rd
  Birmingham, Pype Hayes
    B24............... 57 D5
  Birmingham, Tyburn
    B24............... 57 D3
Springvale Ave
  Bilston WV14 .... 40 B4
  Walsall WS5 .... 43 C7
Springvale Bsns Pk
  WV14...............40 B4
Spring Vale Cl WV14.. 40 A1
Springvale Dr B97... 152 F3
Spring Vale Ind Pk
  WV14............... 40 C5
Spring Vale Island
  WV14............... 40 C4
Springvale Prim Sch
  WS11...............4 E8
Spring Vale Prim Sch
  WV4................39 E4

Springvale Rd B97 .. 152 F2
Spring Vale Rd B65.. 63 A5
Springvale St WV13 .. 27 B3
Springvale Way WV14 40 C4
Springwell Rd CV31. 162 D6
Spring Wlk
  Halesowen B63....... 82 D1
  Oldbury B69 .... 64 A5
  Walsall WS2 .... 28 B3
Sproat Ave WS10 .... 41 C5
Spruce B77 .... 22 B4
Spruce Gr
  Birmingham B24..... 57 B2
  4 Royal Leamington Spa
    CV31............. 161 F5
Spruce Rd
  5 Coventry CV2 .... 96 B2
  Nuneaton CV10...... 72 E7
  Walsall WS5 .... 43 B3
Spruces The DY9 ....98 F4
Spruce Way WV3 .... 24 D1
Spur Tree Ave WV3 .. 24 A1
Squadron Cl B35 .... 58 C4
Square Cl B32 .... 84 C3
Square The
  Aldridge WS9 .... 30 B6
  Alvechurch B48......139 B6
  Birmingham B17..... 85 B7
  3 Birmingham B17.. 85 C5
  2 Birmingham, Ladywood
    B15............... 66 B1
  Brierley Hill DY2 ..... 61 F6
  Coventry CV2 ...... 115 A7
  Fazeley B78......... 35 A8
  Kenilworth CV8......147 E4
  Nuneaton CV11...... 73 E4
  Solihull B91 .... 107 C3
  Tipton DY4 .... 52 D7
  Willenhall WV12 ..... 27 D8
  Wolverhampton WV2 . 163 C1
Squires Croft
  Coventry CV2 .... 96 F1
  Sutton Coldfield B76... 47 A2
Squires Ct DY5 ...... 81 C8
Squires Gate WS7.....7 C8
Squires Gate Rd 4
  WV13 .... 27 B2
Squires Gate Wlk B35 58 A3
Squires Gn LE10......75 F6
Squires Way CV4..... 132 D6
Squire's Wlk **7** WS10 .41 F3
Squirhill Pl **1** CV31. 162 B7
Squirrel Cl
  Cannock WS12 .... 2 D2
  Huntington WS12 .....1 C6
Squirrel Hollow B76... 47 A2
Squirrels Hollow B68. 84 D7
Squirrels The WS14.....9 C7
Squirrel Wlk
  Sutton Coldfield B74... 31 C5
  Wolverhampton WV4 .. 39 A5
Stable Croft B71 .....53 F7
Stable Ct DY3 .... 50 E6
Stableford Cl
  Birmingham B32...... 84 F3
  Redditch B97 ....158 D7
Stables The
  Berkswell CV7........ 110 C4
  Birmingham B29..... 86 A2
  Hinckley LE10 .... 75 D5
  Royal Leamington Spa
    CV32............. 156 C1
Stable Way B60 .... 150 E6
Stable Wlk CV11 .....73 F2
Stacey Cl B64 .... 62 E1
Stacey Dr B13...... 105 A5
Stacey Grange Gdns
  B45..............122 A6
Stackhouse Cl WS9... 16 A4
Stackhouse Dr WS3 .. 15 A4
Stadium Cl
  Coventry CV6 .... 95 D2
  Kidderminster DY10 .. 116 F4
  Willenhall WV13 ..... 27 B3
Stadium Dr B64 ..... 62 C1
Stafford Cl
  Bulkington CV12 ..... 79 C2
  Walsall WS3 .... 14 B2
Stafford Ct
  Birmingham B43..... 54 E7
  Wolverhampton WV10 . 11 C5
Stafford Dr B71 ..... 53 B6
Stafford Ho B33...... 69 E2
Stafford La WS12......2 B5
Stafford Rd
  Birmingham B21..... 65 F8
  Cannock WS11 ...... 1 D1
  Coven Heath WV10... 11 D4
  Darlaston WS10 ..... 41 C6
  Huntington WS11, WS12 .1 C5

Stafford Rd *continued*
  Walsall WS3 .... 14 B4
Staffordshire Pool Cl 2
  B6 .... 55 F1
Staffordshire Univ
  WS13 ....9 B7
Stafford St
  Bilston WV14 .... 40 D5
  Birmingham B5...... 164 D3
  Cannock WS12 ....2 E1
  Dudley DY1 .... 51 B1
  Walsall WS2 .... 28 E3
  Wednesbury WS10 ... 41 F2
  Willenhall WV13 ..... 27 A2
  Wolverhampton WV1 . 163 C4
Stafford Way B43 ... 54 E7
Staff Way B23 ...... 56 E4
Stagborough Way
  WS12 ....2 B4
Stag Cres
  Norton Canes WS11 ....6 A6
  Walsall WS3 .... 28 E6
Stag Dr WS12 ....1 C6
Stag Hill Rd WS3 .... 28 E7
Stag Ind Est WV14 ....40 F4
Stag Wlk B76 .... 57 D7
Staines Cl CV11 ......73 F7
Stainforth Cl CV11 .. 74 A2
Stainsby Ave B19..... 66 C5
Stainsby Croft B90.. 127 B5
Staircase La CV5 .... 112 C7
Stakenbridge La
  DY10 .... 98 D4
Staley Croft WS12.....1 C4
Stalling's La DY6..... 60 D8
Stambermill Cl DY9.. 81 D5
Stambermill Ho DY9.. 81 E5
Stambermill Ind Est
  DY9................ 81 D6
Stamford Ave CV3... 133 C6
Stamford Cres WS7 ...7 A8
Stamford Croft B91.. 107 B2
Stamford Gdns CV32 156 E1
Stamford Gr B20..... 55 C1
Stamford Rd
  Birmingham B20..... 55 C1
  Brierley Hill DY5..... 81 C6
Stamford St DY8.....80 F7
Stamford Way WS9... 16 C1
Stanbrook Rd B90... 127 A5
Stanbury Ave WS10... 41 B6
Stanbury Rd B14..... 105 B4
Stancroft Gr B26..... 89 A8
Standard Ave CV4.... 112 B1
Standard Way B24 ....67 F8
Standbridge Way DY4 52 A5
Standedge B77 ...... 36 B7
Standhills Rd DY6.... 60 E6
Standish Cl CV2...... 114 E2
Standlake Ave B36... 68 D7
Standlake Mews 14
  CV31.............. 162 C6
Standleys Twr B23.... 57 A6
Stand St CV34...... 160 D5
Stanfield Rd
  Birmingham B32..... 84 E6
  Birmingham, Pheasey
    B43............... 44 D5
Stanford Ave B42 ... 55 A7
Stanford Cl B97..... 158 B6
Stanford Dr B65..... 63 B4
Stanford Gr B63..... 82 C1
Stanford Rd WV2... 163 B1
Stanford Way **2** B69. 63 E4
Stanhoe Cl DY5 ..... 81 D8
Stanhope Ho B79 .... 21 A4
Stanhope Rd B67 ....64 F3
Stanhope St
  Birmingham B12..... 86 F7
  Dudley DY2 .... 62 E4
  Wolverhampton WV3 . 163 A2
Stanhope Way B43 ... 44 E4
Stanhurst Way B71... 43 A2
Stanier Ave CV1..... 113 B4
Stanier Cl WS4...... 29 B7
Stanier Gr B20...... 55 B2
Staniforth St B4..... 164 C4
Stanklyn La DY10.... 117 C1
Stanley Ave
  Birmingham B32..... 84 E7
  Solihull B90........ 106 A4
  Sutton Coldfield B75... 46 F4
Stanley Cl
  Birmingham B28..... 106 A5
  Redditch B98 ....154 A5
  Wednesfield WV11 ... 26 E7
Stanley Ct
  9 Birmingham B13... 87 B2
  Perton WV6........ 23 E4

Stanley Ct *continued*
  Royal Leamington Spa
    CV31............. 162 C7
Stanley Gr **2** B11.... 87 B6
Stanley Pl
  Bilston WV14 .... 40 B5
  Birmingham B13..... 86 F5
  Walsall WS4 .... 29 B6
Stanley Rd
  Birmingham B68..... 84 C7
  Birmingham, King's Heath
    B14.............. 104 D7
  Birmingham, Nechells
    B7................ 67 C7
  Cannock WS12 ....2 A6
  Darlaston WS10 ..... 41 D5
  Hinckley LE10 .... 71 C2
  Nuneaton CV11...... 73 C6
  Stourbridge DY8 ..... 80 F3
  Walsall WS3 .... 29 B6
  West Bromwich B71... 53 E7
  Wolverhampton WV10 . 11 D1
Stanley St WS3...... 14 D1
Stanmore Gr B62..... 84 A3
Stanmore Rd B16 .... 65 C1
Stansbury Ho **3** WS2 42 C8
Stansfield Gr CV8... 148 D4
Stanton Ave DY1 .... 51 A4
Stanton Bridge Prim Sch
  CV6............... 113 F6
Stanton Gr
  Birmingham B26..... 88 F8
  Solihull B90........ 106 A4
  Tipton DY4 .... 52 A5
Stanton Ho **2** B71....42 F1
Stanton Rd
  Birmingham B43..... 54 D8
  Royal Leamington Spa
    CV31............. 162 C6
  Solihull B90........ 106 A4
  Wolverhampton WV1 . 25 F2
Stanton Wlk CV34... 155 D1
Stanville Jun & Inf Sch
  B26............... 89 C6
Stanville Rd B26 .... 89 C6
Stanway Gdns B71... 53 D6
Stanway Gr B44......44 F3
Stanway Rd
  Coventry CV5 ...... 133 A8
  Solihull B90........ 106 A4
  West Bromwich B71... 53 D6
Stanwell Gr B23...... 56 E6
Stanwick Ave B33.... 69 E3
Stan Williams Ct
  CV11.............. 73 D4
Stapenhall Rd B90... 127 A5
Stapleford Croft
  B14............... 104 C2
Stapleford Gdns WS7.. 7 D6
Stapleford Gr DY8.... 60 E2
Staple Hall Rd B31... 103 B2
Staplehurst Rd B28 . 105 F8
Staple Lodge Rd
  B31............... 103 C2
Staples Cl CV12 ..... 79 C3
Stapleton Cl
  Redditch B98.......154 D3
  Studley B80.........159 D3
  Sutton Coldfield B76... 58 B6
Stapleton Dr B37..... 70 A4
Stapleton La
  Barwell LE9......... 71 F8
  Hinckley CV13....... 71 A8
Stapleton Rd
  Aldridge WS9 .... 29 F5
  Studley B80.........159 D4
Stapylton Ave B17... 85 B5
Stapylton Ct **5** B17.. 85 B5
Starbank Prim Sch
  B10................ 88 A8
Starbank Prim Sch
  (Annexe) B10 ....68 B1
Starbank Rd B10..... 88 A8
Starbold Cres B93... 128 B5
Starbold Ct B93..... 128 A6
Star City B7 .... 67 D8
Star Cl Tipton DY4.... 52 C5
  Willenhall WS2 ...... 27 F4
Starcrest Ind Est DY5 .61 E1
Starcross Cl CV2..... 114 C2
Starcross Rd B27.... 88 C2
Star Ct B91 .... 107 D2
Stare Gn CV4 .... 132 D5
Stareton Cl CV4..... 132 F6
Star Hill B15........ 86 B8
Star Ind Pk CV2 .... 114 F5
Starkey Croft B37.... 70 D2
Starkie Dr B68...... 64 C4

Starley Ct CV3 ..... 135 A7
Starley Pk CV7 ......96 B8
Starley Rd CV1...... 165 A2
Starley Way B37..... 90 C6
Starling Ct WV10.... 11 B3
Star St Stourbridge DY9 .81 F5
  Wolverhampton WV3 . 38 E8
Startin Cl CV7.......95 F7
Startpoint Trad Est
  B11................ 87 D4
Statham Dr B16..... 65 C2
Station App
  Barnt Green B45..... 138 D8
  Dorridge B93 .... 127 F2
  Kidderminster DY10 . 116 F5
  Lichfield WS13 ....9 C7
  Royal Leamington Spa
    CV31............. 161 F7
  Solihull B91........ 107 A4
  Sutton Coldfield B74... 31 F6
  Sutton Coldfield, Maney
    B73............... 46 B6
Station Ave
  Birmingham B16..... 65 C1
  Coventry CV4 ...... 131 D8
  Warwick CV34 ...... 160 F8
Station Bldgs B46.... 59 B3
Station Cl WS3...... 28 B8
Station Cotts
  Blackwell B60.......138 A4
  Shenstone WS14..... 17 F6
Station Ct WS11.......4 F8
Station Dr
  Blakedown DY10..... 98 C2
  Brierley Hill, Quarry Bank
    DY5.............. 61 E2
  Brierley Hill, Silver End
    DY5.............. 61 B1
  Earlswood B94.......125 D1
  Solihull B92........ 88 E1
  Sutton Coldfield B74... 46 B8
  Tipton DY4 .... 52 B4
  West Hagley DY9 .... 99 A6
Stationfields Park Homes
  B79................ 21 C5
Station La B94....... 144 D3
Station Link Rd B26.. 90 D4
Station Pl WS3...... 28 B8
Station Rd
  Aldridge WS9 .... 30 A5
  Alvechurch B48......139 A5
  Balsall Common CV7.. 130 B7
  Bilston WV14 .... 40 E5
  Birmingham, Acock's Green
    B27............... 88 C3
  Birmingham, Aston B6 . 55 F1
  Birmingham B17..... 85 C6
  Birmingham, Erdington
    B23............... 56 F5
  Birmingham, Handsworth
    B21............... 65 C8
  Birmingham, King's Heath
    B14............... 86 E1
  Birmingham, King's Norton
    B30............... 103 E4
  Birmingham, Marston Green
    B37............... 90 A4
  Birmingham, Northfield
    B31............... 103 A4
  Birmingham, Stechford
    B33............... 68 E3
  Blackwell B60.......138 A5
  Brierley Hill DY5..... 61 C3
  Cannock WS12 ....2 C6
  Coleshill B46........ 59 F1
  Cradley Heath, Haden Cross
    B64............... 83 A8
  Dorridge B93 .... 128 B4
  Great Wyrley WS6......4 F4
  Hammerwich WS7.....7 E3
  Hampton-in-A B92 .. 109 B7
  Hinckley LE10 .... 75 D8
  Kenilworth CV8...... 147 A4
  Kingswood B94......144 D4
  Lichfield WS13 ....9 C7
  Oldbury B69 .... 64 A5
  Rowley Regis B65.... 63 D2
  Shenstone WS14..... 17 F6
  Solihull B91........ 107 B4
  Stourbridge DY9 ..... 81 E6
  Studley B80.........159 D4
  Sutton Coldfield B73... 46 A1
  Walsall, Rushall WS4 .. 29 A7
  Walsall WS3 .... 15 A3
  Warwick CV34 ...... 160 F7
  West Hagley DY9 .... 99 A6
  Wombourne WV5 .... 49 A8
  Wythall B47......... 125 D3
Station Road Ind Est
  B65................ 63 D2

Station St E CV6 .... 113 E7
Station St W CV6.... 113 E7
Station Sq CV1.... 165 B1
Station St
　Birmingham B5.... 164 B2
　Bromsgrove B60.... 136 F1
　Cheslyn Hay WS6.......4 E3
　Cradley Heath B64 .... 82 C8
　Darlaston WS10 .... 41 E7
　Sutton Coldfield B73.. 46 C5
　Tipton DY4 .... 52 B5
　Walsall, Blakenall Heath
　　WS3 .... 28 B8
　Walsall WS2 ...... 28 E1
Station Street W Bsns Pk
　CV6............. 113 D7
Station Villas WS10.. 41 E6
Station Way B97 .. 153 D3
Staulton Gn 5 B69.. 63 E4
Staunton Rd
　Walsall WS3 ...... 14 A3
　Whitnash CV31 .... 162 A5
Staveley Rd
　Birmingham B14.....104 D6
　Wolverhampton WV1 .. 25 C4
Staverton Cl CV5.... 112 A3
Stead Cl Walsall WS2.. 28 C5
　Wednesbury DY4 .... 41 B1
Steadman Croft DY4.. 52 D8
Stechford La B8 .... 68 D5
Stechford Prim Sch
　B33............... 68 D2
Stechford Rd B34 .... 68 E5
Stechford Ret Pk B33 68 E4
Stechford Sta B33 .... 68 D3
Stechford Trad Est
　B33...............68 E3
Steel Bright Rd B66 .. 65 E7
Steel Dr WV10 ...... 25 D8
Steel Gr B25 .... 88 C7
Steelhouse La
　Birmingham B4.....164 C3
　Wolverhampton WV2 .. 39 E8
Steelmans Rd WS10....41 F7
Steelpark Rd B62 .... 83 C7
Steelpark Way WV11 .. 26 E4
Steel Rd B31....... 102 F2
Steel Rdbt WS10 .... 41 E2
Steene Gr B31 ...... 102 D3
Steeplefield Rd CV6. 113 A5
Steeples The DY8 .... 81 B3
Steepwood Croft
　B30.............. 103 D4
Steere Ave B79 ...... 21 C7
Steetley Ind Est WV14 51 C7
Stella Croft B37.... 70 C2
Stella Gr B43 .... 54 C8
Stella Rd DY4 ....51 F6
Stenbury Cl WV10 ....11 F4
Stencills Dr WS4 .... 29 B3
Stencills Rd WS4 .... 29 B4
Stennels Ave B62 .... 83 E4
Stennels Cl CV11 .... 112 F8
Stennels Cres B62... 83 E4
Stephanie Gr B77 .... 22 A6
Stephens Cl WV11.....26 F8
Stephens Ct B73 ..... 46 A6
Stephens Ind Est B11 87 F4
Stephenson Ave WS2. 28 B5
Stephenson Cl
　Royal Leamington Spa
　　CV32......... 156 C1
　Tamworth B77....... 22 A2
Stephenson Dr
　Birmingham B37.... 70 B2
　Perton WV6........ 23 E5
Stephenson Pl B2.. 164 C2
Stephenson Rd
　Bedworth CV7........ 96 C7
　Hinckley LE10 ...... 74 E7
Stephenson Sq WS2.. 28 B5
Stephenson St
　Birmingham B2...... 164 B2
　Wolverhampton WV3 . 163 A4
Stephenson Way WS12 .2 B5
Stephens Rd B76..... 47 A4
Stephens Wlk WS13....3 A2
Stepney Rd CV2 .... 114 A4
Stepping Stone Cl
　WS2.............27 F4
Stepping Stones DY8. 81 B5
Stepping Stones Rd
　CV5............. 112 F4
Steppingstone St DY1 51 B1
Sterling Pk
　Brierley Hill DY5..... 61 F4
　Hinckley LE10 ...... 74 D8
　Tamworth B77....... 35 E7
Sterling Way CV11 ... 78 E8
Sterndale Rd B42 .... 55 C6

Stevenage Wlk 2
　CV2............. 115 A7
Steven Dr WV14...... 40 E1
Stevens Ave B32 .... 84 D2
Stevens Dr WS11 .... 2 D6
Stevens Gate WV2... 163 B1
Stevens Ho CV1 .... 165 C4
Stevenson Rd
　Coventry CV6 ...... 113 A8
　Tamworth B79....... 21 A6
Stevenson Wlk WS14 ...9 B6
Stevens Rd DY9 .... 81 D2
Steve Roberts Ct
　DY11............. 116 A6
Steward St B18 ...... 66 A3
Stewart Cl CV4....... 112 D2
Stewart Ct DY10.... 116 F5
Stewart Rd
　Brownhills WS9 ...... 16 A3
　Kingswinford DY6 .... 60 D4
Stewarts Rd B62 .... 83 D7
Stewart St
　Nuneaton CV11....... 73 C3
　Wolverhampton WV2 . 163 B1
Stewkins DY8 .... 80 E8
Stewkins Ct 4 DY8 .. 80 E8
Steyning Rd B26 .... 88 E5
Stickley La DY3 ..... 50 C4
Stidfall Gr CV31..... 162 D6
Stilehouse Cres B65.. 63 C2
Stilthouse Gr B45... 122 A7
Stirchley Com Sch
　B30............. 104 A6
Stirchley Trad Est
　B30............. 104 B6
Stirling Ave
　Hinckley LE10 ...... 71 A1
　Royal Leamington Spa
　　CV32......... 157 B6
Stirling Cl CV3 ..... 134 F8
Stirling Cres WV12 .. 27 B6
Stirling Ct B16 ....65 F1
Stirling Ho B75 ..... 46 C5
Stirling Pk B90 .... 126 E8
Stirling Pl WS11......4 B8
Stirling Rd
　Bilston WV14 .... 40 F2
　Birmingham B16...... 65 F1
　Dudley DY2 .... 62 E6
　Solihull B90...... 126 E8
　Sutton Coldfield B73... 45 E2
Stirrup Cl WS5 ....42 F4
Stivichall Croft CV3 . 133 B6
Stivichall Prim Sch
　CV3............. 133 A6
Stockbridge Cl WV6.. 23 F2
Stockdale Pl B15..... 85 D8
Stockfield Rd B25,
　B27 .... 88 B5
Stockhay La WS7..... 7 D5
Stockhill Dr B45 .... 121 F6
Stockingford Inf & Jun
　Schs CV10 .... 72 D3
Stocking Leys LE10... 76 A7
Stocking St DY9......81 F5
Stockland Ct B74 ..... 44 F8
Stockland Green Sch
　B23............. 56 C4
Stockland Rd B23.... 56 D4
Stockley Cres B90... 106 D3
Stockley Rd CV6..... 96 C6
Stockmans Cl B38... 123 E8
Stocks Wood B30... 103 F8
Stockton Cl
　Dorridge B93 ..... 128 B4
　Sutton Coldfield B76... 58 C5
　Walsall WS2 .... 28 D4
Stockton Ct WV14.... 51 B8
Stockton Gr
　Birmingham B33.... 69 D1
　2 Royal Leamington Spa
　　CV32............. 157 A2
Stockton Rd CV1.... 165 D4
Stockwell Ave DY5... 81 D8
Stockwell End WV6.. 24 D6
Stockwell Head LE10. 71 D1
Stockwell Rd
　Birmingham B21..... 54 E2
　Wolverhampton WV6 .. 24 D5
Stockwell Rise B92... 107 D7
Stoke Cross B60.... 151 E7
Stoke Gn CV3 .... 114 A2
Stoke Green Cres
　CV3............. 114 B1
Stoke Heath Prim Sch
　CV2............. 114 A6
Stoke La B98....... 154 B7
Stoke Park Mews
　CV2............. 114 A3

Stoke Park Sch & Com
　Tech Coll CV2 ..... 114 B4
Stoke Pound La
　Stoke Pound B60 ... 151 A4
　Stoke Prior B60 .... 150 F3
Stoke Prim Sch CV2 114 A4
Stoke Prior Fst Sch
　B60............. 150 C3
Stoke Rd
　Bromsgrove, Aston Fields
　　B60............151 A7
　Bromsgrove, Charford
　　B60............150 F7
　Hinckley LE10 ...... 71 B4
Stoke Row CV2..... 114 A4
Stokes Ave
　7 Tipton DY4....... 52 A8
　Willenhall WV13 .... 40 F8
Stokesay Ave WV6...23 F3
Stokesay Cl
　Kidderminster DY10 .. 116 E2
　Nuneaton CV11...... 73 A3
　Oldbury B69 .... 63 A8
Stokesay Gr B31 .... 122 F8
Stokesay Ho B33.....56 F6
Stokesay Rise DY1 .. 50 E3
Stoke's La WS11 ....5 F7
Stokes St WS3 ...... 28 B8
Stoke Turn Ct B61... 150 D6
Stoke Way B15...... 66 C1
Stom Rd WV14 ...... 40 B5
Stoneacre Cl WV3.... 24 A1
Stone Ave B75 ...... 47 A5
Stonebow Ave B91 .. 127 B8
Stonebridge Cres B37.69 F4
Stonebridge Highway
　CV3............. 133 E4
Stonebridge Rd
　Birmingham B46.... 91 A7
　Coleshill B46........ 70 F5
Stonebridge Trad Est
　CV3............. 134 B4
Stonebrook Way
　Birmingham B29..... 84 F2
　Coventry CV6 .... 95 F3
Stonebury B15...... 85 D8
Stonebury Ave CV5.. 111 E4
Stone CE Fst Sch
　DY10............. 117 E2
Stonechat Cl DY10.. 117 B2
Stonechat Dr B23... 56 C2
Stone Cl B38....... 103 F2
Stone Cotts B31.... 103 A3
Stonecroft Ave B45.. 122 A7
Stonecrop Cl
　Birmingham B38... 123 F8
　Brownhills WS8 ..... 15 D6
Stone Cross B46 .... 59 B3
Stonedown Cl WV14.. 40 A3
Stonefield Cl CV2 ... 115 A8
Stonefield Dr DY5... 61 A7
Stonefield Rd WV14.. 40 D5
Stoneford Rd B90 ... 106 A4
Stonehaven B77......21 F5
Stonehaven Dr CV3.. 133 C3
Stonehaven Gr B28.. 106 B8
Stonehenge Croft
　B14............. 104 D1
Stone Hill DY10 ..... 117 E2
Stonehill Croft B90.. 126 F6
Stonehill Wlk 5 B77 ..35 F6
Stonehouse Ave
　WV13............26 F4
Stonehouse Cl
　Cubbington CV32 ... 157 B5
　Redditch B97 ..... 153 D1
Stonehouse Cres
　WS10 .... 42 B2
Stonehouse Dr B74... 31 C4
Stonehouse Gr B32 .. 84 D2
Stonehouse Hill B29 . 85 A3
Stonehouse La
　Birmingham B32.... 84 E2
　Birmingham B32.... 84 F3
　Coventry CV3 ..... 134 C4
　Hopwood B48 ..... 123 C1
Stone House La CV7...93 F6
Stonehouse Rd
　Bromsgrove B60.... 137 A1
　Sutton Coldfield B73... 45 F3
Stonehurst Rd B43 .. 44 C3
Stonelea WS9....... 30 B5
Stonelea Cl B71..... 53 E8
Stoneleigh Abbey*
　CV8............. 148 F3
Stoneleigh Ave
　Coventry CV5 ..... 132 F7
　Kenilworth CV8..... 148 A6
Stoneleigh Cl
　Redditch B98 ..... 158 F6

Stoneleigh Cl continued
　Stoneleigh CV8...... 149 B6
　Sutton Coldfield B74... 45 F8
Stoneleigh Ct CV11.. 73 C3
Stoneleigh Deer Park
　Bsns Village CV8 .. 149 D4
Stoneleigh Gdns
　CV11 .... 73 C3
Stoneleigh Ho B32...84 F5
Stoneleigh Park National
　Ag Ctr* CV8....... 149 A4
Stoneleigh Rd
　Baginton CV8 ..... 133 F1
　Birmingham B20.... 55 F3
　Blackdown CV32... 157 A7
　Coventry CV4 ..... 132 E2
　Kenilworth CV8..... 148 A6
　Solihull B91...... 106 C4
　Stoneleigh CV8 ... 149 B3
Stoneleigh Way DY3.. 50 D6
Stone Mdw CV7....... 95 A6
Stone Pine Cl WS12 ...1 F8
Stonepine Pl DY3 .... 50 E6
Stonepit B77........ 21 C1
Stonepits La B97.... 158 D4
Stone Rd B15....... 86 D7
Stonerwood Ave
　B28............. 105 E8
Stones Gn B23...... 56 F6
Stone St Dudley DY1 . 51 C1
　Oldbury B69 .... 64 A7
Stoneton Cres CV7.. 130 A6
Stoneton Gr B29 .... 103 A8
Stoneway Gr CV31 .. 162 D6
Stonewell Cres CV11 . 79 B8
Stoney Cl B92....... 107 E7
Stoney Croft WS11 ....1 F1
Stoneycroft Tower 4
　B36............. 68 E8
Stoney Ct CV3 ..... 135 A7
Stone Yd
　Birmingham B12.... 66 F1
　Cradley Heath B64... 82 C8
Stoneydelph Prim Sch
　B77............. 22 A1
Stoneyfields Cl 8
　WS11 ....1 F2
Stoneyford Gr B14.. 105 B4
Stoneygate Dr LE10 ..71 F3
Stoney Hill Cl B60... 137 A1
Stoneyhurst Rd B24 ...56 F1
Stoney La
　Birmingham B32..... 84 B6
　Birmingham, Balsall Heath
　　B12............. 87 B5
　Birmingham, Stechford
　　B25............. 68 E1
　Blackwell B60 .... 138 C2
　Dudley DY2 .... 62 C3
　Kidderminster DY10 .. 116 E8
　Stakenbridge DY10... 98 E3
　Walsall WS3 .... 14 D3
　West Bromwich B71... 53 D4
　Wolverhampton WV4 . 39 B5
Stoney Lane Ind Est
　DY10............. 116 E8
Stoney Lea Rd WS11....1 F1
Stoneymoor Dr B36... 58 D1
Stoney Rd
　Coventry CV1, CV3 .. 165 B1
　Nuneaton CV10, CV11 . 73 B6
Stoney Stanton Rd CV1,
　CV6............. 113 E5
Stoneythorpe Cl B91 107 B1
Stoneywood Rd CV2.. 114 F8
Stonnal Gr B23 ..... 57 A6
Stonnall Gate WS9 ... 30 C8
Stonnall Rd WS9 .... 30 C8
Stonor Park Rd B91.. 106 F5
Stonor Rd B28 ..... 106 A5
Stonydelph La B77... 36 A7
Stony La B67.........64 F5
Stony St B67.........64 F6
Stoop The CV3 ..... 115 B1
Stornoway Rd B35... 58 B4
Storrage La B48 ... 139 E3
Storrs Cl B9 .... 67 D1
Storrs Pl B10 ...... 67 D1
Storrs Way The B32 . 102 B7
Stotfold Rd B14.... 104 F2
Stour B77......... 36 A5
Stourbridge Coll DY8 81 A4
Stourbridge Coll
　(Longlands Ctr) DY8 80 E5
Stourbridge Juntion Sta
　DY8.............81 B3
Stourbridge Rd
　Brierley Hill DY1, DY2,
　　DY5............. 61 E6
　Catshill B61....... 136 F7

Stourbridge Rd continued
　Churchill DY10 ..... 98 A6
　Clent DY9 .... 99 E3
　Dudley DY1 .... 62 A8
　Fairfield B61...... 120 D2
　Hackman's Gate DY9 . 98 F1
　Hagley DY9 .... 99 C7
　Halesowen B63...... 82 F5
　Kidderminster DY10 .. 116 F8
　Madeley Heath DY9 .. 120 B7
　Stourbridge DY9..... 81 D5
　Wombourne WV5, DY3 . 49 B5
Stourbridge Town Sta
　DY8.............. 81 A5
Stourbridge Trad Est
　DY8.............. 81 A6
Stour Cl Burntwood WS7 7 D6
　Halesowen B63..... 82 E6
Stourdale Rd B64 ... 82 C8
Stourdell Rd B63.... 82 E6
Stour Hill DY5....... 82 A8
Stour Ho 2 B68 ..... 84 B8
Stourminster Specl Sch
　DY10............. 117 B4
Stourmore Cl WV12 .. 27 D6
Stourport Rd DY11 . 116 C2
Stour St
　Birmingham B18.... 66 A3
　West Bromwich B70... 52 E3
Stourton Cl
　Knowle B93......... 128 B7
　Sutton Coldfield B76... 46 F4
Stourton Dr WV4..... 38 C5
Stourton Rd B32..... 84 B5
Stourvale Ind Est DY9 81 F6
Stour Vale Rd DY9....81 F6
Stourvale Trad Est
　B63............. 82 D6
Stour Valley Cl DY5.. 81 D7
Stow Dr DY5 .... 81 B6
Stowecroft WS13.......3 C2
Stowe Hill Gdns WS13 .3 C1
Stowell Rd B44......55 F5
Stowe Pl CV4 ...... 111 C1
Stowe Rd WS13 ......9 C8
Stowe St Lichfield WS13 .9 C8
　Walsall WS3 .... 28 C7
Stow Gr B36 .... 68 E7
Stowheath Ind Est & New
　Ent Ctr WV1....... 40 A8
Stow Heath Jun & Inf
　Schs WV13......... 26 D1
Stow Heath La
　Bilston WV1 .... 40 B8
　Wolverhampton WV1 . 26 C1
Stow Heath Pl WV1 . 40 B7
Stowlawn Jun & Inf Sch
　WV14 .... 40 C8
Stowmans Cl WV14.. 40 B8
Strachey Ave CV32 .. 156 E2
Stradey Cl CV3...... 115 B1
Straight Rd WV12 ... 27 C6
Straits Gn DY3 ...... 50 B4
Straits Prim Sch DY3 .50 B5
Straits Rd DY3 ...... 50 B3
Straits The DY3 ..... 50 A4
Strand The B61 .... 137 A3
Strand Cl DY1 ...... 50 E2
Stratford Cl DY1 .... 50 E2
Stratford Ct B72 .... 46 B3
Stratford Dr WS9.... 30 C8
Stratford Gdns B60.. 137 A2
Stratford Pl B12..... 87 A8
Stratford Rd
　Birmingham, Sparkbrook
　　B11, B28....... 87 B6
　Birmingham, Sparkhill
　　B11............. 87 D3
　Bromsgrove B60..... 137 B3
　Dorridge B94 ..... 127 B3
　Longbridge CV34 ... 160 C3
　Nuthurst B94 ..... 143 C5
　Solihull B90........ 126 D7
Stratford St N B11 ... 87 A8
Stratford St
　Birmingham B11..... 87 C5
　Coventry CV2 ..... 114 A4
　Nuneaton CV11...... 73 B4
Stratford Way WS11.....1 F5
Stratford Wlk B36... 68 C8
Strathdene Gdns B29. 85 C1
Strathdene Rd B29... 85 C1
Strathearn Rd CV32 . 156 E1
Strathern Dr WV14... 40 A1
Strathfield Wlk WV3,
　WV4 .... 38 C6
Strathmore Ave CV1.. 113 E1
Strathmore Cres WV5 38 A1
Strathmore Pl 6 WS11.1 F2
Strathmore Rd
　Hinckley LE10 .... 75 A7

Strathmore Rd continued
　Tipton DY4 .... 52 A8
Stratton St WV10.... 25 E4
Strawberry Cl B69... 63 C7
Strawberry Fields
　CV7 .... 92 B1
Strawberry La
　Great Wyrley WS6..... 13 E8
　Willenhall WV13 ..... 26 D3
Strawberry Lane Ind Est
　WV13............. 26 C2
Strawberry Wlk CV2.. 96 D2
Stray The DY5 ...... 61 C6
Stream Mdw WS4 ... 15 D1
Stream Pk B45 ..... 60 E4
Stream Rd DY6, DY8.. 60 D4
Streamside Cl CV5 .. 112 A8
Streamside Way
　Solihull B92........ 89 D4
　Walsall WS4 .... 29 D8
Streatham Gr B44... 45 A1
Streather Rd B75... 32 C2
Streetly Cres B74 ... 31 D3
Streetly Dr B74 ..... 31 D3
Streetly La B74 ..... 31 D3
Streetly Rd B23 .... 56 D5
Streetly Sch The B74. 45 A4
Streetly Wood B74.. 31 A2
Streetsbrook Inf Sch
　B90............. 106 C4
Streetsbrook Rd B90,
　B91............. 106 D5
Streets Corner Gdns
　WS9............. 16 A4
Streets La WS6.......4 F1
Streetway Rd WS14 .. 18 B7
Strensham Ct B13... 86 E4
Strensham Hill B13.. 86 E4
Strensham Rd B12 .. 86 E5
Stretton Ave CV3.... 134 C6
Stretton Cl LE10..... 75 D6
Stretton Cres CV31 . 162 B5
Stretton Ct
　Birmingham B23.... 56 E2
　Hinckley LE10 ...... 75 D3
Stretton Dr B45 .... 122 A2
Stretton Gr
　2 Birmingham, Lozells
　　B19............. 66 C7
　Birmingham, Sparkbrook
　　B11............. 87 C6
　Birmingham, Stechford
　　B8.............. 68 E1
Stretton Ho 7 B97.. 153 A4
Stretton Pl Dudley DY2 62 D5
　Wolverhampton WV14 . 40 A1
Stretton Rd
　Kidderminster DY11 .. 116 B3
　Nuneaton CV10...... 73 A3
　Solihull B90...... 126 B8
　Willenhall WV12 .... 13 D1
Stretton St B77 ..... 21 E3
Stringer Cl B75 ..... 32 A4
Stringers Hill WS12 .. 2 D7
Stringes Cl WV13.... 27 C3
Stringes La WV13 ... 27 C3
Strode Ho B79 ..... 21 A4
Strode Rd WV2...... 39 C4
Stroma Way CV10 ....72 F2
Stronsay Cl B45..... 101 F1
Stroud Ave WV12.... 27 D5
Stroud Cl WV12 ..... 27 C4
Stroud Rd B90 ..... 105 F2
Strutt Cl B15....... 85 D8
Strutt Rd LE10 ...... 76 A5
Stuart Bathurst RC High
　Sch WS10 ....42 B5
Stuart Cl CV34 .... 160 D3
Stuart Cres DY2..... 51 E1
Stuart Ct
　Coventry CV6 ..... 114 A8
　7 Royal Leamington Spa
　　CV32......... 156 E1
Stuart Rd
　Halesowen B62...... 83 F5
　Rowley Regis B65... 63 C4
Stuarts Ct DY9...... 99 A5
Stuart's Dr B33 ..... 68 D1
Stuarts Gn DY9...... 99 B8
Stuarts Rd B33...... 68 D2
Stuart St
　Birmingham B7...... 67 C7
　Walsall WS3 .... 28 B8
Stuarts Way B32 ... 102 B7
Stubbers Green Rd
　Aldridge WS9 ...... 30 A7
　Walsall WS9 .... 29 E8
Stubbington Cl WV13. 26 D1

Stubbs Cl CV12...... **78** A4
Stubbs Gr CV2 ...... **114** B5
Stubbs Rd WV3 ...... **39** A6
Stubby La WV11 ...... **27** A6
Stud Farm Cotts B78 . **20** E2
Stud La B33............**68** F4
Studland Gn CV2 .... **115** A4
Studland Rd B28 ... **106** A8
Studley Croft B92 ... **89** D3
Studley Dr DY5...... **81** C8
Studley Gate DY8 ... **80** D5
Studley High Sch
B80............... **159** E3
Studley Inf Sch B80. **159** E4
Studley Rd
Redditch B98 .... **154** A2
Wolverhampton WV3 . **38** C8
Studley St Mary's CE Jun
Sch B80 .... **159** E3
Studley St B12....... **87** B5
Studley Twr B12......**86** F7
Sturgeon's Hill WS14...**9** C7
Sturley Cl CV8 ..... **148** B6
Sturman Dr B65...... **63** C1
Sturminster Cl CV2.. **115** A4
Stychbrook Gdns WS13..**3** B2
Styles Cl CV31 ..... **162** A7
Styvechale Ave CV5 . **133** A8
Suckling Green La
WV8 .... **10** A2
Sudbury Cl
Royal Leamington Spa
CV32............. **157** C3
Wednesfield WV11 ... **26** E7
Sudbury Gr B44 ..... **45** B2
Sudeley B77 .... **35** C8
Sudeley Cl B36...... **58** B1
Sudeley Gdns DY1.... **50** D2
Sudeley Rd CV10 .... **78** C8
Suffield Gr B23 ..... **56** B5
Suffolk Cl
Bedworth CV12....... **78** A3
Coventry CV5 .... **112** B3
Nuneaton CV11 ...... **72** E3
Oldbury B68 .... **64** B4
Wolverhampton WV11 . **26** C6
Suffolk Dr DY5 ..... **81** C7
Suffolk Gr WS9...... **30** B8
Suffolk Ho B23......**56** F5
Suffolk Pl
Birmingham B5 ..... **164** B1
Walsall WS2 .... **28** D5
Suffolk Rd Dudley DY2. **62** A7
Wednesbury WS10 ... **42** C3
Suffolk St CV32 .... **157** A1
Suffolk Street
Queensway B1 .... **164** B2
Suffolk Way B78 .... **21** A1
Suffrage St B66...... **65** B4
Sugarbrook Ct **1**
B60 .... **150** F6
Sugarbrook La B60.. **151** A5
Sugarbrook Rd B60 . **151** A7
Sugar Loaf La DY10 .. **98** B7
Sugden Gr B5........ **86** E8
Sulgrave Cl
Coventry CV2 ...... **114** E7
Dudley DY1 .... **51** A4
Sullivan Ct CV6 .... **114** B7
Sullivan Rd CV6..... **114** B7
Sullivan Way WS13....**3** C2
Sullivan Wlk WS13 ...**3** C2
Sumburgh Croft B35 . **58** A3
Summercourt Dr DY6 **60** C6
Summercourt Sq DY6 **60** C5
Summer Croft B19 ... **66** D6
Summer Dr DY3...... **50** C3
Summerfield Ave
Kingswinford DY6..... **60** C7
West Bromwich B70... **53** C4
Summerfield Cl B71.. **21** D4
Summerfield Cres
B16 .... **65** E3
Summerfield Ct B15.. **65** C1
Summerfield Dr **2**
B29 .... **103** A7
Summerfield Gr **5**
B18 .... **65** E4
Summerfield Jun & Inf
Sch B18 ....**65** E4
Summerfield Rd
Birmingham B16...... **65** E3
Burntwood WS7.......**7** A5
Dudley DY2 .... **62** D7
Holy Cross DY9...... **99** E2
Solihull B92........ **89** A1
Tamworth B77....... **21** D4

Summerfield Rd continued
Wolverhampton WV1 .. **25** B2
Summerfields Ave
B62................**83** F7
Summergate DY3 .... **50** C4
Summerhill WS14 .... **16** E8
Summer Hill
6 Halesowen B63..... **83** B3
Kingswinford DY6..... **60** C6
Summerhill Ave
DY11..............**116** A5
Summer Hill Ind Pk **2**
B1.................**66** B3
Summerhill Prim Sch
DY4................ **52** A6
Summerhill Rd
Dudley WV14 .... **40** D1
Tipton DY4 .... **51** F7
Summer Hill Rd B1.. **66** B3
Summerhill Sch The
DY6................**60** B6
Summer Hill St B1.. **66** B3
Summer Hill Terr B1. **66** B3
Summerhouse Cl
B97................**158** A6
Summerhouse Rd
WV14 .... **40** A1
Summer La
Birmingham B19..... **66** D5
Dudley DY3 .... **50** C3
Minworth B76....... **58** D6
Walsall WS4 .... **15** C2
Summerlee Rd B24 .. **57** B2
Summer Pl DY11 ... **116** C5
Summer Rd
Birmingham, Acock's Green
B27................ **88** A2
Birmingham, Edgbaston
B15................ **86** C7
Birmingham, Erddington
B23................ **56** F5
Dudley DY1 .... **51** A4
Kidderminster DY11 . **116** C3
Rowley Regis B65..... **63** D3
Summer Row
Birmingham B3..... **164** A3
Wolverhampton WV2 . **163** B2
Summer St
Kingswinford DY6 .... **60** D6
Redditch B98 ...... **153** E3
Stourbridge DY8 .... **80** F5
Stourbridge, Lye DY9 . **81** E5
West Bromwich B71... **53** D4
Willenhall WV13 .... **26** F2
Summerton Rd
Oldbury B69 .... **52** D1
Whitnash CV31 ..... **162** A3
Summervale Cl DY9 .. **99** A5
Summervale Rd DY9 . **99** A5
Summerville Terr **4**
B17 .... **85** C5
Summit Cres B66 .... **64** E8
Summit Gdns B63....**82** F3
Summit Pl DY3...... **50** B2
Summit The DY9 .... **81** D4
Sumner Rd B46 .....**70** F6
Sunart Way CV10.... **72** C5
Sunbeam B77 .... **21** E3
Sunbeam Cl B36 ....**58** F1
Sunbeam Dr WS6 .....**4** F3
Sunbeam St WV2.... **39** C7
Sunbeam Way B33 ... **69** C2
Sunbury Ave WS14 ....**9** E7
Sunbury Cl WV14 .... **40** E1
Sunbury Cotts B31 . **103** A4
Sunbury Rd
Birmingham B31..... **122** E7
Coventry CV3 ...... **134** C5
Halesowen B63...... **82** F4
Suncliffe Dr CV8 .. **148** A2
Suncroft B32........ **84** C5
Sundbury Rise B31.. **103** B5
Sunderland Dr DY8.. **81** A8
Sunderton Rd B14 .. **104** E4
Sundew Croft B36... **68** D8
Sundew St CV2 ..... **96** D2
Sundial La B43......**43** F1
Sundorne Cl CV5.... **112** A4
Sundour Cres WV11 . **12** B1
Sundridge Prim Sch
B44................**44** E4
Sundridge Rd B44... **44** E4
Sundridge Wlk WV4.. **38** C6
Sunfield Rd WS11 ....**1** B1
Sunningdale
Bromsgrove B60... **137** A1
Halesowen B62...... **83** E4

Sunningdale continued
Sutton Coldfield B73... **46** B1
Tamworth B77........ **22** C5
Sunningdale Ave
Coventry CV6 .... **95** D2
Kenilworth CV8 .... **148** B4
Perton WV6......... **23** D5
Sunningdale Cl
Birmingham B20..... **54** E4
Nuneaton CV11 ..... **74** A1
Redditch B98 ...... **153** F4
Stourbridge DY8 .... **80** F2
Sutton Coldfield B73.. **46** A2
Sunningdale Dr B69.. **63** A7
Sunningdale Rd
Birmingham B11..... **88** A3
Bromsgrove B61.... **150** D8
Sedgley DY3 .... **39** B1
Sunningdale Way
WS3 .... **14** A3
Sunny Ave B12...... **87** A5
Sunny Bank CV1 .... **165** A3
Sunnybank Ave
Birmingham B44..... **56** B7
Coventry CV3 ..... **134** B5
Sunnybank Cl WS9... **30** E2
Sunnybank Rd
Dudley DY3 .... **50** F5
Sutton Coldfield B73... **57** A8
Sunny Bank Rd B68 . **84** C7
Sunnydale Cres LE10 . **75** A4
Sunnydale Rd LE10 . **74** F7
Sunnydale Wlk B71.. **53** C4
Sunnydene B8 ...... **68** A5
Sunnyhill LE10 ..... **75** F7
Sunny Hill Cl WV5.. **49** B6
Sunnyhill S LE10...**75** F6
Sunnymead B60..... **137** A1
Sunnymead Rd
Birmingham B26..... **88** F6
1 Burntwood WS7 .....**7** A8
Sunnymead Way B74..**44** F7
Sunnymede Rd DY6 .. **61** A4
Sunnyside
Brownhills WS9 ..... **16** A2
Hinckley LE10 ...... **71** D3
Oldbury B69 .... **63** B7
Sunnyside Ave B23... **56** F5
Sunnyside Cl
Balsall Common CV7.. **130** C7
Coventry CV5 ..... **112** F3
Sunnyside Ct CV10 .. **72** F3
Sunnyside Hospl
LE10 .... **71** D5
Sunnyside Ind Est
LE10 .... **71** D4
Sunnyside La CV7 .. **130** C7
Sunridge Ave
Birmingham B19..... **66** D6
Wombourne WV5 .... **49** A7
Sunrise Ct B15...... **86** D7
Sunrise Hill WS12 ....**2** B6
Sunrise Wlk B68 .... **64** C3
Sunset Cl
Great Wyrley WS6.....**4** F3
Tamworth B79....... **21** A5
Sunset Pl WV4 ...... **39** F3
Sunshine Cl CV8 .. **148** A4
Sunshine Inf Sch The
WS3 .... **28** C8
Sun St Brierley Hill DY5 . **61** F1
Walsall WS1 .... **42** E7
Wolverhampton
WV10 .... **163** D3
Sunway Gr CV3 .... **133** B6
Surfeit Hill Rd B64.. **82** D8
Surrey Cl Cannock WS11 . **4** F8
Hinckley LE10 ...... **75** E4
Nuneaton CV10...... **72** E3
Surrey Cres B71..... **53** A8
Surrey Ct CV34 .... **160** E8
Surrey Dr
Kingswinford DY6..... **60** F3
Tamworth B78....... **21** A1
Wolverhampton WV3 . **24** E1
Surrey Ho **2** DY8 ....**80** F8
Surrey Rd
Birmingham B44..... **44** F4
Dudley DY2 .... **62** A7
Surrey Wlk WS9..... **16** A1
Sussex Ave
Aldridge WS9 .... **30** A8
Wednesbury WS10 ... **42** D4
West Bromwich B71... **53** C6
Sussex Cl CV10..... **72** E3
Sussex Ct
7 Birmingham B29 .. **103** C7
Warwick CV34 .... **160** E8
Sussex Dr
Cannock WS12 ......**2** B5

Sussex Dr continued
Wolverhampton WV3 . **24** E1
Sussex Rd CV5 ..... **112** F4
Sutherland Ave
Coventry CV5 ...... **112** A4
Solihull B90........ **106** C3
Wolverhampton WV2 . **40** A8
Sutherland Cl
Birmingham B43..... **44** D4
Warwick CV34 .... **155** E1
Sutherland Dr
Bedworth CV12...... **78** A4
Birmingham B13..... **86** F4
Wombourne WV5 .... **38** A1
Sutherland Gr WV6...**23** F4
Sutherland Ho WV1 . **25** A3
Sutherland Pl WV2 . **163** C2
Sutherland Rd
Cheslyn Hay WS6 .....**4** E2
Cradley Heath B64 ... **82** E8
Wolverhampton WV4 . **39** B5
Sutherland St B6.... **67** B8
Sutton App B8 ..... **68** A4
Sutton Ave
Coventry CV5 ...... **111** D4
Tamworth B78....... **21** A2
Sutton Cl
Hinckley LE10 ...... **71** F3
Redditch B98 ...... **154** D2
Sutton Coldfield Coll
B74............... **46** C6
Sutton Coldfield Coll
Design Ctr B72..... **46** C4
Sutton Coldfield Coll
(Erdington Ctr) B24 **57** A4
Sutton Coldfield Coll
(Great Barr Campus)
B44...............**55** E7
Sutton Coldfield Cottage
Hospl B72.........**46** B4
Sutton Coldfield Gram
Sch For Girls B73 .. **46** B3
Sutton Coldfield Sta
B73............... **46** B5
Sutton Cres B70 .... **53** A3
Sutton Ct
Bedworth CV6....... **96** C6
3 Birmingham, Erddington
B24............... **57** B6
Birmingham, Hamstead
B43............... **54** E7
Sutton Coldfield B75.. **46** B7
Wolverhampton WV4 . **39** E2
Sutton Lodge B91... **107** A3
Sutton New Rd B23 .. **56** F4
Sutton Oak Cnr B73.. **45** A5
Sutton Oak Rd B73... **45** A5
Sutton Park Ct B73... **46** B2
Sutton Park Fst Sch
DY11.............. **116** B4
Sutton Park Gr DY11 **116** C3
Sutton Park Rd
DY11.............. **116** B3
Sutton Park Rise
DY11.............. **116** B3
Sutton Park Visitor Ctr*
B74............... **46** A5
Sutton Pk
Nuneaton CV10...... **72** B7
Sutton Coldfield B74.. **45** D6
Sutton Rd
Aldridge WS9 .... **30** A1
Birmingham B23..... **57** B6
Darlaston WS10 ..... **41** A4
Kidderminster DY11 . **116** C4
Mile Oak B78 .... **34** A8
Tamworth B78....... **20** C1
Walsall WS5 .... **43** C8
Sutton's Dr
Birmingham B43..... **44** A4
Walsall B43......... **43** F4
Sutton Specl Sch The
DY1................**61** F8
Sutton Sq B76 ...... **58** E6
Sutton St
Birmingham, Aston B6 . **66** F6
Birmingham B1...... **66** D1
Stourbridge DY8 .... **60** F1
Sutton Stop CV6 .... **96** B5
Swadling St CV31 .. **161** F6
Swaffield Pk WS11 ....**2** B2
Swain Crofts CV31 .. **162** B6
Swains Gn LE10......**75** F6
Swains Gr B44......**44** F4
Swaledale CV4 ..... **132** D6
Swaledale Cl B60 .. **150** E6
Swale Gr
Birmingham B38..... **103** F1
Willenhall WV13 .... **27** D2
Swale Rd B76....... **47** A1

Swallow Ave B36.... **70** A8
Swallow Cl
Birmingham B12..... **87** B5
Dudley DY2 .... **62** D2
Huntington WS12 .....**1** C7
Wednesbury WS10 ... **42** B4
Swallow Croft WS13....**3** A1
Swallow Ct
Bedworth CV12...... **95** C8
Hinckley LE10 ...... **74** F6
Wolverhampton, Fordhouses
WV10 .... **11** B3
Wolverhampton, Low Hill
WV10 .... **25** D7
Swallowdale
Brownhills WS9 ..... **16** B4
Coventry CV5 ...... **112** E8
Swallowdean Rd
CV6............... **112** E8
Swallow Dr DY10 .. **117** A2
Swallowfall Ave DY8 . **80** C4
Swallowfield B79 ... **20** E6
Swallowfields Dr WS12 .**3** B3
Swallowfields Rd DY3 **39** C2
Swallowgate Bsns Pk
CV6............... **95** D1
Swallow Rd CV6 .... **95** C1
Swallows Cl WS3.... **15** A5
Swallows Ind Est The
B90............... **126** D8
Swallows' Mdw B90 . **126** D8
Swallows Rise Bsns Pk
DY5...............**61** E3
Swallow St
Birmingham B2..... **164** B2
West Bromwich B70... **53** A4
Swanage Gn CV2.... **115** A4
Swanage Rd B10.... **87** D8
Swan Ave B66....... **64** E7
Swan Bank WV4.....**38** F4
Swan Cl
Blakedown DY10 .... **98** B1
Cheslyn Hay WS6 ....**4** D2
Swan Copse B25 .... **88** C5
Swan Corner Sh Ctr
WS7...............**7** C6
Swancote Dr WV4... **38** C6
Swancote Rd
Birmingham B33..... **68** F5
Dudley DY1 .... **62** A8
Swancroft Ho **11** DY4. **52** A8
Swancroft Rd
Coventry CV2 ...... **114** A5
Tipton DY4 .... **51** F8
Swan Ctr **7** DY10... **116** E6
Swan Ctyd B25...... **88** D6
Swan Dr WS8 ...... **15** E7
Swanfield Rd DY8 ... **61** A2
Swanfields WS7.......**7** C6
Swan Gdns B23 .....**56** F4
Swan La
Coventry CV2 ...... **113** F4
Fairfield B61........ **120** E3
Stourbridge DY5, DY8.. **61** A2
Upton Warren B61 ... **150** A3
West Bromwich B70... **53** A5
Swan Lane Ind Est
B70............... **53** A5
Swan Mews WS13......**9** A8
Swanmore Cl WV3 .. **38** E8
Swanmote B79......**20** F5
Swann Rd WV14..... **40** A2
Swann Wlk **10** DY4 .. **52** A8
Swan Pk B77........ **21** C3
Swan Pool Gr WS4 .. **15** D1
Swan Rd WS13......**9** A7
Swan Rdbt B70 .....**52** F5
Swansbrook Gdns **4**
B38............... **104** C2
Swanshurst La B13.. **105** C8
Swanshurst Sch B13 **105** B7
Swans Length B48 . **139** A7
Swan St
Alvechurch B48...... **139** B5
Brierley Hill DY5 .... **61** C6
Dudley DY2 .... **62** C6
Royal Leamington Spa
CV32............. **157** A1
Stourbridge DY8 .... **80** E5
Warwick CV34 .... **160** E6
Wolverhampton WV1 . **25** F2
Swanswell Rd B92 .. **106** D7
Swanswell St CV1... **165** C4
Swans Wlk B48 .... **139** A6
Swanswood Gr **3**
B37............... **70** C3
Swan Village Ind Est
B70............... **53** A5

Swarthmore Rd B29. **103** B7
Sweetbriar La WV12. **27** D5
Sweetbriar Rd WV2 . **40** A7
Sweetbriar Way WS12 . **2** D2
Sweetbrier Dr **4** DY8 **60** E1
Sweetman Pl WV6 ... **25** A3
Sweetman St
Wolverhampton WV6 . **24** F4
Wolverhampton WV6 . **25** A4
Sweetmoor Cl B36... **69** C8
Sweetpool La DY8....**98** F5
Swift B77 .... **21** E3
Swift Cl
Birmingham B36..... **70** A8
Bromsgrove B61.... **150** E8
Kenilworth CV8..... **148** A2
Swift Park Gr DY10 . **117** B2
Swift's Cnr CV3 .... **133** E8
Swillington Rd CV6.. **113** B5
Swinbrook Gr B44... **44** E1
Swinbrook Way B90. **106** D4
Swinburne Ave CV2 . **114** D2
Swinburne Cl CV10.. **72** A5
Swinburne Rd
Hinckley LE10 ...... **71** C1
Redditch B97 ...... **158** C2
Swincross Rd DY8... **81** B3
Swindale B77 .... **36** B7
Swindale Croft CV3 . **134** F8
Swindell Rd DY9 .... **81** C1
Swindon Rd
Birmingham B17..... **65** B2
Kingswinford DY6..... **60** B6
Swinfen Broun Rd
WS13...............**9** A8
Swinford Gr B93 .... **127** E3
Swinford Old Hall
B93............... **81** B3
Swinford Rd
Birmingham B29..... **85** B3
Stourbridge DY8 .... **81** A3
Wolverhampton WV10 . **25** B5
Swiss Dr DY8 ....**60** F2
Swiss Lodge Dr B78..**34** F8
Sword Dr LE10 ..... **71** B3
Swynnerton Dr WV11..**12** F4
Sycamore B77 ...... **35** E7
Sycamore Ave
Birmingham B12..... **87** A5
Redditch B98 ...... **153** A6
Sycamore Cl
Birmingham B24..... **56** F3
Hinckley LE10 ...... **75** E5
Kidderminster DY10 . **116** F7
Stourbridge DY8 .... **80** D2
Sutton Coldfield B76.. **46** F2
Walsall WS4 .... **29** B8
Sycamore Cres
Birmingham, Erddington
B24............... **56** F3
Birmingham, Marston Green
B37............... **90** A8
Sycamore Ct
Allesley CV5 ...... **111** F7
Birmingham, Cotteridge
B30............... **103** E4
Birmingham, Perry Common
B23............... **56** C7
Sycamore Dr
Hollywood B47 ..... **125** B6
Wolverhampton WV3 . **24** E1
Sycamore Gn
Cannock WS11 ....**1** E6
Dudley DY1 .... **50** F5
Sycamore Gr CV34 . **156** A1
Sycamore Green Prim
Sch DY1............**50** F5
Sycamore Ho
Birmingham B13..... **87** A3
Redditch B98 ...... **158** F8
Sycamore Ind & Trad Est
B21................ **65** D8
Sycamore Paddock **1**
DY8............... **61** A1
Sycamore Pl
Bilston WV14 .... **41** A3
Burntwood WS7 .....**6** F7
Smethwick B67...... **64** F4
Sycamore Rd
Birmingham, Aston
B6................. **67** A8
Birmingham, Bournville
B30............... **103** F7
Birmingham, Erddington
B23............... **56** F4
Birmingham, Great Barr
B43............... **43** E2
Birmingham, Handsworth
B21................ **65** D7
Burntwood WS7 .....**6** F7

Sycamore Rd *continued*
Cannock WS12 . . . .**2** F4
Coventry CV2 . . . .**96** B2
Kingswinford DY6 . . . . .**60** E6
Nuneaton CV10 . . . . . .**72** D6
Oldbury B69 . . . .**64** A4
Smethwick B66 . . . . . .**65** B3
Tipton DY4 . . . .**51** F7
Walsall, Shelfield WS4 . .**29** B8
Walsall, The Delves
  WS5 . . . .**42** F5
Wednesbury WS10 . . . .**42** A2
Sycamores The
Bedworth CV12 . . . .**77** E2
Lichfield WS14 . . . .**9** B5
2 Sutton Coldfield B74 .**31** F2
West Hagley DY9 . . . . .**98** F5
Wolverhampton, Elston Hall
  WV10 . . . .**25** F8
Wolverhampton WV11 . .**26** B5
Sycamore Terr B14 . .**104** C7
Sycamore Way
1 Birmingham B27 . . .**88** C5
Huntington WS12 . . . . . .**1** D8
Sydenham Dr CV31 . .**162** B6
Sydenham Ind Est
  CV31 . . . .**162** B6
Sydenham Prim Sch
  CV31 . . . .**162** C6
Sydenham Rd
Birmingham B11 . . . .**87** C6
Smethwick B66 . . . . . .**65** A7
Wolverhampton WV1 . . .**26** B2
Sydnall B97 . . . .**152** F2
Sydnall Fields CV6 . . .**95** F4
Sydnall Rd CV6 . . . . .**95** F4
Sydney Cl B70 . . . . . .**53** A7
Sydney Ct 1 CV12 . . .**77** F2
Sydney Ho B34 . . . . .**69** E6
Sydney Rd
Birmingham B9 . . . .**67** C2
Bromsgrove B61 . . . . .**136** E3
Cradley Heath B64 . . . .**82** C8
Smethwick B67 . . . . . .**64** E2
Sykesmoor B77 . . . . . .**36** B7
Sylvan Ave B31 . . . . .**102** F3
Sylvan Dr CV3 . . . . . .**132** F6
Sylvan Gn B62 . . . . . .**83** D5
Sylvan Gr B90 . . . . . .**106** B5
Sylvia Ave B31 . . . . .**123** B8
Symphony Ct B16 . . . .**66** B2
Synkere Cl CV7 . . . . . .**95** A6
Sytch La WV5 . . . .**49** A5

T

Tabbs Gdns DY10 . . . .**117** A6
Table Oak La CV8 . . .**130** B1
Tachbrook Cl CV2 . . . .**96** C2
Tachbrook Link
  CV34 . . . .**161** E4
Tachbrook Park Dr
  CV34 . . . .**161** E5
Tachbrook Rd CV31 . .**161** F4
Tachbrook St CV31 . .**162** A6
Tack Farm Rd DY8 . . . .**60** D1
Tackford Cl B36 . . . . . .**58** D1
Tackford Rd CV6 . . . .**114** A8
Tackley Cl B90 . . . . . .**126** B8
Tadmore Cl WV14 . . . .**40** D5
Tadworth Cl WV1 . . . . .**26** A2
Tainters Hill CV8 . . . .**148** A6
Tait Croft B92 . . . . . .**107** F8
Talaton Cl WV9 . . . . . .**11** A2
Talbot B77 . . . .**21** E3
Talbot Ave B74 . . . . . .**31** B3
Talbot Cl
Birmingham B23 . . . . . .**56** D8
Walsall WS2 . . . .**28** C6
Talbot Ct CV32 . . . . .**157** A1
Talbot Ho
5 Birmingham B24 . . .**56** F4
6 Wednesbury WS10 . .**41** F2
Talbot Pass 6 DY8 . . .**81** A5
Talbot Pl WV14 . . . . . .**40** C6
Talbot Rd
Bromsgrove B60 . . . . .**150** E7
Dudley DY2 . . . .**62** B4
Smethwick B66 . . . . . .**65** A3
Wolverhampton WV2 . . .**39** C6
Talbots La DY5 . . . .**61** F1
Talbot St
Birmingham B18 . . . . . .**65** F6
Brierley Hill DY5 . . . . . .**61** D3
Halesowen B63 . . . . . .**82** C6
Kidderminster DY11 . .**116** C4
Stourbridge, Lye DY9 . . .**81** F5
Stourbridge, Stambermill
  DY8 . . . .**81** A5
Talbot Way B10 . . . . .**87** F7

Talfourd St B9 . . . .**67** D1
Talgarth Covert B38 .**123** E7
Talisman Cl CV8 . . . . .**147** F3
Talisman Sq CV8 . . . .**147** F4
Talke Rd WS5 . . . .**42** F5
Talladale B32 . . . . . .**102** B7
Talland Ave
Coventry CV6 . . . .**114** A6
Tamworth B77 . . . .**21** E5
Tallants Cl CV6 . . . . .**114** A8
Tallants Rd CV6 . . . . .**114** A8
Tallington Rd B33 . . . .**89** D7
Tall Trees Cl
Catshill B61 . . . .**136** F8
Sutton Coldfield B74 . . .**31** D4
Willenhall WV12 . . . . . .**27** D6
Tall Trees Dr DY9 . . . .**81** D2
Talton Cl B90 . . . .**127** A5
Tamar Cl WS8 . . . .**6** C2
Tamar Dr
Birmingham B36 . . . . . .**69** F8
Dudley DY3 . . . .**50** F6
Sutton Coldfield B76 . . .**58** B7
Tamar Gr Perton WV6 .**23** E4
Willenhall WV13 . . . . . .**27** C2
Tamarisk Cl B29 . . . .**103** B8
Tamar Rd
Bulkington CV12 . . . . . .**79** B2
Tamworth B77 . . . .**36** A5
Tamar Rise DY8 . . . . . .**81** A8
Tame Ave
Burntwood WS7 . . . .**7** D6
Wednesbury WS10 . . . .**42** C4
Tamebridge Ind Est
  B42 . . . .**55** E4
Tame Bridge Sta B71 .**42** F2
Tame Cl WS1 . . . .**42** E6
Tame Cres B71 . . . . . .**53** C6
Tame Ct Fazeley B78 . .**35** B8
Tamworth B79 . . . .**21** A5
Tame Dr WS3 . . . .**15** A1
Tamedrive B78, B79 . .**21** A4
Tame Gr WS11 . . . .**4** D8
Tame Rd
Birmingham, Brandhall
  B68 . . . .**84** B8
Birmingham, Witton B6. .**56** A1
Tipton DY4 . . . .**52** C5
Tame Rise B68 . . . . . .**84** B8
Tame Road Ind Est
  B6. . . . .**56** B1
Tamerton Rd B32 . . . .**84** D1
Tame St E WS1 . . . . . .**42** F6
Tameside Dr
Birmingham, Castle
  Bromwich B35 . . . . . .**58** A1
Birmingham, Erdington
  B6 . . . .**56** A3
Tameside Prim Sch
  WS10 . . . .**42** C2
Tame St Bilston WV14 .**40** F5
Tamworth B77 . . . .**21** C3
Walsall WS1 . . . .**42** E6
West Bromwich B70 . . .**52** F8
Tame Valley Bsns Pk
  B77 . . . .**35** E6
Tame Valley Com Sch
  B36 . . . .**68** D8
Tame Valley Ind Est
  B77 . . . .**35** E6
Tame Way LE10 . . . . . .**75** A8
Tamora Cl CV34 . . . . .**161** D3
Tamworth Bsns Ctr
  B77 . . . .**22** B3
Tamworth Bsns Pk
  B77 . . . .**22** B3
Tamworth Castle ★
  B79 . . . .**21** B4
Tamworth Castle Mus ★
  B79 . . . .**21** B4
Tamworth Cl WS8 . . . . .**6** F2
Tamworth Rd Cliff B78 .**35** C2
Keresley CV6, CV7 . . . .**94** D5
Lichfield WS14 . . . .**9** E5
Polesworth B78 . . . . . .**22** E1
Sutton Coldfield B75 . . .**33** A2
Tamworth, Mount Pleasant
  B77 . . . .**21** C1
Tamworth, Two Gates
  B77 . . . .**35** C3
Wood End CV9 . . . .**36** C1
Tamworth Rd (Amington)
  B77 . . . .**21** F5
Tamworth Rd (Dosthill)
  B77 . . . .**35** C6
Tamworth St WS13 . . . .**9** B8
Tamworth Sta B79 . . .**21** C5

Tanacetum Dr WS5 . . .**43** B3
Tancred Cl CV31 . . . .**161** F5
Tandy Ct B14 . . . .**104** F3
Tandy Dr B14 . . . .**104** F3
Tandy's La DY10 . . . .**118** E4
Tanfield Cl WV6 . . . . . .**24** B3
Tanfield Rd
Birmingham B33 . . . . . .**68** F3
Dudley DY2 . . . .**62** B7
Tanford Rd B92 . . . . . .**89** C3
Tanglewood Cl
Birmingham B32 . . . . . .**84** B4
Birmingham, Castle
  Bromwich B34 . . . . . .**69** C5
Blackwell B60 . . . .**138** A5
Tanglewood Gr DY3 . . .**39** C2
Tangmere Cl WV6 . . . .**23** E5
Tangmere Dr B35 . . . . .**58** A3
Tanhill B77 . . . .**36** B7
Tanhouse Ave B43 . . . .**54** C7
Tanhouse Farm Rd
  B92 . . . .**89** C2
Tanhouse La
Halesowen B63 . . . . . .**82** C5
Redditch B98 . . . .**154** C6
Tanners Cl B75 . . . .**46** F7
Tanners Ct WS1 . . . . . .**42** E8
Tanners Ctyd CV34 . .**160** D5
Tanners Gr CV6 . . . . . .**95** D4
Tanners Green La B47,
  B94 . . . .**125** B2
Tanners' La CV4, CV7. .**111** B1
Tannery Cl WS2 . . . . . .**28** D3
Tansey Ct DY5 . . . .**61** B7
Tansey Green Rd
Brierley Hill DY5, DY6. . .**61** B8
Kingswinford DY6 . . . . .**50** A1
Tansley Cl B93 . . . . . .**127** C4
Tansley Gr B44 . . . .**44** F1
Tansley Hill Ave DY2. . .**62** F8
Tansley Hill Rd DY2 . . .**62** E8
Tansley Rd B44 . . . .**55** F8
Tansley View WV2 . . . .**39** D7
Tansy
Sutton Coldfield B74 . . .**31** F4
Tamworth B77 . . . .**21** C3
Tantallon Dr B32 . . . . .**84** D1
Tantany La B71 . . . . . .**53** C4
Tantarra St
Walsall, The Chuckery
  WS1 . . . .**29** A1
Walsall WS1 . . . .**28** F1
Tanwood Barns
  DY10 . . . .**119** B2
Tanwood Cl
Redditch B97 . . . .**158** A6
Solihull B91 . . . .**127** B8
Tanwood Cross
  DY10 . . . .**119** B2
Tanwood La DY10 . . . .**119** A2
Tanworth Gr B12 . . . . . .**86** F6
*Tanworth-in-Arden CE
  Prim Sch* B94 . . . . . .**142** A2
Tanworth La B90 . . . .**126** C5
Tanyard WS13 . . . .**9** C8
Tanyard Cl
Alvechurch B48 . . . . . .**139** B6
Coventry CV4 . . . .**111** D1
Tanyard La B48 . . . . . .**139** B6
Tanyards B27 . . . .**88** D3
Tapcon Way CV2 . . . .**114** F5
Tapestries Ave B70 . . .**53** A4
Taplow Pl WS11 . . . .**1** F4
Tappinger Gr CV8 . . . .**148** C5
Tapster La B94 . . . . . .**143** F2
Tapton Cl WS3 . . . .**14** C3
Tara Ct CV2 . . . .**114** B4
Tardebigge CE Fst Sch
  B60 . . . .**152** B7
Tardebigge Ct B97 . . .**152** C6
Tardebigge Ho B60 . .**137** B3
Tarlington Rd CV6 . . .**112** E6
Tarmac Rd WV14 . . . . .**40** B5
Tarn Cl CV12 . . . .**78** A2
Tarquin Cl CV3 . . . . . .**134** D7
Tarrant B77 . . . .**35** F4
Tarrant Gr B32 . . . .**84** F5
Tarrant Wlk CV2 . . . . .**115** A5
Tarrington Covert 6
  B38 . . . .**123** E8
Tarry Hollow Rd DY5 . .**61** B7
Tarry Rd B8 . . . .**67** E5
Tarvin Mews DY5 . . . . .**61** D1
Taryn Dr WS10 . . . .**41** D7
Tasker St Walsall WS1. .**42** D8
West Bromwich B70 . . .**52** E4
Tasman Gr WV6 . . . . . .**23** E5

Tat Bank Rd B69 . . . . .**64** B6
Tatchbrook Ct 5
  CV31 . . . .**161** F6
Tatnall Gr CV34 . . . . .**160** E8
Taunton Ave WV10 . . . .**11** D4
Taunton Cl B31 . . . . . .**102** C2
Taunton Rd B12 . . . . . .**87** B4
Taunton Way CV6 . . . . .**95** A2
Taverners Cl CV12 . . . .**13** C1
Taverner's Gn B20 . . . .**54** F3
Tavistock Cl B79 . . . . . .**21** C7
Tavistock Rd B27 . . . .**106** C8
Tavistock St CV32 . . . .**156** F1
Tavistock Way CV11 . . .**73** E5
Tavistock Wlk CV2 . . .**114** C2
Taw Cl B36 . . . .**69** F7
Tay Croft B37 . . . .**70** C4
Tay Gr
Birmingham B38 . . . . .**123** F8
Halesowen B62 . . . . . .**83** E8
Taylor Ave
Royal Leamington Spa
  CV32 . . . .**157** B2
Walsall WS3 . . . .**28** D8
Taylor Cl CV8 . . . .**148** B6
Taylor Ct CV34 . . . . . .**160** D7
Taylor Ho 4 WS2 . . . . .**42** C7
Taylor Rd
Birmingham B13 . . . . .**104** F5
Dudley DY2 . . . .**62** E2
Wolverhampton WV4 . . .**39** F5
Taylors La B69 . . . .**63** E7
Taylor's La
Smethwick B67 . . . . . .**64** F5
West Bromwich B71 . . .**53** D4
Taylors Orch B23 . . . . .**56** B4
Taylor St WV11 . . . .**26** D5
Taylor Way B69 . . . . . .**63** B8
Taynton Covert 4
  B30 . . . .**104** C3
Tay Rd
Birmingham B45 . . . . .**102** B1
Coventry CV6 . . . .**113** B6
Taysfield Rd B31 . . . . .**102** E6
Taywood Dr B10 . . . . . .**87** C7
Teachers Cl CV6 . . . . .**113** A5
Tea Gdn The CV12 . . . .**95** E8
Teal Bsns Ctr LE10 . . . .**74** D7
Tealby Gr B29 . . . .**86** A1
Teal Cres DY10 . . . . . .**117** B3
Teal Dr
Birmingham B23 . . . . . .**56** B3
Hinckley LE10 . . . .**75** A6
Teall Ct B27 . . . .**88** C3
Teall Rd B8 . . . .**67** E5
Teal Rd B80 . . . .**159** F4
Tean Cl
Birmingham B11 . . . . . .**88** A3
Burntwood WS7 . . . .**7** D6
Teasdale Way DY9 . . . .**81** D4
Teasel Gr WV10 . . . . . .**12** B7
Teasel Rd WV11 . . . . . .**26** F5
Teazel Ave B30 . . . . . .**103** D6
Tebworth Cl WV9 . . . . .**10** F2
Tedbury Cres B23 . . . . .**56** E6
Tedder Rd WS2 . . . .**27** F2
Teddesley Ct WS11 . . . . .**1** E3
Teddesley Gr B33 . . . . .**69** C4
Teddesley St WS4 . . . . .**28** F3
Teddesley Way WS12 . . .**1** C6
Teddington Cl B73 . . . .**46** A2
Teddington Gr B42 . . . .**55** D3
Tedstone Rd B32 . . . . .**84** E5
Tees Gr B38 . . . .**123** F8
Teeswater Cl B60 . . . .**150** E6
Teign B77 . . . .**36** A5
Teign Bank Cl LE10 . . . .**71** D2
Teign Bank Rd LE10 . . . .**71** D2
Teignmouth Rd B29 . . .**86** A1
Telephone Rd CV3 . . .**114** C2
Telfer Rd CV6 . . . .**113** B7
Telford Ave
Great Wyrley WS6 . . . . . .**4** F3
Royal Leamington Spa
  CV32 . . . .**157** B5
Telford Cl
Burntwood WS7 . . . .**7** C8
Smethwick B67 . . . . . .**64** D1
Walsall WS2 . . . .**28** A5
West Bromwich B71 . . .**53** A8
Telford Gdns WV3 . . . .**38** D7
Telford Gr WS12 . . . . . .**2** B7
Telford Inf & Jun Schs
  CV32 . . . .**157** C5
Telford Rd
Bedworth CV7 . . . .**96** C8

Telford Rd *continued*
Tamworth B79 . . . .**20** F8
Walsall WS2 . . . .**28** A5
Telford Way B66 . . . . . .**64** F8
Teme Ave DY11 . . . . . .**116** B3
Teme Ct B23 . . . .**56** B3
Teme Gr WV13 . . . .**27** D2
Teme Rd
Halesowen B63 . . . . . .**82** B5
Stourbridge DY8 . . . . . .**80** F3
Tempest St
Tamworth B79 . . . .**21** A5
Wolverhampton WV2 . .**163** C2
Templar Ave CV4 . . . .**112** A1
Templar Ct CV11 . . . . . .**73** C3
Templars' Fields
  CV4 . . . .**132** B7
Templars Prim Sch
  CV4. . . . .**112** A1
Templars The
Oldbury B69 . . . .**63** E5
Warwick CV34 . . . .**160** F5
Temple Ave
Balsall Common CV7. . .**129** F6
Birmingham B28 . . . . .**106** A6
Temple Bar WV13 . . . . .**27** A2
Temple Cl B98 . . . .**153** F4
Temple Ct B46. . . . .**59** F1
Temple Gr CV34 . . . . .**160** D5
Temple La B93 . . . .**129** A4
*Temple Meadow Prim
  Sch* B64 . . . .**63** A1
Temple Meadows Rd
  B71 . . . .**53** E6
Templemore Dr B43. . . .**54** E7
Temple Pas B2 . . . . . .**164** B2
Temple Rd
Dorridge B93 . . . .**128** A3
Willenhall WV13 . . . . . .**27** B3
Temple Row B2 . . . . . .**164** C3
Temple Row W B2 . . . .**164** B3
Temple Sq WV13 . . . . . .**27** A3
Temple St
Bilston WV14 . . . .**40** E5
Birmingham B2 . . . . . .**164** B2
Dudley DY3 . . . .**50** D3
West Bromwich B70 . . .**53** C4
Wolverhampton WV2 . .**163** C2
Templeton Cl B93 . . . .**128** A3
Templeton Rd B44 . . . .**44** F2
Temple Way
Coleshill B46 . . . .**59** F1
Oldbury B69 . . . .**52** D2
Temple Wlk WV13 . . . . .**27** A2
Tenacre La B98 . . . . . .**154** F3
Ten Acres End B30 . . .**104** B8
Tenacres Fst Sch
  B98. . . . .**154** F3
Ten Ashes La B45 . . . .**122** C4
Tenbury Cl
Aldridge WS9 . . . .**30** C8
Redditch B98 . . . .**154** C6
Willenhall WS2 . . . .**27** D3
Tenbury Ct WV4 . . . . . .**38** D5
Tenbury Gdns WV4 . . . .**38** D5
Tenbury Ho 2 B63 . . . .**83** A3
Tenbury Rd B14 . . . . . .**104** E6
Tenby Cl CV12. . . . .**77** C1
Tenby Ct CV32 . . . .**161** E8
Tenby Rd B13 . . . .**87** D2
Tenby St N B1 . . . .**66** B4
Tenby St B1. . . . .**66** B4
Tenby Tower 2 B31. . .**103** A1
Teneriffe Rd CV6 . . . . . .**95** F1
Tenlands Rd B63 . . . . . .**82** F3
Tenlons Rd CV10 . . . . . .**72** F2
Tennal Dr B32 . . . .**84** F6
Tennal Gr B32 . . . .**84** F6
Tennal La B32 . . . .**84** F6
Tennal Rd B32 . . . .**84** F6
Tennant St
Birmingham B15 . . . . . .**66** B1
Nuneaton CV11 . . . . . .**73** C3
Tennessee B13 . . . .**86** E2
Tennis Ct B30 . . . .**103** D4
Tennis Ct The B15 . . . .**86** A5
Tennscore Ave WS6 . . . .**4** F3
Tennyson Ave
Sutton Coldfield B74 . . .**31** F6
Tamworth B79 . . . .**21** A6
Warwick CV34 . . . .**160** C4
Tennyson Cl CV8 . . . . .**148** C4
Tennyson Ho
Birmingham B31 . . . . .**123** A8
3 Oldbury B68 . . . . . .**64** C4

Syc–The **245**

Tennyson Rd
Birmingham B10 . . . . . .**87** E7
Coventry CV2 . . . .**114** C3
Dudley DY3 . . . .**50** A4
Hinckley LE10 . . . .**71** C1
Redditch B97 . . . .**158** C8
Walsall WS3 . . . .**28** E8
Willenhall WV12 . . . . . .**27** E8
Wolverhampton WV10 . .**12** A1
Tennyson St DY5 . . . . . .**61** D7
Tennyson Way DY10 . .**117** C6
Ten Shilling Dr CV4 . .**131** E6
Tenter Ct B63 . . . .**83** B4
Tenter Dr B63 . . . .**83** C4
Tenterfields B63 . . . . . .**83** B4
Tenterfields Prim Sch
  B63. . . . .**83** C4
Terminal Rd B26 . . . . . .**89** F3
Tern Cl WV4 . . . .**39** D3
Tern Gr B38 . . . .**103** E1
Terrace Rd
Birmingham B15 . . . . . .**85** F3
Birmingham, Lozells
  B19 . . . .**66** B7
Terrace St
Brierley Hill DY5 . . . . . .**61** E5
Rowley Regis B65 . . . . .**63** B1
Wednesbury WS10 . . . .**42** A3
Terrace The
Cradley Heath B64 . . . .**82** E8
Wolverhampton WV3 . . .**24** C1
Terret Cl WS1 . . . .**28** F2
Terry Ave CV32 . . . . . .**156** C1
Terry Dr B76 . . . .**46** F2
Terry Rd CV1 . . . .**113** F1
Terrys Cl B98 . . . .**153** F5
Terrys La B24 . . . .**57** C3
Terry St DY2 . . . .**51** E1
Tessall La B31 . . . .**102** D2
Tetbury Gr B31 . . . . . .**102** D3
Tetley Ave WS4. . . . .**29** B4
Tetley Rd B11 . . . .**87** E3
Tetnall St DY2 . . . .**62** D8
Tettenhall Arc WV6 . . . .**24** D5
Tettenhall Coll WV6. . . .**24** D4
Tettenhall Gate 9
  WV3 . . . .**25** A2
Tettenhall Rd WV1, WV3,
  WV6 . . . .**24** F4
Tettenhall Wood Sch
  WV6 . . . .**24** B3
Teviot Gdns
Brierley Hill DY5 . . . . . .**61** B6
Wolverhampton WV8 . . .**10** A5
Teviot Gr B38 . . . .**123** F8
Teviot Twr B19 . . . .**66** C5
Tewe Pl WS13. . . . .**9** A6
Tewkesbury Dr
Bedworth CV12 . . . .**78** C3
Dudley DY2 . . . .**62** D3
Tewkesbury Rd
Birmingham B20 . . . . . .**55** E2
Walsall WS3 . . . .**13** E2
Tew Park Rd B21 . . . . . .**65** E7
Thackeray Cl CV10 . . . .**72** A4
Thackeray Dr B79 . . . . .**21** A7
Thackeray Rd B30 . . . .**103** D5
Thackhall St CV2 . . . . .**113** F4
Thame Ct B47 . . . .**124** E2
Thames Cl
Brierley Hill DY5 . . . . . .**61** B7
Bulkington CV12 . . . . . .**79** A3
Thames Ct B73 . . . .**46** B5
Thames Ho DY3 . . . .**50** D3
Thames Rd WS3 . . . . . .**14** E1
Thames Twr B7 . . . .**67** B5
Thamley Rd CV6 . . . . .**113** A4
Thane Cl B80 . . . .**159** F4
Thanet Cl DY6 . . . .**60** C7
Thanet Gr B42 . . . .**55** C4
Thatchers Ct WV5 . . . . .**37** C1
Thatchers The B62 . . . .**83** C4
Thatchway Gdns
  B38 . . . .**123** E7
Thaxted Rd B33 . . . . . .**69** E3
Theatre App B5 . . . . . .**164** C1
Theatre Ct CV34 . . . . .**160** D6
Theatre St CV34 . . . . .**160** D6
Thebes Cl CV5 . . . .**111** B8
Theddingworth Cl
  CV3 . . . .**134** E8
Thelbridge Rd B31 . . .**122** E6
Thelma Rd DY4 . . . .**51** E5
Thelma St 1 WS1. . . . . .**42** D7
Thelsford Way B92 . . .**107** D8
Theodore Cl
4 Birmingham B17 . . .**85** D4
Oldbury B69 . . . .**52** E1

Theresa Rd B11 . . . . . . 87 B7
Thetford Dr DY4. . . . . . 51 D5
Thetford Gdns WV11 . 26 D6
Thetford Rd B42 . . . . . 55 B7
Thetford Way WS5 . . . 43 C3
Thickett Cl WS2 . . . . . 42 B8
Thicknall Dr DY9 . . . . 81 C2
Thicknall La DY9 . . . . 99 B3
Thicknall Rise DY9 . . . 99 B4
Thickthorn Cl CV8. . 148 B2
Thickthorn Mews
  CV8. . . . . 148 B2
Thickthorn Orchs
  CV8. . . . . 148 B2
Thimble Dr B76 . . . . .46 F1
Thimble End Rd B76 . 47 A2
Thimble Mill La B6,
  B7 . . . . 67 B7
Thimblemill Rd B67 . . 64 E3
Thimbler Rd CV4 . . . 132 C7
Thinktank Mus & IMAX
  Theatre★ B4 . . . . . . .66 F3
Third Ave
  Birmingham, Bordesley
    Green B9 . . . . 67 F2
  Birmingham, Selly Oak
    B29. . . . . 86 C3
  Birmingham, Witton B6. 55 F3
  Brownhills WS8 . . . . .7 A1
  Kingswinford DY6 . . . . 60 F8
  Wolverhampton WV10 . 25 F7
Third Exhibition Ave
  B40 . . . . 90 D4
Third Rd B61. . . . . . . 120 F4
Thirlestane Cl CV8 . . 148 C6
Thirlmere Ave CV11 . .73 F6
Thirlmere Cl
  Cannock WS11 . . . . . . .1 E1
  Coventry CV4 . . . . . . 111 E3
  Wolverhampton WV6 . 24 D8
Thirlmere Dr
  Birmingham B13 . . . . 105 D8
  Essington WV11 . . . . . 13 A2
Thirlmere Gr WV6 . .23 F4
Thirlmere Ho 3 B15 . 85 D3
Thirlmere Rd
  Bedworth CV12. . . . . . 78 A2
  Hinckley LE10 . . . . . . 75 A7
  Wolverhampton WV6 . 24 D8
Thirlmere Wlk DY5 . . 81 B7
Thirsk Croft B36 . . . . 68 C8
Thirsk Rd CV3 . . . . . 133 C5
Thirsk Way B61 . . . . . 121 B1
Thirston Cl WV11. . . . 27 A5
Thistle Cl DY3. . . . . . .50 F6
Thistle Croft WV11 . . 26 D5
Thistledown Ave WS7 .7 A6
Thistle Down Cl B74 . 31 A2
Thistledown Dr
  3 Cannock WS12 . . . . . 2 D1
  Featherstone WV10 . . . 12 A7
Thistledown Rd B34. . 69 C7
Thistledown Wlk DY3. 39 C1
Thistle Gn B38 . . . . . 123 E7
Thistlegreen Cl B65 . .62 F5
Thistlegreen Rd DY2 . 62 E4
Thistle Ho B36 . . . . . . 68 D8
Thistle La B32 . . . . . 102 B7
Thistlewood Gr B93 . 145 B6
Thistley Field E CV6. 113 A7
Thistley Field N CV6. 113 A7
Thistley Field S CV6. 112 F6
Thistley Field W CV6 112 F7
Thistley Nook WS13 . .3 A1
Thomas Barnes Prim Sch
  B78. . . . . .20 B7
Thomas Benson Pl 8
  B12 . . . . .86 F7
Thomas Cres 2 B66 . 65 C5
Thomas Greenway
  WS13 . . . . .3 A2
Thomas Guy Rd B70. .52 F6
Thomas Hardy Ct B79 21 A7
Thomas Ho WS3 . . . . 14 D3
Thomas King Ho 6
  CV1 . . . . 113 E4
Thomas Landsdail St
  CV3 . . . . 133 D8
Thomas Lane St CV6 . 96 A1
Thomas Mason Cl
  WV11 . . . . 26 D7
Thomas Naul Croft
  CV4 . . . . 111 F3
Thomas Sharp St
  CV4 . . . . 132 A7
Thomas St
  Bedworth CV12. . . . . . 78 A2
  Birmingham B6. . . . . . 66 F6

Thomas St continued
  Royal Leamington Spa
    CV32. . . . . 157 A1
  Smethwick B66. . . . . . 65 B5
  Tamworth B77. . . . . . . 21 D4
  Walsall WS2 . . . . 28 D2
  West Bromwich B70. . . 53 D2
  Wolverhampton WV2 . 163 B1
Thomas Wlk B35. . . . . 58 B3
Thompson Ave
  Tamworth B77. . . . . . . 21 C3
  Wolverhampton WV2 . 39 E6
Thompson Cl
  Dudley DY2 . . . . 62 B2
  Willenhall WV13 . . . . . 27 A3
Thompson Dr B24. . . .67 F8
Thompson Gdns B67 . .64 F4
Thompson Ho DY4 . . 52 C8
Thompson Rd
  Oldbury B68 . . . . 64 B5
  Smethwick B67 . . . . . . 64 F4
Thompson's La CV7 . . 94 E6
Thompson's Rd CV7. .94 F6
Thompson St
  Bilston WV14 . . . . 40 D5
  Willenhall WV13 . . . . . 27 A3
Thomson Ave B38. . . 103 D1
Thor Cl WS11 . . . . .2 A5
Thoresby B79 . . . . 20 E6
Thoresby Croft DY1 . .50 E7
Thornberry Dr DY1 . . 61 E8
Thornberry Wlk B7. . . 67 C6
Thornbridge Ave B42. 55 D7
Thornbridge Gr WS9 . .15 F3
Thornbrook Ct 1
  WS4 . . . . .28 F3
Thornbury Ct WV6 . . 24 A3
Thornbury Ho CV6 . . 148 A3
Thornbury La B98 . . . 154 C7
Thornbury Rd B20. . . 55 D2
Thornby Ave
  Kenilworth CV8. . . . . 148 B3
  Solihull B91 . . . . 107 B5
  Tamworth B77. . . . . . . 35 E8
Thornby Rd B23. . . . . 56 C8
Thorn Cl WS10 . . . . . .41 F4
Thorncliffe Cl B97 . . 158 A6
Thorncliffe Rd B44. . . 44 E2
Thorncroft Way WS5 . 43 B4
Thorne Ave WV10 . . . 25 E7
Thorne Pl B65 . . . . . . 63 C2
Thorne Rd WV13 . . . . 27 A4
Thornes Croft WS9 . . 16 E4
Thorne St WV2 . . . . . 40 A7
Thorneycroft La
  WV10 . . . . 26 A6
Thorneycroft Pl WV14 41 B3
Thorneycroft Rd
  WV14 . . . . 41 B4
Thorney Rd
  Coventry CV2 . . . . . . 114 B6
  Sutton Coldfield B74. . . 30 F1
Thornfield Cres WS7 . .7 A8
Thornfield Croft DY3 . 50 E7
Thornfield Rd B27. . . 88 D2
Thornfield Way LE10 . 75 E8
Thorngrove Ave 7
  B91 . . . . 127 C8
Thornham Way B14 . . 104 D1
Thornhill Dr CV11 . . . 79 C8
Thornhill Gr B21. . . . .65 F8
Thornhill Pk B74. . . . 45 A8
Thornhill Rd
  Birmingham, Handsworth
    B21. . . . . 65 F8
  Birmingham, Sparkhill
    B11. . . . . 87 D3
  Brierley Hill DY5 . . . . . 81 E8
  Cannock WS12 . . . . . . .1 F7
  Coventry CV1 . . . . . . 113 D5
  Dudley DY1 . . . . 51 C4
  Halesowen B63. . . . . . 82 E3
  Redditch B98 . . . . . . 154 E6
  Solihull B91 . . . . 107 C7
  Sutton Coldfield B74. . . 31 B1
Thornhurst Ave B32. . 84 E7
Thornleigh DY3 . . . . . 50 D5
Thornleigh Trad Est
  DY2. . . . . 62 A7
Thornley Cl
  Birmingham B13. . . . . 87 A1
  Radford Semele CV31. 162 F5
  Wolverhampton WV11. . 12 F1
Thornley Croft WS6 . . 4 D1
Thornley Gr B76 . . . . 58 C6
Thornley Rd WV11. . . 12 F1
Thornley St WV1. . . . 163 C3
Thorn Rd B30. . . . . . 103 D7
Thorns Ave DY5 . . . . 61 E1
Thorns Com Coll DY5 .81 E8

Thorns Com Inf Sch
  CV8. . . . . 148 B4
Thornsett Gr B90. . . . 106 B6
Thorns Prim Sch DY5 81 E7
Thorns Rd DY5. . . . . . 81 E7
Thorn Stile Cl CV32 . 157 E6
Thornthwaite Cl B45 102 B2
Thornton Cl
  Coventry CV5 . . . . . . 111 C4
  Oldbury B69. . . . . . . 52 C2
  Warwick CV34 . . . . . 155 F1
Thornton Dr DY5 . . . . 61 E1
Thornton Ho B19. . . . 66 E5
Thornton Rd
  Birmingham B8. . . . . . 68 B5
  Solihull B90. . . . . . . 126 F6
  Wolverhampton WV1 . 26 B1
Thorntons Way CV10 . 72 A3
Thornton Way B77. . . 35 C8
Thornwood Cl B68. . . 64 C5
Thornycroft Rd LE10 . 75 E8
Thornyfield Cl B90. . 106 D3
Thornyfield Rd B90. . 106 C3
Thornyhurst La WS14. 17 A6
Thorpe Ave WS7 . . . . 6 D8
Thorpe Cl
  Burntwood WS7 . . . . . . 6 D8
  Sutton Coldfield B75. . . 46 C7
Thorpe Ct B91 . . . . . 106 F6
Thorpe Rd WS1 . . . . . 42 E7
Thorpe St WS7 . . . . . . 6 D8
Thorp St B5 . . . . 164 B1
Threadneedle St
  CV1 . . . . 113 D6
Three Acres La B90 . 125 D6
Three Corner Cl B90 125 E8
Three Cornered Cl
  CV32 . . . . 157 E6
Three Crowns Specl Sch
  WS5 . . . . .43 F8
Three Oaks Rd B47. . 125 B4
Three Pots Rd LE10 . . 75 E4
Three Shires Oak Rd
  B67. . . . . .64 F2
Three Spires Ave
  CV6 . . . . 113 A6
Three Spires Ind Est
  CV6. . . . . 96 A5
Three Spires Jct CV6. 95 E1
Three Spires Sch
  CV6. . . . . 112 D6
Three Spires Sh Ctr
  WS13 . . . . .9 B7
Three Tuns La WV10 . 11 D1
Three Tuns Par WV10. 11 C2
Threshers Dr WV12. . 27 D6
Threshers Way WV12. 27 D6
Throckmorton Rd
  B98. . . . . 159 A8
Throne Cl B65 . . . . . . 63 D5
Throne Cres B65. . . . 63 D4
Throne Rd B65. . . . . . 63 D5
Throstles Cl B43 . . . . 54 E7
Thruppence Cl CV4. . 131 E6
Thrushel Wlk WV11 . . 26 C5
Thrush Rd B68. . . . . . .63 F2
Thruxton Cl
  Birmingham B14. . . . . 104 F3
  Redditch B98 . . . . . . 154 E3
Thunderbolt Way
  DY4 . . . . 51 D6
Thurcroft Cl B8 . . . . .67 F4
Thuree Rd B67. . . . . . 64 E2
Thurlby Ct WV1. . . . . 25 A3
Thurleigh Cl DY9. . . . 81 C2
Thurlestone Rd
  Birmingham B31. . . . . 122 E7
  Coventry CV6 . . . . . . 112 F8
Thurloe Cres B45 . . . 101 E1
Thurlston Ave B92 . . . .88 F4
Thurlstone Dr WV4. . .38 F4
Thurlstone Rd WS3. . . 14 B3
Thurne B77 . . . . .35 F8
Thursfield Rd
  Royal Leamington Spa
    CV32. . . . . 157 B3
  Tipton DY4 . . . . 52 A6
  West Bromwich B71. . . 53 E7
Thurso B77 . . . . 21 E5
Thurston Ave B69 . . . .63 F6
Thynne St B70 . . . . . . 53 E2
Tibbats Cl B32 . . . . . 84 C3
Tibberton Cl
  Halesowen B63. . . . . . 83 C4
  Solihull B91 . . . . 127 A8
  Wolverhampton WV3 . 38 D7
Tibberton Ct B60. . . . 150 E7
Tibbets La B17. . . . . . 85 B4
Tibbington Rd DY4 . . 51 E7

Tibbington Terr DY4 . .51 F7
Tibbits Ct 8 CV34. . . 160 E6
Tibbits Ho 1 WS2. . . 28 D3
Tiber Cl CV5 . . . . 111 F4
Tiberius Cl B46. . . . . .59 F1
Tibland Rd B27 . . . . . 88 D2
Ticknall Cl B97 . . . . . 153 A4
Tidbury Cl B97 . . . . . 158 C6
Tidbury Green Sch
  B90. . . . . 125 E4
Tiddington Cl B36. . . 58 B1
Tideswell Cl CV3. . . . 115 A1
Tideswell Rd B42 . . . 55 C7
Tidmarsh Cl CV7 . . . 130 A6
Tidmarsh Rd CV35 . . 156 A7
Tidworth Croft 2
  B14 . . . . 105 A3
Tierney Dr DY4. . . . . 52 C6
Tiffany La WV9. . . . . . . .10 F2
Tiffield Rd B25. . . . . . 88 C5
Tigley Ave B32. . . . . . 84 D1
Tilbury Cl WV3 . . . . . 38 A8
Tilbury Gr B13 . . . . . . 86 D1
Tildasley St B70. . . . . 53 B5
Tildesley Dr WV12. . . 27 B5
Tile Cross Rd B33 . . . 69 E2
Tile Cross Trad Est
  B33. . . . . .69 E1
Tiled House La DY5 . . 61 B6
Tile Gr B37 . . . . 70 C3
Tile Hill La
  Coventry, Allesley CV4,
    CV5. . . . . 112 D2
  Coventry, Tile Hill CV4. 112 B1
Tile Hill Sta CV4 . . . 131 C8
Tile Hill Wood Sch &
  Language Coll CV4 111 D2
Tilehouse B97 . . . . . 153 D2
Tilehouse Green La
  B93. . . . . 127 F6
Tilehouse La B90. . . . 125 E6
Tilehurst Dr CV4 . . . . 111 D1
Tilesford Cl B90. . . . . 127 A6
Tilewood Ave CV5. . . 111 F4
Tilia Rd B77 . . . . 22 B5
Tiller Gr B75. . . . . 32 D4
Tilley St WS10 . . . . . . 41 E6
Tillington Cl B98. . . . 154 E3
Tillyard Croft B29 . . . 85 C1
Tilshead Cl B14 . . . . 104 E3
Tilsley Gr B23. . . . . . . 56 B5
Tilston Dr DY5 . . . . . . 61 D1
Tilton Rd
  Birmingham B9. . . . . . 67 C1
  Hinckley LE10 . . . . . . 75 E6
Timberdine Cl B63. . . 82 D6
Timberhonger La
  B61 . . . . 136 B2
Timberlake Cl B90. . . 127 B6
Timberley Croft B34. . 69 D7
Timberley La B34 . . . 69 C6
Timberley Prim Sch
  B34. . . . . 69 D6
Timber Mill Ct 4 B17 85 B6
Timbers Way
  Birmingham B11. . . . . 87 A6
  Sutton Coldfield B24. . . 57 F4
Timbertree Cres B64. 82 E7
Timbertree Prim Sch
  B64. . . . . .82 E7
Timbertree Rd B64. . .82 F7
Times Square Ave
  DY5 . . . . .61 F2
Timmins Cl B91. . . . . 107 E6
Timmins Cl WV14. . . 40 B3
Timmis Rd DY9 . . . . . 81 C6
Timon View CV34. . . 161 E3
Timothy Gr CV4 . . . . 112 B1
Timothy Rd B69 . . . . 63 D7
Tinacre Hill WV6 . . . 23 E2
Tinchbourne St 1
  DY1 . . . . 51 C1
Tindal Sch B12. . . . . .86 F5
Tindal St B12. . . . . . . .86 F5
Tink-A-Tank CV34 . . 160 E6
Tinkers Farm Gr
  B31. . . . . 102 A3
Tinkers Farm Rd
  B31. . . . . 102 E3
Tinkers Green Rd B77 .35 F6
Tinkers La
  Earlswood B94 . . . . . 142 E7
  Lapworth B94. . . . . . 143 E1
Tinmeadow Cres
  B45 . . . . 122 C7
Tinsley St DY4 . . . . . . 52 E5
Tintagel Cl
  Coventry CV3 . . . . . . 134 D5
  Perton WV6. . . . . 23 F3

Tintagel Dr DY1 . . . . 50 E2
Tintagel Gr CV8 . . . . 148 B4
Tintagel Way
  Nuneaton CV11. . . . . . 74 A5
  Walsall WS9 . . . . 29 E7
Tintern Cl
  Bromsgrove B61. . . . . 136 E1
  Sutton Coldfield B74. . . 45 A7
Tintern Cres WS3 . . . .13 F2
Tintern Ct WV6 . . . . . 23 E4
Tintern Ho B32 . . . . . .84 F5
Tintern Rd B20. . . . . . 55 E1
Tintern Villas 4 B12 . 87 B5
Tintern Way
  Bedworth CV12. . . . . . 78 C3
  Walsall WS3 . . . . 13 F2
Tipperary Cl B36 . . . . 68 D8
Tipperary Wlk 2 B69 .63 F7
Tipper Trad Est DY9. . 82 A5
Tippett Cl CV11 . . . . . 79 A7
Tipping's Hill B97. . . 158 C5
Tippity Gn B65. . . . . . 63 B4
Tipps Stone Cl DY4. . 51 E4
Tipton Green Jun Sch
  DY4. . . . . 51 F4
Tipton Rd
  Dudley, Tipton Green
    DY1. . . . . 51 E3
  Dudley, Woodsetton
    DY3. . . . . 50 F7
  Oldbury B69. . . . . . . 52 C2
Tipton St DY3 . . . . . . 50 E7
Tipton Sta DY4 . . . . . 51 F6
Tirley Rd B33 . . . . . . 69 A4
Tisdale Rise CV8 . . . 148 B6
Titan Bsns Ctr CV34. 161 E4
Titania Cl B45. . . . . . 102 A3
Titan Way WS13 . . . . .9 F8
Titchfield Cl WV10 . . 11 E4
Titford Cl B69. . . . . . .63 F4
Titford La B65 . . . . . . 63 E4
Titford Rd B69 . . . . . .63 F4
Tithe Barn La B94. . . 142 C6
Tithe Croft WV10 . . . .25 F3
Tithe Rd WV11 . . . . . 26 D6
Titterstone Rd B31. . 123 A8
Tiverton Cl DY6 . . . . . 61 A3
Tiverton Dr
  Nuneaton CV11. . . . . . 73 F5
  West Bromwich B71. . . 53 C6
Tiverton Gr
  Coventry CV2 . . . . . . 114 D5
  Smethwick B67. . . . . . 64 F6
Tiverton Jun & Inf Sch
  B29. . . . . .85 F2
Tiverton Rd
  Birmingham B29 . . . . . 85 F2
  Coventry CV2 . . . . . . 114 D5
  Smethwick B67. . . . . . 65 B5
Tiverton Sch CV6 . . . 112 D5
Tiveycourt Rd CV6. . . 96 A3
Tividale Com Arts Coll
  B69. . . . . 52 C1
Tividale Com Prim Sch
  B69. . . . . .52 B2
Tividale Rd B69 . . . . . 52 A2
Tividale St B70 . . . . . 52 A2
Tivoli The B26. . . . . . 88 D6
Tixall Rd B28 . . . . . . 105 E5
Tobruk Wlk
  Brierley Hill DY5 . . . . . 61 D3
  Willenhall WV13 . . . . . 40 E8
Tocil Croft CV4 . . . . . 132 D4
Toledo Cl CV5. . . . . . 112 C1
Toler Rd CV11. . . . . . 73 B5
Tollard Cl CV2 . . . . . 114 F5
Toll End Rd DY4 . . . . 52 C7
Tolley Rd DY11 . . . . . 116 B1
Tollgate Cl B31. . . . . 122 F8
Tollgate Dr B20 . . . . 66 B7
Tollgate Prec B67 . . .64 F6
Tollhouse Rd B60 . . . 150 E6
Toll House Rd B45 . . 122 C7
Tollhouse Way B66. . .64 F6
Tolman Dr B77. . . . . . 21 D3
Tolson Ave B78 . . . . . 35 B8
Tolson Cl B77. . . . . . . 35 D5
Tolworth Gdns WV2 . 39 E7
Tolworth Hall Rd B24. 57 B3
Tom Ellis Ct CV7 . . . . 96 A8
Tomey Rd B11 . . . . . . 87 D5
Tom Henderson Cl
  CV3 . . . . 134 F7
Tom Hill B94. . . . . . . 142 F6
Tomkinson Dr DY11 . 116 B4
Tomkinson Rd CV10 . .72 F4
Tomlan Rd B31. . . . . . 123 C7
Tomlinson Rd B36. . . 58 D1
Tompstone Rd B71. . .53 F8
Tomson Ave CV6 . . . 113 B4

Toms Town La B80 . . 159 E3
Tom Ward Cl CV3 . . . 134 E7
Tonadine Cl WV11. . . 13 A1
Tonbridge Rd
  Birmingham B24. . . . . 57 A1
  Coventry CV3 . . . . . . 134 A6
Tong Ct 9 WV3. . . . . 25 C4
Tong St WS1 . . . . 29 A1
Tongue Ave B78. . . . . 35 A8
Topcliffe Prim Sch
  B35. . . . . 58 A3
Top Croft Rd B23. . . .56 F7
Topfield Ho B14. . . . . 104 F3
Top Field Wlk B14. . . 104 D2
Topland Gr B31. . . . . 102 C2
Topp's Dr CV12. . . . . 77 E1
Topp's Heath CV12. . 77 E1
Top Rd
  Barnacle CV7, CV12. . . 97 B7
  Upper Catshill B61. . . 121 A4
Topsham Croft B14. . 104 D5
Topsham Rd B67 . . . . 64 E6
Torbay B77 . . . . 21 E5
Torbay Rd CV5 . . . . . 112 C4
Torcastle Cl CV6 . . . . 113 F7
Torc Ave B77. . . . . . . 21 E4
Torc High Sch B77. . . 21 F1
Torcross Ave CV2. . . 114 C6
Torfield WV8 . . . . 10 E2
Toronto Gdns B32. . . 84 E6
Torpoint Cl CV2 . . . . 114 C7
Torre Ave B31. . . . . . 102 E2
Torres Cl CV34 . . . . . 160 B4
Torrey Gr B8. . . . . 68 C4
Torridge B77 . . . . 36 A5
Torridge Dr WV11 . . . 26 C5
Torridon Croft B13. . . 86 D3
Torridon Rd WV11 . . . 13 B1
Torridon Way LE10 . . 71 B1
Torrington Ave CV4 . 131 E8
Torrs Cl B97 . . . . 153 D2
Torside B77 . . . . 36 B7
Torvale Rd WV6 . . . . 24 A2
Tor Way WS3. . . . . . .14 F3
Torwood Cl CV4. . . . . 131 F6
Totnes Cl CV2 . . . . . . 114 C7
Totnes Gr 2 B29. . . . .85 F2
Totnes Rd B67 . . . . . .64 F6
Tottenham Cres B44. . 45 B2
Touchstone Rd CV34 . 161 F2
Touchwood Hall Cl
  B91. . . . . 107 C4
Touchwood Sh Ctr 1
  B91. . . . . 107 C3
Towbury Cl B98 . . . . 158 F5
Towcester Croft B36 . 68 D8
Tower Croft B37 . . . . 70 B4
Tower Dr B61. . . . . . . 137 A6
Tower Hill B42 . . . . . 55 A6
Tower Rd
  Bedworth CV12. . . . . . 78 B2
  Birmingham, Aston B6. 67 A7
  Birmingham, Aston New
    Town B6. . . . . 66 F7
  Birmingham B23. . . . . 56 E4
  Oldbury B69 . . . . 63 C7
  Sutton Coldfield B75. . . 32 B3
Tower Rise B69 . . . . . 63 C7
Towers Cl
  Kenilworth CV8. . . . . 147 F2
  Kidderminster DY10 . . 117 B5
Tower St
  Birmingham B19. . . . . 164 B5
  Coventry CV1 . . . . . . 165 B3
  Dudley DY1 . . . . 51 C1
  16 Royal Leamington Spa
    CV31. . . . . 162 A7
  Sedgley DY3 . . . . 39 D1
  Walsall WS1 . . . . 28 E2
  Wolverhampton WV1 . 163 C3
Tower View Cres
  CV10 . . . . 72 B3
Tower View Rd WS6 . .13 F8
Townend St WS2 . . . . 28 E2
Townesend Cl CV34 . 155 F1
Town Feilds Cl CV5. . 112 B7
Townfields WS13. . . . .9 A7
Townfold WS3 . . . . . . 15 A4
Town Gate Retail Pk
  DY1. . . . . .51 F2
Town Jun Sch B72. . . 46 C4
Townley Gdns B6. . . . 55 E1
Townsend Ave
  Bromsgrove B61. . . . . 137 B4
  Sedgley DY3 . . . . 50 D8
Townsend Croft CV3. 133 C7
Townsend Dr
  Nuneaton CV11. . . . . . 73 F3

Townsend Dr continued
Sutton Coldfield B76... **57** F7
Townsend Ho B79..... **21** A4
Townsend Pl DY6..... **60** D6
Townsend Rd WV4... **133** C8
Townsends Cl CV11... **75** A1
Townsend Way 5 B1. **66** B3
Townshend Gr B37...**69** F4
Townson Rd WV11... **27** A8
Townwell Fold WV1. **163** B3
Town Wharf Bsns Pk
WS2.............. **28** D2
Towpath Cl
Bedworth CV6....... **96** B6
Birmingham B9...... **67** B2
Towyn Rd B13...... **87** D2
Toys La B63......... **82** C5
Tozer St DY4.........**51** F7
Traceys Mdw B45... **122** A7
Tractor Spares Ind Est
WV13.............. **26** D2
Trafalgar Cl WS12.....**2** C4
Trafalgar Ct B69.... **52** B1
Trafalgar Gr B25..... **88** A6
Trafalgar Ho
Birmingham B11.... **87** B8
Cannock WS12.......**2** E4
3 Coventry CV1..... **113** B2
Trafalgar Rd
Birmingham, Erdington
B24.............. **56** F3
Birmingham, Handsworth
B21.............. **65** E8
Birmingham, Moseley
B13.............. **86** F4
Oldbury B69........ **52** B1
Smethwick B66....... **65** C4
Trafford Dr CV10.... **72** C6
Trafford Lodge 4
CV31............. **162** B7
Trafford Pk The B98 **153** F3
Trafford Rd LE10....**71** F2
Trajan Hill B46.......**59** F1
Tram St DY10...... **116** E5
Tram Way B66....... **64** C7
Tramway Cl
1 Bilston WV14...... **41** A7
Darlaston WS10..... **41** E7
Tranter Ave B48.... **139** A5
Tranter Cres WS11.....**2** B3
Tranter Rd B8....... **68** A5
Tranwell Cl WV9.....**10** F2
Traquain Dr DY1.... **51** A3
Travellers Cl WS7.....**7** A5
Travellers Way B37... **70** D3
Treaford La B8...... **68** C4
Treasure Cl B77..... **21** E4
Treddles La B70..... **53** D3
Tredington Cl
1 Birmingham B29 .. **103** A7
Redditch B98...... **159** B7
Tredington Rd CV5... **111** F4
Tree Acre Gr B63..... **82** C4
Treedale Cl CV4..... **131** D8
Treeford Cl B91..... **106** F1
Trees Rd WS1........**42** F6
Treeton Croft B33... **69** A2
Treetops Dr WV12.... **27** E4
Trefoil B77......... **22** B5
Trefoil Cl B29...... **103** A7
Treford Ct DY9...... **81** B1
Treforest Rd CV3.... **134** C8
Tregarron Rd B63.... **82** C5
Tregea Rise B43..... **54** C7
Tregony Rise WS14... **9** D6
Tregorrick Rd CV7... **96** A8
Tregullan Rd CV7.... **96** B8
Trehern Cl B93..... **128** A5
Treherne Rd CV6.... **113** B8
Trehernes Dr DY9... **81** B1
Trehurst Ave B42.... **55** C7
Trejon Rd B64....... **82** C4
Trelawney Rd CV7... **96** A7
Tremaine Gdns WV10. **25** E4
Tremont Ho WV10.... **25** E3
Tremont St WV10.... **25** E3
Trenance Cl WS14.... **9** D7
Trenance Rd CV7.... **96** A8
Trenchard Cl B75....**46** F5
Treneere Rd CV7.... **96** A8
Trensale Ave CV6.... **112** F4
Trent Cl Burntwood WS7 **7** C6
Perton WV6......... **23** E4
Stourbridge DY8..... **81** A4
Trent Cres B47..... **124** E2
Trent Ct B73....... **46** B5
Trent Dr B36.......**69** F8
Trentham Ave WV12.. **27** B5
Trentham Cl
Cannock WS11.........**2** B1

Trentham Cl continued
Nuneaton CV11...... **78** F8
Trentham Gdns CV8. **148** C5
Trentham Gr B26.... **88** E5
Trentham Rd CV1... **113** F4
Trentham Rise WV2..**39** F7
Trent Ho Cannock WS12..**2** C5
Dudley DY3......... **50** E3
Trent Pl WS3....... **28** D8
Trent Rd
Bulkington CV12.... **79** A2
Cannock WS11........**1** E5
Hinckley LE10...... **75** A8
Nuneaton CV11..... **73** D5
Walsall WS3....... **15** A1
Trent St B5.........**66** F2
Trent Twr 3 B7..... **67** A4
Trent Valley Cotts
WS13.............**3** F1
Trent Valley Rd WS13,
WS14.............. **9** D8
Trenville Ave B11.... **87** B5
Tresco Cl B45...... **101** E1
Trescott Jun & Inf Sch
B31.............. **102** D3
Trescott Rd
Birmingham B31.... **102** D3
Redditch B98...... **153** F3
Tresham Rd
Birmingham B44.... **44** F1
2 Kingswinford DY6.. **60** D8
Tresillian Rd CV7.... **96** B8
Tressel Croft CV34.. **161** E2
Trevanie Ave B32.... **84** C6
Trevelyan Ho 1 B37. **70** C1
Treville Cl B98..... **154** E3
Treviscoe Cl CV7.... **96** A7
Trevithick Cl WS7.....**7** C8
Trevor Ave WS6......**5** A3
Trevor Cl CV4...... **131** D8
Trevorne Cl B12......**86** F6
Trevor Rd
Hinckley LE10...... **71** F1
Walsall WS3....... **14** F5
Trevor St W B7...... **67** C6
Trevor St B7....... **67** C6
Trevose Ave CV7.... **96** B8
Trevose Cl WS3..... **13** F3
Trevose Retreat B12..**86** F5
Trewint Cl CV7..... **96** A8
Trewman Cl B76.....**57** F8
Treyamon Rd WS5... **43** D7
Treynham Cl WV1... **26** C1
Triangle The
Birmingham B18.... **65** F6
Coventry CV5...... **112** B4
Trianon Rd B60.... **137** C1
Tribune Ho 7 LE10.. **71** D1
Trickley Dr 2 B75...**46** F6
Trident Bsns Pk CV11 **73** D3
Trident Blvd B35.... **58** B2
Trident Cl
Sutton Coldfield, Walmley
B76............. **57** F7
Sutton Coldfield, Wylde
Green B23......... **57** A7
Trident Ct
Birmingham, Coleshill
Heath B37........ **90** E8
Birmingham, Handsworth
Wood B20......... **55** A3
Trident Ctr The DY1.. **51** C1
Trident Dr Oldbury B68 **64** B5
Wednesbury WS10.... **41** D3
Trident Ho 4 B15.... **66** C1
Trident Rd B26..... **90** C4
Trident Ret Pk B9... **67** A2
Trigo Croft B36.... **68** E8
Trimpley Cl B93.... **127** E3
Trimpley Dr
Coventry CV6..... **113** C6
Kidderminster DY11.. **116** A7
Trimpley Gdns WV4.. **38** E3
Trimpley Rd B32.... **84** B1
Trinculo Gr CV34... **161** F2
Trinder Rd B67..... **64** D2
Trindle Rd DY2..... **51** D1
Tring Ct WV6........**24** F4
Trinity CE Prim Sch
WV10.............**25** F4
Trinity Churchyard
CV1.............. **165** B3
Trinity Cl
1 Birmingham B19.. **66** D8
Cannock WS11........**4** E8
Shenstone WS14.... **17** F6
Solihull B92....... **89** B1
Stourbridge DY8.... **60** D2
Trinity Ct
Birmingham B6..... **55** D1

Trinity Ct continued
Bromsgrove B60..... **151** B7
4 Cradley Heath B64. **62** E1
Hinckley LE10...... **75** C8
1 Kidderminster
DY10............. **116** F6
Wolverhampton WV3.. **25** A2
Trinity Ctr 1 B64.... **62** E1
Trinity Dr B79...... **20** D6
Trinity Fields DY10.. **116** F6
Trinity Gr WS10.... **42** A3
Trinity Grange DY10. **116** F7
Trinity High Sch & Sixth
Form Ctr B98..... **153** F4
Trinity Hill B72..... **46** C5
Trinity Ho B70..... **53** E1
Trinity La
Coventry CV1...... **165** B3
Hinckley LE10..... **71** C1
Trinity Pk B40...... **90** D3
Trinity RC Sch CV32. **156** D2
Trinity RC Sch The
CV34............. **161** C6
Trinity Rd
Bilston WV14...... **40** F5
Birmingham B6..... **55** E1
Dudley DY1....... **51** C1
Freasley B78, CV9... **36** B3
Stourbridge DY8.... **81** A8
Sutton Coldfield B75.. **32** C1
Willenhall WV12.... **27** D7
Trinity Road N B70.. **53** D2
Trinity Road S B70.. **53** D1
Trinity St
Brierley Hill DY5... **61** D3
Coventry CV1...... **165** B3
Cradley Heath B64... **62** E1
Oldbury B69...... **64** A6
Royal Leamington Spa
CV32............. **156** F1
Smethwick B67..... **65** A6
West Bromwich B70.. **53** D2
Trinity Terr 2 B11... **87** A8
Trinity Vicarage Rd
LE10.............. **75** C8
Trinity Way B70.... **53** D2
Trinity Way Sta B70. **53** D1
Trinity Wlk CV11... **73** E3
Trippleton Ave B32.. **102** B8
Tristram Ave B31... **103** B1
Triton Cl WS6.......**4** F1
Trittiford Rd B13... **105** C6
Triumph B77....... **21** E3
Triumph Cl CV2.... **114** E3
Triumph Ho CV1.... **165** B2
Triumph Wlk B36... **59** A1
Troilus Ct CV34.... **161** F3
Trojan B77........ **21** E3
Tromans Cl B64..... **82** E7
Tromans Ind Est DY2. **62** D3
Troon B77......... **22** C4
Troon Cl
Sutton Coldfield B75... **46** D8
Walsall WS3....... **14** A3
Troon Ct WV6...... **23** D5
Troon Pl DY8....... **60** C3
Troon Way LE10.... **75** D4
Trossachs Rd CV5... **111** F3
Trotter's La B71.... **53** A7
Troughton Cres CV6.. **113** A5
Trouse La WS10......**41** F3
Troutbeck Ave CV32. **156** C2
Troutbeck Dr DY5... **81** B8
Troutbeck Rd CV5... **111** F4
Troyes Cl CV3...... **133** C7
Troy Gr B14....... **104** D4
Troy Ind Est B96... **159** A3
Truck Stop Bsns Pk
B11..............**88** B5
Truda St 2 WS1.... **42** D7
Trueman Cl CV34... **160** E8
Truemans Heath La B47,
B90............. **125** C7
Truggist La CV7.... **130** E8
Trundalls La B90... **126** A5
Truro Cl Hinckley LE10.. **71** E4
Lichfield WS13........**3** B3
Nuneaton CV11.... **73** F5
Rowley Regis B65... **63** E4
Truro Dr DY11..... **116** A5
Truro Pl WS12.......**5** C8
Truro Rd WS5...... **43** D7
Truro Twr 2 B16.... **66** A2
Truro Wlk B37..... **70** B2
Trustin Cres B92... **107** E8
Tryan Rd CV10..... **72** E4
Tryon Pl WV14..... **40** E6
Tryst The B61...... **137** B5
Trysull Ave B26.... **89** C4
Trysull Gdns WV3... **38** D7

Trysull Holloway WV5. **37** C3
Trysull Rd Orton WV5.. **37** E1
Wolverhampton WV3.. **38** D7
Trysull Way DY2.... **62** C4
Tudbury Rd B31.... **102** E4
Tudman Cl B76..... **58** A7
Tudor Ave CV5..... **111** F4
Tudor Bsns Ctr **9**
B98............. **153** E3
Tudor Cl
Balsall Common CV7.. **130** A6
Birmingham, Highter's Heath
B14............. **105** A1
Birmingham, King's Heath
B13............. **104** F6
Burntwood WS7.....**7** C6
Cheslyn Hay WS6.....**4** E3
Lichfield WS14......**9** F6
Sutton Coldfield B73.. **45** D2
Tudor Cres
Tamworth B77...... **21** F4
Wolverhampton WV2.. **39** B6
Tudor Croft B37....**69** F1
Tudor Ct Bedworth CV7 **95** E7
Coventry CV3..... **133** C8
Essington WV11.... **12** F4
Sutton Coldfield B74.. **32** A2
Tipton DY4....... **52** A4
Warwick CV34..... **160** D5
Tudor Eaves 2 B17.. **85** C5
Tudor Gdns
Birmingham B23.... **56** E3
Stourbridge DY8.... **80** E5
Tudor Gr B74...... **45** A8
Tudor Grange Sch
B91............. **107** A2
Tudor Hill B73..... **46** B6
Tudor Ho Dudley DY2..**61** F6
Walsall WS1....... **28** E2
Tudor Ind Est B11...**88** B5
Tudor Park Ct 2 B74..**31** F3
Tudor Park Gdns WS7.**7** C6
Tudor Pl DY3...... **50** E6
Tudor Rd
Birmingham B13.... **86** F3
Burntwood WS7.....**7** C6
Cannock WS12......**1** F8
Darlaston WV14.... **41** B4
Dudley DY3....... **50** E6
Hinckley LE10..... **71** C3
Nuneaton CV10.... **72** C6
Oldbury B68...... **64** C4
Rowley Regis B65... **63** C5
Sutton Coldfield B73.. **46** B6
Wolverhampton WV10. **26** A4
Tudor Row 3 WS13....**9** B7
Tudors Cl 4 B10.... **87** C8
Tudor St
Birmingham B18.... **65** E4
Tipton DY4....... **52** A4
Tudor Terr
Birmingham B17.... **85** C6
Dudley DY2....... **51** E1
Tudor Vale DY3.... **50** E6
Tudor Way
Cheslyn Hay WS6.....**4** D1
Sutton Coldfield B72.. **46** B2
Tufnell Gr B8...... **68** B7
Tugford Rd B29.... **103** C7
Tuisi Ctr B19...... **164** A4
Tulip Gdns B29.... **102** F7
Tulip Tree Ave CV8.. **148** B5
Tulip Tree Ct CV8... **148** B4
Tulip Wlk B37...... **90** C8
Tulliver Cl CV12.... **78** B3
Tulliver Rd CV10.... **73** C1
Tulliver St CV6.... **113** B5
Tulyar Cl B36...... **68** C8
Tunnel Dr B98..... **153** E2
Tunnel La
Birmingham, Brandwood
End B14........ **104** C4
Birmingham, Lifford
B30............. **104** B4
Tunnel Rd B70..... **53** A7
Tunnel St WV14.... **51** C8
Tunstall Rd DY6.... **61** A5
Turchill Dr B76.... **58** B8
Turf Cl WS11.......**6** A4
Turf Cotts WV4......**38** F2
Turfpits La B23.... **56** D6
Turf Pitts La B75... **32** F4
Turks Head Way B70. **53** C2
Turlands Cl CV2.... **115** A7
Turley St DY1..... **51** A6
Turls Hill Rd
Sedgley DY3...... **50** E8
Sedgley WV14..... **50** F8
Turls St DY3...... **50** E8
Turnberry B77..... **22** C5

Turnberry Dr CV11... **79** C8
Turnberry Gr WV6... **23** D5
Turnberry Rd
Birmingham B42.... **55** B8
Walsall WS3....... **14** A4
Turner Ave WV4,
WV14.............**39** F2
Turner Cl
Bedworth CV12.... **78** A4
Cannock WS11......**2** D2
Warwick CV34..... **160** B4
Turner Dr
Brierley Hill DY5... **81** D7
Hinckley LE10..... **71** A3
Turner Gr WV6..... **24** A4
Turner Rd CV5..... **112** D3
Turners Croft B71... **54** A8
Turner's Gr DY3.... **50** C4
Turner's Hill B65... **63** B6
Turner's Hill Rd DY3.. **50** C4
Turner's La DY5.... **61** D1
Turner St
Birmingham B11.... **87** A6
Dudley, Gornalwood
DY3............. **50** D3
2 Dudley, Old Dock
DY1............. **62** B8
Tipton DY4....... **51** F7
West Bromwich B70.. **53** A4
Turney Rd DY8......**80** F6
Turnham Gn WV6... **23** E3
Turnhouse Rd B35.. **58** B4
Turnley Rd B34.... **69** C6
Turnpike Cl
Balsall Common CV7.. **130** B7
Birmingham B11.... **87** A6
Turnpike Dr B46.... **59** C2
Turnpike La B97.... **153** A4
Turnstone Dr WV10.. **12** B7
Turnstone Rd DY10.. **117** A1
Turpin Ct CV31.... **161** F6
Turquoise Gr WS11....**2** C3
Turton Cl WS3..... **14** A4
Turton Rd Tipton DY4..**40** F1
West Bromwich B70.. **53** B2
Turtons Croft WV14.. **40** B3
Turton St DY10.... **117** A8
Turton Way CV8.... **148** C4
Turves Gn
Birmingham, Turves Green
B31............. **103** A1
Birmingham, West Heath
B31............. **122** F8
Turves Green Boys' Tech
Coll B31......... **123** A8
Turves Green Girls Sch &
Tech Coll B31..... **103** A1
Turves Green Prim Sch
B31............. **103** A1
Turville Cl LE10.....**75** F5
Turville Rd B20.... **55** C1
Tustin Gr B27..... **106** C8
Tutbury B77....... **35** C7
Tutbury Ave
Coventry CV4..... **132** E6
Perton WV6....... **24** A3
Tutbury Cl WS11......**2** C3
Tutehill B77....... **36** B7
Tutnall Cl B60..... **137** F1
Tutnall Dr B94..... **143** B6
Tutnall Grange B60. **138** A1
Tutnall La
Blackwell B60..... **138** A1
Finstall B60....... **137** F1
Tutors Way CV10... **116** E4
Tuttle Hill CV10.....**72** F6
Tuxford Cl WV10.... **25** E4
Twatling Rd B45.... **122** A2
Tweedside Cl LE10... **71** F3
Tweeds Well B32... **102** B7
Tweed Twr B20.... **55** D2
Twickenham Ct DY8. **80** C7
Twickenham Dr B13. **86** E2
Twickenham Prim Sch
B44............. **45** C1
Twickenham Rd B44.. **45** C1
Twickenham Way
CV3............. **115** B1
Twiners Rd B98.... **153** F1
Two Gates B63..... **82** C5
Two Gates Com Prim
Sch
Tamworth B77..... **35** C8
Two Gates Ind Est
B77............. **35** D7
Two Gates La B63... **82** C5
Two Locks DY5..... **62** A4
Two Oaks Ave WS7... **6** D8

Two Trees Cl B78... **20** B6
Two Woods La DY5... **61** E1
Two Woods Trad Est
DY5..............**61** F1
Twycross Gr B36.... **68** D7
Twycross Rd LE10....**75** F6
Twycross Wlk CV34.. **155** D1
Twydale Ave B69.... **52** C2
Twyford Cl WS9.... **30** B5
Twyford Gr WV11....**26** F7
Twyford Rd B8..... **68** C5
Twyning Rd
Birmingham, Edgbaston
B16............. **65** D3
Birmingham, Stirchley
B30............. **104** B7
Tybalt Cl
Coventry CV3..... **134** C5
Royal Leamington Spa
CV34............. **161** D4
Tyber Dr B20...... **55** B3
Tyberry Cl B90.... **106** A1
Tyburn Gr B24..... **57** D3
Tyburn Rd
Birmingham B24.... **57** C2
Wolverhampton WV1.. **26** C2
Tyburn Sq B24..... **57** D3
Tyburn Trad Est B24.. **57** D2
Tyebeams B34..... **69** C5
Tye Gdns DY9...... **81** B1
Tyler Ct B24.......**56** F3
Tyler Gdns WV13... **27** B1
Tyler Gr B43...... **44** A1
Tyler Rd WV13..... **27** B1
Tylers Gn B38..... **104** B1
Tylers Gr B90..... **126** F6
Tylney Cl
Birmingham B5..... **86** D7
Coventry CV3..... **115** B2
Tyndale Cres B43... **44** C3
Tyndall Wlk B32.... **84** A2
Tyne Cl
Birmingham B37.... **70** C4
Brownhills WS8......**6** C2
Tyne Ct B73...... **46** B5
Tynedale Cres WV4.. **39** E3
Tynedale Rd B11....**87** F3
Tyne Gr B25...... **88** D8
Tynemouth Cl CV2.. **96** D5
Tyne Pl DY5.......**61** F2
Tynes The B60.... **150** E7
Tyning Cl WV9..... **11** A2
Tyninghame Ave WV6 **24** D7
Tynings La WS9.... **30** A5
Tynsall Ave B97... **152** F2
Tynward Cl CV3.... **133** B5
Tyrley Cl WV6..... **24** B2
Tyrol Cl DY8...... **80** D6
Tyseley Hill Rd B11.. **88** A4
Tyseley Ind Est B11..**87** E5
Tyseley La B11..... **88** A4
Tyseley Locomotive Wks
Visitor Ctr* B11....**87** F5
Tyseley Sta B11.... **88** A5
Tysoe Cl
Hockley Heath B94.. **143** C6
Redditch B98..... **154** D2
Tysoe Croft CV3.... **134** F8
Tysoe Dr B76......**46** F4
Tysoe Rd B44...... **55** F7
Tythe Barn Cl B60.. **150** D6
Tythebarn Dr DY6... **60** A7
Tythe Barn La B90.. **126** A6
Tyzack Cl DY5..... **61** C2

U

Udall Rd WV14..... **40** D3
Uffculme Rd B30... **104** D8
Uffculme Specl Sch
B13..............**86** E1
Uffmoor Est B63.... **82** E2
Uffmoor La B62.... **100** D7
Ufton Cl B90...... **106** E3
Ufton Cres B90.... **106** D3
Ufton Croft CV5.... **112** A3
Ullapool Cl B97... **158** D5
Ullenhall Rd
Dorridge B93...... **128** A6
Sutton Coldfield B76.. **57** F8
Ullenwood B21..... **65** D7
Ulleries Rd B92.... **89** A2
Ullrik Gn B24......**56** F2
Ullswater B77..... **36** B7
Ullswater Ave
Nuneaton CV11.... **73** F6
Royal Leamington Spa
CV32............. **156** C2

Ullswater Cl B32 . . . . .84 F2
Ullswater Gdns DY6 . . 60 D6
Ullswater Ho **4** B69 . 63 D5
Ullswater Pl WS11 . . . . . .1 E1
Ullswater Rd
　Bedworth CV12 . . . . . . 78 A2
　Coventry CV3 . . . . . . 114 C4
　Willenhall WV11 . . . . . 13 B1
Ullswater Rise DY5 . . . 61 E5
Ulster Cl WS11 . . . . .2 A3
Ulster Dr DY6 . . . . 60 E4
Ulverley Cres B92 . . 106 F8
Ulverley Green Rd
　B92 . . . . .88 F1
Ulverley Sch B92 . . . . . .89 B1
Ulverscroft Rd CV3 . . 133 D7
Ulwine Dr B31 . . . . . . 103 A4
Umberslade Children's
　Farm* B94 . . . . 142 C2
Umberslade Rd
　Birmingham B29 . . . . . 104 A8
　Earlswood B94 . . . . . . 142 C7
　Tanworth-In-A B94 . . . 142 E3
Uncle Ben's Cl **1** B69 .63 F4
Underhill Cl
　Coventry CV3 . . . . 133 D3
　Redditch B98 . . . . 158 F6
Underhill La WV10 . . . 12 A2
Underhill Prim Sch
　WV10 . . . . .12 B1
Underhill Rd
　Birmingham B8 . . . . . . 67 F3
　Tipton DY4 . . . . 52 C6
Underhill St B69 . . . . . 64 A5
Underhill Wlk B69 . . . . 64 A5
Underley Cl DY6 . . . . . 60 B7
Underpass The B40 . . . 90 E4
Underwood Cl
　Birmingham B15 . . . . . 85 D4
　Birmingham, Stockland
　Green B23 . . . . 56 C4
　Redditch B97 . . . . 158 A7
Underwood Rd B20 . . 54 E5
Unett Ct **9** B66 . . . . . 65 C5
Unett St
　Birmingham B19 . . . . . 66 C5
　Smethwick B66 . . . . . . 65 C4
Unett Wlk B19 . . . . . . 66 C5
Unicorn Ave CV5 . . . 111 F4
Unicorn Hill B97 . . . . 153 E4
Unicorn La CV5 . . . . . 111 F4
Union Bldgs CV1 . . . 165 B2
Union Dr B73 . . . . .45 F2
Union Ho B73 . . . . .45 F2
Union La WV5 . . . . 37 D2
Union Mill St WV1 . . 163 D3
Union Pas B2 . . . . . . 164 C2
Union Pl
　Birmingham B29 . . . . . 86 B2
　Coventry CV6 . . . . 95 F4
Union Rd
　Birmingham B6 . . . . . . 67 B8
　Oldbury B69 . . . . 52 E2
　Royal Leamington Spa
　CV32 . . . . 156 E1
　Solihull, Lode Heath
　B91 . . . . 107 C4
　Solihull, Shirley B90 . . 106 C2
　West Bromwich B70 . . . 52 F2
Union Row B21 . . . . . .65 F7
Union St Bilston WV14 . 40 C5
　Birmingham B2 . . . . . . 164 C2
　Burntwood WS7 . . . . . . .6 E5
　Cannock WS11 . . . . . . .4 E6
　6 Dudley DY1 . . . . 51 C1
　Kidderminster DY10 . . 116 E7
　Redditch B98 . . . . 153 F3
　Rowley Regis B65 . . . . 63 C1
　Stourbridge, Lye DY9 . . 81 E5
　Stourbridge, Stambermill
　DY8 . . . . .81 A4
　Tipton, Princes End DY1 51 F8
　Tipton, Tipton Green
　DY4 . . . . 51 F5
　Walsall WS1 . . . . 28 F1
　Wednesbury WS10 . . . . 41 F2
　West Bromwich B70 . . 64 D8
　Willenhall WV13 . . . . . 27 A2
　Wolverhampton WV1 . 163 C3
Unisant Trad Est B64 . .62 F2
United Coll of the
　Ascension B29 . . . . . . 85 C1
Unitt Dr B64 . . . . 82 E8
Unity Cl WS10 . . . . . . 41 C4
Unity Ho CV1 . . . . . . 165 C4
Unity Pl
　9 Birmingham B29 . . 85 F2
　Oldbury B69 . . . . 64 A8

Unity Wlk DY4 . . . . . . .51 F5
University Rd CV4 . . . 132 C5
University Road W
　B15 . . . . .85 F4
University Sta B15 . . . .85 E4
Univ of Birmingham
　B15 . . . . .85 F4
Univ of Birmingham The
　(Halls of Residence)
　B15 . . . . 66 C1
Univ of Central England
　B4 . . . . 164 D4
Univ of Central England
　Edgbaston Ctr B15 . 86 A8
Univ of Central England
　in Birmingham B42. 55 D2
Univ of Warwick
　CV4 . . . . 132 C4
Univ of Warwick (Gibbet
　Hill) CV4 . . . . 132 D3
Univ of Warwick Science
　Pk CV4 . . . . 132 C5
Univ of Warwick
　(Westwood) CV4 . . 132 B6
Univ of Wolverhampton
　(Annexe) WV1 . . . . 163 C3
Univ of Wolverhampton
　(City Campus North)
　WV1 . . . . 163 B4
Univ of Wolverhampton
　(City Campus South)
　WV1 . . . . 163 B3
Univ of Wolverhampton
　Compton Park Campus
　WV6 . . . . .24 E2
Univ of Wolverhampton
　(Walsall Campus)
　WS1 . . . . 43 A7
Unketts Rd B67 . . . . . 64 E3
Unwin Cres DY8 . . . . . 80 E5
Upavon Cl B35 . . . . . . 58 A4
Upfield Cotts WS7 . . . . .7 E7
Upland Gr B61 . . . . . 137 A4
Upland Rd
　Birmingham B29 . . . . . 86 B3
　Bromsgrove B61 . . . . . 137 B4
Uplands Coventry CV2 114 A5
　Halesowen B63 . . . . . . 82 E2
Uplands Ave
　Rowley Regis B65 . . . . 63 D3
　Willenhall WV13 . . . . . 26 D1
　Wolverhampton WV3 . . 38 D8
Uplands Cl DY2 . . . . . 62 E7
Uplands Dr
　Sedgley DY3 . . . . 50 D8
　Wolverhampton WV3 . . 38 E8
　Wombourne WV5 . . . . . 49 A6
Uplands Gr WV13 . . . . 26 C1
Uplands Jun Sch
　WV3 . . . . 38 D8
Uplands Manor Prim Sch
　B67 . . . . .64 F3
Uplands Rd
　Birmingham B21 . . . . . 54 D2
　Dudley DY2 . . . . 62 F7
　Wolverhampton WV13 . 26 C1
Uplands The B67 . . . . .64 F4
Upleadon Cl B97 . . . . 158 A6
Upper Abbey St CV11 . 73 B5
Upper Ashley St B62 . 63 C1
Upper Balsall Heath Rd
　B12 . . . . .86 F6
Upper Bond St LE10 . . 71 D1
Upper Brook St WS2 . . 28 E1
Upper Cape CV34 . . . 160 D8
Upper Chapel St B69 . 52 E2
Upper Church La DY4 52 A6
Upper Cl B32 . . . . 84 D3
Upper Clifton Rd B73 . 46 B6
Upper Conybere St **6**
　B12 . . . . .86 F7
Upper Crossgate Rd
　B98 . . . . 159 C8
Upper Dean St B5 . . . 164 C1
Upper Eastern Green La
　CV5 . . . . 111 E5
Upper Ettingshall Rd
　WV14 . . . . 51 B8
Upperfield Way CV3 . 115 A1
Upper Forster St WS4 .28 F1
Upper Gambolds La
　B60 . . . . 151 C5
Upper Gn WV6 . . . . . . 24 D5
Upper Gough St B1 . 164 B1
Upper Green La WS2 . 28 C4
Upper Grosvenor Rd
　B20 . . . . 55 B2
Upper Grove St **8**
　CV32 . . . . 156 E1

Upper Gungate B79 . . 21 B6
Upper Hall Cl B98 . . . 154 D2
Upper Hall La **6** WS1 . 28 E1
Upper Hattons Cotts
　WV9 . . . . 10 D5
Upper Highgate St
　B12 . . . . .86 F7
Upper High St
　Cradley Heath B64 . . . . 62 D1
　Wednesbury WS10 . . . . 41 F3
Upper Hill St
　Coventry CV1 . . . . 165 A3
　Royal Leamington Spa
　CV32 . . . . 157 A1
Upper Holland Rd
　B72 . . . . 46 C4
Upper Holly Wlk
　CV32 . . . . 157 A1
Upper Keys Bsns Pk
　WS12 . . . . .2 E3
Upper Ladyes Hills
　CV8 . . . . 148 A6
Upper Landywood La
　Cheslyn Hay WS6 . . . . . 4 D1
　Great Wyrley WS6 . . . . 13 D8
Upper Lichfield St
　WV13 . . . . 27 A2
Upper Marshall St
　B1 . . . . 164 B1
Upper Meadow Rd
　B32 . . . . 84 C5
Upper Mill La B5 . . . 164 C1
Upper Navigation St
　WS2 . . . . 28 D2
Upper Norgrove Ho
　B97 . . . . 152 F1
Upper Pk CV3 . . . . . . 134 C8
Upper Portland St B6 67 A7
Upper Prec CV1 . . . . . 165 B3
Upper Ride CV3 . . . . . 134 D5
Upper Rosemary Hill
　CV8 . . . . 147 F5
Upper Rushall St WS1 .28 F1
Upper Russell St **1**
　WS10 . . . . .41 F2
Upper St John St WS14 .9 B4
Upper St Mary's Rd
　B67 . . . . .64 F1
Upper Short St WS2 . . 28 D1
Upper Sneyd Rd
　WV11 . . . . 13 B2
Upper Spon St CV1 . . 113 A3
Upper Spring La
　CV8 . . . . 147 F7
Upper St WV6 . . . . . . 24 D5
Upper Stone Cl B76 . . 46 E4
Upper Sutton St B6 . .66 F7
Upper Thomas St B6 . .66 F7
Upper Trinity St B9 . . 67 A1
Upper Vauxhall WV1 . 25 A2
Upper Villiers St WV2 . 39 C6
Upper Well St CV1 . . 165 B3
Upper William St B1 . 66 C1
Upper York St CV1 . . 113 B2
Upper Zoar St WV3 . . 163 A1
Upton Cl B98 . . . . 154 F3
Upton Ct B23 . . . . 56 B3
Upton Dr CV11 . . . . . .78 F2
Upton Gdns WV14 . . . 40 C5
Upton Gr B33 . . . . 68 C1
Upton Rd B33 . . . . 68 C2
Upton St DY2 . . . . 62 C5
Upwey Ave B91 . . . . . 107 A4
Usam Trad Est WV10 . 11 D2
Usk Cl WS3 . . . . 28 D8
Usk Way B36 . . . . .69 F8
Usmere Rd DY10 . . . . 116 F8
Utrillo Cl CV5 . . . . . . 112 C3
Uttoxeter Cl WV6 . . . . 25 B5
Uxbridge Ave CV3 . . . 114 C2
Uxbridge Cl DY3 . . . . 50 D2
Uxbridge Ct
　Burntwood WS7 . . . . . . 6 F5
　Cannock WS12 . . . . .2 C5
　Kidderminster DY11 . . 116 D5
Uxbridge St
　Birmingham B19 . . . . . 66 D5
　Cannock WS12 . . . . .2 C4

V

Valbourne Rd B14 . . . 104 C4
Vale Ave Aldridge WS9 . 30 D3
　Dudley DY3 . . . . 50 D6
Vale Cl
　Birmingham B32 . . . . . 84 F3
　Lichfield WS13 . . . . .3 B1
Vale Ct B64 . . . . 82 D7
Vale Gr B60 . . . . 151 A7
Vale Head Dr WV6 . . . 24 A2

Vale Ind Est DY11 . . . 116 C1
Valencia Croft B35 . . . 58 B4
Valencia Rd
　Bromsgrove B60 . . . . . 137 D1
　Coventry CV3 . . . . 115 A2
Valentine Cl B74 . . . . .44 F7
Valentine Ct B14 . . . . 86 E1
Valentine Rd
　Birmingham B14 . . . . . 86 F1
　Oldbury B68 . . . . 64 C2
Valepits Rd B33 . . . . . 69 C1
Vale Rd DY2 . . . . 62 E4
Valerian
　Kidderminster DY10 . . 116 C1
　Sutton Coldfield B74 . . 31 F4
Valerie Gr B43 . . . . . . 54 C8
Vale Row DY3 . . . . 50 D5
Vales Cl B76 . . . . 57 E7
Vale St Dudley DY3 . . . 50 D5
　Stourbridge DY8 . . . . . 81 A8
　West Bromwich B71 . . . 53 E6
　Wolverhampton WV2 . . 40 A6
Vale The
　Birmingham, Egbaston
　B15 . . . . 86 A6
　Birmingham, Moseley
　B11 . . . . 87 B2
　Coventry CV3 . . . . 134 C8
Vale View
　Aldridge WS9 . . . . 30 B4
　Nuneaton CV10 . . . . . . 72 E4
Valiant Cl LE10 . . . . . 75 E4
Valley Cl B97 . . . . 158 A6
Valley Farm Rd B45 . 122 A6
Valley Gn WS6 . . . . . . .4 E2
Valley Heritage Ctr*
　WS12 . . . . 2 D6
Valley Inf Sch B92 . . 89 D3
Valley La
　Kingswood B94 . . . . . . 144 E7
　Lichfield WS13 . . . . 9 D8
　Tamworth B77 . . . . 35 E7
Valley Park Nature
　Reserve* WV6 . . . . . . 24 D3
Valley Rd
　Birmingham B43 . . . . . 54 C7
　Bournheath B61 . . . . . 136 E7
　Cannock, Hednesford
　WS12 . . . . 2 D6
　Coventry CV2 . . . . 114 A6
　Cradley Heath B64 . . . . 82 E7
　Dudley DY3 . . . . 50 E6
　Earlswood B94 . . . . . . 126 A1
　Halesowen B62 . . . . . . 83 F8
　Radford Semele CV31 . 162 E4
　Royal Leamington Spa
　CV32 . . . . 157 C3
　Smethwick B67 . . . . . . 64 F3
　Solihull B92 . . . . 89 D4
　Stourbridge DY9 . . . . . 81 F6
　Sutton Coldfield B74 . . 44 F7
　Walsall WS3 . . . . 14 D1
　Wolverhampton WV10 . 25 F5
Valley Side WS3 . . . . .14 F2
Valley Stad (Redditch FC)
　B97 . . . . 153 C4
Valley The
　Burntwood WS7 . . . . . . 6 D8
　Radford Semele CV31 . 162 E4
Valley View WS8 . . . . 16 A7
Vallian Croft B36 . . . .68 F7
Vanborough Wlk DY1 . 51 A2
Vanbrugh Ct WV6 . . . 23 E3
Van Dyke Cl CV5 . . . . 112 C3
Van Gogh Cl WS11 . . . 2 D2
Vanguard B77 . . . . 35 D6
Vanguard Ave CV5 . . 112 C1
Vanguard Cl **1** B36 . . 68 E8
Vanguard Ctr CV4 . . . 132 C6
Vanguard Rd B26 . . . 90 C4
Vann Cl **2** B10 . . . . . 87 C8
Vantage Point **4** B70 53 C2
Varden Croft B5 . . . . . 86 D7
Vardon Dr CV3 . . . . . 133 D4
Vardon Way B38 . . . . 103 D1
Varley Rd B24 . . . . . . 57 D4
Varley Vale B24 . . . . . 57 D4
Varlins Way B38 . . . . 123 C4
Varney Ave B70 . . . . . 53 D2
Vaughan Cl B74 . . . . . .31 F6
Vaughan Rd WV13 . . . 26 E1
Vaughan Trad Est
　DY4 . . . . .52 B3
Vaughton Dr B75 . . . . 46 E6
Vaughton Ho B15 . . . . 86 C7
Vaughton St S B12 . . . 86 E8
Vaughton St B12 . . . . .86 F8
Vauxhall Ave **3** WV1 . 25 A2
Vauxhall Cl **4** CV1 . . 113 E3
Vauxhall Cres B36 . . . .58 F1

Vauxhall Gdns DY2 . . 62 E7
Vauxhall Gr B7 . . . . . . 67 A3
Vauxhall Ho **2** WV1 . . 25 A2
Vauxhall Pl B7 . . . . . . 67 A3
Vauxhall Rd
　Birmingham B7 . . . . . . 67 A3
　Stourbridge DY8 . . . . . 81 A5
Vauxhall St
　Coventry CV1 . . . . 113 E3
　Dudley DY1 . . . . 62 B8
Vauxhall Trad Est B7 .67 B4
Vaynor Dr B97 . . . . . . 158 D8
Vaynor Fst Sch The
　B97 . . . . 158 C7
Veasey Cl CV11 . . . . . 73 E3
Vecqueray St CV1 . . . 113 E2
Vector Ind Pk B71 . . . 53 C6
Velsheda Rd B90 . . . . 106 A2
Venetia Rd B9 . . . . . . 67 C2
Venice Ct **2** B13 . . . . 87 B2
Venning Gr B43 . . . . . 54 D7
Ventnor Ave
　Birmingham, Lozells
　B19 . . . . 66 D7
　Birmingham, Ward End
　B36 . . . . 68 D7
Ventnor Cl
　Birmingham B68 . . . . . 84 C7
　Coventry CV2 . . . . 114 E3
Ventnor Rd B92 . . . . . 89 C3
Ventnor St CV10 . . . . 73 D6
Ventura Park Rd B78 .20 F3
Ventura Pk B78 . . . . . 21 A3
Ventura Pk Rd B78 . . 21 A3
Venture Ct LE10 . . . . 74 E8
Venture Way B7 . . . . .66 F4
Vera Rd B26 . . . . 88 E7
Vera Roberts Way
　DY11 . . . . 116 B3
Verbena Cl
　Coventry CV2 . . . . 96 B1
　Stoke Prior B60 . . . . . 150 C1
Verbena Gdns B7 . . . . 67 A5
Verbena Rd B31 . . . . . 102 F6
Vercourt B74 . . . . 31 B3
Verden Ave CV34 . . . 160 B4
Verdi Ct WS13 . . . . .3 C2
Verdun Cl CV31 . . . . . 162 D2
Verdun Cres DY2 . . . .51 F2
Vere St B5 . . . . 86 D8
Verity Wlk DY8 . . . . . 60 E1
Vermont Gn **4** WS11 . .2 A3
Vermont Gr CV31 . . . 162 D6
Verney Ave B33 . . . . . 89 D7
Vernier Ave DY6 . . . . 61 A5
Vernolds Croft B5 . . . 86 E8
Vernon Ave
　Birmingham B20 . . . . . 54 F4
　Brownhills WS8 . . . . . . 16 A8
　Tipton DY4 . . . . 51 F4
Vernon Cl
　5 Coventry CV1 . . . . 113 E3
　Essington WV11 . . . . . 12 F4
　Halesowen B62 . . . . . . 83 D8
　Redditch B98 . . . . 154 A5
　Royal Leamington Spa
　CV32 . . . . 156 E3
　Sutton Coldfield B74 . . 31 E4
　Willenhall WV13 . . . . . 26 E1
Vernon Ct
　Birmingham B16 . . . . . 65 E1
　9 Coventry CV1 . . . . 113 E4
Vernon Rd
　Bilston WV14 . . . . 40 F6
　Birmingham B16 . . . . . 65 E1
　Halesowen B62 . . . . . . 83 C8
　Oldbury B68 . . . . 64 C6
Vernons Ct CV10 . . . .72 F4
Vernons La CV10, CV11.72 F4
Vernon Mews CV10 . . .72 F4
Vernon St B70 . . . . . . 52 E3
Vernon Trad Est B62 . 83 C8
Vernon Way WS3 . . . . 13 E1
Verona Cl CV11 . . . . . 74 A1
Verona Ct WV10 . . . . . 26 A4
Verona Rd B60 . . . . . . 137 C1
Veronica Ave WV4 . . . 39 E5
Veronica Cl B29 . . . . . 103 A6
Veronica Rd DY6 . . . . 61 A6
Verstone Croft B31 . . 103 A3
Verstone Rd B90 . . . . 106 C4
Verwood Cl WV13 . . . 26 D1
Vesey Cl
　Sutton Coldfield B74 . . 31 F2
　Water Orton B46 . . . . . 59 B2
Vesey Rd B73 . . . . 46 B1
Vesey St B4 . . . . 164 C4
Vestry Ct DY8 . . . . . . 80 E6
Viaduct Dr WV6 . . . . . 25 B6

Viaduct St B7 . . . . 67 A3
Vibart Rd B26 . . . . . . .88 F8
Vicarage Cl
　Birmingham, Great Barr
　B42 . . . . 55 D7
　Birmingham, Stirchley
　B30 . . . . 104 C7
　Brierley Hill DY5 . . . . . 81 C8
　Bromsgrove B60 . . . . . 151 B8
　Brownhills WS8 . . . . . . 16 A7
　Dordon B78 . . . . 36 A5
　Tipton DY4 . . . . 51 E5
Vicarage Cres
　Kidderminster DY10 . . 116 F5
　Redditch B97 . . . . 153 C3
Vicarage Ct WS7 . . . . . .6 F6
Vicarage Field CV34 . 161 B8
Vicarage Gdns
　Halesowen B62 . . . . . . 63 D1
　Sutton Coldfield B76 . . 57 F7
Vicarage Hill
　Middleton B78 . . . . 34 B1
　Tanworth-In-A B94 . . . 141 F3
Vicarage La
　Brierley Hill DY5 . . . . . 61 D7
　Coventry CV7 . . . . 95 D7
　Longbridge CV35 . . . . 160 A1
　Water Orton B46 . . . . . 59 B2
Vicarage Pl WS1 . . . . 28 E1
Vicarage Prospect
　DY1 . . . . 51 B1
Vicarage Rd
　Birmingham, Aston
　B6 . . . . 67 A4
　Birmingham, Chad Valley
　B15 . . . . 85 F8
　Birmingham, Handsworth
　B18 . . . . 66 A7
　Birmingham, Harts Green
　B17 . . . . 85 B5
　Birmingham, King's Heath
　B14 . . . . 104 E8
　Birmingham, Stechford
　B33 . . . . 68 E1
　Brierley Hill DY5 . . . . . 81 C7
　Brownhills WS8 . . . . . . 16 A7
　Cheswick Green B90,
　B94 . . . . 126 C3
　Dudley, West Coseley
　WV14 . . . . 51 C1
　Dudley, Woodsetton
　DY3 . . . . 50 F5
　Halesowen B62 . . . . . . 63 C1
　Hockley Heath B94 . . . 143 F7
　Oldbury B68 . . . . 64 C6
　Royal Leamington Spa
　CV32 . . . . 157 B3
　Smethwick B67 . . . . . . 64 F3
　Stone DY10 . . . . 117 E2
　Stoneleigh CV8 . . . . . 149 B6
　Stourbridge DY8 . . . . . 80 D7
　Stourbridge, Lye DY9 . . 81 F5
　Walsall WS3 . . . . 15 B2
　Wednesbury WS10 . . . . 42 A4
　West Bromwich B71 . . . 53 D6
　Wolverhampton, Blakenhall
　WV2 . . . . 163 C1
　Wolverhampton, Penn
　WV4 . . . . 38 E3
　Wolverhampton WV11 . 26 B6
Vicarage Rd S DY9 . . . 81 E5
Vicarage Rd W DY1 . . 51 C6
Vicarage St
　Nuneaton CV11 . . . . . . 73 C4
　Oldbury B68 . . . . 64 B5
Vicarage Terr **1** WS2 . 42 C1
Vicarage View B97 . . 153 D3
Vicarage Wlk **9** WS1 . 28 E1
Vicar's Cl WS13 . . . . . .9 A4
Vicar St Dudley DY2 . . 62 C8
　Kidderminster DY10 . . 116 E6
　Sedgley DY3 . . . . 50 D8
　Wednesbury WS10 . . . . 42 A3
Vicars Wlk DY9 . . . . . 81 E2
Viceroy Cl
　Birmingham B5 . . . . . . 86 C6
　Kingswinford DY6 . . . . 61 A5
Victor Bsns Ctr B98 . 154 B3
Victor Cl WV2 . . . . . . 40 B6
Victoria Arc WV1 . . . 163 B3
Victoria Ave
　Birmingham B21 . . . . . 65 F6
　Birmingham, Small Heath
　B10 . . . . 87 D8
　Halesowen B62 . . . . . . 83 D6
　Smethwick B66 . . . . . . 65 A5
　Walsall, Blakenall Heath
　WS3 . . . . 28 C1
　Walsall, Wallington Heath
　WS3 . . . . 14 C1

Victoria Bldgs B16 . . . 65 E3
Victoria Bsns Ctr 11
    CV31. . . . . 162 A7
Victoria Colonnade 5
    CV31. . . . . 161 F7
Victoria Com Specl Sch
    B31. . . . . 103 A5
Victoria Ct
    6 Birmingham, Hurst
      Green B62 . . . . 84 A7
    2 Birmingham, Showell
      Green B13 . . . . 86 F4
    Brierley Hill DY5 . . . . . . 61 D3
    Coventry CV5 . . . . 112 C4
    Halesowen B62. . . . . . . 83 F6
    2 Kidderminster
      DY11. . . . . 116 F6
    Norton Canes WS11 . . . . . .6 B5
Victoria Dr B78 . . . . . 35 A8
Victoria Fold WV1. . . 163 B2
Victoria Gdns
    Cradley Heath B64 . . . . 62 F2
    Lichfield WS13 . . . . .8 F6
Victoria Gr
    1 Birmingham B18 . . . 65 E4
    Wombourne WV5 . . . . . 49 A8
Victoria Ho
    2 Birmingham B2 . . . 164 C2
    4 Birmingham, Ladywood
      B16. . . . . 66 B2
    Birmingham, Small Heath
      B10. . . . . 87 D8
    2 Darlaston WS10 . . . 41 C6
Victoria Hospl WS13. . . .9 A6
Victoria Inf Sch DY4 .51 F5
Victoria Law Cts B2. 164 C3
Victoria Mews
    Barnt Green B45. . . . . 138 D8
    Coventry CV3 . . . . . . 114 E2
    Oldbury B69 . . . . 63 F3
    Walsall WS4 . . . . 29 A3
    Warwick CV34 . . . . . . 160 D7
Victoria Park Prim Sch
    B66. . . . . .65 B5
Victoria Park Rd B66. 65 B5
Victoria Pas WV1. . . 163 B3
Victoria Pass 5 DY8 . 81 A5
Victoria Pl DY11. . . . 116 B2
Victoria Rd
    Birmingham, Acock's Green
      B27. . . . . 88 C2
    Birmingham, Aston B6 . 66 F7
    Birmingham B17. . . . . . 85 B5
    Birmingham, Handsworth
      B21. . . . . 65 E7
    Birmingham, Stechford
      B33. . . . . 68 D3
    Birmingham, Stirchley
      B30. . . . . 104 A7
    Birmingham, Stockland
      Green B23 . . . . 56 D3
    Brierley Hill DY5 . . . . . 62 A1
    Bromsgrove B61. . . . . 137 A3
    Cradley Heath B64 . . . . 62 F2
    Darlaston WS10 . . . . . 41 D6
    Dodford B61. . . . . 136 A7
    Halesowen B62. . . . . . . 83 D8
    Hartshill CV10. . . . . . . 72 B8
    Hinckley LE10 . . . . 75 F5
    Oldbury B68 . . . . 64 D6
    Royal Leamington Spa
      CV31. . . . . 161 E8
    Sedgley DY3 . . . . 50 E8
    Sutton Coldfield B72. . . 46 C5
    Tamworth B79. . . . . . . 21 C5
    Tipton DY4 . . . . 52 A4
    Walsall WS3 . . . . 15 A3
    Wolverhampton, Newbolds
      WV10. . . . . 25 F5
    Wolverhampton, New Cross
      WV11. . . . . 26 B6
    Wolverhampton, Oxbarn
      WV3. . . . . 38 E7
    Wolverhampton, Tettenhall
      WV6. . . . . 24 E5
Victoria Sq
    Birmingham B3. . . . . . 164 B2
    Wolverhampton WV1 . 163 C3
Victoria St
    Birmingham B9. . . . . . . 67 D1
    Brierley Hill, Barrow Hill
      DY5. . . . . 61 C7
    Brierley Hill, Merry Hill
      DY5. . . . . 61 D3
    Cannock, Bridgtown
      WS11 . . . . .4 D8
    Cannock, Broomhill
      WS11. . . . . .1 E4
    Cannock WS12 . . . . . . .2 C6
    Coventry CV1 . . . . . . 165 D4

Victoria St continued
    Halesowen B63. . . . . . . 83 A4
    Hinckley LE10 . . . . 71 D1
    Kingswinford DY6 . . . . . 49 B1
    Nuneaton CV11. . . . . . . 73 C4
    7 Redditch B98. . . . . . 153 E4
    Royal Leamington Spa
      CV31. . . . . 161 E8
    Stourbridge DY8 . . . . . . 81 A5
    Warwick CV34 . . . . . . 160 D7
    Wednesbury WS10 . . . . 41 E2
    West Bromwich, Lambert's
      End B70 . . . . 53 C3
    West Bromwich, Swan
      Village B70. . . . . 52 F5
    Willenhall WV13 . . . . . . 27 B3
    Wolverhampton WV1 . 163 B3
Victoria Terr
    Royal Leamington Spa
      CV31. . . . . 161 F7
    4 Walsall WS4 . . . . . . 28 F3
Victor Rd
    Birmingham B18. . . . . . 65 E6
    Solihull B92. . . . . 89 D3
Victor St
    Walsall, Caldmore
      WS1. . . . . 42 E8
    Walsall WS3 . . . . 15 A1
Victor Tower B7. . . . . 67 B6
Victory Ave
    Burntwood WS7 . . . . .6 F7
    Darlaston WS10 . . . . . . 41 C5
Victory Cl WS12 . . . . . . .2 F4
Victory Ho 5 B13. . . . .86 F4
Victory La WS2. . . . . . 28 A4
Victory Rd CV6. . . . . . 95 E1
Victory Rise B71. . . . . 53 D5
Victory Terr B78. . . . . 35 B8
Vienna Ho CV5. . . . . . 112 E2
View Dr DY2 . . . . 62 E8
Viewfield Ave WS12 . . . .1 F7
Viewfield Cres DY3 . . . 50 D6
Viewlands Dr WV6 . . . 24 A2
View Point B69 . . . . . . 63 B7
View St WS12 . . . . .1 F6
Vigo Cl WS9 . . . . .15 F2
Vigo Pl WS9 . . . . 30 A8
Vigo Rd WS9 . . . . .15 F2
Vigo Terr WS9 . . . . . . .15 F2
Viking B77 . . . . 35 D7
Viking Rise B65 . . . . . 63 C4
Vilia Cl LE10 . . . . .75 F4
Villa Cl CV12 . . . . 79 C2
Villa Cotts B19 . . . . . . 66 B7
Villa Cres CV12. . . . . . 79 C1
Villa Cross B20. . . . . . 66 B7
Village Mews The
    WV6 . . . . 24 C5
Village Rd B6 . . . . 56 A1
Village The DY6 . . . . . 60 E7
Village Way WV14 . . . 40 C5
Village Wlk WS10 . . . . 42 B3
Villa Park (Aston Villa
    FC) B6. . . . . .55 F1
Villa Rd
    Birmingham B19. . . . . . 66 B7
    Coventry CV6 . . . . . . 113 B6
Villa St
    Birmingham B19. . . . . . 66 C6
    Stourbridge DY8 . . . . . . 81 A8
Villa Wlk B19 . . . . 66 C6
Villebon Way CV31 . . 162 A2
Villette Gr B14 . . . . . 105 C4
Villiers Ave WV14. . . . 40 D7
Villiers Ind Est WV2. .39 B7
Villiers Jun & Inf Sch
    WV14 . . . . 40 D7
Villiers Rd
    Bromsgrove B60. . . . . 150 E7
    Kenilworth CV8. . . . . . 148 B5
Villiers Sq WV14 . . . . 40 D7
Villiers St
    Birmingham B18. . . . . . 65 E5
    Coventry CV1 . . . . . . 114 A3
    Kidderminster DY10 . . . 117 A5
    Nuneaton CV11. . . . . . . 73 B3
    Royal Leamington Spa
      CV32. . . . . 157 A1
    Walsall WS1 . . . . 42 F7
    Willenhall WV13 . . . . . . 27 B2
Vimy Rd
    Birmingham B13. . . . . 105 B8
    Wednesbury WS10 . . . . 42 A4
Vimy Terr WS10. . . . . . 42 A4
Vincent Cl B12. . . . . . .86 F6
Vincent Dr B15. . . . . . 85 E4
Vincent Par B62. . . . . .86 F6
Vincent Rd B75. . . . . . 46 E7
Vincent St
    Birmingham B12. . . . . . 86 F5

Vincent St continued
    Coventry CV1 . . . . . . 113 B2
    Royal Leamington Spa
      CV32. . . . . 157 A1
    Walsall WS1 . . . . 42 F7
Vincent Wyles Ho
    CV2. . . . . 114 E3
Vince St B66. . . . . 65 A3
Vinculum Way WV13. . 41 A8
Vine Ave B12. . . . . 87 A5
Vine Cl WV10 . . . . 11 D3
Vine Cres B71. . . . . . . 53 D6
Vine Ct
    Cradley Heath B64 . . . . 82 D8
    Warwick CV34 . . . . . . 160 F8
Vine Gdns B64 . . . . . . .62 F2
Vine La Cannock WS11. . . 4 D5
    Clent DY9 . . . . 99 F3
    Halesowen B63. . . . . . . 83 B3
    4 Warwick CV34 . . . . 160 F8
Vineries The B27 . . . . 88 E4
Vine St Birmingham B6. 67 B7
    Brierley Hill DY2, DY5. . 61 E5
    Coventry CV1 . . . . . . 165 C3
    Kidderminster DY10 . . . 117 A8
    Redditch B97. . . . . . . 153 D4
    Stourbridge DY8. . . . . . 60 E1
Vineyard Rd B31 . . . . 102 F5
Vinnall Gr B32. . . . . . 102 B8
Vintage Cl B34. . . . . . 69 A5
Vinyard Cl B18. . . . . . .65 F7
Violet Cl
    Bedworth CV12. . . . . . 77 E2
    Coventry CV2 . . . . 96 C3
Violet Croft DY4. . . . . 41 B1
Violet La DY9 . . . . 99 E4
Virginia Dr WV4. . . . . .38 F4
Virginia Pl CV10. . . . . 72 E3
Virginia Rd CV1 . . . . . 113 E3
Viscount Cl
    Birmingham B35. . . . . . 58 A2
    Royal Leamington Spa
      CV31. . . . . 161 F6
Viscount Dr B35. . . . . 58 B2
Vista Gn B38. . . . . . . 104 B1
Vista The DY3 . . . . 39 D2
Vittle Dr CV34. . . . . . 160 D7
Vittoria St
    Birmingham B1. . . . . . . 66 C4
    Smethwick B66. . . . . . . 65 D6
Vittoria Works B1. . . . 66 C3
Vivian Cl B17. . . . . 85 C5
Vivian Rd B17. . . . . . . 85 C5
Vixen Cl CV11. . . . . . . 78 D7
Vodena Ct 5 CV32. . . 156 E1
Vogue Cl CV1. . . . . . . 165 D3
Vowchurch Cl B97. . . 153 A5
Voyager Dr WS11. . . . . .4 F6
Vulcan Ho B91. . . . . . 107 C6
Vulcan House Ind Est
    B91. . . . . 107 C6
Vulcan Ind Est WS2. . 28 C6
Vulcan Rd
    Bilston WV14 . . . . 40 F5
    Lichfield WS13 . . . . 3 E1
    Solihull B91. . . . . 107 C7
Vulcan Road Island
    WV14 . . . . .40 F5
Vyrnwy Gr B38. . . . . . 123 E8
Vyse St
    Birmingham, Aston B6 . 67 B8
    Birmingham, Hockley
      B18. . . . . 66 C4

W

Wackrill Dr CV32. . . . 157 C3
Wadbarn B90 . . . . . . 126 A5
Waddam's Pool DY2. . 51 D1
Waddell Cl WV14. . . . .39 F7
Waddens Brook La
    WV11. . . . . 26 E5
Waddington Ave B43 . 43 E1
Wade Ave CV3 . . . . . 133 B5
Wadebridge Dr CV11 .73 F5
Wade Gr CV34 . . . . . 155 C2
Wades Cl 3 B90. . . . 51 E5
Wadesmill Lawns
    WV10. . . . . 11 E4
Wade St WS13 . . . . . . .9 B7
Wadham Cl B65. . . . . 63 C6
Wadham Ho B37. . . . . 70 D3
Wadham's Fold WV1 163 B3
Wadhurst Rd B17 . . . . 65 B2
Wadleys Rd B91. . . . . 106 F6
Waen Cl DY4. . . . . 52 B8
Waggestaff Dr CV10. . 72 A7
Waggoners Cl 1
    B60. . . . . 150 E6

Waggoner's La B78. . . 33 E8
Waggon La DY10 . . . . 98 A3
Waggon St B64 . . . . . .62 F2
Waggon Wlk B38. . . . 123 C8
Wagoners Cl B8. . . . . .67 F6
Wagon La B26, B92 . . .88 F4
Wagstaff Cl WV14. . . . 51 D8
Wagstaff Way B37. . . 90 A8
Wainbody Ave N
    CV3 . . . . 133 A6
Wainbody Ave S CV3 132 F5
Wainbody Wood Sch
    CV4. . . . . 132 D2
Wainrigg B77 . . . . 36 B7
Wainwright Cl DY6 . . . 60 A8
Wainwright St B6. . . . 67 A7
Waite Rd WV13. . . . . . 40 E8
Wakefield Cl
    Coventry CV3 . . . . . . 134 F7
    Sutton Coldfield B73. . . 46 A2
Wakefield Ct B13. . . . . 87 B2
Wakefield Gr B46 . . . . 59 B3
Wakeford Rd B31. . . . 103 C1
Wake Gr CV34. . . . . . 160 B5
Wake Green Pk B13 . . 87 B2
Wake Green Rd
    Birmingham B13. . . . . . 87 A2
    Wednesbury DY4 . . . . . 41 A1
Wakehurst Cl CV11. . .78 F8
Wakelam Gdns B43. . . 43 D1
Wakelams Fold DY3. . . 50 C3
Wakeley Hill WV4 . . . .38 F7
Wakelin Rd B90. . . . . 126 B7
Wakeman Cl WV11. . . .12 F3
Wakeman Dr B69. . . . . 63 B8
Wakeman Gr B33. . . . . 89 D7
Wakes Cl WV13. . . . . . 27 B1
Wakes Rd WS10. . . . . . 42 A2
Walcot Cl B75. . . . . . . 32 B3
Walcot Dr B43 . . . . . . 54 F6
Walcote Cl LE10. . . . . .74 F4
Walcot Gdns WV14. . . . 40 B4
Walcot Gn B93. . . . . . 128 A2
Waldale Cl WV11. . . . . 13 C1
Walden Gdns WV4. . . . 38 E6
Walden Rd B11. . . . . . 88 A3
Waldeve Gr B92. . . . . 107 F8
Waldley Gr B24 . . . . . 57 D3
Waldon Wlk B36. . . . . .69 F8
Waldron Ave DY5. . . . . 61 B2
Waldron Cl WS10. . . . .41 F6
Waldrons Moor B14. . 104 C5
Walford Ave WV3. . . . .38 F8
Walford Dr B92. . . . . . 89 D3
Walford Gn B32. . . . . 102 B7
Walford Gr CV34 . . . . 155 F1
Walford Rd B11. . . . . . 87 C6
Walford St B69. . . . . . 52 A2
Walford Wlk 6 B97 . 153 E3
Walhouse CE Jun Sch
    WS11. . . . . .1 C1
Walhouse Cl 6 WS1 .28 F2
Walhouse Rd WS1. . . . 29 A2
Walhouse St WS11 . . . .4 E8
Walker Ave
    Brierley Hill DY5. . . . . . 81 D7
    Oldbury B69 . . . . 63 C7
    Stourbridge DY9. . . . . . 81 E3
    Wolverhampton WV10 . 25 E8
Walker Dr B24 . . . . . . 67 E8
Walker Grange DY4. . . 51 F6
Walker Pl WS3 . . . . . . 28 E8
Walker Rd WS3 . . . . . 28 E8
Walkers Croft WS13 . . .3 C2
Walkers Fold WV12. . . 27 D6
Walkers Heath Rd
    B38. . . . . 104 B1
Walkers Orch CV8. . . 149 B6
Walkers Rd B98. . . . . 154 E6
Walkers Rise 2 B38. . 2 D8
Walker St Dudley DY2 . 62 C4
    Tipton DY4 . . . . 52 C7
Walkers Way
    Bedworth CV12. . . . . . .77 F1
    Kenilworth CV8. . . . . . 147 F2
Walk La WV5. . . . . 49 A6
Walkmill Bsns Pk
    WS11. . . . . .4 D5
Walkmill La WS11 . . . . 4 D5
Walkmill Way WS11. . . 4 D5
Walk The DY3 . . . . 39 D1
Walkwood CE Mid Sch
    B97. . . . . 158 C8
Walkwood Cres B97. . 158 C6
Walkwood Rd B97. . . 158 D6
Wallace Cl
    Norton Canes WS11 . . . . .5 F1
    Oldbury B69 . . . . 63 D6
Wallace Ct WS6 . . . . . . 4 D1

Wallace Ho
    8 Oldbury B69 . . . . . . 63 D5
    Warwick CV34 . . . . . . 160 D7
Wallace Rd
    Bilston WV14 . . . . 41 A2
    Birmingham B29. . . . . . 86 B2
    Brownhills WS8 . . . . . . 15 E8
    Coventry CV6 . . . . . . 113 A8
    Oldbury B69 . . . . 63 D6
Wallace Rise B64. . . . . 82 E7
Wall Ave B46. . . . . . . .70 F5
Wallbank Rd B8. . . . . . 68 A6
Wallbrook Prim Sch
    WV14. . . . . .51 E8
Wallbrook St WV14. . . 51 D8
Wall Croft WS9. . . . . . 30 B7
Wall Dr B74. . . . . .31 F4
Wall End Cl WS2 . . . . . 28 A7
Waller Cl CV35. . . . . . 155 F7
Waller St CV32. . . . . . 157 A2
Wallface B71. . . . . 53 B7
Wallheath Cres WS14. 16 E5
Wallheath La WS14. . . 16 F5
Wall Hill Rd CV5, CV7 . 94 B3
Walling Croft WV14 . . 40 B3
Wallingford Ave CV11 .73 F7
Wallington Cl WS3 . . . 14 B2
Wallington Heath
    WS3 . . . . 14 B2
Wallis Ct 1 B13. . . . . 87 B2
Wall La WS13, WS14. . . 8 D3
Wall (Letocetvm) Roman
    Site (Town)* WS14. . . 8 E2
Wallnut Wlk WS13 . . . .8 F6
Wallows Ind Est The
    DY5. . . . . 61 D5
Wallows La WS1, WS2. 42 C6
Wallows Pl DY5 . . . . . 61 C5
Wallows Rd DY5. . . . . 61 D5
Wallows Wood DY3. . . 50 A4
Wall Roman Site
    (Letocetvm) Mus*
    WS14 . . . . 8 D2
Wallsgrove Cl CV32. . 157 B3
Wall's Rd B60. . . . . . . 150 C3
Wall St WV1 . . . . 26 B2
Wall Well B63. . . . . . .82 F3
Wall Well La B63. . . . .82 F3
Wallwin Ct CV34 . . . . 160 D6
Walmead Croft 1
    B17. . . . . .84 F7
Walmer Ct B16. . . . . . 65 D3
Walmer Gr B23 . . . . . 56 B5
Walmer Mdw WS9. . . . 30 B7
Walmers The WS9 . . . . 30 B7
Walmers Wlk The
    B31. . . . . 102 D1
Walmer Way B37. . . . . 70 C3
Walmesley Way B31. . 102 E3
Walmley Ash Ct B76. .57 F8
Walmley Ash La B76. . 58 C6
Walmley Ash Rd B76 . 58 A7
Walmley Cl
    Halesowen B63. . . . . . . 82 B7
    Sutton Coldfield B76. . . 57 F8
Walmley Jun & Inf Schs
    B76. . . . . 58 A7
Walmley Park Ct B76. .57 F8
Walmley Rd B76. . . . . .46 F2
Walney Cl LE10. . . . . . 71 B1
Walnut Ave WV8 . . . . 10 B3
Walnut Cl
    Birmingham B37. . . . . . 70 B1
    Cannock WS11 . . . . . . .1 F3
    Hartshill CV10. . . . . . . 72 A8
    Nuneaton, Camp Hill
      CV10. . . . . 72 E6
    Stourbridge DY9 . . . . . 81 B1
Walnut Dr
    Cannock WS11 . . . . . . .1 F3
    Royal Leamington Spa
      CV32. . . . . 157 B3
    5 Smethwick B66. . . . 65 B5
    Wolverhampton WV3 . . 24 D1
Walnut Gr WS14. . . . . . 9 F7
Walnut La
    Finstall B60. . . . . 151 D8
    Wednesbury WS10 . . . . 42 A2
Walnut Rd WS5 . . . . . 43 A4
Walnut St CV2 . . . . . . 96 B2
Walnut Tree Cl CV8. . 148 A3
Walnut Way B31 . . . . 122 F6
Walpole Wlk 3 B70. . 53 D1
Walsal End La B92. . . 108 F3
Walsall Acad WS3 . . . 14 C2
Walsall Arboretum*
    WS1. . . . . 29 A2

Walsall Coll of Arts &
    Tech
    Walsall WS1. . . . . 28 E2
    Walsall WS2. . . . . 28 D3
Walsall Coll of Arts &
    Tech (Shelley Campus)
    WS2. . . . . 28 C1
Walsall Ent Pk WS2. . 42 C8
Walsall New Firms Ctr
    WS1. . . . . 42 D8
Walsall Rd
    Aldridge WS9. . . . . 30 A5
    Birmingham B42. . . . . . 55 B6
    Brownhills WS9 . . . . . . 15 E2
    Cannock WS11 . . . . . . .4 E7
    Darlaston WS10 . . . . . . 41 E6
    Great Wyrley WS6. . . . . .5 A2
    Leamonsley WS13. . . . . .8 E6
    Lichfield, Christ Church
      WS13 . . . . .9 A7
    Lichfield, Pipehill WS13,
      WS14. . . . . .8 C5
    Norton Canes WS11. . . .5 F4
    Stonnall WS14 . . . . . . 16 E8
    Sutton Coldfield B74. . . 31 D4
    Walsall, The Delves
      WS5 . . . . 42 F4
    Walsall WS3 . . . . 15 A1
    Wednesbury WS10, B71,
      WS5 . . . . 42 F2
    West Bromwich B71. . . 53 E8
    Willenhall WV13 . . . . . . 27 C2
Walsall St
    Bilston WV14 . . . . 40 D6
    Coventry CV4 . . . . . . 132 B2
    Darlaston WS10 . . . . . . 41 D7
    West Bromwich B70. . . 53 D3
    Willenhall WV13 . . . . . . 27 B1
    Wolverhampton WV1 . 163 D2
Walsall Sta WS2 . . . . .28 E2
Walsall Wood Jun Mix &
    Inf Sch WS8. . . . . 16 A4
Walsall Wood Rd
    WS9. . . . . 30 B7
Walsgrave CE Prim Sch
    CV2. . . . . 115 A6
Walsgrave Cl B92. . . . 107 D6
Walsgrave Dr B92. . . 107 D6
Walsgrave Gdns 5
    CV2. . . . . 115 A7
Walsgrave Hospl
    CV2. . . . . 115 A5
Walsgrave Rd CV2. . . 114 B3
Walsgrave Ret Pk
    CV2. . . . . 115 B7
Walsham Croft B34. . . 69 C5
Walsh Dr B76. . . . . . . .46 F4
Walsh Gr B23 . . . . 56 D8
Walsh La CV7 . . . . 92 E2
Walsingham Dr CV10. 78 A7
Walsingham St WS1. . 29 A1
Walstead Cl WS5. . . . . 43 C5
Walstead Rd WS5 . . . . 43 C5
Walstead Rd W WS5. . 42 E5
Waltdene Cl B43. . . . . 43 E3
Walter Burden Ho
    B66. . . . . 65 C3
Walter Cobb Dr B73. . 46 A1
Walter Ct B20. . . . . . . 55 C2
Walter Nash Rd E
    DY11. . . . . 116 B2
Walter Nash Rd W
    DY11. . . . . 116 A1
Walter Rd
    Bilston WV14 . . . . 40 F3
    Smethwick B67. . . . . . . 64 E6
Walters Cl B31. . . . . . 122 F6
Walter Scott Rd CV12 78 C1
Walters Rd B68. . . . . . 84 B6
Walters Row DY1. . . . . 51 A1
Walter St
    Birmingham B7. . . . . . . 67 B6
    Walsall WS3 . . . . 15 A1
    West Bromwich B70. . . 53 E2
Waltham Cl B61. . . . . 136 E1
Waltham Cres CV10. . . 72 B5
Waltham Gr B44. . . . . 45 B2
Waltham Ho
    Birmingham B38. . . . . 104 B1
    West Bromwich B70. . . 53 D3
Walthamstow Dr DY5. 61 D1
Walton Ave B65. . . . . . 83 B8
Walton Cl
    Coventry CV3 . . . . . . 134 E7
    Halesowen B63. . . . . . . 82 F2
    Kidderminster DY11. . . 116 B2
    Nuneaton CV11. . . . . . . 79 A7
    Redditch B98 . . . . 154 E3

Walton Cl continued
Rowley Regis B65..... **63** A4
Walton Cres WV4...... **39** E5
Walton Croft B91.... **107** B1
Walton Ct B63 ....**82** F3
Walton Dr DY9 .... **81** C5
Walton Gr B30 ...... **104** B2
Walton Heath WS3 ... **13** F3
Walton Pool La DY9 ..**99** F2
Walton Rd
Aldridge WS9 .... **16** A1
Bromsgrove B61..... **137** B4
Oldbury B68 .... **64** C2
Stourbridge DY8 ...... **81** A6
Wednesbury WS10 .... **42** C2
Wolverhampton WV4 .. **39** F5
Walton Rise DY9 .... **100** A3
Walton St DY4 ....**51** F5
Wanderers Ave WV2.. **39** C6
Wanderer Wlk B36 ... **57** E1
Wandle Gr B11........ **88** A3
Wandsbeck B77...... **35** E8
Wandsworth Rd B44...**44** F3
Wanley Rd CV3...... **133** D6
Wannerton Rd DY10.. **98** B3
Wansbeck Gr B38 ... **123** E8
Wansbeck Wlk DY3....**50** F6
Wansfell Cl CV4..... **132** A7
Wanstead Gr B44 .... **45** A1
Wantage Rd B46..... **59** E1
Wappenbury Cl CV2 .. **96** C3
Wappenbury Rd CV2 . **96** D2
Warbage La
Belbroughton DY9.... **119** F1
Dodford B61 .... **136** A7
Warbank Cl B48..... **139** A6
Warbler Pl DY10 .... **117** A2
Ward Cl B8 .... **68** A5
Warden Ave B73.....**56** F8
Ward End Cl B8......**67** F6
Ward End Hall Gr B8 . **68** A6
Ward End Park Rd B8 .**67** F5
Ward End Prim Sch
B8............... **68** B6
Wardend Rd B8 ..... **68** A6
Warden Rd
Coventry CV6 .... **113** B6
Sutton Coldfield B73... **56** F8
Wardens Ave The
CV5.............. **112** B6
Wardens The CV8 .. **148** C5
Ward Gr
Warwick CV34 ..... **161** C7
Wolverhampton WV4 .. **39** F3
Wardle Cl B75 ...... **32** A4
Wardle Pl WS11.......**1** E5
Wardles La WS6.......**4** F2
Wardle St B79 ...... **21** A5
Wardlow Cl WV4 .... **39** B6
Wardlow Rd B7 ..... **67** B4
Wardour Dr B37..... **70** C2
Wardour Gr B44..... **56** C8
Ward Rd WV4 ...... **39** D5
Ward St Bilston WV2 .. **40** B6
Birmingham B19..... **164** C5
Cannock WS12 ....**1** F6
Dudley WV14 ...... **51** B8
Walsall WS1 .... **28** F2
Willenhall WV13 ..... **27** B3
Wolverhampton WV1 . **163** D2
Wareham Cl WS3....**28** F5
Wareham Gn CV2 .. **115** A5
Wareham Ho B28 .. **105** E3
Wareham Rd B45 ... **102** B2
Wareing Dr B23..... **56** D8
Warewell Cl **8** WS1..**28** F2
Warewell St **9** WS1..**28** F2
Waring Cl DY4 ...... **51** E8
Waring Rd DY4...... **52** A8
Warings Green Rd
B94 .... **126** D1
War La B17 .... **85** B5
Warley Croft B68.... **84** E8
Warley Ct B68....... **64** B2
Warley Hall Rd B68.. **64** D1
Warley High Coll of Sport
B68............... **64** A2
Warley Ho B67 .....**64** F2
Warley Inf Sch B68 .. **64** C1
Warley Rd B68 ..... **64** C5
Warmington Cl CV3 . **134** E8
Warmington Dr B73.. **46** B4
Warmington Gr
CV34 .... **160** B8
Warmington Rd
Birmingham B26.... **89** C5
Hollywood B47 ....**125** A6

Warmley Cl
Solihull B91........ **107** D5
Wolverhampton WV6 .. **25** B5
Warmstry Rd B60 ... **137** C1
Warmwell Cl CV2 ... **114** F4
Warneford Mews **9**
CV31 .... **162** A7
Warner Cl CV34 .... **155** D1
Warner Dr DY5...... **61** D1
Warner Pl **1** WS3....**28** F6
Warner Rd
Walsall WS3 .... **29** A6
Wednesbury WS10 ... **42** C2
Warner Row **2** CV6 . **113** F7
Warner St **1** B12 ... **87** A8
Warners Wlk **1** B10.. **87** C8
Warnford Wlk WV4 .. **38** C6
Warple Rd B32...... **84** C5
Warren Ave
Birmingham B13..... **86** F2
Wolverhampton WV10 . **25** F5
Warren Cl
Earlswood B94 .... **142** A8
Lichfield WS14 ....**9** E7
Royal Leamington Spa
CV32............ **157** A3
Ryton-on-D CV8 .... **135** A1
Tipton DY4 .... **52** A7
Warren Dr
Dorridge B93 ...... **128** A3
Rowley Regis B65.... **62** F5
Sedgley DY3 .... **39** C1
Warren Farm Prim Sch
B44............... **56** A8
Warren Farm Rd B44. **56** A8
Warren Field CV8 .. **135** A1
Warren Gdns DY6 ... **60** C6
Warren Gn CV4 .... **131** F7
Warren Hill Rd B44... **56** A7
Warren House Ct B76 .**46** F1
Warren House Wlk
B76.............. **46** F1
Warren La B45...... **122** B3
Warren Pl WS8...... **16** A1
Warren Rd
Birmingham, Perry
B44............... **56** A7
Birmingham, Stirchley
B30............. **104** A6
Birmingham, Washwood
Heath B8 .... **67** E6
Burntwood WS7 ......**7** A5
Warrens Croft WS5.. **43** D5
Warrens End **1** B38. **103** F1
Warrens Hall Rd DY2 . **62** E7
Warrington Cl B76... **47** A1
Warrington Dr B23... **56** D7
Warsash Cl WV1 .... **40** B8
Warstock Cl B14.... **105** A4
Warstock Rd B14.... **105** A3
Warston Ave B32.... **84** D3
Warstone Dr B71.... **53** E4
Warstone La B18.... **66** B4
Warstone Mews **2**
B18.............. **66** C4
Warstone Par E B18.. **66** B4
Warstone Rd WS6... **13** C7
Warstones Cres WV4 . **38** C6
Warstones Dr WV4 .. **38** C6
Warstones Gdns WV4. **38** C6
Warstones Jun & Inf Sch
WV4.............. **38** E6
Warstones Rd WV4 .. **38** D5
Warstone Terr B21... **65** E8
Warstone Tower B36 . **68** D8
Wartell Bank DY6 ... **60** D7
Wartell Bank Ind Est
DY6.............. **60** D7
Warton Cl CV8 ..... **148** C4
Warwards La B29 ... **104** A8
Warwell La B26..... **88** D6
Warwick Ave
Bromsgrove B60..... **151** A8
Coventry CV5 ...... **133** A8
Perton WV6......... **23** F3
Wednesbury WS10 ... **42** C4
Willenhall WV13 ..... **27** D2
Warwick By-Pass
Hampton Magna CV34,
CV35............ **160** A5
Warwick CV34 ..... **161** A1
*Warwick Castle***
Warwick Cl
Cannock WS11 ....**4** F8
Oldbury B68 .... **64** B2
Studley B80........ **159** D3
West Bromwich B70... **52** E7
Warwick Crest B15... **86** B7

Warwick Ct
1 Birmingham, Acock's
Green B27 .... **88** C2
5 Birmingham, Chelmsley
Wood B37........ **70** D2
Birmingham, Moseley
B13............. **87** A2
1 Birmingham, Weoley
Castle B29 ...... **103** C7
Coventry CV3 ..... **165** B1
Dudley DY3 .... **50** D3
5 Solihull B91..... **107** C3
Solihull, Lode Heath
B91............. **107** B4
6 Wolverhampton
WV4 .... **39** F4
Warwick Gdns
Hinckley LE10 ...... **71** E3
Nuneaton CV10 ..... **72** E4
Oldbury B69 .... **52** C2
Willenhall WV13 ..... **27** D2
Warwick Gn CV12 ... **79** C1
Warwick Gr B92..... **88** E1
Warwick Grange
B91............. **106** F7
Warwick Hall Gdns
B60............. **151** A8
Warwick Highway
B98............. **154** C2
Warwick Ho
6 Birmingham B24... **56** F4
Sutton Coldfield B73.. **46** A3
Warwick Hospl CV34 **160** E8
Warwick La CV1..... **165** B2
Warwick New Rd
CV32............ **161** C8
Warwick Park Ct
B92............. **106** F8
Warwick Parkway
CV35............. **160** A7
Warwick Pas **3** B2.. **164** C2
Warwick Pl CV32.... **156** E1
Warwick Race Course
CV34............ **160** C6
Warwick Rd
Birmingham, Birchfield
B42............. **55** E2
Birmingham, Sparkhill
B11............. **87** D4
Birmingham, Warley Woods
B68............. **84** D7
Chadwick End B93 .. **145** A7
Coventry CV3 ..... **165** B1
Dudley DY2 .... **62** E3
Kenilworth CV8..... **148** A1
Knowle B93........ **128** D3
Leek Wootton CV35 .. **155** F7
Solihull B27, B91, B92 **106** F7
Stourbridge DY8...... **60** D1
Sutton Coldfield B73... **45** C2
Tamworth B77....... **21** E4
Wolston CV8 ...... **135** F3
Warwick Road Trad Est
B11............. **87** D4
Warwick Row CV1... **165** B2
Warwick Sch CV34 .. **161** A6
Warwickshire Coll
CV32............ **161** D8
*Warwickshire Mus***
CV34............ **160** E6
*Warwickshire Nuffield
Hospl The* CV32 ... **156** E5
Warwick St
Bilston WV14 .... **40** E5
Birmingham B12...... **67** A1
Coventry CV5 ...... **112** F1
Royal Leamington Spa
CV32............ **156** F1
Walsall WS4 .... **28** F3
Wolverhampton WV1 . **163** D2
Warwick Sta CV34 .. **160** F7
Warwick Tech Pk
CV34............ **161** B5
Warwick Terr CV32 . **156** E1
Warwick Way WS9 .. **16** A1
Wasdale Cl CV32 ... **156** C1
Wasdale Dr DY6..... **60** E6
Wasdale Rd
Birmingham B31..... **102** F4
Brownhills WS8 ..... **15** D6
Waseley Hills Country
Pk* B45 .... **121** C1
*Waseley Hills High Sch &
Sixth Form Ctr* B45 **121** D7
*Waseley Hills Visitor
Ctr** B45 .... **101** C1
Waseley Rd B45.... **121** E8
Washbourne Rd
CV31............ **162** A2

Washbrook La
Hawkes End CV5..... **94** A1
Norton Canes WS11 ...**5** D5
Washbrook Rd B8... **68** A6
Washford Dr B98.... **159** D7
Washford Gr B25.... **88** B8
Washford Ind Est
B98.............. **159** E8
Washford La B98.... **159** D8
Washington Ct
Birmingham B1..... **164** A1
Wolverhampton WV3 . **24** D1
Washington Ctr DY2 . **62** D4
Washington Dr B20.. **55** B3
Washington St
Birmingham B1..... **164** A1
Dudley DY2 .... **62** D3
Kidderminster DY11.. **116** C5
Washington Wharf
B1.............. **164** A1
Wash La B25....... **88** C8
Washwood Heath Rd
B8............... **67** E6
*Washwood Heath Tech
Coll* B8 .... **68** C5
Wasperton Cl B36... **69** B8
6 Coventry CV3..... **134** F8
Wassell Ct B63...... **82** E2
Wassell Grove Bsns Ctr
DY9.............. **82** A2
Wassell Grove Rd
Hagley DY9........ **99** F8
Halesowen B63...... **82** A2
Wassell Rd
Bilston WV14 .... **40** D7
Halesowen B63...... **82** E2
Stourbridge DY9..... **81** E2
Waste La
Balsall Common CV7.. **130** F5
Coventry CV6 ...... **94** F1
Wastwater Ct WV6 ..**23** F4
Watchbury Cl B36... **58** C1
Watch Cl CV1...... **165** A3
Watchmaker Ct CV1 . **165** A2
Watchman Ave DY5 ..**81** F7
Watcombe Rd CV2 . **114** E8
Waterbrook Way WS11 .**4** E6
Watercall Ave CV3 . **133** C6
Waterdale B90..... **126** D5
Water Dale WV3 .... **24** E2
Waterfall Cl
Meriden CV7........ **92** C1
Smethwick B66...... **64** E7
Waterfall La B64 .... **63** A1
Waterfall Lane Ind Est
B64.............. **63** A1
Waterfall Rd DY5.... **81** D7
Waterfall Way LE9...**71** F5
Waterfield Cl DY4... **51** D5
Waterfield Gdns
CV31............ **162** C7
Waterfield Way
Birmingham B26..... **89** C7
Hinckley LE10 ...... **75** C5
Waterford Ct B23 ... **56** B4
Waterford Pl B33 ... **69** D3
Waterford Rd DY6... **60** D7
Waterford Way CV3 . **114** C1
Waterfront Bsns Pk
DY5.............. **61** E4
Waterfront E DY5.... **61** E4
Waterfront W DY5... **61** E4
Waterfront Way
Brierley Hill DY2, DY5.. **61** F4
2 Walsall WS2 ...... **28** D2
Waterglade La WV13 . **27** A1
Waterhaynes Cl B45. **122** A6
Waterhead Cl WV10 . **12** A2
Waterhead Dr WV10.. **12** B2
Water La B71 ....**53** F7
Waterlily Cl WS12 .....**2** E4
Water Lily Gr WS8... **15** E7
Water Lily Way WV10 . **78** A8
Waterlinks Bvd B6... **67** A7
Waterloo Ave B37.... **70** B4
Waterloo Bvd WS12 ...**2** E4
Waterloo Ct CV34 ... **161** A8
Waterloo Ind Est B37 .**70** B5
Waterloo Pl **5** CV32. **156** F1
Waterloo Rd
Birmingham, King's Heath
B14............. **104** E8
Birmingham, South Yardley
B25............. **88** C6
Hinckley LE10 ...... **75** D8
Smethwick B66...... **65** A3
Wolverhampton WV1 . **163** B4

Waterloo St E DY4 ...**51** F5
Waterloo St
Birmingham B2..... **164** B2
8 Coventry CV1..... **113** E4
Dudley DY1 .... **62** B8
Kidderminster DY10. **116** E6
Royal Leamington Spa
CV31............ **162** B7
Tipton DY4 .... **51** F5
Waterloo Terr WV1 . **163** A4
Waterman Rd CV6... **113** F6
Watermarque **2** B16. **66** B2
Watermead Grange
WS8.............. **15** E7
Watermeadow Dr
WS4.............. **15** D1
Watermere WS4..... **29** D8
Watermill Cl WV10 .. **11** D3
Water Mill Cl B29.... **85** D3
Water Mill Cres B76..**46** F1
Water Mill Prim Sch
B29.............. **85** D3
Watermint Cl WS12.....**2** E4
Water Orton La B46,
B76.............. **58** E4
Water Orton Prim Sch
B46..............**59** D2
Water Orton Rd B36.. **58** E1
Water Orton Sta B46. **59** A3
Water Rd DY3....... **50** C2
Watersbridge Gdns
CV10............. **73** C1
Waters Dr B74 ...... **31** D3
Waters Edge The B1.. **66** C2
Waterside
Bedworth CV6....... **96** C6
1 Birmingham B15... **66** C1
Birmingham, Egdbaston
B15............. **86** C8
Birmingham, Hamstead
B43............. **54** E7
Royal Leamington Spa
CV31............ **161** D7
Waterside Cl
Birmingham, Bordesley
B9............... **67** B2
Birmingham, Pype Hayes
B24............. **58** A8
Wolverhampton WV2 . **39** D7
Waterside Ct
6 Birmingham B16... **66** B2
Hinckley LE10 ...... **74** B4
Royal Leamington Spa
CV31............ **162** B6
Tamworth B77....... **21** F5
Waterside Dr B18.... **65** F5
Waterside Est DY2... **62** C3
Waterside Grange
DY10............ **116** B2
Waterside Ind Est
Rowley Regis B65.... **62** F4
Wolverhampton WV2 . **40** A6
Waterside Orch B48. **123** B2
Waterside View
Birmingham B18..... **66** A5
Brierley Hill DY5..... **81** B8
Waterside Way
Brownhills WS8 ....**6** D2
Wolverhampton WV9 . **11** A3
Watersmead Cl WS12...**2** F4
Watersmeet Gr CV2 . **114** B6
Watersmeet Ho B78.. **35** E8
Watersmeet Rd CV2 . **114** B6
Waterson Croft B37.. **70** D3
Water St
Birmingham B3..... **164** B3
Burntwood WS7 ......**6** E8
Kingswinford DY6.... **60** D7
West Bromwich B70... **53** D2
Wolverhampton
WV10 .... **163** D4
Waters View WS3.... **15** B5
Water Tower La CV8. **147** F6
Waterward Cl B17.... **85** C5
Waterway Cl B14.... **105** C3
Waterways Dr B69... **63** B8
Waterways Gdns DY8. **60** E1
Waterworks Dr B31.. **102** D4
Waterworks Rd B16.. **65** F1
Waterworks St B6... **67** B8
Watery La
Alvechurch B48..... **124** C1
Birmingham B62..... **84** A3
Blakedown DY9..... **118** F3
Cheswick Green B90 . **126** D4
Codsall WV8 .... **10** A5
Corley Moor CV7..... **93** D5
Coventry CV6 ...... **95** A4
Hopwood B48...... **123** F2
Keresley CV7 .... **94** F4

Watery La continued
Knowle B93......... **128** E4
Lichfield WS13 ....**3** C4
Longbridge CV35 ... **160** A1
Portway B47, B48... **140** D7
Redditch B98 ...... **154** B2
Smethwick B67...... **65** A5
Stourbridge DY8 .... **60** E2
Tipton DY4 .... **51** F5
Walsall WS1 .... **42** E8
Willenhall WV13 .... **26** E3
Watery Lane Ind Est
WV13............. **26** E3
Watery Lane Middleway
B9............... **67** B2
Watford Gap WS14 .. **32** A7
Watford Gap Rd
WS14............. **32** A7
Watford Rd B30..... **103** F5
Wathan Ave WV14.....**39** F1
Wathen Rd
Royal Leamington Spa
CV32............ **157** A2
Warwick CV34 ..... **160** E8
Watkins Gdns B31... **103** C4
Watkins Rd WV12 ... **27** C5
Watland Gn B34..... **69** B5
Watling Cl LE10 .... **75** C4
Watling Ct CV11......**73** F3
Watling Dr LE10..... **75** C4
Watling Rd CV8 .... **148** B6
Watling St
Brownhills WS8 ....**6** D1
Cannock WS11 ....**4** D6
Dordon B77, B78 .... **36** D6
Hinckley CV11, LE10.. **74** C8
Hints B78 .... **19** D3
Norton Canes WS11 ...**5** D3
Tamworth, Bonehill B78 **20** D1
Tamworth, Wilnecote
B77............. **35** E7
Watling Street Bsns Pk
WS11..............**6** A2
Watling Street Prim Sch
WS8................**6** E1
Watney Gr B44...... **56** C8
Watson Cl
Sutton Coldfield B72... **46** C2
3 Warwick CV34.... **155** E1
Watson Rd
Birmingham B7...... **67** D7
Birmingham, Nechells
B24............. **67** D8
Birmingham, Saltley B8 **67** F5
Coventry CV5 ...... **112** D2
Darlaston WS10 ..... **41** A5
Wolverhampton, Pendeford
WV10 .... **11** B2
Wolverhampton WV14 . **39** D7
Watson Rd E B7..... **67** D7
Watsons Cl DY2..... **62** E8
Watson's Green Fields
DY2..............**62** F8
Watson's Green Rd
DY2.............. **51** E1
Watson Way CV7 ... **130** C8
Watt Cl B60........ **136** F1
Watt Ho DY6........**60** F7
Wattisham Sq B35... **58** A4
Wattis Rd B67....... **65** A2
Wattle Gn B70...... **53** A3
Wattle Rd B70 ...... **53** A4
Watton Cl WV14..... **40** A1
Watton Ct B6....... **66** E8
Watton Gn B35...... **58** A2
Watton La B46...... **59** D2
Watton St B70...... **53** D2
Watt Rd
Birmingham B23..... **56** E4
Tipton DY4 .... **52** B8
Watts Cl DY4....... **51** D5
Watts Rd B80 ...... **159** E2
Watt's Rd B10...... **87** D8
Watt St
Birmingham B21..... **65** D7
Smethwick B66...... **65** B6
Wattville Ave B21... **65** C8
Wattville Prim Sch
B21...............**65** B8
Wattville Rd B21.... **65** C8
Watwood Rd B28,
B90............. **105** F3
Waugh Cl B37....... **70** B2
Waugh Dr B63...... **100** D8
Waveley Rd CV1.... **113** A3
Wavell Rd
Birmingham B8...... **67** E5
Brierley Hill DY5..... **81** F7
Walsall WS2 .... **27** E2
Wavendon Cl CV2 ....**96** C1

Waveney B77 35 E8
Waveney Ave WV6 23 E4
Waveney Cl LE10 75 A8
Waveney Croft B36 69 F8
Waveney Gr WS11 1 B1
Wavenham Cl B74 31 E5
Waverhill Rd B21 65 F7
Waverley Ave
Birmingham B43 44 B4
Nuneaton CV11 73 F1
Waverley Cl DY10 117 A8
Waverley Cres
Romsley B62 100 F4
Wolverhampton, Goldthorn Hill WV4 39 B6
Wolverhampton, Lanesfield WV4 39 F3
Waverley Gdns WV5 49 B7
Waverley Gr B91 106 F3
Waverley Rd
Birmingham B10 87 D7
Darlaston WS10 41 D6
Kenilworth CV8 148 A4
Royal Leamington Spa CV31 162 B6
Walsall WS3 13 F2
Waverley Sch B10 88 A8
Waverley Sq CV11 73 F1
Waverley St DY2 62 A8
Waverley Wlk WS14 9 B6
Wavers Marston B37 90 A8
Waverton Mews [15] CV31 162 C6
Wavytree Cl CV34 160 D7
Waxland Rd B63 83 B2
Wayfield Cl B90 106 C3
Wayfield Rd B90 106 C3
Wayford Dr B72 57 D7
Wayford Glade WV13 40 F8
Wayford Gr B8 68 B4
Waynecroft Rd B43 43 E2
Wayside
Birmingham B37 90 A8
Wolverhampton WV8 10 F2
Wayside Dr B74 31 C3
Wayside Gdns WV12 27 E5
Wayside Wlk WS2 28 A3
Waystone La DY9 119 D4
Wealden Hatch WV10 11 E4
Wealdstone Dr DY3 50 D2
Weale Gr CV34 155 F2
Weaman St B4 164 C3
Weates Yd B27 88 C4
Weatheroak Cl B97 153 A1
Weatheroak Hill B48 124 B1
Weatheroak Rd B11 87 C5
Weatheroaks
Birmingham B62 84 A7
Brownhills WS9 16 B4
Weather Oaks B17 85 B6
Weaver Ave
Birmingham B26 89 B6
Sutton Coldfield B76 47 A1
Weaver Cl DY5 61 B6
Weaver Ct [8] B75 32 E3
Weaver Gr WV13 27 D2
Weavers Cl B97 158 D4
Weavers Hill B97 158 D4
Weavers Rise DY2 62 D3
Weavers Wharf DY10 116 D6
Weavers Wlk CV6 114 B8
Weaving Gdns [1] WS11 1 E1
Webb Ave WV6 23 E5
Webbcroft Rd B33 68 F4
Webb La B28 105 E6
Webb Rd DY4 52 C7
Webb St Dudley WV14 40 C1
Nuneaton CV10 72 D3
Willenhall WV13 26 F2
Webheath Fst Sch B97 153 A2
Webley Rise WV10 11 F4
Webner Ind Est WV2 40 A6
Webster Ave CV8 148 B5
Webster Cl
Birmingham B11 87 B6
Sutton Coldfield B72 57 B7
Webster Rd
Walsall WS2 28 E5
Willenhall WV13 27 A3
Webster St CV6 113 E7
Webster Way B76 58 B8
Webster Wlk WS11 2 A4
Weddell Wynd WV14 40 F1
Weddington Ctry Wlk* CV10 73 B8
Weddington Prim Sch CV10 73 D7
Weddington Rd CV10 73 C7
Weddington Terr CV10 73 D5
Wedgbury Cl WS10 42 A1
Wedgbury Way DY5 61 B1
Wedge St [10] WS1 28 F2
Wedgewood Ave B70 52 F7
Wedgewood Cl
Burntwood WS7 7 C7
Coventry CV2 114 E8
Wedgewood Ct WS4 15 C1
Wedgewood Dr B20 55 B2
Wedgewood Ho B37 70 B4
Wedgewood Pl B70 52 F7
Wedgewood Rd B32 84 D5
Wedge-Woods CV5 132 F8
Wedgnock Gn CV34 160 D8
Wedgnock Ind Est CV34 160 C8
Wedgnock La CV34 155 C1
Wedgwood Cl WV1 26 A1
Wedmore Rd B73 45 F1
Wednesbury, Great Western Street Sta WS10 41 E2
Wednesbury Mus & Art Gall* WS10 41 F2
Wednesbury Oak Prim Sch DY4 41 A1
Wednesbury Oak Rd DY4 41 A1
Wednesbury Parkway Sta WS10 41 D2
Wednesbury Rd WS1 42 D7
Wednesbury Trad Est WS10 41 E4
Wednesfield High Sch Specialist Engineering Sch WV11 26 E5
Wednesfield Rd
Willenhall WV13 27 A3
Wolverhampton WV1, WV10 163 D4
Wednesfield Village Prim Sch WV11 26 D5
Wednesfield Way WV11 26 D4
Wednesfield Way Ind Est WV11 26 D4
Wedon Cl CV4 131 E7
Weeford Dell [2] B75 32 E3
Weeford Dr B20 54 F4
Weeford Rd B75 32 F3
Weethley Ho [6] B97 153 A4
Weights Farm B97 153 C7
Weights La B97 153 C7
Weilerswist Dr CV31 161 F4
Weirbrook Cl B29 103 C7
Weland Cl B46 59 B2
Weland Ct B46 59 B2
Welbeck Ave
Hinckley LE10 75 D4
Wolverhampton WV10 25 D7
Welbeck Cl B62 83 E6
Welbeck Dr
Kidderminster DY11 116 B5
Walsall WS4 29 D7
Welbeck Gr B23 56 B5
Welbury Gdns WV6 24 F5
Welby Gate CV7 130 B5
Welby Rd B28 87 F1
Welch Cl DY4 52 B7
Welches Cl B31 103 B5
Welcombe Dr B76 57 F7
Welcombe Gr B91 106 F4
Welcome Dr B61 121 A1
Welford Ave B26 88 F8
Welford Cl B98 158 F5
Welford Gr B74 31 F3
Welford Pl CV6 113 D7
Welford Prim Sch B20 66 A8
Welford Rd
Birmingham B20 66 A8
Solihull B90 106 C4
Sutton Coldfield B73 45 E1
Tamworth B77 35 C5
Welgarth Ave CV6 112 F6
Welham Croft B90 127 A6
Welland Dr DY8 81 A8
Welland Gr
Birmingham B24 57 D3
Willenhall WV13 27 C2
Welland Rd
Coventry CV1 113 F1
Halesowen B63 83 A2
Welland Way B76 58 A7
Well Cl
Birmingham B36 68 E8
Redditch B97 158 E5
Wellcroft Rd B34 69 A7
Wellcroft St WS10 41 F3
Weller Ct WV3 24 D1
Wellesbourne B79 21 C8
Wellesbourne Cl
Redditch B98 153 E4
Wolverhampton WV3 38 B8
Wellesbourne Dr WV14 51 B7
Wellesbourne Rd
Birmingham B20 55 B1
Coventry CV5 112 A3
Wellesbourne Twr [3] B5 86 E8
Wellesley Dr DY4 51 F5
Wellesley Gdns B13 87 D1
Wellesley Rd B68 64 B6
Wellfield Cl
Balsall Common CV7 130 D5
Cannock WS11 4 B7
Wellfield Gdns DY2 62 E6
Wellfield Rd
Aldridge WS9 30 B8
Birmingham B28 106 B6
Wellhead La B42 55 E3
Wellhead Way B42 55 F2
Wellington Ave WV3 38 F7
Wellington Cl
Hinckley LE10 75 E4
Kingswinford DY6 60 E4
Wellington Cres B20 55 B2
Wellington Ct
Birmingham B32 84 F5
Birmingham, Handsworth Wood B20 55 C2
Cradley Heath B64 62 F2
Kidderminster DY11 116 C5
Willenhall WV13 26 F3
Wellington Dr WS11 4 B8
Wellington Gdns [1] CV1 113 B2
Wellington Gr B91 106 F6
Wellington Ho B32 84 F4
Wellington Ind Est WV14 51 C7
Wellington Pl WV13 26 F3
Wellington Rd
Bilston WV14 40 D6
Birmingham B20 55 C2
Birmingham, Edgbaston B15 86 C7
Bromsgrove B60 151 A8
Dudley DY1 51 B1
Royal Leamington Spa CV32 157 C2
Smethwick B67 65 A3
Tipton DY4 52 A4
Walsall WS5 43 C6
Wellington St S B70 53 C4
Wellington St
Birmingham B18 65 D5
Coventry CV1 165 D4
Cradley Heath B64 62 F2
Oldbury B69 64 B6
[6] Redditch B98 153 E4
Walsall WS2 42 B7
West Bromwich B71 53 C4
Wellington Terr [3] B19 66 B7
Wellington Tower [4] B31 103 A1
Wellington Way B35 58 B2
Well La
Birmingham B5 164 D2
Great Wyrley WS6 5 A1
Hinckley LE10 71 D1
Tanworth-In-A B94 142 A1
Walsall, Harden WS3 28 D7
Walsall WS3 28 E8
Wolverhampton WV11 26 C4
Wellman Croft B29 85 D1
Wellman's Rd WV13 27 C1
Well Mdw B45 122 A6
Wellmeadow Gr B92 109 A7
Wellmead Wlk B45 121 F8
Well Pl WS3 28 E8
Wells Ave WS10 41 B6
Wells Cl Cannock WS11 1 E6
Kidderminster DY11 116 A6
Perton WV6 23 D4
Wednesbury DY4 41 A1
West Bromwich B71 53 D8
Wells Ct Coventry CV3 133 F7
Dudley DY2 62 C5
Wellsford Ave B92 89 B4
Wells Green Rd B92 89 A4
Wells Rd Bilston WV14 40 E3
Brierley Hill DY5 61 B3
Rowley Regis B65 63 E4
Solihull B92 89 C4
Wells Rd *continued*
Wolverhampton WV4 38 F5
Well St
Birmingham B19 66 C5
Coventry CV1 165 B3
Darlaston WS10 41 E6
Wells Twr B16 66 A2
Wells Wlk B37 70 A1
Welney Gdns WV9 11 A3
Welsby Ave B43 54 E7
Welsh Cl CV34 155 E2
Welsh House Farm Com Sch B32 84 F4
Welsh House Farm Rd B32 84 F4
Welshmans Hill B73 45 C3
Welsh Rd
Coventry CV2 114 B4
Cubbington CV32, CV33 157 F2
Welton Cl B76 47 A2
Welton Rd CV34 155 D1
Welwyndale Rd B72 57 C6
Welwyn Rd LE10 71 F1
Wembley Gr B25 88 C8
Wembley La WS7 6 D8
Wembrook Cl CV11 73 D2
Wembrook Ho CV11 73 E2
Wembrook Prim Sch CV11 73 C2
Wembury B77 21 E5
Wem Gdns WV11 26 D6
Wendell Crest WV10 11 F4
Wendiburgh St CV4 132 B7
Wendover Dr LE10 71 E4
Wendover Rd
Birmingham B23 56 C7
Rowley Regis B65 63 A5
Wolverhampton WV4 39 F2
Wendover Rise CV5 112 C4
Wendron Cl B60 137 B2
Wendron Gr B14 104 D4
Wenlock B77 21 D3
Wenlock Ave WV3 38 E8
Wenlock Cl
Halesowen B63 82 D2
Sedgley DY3 50 C7
Wenlock Dr B61 137 A5
Wenlock Gdns WS3 28 E5
Wenlock Rd
Birmingham B20 55 F1
Stourbridge DY8 81 B6
Wenlock Way CV10 72 B3
Wenman St B12 86 F6
Wensley Croft B90 106 B6
Wensleydale Rd B42 55 B6
Wensley Rd B26 88 F6
Wensum Cl LE10 75 B8
Wentbridge Rd WV1 26 C1
Wentworth Ave B36 69 B8
Wentworth Cl
Burntwood WS7 7 C7
Hinckley LE10 71 E3
Wentworth Ct
Birmingham B24 56 F2
Sutton Coldfield B75 32 B1
Wentworth Dr
Blackwell B60 138 A5
Coventry CV6 95 B4
Lichfield WS14 9 D5
Nuneaton CV11 74 A1
Oldbury B69 63 A7
Wentworth Gate B17 85 B6
Wentworth Gr WV6 23 D5
Wentworth Park Ave B17 85 B6
Wentworth Rd
Birmingham B17 85 B6
Royal Leamington Spa CV31 162 D6
Solihull B92 88 F3
Stourbridge DY8 80 E7
Sutton Coldfield B74 46 A8
Walsall WS3 13 F3
Wolverhampton WV10 11 F3
Wentworth Rise B62 83 D3
Wentworth Way B32 84 F3
Wenyon Cl DY4 52 B4
Weoley Ave B29 85 C2
Weoley Castle Rd B29 84 F1
Weoley Hill B29 103 C8
Weoley Park Rd B29 85 C1
Wergs Dr WV6 24 A7
Wergs Hall WV8 23 F7
Wergs Hall Rd WV6, WV8 24 A7
Wergs Rd Codsall WV6 23 F7
Wolverhampton WV6 24 B6
Werneth Gr WS3 14 A4
Wesleyan Ct WS4 29 A4
Wesley Ave
Cheslyn Hay WS6 4 D3
Codsall WV8 10 B2
Halesowen B63 82 B8
Wesley Cl B64 62 F1
Wesley Ct
Birmingham B16 65 C2
Cannock WS11 1 E1
[4] Cradley Heath B64 82 F8
[5] Wolverhampton WV4 39 F4
Wesley Gr WS10 41 E3
Wesley Ho [3] WS2 42 C7
Wesley Pl
Cannock WS12 2 C7
Tipton DY4 52 C7
Wesley Rd
Birmingham B23 56 F5
Brierley Hill DY5 61 B5
Codsall WV8 10 B2
Willenhall WV12 27 C6
Wesley's Fold WS10 41 D6
Wesley St
Bilston WV14 40 E2
Oldbury B69 64 A8
West Bromwich B70 53 B3
Wolverhampton WV2 40 A6
Wesley Way B77 21 F4
Wesley Wlk B60 150 E7
Wessenden B77 36 B7
Wessex Cl
Bedworth CV12 78 A4
Brownhills WS8 15 F7
Wessex Ct B79 22 F7
Wessex Dr WS11 1 F2
Wessex Rd WV2 39 F8
Wesson Gdns B63 83 A3
Wesson Rd WS10 41 C8
West Acre WV13 26 F1
Westacre Cres WV3 24 C1
Westacre Dr DY5 81 F8
Westacre Gdns B33 68 F3
Westacre Inf Sch WV3 24 C1
West Ave
Bedworth CV12 78 D2
Birmingham, Castle Bromwich B36 69 D8
Birmingham, Handsworth B20 55 A4
Coventry CV6, CV7 95 A5
Coventry, Middle Stoke CV2 114 A2
Oldbury B69 63 B7
Redditch B98 153 E3
Wolverhampton WV11 26 C6
Westbourne Ave
Birmingham B34 68 E6
Cannock WS11 1 D3
Cheslyn Hay WS6 4 E3
Westbourne Cl [3] B61 136 E1
Westbourne Cres
Birmingham B15 86 A8
Burntwood WS7 7 B7
Westbourne Ct
Darlaston WS10 41 F7
Walsall WS4 29 A3
Westbourne Gdns B15 86 A7
Westbourne Gr B21 65 F7
Westbourne Rd
Birmingham, Edgbaston B15 86 A8
Birmingham, Handsworth B21 54 D1
Darlaston WS10 41 F7
Halesowen B62 83 E7
Solihull B92 106 F8
Walsall, Ryecroft WS4 28 F4
Walsall WS4 29 A4
West Bromwich B70 53 B2
Wolverhampton WV4 39 A5
Westbourne St WS4 28 F3
Westbourne Terr [2] B61 136 E1
West Bromwich Central Sta B70 53 C2
West Bromwich Rd WS5 42 F5
West Bromwich Ringway B70 53 D2
West Bromwich St
Oldbury B69 52 F1
Walsall WS1 42 E7
Westbrook Ave
Aldridge WS9 29 F5
Aldridge WS9 30 A5
Westbrook Ct CV5 112 A4
Westbury Ave WS10 41 F6
Westbury Ct
[22] Brierley Hill DY5 61 D2
Coventry CV2 114 A3
Warwick CV34 161 A7
Westbury Ho B97 153 B2
Westbury Rd
Coventry CV5 112 D5
Nuneaton CV10 72 D3
Smethwick B17 65 B3
Wednesbury WS10 41 F6
Westbury St WV1 163 C3
West Bvd B32 84 F4
West Cl LE10 75 D7
Westcliff Dr CV34 155 E2
Westcliffe Dr CV3 133 B5
Westcliff Pl B31 102 F4
Westcombe Gr B32 84 A1
West Coppice Rd WS8 15 C8
Westcote Ave B31 102 C2
Westcote Cl B92 89 A2
Westcotes CV4 112 B1
Westcott Cl DY6 60 F3
Westcott Rd B26 89 A8
Westcroft Ave WV10 12 A1
Westcroft Gr B38 103 D3
Westcroft Rd
Sedgley DY3 39 B2
Wolverhampton WV6 23 F6
Westcroft Sch & Sports Coll WV10 12 B2
Westcroft Way B14 105 B1
West Cross Sh Ctr B66 64 D7
West Ct B60 150 F6
Westdean Cl B62 83 C4
West Dr
Birmingham, Edgbaston B5 86 C5
Birmingham, Handsworth B20 66 B8
Fazeley B78 20 E2
West End Ave B66 64 D7
West End Ct CV34 160 D6
West End Villas B38 103 F2
Westerdale Cl DY3 51 A7
Westerham Cl B93 127 F6
Westerhope Gr B19 66 C5
Westeria Cl B36 69 C8
Westeria Ho B36 69 C8
Westering Parkway WV10 11 F4
Westerings B20 55 C2
Western Ave
Brierley Hill DY5 61 B2
Halesowen B62 83 E4
Sedgley DY3 50 B8
Willenhall WS2 27 D3
Western Bsns Pk
Birmingham B18 65 E6
Halesowen B62 83 B7
Western By-Pass WS13 8 F8
Western Cl WS2 27 D3
Western Hill Cl B96 158 E1
Western Rd
Birmingham, Edgbaston B18 65 F4
Birmingham, Erdington B24 57 A3
Cannock WS12 2 B6
Cradley Heath B64 82 E8
Oldbury B69 64 B5
Stourbridge DY8 80 F4
Sutton Coldfield B73 46 A1
West Hagley DY9 99 B4
Western Way
Darlaston WS10 41 C3
Kidderminster DY11 116 A5
Westfield Ave B14 105 B1
Westfield Cl
Dorridge B93 127 F2
Nuneaton CV10 73 D5
Westfield Ct LE10 75 C7
Westfield Dr WS9 30 A6
Westfield Gr WV3 38 C8
Westfield Grange B14 86 E1
Westfield Hall [2] B16 65 D1
Westfield Ho B36 70 A7
Westfield Inf Sch LE10 75 B7
Westfield Jun Sch LE10 75 B7
Westfield Manor B75 32 A4
Westfield Prim Sch WV5 49 A7
Westfield Rd
Bilston WV14 40 B7

Westfield Rd continued
Birmingham, Acock's Green
B27 . . . . **88** B3
Birmingham B15 . . . . **85** D7
Birmingham, Moseley
B14 . . . . **86** E1
Brierley Hill DY5 . . . . . **81** F8
Dudley DY2 . . . . **62** D7
Halesowen B62 . . . . . . **63** E1
Hinckley LE10 . . . . **75** B7
Sedgley DY3 . . . . **39** E1
Smethwick B67 . . . . . . **64** F5
Willenhall WV13 . . . . **40** E8
Westfields
Birchmoor B78 . . . . . . **36** D8
Catshill B61 . . . . **136** F8
Westford Gr B28 . . . . **105** E3
Westgate
Aldridge WS9 . . . . **29** E6
Birmingham B15 . . . . . **85** E4
Cannock WS12 . . . . **2** F6
Oldbury B65 . . . . **63** E4
West Gate B16 . . . . . . **65** E3
Westgate CI
Sedgley DY3 . . . . **50** E7
Warwick CV34 . . . . . . **160** D6
Westgate Ho 10
CV34 . . . . **160** E6
Westgate Prim Sch
CV34 . . . . **160** D6
Westgate Trad Est
WS9 . . . . **29** E6
West Gn WV4 . . . . . . **38** C5
West Green CI B15 . . **86** B8
Westgrove Ave 6
B90 . . . . **127** A6
Westgrove Terr 1
CV32 . . . . **161** D8
Westhall Gate WS3 . . . **14** B2
Westham Ho B37 . . . . **70** B4
Westhaven Dr B31 . . **102** E7
Westhaven Rd B72 . . **46** C5
Westhay Rd B28 . . . . **106** B7
West Heath Hospl
B38 . . . . **123** C8
West Heath Prim Sch
B38 . . . . **123** C8
West Heath Rd
2 Birmingham, Edgbaston
B18 . . . . **65** D4
Birmingham, Northfield
B31 . . . . **103** B1
Westhill WV3 . . . . . . **24** C2
West Hill Ave WS12 . . . . **2** B6
Westhill CI B92 . . . . **106** E8
Westhill Coll of H Ed
B29 . . . . **85** D1
Westhill Coll (Univ
Birmingham) B29 . **103** D8
West Hill Ct B14 . . . **104** C4
West Hill Prim Sch
WS12 . . . . **2** B6
Westhill Rd
Birmingham B38 . . . . **103** F3
Blackdown CV32 . . . . **157** A6
Coventry CV6 . . . . . . **112** F6
West Holme B9 . . . . . **67** C2
Westholme Croft
B30 . . . . **103** E8
Westhouse Ct B14 . . **104** D4
Westhouse Gr B14 . . **104** D4
West House Sch B15 . **86** C8
West Hyde LE10 . . . . . . **74** F7
Westland Ave WV3 . . **24** F2
Westland CI B23 . . . . **56** F5
Westland Gdns
Stourbridge DY8 . . . . . **80** F7
6 Wolverhampton
WV3 . . . . **25** A2
Westland Rd WV6 . . . **24** F2
Westlands Rd
Birmingham B13 . . . . . **87** A1
Sutton Coldfield B76 . . **57** F6
Westland Wlk B35 . . . **57** F2
Westlea Rd CV31 . . . **161** E6
Westleigh Ave CV5 . . **132** F7
Westley Brook CI B26 **89** B5
Westley CI B28 . . . . **106** B6
Westley Rd B27 . . . . . **88** B3
Westley St
Birmingham B9 . . . . . . **67** A2
6 Dudley DY1 . . . . . . **62** B8
West Lodge WV1 . . . . **25** A3
Westmead Ave B80 . **159** E4
Westmead Cres B24 . . **57** C4
Westmead Dr B68 . . . **64** B4
West Mead Dr B14 . . **104** E6

Westmede Ctr CV5 . . **112** C4
West Mews B44 . . . . . . **44** D2
West Midlands Hospl
B63 . . . . **82** D5
West Mill Croft B38 . **123** E7
Westminster B37 . . . . . **69** F5
Westminster Ave
WV4 . . . . **39** B5
Westminster CI
Bromsgrove B61 . . . . **136** D1
Dudley DY1 . . . . **51** A2
Westminster Ct
Birmingham B20 . . . . . **55** C2
3 Bromsgrove B60 . . **137** A2
Westminster Dr
Birmingham B14 . . . . **104** E6
Hinckley LE10 . . . . **75** F4
Nuneaton CV10 . . . . . . **72** B7
Westminster Ind Est
DY2 . . . . **62** D2
Westminster Prim Sch
B20 . . . . **55** C1
Westminster Rd
Birmingham, Handsworth
B20 . . . . **55** C1
Birmingham, Stirchley
B29 . . . . **104** A8
Cannock WS11 . . . . **1** E6
Coventry CV1 . . . . . . **165** A1
Kidderminster DY11 . **116** A6
Stourbridge DY8 . . . . . **60** D2
Walsall WS4 . . . . **29** B7
West Bromwich B71 . . **53** D8
Westminster Sch The
Smethwick B67 . . . . . . **65** A5
West Bromwich B71 . . **53** D8
Westmoreland Ave
CV10 . . . . **72** E4
Westmore Way WS10 . **42** D5
Westmorland CI B78 . **21** A1
Westmorland Ct B71 . **53** D7
Westmorland Rd
Coventry CV2 . . . . . . **114** F4
West Bromwich B71 . . **53** D7
Weston Ave
6 Birmingham, Lozells
B19 . . . . **66** C7
Birmingham, Sparkbrook
B11 . . . . **87** C6
Oldbury B69 . . . . **52** B1
Westonbirt CI CV8 . . **148** C6
Weston CI
Cannock WS11 . . . . **2** C1
Dorridge B93 . . . . . . **128** A2
Hinckley LE10 . . . . **71** A1
5 Royal Leamington Spa
CV31 . . . . **162** C6
Walsall WS1 . . . . **42** E6
Warwick CV34 . . . . . . **160** F7
Weston Cres WS9 . . . . **30** B4
Weston CI 10 WV3 . . . **25** C4
Weston Dr
Bilston WV14 . . . . **40** B5
Great Wyrley WS6 . . . . . . **4** F1
Wednesbury DY4 . . . . . **41** C2
Westonhall Rd B60 . . **150** D1
Weston Hall Stables
CV12 . . . . **79** A3
Weston Ho
Birmingham B19 . . . . . **66** E6
Wolverhampton WV6 . . **24** E5
Weston Ind Est B11 . . **87** E4
Weston La
Birmingham B11 . . . . . **87** E4
Bulkington CV12 . . . . . **79** B3
Weston Rd
Birmingham B19 . . . . . **66** B7
Lichfield WS13 . . . . **3** A2
Smethwick B67 . . . . . . **64** F2
Weston St
Coventry CV1 . . . . . . **165** C4
Walsall WS1 . . . . **42** E7
Weston Terr 3 B19 . . **66** D8
West Orchards Sh Ctr
CV1 . . . . **165** B3
Westover Rd B20 . . . . **54** E4
West Park Ave B31 . . **102** E2
West Park CI WS9 . . . . **29** E5
West Park Ct WV1 . . . . **25** A2
West Park Hospl WV1 **25** A2
West Park Prim Sch
WV1 . . . . **163** A4
West Park Rd B67 . . . . **64** D6
West Pathway B17 . . . **85** C6
West Point B17 . . . . . . **85** C8
Westport Cres WV11 . . **26** F5
Westray CI B45 . . . . . **101** F1
Westray Dr LE10 . . . . . **71** C1

West Rd
Birmingham, Hamstead
B43 . . . . **54** E7
Birmingham, Handsworth
B6 . . . . **55** E2
Bromsgrove B60 . . . . . **137** A2
Halesowen B63 . . . . . . **82** B6
Tipton DY4 . . . . **52** B8
Wolverhampton WV4 . . **39** F5
West Rd S B63 . . . . . . **82** B6
Westridge DY3 . . . . . . **50** C8
West Ridge CV5 . . . . **112** A5
Westridge Rd B13 . . **105** C6
West Rise B75 . . . . . . **46** C6
West Rock CV34 . . . . **160** D7
West Side Bsns Ctr
CV4 . . . . **131** F8
Westside Dr B32 . . . . **84** D1
West St
Brierley Hill DY5 . . . . . **81** F8
Cannock WS11 . . . . **4** E6
Coventry CV1 . . . . . . **113** E3
Redditch B98 . . . . . . **153** E3
Rowley Regis B65 . . . . **63** C1
17 Royal Leamington Spa
CV31 . . . . **162** A7
Stourbridge DY8 . . . . . **80** F5
Tamworth B79 . . . . **21** C5
Tamworth, Kettlebrook
B77 . . . . **21** C3
Walsall WS3 . . . . **28** C7
Warwick CV34 . . . . . . **160** D5
Wolverhampton WV6 . . **25** C5
West View B8 . . . . . . **68** C4
West View Ct B75 . . . . **46** E6
West View Dr DY6 . . . **60** E5
West View Rd
Royal Leamington Spa
CV32 . . . . **157** C5
Sutton Coldfield B75 . . **46** E6
Westville Ave DY11 . . **116** A5
Westville Rd WS2 . . . . **28** A3
Westward CI B44 . . . . . **55** F8
West Way
Birmingham B31 . . . . **123** B7
Walsall WS4 . . . . **15** B2
Westway Ho WS4 . . . . **15** B1
Westwick CI WS9 . . . . **16** E4
West Winds WV10 . . . **12** C7
Westwood Ave
Birmingham B11 . . . . . **87** D4
Stourbridge DY8 . . . . . **80** D3
Westwood Bsns Pk
Birmingham B6 . . . . . . **56** B1
Coventry CV4 . . . . . . **131** F6
Westwood CI CV10 . . . **72** E3
Westwood Ct B73 . . . . **45** B4
Westwood Dr B45 . . . **102** B1
Westwood Gr B91 . . . **106** F2
Westwood Heath Rd
CV4 . . . . **131** E6
Westwood Holdings
WS12 . . . . **1** B6
Westwood Rd
Birmingham, Aston
B6 . . . . **56** A2
Coventry CV5 . . . . . . **113** A1
Sutton Coldfield B73 . . **45** A4
Westwoods Hollow
WS7 . . . . **7** B8
Westwood St DY5 . . . . **61** A1
Westwood View B24 . . **57** C3
Westwood Way CV4 . **132** A6
Wetherby CI
Birmingham B36 . . . . . **68** D8
Wolverhampton WV10 . **11** D5
Wetherby Rd
Birmingham B27 . . . . . **88** C2
Walsall WS3 . . . . **14** A4
Wetherfield Rd B11 . . **88** A3
Wexford CI DY1 . . . . . . **50** F7
Wexford Rd CV2 . . . . . **96** D1
Weybourne Rd B44 . . . **44** E2
Weycroft Rd B23 . . . . **56** B7
Weyhill CI WV9 . . . . . . **10** F2
Weymoor Rd B17 . . . . **85** B3
Weymouth CI CV3 . . . **134** D5
Weymouth Dr B74 . . . . **31** F4
Weymouth Ho B79 . . . **21** B5
Whaley's Croft CV6 . . **113** B4
Wharf App WS9 . . . . . **29** F7
Wharf CI WS14 . . . . **9** C7
Wharfdale Rd B11 . . . . **88** A5
Wharfedale CI DY6 . . . **60** B7
Wharfedale St WS10 . . **42** A2
Wharf La
Birmingham B18 . . . . . **66** A6
Burntwood WS8 . . . . **6** F3
Nuthurst B94 . . . . . . **143** D4
Solihull B91 . . . . **107** D6

Wharf La continued
Tardebigge B60 . . . . . **138** B1
Wharf Lodge CV31 . . **161** D7
Wharf Rd
Birmingham, King's Norton
B30 . . . . **104** A2
Birmingham, Tyseley
B11 . . . . **88** B5
Coventry CV6 . . . . . . **113** F5
Wharfside B69 . . . . . . **63** F7
Wharf St
Birmingham, Aston
B6 . . . . **67** A7
Birmingham, Hockley
B18 . . . . **66** A6
Walsall WS2 . . . . **28** C1
Warwick CV34 . . . . . . **161** A8
Wolverhampton WV1 . **163** D2
Wharf The B1 . . . . . . **164** A2
Wharf Yd LE10 . . . . . . **75** A7
Whar Hall Rd B92 . . . **107** E8
Wharrington CI B98 . **159** A8
Wharrington Hill
B98 . . . . **159** A8
Wharton Ave B92 . . . **107** E7
Wharton St Ind Est
B7 . . . . **67** D8
Wharton St B7 . . . . . . **67** D8
Wharwell La WS6 . . . . . **5** A1
Whatcote Gn B92 . . . **107** E8
Whatecroft The 3
B17 . . . . **85** B6
Whateley Ave WS3 . . . **28** F6
Whateley Cres B36 . . . **69** D8
Whateley CI CV11 . . . . **73** B4
Whateley Gn B74 . . . . **46** A8
Whateley Hall CI
B93 . . . . **128** C7
Whateley Hall Rd
B93 . . . . **128** C7
Whateley La B77, B78 . **35** F4
Whateley Lodge Dr
B36 . . . . **69** C8
Whateley PI WS3 . . . . . **28** F6
Whateley Rd
Birmingham B21 . . . . . **65** E8
Walsall WS3 . . . . **28** F6
Whateley's Dr CV8 . . **148** A5
Whateley Villas CV9 . . **36** A2
Wheatcroft CI
Burntwood WS7 . . . . **7** A5
Halesowen B62 . . . . . . **83** F8
Redditch B97 . . . . . . **153** A5
3 Sutton Coldfield B75 **32** E3
Wheatcroft Dr B37 . . . **70** C1
Wheatcroft Gr DY2 . . . **51** F1
Wheatcroft Rd B33 . . . **68** F2
Wheate Croft CV4 . . . **111** F2
Wheaten CI B37 . . . . . **70** D3
Wheatfield CI B36 . . . . **70** D1
Wheatfield View
B31 . . . . **102** D6
Wheatfield Way LE10 . **71** C4
Wheat Hill WS5 . . . . . **43** E8
Wheathill CI
Royal Leamington Spa
CV32 . . . . **156** E2
Wolverhampton WV4 . . **38** E3
Wheatland Gr WS9 . . . **30** B4
Wheatlands CI
WS12 . . . . **2** C1
Wheatlands Croft B33 **69** E3
Wheatlands The WV6 . **23** D3
Wheatley CI
Birmingham B68 . . . . . **84** C8
Solihull B92 . . . . **107** E8
Sutton Coldfield B75 . . **32** C3
Wheatley Gr WS6 . . . . . **5** A2
Wheatley Grange B46 . **70** F6
Wheatley Rd B68 . . . . **84** D8
Wheatley St
West Bromwich B70 . . **53** A3
Wolverhampton WV2 . . **39** F6
Wheatmill CI DY10 . . . **98** B2
Wheatmoor Rd B75 . . . **47** A6
Wheatmoor Rise B75 . **46** E6
Wheaton CI WV10 . . . . **25** C7
Wheaton Vale B20 . . . . **54** E3
Wheatridge CI DY6 . . . **60** A8
Wheatridge Rd B60 . . **150** E6
Wheats Ave B17 . . . . . **85** B3
Wheatsheaf CI B75 . . . **32** E4
Wheatsheaf Rd
Birmingham B16 . . . . . **65** D2
Oldbury B69 . . . . **63** A8
Wolverhampton WV8 . . **10** E1
Wheat St CV11 . . . . . . **73** D4
Wheatstone CI DY3 . . . **50** E6
Wheatstone Gr B33 . . **68** F5
Wheeldon Ho B26 . . . . **88** E4

Wheeler CI B93 . . . . . **145** B7
Wheeler Ho 12 B69 . . **64** A7
Wheeler Rd WV11 . . . . **26** C8
Wheeler's Fold WV1 . **163** C3
Wheelers La
Birmingham B13 . . . . **104** F7
Redditch B97 . . . . . . **153** C6
Wheeler's La B13 . . . **105** A7
Wheelers Lane Prim Sch
B13 . . . . **104** F7
Wheelers Lane Prim Sch
(Annexe) B13 . . . . . **105** A6
Wheelers Lane Tech Coll
B13 . . . . **104** F7
Wheeler St
Birmingham B19 . . . . . **66** D7
Stourbridge DY8 . . . . . **80** F5
Wheeler Street Sh Ctr
B19 . . . . **66** D6
Wheeley Moor Rd
B37 . . . . **70** A5
Wheeley Rd
Alvechurch B48 . . . . . **138** D5
Solihull B92 . . . . **107** D7
Wheeley's La B15 . . . . **66** C1
Wheeleys Rd B15 . . . . **86** B8
Wheelock CI B74 . . . . . **44** F7
Wheelwright CI
Bromsgrove B60 . . . . **150** E6
4 Darlaston WS10 . . . **41** C6
Wheelwright Ct 5
B24 . . . . **56** E2
Wheelwright La CV6,
CV7 . . . . **95** C4
Wheelwright Lane Prim
Sch CV7 . . . . **95** D5
Wheelwright Rd B24 . **56** F1
Wheldrake Ave B34 . . **69** C6
Wheler Rd CV3 . . . . . **134** A7
Whernside Dr WV6 . . . **25** A5
Wherretts Well La
B91 . . . . **107** E6
Whetstone CI B15 . . . . **85** F5
Whetstone Field Prim
Sch WS9 . . . . **30** B4
Whetstone Gn WV10 . . **11** D1
Whetstone Gr WV10 . . **25** D8
Whetstone La WS9 . . . **30** B4
Whetstone Rd WV10 . . **25** D8
Whettybridge Rd
B45 . . . . **121** E6
Whetty La B45 . . . . . . **121** F7
Whichcote Ave CV7 . . **92** C1
Whichford CI B76 . . . . **57** D6
Whichford Gr B9 . . . . . **68** C2
While Rd B72 . . . . **46** B4
Whilmot CI WV10 . . . . **12** B6
Whimbrel Gr DY10 . . **117** A1
Whinberry Rise DY5 . . **50** C1
Whinchat Gr DY10 . . **117** A2
Whinfield Rd B61 . . . **136** B6
Whinyates Rise WS11 . . **4** F8
Whisley Brook La B28 **87** F2
Whistler Gr WV10 . . . . **26** A8
Whiston Ave WV11 . . . **27** A7
Whiston Gr B29 . . . . . **103** B8
Whiston Ho 9 WS1 . . **28** F1
Whitacre La WS14 . . . . **16** E7
Whitacre Rd
Birmingham B9 . . . . . . **67** F3
Knowle B93 . . . . **128** B7
Nuneaton CV11 . . . . . . **73** E4
3 Royal Leamington Spa
CV32 . . . . **157** A2
Whitacre Rd Ind Est
CV11 . . . . **73** E4
Whitaker Rd CV5 . . . **112** C3
Whitbourne CI B12 . . . **87** B5
Whitburn Ave B42 . . . **55** A5
Whitburn CI
Kidderminster DY11 . **116** B6
Wolverhampton WV9 . . **11** A2
Whitburn Rd CV12 . . . **77** C1
Whitby CI WS3 . . . . . . **13** F3
Whitby Rd B12 . . . . . . **87** A4
Whitby Way WS11 . . . . . **4** C8
Whitchurch CI B98 . . **158** F6
Whitchurch Way
CV4 . . . . **131** F6
Whitcot Gr B31 . . . . . **122** F8
White Bark CI WS12 . . . **2** A8
Whitebeam CI
Brownhills WS8 . . . . . . **15** E6
Coventry CV4 . . . . . . **111** D1
Dudley DY3 . . . . **50** C4
Whitebeam Croft 3
B38 . . . . **103** E1
White Beam Rd B37 . . **90** D8
Whitebeam Way
CV10 . . . . **72** D7

White City Rd DY5 . . . **62** A1
White CI DY9 . . . . **81** C2
Whitecrest B43 . . . . . . **44** A2
Whitecrest Jun & Inf Sch
B43 . . . . **44** A2
Whitecroft Rd B26 . . . **89** D5
White Falcon Ct B91 **106** F2
White Farm Rd B74 . . **31** E4
White Field Ave B17 . . **85** A6
Whitefield CI
Codsall WV8 . . . . **10** B2
Coventry CV4 . . . . . . **131** D6
Whitefields Cres
B91 . . . . **107** B2
Whitefields Gate
B91 . . . . **107** A1
Whitefields Rd B91 . **107** B2
Whitefriars CI B63 . . . **83** A4
White Friars La CV1 . **165** C2
White Friars St CV1 . **165** C2
Whitegate Dr DY11 . . **116** A3
Whitegates Rd WV14 . **40** D2
Whitehall Ct WV3 . . . . **38** F7
Whitehall Dr
Dudley DY1 . . . . **51** A2
Halesowen B63 . . . . . . **83** B4
Whitehall Ind Pk DY4 . **52** E5
Whitehall Inf Sch
WS1 . . . . **42** E7
Whitehall Jun Sch
WS1 . . . . **42** F7
Whitehall Rd
Birmingham, Bordesley
Green B9 . . . . **67** E1
Birmingham, Handsworth
B21 . . . . **66** A8
Cradley Heath B64 . . . . **82** C8
Halesowen B63 . . . . . . **83** B4
Kingswinford DY6 . . . . **60** C6
Stourbridge DY8 . . . . . **81** B2
Tipton DY4, B70 . . . . . **52** E4
2 Walsall WS1 . . . . . **42** F4
Wolverhampton WV4 . . **39** B4
White Hart The 8
WS1 . . . . **42** E8
Whitehead Dr
Kenilworth CV8 . . . . . **148** C7
Minworth B76 . . . . **58** D6
Whitehead Gr CV7 . . **130** F3
Whitehead Rd B6 . . . . **66** D8
Whiteheads Ct 17
CV32 . . . . **156** F1
Whiteheath Ct 6 B65 **63** E4
Whiteheath PRU B65 . **63** D4
White Hill B31 . . . . . **103** B6
Whitehill La B29,
B31 . . . . **103** A5
Whitehill Rd DY11 . . **116** A4
White Hollies WS3 . . . **14** A1
Whitehorse CI CV6 . . . **96** B6
White Horse Rd WS8 . . **6** E2
Whitehouse Ave
Darlaston WS10 . . . . . . **41** A4
Wednesbury WS10 . . . . **41** F3
Wolverhampton WV3 . . **38** D7
White House Ave
WV11 . . . . **26** H1
White House CI B91 . **106** F2
Whitehouse Common
Prim Sch B75 . . . . . . **46** F6
Whitehouse Common Rd
B75 . . . . **46** F6
Whitehouse Cres
Burntwood WS7 . . . . **7** B7
Nuneaton CV10 . . . . . . **72** D3
Sutton Coldfield B75 . . **46** F8
Wolverhampton WV11 . **12** F1
Whitehouse Ct 8 B75 **46** F6
Whitehouse Dr
Lichfield WS13 . . . . **8** F6
Smethwick B66 . . . . . . **65** A7
White House Dr B45 . **122** A2
White House Gn B91 **106** F3
Whitehouse La
Codsall WV8 . . . . **10** A6
Redditch B98 . . . . . . **154** E4
Whitehouse PI B45 . . **121** F6
Whitehouse Rd
Kidderminster DY10 . **116** D4
Polesworth B78 . . . . . . **36** F7
White Houses La
WV10 . . . . **12** B5
Whitehouse St
Birmingham B6 . . . . . . **66** F6
Tipton, Burnt Tree DY4 . **52** A2
Tipton, Wallbrook
WV14 . . . . **51** D8
Walsall WS2 . . . . **28** D3
Whitehouse Way WS9 . **29** F4

White House Way
B91. . . . . 107 A3
Whitelaw Cres CV5. . 112 C6
Whitemoor Dr B90. . 127 A7
Whitemoor Rd CV8. . 148 B5
White Oak Dr
Kingswinford DY6. . . . . 60 C6
Wolverhampton WV3. . 24 C1
Whitepits La B48. . . 140 F4
Whitepoplars Cl DY5. 61 C4
White Rd
Birmingham B32. . . . . 84 D6
Birmingham, Sparkbrook
B11. . . . . 87 C7
Smethwick B67. . . . . . 64 F6
White Rose Ho 4
CV32. . . . . 156 F2
White Row WV5. . . . . 37 C1
Whitesands Cl B77. . . 21 E5
White's Dr DY3. . . . . 50 E8
Whiteside Cl CV3 . . 134 F8
Whiteslade Cl B93. . 128 A7
Whitesmith Croft
B14. . . . . 104 E8
Whitesmiths Cl DY3. 50 D8
Whitesmore Sch B37. 69 F1
White's Rd B71. . . . . 53 C6
Whites Row CV8 . . . 148 A3
White St
Birmingham B12. . . . . 87 A5
Coventry CV1 . . . . . . 165 C3
Walsall WS1 . . . . 42 E8
Whitestitch La CV7. . . 92 C3
Whitestone Inf Sch
CV11. . . . . 79 A8
Whitestone Rd
Halesowen B63. . . . . . 83 A6
Nuneaton CV11. . . . . 79 B7
Whites Wood WV5 . . . 49 A5
Whitethorn Cl WS12. . . .2 A8
Whitethorn Cres B74. 30 D1
Whitethorn Dr CV32. 157 B2
Whitethorn Rd DY8. . 61 A1
Whitewood Glade
WV12. . . . . 27 E4
Whitfield Gr B15. . . . 86 D8
Whitfield Rd WS12. . . . .2 C7
Whitford Bridge Rd
B60. . . . . 151 A2
Whitford Cl B61. . . . 150 D8
Whitford Dr B90 . . . 127 C7
Whitford Gdns B61. . 136 D2
Whitford Rd B61. . . . 136 D2
Whitgreave Ave
Featherstone WV10 . . . 12 B7
Wolverhampton WV10 . 25 F8
Whitgreave Ct WV10 . 12 B6
Whitgreave Inf Sch
WV10. . . . . .25 E8
Whitgreave Jun Sch
WV10. . . . . .25 E8
Whitgreave Prim Sch
WV10. . . . . .12 B7
Whitgreave St B70 . . 52 E3
Whiting B77. . . . . 35 D7
Whitland Cl B45 . . . . 122 B6
Whitland Dr B14 . . . 104 F3
Whitley Abbey Com Sch
CV3. . . . . 133 F6
Whitley Abbey Prim Sch
CV3. . . . . 134 A6
Whitley Ave B77 . . . . 21 E5
Whitley Cl WV6 . . . . 24 B2
Whitley Court Rd B32 84 C6
Whitley Ct
Birmingham B20. . . . . 54 E3
Coventry CV3 . . . . . . 133 F7
Whitley Dr B74. . . . . 45 A8
Whitley St WS10 . . . . 41 E3
Whitley Village CV3 . 133 F7
Whitlock Gr B14 . . . 105 A3
Whitlocks End Halt
B90. . . . . 125 E7
Whitminster Ave B24. 57 B3
Whitminster Cl WV12. 27 C4
Whitmore Hill WV1. . 163 B3
Whitmore Ho WV6 . . 25 A4
Whitmore Park Prim Sch
CV6. . . . . 95 A1
Whitmore Park Rd
CV6. . . . . 95 D3
Whitmore Rd
Birmingham B10. . . . . 87 C8
Stourbridge DY8. . . . . 80 D5
Whitnash CV31. . . . . 162 A3
Whitmore St
Birmingham B18. . . . . 66 B6
Walsall WS1 . . . . 42 D7
Wolverhampton WV1. 163 C3
Whitnash Cl CV7. . . . 130 A6

Whitnash Gr CV2. . . . 114 D5
Whitnash Prim Sch
CV31. . . . . 162 A4
Whitnash Rd CV31. . 162 B4
Whitney Ave DY8. . . . 80 D6
Whittaker St WV2 . . . 39 E6
Whittall Dr E DY11. . 116 B1
Whittall Dr W DY11. . 116 A1
Whittall St B4. . . . . . 164 C3
Whittimere St WS1. . .28 F2
Whittingham Gr
WV11 . . . . .26 F6
Whittingham Rd B63. 83 A5
Whittington Cl
Birmingham B14. . . . 104 C5
4 Warwick CV34. . . 161 B8
West Bromwich B71. . 53 F8
Whittington Gr B33. . .68 F2
Whittington Hall La
DY7. . . . . 80 B3
Whittington Ho WS13. .3 E1
Whittington Oval B33. 69 A2
Whittington Rd DY8. . 80 C3
Whittle Cl CV3 . . . . . 134 F8
Whittle Croft B35 . . . .57 F3
Whittle Ct 9 CV32. . 157 A1
Whittleford Gr B36. . 58 C1
Whittleford Rd CV10. 72 C4
Whittle Rd LE10. . . . . 74 E7
Whittles St DY11. . . . 116 B8
Whitton St WS10. . . . 41 E6
Whitville Cl DY11. . . 116 C7
Whitwell Cl B90. . . . 127 A6
Whitworth Ave
Coventry CV3. . . . . . 114 B1
Hinckley LE10 . . . . . . 74 F7
Whitworth Cl WS10. . 41 E7
Whitworth Dr B71. . . 42 E1
Whitworth Ind Pk B9 67 C2
Whoberley Ave CV5. . 112 D2
Whoberley Hall Prim Sch
CV5. . . . . 112 C3
Whyley St B70 . . . . . 53 A4
Whyley Wlk B69. . . . 64 A5
Whynot Cl B60. . . . . 150 C2
Whynot St B63. . . . . 82 B5
Whytmore The WS13 . .8 F5
Wibert Cl B29. . . . . . 86 A1
Wichnor Rd B92. . . . .88 F5
Wickets Twr B5 . . . . 86 C5
Wickham Cl CV6 . . . .94 F2
Wickham Ct B32. . . . 157 B3
Wickham Gdns WV11. 26 A6
Wickham Rd B80. . . . 159 F4
Wickham Sq B70. . . . 53 B2
Wicklow Cl B63. . . . . 82 D1
Wickmans Dr CV4. . . 111 C2
Wiclif Way CV10. . . . 72 B3
Widdecombe Cl CV2 114 D7
Widdrington Rd CV1 113 C5
Wideacre Dr B44. . . . 55 E7
Wide Acres B45. . . . . 101 E7
Widgeon Gr WV10. . . 12 B7
Widney Ave
Aldridge WS9 . . . . . . 16 B1
Birmingham B29. . . . . 85 C1
Widney Cl B93 . . . . . 127 F5
Widney Ho B97 . . . . 153 C4
Widney Jun Sch B91 106 F1
Widney La B91. . . . . 127 B8
Widney Manor Rd B91,
B93. . . . . 127 D7
Widney Manor Sta
B91. . . . . 127 C8
Widney Rd B93. . . . . 127 F5
Wigford Rd DY8. . . . . 35 C5
Wiggin Cotts 5 B17. 85 C5
Wiggin Ho WS3 . . . . 14 C3
Wiggins Croft B76. . . .46 F1
Wiggins Hill Rd B76. . 58 F1
Wigginsmill Rd WS10. 41 D1
Wiggin St B16. . . . . . 65 F3
Wigginton Rd B79. . . 21 B7
Wight Croft B36. . . . . 70 B6
Wightman Cl WS14. . .9 E6
Wightwick Bank WV6. 24 A2
Wightwick Cl WS3. . . 14 B1
Wightwick Ct WV6 . . 24 A2
Wightwick Gr WV6 . . 24 A2
Wightwick Hall Rd
WV6 . . . . 23 E1
Wightwick Hall Sch
WV6 . . . . .23 E2
Wightwick Manor*
WV6 . . . . .23 F1
Wigland Way B38 . . . 104 A1
Wigmore Gr B44. . . . 56 B8
Wigmore La B71. . . . 54 E3
Wigorn Ho B67. . . . . .84 F3
Wigorn La DY9. . . . . 99 B8

Wigorn Rd B67. . . . . . .64 F1
Wigston Rd CV2. . . . . 96 F1
Wilberforce Way
B92. . . . . 107 F7
Wilbraham Rd WS2. . 28 C1
Wilcote Gr B27. . . . . 106 C8
Wilcox Ave WS12. . . .2 B7
Wilday Cl DY4. . . . . . 52 A5
Wildcroft Rd CV5. . . 112 C3
Wilde Cl B14. . . . . . . 104 D4
Wilden Cl B31. . . . . . 102 C3
Wilden La DY10. . . . . 116 E1
Wilderness La B43. . . 43 D3
Wildey Rd 1 CV12 . . 77 D2
Wildfell Rd B27. . . . . 88 D2
Wild Goose La B98. . 159 D8
Wildmoor Cl CV2. . . . 96 B4
Wildmoor La B61. . . . 121 A4
Wildmoor Rd B90. . . 106 B5
Wildtree Ave WV10. . 12 A2
Wiley Ave WS10. . . . 41 C5
Wiley Ave S WS10. . . 41 C5
Wilford Gr
Solihull B91. . . . . 107 B2
Sutton Coldfield B76. . 58 B6
Wilford Rd B71. . . . . 53 D6
Wilhelmina Cl CV32. 161 E8
Wilkes Ave WS2. . . . .27 F2
Wilkes Cl WS3 . . . . . 14 E3
Wilkes Croft DY3 . . . 50 D7
Wilkes Green Jun & Inf
Sch B21. . . . . .54 E1
Wilkes St
West Bromwich B71. . 53 E7
Willenhall WV13. . . . . 27 A1
Wilkin Rd WS8 . . . . . .6 C2
Wilkins Ho WS3 . . . . 14 A1
Wilkinson Ave WV14. . 40 E3
Wilkinson Cl
Burntwood WS7 . . . . . .7 B8
Sutton Coldfield B73. . 46 A2
Wilkinson Croft B8. . 68 C6
Wilkinson Jun & Inf Sch
WV14. . . . . .40 F3
Wilkinson Rd WS10. . 41 A4
Wilkins Rd WV14. . . . 40 D7
Wilks Gn B21. . . . . . . 54 D3
Willard Rd B25. . . . . 88 C6
Willaston Rd B33. . . . 89 D7
Willclare Rd B26. . . . 89 A6
Willcock Rd WV2. . . . 39 E7
Willenhall Ind Est
WV13. . . . . 27 C3
Willenhall La
Coventry CV3 . . . . . . 134 F7
Walsall WS3 . . . . 28 A8
Willenhall Lane Cvn Site
WS2 . . . . .27 F7
Willenhall Lane Ind Est
WS3. . . . . 28 A8
Willenhall Mus*
WV13. . . . . 27 B1
Willenhall Rd
Bilston WV14. . . . . . . 40 F7
Darlaston WS10 . . . . 41 D8
Wolverhampton WV1,
WV13. . . . . 26 C1
Willenhall Sch Sports
Coll WV12. . . . . .27 E5
Willenhall St WS10. . 41 C7
Willenhall Trad Est
WV13. . . . . 27 A1
Willenhall Wood Prim
Sch CV3 . . . . 134 D6
Willerby Fold WV10. .11 F4
Willersey Rd B13. . . 105 D8
Willes Ct
2 Birmingham B62 . . 84 A7
2 Royal Leamington Spa
CV31. . . . . 162 B7
Willes Rd
Birmingham B18. . . . . 65 E6
Royal Leamington Spa CV31,
CV32. . . . . 162 A8
Willes Terr CV31. . . . 162 B8
Willett Ave WS7. . . . .6 E5
Willett Rd B71. . . . . . 53 E8
Willetts Dr B63 . . . . 82 B4
Willetts Rd B31. . . . . 103 A1
Willetts Way B64. . . .62 F2
Willey Gr B24. . . . . . 57 B2
William Arnold Cl
CV2. . . . . 114 A4
William Batchelor Ho
CV1. . . . . 165 B4
William Baxter Sch
WS12. . . . . .2 A6
William Beesley Cres
CV11. . . . . 79 E6

William Bentley Ct
WV11 . . . . 26 C5
William Booth La B4 164 B4
William Bree Rd
CV5 . . . . 111 C5
William Bristow Rd
CV3. . . . . 133 E7
William Cook Rd B8. . 68 B5
William Cowper Prim Sch
B19. . . . . .66 E6
William Cree Cl CV8. 135 F3
William Ct
Birmingham, Rotton Park
B16. . . . . 65 E1
7 Birmingham, Showell
Green B13 . . . . 86 F4
William Edward St 1
B12. . . . . .86 F7
William Green Rd
WS10 . . . . 42 C3
William Groubb Cl
CV3 . . . . 134 D7
William Hanke Ind Est
DY5. . . . . .61 E1
William Harper Rd
WV13 . . . . 27 B1
William Henry St B7 . 67 A6
William Iliffe St LE10. 75 B7
William Ker Rd DY4. . 52 C5
William Kirby Cl
CV4. . . . . 112 A1
William Lunn's Homes 2
WS14 . . . . .9 C8
William McCool Cl
CV3. . . . . 134 F7
William MacGregor Prim
Sch B77. . . . . 21 D4
William McKee Cl
CV3. . . . . 134 E7
William Malcolm Ho
CV2. . . . . 114 E3
William Morris Gr
WS11 . . . . 1 E4
William Rd
Birmingham B31. . . . . 102 F1
Smethwick B67. . . . . . 64 D3
William St N B19. . . . 164 B4
William St W B66. . . . 65 B7
Williams Cl WV12. . . 27 C5
William Sheriden Ho
CV2. . . . . 114 E3
Williamson St WV3. . 163 A2
Williams Rd CV31. . . 162 E4
William St
Bedworth CV12. . . . . 78 D2
Birmingham B15. . . . . 66 C1
Brierley Hill DY5. . . . 61 C1
Nuneaton CV11. . . . . 73 E3
Redditch B97 . . . . . 153 E4
Royal Leamington Spa
CV32. . . . . 162 A8
Walsall WS4 . . . . 28 F3
West Bromwich B70. . 52 E5
William Tarver Cl
CV34. . . . . 161 A7
William Thomas Ho 7
CV32. . . . . 157 A1
William Thomson Ho 2
CV1. . . . . 165 D4
William Tolson's Ind Est
B78. . . . . .35 A8
William Wiggin Ave
WS3 . . . . 14 B2
Willingsworth High Sch
DY4. . . . . .41 B2
Willingsworth Rd
WS10 . . . . 41 D1
Willington Rd B79. . . 21 B7
Willington St CV11 . . 73 B5
Willingworth Cl WV14 40 A3
Willis Gr CV12. . . . . . 78 C3
Willis Ho CV11 . . . . . 73 E1
Willis Pearson Ave
WV14. . . . . 41 A3
Willis St DY11. . . . . . 116 C5
Willmore Gr 4 B38 . 123 F8
Willmore Rd B20. . . . 55 D2
Willmott Cl B75. . . . . 32 D3
Willmott Rd B75. . . . 32 D3
Willoughby Ave CV8. 147 E3
Willoughby Cl CV3 . . 134 E8
Willoughby Ct B76. . .46 F2
Willoughby Dr B91. . 107 B1
Willoughby Gr B29. . 85 A1
Willoughby Rd B79. . 20 E7
Willow Ave
Birmingham B17. . . . . 65 A2
Burntwood WS7 . . . . .7 C6
Wednesbury WS10. . . 41 F4
Wolverhampton WV11 . 26 B8

Willowbank B78. . . . . 21 B1
Willow Bank WV3 . . . 24 C1
Willowbank Rd LE10. 75 C7
Willow Bank Rd B93. 127 F6
Willow Brook Rd
B48. . . . . 139 A7
Willowbud Ho B98. . 158 F8
Willow Cl
Bedworth CV12. . . . . 78 A5
Bromsgrove B61. . . . 136 E2
Cradley Heath B64. . . 62 E1
Hinckley LE10 . . . . . . 75 E5
Nuneaton CV10. . . . . 72 A7
West Hagley DY9 . . . 98 F5
Whitnash CV31. . . . . 162 B2
Willow Coppice B32. 84 C1
Willow Ct
Birmingham B13. . . . . 87 A3
Bromsgrove B61. . . . 136 E3
Lichfield WS14 . . . . . .9 C5
Oldbury B66 . . . . 64 D8
Smethwick B67. . . . . 65 A2
Willow Ctyd CV2 . . . 114 D7
Willowdale LE10. . . . 75 A7
Willowdale Grange
WV6 . . . . 24 E5
Willow Dr
Birmingham B21. . . . . 54 C1
Cheswick Green B90 . 126 D4
Codsall WV8 . . . . 10 B3
Oldbury B69 . . . . 63 C7
Willow End DY9. . . . . 81 D3
Willowfield Dr DY11. 116 C8
Willowfields Rd CV11. 74 A1
Willow Gdns
Birmingham B16. . . . . 65 F4
Bromsgrove B61. . . . 136 E3
Willow Gr
Coventry CV4 . . . . . . 112 B2
Essington WV11 . . . . 13 B3
Willenhall WV13 . . . . 27 B1
Willow Ho
Birmingham B7. . . . . . 67 B4
Walsall WS4 . . . . 15 D1
11 Warwick CV34. . . 161 D8
Willow Hts B64 . . . . . 83 A8
Willow Meer CV8. . . 148 B5
Willow Mews B29. . . 85 B1
Willow Park Dr DY8 . 81 B2
Willow Rd
Birmingham, Bournville B29,
B30. . . . . 103 F8
Birmingham, Great Barr
B43. . . . . 44 A2
Bromsgrove B61. . . . 136 E3
Dudley DY1 . . . . 51 A4
Nuneaton CV10. . . . . 72 F5
Solihull B91. . . . . 106 E2
Wolverhampton WV3 . 38 D8
Willow Rise DY5 . . . . 61 C1
Willowsbrook Rd B62 .83 F8
Willows Cres B12 . . . 86 E5
Willow Sheets Mdw
CV32. . . . . 157 E6
Willowside WS4. . . . . 29 C8
Willowsmere Dr WS14. .9 F7
Willows Prim Sch
WS13. . . . . .3 B2
Willows Rd
Birmingham B12. . . . . 86 E5
Walsall, Shelfield WS4 . 29 C8
Walsall, The Chuckery
WS1 . . . . 29 A1
Willows The
Bedworth CV12. . . . . 77 E2
Birmingham B27. . . . . 88 B2
Cannock WS11 . . . . . .1 C1
Dudley DY2 . . . . 62 E5
Hollywood B47. . . . . 125 A6
Portway B47. . . . . . . 140 F7
10 Sutton Coldfield B74 31 F2
Sutton Coldfield, Walmley
B76. . . . . .46 F2
Wolverhampton WV11 . 26 B5
Willowtree Cl WS13. . . .3 B2
Willow Tree Dr B45. . 138 D8
Willow Way
Birmingham B37. . . . . 70 B1
Redditch B97 . . . . . 153 B4
Studley B80. . . . . 159 E2
Wills Ave B71. . . . . . . 53 B7
Willsbridge Covert 8
B14. . . . . 104 C2

Whi–Win 253

Wills Ho B70. . . . . . . 53 C2
Willson Croft B28. . . 105 D3
Wills St B19. . . . . . . 66 C7
Wills Way B66. . . . . . 65 C4
Wilmcote Cl B12. . . . 86 E6
Wilmcote Ct B61. . . . 150 D8
Wilmcote Dr B75. . . . 32 B3
Wilmcote Gn CV5 . . . 112 A3
Wilmcote Ho B97. . . 153 B4
Wilmcote Rd B91. . . 106 F6
Wilmcote Twr 5 B12. .86 F7
Wilmhurst Rd CV34. . 160 C8
Wilmington Rd B32. . 84 B6
Wilmore Ho B20. . . . 55 D1
Wilmore La B47. . . . . 124 F4
Wilmot Ave B46. . . . . 70 F6
Wilmot Cl CV7 . . . . . 130 B8
Wilmot Dr
Birmingham B23. . . . . 57 A6
Tipton DY4. . . . . 51 E6
Wilmot Gdns DY1. . . 51 A2
Wilmott Cl WS13. . . . .9 A7
Wilncote Gr
Birmingham B42. . . . . 55 D4
Whitnash CV31. . . . . 162 B5
Wilncote High Sch
B77. . . . . .35 F6
Wilncote Jun Sch
B77. . . . . .35 F7
Wilncote La B77. . . . 21 D2
Wilncote Sta B77. . . . 35 D7
Wilner's View WS3 . . 14 F5
Wilsford Cl
Birmingham B14. . . . . 104 D1
Walsall WS4 . . . . 29 C8
Wilsford Gn B15. . . . 85 E7
Wilson Dr B75. . . . . . 47 A5
Wilson Gn CV3 . . . . . 114 F1
Wilson Gr
Cannock WS11 . . . . . . .2 C2
Kenilworth CV8. . . . . 148 C4
Wilson Rd
Birmingham B19. . . . . 66 D8
Brierley Hill DY5. . . . 61 C4
Dudley WV14. . . . . . . 51 C7
Oldbury B68. . . . . 64 D1
Smethwick B66. . . . . . 65 B3
Wilsons La CV7 . . . . . 96 A6
Wilson's La CV6. . . . . .95 F5
Wilsons Rd B93. . . . . 128 C6
Wilson St Tipton DY4. . 52 A5
Wolverhampton WV1. 163 C4
Wilson Stuart Sch
B23. . . . . .56 C6
Wiltell Rd WS14. . . . .9 B6
Wiltell Rd Ind Est
WS14. . . . . .9 B7
Wilton Ave DY11. . . . 116 B8
Wilton Cl DY3. . . . . . 50 E7
Wilton Rd
Balsall Common CV7. . 130 B5
Birmingham, Balsall Heath
B11. . . . . 87 B5
Birmingham, Erdington
B23. . . . . 57 A5
Birmingham, Handsworth
B20. . . . . 55 B1
Wilton St B19. . . . . . 66 D8
Wiltshire Cl
Bedworth CV12. . . . . 78 A3
Coventry CV5 . . . . . . 112 B3
Walsall WS2 . . . . 28 D4
Wiltshire Ct 10 B29. . 103 C7
Wiltshire Dr B63. . . . 82 B7
Wiltshire Ho 3 DY8. .80 F8
Wiltshire Way B71. . . 53 C7
Wimberger Ho 2
B71. . . . . .53 D4
Wimblebury Rd WS12 .2 F2
Wimbledon Dr DY8. . 81 B2
Wimborne Dr CV2. . . 115 A4
Wimborne Rd WV10. 26 A6
Wimbourne Cl CV10. 72 B5
Wimbourne Rd
Birmingham B16. . . . . 65 D3
Sutton Coldfield B76. . 47 A4
Wimperis Way B43. . 44 C4
Wimpole Gr B44. . . . 56 B7
Wimshurst Mdw
WV10. . . . . .11 F4
Wincanton Croft B36. 68 C8
Winceby Pl CV4. . . . 111 D1
Winceby Rd WV6. . . .23 F3
Winchat Cl CV3 . . . . 114 F1
Winchcombe Cl
Dudley DY1. . . . . 50 E3
Solihull B92. . . . . 89 B2
Winchcombe Rd B92. 89 B2

Winchester Ave
Kidderminster DY11 . . **116** A6
Nuneaton CV10 . . . . **73** C7
Winchester Cl
Lichfield WS13 . . . . **3** C3
8 Rowley Regis B65 . . **63** E4
West Hagley DY9 . . . . . **99** A6
Winchester Ct 4 B74 . **31** F2
Winchester Dr
Birmingham B37 . . . . . . **70** A2
Hinckley LE10 . . . . **76** B7
Stourbridge DY8 . . . . . . **81** A3
Winchester Gdns
B31 . . . . **103** A3
Winchester Gr B21 . . **65** C8
Winchester Mews
WS9 . . . . **30** B4
Winchester Rd
Birmingham B20 . . . . . . **55** D1
Cannock WS11 . . . .**2** A3
Tamworth B78 . . . . **20** F3
West Bromwich B71 . . . **53** B8
Wolverhampton WV10 . **11** C3
Winchester Rise DY1 . **51** A2
Winchester St CV1 . . **113** E3
Winchfield Dr B17 . . . .**84** F7
Wincote Dr WV6 . . . . . **24** C4
Wincrest Way B34 . . . **69** C5
Windermere B77 . . . . . **36** A7
Windermere Ave
Coventry, Binley CV3 . . **114** E1
Coventry, Upper Eastern
Green CV11 . . . . **111** E4
Nuneaton CV11 . . . . **73** F6
Windermere Dr
Kingswinford DY6 . . . . . **60** D6
Royal Leamington Spa
CV32 . . . . **156** D2
Sutton Coldfield B74 . . . **30** F3
Windermere Ho
Kidderminster DY10 . . **116** E7
11 Oldbury B69 . . . . **63** D5
Windermere Pl WS11 . . .**1** E1
Windermere Rd
Birmingham, Handsworth
B21 . . . . **54** E2
Birmingham, Moseley
B13 . . . . **87** B1
Wolverhampton WV6 . . **24** D8
Windermre Ho 2
B15 . . . . **85** D3
Windfall Ct B24 . . . . . **57** D4
Winding House La CV6,
CV7 . . . . **95** C4
Winding Mill N DY5 . . **81** E7
Winding Mill S DY5 . . **81** E7
Windings The WS13 . . .**3** A1
Windleaves Rd B36 . . . **69** E8
Windley Ho B73 . . . . . . **45** C2
Windmill Ave
Birmingham B45 . . . . . **121** E8
4 Coleshill B46 . . . . . . **70** F7
Windmill Bank WV5 . . **49** A7
Windmill Cl
Birmingham B31 . . . . . **103** C5
Kenilworth CV8 . . . . . . **148** A6
Lichfield WS13 . . . .**3** A2
Tamworth B79 . . . . **21** A8
Windmill Cres
Smethwick B66 . . . . . . **65** C5
Wolverhampton WV3 . . **24** A1
Windmill Croft CV32. **157** D5
Windmill Ct CV6 . . . . **96** A3
Windmill Dr B97 . . . . **158** C6
Windmill End DY2 . . . . **62** E5
Windmill Gdns B97 . . **158** B6
Windmill Gr DY6 . . . . **60** B8
Windmill Hill
Birmingham B31 . . . . . **103** B5
Cubbington CV32 . . . . . **157** D5
Halesowen B63 . . . . **82** D5
Windmill Hill The
CV5 . . . . **112** A7
Windmill Ind Est
CV5 . . . . **111** F7
Windmill La
Balsall Common CV7. . **130** D4
Corley Moor CV7 . . . . . . **93** D6
Dorridge B93 . . . . **127** F1
Lichfield WS13 . . . .**3** A2
Smethwick B66 . . . . **65** B5
Tanworth-in-A B94 . . . **144** A8
Wolverhampton WV3 . . **24** A1
Windmill Prec B66 . . **65** C5
Windmill Rd
Bedworth CV7 . . . . **96** A8
Coventry CV6 . . . . **96** A3

Windmill Rd continued
Nuneaton CV10 . . . . . . **72** D7
Solihull B90 . . . . **105** E2
Whitnash CV31 . . . . . . **161** F5
Windmill St
Birmingham B1 . . . . . . **164** B1
Dudley DY1 . . . . **51** A2
Dudley, Gornalwood
DY3 . . . . **50** D5
Walsall WS1 . . . . **42** F8
Wednesbury WS10 . . . . **42** A3
Windmill Terr WS10 . . **42** A3
Windmill View DY1 . . **51** B7
Windmill Works Ind Pk
DY2 . . . .**62** B6
Windridge Cl CV3 . . **134** C6
Windridge Cres B92. **107** F8
Windrow The WV6 . . . **23** D4
Windrush Cl
Redditch B97 . . . . **158** D6
Solihull B92 . . . . **89** A2
Walsall WS3 . . . . **15** A1
Windrush Dr LE10 . . . **75** A8
Windrush Gr B29 . . . **104** A8
Windrush Rd
Cannock WS11 . . . .**1** E6
Hollywood B47 . . . . . . **125** B7
Windsor Arc B2 . . . . . **164** C3
Windsor Ave
Cannock WS12 . . . .**2** B6
Oldbury B68 . . . . **64** A3
Wolverhampton WV4 . . **38** E6
Windsor Cl
Birmingham, Coft Common
B31 . . . . **123** A6
Birmingham, Frankley
B45 . . . . **102** A2
Dudley DY3 . . . . **50** B2
Halesowen B63 . . . . **82** F3
Rowley Regis B65 . . . . . **63** C4
Tamworth B79 . . . . **21** C7
Windsor Cres DY2 . . . **62** D6
Windsor Ct
Birmingham B38 . . . . . **103** F1
Cannock WS12 . . . .**2** B6
Coventry CV4 . . . . **112** B2
Hinckley LE10 . . . . **76** A5
Lichfield WS14 . . . .**9** B6
Nuneaton CV10 . . . . . . **72** E6
12 Royal Leamington Spa
CV32 . . . . **161** F8
Windsor Dr
Birmingham B24 . . . . . **57** C5
Kidderminster DY10 . . **116** E7
Solihull B92 . . . . **89** B2
Windsor Gate WV12 . . **27** C4
Windsor Gdns
Bromsgrove B60 . . . . . **137** A2
Nuneaton CV10 . . . . . . **72** E4
Wolverhampton WV3 . . **38** A4
Windsor Gr
Stourbridge DY8 . . . . . . **60** E1
Walsall WS4 . . . . **15** C2
Windsor High Sch
B63 . . . .**82** F4
Windsor Ho
Birmingham B23 . . . . . **56** F6
Dudley DY2 . . . . **61** F7
Wolverhampton WV3 . **163** A1
Windsor Ind Est B7 . . **67** A5
Windsor Lodge B92 . **106** D8
Windsor Pl
Birmingham B7 . . . . . . **67** A3
Birmingham, Erdington
B23 . . . . **56** E3
10 Royal Leamington Spa
CV32 . . . . **156** F1
Windsor Rd
Birmingham, Castle
Bromwich B36 . . . . . . **69** F7
Birmingham, New Oscott
B73 . . . . **45** D1
Birmingham, Stirchley
B30 . . . . **104** B5
Cheslyn Hay WS6 . . . . . **4** F2
Halesowen B63 . . . . **82** F4
Oldbury B68 . . . . **64** A3
Redditch B97 . . . . **153** D5
Rowley Regis B65 . . . . . **63** C5
Stourbridge DY8 . . . . . . **80** E3
Tipton DY4 . . . . **52** A8
West Bromwich B71 . . . **42** B1
Wolverhampton WV4 . . **39** B7
Windsor St S B7 . . . . . **67** A4
Windsor St
Bilston WV14 . . . . **40** C6
Birmingham B7 . . . . . . **67** A4
Bromsgrove B60 . . . . . **137** A2
Coventry CV1 . . . . **113** B2
Hinckley LE10 . . . . **76** A5

Windsor St continued
Nuneaton CV11 . . . . . . **73** B4
Royal Leamington Spa
CV32 . . . . **161** F8
Walsall WS1 . . . . **42** F7
Windsor Terr 5 B16. . **65** F1
Windsor View B32 . . . **102** B7
Windsor Way WS4 . . . **29** D7
Windsor Wlk WS10 . . . **41** D8
Winds Point WV9 . . . . **99** A6
Windward Way B36 . . **70** B6
Windward Way Ind Est
B36 . . . .**69** F8
Windy Arbor Prim Sch
B37 . . . . **70** D2
Windy Arbour CV8 . . **148** B4
Windyridge Rd B76. . . **58** A6
Winfield Rd CV11 . . . . **73** B5
Winford Ave DY6 . . . . **60** E4
Winforton Cl B98 . . . **154** E3
Wingate Cl B30 . . . . . **103** F4
Wingate Ct B74 . . . . . **31** E4
Wingate Rd WS2 . . . . . **27** E2
Wing Cl WS2 . . . .**27** F4
Wingfield Cl B37 . . . . .**69** F3
Wingfield Ho B37 . . . . .**69** F5
Wingfield Rd
Birmingham B42 . . . . . **55** C7
Coleshill B46 . . . . **70** F5
Wingfield Way CV6 . . . **95** A2
Wingfoot Ave WV10 . . **25** E8
Wingrave Cl CV5 . . . . **112** A6
Winifred Ave CV5 . . . **113** A1
Winifride Ct B17 . . . . **85** B5
Winkle St B70 . . . . **53** B4
Winleigh Rd B20 . . . . .**54** F7
Winnall Cl WV14 . . . . **40** D2
Winnallthorpe CV3 . . **134** E6
Winn Ho 3 WS2 . . . . . **28** D3
Winnie Rd B29 . . . . . . **85** E1
Winnington Rd B8 . . . **68** A7
Winnipeg Rd B38 . . . **124** A8
Winrush Cl DY3 . . . . . . **50** D3
Winscar Croft DY3 . . . **50** D3
Winsford Ave CV5 . . . **112** B4
Winsford Cl
Balsall Common CV7. . **130** A6
Halesowen B63 . . . . **83** A6
Sutton Coldfield B76 . . . **46** E3
Winsford Ct CV5 . . . . **112** C4
Winsham Gr B21 . . . . . **65** E8
Winsham Wlk CV3 . . . **133** C3
Winslow Ave B8 . . . . . **68** B4
Winslow Cl
Coventry CV5 . . . . **112** B3
Redditch B98 . . . . **154** F3
Royal Leamington Spa
CV32 . . . . **156** C1
Winslow Dr WV6 . . . . . **24** E4
Winslow Ho 11 CV1 . . **113** B2
Winson Green, Outer
Circle Sta B21 . . . .**65** E7
Winson Green Rd B18 **65** E5
Winson St B18 . . . . . . **65** D4
Winsor Ave WS12 . . . . .**2** B6
Winspear Cl CV7 . . . . **92** B1
Winstanley Rd B33 . . . **68** D2
Winster Ave B93 . . . . **127** E4
Winster Cl CV7 . . . . . . **95** A4
Winster Gr B44 . . . . . . **44** D2
Winster Rd
Birmingham B43 . . . . . **54** D8
Wolverhampton WV1 . . **26** B1
Winston Ave CV2 . . . . **114** D8
Winston Churchill Ct
WV14 . . . . **40** C8
Winston Cl CV2 . . . . . **114** D8
Winston Dr
Birmingham B20 . . . . . **55** B4
Romsley B62 . . . . **101** A4
Winstone Cl B98 . . . . **154** A4
Winterborne Gdns
CV10 . . . . **73** A2
Winterbourne Botanic
Gdn* B15 . . . . **86** A5
Winterbourne Croft
B14 . . . . **104** C1
Winterbourne Rd
B91 . . . . **106** F4
Winter Cl WS13 . . . . . . **3** D2
Winterdene CV7 . . . . . **130** B7
Winterfold Cl DY10 . . **117** B6
Winterley Gdns DY3 . . **50** E6
Winterley La WS4 . . . . **29** C6
Winterton Rd
Birmingham B44 . . . . . **45** A3
Bulkington CV12 . . . . . . **79** C2
Winthorpe Dr B91. . . **127** C8

Wintney Cl B17 . . . . . . **85** A7
Winton Gr B76 . . . . . . **58** A6
Wintour Wlk B60 . . . . **150** E7
Winward Rd B98 . . . . **154** F1
Winwood Ct DY8 . . . . . **80** F4
Winwood Heath Rd
B62 . . . . **100** A1
Winwood Rd B65 . . . . . **63** E3
Winwoods Gr B32 . . . **102** A8
Winyate Hill B98 . . . . **154** A2
Winyates Crafts Ctr
B98 . . . . **154** E3
Winyates Ctr B98 . . . **154** E3
Winyates Way B98 . . **154** E4
Wirehill Dr B98 . . . . . **153** F1
Wiremill Cl B44 . . . . . **55** E6
Wirral Rd B31 . . . . . . **102** F6
Wiseacre Croft B90 . **105** E2
Wise Gr CV34 . . . . . . **155** E2
Wiseman Gr B23 . . . . **45** D1
Wisemore WS2 . . . . . . **28** E2
Wise St CV31 . . . . . . **161** F7
Wise Terr CV31 . . . . . **161** F7
Wishaw Cl
Redditch B98 . . . . **159** A8
Solihull B90 . . . . **105** E2
Wishaw Gr B37 . . . .**69** F5
Wishaw La
Curdworth B76 . . . . . . **59** A7
Middleton B76, B78 . . . **48** C6
Minworth B76 . . . . **58** E7
Wisley Gr CV8 . . . . . . **148** C5
Wisley Way B32 . . . . . .**84** F5
Wissage Ct WS13 . . . . . **9** D8
Wissage La WS13 . . . . . **3** D1
Wissage Rd WS13 . . . . . **9** D8
Wistaria Cl
Birmingham B31 . . . . . **103** A6
2 Coventry CV2 . . . . . **96** B2
Wisteria Dr
Brownhills WS8 . . . .**6** C2
Wisteria Gr B44 . . . . . **44** E2
Wistmans Cl DY1 . . . . **50** E2
Wistwood Hayes
WV10 . . . . **11** F4
Witham Cl B76 . . . . . . **47** A1
Witham Croft B91 . . . **107** C1
Withdean Cl B11 . . . . . **87** D6
Witherford Cl B29 . . . **103** C8
Witherford Croft
B91 . . . . **106** E2
Witherford Way B29. . **103** C8
Withern Way DY3 . . . . **50** D3
Withers Rd WV8 . . . . . **10** B3
Withers Way B71 . . . . . **53** D4
Withington Covert
B14 . . . . **104** D2
Withington Gr B93 . . **127** E4
Withybed Cl B48 . . . . **139** A6
Withybed La B48 . . . . **139** A6
Withybrook Cl CV2 . . . **96** D2
Withybrook La CV7 . . . **97** F5
Withybrook Rd
Bulkington CV12 . . . . . . **79** D2
Solihull B90 . . . . **126** B8
Withy Gr B37 . . . .**69** F5
Withy Hill Rd B75 . . . . **47** B8
Withymere La WV5 . . . **49** C8
Withymoor Prim Sch
DY5 . . . . **61** D1
Withymoor Rd
Dudley DY2 . . . . **62** E4
Stourbridge DY8 . . . . . . **81** A7
Withymore Ct WV3 . . . **25** A1
Withy Rd WV14 . . . . . . **40** C3
Withy Road Ind Est
WV14 . . . . **40** C3
Withywood Cl WV12. . . **13** C1
Witley Ave
Halesowen B63 . . . . **82** E4
Solihull B91 . . . . **107** C2
Witley Cl DY11 . . . . . . **116** B2
Witley Cres B69 . . . . . **63** E5
Witley Dr 1 B31 . . . . **103** D2
Witley Farm Cl B91. . **107** C2
Witley Rd 1 B31 . . . . **103** D2
Witnell Rd CV6 . . . . . **113** C6
Witney Cl B79 . . . . **20** F7
Witney Dr B37 . . . .**69** F2
Witney Gr WV10 . . . . . **11** B3
Wittersham Ct 5
WV13 . . . . **27** B2
Witton Bank B62 . . . . .**83** F7
Witton La
Birmingham B6 . . . . . . **55** F1
West Bromwich B71 . . . **53** F4
Witton Lodge Rd B23. **56** D7
Witton Rd
Birmingham B6 . . . . . . **66** E8

Witton Rd continued
Wolverhampton WV4 . . **39** A6
Witton St
Birmingham B9 . . . . . . **67** B2
Stourbridge DY8 . . . . . . **80** F4
Witton Sta B6 . . . . **55** F1
Wixford Gr B90 . . . . . **106** D2
Wobaston Ct WV10 . . . **11** B3
Wobaston Rd
Codsall WV9 . . . . **10** E4
Wolverhampton WV9,
WV10 . . . . **11** B4
Woburn B77 . . . . **21** D3
Woburn Ave WV12 . . . **27** B6
Woburn Cl
Bromsgrove B61 . . . . . **136** D1
Hinckley LE10 . . . . **71** E3
Royal Leamington Spa
CV31 . . . . **162** D1
Woburn Cres B43 . . . . **43** D1
Woburn Dr
Brierley Hill DY5 . . . . . **81** B8
Cradley Heath B62 . . . . **83** B7
Nuneaton CV10 . . . . . . **73** A2
Woburn Gr B27 . . . . . . **88** C1
Woburn Ho B15 . . . . . . **86** C7
Wodehouse Cotts
WV5 . . . . **49** D8
Wodehouse La WV5,
DY3 . . . . **49** E8
Woden Ave WV11 . . . . **26** C6
Woden Cres WV11 . . . . **26** C6
Woden Prim Sch
WV10 . . . .**25** E4
Woden Rd WV10 . . . . . **25** F4
Woden Rd E WS10 . . . . **42** B4
Woden Rd N WS10 . . . .**41** F5
Woden Rd S WS10. . . . **42** A1
Woden Rd W WS10 . . . **41** D4
Wodensborough Com
Tech Coll WS10 . . . . . .**42** B2
Wodensfield Prim Sch
WV11 . . . .**26** B6
Wodensfield Twr
WV11 . . . . **26** C5
Woden Way WV11 . . . . **26** C6
Wold Wlk
Birmingham B13 . . . . . **105** C6
Birmingham B13 . . . . . **105** C6
Wolfe Rd CV4 . . . . **131** F8
Wolfsbane Dr WS5 . . . **43** A3
Wolfson Dr B15 . . . . . . **85** E4
Wollaston Cres WV11. **26** D6
Wollaston Ct
Stourbridge DY8 . . . . . . **80** C6
1 Walsall WS1 . . . . **28** F2
Wollaston Rd
Stourbridge DY7 . . . . . . **80** C7
Stourbridge DY8 . . . . . . **80** E8
Wollerton Gr B75. . . . . **46** F6
Wollescote Bsns Pk 6
DY9 . . . .**81** F5
Wollescote Dr B91 . . . **107** B2
Wollescote Prim Sch
DY9 . . . .**81** F5
Wollescote Rd DY9 . . . **81** D3
Wolmer Rd WV11 . . . . . **13** A2
Wolseley B77 . . . . **21** F3
Wolseley Ave B27 . . . . **88** D4
Wolseley Bank WV10 . **25** F7
Wolseley Cl
Birmingham B36 . . . . . **59** A1
Wolverhampton WV10 . **25** F7
Wolseley Dr B8 . . . . . . **68** A7
Wolseley Gate WV10. . **25** F7
Wolseley Rd
Bilston WV14 . . . . **40** C7
West Bromwich B70 . . . **52** F6
Wolseley St B9 . . . . . . **67** B2
Wolston Cl B90 . . . . . **106** B5
Wolston La CV8 . . . . . **135** E2
Wolston Way CV3 . . . **134** C4
Wolverhampton Coll
Wulfrun Campus
WV6 . . . .**24** E4
Wolverhampton (Dunstall
Park) Race Course
WV6 . . . . **25** A6
Wolverhampton Girls'
High Sch WV6 . . . .**24** F2
Wolverhampton Gram
Sch WV3 . . . .**24** F2
Wolverhampton &
Midland Cties Eye Infmy
WV3 . . . . **25** A2
Wolverhampton Mus &
Art Gall* WV1 . . . . . **163** B3
Wolverhampton Rd
Cannock WS11 . . . . **4** D8
Cheslyn Hay WV10, WS6 . **4** B2

Wolverhampton Rd
continued
Codsall WV8 . . . . **10** A3
Essington WV11 . . . . . . **13** A3
Kingswinford DY6 . . . . **49** C1
Nurton WV6 . . . . **23** A3
Oldbury B69 . . . . **63** F4
Sedgley DY3 . . . . **39** D2
Walsall, Birchills WS2. . **28** B2
Walsall, Pelsall WS3. . . **14** F3
Walsall, Wallington Heath
WS3 . . . . **14** B1
Wedges Mills WS11 . . . . **4** B6
Wolverhampton WV10,
WV11 . . . . **26** B4
Wolverhampton Rd E
WV4 . . . . **39** D5
Wolverhampton Rd S
B32 . . . . **84** E7
Wolverhampton Rd W
WV13, WS2 . . . . **27** D2
Wolverhampton St
Bilston WV14 . . . . **40** C6
Darlaston WS10 . . . . . . **41** C6
Dudley DY1 . . . . **51** B1
Walsall WS2 . . . . **28** D2
Willenhall WV13 . . . . . **27** A1
Wolverhampton Sta
WV1 . . . . **163** C3
Wolverley Ave
Stourbridge DY8 . . . . . . **80** C6
Wolverhampton WV4 . . **38** D5
Wolverley Cres B69 . . **63** E5
Wolverley Rd
Birmingham B32 . . . . . **102** B8
Halesowen B63 . . . . **82** F2
Solihull B92 . . . . **89** D2
Wolverson Cl WV12 . . **27** C4
Wolverson Rd WS9 . . . **16** A4
Wolverton Cl B98 . . . **154** E2
Wolverton Rd
Birmingham, Marston
Green B37 . . . . **90** B7
Birmingham, Rednal
B45 . . . . **122** C6
Coventry CV5 . . . . **112** A3
Dudley DY2 . . . . **51** B7
Wolvey Rd
Bulkington CV12 . . . . . . **79** E2
Hinckley LE10 . . . . **75** E4
Wombourne Cl DY3 . . . **50** E8
Woodacre Rd B24 . . . . **57** C4
Woodall Ho WS3 . . . . . **28** C8
Woodall Rd B6 . . . .**55** F1
Woodall St
Cradley Heath B64 . . . . **62** C1
Walsall WS3 . . . . **28** C8
Woodard Rd DY4 . . . . . **52** C7
Wood Ave Dudley DY3 . **50** C7
Wednesfield WV11 . . . . **26** D6
Woodbank LE10 . . . . . . **76** A7
Woodbank Dr B61. . . . **136** F8
Woodbank Rd DY3 . . . . **50** C7
Wood Bank Rd WV3 . . **38** A8
Woodberrow La B97 . . **158** D6
Woodberry Dr B76 . . . **47** A2
Woodberry Wlk B27 . . **88** D3
Woodbine Ave B10 . . . **87** D8
Woodbine Cotts
Kingswood CV35 . . . . . **144** D3
2 Royal Leamington Spa
CV32 . . . . **161** E8
Woodbine Croft B26. . **89** A6
Woodbine St 1
CV32 . . . . **161** E8
Woodbine Wlk B37 . . . **70** D2
Woodbourne B15 . . . . . **85** D8
Woodbourne Rd
Birmingham B15, B16. . **85** C8
Smethwick B67 . . . . **64** E2
Woodbridge Cl
Walsall, Wallington Heath
WS3 . . . . **14** A3
Walsall WS4 . . . . **15** D1
Woodbridge Rd B13. . .**86** F7
Woodbrooke Gr B31. . **103** C6
Woodbrooke Rd B30 . **103** E7
Woodbrook Ho 9
B37 . . . . **70** B2
Woodburn Cl CV5 . . . **112** B4
Woodburn Rd B66. . . . **65** D7
Woodbury Cl
Brierley Hill DY5 . . . . . **61** D2
Halesowen B62 . . . . **83** F8
Redditch B97 . . . . **158** A6
Woodbury Gr B91 . . . **107** B1
Woodbury Rd
Birmingham B62 . . . . . **84** A8
Kidderminster DY11 . . **116** B2
Woodchester DY9 . . . . **99** B4

Woodchester Rd
B93 . . . . 127 E2
Woodchurch Grange
B73 . . . . .56 F8
Wood Cl B46. . . . . . . .70 F7
Woodclose Ave CV6 . 112 F6
Woodclose Rd B37 . . .69 F3
Woodcock Cl
Birmingham B31. . . . . . 102 C1
Tanworth-In-A B94 . . . 141 E3
Woodcock Gdns
WV10 . . . . 12 B7
Woodcock Hill Jun & Inf
Sch B31 . . . . 102 E7
Woodcock La
Birmingham, Acock's Green
B27. . . . . 88 D3
Birmingham, Northfield
B31. . . . . 102 E8
Woodcock La N B27. . 88 D4
Woodcock St B7 . . . . .66 F4
Woodcombe Cl DY5 . . 81 B7
Wood Common Grange
WS3 . . . . .14 F4
Woodcote Ave
Kenilworth CV8. . . . . . 147 D6
Nuneaton CV11. . . . . . 73 F8
Woodcote Cl B98 . . . 154 E3
Woodcote Dr
Birmingham B8 . . . . . . 67 F5
Dorridge B93 . . . . 128 B2
Leek Wootton CV35 . . 155 F7
Woodcote La
Belbroughton DY9. . . . 119 E1
Leek Wootton CV8,
CV35. . . . . 155 F7
Woodcote Rd
Birmingham B24. . . . . . 57 D5
Royal Leamington Spa
CV32. . . . . 156 F3
Warwick CV34 . . . . . . 160 F8
Wolverhampton WV6 . . 24 C4
Woodcote Way
Birmingham B18. . . . . . 66 A4
Sutton Coldfield B74. . . 44 F6
Woodcraft Cl CV4 . . 112 A2
Wood Croft B47. . . . 125 B6
Woodcroft Ave
Birmingham B20. . . . . . 54 E3
Dudley DY4 . . . . 51 C4
Tamworth B77. . . . . . . 21 B6
Woodcroft Cl
Blackwell B60. . . . . . . 137 F5
Cradley Heath B64 . . . . 82 F8
Woodcross La WV14. . 40 A2
Woodcross St WV14 . . .39 F2
Wood Ct
Birmingham B20. . . . . . 55 A2
Coventry CV2 . . . . 114 D7
Redditch B97 . . . . 153 C1
Woodend B20. . . . . . . 54 E6
Woodend Cl B97. . . . . 153 B2
Woodend Croft CV4 . 131 E8
Wood End Dr B45. . . 138 A8
Wood End La
Birmingham B24. . . . . . 56 F3
Lichfield WS13 . . . . . . .3 B7
Tanworth-In-A B94 . . . 141 F5
Woodend Pl WV6 . . . . 24 B4
Wood End Prim Sch
Wolverhampton
WV11 . . . . 26 C7
Wood End CV9 . . . . . . 36 C1
Wood End Rd
Birmingham B24. . . . . . 56 F3
Walsall WS5 . . . . 43 D8
Wednesfield WV11 . . . . 26 C7
Wolverhampton WV11 . 12 C1
Wood End Sta B94. . . 141 F4
Wood End Way WS9. . . 16 B3
Woodfall Ave B30. . . 103 F5
Woodfield DY9 . . . . . 119 E7
Woodfield Ave
Brierley Hill DY5 . . . . . 61 B7
Cradley Heath B64 . . . . 82 D8
Oldbury B69 . . . . 64 A4
Stourbridge DY9. . . . . . 81 F2
Wolverhampton WV4 . . 38 F6
Woodfield Cl
Norton Canes WS11. . . . .5 F7
Redditch B98 . . . . 154 A5
Sutton Coldfield B74. . . 46 B8
Walsall WS5 . . . . 43 E5
Woodfield Cres
Birmingham B12. . . . . . 87 A6
Kidderminster DY11. . . 116 D5
Woodfield Ct B14 . . . 104 F8
Woodfield Dr WS11 . . . .5 F7
Woodfield Ho WS3 . . . 15 B3
Woodfield Hts WV6. . . 24 D4

Woodfield Jun & Inf Schs
WV4 . . . . .38 F6
Woodfield La B62 . . . 120 D8
Woodfield Mid Sch
B98. . . . . 154 A2
Woodfield Rd
Birmingham, Balsall Heath
B12. . . . . 87 A6
Birmingham, King's Heath
B13. . . . . 104 F8
Coventry CV5 . . . . 132 E8
Dudley DY3 . . . . 50 C4
Hinckley LE10 . . . . 75 C6
Solihull B91. . . . . 107 B6
Woodfield St 4
DY11 . . . . 116 C6
Woodfold Croft WS9 . . 30 B7
Woodford Ave B36. . . 69 B8
Woodford Cl
Coventry CV7 . . . . 95 D5
Nuneaton CV10. . . . . . 72 D4
Wolverhampton WV9 . . 10 F7
Woodford Cres WS7. . . .7 B7
Woodford End 1
WS11 . . . . .1 F4
Woodford Green Rd
B28 . . . . 106 B8
Woodford Way WS12 . . .2 D1
Woodfort Rd B43. . . . 54 E7
Woodgate Bsns Pk
B32. . . . . .84 B2
Woodgate Dr B32 . . . 84 A1
Woodgate Gdns B32 . 84 A2
Woodgate Ho B97. . . . 153 B4
Woodgate La B32. . . . 84 A2
Woodgate Prim Sch
B32. . . . . .84 B1
Woodgate Rd
Hinckley LE10 . . . . 76 A8
Stoke Prior B60 . . . . . 151 B1
Woodgate Valley Ctry
Pk★ B32 . . . . 84 D3
Woodgate Way DY9 . . 119 E7
Woodglade Croft
B38 . . . . 103 E2
Woodgreen WS6 . . . . . 4 E5
Woodgreen Cl B97 . . . 158 B7
Woodgreen Croft B68 84 C7
Wood Green High Sch
WS10 . . . . .42 B5
Wood Green Jun Sch
WS10 . . . . 42 A4
Woodgreen Rd B68 . . 84 C7
Wood Green Rd
Birmingham B18. . . . . . 65 D4
Wednesbury WS10. . . . 42 B4
Woodhall Cl
Nuneaton CV11. . . . . . 74 A2
Tipton DY4 . . . . 52 A8
Woodhall Croft B92 . .88 F3
Woodhall Rd WV4. . . . 38 E5
Woodham Cl B45. . . . 101 E1
Woodhams Rd CV3 . . 134 C3
Woodhaven
Walsall WS4 . . . . 15 D1
Wedges Mills WS11 . . . .4 B5
Wood Hayes Croft
WV10 . . . . 12 C2
Wood Hayes Rd
WV11 . . . . 12 C1
Wood Hill Rise CV6. . . 95 D2
Wood Ho 1 WS1. . . . . 42 E7
Woodhouse Cl CV3. . . 134 C8
Woodhouse Fold
WV11 . . . . 26 D5
Woodhouse High Sch
B77. . . . . .21 F4
Woodhouse La B77. . . 22 A5
Woodhouse Orch
DY9 . . . . 119 E7
Woodhouse Prim Sch
B32. . . . . .84 E6
Woodhouse Rd
Birmingham B32. . . . . . 84 E5
Wolverhampton WV6 . . 24 B4
Woodhouse Rd N
WV6 . . . . 24 B4
Woodhouses La WS7 . . .7 F6
Woodhouses Rd WS7. . .8 A7
Woodhouse St CV34. . . 160 D6
Woodhouse Way B64. . 62 C1
Woodhurst Cl B77. . . .21 F5
Woodhurst Rd B13. . . 87 A4
Wooding Cres DY4 . . . 41 B1
Woodington Rd B75. . . 47 B5
Wood La
Birmingham, Erdington
B24. . . . . 57 C1

Wood La continued
Birmingham, Handsworth
B20. . . . . 55 B2
Birmingham, Marston Green
B37. . . . . 90 A8
Birmingham, Queen's Park
B17. . . . . 85 A6
Birmingham, Woodgate
B32. . . . . 84 A1
Cannock WS12 . . . . . . .2 C4
Earlswood B94 . . . . . . 125 E1
Eastcote B92. . . . . . . 108 F2
Fairfield B61. . . . . . . 120 C3
Hartshill CV10. . . . . . . 72 A8
Shenstone WS14. . . . . . 17 B2
Shilton CV7 . . . . 97 D5
Sutton Coldfield B74. . . 30 E2
Walsall WS3 . . . . 14 F4
Wedges Mills WS11 . . . .4 A6
West Bromwich B70. . . 53 A3
Willenhall WV12 . . . . . 27 E7
Wolverhampton WV10 . 11 D2
Woodland Ave
Brierley Hill DY5 . . . . . 62 A1
Coventry CV5 . . . . 132 F7
Dudley DY1 . . . . 51 C3
Hinckley LE10 . . . . 76 A7
Kidderminster DY11 . . . 116 C7
West Hagley DY8 . . . . . 98 F5
Wolverhampton WV6 . . 24 B3
Woodland Cl
Cannock WS12 . . . . . . .2 B8
Stourbridge DY9 . . . . . 81 D2
Willenhall WV12 . . . . . 27 D6
Woodland Cres WV3. . 38 D7
Woodland Ct
Cannock WS12 . . . . . . .1 C4
Shenstone WS14. . . . . . 32 A7
Woodland Dr
Barnt Green B45. . . . . 122 A2
Cheslyn Hay WS6 . . . . . .4 E4
Smethwick B66. . . . . . 64 E7
Woodland Gr
Birmingham B43. . . . . . 43 E3
Dudley DY3 . . . . 50 B3
Woodland Rd
Birmingham, Handsworth
B21. . . . . 65 C8
Birmingham, Northfield
B31. . . . . 103 B3
Dodford B61. . . . . 136 A7
Halesowen B62. . . . . . 83 D8
Hinckley LE10 . . . . 71 F1
Kenilworth CV8. . . . . . 148 B7
Redditch B97 . . . . 153 B3
Tamworth B77. . . . . . . 22 A4
Wolverhampton WV3 . . 38 D7
Woodland Rise
Cradley Heath B64 . . . . 82 F8
Sutton Coldfield B73. . . 46 B4
Woodlands Ave
Walsall WS5 . . . . 43 E5
Water Orton B46. . . . . 59 B2
Woodlands Com Prim
Sch The B77. . . . . .21 E4
Woodlands Cotts
WV4 . . . . .38 F4
Woodlands Cres WS3. .14 F5
Woodlands Ct
Binley Woods CV3. . . . 135 D7
Coventry CV5 . . . . 133 A8
Woodlands Farm Rd
B24 . . . . .57 F4
Woodlands Inf Sch
B90. . . . . 126 B8
Woodlands La
Bedworth CV12. . . . . . 77 E4
Solihull B90. . . . . 126 B8
Woodlands Paddock
WV4 . . . . 38 E4
Woodlands Park Rd
B30 . . . . 103 C5
Woodlands Prim Sch
WV12. . . . . 27 D6
Woodlands Rd
Bedworth CV12. . . . . . 77 F3
Binley Woods CV3. . . . 135 D7
Birmingham B45. . . . . 121 D7
Birmingham, Moseley
B11. . . . . 87 C2
Birmingham, Saltley B8 . 67 F3
Wombourne WV5 . . . . . 49 A5
Woodlands Sch The
CV5. . . . . 111 D3
Woodlands St B66 . . . 65 C5
Woodlands The
Cradley Heath B64 . . . . 83 A7
Hartshill CV10. . . . . . . 72 A8
Lichfield WS13 . . . . . . .9 D8
Stourbridge DY8 . . . . . 81 A2

Woodlands The continued
Sutton Coldfield B75. . . 47 A6
Wood End CV9 . . . . . . 36 C1
Woodlands Way B37 . . 70 D3
Woodland Way
Burntwood WS7 . . . . . .7 A6
Polesworth B78 . . . . . . 36 F8
Wood Lane Cl WV12. . 27 E7
Woodlawn B91. . . . . . 107 E4
Woodlawn Gr DY6. . . . 60 D5
Woodlea Dr
Birmingham B24. . . . . . 56 F2
Solihull B91. . . . . 106 E4
Wood Leasow B32 . . . 84 D2
Woodleaves B47. . . . . 124 F8
Woodleigh Ave B17. . . 85 D4
Wood Leigh Cl B63. . . 83 A6
Woodleigh Ct B38. . . . 103 F1
Woodleigh Rd
Coventry CV4 . . . . 131 F5
Sutton Coldfield B72. . . 46 C1
Woodleys The B14. . . . 105 B4
Woodloes Ave N
CV34 . . . . 155 F2
Woodloes Ave S
CV34 . . . . 155 F1
Woodloes Inf Sch
CV34. . . . . 155 E1
Woodloes Jun Sch
CV34. . . . . 155 E1
Woodloes La CV34,
CV35. . . . . 155 F2
Woodloes Rd B90. . . . 126 B7
Woodman Cl
Halesowen B63. . . . . . 83 C3
Wednesbury WS10 . . . . 42 B4
Woodman Gr 5 B75 . 32 E3
Woodman La
Cheslyn Hay WS6 . . . . . .4 E4
Clent DY9 . . . . 99 E4
Woodman Rd
Birmingham B14. . . . . 105 A1
Halesowen B63. . . . . . 83 C3
Woodman Wlk B23. . . 56 A5
Woodmeadow Rd
B30 . . . . 104 B3
Woodmill Mdw CV8 . . 148 B6
Woodnorton Dr B13. . 86 E2
Woodnorton Rd B65. . .63 F2
Woodpecker Gr
Birmingham B36. . . . . . 70 A7
Kidderminster DY10 . . . 117 B2
Woodpecker Way
WS11 . . . . .2 C3
Woodperry Ave B91. . 107 C1
Wood Piece La B98 . . 154 D7
Wood Rd Dudley DY3. . 50 C4
Wolverhampton WV6 . . 24 C3
Wombourne WV5 . . . . . 49 B7
Woodridge B6 . . . . . . 55 E1
Woodridge Ave
Birmingham B32. . . . . . 84 B4
Coventry CV5 . . . . 112 A6
Woodridge Rd B63. . . 83 A5
Wood Ridings WS13. . . .3 A1
Woodroffe Wlk CV6 . . 96 A4
Woodrough Dr B13. . . .86 F2
Woodrow Cl B61. . . . . 120 F1
Woodrow Cres B93. . . 128 A5
Woodrow Ctr B98. . . . 159 B8
Woodrow Dr B98. . . . . 159 B6
Woodrow Fst Sch
B98. . . . . 159 B7
Woodrow La
Bluntington DY10 . . . . 118 E3
Lower Marlbrook B61. . . 121 B2
Woodrow N B98. . . . . 159 A7
Woodrow S B98. . . . . 159 A7
Woodrow Wlk B98. . . . 159 A7
Woodruff Way WS5. . . 43 A3
Woodrush Com High Sch
The B47. . . . . 125 A6
Woodrush Dr B47. . . . 125 A5
Woodsbank Ind Est The
WS10 . . . . 41 D4
Woods Bank Terr
WS10 . . . . 41 C5
Woods Cres DY5 . . . . . 62 A1
Woods Croft WS13 . . . .3 A1
Woodsetton Cl DY1. . . 51 B6
Woodsetton Sch The
DY3. . . . . .50 F7
Woodshill Ave B45. . . 122 A2
Woodshires Rd
Coventry CV6 . . . . 95 F5
Solihull B92. . . . . 106 E7
Woodside
Birmingham B37. . . . . . 69 E4
Sutton Coldfield B74. . . 31 E2
Wood Side WV11. . . . . 27 A8

Woodside Ave B97 . . 153 B2
Woodside Ave N
CV3 . . . . 132 F6
Woodside Ave S CV3 . 132 F5
Woodside Cl
Walsall WS5 . . . . 43 D6
Wood End CV9 . . . . . . 36 C1
Woodside Cres B93 . 128 B4
Woodside Dr
Barnt Green B45. . . . . 138 B8
Sutton Coldfield B74. . . 31 C5
Woodside Gr WV8. . . . 10 B2
Woodside Ind Est DY2 61 F5
Woodside Pk Mobile
Homes Pk B94. . . . . . 141 B7
Woodside Pl WS11 . . . .1 E5
Woodside Rd
Birmingham B29. . . . . . 86 A1
Dudley DY2 . . . . 61 F7
Walsall WS5 . . . . 43 E6
Woodside Way
Aldridge WS9 . . . . 30 B5
Birmingham B32. . . . . 102 A8
Solihull B91. . . . . 106 E5
Willenhall WV12 . . . . . 27 E7
Woods La
Brierley Hill DY5 . . . . . 81 D7
Cradley Heath B64 . . . . 82 C8
Woodsome Gr B23 . . . 56 C7
Woodsorrel Rd DY1 . . .50 F4
Woods Piece CV7 . . . .94 F6
Wood St
Bedworth CV12. . . . . . 78 B5
Bilston WV14 . . . . 40 D5
Birmingham B16. . . . . . 66 A2
Darlaston WS10 . . . . . . 41 F6
Dudley DY2 . . . . 61 F6
Hinckley LE10 . . . . 71 D1
Kidderminster DY11 . . . 116 D5
Nuneaton CV10. . . . . . 72 F4
Royal Leamington Spa
CV32. . . . . 162 A8
Stourbridge DY8 . . . . . 80 D6
Stourbridge, Lye DY9 . . 81 F5
Tipton DY4 . . . . 51 E5
Willenhall WV13 . . . . . 27 B2
Wolverhampton, Park Village
WV10 . . . . 25 F5
Woodcross WV4 . . . . . . 40 A3
Wood End CV9 . . . . . . 36 C1
Woods The B14 . . . . . .86 F1
Woodstile B34 . . . . . . 69 B6
Woodstile Cl B75. . . . . 32 D3
Woodstock Cl
Dudley DY1 . . . . 62 A8
Hinckley LE10 . . . . 76 A5
Stourbridge DY8 . . . . . 60 C1
2 Walsall WS5 . . . . . . 43 A3
Woodstock Cres B93 127 F3
Woodstock Ct B13 . . . 87 B4
Woodstock Dr
Huntington WS12 . . . . .1 C7
Stourbridge DY8 . . . . . 60 C2
Sutton Coldfield B74. . . 31 D4
Woodstock Ho B13. . . 105 A7
Woodstock Rd
Birmingham, Handsworth
B21. . . . . 65 D8
Birmingham, Moseley
B13. . . . . 87 B3
Coventry CV3 . . . . 133 D7
Nuneaton CV11. . . . . . 73 E1
Wolverhampton WV1 . . 26 B1
Woodston Gr B91 . . . 127 C8
Wood Street Cl LE10 . 71 E1
Wood Terr B96 . . . . . . 159 B1
Woodthorne Cl DY1. . . 50 D2
Woodthorne Prim Sch
WV6 . . . . 24 A4
Woodthorne Rd WV6. . 24 A6
Woodthorne Rd S
WV6 . . . . 24 A5
Woodthorpe Dr DY9. . 81 D3
Woodthorpe Gdns
B14. . . . . 104 E5
Woodthorpe Jun & Inf
Sch B14. . . . . 104 E5
Woodthorpe Rd B14. . 104 E5
Woodvale Cl B13 . . . . 87 A4
Woodvale Dr B28 . . . . 105 E4
Woodvale Rd
Birmingham B32. . . . . . 84 A1
Birmingham, Yardley Wood
B28 . . . . 105 E4
Woodview Primary Sch
B15. . . . . 86 C7
Woodville Ct
3 Birmingham B23 . . 56 E2

Woodville Ct continued
Warwick CV34 . . . . . . 160 F7
Woodville Gdns DY3. .39 F1
Woodville Rd
Birmingham, King's Heath
B14. . . . . 104 F8
Warwick CV34 . . . . . . 160 E8
Woodward Cl CV31. . . 162 A2
Woodward Pl DY9. . . . 81 C4
Woodward Rd DY11. . . 116 C4
Woodwards Cl WS2 . . 42 B8
Woodwards Pl WS2 . . 42 B8
Woodwards Rd WS2. . 42 B8
Woodward St B71. . . . 53 E4
Woodway B24. . . . . . . 57 B5
Woodway Cl CV2. . . . 114 F8
Woodway La CV2. . . . .96 F1
Woodway Park Sch &
Com Coll CV2. . . . . . .96 F1
Woodway Wlk CV2 . . . 114 E8
Woodwells Rd B8 . . . . 68 B5
Woody Bank WS6 . . . . 4 E2
Woolacombe Lodge Rd
B29 . . . . 85 C2
Woolaston Rd B98 . . . 159 A3
Woolgrove St CV6 . . . 96 A3
Woolhope Cl B98 . . . . 154 F3
Woolmore Rd B23. . . . 56 C5
Woolpack Cl B65. . . . . 63 A4
Woolpack St WV1 . . . 163 B3
Woolpack The 9
CV34. . . . . 160 E6
Woolwich Rd CV11. . . .79 F4
Wooton Cl B97. . . . . . 153 A4
Wootton Gr B44. . . . . 56 C8
Wootton Ave WV11. . . 26 D7
Wootton Cl WS11 . . . . .2 B3
Wootton Ct
Coventry CV2 . . . . 114 D7
6 Royal Leamington Spa
CV32. . . . . 156 F2
Wootton Green La
CV7 . . . . 130 A8
Wootton La CV7. . . . . 109 E1
Wootton Rd
Birmingham B31. . . . . 123 A6
Wolverhampton WV3 . . 38 D8
Woottons Ct WS11 . . . .1 F1
Wootton's Sq WV14 . . 40 E2
Wootton St CV12. . . . . 78 D3
Worcester Cl
Allesley CV5 . . . . 112 F8
Cannock WS11 . . . . . . .4 F8
Lichfield WS13 . . . . . . .3 C3
Sutton Coldfield B75. . . 32 D3
West Hagley DY9 . . . . . 99 A5
Worcester Cross 3
DY10 . . . . 116 E5
Worcester Ct
Coventry CV6 . . . . 96 B4
Wolverhampton WV3 . . 39 A6
Worcester Gn B71. . . . 53 C7
Worcester Gr WV6 . . . 23 D4
Worcester Ho
Birmingham B36. . . . . . 70 A8
4 Halesowen B63. . . . 83 A3
Worcester La
Stourbridge DY9 . . . . . 99 B7
Sutton Coldfield B75. . . 32 D4
Worcester Rd
Birmingham, Birchfield
B6. . . . . 55 F2
Birmingham, Brandhall
B68. . . . . 84 A8
Bromsgrove B61. . . . . . 136 F1
Dudley DY2 . . . . 62 E3
Harvington B9, DY10 . . 118 C4
Kenilworth CV8. . . . . . 148 B3
Kidderminster DY10 . . . 116 E2
Mustow Green DY10. . . 117 F1
Stoke Heath B61. . . . . 150 B4
West Hagley DY9 . . . . . 99 A5
Willenhall WV13 . . . . . 27 D2
Worcester Rise B29 . . 86 B1
Worcester Sq 1
B97. . . . . 153 E4
Worcester St
Birmingham B2. . . . . . 164 C2
Kidderminster DY10 . . . 116 E6
Stourbridge DY8 . . . . . 81 A4
Wolverhampton WV2 . . 163 B2
Worcester Wlk B37. . . 70 A1
Word Hill B17. . . . . . . .84 F7
Wordsley Ct DY8 . . . . 154 B7
Wordsley Ct DY8 . . . . 60 E3
Wordsley Green Sh Ctr
DY8. . . . . 60 D2

Wordsley Hospl DY8 . .**60** E3
Wordsley Sch The
DY8 . . . .**60** F3
Wordsworth Ave
Redditch B97 . . . . **158** C8
Tamworth B79 . . . . **21** A6
Warwick CV34 . . . . . . **160** D5
Wolverhampton WV4 . . **39** F4
Wordsworth Cl
Cannock WS11 . . . . **1** D4
Lichfield WS14 . . . .**9** B5
Tipton DY4 . . . . **52** A8
Wordsworth Cres
DY10 . . . . **117** B6
Wordsworth Ct WV6 . . **23** E4
Wordsworth Dr CV8 . **148** C4
Wordsworth Ho
Birmingham B31 . . . . . **123** A8
Halesowen B63 . . . . **82** B5
4 Oldbury B68 . . . . **64** C4
Wordsworth Rd
Bedworth CV12 . . . . . . **78** D1
Birmingham B10 . . . . . . **87** D7
Burntwood WS7 . . . . . .**7** A8
Coventry CV2 . . . . **114** C4
Dudley DY3 . . . . **50** B5
Walsall WS3 . . . . **28** E8
Willenhall WV12 . . . . . . **27** E7
Wolverhampton WV10 . . **26** A8
Wordsworth St B71 . . **53** C5
Worfield Cl WS4 . . . . . **29** A4
Worfield Gdns WV3 . .**38** F6
Workhouse La LE10 . . **76** A4
Works Rd B26 . . . . **90** A3
World's End Ave B32 . . **84** D6
World's End Jun Sch
B32 . . . . **84** D5
World's End La B32 . . **84** D5
Worlds End Rd B20 . . . **55** A3
Worleys Wharf Ave
WS10 . . . . **42** E2
Worsdell Cl CV1 . . . . . **113** B4
Worsey Dr DY4 . . . . . . **52** D6
Worsfold Cl CV5 . . . . . **112** A7
Worthen Gr B31 . . . . . **123** A8
Worthings The B30 . . **104** B6
Worthy Down WV11 . . **26** F5
Worthy Down Wlk
B35 . . . . **58** B3
Wortley Ave WV10 . . . **25** E6
Worton Rd DY9 . . . .**81** F2
Wragby Cl WV9 . . . . . **11** B3
Wrekin Cl
Halesowen B63 . . . . **82** C1
Kidderminster DY11 . . **116** B2
Wrekin Ct 9 B74 . . . . .**31** F2
Wrekin Dr
Bromsgrove B61 . . . . . **137** A5
Stourbridge DY9 . . . . . . **81** D4
Wolverhampton, Bradmore
WV3 . . . . **38** E8
Wolverhampton, Wergs
WV6 . . . . **24** A5
Wrekin Gr WV11 . . . . . **13** B1
Wrekin La WV6 . . . . . . **24** A5
Wrekin Rd
Birmingham B44 . . . . . . **56** A6
Sutton Coldfield B73 . . . **46** A1
Wrekin View
Brownhills WS8 . . . . . . **16** A5
Huntington WS12 . . . . . .**1** C7
Wolverhampton WV1 . . **163** B3
Wrekin View Rd DY3 . . **50** C8
Wren Ave WV6 . . . . . . **23** D3
Wrenbury Dr
Bilston WV14 . . . . **41** A7
Coventry CV6 . . . . **96** A4
Wrens Ave
Kingswinford DY6 . . . . . **61** A4
Tipton DY4 . . . . **51** D4
Wrens Croft WS11 . . . . . .**2** B1
Wrens Hill Rd DY1 . . . **51** B5
Wren's Nest Cl B90 . **126** A6
Wren's Nest Nature
Reserve* DY1 . . . . . **51** B4
Wrens Nest Pl DY1 . . . **51** A5

Wren's Nest Prim Sch
DY1 . . . . **51** A4
Wrens Nest Rd DY1 . . **51** A4
Wren's Nest Rd DY1 . . **51** A5
Wrens Park Ave B76 . . **57** E7
Wren St Coventry CV2 **113** F3
Dudley DY1 . . . . **51** C6
Dudley, Netherton DY2 . **62** B5
Wrentham St B5 . . . . . **86** E8
Wretham Ct B19 . . . . . **66** B7
Wretham Rd B19 . . . . . **66** B6
Wrexham Ave WS2 . . . .**27** F1
Wright Ave WV11 . . . . **26** E7
Wrighton Cl WV12 . . . . **27** C8
Wrighton Dr DY5 . . . . . **50** C1
Wrighton Gr B78 . . . . . **35** A8
Wright Rd B8 . . . . **67** E5
Wright's Ave WS11 . . . . . .**1** F5
Wright's La B64 . . . . . . **63** A1
Wright St
Bilston WV14 . . . . **40** E4
Birmingham B10 . . . . . . **87** D8
Coventry CV1 . . . . **113** E4
Halesowen B63 . . . . **83** B4
Wolverhampton WV10 . . **25** D4
Wrigsham St CV3 . . . **133** D8
Wrottesley Ct WV8 . . . **23** C8
Wrottesley Park Rd WV6,
WV8 . . . . **23** D5
Wrottesley Rd
Birmingham B43 . . . . . . **43** D1
Wolverhampton WV6 . . **24** B5
Wrottesley Rd W
Perton WV6 . . . . **23** F6
Wolverhampton WV6 . . **24** A6
Wrottesley St B5 . . . . **164** C1
Wroxall Cl DY5 . . . . . . **81** C8
Wroxall Dr CV3 . . . . . **134** D5
Wroxall Gr B13 . . . . . . **105** A6
Wroxall Rd B91 . . . . . **106** E6
Wroxham Glen WV13 . .**40** F8
Wroxton Rd B26 . . . . . **88** E8
Wulfruna Ct WV3 . . . **163** A2
Wulfruna Gdns WV3 . .**24** F1
Wulfruna St WV1 . . . **163** B3
Wulfrun Coll Annexe,
Newhampton Ctr
WV1 . . . . **163** B4
Wulfrun Ctr WV1 . . . **163** C2
Wulfrun Hall* WV1 . **163** B3
Wulfrun Sq WV1 . . . **163** C2
Wulfrun Trad Est
WV6 . . . . **25** C5
Wulfrun Way WV1 . . **163** B2
Wyatt Cl B5 . . . . **86** C5
Wyatt Ho CV2 . . . . . . **114** D7
Wyatt Rd B75 . . . . **47** B5
Wyatts Ct CV12 . . . . . . **78** B3
Wychall Dr WV10 . . . . **11** E4
Wychall La B38 . . . . . **103** E2
Wychall Park Gr
B38 . . . . **103** D2
Wychall Prim Sch
B31 . . . . **103** C2
Wychall Rd B31 . . . . . **103** C3
Wychbold Cl
Redditch B97 . . . . **158** A6
Willenhall WV12 . . . . . . **13** D1
Wychbold Cres B33 . . **69** C3
Wychbold Ct DY9 . . . . **99** C8
Wychbold Way WV12 . **13** D1
Wychbury B76 . . . . **47** A1
Wychbury Ct B63 . . . . . **83** A3
Wychbury Dr DY9 . . . . **99** C7
Wychbury Grange
DY9 . . . . **81** C1
Wychbury Rd
Birmingham B32 . . . . . **102** B7
Brierley Hill DY5 . . . . . . **81** E8
Stourbridge DY9 . . . . . . **81** E2
Wolverhampton WV3 . . **38** C7
Wyche Ave B14 . . . . . **104** D4
Wyche Cotts B60 . . . . **150** C1
Wych Elm Dr 6
CV31 . . . . **161** F5
Wychelm Farm Rd
B14 . . . . **105** A1
Wych Elm Rd WS8 . . . **15** E5
Wycherley Way B64 . . **82** E8

Wychnor Gr B71 . . . . . **42** E2
Wychwood Ave
Coventry CV3 . . . . **133** C3
Knowle B93 . . . . **128** B8
Wychwood Cres B26 . . **89** A6
Wychwood Dr B97 . . **158** D6
Wyckham Cl B17 . . . . . **85** A4
Wyckham Rd B36 . . . . .**69** F8
Wycliffe Gr CV2 . . . . **114** B5
Wycliffe Rd W CV2 . . **114** C5
Wycome Rd B28 . . . . **106** A7
Wye Cl Bulkington CV12 **79** B2
Hinckley LE10 . . . . **75** A8
Perton WV6 . . . . **23** F4
Royal Leamington Spa
CV32 . . . . **157** C3
Sutton Coldfield B76 . . . **58** B7
Wye Cliff Rd B20 . . . . . **66** B8
Wyegate Cl B36 . . . . . .**69** F8
Wye Ho DY3 . . . . **50** D3
Wyemanton Cl B43 . . . **43** C1
Wye Rd WS3 . . . . **14** E1
Wykeham Gr WV6 . . . . **23** D3
Wykeley Rd CV2 . . . . **114** C4
Wyken Ave CV2 . . . . . **114** D5
Wyken Cl B93 . . . . **127** E2
Wyken Croft CV2 . . . . **114** D6
Wyken Croft Nature Pk*
CV2 . . . . **114** D6
Wyken Croft Prim Sch
CV2 . . . . **114** E5
Wyken Grange Rd
CV2 . . . . **114** C5
Wyken Way CV2 . . . . . **114** B5
Wyke Rd CV2 . . . . **114** C4
Wykin Rd LE10 . . . . . . **71** A3
Wyld Cl B71 . . . . **53** A8
Wyld Ct CV5 . . . . **112** B5
Wylde Cres B65 . . . . . . **63** C4
Wylde Green Coll
B72 . . . . **46** C1
Wylde Green Prim Sch
B73 . . . .**57** B7
Wylde Green Rd B72,
B76 . . . . **46** D1
Wylde Green Sta B73 . **46** B1
Wyley Rd CV6 . . . . . . **113** B5
Wymering Ave WV11 . .**26** F7
Wynall La DY9 . . . .**81** F3
Wynall La S DY9 . . . . . **82** A3
Wynbrook Gr B90 . . . **127** A6
Wynchcombe Ave
WV4 . . . . **38** D4
Wyncote Cl CV8 . . . . . **148** A4
Wyndcliffe Prim Sch
Birmingham B9 . . . . **67** C1
Birmingham B9 . . . . **67** D1
Wyndcliff Rd B9 . . . . . **67** D1
Wyndham Gdns B30 . **103** D4
Wyndham Rd B16 . . . . .**65** F1
Wyndhurst Rd B33 . . **68** E5
Wyndley Cl B74 . . . .**31** F6
Wyndley Dr B73 . . . . . **46** B4
Wyndley Gr B72 . . . . . **46** C2
Wyndley La B73 . . . . . **46** A4
Wyndley L Ctr B73 . . **46** A5
Wyndley Manor B74 . . **32** A6
Wyndmill Cres B71 . . .**42** F1
Wynds Covert B14 . . . **104** D2
Wynds Point B31 . . . **103** B5
Wynd The DY3 . . . . **39** D1
Wynfield Gdns B14 . . **104** F5
Wynford Rd B27 . . . . . **88** C5
Wynford Road Ind Est
B27 . . . . **88** C5
Wyn-Griffith Dr DY4 . . **52** A3
Wynne Cres WV4 . . . . **38** C3
Wynn Rd WV4 . . . .**38** F5
Wynn St B15 . . . . **86** D8
Wynstead Covert 6
B14 . . . . **104** C2
Wyntor La B71 . . . . **53** B8
Wynyates B79 . . . . **20** E6
Wyre Cl
Birmingham B45 . . . . . **102** B1
Brownhills WS9 . . . . **15** F4
Wyre Rd DY8 . . . . **80** E7
Wyrley Brook Pk WS11 **4** D5

Wyrley Brook Ret Pk
WS11 . . . .**4** D6
Wyrley Cl
Burntwood WS8 . . . .**6** F3
Lichfield WS14 . . . .**9** A5
Willenhall WV12 . . . . . . **27** D7
Wyrley Ho
Birmingham B23 . . . . . . **56** C6
Tipton DY4 . . . . **52** B3
Wyrley La WS3 . . . . **14** E8
Wyrley Rd
Birmingham B6 . . . . **56** A2
Sutton Coldfield B75 . . . **32** D1
Wednesfield WV11 . . . . **27** A6
Wyrley St WV10 . . . .**25** F2
Wyrley Trad Est B6 . . .**56** B2
Wyrley Way B23 . . . . . **56** A6
Wythall Green Way
B47 . . . . **124** E3
Wythall Rd B63 . . . . . . **83** A2
Wythall Sta B47 . . . . . **125** C4
Wythwood Gr
Hollywood B47 . . . . . . **125** C6
Tipton DY4 . . . . **52** A8
Wythwood Gr
Hollywood B47 . . . . . . **125** C6
Wyton Ave B68 . . . . . . **64** C2
Wyver Cres CV2 . . . . . **114** C3
Wyvern B77 . . . .**21** F3
Wyvern Cl
Hinckley LE10 . . . . **75** E4
Oldbury B68 . . . . **64** B4
Sutton Coldfield B74 . . . **46** B7
Wednesfield WV12 . . . . **27** A7
Wyvern Gr
Birmingham B29 . . . . . . **85** C2
Cannock WS12 . . . .**2** A5
Wyvern Rd B74 . . . . . . **46** B7
Wyvis Cl WV6 . . . . **24** E2

Y

Yale Dr WV11 . . . . **26** E5
Yale Rd WV13 . . . . **41** A7
Yardley Cl Oldbury B68 **64** B1
Redditch B98 . . . . **154** E3
Warwick CV34 . . . . **155** F2
Yardley Fields Rd B33 **68** E2
Yardley Green Rd B9, B25,
B33 . . . . **68** A2
Yardley Prim Sch
B26 . . . . **88** D7
Yardley Rd B27 . . . . . . **88** C5
Yardleys Sch B11 . . .**87** F4
Yardley St
Coventry CV1 . . . . **113** E4
Darlaston WS10 . . . . . . **41** C7
Stourbridge DY9 . . . . . . **81** C6
Yardley Wood Com Prim
Sch B14 . . . . **105** D4
Yardley Wood Rd B13,
B14 . . . . **105** B5
Yardley Wood Sta
B28 . . . . **105** D5
Yardley Works DY9 . . **81** C5
Yare Gr WV13 . . . . **27** D1
Yarmouth Gn CV4 . . . **131** E8
Yarnborough Hill DY8 . **81** A2
Yarnbury Cl B14 . . . . . **104** E1
Yarn Cl B47 . . . . **125** A5
Yarner Cl DY1 . . . . **50** E2
Yarnfield Prim Sch
B11 . . . . **88** A3
Yarnfield Rd B11 . . . . . **88** A3
Yarningale Cl B98 . . . **158** F6
Yarningale Rd
Birmingham B14 . . . . . **104** D5
Coventry CV3 . . . . **134** D5
Yarningdale 7 B90 . . **126** C8
Yarn La B90 . . . . **126** A6
Yarnold La
Bournheath B61 . . . . . **136** C8
Fairfield B61 . . . . **120** C1
Yarrow Cl Walsall WS3 . **15** A5
Wednesfield WV11 . . . . **26** F5
Yarrow Dr B38 . . . . . . **123** F8
Yarwell Cl WV10 . . . . **163** C4
Yateley Ave B42 . . . . . **55** A7
Yateley Cres B42 . . . . **55** A7

Yateley Rd B15 . . . . . . **85** E7
Yatesbury Ave B35 . . . **58** A3
Yates Croft B74 . . . . . .**31** F6
Yates Ind Est WS3 . . . .**5** F2
Yates La B65 . . . .**63** F2
Yeadon Cl B97 . . . . . . **153** A1
Yeadon Gdns WV3 . . . **38** D8
Yeames Cl B43 . . . . . . **44** C4
Yellowhammer Ct
DY10 . . . . **117** A1
Yelverton Cl WS3 . . . . **14** B4
Yelverton Dr B15 . . . . . **85** E8
Yelverton Rd CV6 . . . **113** D8
Yeman Rd B68 . . . . **64** D3
Yemscroft WS6 . . . . . . **14** A8
Yems Croft WS4 . . . . . **29** A6
Yenton Cl B78 . . . . **21** A1
Yenton Gr B24 . . . . **57** C6
Yenton Prim Sch B24 **57** C6
Yeoman Cl DY10 . . . . . **116** E3
Yeomanry Cl
Sutton Coldfield B75 . . . **47** A6
12 Warwick CV34 . . . **160** F7
Yeomans Grange 5
B75 . . . . **46** F6
Yeomans Way B75 . . . **46** F6
Yeomans Wlk B60 . . . **150** E8
Yeovil Ct 15 DY5 . . . . . **61** D2
Yerbury Gr B23 . . . . . . **56** B4
Yew Cl CV3 . . . . **114** C1
Yew Croft Ave B17 . . . **85** B6
Yewdale B17 . . . . **85** C4
Yewdale Cres CV2 . . . . **96** E1
Yewdale Ct CV2 . . . . . . **96** F1
Yewhurst Rd B91 . . . . **106** E4
Yew St WV3 . . . . **25** A1
Yews The CV12 . . . . . . **77** E2
Yew Tree Ave
Belbroughton DY9 . . . . **119** D8
Birmingham B26 . . . . . . **88** E7
Lichfield WS14 . . . .**9** E8
Yew Tree Cl
Kingswood B94 . . . . . . **144** D3
Norton Canes WS11 . . . . .**6** A5
Redditch B97 . . . . **153** A4
Yew Tree Com Jun & Inf
Sch B6 . . . . **56** A1
Yew Tree Ct 1 CV31 . **161** F5
Yewtree Dr B60 . . . . . **137** B2
Yew Tree Gdns WV8 . . **10** A4
Yew Tree Hills DY2 . . . **62** C4
Yew Tree Inf & Jun Sch
B91 . . . . **107** E6
Yewtree La B65 . . . . . . **63** B2
Yew Tree La
Birmingham, Frankley
B32 . . . . **101** E3
Birmingham, Yardley
B26 . . . . **88** E7
Dudley WV14 . . . . **40** D1
Fairfield B61 . . . . **120** D2
Lapworth B94 . . . . **144** B1
Solihull B91 . . . . **107** E5
Wednesbury WS10 . . . . **42** A2
Wolverhampton WV6 . . **24** A5
Yew Tree Pl
Romsley B62 . . . . **101** A5
Walsall WS3 . . . . **14** D3
Yew Tree Prim Sch
WS5 . . . . **43** C4
Yewtree Rd
Sutton Coldfield, Boldmere
B73 . . . . **57** A7
Sutton Coldfield, Streetly
B74 . . . . **44** D8
Yew Tree Rd
Birmingham, Castle
Bromwich B36 . . . . . . **69** E8
Birmingham, Edgbaston
B15 . . . . **86** C8
Birmingham, Handsworth
B6 . . . . **56** A1
Birmingham, Moseley
B13 . . . . **86** D2
Dudley DY2 . . . . **62** C4
Halesowen B63 . . . . **82** F3
Kidderminster DY10 . . . **116** F5
Smethwick B67 . . . . **64** E4

Yew Tree Rd continued
Walsall, The Delves
WS5 . . . . **43** A5
Walsall WS4 . . . . **15** B1
Yew Tree Rise B76 . . . .**46** F3
Yew Tree Villas B73 . . . **57** A7
Yew Wlk B37 . . . . **70** B2
Yockleton Rd B33 . . . . **69** C3
York Ave
Bedworth CV12 . . . . **78** D2
Bromsgrove B61 . . . . . **136** E4
Walsall WS2 . . . . **28** B2
Willenhall WV13 . . . . . . **27** D2
Wolverhampton WV3 . . **24** E1
Yorkbrooke Dr B26 . . . **89** B5
York Cl
Birmingham B30 . . . . . **104** A6
Bromsgrove B61 . . . . . **136** E4
Coventry CV3 . . . . **134** C5
Lichfield WS13 . . . .**3** C3
Studley B80 . . . . **159** C4
Tipton DY4 . . . . **51** D4
York Cres
Birmingham B34 . . . . . . **69** E6
Darlaston WS10 . . . . . . **41** D6
Stourbridge DY8 . . . . . . **80** D7
West Bromwich B70 . . . **53** A6
Wolverhampton WV3 . . **24** E1
York Ct DY10 . . . . **116** F2
Yorkdale Cl DY3 . . . . . **50** D3
York Dr B36 . . . . **68** B8
Yorke Ave DY5 . . . . **61** A1
York Gdns WV3 . . . . . . **24** E1
Yorklea Croft B37 . . . . .**69** F2
Yorkmead Jun & Inf Sch
B28 . . . .**87** F2
Yorkminster Dr B37 . . **70** D3
York Rd
Birmingham B23 . . . . . . **56** F4
Birmingham, Edgbaston
B16 . . . . **65** E1
Birmingham, Handsworth
B21 . . . . **65** F8
Birmingham, King's Heath
B14 . . . . **104** E8
Birmingham, Tyseley
B28 . . . .**87** F2
Bromsgrove B61 . . . . . **136** F4
Cannock WS11 . . . .**4** F7
Dudley DY2 . . . . **62** E3
Hinckley LE10 . . . . **71** D3
Rowley Regis B65 . . . . . **63** E3
Royal Leamington Spa
CV31 . . . . **161** F8
Walsall WS4 . . . . **29** D7
Wolverhampton WV3 . . **38** B8
Yorksand Rd B78 . . . . .**34** F8
Yorkshire Way WS7 . . . .**7** F8
York St
Birmingham B17 . . . . . . **85** D6
Coventry CV1 . . . . **113** B2
Kidderminster DY10 . . **116** F2
Nuneaton CV11 . . . . . . **73** A4
Wolverhampton WV1 . . **163** D2
Yorks Wood Dr B37 . . . **69** E5
Yorkswood Prim Sch
B37 . . . .**69** F5
York Terr B18 . . . . **66** C5
Young Cl CV34 . . . . . . **160** B5
Young St B70 . . . . **53** A3
Yoxall Gr B33 . . . . **69** A3
Yoxall Rd B90 . . . . **106** D2
Yule Rd CV2 . . . . **114** D5
Yvonne Rd B97 . . . . . . **158** D7

Z

Zealand Cl LE10 . . . . . .**71** F3
Zion Cl WS6 . . . .**4** D3
Zions Cl B64 . . . .**62** C1
Zion St DY4 . . . .**51** F8
Zoar St Dudley DY3 . . . **50** C3
Wolverhampton WV3 . . **25** B1
Zorrina Cl CV10 . . . . . . **72** B1
Zouche Cl DY8 . . . . **80** E8